The Changing Newspaper

Typographic Trends in Britain and America 1622–1972

Numb.

The Daily Courant.

Wednesday, March 11, 1702.

From the Harlem Courant, Dated March 18. N. S.

Flanders under the Duke of Burgundy; and the Duke of Maine is to Command upon the Rhine.

The Pennsylvania Packet, *and Daily Advertiser.*

Price Four Pence.] TUESDAY, SEPTEMBER 21, 1784. [No. 1755.

For Liverpool.

This Morning

The Times.

NUMBER 6572. LONDON, THURSDAY, NOVEMBER 7, 1805. PRICE SIXPENCE.

The Manchester Guardian.

No. 1. SATURDAY, MAY 5, 1821. PRICE SEVEN-PENCE.

LLOYD'S WEEKLY NEWSPAPER.

SUNDAY, ["MEASURES NOT MEN."] JANUARY 6, 1850.

No. 372. PUBLISHED AT THE OFFICE, 12, SALISBURY-SQUARE, FLEET-STREET. Price 3d.

THE NEW YORK HERALD.

WHOLE NO. 10,456. NEW YORK, SATURDAY, APRIL 15, 1865. PRICE FOUR CENTS.

IMPORTANT.

ASSASSINATION

THE REBELS.

JEFF. DAVIS AT DANVILLE.

LATE LONDON EDITION.

Will the Millennium Work? Page 10.

Daily Herald

THE LABOUR DAILY NEWSPAPER.

Socialists and Socialism. Page 10.

NO. 231. [REGISTERED AT THE G.P.O. AS A NEWSPAPER.] MONDAY, JANUARY 13, 1913. ONE HALFPENNY.

ASSUITH'S LAST CHANCE. | HUNDREDS | Millerand's Exit. | LIVES LOST IN

"All the News That's Fit to Print."

The New York Times.

THE WEATHER.

NEW YORK, TUESDAY, APRIL 16, 1912—TWENTY-FOUR PAGES. ONE CENT

TITANIC SINKS FOUR HOURS AFTER HITTING ICEBERG;
866 RESCUED BY CARPATHIA, PROBABLY 1250 PERISH;

MEN'S SUITS Ready to Wear or Made to Measure Anderson's 14-16 GEORGE STREET, EDINBURGH

THE SCOTSMAN

CRAIGIEBIELD HOTEL

No. 40,278 EDINBURGH, FRIDAY, JUNE 30, 1972 3 a.m. news PRICE 4p

Seven killed as blazing

Newsday

THE LONG ISLAND NEWSPAPER

10 CENTS MONDAY JAN. 22, 1973

Daily Mirror

Chaos on the railways

MISERY

The Changing Newspaper

Typographic Trends in Britain and America 1622–1972

Allen Hutt RDI

GORDON FRASER
London 1973

The Gordon Fraser Gallery Limited
London and Bedford
First published 1973

ISBN 0 900406 22 4

Published in the U.S.A. by
The Sandstone Press
New York
(ISBN 0-913720-34-8)

Set in 'Monophoto' Century Schoolbook 227
Printed and bound by W. S. Cowell Ltd, Ipswich

Contents

NOTE: footnotes are keyed with an asterisk and appear in the margin on the relevant text page; bibliographical references are keyed with a superior figure and appear on page 220.

Acknowledgements

The publishers are grateful to newspapers for giving permission to reproduce material still in copyright. In addition to those bodies especially mentioned by the author in his preface thanks are also due to Associated Newspapers, Beaverbrook Newspapers, Beckett Newspapers, the *News of the World, Northern Echo,* the *Observer,* Slough *Evening Mail,* the *Sunday Telegraph,* the *Yorkshire Post,* the Hearst Corporation, the *Los Angeles Times,* the *New York Times* (illustrations © 1931/1944/1973 by The New York Times Company. Reprinted by permission), the *Washington Post,* the *Minneapolis Tribune.* The St Bride Printing Library provided illustrations for Napier double-cylinder 1824 – p. 54, Applegath & Cowper four-feeder 1828 and Applegath vertical type-revolver 1848 – p. 44, Walter rotary 1868 and Hoe rotary – p. 63.

Preface

THIS book began with the notion that it would simply supplement Stanley Morison's *The English Newspaper* (1932). That classic, while it purported to discuss developments in the typography of the London nationals up to its time of publication, effectively stopped at the First World War. None of the numerous facsimiles it presented were later than 1914. Thus there was a gap of over half-a-century to fill if the story of the 'physical development' of our newspapers was to be brought up to the opening years of the 1970s.

On reflection, however, it was not thought possible to limit the work to a mere supplementary function. For this there were two compelling reasons.

First, it was felt necessary to traverse again, at least in essential outline, the ground that Morison had already covered in detail. Morison's book is now only available in major libraries; long out of print, it has become an item of great rarity and high price. When it appears in antiquarian booksellers' catalogues it commands more than twenty times the 50s at which it was published. Thus the first four chapters of the present work summarise Morison, though with certain corrections and changes of emphasis.

Second, it was thought only reasonable to widen the book's scope to cover at least the main trends in American newspaper development. The United States, after all, has by far the largest English-language Press in the world. The pages that follow do not attempt to do more than sketch American developments in bare outline. The amazing complexity and variety in the typographic history of U.S. newspapers, even in the present century, can be instantly perceived by anyone who glances through the page facsimiles in the remarkable compilation *America's Front Page News 1690–1970*, edited by Michael C. Emery, R. Smith Schunemann and Edwin Emery (New York: Doubleday, 1970).

For further British and American examples from one important period the reader may be referred to the facsimiles in *Newspapers of the First World War*, edited by Ian Williams (Times Newspapers Ltd: David and Charles, 1970). Many others are facsimiled and discussed in Harold Evans's *Newspaper Design* (Heinemann, 1973), the fifth and final book in his five-volume manual *Editing and Design*.

Newspaper files in many great libraries have had to be drawn on for the facsimiles that illustrate this book; and, like Morison, I have to note that the rigid binding of many of these files often results in a curved distortion of the lefthand columns. The co-operation of the British Museum Newspaper Library (Colindale), the New York Public Library, the Library of Congress (Washington, DC) and the American Antiquarian Society (Worcester, Mass.) is warmly acknowledged.

Sir William Richardson (Co-operative Press) and John J. Horton (Social Sciences Librarian, University of Bradford) took extraordinary pains to provide a photoprint of an edition of *Reynolds News* not in the British Museum file. Among the editorial and managerial authorities of many newspapers who have been most helpful were Victor Clark (*Financial Times*), John Coote (*Daily Express*), Maurice Green (*Daily Telegraph*), Ernest Greenwood (*Morning Star*), Alastair Hetherington and John Ryan (*Guardian*), Denis Holmes and S. Pryor (*Daily Mail*), David Hopkinson (*Birmingham Post*), Jack Lonsdale (*The Times*), Eric B. Mackay (*Scotsman*), Ian Park (*Liverpool Daily*

Post), Eric Price (*Western Daily Press*), Percy Roberts and Douglas Long (*IPC*).

In varied ways I have had welcome assistance from Matthew Carter, Harold Evans, James Moran, Sir James Richards, Walter Tracy. John C. Tarr and Mrs Enid Broomfield strove to unravel the obscurity which surrounds the origin of Times Bold and the Times Titlings. Clive Irving and Paul Back provided invaluable information about *Newsday*. Robert Harling, Ralph McCarthy, Sir Paul Reilly and Tangye Lean illuminated a dark passage in the typographic history of the *News Chronicle*.

Of New York friends who have hastened to help I must mention Eric Frankland and more especially Horace Hart, who spared no effort in speeding-up the dispatch of illustration material. My warmest final thanks go to Peter Guy for the exemplary energy and skill he has applied to the production of an unusually complicated work.

G.A.H.

Camden Town
July 1973

1: The Beginnings

THE prehistory of the English-language newspaper begins in the early 1620s. I say prehistory because we are not yet concerned with the newspaper – that is, the sheet of two or four pages, made up in two or more columns – but with the news-book, or more properly news-pamphlet. One-off, or irregular and occasional, news-pamphlets date back to the sixteenth century; our story only starts when periodicity has become both regular and reasonably frequent. There is some obscurity about those early days, giving rise to learned discussion.[1] A substantial number of news-sheets or pamphlets in English were published in Holland (mostly in Amsterdam) in 1620–21; the argument has related to the primacy of actual London printing and publishing. The first unquestioned London publication appears to be the *Corante, or Newes from Italy, Germany* &c 'printed for N.B.' 24 September 1621 and describing itself as a translation from the German copy printed at Frankfurt. 'N.B.' would have been either Nathaniel Butter or Nicholas Bourne, two London printer-booksellers who were to be leaders in the news trade. Seven issues of this *Corante* have survived, its second issue adding the subtitle *Weekely Newes*; the extant run finished with the copy of 22 October 1621. No. 1 was set in roman, with italic for datelines and proper names; the remaining six somewhat inexplicably went over to blackletter for text, with datelines and proper names in roman. Throughout the run separate items were each introduced with a two-line roman drop initial.

The 1621 *Corante* notwithstanding, it seems fair to take 1622 for our effective starting date, as indicated on the title-page of the present work, following the example of Stanley Morison's *The English Newspaper* (1932). In that year the first officially licensed weekly news-pamphlets, dated and numbered, made their appearance. Nicholas Bourne and Thomas Archer were the publishers of the *Weekely Newes* – from Italy, Germany, Hungary, Bohemia, the Palatinate, France and the Low Countries, 'translated out of the Dutch copie' – whose first issue was on 23 May 1622; issue No. 2, on 30 May, had changed its printer and *Weekly* was spelt in modern fashion. Later in the year Bourne and Butter joined forces to produce the first numbered weekly publication, No. 1 appearing on 15 October. Initially this publication dropped the word 'news' from its title, using the older term *A Relation* &c; this was then varied to *A Continuation of the Weekely Newes* and No. 6 (7 November) titled itself *A Coranto*.

Another significant point about 1622 was that the news-periodicals then started adopted the book/pamphlet style of presentation, abandoning for over forty years the Dutch 'newspaper' style – a sheet made up in two columns – which the *Corante* of 1621 had followed. Thus the front page, as the facsimiles show, was displayed in the normal manner of a book title-page; and the matter throughout was set, book fashion, to the type-area of the format, usually quarto. Arrangement of the various items within this simplest of typographical forms was haphazard. Letters from abroad and foreign publications provided matter which was culled as it came; whole items were lifted and translated from the Dutch or German, as the title-pages acknowledged.

The concept of make-up really did not arise in these early book-style news-pamphlets, though some faint stirrings were perceptible on the continent. An early Dutch coranto had shoulder-notes as did the first French news-pamphlet, Dr Renaudot's *Gazette* of 1631. Published first

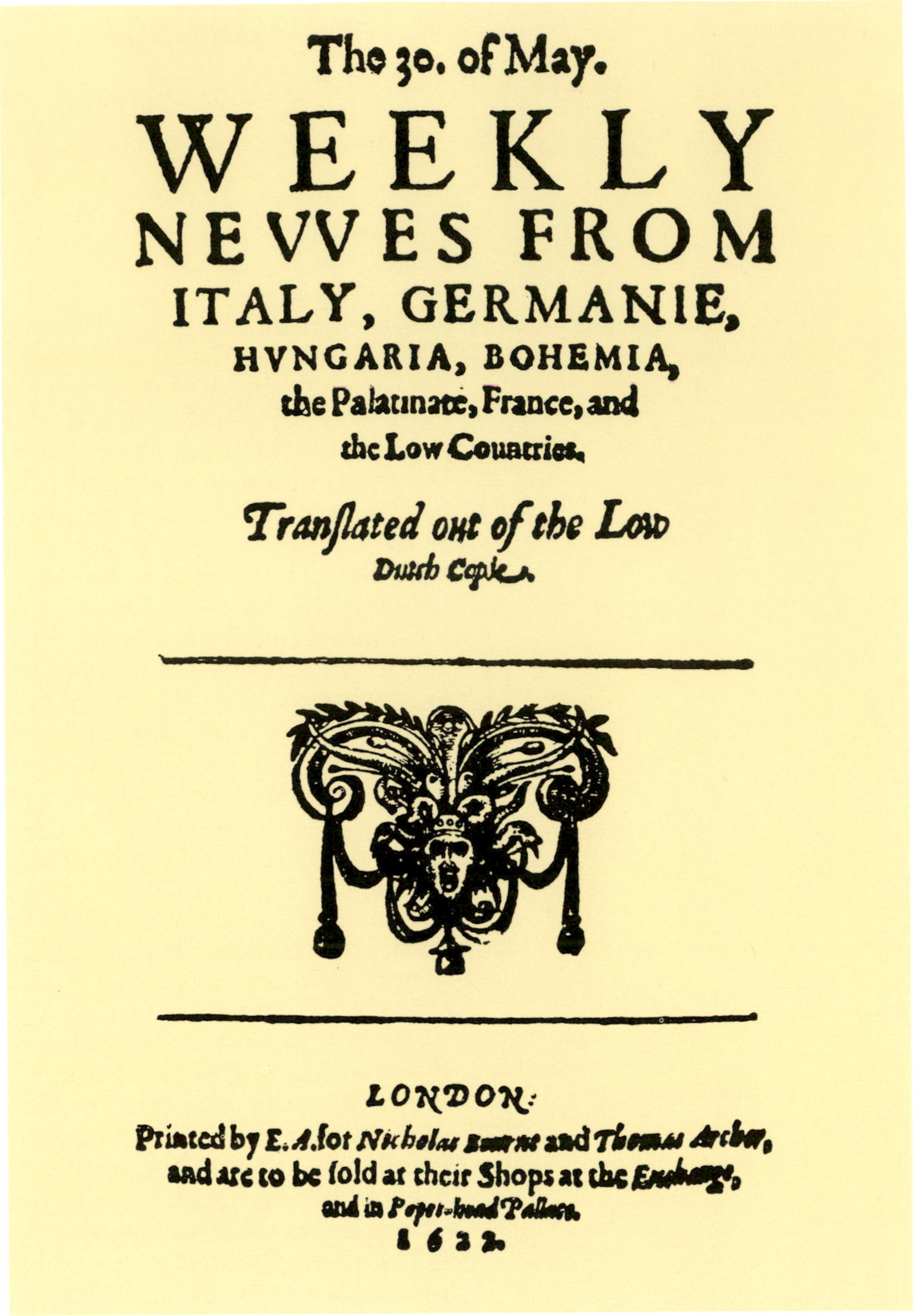
The 30. of May.

WEEKLY NEVVES FROM ITALY, GERMANIE, HVNGARIA, BOHEMIA, the Palatinate, France, and the Low Countries.

Translated out of the Low Dutch Copie.

LONDON:
Printed by E. A. for *Nicholas Bourne* and *Thomas Archer*, and are to be sold at their Shops at the *Exchange*, and in *Popes-head Pallace*.
1622.

One of the first of the officially-licensed, dated London weekly news-pamphlets.

weekly and then bi-weekly (as the postal services developed) the *Gazette* was backed by Richelieu and functioned from the start as a semi-official organ. Its four quarto pages were set book-style but the datelines, in italic, were set as side-notes in the margin to line up with the opening of each item; they thus served as a kind of embryonic headline. At the same time the front page eschewed the book-title style and approached later newspaper style; the title GAZETTE, in large capitals, letter-spaced, ran right across the page and was immediately followed by news. This practical French approach, however, was a good generation ahead of English conventions.

While make-up and typography – using the imported French/Dutch types then common in London – did not concern these earliest English journalists they soon began to take pains with the orderly presentation of text; or, as we would say, with the whole problem of sub-editing. In 1623 Butter, Bourne and Archer jointly produced *More Newes from Europe*; and in several issues an anonymous news-writer took the readers into his confidence in these matters.[2] Of the news as received, he explained, 'they that writ these letters had them by snatches' but he has 'brought them as it were into a continued relation', by which he clearly meant a consistent account which also pro-

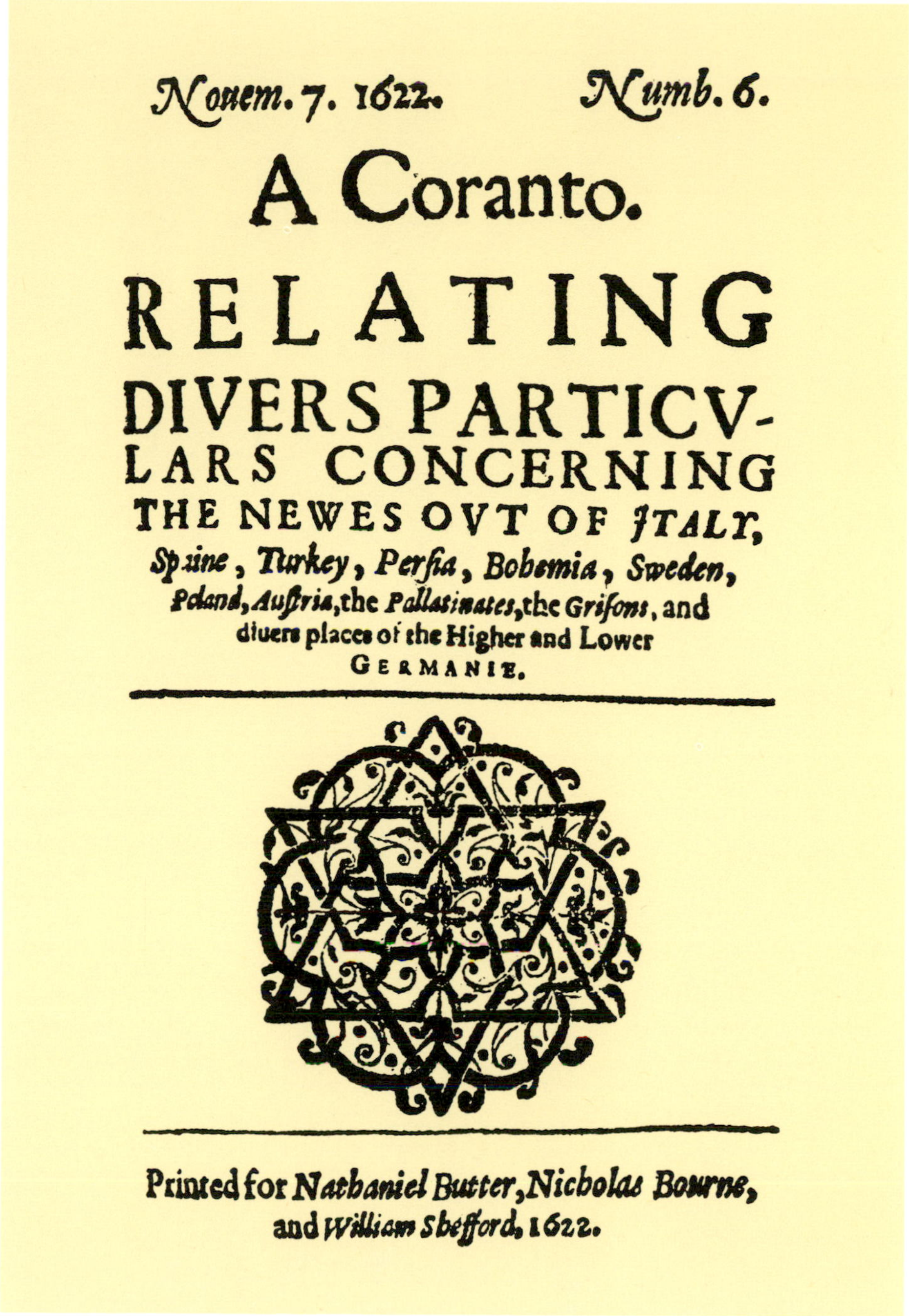

Nouem. 7. 1622. Numb. 6.

A Coranto.

RELATING DIVERS PARTICV-LARS CONCERNING THE NEWES OVT OF ITALY, Spaine, Turkey, Persia, Bohemia, Sweden, Poland, Austria, the Pallatinates, the Grisons, and diuers places of the Higher and Lower GERMANIE.

Printed for Nathaniel Butter, Nicholas Bourne, and William Sheffard. 1622.

A typical weekly *Coranto* of the 1620s, serial numbered as well as dated.

vided the necessary recapping of earlier news ('it will be the pleasanter, because you need not trouble your remembrance with looking backe after former matters') – a very early adumbration of a still sound journalistic practice. He did not think that his readers were always right; he bluntly chided them, saying 'if wee afforde you plaine stuffe you complain', but 'if wee add some exornation then are you curious to examine the method and coherence, and are forward in saying the sentences are not well adapted'.

The Thirty Years War was then raging in Europe and formed a major staple of news; so the Butter-Bourne-Archer editorial man assured readers that, directly decisive war news was available 'I will come towards you with honest information', adding quaintly 'I will not hide my talent in a Napkin, but acquaint you with as much as falls to my poore portion to know'. This seems to have been a false modesty, for later he did not hesitate to knock his competitors, who 'have not taken the paines, had the meanes, or been willing to beare the charges which we undergoe to get newes and intelligences'. He was frank about his correspondents and their limitations: 'our Courantiers cannot so readily guesse right what a General intends'.

These editorial discourses also point to the early emergence of short

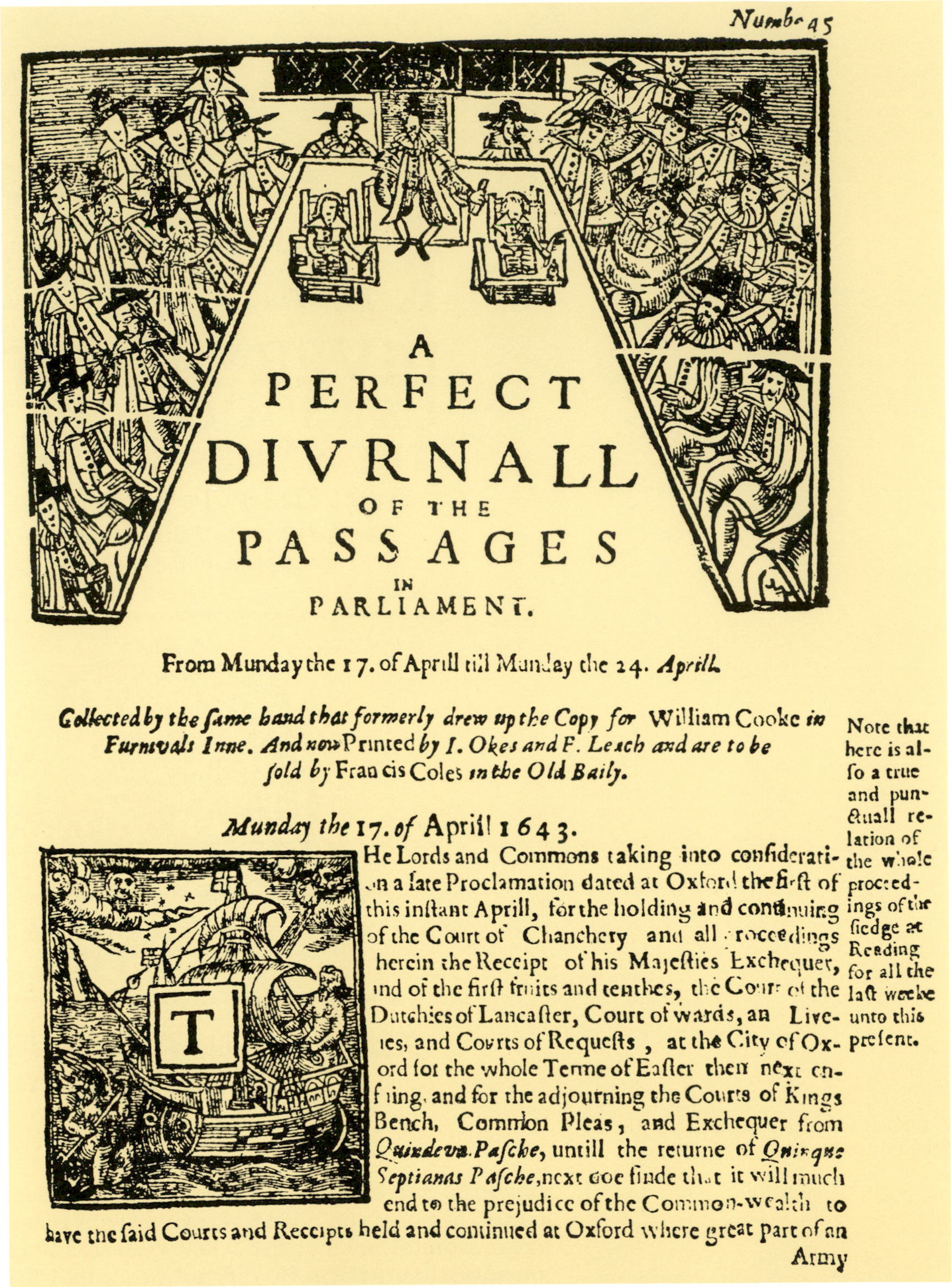
Numb^r 45

A PERFECT DIVRNALL OF THE PASSAGES IN PARLIAMENT.

From Munday the 17. of Aprill till Munday the 24. Aprill.

Collected by the same hand that formerly drew up the Copy for William Cooke *in Furnivals Inne. And now* Printed *by I. Okes and F. Leach and are to be sold by* Francis Coles *in the Old Baily.*

Munday the 17. *of* Aprill 1643.

THe Lords and Commons taking into consideration a late Proclamation dated at Oxford the first of this instant Aprill, for the holding and continuing of the Court of Chanchery and all proceedings herein the Receipt of his Majesties Exchequer, and of the first fruits and tenthes, the Court of the Dutchies of Lancaster, Court of wards, and Liveries, and Courts of Requests, at the City of Oxford for the whole Terme of Easter then next ensuing, and for the adjourning the Courts of Kings Bench, Common Pleas, and Exchequer from *Quindena Pasche*, untill the returne of *Quinque Septianas Pasche*, next doe finde that it will much end to the prejudice of the Common-wealth to have the said Courts and Receipts held and continued at Oxford where great part of an Army

Note that here is also a true and punctuall relation of the whole proceedings of the siedge at Reading for all the last weeke unto this present.

news items which did not fit in to the longer 'relation'. The writer called them 'broken stuffe', not coming 'within the compasse of our continued discourse', and therefore gathered together in a separate position, somewhat in the later manner of News in Brief.

The news-pamphlets of the 1620s, it will have been gathered, dealt exclusively with foreign news, of which there was no dearth. Home news was unknown. But the publication of foreign news was not without its internal hazards. In 1632, following a *démarche* by the Spanish Ambassador, Charles I's Star Chamber withdrew all news-publication licenses. The ban remained until 1638, when Butter was granted a monopoly license for news-publication. But great events were at hand which entirely changed the publication picture and forced news of home events to the front. Once the struggle between King and Parliament had erupted into civil war – the Star Chamber having been abolished in 1641 – news-pamphlets, and news-pamphlets of a new type, proliferated.

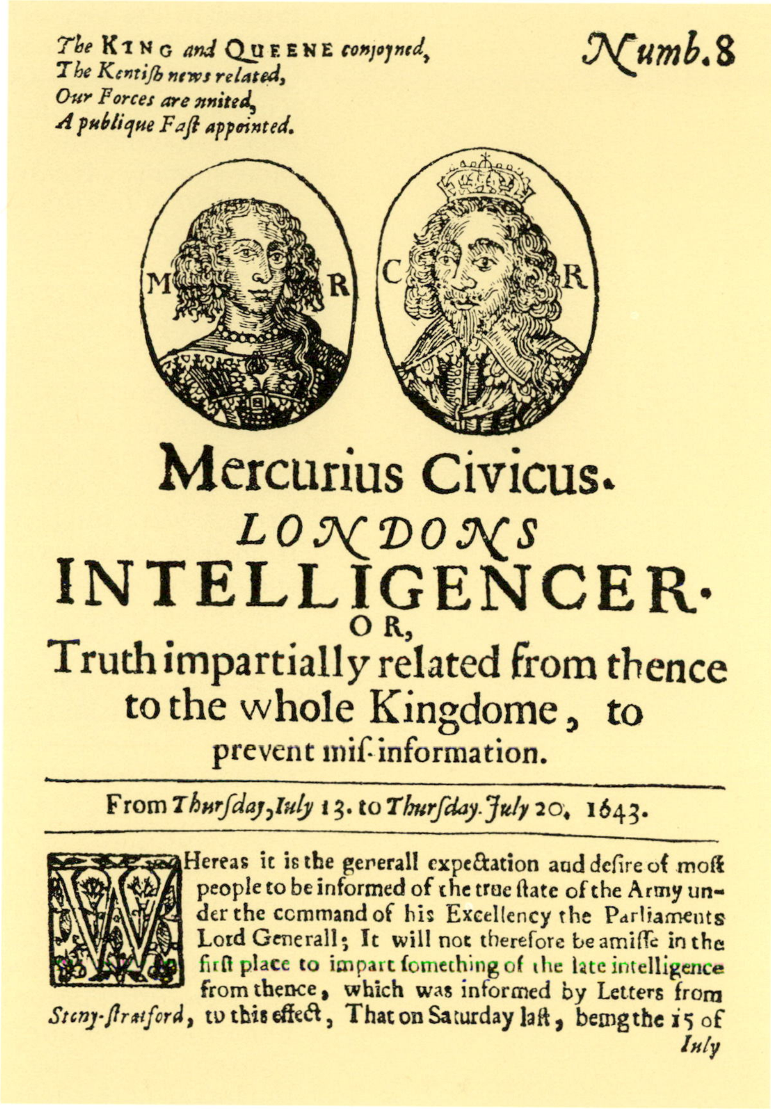

The KING *and* QUEENE *conjoyned,*
The Kentish news related,
Our Forces are united,
A publique Fast appointed.

Numb. 8

M R

C R

Mercurius Civicus.

LONDONS

INTELLIGENCER.

OR,

Truth impartially related from thence to the whole Kingdome, to prevent mis-information.

From *Thursday, July* 13. to *Thursday. July* 20. 1643.

WHereas it is the generall expectation and desire of most people to be informed of the true state of the Army under the command of his Excellency the Parliaments Lord Generall; It will not therefore be amisse in the first place to impart something of the late intelligence from thence, which was informed by Letters from *Stony-Stratford*, to this effect, That on Saturday last, being the 15 of *July*

◀ A Civil War *Diurnall*, the weekly publication reporting the daily proceedings of Parliament, with woodcut illustration.

In addition to the Royal effigies this 1643 news-pamphlet for the first time introduced the significant title-word *Intelligencer*. ▶

New titles came into vogue for these new publications, reflecting their new-found preoccupation with domestic news. This meant news of proceedings in Parliament and (as the war progressed and the New Model emerged) those of the Army. Thus we have the *Diurnalls* – not, as the word might suggest, daily issues, but weekly reports of daily affairs in Parliament – *Passages* – of Parliamentary proceedings – and *Mercuries*. The Royalist *Mercurius Aulicus* (the Court Mercury) was matched by the Cromwellian *Mercurius Britannicus*. A new title-word was introduced in *Mercurius Civicus: London's Intelligencer* (1643), the INTELLIGENCER, set in roman capitals to the full measure, being the most prominent line in the title-piece. This *Intelligencer* struck a novel note by printing woodcut illustrations (of the King and Queen) on its front page; that same year the outstanding *Perfect Diurnall* edited by Samuel Pecke livened its front page with an elaborate woodcut headpiece representing the Commons in session, and introduced its lead item with a two-inch square decorative initial.

One important feature was common to all the civil war news-pamphlets; they abandoned the book-style title-page, reduced the depth of the title-matter and got as much of their principal news as they could on to the front page. It is an important sign of growth away from the news-book to the newspaper. There were other signs of this trend. A new *Perfect Diurnal* of 1643 used italic shoulder-lines over its different items, a modest beginning of something like headlining. In 1644 the *Perfect Occurrences of Parliament*, with a format substantially larger than the usual news-pamphlet quarto, ran a whole series of summary points, in italic, immediately under its title. Separated by full points, these amounted to headlines strung together in summary form, enabling the reader to see at a glance the pieces of news contained in the issue. Thus, for example, 'The King's speech to Capt Blythe', 'The Queen sick again in France', 'A great victory at Pomfret Castle', 'The Lord General relieved by sea, and his beating of the King's forces at Blazey Bridge', 'A Dam made to hinder the enemy from relieving their forces at Lestitheel (Lostwithiel) Castle'. The same summary technique was used in the *London Post*, *True Informer* and *Weekly Intelligencer*.[3]

This study is concerned with form, not content; but it is impossible not to note the lead story in *A Perfect Diurnall of Some Passages in Parliament and the Daily Proceedings of the Army* (1649) which opened: 'Tuesday, January 30. This day the King was beheaded, over against the Banquetting house by Whitehall.' There followed a piece of news-reporting as tight as it was vivid; a quite remarkable journalistic *tour de force*.[4] Here, further, it may not be out of place to remark the efforts made in London during this whole period to 'impart beyond seas the certain condition of affairs here'. News-pamphlets in French were published for this purpose. The *Mercure Anglois* ran from 1644–48 and was succeeded under the Commonwealth (1650) by the *Nouvelles Ordinaires de Londres*, which was so successful that it continued under the Restoration; its last known issue was No. 567 of 1663.

At this point, with the news-pamphlets breaking out of their bookish framework and beginning to foreshadow the coming newspaper, it may be convenient to review the different titles that had established themselves for news-publications. Many of these, indeed, have continued unchanged as titles up to the present day and show every sign of so continuing into the far future. The plain descriptive word *News* had clearly come to stay. Titles that suggested the keen ferreting out and transmission of news, like *Intelligencer*, *Spy*, *Scout*, were shorter lived (though the first two were to reappear prominently in the United States in its early days and the later *Observer* or *Argus* were of the same genre). *Coranto* (*Corante* or even *Currant*), implying continuous handling of running or current news survived with a change to *Courant*. *Mercurius*, anglicised to *Mercury* was another permanency; the image of the fleet-footed messenger of the gods usefully combined the concepts of speed (as, later, in *Dispatch* or *Express*) and the bearing of tidings (as in *Herald* or *Messenger*). *Post* was a civil war innovation which, in varying combinations, became one of the commonest title-words (the variant *Mail* was to come).

Gazette, about to become the title of the first English newspaper, and to start a wide career in Britain and America, is a fascinating word whose derivation has been variously debated. There is no doubt of its Italian origin in the word *gazzetta*; most dictionaries say that this is the Venetian word *gazeta*, a small coin that was the sum demanded for the official *Notizie Scritte* first issued in Venice in the mid-sixteenth century.*

Of the other titles yet to emerge we may note here just one, but that one to attain particular fame, the *Times*. The German word for newspaper, *zeitung*, whose use can be traced back to the beginning of the sixteenth century, has surely that connotation (*zeit*=time, epoch). I do not know why Morison equated *zeitung* with *tidings*, since in normal German usage that word would be rendered *nachrichten*. *Zeitung* was well established as a title for German news-publications by the early seventeenth century, as in the *Aviso oder Zeitung* (ascribed to Augsburg) of 1609; the un-Germanic *Aviso* is interesting, recalling the secondary meaning of the French *avis* as 'information', and conveying some idea of speed (the word *aviso* is the French naval term for a fast dispatch-boat). *Tidings*, incidentally, was to be of extreme rarity in English news-titles, though common in Scandinavia (Danish *Tidende*, Swedish *Tidning*): of my own knowledge I can only recall the quaint and tiny Penzance daily, the *Cornish Evening Tidings*, whose seventy-year life ended with the outbreak of the Second World War.

* This is the derivation given in Onions, *Oxford Dictionary of English Etymology* (1966) or Italian authorities like Devoto, *Avviamento alla etimologia italiana* (1967). I confess to a romantic leaning to a derivation from *gazza*, the chattering magpie; a century ago this was cited as a possible origin of the word by Frederic Hudson, an early historian of American journalism. Morison's derivation from 'the Greek word *gaza*, meaning a treasury of news' (*Origins*, pp. 3–4) appears to have no authority whatever, though it was repeated by P. M. Handover in her official *History of the London Gazette* (HMSO, 1965), p. 9. The Liddell and Hart Lexicon gives *gaza* as 'treasure . . . large sum of money', not 'treasury or store' (Handover).

2: The Birth of the Newspaper

THE establishment of the first English newspaper was politically motivated, arising directly from the circumstances of the Restoration (1660). Two years after Charles II resumed the throne a control of news-publication as tight as in the days of the Star Chamber was introduced. To enforce this control a Surveyor of the Press was appointed, in the person of Sir Roger L'Estrange, an old Royalist hack of notable professional incompetence and brutal disposition. Typical of his ruthless exercise of his office was the railroading to the gallows – for the full horror of hanging, disembowelling and quartering – of a London printer named John Twyn, found guilty of producing unlicensed work of radical sentiment. Not surprisingly, perhaps, that arch-Royalist historian the first Earl of Clarendon thought L'Estrange 'a man of a good wit . . . and of an enterprising nature'.

In 1663 L'Estrange was granted the monopoly of news-publication, thus ending the publishing activity of Henry Muddiman, an able journalist ('a good scholar and an arch-rogue', said Pepys) who had been till then the principal news-pamphlet producer of the Restoration. Muddiman, however, was not only a publisher; he specialised in the production of manuscript news-letters, which had been popular since the sixteenth century. Since L'Estrange's monopoly specifically excluded handwritten news – to his considerable chagrin – Muddiman agreed to co-operate in the production of the monopoly *Intelligencer* and the *News*; for Muddiman this meant continued access to news-sources and the ability to circulate postally his expensive manuscript news-letters – the subscription was £5 a year, an immense sum for those days – with the L'Estrange journals.

To Joseph Williamson, the ambitious Under-Secretary of State for the Southern Department (in theory the division concerned with the Catholic Powers), this arrangement had obvious defects. He was impressed by the possibilities of a direct Government news-publication, like the official *Gazettes* of Paris and Amsterdam. To achieve this he had to circumvent the L'Estrange monopoly and attract the editorial services of Muddiman. The opportunity arose in 1665, when the Great Plague in London drove the Court and the principal Government officials to Oxford. Muddiman went to Oxford, too, and without his skilled collaboration L'Estrange's *Intelligencer* and *News* were so feeble that Williamson had his excuse. Vainly protesting, L'Estrange found himself compelled to relinquish his monopoly in return for a pension of £100; taking on Muddiman as editor, Williamson set about the launching of the *Oxford Gazette*; the first number 'Published by Authority' appeared on 16 November 1665.

The title was foreign and novel; so was the format. Gone was the book format supreme since 1622. The *Gazette* returned to the style of the early Dutch corantos; it was a substantial half-sheet, $11\frac{1}{4}$-by-$6\frac{3}{4}$-inches, printed both sides, each made up in two 17-pica columns separated by a fine rule. Instead of the pica or small pica (12pt, 11pt) text common in the news-pamphlets the body size was dropped to bourgeois (9pt), then more usual for Bible composition. Not only did the 9pt text enable more news to be accommodated; the space-consuming top-hamper of so many of the old news-pamphlets gave way to a simple three-word title right across the page, immediately followed by the 'Authority' line between transverse fine rules, with the date, or rather dates (*from . . . to*) in the italic of the 9pt text.

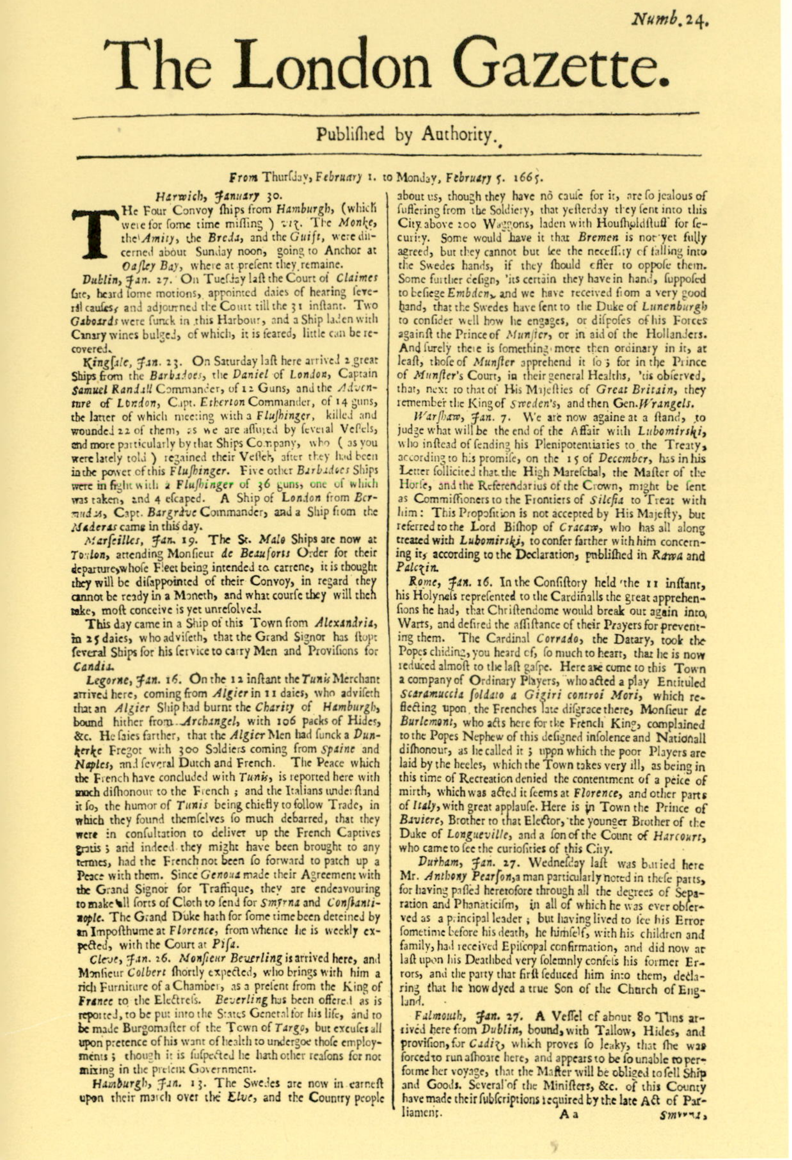

Numb. 24.

The London Gazette.

Publiſhed by Authority.

From Thurſday, February 1. to Monday, February 5. 1665.

Harwich, January 30.

THe Four Convoy ſhips from Hamburgh, (which were for ſome time miſſing) viz. The Monke, the Amity, the Breda, and the Guift, were diſcerned about Sunday noon, going to Anchor at Oaſley Bay, where at preſent they remaine.

Dublin, Jan. 27. On Tueſday laſt the Court of Claimes ſate, heard ſome motions, appointed daies of hearing ſeveral cauſes, and adjourned the Court till the 31 inſtant. Two Gaboards were ſunck in this Harbour, and a Ship laden with Canary wines bulged, of which, it is feared, little can be recovered.

Kingſale, Jan. 23. On Saturday laſt here arrived 2 great Ships from the Barbadoes, the Daniel of London, Captain Samuel Randall Commander, of 12 Guns, and the Adventure of London, Capt. Etherton Commander, of 14 guns, the latter of which meeting with a Fluſhinger, killed and wounded 22 of them, as we are aſſured by ſeveral Veſſels, and more particularly by that Ships Company, who (as you were lately told) regained their Veſſel, after they had been in the power of this Fluſhinger. Five other Barbadoes Ships were in fight with a Fluſhinger of 36 guns, one of which was taken, and 4 eſcaped. A Ship of London from Bermudas, Capt. Bargrave Commander, and a Ship from the Maderas came in this day.

Marſeilles, Jan. 19. The St. Malo Ships are now at Toulon, attending Monſieur de Beauforts Order for their departure, whoſe Fleet being intended to carrene, it is thought they will be diſappointed of their Convoy, in regard they cannot be ready in a Moneth, and what courſe they will then take, moſt conceive is yet unreſolved.

This day came in a Ship of this Town from Alexandria, in 25 daies, who adviſeth, that the Grand Signor has ſtopt ſeveral Ships for his ſervice to carry Men and Proviſions for Candia.

Legorne, Jan. 16. On the 12 inſtant the Tunis Merchant arrived here, coming from Algier in 11 daies, who adviſeth that an Algier Ship had burnt the Charity of Hamburgh, bound hither from Archangel, with 106 packs of Hides, &c. He ſaies farther, that the Algier Men had ſunck a Dunkerke Fregot with 300 Soldiers coming from Spaine and Naples, and ſeveral Dutch and French. The Peace which the French have concluded with Tunis, is reported here with much diſhonour to the French; and the Italians underſtand it ſo, the humor of Tunis being chiefly to follow Trade, in which they found themſelves ſo much debarred, that they were in conſultation to deliver up the French Captives gratis; and indeed they might have been brought to any termes, had the French not been ſo forward to patch up a Peace with them. Since Genoua made their Agreement with the Grand Signor for Traffique, they are endeavouring to make all ſorts of Cloth to ſend for Smyrna and Conſtantinople. The Grand Duke hath for ſome time been deteined by an Impoſthume at Florence, from whence he is weekly expected, with the Court at Piſa.

Cleve, Jan. 26. Monſieur Beverling is arrived here, and Monſieur Colbert ſhortly expected, who brings with him a rich Furniture of a Chamber, as a preſent from the King of France to the Electreſs. Beverling has been offered as is reported, to be put into the States General for his life, and to be made Burgomaſter of the Town of Targo, but excuſes all upon pretence of his want of health to undergoe thoſe employments; though it is ſuſpected he hath other reaſons for not mixing in the preſent Government.

Hamburgh, Jan. 13. The Swedes are now in earneſt upon their march over the Elve, and the Country people about us, though they have no cauſe for it, are ſo jealous of ſuffering from the Soldiery, that yeſterday they ſent into this City above 200 Waggons, laden with Houſholdſtuff for ſecurity. Some would have it that Bremen is not yet fully agreed, but they cannot but ſee the neceſſity of falling into the Swedes hands, if they ſhould offer to oppoſe them. Some further deſign, 'tis certain they have in hand, ſuppoſed to beſiege Embden, and we have received from a very good hand, that the Swedes have ſent to the Duke of Lunenburgh to conſider well how he engages, or diſpoſes of his Forces againſt the Prince of Munſter, or in aid of the Hollanders. And ſurely there is ſomething more then ordinary in it, at leaſt, thoſe of Munſter apprehend it ſo; for in the Prince of Munſter's Court, in their general Healths, 'tis obſerved, that, next to that of His Majeſties of Great Britain, they remember the King of Sweden's, and then Gen. Wrangels.

Warſhaw, Jan. 7. We are now againe at a ſtand, to judge what will be the end of the Affair with Lubomirski, who inſtead of ſending his Plenipotentiaries to the Treaty, according to his promiſe, on the 15 of December, has in his Letter ſollicited that the High Mareſchal, the Maſter of the Horſe, and the Referendarius of the Crown, might be ſent as Commiſſioners to the Frontiers of Sileſia to Treat with him: This Propoſition is not accepted by His Majeſty, but referred to the Lord Biſhop of Cracaw, who has all along treated with Lubomirski, to confer farther with him concerning it, according to the Declaration, publiſhed in Rawa and Palczin.

Rome, Jan. 16. In the Conſiſtory held the 11 inſtant, his Holyneſs repreſented to the Cardinalls the great apprehenſions he had, that Chriſtendome would break out again into Warrs, and deſired the aſſiſtance of their Prayers for preventing them. The Cardinal Corrado, the Datary, took the Popes chiding, you heard of, ſo much to heart, that he is now reduced almoſt to the laſt gaſpe. Here are come to this Town a company of Ordinary Players, who acted a play Entituled Scaramuccia ſoldato a Gigiri controi Mori, which reflecting upon the Frenches late diſgrace there, Monſieur de Burlemont, who acts here for the French King, complained to the Popes Nephew of this deſigned inſolence and Nationall diſhonour, as he called it; upon which the poor Players are laid by the heeles, which the Town takes very ill, as being in this time of Recreation denied the contentment of a peice of mirth, which was acted it ſeems at Florence, and other parts of Italy, with great applauſe. Here is in Town the Prince of Baviere, Brother to that Elector, the younger Brother of the Duke of Longueville, and a ſon of the Count of Harcourt, who came to ſee the curioſities of this City.

Durham, Jan. 27. Wedneſday laſt was buried here Mr. Anthony Pearſon, a man particularly noted in theſe parts, for having paſſed heretofore through all the degrees of Separation and Phanaticiſm, in all of which he was ever obſerved as a principal leader; but having lived to ſee his Error ſometime before his death, he himſelf, with his children and family, had received Epiſcopal confirmation, and did now at laſt upon his Deathbed very ſolemnly confeſs his former Errors, and the party that firſt ſeduced him into them, declaring that he now dyed a true Son of the Church of England.

Falmouth, Jan. 27. A Veſſel of about 80 Tuns arrived here from Dublin, bound, with Tallow, Hides, and proviſion, for Cadiz, which proves ſo leaky, that ſhe was forced to run aſhoare here, and appears to be ſo unable to performe her voyage, that the Maſter will be obliged to ſell Ship and Goods. Several of the Miniſters, &c. of this County have made their ſubſcriptions required by the late Act of Parliament.

A a Smyrna,

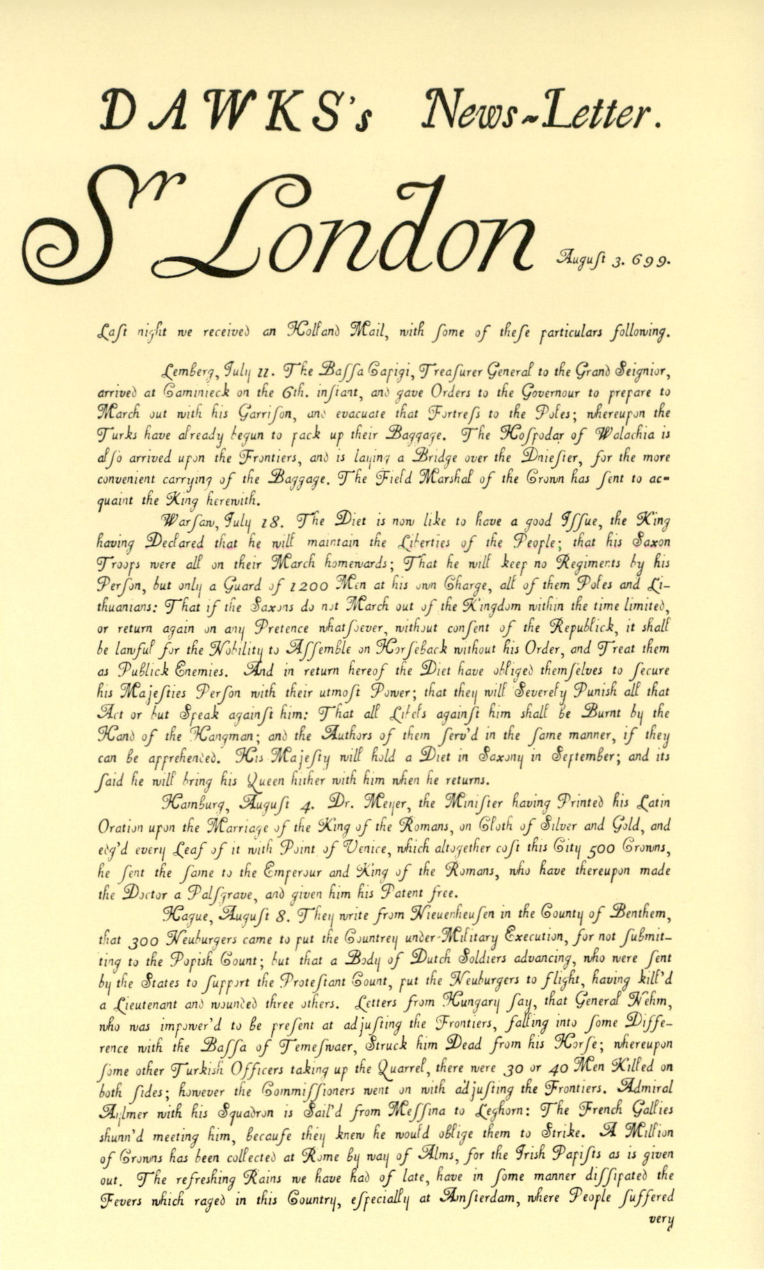

DAWKS's News-Letter.

Sr London August 3. 699.

Laſt night we received an Holland Mail, with ſome of theſe particulars following.

Lemberg, July 11. The Baſſa Capigi, Treaſurer General to the Grand Seignior, arrived at Caminieck on the 6th. inſtant, and gave Orders to the Governour to prepare to March out with his Garriſon, and evacuate that Fortreſs to the Poles; whereupon the Turks have already begun to pack up their Baggage. The Hoſpodar of Walachia is alſo arrived upon the Frontiers, and is laying a Bridge over the Dnieſter, for the more convenient carrying of the Baggage. The Field Marſhal of the Crown has ſent to acquaint the King herewith.

Warſaw, July 18. The Diet is now like to have a good Iſſue, the King having Declared that he will maintain the Liberties of the People; that his Saxon Troops were all on their March homewards; That he will keep no Regiments by his Perſon, but only a Guard of 1200 Men at his own Charge, all of them Poles and Lithuanians: That if the Saxons do not March out of the Kingdom within the time limited, or return again on any Pretence whatſoever, without conſent of the Republick, it shall be lawful for the Nobility to Aſſemble on Horſeback without his Order, and Treat them as Publick Enemies. And in return hereof the Diet have obliged themſelves to ſecure his Majeſties Perſon with their utmoſt Power; that they will Severely Puniſh all that Act or but Speak againſt him: That all Libels againſt him shall be Burnt by the Hand of the Hangman; and the Authors of them ſerv'd in the ſame manner, if they can be apprehended. His Majeſty will hold a Diet in Saxony in September; and its ſaid he will bring his Queen hither with him when he returns.

Hamburg, Auguſt 4. Dr. Meyer, the Miniſter having Printed his Latin Oration upon the Marriage of the King of the Romans, on Cloth of Silver and Gold, and edg'd every Leaf of it with Point of Venice, which altogether coſt this City 500 Crowns, he ſent the ſame to the Emperour and King of the Romans, who have thereupon made the Doctor a Palſgrave, and given him his Patent free.

Hague, Auguſt 8. They write from Nieuenheuſen in the County of Benthem, that 300 Neuburgers came to put the Countrey under Military Execution, for not ſubmitting to the Popish Count; but that a Body of Dutch Soldiers advancing, who were ſent by the States to ſupport the Proteſtant Count, put the Neuburgers to flight, having kill'd a Lieutenant and wounded three others. Letters from Hungary ſay, that General Nehm, who was impower'd to be preſent at adjuſting the Frontiers, falling into ſome Difference with the Baſſa of Temeſwaer, Struck him Dead from his Horſe; whereupon ſome other Turkish Officers taking up the Quarrel, there were 30 or 40 Men Killed on both ſides; however the Commiſſioners went on with adjuſting the Frontiers. Admiral Aylmer with his Squadron is Sail'd from Meſſina to Leghorn: The French Gallies shunn'd meeting him, becauſe they knew he would oblige them to Strike. A Million of Crowns has been collected at Rome by way of Alms, for the Irish Papiſts as is given out. The refreshing Rains we have had of late, have in ſome manner diſſipated the Fevers which raged in this Country, eſpecially at Amſterdam, where People ſuffered very

▲ First issue of the official *London Gazette*, after the removal from Oxford, where its initial twenty-three numbers appeared.

The first twenty-three numbers of the *Oxford Gazette* were printed by Leonard Lichfield, selected printer of the University since 1657 (there was not yet a University Press), each being reprinted in London by Thomas Newcomb. Apart from a small variation in the opening drop initial, from a two-line to a three-line, the most obvious difference was in the style of the title-line. Lichfield used a light roman upper- and lower-case in the size then called great canon (the French *gros canon*), approximating 44pt, and shortly to be designated double small pica, canon (the French *double canon*) becoming the description of the next size up (48pt). Lichfield's letter had a French/Dutch aspect, as did Newcomb's similarly light line for *The London Gazette* when, with its twenty-fourth number and the return of the Court to St James's early in 1666, the paper was finally domiciled in the metropolis. Newcomb's title-line for his reprints of the *Oxford Gazette*, however, was markedly heavier and I suspect was the reason why Morison said the *Gazette* title 'was, in all probability, cut by Moxon'. The great canon in Moxon's 1669 specimen, to which Morison referred, makes it plain that, despite comparable colour, the type is not the same.[1]

The *Gazette's* simplification of its title to a single line brought one typographic item into new prominence – the full point at the end of the line. This superfluous point at the end of title-lines and display headings, a curious piece of compositorial conservatism, remained until well into my lifetime; the *New York Times* did not abolish the full point after its title until 1967. A device introduced by the *Gazette* after its arrival in London in 1666, and which lived for centuries, was to emphasise the Published by Authority line by setting it in blackletter, while the days of the week in the dateline – now set in roman a size

◀ The weekly *News Letter* of Ichabod Dawks, set in the script specially cut for it, to imitate the handwritten news-letters.

larger than the text – were similarly differentiated.

Thirty years after the founding of the *Gazette* and seven years after the Revolution of 1688, the Press suddenly found itself free. In 1695 Parliament refused to renew the Restoration's Licensing Act and thus removed all obstacles, other than economic and technical, to the multiplication and expansion of newspapers (until the imposition of new restrictions in the shape of the first Stamp Duty in 1712).

The effect of the 1695 emancipation was twofold. It was a mortal blow to the manuscript news-letters. One news-writer, Frederick Leach, wrote: 'The Trade of writing News . . . being now quite out of doors, I am forced against my own inclination to appear in Print, to recover, if I can, my former customers and preserve those few I have left.' Edward Lloyd, the Lombard Street coffee-house proprietor immortalised in 'Lloyd's', tried in his *Lloyd's News* to imitate a handwritten news-letter by setting it in a large size of italic; but its look was neither that of a news-letter nor a newspaper, and it failed. Most famous of the news-writers of the time, Ichabod Dawks showed real ingenuity in his changeover from manuscript to printing. He had a fount of an unusual script type specially cut and was careful to retain the heading and presentation style of the handwritten news-letter. *Dawks's News Letter* continued to prosper for many years.

The second effect of the new freedom was the sprouting of weeklies in the provinces – of which the still extant *Berrow's Worcester Journal* and the *Stamford Mercury* are the oldest – and the starting of a whole string of thrice-weekly London papers, taking advantage of the extended postal service and all incorporating *Post* in their titles, which additionally were livened with woodcuts representing mounted post-boys trumpeting GREAT NEWS and the like. Marlborough's war brought plenty of late news and these sheets issued 'extras', called *Postscripts*, set in large type on one side of a small sheet. Otherwise they made no change in the solid, double-column text presentation, though they gained a bad reputation for exaggeration and sensationalism. In *The Tatler* (21 May 1709) Addison jeered 'They have made us masters of several strong towns many weeks before our generals could do it, and completed victories when our courageous captains have been content to come off with a drawn battle. Where Prince Eugene has slain his thousands, Boyer [publisher of the *Post Boy*] has slain his ten thousands.'

From thrice-weekly to daily is a short step; and on 11 March 1702, the first daily newspaper appeared – the *Daily Courant*. Printed on one side of a half-sheet by Edward Mallet in an office at the foot of Ludgate Hill, its double-column format was virtually identical with that of the *Gazette* thirty-seven years before. There was the full-width great canon title in lower-case, the transverse rules (enclosing the dateline instead of the Authority line) and indeed the only difference appeared in the substitution of white for the vertical column rule.

After its first nine issues the paper was taken over by Samuel Buckley, who continued it successfully until he retired in 1735 (the last known issue of the *Courant* is No. 6002 of that year). He died in 1741, aged sixty-eight, having begun his career as the first daily paper publisher when he was thirty; among his other enterprises was the printing and publishing of *The Spectator* from its start in 1711.

Under Buckley the *Courant* soon filled its second page, expanded to four pages and (from 1710) occasionally six pages. Buckley made a break with the flamboyance and exaggeration of the *Posts*; he explained the care he took with the foreign news which mainly filled the paper, 'preferring what is probable . . . to what is more surprising and unlikely or founded only on Rumour'. He related paging to news, since he did not believe in dressing the paper 'with an air of news when there can be none' (an example rarely emulated by later journalists!); and I have seen issues of the *Courant* as late as 1720 of a single sheet, the front giving the news, the back full of advertisements – another significant development.*

* By the beginning of the eighteenth century, Morison wrily remarked, 'the Press had acquired diplomatic and professional status'. He quoted, from the bill of Sir Lambert Blackwell, Ambassador to Genoa, the 1705 item of £66 to cover, *inter alia*, 'regalers to news writers', at Christmas, 'as customary' (*Origins*, p. 43).

(Numb. 1.)

The Old Post-Master.

WITH THE

Occurrences of GREAT BRITTAIN and IRELAND, and from Foreign Parts; Collected and Publiſhed.

From Saturday *June* the 20th. to Tueſday *June* the 23th. 1696.

THIS Paper is intended conſtantly to be Publiſhed Three Days in the Week, viz. Tueſdays, Thurſdays *and* Saturdays; *and to contain only matters of Fact, without Reflections on Perſons or Things: As alſo ſuch other matters as will be found Uſeful for the Trading part of Mankind, as well Merchants as Mechanicks, &c. So many News Papers (or ſo called) are daily Publiſhed, that it would ſeem needleſs to trouble the World with more; but the difference of this Paper from thoſe others Publiſhed, is with all modeſty ſubmitted to the judgment of every Judicious and Impartial Reader.*

THE Advices from His Majeſty's Camp, by the *Holland* Mail, which came in on *Saturday*, being in the Gazett and other Prints, I ſhall only add as follows, *viz.*

Paris June 21. We are extreamly ſurprized here, to hear of no action from any place, which makes News very bare; all our attention is on the ſide of *Piedmont*, being very impatient to ſee the iſſue of all our Negotiations with the Duke of *Savoy*: Couriers paſs and repaſs the Mountains continually, and that which makes us the more uneaſie, to know how the Affairs will be managed on that ſide, is, by reaſon of the Numerous Army that is kept there with ſo vaſt Expences and Charges, and great ſcarcity of Proviſions, which cannot be ſent to M. *de Catinat*'s Camp without exceſſive Coſts; but it was abſolutely neceſſary to be Superiour in Forces to the Duke of *Savoy*, to Intimidate him, and to oblige him to come to a compoſition, and in that caſe, to turn with thoſe Troops the *Spaniards* and *Germans* out of his Dominions, which was the only obſtacle lookt upon at Court, that could hinder His Royal Highneſs from accepting the Advantageous Propoſals which would be offered him for a Separate Peace.— The laſt Letters from the Army are of the 16*th*, but bring no News; they ſay only, that M. *de Catinat*, before he enters upon action, ſtays for an anſwer from the Duke of *Savoy*, about the preſſing Solicitations made him from the King and the Pope. His Majeſty ſent an Expreſs yeſterday with his laſt Reſolutions, at the inſtances of the Duke of *Orleans*, and gives that Prince time, till the end of this month to declare himſelf; and if he continues to reject the Kings offers, the M. *de Catinat* will go on, either to Bombard *Turin*, or to ruine the Plain, which he can reduce to ſuch a Deplorable Condition, that the damage will not be made good in 30 years, which would be the utter ruine of *Piedmont*; the more, by reaſon that its chief Commerce conſiſts in Silk, and that the Plain is full of Mulberry-Trees; a few days will make us wiſe, and learn its deſtiny: The mean while they write from *Turin* of the 12*th*, that M. *de Catinat* obſerves at preſent a very ſtrict diſcipline in his Army, and does not tolerate the leaſt vexation, though the Scarcity of Proviſions begins a new in his Camp; we cannot imagine the reaſon of it, they pretend that he ſtays for his Artillery; but we are perſwaded that ſuch a General as M. *de Catinat*, would cauſe his orders to be better obſerved than ſo, if there were not ſome very important reaſons that hindred it hitherto, which are unknown to us: They that come from Court aſſure, that 'tis diſcourſed there, that all the Articles of Compoſition between His Majeſty and the Duke of *Savoy*, are agreed on by his Royal Highneſs, that there remains no other difficulty, than to make good the damage ſuſtained by that Prince, which will be eaſily compoſed by the Pope's means, who labours hard to procure a Peace to *Italy*. An Expreſs is arrived from *Breſt*, diſpatched by M. *de Chateau Renaud*, to know his Majeſty's laſt reſolution concerning the Squadron of 12 Men of War, which he is to command; they ſay at Court, that he is deſigned for Cruiſing on the *Iriſh* Coaſt, to Sail thence for *Cape Finiſterre*, to paſs the *Streight*, and to joyn the *Mediterranean* Men of War and Galleys that are arming with a deſign to beſieg *Barcelona* by Sea, whilſt the Duke *de Vendome* ſhall Attack it by Land; the great quantity of Ammunition and Proviſion that are laying up in *Provence*, together with the Detachments that are to be ſent from *Catinat*'s Army, after his Expedition in *Piedmont*, for *Catalonia*; confirm the opinion of the Sieg of that Important Place, after the great heats are over. 'Tis ſaid that the Squadron of M. *Dandenne* is gone for the *Eaſt-Indies*; and that of Capt. *de Genes*, to cruiſe on the *Engliſh* and *Dutch* Colonies: and tho' ſome think that all our Naval Forces will act in ſeveral Squadrons; yet ſome are of opinion, that the Grand Fleet will put to Sea in *Auguſt* next, and that all the Privateers are to be called in, and ordered to come in Port by the end of *July*, in order to make uſe of their Equipages, as occaſion ſhall require.

We have advice from *Stockholm*, that ſeveral Conferences have been held there with Count *d' Avaux*, about Peace, of which the King of *Suedeland* would fain be the only Mediator; and that the ſame might be Negociated in that Place; but that the ſaid Count *d' Avaux* has declared, the King his Maſter not to be of that opinion; and that it will be convenient to regulate matters with *England* and the States of *Holland*, as to the quality King *William* muſt be treated with, before he enters upon any Negotiation.

Its wrote from *Collogne*, that the French have burnt *Treves*; but we hope it will need a confirmation.

Francfort June the 20*th*. The Allies on the upper *Rhine* have now finiſhed their Line, which, when their Army paſſes that River, is to be guarded by 12 or 15000 of the Militia, to ſecure the Countrey of *Wirtemberg* from a French Invaſion. The French continue to deſert in great numbers, and their Army is ſtill in the ſame

Moving towards the daily paper, this thrice-weekly was typical of many *Posts* which followed the new freedom of 1695; it is also the first example of the flying post-boy as a device.

Numb.

The Daily Courant.

Wedneſday, March 11. 1702.

From the Harlem Courant, Dated March 18. N. S.

Naples, Feb. 22.

ON Wedneſday laſt, our New Viceroy, the Duke of Eſcalona, arriv'd here with a Squadron of the Galleys of Sicily. He made his Entrance dreſt in a French habit; and to give us the greater Hopes of the King's coming hither, went to Lodge in one of the little Palaces, leaving the Royal one for his Majeſty. The Marquis of Grigni is alſo arriv'd here with a Regiment of French.

Rome, Feb. 25. In a Military Congregation of State that was held here, it was Reſolv'd to draw a Line from Aſcoli to the Borders of the Eccleſiaſtical State, thereby to hinder the Incurſions of the Tranſalpine Troops. Orders are ſent to Civita Vecchia to fit out the Galleys, and to ſtrengthen the Garriſon of that Place. Signior Caſali is made Governor of Perugia. The Marquis del Vaſto, and the Prince de Caſerta continue ſtill in the Imperial Embaſſador's Palace; where his Excellency has a Guard of 50 Men every Night in Arms. The King of Portugal has deſir'd the Arch-Biſhoprick of Lisbon, vacant by the Death of Cardinal Souſa, for the Infante his ſecond Son, who is about 11 Years old.

Vienna, Mar. 4. Orders are ſent to the 4 Regiments of Foot, the 2 of Cuiraſſiers, and to that of Dragoons, which are broke up from Hungary, and are on their way to Italy, and which conſiſt of about 14 or 15000 Men, to haſten their March thither with all Expedition. The 6 new Regiments of Huſſars that are now raiſing, are in ſo great a forwardneſs, that they will be compleat, and in a Condition to March by the middle of May. Prince Lewis of Baden has written to Court, to excuſe himſelf from coming thither, his Preſence being ſo very neceſſary, and ſo much deſir'd on the Upper-Rhine.

Francfort, Mar. 12. The Marquiſs d' Uxelles is come to Straſburg, and is to draw together a Body of ſome Regiments of Horſe and Foot from the Gariſons of Alſace; but will not leſſen thoſe of Straſburg and Landau, which are already very weak. On the other hand, the Troops of His Imperial Majeſty, and his Allies, are going to form a Body near Germeſhein in the Palatinate, of which Place, as well as of the Lines at Spires, Prince Lewis of Baden is expected to take a View, in three or four days. The Engliſh and Dutch Miniſters, the Count of Friſe, and the Baron Vander Meer, and likewiſe the Imperial Envoy Count Lowenſtein, are gone to Nordlingen, and it is hop'd that in a ſhort time we ſhall hear from thence of ſome favourable Reſolutions for the Security of the Empire.

Liege, Mar. 14. The French have taken the Cannon de Longie, who was Secretary to the Dean de Mean, out of our Caſtle, where he has been for ſome time a Priſoner, and have deliver'd him to the Provoſt of Maubeuge, who has carry'd him from hence, but we do not know whither.

Paris, Mar. 13. Our Letters from Italy ſay, That moſt of our Reinforcements were Landed there; that the Imperial and Eccleſiaſtical Troops ſeem to live very peaceably with one another in the Country of Parma, and that the Duke of Vendome, as he was viſiting ſeveral Poſts, was within 100 Paces of falling into the Hands of the Germans. The Duke of Chartres, the Prince of Conti, and ſeveral other Princes of the Blood, are to make the Campaign in Flanders under the Duke of Burgundy; and the Duke of Maine is to Command upon the Rhine.

From the Amſterdam Courant, Dated Mar. 18.

Rome, Feb. 25. We are taking here all poſſible Precautions for the Security of the Eccleſiaſtical State in this preſent Conjuncture, and have deſir'd to raiſe 3000 Men in the Cantons of Switzerland. The Pope has appointed the Duke of Berwick to be his Lieutenant-General, and he is to Command 6000 Men on the Frontiers of Naples: He has alſo ſettled upon him a Penſion of 6000 Crowns a year during Life.

From the Paris Gazette, Dated Mar. 18. 1702.

Naples, Febr. 17. 600 French Soldiers are arrived here, and are expected to be follow'd by 3400 more. A Courier that came hither on the 14th. has brought Letters by which we are aſſur'd that the King of Spain deſigns to be here towards the end of March; and accordingly Orders are given to make the neceſſary Preparations againſt his Arrival. The two Troops of Horſe that were Commanded to the Abruzzo are poſted at Peſcara with a Body of Spaniſh Foot, and others in the Fort of Montorio.

Paris, March. 18. We have Advice from Toulon of the 5th inſtant, that the Wind having long ſtood favourable, 22000 Men were already ſail'd for Italy, that 2500 more were Embarking, and that by the 15th it was hoped they might all get thither. The Count d' Eſtrees arriv'd there on the Third inſtant, and ſet all hands at work to fit out the Squadron of 9 Men of War and ſome Fregats, that are appointed to carry the King of Spain to Naples. His Catholick Majeſty will go on Board the *Thunderer*, of 110 Guns.

We have Advice by an Expreſs from Rome of the 18th of February, That notwithſtanding the preſſing Inſtances of the Imperial Embaſſadour, the Pope had Condemn'd the Marquis del Vaſto to loſe his Head and his Eſtate to be confiſcated, for not appearing to Anſwer the Charge againſt him of Publickly Scandalizing Cardinal Janſon.

ADVERTISEMENT.

IT will be found from the Foreign Prints, which from time to time, as Occaſion offers, will be mention'd in this Paper, that the Author has taken Care to be duly furniſh'd with all that comes from Abroad in any Language. And for an Aſſurance that he will not, under Pretence of having Private Intelligence, impoſe any Additions of feign'd Circumſtances to an Action, but give his Extracts fairly and Impartially; at the beginning of each Article he will quote the Foreign Paper from whence 'tis taken, that the Publick, ſeeing from what Country a piece of News comes with the Allowance of that Government, may be better able to Judge of the Credibility and Fairneſs of the Relation: Nor will he take upon him to give any Comments or Conjectures of his own, but will relate only Matter of Fact; ſuppoſing other People to have Senſe enough to make Reflections for themſelves.

This Courant (as the Title ſhews) will be Publiſh'd Daily: being deſign'd to give all the Material News as ſoon as every Poſt arrives: and is confin'd to half the Compaſs, to ſave the Publick at leaſt half the Impertinences, of ordinary News-Papers.

LONDON. Sold by *E. Mallet*, next Door to the *King's-Arms* Tavern at *Fleet-Bridge*.

Front page of the first daily newspaper.

Henceforth attention concentrates on the development of the daily newspaper, at least so far as Britain is concerned, though the Sunday papers will later be seen to be a special case calling for separate consideration. This is not to say that the weekly journals lack typographic interest, as readers of chapters V and VI in Morison's *The English Newspaper* will readily perceive; following the early *Posts* the weeklies of the first third of the eighteenth century developed highly decorative title-pieces and began to turn to three-column make-up.

The pioneer of three-column make-up appears to have been the *Daily Journal* (1720) but a more famous exponent was the *Daily Advertiser* (1730), which was to survive until 1807. The importance of the paper's title was obvious, reflecting the country's rapid economic expansion and the role that advertising was to play in the contents of a newspaper. Henceforth the advertising concept was to be more and more featured in newspaper titles; when the *Morning Post* was founded in 1772 it had the sub-title *And Daily Advertising Pamphlet* (an attempt, rapidly proved vain, to circumvent the Stamp Acts), later changed to *Daily Advertiser*. The *Daily Advertiser* itself began on

3 February 1730 as an advertising sheet only, initially 'given gratis to all Coffee Houses' as a promotion measure. In three weeks, however, its No. 21 included news and trade figures, 'the best and freshest accounts of all occurrences both foreign and domestick', with which it made up its front page. Foreign news came first, each item label-headed with the name of the country in letter-spaced capitals, the following home news was simply headed LONDON.

The *Daily Advertiser* printed and published throughout its seventy-seven-year career by the Jenour family (in Fleet Street, opposite St Dunstan's), adhered to the title-style of its predecessor the *Courant*, namely a simple line in roman upper- and lower-case across the page. Blackletter, apart from its early outcrop in the *Posts* and later occasionally in some weeklies, was unknown in daily paper titles until well after mid-century, when the *Public Ledger* (1769) and the *Morning Post* (1772) turned to blackletter for their main line, the sub-titles continuing in roman. The white-lined blackletter for titles so long believed to be an ancient 'tradition' came still later and will be considered in its due place.

By the time the two last-named papers appeared a further format was steadily gaining ground – the change to four columns in place of three; this was long to remain the standard. Indeed, it represented the effective size limit of the wooden hand-press, printing two folio pages

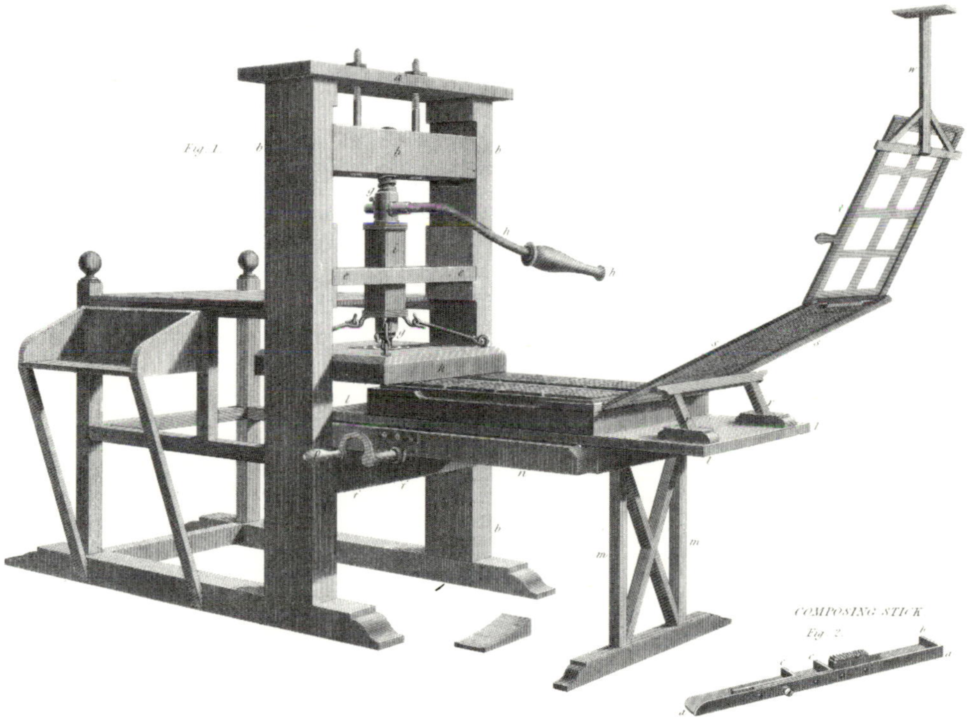

A wooden hand-press.

at a time and backing-up on another press to produce a four-pager. Column measures varied, on a four-column make-up, from 14 to 16 picas; the resultant type-area, given a depth proportionate to its width, and allowing for column rules, would be consistent with the folio of a demy ($17\frac{1}{2}$-by-$22\frac{1}{2}$-inch) or royal (20-by-25-inch) sheet. The maximum sheet accommodated by the presses of those days was double crown (20-by-30-inch) and from demy upwards two pulls were needed to make one impression, in view of the inadequate size of the platen. This suggests something of the slowness of newspaper production when the daily paper had already become well established.*

* With the wooden hand-press some half-dozen operations were needed for one pull; inking, too, was performed by dabbing the forme with a pair of leather ink-balls, a clumsy and exacting business. To get, say, 200 impressions an hour (the figure of 250 is sometimes mentioned) allowed not much more than 15 seconds a pull. Hence, when circulations first began to rise into four figures duplicate setting became necessary. A case of quadruplicate setting is recorded; in Restoration France the Paris *Constitutionnel*, a four-page crown folio, four columns a page set in 8pt, reached the then fabulous circulation of 20,000 copies a day. Printed on ten wooden hand-presses, it was set four times by four companionships each of eight compositors, including the clicker who made up the pages (Raymond Manevy, *L'Evolution des Formules de Présentation de la Presse Quotidienne*, Paris, 1956, p. 21).

By the middle of the century the London morning and evening papers (the last still a misnomer in our terms, since they did not publish every evening, but *in* the evening three times a week to catch the latest possible news of the day before the departure of the country posts) benefited from the extension of the postal services. In 1741 the main east and west posts from London – to Cambridge, King's Lynn and Norwich, to Bath, Bristol and Gloucester – were increased from three to six nights a week; and later there was a substantial development of cross-country services.

Noteworthy among the evening papers of this period was the *St James's Chronicle* (1761), which began with the four-column format. Its setting was better whited than that of its competitors and it pioneered the device – to be emulated by other papers – of using a bold treble rule to separate major items on its front page. Its elegant title incorporated a floriated G R Royal monogram; not till much later did the centring of the full Royal arms in newspaper title-pieces become customary, though one early eighteenth-century evening paper had done so, initially without the Lion and Unicorn supporters.

Enterprising, too, was the radical evening the *Middlesex Journal or, Chronicle of Liberty*, started in 1769 to back John Wilkes's Parliamentary election campaign for Middlesex. It ran a leading article in column one of its front page and used simple headlines, like COUNTRY NEWS in letter-spaced capitals over provincial items. By 1773 its political appeal had been broadened a good deal; its sub-title changed to the *Evening Advertiser*, set in roman lower-case and running on from the main title reset in blackletter in the style of the *Morning Post* (not surprisingly, since it had passed into the hands of the *Post's* publisher). Its most unusual feat began in April 1773 when it introduced a weekly, later bi-weekly, feature ('never before attempted in a newspaper') of a song 'catch, glee or minuet' set to music – 'printed in Falkner's (*sic*) new-invented Music Types . . . the best hitherto projected.' Robert Faulkener was in fact only the entrepreneur; the 'new-invented music types' were those of the Swede Henric Fougt, the third great music-type innovator of the eighteenth century after Breitkopf and Fournier. Frustrated in Stockholm, Fougt brought his material to London in 1767, obtained a fourteen-year patent for his types, and conducted a music-printing business – anglicising his name to Henry Fought – until he returned to Sweden in 1770. Faulkener had then bought his plant and types. Morison commented that 'the music type is a very remarkable fount, well cast and composed with good alignment' though he was not aware that it was Fougt's.

At this point it seems convenient to take one look back, and another forward, before proceeding to a survey of American newspaper developments. John Payne's *Universal Chronicle* (1758), in which Dr Johnson published his celebrated 'Idler' essays, was an open-looking sheet, its text judiciously leaded, with a line of printers' flowers to divide main items. Prominent in the centre of its first front page was a headline, in italics and caps and smalls – *Of the Duty of a* JOURNALIST – which opined that 'a journalist is an Historian . . . He ought therefore to consider himself as subject at least to the first law of History, the Obligation to tell Truth', though too often there were 'violations of truth admitted only to gratify idle curiosity'. Well-leaded and easy on the eye also, boldly using treble rule cut-offs, was the *Noon Gazette and Daily Spy* (1781) of which only two copies survive.

The *Noon Gazette* was an afternoon paper, published at midday 'and contains all the actual news of the Nine Morning Papers'. Of the extant copies that for 10 December 1781 was sensational for its deep full-width woodcut showing the Rock of Gibraltar under bombardment by Spanish warships. For its time this was an exceptional technical feat. The only other recorded fact from the *Noon Gazette's* obscure career is that, in common with five other leading London papers in 1781, it was savagely penalised for a paragraph held to be a libel on the Russian Ambassador. Under the monstrous libel laws of that day it was the Crown that determined whether a publication was libellous or not; the jury merely had to decide whether the accused had published it. The six printers received various sentences, of fines and im-

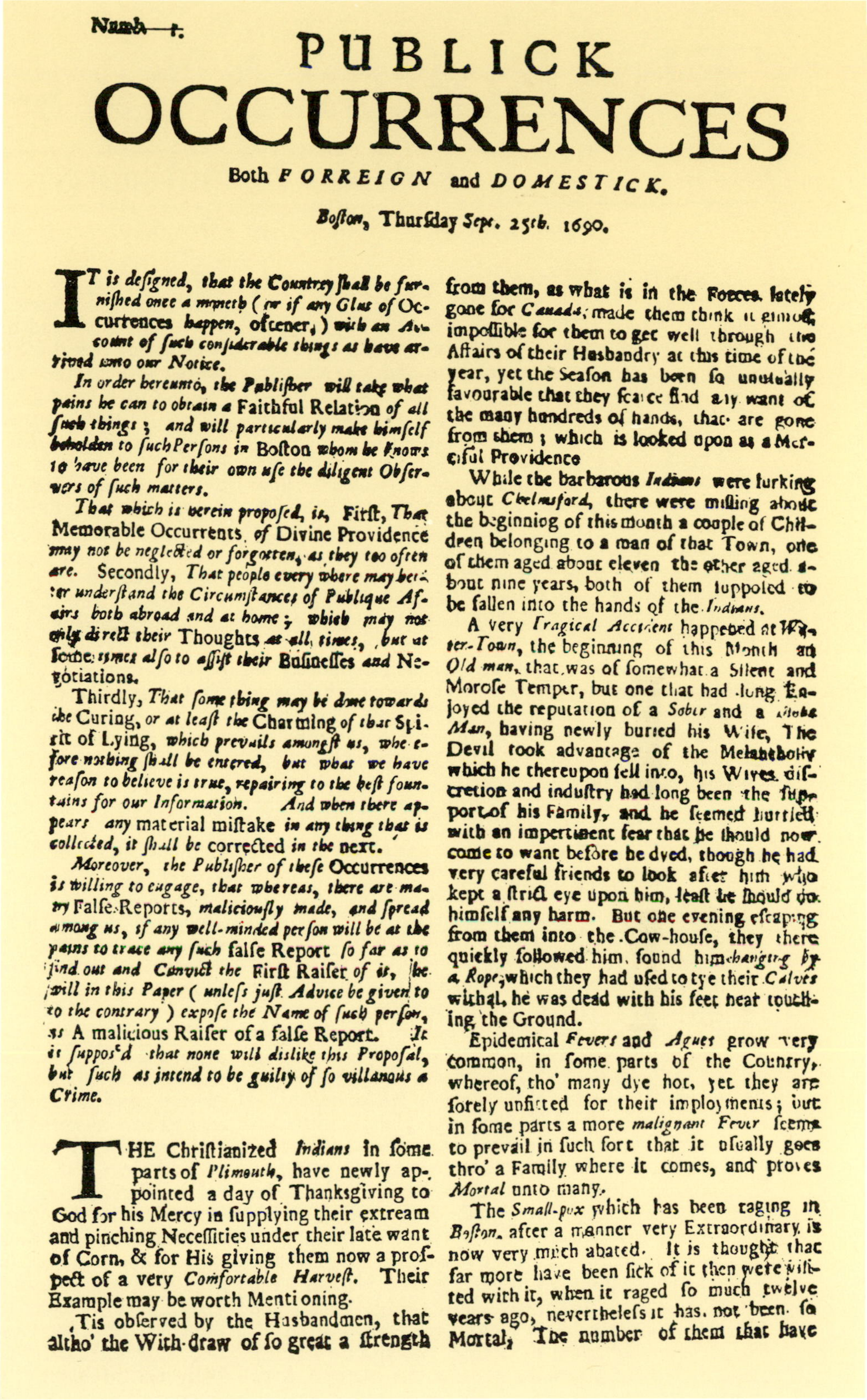

Numb. 1.

PUBLICK OCCURRENCES

Both FORREIGN and DOMESTICK.

Boston, Thursday *Sept.* 25th. 1690.

IT is designed, that the Countrey shall be furnished once a moneth (or if any Glut of Occurrences happen, oftener,) with an Account of such considerable things as have arrived unto our Notice.

In order hereunto, the Publisher will take what pains he can to obtain a Faithful Relation of all such things; and will particularly make himself beholden to such Persons in Boston whom he knows to have been for their own use the diligent Observers of such matters.

That which is herein proposed, is, First, That Memorable Occurrents of Divine Providence may not be neglected or forgotten, as they too often are. Secondly, That people every where may better understand the Circumstances of Publique Afairs, both abroad and at home; which may not only direct their Thoughts at all times, but at some times also to assist their Businesses and Negotiations.

Thirdly, That some thing may be done towards the Curing, or at least the Charming of that Spirit of Lying, which prevails amongst us, wherefore nothing shall be entered, but what we have reason to believe is true, repairing to the best fountains for our Information. And when there appears any material mistake in any thing that is collected, it shall be corrected in the next.

Moreover, the Publisher of these Occurrences is willing to engage, that whereas, there are many False Reports, maliciously made, and spread among us, if any well-minded person will be at the pains to trace any such false Report so far as to find out and Convict the First Raiser of it, he will in this Paper (unless just Advice be given to the contrary) expose the Name of such person, as A malicious Raiser of a false Report. It is suppos'd that none will dislike this Proposal, but such as intend to be guilty of so villanous a Crime.

THE Christianized *Indians* in some parts of *Plimouth*, have newly appointed a day of Thanksgiving to God for his Mercy in supplying their extream and pinching Necessities under their late want of Corn, & for His giving them now a prospect of a very *Comfortable Harvest*. Their Example may be worth Mentioning.

'Tis observed by the Husbandmen, that altho' the With-draw of so great a strength from them, as what is in the Forces lately gone for *Canada*; made them think it almost impossible for them to get well through the Affairs of their Husbandry at this time of the year, yet the Season has been so unusually favourable that they scarce find any want of the many hundreds of hands, that are gone from them; which is looked upon as a Merciful Providence

While the barbarous *Indians* were lurking about *Chelmsford*, there were missing about the beginning of this month a couple of Children belonging to a man of that Town, one of them aged about eleven the other aged about nine years, both of them supposed to be fallen into the hands of the *Indians*.

A very *Tragical Accident* happened at *Water-Town*, the beginning of this Month an *Old man*, that was of somewhat a Silent and Morose Temper, but one that had long Enjoyed the reputation of a *Sober* and a *Pious Man*, having newly buried his Wife, The Devil took advantage of the Melancholly which he thereupon fell into, his Wives discretion and industry had long been the support of his Family, and he seemed hurried with an impertinent fear that he should now come to want before he dyed, though he had very careful friends to look after him who kept a strict eye upon him, least he should do himself any harm. But one evening escaping from them into the Cow-house, they there quickly followed him, found him hanging by a Rope, which they had used to tye their *Calves* withal, he was dead with his feet near touching the Ground.

Epidemical *Fevers* and *Agues* grow very common, in some parts of the Country, whereof, tho' many dye not, yet they are sorely unfitted for their imployments; but in some parts a more *malignant Fever* seems to prevail in such sort that it usually goes thro' a Family where it comes, and proves *Mortal* unto many.

The *Small-pox* which has been raging in *Boston*, after a manner very Extraordinary is now very much abated. It is thought that far more have been sick of it then were visited with it, when it raged so much twelve years ago, nevertheless it has not been so Mortal, The number of them that have

The first American newspaper, instantly suppressed by Governor Winthrop of the Colony of Massachusetts.

prisonment; the *Noon Gazette* man went down for eighteen months and was fined £200.

The early American newspapers naturally followed the style of their English contemporaries. Their printers and publishers were English immigrants, or the descendants of English immigrants, and thought of themselves as English. Their type and materials were imported from London (there was no American typefoundry until the very end of the eighteenth century). Repressive English laws against the Press were not operated any more gently by colonial Governors. Thus the first of the many, the *Publick Occurrences* of Boston, never survived its first issue of 25 September 1690. It was instantly sup-

N. E. Numb. 17

The Boston News-Letter.

Published by Authority.

From Monday April 17. to Monday April 24. 1704.

London Flying-Post from *Decemb.* 2*d.* to 4*th.* 1703.

Letters from *Scotland* bring us the Copy of a Sheet lately Printed there, Intituled, *A seasonable Alarm for* Scotland. *In a Letter from a Gentleman in the City, to his Friend in the Country, concerning the present Danger of the Kingdom and of the Protestant Religion.*

This Letter takes Notice, That Papists swarm in that Nation, that they traffick more avowedly than formerly, and that of late many Scores of Priests & Jesuites are come thither from France, and gone to the North, to the Highlands & other places of the Country. That the Ministers of the Highlands and North gave in large Lists of them to the Committee of the General Assembly, to be laid before the Privy-Council.

It likewise observes, that a great Number of other ill-affected persons are come over from *France*, under pretence of accepting her Majesty's Gracious Indemnity; but, in reality, to increase Divisions in the Nation, and to entertain a Correspondence with *France*: That their ill Intentions are evident from their talking big, their owning the Interest of the pretended King *James* VIII. their secret Cabals, and their buying up of Arms and Ammunition, wherever they can find them.

To this he adds the late Writinge and Actings of some disaffected persons, many of whom are for that Pretender: that several of them have declar'd they had rather embrace Popery than conform to the present Government; that they refuse to pray for the Queen, but use the ambiguous word Soveraign, and some of them pray in express Words for the King and Royal Family; and the charitable and generous Prince who has shew'd them so much Kindness. He likewise takes notice of Letters, not long ago found in Cypher, & directed to a Person lately come thither from St. *Germains*.

He says that the greatest Jacobites, who will not qualifie themselves by taking the Oaths to Her Majesty, do now with the Papists and their Companions from St. *Germains* set up for the Liberty of the Subject, contrary to their own Principles, but meerly to keep up a Division in the Nation. He adds, that they aggravate those things which the People complain of, as to *England's* refusing to allow them a freedom of Trade, *&c.* and do all they can to foment Divisions betwixt the Nations, & to obstruct a Redress of those things complain'd of.

The Jacobites, he says, do all they can to perswade the Nation that their pretended King is a Protestant in his Heart, tho' he dares not declare it while under the Power of *France*; that he is acquainted with the Mistakes of his Father's Government, will govern us more according to Law, and endear himself to his Subjects.

They magnifie the Strength of their own Party, and the Weakness and Divisions of the other, in order to facilitate and hasten their Undertaking; they argue themselves out of their Fears, and into the highest assurance of accomplishing their purpose.

From all this he infers, That they have hopes of Assistance from *France*, otherwise they would never be so impudent; and he gives Reasons for his Apprehensions that the *French* King may send Troops thither this Winter, 1. Because the *English* & *Dutch* will not then be at Sea to oppose them. 2. He can then best spare them, the Season of Action beyond Sea being over. 3. The Expectation given him of a considerable number to joyn them, may incourage him to the undertaking with fewer Men, if he can but send over a sufficient number of Officers with Arms and Ammunition.

He endeavours in the rest of his Letters to answer the foolish Pretences of the Pretender's being a Protestant and that he will govern us according to Law. He says, that being bred up in the Religion and Politicks of *France*, he is by Education a stated Enemy to our Liberty and Religion. That the Obligations which he and his Family owe to the *French* King must necessarily make him to be wholly at his Devotion, and to follow his Example; that if he sit upon the Throne, the three Nations must be oblig'd to pay the Debt which he owes the *French* King for the Education of himself, and for Entertaining his supposed Father and his Family. And since the King must restore him by his Troops, if ever he be restored, he will see to secure his own Debt, before those Troops leave *Britain*. The Pretender being a good Proficient in the *French* and *Romish* Schools, he will never think himself sufficiently aveng'd, but by the utter Ruine of his Protestant Subjects, both as Hereticks and Traitors. The late Queen, his pretended Mother, who in cold Blood when she was Queen of *Britain*, advis'd to turn the West of *Scotland* into a hunting Field, will be then for doing so by the greatest part of the Nation; and, no doubt, is at Pains to have her pretended Son educated to her own Mind: Therefore, he says, it were a great Madness in the Nation to take a Prince bred up in the horrid School of Ingratitude, Persecution and Cruelty, and filled with Rage and Envy. The *Jacobites*, he says, both in *Scotland* and at St. *Germains*, are impatient under their present Straits, and knowing their Circumstances cannot be much worse than they are, at present, are the more inclinable to the Undertaking. He adds, That the *French* King knows there cannot be a more effectual way for himself to arrive at the Universal Monarchy, and to ruine the Protestant Interest, than by setting up the Pretender upon the Throne of Great *Britain*, he will in all probability attempt it; and tho' he should be perswaded that the Design would miscarry in the close, yet he cannot but reap some Advantage by imbroiling the three Nations.

From all this the Author concludes it to be the Interest of the Nation, to provide for Self-defence; and says, that as many have already taken the Alarm, and are furnishing themselves with Arms and Ammunition, he hopes the Government will not only allow it, but encourage it, since the Nation ought all to appear as one Man in the Defence pressed by Governor Winthrop of Massachusetts under the Press-licensing laws and the only copy extant is in the Public Record Office in London. The colonial regime objected to the paper's criticism of the conduct of the war against the Mohawks and its exposure of the atrocities perpetrated on French-Canadian prisoners by the Indian allies of the colonial forces.

For its day the *Occurrences* was not undistinguished in its typography. The title-lines were set in a well-cut, well-aligned fount of roman capitals, neatly graded in the equivalent of 24pt and 36pt; the italic sub-title and the dateline were decently whited away from the title and the matter. This was set in 12pt made up in the customary two columns (of 17-pica measure) separated by a pica white instead of a column rule. Large drop letters opened the publisher's italic manifesto or introductory address – the type badly worn – and the start of the news items towards the foot of the first column. These then ran steadily and disparately on, in the fashion of the times, until they had filled three of the paper's four small folio pages, the fourth being blank.

The publisher of the abortive *Occurrences*, Benjamin Harris, was a considerable character. Harris was a London bookseller and newspaper publisher of strong Whig and anti-Popish leanings who had been pilloried and jailed for two years in 1680 for publishing a 'seditious libel' (under the outrageous procedure already described, whereby the jury could not adjudicate on the libel but only on the fact of publication). When, after his release and resumption of his publishing activity, he was subject to further persecution – a warrant for his arrest was issued in 1686, the year after the accession of the ultra-reactionary James II – he took ship for New England. He did well in Boston, where he opened 'The London Coffee, Tea and Chaucaletto Shop', to which a year later he added a printing office. Despite the suppression of his newspaper his business flourished. In 1692 he was named Public Printer to 'Their Majesties' Province of Massachusetts-Bay in New England'. He appears, however, to have regarded America as only a temporary refuge; when 1695 brought Press freedom in England, as mentioned above, he returned to London to publish the *London Post*, one of the thrice-weekly *Posts* that then sprang up and that we have already discussed.

For nearly fourteen years no further attempt was made to launch a newspaper in America. Then an official personage, Postmaster John Campbell of Boston, first assuring himself of official approval, launched the *Boston News-Letter* in April 1704. For some time Campbell had been plying the trade of news-writer; his manuscript news-letters were circulated to all the colonial Governors, including the Governor Winthrop who had suppressed Harris's paper. Thus it was reasonable both for him to turn to printing and to choose the title he did. Campbell made no bones about the fact that his paper was subject to preliminary censorship; in the issue for the week ending 9 April 1705 he explained that he was accustomed to 'waiting on His Excellency or Secretary for approbation of what is Collected'.

No wonder the early *News-Letter* looked like a facsimile of the *London Gazette*. There was the full-width title in roman upper- and lower-case, the 'Published by Authority' line between transverse rule, in blackletter, also used for emphasising the days of the week in the dateline. Like the *Gazette*, too, was the solid two-column make-up, set in 11pt to 19-pica measure and filling two sides of a folio sheet. As in London, foreign news came first though shipping news understandably found a considerable place; the departure of the 60-ton *Adventure* for London was announced, as was the arrival of a vessel, taken prize in the Caribbean, and 'loaden with Cocco'.

Though two years junior to London's first daily, Campbell's *News-Letter* remained a weekly throughout its long life; for many years there were no American dailies. His ultimate successors made the fatal error of espousing the British colonialist side when the Revolu-

◀ America's second newspaper, but the first to last, published by Boston Postmaster John Campbell.

THE [No 80

New-England Courant.

From MONDAY February 4. to MONDAY February 11. 1 7 2 3.

The late Publiſher of this Paper, finding ſo many Inconveniencies would ariſe by his carrying the Manuſcripts and publick News to be ſuperviſ'd by the Secretary, as to render his carrying it on unprofitable, has intirely dropt the Undertaking. The preſent Publiſher having receiv'd the following Piece, deſires the Readers to accept of it as a Preface to what they may hereafter meet with in this Paper.

Non ego mordaci diſtrinxi Carmine quenquam,
Nulla venenato Litera mixta Joco eſt.

LONG has the Preſs groaned in bringing forth an hateful, but numerous Brood of Party Pamphlets, malicious Scribbles, and Billingſgate Ribaldry. The Rancour and bitterneſs it has unhappily infuſed into Mens minds, and to what a Degree it has ſowred and leaven'd the Tempers of Perſons formerly eſteemed ſome of the moſt ſweet and affable, is too well known here, to need any further Proof or Repreſentation of the Matter.

No generous and impartial Perſon then can blame the preſent Undertaking, which is deſigned purely for the Diverſion and Merriment of the Reader. Pieces of Pleaſancy and Mirth have a ſecret Charm in them to allay the Heats and Tumors of our Spirits, and to make a Man forget his reſtleſs Reſentments. They have a ſtrange Power to tune the harſh Diſorders of the Soul, and reduce us to a ſerene and placid State of Mind.

The main Deſign of this Weekly Paper will be to entertain the Town with the moſt comical and diverting Incidents of Humane Life, which in ſo large a Place as *Boſton*, will not fail of a univerſal Exemplification: Nor ſhall we be wanting to fill up theſe Papers with a grateful Interſperſion of more ſerious Morals, which may be drawn from the moſt ludicrous and odd Parts of Life.

As for the Author, that is the next Queſtion. But tho' we profeſs our ſelves ready to oblige the ingenious and courteous Reader with moſt Sorts of Intelligence, yet here we beg a Reſerve. Nor will it be of any Manner of Advantage either to them or to the Writers, that their Names ſhould be publiſhed; and therefore in this Matter we deſire the Favour of you to ſuffer us to hold our Tongues: Which tho' at this Time of Day it may ſound like a very uncommon Requeſt, yet it proceeds from the very Hearts of your Humble Servants.

By this Time the Reader perceives that more than one are engaged in the preſent Undertaking. Yet is there one Perſon, an Inhabitant of this Town of *Boſton*, whom we honour as a Doctor in the Chair, or a perpetual Dictator.

The Society had deſign'd to preſent the Publick with his Effigies, but that the Limner, to whom he was preſented for a Draught of his Countenance, deſcryed (and this he is ready to offer upon Oath) Nineteen Features in his Face, more than ever he beheld in any Humane Viſage before; which ſo raiſed the Price of his Picture, that our Maſter himſelf forbid the Extravagance of coming up to it. And then beſides, the Limner objected a Schiſm in his Face, which ſplits it from his Forehead in a ſtrait Line down to his Chin, in ſuch ſort, that Mr. Painter proteſts it is a double Face, and he'll have *Four Pounds* for the Pourtraiture. However, tho' this double Face has ſpoilt us of a pretty Picture, yet we all rejoiced to ſee old *Janus* in our Company.

There is no Man in *Boſton* better qualified than old *Janus* for a *Couranteer*, or if you pleaſe, an *Obſervator*, being a Man of ſuch remarkable *Opticks*, as to look two ways at once.

As for his Morals, he is a chearly Chiſtian, as the Country Phraſe expreſſes it. A Man of good Temper, courteous Deportment, ſound Judgment; a mortal Hater of Nonſenſe, Foppery, Formality, and endleſs Ceremony.

As for his Club, they aim at no greater Happineſs or Honour, than the Publick be made to know, that it is the utmoſt of their Ambition to attend upon and do all imaginable good Offices to good Old *Janus* the Couranteer, who is and always will be the Readers humble Servant.

P. S. Gentle Readers, we deſign never to let a Paper paſs without a Latin Motto if we can poſſibly pick one up, which carries a Charm in it to the Vulgar, and the learned admire the pleaſure of Conſtruing. We ſhould have obliged the World with a Greek ſcrap or two, but the Printer has no Types, and therefore we intreat the candid Reader not to impute the defect to our Ignorance, for our Doctor can ſay all the *Greek* Letters by heart.

His Majeſty's Speech to the Parliament, October 11. tho' already publiſh'd, may perhaps be new to many of our Country Readers; we ſhall therefore inſert it in this Day's Paper.

His MAJESTY's moſt Gracious SPEECH to both Houſes of Parliament, on Thursday *October* 11. 1722.

My Lords and Gentlemen,

I Am ſorry to find my ſelf obliged, at the Opening of this Parliament, to acquaint you, That a dangerous Conſpiracy has been for ſome time formed, and is ſtill carrying on againſt my Perſon and Government, in Favour of a Popiſh Pretender.

The Diſcoveries I have made here, the Informations I have received from my Miniſters abroad, and the Intelligences I have had from the Powers in Alliance with me, and indeed from moſt parts of Europe, have given me moſt ample and current Proofs of this wicked Deſign.

The Conſpirators have, by their Emiſſaries, made the ſtrongeſt Inſtances for Aſſiſtance from Foreign Powers, but were diſappointed in their Expectations: However, confiding in their Numbers, and not diſcouraged by their former ill Succeſs, they reſolved once more, upon their own ſtrength, to attempt the ſubverſion of my Government.

To this End they provided conſiderable Sums of Money, engaged great Numbers of Officers from abroad, ſecured large Quantities of Arms and Ammunition, and thought themſelves in ſuch Readineſs, that had not the Conſpiracy been timely diſcovered, we ſhould, without doubt, before now have ſeen the whole Nation, and particularly the City of London, involved in Blood and Confuſion.

The Care I have taken has, by the Bleſſing of God, hitherto prevented the Execution of their trayterous Projects. The Troops have been incamped all this Summer; ſix Regiments (though very neceſſary for the Security of that Kingdom) have been brought over from *Ireland*; The States General have given me aſſurances that they would keep a conſiderable Body of Forces in readineſs to embark on the firſt Notice tionary War began, even going so far as to conduct a smear campaign against George Washington on the grounds of his 'immorality'. The paper died in 1776, the year of the Declaration of Independence. During his years of control (he sold the *News-Letter* in 1721) Campbell showed no interest in unusual graphic presentation, with the exception of one issue in January 1708 when he ran a woodcut of the new flag arising from the Act of Union between England and Scotland.

Campbell was a most meticulous editor and an ingenious businessman. Under the first head it may suffice to cite one of his corrections following a report of a local fire ('Whereas it said Flame covering the Barn, it should be said Smoak'). Of the second his concern to attract advertising gave ample testimony. He did this in his first issue, with the novel suggestion that advertisers could negotiate the appropriate rate for their announcement (apart from the usual buying and selling, 'runaway servants' was a category indicated) between the lower and upper limits of twelve pence and five shillings. The subscription rate for the *News-Letter* was likewise negotiable.

As America's newspaper Press grew, advertising flooded in at least as much as, if not more than, in the London papers. In a developing country this was not surprising. As early as 1743 John Peter Zenger's *New York Journal* carried the first double-column advertisement. Nine years before, Zenger was the central figure (in 1734) in a seditious libel *cause célèbre* which both sharpened the struggle for Press freedom in America and fanned the colonists' resentment against the automatic and arbitrary operation of English repressive laws and English imposts.

This spirit of independence was most marked in the newspaper printing and publishing enterprises of the Brothers Franklin. James, the elder, to whom the more famous Benjamin was apprenticed, launched his *New England Courant* in August 1721. He proclaimed his intention to compete with the 'dull' and official *News-Letter*. He made himself suspect by opposing the still strict Puritan domination in Massachusetts; he campaigned against smallpox vaccination; but most of all he fell foul of the authorities through his criticism of Government shortcomings. This soon earned him a prison sentence, during which the paper was edited and printed by apprentice Benjamin, then only sixteen. 'Private differences' between the brothers led to Benjamin leaving Boston for Philadelphia in 1723 where, in his early twenties, he became a newspaper publisher in his own right. The *Pennsylvania Gazette* developed into a real power in the largest and

◀ Competition in Boston: the *Courant* founded by James Franklin, elder brother of Benjamin.

▼ Benjamin Franklin's Philadelphia weekly, founded 1728, which became a real power in colonial America's most important city.

May 9, 1754. NUMB. 1324.

The PENNSYLVANIA GAZETTE.

Containing the Freſheſt Advices, Foreign and Domeſtick.

The SPEECH of his Excellency *WILLIAM SHIRLEY*, Eſq; To the Great and General Court or Aſſembly of the Province of the *Maſſachuſetts Bay*, in *New-England*, *March* 28. 1754.

Gentlemen of the Council, and Houſe of Repreſentatives,

HAVING received in the Receſs of the Court ſome Diſpatches, which nearly concern the Welfare of the Province: I thought it neceſſary to require a general Attendance of the Members of both Houſes at this Meeting of the Aſſembly, that the Matters contain'd in them may have as full and ſpeedy a Conſideration, as the Importance of them ſeems to demand.

By Accounts ſent from *Richmond* Fort, and Declarations made before me and His Majeſty's Council, by two of the Settlers at *Frankfort*, upon the River *Kennebeck*, I am inform'd, that in the Summer before laſt a conſiderable Number of *French* ſettled themſelves on a noted Carrying-Place, made Uſe of by the ſeveral *Indian* Tribes inhabiting that Part of the Country, in their Paſſage to and from *Canada*, which ſeparates the Head of the aforeſaid River from that of the River *Chaudiere*, which laſt falls into the great River St. *Lawrence*, at Four Miles and a Half above the City of *Quebeck*.

And I have received further Intelligence, that the *French* are ſettled very thick for 12 Miles on each Side of the ſaid River *Chaudiere*.

Lewis, the Tribe of St. *Francis* (or *Arreſſigunticooks*) and the *Indians* of the *Seignorie* (as the *French* call them) of *Becancour* on the one Hand, uſed to aſſemble with the *Norridgwalks* here, from their ſeveral Settlements, and the *Penobſcots* from their River, on the other: Here they held their Conſultations, and from hence iſſued out in Parties united or ſeparate, as beſt ſuited them, againſt the *Engliſh*; hither they retired after Action, and brought their Wounded for Relief; and here, if they met with Proviſions, they far'd well; if not, they ſuffer'd greatly for Want of them.

It appears further from theſe Letters, that the ſeveral *French* Miſſionaries chiefly conducted and managed this War; that they had the Care of ſupplying the *Indians* with the neceſſary Proviſions and Stores for carrying it on; were employed to make them perſevere in it, and to puſh them on to their boldeſt Enterprizes; that they tranſmitted Accounts of their Proceedings to the Government of *Canada* thro' the Hands of the Superior of the Jeſuits at *Quebeck*, thro' whom likewiſe they received *their* Directions from thence; as the Governor of *Canada* ſeems to have done *his*, upon this Occaſion, from the Court of *France*.

And I would further obſerve, that this Route affords the *French* a ſhorter Paſſage for making Deſcents from *Quebeck* upon this Province, and deſtroying the whole Province of *Maine*, with the King's

to lay before you the following Letters: One from the Right Hon. the Earl of *Holderneſſe*, one of His Majeſty's principal Secretaries of State, dated *Whitehall*, *Auguſt* 28, 1753: And another from the Right Hon. the Lords Commiſſioners for Trade and Plantations, dated *Whitehall*, *September* 18, 1753. The firſt Letter you will ſee, relates to any hoſtile Attempts or Incroachments that ſhould be made on the Limits of the King's Dominions. And the other reſpects an Interview that is to be held, the Middle of *June* next, with the Chiefs of the *Six Nations* at *Albany*.

I have alſo ordered to be communicated to you, three Letters from the Honourable Mr. *Dinwiddie*, Lieutenant Governor and Commander in Chief of His Majeſty's Territory and Dominion of *Virginia*; which gave you the Particulars of the Invaſion and Depredations made by a Body of *French* and *Indians*, on the King's Lands; and of the cruel Barbarities and Murders committed by them, on His good Subjects; and all done in Infraction of the Treaties of Peace, made between His *Britiſh* Majeſty and the *French* King.

I alſo ſend, with the other Letters mentioned, One from his Excellency Mr. *Shirley*, Governor of His Majeſty's Province of the *Maſſachuſetts Bay*, in *New-England*: Another from the Honourable Mr. *De Lancey*, Lieutenant Governor and Commander in Chief of His Majeſty's Colony of *New-York*.

THE
Boſton-
AND
COUNTRY

Gazette,
JOURNAL.

No. 779.

Containing the freſheſt Advices, Foreign and Domeſtic.

M O N D A Y, March 12, 1770.

Like a ſcurvy politician ſeem,
To ſee the things thou doſt not.
SHAKESPEARE.

A Writer, in the Boſton Chronicle, has not only been charged, in direct terms, but *proved*, by irreſiſtable demonſtration, guilty of *impertinence, abſurdity, ſophiſtry* & *falſehood*. That, all this has been done, with fair argument and good manners, the BOSTONIAN ought, with bluſhes, to concede. But ſhould that gentleman think ſuch a conceſſion too great a ſacrifice to truth and juſtice, it is then hoped, that his future publications, *tho' unanſwer'd*, will meet little attention, and leſs credit. For, ſurely, when a writer, after ſuch *charges* and ſuch *proofs*, continues to *vapour* and *froth*, in futile ſtrains and indeterminate expreſſions, devoid of reaſon or excuſe, he cannot rationally hope even the countenance of *a party*.

Such a *profound ignorance* of the laws and conſtitution of our government is diſplayed in the laſt publication, ſigned A BOSTONIAN, that it is very difficult to refrain, from expreſſions of contempt; ſuch trifling evaſion and deſpicable argument are below ſerious confutation.

"To acknowledge *allegiance* to the *King*, and deny obedience to the *laws* of *Great-Britain*, the BOSTONIAN ſays would be prepoſterous." As well might he aſſert, that an acknowledgment of DUTY to a *natural* parent was incompatible with an abſolute denial of obedience to his *unnatural* demands. But the weakneſs of what is, here, called, "prepoſterous", muſt be peculiarly evident to thoſe,who are acquainted with the ſpirit of our laws: And if fame ſays true, our BOSTONIAN ought to be *much aſhamed* of his defects, in handling this ſubject.

I would chuſe to treat every publick writer with politeneſs, but when palpable lies are aſſerted, for truth, in the face of all mankind, it is difficult to abſtain from an appearance of incivility.——The BOSTONIAN is called upon to offer the *leaſt* ſhadow of evidence, that——"the Independant would convert *every* province or iſland, *however inſignificant* ſome of them may be, into *ſeperate* and *diſtinct* ſtates:"--

It would require little leſs than a ſpirit of divination to find out, what reaſon or propriety there was in the ſtated ſuppoſition, about "the people of Main". The BOSTONIAN ſurely expoſes himſelf to very juſt ridicule! Matters of greater importance, than viewing the defects and deformities of the BOSTONIAN, demand our inſtant attention. I therefore, cloſe with the very applicable ſentiments of an author, whoſe ſtrength and life were ſpent in the ſervice of his GOD and his country.

"Few words, well conſidered; few and eaſy things, now ſeaſonably done; will ſave us. But if the people be ſo affected,as to proſtitute religion and liberty, to the vain and groundleſs apprehenſion, that nothing, but a lucrative trade can make them happy; and if trade be grown ſo craving and importunate thro' the profuſion of men, that nothing can ſupport it, but the luxurious expences of the community upon trifles or ſuperfluities, ſo as if the people ſhould generally betake themſelves to frugality, it might prove a dangerous matter, leſt tradeſmen ſhould mutiny, for want of trading; and that, therefore, we muſt forego and ſet to ſale, religion, liberty, honour, ſafety, all concernment divine or human, to keep up trading; if, laſtly, after all this light among us, the ſame reaſon ſhall paſs for current to fix our necks under illegal impoſitions, as was made uſe of, by the Jews, to return back to Egypt, becauſe they fooliſhly imagined, that they would then live in more plenty and proſperity; our condition is not ſound but rotten, both in religion and all civil prudence; and we ſhall ſoon be brought to thoſe calamities, which attend always and unavoidably on luxury, that is to ſay, all national judgments under foreign and domeſtic ſlavery.

Thus, with hazard, I have ventured, what I thought my duty, to ſpeak in ſeaſon, and to fore warn my country in time. Many circumſtances and particulars I could have added; but a few *main matters*, now put ſpeedily into execution, will ſuffice to recover us from bondage, and ſet all right.—What I have ſaid, is the language of the GOOD OLD CAUSE: If it ſeem ſtrange to any, it will not ſeem more ſtrange I hope than convincing to backſliders. Thus much I ſhould perhaps have ſaid, tho' ſure I ſhould have ſpoken, only, to trees and ſtones, and had none to hear, but with the prophet; *O earth, earth, earth!* But, I truſt, I ſhall have ſpoken perſuaſion to abundance of ſenſible and ingenuous men: to ſome,perhaps, whom GOD may raiſe of theſe ſtones, to become children of liberty: and may enable and unite in noble reſolution to give a full ſtay to the ruinous proceedings of tyranny and rapine."

AN INDEPENDANT.

At a Meeting of the Freeholders and other Inhabitants of the Town of Roxbury, legally aſſembled, on Monday the 5th Day of March, 1770, the Inhabitants taking into Conſideration a Clauſe in the Warrant for calling ſaid Meeting, viz. And to know the Minds of the Town, whether they will do any Thing to ſtrengthen the Hands of the Merchants in their Non-Importation Agreement.

V O T E D,

THAT Capt. William Heath, Col. Joſeph Williams, Mr. Eleazer Weld, Capt. Joſeph Mayo, and Doctor Thomas Williams, be a Committee to take this Matter into Conſideration, and report to the Town what they ſhall think proper to be done thereon.

The Meeting was then adjourn'd to the 8th Inſtant, Two o'Clock Afternoon; at which Time the Inhabitants being again aſſembled, the Committee made the following Report, viz.

WHEREAS the Merchants and Traders of the Town of Boſton, and almoſt all the Maritime Towns on the Continent, from a principle truly noble and generous, and to the ſacrificing of their own private Intereſts, have entred into an Agreement not to import Britiſh Goods (a few neceſſary Articles excepted) until the Act of Parliament impoſing certain Duties on Tea, Glaſs, Paper, Painters Colours, Oyl, &c. for the expreſs Purpoſe of raiſing a Revenue in America, be repealed; which Agreement, if ſtrictly adhered to, will not fail to produce the moſt ſalutary Effects. Therefore,

VOTED, That the Inhabitants of this Town do highly applaud the Conduct and Reſolution to ſaid Merchants and Traders: And we do take this Opportunity to expreſs our warmeſt Gratitude to ſaid Merchants, for the ſpirited Meaſures which they have taken. And we do hereby declare,that we will, to the utmoſt of our power, aid and aſſiſt ſaid Merchants, in every conſtitutional Way, to render ſaid Agreement effectual.

VOTED, That we do with the utmoſt Abhorrence and Deteſtation, view the little, mean and ſordid Conduct of a few Traders in this Province, who have and ſtill do import Britiſh Goods contrary to ſaid Agreement, and have thereby diſcovered that they are governed by a ſelfiſh Spirit,and are regardleſs of, and deaf to, the Miſeries and Calamities which threaten this people.

VOTED, That whereas *John Barnard, James McMaſters, Patrick McMaſters, John Mein, Nathaniel Rogers, William Jackſon, Theophilus Lillie, John Taylor*, and *Ame* & *Elizabeth Cummings*, all of Boſton; *Iſrael Williams* Eſq; & *Son* of Hatfield; & *Henry Barnes* of Marlboro', are of this Number; and do import contrary to ſaid Agreement: We do hereby declare, that we will not buy the leaſt Article of any of ſaid perſons ourſelves, or ſuffer any acting for or under us, to buy of them; neither will we buy of thoſe that ſhall buy or exchange any articles of Goods with them.

VOTED, That to the End the Generations which are yet unborn, may know who they were that laughed at the Diſtreſſes and Calamities of this people; and inſtead of ſtriving to ſave their Country when in imminent Danger, did ſtrive to render ineffectual a virtuous and commendable Plan; the Names of theſe Importers ſhall be annually read at March Meeting.

VOTED, That we will not make uſe of any Foreign Teas in our ſeveral Families, until the Revenue Acts are repealed (Caſe of Sickneſs excepted.)

VOTED, That a Committee of Inſpection be choſen, to make Enquiry from Time to Time,how far theſe votes are complied with.

VOTED, That a Copy of theſe Votes be tranſmitted to the Committee of Inſpection in the Town of Boſton.

At a Meeting of the Inhabitants of the Town of Littleton, in the County of Middleſex, on Monday March 5th, 1770, a Committee was choſen to prepare certain Votes to be paſſed by the Town relating to the Importation of Britiſh Goods, who after retiring a ſhort Time into a private Room, returned, and reported the following, which was unanimouſly Voted.

THE grievous Impoſitions the Inhabitants of the Britiſh Colonies have long ſuffered from their Mother Country, ſtrongly claim their Attention to every legal Method for their Removal.

WE eſteem the Meaſure already propoſed, viz. the withdrawing our Trade from England, both œconomical and effectual.

WE do therefore Vote,

1. THAT we will not (knowingly) directly or indirectly, purchaſe any Goods which now are or hereafter may be imported contrary to the Agreement of the Merchants of the Town of Boſton.

2. That if any Inhabitant of the Town of Littleton, ſhall be known to purchaſe any one Article of any Importer of Goods contrary to the before-mentioned Agreement, or of any one who ſhall buy of any ſuch Importer, he ſhall ſuffer our high Diſpleaſure and Contempt.

3. That a Committee be choſen to inſpect the Conduct of all Buyers and Sellers of Goods in this Town, and report the Names of all (if any ſuch there ſhould be) who ſhall violate the true Spirit and Intention of the above-mentioned Votes and Reſolutions.

4. That we will not drink or purchaſe any foreign Tea, howſoever Imported, until a general Importation of Britiſh Goods ſhall take Place.

THE Inhabitants of the Town of *Acton*, at their annual Town Meeting on the firſt Monday of March, 1770, taking into Conſideration the diſtreſſed circumſtances, that this Province and all North-America are involv'd in, by reaſon of the acts of Parliament impoſing Duties and Taxes, upon the Inhabitants of North-America, for the ſole purpoſe to raiſe a Revenue, and when the Royal Ear ſeems to be ſtopt againſt all our humble Prayers, and Petitions, for redreſs of Grievances, that this Land is involv'd in, and conſidering the ſalutary Meaſures that the Body of Merchants and Traders in this province have come into, in order for the redreſs of the many troubles that we are involv'd in, and to ſupport and maintain our Charter Rights, and Privileges, and to prevent our total Ruin and Deſtruction: Making all theſe things into ſerious Conſideration; came into the following Votes.

VOTED, That we will uſe our utmoſt Endeavours to encourage and ſupport the Body of Merchants and Traders, in their ſalutary Endeavours to retrieve this Province out of its preſent Diſtreſſes, to whom this Town vote their Thanks for the conſtitutional and ſpirited Meaſures purſued by them for the good of this Province.

Voted, That from this Time, we will have no commercial, or ſocial connection with thoſe, who at this Time do refuſe to contribute to the relief of this abuſed Country, eſpecially, thoſe that import Britiſh Goods, contrary to the Agreement of the Body of Merchants in Boſton, or elſewhere, that we will not afford them our Cuſtom, but treat them with the utmoſt Neglect, and all thoſe who countenance them.

VOTED, That we will uſe our utmoſt Endeavours, to prevent the Conſumption of all foreign Superfluities, and that we will uſe our utmoſt Endeavours, to promote and encourage our own Manufactures.

VOTED, That the Town Clerk tranſmit a Copy of theſe votes of the Town, to the Committee of Merchants of Inſpection at Boſton.

A true Copy Atteſted,

FRANCIS FAULKNER, *Town Clerk.*

▲The 'snake' cartoon from Franklin's *Pennsylvania Gazette* of May 1754, symbolising the division of the colonies – New England, New York, New Jersey, Pennsylvania, Virginia, North and South Carolina – and urging them to 'join', i.e. unite.

most important city in America. From the start the *Gazette* was notable for its multiplicity of brief news-paragraphs. Franklin had disciplined himself to write clearly and plainly ('If a man would that his writings have an effect on the generality of readers', he said, 'he had better imitate that gentleman who would use no word in his works that was not well understood by his cookmaid.')

Franklin had been at the helm of the *Gazette* when he ran what has been called the first cartoon to appear in an American paper. On 9 May 1754 page two of the *Gazette* was adorned with a woodcut depicting a dismembered snake, each portion labelled with the initials for New England, New York, New Jersey, Pennsylvania, Virginia, North and South Carolina, with a large-type caption 'JOIN (i.e. *unite*) or DIE'. The purpose of the cartoon was to urge unity of the colonies in the face of the then anticipated war with the French and the Indians. It evoked a remarkable response, was largely copied and was frequently revived to symbolise the need for unity of the colonies, especially against exactions imposed by the mother-country. From it stemmed the later American Revolutionary symbol of the rattlesnake with the legend 'Don't tread on me!'

In 1765, when opposition to the subjecting of the American Press to the Stamp Act swept the colonies, the snake cartoon was extensively reprinted. The Stamp Act was the occasion of Patrick Henry's famous 'if this be treason' speech in the Virginia House of Burgesses, when he moved his resolutions that the exclusive right to levy taxes in the colonies should rest with the elected colonial assemblies. But it was the 'tombstone' edition of Franklin's contemporary, the *Pennsylvania Journal* of William Bradford that made the most extraordinary impact. On 31 October 1765 the *Journal* appeared in the full funereal panoply of heavy mourning rules through its four folio, three-column pages. The front page was topped with a curved rule and ornament contrivance – plus a skull and crossbones – to produce the tombstone effect. Legends like 'EXPIRING: in Hope of a Resurrection' and 'Adieu, Adieu, to the LIBERTY of the PRESS' (a read-down line in the fore-edge margin) were duly displayed. It was an outstanding and startling use of purely typographic means to secure an agitational effect; it was to be echoed elsewhere, as we shall see in the case of the *Massachusetts Spy*.[2]

As the break with Britain, and the start of the War of Independence, drew nearer it was Boston that emerged as the principal political and journalistic centre. Friction between Bostonians and the British garrison culminated in the 'Boston Massacre' of 5 March 1770, when troops of the twenty-ninth Foot fired on a crowd of demonstrators, killing five and wounding several more. First to react was the *Boston Gazette*, an old-established sheet which had had new, militant life imparted to it since being taken over some years before by Benjamin Edes and John Gill.

The *Boston Gazette* of 1770, a four-page folio with three-column make-up and nothing more than an occasional italic intro or small drop letter to break its solid text, had the general air of a London paper of forty years before. The title, in Caslon italic and roman, was attractively displayed, disposed round a centre-block that appeared to show Britannia (though with a cap of liberty instead of the trident) and a Dove, with double rules separating off the tag-line 'Containing the freshest Advices/Foreign and Domestic' and the dateline. The *Gazette's* austere look, however, belied both the activity of its associates and the radical nature of its content. The Boston Tea Party, that climax of colonial defiance short of war, was planned in the *Gazette* office; and in the autumn of 1773 it carried the calls by Samuel Adams, later reinforced by his remote kinsman the lawyer John Adams, for the assembling of a 'Congress of American States' – *not* 'colonies' – to form an independent 'American Commonwealth'. The *Gazette* campaign resulted in the summoning of the Continental Congress which led America to independence.

◀ Edes and Gill's *Boston Gazette*, a radical campaigner against the colonial regime.

Americans !---Liberty or Death !---Join or Die !

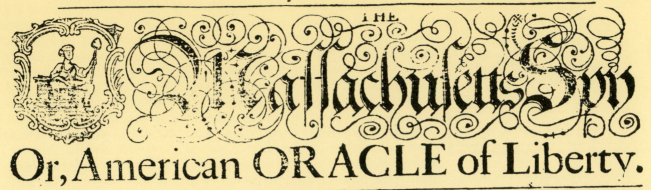

THE Maſſachuſetts Spy

Or, American ORACLE of Liberty.

VOL. V.) WORCESTER, WEDNESDAY, MAY 3, 1775. (NUMB. 210.

To the PUBLIC.

THE good People of this County, at a Meeting ſome Time ſince, voted to encourage the Eſtabliſhment of a Printing-Office in this Place: In Conſequence thereof, Application was made to me, then in Boſton, to iſſue Propoſals for publiſhing a weekly NEWS-PAPER in this Town, to be entitled, The WORCESTER GAZETTE, or AMERICAN ORACLE of LIBERTY: This I accordingly did; ſince that Time, Things have worn a different Face in our diſtreſſed Capital, and it was thought highly neceſſary that I ſhould remove my Printing Materials from Boſton to this Place, and inſtead of publiſhing the intended WORCESTER GAZETTE, &c. continue the Publication of the well-known MASSACHUSETTS SPY, or THOMAS's BOSTON JOURNAL: I accordingly removed my Printing Utenſils to this Place, and eſcaped myſelf from Boſton on the memorable 19th of April, 1775, which will be remembered in future as the Anniverſary of the BATTLE of LEXINGTON! I intend publiſhing this Paper regularly every Wedneſday, and have made an Alteration in the Title, in order to take in Part of that intended for the Gazette.

I beg the Aſſiſtance of all the Friends to our righteous Cauſe to circulate this Paper.—They may rely that the utmoſt of my poor Endeavours ſhall be uſed to maintain thoſe Rights and Privileges for which we and *our Fathers have bled*! and that all poſſible Care will be taken to procure the moſt intereſting and authentic Intelligence.

I am the Public's moſt obedient Servant,

ISAIAH THOMAS.

Worceſter, May 2d, 1775.

PROPOSLAS

For continuing the Publication of

THE MASSACHUSETTS SPY,

OR,

AMERICAN ORACLE of LIBERTY.

CONDITIONS.

I. The MASSACHUSETTS SPY, or AMERICAN ORACLE of LIBERTY, ſhall be printed on good paper, manufactured in this province, with a neat type.

II. It ſhall contain four pages, large folio, of the ſame ſize of the Boſton news-papers.

III. To be publiſhed every WEDNESDAY Morning, as early as poſſible, and delivered to the Subſcribers in Worceſter at their houſes, and ſent by the firſt opportunity to ſuch as are at a greater diſtance.

IV. Every ſubſcriber to pay Three Shillings and Four Pence, Lawful Money, at the time of ſubſcribing, and Three Shillings and Four Pence more at the expiration of Twelve Months. The price being Six Shillings and Eight Pence *per annum*, the ſame as the Boſton news-papers.

VI. Advertiſements to be inſerted in a neat and conſpicuous manner at the loweſt rate.

SUBSCRIPTIONS are taken in by the Publiſher in *Worceſter*, and by the following Gentlemen, viz. Capt. Aſa Whitcomb, and Dr. William Dunſmore, *Lancaſter*; Dr. William Jenneſon, *Mendon*; Jedediah Foſter, Eſq; *Brookfield*; Col. Learned, *Oxford*; Capt. Jonathan Tucker, *Charlton*; Capt. Henry King, and Mr. Amos Singleterry, *Sutton*; Col. Joſhua Henſhaw, and Mr. J. Allen, *Leiceſter*; Mr. Jonas How, *Rutland*; Mr. John Maſon, *Hutchinſon*; Capt. Iſaac Stone, *Oakham*; Mr. Levi Brigham, *Northborough*; Capt. Stephen Maynard, *Weſtborough*; Hon. Artemas Ward, *Shrewſbury*; Dr. John Taylor, *Lunenburgh*; Capt. David Goodridge, *Fitchburgh*; Mr. Benjamin Green, *Uxbridge*; Capt. Samuel Baker, *Bolton*; Col. Jonathan Grout, *Peterſham*; Capt. Joſiah Fay, *Southborough*; Col. Paul Mendall, *Hardwich*; Simeon Dwight, Eſq; *Weſtern*; Capt. Timothy Newell *Sturbridge*; Mr. Iſrael Nichols, *Leominſter*; Mr. Abiel Sadler, *Upton*; Capt. James Woods, *New-Braintree*; Mr. John Child, *Holden*; Capt. Samuel Jenneſon, *Douglaſs*; Mr. John Sherman, *Grafton*; Mr. Naham Green, *Royalſton*; Mr. Nathan Wood, *Weſtminſter*; Mr. Jonathan Baldwin, *Templeton*; Mr. William Bigelow, *Athol*; Mr. Samuel Eaſterbrook, *Princetown*; (all in Worceſter County) and by many other Gentlemen in ſeveral parts of the province.

For the MASSACHUSETTS SPY.

NUMBER VII.

To the INHABITANTS *of the* MASSACHUSETTS-BAY.

(Continued from our laſt.)

My Friends and Fellow Countrymen,

AFTER making ſome obſervations which are nothing to the purpoſe, unleſs the colonies are annexed to the realm, which is not the caſe, nor ever will be, and if they were, it would not follow if Guernſey and Jerſey are enſlaved, that the Americans muſt be ſo too—A clauſe from our firſt charter too long to be repeated, reſpecting incorporation, is recited by our author; upon which he gravely aſks this ſimple queſtion, "Whether it looks like a diſtinct or independent ſtate?" We may fully anſwer him by another queſtion equally ſimple, viz. Is there a ſingle word in it that looks like uniting us to the Britiſh empire, or ſubjecting us to the authority of Parliament? If it has not this look, it does not look to the point: For it is demonſtration, as there was a time when the colonies were diſunited from the realm, and the ſupreme authority of the parent ſtate, that they are ſo now unleſs there is evidence of a ſubſequent connexion. It is to be wiſhed that thoſe who keep eternally harping upon our being annexed to the Britiſh realm would point out the proceſs that united us.—There is none in nature: I challenge them to produce any.

The two next adduced paragraphs from our firſt charter, we have examined in our third and fourth numbers, and have ſhewn the firſt exactly to correſpond with the rights we contend for, and the latter to be abſolutely inconſiſtent with, and repugnant to, every principle and idea of our being a part of the Britiſh empire and ſubject to its ſovereign power.—It is therefore unneceſſary to take them up in this place.

The laſt recited clauſe from this charter, we have alſo conſidered, the ſubſtance of which is, that all and every of the ſubjects of the King of England, his heirs and ſucceſſors, who ſhould go to and inhabit in the Maſſachuſetts colony, and all their children, born in the ſaid colony, or on the ſeas ſhould *have and enjoy all the liberties and immunities of free and natural born ſubjects* within any of the dominions of the King, his heirs and ſucceſſors to *all intents* and *purpoſes* whatſoever, as if they were, and every of them, born within the realm.

"It is upon this clauſe, or a ſimilar one in the charter of William and Mary that our patriots have built up the ſtupendous fabric of American independence." Be it ſo: The foundation were there no other would ſuſtain the building. It is impoſſible to undermine it or explain it away.

"I have already, ſays our writer, ſhewn that the ſuppoſition of our being exempted from the authority of Parliament, is pregnant with the groſſeſt abſurdities."—No mortal excepting himſelf has ever been able to ſee thoſe abſurdities. We have ſeen what ſuch empty pretenſions amounted to in a paſt paper, and to whom the abſurdities were imputable.——"Let us now, ſays he, conſider this clauſe in connexion with other parts of the charter."—Here we are led to expect ſome important reaſoning; however a recital of his argument is its beſt confutation. "If, ſays he, we ſuppoſe this clauſe to exempt us from the authority of Parliament, we muſt throw away all the reſt of the charter, *for every other part indicates the contrary as plainly as words can do.*" This is conſidering the clauſe in connexion with other parts. There is no end in contradicting the mere aſſertions of one who *lets his pen run ſo freely*. Read the charter, and ſee if any part indicates the contrary, unleſs profound ſilence upon the ſubject is taken for ſuch an indication.

"What is ſtill worſe, this clauſe becomes *felo de ſe*, and deſtroys itſelf; for if we are not annexed to the realm we are aliens, and no charter, grant, or other act of the crown can naturalize us, or entitle us to the liberties and immunities of Engliſhmen." This is begging the queſtion; it goes upon the old Jacobitiſh ſuppoſition deteriorated: It ſuppoſes, that within the realm the ſubject holds all his rights and liberties of the King, as the original poſſeſſor; and that perſons out of the realm, in a ſtate of nature poſſeſs no rights and liberties as men.—In ſhort, it ſuppoſes Great-Britain to be the grand and only ſtore-houſe of Freedom, the diſpenſor of civil Bleſſings, and that no part of the wide world can be entitled to any liberties or immunities but what ſhe, of her ſpecial grace and mere bounty, is pleaſed to grant them; whereas the truth is, we were entitled to all the rights of Engliſhmen independent of any charters or realms under Heaven, and ſurely we are not the leſs ſo for having them confirmed by compact.

We ſhall wave what might be offered reſpecting aliens allegiance to the King, and the relation that Wales, Jerſey, Guernſey and Ireland ſtand in to the realm of England, as they do not effect the ſolution of our preſent queſtion.

More diſtortions, windings and twiſtings, were never crowded into ſo ſmall a compaſs as in the paragraph we are now conſidering.—The following is diverting enough: "If a perſon born in England removes to Ireland, Jerſey, or Guernſey, and ſettles there, he is then no longer repreſented in the Britiſh Parliament, but he and his poſterity are, and will ever be, ſubject to its authority. So that the inhabitants of the American colonies, do in fact enjoy all the liberties and immunities of natural born ſubjects. We are entitled to no greater privileges than thoſe who are born within the realm: And they can enjoy no other than we do when they reſide out of it. Thus it is evident that this clauſe amounts to no more than the royal aſſurance that we are a part of the Britiſh empire, and natural born ſubjects, and as ſuch bound to obey the ſupreme power of the ſtate." Such a concatenation of ideas we never jumbled up together before. The clauſe grants to all perſons, who were born within the realm, and ſhould come and inhabit in this province from time to time, as well as to all their children born on the ſeas, or in this colony, all the liberties and immunities of free natural born ſubjects within any of the King's dominions to all intents and purpoſes whatſoever, as if they were born within the realm of England. The language of this clauſe then, according to our myſterious interpreter, to all thoſe who come from England here, would be this, viz. You who are born within the realm of England, and ſhall go and inhabit in the Maſſachuſetts colony ſhall have and enjoy all the liberties and immunities that thoſe have and enjoy who are born within the realm of England, and ſhall go and inhabit in America. As great a ſolecism as ever entered the head of man. If the accidental liberties that thoſe perſons enjoy, who are only born within the realm and remove to foreign parts, are to meaſure and point out ours, how ſhall we ever know them? Is Ireland, Guernſey, the Eaſt and Weſt-Indias, or Turkey, to decide the queſtion and define the rights of all America: For thoſe born in England have gone to, and enjoy different liberties in all theſe places: And, according to our Logician, if the Americans enjoy as much liberty as thoſe who were born in England enjoy in any of theſe dominions, even if it be in Turkey, we are entitled to no more.

From 1771, however, the Boston newspaper which took the lead alike in circulation and in the independence struggle was the newly-founded *Massachusetts Spy*. This was printed and published by Isaiah Thomas, easily the most remarkable of American printers and publishers of his period, and perhaps of any period.[3] Of Welsh extraction – his great-great-grandfather, a merchant in Boston in 1640, was Evan Thomas – he was born in Boston in 1749, his spendthrift father dying when he was three. At seven he was apprenticed to an indifferent local printer named Zechariah Fowle; by his early 'teens he was a skilled journeyman and at sixteen moved to Nova Scotia to work in effect as printer of the official *Gazette* in Halifax. But the young New Englander was soon too much for the Nova Scotian administration; and after further peregrinations he came back to Boston in 1770. Now twenty-one, he promptly issued a prospectus for the *Massachusetts Spy*, starting it as a thrice-weekly, later bi-weekly, quarto.

The sensational success story of the *Spy* dated from March 1771, when Thomas transformed it from the smallest to the largest sheet ever seen in a Boston newspaper. A four-page royal folio (20-by-12½-inches) weekly, it adopted the current London fashion of four-column make-up and of treble rule cut-offs between major items. Important advertisements were given a semi-display appearance by setting main lines in larger-than-text sizes. The issue (of 7 March) marked the first anniversary of the 'Boston Massacre', which was commemorated prominently with an adaptation of the 'tombstone' technique. A mourning-bordered box, with a skull-and-crossbones cut, was run down column one 'as a solemn and perpetual memorial'.

The deep title-piece, in an engrossing-style blackletter extravagently scrolled, was of a degree of elaboration and fine engraving unprecedented in a newspaper title. As tension grew Thomas adapted his title, adding a cut of the goddess of liberty and for a time in 1774 running a modification of Franklin's dismembered snake of twenty years before right across the top. But Boston was now becoming too hot for Thomas; with Edes and Gill of the *Gazette*, and Samuel Adams, he was on the black list of twelve 'trumpeters of sedition' liable to summary execution if they fell into the hands of the British forces. So in April 1775, just before the armed clashes at Lexington and Concord opened the Revolutionary War, Thomas managed to evacuate his presses and equipment inland to the safety of Worcester, which was to remain the headquarters of his newspaper and of the general printing and publishing business which, with its peak workforce of 1,200, was to become by far the largest of its kind in post-independence America.

On 3 May 1775 Thomas produced the first of the war issues of the *Spy* in Worcester (and it was the first piece of printing ever to be done in the little town). The title-piece, with the blackletter now carrying a fine white inline and the goddess of liberty medallioned at the left, was even more elaborate than in 1771. Across the top, in 24pt upper- and lower-case underscored, ran the slogan 'Americans! – Liberty or Death! – Join or Die!'; below the engraving a full-width sub-title in still larger Caslon (resembling the later 42pt) read 'Or, American ORACLE of Liberty.' The treble rule cut-offs continued and there was modest headlining of the PROPOSALS for the continuance of the *Spy*. The sheet was smaller and the format dropped to three columns, since Thomas had to wrestle with an acute shortage of paper and ink and the impossibility of renewing his founts of type, since imports from London had naturally ceased.

With the War of Independence won, Thomas was able to extend his general business (which included Bibles and magazines, children's books and almanacs), later turning to write his classic *History of Printing in America* and to found the American Antiquarian Society, whose headquarters and fine library are still at Worcester. He was able to resume his type imports, mainly from Caslons but with some founts from Fry in London and Wilson in Glasgow; thus replenished,

◀ First War of Independence issue of Isaiah Thomas's *Massachusetts Spy*, after its evacuation from British-occupied Boston to Worcester (Mass).

The Pennſylvania Packet, *and Daily Advertiſer*.

Price Four Pence.] TUESDAY, September 21, 1784. [No. 1755.

For Liverpool.

The good Ship CASTOR, DANIEL BROCKLEBANKS, Maſter; BURTHEN about 300 tons; will ſail with all expedition, the greater part of her cargo being engaged; ſhe lies at the wharf of the ſubſcribers. For Freight or Paſſage apply to WILLING, MORRIS & SWANWICK.

For Dublin,

The Ship DUBLIN PACKET, ROBERT ALCORN, Maſter; WILL ſail about the 20th October. For Freight or Paſſage apply to HAYNES & CRAWFORD, or the Captain on board. This ſhip is intended for the Dublin trade, has exceeding good accommodations for paſſengers, and will return here early in the ſpring.

For CORK,

The new Ship PENELOPE, Captain GEORGE PARKER; WILL be ready to ſail in about 10 days, one half her cargo being engaged. For Freight or Paſſage apply to the Captain on board, or CAMPBELL & KINGSTON, on Walnut-ſtreet wharf.

N. B. She has elegant accommodations for about ſix paſſengers. Sept. 12

For Gottenburgh,

The Brig ELIZA, ANDREAS LUNDBERG, Commander: WILL ſail the 1ſt of October, having the greateſt part of her cargo on board. For Freight or Paſſage apply to HAYNES & CRAWFORD, or the Captain on board, at Race-ſtreet wharf. Sept. 15. td.

For LONDON,

The Ship COMMERCE, ROBERT MERCER, Commander: WILL poſitively ſail by the 20th of October, at fartheſt. For Freight or Paſſage apply to COLLINS & TRUXTUN, or the Commander.

FOR SALE, The good Hermaphrodite BRIGANTINE

Bermudas Packet

An Engliſh bottom, a prime ſailer, and about two years old. Apply to COXE & FRAZIER. Sept. 17.

Philadelphia, September 17, 1784.

Sixty Dollars Reward.

THE STORE of the ſubſcribers was broke open laſt night, and the undermentioned Articles were ſtolen. The above reward will be paid to any perſon who ſhall diſcover the Goods, and proſecute to conviction the Thief or Thieves, or Thirty Dollars for diſcovering the Goods only.

BACHE & SHEE.

- 13 dozen mens and womens ſilk ſtockings
- 6 pair cotton ſtockings
- 21 breeches patterns
- 10 pieces gauze
- 2 pieces Mancheſter ſtuff
- 1 piece chintz, green ground with red flowers
- 6 patterns ſilk for gowns
- 2 pieces fine cambrick :—

Perhaps other Articles yet unknown.

Peter Whiteſide & Co.

HAVE FOR SALE,

COARSE and fine blankets,
Baize, coatings,
Yorkſhire clothes,
Britannias,
Dowlas ſheetings,
Ruſſia ſail duck,
Hyſon, ſouchong and green tea, Sept. 1.

Juſt Imported and to be Sold by HENRY LISLE in Second-ſtreet, below the Drawbridge,

Muſcovado Sugars of the firſt

and ſecond quality, in hogſheads and barrels, and very fine cotton, in large and ſmall bags. Sept. 18.

DELAWARE STATE.

BY virtue of an order of the Orphans court for the county of Kent, there will be ſold on *Thurſday* the 23d. of this inſt. September, on the premiſes, a tract of land containing about four hundred acres, including a very fine plantation, with a large brick dwelling houſe and kitchen, a large barn, ſtables, coach houſe, ſmoak houſe and other neceſſary out buildings, ſituate about five miles from Duck-creek, Croſs Roads, on the road to Georgetown, being the real eſtate of Benjamin Haret deceaſed, and to be ſold for the payment of his debts.

Attendance will be given at the time and place of ſale, by *Charles Nixon*, Executor.

By order of the court, THOMAS RODNEY, *Clerk.*

Dover, September 1.

NOTICE is hereby given to the Collectors who are in arrears for the Effective Supply Sinking Fund and County Taxes, for the year 1782, that unleſs they ſettle and pay their reſpective balances to the county treaſurer, on or before the 8th day of October next, the commiſſioners are determined to proceed againſt ſuch delinquent collectors as the law directs.

NATHAN GIBSON, MICHAEL SHUBART, JOHN BROOKE, } Commiſſioners.

Philadelphia, September 1, 1784. eptd.

Jones and Foulke,

Have for SALE, at their STORE, in Market-ſtreet, between Third and Fourth ſtreets,

A general aſſortment of GOODS, imported in the laſt veſſels from London and Amſterdam: among which are, a large Quantity of

German DOWLAS,

Which they will ſell very reaſonable by the bale, or [illegible]

To the Reſpectable FREEMEN, ELECTORS for the City, Liberties, and County of PHILADELPHIA.

GENTLEMEN.

ENCOURAGED by the honor done me the laſt election, in returning me your ſheriff, I am induced to requeſt the continuance of your votes and intereſts at the next general election, in October; your favors again beſtowed upon me, ſhall be gratefully acknowledged by the moſt particular attention to the duties of the office, by Gentlemen,

Your moſt obliged, and Moſt obedient humble ſervant, THOMAS PROCTER, Sheriff.

Philadelphia, Sept. 13, 1784.

The Sale of Public Stores

at Carpenters-Hall, commences again on TUESDAY the 21ſt inſtant, at 10 o'Clock, A. M. when a great Variety will be expoſed to Sale, for Public Securities, agreeable to the former Advertiſement.

SAMUEL HODGDON, Com. Mil. Stores.

September 15, 1784.

Hiſtory of the Bible

This Day is publiſhed, in one Volume Octavo, (*Price, bound and lettered, Two Dollars*)

THE Hiſtory of the OLD and NEW TESTAMENT, interſperſed with moral and inſtructive REFLECTIONS, chiefly taken from the Holy Fathers.—From the French, by *J. Reeve*. Philadelphia: Printed for C. TALBOT, late of Dublin, Printer and Bookſeller, and ſold by him at the French-Arms, in Second ſtreet, between Union and Pine ſtreets; likewiſe at Mr. BELL's Book-ſtore, Third ſtreet; by Mr. SEDDON, Mr. PRICHARD, and Mr. RICE, in Market-ſtreet; Mr. BUCKLASS, Front-ſtreet; and by moſt of the other Bookſellers in this city.

N. B. The Subſcribers are requeſted to pay in their ſecond Subſcriptions, and take up their Books. Aug. 3.

THE Partnerſhip of WILLIAM & JAMES MILLER, being diſſolved by the death of William Miller, all perſons who are anyway indebted to the ſaid Partnerſhip, or to the Eſtate of William Miller are requeſted to diſcharge the ſame as ſoon as poſſible; and all thoſe who have any demands againſt the ſaid Partnerſhip or Eſtate, are deſired to bring them in to the ſubſcribers for ſettlement.

JAMES MILLER, JOHN MILLER, jun. } Adminiſtrators.

Philadelphia, Auguſt 19, 1784.

JAMES MILLER ſtill continues the buſineſs at his ſtore in Front-ſtreet the corner of Gray's alley, between Cheſnut and Walnut ſtreets, and has for Sale, a general aſſortment of MERCHANDIZE, and expects a large importation by the firſt veſſels from Europe. eptf.

TO BE SOLD.

Either together or divided, or LET on Leaſe for YEARS,

The Iſland of Bombay-Hook,

in New-Caſtle county, at the mouth of Duck-creek, having the advantage of a very extenſive range of marſh, a conſiderable part of which may be eaſily improved at a ſmall expence. Being at the head of the Bay and mouth of the river Delaware, it has ever commanded the ſupply to ſhipping of live ſtock and proviſions, and will be of growing importance. Its ſituation with reſpect to the country adjoining is advantageous, having an eaſy and accuſtomed communication with the waters of the Cheſapeak. The ſoil is excellent, and capable of any cultivation. The timber is plenty and of ſtrong growth. Fiſh and wild fowl abound, and the tenants have been healthy.

Alſo, about 50 acres of Land on the Old York road, 5 miles from the city, in an elegant and healthy ſituation, and newly fenced with cedar. On the place are a ſtone dwelling houſe and milk houſe, a log tenement, a great plenty and variety of fruit, ſome meadow and woodland, and a quantity of building ſtone.

Government ſecurities or real eſtate in Philadelphia, will be received in part of the conſideration. Enquire of the Printer.

ISAAC FRANKS, Broker,

At his OFFICE on the ſouth ſide of Market-ſtreet, between Second and Third ſtreets, two doors below the Preſbyterian Meeting, Philadelphia,

BUYS and ſells on Commiſſion, all kinds of Merchandize, Bills of Exchange, Continental Loan-Office Certificates, State Money, Officers and Soldiers Certificates, and every other kind of Paper Security of the United States, or of any particular State: he procures Money on Loan, diſcounts Notes, Bonds and Bills of all ſorts, Lets out Money, diſpoſes of, and purchaſes Real Eſtates, and every other kind of transferable property: he procures Freight or Charter for Veſſels, at the ſhorteſt notice; and tranſacts every other kind of Buſineſs as a Broker, with fidelity, care and diſpatch.

He has for SALE, a Variety of

Well Aſſorted MERCHANDIZE,

Wholeſale and Retail, upon eaſy terms for Caſh or Public Securities. Feb. 6.

Benjamin Nones & Co.

BROKERS.

ACQUAINT their friends and the public in general, that they intend carrying on the Commiſſion, Factorage and brokers Buſineſs in their various branches, at the houſe of Benjamin Nones, in Front-ſtreet, next door to the Poſt-Office, and formerly occupied by Mr. Philip Syng: Where they have provided ſtores for the reception of all kind of Goods to ſell on Commiſſion: will purchaſe on the ſhorteſt notice and moſt advantageous terms, all kind of merchandize or produce, for ſuch as pleaſe to employ them as Factors. Buy and ſell Bills of Exchange on France, Spain, Holland and other parts. Likewiſe Loan-Office and other Certificates, State and Continental Money, &c.

They flatter themſelves that by ſteady attention, ſecrecy, punctuality and diſpatch, which ſhall be their earneſt endeavours, to give general ſatisfaction to ſuch as pleaſe to employ them in all or either of the above branches.

LION MOSES, Broker,

BEGS leave to acquaint the Public in general, and his friends in particular, that he carries on the buſineſs of BROKERAGE in all its various branches, at his houſe in Race-ſtreet oppoſite the King of Pruſſia tavern, between Third and Fourth ſtreets. Negociates bills of exchange on Europe, the continent of America, or the Weſt Indies, loan-office and ſtate certificates and notes, takes goods for ſale on commiſſion, buys and ſells houſes, lands, ſhipping, &c. Thoſe that pleaſe to employ him may depend on the ſtricteſt punctuality, diſpatch and ſecrecy. It will be his conſtant ſtudy to merit the confidence of a diſcerning public, and will gratefully acknowledge all favors conferred on him. eptf.

To the Free and Independent ELECTORS of the City, Liberties and County of Philadelphia.

GENTLEMEN,

THE honor you conferred by placing me on the return at the late election, for Sheriff, lays me under many obligations, and induces me to ſolicit your further favors at the enſuing election, by continuing me on the return with the preſent ſheriff; which favor will be gratefully acknowledged by the public's humble ſervant,

JOSEPH COWPERTHWAIT.

Philadelphia, September 13, 1784.

Philadelphia, 13th September, 1784.

Grand Lodge.

THE quarterly communication of the Grand Lodge of Pennſylvania, will meet at their room in Lodge Alley, on Monday the 27th Inſt. at ten o'clock A. M. at which time and place the officers of the ſeveral Lodges under this juriſdiction, are requeſted punctually to attend. By Order of the R. W. Grand Maſter.

JOSEPH HOWELL, Jun. Grand Sec'ry.

Reed & Forde

HAVE removed their STORE to the bank ſide of Front-ſtreet, half way between Market and Cheſnut ſtreets, where they are opening a freſh aſſortment of Seaſonable GOODS, received by the laſt veſſels from England, France and Holland, which they are determined to ſell on the very loweſt terms.

N. B. Tobacco, flour, iron, ginſang and ſnakeroot, are received at the market price; alſo, public ſecurities of all kinds at their current value.

For SALE by

LACAZE *and* MALLET,

At their STORES in Water-ſtreet, between Arch and Race-ſtreets,

CLARET in hogſheads,
Ditto of ſuperfine quality,
Old Medoc ditto in boxes of 12, 24, and 36 bottles,
White and Red Burgundy in bottles,
Sherry in quarter caſks,
A few pipes of the beſt Teneriffe wine,
Old Cognac Brandy in boxes of 12 bottles each,
Sweet Oil in boxes,
Old Engliſh Beer in hogſheads. ALSO,
A large aſſortment of Dry Goods.
One hundred and nine tierces of beſt Carolina RICE, juſt arrived in the ſhip Philadelphia, captain Strong, from Charleſton. For ſale, a cargo of Havanna box Sugars, juſt arrived.

Juſt Imported in the laſt Veſſels from Nantz, and to be Sold on reaſonable Terms for Caſh or ſhort Credit by

P. D. Robert,

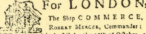

In Water-ſtreet, three Doors above Market-ſtreet,

BOHEA and hyſon tea,
Chintzes and callicoes,
Madder,
Old bourdeaux claret in bottles;
White Burgundy wine in barrels,
Alſo, a large Aſſortment of DRY GOODS to be ſold at low Prices, viz.

Several kinds of broad and narrow cloths, ſhalloons, pluſhes, velvets, corduroys, ſilke cloth, [illegible], callimanco, buckram, cambricks, half-[illegible], prunellas, [illegible], everlaſting, flowered flannels, linens, black ſilk ſtuffs, ſilk ſtockings, [illegible] gauze handkerchiefs and aprons, printed handkerchiefs, ſuperfine cotton [illegible] coverlets adorned with ribbons and fringes, and various other articles.

Likewiſe, ſeveral muſquets and piſtols, [illegible] in barrels, twine, &c. June 28. eod

Juſt Imported, and to be Sold by

Onfray Painniere,

At his Store the weſt ſide of Front-ſtreet, five doors above the Drawbridge,

SUPERFINE and ſecond broadcloths, pluſhes, caſſimers, ſileſia cloths, prunellas, ſilk ribbons, gauzes, ſilk ſtockings; thread, cotton and woolen ditto, ſilk gloves; lawns and cambricks, ſilk handkerchiefs, taffities, chintzes, linen and cotton handkerchiefs, ſewing ſilk, cotton ſtripes, threads, oznaburgs, ſailcloths, ſmall cordage; twine, writing paper, ſtuff for curtains, ticken, white and brown linen, Britania and Laval linen, delph ware, nails, ſalt; lampblack, red and yellow oacre, copperas, claret in hogſheads and boxes, Port wine in pipes and quarter pipes, Malaga and Champaigne in boxes, cordials and ſweet oil in boxes, brown ſugar, of the firſt quality in hogſheads and barrels.

ALL perſons indebted to the houſe of JAMES CUMMING, or CUMMING & MACARTY, of l'Orient; or to *James Cumming* acting for *Cumming & Macarty* at Philadelphia, in the year 1783, are deſired, to make immediate payment to the ſubſcriber, attorney to *William Macarty*, ſurviving partner of ſaid houſe.

Philad. Sept. 12. JOHN CHALONER.

Matthew M'Connell,

Lately removed into Second-ſtreet, between Market and Cheſnut ſtreets, on the eaſt ſide, ſeven doors below Black-horſe-alley, hath for SALE,

A General ASSORTMENT of

DRY GOODS,

At the loweſt Prices:

And will receive in payment, notes of the financier and treaſurer of this ſtate; alſo, depreciation, loan-office, and different kinds of certificates or public ſecurities, at their current value:

And will purchaſe *Final Settlements*, and give either Caſh or Goods, as may be moſt agreeable.

Perſons wanting Certificates or State Money to make payments in the *Land-Office*, may be ſupplied as above.

Philadelphia, September 3.

Two Dollars Reward.

LOST a few days ago, a RED COW with ſhort horns, white face, white feet, and large eyes. Whoever takes up ſaid Cow, and brings her to the Printer hereof, ſhall have the above reward. Sept. 15.

Five Pounds Reward.

LOST this day, at the Coffee-houſe, a LEATHER PURSE, containing a Sum of MONEY in Gold, about 23l. Whoever has found the ſame, and will bring it to the Printer hereof, ſhall have the above reward.

Sept. [illegible]

This Morning

At TEN o'Clock, at the CITY VENDUE-STORE, Will begin the SALE of a Large and [illegible] Aſſortment of Merchandize, Houſhold and Kitchen FURNITURE.

PUBLIC GOODS

On Thurſday, the twenty third inſtant, at ten o'clock in the morning, will commence the ſale by auction (at the office of finance, in Market-ſtreet) of the following articles, which are the property of the United States, viz.

FINE and coarſe Blankets,
Seal Leather,
Calf Skins,
Worſted Stockings,
Thread ditto,
Coarſe Hats,
Iron Wire,
Brown Linen,

Caſh, bank notes, and notes ſigned by the Superintendent of finance, will be received in payment.

ARTHUR St. CLAIR and Co. Auctioneers.

Jackſon & Dunn

Inform the Gentlemen of the Faculty and the Public,

THAT amongſt a large Collection of valuable books (a Catalogue of which is preparing) they have juſt opened for Sale, at their Store in Front-ſtreet, near the Coffee houſe, a few Copies of Doctor CULLEN's COMPLETE PRACTICE; publiſhed in May, 1784. This edition is immediately from the perſon who purchaſed the Copy-right, and will be ſold on very reaſonable terms.—Several other Books on Phyſic and Surgery, by the moſt approved Writers, have been received in this Collection. Sept. 15.

ALL perſons indebted to the eſtate of JOSHUA ASH, late of the Northern-liberties of Philadelphia, victualler, deceaſed, are hereby requeſted to make immediate payment; and all thoſe who have any demands againſt the ſaid eſtate, are deſired to bring in their accounts, duly atteſted, that they may be ſettled by

ABIGAIL ASH, THOMAS BRITTON, AARON OAKFORD. } Adminiſtrators.

Sept. 10.

To be ſold by public Vendue,

On the 23d inſtant, at the late Houſe of Joſhua [Ash] deceaſed, in Darby townſhip, Cheſter county,

ALL the Houſhold Goods and Kitchen Furniture; alſo, a number of blooded mares and colts, likewiſe working oxen, milch cows, and other cattle, a quantity of good hay, wheat, rye, barley and oats, in the ſheaf, indian corn and potatoes in the ground, a waggon, cart, plough and harrow, and other farming utenſils. The ſale to begin at 10 o'clock in the forenoon where attendance will be given by

ABIGAIL ASH, THOMAS BRITTON, AARON OAKFORD, } Adminiſtrators.

Sept. 10.

PROCLAMATION.

WHEREAS the honorable Thomas M'Kean, eſq. doctor of laws, chief juſtice of the ſupreme court of the ſtate of Pennſylvania; the honorable Francis Hopkinſon, eſq. judge of the admiralty of Pennſylvania, and the honorable George Bryan, eſq. one of the juſtices of ſaid court, have iſſued their precept bearing date the eighth day of September, (inſtant) to me directed, for holding a Court of Admiralty Seſſions, for the United States of America, at the State-houſe in the city of Philadelphia, on Friday the twenty-fourth inſt.

And whereas the honorable Thomas M'Kean, and the honorable George Bryan, eſqs. juſtices as aforeſaid, have alſo iſſued their precept to me directed the ſaid eighth day of September, for holding a Court of Admiralty Seſſions, for the ſtate of Pennſylvania, at the State-houſe, on the ſaid 24th day of Sept. (inſtant).

NOTICE is hereby given, to all juſtices of the peace, coroners and conſtables within the city and county of Philadelphia, that they be then and there in their own perſons, with their rolls, records, inquiſitions and other remembrances, to do thoſe things which to their offices on that behalf appertain to be done; and alſo all they who will proſecute againſt the priſoners that are or then ſhall be in the gaol of the ſaid city or county, are to be then and there, to proſecute againſt them as ſhall be juſt.

Dated at Philadelphia the eighth day of September, in the year of our Lord one thouſand ſeven hundred and eighty-four, and in the ninth year of American Independence.

THOMAS PROCTER, Sheriff.

GOD SAVE THE COMMONWEALTH!

Louis D'Orſiere,

WILL open his dancing ſchool the 1ſt of October next, in the Lodge room, in Lodge-alley, as he has done for this two years paſt, in partnerſhip with Mr Queſnay; but now as their partnerſhip has diſſolved; willing to carry on the dancing ſchool on his own account he offers his ſervices to the public in general, and his former ſcholars in particular, and expects the continuation of their favors.

N. B. It will be M. D'Orſiere's conſtant ſtudy to take none into his ſchool but perſons known by their good behavior, and he will take care that good order and decency is maintained in it. Sept. 14.

LOTS to be LET

on Ground-Rent forever on the bank between Callowhill ſtreet and Pool's bridge. Enquire of

THOMAS and ANTHONY CUTHBERT.

N. B. Stolen out of the houſe of Thomas Cuthbert, three ſilver Table Spoons, two of them marked S. L. and ſtamped I. David, the other marked T. C. and ſtamped W. B. All Silverſmiths are requeſted to ſtop them if offered for ſale. Sept. 20, 1784.

ALL perſons indebted to the eſtate of William Garwood, deceaſed, are deſired to make payment immediately to the ſubſcribers, in order that they may be enabled to diſcharge the demands upon ſaid eſtate. Likewiſe—All perſons having demands are requeſted to ſend them in in three weeks from this date, that they may be adjuſted and paid, by

WILLIAM GARWOOD, JOSEPH GARWOOD, } Executors.

Philadelphia, September 14.

CAME to the plantation of the ſubſcriber, living in Springfield townſhip, Cheſter county, a ſmall Sorrel HORSE, 10 years old, about 14 hands and a half high, the near hind foot white and ſome white ſpots on his back. The owner is deſired to come, prove property, pay charges and take him away.

Sept. [illegible] [illegible]

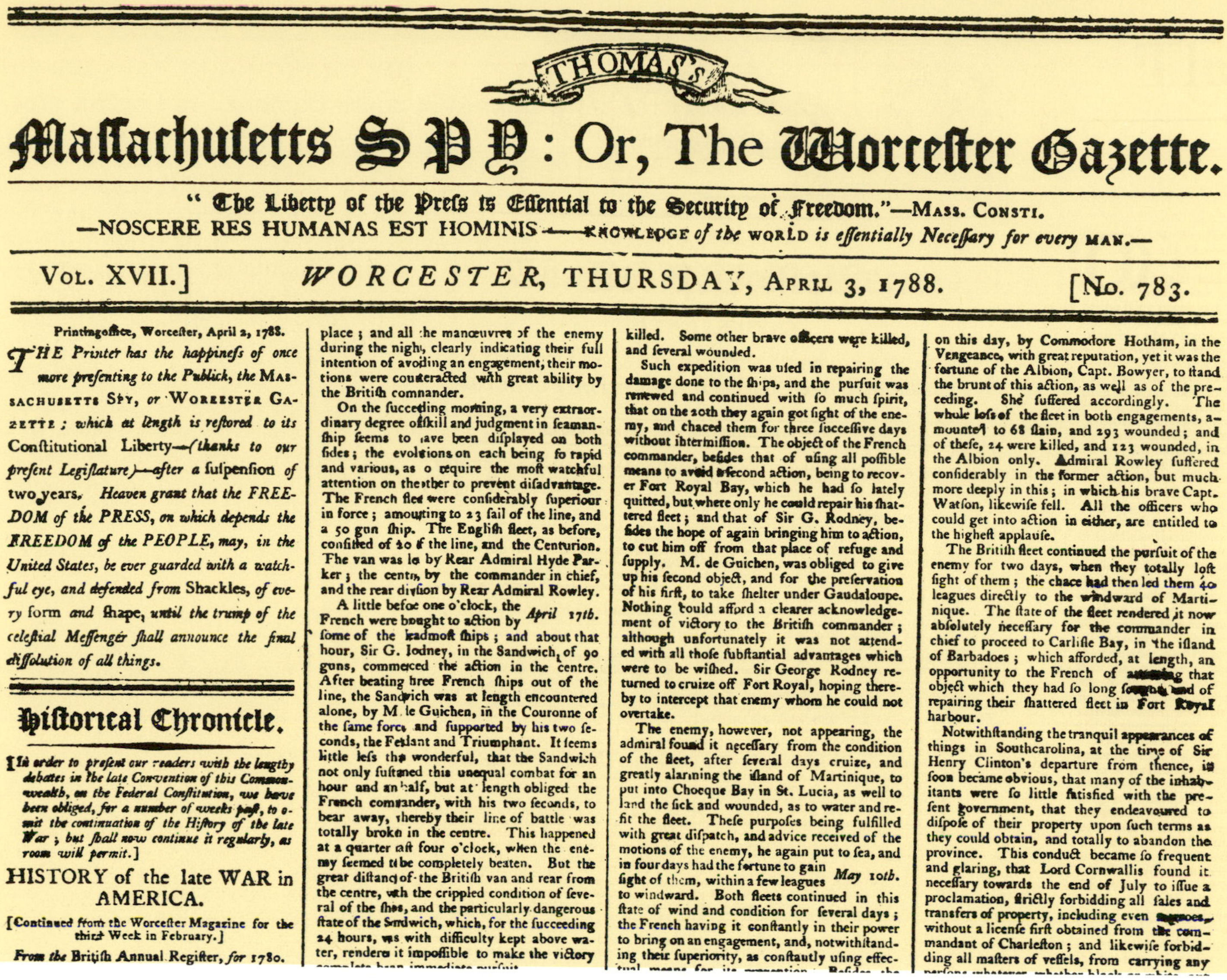

THOMAS'S

Massachusetts SPY: Or, The Worcester Gazette.

"The Liberty of the Press is Essential to the Security of Freedom."—Mass. Consti.

—NOSCERE RES HUMANAS EST HOMINIS——KNOWLEDGE *of the* WORLD *is essentially Necessary for every* MAN.—

Vol. XVII.] *WORCESTER*, THURSDAY, April 3, 1788. [No. 783.

Printingoffice, Worcester, April 2, 1788.

THE Printer has the happiness of once more presenting to the Publick, the Massachusetts Spy, *or* Worcester Gazette; *which at length is restored to its* Constitutional Liberty—*(thanks to our present Legislature)—after a* suspension *of* two years. *Heaven grant that the FREEDOM of the PRESS, on which depends the FREEDOM of the PEOPLE, may, in the United States, be ever guarded with a watchful eye, and defended from* Shackles, *of every* form *and* shape, *until the trump of the celestial Messenger shall announce the final dissolution of all things.*

Historical Chronicle.

[*In order to present our readers with the lengthy debates in the late Convention of this Commonwealth, on the Federal Constitution, we have been obliged, for a number of weeks past, to omit the continuation of the History of the late War; but shall now continue it regularly, as room will permit.*]

HISTORY of the late WAR in AMERICA.

[Continued from the Worcester Magazine for the third Week in February.]

From the British Annual Register, *for* 1780.

place; and all the manœuvres of the enemy during the night, clearly indicating their full intention of avoiding an engagement, their motions were counteracted with great ability by the British commander.

On the succeeding morning, a very extraordinary degree of skill and judgment in seamanship seems to have been displayed on both sides; the evolutions on each being so rapid and various, as to require the most watchful attention on the other to prevent disadvantage. The French fleet were considerably superiour in force; amounting to 23 sail of the line, and a 50 gun ship. The English fleet, as before, consisted of 20 of the line, and the Centurion. The van was led by Rear Admiral Hyde Parker; the centre, by the commander in chief, and the rear division by Rear Admiral Rowley.

A little before one o'clock, the French were brought to action by some of the leadmost ships; and about that hour, Sir G. Rodney, in the Sandwich, of 90 guns, commenced the action in the centre. After beating three French ships out of the line, the Sandwich was at length encountered alone, by M. le Guichen, in the Couronne of the same force, and supported by his two seconds, the Fendant and Triumphant. It seems little less than wonderful, that the Sandwich not only sustained this unequal combat for an hour and an half, but at length obliged the French commander, with his two seconds, to bear away, thereby their line of battle was totally broken in the centre. This happened at a quarter past four o'clock, when the enemy seemed to be completely beaten. But the great distance of the British van and rear from the centre, with the crippled condition of several of the ships, and the particularly dangerous state of the Sandwich, which, for the succeeding 24 hours, was with difficulty kept above water, rendered it impossible to make the victory complete by an immediate pursuit. *April 17th.*

killed. Some other brave officers were killed, and several wounded.

Such expedition was used in repairing the damage done to the ships, and the pursuit was renewed and continued with so much spirit, that on the 20th they again got sight of the enemy, and chaced them for three successive days without intermission. The object of the French commander, besides that of using all possible means to avoid a second action, being to recover Fort Royal Bay, which he had so lately quitted, but where only he could repair his shattered fleet; and that of Sir G. Rodney, besides the hope of again bringing him to action, to cut him off from that place of refuge and supply. M. de Guichen, was obliged to give up his second object, and for the preservation of his first, to take shelter under Gaudaloupe. Nothing could afford a clearer acknowledgement of victory to the British commander; although unfortunately it was not attended with all those substantial advantages which were to be wished. Sir George Rodney returned to cruize off Fort Royal, hoping thereby to intercept that enemy whom he could not overtake.

The enemy, however, not appearing, the admiral found it necessary from the condition of the fleet, after several days cruize, and greatly alarming the island of Martinique, to put into Chocque Bay in St. Lucia, as well to land the sick and wounded, as to water and refit the fleet. These purposes being fulfilled with great dispatch, and advice received of the motions of the enemy, he again put to sea, and in four days had the fortune to gain sight of them, within a few leagues to windward. Both fleets continued in this state of wind and condition for several days; the French having it constantly in their power to bring on an engagement, and, notwithstanding their superiority, as constantly using effectual means for its prevention. Besides the *May 10th.*

on this day, by Commodore Hotham, in the Vengeance, with great reputation, yet it was the fortune of the Albion, Capt. Bowyer, to stand the brunt of this action, as well as of the preceding. She suffered accordingly. The whole loss of the fleet in both engagements, amounted to 68 slain, and 293 wounded; and of these, 24 were killed, and 123 wounded, in the Albion only. Admiral Rowley suffered considerably in the former action, but much more deeply in this; in which his brave Capt. Watson, likewise fell. All the officers who could get into action in either, are entitled to the highest applause.

The British fleet continued the pursuit of the enemy for two days, when they totally lost sight of them; the chace had then led them 40 leagues directly to the windward of Martinique. The state of the fleet rendered it now absolutely necessary for the commander in chief to proceed to Carlisle Bay, in the island of Barbadoes; which afforded, at length, an opportunity to the French of attaining that object which they had so long sought, and of repairing their shattered fleet in Fort Royal harbour.

Notwithstanding the tranquil appearances of things in Southcarolina, at the time of Sir Henry Clinton's departure from thence, it soon became obvious, that many of the inhabitants were so little satisfied with the present government, that they endeavoured to dispose of their property upon such terms as they could obtain, and totally to abandon the province. This conduct became so frequent and glaring, that Lord Cornwallis found it necessary towards the end of July to issue a proclamation, strictly forbidding all sales and transfers of property, including even negroes, without a license first obtained from the commandant of Charleston; and likewise forbidding all masters of vessels, from carrying any persons whatever, whether black or white, out

▲ The changed style of the *Massachusetts Spy* in the years after independence.

◀ America's first daily paper; before its conversion from weekly (later thrice-weekly) publication in Philadelphia the *Packet* carried an elaborately-scrolled title in the manner of the 1775 *Massachusetts Spy*.

he issued an impressive specimen book in 1785, rightly claiming that it was 'as *large* and *complete* an ASSORTMENT as is to be met with in any one Printing-Office in AMERICA'. The types shown, his title-page added, were 'Chiefly MANUFACTURED by that great Artist, WILLIAM CASLON Esq of LONDON'.

The new types gave a smart look to the *Spy* when Thomas revived it as a local Worcester paper; for a while he had turned it into a magazine, to avoid a Massachusetts newspaper tax, repealed in 1788. It was now titled, in blackletter, *Massachusetts* SPY Or, The *Worcester Gazette*, with THOMAS's scrolled above the title, the whole piece (including the dateline) enclosed between full-page treble rules, which also appeared in their customary style as single-column cut-offs. The format returned to four columns and there was elementary headlining in capitals a size up from the text. Sections were handsomely signalised with blackletter heads, followed by swelled rules ('French dashes').

As already indicated, no American dailies appeared until after independence. With the recognition of independence by Britain in 1782 and the conclusion of the formal treaty the following year the way was clear for daily papers, particularly in the new Republic's main commercial centre, Philadelphia. In September 1784 John Dunlap and David Claypoole successfully converted their thrice-weekly *Pennsylvania Packet* into a daily, changing its former sub-title to *Daily Advertiser*. It was a four-page folio, with four-column make-up, and altogether a distinguished-looking sheet, of Caslon Old Face aspect. The title, in large roman and italic upper- and lower-case, ran the full width of the page. As was by this time the London custom – for reasons analysed below – advertisements filled the front and back pages; but the typography of what we would now call the *Packet's* semi-display front page was superior to that of its London contemporaries.

A short-lived daily followed in South Carolina. An English expatriate publisher in Charleston, John Miller, converted his bi-weekly *Gazette* to daily publication in December 1784. The next stable daily, however, was in New York where, in March 1785 Francis Childs launched the *Daily Advertiser*. It was a more modest sheet than the *Packet*, reflecting the minor commercial status of the New York of those days. Smaller in format than its Philadelphia contemporary, with narrower columns and larger body type (indicating a lesser volume of advertising) the New York *Advertiser* nevertheless exhibited the same handsome Caslon look. Massachusetts, as it happened, did not get a daily until 1813, when John Burke, one of the early Boston Irish, started the *Polar Star and Boston Daily Advertiser*; the following year the editorship was taken over by Nathan Hale, nephew of a famous figure of the independence struggle, who proved to be one of the most articulate and forthright of early American daily paper journalists.

▼ The first daily in Manhattan: a neat 1785 display of the types of 'that great artist, William Caslon Esq, of London'. Twenty years later (below) New York titles had been notably 'modernised'.

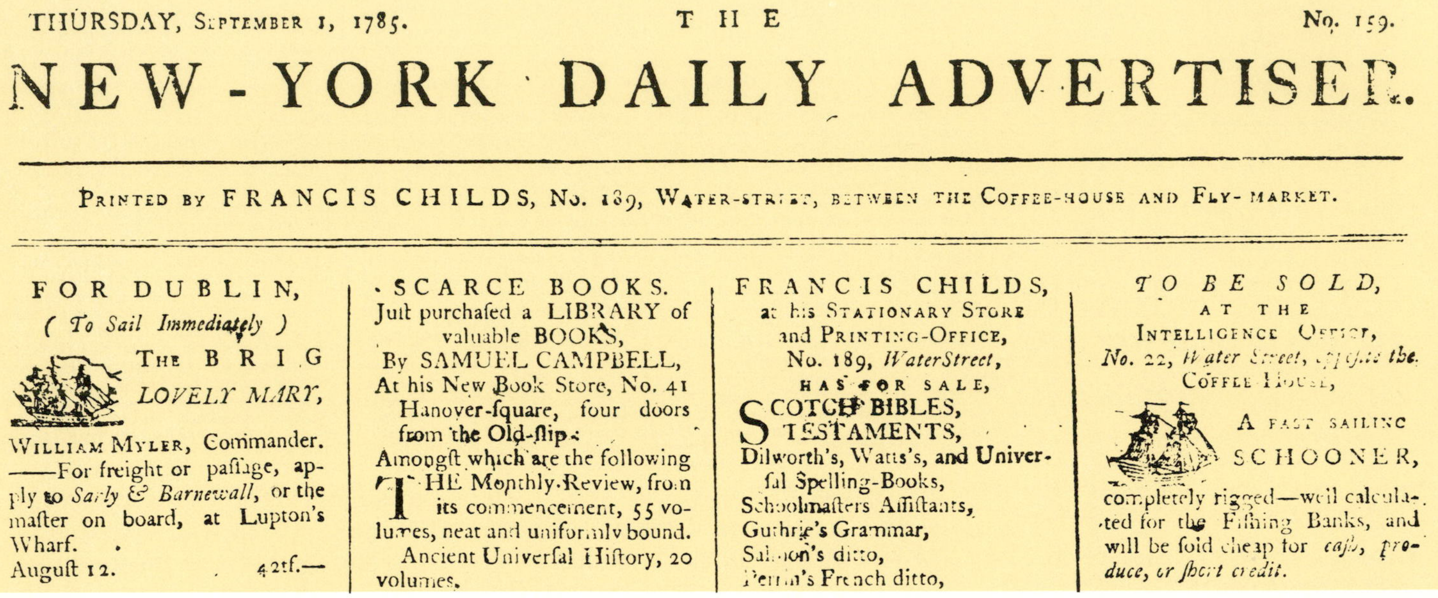
THURSDAY, SEPTEMBER 1, 1785. THE No. 159.

NEW-YORK DAILY ADVERTISER.

PRINTED BY FRANCIS CHILDS, No. 189, WATER-STREET, BETWEEN THE COFFEE-HOUSE AND FLY-MARKET.

FOR DUBLIN, (*To Sail Immediately*) THE BRIG *LOVELY MARY*, WILLIAM MYLER, Commander. ——For freight or passage, apply to *Sarly & Barnewall*, or the master on board, at Lupton's Wharf. August 12. 42tf.—

SCARCE BOOKS. Just purchased a LIBRARY of valuable BOOKS, By SAMUEL CAMPBELL, At his New Book Store, No. 41 Hanover-square, four doors from the Old-slip. Amongst which are the following THE Monthly-Review, from its commencement, 55 volumes, neat and uniformly bound. Ancient Universal History, 20 volumes.

FRANCIS CHILDS, at his STATIONARY STORE and PRINTING-OFFICE, No. 189, *WaterStreet*, HAS FOR SALE, SCOTCH BIBLES, TESTAMENTS, Dilworth's, Watts's, and Universal Spelling-Books, Schoolmasters Assistants, Guthrie's Grammar, Salmon's ditto, Perrin's French ditto,

TO BE SOLD, AT THE INTELLIGENCE OFFICE, *No. 22, Water Street, opposite the* COFFEE HOUSE, A FAST SAILING SCHOONER, completely rigged—well calculated for the Fishing Banks, and will be sold cheap for *cash*, *produce*, *or short credit*.

NEW-YORK GAZETTE & GENERAL ADVERTISER.

[TUESDAY, MAY ... 180..] Published (Daily) by JOHN LANG & Co. [Franklin's Head] No. 116 Pearl-street. [No. 5134......Vol XVI.]

For Liverpool, ... For Baltimore. ... For Savannah, ...

For Liverpool. ... For Liverpool. ...

FLOUR, PORK, LARD, &c. ...

PAINTS, &c. ...

CAIRNS, Frears, Halliday and Co. ...

It is now time to resume the story of the London newspaper developments; the last quarter of the eighteenth century was particularly productive. The establishment of the *Morning Post* has already been mentioned; it was to survive until well into this century, being absorbed by the *Daily Telegraph* only in 1937. Other long-lived and in their day famous papers were the *Morning Chronicle* (1770–1862), which employed Dickens as a reporter, and the *Morning Herald* (1780–1869). In 1788 Peter Stuart launched *The Star*, the first true evening paper (i.e. appearing every evening); later he produced a short-lived *Morning Star*. Of central importance was the founding of *The Times* (first as the *Daily Universal Register*) on 1 January 1785, the change to the noted name taking place three years later; under the headline

▶ Forerunner of *The Times*, John Walter's *Daily Universal Register* of 1785.

THE *Univerſal* DAILY *Regiſter,*

Printed Logographically — *By His Majeſty's* Patent.

NUMB. 1.] SATURDAY, JANUARY 1, 1785. [Price Two-pence Halfpenny.

The SIXTH NIGHT.
By His MAJESTY's Company

AT the THEATRE ROYAL in DRURY-LANE, this preſent SATURDAY, will be performed

A New COMEDY, called
The NATURAL SON.

The characters by Mr. King, Mr. Parſons, Mr. Benſley, Mr. Moody, Mr. Baddeley, Mr. Wrighten, and Mr. Palmer. Miſs Pope, Miſs Tidſwell, and Miſs Farren.

With new Scenes and Dreſſes.
The Prologue to be ſpoken by Mr. Banniſter, jun.
And the Epilogue by Miſs Farren.

After which will be performed the laſt New Pantomime Entertainment, in two Parts, called

HARLEQUIN JUNIOR;
Or, The MAGIC CESTUS.

The Characters of the Pantomime, by Mr. Wright, Mr. Williamſon, Mr. Burton, Mr. Staunton, Mr. Williames, Mr. Palmer, Mr. Waldron, Mr. Fawcett, Mr. Chaplin, Mr. Phillimore, Mr. Wilſon, Mr. Alfred, Mr. Spencer, Mr. Chapman, and Mr. Grimaldi. Mrs. Burnet, Miſs Burnett, Miſs Tidiwell, Miſs Barnes, Miſs Cranford, and Miſs Stageldoir.

To conclude with the Repulſe of the Spaniards before The ROCK of GIBRALTAR.

To-morrow, by particular deſire, (for the 4th time) the revived Comedy of the DOUBLE DEALER, with the favorite Maſque of ARTHUR and EMMELINE.

On Tueſday the Tragedy of VENICE PRESERVED: Jaffier by Mr. Brereton, Pierre by Mr. Benſley, and Belvidera, by Mrs. Siddons: And on Friday the Carmelite. Maſſinger's Play of the MAID of HONOUR, (with alterations and Additions) is in Rehearſal and will ſoon be produced.

NINTH NIGHT. FOR THE AUTHOR.

AT the THEATRE-ROYAL, COVENT-GARDEN, this preſent SATURDAY, January 1, 1785, will be performed, a New Comedy, called

The FOLLIES of a DAY,
Or, The Marriage of Figaro.
With new Dreſſes, Decorations, &c.

The principal characters by Mr. Lewis, Mr. Quick, Mr. Edwin, Mr. Wilſon, Mr. Wewitzer, Mr. Bonnor, Mr. Thompſon, and Mrs. Martyr; Mrs. Bates, Mrs. Webb, Miſs Wewitzer, and Miſs Younge.

With a new Prologue, to be ſpoken by Mr. Davies.
To which will be added, for the the ſixth time,
A new Pantomime, called,

The MAGIC CAVERN,
Or, VIRTUE's TRIUMPH.

With new Scenery, Machinery, Muſic, Dreſſes, and Decorations.

The Scenes chiefly deſigned by Mr. Richards, and executed by him, Mr. Carver, Mr. Hodgins, and Aſſiſtants.

The Overture, Songs, Choruſſes, and the Muſic of the new Pantomime, and compoſed by Mr. Shield.

Nothing under full Price will be taken.
The Words of the Songs, &c. to be had at the Theatre.

MR. WALTER returns his thanks to his Friends and the Public for the great encouragement and generous ſupport he has already received from them to his new improvement in Printing, by the readineſs with which they have ſubſcribed to his intended publication of the works of ſome eminent Authors; and whilſt he ſolicits a continuance of their favours, begs leave to acquaint them that by

The middle of January will be publiſhed,
In One Volume 12mo,
MISCELLANIES IN VERSE AND PROSE,

Intended as a Specimen of his Printing Types at the Logographic Office, Printing-Houſe Square, Blackfriars.—And by the beginning of February, his firſt volume, containing Watts's Improvement of the Mind, with an Introduction written on the occaſion, will be ready to be delivered to the ſubſcribers.

This Day is publiſhed, Price 6d.

PLAN of the CHAMBER of COMMERCE, King's-Arms Buildings, Cornhill, London; which is open every day, for Conſultation, Opinion, and Adice (verbal or in Writing) Mediation, Aſſiſtance, Arbitration, &c. in all *Commercial, Maritime,* and *Inſurance* Affairs, and matters of *Trade* in general; and the *Laws* and *Uſages* relating thereto.——The Addreſs is, To the Director of the Chamber of Commerce, as above.

To be had of Richardſon and Urquhart, Royal Exchange; J. Sewell, Cornhill; T. Whieldon, Fleet-ſtreet; W. Flexney, Holborn; and at the aforeſaid Chamber.

Where may alſo be had, in one Volume Folio;
Mr. Weſkett's COMPLETE DIGEST of the THEORY, LAWS and PRACTICE of INSURANCE; an entire new and comprehenſive work, including all the adjudged Caſes extant, with ſeveral never before printed; Extracts from the Statutes, foreign Ordinances, and marine Treaties; accounts of all the Inſurance Companies the MaritimeCourts, the commercial and maritime Laws, the Law of Nations, &c. the whole forming (alphabetically) a new *Lex Mercatoria.*

☞ "This Work has been compiled with great Care and Induſtry, by one who is evidently a Maſter of the Subject. It abounds with Proofs of extenſive Reading, as well as mature Reflection, and judicious Remarks; and if the completeſt Syſtem of Inſurance that has hitherto been compoſed be entitled to Praiſe, the preſent uſeful Digeſt muſt meet with the Approbation of the commercial World." Crit. Rev. Vol. 52, p. 443.—All the other Literary Journals ſpeak in ſimilar Terms of this Book; which had already been tranſlated abroad.

This Day is publiſhed, in 3 Vols. Price 9s. ſewed.
By the LITERARY SOCIETY,

MODERN TIMES: or The ADVENTURES of GABRIEL OUTCAST. A Novel, in Imitation of Gil Blas.

"Qui capit ille facit."

Printed for the Author, and ſold by J. Walter, Printing-houſe Square, Black-friars; where may be had, gratis, the Plan of this Society, aſſociated for the Encouragement of Literature, who propoſe to print and publiſh at their own Riſk and Expence ſuch original Works as they may approve of, and give their Authors all Profits ariſing from the ſame.

MRS. KING begs leave to acquaint her Friends ſhe opens her SCHOOL at CHIGWELL in ESSEX, on Monday, the 10th of January, for the EDUCATION of YOUNG LADIES: as ſhe has always been accuſtomed to watch and improve the opening mind, hopes to give ſatisfaction to thoſe who truſt her with ſo important a charge.

Till the 10th of January Mrs. King may be ſpoke with at Mr. Kerr's, Bitt-maker to his Majeſty, in the Mews, Charing-croſs.

N. B. Wanted an Apprentice and Half-boarder.

SHIPPING ADVERTISEMENTS

For NICE, GENOA, and LEGHORN,
(With Liberty to touch at One Port in the Channel,)
The NANCY.
THOMAS WHITE, Commander,

BURTHEN 160 Tons; Guns and Men anſwerable. Lying off the Tower, and will abſolutely depart on Saturday the 8th inſtant.

The ſaid Commander to be ſpoken with every morning at Sam's Coffee-houſe, near the Cuſtom-houſe; at Will's Coffee-houſe, in Cornhill; and at Exchange hours on the French and Italian Walk, or

WILLIAM ELYARD, for the ſaid Commander,
No. 16, Savage-Gardens.

Direct for LISBON,
The NANCY.
JOHN RACKHAM, Commander,

BURTHEN 300 Tons, Men anſwerable. Lying off Horſlydown Chain; Seven-eighths of her Cargo abſolutely engaged, and is obliged by Charter-party to depart on Saturday the 8th inſtant.

The ſaid Commander to be ſpoken with every morning at Sam's Coffee-houſe, near the Cuſtom-houſe; at Will's Coffee-houſe, in Cornhill; and in Exchange hours in the French and Italian Walk; or

WILLIAM ELYARD, for the ſaid Commander,
No. 16, Savage-Gardens.

For NICE, GENOA, and LEGHORN.
(With Liberty to Touch at One Port in the Channel.)
The LIVELY,
ROBERT BRINE, Commander,

BURTHEN 209 Tons, Guns and Men anſwerable. Lying off Iron Gate.

The ſaid Commander to be ſpoke with every Morning at Sam's Coffee-houſe, near the Cuſtom-houſe; at Will's Coffee-houſe in Cornhill; and in Exchange Hours in the French and Italian Walk; or

WILLIAM ELYARD, for the ſaid Commander,
No. 16, Savage-Gardens.

For CONSTANTINOPLE and SMYRNA, or SMYRNA and CONSTANTINOPLE,
(With Liberty to Touch at One Port in the Channel,)
The BETSEY,
ROBERT LANCASTER, Commander,

BURTHEN 200 Tons, Men anſwerable. Lying at Iron-Gate. Two-thirds of her Cargo engaged, and is obliged to depart by Charterparty, in all the preſent Month of January.

The ſaid Commander to be ſpoke with every Morning at Sam's Coffee-houſe, near the Cuſtom-houſe; at Will's Coffee-houſe in Cornhill; and in Exchange Hours in the French and Italian Walk; or

WILLIAM ELYARD, for the ſaid Commender,
No. 16, Savage-Gardens.

N. B. No Goods to be taken on Board the Veſſel without an Order from the Broker.

NEW NOVELS.

This Day are publiſhed, (in two Volumes, price 5s. ſewed,)

THE YOUNG WIDOW; or, the HISTORY of Mrs. LEDWICH.

The HISTORY of Lord BELFORD and Miſs SOPHIA WOODLEY, 3 vol. 9s. bound.

Printed for the Editor, and ſold by F. Noble, in Holborn;
Where may be had lately publiſhed,

St. Ruthin's Abbey, a Novel, 3 vols. 9s. bound.

The Woman of Letters; or, Hiſtory of Fanny Belton, 2 vol. 7s. bound.

A Leſſon for Lovers; or, Hiſtory of Col. Melville and Lady Richly, 2 vols. 7s. bound.

Literary Amuſements; or, Evening Entertainer, 2 vol. 7s. bound.

Adventures of a Cavalier, by Daniel Defoe, 3 vols. 9s bound.

T. RICKABY, PRINTER,
No. 15, Duke's Court, Drury Lane;

REſpectfully informs his Friends and the Public in general, that the Partnerſhip between him and Mr. Moore being entirely diſſolved, he now intends to carry on every branch of the PRINTING BUSINESS upon his own account;—and having purchaſed a complete aſſortment of the neateſt and beſt materials, is determined to purſue a Mode of Printing which he hopes will meet with the approbation of his employers.

N.B. Cards, Hand-Bills, Circular Letters, and all articles of the kind, accurately printed at a few hours notice. in a manner particularly neat, and at the loweſt prices.

⁂ An Apprentice wanted.

To the Readers of the London Medical Journal.
This day is firſt publiſhed, price 1s.

SYMPATHY DEFENDED; or, the State MEDICAL CRITICISM in London; written to improve the Principles and Manners of the Editor of the London Medical Journal: To which are added the Contents of the Treatiſe on Medical Sympathy, and a Poſtſcript, on account of a premature Review in a late Number of the London Medical Journal.

By a Society of Faculties;
Friends to the Public and Enemies to Impoſition.

"Cum tua non edas, carpis mea carmina, Laeli,
"Carp re vel noli noſtra, ede tua."

MART. Epig.

This pamphlet has been hitherto diſtributed gratuitouſly. The repeated applications for them, particularly from the country, have become ſo numerous, that the Society feel themſelves under the neceſſity of putting them into the hands of a publiſher.

Sold by J. Murray, Bookſeller, Fleet-ſtreet.

Nondum lingua ſilet dextra, peregit opus.
MART.

SHORT-HAND, on the lateſt and moſt approved Principles taught by J. LARKHAM, No 11, Roſe Alley, Biſhopſgate Street.

It would exceed the limits of an advertiſement merely to mention the various errors either in the *plan* or the *execution* of the different ſchemes of Short-hand hitherto made public, or to point out the peculiarities and excellencies of the preſent: Mr. L. therefore only begs leave to obſerve, that the approbation of many gentlemen well known in the literary world, and well verſed in the *Theory* and *Practice* of Short-hand, expreſſed in ſtronger terms than delicacy will permit him to repeat, warrants him in ſaying *his* will be found a ſyſtem of ſhort and ſwift writing; more *eaſy* to acquire and retain, more *expeditiouſly*, more *legible* and more *regular* than any ever yet offered to the Public.

The terms of teaching *one* Guinea, the *uſual* time of learning *ſeven* leſſons.

To the Public.

TO bring out a New Paper at the preſent day; when ſo many others are already eſtabliſhed and confirmed in the public opinion, is certainly an arduous undertaking; and no one can be more fully aware of its difficulties than I am: I, nevertheleſs, entertain very ſanguine hopes, that the nature of the plan on which this paper will be conducted, will enſure it a moderate ſhare at leaſt of public favour; but my pretenſions to encouragement, however ſtrong they may appear in my own eyes, muſt be tried before a tribunal not liable to be blinded by *ſelf-opinion*: to that tribunal I ſhall now, as I am bound to do, ſubmit theſe pretenſions with deference, and the public will judge whether they are well or ill founded.

It is very far from my intention to detract from the acknowledged merit of the Daily Papers now in exiſtence; it is ſufficient that they pleaſe the claſs of readers whoſe approbation their conductors are ambitious to deſerve; nevertheleſs it is certain ſome of the beſt, ſome of the moſt reſpectable, and ſome of the moſt uſeful members of the community, have frequently complained (and the cauſes of their complaints ſtill exiſt) that by radical defects in the plans of the preſent eſtabliſhed papers, they were deprived of many advantages, which ought naturally to reſult from daily publications. Of theſe ſome build their fame on the length and accuracy of parliamentary reports, which unqueſtionably are given with great ability, and with a laudable zeal to pleaſe thoſe, who can ſpare time to read ten or twelve columns of debates. Others are principally attentive to the politics of the day, and make it their ſtudy to give ſatisfaction to the numerous claſs of politicians, who, bleſſed with eaſy circumſtances, have nothing better to do, than to amuſe themſelves with watching the motions of miniſters both at home and abroad; and endeavouring to find out the ſecret ſprings that ſet in motion the great machine of government in every ſtate and empire in the world. There is one paper which in no degree interferes with the purſuits of its cotemporaries; it looks upon parliamentary debates as ſacred myſteries, that cannot be ſubmitted to vulgar eyes without profanation; political inveſtigations it apprehends to be little ſhort of treaſon, and therefore *loyally* abſtains from them; it deals almoſt ſolely in advertiſements; and conſequently, though a very uſeful, it is by no means an entertaining paper. Thus it would ſeem that every News-Paper publiſhed in London is calculated for a particular ſet of readers only; ſo that if each ſet were to change its favourite publication for another, the commutation would produce diſguſt, and diſſatisfaction to all; the politician would then find nothing to amuſe him but long accounts of petty ſquabbles about trifles in Parliament, or panegyrics on the men and meaſures that he moſt diſliked; or libels on thoſe whom he moſt revered. The perſon to whom parliamentary debates afford unſpeakable delight, would find himſelf bored with political ſpeculations about the meaſures that the different courts in Europe might probably adopt; or diſguſted with whole pages of advertiſements, in which he felt no concern;—whilſt the plain ſhop-keeper who wanted to find a convenient houſe for his buſineſs, and the ſervant who purchaſed his paper in hopes of ſeeing in it an advertiſement directing where he might find a place to ſuit him, would have their labour for their pains, in peruſing publications, filled with ſenatorial debates, or political eſſays and remarks, which would direct them to nothing leſs than the houſe or place they wanted.—A News-Paper, conducted on the true and natural principles of ſuch a publication, ought to be the Regiſter of the times, and faithful recorder of every ſpecies of intelligence; it ought not to be engroſſed by any particular object; but, like a well covered table, it ſhould contain ſomething ſuited to every palate: obſervations on the diſpoſitions of our own and of foreign courts ſhould be provided for the political reader; debates ſhould be reported for the amuſement or information of thoſe who may be particularly fond of them; and a due attention ſhould be paid to the intereſts of trade, which are ſo greatly promoted by advertiſements.—A paper that ſhould blend all theſe advantages, and by ſteering clear of extremes, hit the happy medium, has long been expected by the public.—Such, it is intended, ſhall be the UNIVERSAL REGISTER, the great objects of which will be to facilitate the *commercial* intercourſe between the different parts of the community, through the channel of *Advertiſements*; to record the principal occurrences of the times; and to abridge the account of debates during the ſitting of Parliament.

It is no leſs the intereſt of the proprietors of News-Papers, than of the public, that every encouragement ſhould be given to advertiſing correſpondents; yet this private intereſt of the proprietors is frequently ſacrificed to the rage for parliamentary debates, to the great injury of trade; for the extreme length of theſe debates ſo greatly retards the publication of the New-Papers which are noted for detailed accounts of them, that the advantages ariſing from this ſpecies of intelligence, though highly acceptable in itſelf, are frequently over-balanced by the inconvienences occaſioned to people in buſineſs by the delay. Theſe inconveniences are great and many; it generally happens, that when either Houſe of Parliament has been engaged in the diſcuſſion of an important queſtion till after midnight, the papers in which the ſpeeches of the Members are reported at large, cannot be publiſhed before noon; nay, they ſometimes are not even ſent to preſs ſo ſoon; conſequently parties intereſted in *ſales* are eſſentially injured, as the advertiſements, inviting the public to attend them at *ten* or *twelve* o'clock, do not appear, on account of a late publication, till ſome hours after.—From the ſame ſource flows another inconvenience; it is ſometimes found neceſſary to *defer* ſales, after they have been advertiſed for a particular day; but the notice of putting them off not appearing early enough, on account of the late hour at which the papers containing it are publiſhed, numbers of people, acting under the impreſſion of former advertiſements, are unneceſſarily put to the trouble of attending.—It will be the object of the *Univerſal Regiſter* to guard againſt theſe great inconveniences, without depriving its readers of the pleaſure of learning what paſſes in Parliament.—It is intended, then, that the debates ſhall be regularly reported in it; but on the other hand, that the publication may not be delayed to the prejudice of people in trade, the ſpeeches will not be given on a large ſcale; the *ſubſtance* ſhall be faithfully preſerved; but all the unintereſting parts will be omitted. I ſhall thus be enabled to publiſh this paper at an early hour; and I propoſe to bring it out *regularly* every morning at *ſix* o'clock. The *Univerſal Regiſter* will therefore have this advantage over the *Daily Advertiſer*, that, though publiſhed as early, it will contain a ſubſtantial account of the proceedings in Parliament the preceding night, which is never to be found in that paper; and compared with the other morning papers it will be found to have the merit of containing in ſubſtance, what they give in long detail (which men in buſineſs cannot well ſpare time to read) and, nevertheleſs, of being publiſhed much ſooner. Theſe circumſtances, it is hoped, will give the *Univerſal Regiſter* at leaſt an *equal* claim to public favour with the parliamentary papers, and the *trading* part of the metropolis, it is preſumed, will find it their advantage to give it the preference.

An eſſential part of the plan of this new paper is, that, for the convenience of advertiſing correſpondents, their favours ſhall, *to a certainty*, be inſerted on the very day that they ſhall direct; provided they deliver them at the office in due time. For the *ſtrict* obſervance of this rule, the credit of the paper ſhall ſtand pledged; and its pretenſions to public countenance will be renounced, if this fundamental principle in its inſtitution ſhall ever be violated, except in caſes of abſolute neceſſity, which human prudence cannot prevent.—And here I beg it may be underſtood that I do not make uſe of the word *neceſſity* as a reſerve, under colour of which, I may, whenever I think fit, be releaſed from my engagements; I mean by that word a neceſſity ariſing from accidents that ſometimes happen in the printing buſineſs, and from which, the moſt careful man cannot, at all times, be ſecure. But ſo far from wiſhing to ſhrink from my engagements, I intend, whenever the length of the Gazette, Parliamentary Debates, &c. ſhall render it impoſſible for me to inſert all the advertiſements promiſed for the day, in *one* ſheet, to print an additional half ſheet, and publiſh it with the ordinary paper without any additional charge to my cuſtomers.—From the difficulty that people experience in procuring the inſertion of their advertiſements even in the *Daily Advertiſer*; and particularly from the impoſſibility of obtaining an *early* inſertion at ſome periods of the year, it may be preſumed that this regulation will greatly recommend the UNIVERSAL REGISTER to public notice, and procure it ſupport.

Theſe, though in my opinion good, are not the *only* grounds on which I build my hopes of ſucceſs. I flatter myſelf, I have ſome claim to public encouragement, on account of a great improvement which I have made in the art of printing. The inconveniences attending the old and tedious mode of compoſing with letters taken up *ſingly*, firſt ſuggeſted the idea of deviſing ſome more expeditious method. The cementing of ſeveral letters together, ſo as that the type of a *whole word* might be taken up in as ſhort a time as that of a *ſingle letter*, was the reſult of much reflection on that ſubject. But the bare idea of cementing was merely the opening, not the accompliſhment or perfection of the improvement. The fount conſiſting of types of words, and not of letters, was to be ſo arranged, as that a compoſitor ſhould be able to find the former with as much facility as he can the latter. This was a work of inconceivable difficulty. I undertook it however, and was fortunate enough, after an infinite number of experiments, and great labour, to bring it to a happy concluſion. The whole Engliſh language is now methodically and ſyſtematically arranged at my fount: ſo that printing can now be performed with greater diſpatch, and at leſs expence, than according to the mode hitherto in uſe.

In bringing this work to perfection, I had not my own advantage ſolely in view; I wiſhed to be uſeful to the community; and it is with pleaſure I ſee that the public will derive conſiderable benefit from my induſtry; for I have reſolved to ſell the REGISTER *One halfpenny* UNDER the price paid for ſeven out of eight of the morning

The Times.

NUMBER 6572. LONDON, THURSDAY, NOVEMBER 7, 1805. PRICE SIXPENCE.

The LONDON GAZETTE EXTRAORDINARY.

WEDNESDAY, Nov 6, 1805.

ADMIRALTY-OFFICE, Nov. 6.

Dispatches, of which the following are Copies, were received at the Admiralty this day, at one o'clock A. M. from Vice-Admiral Collingwood, Commander in Chief of his Majesty's ships and vessels off Cadiz:—

SIR, *Euryalus, off Cape Trafalgar, Oct. 22, 1805.*

The ever-to-be-lamented death of Vice-Admiral Lord Viscount Nelson, who, in the late conflict with the enemy, fell in the hour of victory, leaves to me the duty of informing my Lords Commissioners of the Admiralty, that on the 19th instant, it was communicated to the Commander in Chief, from the ships watching the motions of the enemy in Cadiz, that the Combined Fleet had put to sea; as they sailed with light winds westerly, his Lordship concluded their destination was the Mediterranean, and immediately made all sail for the Streights' entrance, with the British Squadron, consisting of twenty-seven ships, three of them sixty-fours, where his Lordship was informed, by Captain Blackwood (whose vigilance in watching, and giving notice of the enemy's movements, has been highly meritorious), that they had not yet passed the Streights.

On Monday the 21st instant, at day-light, when Cape Trafalgar bore E. by S. about seven leagues, the enemy was discovered six or seven miles to the Eastward, the wind about West, and very light; the Commander in Chief immediately made the signal for the fleet to bear up in two columns, as they are formed in order of sailing; a mode of attack his Lordship had previously directed, to avoid the inconvenience and delay in forming a line of battle in the usual manner. The enemy's line consisted of thirty-three ships (of which eighteen were French, and fifteen Spanish), commanded in Chief by Admiral Villeneuve: the Spaniards, under the direction of Gravina, wore, with their heads to the Northward, and formed their line of battle with great closeness and correctness; but as the mode of attack was unusual, so the structure of their line was new; it formed a crescent, convexing to leeward, so that, in leading down to their centre, I had both their van and rear abaft the beam; before the fire opened, every alternate ship was about a cable's length to windward of her second a-head and a-stern, forming a kind of double line, and appeared, when on their beam, to leave a very little interval between them; and this without crowding their ships. Admiral Villeneuve was in the Bucentaure, in the centre, and the Prince of Asturias bore Gravina's flag in the rear, but the French and Spanish ships were mixed without any apparent regard to order of national squadron.

As the mode of our attack had been previously determined on, and communicated to the Flag-Officers, and Captains, few signals were necessary, and none were made, except to direct close order as the lines bore down.

The Commander in Chief, in the Victory, led the weather column, and the Royal Sovereign, which bore my flag, the lee.

The action began at twelve o'clock, by the leading ships of the columns breaking through the enemy's line, the Commander in Chief about the tenth ship from the van, the Second in Command about the twelfth from the rear, leaving the van of the enemy unoccupied; the succeeding ships breaking through, in all parts, astern of their leaders, and engaging the enemy at the muzzles of their guns; the conflict was severe; the enemy's ships were fought with a gallantry highly honourable to their Officers; but the attack on them was irresistible, and it pleased the Almighty Disposer of all events to grant his Majesty's arms a complete and glorious victory. About three P. M. many of the enemy's ships having struck their colours, their line gave way; Admiral Gravina, with ten ships joining their frigates to leeward, stood towards Cadiz. The five headmost ships in their van tacked, and standing to the Southward, to windward of the British line, were engaged, and the sternmost of them taken; the others went off, leaving to his Majesty's squadron nineteen ships of the line (of which two are first rates, the Santissima Trinidad and the Santa Anna,) with three Flag Officers, viz. Admiral Villeneuve, the Commander in Chief; Don Ignatio Maria D'Aliva, Vice Admiral; and the Spanish Rear-Admiral, Don Baltazar Hidalgo Cisneros.

After such a Victory, it may appear unnecessary to enter into encomiums on the particular parts taken by the several Commanders; the conclusion says more on the subject than I have language to express; the spirit which animated all was the same: when all exert themselves zealously in their country's service, all deserve that their high merits should stand recorded; and never was high merit more conspicuous than in the battle I have described.

The Achille (a French 74), after having surrendered, by some mismanagement of the Frenchmen, took fire and blew up; two hundred of her men were saved by the Tenders.

A circumstance occurred during the action, which so strongly marks the invincible spirit of British seamen, when engaging the enemies of their country, that I cannot resist the pleasure I have in making it known to their Lordships; the Temeraire was boarded by accident, or design, by a French ship on one side, and a Spaniard on the other; the contest was vigorous, but, in the end, the Combined Ensigns were torn from the poop, and the British hoisted in their places.

Such a battle could not be fought without sustaining a great loss of men. I have not only to lament, in common with the British Navy, and the British Nation, in the Fall of the Commander in Chief, the loss of a Hero, whose name will be immortal, and his memory ever dear to his country; but my heart is rent with the most poignant grief for the death of a friend, to whom, by many years intimacy, and a perfect knowledge of the virtues of his mind, which inspired ideas superior to the common race of men, I was bound by the strongest ties of affection; a grief to which even the glorious occasion in which he fell, does not bring the consolation which, perhaps, it ought: his Lordship received a musket ball in his left breast, about the middle of the action, and sent an Officer to me immediately with his last farewell; and soon after expired.

I have also to lament the loss of those excellent Officers, Captains Duff, of the Mars, and Cooke, of the Bellerophon; I have yet heard of none others.

I fear the numbers that have fallen will be found very great, when the returns come to me; but it having blown a gale of wind ever since the action, I have not yet had it in my power to collect any reports from the ships.

The Royal Sovereign having lost her masts, except the tottering foremast, I called the Euryalus to me, while the action continued, which ship lying within hail, made my signals—a service Captain Blackwood performed with great attention: after the action, I shifted my flag to her, that I might more easily communicate any orders to, and collect the ships, and towed the Royal Sovereign out to Seaward. The whole fleet were now in a very perilous situation, many dismasted, all shattered, in thirteen fathom water, off the shoals of Trafalgar; and when I made the signal to prepare to anchor, few of the ships had an anchor to let go, their cables being shot; but the same good Providence which aided us through such a day preserved us in the night, by the wind shifting a few points, and drifting the ships off the land, except four of the captured dismasted ships, which are now at anchor off Trafalgar, and I hope will ride safe until those gales are over.

Having thus detailed the proceedings of the fleet on this occasion, I beg to congratulate their Lordships on a victory which, I hope, will add a ray to the glory of his Majesty's crown, and be attended with public benefit to our country. I am, &c.

(Signed) C. COLLINGWOOD.

William Marsden, Esq.

The order in which the Ships of the British Squadron attacked the Combined Fleets, on the 21st of October, 1805.

VAN.	REAR.
Victory,	Royal Sovereign,
Temeraire,	Mars,
Neptune,	Belleisle,
Conqueror,	Tonnant,
Leviathan,	Bellerophon,
Ajax,	Colossus,
Orion,	Achille,
Agamemnon,	Polyphemus,
Minotaur,	Revenge,
Spartiate,	Swiftsure,
Britannia,	Defence,
Africa,	Thunderer,
Euryalus,	Defiance,
Sirius,	Prince,
Phœbe,	Dreadnought.
Naiad,	
Pickle Schooner,	
Entrepenante Cutter.	

(Signed) C. COLLINGWOOD.

GENERAL ORDER.

Euryalus, October 22, 1805.

The ever-to-be-lamented death of Lord Viscount Nelson, Duke of Bronté, the Commander in Chief, who fell in the action of the twenty-first, in the arms of victory, covered with glory; whose memory will be ever dear to the British Navy, and the British Nation; whose zeal for the honour of his King, and for the interests of his Country, will be ever held up as a shining example for a British Seaman—leaves to me a duty to return my thanks to the Right Honourable Rear-Admiral, the Captains, Officers, Seamen, and detachments of Royal Marines serving on board his Majesty's Squadron now under my command, for their conduct on that day; but where can I find language to express my sentiments of the valour and skill which were displayed by the Officers the Seamen, and Marines in the battle with the enemy, where every individual appeared an Hero, on whom the Glory of his Country depended; the attack was irresistible, and the issue of it adds to the page of Naval Annals a brilliant instance of what Britons can do, when their King and their Country need their service.

To the Right Honourable Rear-Admiral the Earl of Northesk, to the Captains, Officers, and Seamen and to the Officers, Non-commissioned Officers, and Privates of the Royal Marines, I beg to give my sincere and hearty thanks for their highly meritorious conduct, both in the action, and in their zeal and activity in bringing the captured ships out from the perilous situation in which they were after their surrender, among the shoals of Trafalgar, in boisterous weather.

And I desire that the respective Captains will be pleased to communicate to the Officers, Seamen, and Royal Marines, this public testimony of my high approbation of their conduct, and my thanks for it. (Signed) C. COLLINGWOOD

To the Right Honorable Rear-Admiral the Earl of Northesk, and the respective Captains and Commanders.

GENERAL ORDER.

The Almighty God, whose arm is strength, having of his great mercy been pleased to crown the exertion of his Majesty's fleet with success, in giving them a complete victory over their enemies, on 21st of this month: and that all praise and thanksgiving may be offered up to the Throne of Grace for the great benefits to our country and to mankind:

I have thought proper, that a day should be appointed of general humiliation before God, and thanksgiving for this his merciful goodness, imploring forgiveness of sins, a continuation of his divine mercy, and his constant aid to us, in the defence of our country's liberties and laws, without which the utmost efforts of man are nought; and direct, therefore, that be appointed for this holy purpose.

Given on board the Euryalus, off Cape Trafalgar, 22d Oct. 1805

(Signed) C. COLLINGWOOD.

To the respective Captains and Commanders.

N. B. The fleet having been dispersed by a gale of wind, no day has yet been able to be appointed for the above purpose.

SIR, *Euryalus, off Cadiz, Oct. 24. 1805.*

In my letter of the 22d, I detailed to you, for the information of my Lords Commissioners of the Admiralty, the proceedings of his Majesty's squadron on the day of the action, and that preceding it, since which I have had a continued series of misfortunes; but they are of a kind that human prudence could not possibly provide against, or my skill prevent.

On the 22d, in the morning, a strong southerly wind blew, with squally weather, which. however, did not prevent the activity of the Officers and Seamen of such ships as were manageable, from getting hold of many of the prizes (thirteen or fourteen), and towing them off to the Westward, where I ordered them to rendezvous round the Royal Sovereign, in tow by the Neptune: but on the 23d the gale increased, and the sea ran so high that many of them broke the tow-rope, and drifted far to leeward before they were got hold of again; and some of them, taking advantage in the dark and boisterous night, got before the wind, and have, perhaps, drifted upon the shore and sunk; on the afternoon of that day the remnant of the Combined Fleet, ten sail of ships, who had not been much engaged, stood up to leeward of my shattered and straggled charge, as if meaning to attack them, which obliged me to collect a force out of the least injured ships, and form to leeward for their defence; all this retarded the progress of the hulks, and the bad weather continuing, determined me to destroy all the leewardmost that could be cleared of the men, considering that keeping possession of the ships was a matter of little consequence, compared with the chance of their falling again into the hands of the enemy; but even this was an arduous task in the high sea which was running. I hope, however, it has been accomplished to a considerable extent; I entrusted it to skilful Officers, who would spare no pains to execute what was possible. The Captains of the Prince and Neptune cleared the Trinidad and sunk her Captains Hope, Bayntun, and Malcolm, who joined the fleet this moment from Gibraltar, had the charge of destroying four others. The Redoubtable sunk astern of the Swiftsure while in tow. The Santa Anna, I have no doubt, is sunk, as her side was almost entirely beat in; and such is the shattered condition of the whole of them, that unless the weather moderates I doubt whether I shall be able to carry a ship of them into port. I hope their Lordships will approve of what I (having only in consideration the destruction of the enemy's fleet) have thought a measure of absolute necessity.

I have taken Admiral Villeneuve into this ship; Vice-Admiral Don Aliva is dead. Whenever the temper of the weather will permit, and I can spare a frigate (for there were only four in the action with the fleet, Euryalus, Sirius, Phœbe, and Naiad; the Melpomene joined the 22d, and the Eurydice and Scout the 23d,) I shall collect the other flag officers, and send them to England, with their flags, (if they do not all go to the bottom), to be laid at his Majesty's feet.

There were four thousand troops embarked, under

'Why change the head?' the advantage of the shorter and more distinctive title was expounded in a lengthy and even skittish editorial column and a half.

By the 1780s the format of the London dailies was firmly set at four four-column pages with advertisements occupying the whole of the front page. Several factors combined to make the ad-front-page a peculiar and persistent institution of the British Press (it was not the custom in America or in Europe). It has been gradually abandoned only during the past thirty-odd years, *The Times* itself clinging to the antique practice until May 1966. To the eighteenth-century London daily the theatrical announcements (the 'bills') were of major importance and thus had an instant claim to front-page disposition.* As dailies developed many of them – witness the 'Advertiser' in their titles – put advertising first and, initially at least, regarded news as filler; advertising therefore had the front-page preference. Finally, it was a matter of technical convenience and prudence to work off the outer sheet, i.e. pages one and four, first; so these pages were filled with the early, and controllable, advertising copy, leaving the back-up pages two and three to await the later news copy – plus, of course, such advertising as might have come in too late for the front or the back. This arrangement, there seems no doubt, was understood and accepted by the newspaper readers of those days.

The tale of *The Times* – and its birth as a promotion sideline of the 'Logographic Press', set up by a failed coal merchant, John Walter I, has often been told. It will not be re-traversed here, since our purpose is simply to consider the paper's typographic aspect, and the 'logographic' gimmick – in which commonly-used words were cast as logotypes – soon proved to be of no practical utility. Far more important was the influence and example of a rival publisher, John Bell, who was also a printer of distinction and had, further, just started as a typefounder. Bell was associated with two dailies, *The World* (1787) and *The Oracle* (1789), which between them brought significant changes in London newspaper typography.

These were firstly, the use of an entirely new style of white-lined blackletter for title-lines; secondly, leading between paragraphs in the editorial columns, which much aided ease of reading; thirdly, abandonment of the old-fashioned long 's' in text; fourthly, the introduction of a new 'modern' type-face specifically for newspaper text. The first and the fourth innovations were the most important to the look of the newspaper; the paragraph-leading did not long survive the increasing pressure of the Stamp Acts, which made every fragment of newspaper space more expensive and more precious, thus encouraging the ruthless shoehorning-in of matter to the last degree of overcrowding.

As we have seen, blackletter had made its appearance from time to time in newspaper titles, but it was always a normal, solid blackletter. The title of *The World* was a blackletter 'tricked out', as Morison said, 'with a white line drawn or "tooled" upon every letter – thus making a namby-pamby, artificial affair of it', a mannerism redolent of the

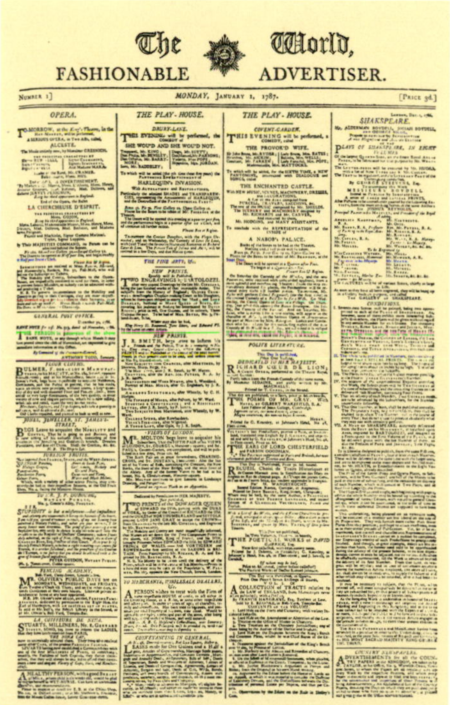

▲ John Bell's *The World* (1787), showing the 'Strawberry Hill' white-lined blackletter promptly imitated by *The Times* for its title-line.

◀ *The Times* well-established (1805): note the continuing 'Strawberry Hill' white-lined blackletter title, just about to change to a stouter version.

'Gothick' of Horace Walpole's Strawberry Hill style. But this 'mock-antique' Strawberry Hill Gothic took the trade by storm. *The Times* began on 1 January 1788 with its new title in decent roman capitals; but it capitulated by mid-March, going over to an exact copy of the 'namby-pamby' *World* blackletter. Not till 1805 did it adopt the stouter white-lined blackletter which was thereafter to be largely accepted as standard, 'traditional' news-title style (in America, too, though there

* Subsequently there was a tendency to put the theatre 'bills' on the inside pages, since they frequently came in very late; hence the term 'the bill page' for the centre-spread page of *The Times* facing the leader page.

solid blackletter was more often to be met with). The difference between Bell's blackletter title and its stouter successors was that, whereas the first weakened the letter by tooling a white *inline*, the second (as shown in the Caslon specimen of 1808, for example) added a white *outline*, thus retaining the original strength and colour of the letter. A later development came with the spread of the Regency Fat Face vogue to blackletter. The fat Blacks, starting with Figgins in 1815, had what I once called 'a jovial, Falstaffian quality', whether solid or white-lined. In the latter form they made vigorous titles for the *Manchester Guardian* (1821) and *The Standard* (1827).[4]

Bell's news-text innovation arose directly from his establishment of the British Letter Foundry in the late 1780s. He employed a talented punch-cutter, Richard Austin, who produced the first British 'modern' face; it was hardly accidental that it closely followed what is generally held to be the true pioneer of the 'modern' style – with vertical stress, unbracketed serifs and strong thick-thin contrast – the Didot roman of 1784. Bell used Austin's elegant letter for some of his bookwork; but most important was his employment of it to transform the text of *The Oracle* in 1792. This started a revolution which was to spread rapidly. Newspaper text was given its own distinctive flavour instead of being a narrow-measure version of book typography, using the familiar classic type-faces of the book printer.

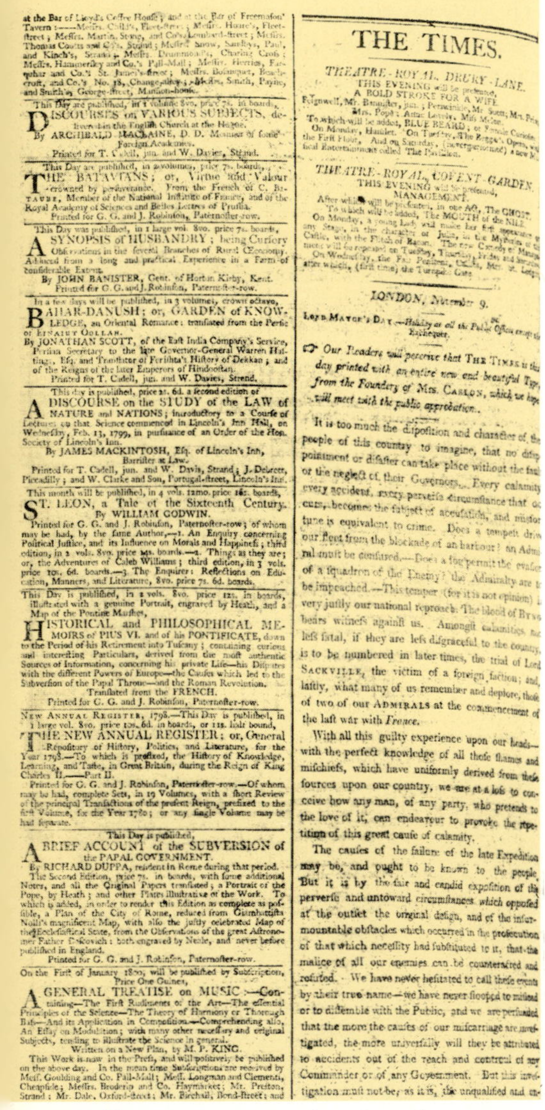
at the Bar of Lloyd's Coffee House; and at the Bar of Freemason' Tavern :——Messrs. Child's, Fleet-street; Messrs. Hoare's, Fleet-street; Messrs. Martin, Stone, and Co's Lombard-street; Messrs. Thomas Coutts and Co's. Strand; Messrs. Snow, Sandbys, Paul, and Kinch's, Strand; Messrs. Drummond's, Charing Cross; Messrs. Hammersley and Co.'s Pall-Mall; Messrs. Herries, Farquhar and Co.'s St. James's-street; Messrs. Bosanquet, Beachcroft, and Co.'s No. 18, Change-alley; Messrs. Smith, Payne, and Smith's, George-street, Mansion-house.

This Day are published, in 1 volume 8vo. price 7s. in boards,
DISCOURSES on VARIOUS SUBJECTS, delivered in the English Church at the Hague.
By ARCHIBALD MACLAINE, D. D. Member of some Foreign Academies.
Printed for T. Cadell, jun. and W. Davies, Strand.

This Day are published, in 2 volumes, price 7s. boards,
THE BATAVIANS; or, Virtue and Valour crowned by perseverance. From the French of C. Bitaube, Member of the National Institute of France, and of the Royal Academy of Sciences and Belles Lettres of Prussia.
Printed for G. G. and J. Robinson, Paternoster-row.

This Day was published, in 1 large vol. 8vo. price 7s. boards,
A SYNOPSIS of HUSBANDRY; being Cursory Observations in the several Branches of Rural Œconomy. Adduced from a long and practical Experience in a Farm of considerable Extent.
By JOHN BANISTER, Gent. of Horton Kirby, Kent.
Printed for G. G. and J. Robinson, Paternoster-row.

In a few days will be published, in 3 volumes, crown octavo,
BAHAR-DANUSH; or, GARDEN of KNOWLEDGE, an Oriental Romance: translated from the Persic of Einaiut Oollah.
By JONATHAN SCOTT, of the East India Company's Service, Persian Secretary to the late Governor-General Warren Hastings, Esq. and Translator of Ferishta's History of Dekkan; and of the Reigns of the later Emperors of Hindoostan.
Printed for T. Cadell, jun. and W. Davies, Strand.

This day is published, price 2s. 6d. a second edition of
A DISCOURSE on the STUDY of the LAW of NATURE and NATIONS; introductory to a Course of Lectures on that Science commenced in Lincoln's Inn Hall, on Wednesday, Feb. 13, 1799, in pursuance of an Order of the Hon. Society of Lincoln's Inn.
By JAMES MACKINTOSH, Esq. of Lincoln's Inn, Barrister at Law.
Printed for T. Cadell, jun. and W. Davis, Strand; J. Debrett, Piccadilly; and W. Clarke and Son, Portugal-street, Lincoln's Inn.

This month will be published, in 4 vols. 12mo. price 16s. boards,
ST. LEON, a Tale of the Sixteenth Century.
By WILLIAM GODWIN.
Printed for G. G. and J. Robinson, Paternoster-row; of whom may be had, by the same Author,—1. An Enquiry concerning Political Justice, and its Influence on Morals and Happiness; third edition, in 2 vols. 8vo. price [illegible] boards.—2. Things as they are; or, the Adventures of Caleb Williams; third edition, in 3 vols. price 10s. 6d. boards.—3. The Enquirer: Reflections on Education, Manners, and Literature, 8vo. price 7s. 6d. boards.

This Day is published, in 2 vols. 8vo. price 12s. in boards, illustrated with a genuine Portrait, engraved by Heath, and a Map of the Pontine Marshes,
HISTORICAL and PHILOSOPHICAL MEMOIRS of PIUS VI. and of his PONTIFICATE, down to the Period of his Retirement into Tuscany; containing curious and interesting Particulars, derived from the most authentic Sources of Information, concerning his private Life—his Disputes with the different Powers of Europe—the Causes which led to the Subversion of the Papal Throne—and the Roman Revolution.
Translated from the FRENCH.
Printed for G. G. and J. Robinson, Paternoster-row.

New Annual Register, 1798.—This Day is published, in 1 large vol. 8vo. price 10s. 6d. in boards, or 11s. half bound,
THE NEW ANNUAL REGISTER; or, General Repository of History, Politics, and Literature, for the Year 1798.—To which is prefixed, the History of Knowledge, Learning, and Taste, in Great Britain, during the Reign of King Charles II.——Part II.
Printed for G. G. and J. Robinson, Paternoster-row.—Of whom may be had, complete Sets, in 19 Volumes, with a short Review of the principal Transactions of the present Reign, prefixed to the first Volume, for the Year 1780; or any single Volume may be had separate.

This Day is published,
A BRIEF ACCOUNT of the SUBVERSION of the PAPAL GOVERNMENT.
By RICHARD DUPPA, resident in Rome during that period.
The Second Edition, price 7s. in boards, with some additional Notes, and all the Original Papers translated; a Portrait of the Pope, by Heath; and other Plates illustrative of the Work. To which is added, in order to render this Edition as complete as possible, a Plan of the City of Rome, reduced from Giambattista Nolli's magnificent Map, with also the justly celebrated Map of the Ecclesiastical State, from the Observations of the great Astronomer Father Boscovich: both engraved by Neale, and never before published in England.
Printed for G. G. and J. Robinson, Paternoster-row.

On the First of January 1800, will be published by Subscription, Price One Guinea,
A GENERAL TREATISE on MUSIC:—Containing—The First Rudiments of the Art—The essential Principles of the Science—The Theory of Harmony or Thorough Bass—And its Application in Composition.—Comprehending also, An Essay on Modulation; with many other necessary and original Subjects, tending to illustrate the Science in general.
Written on a New Plan, by M. P. KING.
This Work is now in the Press, and will positively be published on the above day. In the mean time Subscriptions are received by Mess. Goulding and Co. Pall-Mall; Mess. Longman and Clementi, Cheapside; Messrs. Broderip and Co. Haymarket; Mr. Preston, Strand; Mr. Dale, Oxford-street; Mr. Birchall, Bond-street; and

THE TIMES.

THEATRE-ROYAL, DRURY-LANE.
THIS EVENING will be presented,
A BOLD STROKE FOR A WIFE.
Feignwell, Mr. Bannister, jun.; Periwinkle, Mr Suett; Mrs. Pri[illegible] Mrs. Pope; Anne Lovely, Miss Mellon.
To which will be added, BLUE BEARD; or Female Curiosity.
On Monday, Hamlet. On Tuesday, The Beggar's Opera, [illegible] the First Floor. And on Saturday, (never performed) a new M[illegible] sical Entertainment called The Pavilion.

THEATRE-ROYAL, COVENT-GARDEN.
THIS EVENING will be presented,
MANAGEMENT.
After which will be presented, in one Act, The GHOST.
To which will be added, The MOUTH of the NILE.
On Monday, a young Lady will make her first appearance [illegible] any Stage, in the character of Julia, in the Mysteries of the Castle, with the Flitch of Bacon. The new Comedy of Manage[illegible] ment will be repeated on Tuesday, Thursday, Friday and [illegible] On Wednesday, the Fair Penitent, [illegible], Mrs. St. Leger, after which, (first time) the Turnpike Gate.

LONDON, November 9.

Lord Mayor's Day.—Holiday at all the Public Offices except the Exchequer.

Our Readers will perceive that The Times is this day printed with an entire new and beautiful Type, from the Foundery of Mrs. Caslon, which we hope will meet with the public approbation.

It is too much the disposition and character of the people of this country to imagine, that no disappointment or disaster can take place without the fault or the neglect of their Governors. Every calamity, every accident, every perverse circumstance that occurs, becomes the subject of accusation, and misfortune is equivalent to crime. Does a tempest drive our fleet from the blockade of an harbour? an Admiral must be censured.—Does a fog permit the evasion of a squadron of the Enemy? the Admiralty are to be impeached.—This temper (for it is not opinion) is very justly our national reproach. The blood of Byng bears witness against us. Amongst calamities not less fatal, if they are less disgraceful to the country, is to be numbered in later times, the trial of Lord Sackville, the victim of a foreign faction; and, lastly, what many of us remember and deplore, those of two of our Admirals at the commencement of the last war with *France*.

With all this guilty experience upon our heads—with the perfect knowledge of all those flames and mischiefs, which have uniformly derived from these sources upon our country, we are at a loss to conceive how any man, of any party, who pretends to the love of it, can endeavour to provoke the repetition of this great cause of calamity.

The causes of the failure of the late Expedition may be, and ought to be known to the people. But it is by the fair and candid exposition of the perverse and untoward circumstances which opposed at the outset the original design, and of the insurmountable obstacles which occurred in the prosecution of that which necessity had substituted to it, that the malice of all our enemies can be counteracted and refuted. We have never hesitated to call these events by their true name—we have never stooped to mislead or to dissemble with the Public, and we are persuaded that the more the causes of our miscarriage are investigated, the more universally will they be attributed to accidents out of the reach and controul of any Commander or of any Government. But this investigation must not be, as it is, the unqualified and un-

First appearance of modern-face text in *The Times* (1799).

The Times followed suit in November 1799, when it 'went modern' with 'a new and beautiful type from the Foundery of Mrs Caslon'. This was Mrs Elizabeth Caslon the Second, widow of the original Caslon's grandson Henry; finding the foundry's sales seriously declining, because it only had the classic Old Face to offer, she had just commissioned the cutting of a range of roman to accord with the 'modern' style made high fashion, notably by Bodoni. *The Times* appears to have been one of the earliest beneficiaries of her enterprise.

Argument over the Didot provenance of Bell's new roman and the Bodoni provenance of the Caslon new roman seems to me unprofitable to pursue. Broadly the two ascriptions appear to be correct; but Bell's letter (which we have known for the past forty years in the Monotype re-cutting as Bell series 341) had, and has, a character and brilliance of its own, due to the taste and skill of Richard Austin and not to any French or Italian inspiration. The same applies to William Martin's book-type cut in the 1790s for William Bulmer's Shakespeare Printing Office, a stately face which we know as Bulmer (Monotype series 469). Martin anyhow was much influenced by Baskerville, for whom his brother Robert had worked, and the 'transitional' flavour of the Birmingham maestro was strong in Martin's type. Thus I find it peculiar that Stanley Morison, after conceding the Bodoni origin of the Caslon type for *The Times*, should add 'it is, however, immediately based on the book-type cut by William Martin', concluding that British 'modern' was henceforth to 'take the Martin rather than the Bell line'.[5] A glance at specimens of the Caslon new roman is enough to suggest its direct Bodoni descent without intermediary, for what that is worth. In fact the one serious conclusion to be drawn is that the 'moderns', and the Caslon more than the Bell, had a degree of condensation which was of practical value in economising space.

The 'modern' revolution in newspaper text – which was to be complete in both Britain and America and to remain unchallenged until the 1920s – was accompanied by other technical changes. First of these was the substitution of the iron press for the traditional wooden press, Lord Stanhope's invention being completed in 1800. The Stanhope iron press and its successors were of special importance for newspaper production firstly because they allowed a larger sheet to be worked, and secondly because they took the impression at a single pull, since it was possible to make the metal platen of an appropriate size, which was not practicable with the old wooden platen. The Stanhope went up to a 'newspaper' size, with a platen of 36-by-23½-inches (compared with maximum 30-by-20-inches of the wooden press). When the American George Clymer's Columbian iron press was introduced in 1813 it had a model which could exceed Double Royal (40-by-25-inches). The effect of the iron press on format was seen in 1808, when *The Times* first introduced a five-column page – admittedly somewhat square-looking and ungainly – and in 1811 this was adopted as its regular make-up.

This extra capacity, however, came at a time when the pressure of the newspaper taxes on space, mentioned above, was reinforced by an unprecedented pressure of news. As the Napoleonic wars rolled on year after year this chronic double pressure became acute and was reflected in all details of newspaper make-up, both in the advertising and the editorial columns. Thus the fairly open, semi-display style of advertisement setting gave place to tight, run-on 'smalls', each opening with a drop initial and packed as close as possible in the page with minimal-measure column rules instead of the former generous rule-work. Where column rules had gauged not less than long primer (10pt), yielding a series of agreeable vertical whites in the page, they were now reduced to not more than four-to-pica (3pt). These tight-packing trends, already apparent in *The Times* by 1806, were complete by 1808 and continued when (in 1812) substantially more space was created by adding two inches to the depth of each column.

Thus any attempts at display, any exploitation of typographic art, vanished from *The Times* just as, under its first outstanding publisher, John Walter II and its first independent editor, Thomas Barnes (the 'Thunderer'), it began to forge ahead to its extraordinary position of journalistic and political near-monopoly. In the earlier war years there had been striking efforts at woodcut illustration – of Nelson's funeral car, for instance, or maps of the battle zones. Big events had even called forth headlines of a certain size, as this four-liner, in 12pt and 18pt full-face capitals, of 16 September 1807:

SURRENDER OF
COPENHAGEN,
AND THE
DANISH FLEET.

Now there were to be no more than one-line labels in italic capitals of the body of the paper. The smallest text size was to drop from minion (7pt) to nonpareil (6pt), despite compositorial opposition. In the 1820s the decent look of the front-page title was spoiled by allowing the 'smalls' to climb to the top of each end column.

During the Napoleonic days the conductors of *The Times* had, in addition to the constricting circumstances described above, a major mechanical preoccupation. Their rising circulation could not be met efficiently and economically by hand-press working, even with multiple setting. The problem was solved when the first power-driven printing machines were introduced in Printing House Square in November 1814. It is not necessary to stress the revolutionary importance in printing technology of the Koenig and Bauer cylinder machine, with its quintupling of the output of the hand-press. For newspaper production it was by far the biggest single step forward; its development and effects will be considered in detail in the next chapter. Here it may be noted that by 1817, when Barnes was named editor, the Koenig machine enabled *The Times* to cope with a circulation of no less than 7,000 a day (at the turn of the century it had been appreciably under 2,000).

One of the early visitors to *The Times* to see the Koenig machine at work was a Lancashire-born printer, Edward Baines, who, since 1801, had been editor of the weekly *Leeds Mercury*. The *Mercury*, an early eighteenth-century foundation, was not to be printed by a steam-powered cylinder machine until 1837; but Baines, a solid Whig reform-

A reconstruction of the Koenig machine of *The Times* (1814).

THE LEEDS MERCURY.

Printed by JAMES BOWLING, in BOAR-LANE.

Nº 1045. Vol. XX. TUESDAY, FEBRUARY 20, 1787. [Price THREE-PENCE.]

☞ THIS PAPER may Conſtantly be ſeen at the CHAPTER Coffee-Houſe, St. Paul's Church-Yard; at the LONDON Coffee-Houſe, Ludgate-ſtreet; at PEELE'S Coffee-Houſe, Fleet-ſtreet, and at Mr. TAYLER'S, Nº. 5, Warwick-Court, LONDON.

Pontefract Cocking.
To be FOUGHT,
At Mr. William Lodge's Pit, the Red-Lion, in Pontefract,
A MAIN of COCKS, betwixt the Right Honourable the EARL of MEXBOROUGH, and WILLIAM SOTHERON, Eſquire, for TEN GUINEAS a Battle, and ONE HUNDRED the Main or Odd Battle. To ſhew 46 Cocks on each Side, weigh on Saturday the 24th of March next, and fight Monday, Tueſday, and Wedneſday following.
FEEDERS. BASTALL and SMITH.

KIGHLEY, 6th Feb. 1787.
ISAAC UMPLEBY,
TAKES this Method of informing his Ac-

LEEDS, Feb. 12, 1787.
Sun Fire-Office.
WHEREAS Agents of the ROYAL EXCHANGE ASSURANCE-OFFICE and the PHOENIX FIRE-OFFICE have, in different Parts of the Kingdom, advertiſed the giving of POLICIES GRATIS to all Perſons removing from any other Office, whereby ſome Perſons have been induced to leave this Office:
NOTICE is hereby given,
That the SUN FIRE-OFFICE will henceforth give POLICIES GRATIS to all Perſons already inſured in this Office, who have Occaſion to alter their INSURANCE; and likewiſe POLICIES GRATIS to any Perſons removing their INSURANCES from any other Office.
The Public will pleaſe to obſerve, That the LARGE FIRE-ENGINE for the Uſe of the Town of Leeds, was preſented by this Office; and if the Town is deſirous of having another Engine equally powerful, this Office will ſubſcribe towards the Expence thereof; alſo for Ladders, Buckets, or other uſeful

To be SOLD,
About One Hundred Tons of exceeding Fine HAY.
For Particulars apply to Mr. Chriſtopher Johnſton, Mill-Hill, Leeds.

To be SOLD by AUCTION,
(Together or in Separate Lots,)
At the White-Lion in Halifax, on Monday the 26th Day of February Inſt. at Four in the Afternoon,
(Situate in SOUTHOWRAM, near HALIFAX,)
A MESSUAGE and FARM-HOUSE, with the Barns, Stables, Cow-Houſes, and other convenient Outbuildings, and Five Cloſes of Land contiguous and near thereto, containing together about Twenty-one Days Work, in the Poſſeſſion of Abraham Fox.
Alſo, Several HOUSES, in the Poſſeſſion of Thomas Turner,

pedient by which ſhe thought to bubble us, and all is well; otherwiſe, by G—d, both they and we are undone. So my comps. to M. de Torcy, and let him know, that if they do not agree with the Queen I may be a refugee. Do pray make the French aſhamed of their ſneaking chicane. By heaven, they treat like pedlars; or, which is worſe, like attornies.
On Saturday evening there was a numerous and reſpectable meeting of the Chamber of Manufacturers, Thomas Walker, Eſq; of Mancheſter, in the chair, when, after ſpeeches that laſted above three hours, it was unanimouſly agreed, that a petition ſhould be immediately preſented to the Houſe of Commons, praying for time to inveſtigate into a meaſure which clearly appeared to them to be ſo fraught with miſchief to the intereſt of this country, as the Commercial Treaty now depending between

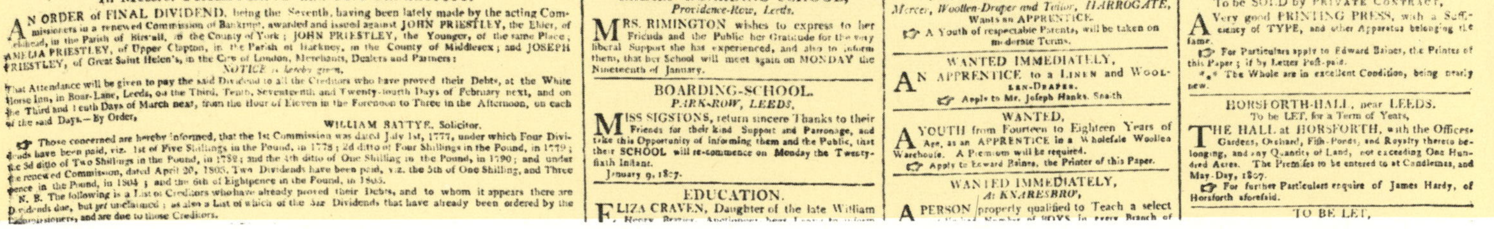

The Leeds Mercury.

PRINTED AND PUBLISHED BY EDWARD BAINES, AT HIS OFFICE IN BRIGGATE.

VOL. XL.—No. 2162.] SATURDAY, JANUARY 17, 1807. [PRICE SIX-PENCE.

In Messrs. PRIESTLEYS' and Co.'s BANKRUPTCY.
AN ORDER of FINAL DIVIDEND, being the Seventh, having been lately made by the acting Commissioners in a renewed Commission of Bankrupt, awarded and issued against JOHN PRIESTLEY, the Elder, of ... in the Parish of Birstall, in the County of York; JOHN PRIESTLEY, the Younger, of the same Place, ... AMELIA PRIESTLEY, of Upper Clapton, in the Parish of Hackney, in the County of Middlesex; and JOSEPH PRIESTLEY, of Great Saint Helen's, in the City of London, Merchants, Dealers and Partners:
NOTICE is hereby given,
That Attendance will be given to pay the said Dividend to all the Creditors who have proved their Debts, at the White Horse Inn, in Boar-Lane, Leeds, on the Third, Tenth, Seventeenth and Twenty-fourth Days of February next, and on the Third and Tenth Days of March next, from the Hour of Eleven in the Forenoon to Three in the Afternoon, on each of the said Days.—By Order,
WILLIAM BATTYE, Solicitor.
☞ Those concerned are hereby informed, that the 1st Commission was dated July 1st, 1777, under which Four Dividends have been paid, viz. 1st of Five Shillings in the Pound, in 1778; 2d ditto of Four Shillings in the Pound, in 1779; the 3d ditto of Two Shillings in the Pound, in 1782; and the 4th ditto of One Shilling in the Pound, in 1790; and under the renewed Commission, dated April 20, 1803, Two Dividends have been paid, viz. the 5th of One Shilling, and Three pence in the Pound, in 1804; and the 6th of Eightpence in the Pound, in 1805.
N. B. The following is a List of Creditors who have already proved their Debts, and to whom it appears there are Dividends due, but yet unclaimed; as also a List of which of the Six Dividends that have already been ordered by the Commissioners, and are due to those Creditors.

LADIES' BOARDING SCHOOL,
Providence-Row, Leeds.
MRS. RIMINGTON wishes to express to her Friends and the Public her Gratitude for the very liberal Support she has experienced, and also to inform them, that her School will meet again on MONDAY the Nineteenth of January.

BOARDING-SCHOOL,
PARK-ROW, LEEDS.
MISS SIGSTONS, return sincere Thanks to their Friends for their kind Support and Patronage, and take this Opportunity of informing them and the Public, that their SCHOOL will re-commence on Monday the Twenty-sixth Instant.
January 9, 1807.

EDUCATION.
ELIZA CRAVEN, Daughter of the late William

JONATHAN GILBERTSON,
Mercer, Woollen-Draper and Tailor, HARROGATE,
Wants an APPRENTICE.
☞ A Youth of respectable Parents, will be taken on moderate Terms.

WANTED IMMEDIATELY,
AN APPRENTICE to a LINEN and WOOLLEN-DRAPER.
☞ Apply to Mr. Joseph Hanks, Snaith.

WANTED,
A YOUTH from Fourteen to Eighteen Years of Age, as an APPRENTICE in a Wholesale Woollen Warehouse. A Premium will be required.
☞ Apply to Edward Baines, the Printer of this Paper.

WANTED IMMEDIATELY,
At KNARESBRO',
A PERSON properly qualified to Teach a select

To PRINTERS.
To be SOLD by PRIVATE CONTRACT,
A Very good PRINTING PRESS, with a Sufficiency of TYPE, and other Apparatus belonging the same.
☞ For Particulars apply to Edward Baines, the Printer of this Paper; if by Letter Post-paid.
** The Whole are in excellent Condition, being nearly new.

HORSFORTH-HALL, near LEEDS.
To be LET, for a Term of Years,
THE HALL at HORSFORTH, with the Offices, Gardens, Orchard, Fish-Ponds, and Royalty thereto belonging, and any Quantity of Land, not exceeding One Hundred Acres. The Premises to be entered to at Candlemas, and May-Day, 1807.
☞ For further Particulars enquire of James Hardy, of Horsforth aforesaid.

TO BE LET,

▲ The *Leeds Mercury* of 1807 exemplified the conversion of a leading provincial paper to the blackletter title from its previous roman capitals (above).

er, was already developing the paper as a powerful local campaigner and made it an outstanding organ of Yorkshire opinion (it was later to be one of the most notable provincial dailies, surviving until November 1939, when it was merged with its contemporary the *Yorkshire Post*). The other great provincial city, Manchester, had a succession of weeklies from 1719 onwards; the most famous, the *Manchester Guardian*, to become in time unique among the British daily Press, was not founded until 1821. No. 1 of the *Guardian* had a handsome,

The Manchester Guardian.

Manchester: Printed and Published by J. GARNETT, No. 29, Market-street.

No. 1. SATURDAY, MAY 5, 1821. PRICE SEVEN-PENCE.

▲ Number one of the *Manchester Guardian*, started as a 1,000-circulation weekly in 1821.

white-lined fat Black title of the kind already mentioned, a six-column make-up, and a front page of advertisements – helped by a number of woodcut blocks – a good deal more open and easy on the eye than that of *The Times*. I imagine that initially the paper must have been worked at press, not by machine; at the end of its first year its circulation was only 1,000 and did not pass the 2,000 mark until 1824.

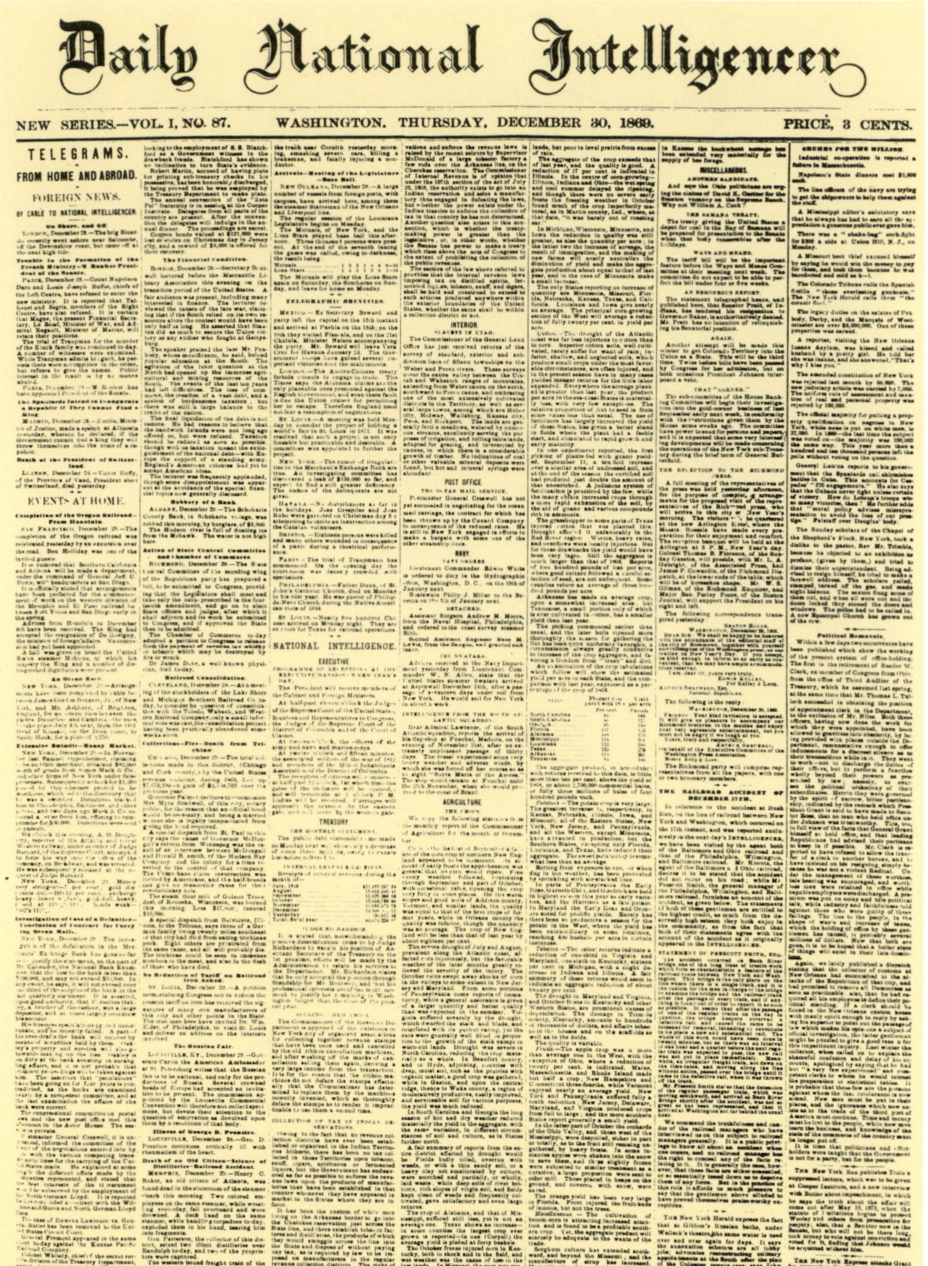
Daily National Intelligencer

NEW SERIES.—VOL. I, NO. 87. WASHINGTON, THURSDAY, DECEMBER 30, 1869. PRICE, 3 CENTS.

TELEGRAMS. FROM HOME AND ABROAD.

FOREIGN NEWS.

EVENTS AT HOME.

NATIONAL INTELLIGENCER.

The first newspaper in Washington (D.C.) the *National Intelligencer* became a daily in 1813: the only 'official' paper in American history, sustained by Federal funds, it had long passed its prime by the time of the Civil War and finally faded away in 1869.

In the American newspaper field the opening decades of the last century were not uneventful. Two features may be singled out. One was the founding of the first newspaper in Washington, DC, the new and raw Federal capital, the other was the extension of what may be called the newspaper frontier as the tide of settlement flowed faster and further into the vast virgin lands of the West.

It was in 1800 that Samuel Harrison Smith, a young Philadelphia publisher, rode into Washington, still a jumble of building sites, frame houses and shacks, to start his *National Intelligencer* (it became a daily in 1813). Never before or since did the United States have another paper like it. Smith had a rigid concept of his paper, faithfully followed until its demise in 1869, as a sheet of public record. By this he meant full reports of Congress debates – in this regard the *Intelligencer* attained virtually the authority of Hansard – together with Federal Government reports and statements. Contrary to all American tradition and practice, the *Intelligencer* functioned as an 'official' journal; it was sustained by Federal funds, through the award of lucrative Government printing contracts to its publishers. It became an accepted Presidential mouthpiece, notably for Jefferson. But with its tiny, bald label heads and text largely in 6pt it was even more stodgily solid than *The Times*; and its restriction of interest made it in many ways more of an American approximation to the *London Gazette*. Its

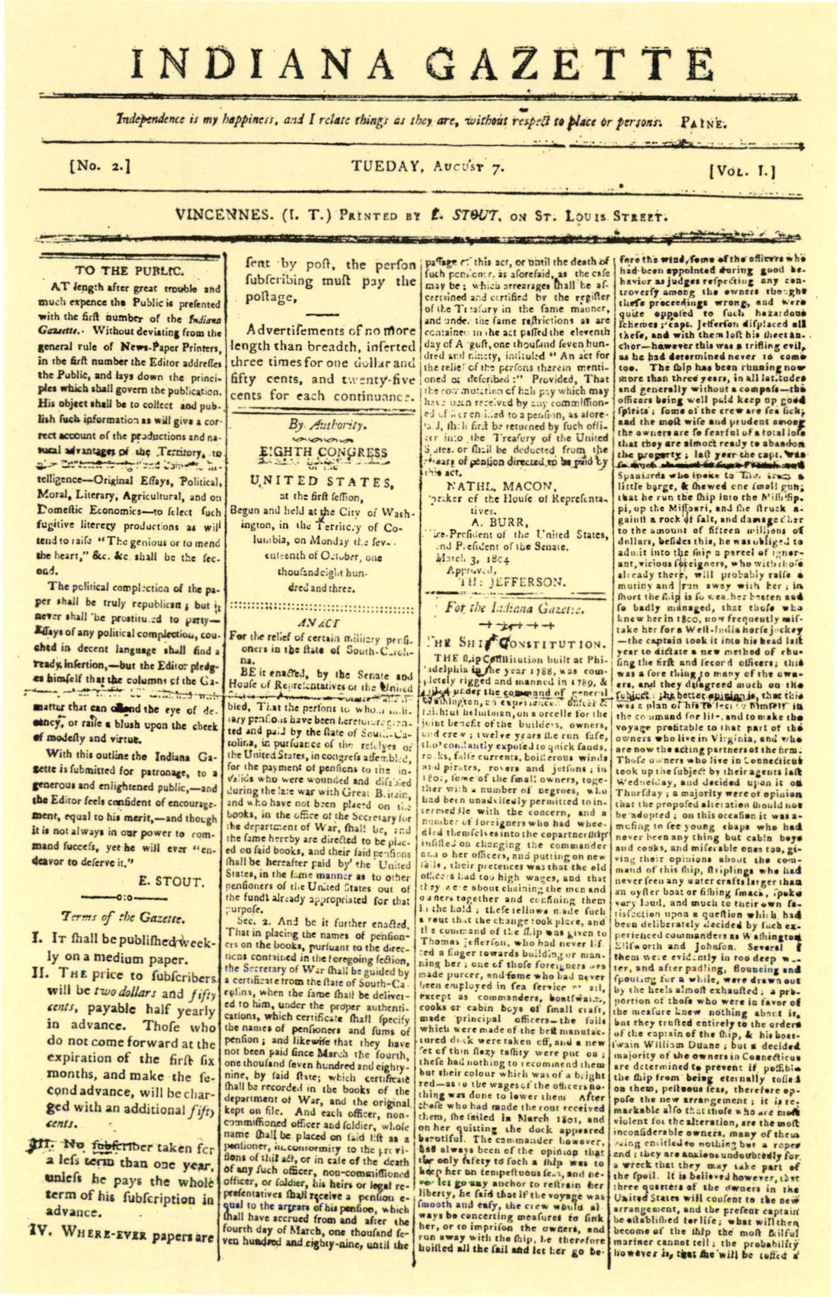

INDIANA GAZETTE

Independence is my happiness, and I relate things as they are, without reſpect to place or perſons. PAINE.

[No. 2.] TUEDAY, AUGUST 7. [VOL. I.]

VINCENNES. (I. T.) PRINTED BY E. STOUT, ON ST. LOUIS STREET.

TO THE PUBLIC.

AT length after great trouble and much expence the Public is preſented with the firſt number of the *Indiana Gazette.* Without deviating from the general rule of News-Paper Printers, in the firſt number the Editor addreſſes the Public, and lays down the principles which ſhall govern the publication. His object ſhall be to collect and publiſh ſuch information as will give a correct account of the productions and natural advantages of the Territory, to [illegible] intelligence—Original Eſſays, Political, Moral, Literary, Agricultural, and on Domeſtic Economics—to ſelect ſuch fugitive literery productions as will tend to raiſe "The genious or to mend the heart," &c. &c. ſhall be the ſecond.

The political complection of the paper ſhall be truly republican; but it never ſhall be proſtituted to party—Eſſays of any political complection, couched in decent language ſhall find a ready inſertion,—but the Editor pledges himſelf that the columns of the Ga[illegible] matter that can offend the eye of decency, or raiſe a bluſh upon the cheek of modeſty and virtue.

With this outline the Indiana Gazette is ſubmitted for patronage, to a generous and enlightened public,—and the Editor feels confident of encouragement, equal to his merit,—and though it is not always in our power to command ſucceſs, yet he will ever "endeavor to deſerve it."

E. STOUT.

Terms of the Gazette.

I. IT ſhall be publiſhed weekly on a medium paper.

II. THE price to ſubſcribers will be *two dollars* and *fifty cents*, payable half yearly in advance. Thoſe who do not come forward at the expiration of the firſt ſix months, and make the ſecond advance, will be charged with an additional *fifty cents*.

III. No ſubſcriber taken for a leſs term than one year, unleſs he pays the whole term of his ſubſcription in advance.

IV. WHERE-EVER papers are ſent by poſt, the perſon ſubſcribing muſt pay the poſtage,

Advertiſements of no more length than breadth, inſerted three times for one dollar and fifty cents, and twenty-five cents for each continuance.

By Authority.

EIGHTH CONGRESS

OF THE

UNITED STATES,

at the firſt ſeſſion,

Begun and held at the City of Waſhington, in the Territory of Columbia, on Monday the ſeventeenth of October, one thouſand eight hundred and three.

AN ACT

For the relief of certain military penſioners in the ſtate of South-Carolina.

BE it enacted, by the Senate and Houſe of Repreſentatives of the United [illegible] bled, That the perſons to whom military penſions have been heretofore granted and paid by the ſtate of South-Carolina, in purſuance of the reſolves of the United States, in congreſs aſſembled, for the payment of penſions to the invalids who were wounded and diſabled during the late war with Great Britain, and who have not been placed on the books, in the office of the Secretary for the department of War, ſhall be, and the ſame hereby are directed to be placed on ſaid books, and their ſaid penſions ſhall be hereafter paid by the United States, in the ſame manner as to other penſioners of the United States out of the funds already appropriated for that purpoſe.

Sec. 2. And be it further enacted, That in placing the names of penſioners on the books, purſuant to the directions contained in the foregoing ſection, the Secretary of War ſhall be guided by a certificate from the ſtate of South-Carolina, when the ſame ſhall be delivered to him, under the proper authentications, which certificate ſhall ſpecify the names of penſioners and ſums of penſion; and likewiſe that they have not been paid ſince March the fourth, one thouſand ſeven hundred and eighty-nine, by ſaid ſtate; which certificate ſhall be recorded in the books of the department of War, and the original kept on file. And each officer, non-commiſſioned officer and ſoldier, whoſe name ſhall be placed on ſaid liſt as a penſioner, in conformity to the proviſions of this act, or in caſe of the death of any ſuch officer, non-commiſſioned officer, or ſoldier, his heirs or legal repreſentatives ſhall receive a penſion equal to the arrears of his penſion, which ſhall have accrued from and after the fourth day of March, one thouſand ſeven hundred and eighty-nine, until the paſſage of this act, or until the death of ſuch penſioner, as aforeſaid, as the caſe may be; which arrearages ſhall be aſcertained and certified by the regiſter of the Treaſury in the ſame manner, and under the ſame reſtrictions as are contained in the act paſſed the eleventh day of Auguſt, one thouſand ſeven hundred and ninety, intituled "An act for the relief of the perſons therein mentioned or deſcribed:" Provided, That the commutation of half pay which may have been received by any commiſſioned officer entitled to a penſion, as aforeſaid, ſhall firſt be returned by ſuch officer into the Treaſury of the United States, or ſhall be deducted from the arrears of penſion directed to be paid by this act.

NATHL. MACON,
Speaker of the Houſe of Repreſentatives.
A. BURR,
Vice-Preſident of the United States, and Preſident of the Senate.
March 3, 1804
Approved,
TH: JEFFERSON.

For the Indiana Gazette.

THE SHIP CONSTITUTION.

THE ſhip Conſtitution built at Philadelphia in the year 1788, was completely rigged and manned in 1789, & ſailed under the command of general Waſhington, an experienced officer & faithful helmſman, on a orcelle for the joint benefit of the builders, owners, and crew; twelve years ſhe run ſafe, tho' conſtantly expoſed to quick ſands, rocks, falſe currents, boiſterous winds and pirates, rovers and jetſons; in 1801, ſome of the ſmall owners, together with a number of negroes, who had been unadviſedly permitted to intermeddle with the concern, and a number of foreigners who had wheedled themſelves into the copartnerſhip inſiſted on changing the commander and other officers, and putting on new ſails, their pretences was that the old officers had too high wages, and that they were about chaining the men and owners together and confining them in the hold; theſe fellows made ſuch a rout that the change took place, and the command of the ſhip was given to Thomas Jefferſon, who had never lifted a finger towards building or manning her; one of thoſe foreigners was made purcer, and ſome who had never been employed in ſea ſervice [illegible], except as commanders, boatſwains, cooks or cabin boys of ſmall craft, made principal officers—the ſails which were made of the beſt manufactured duck were taken off, and a new ſet of thin flazy taſſity were put on; theſe had nothing to recommend them but their colour which was of a bright red—as to the wages of the officers nothing was done to lower them. After thoſe who had made the rout received them, ſhe ſailed in March 1801, and on her quitting the dock appeared beautiful. The commander however, had always been of the opinion that the only ſafety to ſuch a ſhip was to keep her on tempeſtuous ſeas, and never let go any anchor to reſtrain her liberty, he ſaid that if the voyage was ſmooth and eaſy, the crew would always be concerting meaſures to ſink her, or to impriſon the owners, and run away with the ſhip, he therefore hoiſted all the ſail and let her go before the wind, ſome of the officers who had been appointed during good behavior as judges reſpecting any controverſy among the owners thought theſe proceedings wrong, and were quite oppoſed to ſuch hazardous ſchemes; capt. Jefferſon diſplaced all theſe, and with them loſt his ſheet anchor—however this was a trifling evil, as he had determined never to come too. The ſhip has been running now more than three years, in all latitudes and generally without a compaſs—the officers being well paid keep up good ſpirits; ſome of the crew are ſea ſick; and the moſt wiſe and prudent among the owners are ſo fearful of a total loſs that they are almoſt ready to abandon the property; laſt year the capt. was [illegible] Spaniards who ſpoke to him [illegible] a little barge, & ſhewed one ſmall gun; that he run the ſhip into the Miſſiſſippi, up the Miſſouri, and ſhe ſtruck againſt a rock of ſalt, and damaged her to the amount of fifteen millions of dollars, beſides this, he was obliged to admit into the ſhip a parcel of ignorant, vicious foreigners, who with thoſe already there, will probably raiſe a mutiny and run away with her; in ſhort the ſhip is ſo weather beaten and ſo badly managed, that thoſe who knew her in 1800, now frequently miſtake her for a Weſt-India horſe jockey—the captain took it into his head laſt year to dictate a new method of chuſing the firſt and ſecond officers; this was a ſore thing to many of the owners, and they diſagreed much on the ſubject: the better opinion is, that this was a plan of his to ſecure to himſelf the command for life, and to make the voyage profitable to that part of the owners who live in Virginia, and who are now the acting partners of the firm. Thoſe owners who live in Connecticut took up the ſubject by their agents laſt Wedneſday, and decided upon it on Thurſday; a majority were of opinion that the propoſed alteration ſhould not be adopted; on this occaſion it was amuſing to ſee young chaps who had never been any thing but cabin boys and cooks, and miſerable ones too, giving their opinions about the command of this ſhip, ſtriplings who had never ſeen any water crafts larger than an oyſter boat or fiſhing ſmack, ſpoke very loud, and much to their own ſatisfaction upon a queſtion which had been deliberately decided by ſuch experienced commanders as Waſhington, Ellſworth and Johnſon. Several of them were evidently in too deep water, and after padling, flouncing and ſpouting for a while, were drawn out by the heels almoſt exhauſted; a proportion of thoſe who were in favor of the meaſure knew nothing about it, but they truſted entirely to the orders of the captain of the ſhip, & his boatſwain William Duane; but a decided majority of the owners in Connecticut are determined to prevent if poſſible the ſhip from being eternally toſſed on them, peſtuous ſeas, therefore oppoſe the new arrangement; it is remarkable alſo that thoſe who are moſt violent for the alteration, are the moſt inconſiderable owners, many of them being entitled to nothing but a ropes end; they are anxious undoubtedly for a wreck that they may take part of the ſpoil. It is believed however, that three quarters of the owners in the United States will conſent to the new arrangement, and the preſent captain be eſtabliſhed for life; what will then become of the ſhip the moſt ſkilful mariner cannot tell; the probability however is, that ſhe will be toſſed a

An early 'frontier' newspaper, the *Indiana Gazette* was launched in 1804: despite the remoteness of Indiana Territory it was a neat piece of old face setting.

epitaph was pronounced by one of Smith's successors when he contemptuously referred to his contemporaries as 'mere news and advertising sheets'.[6]

Of the 'frontier' newspapers two samples may be taken, one a good deal more sophisticated than the other. The *Indiana Gazette* was launched in Vincennes, then capital of Indiana Territory (Statehood was not attained until 1816) on 7 August 1804. Small by metropolitan standards, it was a neat-looking four-page sheet with a four-column make-up, the 14-inch columns set in old face (with the long 's' still surviving) to the then narrow measure of 13½ picas. The title-line, in letter-spaced roman capitals, was followed by a series of full transverse rules enclosing a motto from Tom Paine, the date and publication lines. Advertisements were solicited, at the rate of $1.50 for three insertions, if 'of no more length than breadth', but there were none on the front page, which was exclusively editorial. News proper, ranging from accounts of Napoleon's proclamation as Emperor to a highly premature report of the death of Nelson, and from the arrival of German immigrants in Ohio to a landslide in Virginia, appeared in inside pages. The editorial matter on the front, apart from a tolerably displayed Act of Congress, comprised the publisher's opening promotion pieces and a long political essay, strongly Federalist in sentiment, modestly headed 'THE SHIP CONSTITUTION' in caps and smalls.

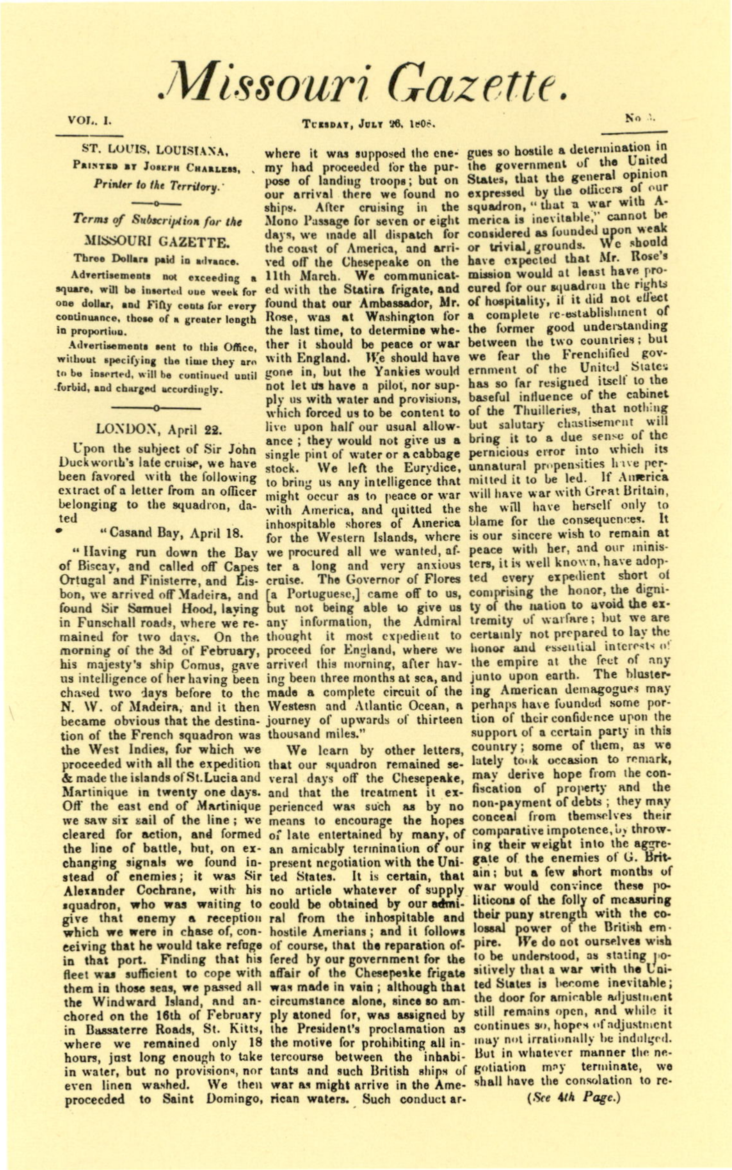

Missouri Gazette.

VOL. I. TUESDAY, JULY 26, 1808. No 3.

ST. LOUIS, LOUISIANA,
PRINTED BY JOSEPH CHARLESS,
Printer to the Territory.

Terms of Subscription for the
MISSOURI GAZETTE.

Three Dollars paid in advance.

Advertisements not exceeding a square, will be inserted one week for one dollar, and Fifty cents for every continuance, those of a greater length in proportion.

Advertisements sent to this Office, without specifying the time they are to be inserted, will be continued until forbid, and charged accordingly.

LONDON, April 22.

Upon the subject of Sir John Duckworth's late cruise, we have been favored with the following extract of a letter from an officer belonging to the squadron, dated

"Casand Bay, April 18.

"Having run down the Bay of Biscay, and called off Capes Ortugal and Finisterre, and Lisbon, we arrived off Madeira, and found Sir Samuel Hood, laying in Funschall roads, where we remained for two days. On the morning of the 3d of February, his majesty's ship Comus, gave us intelligence of her having been chased two days before to the N. W. of Madeira, and it then became obvious that the destination of the French squadron was the West Indies, for which we proceeded with all the expedition & made the islands of St. Lucia and Martinique in twenty one days. Off the east end of Martinique we saw six sail of the line; we cleared for action, and formed the line of battle, but, on exchanging signals we found instead of enemies; it was Sir Alexander Cochrane, with his squadron, who was waiting to give that enemy a reception which we were in chase of, conceiving that he would take refuge in that port. Finding that his fleet was sufficient to cope with them in those seas, we passed all the Windward Island, and anchored on the 16th of February in Bassaterre Roads, St. Kitts, where we remained only 18 hours, just long enough to take in water, but no provisions, nor even linen washed. We then proceeded to Saint Domingo, where it was supposed the enemy had proceeded for the purpose of landing troops; but on our arrival there we found no ships. After cruising in the Mono Passage for seven or eight days, we made all dispatch for the coast of America, and arrived off the Chesepeake on the 11th March. We communicated with the Statira frigate, and found that our Ambassador, Mr. Rose, was at Washington for the last time, to determine whether it should be peace or war with England. We should have gone in, but the Yankies would not let us have a pilot, nor supply us with water and provisions, which forced us to be content to live upon half our usual allowance; they would not give us a single pint of water or a cabbage stock. We left the Eurydice, to bring us any intelligence that might occur as to peace or war with America, and quitted the inhospitable shores of America for the Western Islands, where we procured all we wanted, after a long and very anxious cruise. The Governor of Flores [a Portuguese,] came off to us, but not being able to give us any information, the Admiral thought it most expedient to proceed for England, where we arrived this morning, after having been three months at sea, and made a complete circuit of the Westesn and Atlantic Ocean, a journey of upwards of thirteen thousand miles."

We learn by other letters, that our squadron remained several days off the Chesepeake, and that the treatment it experienced was such as by no means to encourage the hopes of late entertained by many, of an amicably termination of our present negotiation with the United States. It is certain, that no article whatever of supply could be obtained by our admiral from the inhospitable and hostile Amerians; and it follows of course, that the reparation offered by our government for the affair of the Chesepeake frigate was made in vain; although that circumstance alone, since so amply atoned for, was assigned by the President's proclamation as the motive for prohibiting all intercourse between the inhabitants and such British ships of war as might arrive in the American waters. Such conduct argues so hostile a determination in the government of the United States, that the general opinion expressed by the officers of our squadron, "that a war with America is inevitable," cannot be considered as founded upon weak or trivial grounds. We should have expected that Mr. Rose's mission would at least have procured for our squadron the rights of hospitality, if it did not effect a complete re-establishment of the former good understanding between the two countries; but we fear the Frenchified government of the United States has so far resigned itself to the baseful influence of the cabinet of the Thuilleries, that nothing but salutary chastisement will bring it to a due sense of the pernicious error into which its unnatural propensities have permitted it to be led. If America will have war with Great Britain, she will have herself only to blame for the consequences. It is our sincere wish to remain at peace with her, and our ministers, it is well known, have adopted every expedient short of comprising the honor, the dignity of the nation to avoid the extremity of warfare; but we are certainly not prepared to lay the honor and essential interests of the empire at the feet of any junto upon earth. The blustering American demagogues may perhaps have founded some portion of their confidence upon the support of a certain party in this country; some of them, as we lately took occasion to remark, may derive hope from the confiscation of property and the non-payment of debts; they may conceal from themselves their comparative impotence, by throwing their weight into the aggregate of the enemies of G. Britain; but a few short months of war would convince these politicons of the folly of measuring their puny strength with the colossal power of the British empire. We do not ourselves wish to be understood, as stating positively that a war with the United States is become inevitable; the door for amicable adjustment still remains open, and while it continues so, hopes of adjustment may not irrationally be indulged. But in whatever manner the negotiation may terminate, we shall have the consolation to re-

(*See 4th Page.*)

The first newspaper to appear west of the Mississippi, the *Missouri Gazette* was a small and simple sheet: the lower-case italic title, in a face of transitional-modern cut, is unusual. When the *Gazette* started in 1808 St Louis was a place in 'Louisiana', the vast territory purchased from Napoleonic France only five years before: the State of Missouri only dated from 1821.

The *Missouri Gazette*, the first paper to be published west of the Mississippi, was a smaller and simpler sheet. Appearing in St Louis on 12 July 1808, its four pages were made up in three 13-pica columns 11-inches deep; white was used instead of column rules. Rules were no doubt in short supply in the stock of the paper's editor-printer-publisher, thirty-six-year-old Irish immigrant Joseph Charless; he had taken off for Philadelphia a couple of years before the '98 and worked his way westwards via Kentucky, transporting his small press and cases of type by river boat down the Ohio and up the Mississippi to St Louis. Thus the *Missouri Gazette* had white space only, and the simplest of date-lines, under its title in an upper- and lower-case italic of transitional character. Again the front page was entirely editorial and, though lacking any display, news as well; for it contained a detailed account of British naval moves presaging what was to be the War of 1812 – so detailed that it 'turned' to the back page.

In a dozen years Charless built up his subscribers from 170 to 1,000; on which it is worth noting his call to 'those of his subscribers who gave their notes or word of honour to pay in flour or corn to bring it in directly. Others who promised to pay in beef or pork, to deliver it as soon as possible'. The *Gazette* made a good show from the start of St Louis local news, though its headlining was no more than the one-line label. An inside page lead, on a Fourth of July celebration, was labelled PATRIOTIC EFFUSIONS; it was an apt line, since there were a score of toasts, including one to 'The American Fair' – 'May they press to their bosoms none but freemen and spurn from their embraces the followers of vice and corruption'.

3: The Mid-Nineteenth Century Daily

THE mechanisation both of printing and paper-making lies at the heart of the newspaper developments that now have to be considered. It should be made plain that the 'mid' of this chapter's title does not mean some point in mid-century but a whole period – the four middle decades from the 1830s to the 1860s inclusive. In a way it could be called the prerotary period, using the word 'rotary' in our accepted sense of a web-fed press printing from stereotype plates and delivering 'perfected' (completely printed) copies of a newspaper. The period's advances in newspaper printing techniques, which were very great, were nevertheless limited to production from paper in sheet form and no machine could 'perfect' the sheets, i.e. all machines printed one side of the paper only. To produce a complete paper, therefore, a pair of machines were always required – as with the original Koenig and Bauer of 1814.

The preceding chapter noted how the introduction of the iron press enabled larger sheets to be handled; these larger sheets, however, were small in comparison with the sheet sizes that the machine could tackle, sizes that grew as larger and larger machines were devised. Here is the point at which the development of the paper-making machine became of primary importance. Without the larger sheets that could be mechanically produced, the printing machine could have done no more than run off faster the small four-page folio or eight-page quarto papers of the hand-press. Handmade paper was naturally limited by the size of mould that the vatman was physically able to lift, with its weighty content of pulp. Machine-made paper had no such limitation; it thus provided the printing machine with the material without which neither newspaper format nor paging could be increased.

The first effective paper-making machine, sponsored by the brothers Fourdrinier, was erected by the ingenious engineer Bryan Donkin in Hertfordshire in 1803. While progress was patchy – the first Fourdrinier was not set up in the United States, also by Donkin, until 1827 – and the handmade mills fought a long battle for the quality market, machine-made paper must have been generally available to the larger newspapers by the opening of the period we are discussing. By the 1850s British mills had over 400 Fourdrinier machines at work, though struggling with the long-standing and chronic shortage of the linen and cotton 'rag' which was then still the sole source of paper-making pulp. It is unnesessary here to go into the elaborate story of last century's search for alternative paper-making materials; from the newspaper standpoint the real breakthrough did not come until the 1870s, when newsprint was first made from wood-pulp, and not till the following decade did this cheap and quickly-produced newsprint finally become the norm.

Before turning now to examine newspaper printing developments we must recall that the peculiar pressure of the Stamp Acts, already adverted to, continued to affect the London dailies until 1855. Nor was news pressure light in a period which included, for instance, the Reform crisis of 1831–32, the Chartist campaigns of 1839–48, the agitation which culminated in the repeal of the Corn Laws in 1846, Europe's revolutionary year of 1848, the Crimean War. The factors which had produced tight-packed papers with minimal headlining continued to be valid, or were thought to be valid, despite increases in format and

The Applegath 4-cylinder press.

The Applegath type revolver.

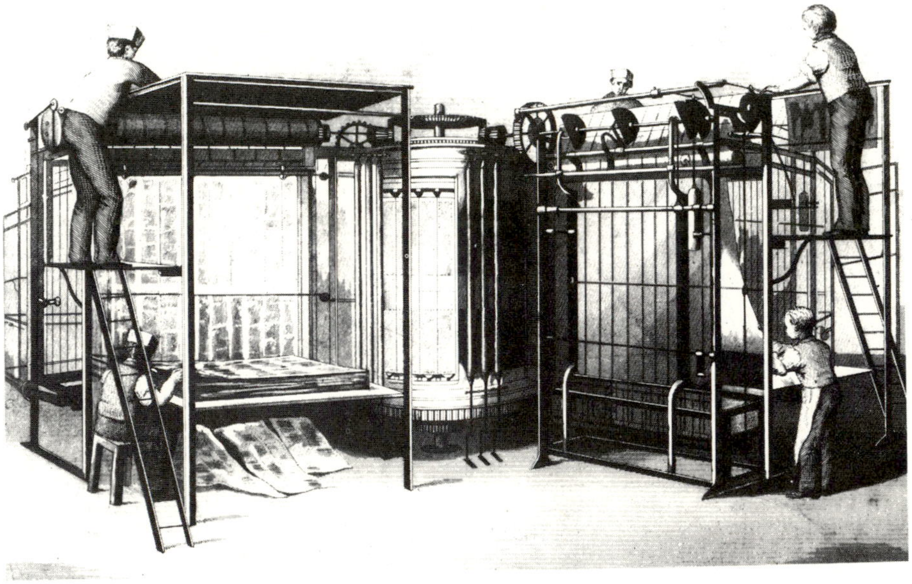

The Hoe type revolver.

paging. *The Times* adopted six-column make-up in 1825 (this was long to be standard format for all London dailies) and increased its basic paging to eight from 1833.

The first step in mechanical advance had been the simplification and improvement of the original Koenig and Bauer cylinder machines at *The Times*. This was achieved by a talented pair of engineers, Augustus Applegath and his brother-in-law Edward Cowper, who had been engaged by John Walter II as consultants and supervisors when the Koenig machines went in. Applegath and Cowper, two of the most interesting characters in the history of printing technology, had previously experimented with rotary note-printing, from curved stereotypes, for the Bank of England. They ironed out mechanical troubles that had developed in the Koenig machines and secured some increase in output; but this was quite insufficient to cope with the steadily-rising *Times* circulation.

Applegath and Cowper therefore addressed themselves to the problem of how to achieve a spectacular output increase from a flatbed cylinder machine, where the impression was taken by a rotating cylinder from a reciprocating forme on the bed of the machine. Since the reciprocating speed of the heavy forme had reached its practical limit what was to be done? The answer was to make the machine a four-feeder, in effect four machines built into a single unit and printing from the one forme. The four-feeder required four layers-on, stroking in a sheet every $3\frac{1}{2}$ seconds when the machine was at full speed, and four boys to take off the printed sheets. Producing 4,000 impressions an hour (one side only) the Applegath four-feeder served *The Times* well for a score of years from its inception in 1828. Machines of similar type were made by Koenig and Bauer in Germany and were long standard in many newspaper pressrooms.

By the mid-1840s, however, with circulations continuing to rise and advertising pressure demanding higher paging, the capacity of the multi-feeder flatbed was being outstripped. Clearly a revolutionary change in the mechanical technique of printing was called for. To this problem two men independently addressed themselves – Applegath in London and Hoe, an American printing-machine maker, in New York. They both hit on the same solution, namely to turn the printing surface itself from a flat reciprocating forme to a rotating cylinder; this was the basic invention of the rotary press, since whether the rotary is sheet-fed or reel-fed is quite incidental to its central principle.

The 'rotaries' that Applegath and Hoe produced were both type-revolving machines. Though the papier-mâché mode of stereotyping had been invented, and it was thus possible to visualise the casting of curved printing plates from a curved flexible mould, this did not appear technically practical at that stage, though it may well have occurred to Applegath in the light of his banknote experiments. So both inventors devised methods of converting pages set in movable type into segments of a circle, securing those segments to the huge cylinder or drum which was their operative unit, combining ink-distribution and the actual printing. Hoe's drum was $6\frac{1}{2}$ feet in diameter, Applegath's $5\frac{1}{2}$ feet, so the curve of the segmental chases, which the Americans called 'turtles', was not great.

The individual columns of each page were slid into position on the 'turtle' and secured by wedge-shaped column rules, themselves held in position by a tongue and groove system. Sliding blocks and screws at the ends and sides then locked the whole page. While it was claimed that the polygonal mass of types was thus as secure as in the flat forme there was an ever-present risk that an imperfect lock-up, coupled with the centrifugal force generated by the rotary action, could bring disaster. In any event, it will be appreciated that this mode of production rendered impossible any setting beyond single-column, which had an important effect on the development of headline display, as will be seen.

Output of the type-revolving presses was determined by the number of impression cylinders, which could step by twos up to ten, each with its feeding position for the sheet-feeding of the machine. Here the Hoe type-revolver had an advantage in an ingenious cam-operated sheet-delivery system which dispensed with the boy takers-off needed by the Applegath machine. There was also another marked difference between the machines. Applegath's giant drum was vertical, Hoe's horizontal. The backed-up, complete paper came from the type-revolver as a flat sheet, which was then hand-folded; this left the 'bolts' (the top edge) uncut, and thus it was said that in the houses of the gentry the butler's first morning duty was to slit the bolts of his master's paper.

Hoe was quicker off the mark than Applegath in completing his type-revolver. His first machine, a four-feeder with a reputed output of 8,000 impressions an hour, was installed at the Philadelphia *Public Ledger* in 1847. Applegath, though his patent specification for his machine dated from December 1846, did not have his first two eight-feeders running at *The Times* till October 1848; their output has generally been rated at 10,000 impressions an hour.* *The Times* itself initially claimed an hourly output of 8,000 impressions, while looking to an 'ultimate' 12,000; these figures were given in the first leader of 29 December 1848, when the new type-revolvers had had three months to run-in. The leader, a remarkable piece of simple technical exposition, offered a detailed comparison of the old multi-feeder flatbeds and the new machines; it noted that Applegath's 'great improvement' was 'the substitution of a uniform rotatory motion for the horizontal reciprocating motion of the old machine'. It further argued that types would be more secure on Applegath's vertical drum than on horizontal-drum machines, since they would not be subject to the effects of gravity as well as to those of centrifugal force.

As the Applegath and Hoe machines settled down to work, some controversy developed over output figures. The customary urges of manufacturers' publicity led the Hoe firm to make claims that Applegath not unreasonably contested. Thus the Hoe assertion that the *Public Ledger* produced 8,000 impressions an hour meant that each feeder was laying-on sheets at a rate of 2,000 an hour, or under two seconds a sheet. Even if such a breakneck pace could be reached it could scarcely be maintained; and when Hoes went further, boasting that an eight-feeder could produce 20,000 impressions an hour (i.e. laying-on at 2,500 sheets an hour), Applegath commented that 1,500 sheets an hour was the maximum that could be got from London layers-on. On an eight-feeder that last figure would produce the 12,000 an hour foreseen by *The Times*; a steady laying-on rate of somewhere between 1,000 and 1,500 sheets an hour would produce the 10,000 impression with which the Applegath is normally credited.

Despite the editorialising in *The Times* about the effects of gravity, there were soon signs that the future lay with the horizontal type-revolver. Applegath himself was converted and was anxious to build horizontal machines; indeed, he took out a patent in 1858 and built a ten-feeder for the old *Morning Herald*, which had not long to live. But it was too late. Hoe had been in the field too long, and too soon. In 1848 he had installed a horizontal type-revolver for *La Patrie* in Paris, the first machine of its kind in Europe; this installation was visited by Edward Lloyd, a keen Sunday paper publisher whose *Lloyd's Weekly News* had begun to boom, and he ordered a six-feeder Hoe, eventually installed in his London plant in 1856. This news alarmed John Walter III, who succeeded to the Chief Proprietorship of *The Times* in 1847; no doubt he was also concerned because, even with the Applegath verticals, the paper had been barely able to cope with its Crimean War circulation boost (1854–56). Though his manager, Mowbray Morris, had told a Government Committee in 1851 that no machine in America could equal Applegath's, which was 'superior to anything in use in any part of the world', Walter journeyed to Philadelphia to see the Hoes at work and promptly ordered two ten-feeders.

These machines, costing the then formidable sum of £6,000 each

* Applegath supplied a smaller version of his machine to the *Illustrated London News*; this was shown at the Great Exhibition of 1851 and attracted immense attention. Applegath demonstrated the machine to the Queen and the Prince Consort (W. Turner Berry, *Augustus Applegath* in the *Journal of the Printing Historical Society*, No. 2, 1966, pp. 49–57).

(later reduced to £10,000 for the two) were made in this country under licence at the famous Whitworth engineering works in Manchester; the order made Hoes realise the potentialities of the British market and led to their establishment of a London office in 1865. The Hoe ten-feeders went on edition in Printing House Square in August 1858 and the Applegath verticals were shortly after broken up. What a contemporary observer called 'the cheap daily newspapers' – those which, after 1855, dropped their price to a penny – followed suit by installing 'the American machines'. By 1866 the rising *Daily Telegraph* had four Hoe ten-feeders, the *Standard* (which turned from an evening into a morning in 1857) had five, the *Daily News* (whose modest circulation had been catered for, since its foundation in 1846, by four-feeder flat-beds) put in two eight-feeders in 1868. While the Hoe ten-feeder was rated at 20,000 impressions an hour, the highest actual running speed in London appears to have been the *Telegraph* at 18,000 an hour; on *The Times* 13,000 was regarded as the safe maximum, while the contemporary observer already cited referred to 'rates varying from 12–15,000 in an hour'.

The type-revolving machines, for obvious reasons, gave a new impetus to the examination of stereotyping possibilities. Could a suitably curved plate be cast from each page to take the place of the 'turtle' on the type-revolver's drum? The problem, which involved exploiting the papier-mâché mould to make a cast of an entire page, was solved by the brothers Dellagana in London (whither they had fled after the 1848 Revolution in France, where they had been working on the Paris *Constitutionnel*) and by Charles Craske in New York (whither he had emigrated from London in 1837). Craske was casting curved plates for the *New York Herald's* type-revolvers by 1854 and the *New York Tribune* by 1861. James Dellagana had his first curved plates running on the Applegath vertical in December 1857; by 1860 the Hoe horizontals in Printing House Square were printing entirely from stereo plates, Dellagana having set up a stereo foundry as an integral part of the mechanical establishment of *The Times* in March of that year. The Dellaganas also made plates for the *Daily Telegraph* – up to 96 a night by 1867.

By now enough has been said of the mechanical developments of the period to permit some discussion of their implications for newspaper typography. In practice these amounted to very little. Let us again recall the oppressive Stamp Acts and the premium they put on space, which produced a species of conditioning that the emancipation of 1855 by no means speedily removed. The consequent tight-packing of their papers apart, publishers were preoccupied with the problems of news-getting (whether by 'extraordinary express' or the new-fangled electric telegraph when it began in the 1840s), faster presswork, and the handling of an ever-growing mass of close-set advertisements, mainly in the form of run-on 'smalls'. When *The Times* produced its first twenty-four-page issue, on 21 June 1861, announcing that this mammoth issue was due to the 'extraordinary pressure of advertisements', it noted that whereas half-a-century before the paper's daily average of advertisements was 150, that day's issue carried 4,000.

In such circumstances typography was likely to take a back seat, whatever the technical advances in newspaper production. By this time, too, there was a total cleavage between the book trade, with its traditionally high typographic standards, and the news trade. News compositors in London became a race apart from their fellows in the general trade, even their union organisation (such as it was) remaining separate until mid-century. Morison aptly summed it up thus: 'While the news trade expanded economically as the handmaid and sometimes slave of commercial publicity, the newspapers fell backward as pieces of typography and their staffs as skilled designers of print.'[1] For generations newspaper head printers and their men remained pillars of typographical conservatism, ensuring that what had always been done would always be done; journalists were writing

ENTRE DEUX VERRES A VIN DE CHAMPAGNE

NOUVEAU MONDE — LOUIS BLANC

L'ÉTAT-ANARCHIE

DU CITOYEN PROUDHON.

LES INSTITUTEURS PRIMAIRES.

NAPOLÉON.

SANG.

2 ET 3 DÉPARTS: CALIFORNIE

▲ Multi-column advertising display in a Parisian daily of 1850.

men, indifferent to the graphic look of their paper; a functionary called 'the sub-editor' (singular) checked the copy and wrote the one-line label headings; the printer did the page make-up.

The traditionalist, pack-it-in, single-column approach was reinforced by the type-revolving machine, as already noted. So long as the Applegath or the Hoe operated with type locked in 'turtles' anything other than single-column working was out of the question; that this restriction was removed when curved stereoplates were introduced was of no practical consequence, since attitudes had become so firmly fixed. Only the largest newspapers, anyhow, plated their type-revolvers; and not only did all other newspapers continue to use 'turtles' of wedged single-column type on their type-revolvers, but one of the early web-fed rotaries (the Foster 'Prestonian') was designed to run either from type or plates. Any sort of multi-column display would clearly have been a totally foreign concept to any newspaper printer. In fact, of course, any working from the flat forme, whether direct or plated, permitted multi-column display. A Parisian example of this, within the period, can be seen in Victor Hugo's daily *L'Évènement* (1850); this would have been printed on a multi-feeder flatbed and, while its front page was a solid, minimal-headed, set of editorial columns, its advertising back page presented a sledge-hammer spread of big, bold display type; but such French flamboyance was quite incompatible with English-phlegm.

For the London dailies the period was indeed one of *plus ça change* (mechanically) *plus c'est la même chose* (typographically). Front pages remained a wilderness of 'smalls'. The unrelieved solidity of the news pages was crushing (or would have appeared so to later generations). A page of the first number, 21 January 1846, of the radical *Daily News*, edited by that dynamic reporter Charles Dickens, could be cited as a classic monolith of Victorian news-text – not merely no crossheads but no paragraphs; the standing instruction to news compositors as they lifted their short 'takes' was 'end even', i.e. make the last line set a full line, whatever the spacing. In fact the only piece of textual relief emerging during the period was in *The Times* which began, in 1840, to let a tiny chink of light into its columns by leading some of its minion (7pt) body type. But a great deal of too, too solid minion remained; and, even in leaded columns, an important news-story could still be headed, in small italic capitals, *EXPRESS FROM FALMOUTH*.

The universally-established Modern face typography of news-text was paralleled in the headline typography, such as it was. Two weights of Modern roman capitals formed the main headline ingredient; they were cast as 'titling' letters, namely full-face capitals without beard or shoulder, and began to be called 'news titlings'. Suitable sizes of these titlings were also used as drop initials (in the small advertisements, for instance): hence they were classed as 'two-line' letters and their sizes so expressed – two-line pearl (10pt), two-line nonpareil (12pt), two-line minion (14pt). They were in the main unsatisfactory versions of the Modern face, much debased from the standards of Bodoni or Didot; the lighter weight in particular was a spindly and colourless affair, grey and weak in appearance when printed. It had a condensed version, rare at this time, but popular later.

The Times used the bold titling, in 14pt, for standing lines like SECOND EDITION (which early in the century had been in 24pt Caslon Old Face upper- and lower-case) and for the labels to main foreign news – INDIA, AMERICA and so on – which on great occasions might be followed by a deck in 10pt light titling (as when the S.S. *Great Western* successfully completed its Atlantic crossing in 1842). From time to time in the 1840s the 14pt bold titling was also used as the main heading to big news stories. Thus in 1842 the DEATH OF THE / DUKE OF / ORLEANS rated a solid three-liner; with equine aptness – since the Duke had been thrown from his horse-carriage in the Bois – the brief,

Big news in *The Times* 1840-4 (below and top of facing page).

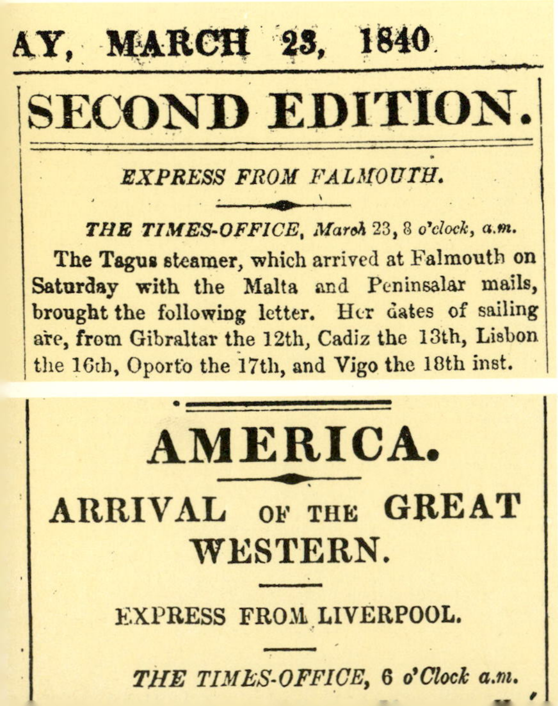

AY, MARCH 23, 1840

SECOND EDITION.

EXPRESS FROM FALMOUTH.

THE TIMES-OFFICE, March 23, 8 o'clock, a.m.

The Tagus steamer, which arrived at Falmouth on Saturday with the Malta and Peninsular mails, brought the following letter. Her dates of sailing are, from Gibraltar the 12th, Cadiz the 13th, Lisbon the 16th, Oporto the 17th, and Vigo the 18th inst.

AMERICA.

ARRIVAL OF THE GREAT WESTERN.

EXPRESS FROM LIVERPOOL.

THE TIMES-OFFICE, 6 o'Clock a.m.

DAY, AUGUST 6, 1844.

SECOND EDITION.

EXTRAORDINARY EXPRESS.

THE TIMES-OFFICE, 11 *o'clock*.

DEATH OF THE DUKE OF ORLEANS.

PARIS, 6 o'CLOCK WEDNESDAY EVENING.

An extraordinary dispatch announces the melancholy intelligence of the death of the Duke of Orleans. His Royal Highness was thrown from his cabriolet in the Bois de Boulogne about 12 o'clock, and although no danger was apprehended from the accident at first alarming symptoms appeared, and the Duke breathed his last about half past 4 o'clock.

LIVERPOOL RACES.

(BY EXPRESS.)

THE TIMES-OFFICE, 6 *o'Clock a.m.*

LIVERPOOL JULY MEETING, WEDNESDAY.

The CROXTETH STAKES were won easily by Lord Westminster's Satirist (Marson), beating The Shadow, Currier, and Meal.

The PRODUCE STAKES were won by Lord Derby's Fortune-teller (Helmes), beating Sir R. Bulkeley's c. by Beagle, by a head.

The BICKERSTAFFE STAKES were won by Lord Westminster's Candahar (Marson), beating Lord G. Bentinck's Peloponnesus, by a head.

The SEFTON STAKES, for fillies, were won by Mr. Meik-

THE

ACCOUCHEMENT

OF

HER MAJESTY.

BIRTH OF A PRINCE.

THE TIMES-OFFICE, *Tuesday Morning*, *Half-past* 8 *o'Clock.*

We have the happiness to announce that the Queen has been safely delivered of a PRINCE.

We are happy to state that Her Majesty is doing well.

We are indebted to the extraordinary power of the Electro-Magnetic Telegraph for the rapid communication of this important announcement.

COURT CIRCULAR.

WINDSOR, MONDAY.

The Queen and Prince Albert walked this morning in the

SECOND EDITION.

THE

ACCOUCHEMENT

OF

HER MAJESTY.

EXPRESS FROM WINDSOR.

THE TIMES-OFFICE, Tuesday Morning, Half-past 10 *o'Clock a.m.*

In addition to the intelligence of the auspicious event which we published at half-past 8 o'clock, we have just received the following

OFFICIAL DESPATCH.

" WINDSOR CASTLE, AUGUST 6, 1844.

" *Half-past* 8 *o'Clock a.m.*

" The Queen was safely delivered of a PRINCE this morning at 50 minutes past 7 o'clock.

" Her Majesty and Infant are perfectly well.

" JAMES CLARK, M.D.

" CHARLES LOCOCK, M.D.

" ROBERT FERGUSON, M.D."

Intimation of Her Majesty's illness was forwarded

heavily-leaded seven-line dispatch from Paris was followed by the racing results, with a one-line 8pt italic capitals heading *LIVERPOOL RACES*. Two years later, aroused by loyal fervour and electrified by the new-fangled telegraph ('we are indebted to the extraordinary power of the Electro-Magnetic Telegraph for the rapid communication of this important announcement' *The Times* gave the 14pt bold titling, amply whited, to the news of the birth of Queen Victoria's second son, Prince Alfred Ernest. The ACCOUCHEMENT of HER MAJESTY, with the 10pt light titling deck BIRTH OF A PRINCE made a brave show: the second edition's juxtaposed repetition of the main deck, with slightly reduced spacing, over the later 'Official Dispatch' from Windsor is without doubt the most amazing deliberate 'double' in the history of journalism.

Bold aberrations of this sort, however, did not long survive; by the end of the 1850s a minimal-heading style, based on the 10pt light titling, had been evolved which was to remain unchanged in *The Times* for half a century, spacing becoming somewhat more generous as time went on. What we would now call lead stories bore the label LATEST INTELLIGENCE in 10pt light titling, followed by a French dash and then the news headline, usually one line, in the same type, with a three-em rule before the opening of text. In this style THE WAR IN ITALY sufficed in 1859 for the news of the Solferino campaign; identical typography served in 1871 for the capitulation of Paris in the Franco-Prussian war and in 1907 for the assassination of the King of Portugal. It was not the only example of the institutional inertia of

▼'Latest Intelligence' in *The Times*: left to right 1859, 1871, 1907.

LATEST INTELLIGENCE.

THE WAR IN ITALY.

[A portion of the following appeared in our second edition of yesterday:—]

The following telegram was received at Mr. Reuter's office May 24:—

" PARIS, TUESDAY, MAY 24.

" The *Moniteur* of this morning publishes the

LATEST INTELLIGENCE.

THE WAR.

THE

CAPITULATION OF PARIS.

(BY TELEGRAPH.)

(FROM OUR SPECIAL CORRESPONDENT.)

IMPERIAL AND FOREIGN INTELLIGENCE.

ASSASSINATION OF

THE KING OF PORTUGAL

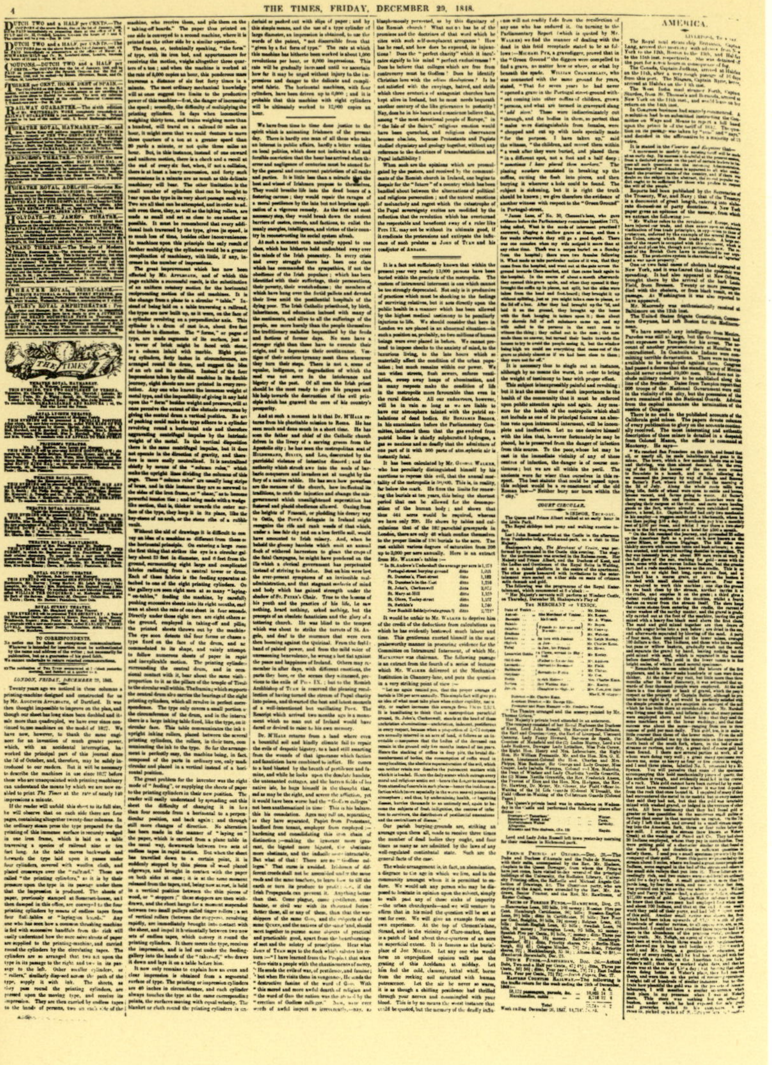
THE TIMES, FRIDAY, DECEMBER 29, 1848.

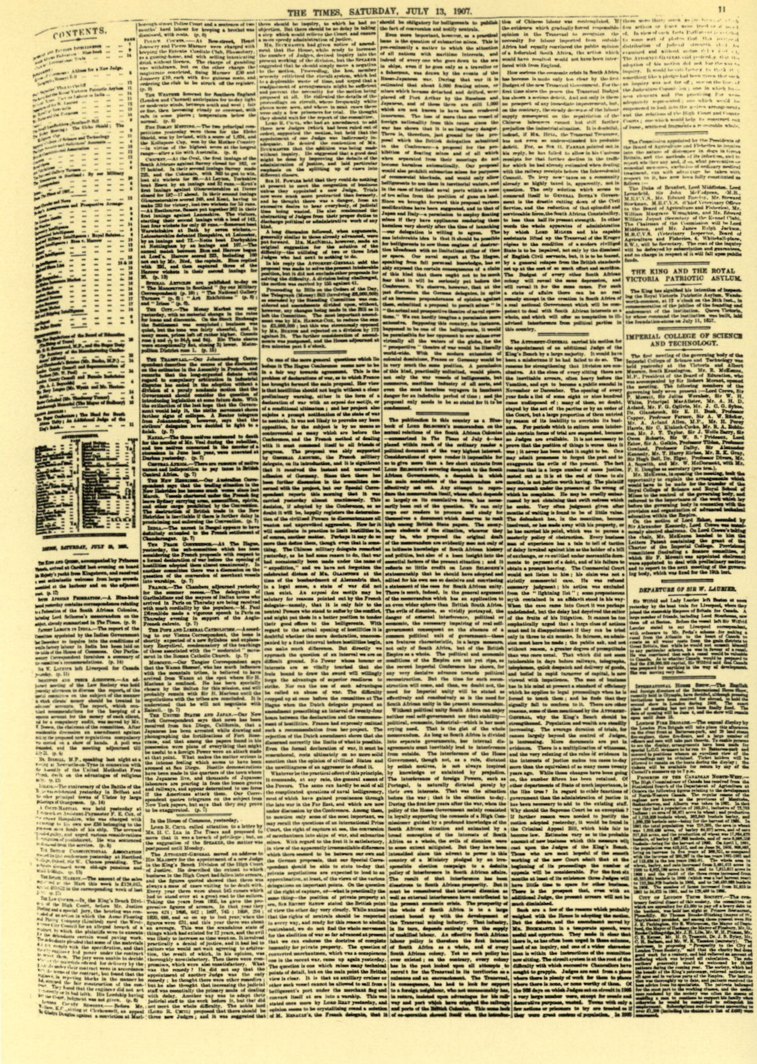
THE TIMES, SATURDAY, JULY 13, 1907.

▲ *Plus ça change . . . The Times* leader page in 1848 and 1907.

The Times, as may be seen from a comparison of the leader page in 1848 and 1907 (though later that year leader headings were at last introduced).

The essential point to grasp about the evolution of the mid-nineteenth-century minimal-size, single-column, news titling headline is that, far from being confined to *The Times*, it became the universal morning paper style, in the provinces (where dailies were launched everywhere after 1855) as well as in London. Occasionally in the beginning the provinces exhibited survivals of earlier styles; thus the *Birmingham Post* (1857) dressed the five wide columns of its big sheet with blackletter for all section headings – Foreign Intelligence, The Provinces, District News and the like – with titling news headlines even smaller than the 10pt of *The Times*. But the big city dailies soon approximated to the London style. The penny rivals of *The Times*, like the *Daily Telegraph* and the *Standard*, were indistinguishable in their headline typography from the old giant of the trade whom they were soon to leave hopelessly behind in the circulation race which it had so long and so impressively led (by 1880 the *Telegraph* was selling 217,000, the *Standard* 200,000 compared to the 50,000 of *The Times*). Indeed, this mid-nineteenth-century determination of news headline style was to become the overall British newspaper style and to last right through the following period, as will be seen, and even beyond.

A special place in British nineteenth-century newspaper development was occupied by the separate Sunday papers, a separation in which Britain was unique. In fact the Sunday Press dated back to the eighteenth century, the first being Mrs Elizabeth Johnson's *British Gazette and Sunday Monitor* of 1779; during the following forty years a number of others followed, including the still extant *Observer* (1791) and *Sunday Times* (1822). These papers, however, were in effect daily papers published on Sunday; their typographic conventions were the same as those of their daily contemporaries and their readership was similarly selective and limited. An entirely different approach began

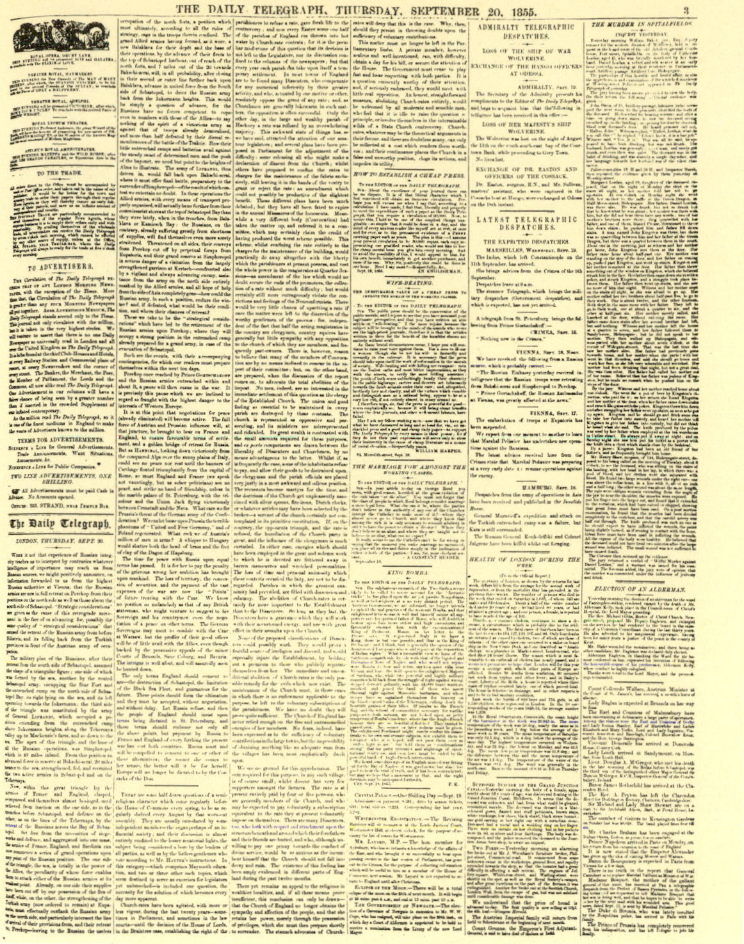
THE DAILY TELEGRAPH, THURSDAY, SEPTEMBER 20, 1855.

The Daily Telegraph.

▲ Main news page of the *Daily Telegraph* (1855), penny rival of *The Times*.

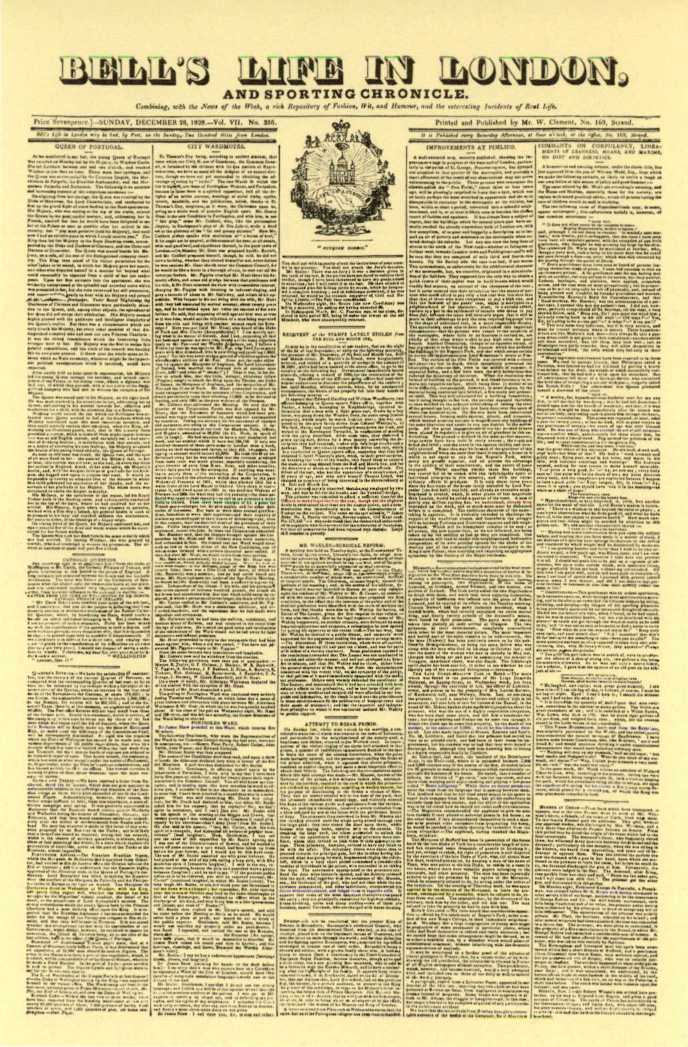
BELL'S LIFE IN LONDON,
AND SPORTING CHRONICLE.

▲ An elegant shaded title adorned this sporting Sunday (1828): it survived until 1886.

with *Bell's Weekly Messenger*, founded in 1796 by the enterprising John Bell we have already met.

Bell produced a Sunday newspaper with a fully editorial front page (mainly commercial and market news) and arranged the three 18½-pica columns of his three-column quarto eight-pager with neat headlines following 'half-double' rules and opened with French dashes. Later he went to a Monday edition to give provincial readers the latest weekend news. This was the start of the most important nineteenth-century Sunday paper tradition, namely that of the paper which rounded up the week's news for those humble folk who could not afford a daily paper; a Sunday paper poster of 1865, listing no fewer than fifty-seven items, concluded with the line AND ALL THE NEWS OF THE WEEK.

These popular nineteenth-century Sundays were uniformly radical in tone, appealed to the working-class reader and were generally at odds with the Establishment. The stricter Victorian sabbatarians regarded the purchase and perusal of a newspaper on Sunday as sinful in itself; as late as 1939 Sunday papers used to run a 'Saturday morning edition', so labelled, on Friday nights for pre-Sabbath sale to the unco guid. After John Bell two other Bells (both Robert, and both different) were respectively associated with the *Weekly Dispatch* – which survived, re-named the *Sunday Dispatch*, until 1961 – and the sporting *Bell's Life in London*. These had news front pages and in the 1820s the *Dispatch* was boldly headlining its news with the then new slab-seriffed 'Egyptian' (first shown in Vincent Figgins's specimen book in 1815), which it also used for crossheading long stories.

▼ A typical early nineteenth-century popular Sunday (issues from 1824 and 1836) showing bold Egyptian headlines and Fat Face title.

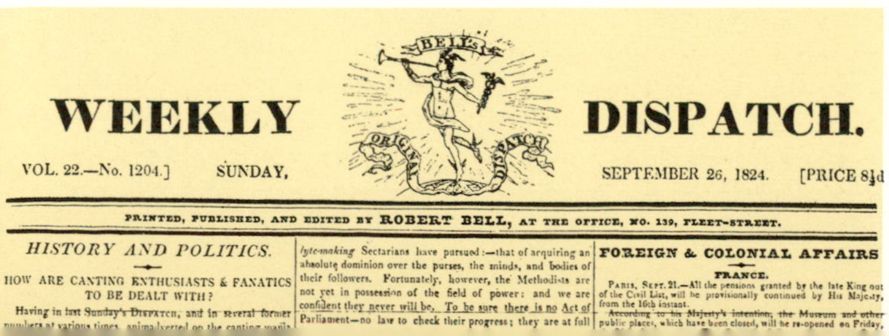
WEEKLY DISPATCH.
VOL. 22.—No. 1204.] SUNDAY, SEPTEMBER 26, 1824. [PRICE 8½d
PRINTED, PUBLISHED, AND EDITED BY ROBERT BELL, AT THE OFFICE, NO. 139, FLEET-STREET.
HISTORY AND POLITICS.
HOW ARE CANTING ENTHUSIASTS & FANATICS TO BE DEALT WITH?
FOREIGN & COLONIAL AFFAIRS
FRANCE.

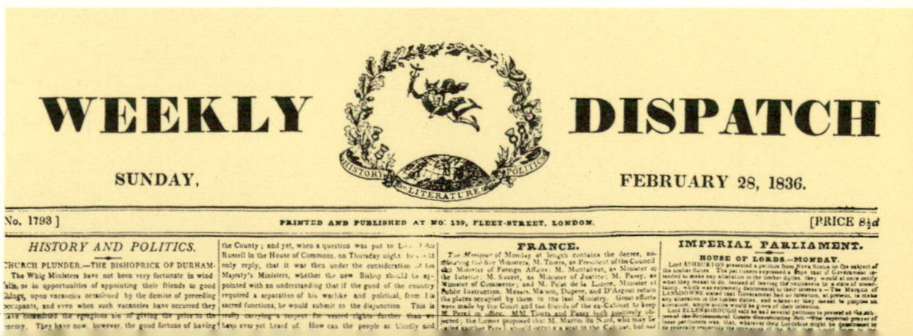
WEEKLY DISPATCH
SUNDAY, FEBRUARY 28, 1836.
HISTORY AND POLITICS.
FRANCE.
IMPERIAL PARLIAMENT.

REYNOLDS'S WEEKLY NEWSPAPER;

A JOURNAL OF DEMOCRATIC PROGRESS AND GENERAL INTELLIGENCE.

No. 1. LONDON: SUNDAY, MAY 5, 1850. Price Fourpence.

THE PROSPECTS OF THE DEMOCRATIC CAUSE.

Another glorious victory is gained by the cause of True Freedom: Eugene Sue, the Red Republican and Socialist Candidate, has triumphed by an immense majority of votes over the favourite of the Reactionaries. The writer of tales which everybody has read, has beaten the hero of a romance for which no one could vouch. In spite of the sickening, nauseating, mendacious accounts of Leclerc's bravery at the barricades,—in spite of the maudlin sympathy which it was the endeavour to create on behalf of the shop-keeper by the representation of his stoic patriotism in fetching out one son to avenge another's death,—in spite of all the diabolical attempts made by the ruffian Prefect of Police to put down the public meetings of the veritable Democrats,—in spite of all these influences, I say, truth has prevailed and Eugene Sue is triumphant. Now what will the *Times* newspaper say? How will it account for its prophecies of the inevitable success of M. Leclerc? Never was there a public print so cursed by a misinformed, pig-headed, and purblind Paris correspondent as this unfortunate *Times* which dares to call itself the "leading journal of Europe!" Its predicament was as ludicrously miserable on the occasion of the last elections as it is in the present instance. Both then and now its readers were assured—most positively assured—that the Red Republicans and Socialists had not a chance. What do the aristocracy and middle-classes of England think of their favourite journal *now?* Will they still look upon its opinions as gospel? will they still regard its prescience as infallible? Poor wretched drivelling *Times*—it is not even so truthful, so sapient, or so far-seeing as the "Grandmamma" *Herald!*

Let the Democrats of England rejoice at the victory which their cause has obtained in France. *Again* is the grand truth made patent to all the world, that two-thirds of the French nation, judged by any test that may be put, are Red Republican and Socialist. Who, then, shall dare to say that millions and millions of the most intelligent, enlightened, and logical people on the face of God's earth, are all in error and that they have adopted opinions which will prove subversive of society? A year and a half ago the *Times* ridiculed the French by the averment that "they had a Republic without a single partizan of Republicanism." Wondrous, indeed, then, must be the truthfulness of Red Republican and Social doctrines, when they can make millions of proselytes in so short a space! And now observe, that the middle-classes in France must be deeply imbued with those principles, in order to enable them *again and again* to achieve so signal a triumph. And yet in England the leaders of the middle-classes will not even grant universal suffrage to the nation!

I cannot for the moment take leave of the *Times* without reminding my readers that, after the last elections, which resulted in the triumph of the glorious patriots, Carnot, Vidal, and De Flotte, the Paris Correspondent of the English journal just mentioned, wrote day after day to insist that the French shop-keepers bitterly repented of the votes they had given and had merely purposed to give the Government a lesson. Now, either the *Times* must have made the scandalous misrepresentations wilfully, or it must have been so badly informed as to destroy for ever its authority as an organ of intelligence. For, so far from the Parisian middle-classes being sorry for their recent conduct, they have deliberately, intentionally, and nobly enacted the same admirable part over again. In a word, the great majority of the French people are Red Republican and Socialist: and as France is the nation which moves the world, the progress of true democracy throughout Europe cannot be for a moment doubtful.

What dismay—what terror—what dread alarms, has the result of the Paris election created amongst the tyrants and oppressors of the people in all countries which the glorious intelligence has yet reached!—and what rage, despair, and apprehension must now rack the soul of Louis Napoleon Bonaparte! The Army is against him—the Middle-classes are against him—the Millions are against him: and the wretched knot of drivellers, traitors, and intriguers who constitute the "Party of Order," are *alone* for him.

There never was a period in the annals of the civilised world more solemnly or sublimely interesting than the present one. It is fraught with materials for the study of the philosopher—with striking events for the narrative of the historian—with wondrous phases for the contemplation of the social reformer—and with the gravest subjects for the pen of the journalist and the oratory of the politician. And more than all these, it is pregnant with terror for the oppressor and with hope for the oppressed. Everywhere have worn-out institutions been shaken, and the old systems of society subjected to a scrutiny and an exposure which they cannot long survive. Their iniquity, their corruption, and their injustice have been rendered so apparent, that the next revolutionary convulsion on the Continent will be the signal for their utter annihilation. In some countries this result will be brought about by violence: in others by moral means. Where the possessors of power and the privileged orders persist in clinging to the very last unto those systems which benefit the few to the prejudice of the many, torrents of blood will inevitably flow: but where the rulers and the aristocratic exclusives yield in time, freedom may be gained without the loss of a single life.

It is easy to distinguish and point out the countries that will have to pass through a fiery ordeal, and those which will change by peaceful transitions from a state of corruption and danger to a condition of health and security. In England, the grandest reforms may be accomplished by moral means, because the very nature of our institutions is such that those which are objectionable are either perishing by their own intrinsic rottenness, or are ready to fall by their own weight. It only requires that continual pressure of truth which the growing intelligence of the millions has brought to bear upon such institutions, to hasten their decay and accelerate their fall. For instance, the bloated Church Establishment, so flagrantly at variance with the true spirit of Christianity, cannot possibly maintain itself much longer. The dissenters and nonconformists of all sects, grades, and opinions, are the really intellectual and the most enlightened religionists in the country; and they constitute an overwhelming majority in comparison with the votaries and adherents of that Church Establishment. Then again, the Hereditary Aristocracy is perishing by a suicidal process; its avowed antagonism to all real progress—its hatred of the masses generally—its arrogance, greed, ignorance, selfishness, and all the other bad passions which inspire its exclusive mind, are so many weapons which it is in reality turning against itself. Next come the great Landowners—the monopolists of that garden which God Almighty gave for the benefit of all, and not for the advantage of a favoured few: *their* tremendous privileges received a heavy blow by the abolition of the Corn-Laws—and the destruction of the far more infamous feudalisms of primogeniture, mortmain, and entail, would speedily break up their monopoly altogether. The ridiculous pomp, ostentation, and pageantry connected with the Court have even become obnoxious to middle-class leaders; and such men as Hume, Bright, Cobden, Walmsley, and others of the same school, have not hesitated to denounce that extravagant [illegible] in the strongest terms. The Chancery and Ecclesiastical Courts,—the Navy and the Army,—the Crown Lands and the Colonies,—the Government [illegible] and the Diplomatic Departments,—all these have received such a showing-up that to maintain them on their present basis and in their existing condition [illegible] length of time, is a hope in which none but the [illegible] drivelling old Tory can possibly indulge. Then [illegible] Parliamentary Reform and the remodelling of [illegible] whole representative system,—these are certainties [illegible] the range of prophecy,—not only because the [illegible] are resolute on these points, but also because [illegible] is such a complete break-up of all the old political parties in the House of Commons that no strong [ministry] can now be formed upon the present system. [illegible], with the Whigs continuing to hold power upon [the] most precarious tenure,—with Peel's party utterly unable to take their place,—with the Protectionists notoriously incompetent to retain office for three months, even if their opponents should allow them to slip into —the state of parties is such that confusion and anarchy must follow unless some influential leader suddenly and promptly takes up the cry of "Reform." England, then, is in that position which must shortly *compel* the adoption of a progressive policy, however unwillingly it may be taken up by those time-servers who are likely to yield through selfish expediency rather than from conscientious motives. It requires but a vigorous agitation on the part of the industrious classes throughout the country to evoke that spirit of pliancy: let the seed be sown now—and the harvest will be reaped abundantly in a very short time.

Such is the position of England—a position which guarantees a bloodless triumph for the true votaries of Democracy. In the United States of America, a happy and prosperous people will pass by rapid transitions, easily and without convulsive shocks, from the enjoyment of those glorious political rights which they now possess, to the attainment of those social blessings which constitute the true meaning of liberty, fraternity, and equality. In Sweden and Norway, there is likewise every prospect of the masses obtaining their rights and privileges without insurrectionary means:—and the same may be said of Switzerland. But now the picture becomes reversed;—and in pointing to France, the German States, Prussia, Austria, Italy, Spain, Portugal, and glorious Hungary, it becomes lamentably evident that the atrocious tyranny of despots or the oppression of worn-out institutions can only be shaken off by violence.

In France the existing government stands upon a mine which the most trivial accident may cause to explode at any moment. Louis Napoleon Bonaparte has become not only obnoxious—but what is infinitely worse for his prospects, he has grown contemptible. The French might endure the real lion for a season: but it is against all experience to believe that they can long tolerate the ass in the lion's skin. Not even the great name of Bonaparte can serve as a cloak, much less as an apology, for the most impudent charlatanism. The hand has gone forth—the writing is upon the wall—and the fingers of Red Republicanism have traced the *Upharsin* of the presidential career of special-constable Louis Napoleon. He is falling—he will fall: and on the ruins of his insane hopes and ambitious prospects, will be established the veritable Social and Democratic Republic.

In Spain and Portugal the aspect of affairs is by no means encouraging to the "party of order." The Queens of those countries have done all that they possibly could to render monarchical institutions odious, scandalous, and infamous in the eyes of their subjects. I know not how true it may be, but the *Morning Post* has openly and fearlessly accused the Portuguese Queen of adultery with the Count de Thomar, her favorite minister;—and a reference to the letter of my Spanish Correspondent in another column, will furnish an idea of the estimation in which the Spaniards must now hold the young woman who reigns over them. But, whether these Queens be calumniated or guilty, matters little to the argument. It is enough for the true friends of Democracy to know that Isabella of Spain and Maria of Portugal are regarded with very unloving eyes by their subjects. Whatever their private characters may really be, it is certain enough that the tyranny which they either practise or countenance has goaded their people to the very verge of desperation;—and the instant that the thrilling cry of "Paris is again in revolution!" shall once more echo across the Pyrenees, the Democrats of Spain and Portugal will not look idly or quietly on.

And who does not know—who does not feel convinced beyond all possibility of doubt, that the moment the brave Republicans of Paris shall rise again, the cowardly old Pope will decamp from Rome with a greater precipitation than ever, to make room for the glorious Mazzini? The miserable, narrow-minded, bigotted ecclesiastic, who dares to call himself the Apostle of that Christ whose worshippers he instigated the Franco-Algerine marauders to butcher and massacre—who returns to his States through pools of blood shed to minister to his ambition and worldly-mindedness,—and who has the impiety to pronounce blessings where the widows and orphans of murdered or exiled patriots are invoking curses upon his head,—this old man who has so much to answer for, will not retain his ill-recovered power a single week after the coming overthrow of Louis Napoleon Bonaparte. With the downfall of the Popedom, adieu to tyranny in Naples—farewell to Royalty in Sardinia. Italy will be emancipated; and from the Alps to the Gulf of Tarento, the pæans of an enfranchised people shall gladden the hearts of Garibaldi the brave and Mazzini the incorruptible.

Then, too, in that good time which is fast approaching, the banner of the Magyar shall be again fanned by the breath of Liberty. A day of terrible retribution will it be for the Austrian miscreants who hanged the patriots, scourged the women, and massacred the innocent children of Hungary. But a glorious day will it be for European democracy, when the admirable Kossuth, whom the villainous scavengers of a hireling press have dared to calumniate, shall once more preside over the councils of the nation that he loves so well. Then, despite the execrable perfidy of Georgey—despite the sanguinary policy of the Austrian Kaiser—despite the sword of the blood-stained fiend Haynau—and despite also the English *Times*, Kossuth shall become the regenerator and the avenger of his country.

Austria, deprived of Hungary and the Italian provinces, will be reduced to a fifth-rate power—its limits circumscribed to those of the mediæval Duchy ere its rulers placed the crown of the Cæsars on their brow. But the brave Viennese will not tolerate any imperial, nor royal, nor ducal authority: they will remember the atrocities of Windischgratz and the cruelties of the Ban Jellachich—and they will hoist the banner of democracy on the summit of Saint Stephen's.

But when all these grand events are occurring in the countries already named, Prussia and the German States will not remain tranquil. The citizens of Berlin have not forgotten the cannonading with which their king, who rules "by the grace of God," treated them in the month of March, 1848: neither have they lost sight of his numerous oaths glibly pronounced and as readily broken—his impudence in octroying them a constitution, instead of allowing the national representatives to form one—his treachery towards the Frankfort Parliament, and his miserable trickery in establishing the Erfurt farce,—nothing of all this will the Prussians forget when the proper time arrives for them to proclaim how deeply the remembrance of their wrongs is seared upon their hearts. As for the petty kings and trumpery dukes of the smaller states, they only retain their power at this moment through the protection of Prussia; and when the cause of democracy triumphs at Berlin, it will spread like wild-fire throughout the Germanic Confederation.

All these results are inevitable. Nor are they far distant. The experience of 1848, and the teachings of the *seventeen revolutions* which occurred in Europe at that epoch, warrant all the predictions which I have hastily sketched. Prior to the glorious days of February in the above-mentioned year, had any man written or spoken prophetically of an Emperor of Austria running away from his capital—of a King of Prussia remaining a prisoner, with paralysed energies, in his palace—of a King of Naples granting a Constitution—of a Baden army laying down its muskets to a man—of a Tuscan Grand Duke flying from the presence of democracy—or of a Pope bolting in the most ignominious and cowardly manner possible, while a modern Rienzi arose in his place,—had all these things been predicted even a week before they began to happen, the prophet would have been laughed at as a madman. But they did all happen, nevertheless. Aye—and they shall happen again too, within a very short time. But the results may not prove quite so satisfactory to the "party of order" on a future occasion as they did on the last. For inasmuch as most of the fugitive monarchs have now returned to the seats of their tyranny, when they run off or are driven away the next time, *they shall never come back!* The democrats of the Continent have been duped once: they will be deceived no more.

But while waiting to become the spectators of those glorious deeds that are soon to be enacted on the theatre of Europe, let the industrious classes of England remember that if their democratic brethren *abroad* are compelled to bide their time, they may nevertheless be agitating *at home.* Because the former struggle will be one of violence, for which a favourable opportunity must be awaited: whereas the movement here is a peaceful, a legal, and a constitutional one, relying only on moral means and bloodless agencies, and therefore fitted for all seasons and all occasions. Let meetings be held—let tracts be circulated—let cheap political periodicals be established—and let the working men assemble of an evening to read or hear read the journals that are favourable to their cause. Especially let them study foreign politics, which open so vast a field for their enlightenment and furnish so many glorious champions worthy of their admiration. Let them teach their children to mingle in their prayers the names of Kossuth, Mazzini, Ledru-Rollin, and Louis Blanc: let them rear their offspring in adoration of the nobles of nature, instead of teaching them to cringe and bow to the aristocracy created by title and by privilege. In conclusion, let them remember that MAN is the highest distinction which God recognised when He made all living things—and that there is no real or estimable aristocracy save that of Mind and of Virtue.

GEORGE W. M. REYNOLDS.

FOREIGN INTELLIGENCE.

FRANCE.

It would appear, by the daily accounts received from France, that all parties are at length convinced a crisis is rapidly approaching, and that neither Louis Bonaparte or his Ministers are at all capable of meeting it. The ridiculous incapacity of the Ministry has been so long apparent, that even the middle-classes, "the friends of quiet and order," at length declare that fresh measures and men must be found to tranquillise and satisfy the country. The blusterings and vapouring of the Minister of War, the portly General D'Hautpoul, when, with unbecoming and laughable irascibility, he invited the Members of the Mountain to descend into the street and settle political questions, not by argument, but by bayonets and cannon-shot, have rendered him extremely unpopular with all parties in France, excepting those whose deep-rooted bigotry sees no hopes for the future, unless by general anarchy and bloodshed, opening a pathway for the pudding-headed representative of the elder Bourbons. The policy of the Legitimists has been, not openly to oppose the Republic, but by underhand measures to render it unsatisfactory to the majority of the French people. They well know that Louis Bonaparte is utterly incapable of governing, that his residence amongst the aristocracy of England has rendered a tyrannical disposition yet more arbitrary, and that at the end of his presidential term, desperation and the prospect of a debtor's prison will induce him to strike some blow which may again convulse France, and afford a chance for despotism to raise its head. The festivities of the Elysée are his delight, and business is with Louis Napoleon a secondary consideration to pleasure. France feels he is not the man for a crisis, and even the peasantry, who voted for a puppet merely because he was the nephew of their idol Emperor, now look upon their President as an ass who has unworthily assumed the lion's skin.

The *Chronicle*, in its Paris correspondence of Monday, is thus preparing the way for fresh outbreaks against the weak and imbecile Government of Louis Napoleon:—"It is impossible to shut one's ears to what is the general subject of conversation around, and very difficult to avoid being carried away by what seems to be the general opinion. It must be admitted that, for some days past, the feeling is rapidly gaining ground that France is on the eve of some important event or frightful convulsion. It is, in short, firmly believed, and that in some of the highest and best-informed quarters, that the parties at the head of the Government, despairing of inducing any of the great sections of the Conservative party to join in procuring the sanction of the country to a prolongation of Louis Napoleon's tenure of the Presidency, have determined to risk everything on a cast of the dice, and to triumph by a *coup d'etat* or perish in the attempt." One thing is very certain; the present extraordinary and anomalous state of affairs cannot much longer exist; we have Universal Suffrage on one hand, and on the other we find the Government suppressing all election meetings, and seizing upon every journal favourable to one candidate's claims, simply because his opinions differ from its own. Again we have the French army thoroughly *demoralised*, as the re-actionary party are pleased to term republican soldiers who presume to entertain republican notions. Banishment to Algeria is the fate awaiting those men who dare profess doctrines in accordance with the institutions they serve.

The ministerial journals of Sunday last were in high glee at a fresh outrage committed on the liberty of the press by the officious Monsieur Carlier, the Prefect of Police. They contained the following paragraph:—"The Court of Cassation has decided that the sale of newspapers, except with the express authorisation of the Prefect of Police, is as illegal in the interior of a shop as in the public street." The ever active Carlier, eager to hasten the approaching collision betwixt the Government and the people, pounced upon those newspapers advocating a liberal policy, and forbade the sale of the most extensively circulated journals in France: amongst others are Girardin's *Presse*, Proudhon's *Voix du Peuple*, Victor Hugo's *Evenement*, and Marrast's *National*. Yet strange to say, with all these unmistakable signs of approaching civil war, dancing, singing, and feasting is maintained right royally at the Elysée; who pays the bills, or if they are ever paid at all, remains a profound mystery. Certain it is, that Louis Napoleon's state income, together with his private fortune, both scarcely forming a total of fifty thousand a-year, cannot maintain an expense of more than treble that amount. People wonder, shake their heads, and openly talk of the necessity for a *coup d'etat*, even if only to save the Presidential person from the ignominious touch of a sheriff's officer at the expiration of his four years' term of office. The President himself is gratifying his childish vanity by publishing in his own organ, the *Napoleon*, the ordinances issued previous to the time when his uncle assumed the direction of affairs. The object of this proceeding is evident; for the situation of the country when they were found necessary to be promulgated by the Emperor, is compared to the present state of France; and we suppose the ape now governing that nation, presumptuously means to imply that *he* is the man about to fulfil the same mighty destiny as the great Napoleon. It has been ascertained that Leclerc's nephew is a clerk in Carlier's office, and that it was at the Prefect's instigation his uncle was brought forward to oppose M. Eugene Sue. Certainly, there was some *prestige* attached to the defeated candidate's name, which might have commanded success, had victory been attainable by the party of order. The truth however is, that the middle classes have more confidence in Socialist than Bonapartist policy; the former party is daily becoming stronger, whilst the latter is hourly sinking under the most formidable weapon in France—ridicule. The Mountain, throughout the whole of this momentous struggle in Paris, has maintained a calm and dignified attitude; it had not, like the order party, recourse to lying or trickery for the purpose of procuring votes for a democratic candidate; on the contrary, relying upon the people's discrimination, the Mountain tranquilly and confidently awaited the *issue*. France has appreciated this forbearance, and contrasted the noble conduct of the democratic party with the shuffling, overbearing demeanour of the reactionists. The Parisians have, in selecting M. Sue as their representative, strongly protested against the barbarous Cavaignac butchery of June, 1848. The reactionists are overwhelmed with consternation; their defeat has been the more decisive, because, on this occasion, they were supported by a party that seldom sanctions their obstructive policy—the moderate republicans, led by Generals Cavaignac, Lamoriciere, and Bedeau, with Messrs. Dufaure, De Beaumont, Marie, &c. Lord Brougham discovering that his eloquence would not be tolerated in a republican National Assembly, all the time he chose to remain a peer of England, has been giving the provincial bar of France a touch of his oratorical powers. The question at issue, and to be argued before one of the most obscure law-courts in the department of the bar, related to the building of a cistern to supply his lordship's chateau of Cannes with water. The ex-chancellor pleaded his own cause in person, first apologising for having inconsiderately left his wig and gown in England. The little court-room, generally deserted, was on this occasion crammed to suffocation; his lordship soon forgot his cistern, and read the auditory a long lecture on the danger and immorality of Socialist doctrines; arguing lengthily upon the inviolability and sacredness of property and privileges; hinting, in pretty broad terms, that some of his Socialist listeners had been found looking, with longing eyes, upon citizen Brougham's splendid property at Cannes, and had even gone so far as to question his right of possession. In the cistern affair, however, his lordship was beat hollow by a young and unknown lawyer, who plainly demonstrated that the ex-lord chancellor of England was totally ignorant of French law. A verdict was given against Lord Brougham.

Consternation prevails in the re-actionary ranks at Eugene Sue's glorious triumph. Monarchy and Imperialism have received a terrible blow by the illustrious author's tremendous success. Re-actionary journals again raise a shout of despair, and endeavour to spread alarm at an event which, in truth, should be considered as adding stability to the Republic. The *Assemblee National*, an influential organ of re-actionary policy, thus croaks forth its disappointment and rage in the most absurd and doleful prognostics:—"To-morrow strangers will fly this city; to-morrow the manufacturers will see their orders diminish; to-morrow property will have lost a fifth of its value; to-morrow the funds will have fallen considerably; to-morrow the *employes* who have voted for the Reds may lose their places; to-morrow gloom and disquietude will prevail over every point of France. Let the Democrats thunder out their songs of victory; their triumph is a cause of mourning for France." A change of ministry, and that an immediate one, must necessarily follow M. Sue's magnificent victory; even General Changarnier is said to be disgusted, not only with the incompetency of the President's ministry, but likewise disapproves and ridicules Louis Napoleon's own conduct relative to the publication of his uncle's ordinances in the columns of the *Napoleon*. It is said that, in allusion to these impolitic outbursts of the President, General Changarnier, when jocularly addressing a member of the extreme left, remarked, "Why, it appears they are about to transport you all; but, as we are generous in prosperity, you shall at all events choose a place for transportation." And then significantly shrugging his shoulders, added, "What stupidity." Two sorts of combinations are spoken of to form a ministry; one energetic and re-actionary, the other liberal and conciliatory,—the first to be composed of such men as Messrs. Baroche, d'Hautpoul, with old Molé in the background; the latter would comprise a few semi-liberal nonentities, personal friends of the President's, as Messrs. Persigny and Moskawa, with perhaps one or two names of importance, like those of Dufaure or Lamartine. The only thing that appears pretty certain is, that the present ministry, should it remain in power, has determined to bring forward a measure for the modification of the law of universal suffrage. Fifteen of the Moderate representatives, foreseeing the success of M. Eugene Sue, expressed a wish to present a bill beforehand, having for its object the regulation of the exercise of universal suffrage; but they were prevented by the Minister of the Interior, who stated that, in case of necessity, he was ready to bring forward a project of law. Acting upon the advice of some sagacious friends, the President has unwillingly consented to stop the *Napoleon's* publication.

Ministers are now busily occupied, and have been for the last two or three days, in framing a new electoral law or a reform of the existing one. It is proposed that the age at which a man can exercise the franchise will be fixed at 25 years instead of 21; a residence of three years in the same commune; and, perhaps, (and this is the most just of all,) the imposition of a penalty, similar to the fine imposed for non-attendance on a jury, on any man who absents himself from the poll without sufficient cause. The extension to 25 years, if forming part of the law, will have the effect of withdrawing the franchise from a considerable number of soldiers, and the result of such an impolitic measure will be a revolt in the whole army. These are some of the principal changes that will probably be made, in addition to some minor details.

The 25th article of the constitution specifies that 21 years as the age when the franchise can be exercised; but the 27th article says, 'The Electoral Law shall determine the causes which may deprive a French citizen of the right to elect and of being elected.' This law will be presented without delay; and it remains to be seen whether resistance in any other quarter has to be dreaded. No doubt these harsh measures will still further irritate the Republicans, who, it is perhaps hoped, will take to the streets, and thereby afford the President the long-wished-for opportunity to assume the Imperial purple, of which he would soon be stripped and sent naked back to his dear friends the aristocratic dandies of St. James's. The President is disposed to adopt the advice of M. Molé, and those who advise rigour instead of conciliation. Among those who strongly recommend a cabinet chosen from the party of the moderate Republicans or Dufaure party, is, singular enough, M. Dupin, the President of the Assembly. He declares himself warmly in favour of a liberal policy. He says that the time has arrived when all the friends of France should take up their stand on the ground of an "honest and moderate Republic," and that the Government should be composed of "honest and moderate men." He adds, that in these times everything soon becomes stale; that General Changarnier himself is subject to the same universal law; and that there is no faith to be put in the continuance of his popularity, even among the friends of order.

MM. Thiers, Molé, Montalembert, Berryer, de Broglie, and Gen. Changarnier did not attend the Assembly on Wednesday, and it is said that they have been all day in consultation with the President of the Republic, at the Palace of the Elysée.

The number polled by the two candidates for Paris, and which ended in the glorious triumph of principle in the person of Eugene Sue are as follows:—

EUGENE SUE	127,927
Leclerc	117,711

The whole of the democratic social candidates are returned by immense majorities. The sitting of Wednesday, in the Assembly, was devoid of interest.

SPAIN.

Nothing can be more demoralizing to the Spanish nation, nor more scandalous to the whole civilised world, than the disgusting scenes which are in constant occurrence at the palace. It will be remembered that Queen Isabella, the reigning sovereign, was forced by her shameless mother, the Queen-Dowager Christina, to marry her cousin, Don Francisco D'Assis. This prince is half an imbecile, and half a bigot; and moreover it has always been doubted whether he ought to have entered the marriage state at all, inasmuch as it was believed that no genuine issue could result from such an union. But the atrocious intrigues of Louis Philippe, who, thank God! no longer has the power to tyrannise over any one, and the inhuman coercion practised by Queen Christina, forced the young and hapless Isabella into that most unfortunate marriage. At the same time, Isabella's younger sister, the Princess Louisa, a mere child of thirteen, was compelled to espouse the Duke of Montpensier, one of Louis Philippe's precious progeny. But Isabella and Don Francisco D'Assis had not been married four days, when the King-Consort insisted upon sleeping in a separate apartment; and a few months afterwards he actually quitted the royal palace and remained in complete seclusion for a long time at the country-palace of the Prado. Then came all the scandalous scenes relative to the handsome General Serrano, who was said to have ingratiated himself so intimately into Isabella's favour: and when he was either compelled to leave the capital, or else the Queen was tired of him, fresh scandals arose respecting her Majesty and the young and handsome Marquis of Bedmar. This nobleman, though ordered by General Narvaez (Duke of Valencia), the Prime Minister, to quit Madrid, was actually found concealed in the royal palace; and on one occasion, Narvaez not only threatened to "spill his aristocratic blood," but called his uncle, the Marquis of Miraflores, "a pimp,"—the said respectable Marquis having introduced Bedmar by stealth into the palace. After a time the King-Consort was induced to return to his royal wife: but this he did with a very bad grace indeed, doubtless not admiring the Serrano and Bedmar affairs.

And here it may be as well to remind our readers that the Queen-Dowager Christina, Isabella's mother, is a woman of notoriously profligate character, and that she not only committed adultery with Munoz, the guardsman, during the latter period of her husband, King Ferdinand's, life-time, but lived openly with him after that monarch's death. A numerous family has sprung from this amour, at which the pious Louis Philippe and his religious wife, Queen Amelie (Christina's aunt) were pleased to wink. At length, that strumpet-life which Christina was leading became such a scandal, that, about four or five years ago, she was married to Munoz, who was created Duke of Rianzares. We have only recalled these facts to the mind of our readers in order to show them how shocking an example the lascivious Christina must have proved to her daughter Isabella.

Within the last few months it has been paraded forth to the world, with disgusting minuteness of detail that Queen Isabella is in a way to become a mother; and perhaps Don Francisco has been not highly pleased at the prospect of receiving the "honours" of such paternity. At all events, he has recently shown much irritation and uneasiness, and on one occasion endeavoured to upset the Narvaez Cabinet, by getting his wife (by means of mingled coaxing and threats) to sign a decree dismissing that ministry and calling Senor Cleonard and a few other political nonentities into office. But this ministry only lasted a day; and through the secret influence of Christina with her daughter, Narvaez was reinstated. Matters have been thus going on, like the uneven and turbid flow of a troubled river, until things again appeared to reach a crisis on the 23rd of April. On that day the King-Consort Don Francisco suddenly notified to General Narvaez and the rest of the Cabinet his intention of quitting Madrid in order not to be present at the *accouchement* of the Queen. After exhausting all means of persuasion to induce him to change his purpose, but which were of no avail, a Council of Ministers was held, in which it was decided to oppose, by force, the King's departure. Accordingly it was announced to His Majesty that he must be placed under arrest. Sentries were stationed at the door of his apartment, and the King remained a prisoner during four hours, at the end of which time His Majesty capitulated, and even consented to accompany the Queen in an open carriage in her usual evening drive on the Prado. To such trumpery uses have continental kings come at last! Who does not despise such a wretched imbecile, and loathe the system which tolerates and maintains such scandalous folly?

It appears, in addition to the above particulars, that previously to the King being reduced to obedience, he declared his firm intention to publish, immediately on leaving his Consort, a manifesto to the nation, explaining clearly his reasons for taking such a step, and for not choosing to be present at the birth of the Royal infant. His Majesty added, that in the manifesto referred to, he should recount all the incidents, however strange they may be, that have occurred, and which forced him to the step referred to. The Queen was much excited on learning the determination of her Consort; and the Ministers, after repeated consultations, came to the resolution of adopting some very energetic measures to "save the honour of the Crown;" for Don Francisco told the Ministers as plainly as plainness could possibly be, that the expected child was not his own, and that he would not acknowledge it. He also said, that he had in his possession certain intercepted letters, addressed to the Queen at different times by Serrano and Bedmar, and also by a certain stage actor who had once been particularly patronized by Her Majesty; and these documents Don Francisco was resolved to make public. However, the result was the capitulation of the King, as above noticed; and thus has ended that scandalous episode in the annals of the present Royalty of Spain.

The unpleasant affair has, however, been patched up, and the cuckold King is about being re-appointed to the government of the Palace. A grand banquet is to be given by the Pope's Nuncio, in honour of his master's return to Rome; it will include the Ministers, the *corps diplomatique*, the Archbishop of Toledo, the Presidents of the two Chambers, the Duke of Rianzares, General Cordova, and several members of the household. Senor Martinez de la Rosa, Spanish ambassador at Rome, has written a flaming account of his reception by the Pope; this frivolous circumstance has caused immense delight to the Government and to Queen Christina, whose religious bigotry equals, if not exceeds, her amorous propensities. The young Queen Isabella is much annoyed that her present "interesting" condition partly prevents her enjoying the favourite amusement of dancing, and she appears to think more of the balls and festivities missed, than of giving birth to a royal bantling.

General Narvaez has been confined to his house by a bilious attack, brought on, it is said, by vexation at the King's obstinacy, and constant opposition to his, Narvaez's will. The palace question, as it is called in Madrid, has been adjourned for a few days. The partisans of the ministry give out that it has been resolved in their favour, and that the misunderstanding between them and the King-Consort has disappeared, that the Queen gives them every mark of confidence, and that Queen Christina has managed, as before, to impose upon the King-Consort with promises made merely to gain time. On the other hand, the opposition shows equal confidence in the approaching downfall of the ministry, assailed as it is both in public and private. Be that as it may, there can be no doubt but what the King-Consort displays a determined repugnance to acknowledge a child, upon the paternity of which so many doubts have been thrown; and could he have his own way, there is no doubt but what the example set by the Foreign Ambassadors of absenting themselves during the interesting event would be eagerly followed by Don Francisco, the Queen's-Consort.

The palace-plot has had a most ridiculous and unimportant conclusion: the Marquis of Alcanzes and the Duke of Conquista—two stiff-backed buckram grandees, have been dismissed—or, rather, called upon to resign their offices of chamberlains. The 27th of April was Queen Christina's birth-day, and she gave a grand dinner to celebrate the auspicious occasion! M. and Madame Montpensier are expected at Madrid: M. and Madame Joinville are to embark at Cadiz for London.

AUSTRIA.

Intrigues are being carried on by the cabinet of Vienna, to place the Hungarian exiles, at present in Turkey, entirely under the surveillance of the Austrian ambassador at Constantinople. So long as Kossuth, Dembinski, and Bem remain alive, and comparatively free, the government of Austria will spare no effort, or stop at no means, to rid itself of such formidable adversaries. Report says that although the illustrious exiles are kept under the strictest *surveillance*, in other respects they are hospitably and honourably treated by the Sultan. Kossuth is allowed 10,000 piastres a month (equal to 100*l*), whilst the other exile generals receive 4,000. The wife of the late Vicar of the Empire, the Archduke John, has, by letters patent, been raised to the rank of Countess, as reward, we suppose, for the traitorous conduct of her husband in assisting to "burke" the Frankfort Parliament. This lady, whose romantic history was a general theme of conversation during the unfortunate administration of the archduke, was known as Baroness Brandhof, and is now Countess of Meran. She was the daughter of a postmaster, and on an occasion when her present husband, travelling in his carriage, was delayed at the post-house for want of a postilion, the present Countess of Meran instantly mounted the saddle and performed the functions of one; either her equestrian grace, or personal charms so pleased the royal prince, that a morganatic marriage ensued, and the lady shared the Archduke's honours as head of the German government, which he so effectually contrived to overthrow.

GERMANY.

ERFURT.—The Parliament of Erfurt is pursuing a career of legislation as though the King of Prussia, its master, was close at hand, overawing the deliberations by his armed forces. To whatever decision this assemblage may come as to the centralisation of Germany, it is pretty certain that nothing but absolutism is intended for the people, the struggle for preponderance will rest betwixt Austria and Prussia. The former is fearfully weakened by the insurrection of Hungary, and by the officious friendship of Russia; the latter has acquired more influence in the affairs of Germany than formerly, owing to the cunning policy pursued by King William towards the Frankfort Parliament. He affected to consider that liberal assemblage of statesmen as constituting the only hope for what he hypocritically denominated "his dearest wish—the centralisation and independence of Germany." These words, it must be remembered, were uttered when revolutions were rife in Europe, and when the Frankfort Parliament, with such men as the noble-hearted and patriotic Robert Blum, was far more influential than his Majesty of Prussia. A temporary change has come over the surface of affairs, and we now have a "College of Princes" all paramount in the affairs of Germany. The Committee of the House of the People has completed its revision of the draft concerning the organisation of the Imperial Court of Judicature, subject always to the approval of the "College of Princes." The twelve judges are to be elected, half by the "College of Princes," a fourth part by the House of States, and the remaining fourth by the House of the People. So that the Princes of Germany will, in fact, control the appointments of three-fourths of the judges. Report says the Parliament of Erfurt is about being adjourned, and it is questionable whether to meet again. Something, however, must be done to supply the absence of the Frankfort Parliament; Germany cannot be left without any governing powers whatever. In the Erfurt Parliament the domineering tone assumed by Prussia has given much offence, and caused her intentions to be looked upon with very great suspicion. Erfurt letters describe the Deputies as so exhausted and sickened with the monotonous farce they have been performing, that the ablest speeches are listened to with indifference, and the sitting put an end to as speedily as decency will permit of. During the month the Parliament has been assembled, its sittings have been very irregular, and seldom lasted longer than five hours.

A quarrel has taken place between the Presidency of the Chamber and of all the representatives of the German press, who have returned their cards of admission *en masse*. The dispute has arisen from the officers of the Chamber attempting to enforce what the representatives of the press consider an undue control over their liberty of opinion and expression, which would amount to a censorship, and they are resolved, though the measure affects only two of their number, to resist the attempt as a body. No more reports of the last sitting will be published, unless an amicable arrangement is come to.

FRANKFORT.—It will be recollected that two of the re-actionary or Conservative members in the Frankfort Assembly were discovered plotting against the liberty of the people, and fell victims to popular indignation. These persons were Prince Lichnowski and General Averswald; the trial of the persons charged with their murder has concluded. The prisoner Ludwig was condemned to imprisonment for life, Georg to twenty years, and Pflug to five years and a half's imprisonment in irons. Dietrich was sentenced to the House of Correction for one year, and Korber for six months. Schmidt and Gomble were acquitted.

SCHLESWIG.—All amicable arrangements between the Danes and Schleswigers appear as far distant as ever. Preparations for war are actively carried on by the latter under their new General, Willisen, who has resigned his appointments in the Prussian army to take command of that of Schleswig. General Willisen has reported that he shall be able to bring 36,000 effectives into the field within the course of a fortnight or three weeks. The mission of the "confederated agents," as anticipated, will prove to be a complete failure. It must, therefore, be expected that their return will be the signal for the outbreak, which General Willisen seems most anxious to promote. M. de Reedtz, one of the Danish plenipotentiaries, proceeds to Copenhagen to-morrow, for the purpose of giving explanations relative to the state of the negotiations to his Government. He will probably be the bearer of the new propositions for a mixed commission, and will return in the course of ten days with the replies.

ROME.

The Pope's return to his capital has been far from a triumphal entry; some hired devotees shouted at the signal given by Baraguay d'Hilliers, the French general; but all enthusiasm, if any ever existed, has dropt down to a chill and suspicious coldness. The truth is, Pius dreads assassination—Rossi's fate is ever before his eyes, and he feels the dagger always at his heart. The Pope blessed, on April the 18th, ten thousand of the French troops; his Eminence was attended by his Cardinals, and carefully surrounded by followers and soldiers. An air of ominous gloom and anger was easily perceptible on the visages of the people; and had it not been for the 10,000 French bayonets bristling in the square some outbreak might have occurred. As it was, there were many isolated shouts of *Viva Mazzini!* and on these unwelcome sounds reaching the papal ears, that old man was observed to shudder and frown. Last Monday his Holiness left the Vatican, simply accompanied by his body-guard of eight cavalry soldiers, and proceeded unexpectedly to visit the French Military Hospital. His Holiness passed through the streets almost unobserved; and many of the people who had seen him approaching, positively ran under doorways and into shops to avoid him. In short, dislike would have been shown in a strong manner had not fear of imprisonment prevented them. It is really absurd and humiliating to see the brave French soldiers, by order of their general, kissing the Pope's toe, buying chaplets, procuring a blessing, &c., whilst his own subjects assume an attitude, if not of absolute hatred, at all events of contempt and disgust. Since Pius's return to his capital, no steps have been taken to alleviate the sufferings of his subjects; and throwing himself entirely into the arms of priests, Jesuits, and inquisitors, seems determined to pursue a course of policy which sad experience has not yet convinced him of its errors. General Baraguay d'Hilliers, who is about returning to France, looks on, shrugs his shoulders, and says nothing. In fact, the Pope's return is now generally considered as an "untoward event."

It was generally expected that an amnesty would have been granted by his Holiness on his return to Rome; but, quite contrary to the public expectation, arrests continue, and dismissals from office daily take place. Three or four persons only have been liberated from prison—*i. e.*, young Clarisse, son of a French milliner; and the family of Castellani, who had been imprisoned for several months, their crime being that of exclaiming in the Church, "Peace to the souls of the Italian martyrs!" The refusal of the Rothschilds to pay the second and third instalments of the loan, which they had the option to refuse or accept, has caused great embarrassment to the Roman Government.

SICILY.

A shock of earthquake took place on the 11th instant at Ragusa, which exceeded in violence and duration that of 1848, and threw the inhabitants into a perfect state of consternation. The undulatory movement first began at one o'clock in the day, and was preceded by a bright light, which soon disappeared. The gates of the city were opened in order to give egress to the inhabitants in case of need. Many of the walls and roofs of the houses were damaged, and the furniture in some of them thrown down and broken. Similar shocks were felt at the same time at Jara and at Stagno; at the latter place several houses were thrown down.

GREECE.

After a series of conferences, which continued for eight days, and the last of which was held on the 13th, the representative of Great Britain and the French mediator were as far from anything like an understanding as they could possibly be. M. Gros thought it irreconcileable with his convictions and with his instructions, with the dignity of France and the independence of Greece, to make and to submit proposals of any kind to the Hellenic Government. The negotiations were discontinued for two days, at the termination of which period Mr. Wyse, the English ambassador, invited the French mediator to meet him again on board the French line-of-battle ship *L'Inflexible*.

On the 12th inst. a conference took place between Mr. Wyse and M. Gros on board the French ship of the line the Inflexible, stationed in the Piræus. Before his interview with the British Minister, M. Gros made known to the Greek government the propositions which on that day he intended to make to Mr. Wyse for the final adjustment of the question. After a long conference the Ministers separated without having agreed, and as it was supposed to be a final meeting. Mr. Wyse announced his intention of putting certain measures into execution. On his return to Athens, however, M. Gros had an interview with M. Londos, after which he wrote to Mr. Wyse, requesting another conference on the 14th, to which the British Mi[nister] at[illegible] acceded. By a mistake, however, on the part of Baron Gros, the interview did not take place till the 15th. On the morning of that day, for the purpose of repairing his error as to the date of the conference, and to show his anxiety to meet the wishes of Mr Wyse in every particular, M. Gros went to Salamis in the French war steamer La Vidette, and paid a visit to the English Minister on board the Queen, after which both Envoys repaired to the Inflexible. The conference lasted some time, but proved as unsatisfactory as the preceding. On the following day, however, Mr. Wyse and M. Gros met again, and you will be surprised on hearing the tenor of the propositions made by the French Envoy that they were rejected by Her Majesty's representative.

On the part of the Greek Government M. Gros offered the amplest apology for the insult given to Mr Brown, the midshipman of the Fantome. He offered to pay the indemnity demanded for the Ionians who had been imprisoned, and for those whose ships had been plundered. He offered to pay Mr Finlay the value of his garden; and also offered, from the Greek Government, what I feel convinced the English people will consider a fair remuneration to Don Pacifico for the losses he sustained when his house was attacked by the mob. 50,000 drachmas is the sum offered by the Greek Government as an indemnity to the ex-Portuguese Consul. This sum, however, Don Pacifico has indignantly rejected; and because the terms of his bond are not complied with, a British Admiral and a British Minister threaten to ruin an already bankrupt country with utter annihilation. Mr. Wyse, however, has granted a short delay before putting hostile measures into execution. He has agreed to wait till after the arrival of the steamer from France, which ought to have come in this morning, but which has not yet appeared.

AMERICA.

Letters from Cuba state, that American visitors are under the strictest surveillance, for fear of an invasion by the projected expedition. The military of the island is increased, and robberies and murders by some of the soldiery are not uncommon. Don Fernandez de Abuja was recently robbed and assassinated by one Antonio Balero, who was tried and garotted in a few days. Thirty soldiers died towards the close of March at Havana, having been accidentally poisoned, owing to their food having been prepared in unclean copper kettles.

We have the sad intelligence of the destruction of the greater part of the port of La Guayra by fire: loss 2,000,000 of dollars.

The cholera prevails to a rather fearful extent on the western and southern rivers, and at New Orleans. Out of 234 deaths in New Orleans the week before last, 141 were from cholera. The steamer Washington had recently ten cholera deaths on board. Between New Orleans and Saint Louis, the Cincinnatus, to Louisville, lost ten passengers; and deaths on the Mississippi plantations have been numerous.

In the senate of the United States, on the 17th ultimo, during a debate on California and slavery, a violent altercation occurred between Benton and Foote, in the course of which Foote drew a pistol and aimed at Benton. Foote was immediately disarmed, and a committee of investigation appointed. On the 18th a resolution was passed in the Senate, referring the whole question of California and the territories to a committee of 13, to report a plan for compromise. The committee is not yet appointed. It is settled the cabinet will not be dissolved.

CALIFORNIA.

There have been two late arrivals from California, namely, the steamers Cherokee and Empire City, via Chagres. These vessels brought rich and welcome contributions of gold dust, amounting to 2,000,000 dollars, and several hundreds of passengers.

Letters have been received announcing the destruction of half the town of Chagres by fire; but it should be remembered that all such towns are mere collections of huts, made of adobe, or palm leaves, or bark. A post-office has been established at Chagres to meet American emergencies, but the Panama authorities intend to introduce the passport system on the Isthmus, in consequence, as they say, of riots by the Americans, but no doubt the real object is, to collect fees. This vexatious policy will lead to quarrels. Only a day or two before the last steamer left Chagres, an American was killed by an attack of natives on the Isthmus, and a few days before that event another sanguinary riot occurred between the Americans and the people.

A PARSON IN TROUBLE.—On Friday, at the Marlborough-street, Police-office, the *Rev. John Berrington* appeared to meet a charge on which he had been remanded, of having fraudulently obtained from Mary Ann Oakley a sum of 4*l.*, under pretence of giving her the situation of housekeeper. Mr. Clarkson, who appeared for the defendant, contended that the alleged offence imputed to his client merely amounted to this, that being desirous to engage the services of Mrs. Oakley, he borrowed from her 4*l.*, which he was prepared to pay whenever called upon. It would be impossible to frame any indictment on the evidence before the court, and he therefore prayed the magistrate to dismiss the defendant from the charge of having attempted to obtain money under false pretences. In reply to Mr. Hardwick, the defendant said he was in holy orders, having been ordained by the Archbishop of York. Mr. Hardwick said, far as the evidence went on this charge it did not go far enough to enable him to send the case for trial. With the utmost reluctance, therefore, he must discharge him. The defendant said he was willing and ready to pay back the money he had borrowed from Mrs. Oakley. Mr. Clarkson advised him to do so without delay. The defendant produced four sovereigns and some silver, and gave them to Mrs. Oakley. A chorus of creditors immediately petitioned for prompt payment. The Rev. Gentleman turned round, and smilingly assured them they should all be paid as soon as he could make proper arrangements. The defendant was then discharged.

EXTRAORDINARY CASE AT THE INSOLVENTS' COURT.—On Friday the case of Josiah Wilson, which had occupied three days' hearing, at the Insolvents' Court, was brought to a close. The leading features are mainly these. The insolvent is a young man, the son of a farmer at Osmanthorpe, near Leeds; the opposing creditor is a female of the name of Jane Dunn, apparently a few years his senior. Her ground of complaint was that, after the insolvent had many years paid his addresses to her, she lent him a sum of 27*l.* Instead of fulfilling his engagements to her, the insolvent had married a fresh love in London. She thereupon, brought an action for the 27*l.* The insolvent allowed judgment to go by default, and came to this court for protection against arrest for the debt. He now swore that he had maintained an illicit connexion with the opposing creditor for seven years; that she had been *enceinte*; that she was a female of abandoned character; that during the seven years' connexion he had never given her any money, but that she had, at various times, robbed him of sums amounting to about 70*l.*; that she had never lent him the 27*l.*; that he had allowed judgment to go by default on account of the difficulty of defending the action when his own evidence could not be received, and the expense which would attend it. He also said that she had been employed on his father's farm at the rate of 10*d.* per day; that she had slept with him at Scarborough, York, and elsewhere; and, in short, that she was an immoral character undeserving of credit, and that no debt whatever existed. His case was concluded by calling witnesses to show that he had slept with Dunn, at York. On the other hand, she swore with equal distinctness that no immoral connexion had ever taken place between herself and the insolvent, or any other person: that he had paid his addresses to her for years; that the money had been lent to him; that she had not slept with him at Scarborough, but had spent the evening in question at another house in Scarborough with friends. She acknowledged that she had spent the night with him alone at the tavern, at York, to which the witness had deposed; but the insolvent, she stated, had alone occupied the only bed that was in the room, and she had sat in a chair in the same room all night. She called a witness who deposed to the 27*l.* having been advanced to the insolvent in her presence. The insolvent had counted the money, note by note, and the witness had seen him put it into his pocket. A book was also produced to show that the opposing creditor had the money to advance. The Commissioner commented upon the painful position in which he was placed, in having to decide where the evidence was so conflicting. The account given by the opposing creditor respecting the manner in which she had passed the night at York was a very strange one. He could not, however, say that it might not be true. There was, however, the evidence of another witness, as well as herself, to substantiate the statement with respect to the advance of the money. That was the point which he was called upon to decide. He should decide it by refusing to accede to the insolvent's application for protection. His petition must be dismissed.

LOVE AND DESPERATION.—On Friday, at the Southwark Police Court, George Ferry, a man of respectable appearance, was brought before Mr. Hammill charged with sending a letter to Miss Mary Franklin, containing threats against her life. The complainant handed a letter to the magistrate, which she said was written by the prisoner, and from which she apprehended her life was in danger. It ran thus:—"You threaten to complain to a magistrate—that threat has no terrors for me. I again swear, by Heaven, that if I see you in the company of any other man, I shall stab you to the heart. Depend upon it I shall not depart from my words. You know that I love you, and sooner than see you with any other, I should prefer dying on the scaffold. You had better let me have killed myself last night, and all would be over now, than have wrested the knife out of my hand." Mr Hammill inquired what the writer meant by his allusion to complainant having prevented him from committing self-destruction? The complainant in reply said that she certainly did prevent the prisoner from cutting his throat. Mr Hammill asked what was the cause of all this desperation on the part of the prisoner? The complainant proceeded to state that she was acquainted with the prisoner's family, who were highly respectable, and although she had never given him the slightest encouragement, he annoyed her with his attentions. That he came to the house where she lived on a recent occasion, and in consequence of her refusal to comply with his wishes with respect to her breaking off all intercourse with any other man, he took a knife from his pocket, tore his shirt open, and was in the act of plunging the point of it into his throat, when she rushed towards him, grasped the hand that held the weapon, wrested it from him, and dashed it out of the window. Mr Hammill said that he should call upon the prisoner to find ample sureties to keep the peace; and that until then he should be committed to prison. The prisoner was locked up in default of finding the required bail, and sent off in the van to gaol at five o'clock.

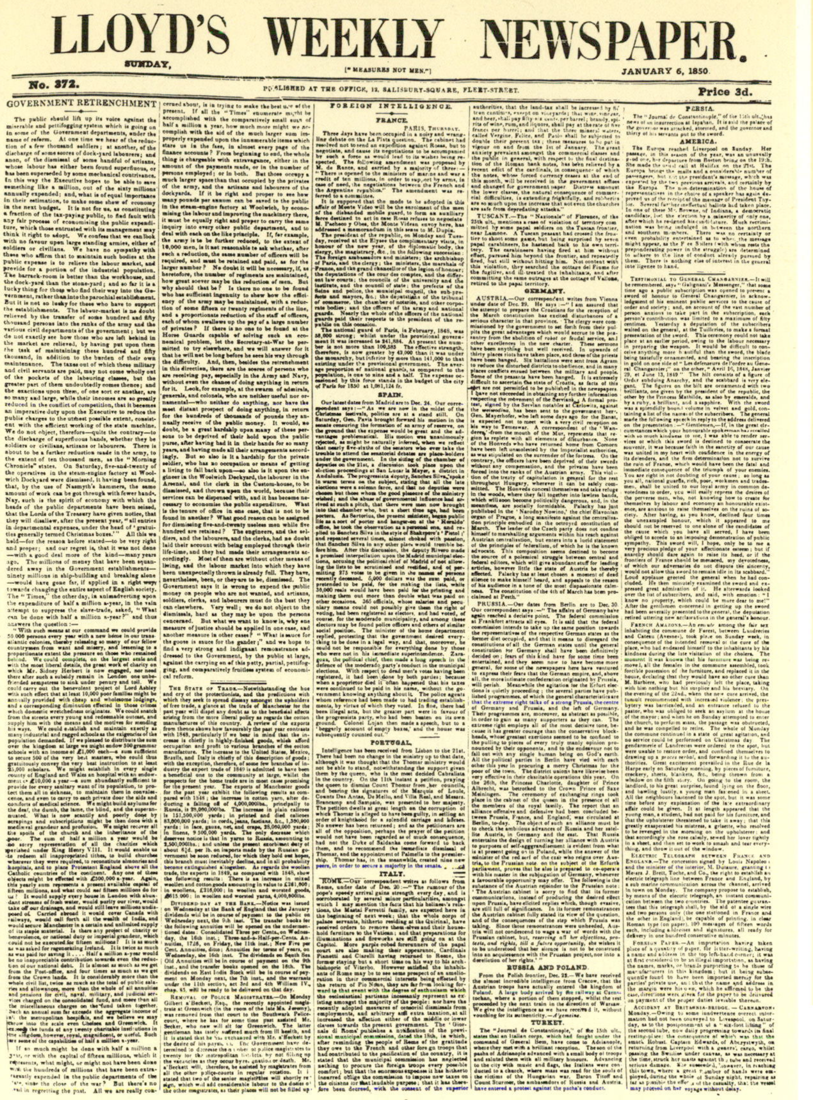

LLOYD'S WEEKLY NEWSPAPER.

SUNDAY, ["MEASURES NOT MEN."] JANUARY 6, 1850

No. 372. PUBLISHED AT THE OFFICE, 12, SALISBURY-SQUARE, FLEET-STREET. Price 3d.

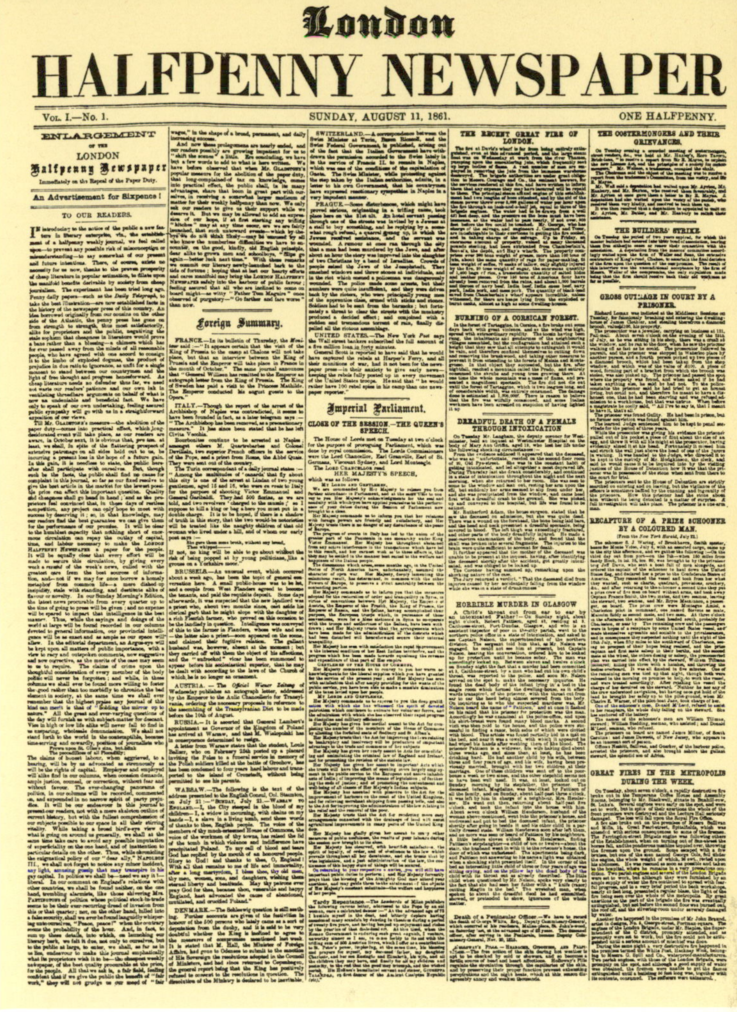

London

HALFPENNY NEWSPAPER

VOL. I.—No. 1. SUNDAY, AUGUST 11, 1861. ONE HALFPENNY.

▲ First of the halfpenny newspapers, this short-lived Sunday of 1861 combined blackletter and condensed Clarendon in its headlining.

▲ An 1850 issue of *Lloyd's Weekly News*, which by the 1870s had become the Sunday circulation leader. Note the similarity of its bold headline style to that of the *Weekly Dispatch* and *Reynolds's*.

◀ Number one of *Reynolds's*, which developed into the leading radical and republican journal of the late nineteenth century: note the bold headings.

The politically and socially tense 1840s saw the birth of a batch of influential radical Sunday papers. In 1842 Edward Lloyd launched *Lloyd's Weekly News* (for which he later put in the first Hoe type-revolver in London, as we have seen). In 1843 John Browne Bell, son of John Bell, started the fabulous *News of the World*, still the biggest-selling Sunday. In 1850 George W. M. Reynolds, one of the later Chartist leaders, began *Reynolds's Newspaper*, long famous as *Reynolds News* and surviving (re-named the *Sunday Citizen*) till 1967. These papers began with bolder headlining than the dailies, reaching a mass market then far beyond the dailies' scope (in 1874 the circulation of *Lloyd's Weekly News* was 600,000). The bold headline style was not to last, however. Last of the breed were the ephemeral Sundays of an enterprising but unsuccessful publisher, John Bastow; in 1860 he brought out his *Penny Newsman*, headed in bold Egyptians, and the following year the *London Halfpenny Newspaper*, the first of all halfpenny newspapers, attractively headed in blackletter and Clarendon condensed. But his unusually busy-looking venture did not last; and the Sundays sank gradually into the feeble news-titling style of the dailies.

One feature of nineteenth-century popular Sundays, sharply differentiating them from the dailies, remains to be noted. That feature was the title-piece. The Sundays steered clear of the white-lined blackletter, of whatever weight or style, that, as we have seen, became the London dailies' title uniform. The Sundays mostly went for roman capitals, ranging from Bell's elegant line for his *Messenger* (with its central device of the horn-boy, the traditional Sunday paper vendor), the handsome shaded of *Bell's Life*, and the fat face of the *Weekly Dispatch* to the modern of *Reynolds's*. The *News of the World* was highly individualistic, with what has been called its 'music-hall' style – the Britannia-dominated scroll of decorative sign-writer's lettering which survived with little modification until 1960. The sole appearance of white-lined blackletter was in the 'London' of the *London Halfpenny Newspaper*; and that was more than offset by the Didot-style, sharp-cut, hairline-seriffed roman capitals of the full-measure line HALFPENNY NEWSPAPER.

Across the Atlantic, the opening of this chapter's period found American newspaper production techniques less advanced than those of London and depending, indeed, on imports of British machinery. As earlier remarked, the first Fourdrinier papermaking machine in America was installed in 1827. London-built, it was erected at Saugerties (New York) by a British engineer, Donkin; it is true that Thomas Gilpin had devised a papermaking machine at his Delaware mill ten years earlier – but this was a cylinder-type machine, resembling John Dickinson's invention that had been successfully running in Hertfordshire since 1809, and not suited or intended to produce cheap news-printing paper. As to printing plant, the first cylinder printing machine used by a U.S. daily appears to have been a Napier imported from London jointly by the morning *Daily Advertiser* and the evening *American*, of New York, in 1825. Other American papers followed suit, including the Washington *National Intelligencer* (in 1829). These imports encouraged engineering firms like Hoe and others to start making printing machines on the Napier model (the first American cylinder machines were generically called 'Napiers').[2]

The London firm of David Napier and Son, famous in this century for their automobiles and aero engines, were printing machine pioneers. In 1824 they introduced their first perfector, which they punningly called the 'Nay-Peer'; this was a slow machine, producing around 800 complete copies an hour. The machine imported by the Americans was evidently the Napier double-cylinder (i.e. two-feeder) machine, producing 2,000 or more sheets an hour, printed one side only; the first American users complained that because of poor paper their initial output was only some 1,400 sheets an hour. London papers were said to be getting 2,400 an hour from their Napiers.

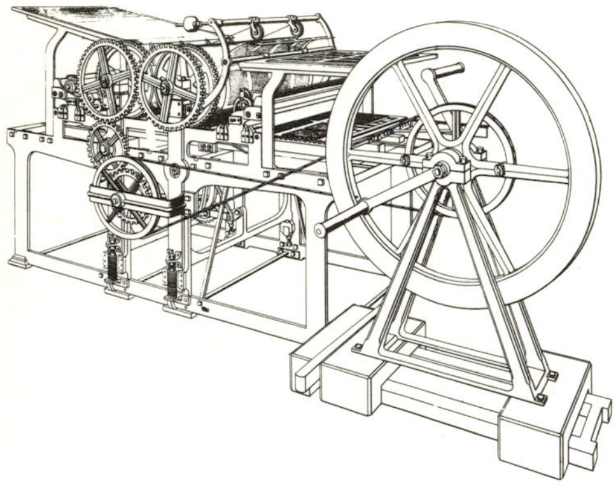

A Napier cylinder machine with crank and flywheel for manual operation.

Contemporary references indicate that in the 1830s New York dailies were generally using Napier double-cylinder machines, and manually-operated, by crank and flywheel, at that. When, in 1835, Manhattan's first penny paper, *The Sun*, began to drive its Napiers by steam-power it was considered a sensational event.[3] But *The Sun* must now form the starting-point for our examination of American newspaper developments other than in the sphere of mechanical production.

It is hardly necessary to stress the great differences between British and American society at this time. These differences were reflected in the character of the daily newspapers, which in the U.S. were significantly free of Stamp Act oppression and restriction. The popular New York dailies which sprouted so fast in the period under discussion were quite unlike their London counterparts; their overall appearance and style resembled much more that of the radical London Sundays, even to the use of roman capitals for their titles instead of lower-case blackletter. Front pages were either exclusively or mainly editorial, the London small-advertisement fronts being unknown.

At this early stage, however, there were two similarities between New York and London – minimal headlining (10pt capitals the maximum) and close-packing of the text, usually even more than was customary with the mainly minion (7pt) Londoners. Nonpareil and even agate (the American trade name for ruby, or $5\frac{1}{2}$pt) were largely used in the U.S., so that agate thereafter became the unit for expressing depths of newspaper matter and advertisements. These factors operated in *The Sun* when it was launched in September 1833 by a twenty-three-year-old compositor, Benjamin H. Day. To start with it was an almost midget four-page sheet, made up in three $14\frac{1}{2}$-pica columns. But Ben Day knew what he was about. He realised that the readers he was after preferred a mass of short news items to long slabs of matter; so he filled *The Sun* with heavily-condensed briefs, each

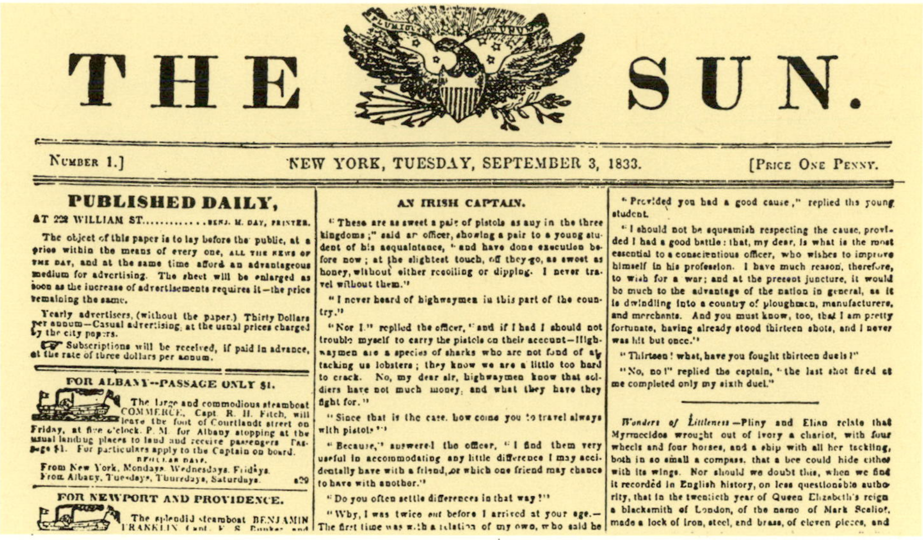

THE SUN.

NUMBER 1.] NEW YORK, TUESDAY, SEPTEMBER 3, 1833. [PRICE ONE PENNY.

PUBLISHED DAILY,

AT 222 WILLIAM ST............BENJ. H. DAY, PRINTER.

The object of this paper is to lay before the public, at a price within the means of every one, ALL THE NEWS OF THE DAY, and at the same time afford an advantageous medium for advertising. The sheet will be enlarged as soon as the increase of advertisements requires it—the price remaining the same.

Yearly advertisers, (without the paper.) Thirty Dollars per annum—Casual advertising, at the usual prices charged by the city papers.

☞ Subscriptions will be received, if paid in advance, at the rate of three dollars per annum.

FOR ALBANY--PASSAGE ONLY $1.

The large and commodious steamboat COMMERCE, Capt. R. H. Fitch, will leave the foot of Courtlandt street on Friday, at five o'clock. P. M. for Albany stopping at the usual landing places to land and receive passengers. Passage $1. For particulars apply to the Captain on board.

REGULAR DAYS.

From New York, Mondays. Wednesdays. Fridays.
From Albany, Tuesdays, Thursdays, Saturdays. a29

FOR NEWPORT AND PROVIDENCE.

The splendid steamboat BENJAMIN FRANKLIN Capt. E. S. Bunker and

AN IRISH CAPTAIN.

"These are as sweet a pair of pistols as any in the three kingdoms;" said an officer, showing a pair to a young student of his acquaintance, "and have done execution before now; at the slightest touch, off they go, as sweet as honey, without either recoiling or dipping. I never travel without them."

"I never heard of highwaymen in this part of the country."

"Nor I." replied the officer, "and if I had I should not trouble myself to carry the pistols on their account—Highwaymen are a species of sharks who are not fond of attacking us lobsters; they know we are a little too hard to crack. No, my dear sir, highwaymen know that soldiers have not much money, and what they have they fight for."

"Since that is the case, how come you to travel always with pistols?"

"Because," answered the officer, "I find them very useful in accommodating any little difference I may accidentally have with a friend, or which one friend may chance to have with another."

"Do you often settle differences in that way?"

"Why, I was twice *out* before I arrived at your age.—The first time was with a relation of my own, who said he

"Provided you had a good cause," replied the young student.

"I should not be squeamish respecting the cause, provided I had a good battle: that, my dear, is what is the most essential to a conscientious officer, who wishes to improve himself in his profession. I have much reason, therefore, to wish for a war; and at the present juncture, it would be much to the advantage of the nation in general, as it is dwindling into a country of ploughmen, manufacturers, and merchants. And you must know, too, that I am pretty fortunate, having already stood thirteen shots, and I never was hit but once."

"Thirteen! what, have you fought thirteen duels?"

"No, no!" replied the captain, "the last shot fired at me completed only my sixth duel."

Wonders of Littleness—Pliny and Elian relate that Myrmecides wrought out of ivory a chariot, with four wheels and four horses, and a ship with all her tackling, both in so small a compass, that a bee could hide either with its wings. Nor should we doubt this, when we find it recorded in English history, on less questionable authority, that in the twentieth year of Queen Elizabeth's reign a blacksmith of London, of the name of Mark Scaliot, made a lock of iron, steel, and brass, of eleven pieces, and

New York's first penny daily, *The Sun* (1833): later in the century the title was changed to blackletter.

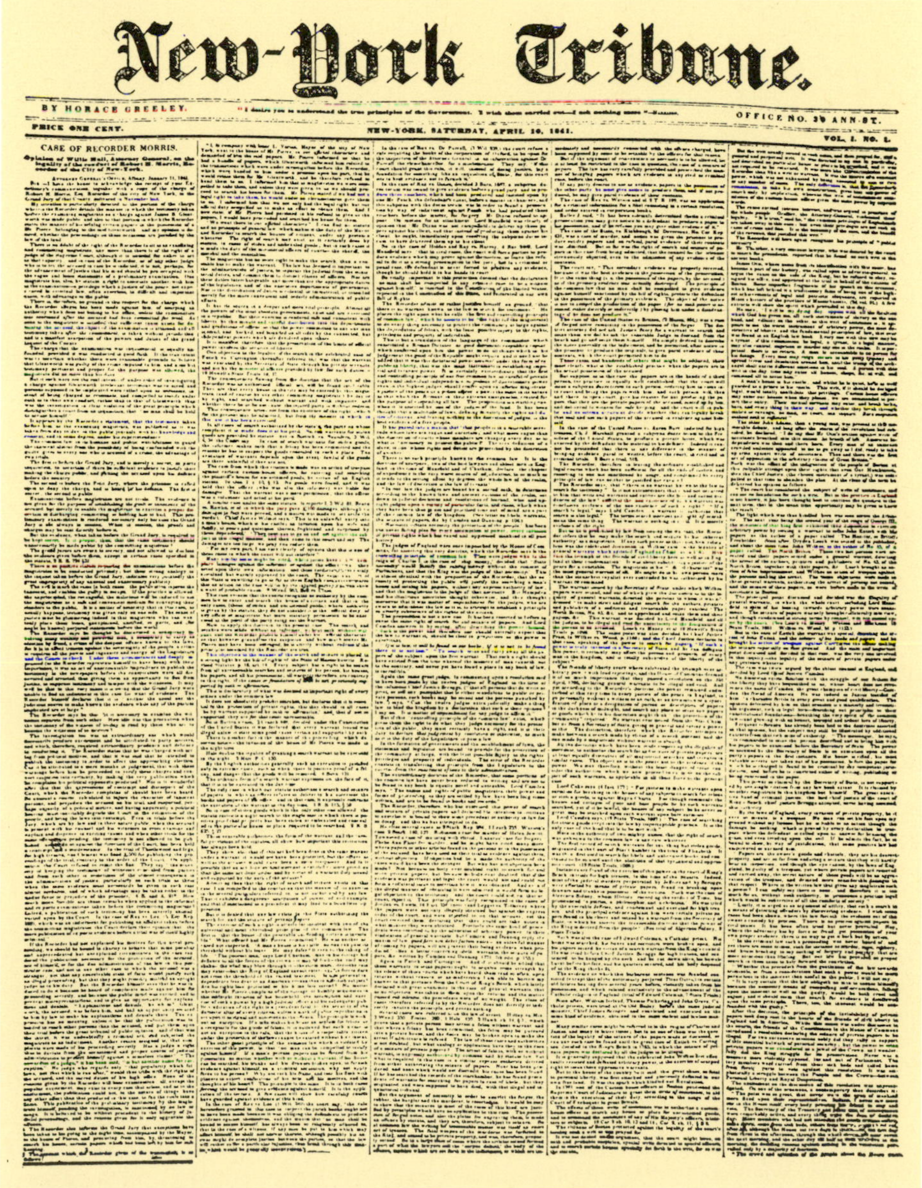

New-York Tribune.

BY HORACE GREELEY. OFFICE NO. 30 ANN-ST.

PRICE ONE CENT. NEW-YORK, SATURDAY, APRIL 10, 1841. VOL. I. NO. 1.

CASE OF RECORDER MORRIS.

The 1841 debut of Horace Greeley's famous *New York Tribune*; five months later the title was changed from blackletter to condensed roman capitals, reverting to blackletter again in 1853. The *Tribune* was an American pioneer of curved-plate stereotyping (1861) and the world pioneer of the Linotype (1886).

'headlined' with a couple of words in italic lower-case from which the text ran on. Day was not averse to hoaxes as circulation-builders, as will be seen below.

The next two major foundations, that of the *New York Herald* by James Gordon Bennett in 1835, and of the *New York Tribune* by Horace Greeley in 1841, adhered to the typography already described. Indeed, No. 1 of Greeley's *Tribune* can only be compared for unrelieved solidity with the *Daily News* page of 1846 described earlier in

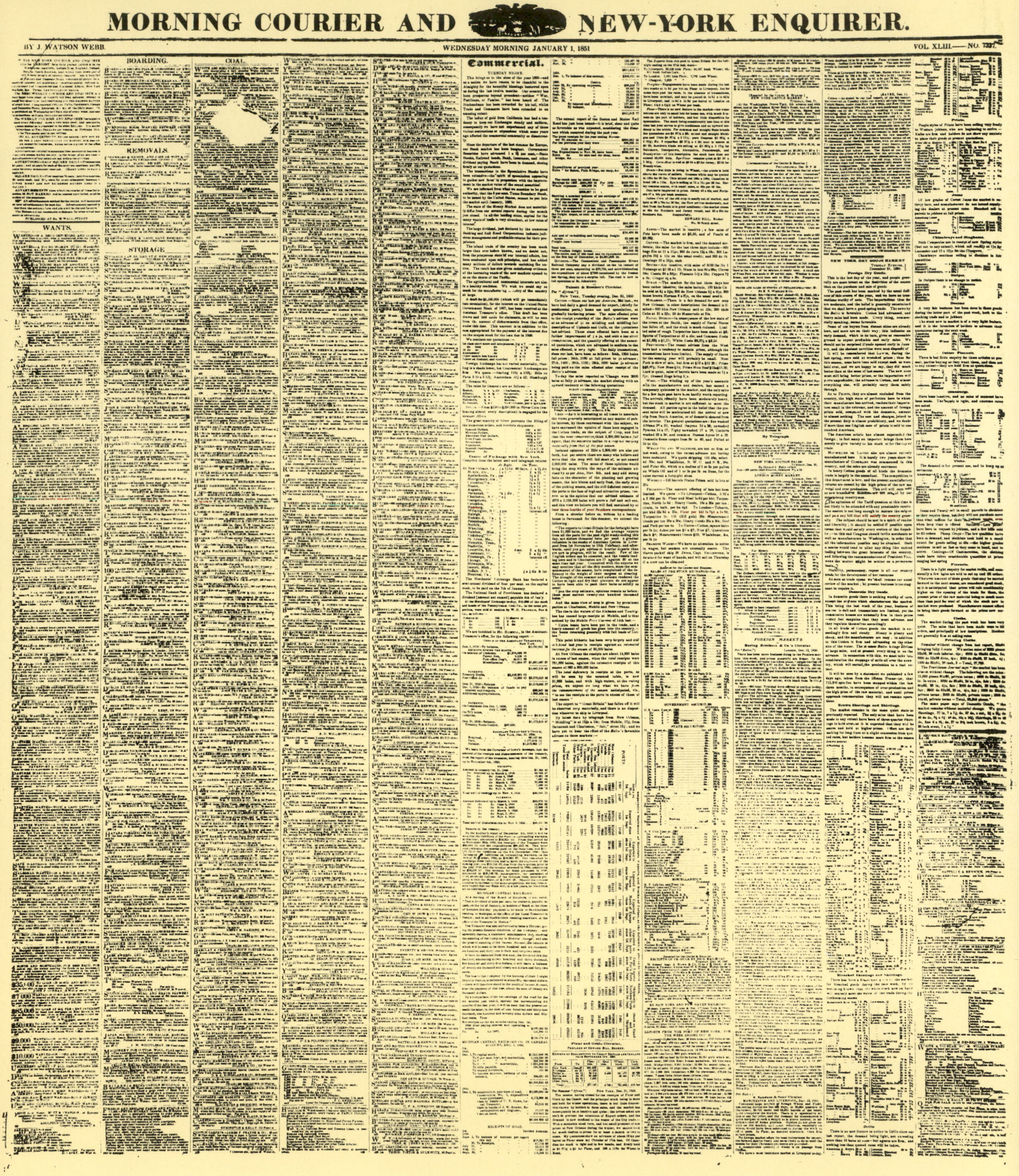
MORNING COURIER AND NEW-YORK ENQUIRER.

BY J. WATSON WEBB. WEDNESDAY MORNING, JANUARY 1, 1851. VOL. XLIII.—NO. 7337.

BOARDING. COAL. REMOVALS. STORAGE. WANTS.

Commercial.

A 'blanket sheet' – the eleven-column New York *Morning Courier* of 1851 with a page measuring 27-by-$32\frac{1}{2}$-inches.

this chapter, though at least it had more paragraphs. The whole of the five $16\frac{1}{4}$-pica columns, on a page $20\frac{1}{2}$ inches deep, were occupied by a single story (concerned with a local judicial scandal), minutely headed in column one only. The blackletter title, incidentally, was changed in a few months to condensed roman capitals, flanking a pictorial device, while a six-column make-up, with advertisements admitted to the last three columns, was introduced. In April 1844 format was again changed, to seven $13\frac{1}{2}$-pica columns (as late as 1939 this was to remain the standard measure for British seven-column papers).

Greeley was the outstanding editor of all American newspaper history and under him the *Tribune* became a major political force, largely responsible for making Abraham Lincoln President. A radical of firm principles, Greeley assembled a remarkable body of contributors and correspondents, including Karl Marx himself as principal European correspondent. Marx was taken on by managing editor Charles A. Dana, who was keenly interested in socialism, on the recommendation of the revolutionary poet Ferdinand Freiligrath (a noted contributor to Marx's *Neue Rheinische Zeitung* in 1848–9). Marx's correspondence was a feature of the *Tribune* for the ten years from 1851, when he began with the famous 'Revolution and Counter-Revolution in Germany' series – actually written by Engels, since at that time Marx's English was not quite up to the task. Typical of Greeley's regard for Marx was the editorial note in the *Tribune* in 1853: 'Mr Marx has indeed opinions of his own, with some of which we are far from agreeing; but those who do not read his letters neglect one of the most instructive sources of information on the great questions of European politics.'

Representing as he did the serious, responsible, socially-conscious tradition in American journalism, Greeley always fell foul of Bennett, the cynical and reckless founder of the opposite, demagogic 'yellow' tradition. Bennett's own prescription for journalism was 'light and spicy' (though 'earliest of the early' with the news). He was the first to start a financial page but stuck at nothing in brash self-advertisement. When he was married in June 1840, he ran a story in the *Herald* headed thus:

TO THE READERS OF THE HERALD
Declaration of Love – Caught at Last – Going to be Married – New Movement in Civilisation

It will be recalled that reference has already been made to the effect on newspaper format of the larger sheet that machine-printing made possible. So developed the trend to the 'blanket sheets', papers with gargantuan pages which proved far too unwieldy for reader-comfort; and with the extra paging made possible by improved machinery, publishers realised that smaller pages, and more of them, better solved the problem. For a time America developed the 'blanket sheet' to a much more extreme point than was ever known in Britain. Thus in 1851 the four-page New York *Morning Courier* had a page 27 inches wide by $32\frac{1}{2}$ inches deep (no less than 9 inches deeper than the standard newspaper page today); it was made up with eleven columns of 14-picas measure and carried five columns of small advertisements on the front page. The 'blanket' ultimate appeared in New York as a one-off stunt for the Fourth of July, 1859. *The Constellation*, described as an 'Illuminated Quadruple Sheet', was an eight-pager with a thirteen-column format (of $13\frac{1}{2}$-pica columns) on a page 35 inches wide, 50 inches deep; it was spattered with big, multi-column woodcuts, indicating that it must have been printed flatbed from the forme. The editor and publisher, a Bostonian named George Roberts, enthused about his 'magnificent sheet' in flowery language. 'It is', he wrote, 'the offspring of Invention, Taste, Enterprise and herculean Industry. . . . It cannot be excelled in its general imperialism of thought and design. It will be the pride of every true-hearted American and the wonder of Europe.' It never appeared again.

The circulation-building hoaxes perpetrated by *The Sun* have already been mentioned. The first, the 'moon hoax', was in 1835; deliberately faked by a *Sun* reporter, with Ben Day's approval, it purported to recount detailed telescopic observations of animals and men on the moon by the great astronomer Sir John Herschel from his new observatory in South Africa. The hoax pushed up the circulation of *The Sun* to over 19,000 and this was held despite the general outcry when the fraud was exposed. Nine years later came the second, the 'balloon hoax', which was the work of Edgar Allan Poe; purporting to describe a three-day crossing of the Atlantic by an aeronaut named Monck Mason in 'the steering balloon Victoria', it is of interest to us

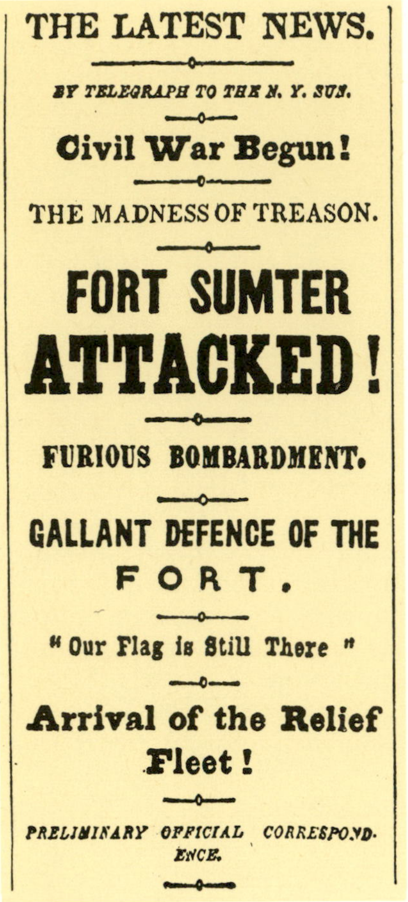
THE LATEST NEWS.

BY TELEGRAPH TO THE N. Y. SUN.

Civil War Begun!

THE MADNESS OF TREASON.

FORT SUMTER ATTACKED!

FURIOUS BOMBARDMENT.

GALLANT DEFENCE OF THE FORT.

"Our Flag is Still There"

Arrival of the Relief Fleet!

PRELIMINARY OFFICIAL CORRESPONDENCE.

▲ Civil War: the 1861 multi-decker reaction of *The Sun*.

because *The Sun* of 13 April 1844 presented it with a five-decker single-column heading, aggregating 25 lines of type in display. The typography was mixed, but the main flavour was contributed by fat face roman and italic capitals, with the main line, ending in three exclamation marks, in an unprecedentedly large 30pt (or 24pt titling) heavy Condensed Egyptian.

Reality, not fantasy, was now to spread the multi-decker display headline through the American Press. The outbreak of the Mexican War in the spring of 1846, after the previous year's admission of Texas as the twenty-eighth State of the Union, was followed by the completion of the direct telegraph line between Washington and New York that summer; it met with an excited newspaper and popular response. The *New York Herald* of 6 June 1846 greeted the opening of the Washington telegraph, and the consequent prompt receipt of the latest war news ('18 hours in advance of the mail') with a six-decker headline.

So by the time the Civil War began in 1861 displayed headlines had become normal in the American dailies; and the four years of that colossal conflict completed the process. Headings now ran up to as many as a dozen decks, according to the weight of the news; the favoured types were slab-seriffed Egyptians or 'Antiques', bold or bold condensed, though sanserifs also began to appear. The seven-decker in *The Sun* of 13 April 1861, reporting the bombardment of Fort Sumter and the beginning of the war, had one main line in bold condensed sans; three of the decks, too, were in lower-case and the use of lower-case in decker headings extended as time went on. The use of dashes, or three-em rules, between decks was general. A striking comparison of the developed American decker headline and the minimal news-titling presentation still prevailing in the London dailies is afforded by the issue of the *New York Herald* (April 1865) reporting the assassination of Lincoln and the *Daily Telegraph's* presentation of the same world-shaking event.

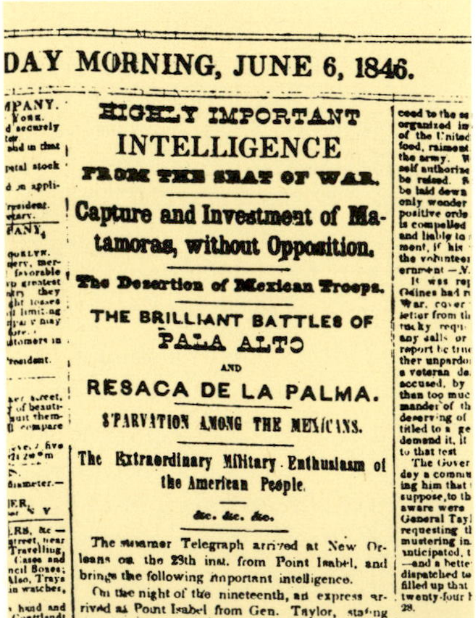
DAY MORNING, JUNE 6, 1846.

HIGHLY IMPORTANT INTELLIGENCE FROM THE SEAT OF WAR.

Capture and Investment of Matamoras, without Opposition.

The Desertion of Mexican Troops.

THE BRILLIANT BATTLES OF PALA ALTO AND RESACA DE LA PALMA.

STARVATION AMONG THE MEXICANS.

The Extraordinary Military Enthusiasm of the American People.

&c. &c. &c.

▲ The Mexican War and the newly-completed telegraph line from Washington to New York brought the first multi-decker, bold headlines, as in this 6 June 1846 issue of James Gordon Bennett's *New York Herald*: note the lower-case decks.

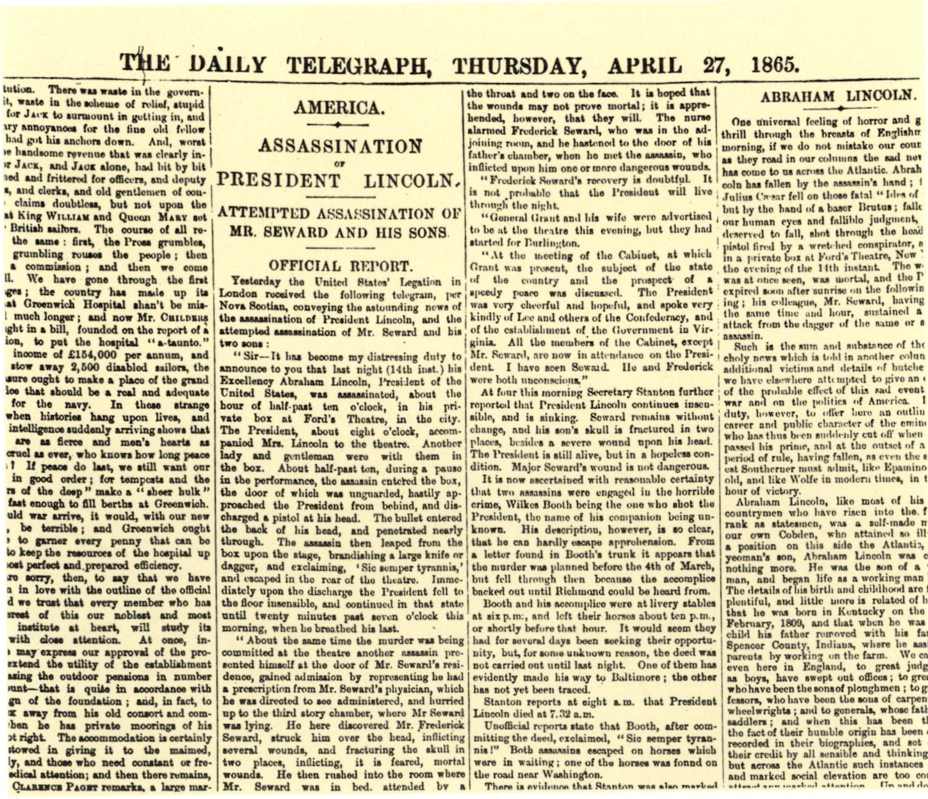
THE DAILY TELEGRAPH, THURSDAY, APRIL 27, 1865.

AMERICA.

ASSASSINATION OF PRESIDENT LINCOLN.

ATTEMPTED ASSASSINATION OF MR. SEWARD AND HIS SONS.

OFFICIAL REPORT.

ABRAHAM LINCOLN.

The decker headline as developed by four years of war: the massive display of the *New York Herald* (15 April 1865) ▶ on the assassination of Abraham Lincoln (right), compared (above) with ▲ the London *Daily Telegraph's* minimal headlining of the same event.

THE NEW YORK HERALD.

WHOLE NO. 10,456. NEW YORK, SATURDAY, APRIL 15, 1865. PRICE FOUR CENTS.

IMPORTANT.

ASSASSINATION OF PRESIDENT LINCOLN.

The President Shot at the Theatre Last Evening.

SECRETARY SEWARD DAGGERED IN HIS BED, BUT NOT MORTALLY WOUNDED.

Clarence and Frederick Seward Badly Hurt.

ESCAPE OF THE ASSASSINS.

Intense Excitement in Washington.

Scene at the Deathbed of Mr. Lincoln.

J. Wilkes Booth, the Actor, the Alleged Assassin of the President,

&c., &c., &c.

THE OFFICIAL DESPATCH.

WAR DEPARTMENT, WASHINGTON, April 15—1:30 A. M.

Major General Dix, New York:—

This evening at about 9:30 P. M., at Ford's Theatre, the President, while sitting in his private box with Mrs. Lincoln, Mrs. Harris and Major Rathburn, was shot by an assassin, who suddenly entered the box and approached behind the President.

The assassin then leaped upon the stage, brandishing a large dagger or knife, and made his escape in the rear of the theatre.

The pistol ball entered the back of the President's head and penetrated nearly through the head. The wound is mortal.

The President has been insensible ever since it was inflicted, and is now dying.

About the same hour an assassin, whether the same or not, entered Mr. Seward's apartments, and under pretence of having a prescription was shown to the Secretary's sick chamber. The assassin immediately rushed to the bed and inflicted two or three stabs on the throat and two on the face.

It is hoped the wounds may not be mortal. My apprehension is that they will prove fatal.

The nurse alarmed Mr. Frederick Seward, who was in an adjoining room, and he hastened to the door of his father's room, when he met the assassin, who inflicted upon him one or more dangerous wounds. The recovery of Frederick Seward is doubtful.

It is not probable that the President will live through the night.

General Grant and wife were advertised to be at the theatre this evening, but he started to Burlington at six o'clock this evening.

At a Cabinet meeting, at which General Grant was present, the subject of the state of the country and the prospect of a speedy peace were discussed. The President was very cheerful and hopeful, and spoke very kindly of General Lee and others of the confederacy, and of the establishment of government in Virginia.

All the members of the Cabinet except Mr. Seward, are now in attendance upon the President.

I have seen Mr. Seward, but he and Frederick were both unconscious.

EDWIN M. STANTON, Secretary of War.

THE HERALD DESPATCHES.

WASHINGTON, April 14, 1865.

Assassination has been inaugurated in Washington. The bowie knife and pistol have been applied to President Lincoln and Secretary Seward. The former was shot in the throat, while at Ford's theatre to-night. Mr. Seward was badly cut about the neck, while in his bed at his residence.

SECOND DESPATCH.

WASHINGTON, April 14, 1865.

An attempt was made about ten o'clock this evening to assassinate the President and Secretary Seward. The President was shot at Ford's Theatre. Result not yet known. Mr. Seward's throat was cut, and his son badly wounded.

There is intense excitement here.

Details of the Assassination.

WASHINGTON, April 14, 1865.

Washington was thrown into an intense excitement a few minutes before eleven o'clock this evening, by the announcement that the President and Secretary Seward had been assassinated and were dead.

The wildest excitement prevailed in all parts of the city. Men, women and children, old and young, rushed to and fro, and the rumors were magnified until we had nearly every member of the Cabinet killed. Some time elapsed before authentic data could be ascertained in regard to the affair.

About half-past ten o'clock this evening a tall, well dressed man made his appearance at Secretary Seward's residence, and applied for admission. He was refused admission by the servant, when the desperado stated that he had a prescription from the Surgeon General, and that he was ordered to deliver it in person. He was still refused, except upon the written order of the physician. This he pretended to show, and pushed by the servant and rushed up stairs to Mr. Seward's room. He was met at the door by Mr. Fred Seward, who notified him that he was master of the house, and would take charge of the medicine. After a few words had passed between them he dodged by Fred Seward and rushed to the Secretary's bed, and struck him in the neck with a dagger, and also in the breast.

It was supposed at first that Mr. Seward was killed instantly, but it was found afterwards that the wound was not mortal.

Major Wm. H. Seward, Jr., paymaster, was in the room, and rushed to the defence of his father, and was badly cut in the mêlée with the assassin, but not fatally.

The desperado managed to escape from the house, and was prepared for escape by having a horse at the door. He immediately mounted his horse, and sung out the motto of the State of Virginia, "*Sic Semper Tyrannis!*" and rode off.

Surgeon General Barnes was immediately sent for, and he *examined Mr. Seward and pronounced him safe.* His wounds were not fatal. The jugular vein was not cut, nor the wound in the breast deep enough to be fatal.

The President and Mrs. Lincoln were at Ford's theatre, listening to the performance of the American Cousin, occupying a box in the second tier. At the close of the third act a person entered the box occupied by the President, and shot Mr. Lincoln in the head. The shot entered the back of his head, and came out above the temple.

The assassin then jumped from the box upon the stage and ran across to the other side, exhibiting a dagger in his hand, flourishing it in a tragical manner, shouting the same words repeated by the desperado at Mr. Seward's house, adding to it, "The South is avenged," and then escaped from the back entrance to the stage, but in his passage dropped his pistol and his hat.

Mr. Lincoln fell forward from his seat, and Mrs. Lincoln fainted.

The moment the astonished audience could realize what had happened, the President was taken and carried to Mr. Petersen's house, in Tenth street, opposite to the theatre. Medical aid was immediately sent for, and the wound was at first supposed to be fatal, and it was announced that he could not live; but at half-past twelve he is still alive, though in a precarious condition.

As the assassin ran across the stage, Colonel J. B. Stewart, of this city, who was occupying one of the front seats in the orchestra, on the same side of the house as the box occupied by Mr. Lincoln, sprang to the stage and followed him; but he was obstructed in his passage across the stage by the fright of the actors, and reached the back door about three seconds after the assassin had passed out. Colonel Stewart got to the street just in time to see him mount his horse and ride away.

This operation shows that the whole thing was a preconcerted plan. The person who fired the pistol was a man about thirty years of age, about five feet nine, spare built, fair skin, dark hair, apparently bushy, with a large mustache. Laura Keene and the leader of the orchestra declare that they recognized him as J. Wilkes Booth the actor, and a rabid secessionist. Whoever he was, it is plainly evident that he thoroughly understood the theatre and all the approaches and modes of escape to the stage. A person not familiar with the theatre could not have possibly made his escape so well and quickly.

The alarm was sounded in every quarter. Mr. Stanton was notified, and immediately left his house.

All the other members of the Cabinet escaped attack.

Cavalrymen were sent out in all directions, and despatches sent to all the fortifications, and it is thought they will be captured.

WASHINGTON, April 15—1 A. M.

The streets in the vicinity of Ford's Theatre are densely crowded by an anxious and excited crowd. A guard has been placed across Tenth street and F and E streets, and only official persons and particular friends of the President are allowed to pass.

The popular heart is deeply stirred, and the deepest indignation against leading rebels is freely expressed.

The scene at the house where the President lies *in extremis* is very affecting. Even Secretary Stanton is affected to tears.

When the news spread through the city that the President had been shot, the people, with pale faces and compressed lips, crowded every place where there was the slightest chance of obtaining information in regard to the affair.

After the President was shot, Lieutenant Rathbun, caught the assassin by the arm, who immediately struck him with a knife, and jumped from the box, as before stated.

The popular affection for Mr. Lincoln has been shown by this diabolical assassination, which will bring eternal infamy, not only upon its authors, but upon the hellish cause which they desire to avenge.

Vice President Johnson arrived at the White House, where the President lies, about one o'clock, and will remain with him to the last.

The President's family are in attendance upon him also.

As soon as intelligence could be got to the War Department, the electric telegraph and the Signal corps were put in requisition to endeavor to prevent the escape of the assassins, and all the troops around Washington are under arms.

Popular report points to a somewhat celebrated actor of known secession proclivities as the assassin; but it would be unjust to name him until some further evidence of his guilt is obtained. It is rumored that the person alluded to is in custody.

The latest advices from Secretary Seward reveals more desperate work there than at first supposed. Seward's wounds are not in themselves fatal; but, in connection with his recent injuries, and the great loss of blood he has sustained, his recovery is questionable.

It was Clarence A. Seward, instead of Wm. H. Seward, Jr., who was wounded. Fred. Seward was also badly cut, as were also three nurses, who were in attendance upon the Secretary, showing that a desperate struggle took place there. The wounds of the whole party were dressed.

ONE O'CLOCK A. M.

The President is perfectly senseless, and there is not the slightest hope of his surviving. Physicians believe that he will die before morning. All of his Cabinet, except Secretary Seward, are with him. Speaker Colfax, Senator Farwell, of Maine, and many other gentlemen, are also at the house awaiting the termination.

The scene at the President's bedside is described by one who witnessed it as most affecting. It was surrounded by his Cabinet ministers, all of whom were bathed in tears, not even excepting Mr. Stanton, who, when informed by Surgeon General Barnes, that the President could not live until morning, exclaimed, "Oh, no, General; no—no;" and with an impulse, natural as it was unaffected, immediately sat down on a chair near his bedside and wept like a child.

Senator Sumner was seated on the right of the President's couch, near the head, holding the right hand of the President in his own. He was sobbing like a woman, with his head bowed down almost on the pillow of the bed on which the President was lying.

TWO O'CLOCK A. M.

The President is still alive, but there is no improvement in his condition.

THE PRESS DESPATCHES.

WASHINGTON, April 15—12:30 A. M.

The President was shot in a theatre to-night, and is perhaps mortally wounded.

SECOND DESPATCH.

WASHINGTON, April 15—1 A. M.

The President is not expected to live through the night. He was shot at a theatre.

Secretary Seward was also assassinated. No arteries were cut.

Additional Details of the Assassination.

WASHINGTON, April 15—1:30 A. M.

President Lincoln and wife, with other friends, this evening visited Ford's theatre, for the purpose of witnessing the performance of the American Cousin.

It was announced in the papers that General Grant would also be present; but that gentleman took the late train of cars for New Jersey.

The theatre was densely crowded, and all seemed delighted with the scene before them. During the third act, and while there was a temporary pause for one of the actors to enter, a sharp report of a pistol was heard, which merely attracted attention, but suggested nothing serious, until a man rushed to the front of the President's box, waving a long dagger in his right hand, and exclaiming "*Sic semper tyrannis!*" and immediately leaped from the box, which was in the second tier, to the stage beneath, and ran across to the opposite side, making his escape, amid the bewilderment of the audience, from the rear of the theatre, and, mounting a horse, fled.

The screams of Mrs. Lincoln first disclosed the fact to the audience that the President had been shot, when all present rose to their feet, rushing towards the stage, many exclaiming "Hang him! Hang him!"

The excitement was of the wildest possible description, and of course there was an abrupt termination of the theatrical performance.

There was a rush toward the President's box, when cries were heard:—"Stand back and give him air." "Has any one stimulants?"

On a hasty examination it was found that the President had been shot through the head, above and back of the temporal bone, and that some of the brain was oozing out.

He was removed to a private house opposite to the theatre, and the Surgeon General of the army and other surgeons sent for to attend to his condition.

On an examination of the private box blood was discovered on the back of the cushioned rocking chair on which the President had been sitting, also on the partition and on the floor. A common single barreled pocket pistol was found on the carpet.

A military guard was placed in front of the private residence to which the President had been conveyed. An immense crowd was in front of it, all deeply anxious to learn the condition of the President. It had been previously announced that the wound was mortal, but all hoped otherwise. The shock to the community was terrible.

At midnight the Cabinet, with Messrs. Sumner, Colfax and Farnsworth, Judge Curtis, Governor Oglesby, General Meigs, Colonel Hay, and a few personal friends, with Surgeon General Barnes and his immediate assistants, were around his bedside.

The President was in a state of syncope, totally insensible, and breathing slowly. The blood oozed from the wound at the back of his head.

The surgeons exhausted every possible effort of medicinal skill; but all hope was gone.

The parting of his family with the dying President is too sad for description.

The President and Mrs. Lincoln did not start for the theatre until fifteen minutes after eight o'clock. Speaker Colfax was at the White House at the time, and the President stated to him that he was going. Mrs. Lincoln had not been well, because the papers had announced that General Grant and they were to be present, and, as General Grant had gone North, he did not wish the audience to be disappointed.

He went with apparent reluctance, and urged Mr. Colfax to go with him; but that gentleman had made other engagements, and, with Mr. Ashmun, of Massachusetts, bid him goodby.

When the excitement at the theatre was at its wildest height reports were circulated that Secretary Seward had also been assassinated.

On reaching this gentleman's residence a crowd and a military guard were found at the door, and on entering it was ascertained that the reports were based on truth.

Everybody there was so excited that scarcely an intelligible word could be gathered. But the facts are substantially as follows:—

About ten o'clock a man rang the bell, and the call having been answered by a colored servant, he said he had come from Dr. Verdi, Secretary Seward's family physician, with a prescription, at the same time holding in his hand a small piece of folded paper, and saying, in answer to a refusal, that he must see the Secretary, as he was entrusted with particular directions concerning the medicine.

He still insisted on going up, although repeatedly informed that no one could enter the chamber. The man pushed the servant aside, and walked hastily towards the Secretary's room, and was then met by Mr. Frederick Seward, of whom he demanded to see the Secretary, making the same representation which he did to the servant.

What further passed in the way of colloquy is not known; but the man struck him on the head with a billy, severely injuring the skull and felling him almost senseless.

The assassin then rushed into the chamber and attacked Major Seward, Paymaster United States Army, and Mr. Hansell, a messenger of the State Department, and two male nurses, disabling them all.

He then rushed upon the Secretary, who was lying in bed in the same room, and inflicted three stabs in the neck, but severing, it is thought and hoped, no arteries, though he bled profusely.

The assassin then rushed down stairs, mounted his horse at the door, and rode off before an alarm could be sounded, and in the same manner as the assassin of the President.

It is believed that the injuries of the Secretary are not fatal, nor those of either of the others, although both the Secretary and the Assistant Secretary are very seriously injured.

Secretaries Stanton and Welles, and other prominent officers of the Government, called at Secretary Seward's house to inquire into his condition, and there heard of the assassination of the President.

They then proceeded to the house where he was lying, exhibiting of course intense anxiety and solicitude.

An immense crowd was gathered in front of the President's house, and a strong guard was also stationed there. Many persons evidently supposing he would be brought to his home.

The entire city to-night presents a scene of wild excitement, accompanied by violent expression of indignation and the profoundest sorrow; many shed tears.

The military authorities have despatched mounted patrols in every direction, in order, if possible, to arrest the assassins. The whole metropolitan police are likewise vigilant for the same purpose.

The attacks, both at the theatre and at Secretary Seward's house, took place at about the same hour—ten o'clock—thus showing a preconcerted plan to assassinate those gentlemen. Some evidences of the guilt of the party who attacked the President are in the possession of the police.

Vice President Johnson is in the city, and his head-quarters are guarded by troops.

THE LATEST NEWS.

Secretary Stanton to General Dix.

WAR DEPARTMENT, WASHINGTON, April 15—3 A. M.

Major General Dix, New York:—

The President still breathes, but is quite insensible, as he has been ever since he was shot. He evidently did not see the person who shot him, but was looking on the stage, as he was approached from behind.

Mr. Seward has rallied, and it is hoped he may live.

Frederick Seward's condition is very critical.

The attendant who was present was shot through the lungs, and is not expected to live.

The wounds of Major Seward are not serious.

Investigation strongly indicates J. Wilkes Booth as the assassin of the President. Whether it was the same or a different person that attempted to murder Mr. Seward remains in doubt.

Chief Justice Cartter is engaged in taking the evidence.

Every exertion has been made to prevent the escape of the murderer. His horse has been found on the road near Washington.

EDWIN M. STANTON, Secretary of War.

Our Special Washington Despatch.

WASHINGTON, April 15, 1865.

When the fatal shot was fired, Mrs. Lincoln, who was alongside of her husband, exclaimed, "Oh! why didn't they shoot me—why didn't they shoot me?"

There is evidence that Secretary Stanton was also marked for assassination. On receipt of intelligence at the War Department of the attack on the President, two employes of the department were sent to summon the Secretary. Just as they approached his house, a man jumped out from behind a tree box in front of the house and ran away. It is well known to be the custom of the Secretary to go from the department to his house between nine and twelve P. M., and usually unattended. It is supposed that the assassin intended to shoot him as he entered the house, but failed from the fact that Mr. Stanton remained at home during the evening.

The circumstantial evidence is very strong that J. Wilkes Booth is the person who shot the President. Several parties who are well acquainted with him, and saw the assassin when he jumped from the box, are positive that he is the man. It is also reported that Booth's horse was saddled at the side door of the theatre, and was rode off by the assassin. If he is the man, it is impossible for him to escape. The horse of the man who made the attack on Secretary Seward has been found near the Lincoln Hospital, bathed in sweat, and with blood upon the saddle cloths.

SEVEN O'CLOCK A. M.

There is up to this time no material change in the President's condition.

The Press Despatch.

WASHINGTON, April 15—[illegible]

The President is still alive, but he is growing weaker. The ball is lodged in his brain, three inches from where it entered the skull. He remains insensible, and his condition is utterly helpless.

The Vice President has been to see him, but all company except the members of the Cabinet and of the family is rigidly excluded.

Large crowds still continue in the street, as near the house as the line of guards allow.

IMPORTANT FROM SOUTH AMERICA.

Surrender of Montevideo to Gen. Flores—Brazil in Possession of the City, &c.

The Brazilian mail arrived at Lisbon April 2, bringing the following advices:—

Montevideo has surrendered to General Flores.

The Brazilians now (March 11) occupy the city.

RIO JANEIRO, March 11, 1865.

Exchange 25½ a 26¼.

Coffee—Sales of good firsts at 6s. 6d. Shipments, 100,000 bags. Stock, 100,000 bags. Freights, 50.62½.

BAHIA, March 11, 1865.

Exchange 26¼. Cotton nominal.

News from San Francisco.

SAN FRANCISCO, April 13, 1865.

The exports of treasure for the quarter just ended show a falling off of about six and a half millions as compared with the same period last year.

City Intelligence.

EASTER SUNDAY AT ST. ANN'S CHURCH.—The admirers of sacred music, made truly effective by a well trained choir, have an opportunity of indulging their taste by repairing to St. Ann's church on Easter Sunday evening, the doors opening at seven, the concert beginning at eight. Three of the pieces are from Gordigiani, three from Rossini and one from each of the composers Verdi, Donizetti, Verrimst, Dachauer and Gounod. We need only mention the names of Signor Remi and Messrs. Schmitz, Schubert and Dachauer to insure confidence in the vocal results. The ladies are quite distinguished for contralto and soprano execution, and no exertion will be spared to make the musical feast worthy of the day.

A NEW CHURCH.—An advertisement among our religious notices announces the opening of the new Church of the Holy Trinity, Madison avenue, corner of Forty-second street, on Sunday. Sermons will be preached at the three sessions by Rev. Dr. Tyng, of St. George's; Rev. Dr. Dyer, and the Rev. Stephen H. Tyng, Jr., the pastor of the church. It promises to be an occasion of great interest to residents on Murray Hill.

MISS EMMA HARDINGE delivers her able lecture on "Politics in the Pulpit" this evening, at Dodworth Hall. To test the lady's ability, any questions the audience desire to ask will be answered.

MAN DROWNED.—On the morning of the 13th instant a journeyman housepainter, whose name is believed to be Barnard Burns, was accidentally drowned at Guntherville, Long Island. His body has not yet been claimed by his friends. Mr. J. B. Acker, of No. 9 Macdougal street, will give facilities to any one who can identify the corpse.

THE REBELS.

JEFF. DAVIS AT DANVILLE.

His Latest Appeal to His Deluded Followers.

He Thinks the Fall of Richmond a Blessing in Disguise, as it Leaves the Rebel Armies Free to Move from Point to Point.

He Vainly Promises to Hold Virginia at All Hazards.

Lee and His Army Supposed to be Safe.

Breckinridge and the Rest of Davis' Cabinet Reach Danville Safely.

The Organ of Governor Vance, of North Carolina, Advises the Submission of the Rebels to President Lincoln's Terms,

&c., &c., &c.

Jeff. Davis' Last Proclamation.

VIRGINIA TO BE HELD BY THE REBELS AT ALL HAZARDS.

DANVILLE, Va., April 5, 1865.

The General-in-Chief found it necessary to make such movements of his troops as to uncover the capital. It would be unwise to conceal the *moral and material injury to our cause resulting from the occupation of our capital* by the enemy. It is equally unwise and unworthy of us to allow our own energies to falter and our efforts to become relaxed under adverses, however calamitous they may be. For many months *the largest and finest army* of the confederacy, under command of a leader whose presence inspires equal confidence in the troops and the people, has been greatly trammelled by the necessity of keeping constant watch over the approaches to the capital, and has thus been forced to forego more than one opportunity for promising enterprise. It is for us, my countrymen, to show by our bearing under reverses how wretched has been the self-deception of those who have believed us less able to endure misfortune with fortitude than to encounter dangers with courage.

We have now entered upon a new phase of the struggle. Relieved from the necessity of guarding particular points, *our army will be free to move from point to point* to strike the enemy in detail far from his base. *Let us but will it and we are free.*

Animated by that confidence in spirit and fortitude which never yet failed me, I announce to you, fellow countrymen, that it is my purpose to maintain your cause with my whole heart and soul; that I will never consent to abandon to the enemy one foot of the soil of any one of the States of the confederacy. That Virginia—noble State—whose ancient renown has been eclipsed by her still more glorious recent history; whose bosom has been bared to receive the main shock of this war; whose sons and daughters have exhibited heroism so sublime as to render her illustrious in all time to come—that Virginia, with the help of the people and by the blessing of Providence, *shall be held and defended*, and no peace ever be made with the infamous invaders of her territory.

If by the stress of numbers we should ever be compelled to a temporary withdrawal from her limits, or those of any other border State, again and again will we return, until the baffled and exhausted enemy shall abandon in despair his endless and impossible task of making slaves of a people resolved to be free.

Let us, then, not despond, my countrymen; but, relying on God, meet the foe with fresh defiance and with unconquered and unconquerable hearts.

JEFFERSON DAVIS.

The Evacuation of the Rebel Capital.

THE FIRST REBEL ACCOUNT OF HOW THE CITY WAS ABANDONED.

[From the Danville (Va.) Register, April 5.]

Persons who left the capital Sunday night and Monday morning represent that the scene which followed the evacuation of the city by our troops beggars description. To preserve order and protect the property of the citizens who unavoidably remained there, as far as could be done, the Nineteenth Virginia militia, under Colonel Evans, was placed on police duty in the city, to await the coming of the enemy; but accounts state that they failed to render any aid or protection to the people whatever. On Sunday night a mob of the lower classes of the city, composed, it is said, mostly of the foreign element, visited a number of the largest storehouses of the city and robbed them of their contents. It is affirmed that Main street was pillaged, and then burned, and that some of the milling establishments were also committed to the flames. We have no doubt that a considerable portion of that brave city has been laid in ashes, and a number of its people insulted, outraged, robbed and massacred. How painful the thought that the place should be given over to rapine and plunder, even before the public enemy entered its limits. But the fact only proves that the people of Richmond have had secret enemies in their own midst scarcely less savage and even more treacherous and vindictive than the open foe.

We are told that the people banded together during the violent proceeding of the mob and resisted them with force, a street fight ensuing, in which several persons were killed.

No intelligence has reached us of the enemy's troops occupying the city. The last trains on the Danville railroad which came out of the place left Monday morning, and passengers upon them had heard nothing from the enemy. The greater portion of Grant's army was transferred to the south side of James river some days ago, only the command of General Ord, which is composed mostly, if not entirely, of negro troops, being left on the north side. This command will enter and occupy the city. Some of our people who are acquainted with the character of General Ord think they have reason to hope that his treatment of the unfortunate people of Richmond will not be so hard, and cruel and inhuman as that which has fallen upon the heads of our fellow citizens in some other captured cities.

The newspapers of Richmond, we suppose, all fell into the hands of the enemy. The evacuation of the city was so sudden and unexpected—scarcely any one being prepared for it—that no time was left for the removal of so cumbrous an establishment as a city newspaper office. In a few days we may expect to hear that the *Enquirer* or the *Whig* or the *Examiner* is issued as a Yankee paper.

All the rolling stock of the Richmond and Danville Railroad in running order was saved on the retreat from Richmond. A few old cars, not in a movable condition, were left at Manchester. No train was captured by the enemy near the junction, as was at one time reported; and, indeed, we do not believe that any body of Yankees had struck the road at any point up to yesterday evening.

The Secretary of War, the Quartermaster General, Commissary General and a number of other officers of the government, left Richmond on horseback, and will probably arrive at this place to-morrow.

Should General Lee establish his lines east of the junction, we suppose the State Legislature will be convened at Lynchburg.

All the specie and other valuables belonging to the banks in Richmond were removed from the city on Sunday, and have been carried to places of safety.

A considerable amount of goods purchased by the State for distribution to the people, we regret to learn had to be left behind. Also the State archives remained in the city; but we perceive no motive the enemy can have in destroying them, as they will, no doubt, endeavor to occupy the city permanently, and establish a State government at Richmond under the federal Union.

Lee's Army Supposed to be in a Safe Position.

[From the Raleigh Confederate, April 7.]

This is the time for rumor manufacturers who are engaged in a wholesale business. Sometimes they have it that whole brigades deserted in the last great battle; among others, Cook's brigade is selected as the bearer of this stigma. We are assured that such a statement has no foundation whatever; that no treachery induced the disaster at Petersburg; that our forces fought splendidly, and the enemy only succeeded by overwhelming numbers. We are convinced, too, from facts which we cannot mention, that *Lee's army is in a safe position, and that his future movements will be directed with the skill and energy which distinguish this great captain.*

Having anticipated the probable loss of Richmond, and fully recognizing the importance of the disaster, we are, nevertheless, not of the number of those who give up the cause. In the Southern confederacy this day there is military strength of men, material and supplies to make independence certain. It is with the *people themselves* whether they secure or lose their liberties.

Rebel Particulars of the Battle at Petersburg.

[From the Raleigh Confederate, April 7.]

An officer who left Richmond at nine o'clock on Monday morning last informs us that at the time he left the city was in flames from Cary to Canal streets. The Shockoe warehouse and other entrepots of supplies were burning. The bridges also had been fired.

No mob or violence of any kind had occurred up to the period when he left, so that the reports of a destructive mob on Sunday night are untrue. The enemy's cavalry entered the city as the train moved off that he came out in. The story of the mob, therefore, we hope, is entirely erroneous.

This officer describes the fighting on Saturday as terrific beyond description. The enemy forced column after column on our works, lapping our lines on the extreme right. They came nine columns deep. Eight lines faltered and were broken by the obstinacy of our defences; but the ninth broke over our forces like a whirlwind. He says the destruction of the enemy was immense. Our loss, we think, consisted mainly in the prisoners taken by the enemy. All the prisoners whom we captured were drunk, having been prepared according to Yankee tactics for this dreadful ordeal. Lieutenant General A. P. Hill was certainly killed. General Fitz. Lee was not killed, as reported, nor General W. H. F. Lee. No general officer from North Carolina was killed, as far as he heard. On Monday Sheridan attacked Fitz. Lee and was handsomely repulsed.

The Organ of Governor Vance, of North Carolina, Advising General Lee to Submit on Mr. Lincoln's Terms.

[From the Raleigh Confederate, April 7.]

The *Conservative* occasionally seems to fall into very mysterious hands, and to come under the control of an incomprehensible influence. On the day before yesterday that paper availed itself of a period of extreme reverse and disaster to renew the attempt to cast odium on a portion of our own citizens, which has been a favorite policy with its political leaders ever since the reverses began, and after it was no longer politic to claim that they "made the revolution." Yesterday it sends to the public a leader of still more extraordinary import. From what we comprehend of it, it seems to be a *distinct proposition to submit and surrender upon the terms proposed by Lincoln.* This has never yet, that we recollect of, been more distinctly proposed, even by journals whose loyalty has been called in question. The *Conservative* says:—"It is nonsense to propose to treat with the North with any expectation of the concession that the confederacy is a government," and hence, says the *Conservative*, "if our authorities are determined to force this condition upon the North, as a basis of negotiation, then the North will never negotiate." What is this but surrender? Not only surrender, but an assertion to the world that the defence of the last four years has been of a position which is one of sheer nonsense—one which the North "never could admit!" We have not seen in this controversy so bold and unconditional a justification of the Northern invasion; for, if we sought to force a claim inconsistent with reason, and to demand an "admission" which "is an absurdity in anything like government," and the North only resisted such claim and refused such admission, then we are in the wrong and the Yankee government is right, and the writer of the article to which we are replying does well when he advises General Lee not to "block up his way, *at the threshold, by presenting a basis to which he knows the enemy will not yield,*" but "to meet him on his own ground," as "the only way to open the negotiation." When we remember what "his own ground" is, upon which the *Conservative* proposes to meet the enemy, we may readily understand how much it is prepared to concede. "His own ground" measured the length of three propositions; submission to the laws and constitution of the United States, the laying down of our arms, and acquiescence in Lincoln's proclamations. This is the ground on which the author of the editorial desires General Lee to meet Lincoln and "secure a talk about peace." We have no idea that Governor Vance will support this idea; but it is very unfortunate that now, in the very moment when everything should be said to uphold the hopes and confidence of the army and people, such sentiments should obtain publication in the organ of the Governor.

High Prices in an Overstocked Market.

[From the Raleigh Confederate, April 7.]

Our market, on the arrival of the Weldon train, on yesterday, *became overstocked* with shad; *they went off slowly at $50 per pair.*

THE STATE CAPITAL.

Rejection of the New York Fire Commissioners—Passage of the Central Railroad Fare Bill—Great Excitement Over the Health Bill, &c.

ALBANY, April 14—11:40 P. M.

Legislation each day is now so rapid here that a detail or analysis of its progress is out of the question. To-day the long pending Central Railroad bill passed the Senate, and is virtually a law if the Governor does [illegible]. But the result may be foreshadowed in the [illegible] to-day of the Dry Dock and Battery Railroad [illegible].

The Health bill, which two days since was [illegible] caucus rules to have a sure passage, was to-night defeated by republican votes. The Collector of the port of New York, who has had an elaborate organization up for his retention in the office of Commissioner of Charities, was thrown overboard and the power of all his patronage disregarded in the strife to secure this position, which has been his pet desire and speciality for many years.

A final vote was forced upon the friends of the bill at a late hour. Sixty-one voted for the bill and fifty-one against it. Sixty-five votes being necessary to its passage, it was lost. Mr. Salmon, of New York, who had made himself obnoxious by the vehemency of his opposition to the bill, was sought to be involved in proceedings before the bar of the House; but the Speaker was evidently discouraged from any such attempts. The management for the bill on the floor of the House was understood to be in the hands of the radicals, under the lead of Fields. Boole was in the lobby in person. Mayor Gunther, Carr and others of his opponents were here yesterday to urge on the passage of the bill. It is alleged that the republican interest was sold out by the radicals.

The Fire Commissioners encountered a decided capsize in executive session. The defeat of the Health bill was pending on the [illegible], and the Assembly had adjourned in the excitement [illegible] manner of the morning. The names were at first confirmed. Senator Laimbier, who had made the chief opposition, moving the confirmation. This action was, however, reconsidered on motion of Senator Andrews, on the ground of the promises made in the Assembly to the democrats, who passed it, that the Commission would comprise two democrats. The names were accordingly sent back to the Governor.

The continuation of [illegible] in office by the defeat of the [illegible] passage of a resolution [illegible] the investigating committee, to sit during the summer [illegible] the other departments. The [illegible] and [illegible] exception and [illegible].

The action [illegible] in regard to Draper and the Board of [illegible] was decided by resolution to day, [illegible] the [illegible] and [illegible] District Attorney at New York, as a satisfactory manifestation of Thurlow Weed's power.

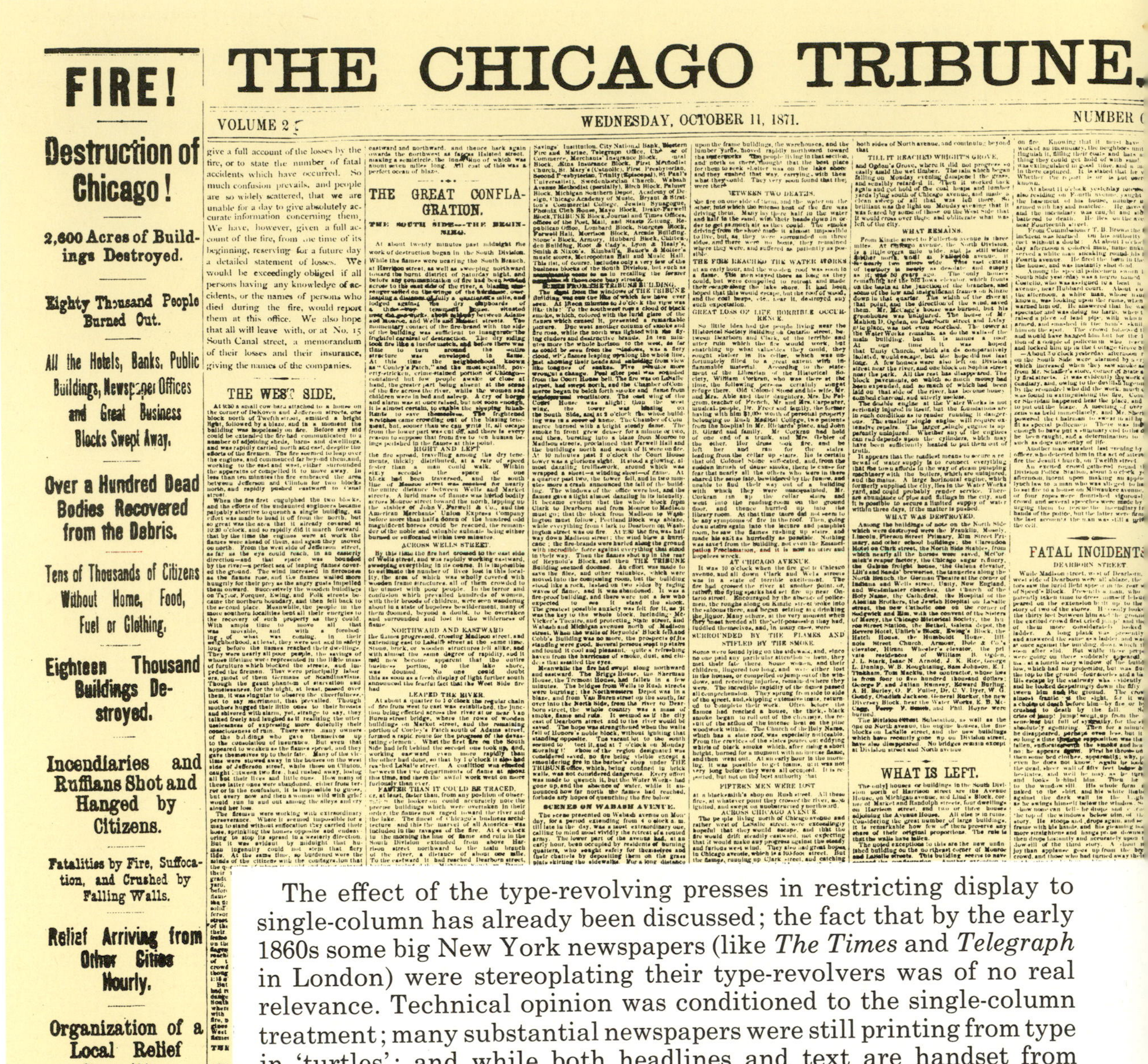

THE CHICAGO TRIBUNE.

VOLUME 25 — WEDNESDAY, OCTOBER 11, 1871. — NUMBER

FIRE!

Destruction of Chicago!

2,600 Acres of Buildings Destroyed.

Eighty Thousand People Burned Out.

All the Hotels, Banks, Public Buildings, Newspaper Offices and Great Business Blocks Swept Away.

Over a Hundred Dead Bodies Recovered from the Debris.

Tens of Thousands of Citizens Without Home, Food, Fuel or Clothing.

Eighteen Thousand Buildings Destroyed.

Incendiaries and Ruffians Shot and Hanged by Citizens.

Fatalities by Fire, Suffocation, and Crushed by Falling Walls.

Relief Arriving from Other Cities Hourly.

Organization of a Local Relief Committee.

List of Names of Over Two Hundred Missing Men, Women, and Children.

The City Without Light or Water.

Crosby's and Hooley's Opera Houses, McVicker's and the Dearborn Theatres, Wood's Museum, and all the Art Galleries in Ashes.

During Sunday night, Monday, and Tuesday, this city has been swept by a conflagration which has no parallel in the annals of history, for the quantity of property destroyed, and the utter and almost irremediable ruin which it wrought. A fire in a barn on the West Side was the insignificant cause of a conflagration which has swept out of existence hundreds of millions of property, has reduced to poverty thousands who, the day before, were in a state of opulence, has covered the prairies, now swept by the cold southwest wind, with thousands of homeless unfortunates, which has stripped 2,600 acres of buildings, which has destroyed public improvements that it has taken years of patient labor to build up, and which has set back for years the progress of the city, diminished her population, and crushed her resources. But to a blow, no matter how terrible, Chicago will not succumb. Late as it is in the season, general as the ruin is, the spirit of her citizens has not given way, and before the smoke has cleared away, and the ruins are cold, they are beginning to plan for the future. Though so many have been deprived of homes and sustenance, aid in money and provisions is flowing in from all quarters, and much of the present distress will be alleviated before another day has gone by.

It is at this moment impossible to give a full account of the losses by the fire, or to state the number of fatal accidents which have occurred. So much confusion prevails, and people are so widely scattered, that we are unable for a day to give absolutely accurate information concerning them. We have, however, given a full account of the fire, from the time of its beginning, reserving for a future day a detailed statement of losses. We would be exceedingly obliged if all persons having any knowledge of accidents, or the names of persons who died during the fire, would report them at this office. We also hope that all will leave with, or at No. 15 South Canal street, a memorandum of their losses and their insurance, giving the names of the companies.

THE WEST SIDE.

THE GREAT CONFLAGRATION.

The effect of the type-revolving presses in restricting display to single-column has already been discussed; the fact that by the early 1860s some big New York newspapers (like *The Times* and *Telegraph* in London) were stereoplating their type-revolvers was of no real relevance. Technical opinion was conditioned to the single-column treatment; many substantial newspapers were still printing from type in 'turtles'; and while both headlines and text are handset from movable type the only safe and speedy procedure is to make-up, column by column, in separate galleys whence the matter can be slid on to the stone to complete the forme.

Thus, whereas the modern newspaper gains emphasis by increasing horizontal display, the mid-nineteenth-century paper could only gain emphasis by increasing vertical display. Of the lengths to which the American single-column decker could go the most extraordinary example was the front page of the *Chicago Tribune* of 11 October 1871, reporting the appalling conflagration which virtually destroyed the great western metropolis. Apart from minor one-line headings here and there, and a number of crossheads in text, the eight-column page was dominated by a single-column fifteen-decker, descending over three-quarters of the way down column one. Every other column was 'blind', matter running to the head of each. The first deck, the one word FIRE! in bold condensed sans, was followed by exclusively upper- and lower-case decks, varying between antique or sans condensed, some of them running to as many as four lines, and all of them displayed in inverted pyramid style. It was the sledge-hammer ultimate of the single-column decker.

The mightiest of all single-column decker headings – column one of the front page of the *Chicago Tribune*, 11 October 1871. The remaining columns all ran 'blind' (as in *The Sun* of 1888, see p. 79).

4: The Rotary Age and News Display

From 1870 onwards the web-fed rotary perfector, printing from curved stereo-plates, progressively took over as the machine producing the larger daily papers. The change was gradual, of course; type-revolvers, whether printing from plates or type, continued in use, especially on smaller papers. By the 1890s, indeed, a different trend developed, which we need do no more than mention here; this was the web-fed flatbed press, printing direct from the forme and thus popular with papers of modest circulation, glad to avoid the complications and expense of stereotyping. These machines were slow, despite their makers' boasts (3,000 copies an hour was a fair average output), but they delivered perfected and folded papers. In Britain the Cossar, the latest of the type to emerge, and in America the Duplex, typified these still extant machines.

The advent of the paper-making machine, delivering its product in an endless web, soon turned ingenious minds to considering the possibility of printing from the web. There were some interesting early experiments in America and in 1841 a trial issue of the New York *Sun* was run on the 'Rotary Cylindrical Printing Press' – a web-fed type-revolver – invented by Jeptha A. Wilkinson (appreciably antedating Hoe's first type-revolver, it will be noted). That the invention evidently did not catch on was no bar to continued pursuit of the possibilities of web-feeding.[1]

Thomas Nelson (of the Edinburgh printers and publishers) designed a model of a web-fed press which was shown at the Great Exhibition of 1851. Applegath himself, in his 1847 patent specification for his vertical type-revolver, said: 'It is possible that a still greater production and more economy may be obtained by a machine in which the paper is supplied in rolls . . . in which case the paper must have an uninterrupted motion.' He added the significant proviso that web-feeding would not be possible unless the authorities 'shall think fit to grant the necessary concession as to the stamping'. This indicates how, up to 1855, the Stamp Acts, requiring the impression of the tax stamp on every *sheet* of paper used, could hamper technical progress.

The problem facing newspaper production technicians during the 1860s was not simply one of marrying the two principles of web-feeding and rotary printing. They needed a machine which would be a perfector, producing complete copies of the paper printed both sides at a single pass, and equally a machine which would cut the heavy labour costs of the multi-feeder type-revolver. Two ten-feeder Hoes required a total crew of twenty-eight men. When *The Times* designed and built its own web-fed rotary perfector, the Walter press, which started working in 1868 and took over the printing entirely the following year, the redundancy was formidable; two Walter presses required a total crew of only seven men. Since one Walter press, with an output of something over 10,000 copies an hour (later improved to 12,000), was not so far behind the effective output of two Hoe ten-feeders, two Walter presses clearly gave *The Times* great advantages in speed (and thus later edition schedules) as well as in economy.

The complex story of the genesis and growth of rotary press design and manufacture is beyond the scope of this book. The Walter press was rapidly rivalled by the American Hoe – which indeed surpassed it and became for many years the standard machine – and by the French Marinoni and a whole string of British engineering firms of

THE NEWS OF THE WORLD.

No. 1. LONDON:—SUNDAY, OCTOBER 1, 1843. PRICE THREEPENCE

THE CHEAPEST AND BEST MODE OF ADVERTISING.

TO BOOKSELLERS, PUBLISHERS, AND THE ADVERTISING WORLD IN GENERAL.

Scale of Prices for Advertisements IN "THE NEWS OF THE WORLD."

*** It will be perceived from the following Scale, that the Charge for Advertisements will be—Seven Lines, Three Shillings; and every Three additional Lines, Sixpence Only. Ten Words in a line, and every additional line will be charged only 2d.

	£	s.	d.		£	s.	d.
7 Lines	0	3	0	64 Lines	0	12	6
10	0	3	6	67	0	13	0
13	0	4	0	70	0	13	6
16	0	4	6	73	0	14	0
19	0	5	0	76	0	14	6
22	0	5	6	79	0	15	0
25	0	6	0	82	0	15	6
28	0	6	6	85	0	16	0
31	0	7	0	88	0	16	6
34	0	7	6	91	0	17	0
37	0	8	0	94	0	17	6
40	0	8	6	97	0	18	0
43	0	9	0	100	0	18	6
46	0	9	6	103	0	19	0
49	0	10	0	106	0	19	6
52	0	10	6	109	1	0	0
55	0	11	0	112	1	0	6
58	0	11	6	115	1	1	0
61	0	12	0	118	1	1	6

THE GREAT WARRIOR OF THE AGE.—Just Published,

A Portrait of the Duke of Wellington.

It must be in the desire of every individual in the kingdom to have a faithful Portrait of this great Warrior and Statesman, as a memorial of his wonderful career, and as an Illustration of the most important events of modern history. The publisher has caused a splendid Whole-length Portrait of the Noble Duke to be Engraved on Steel, in the First Style of Art, impressions

81. Paganini, price 3d.
82. Portraits of Madame Grisi, Signors Tamburini, Rubini, Salabert, &c. &c., in the Grand Serious Opera, called "I Briganti," as performed at the Queen's Theatre, Haymarket.
83. Madame Grisi, price 3d.
84. Pauline Duvernay, price 3d.
85. Mrs. Nisbett, in Zarah, price 3d.
86. Miss Sheriff, as Clara, price 3d.
87. Madame Rachel, price 3d.
88. Carlotta Grisi and Perrot, price 3d.
89. Six Portraits of celebrated French Actresses, viz. —1. Mdlle. Mars 2. Mdlle. Sontag 3. Mme. Malibran Garcia 4. Mme. Damoreau Cinti 5. Mme. Pasta 6. Mdlle. Georges, price 3d.
90. Six more Portraits of celebrated French Actresses, viz. —1. Mdlle. Taglioni 2. Mdlle. Nobiet 3. Mdlle. Julia 4. Mme. Montesqu 5. Mdll Legallois 6. Mme. Alexis, price 3d.
91. Popular Musicians — Rubini, Donizetti, and Lablache, price 3d.

Panoramas.

92, 93, 94, 95. A Correct Panoramic View of Paris, four plates one yard long, price 1s.
96, 97, 98. A Correct Panoramic View of Venice, three plates, two feet three inches long, price 9d.

Historical Career of the Duchess de Berri.

99. S.A.R. Monsieur Le Duc de Bordeaux, S.A.R. Madam Duchess de Berri, price 3d.
100. Last Interview of the Duchess de Berri, with her Betrayer, Deutz.—Refusal of Marie Bossy to be bribed.—Arrest of the Duchess de Berri, and Entry of the Duchess into Nantes.—All in one plate, price 3d.
101. Consultation in the bed-room of Mademoiselle Pauline Duguiny, and Departure of the Duchess from Nantes.—One plate, price 3d.
102. Embarkation of the Duchess de Berri, and Storm at Sea; and Landing of the Duchess de Berri, at Blaye.—One plate, price 3d.
103. The Capture of the Duchess de Berri, at Nantes, on November 7, 1832.—One plate, price 3d.

*** The whole of the above Historical Engravings are printed on a uniform size paper, so as to form a Complete Album and Scrap Book, the whole Collection, consisting of ONE HUNDRED AND FOUR PLATES, will only cost the very moderate price of ONE POUND SIX SHILLINGS; and may be had, elegantly Bound into a Volume, at 3s. 6d. extra.

PUBLISHED at the Office of THIS PAPER; and may be had, by giving Orders, of all Booksellers and Printsellers, wherever residing.

THE POLITICIAN.

THE STATE OF THE NATION.

In presenting to the public, the first number of this paper, it will naturally be expected that a few words should be addressed by its conductors to those whose patronage it claims, and to whose favour it is confidently hoped, it will prove itself entitled. The general utility of all classes, is the idea with which this paper originated. To give to the poorer classes of society a paper that would suit their means, and to the middle, as well as the rich, a journal, which from its immense circulation, should command their attention, have been the influencing motives that have caused the appearance of "THE NEWS OF THE WORLD." We shall make no apology for those motives, because, we conceive, that in their accomplishment we shall attain an end, that in the present state of England is not only desirable, but absolutely necessary. Journalism for the rich man, and journalism for the poor, has up to this time, been as broadly and distinctly marked, as the manners, the dress, and the habitations of the rich, are from the customs, the squalor, and the dens of the poor. The paper for the wealthy classes is high priced, it is paid for by them, and it helps to lull them in the security of their prejudices. The paper for the poorer classes is on the other hand, low priced, and it is paid for by them; it feels bound to pander to their passions. TRUTH, when it offends a prejudice, and shews the evil of passion, is frequently excluded from both. The first is often as remarkable for its talent, for its early intelligence, as the other, we regret to say, is for the absence of talent, and the stale-people, what it behoves them to do, and what it might be dangerous for them to attempt.

It is, for instance, manifest, that the present state of poverty will be aggravated, and not ameliorated, in the course of a few weeks. Greater demands will be made for relief upon the poor-rates, and many more applicants will knock at the doors of the Union-workhouses. Is there, then, we ask, any one who has looked into the working of the new Poor-law, as it has been administered by the Poor-law Commissioners, who must not be convinced, that its provisions have been unnecessarily harsh upon the distressed? Who is there, that has heard of that cruel clause, which compels an entire family to become the inmates of a Workhouse, if the hard industry of the father and mother cannot support all their children, who must not be convinced that such a provision ought to be relaxed? Who is there, that has heard of the shocking rule of placing a prison dress upon the pauper, who must not think, that such an infamous regulation ought not to be abolished? Who is there, that has read the pitiable tale some time since disclosed at one of the Police-offices, of a man being denied the opportunity of offering consolation to his sick wife, upon hearing of the death of his child, who must not be convinced, that the separation of husband and wife, in their sorrow and their misery, ought not to be put an end to? *Here* is a neutral ground—it is that of humanity, and of charity—on which the rich and the poor—the Whig, the Tory, and the Radical can meet together—can make their voices heard by the Government, and on which, it may be remarked, the Government *has the power* to interfere for a Proclamation from the Crown, on the advice of the Secretary of the

EXTRAORDINARY CHARGE OF DRUGGING AND VIOLATION.

EXTRAORDINARY OCCURRENCE.—Much sensation was created in Lambeth throughout the whole of Sunday under the following circumstances:—A servant named Emma Munton, a very handsome young woman, 17 years of age, in the service of Mr. Wood, one of the deputy registrars of Lambeth, and who resides at No. 144, Prince's-road, went to a surgeon in Kennington Lane, for some medicine for her mistress's child, who was ill with the hooping cough. On her arrival she was asked to partake of something which she supposed to be wine. She did so, but soon afterwards became insensible. At a later period of the evening, but at present the precise time cannot be ascertained, a cab was obtained from a neighbouring stand, by a bricklayer, but just as he was about to drive off with it, the driver, who was the worse for liquor in the public house, came out and drove it (the cab) to the surgeon's door, where two women were placed inside, and it is believed that the surgeon got in also. The cabman, after driving to various places, returned once more to the surgery, was demanded 4s. as his fare; 2s., however, were offered and refused, and the cabman become ing abusive, he was given into custody, and the cab conveyed to the Green yard. Shortly before 12 o'clock the same night the surgeon was seen near his own residence in the company of two women, one of whom is supposed to be his servant, and the other the person above alluded to. The most mysterious part of this extraordinary story is that shortly before 1 o'clock on Friday morning some men at work at Mr. Davies's coal wharf, opposite Lambeth Church, observed a woman struggling in the water; they called out to her, but received no answer, she went down twice, and on coming to the surface seized hold of the side of one of the barges, but her bonnet and shawl floated away with the tide. She was immediately extricated from her perilous situation, and conveyed to the station house in High street, where, strange to relate, her uncle, police constable 136 L, was on duty, who immediately recognized her, but was of course ignorant of the cause of her being found under such circumstances. From the state of insensibility in which she was, it was deemed advisable to lose no time in conveying her to Lambeth workhouse. Mr. Duke, one of the medi-

JOKES.

(From Punch of Yesterday.)

A DANGEROUS PRECEDENT.—Two or three days ago a verdict of "unsoundness of mind" was found against a man; for, in the first place that "he was ignorant of the value of money;" and secondly, that all he cared for, was—"Comfortable eating, comfortable drinking, comfortable lodging, comfortable clothing, and a comfortable pipe. The word 'comfortable' was invariably in his mouth." If a man is to be found lunatic for this last peculiarity, we ask—is every placeman, every bishop safe?

A SHOWER OF PUPPIES.—A *Paris Paper* states that—"This morning, the 9th of September, 1843, a shower of puppies fell from the heaven in an orchard of the parish of Saint Giles de Livet." *Punch* has since ascertained that the said puppies, for bad behaviour, were kicked out of the dog star. Pots of bears' grease may every day be expected from Ursa Major.

LIFTS TO LAZY LAWYERS.—*Q.* What is a Feme Sole? *A.* Don't know, but think it may be a mermaid.—*Q.* What are appurtenances? *A.* Trimmings to a leg of mutton.—*Q.* What is Summary Process? *A.* Bathing and eating ices.—*Q.* What is a rejoinder? *A.* It is when any one asks you "If your mother has sold her mangle?" and you reply, "Yes, and bought an enterprise on"—*Q.* What is understood in law by the term "Mystery?" *A.* That Lord Brougham should ever have been Chancellor.—*Q.* What is a maxim in law? *A.* "Do, and don't be done."

THE REGISTRATION COURTS.—Mr. T. J. Chickabiddy, the revising barrister, had a private sitting in his own chambers, a few days ago, when several claims were brought under his notice. He objected to most of them, but the claimants becoming rather vehement, he promised on a future day to look further into them. The learned gentleman takes in several districts.

A CARD.—Signor Browni (the celebrated *singing mouse*) begs to announce for the benefit of families, that he has instituted a singing class for all kinds of vermin.

The Boy that alternated between the Nelson Pillar and the Hungerford Suspension Bridge, has gone home for the Michaelmas holidays.

THE NEWS OF THE WORLD.

NO. 2,421. SPECIAL SUNDAY EDITION. {REGISTERED FOR CIRCULATION IN THE UNITED KINGDOM AND ABROAD.} LONDON: SUNDAY, FEBRUARY 16, 1890. ONE PENNY. {POST-FREE THREE-HALFPENCE.

THE POLITICIAN.

OPENING OF PARLIAMENT—THE QUEEN'S SPEECH.

PARLIAMENT was opened for the despatch of business on Tuesday afternoon, the occasion being signalised by a Speech from the Throne by Commission, in which the deliberations of Ministers and their results are mentioned, leading to conclusions of what will be comprehended in the proceedings of the Session. The subjects are of interest both foreign and domestic, but between the lines may be recognised probabilities of deep interest, which in due course will be developed and give rise to animated debates and contests. The British public will receive satisfaction in learning that the difficulty with Portugal is settled, the Ministers of both countries having found grounds of arrangement, which it is hoped will be serviceable to the interests of both countries, and so re-establish the mutual good feeling which existed between them and soften the rancour shown by the Portuguese public when the submission of some of their ill-conditioned politicians and populace to the British views became known. The Speech from the Throne also adverts to the Treaty whereby the relative arrangements between the United Kingdom, the United States, and the German Empire with Samoa are made, and satisfaction is justly expressed that by the Conference at Brussels another heavy blow and sore discouragement will be given to the practice of human slavery. Much more may remain to be done by Governments and humanitarians before that diabolical traffic is abolished, but every conquest marks an advance and

fourth book of the 'Odyssey,' and in the account of Menelaus's travels all the world known to him was alluded to." One might, perhaps, say that if any hon. member were to rise in the midst and ask for information who was the gentleman named Menelaus, a sensation might occur in a debate. The right hon. gentleman said he believed Homer intended to describe the figures of the Palace of Antinous and the shield of Achilles as alive; and he recommended his audience to look deeply into anything curious in Homer, for nothing came into his writing by chance, even less than in Shakespeare; for Shakespeare wrote for a different and he thought an inferior audience. A learned man's thoughts deserve respect; but we might consider the beautiful figures on the Prince Consort's Memorial in Hyde Park as much entitled to be thought alive. The Session has begun with promise of much animated discussion, but without material injury to the Liberal Opposition. The great object is to prevent the national dismemberment and disorganisation.

JOKES OF THE DAY.

From "Punch."

A DIAGNOSIS.—"It says 'ere, as your old boss, Colonel M'Whuskey, has been took ill."—"Ah! so I 'erd!"—"Russian epidemic?"—"No, Scotch."

MISUNDERSTOOD!—(Annals of a Quiet Neighbourhood.)—Daughter of the house (anxious to introduce partners to each other): "Is your card quite full, Mr. M'Sawney?"—Mr. M'Sawney: "Oh dear, no! Which dance shall I give you?"

ULTIMA RATIO.—Small Rustic: "Yeou can't go that way."—Stalwart Young Lady (out sketching): "Why not?"—Small Rustic: "'Cause there's ...

SUNDAY SPECIAL

NEWS OF THE WORLD.

No. 4,513. [Estab. 1843.] Telephones: Central 5561. SUNDAY, APRIL 27, 1930. Telegrams: Worldly, Fleet, London. 16 PAGES—TWOPENCE.

NET CERTIFIED SALE EXCEEDS 3,000,000 COPIES.

STORMY OUTLOOK FOR CHANCELLOR.

Stubborn Opposition to Budget Proposals.

MR. PHILIP SNOWDEN, Chancellor of the Exchequer.

COMPANIES AND SURTAX.

(By Our Political Correspondent.)

Parliament meets on Tuesday, and already it is clear that if the Government are to bring the Session to an end in July there will have to be a wholesale "slaughter of the innocents."

The Budget resolutions will be taken on Wednesday and

MAROONED!

JOHN CITIZEN (sailing with representatives of Naval Conference): "Good-bye! 'It may be for years, and it may be for ever.'"

The Naval Conference has been brought to a close with the signing of a Treaty making provision for important measures of disarmament.

ZEPPELIN COMES TO CUP FINAL.

An "Extra Turn" For Wembley's Frenzied Thousands.

PARKER, Arsenal's winning captain.

KING SEES ARSENAL WIN.

("News of the World" Special.)

In a memorable game on a memorable afternoon the Arsenal won the English Football Cup on the classic turf of Wembley yesterday.

The Hoe press; this is the 'Double Supplement' model of 1885.

The Walter press.

whom only Fosters of Preston (already mentioned) and the Liverpool makers of the Victory press, survived into the present century; the Victory, the first rotary to be fitted with a folder – the Walter and the early Hoes delivered flat sheets, which had to be hand-folded – could boast of fifty-four installations by the late 1870s.* All these machines had been preceded by the web-fed press invented by William H. Bullock in Philadelphia in 1865; but the Bullock, slower and less efficient than its immediately following rivals, did not long survive. It had the unique, and unsatisfactory, feature of slitting the sheet from the web before printing instead of after, and its sales were further bedevilled by litigation. The *Daily Telegraph* appears to have been the only London paper to install a Bullock (1870) and it soon switched to Hoes.

It was something of a historic irony that *The Times* should have pioneered the web-fed rotary press when in fact it had lost its old dominant position, when its penny rivals, as recounted in the previous chapter, were to win circulations four times as large, when it was to slide, by way of the disaster of the Pigott forgeries and the Parnell Commission, into the moribundity from which it was only rescued in 1908 when Northcliffe took it over. The curious thing was the remarkable longevity, and universality, of the minimal news-titling headline style which *The Times* had evolved, and which has been already described. The popular Sundays showed no signs of striking a bolder note. The *News of the World*, sporting its splendid scrolled title, made a fine art of squeezing the last drop of dirt out of the more squalid court cases, a process that continued unabated until the Judicial Proceedings Act of 1925; but there was nothing novel about its display, apart from the strange device of the 'read-through' crosshead; this breaking of solid columns by picking out two or three words

◀ The *News of the World* of 1890 showed little change from its original aspect of 1843 (top); while forty years later the 1930 paper, despite heavy display (bottom), still clung to antique devices like the 'read-through' crosshead; these survived in the first *Daily Mail* (see p. 70).

* A Victory rotary, believed to be of the earliest (1869) vintage was still printing the *Wigan Observer* when that paper changed over to web-offset in 1966. Attempts to preserve this unique relic proved unsuccessful.

of text, centring them in capitals, and then reading on, long continued. In 1900 a radical sheet like *Reynolds News* still went no further with main news stories than crowded decker headings in news-titlings of 12pt and below.

At the stage now reached, or roughly by the early 1880s, not only had the web-fed rotary conquered the big daily paper field, but its basic raw material had become cheaper and more plentiful with the development of wood-pulp for paper-making. Tightness in newsprint supply no longer restricted circulation and/or paging, though actually both were to grow slowly, more slowly in Britain than in America. It is worth noting that the newsprint of eighty years ago was often of higher quality than we have been accustomed to regard as normal. The percentage of mechanical wood in the furnish was offset by as much as twenty per cent esparto, according to a description in 1892 of the newsprint manufactured at the Lloyd mills at Sittingbourne, Kent, then Britain's largest paper-maker.

The rotary set certain limits to format which the flatbed did not; the depth of a broadsheet page was fixed by the 'cutoff' of the machine, a dimension itself determined by the circumference of the plate cylinder; on the other hand, the page-width could be varied by varying the width of the newsprint reel. In the early days the comparative standardisation of cutoff with which we are familiar – though variations to meet special needs still inevitably remain – did not operate. Though standardisation was clearly advantageous with a machine as complicated as a web-fed rotary and its attendant plate-casting equipment, newspapers ordered machines with cutoffs designed to produce the size of sheet to which they had been accustomed. Initially this meant a trend to deep cutoffs ($26\frac{1}{4}$ inches was common – $27\frac{3}{4}$ inches not unknown) which with wide reels yielded vast 'blanket' sheets; with this cutoff, and eight 15-pica columns, *The Standard* of 1897 was such a sheet (ten years later it had dropped to seven columns, but with a fractional increase in measure to $15\frac{1}{2}$-picas). An eight-column page was quite exceptional, however. There could be fives and sevens, but the long-established six-column make-up was still the commonest. By the 1890s, however, this was a broad gauge (*The Times* column measure was $16\frac{1}{2}$-picas), becoming outmoded as rapidly as Brunel's 7-foot gauge on the Great Western. When Northcliffe's revolutionary *Daily Mail* appeared in 1896 it had a seven-column page with a $13\frac{1}{2}$-pica measure; this set a trend, both in format and measure, which was to remain standard for the British national broadsheets until the outbreak of the Second World War. Not less significant was the *Mail's* adoption of a cutoff nearly 3 inches less than that of the 'blankets'. This $23\frac{9}{16}$-inch cutoff yielded a much less cumbersome broadsheet, as well as making savings in newsprint which grew more and more important as circulation rose. Gradually it became the standard cutoff for broadsheet British papers, whether London or provincial, so that today there are few exceptions.

Stanley Morison said that 'the "New Journalism", so called by Matthew Arnold, made its entry into the English newspaper world by way of the evening papers.'[2] We must now examine the implications of this observation for the general development of headlining and make-up. In those days London had an extraordinary string of evenings; the gentlemanly 'pennies', of which the most important were the *Pall Mall Gazette* (1865), the *St James's Gazette* (1880), *The Globe* and (after an internal revolution on the *PMG* in 1893) the *Westminster Gazette*, plus the popular 'halfpennies', *The Echo* (1868), the *Evening News* (1881) and *The Star* (1888).

Of the papers named neither *The Globe* nor *The Echo* were of serious importance in terms of the present inquiry. Though *The Globe* was by far the oldest London evening then extant (it had been founded in 1802) its career was chequered, its policy old-world Tory, and its sole claim to fame at the time we are discussing was the technical ingenuity of its manager, W. A. Madge, who found a way of constructing

◀ A political exclusive forced the *Pall Mall Gazette* away from its genteel old style headlining to condensed and square grot, with bold text.

punchy news-story set in heavily-leaded bold face; set against the modest headlines of the rest of the page, in old style capitals, this scoop had imposing impact.

Both the *Evening News* and *The Star* came into being with a mass public in view. This public was interested in the rapidly-developing sport of Association Football and with betting on horse-racing, aided by the now universal telegraph system. It likewise had an appetite for sensational crime; the worst of the series of notorious Jack the Ripper murders in Whitechapel in 1888–9 brought both papers nights with the then unprecedented circulation of over 300,000. Both of them started as four-pagers with a six-column make-up; they adopted conventional blackletter titles and split their front pages half-and-half between classified and semi-display advertisements and editorial, giving preference to gossip columns and items. The *Evening News*, which ran its first edition on blue-tinted newsprint, with yellow and then green for later editions, started in 1881, with news-titling headings as light and small as those of the mornings; but the following year it turned to eye-catching condensed Grot capitals. When Alfred Harmsworth (Northcliffe) and his coadjutor Kennedy Jones got control of the paper in the 1890s headline development was soon speeded up; double-column headings appeared and in 1895 a multi-column banner, one of the first to appear in any London paper.

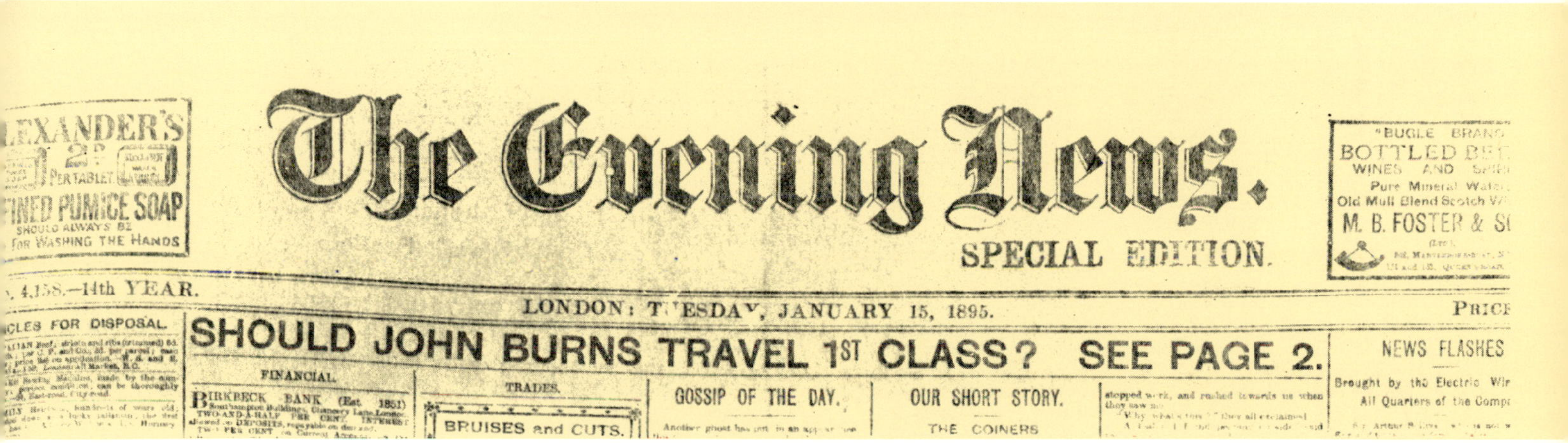
The Evening News.
SPECIAL EDITION.
LONDON: T. ESDAY, JANUARY 15, 1895.
SHOULD JOHN BURNS TRAVEL 1ST CLASS? SEE PAGE 2.
FINANCIAL. TRADES. GOSSIP OF THE DAY. OUR SHORT STORY. NEWS FLASHES
FINED PUMICE SOAP SHOULD ALWAYS BE FOR WASHING THE HANDS
BOTTLED BE... WINES AND SPI... M. B. FOSTER & S...

▲ Britain's first multi-column streamer in the *Evening News* of 15 January 1895.

The Star was quicker off the mark, as befitted a radical paper which helped to organise the Progressive majority in the first London County Council election, and which did much to reflect the aspirations of the 'New Unionism', the transformed trade unionism which emerged after the great dock strike of 1889. Within a few months of its launching in January 1888 *The Star* introduced American-style headings, in which a first deck in capitals was followed by a second deck in upper- and lower-case, giving sufficient wordage for the effective summary of the following news-story. This was a real revolution, since hitherto British newspaper headlines had never been set other than in capitals. *The Star* went further; by using this second-deck style as the sole heading for down-page shorts, it was the first paper to propagate the notion of the all upper- and lower-case headline. It had already broken with morning paper tradition by using multi-column heads and by breaking long stories with crossheads (not yet bold, but set in the capitals of the text). Founding editor O'Connor's remark about taking American papers as his model was carried through by his successors H. W. Massingham and Ernest Parke.

Here we may pause to consider the importance of the new techniques that were becoming available to newspapers in the 1890s. Outstanding was the introduction of the linecaster. Mergenthaler's first Linotype – the 'blower' – had been installed at the *New York Tribune* in 1886. An improved version shortly followed, the 'square base', which was basically the Linotype as we know it; instead of the compressed-air blast to assemble the circulating matrices (whence the first model's nickname), this was achieved by gravity fall from a

In order to cope with the unprecedented demand for this first issue we are obliged to go to Press earlier than usual. Four editions will be published during this morning, the first at two o'clock, the last at seven.

In the event of any late news arriving it will be inserted in the remaining editions.

This is a Copy of the FIRST EDITION.

BULAWAYO.

QUIET REIGNING.

SLIGHT BRUSH WITH THE ENEMY.

BRAVE MAN'S FUNERAL.

RHODES' COLUMN ATTACKED.

(SPECIAL CABLE TO THE "DAILY MAIL.")

BULAWAYO, May 1, 11.40 p.m.

A quiet confidence has returned to the camp, and the anxiety that disturbed the settlement a few weeks ago is no longer apparent.

The signal defeat of the rebels a week ago has done much to bring about this improved state of affairs, and the arrival of Earl Grey has increased the feeling of security.

The local news sheets here speak highly of the new Administrator, and there is no question but that on all hands he will be accorded a hearty support. The citizens are not disposed to regard recent events as an unmixed evil. They are determined that good shall come of it, and are working like Englishmen to bring it about.

Earl Grey has to-day chiefly devoted himself to consulting the civil and military authorities in regard to the present position of the town and arrangements for the future. He has inspired his staff with his own spirit and energy, and every one feels that whatever is now attempted will be effectively carried out.

The services of the Public Committee of Safety and Defence have been dispensed with, the members being warmly thanked by Earl Grey for the patriotism they had shown at a critical time. The committee will now devote itself to the relief of those impoverished by the revolt, and providing work for those unable at present to follow their usual pursuits.

Scouts Burnham and Swinburn came in to-day from the new fort which has been constructed at Matabele Wilson's on Six Mile Spruit. They say that whilst strengthening the works yesterday afternoon they were completely surrounded by an impi. The rebels advanced on all sides as though to rush upon the fort, but the whites and their native allies opened fire when the enemy got to 700 yards, and this stopped them. The indunas, who directed the operations from horseback, then called upon their warriors to retreat, and the whole force fell back to the Khami River. Their losses are unknown. No one on our side was hit.

There was another little brush this afternoon, when a small body of rebels sought to capture a number of forage waggons on their way to Hope Fountain Station. The train was guarded by forty mounted troopers of Gifford's force, and the patrol proved too smart for the natives. The waggons were brought round into laager long before the rebels got anywhere near them, and a brisk fire caused them to rapidly disperse. There were no casualties on our side, but the rebels lost severely.

A few of the enemy were also seen today between Government House and Gifford's House. Undoubtedly they were spying, the number being too small for active hostilities. They seem to be recovering heart, but the garrison here is ample to guard against attack. It is evident that a crushing blow will have to be inflicted upon them before they are thoroughly cowed.

AN IMPRESSIVE FUNERAL.

Trooper R. V. Lovett, of Grey's Scouts, who died from the wounds that he received in the smart fighting on Saturday, was buried to-day in the little cemetery outside the town. Earl Grey, Captain Duncan, and all the members of the staff attended. The spectacle was weird and awe-inspiring. There was not a man in the procession but carried rifle or revolver. Mounted scouts, with rifles ready in hand, were thrown out in advance. Either flank was similarly guarded and the rear was likewise protected by mounted riflemen.

The coffin was borne by the men of his own company, and even these were prepared to drop their burden and fight if occasion arose. But we were not molested. The comrades of the deceased man fired three rounds over his grave, and then we all marched silently back to camp again, praying that when our time came we might also play the man as he who was gone.

Some natives have reported that the enemy were present in some force on the Umguza last night. A small patrol has been despatched to feel the enemy's position, but no vigorous military initiative will be undertaken until the reinforcements come up. Then we hope to make short work of it.

The coach came in from the south safely to-day, bringing mails and a few travellers. We greeted them with loud cheers. Amongst the passengers were Father Prestage and Nurse Clarke of the Red Cross Society.

All the wounded now in hospital are doing well.

RHODES'S COLUMN ENGAGED.

(FROM OUR OWN CORRESPONDENT.)

GWELO, May 1.

A message has just come through stating Cecil Rhodes's column has been attacked at Makalala Kop. The enemy showed some hesitancy in coming to close quarters, and meantime the white column rapidly formed into laager. A hot fire was opened directly the rebels came within range, and seeing that the camp was prepared for them, they rapidly retired.

Their loss is estimated at fifty killed. The white column had no casualties, and arrived that night on the Que Que River.

A large accession of strength is expected here from Fort Charter to-day.

The march of Mr. Rhodes's column has been hampered greatly by cattle disease and the tsetze fly. Whilst at Iron Mine Hill he was losing oxen at the rate of thirty per day, and it was found impossible to make a decent day's march. He will be in touch with this camp very shortly now.

Scouts have returned here from the Shangani. They report that there is no sign of natives there now, but that at a settlement in the new Sombula Forest they found that a coach and stable had been burned by the enemy. The place had been abandoned by the owners when this trouble broke out.

No less than two hundred head of cattle have died here from rinderpest since the inhabitants of the town were compelled to camp in laager.

Trooper Archibald Maclean, who was wounded in a fight with natives recently, has died in hospital.

PRETORIA PRISONERS.

SEARCHED BY THE BOERS.

PUBLIC SYMPATHY.

(SPECIAL TO THE "DAILY MAIL.")

PRETORIA, May 1, 11.30 p.m.

It is stated that the Boer Executive has asked each of the prisoners charged with taking part in the Johannesburg rebellion to make a separate statement of their reasons why the sentences passed upon them should be reduced. It is significant that the four leaders condemned to death and whose sentences were respited have not been asked to make such a statement.

All the prisoners were searched to-day, and everything was taken from them. There is no relaxation of gaol rules in their favour. They are kept strictly to prison fare.

Mr. George Becker, a well-known geologist of the United States, has cabled to Mr. Olney pointing out that, when in December last a proposal was made to raise a foreign flag at Johannesburg, Mr. Hays Hammond, the American, demanded and obtained from the members of the Reform Committee an oath of allegiance to the Transvaal flag. He contends that this conclusively shows that the sole purpose of forming the committee was for the protection of their homes, and not for revolution.

Mr. Barnato has not only offered his Transvaal property for sale, but prominent financiers have made a bid for it.

Petitions are being everywhere framed and signed in favour of the Reform prisoners. Hosts of visitors are calling at the gaol daily, and many are allowed to see the prisoners.

(REUTER'S CABLEGRAMS.)

PRETORIA, May 2.

The decision as to any change in the sentences passed on the fifty-nine Johannesburg prisoners who were not condemned to death has been postponed until early next week. To-day no permits were issued to visitors desiring to see the prisoners. The improvements in the gaol arrangements have now been completed. The Rev. Mr. Batts, chairman of the Baptist Union, will hold Divine service for the prisoners to-morrow. The strongest influences in South Africa have been brought to bear on the Government to deal leniently with the majority of the prisoners, and the outlook is hopeful.

(FROM OUR OWN CORRESPONDENT.)

CAPETOWN, Saturday.

The action of the Orange Free State judge, Gregorowski, in going to Pretoria to condemn the Reform leaders to death, has called forth fierce denunciation and intense loathing. One Cape paper says:—"Gregorowski ranks with such men as Judge Jefferies, of Bloody Assize fame, and with the presidents of the Spanish Inquisition. A proper tool to do the work of the Boer Government."

The High Commissioner will leave for England before the end of the month. There is no foundation for the statement that he has been recalled.

It is generally understood to-day that a debate will be opened in the Cape Parliament on Monday, on recent events in the Transvaal. The sentences at Johannesburg will not serve to restore good relations between the English and Dutch sections in the House.

Mr. J. S. Curtis, one of the Reform leaders, who escaped from Johannesburg at the time of the raid, is still lying very ill near Capetown. It is possible that he will be tried separately when he has sufficiently recovered.

(REUTER'S CABLEGRAM.)

CAPETOWN, May 1.

The Volksraad of the Orange Free State has adopted a resolution instructing the Government to notify the High Commissioner of the termination by the Free State of the extradition treaty with the Chartered Company, as the Volksraad declines to recognise the company as a Government.

NEW YORK, May 2.

The petition, signed by many members of Congress, asking President Kruger to pardon Mr. Hays Hammond is being taken to the Cape by Mr. and Mrs. Jewell, of Johannesburg.

They were received to-day by President Cleveland, who showed great interest in their mission, and expressed his appreciation of President Kruger, and the latter's ability to cope with the affairs of his country.

CAPE PARLIAMENT OPENED.

RECENT TRANSVAAL EVENTS.

(REUTER'S TELEGRAM.)

CAPE TOWN, May 1.

The Cape Parliament was opened to-day. The Governor's speech first dealt with the entry of an armed force into the Transvaal contrary to international law. Such entry, the Governor said, was deeply deplored by every right-minded colonist, and had produced the most lamentable results.

"My advisers," the speech continued, "have entire confidence in her Majesty's Government taking steps which shall prevent the recurrence of a calamity which stirred so deeply the sentiments of all people in Africa, and so gravely endangered the friendly relationship between British colonists and the adjoining States. My Ministers, while recognising the advantage of maintaining unimpaired the existing authority of the Crown, are directing their best efforts to the promotion and the maintenance of a cordial understanding with neighbouring States and colonies. I trust that the troubled state of affairs in the Transvaal, which necessarily agitates the people of this colony, will, by the exercise of a wise spirit of moderation and conciliation on the part of all concerned, present before long a calmer aspect. The colony is so materially interested in the development of the interior that the recent rising of the natives in Rhodesia is viewed with extreme concern. My sympathies are with my fellow countrymen in their time of peril, and my fervent hope is that the forces now marching to relieve the beleaguered settlers will reach the seat of danger in time to prevent further serious loss of life and property, and that the strenuous efforts now being employed to quell the rising and to restore peace may be successful.

LORD LOCH INTERVIEWED.

Lord Loch was seen by a "DAILY MAIL" reporter, in Elm Park-gardens, last night, in regard to his views concerning his recent utterances.

His lordship was asked directly if, were he placed in the same position as Dr. Jameson was in the last days of the year 1895, believing that Englishmen and women at Johannesburg were in danger of outrage and murder at the hands of Boers and savages, would he not have taken the very steps that Dr. Jameson did? His lordship paced up and down the room for a moment before replying, and then burst out:

"Why, I can't see how any one that has read the accounts of the whole affair can have any doubts in the matter. I can't say any more plainly than I did in the House what I would have done had things taken the turn you suggest. I can't talk of a case that is before the courts, but any one ought to know what steps it would have been my duty to take; but, there, I won't be interviewed. I have said I could not discuss the Jameson matter under any shape or form; and then the positions were so very different."

His lordship then declared that he would make no further statement than he had already made before the House of Lords, and that the report of his speech contained in the "Times" ought to be as clear and convincing as any man not born deaf and blind could desire.

AMERICA.

NEW YORK PRESS AND THE TRANSVAAL.

THE CASE OF MR. HAMMOND.

(SPECIAL CABLES TO THE "DAILY MAIL.")

NEW YORK, Sunday.

All the morning papers devote considerable space to the Transvaal question, and unite in praising the temperate and humane conduct of the Boer Government, while severely criticising the recent attitude of the English Press in upholding Dr. Jameson's raiders.

The "Sun" says it is the manifest duty of the British Government to arrest and try Mr. Rhodes for inciting war against a friendly State, and however subtle and sly the Colonial Secretary may be, he can hardly shirk that duty.

The "Recorder," however, insists that the State Department should demand Hammond's instant release, his only offence having been to accept employment in the Transvaal and he not being identified with raiders or as accessory to British aggression. Kruger must be made to see the distinction between Hammond's case and that of the British prisoners.

Washington advices state that Cleveland has refused to officially intervene in Hammond's case.

MISS EVA BOOTH.

(SPECIAL CABLE TO THE "DAILY MAIL.")

NEW YORK, Sunday.

Miss Eva Booth, the Canadian commander of the Salvation Army, sailed for Liverpool on the Umbria yesterday. Crowds of Salvationists witnessed her departure.

Another Umbria passenger was Mr. Parnell, M.P., who has been making an extended American tour, and has obtained valuable assistance for the establishment of productive industries in Ireland.

MR. HARE IN NEW YORK.

(SPECIAL CABLE TO THE "DAILY MAIL.")

NEW YORK, Sunday.

Mr. Hare made his farewell appearance at Abbey's last night in "A Pair of Spectacles." He received four curtain calls, and made a speech expressing his appreciation of the American reception. Mr. Henry Irving and Miss Terry begin a two-weeks engagement at Abbey's on Monday, and on closing leave for London. They have no settled plans for their next American tour.

ATROCITIES IN CUBA.

WOMEN AND CHILDREN SHOT BY SPANISH.

(SPECIAL CABLE TO THE "DAILY MAIL."

NEW YORK, Sunday.

The Reverend Alberto Diaz, a Protestant missionary, who was expelled from Cuba by General Weyler, arrived at Tampa yesterday. He gives an awful account of Spanish atrocities, which took place recently by order of Colonel Fondeville. Many poor Cubans, men, women, and children, were made to dig their own graves, and then riddled with bullets by the Spanish. They were afterwards falsely reported killed in battle. The horrors, he says, rival the Armenian. The "New York World's" correspondent has been threatened with expulsion from Cuba for reporting those facts.

I am told by a reliable newspaper representative who has just returned from Cuba, that General Weyler's forces are hopelessly "bottled up" in an attempt to keep one division of the patriot army where it is, while the other leaders are left to push the war and rule the island elsewhere. As soon as the rainy season sets in everything will be in favour of the insurgents, and the Spanish will have to give up the fight. The reports telegraphed from Havanna are unreliable, as they are doctored by the Government censors, who alter the language, and make it appear that the Spanish army is carrying everything before it.

(REUTER'S TELEGRAM.)

MADRID, May 3.

A telegram from Havana states that General Tuclan has defeated 1,500 insurgents at Cararajicaras, on the north coast of the Province of Pinar del Rio, and has captured the insurgent fort at that place. Two hundred rebels were killed.

(CENTRAL NEWS CABLEGRAM.)

NEW YORK, Saturday.

A large quantity of contraband of war has been successfully shipped from Jamaica to Cuba.

MAJOR LOTHAIRE.

HIS DEFENCE AND ACQUITTAL.

An official telegram from Boma confirms the announcement that Major Lothaire has been acquitted.

The Court was presided over by Judge Fuchs and four assessors.

Major Lothaire stated that after the campaign against Rumaliza he advanced against the chief Kibonghe, who was captured at Lindi by Lieut. Henry's troops and shot by his (Major Lothaire's) orders. On January 1, 1895, he discovered at Lindi proofs of an alliance between the late Mr. Stokes and Kibonghe. He therefore ordered Mr. Stokes's arrest, and Lieutenant Henry was sent in search of him. On his way that officer gained possession of a letter dated January 7 from Mr. Stokes to Kibonghe saying, "I can help you. Have no fear. I am coming." Mr. Stokes was tried as a soldier, and executed within four and twenty hours in conformity with the Coquilhat statute. There was no clerk at the court-martial. Counsel for Lothaire instanced precedents for Major Lothaire's action in the cases of Governor Eyre and Nelson, who had both been acquitted on a similar charge being brought against them, and concluded by demanding the acquittal of the accused. The Public Prosecutor thereupon withdrew from the case, and after deliberating for forty minutes the Court acquitted the prisoner. The British Consul attended all the sittings of the Court, and no difference arose between him and the Public Prosecutor.

DEATH OF PROFESSOR GEFFCKEN.

The death of Professor Geffcken has taken place in Munich under shocking circumstances. Geffcken was in the habit of reading by a lamp placed at his bedside, and is supposed to have upset the lamp in his sleep, setting the room on fire, with the result that he was suffocated before help arrived.

Friedrich Heinrich Geffcken was born at Hamburg on December 9, 1830. Having studied law at the Universities of Bonn, Gottingen, and Berlin, he entered the foreign service of the Hanseatic towns, and was sent to Paris as Secretary of Legation. In 1866 he became resident Minister in London, and in 1869 he was elected Senator of Hamburg. He accepted the Chair of Law in the University of Strasburg in 1872. Ill-health caused him to abandon this position in 1882, and, having fixed his residence at Munich, he gave himself up to his historical work. In September, 1888, he published in the "Deutsche Rundschau" the Emperor Frederick's Private Diary. This caused him to be arrested for high treason. For several months he endured imprisonment and was subjected to a rigorous magisterial examination, whilst Prince Bismarck's agents conducted a futile search for the manuscript of the diary. On September 4, 1889, he was brought before the High Court of the Empire. The charge of high treason failed and he was set at liberty, being condemned, however, to pay the costs of the trial. Since then he lived in retirement in Switzerland. The works of Professor Geffcken have relation principally to international law.

SOUDAN

BRILLIANT BRITISH VICTORY.

TERRIBLE HEAT.

(REUTER'S SPECIAL TO THE "DAILY MAIL.")

WADY HALFA, May 2.

Yesterday morning a force of Dervish horse and camel men was observed about four miles from Akasheh. The Sirdah at once despatched Major Burn-Murdoch and three squadrons of cavalry, with the Eleventh Soudanese battalion in support, to establish touch with the enemy. The troops came up with a body of 300 camelmen and riflemen, and, attacking vigorously, soon drove them back on their supports.

Our men fought with conspicuous gallantry. They boldly charged the enemy's horse, driving them back through the footmen, who were in considerable force in the rear. The ground then became exceedingly difficult for cavalry movements, and the troopers, dismounting, continued the fight on foot. Eventually the Dervishes were completely dispersed, and retired under a heavy fire.

The force of the enemy engaged numbered altogether about a thousand foot and 250 cavalry. Our loss was one cavalryman and one intelligence scout killed, and ten men wounded. Among the latter was Captain H. G. Fitton, of the Intelligence Department, but his wound was very slight, a bullet having grazed one of his left ribs. He was not placed on the sick list.

The enemy's loss was estimated at about fifty men. Six horses were captured, and the enemy also left behind a large number of spears and swords.

Owing to the rapidity with which the Dervishes retreated, the Eleventh Soudanese infantry battalion, supporting the cavalry, did not arrive in time to take part in the action. Had they done so the Dervish loss would doubtless have been enormous, and their force in that region utterly broken.

116 IN THE SHADE.

During the action the heat was terribly trying. The operation took place partly in a khor, or nullah, where the thermometer registered 116deg. in the shade. Out in the open desert, however, owing to the radiation of the heat from the sand and rocks, the temperature, it was estimated, was over 150deg. Both horses and men suffered considerably from this cause.

It is believed that the enemy were attempting a turning movement with a view to interfere with the Egyptian lines of communication, but the prompt action of our cavalry totally defeated this object.

In his report on the action Major Burn-Murdoch speaks in the most flattering terms of the behaviour of our men, who, he says, displayed great steadiness.

The liveliest satisfaction is expressed here at the result of the fight. All the troops are in the best of spirits, and anxious to meet the enemy.

The heat at Wady Halfa continues to be terrible. One man has died of heat apoplexy.

THE TRANSPORT DIFFICULTY.

(REUTER'S SPECIAL TO THE "DAILY MAIL.")

WADY HALFA, May 3.

Nothing more has been seen of the Dervishes since the skirmish near Akasheh on Friday. The Sirdar is now on his way back to Wady Halfa.

Major Benson has arrived, and has been attached to the Intelligence Department. Captain B. R. Mitford and Lieutenant H. V. Ravenscroft have also come in. The former has been attached to General Hunter's staff.

Owing to the difficulty experienced in getting the natives to take boats through the cataracts, an attempt is being made to carry a few boats by rail to Sarras. A fatigue party succeeded in hauling a large and heavy craft up to the top of the bank, where it will be placed on a railway waggon.

The Camel Corps is now amply provided with camels.

The Court.

WINDSOR CASTLE, May 2.

The Queen, accompanied by her Royal Highness Princess Christian of Schleswig-Holstein, her Highness Princess Victoria of Schleswig-Holstein, and her Royal Highness Princess Henry of Battenberg, with their Highnesses Prince Leopold and Prince Maurice of Battenberg, arrived at the Castle shortly after eight o'clock last evening from Cimiez, Nice.

The suite in attendance consisted of Lady Southampton, the Hon. Harriet Phipps, Lieut.-Colonel the Right Hon. Sir Fleetwood Edwards, Lieut.-Colonel the Hon. W. Carrington, Lieut. F. Ponsonby, and Sir James Reid.

Their Highnesses Prince Alexander and Princess Victoria Eugénie of Battenberg, attended by Mlle. du Perrut, Lieut.-Colonel Clerk, and Mr. Tufnell, arrived at the Castle on Wednesday last.

Her Majesty received this morning the gratifying intelligence that her granddaughter, the Crown Princess of the Hellenes, had given birth to a daughter, and that both mother and child are doing well.

The Queen went out, accompanied by her Royal Highness Princess Henry of Battenberg.

Her Royal Highness Princess Christian of Schleswig-Holstein, with her Highness Princess Victoria of Schleswig-Holstein, returned to Cumberland Lodge.

The Hon. Evelyn Moore and the Hon. Bertha Lambart have arrived as maids of honour in waiting to her Majesty.

The Earl of Ranfurly, Admiral of the Fleet Sir Edmund Commerell, and Major the Hon H. C. Legge have arrived as lord, groom, and equerry-in-waiting to the Queen.

Lieut. F. Ponsonby has left the Castle.

May 2.

The Queen drove out yesterday afternoon attended by the Hon. Harriet Phipps and the Hon. Bertha Lambart.

The Bishop of Winchester arrived at the Castle, and had the honour of dining with her Majesty and her Royal Highness Princess Henry of Battenberg.

The Queen and the Royal Family, as well as the members of the Royal Household, attended divine service in the private chapel this morning.

The Lord Bishop of Winchester, Clerk of the Closet to the Queen, officiated, assisted by the Very Rev. the Dean of Windsor.

The Bishop of Winchester preached the sermon.

Lady Southampton has been succeeded by Lady Ampthill as Lady-in-Waiting to her Majesty.

The King and Queen of Saxony will leave Dresden in June for England. Their Majesties intend to pass some weeks at one of the watering places on the English coast.

The Crown Princess of Greece, sister of the German Emperor, gave birth to a daughter on Saturday. The little princess has already received the name of Helene.

Owing to very disquieting news concerning the condition of the eldest son of the Duke of Cumberland, the Royal ball and the gala performance at the Copenhagen Theatre, which were to have taken place on Wednesday, on the occasion of the marriage of Princess Louise to Prince Friedrich of Schaumburg-Lippe, have been countermanded.

OMNIBUS ROUTES.

In accordance with instructions from the authorities, the various omnibus companies have, with a view to relieve the congestion of street traffic, arranged that on and after to-day all omnibus traffic going south, via the Tower Bridge, will proceed via Bishopsgate-street, Wide Gate-street, Sandy-row, and Middlesex-street, formerly Petticoat-lane, into Aldgate and Minories. On their return journey the 'buses will drive through Houndsditch as heretofore.

DARING ROBBERY.

The police are investigating a daring case of robbery which was perpetrated by two young men on a Woolwich tradesman a day or two ago. It appears one of the men induced a shopkeeper to leave his premises for a few moments, and while absent the other man entered and made off with a cash box containing £60 in Bank of England notes and £20 in gold and silver. No arrest has yet been made.

THE ASHANTIS.

NEWS FROM KUMASI.

(FROM OUR SPECIAL CORRESPONDENT.)

CAPE COAST, Saturday.

Since the departure of Prempeh from Kumasi the Ashantis have entirely deserted their capital, and the British Resident, Major Piggott, is left in undisputed possession. The men in his charge have to forage among the surrounding towns for their food, and all labour required for building operations is obtained from here.

Every effort, however, is being made to induce the Ashantis to gain confidence in the friendly intentions of the British Government, and to return to their homes, and it is hoped that this result will soon be brought about.

KUMASI UNDER THE BRITISH.

The Rev. Denis Kemp, general superintendent of the Wesleyan Missionary Society at the Gold Coast, was a passenger by the British and African Royal Mail steamer Bathurst, which arrived at Liverpool on May 1 from West Africa. He visited the Ashanti capital just before leaving the coast.

On the 9th ult. Major Pigott, D.S.O. (the British Resident, pro. tem., of Kumasi) was on his way to the coast ill. When Mr. Kemp left Kumasi Major Pigott was unwell, though he frequently persisted in coming out to supervise the Government work in progress. The chief operation then being carried on was the erection of a fort in the centre of the town. The notorious execution grove is now a thing of the past, and although skulls and bones are still to be met with, the great majority of them had been buried by the British. A space of 200 yards is being speedily cleared around the fort, and in this area no buildings will be permitted, nor trees grown. A turret is being erected on each of the four corners of the fort, and on these Maxim guns are to be mounted. The town has been portioned out for the residence of the various people—traders, natives, and others. There were two former executioners in the King's palace, they were prisoners, and did not know what fate awaited them. The elder one, who was about seventy years old, modestly claimed to be but a "small" executioner, having carried out only fifty executions. As, however, many of those fiendish customs meant the sacrifice of some 400 people, the extent of this "little" man's work must have been terrible.

Shortly a magnificent road will be made, not merely between the Gold Coast proper and the Ashanti capital, but also to the famous Nooranza country. Governor Maxwell had intimated to all the chiefs that all their instruments of torture must be given up. This collection will doubtless form the most important of any yet brought from the district, and possibly his Excellency is bringing them to England. The Government has undertaken to furnish a new plot of land for a Wesleyan mission. At Bekwai and Abodom the kings and chiefs have most gladly given sites for mission work, and are greatly helping the missionaries. The Rev. W. F. Somerville, a native of Weston Runcorn, is in charge of the Wesleyan mission, and is aided by two experienced Fanti ministers, in whom the Ashantis have the greatest confidence.

There seems every prospect that Kumasi will form an important centre for British trade relations with the far interior. Rest houses are being erected by the British at Dunqual, Mansu, and Fesu. These are for expeditions and parties going up to Kumasi. Hitherto the only rest house was at Prahsu. It is four days' journey to Prahsu, and the four rest houses are at the end of each day's journey. A permanent telegraph was being erected to replace the temporary military one.

All through the districts traversed, the kings expressed the liveliest satisfaction at the overthrow of the Prempeh dynasty.

Mr. Kemp learned that Prempeh's mother, now a prisoner with him at Elmina, had had fifty husbands, all of whom had been put to death by her orders except Prempeh's father.

NIZHNY-NOVGOROD EXHIBITION.

HOUSEHOLDERS RAPACITY.

Our St. Petersburg correspondent writes:—In view of the approaching exhibition, the householders of Nizhny have raised the price of lodgings to almost prohibitive rates. Residents of slender means find themselves practically turned out into the street. The officers of the garrison are obliged to stand on their right of having free quarters provided for them by the town, instead of receiving a lodging allowance.

The greedy householders have been denounced from the pulpit without effect. The governor of the province is, however, now taking steps which will probably meet with success. In an open letter to the Mayor he calls the attention of the Town Council to the question, and suggests that in cases where the rent has been raised more than 30 per cent. next year's valuation of the property for rating purposes shall be based on the increased rental. He winds up, with apparent irrelevance: "I need hardly add that I shall be only too glad to lend you my assistance and that of the police under my command should you require it."

INTERNATIONAL CYCLING.

FRENCH VICTORY.

(REUTER'S TELEGRAM.)

PARIS, May 3.

At the Velodrome de la Seine to-day a two kilometres match between Jacquelin and Macdonald, the French and American cyclists respectively, was won very easily by the former, who came in first in both heats. He led in the first heat by twenty yards, and in the second by fifty yards.

In an international eight days' race for ladies (one hour a day), Mlles. Dutrieux, Savigny, Reills, to-day each covered 33 kilometres, 181 metres; Mrs. Grace, the English lady champion, 33 kilometres 778 metres; and Mlle. Lisette, 32 kilometres 728 metres.

In the race for male cyclists under similar conditions Tom Linton covered 46 kilometres 778 metres; and Sesna 45 kilometres 860 metres, Nelson and Macgregor, both British, coming next with forty-one kilometres British, coming next with 45 kilometres each.

SUICIDE OF A SOLDIER.

A sentry at Elizavetpol the other day fell asleep at his post. While he was asleep an officer who was driving by noticed him, came and stealthily took from him his sword and cap, and carried them off as "pieces de conviction." When the sentry awoke and saw that he had been detected in his breach of duty, he put the muzzle of his rifle to his head and blew his brains out.

FEEDING THE POOR.

Whilst the Czar remains in Moscow for the coronation fetes, 5,000 dinners will be gratuitously given daily to the poor, and on the day of coronation 10,000 dinners will be the Imperial souvenir by which the poor will remember his visit.

CANADIAN HIGH COMMISSIONER.

(CENTRAL NEWS TELEGRAM.)

NEW YORK, Saturday.

It is stated in a report from Montreal that Sir Donald Smith will resign the office of High Commissioner in London.

THE CZAREVITCH.

(REUTER'S TELEGRAM.)

NICE, May 2.

The Czarevitch passed an uneasy, feverish night, and the Dowager Empress remained for several hours at his bedside. The physicians in attendance have decided that a change of air is desirable, but the present condition of his Imperial Highness prevents his being moved. The Dowager Empress expects to start from Nice about the 8th or 10th inst., and the Czarevitch will leave as soon as possible after that date, providing his health permits and the weather is favourable.

SEAMAN IN HOLLOWAY.

On inquiry last night at Holloway it was stated that Seaman, who is charged with the murders in Stepney, had had a slight relapse, probably due to the strain of the magisterial examination on Friday, and he is now under the special care of Dr. Pitcairn, the assistant medical officer. The doctor, however, does not anticipate any serious result, and in a few days the prisoner will regain his strength. The injury he received was a very unusual one, and that accounts for the length of time which his wounds have taken to heal. It is stated that he has intimated to the police his refusal to be professionally represented at his trial, and declines to aid the police in tracing out the truth of his statements as to his connection with the deceased Mr. Levy.

THE LATE SHAH.

DETAILS OF THE ASSASSINATION.

QUEEN'S MESSAGE.

SUCCESSOR PROCLAIMED.

(REUTER'S CABLEGRAM.)

TEHERAN, May 2.

Further particulars have been received of the circumstances attending the assassination of the Shah. His Majesty, accompanied by the Grand Vizier and several attendants, shortly before two o'clock yesterday afternoon walked through the outer court of the shrine of Shah Abdul Azim, where he gave a bank note to an Arab and spoke kindly to a water carrier. The entrance to the inner court is closed by two chains, and the Shah had just passed the first when the assassin, armed with a revolver, approached, and fired within a few feet of his Majesty, who fell forward on his knees. Then rising, the Shah walked a few paces and fell again. The assassin was immediately arrested. His Majesty was taken in an unconscious condition to his carriage, and conveyed to the Palace at Teheran. When the doctors arrived life was found to be extinct. The medical certificate says that death was caused by the bullet entering the pericardial region between the sixth and seventh ribs. Authentic information regarding the nature of the wound was at first withheld, as the attendants hoped that it would not prove serious.

(REUTER'S CABLEGRAM.)

TIFLIS, May 2.

A despatch from Teheran announces that immediately after the Shah's death, Mozaffer-ed-Din Vali Ahd, second son of his late Majesty, and at present Governor of Azerbaijan, was proclaimed successor to the throne. Mozaffer-ed-Din was recognised as the heir-apparent in 1858 by Great Britain and Russia. All is quiet at Teheran. The Grand Vizier will carry on the Government until the arrival of the new Sovereign.

On the Queen's behalf Lord Salisbury on Saturday sent through the British Minister at Teheran the foregoing telegraphic despatch to Mozaffer-ed-Din, the veliahd who has succeeded to the throne:—

"By direction of the Queen-Empress, my gracious Sovereign, I have the honour to convey to you her deep sympathy on the great loss you have sustained by the lamentable death of the late Shah. At the same time I am on her behalf to congratulate Persia and your Majesty that so worthy and illustrious a successor is at hand to take up the sovereignty of the late Shah. She hopes with the help of the distinguished Minister, the Sadr Azam, on whom the late Shah relied so much, your Majesty will enjoy a glorious reign which will reflect honour on your own name and bring happiness to the great people over whom you rule."

TEHERAN, May 3.

Mozaffer-ed-Din was yesterday morning enthroned at Tabriz under the style and title of Mozaffer-ed-Din Shâhinshâh, or King of Kings. His Majesty is leaving for Teheran.

The body of the late Shah has been embalmed and will be taken to Koom for burial after the arrival of the Shah.

All State affairs have been entrusted to Mirza Ali Asghar Khan Amin-es-Sultan, the Grand Vizier, who has occupied this position for the last ten years or more.

All the Princes, Governors, Ministers, and Persian officials have telegraphed congratulatory messages to the Shah at Tabriz, and, it has been remarked, his Majesty, in replying to the congratulations, was very gracious, particularly so to Mas-ud-Mirza Zil-es-Sultan, the eldest son of the late Shah, and Governor of Ispahan.

CONSTANTINOPLE, May 2.

The assassination of the Shah has produced a profound impression in Turkish circles here.

The Press Association says: The Anguman-i-Islam, London, met on Saturday in Northumberland-avenue, and passed the following resolution of condolence: "The Anguman-i-Islam, London, representing the Moslems in Great Britain, expresses its deep regret and sorrow at the outrageous assassination of H.I.M. the Shah of Persia, and tenders its heartfelt sympathy with the Royal family."

HUNGARIAN MILLENNIUM

EXHIBITION OPENED BY THE EMPEROR.

A BRILLIANT CELEBRATION.

(REUTER'S TELEGRAM.)

BUDAPEST, May 2.

The fetes connected with the thousandth anniversary of the foundation of the Hungarian State began this morning with the opening of the Millennial Exhibition by the Emperor Francis Joseph. The Emperor was accompanied to the exhibition by the Empress, where an address was presented to him, which among other things stated that the present generation has a double cause for rejoicing in that Providence has permitted it to celebrate the millennium of the beloved fatherland under the sceptre of the Prince in whose reign the constitutional life of the country has attained its highest perfection, and civilisation has received the most powerful impulse. In his reply the King hoped that the exhibition would prove to the whole world that the Hungarian nation, which has gloriously upheld the State for a thousand years under many adverse circumstances, had not only defended at all times the throne of the fatherland with valour on the battlefield, but had won a worthy place in the field of culture, and takes her due rank among the civilised peoples.

(REUTER'S TELEGRAM.)

BUDAPEST, May 3.

A solemn thanksgiving service was celebrated in the Mathias Church here to-day in connection with the millennial celebrations. The audience included the Emperor and Empress of Austria-Hungary, the Archdukes and Archduchesses, the diplomatic corps, and the members of the Hungarian aristocracy. No spectacle of equal brilliance has ever been witnessed in the Hungarian capital since the coronation of the King. All the ladies wore the national Magyar Festival costume, the distinctive features of which are a high-laced bodice and apron and veil and diadem.

An enormous concourse of spectators witnessed the procession to and return from the church. The greatest order everywhere prevailed. In the evening the city was beautifully illuminated.

(CENTRAL NEWS TELEGRAM.)

BELGRADE, Sunday.

In consequence of the employment yesterday at the Budapest Exhibition of the Servian flag, which was, however, carried merely as a historical emblem, a riotous anti-Hungarian demonstration took place here last night before the Austrian legation, the windows of which were broken by stones. The gendarmerie intervened, with drawn swords, and several persons were killed and wounded. The Prefect and the Commandant of the Gendarmerie have both been deprived of their positions. There is a Ministerial crisis, and popular excitement is running very high.

A DUSTMAN'S WEDDING.

The riverside district between Blackfriars and Waterloo Bridges was yesterday the scene of much rejoicing, the occasion being the wedding of a young dustman named Reed, who is a much respected employé of the Clerkenwell Vestry. The ceremony was performed at Christ Church, Blackfriars-road, and the happy couple came in for a rather novel reception on leaving the church. Outside a large concourse of neighbours and spectators had collected; and upon the bridal party entering their four wheeler a procession of an extraordinary character was formed, and headed by a band of Reed's associates in their ordinary working attire—some of them in their shirt sleeves—they marched to the residence of the bride's friends in Prince's-square, Commercial-road. The youths heading the strange array were armed with old tin plates, trays, and kettles, which they performed upon with vigour. The unusual din brought numbers of spectators, and the crowd had swollen to large proportions by the time Prince's-square was reached.

READING MU

SENSATIONAL LETT

CONFESSION

HOW MRS. DYER

MRS. PALMER'S ST EVIDENCE.

"Nothing so commonplace as was the impression that was con itself on my mind at the Readin on Saturday, both before and dur Mrs. Dyer.

Palmer was the first to make in the dock. Previous to his en the ordinary business of the court through—the usual "drunk and d before knowing that the man who his seat was Palmer, I imagined h clerk who had been taking a nigh well-dressed, rather pale and h look about the eye that suggeste that of a hunted animal. Im taking his seat, however, Palmer to recover his serenity, and, supp comfort, gazed steadily round th

There was nothing to distinguish from that of hundreds of other men or clerks one might meet London. His head was well-shap regular, and his expression mi weak; his hair, carefully brus light chestnut colour, his moust sandy hue, and he seemed to ha night's growth of sandy beard.

His figure was rather slight, an active and athletic young m high collar, a neat-fitting bow, a A second impression confirmed t was really just

LIKE A CITY CLER

who had had a night out, and prised and very much disgusted in the dock of a police court, bu well to put on the best face pos

Palmer did not remain long his lawyer asked for his discharg cuting counsel making no opposi tired quickly, and as though with relief walked past Mrs. Dyer, meantime been ushered into the the slightest notice of her, and taking not the slightest notice o

Mrs. Dyer's entry had not b degree sensational. Unexpected been opened and she walked looking round simply plumped of the seat adjacent to the door

It was in vain that I endea that this woman was the autho incredible crimes, crimes whic made her name notorious throug world, and which will raise her nence for ever in the history o ness.

Mrs. Dyer is a type of woma see anywhere in any of the p London suburbs. She look typical professional midwif motherly, rather heavy, but w expression of experience.

She is a stout, dull-faced w little colour in her cheeks, and the tinge of putty. Her hair tween grey and white, draw from a forehead neither high void of any particular charact neither bright nor dull, her sharp nor slow. The nose is bad, the lips rather thin, and th The whole face is simply

COMMONPLACE, FAT, A

but precisely answering to t spectable middle-aged woman for her living, but always " The only sign of emotion th long time was in the nervo lips, and in the flickering of once did she look round with but for the most part she sat eyes cast down, and face wea less.

Mrs. Dyer's dress was exact the idea of her respectabilit heavy, shapeless black bonnet, and trimmings, and with bla down behind her ears and Around her neck was a black ever, she took off almost im dress was of black linsey, clea

Looking at her, one could appearance any very terrible like a woman who had strugg sordid circumstances, clingin deeply-engrained idea of r taking to the trade of murd sibly because that was a busin something about, and because a simple and fairly commonpla

Imagine for a moment the s Station when one of the little to her care. Mrs. Sargent, child over to her, is all of a a thousand fears and a thous child from which she finds it She is sure it is in good han the typical, respectable, moth She will take care of the l him, and the woman, who ha the child to her, runs after kisses him tenderly, passionate self away, and wishes her go

How is Mrs. Dyer touched Simply not at all. She is a d unsympathetic woman. She with but one thought in her m murder.

SHE WILL MAKE £5

Yet she had a great love for and her son-in-law. She brok her great efforts at self-contr of confession was being read ferred to "Polly" and Palmer sight—this woman with so m cent babes on her head, listeni fession, garnished with the usu declaring her readiness to m sobbing with the tenderness her own children.

Even her grief was commo and the picture was compl her large, coarsely gloved han covered her face with her wh chief.

Mrs. Palmer, who gave evi the crowded court, looks abo and at first glance has decid pearance—rather tall, of go riage, plainly dressed, but wi neat black bonnet was trimm her black veil drawn along th Her tailor-made and well-fit bluish-grey cloth, with black the wide sleeves that are now features are well-marked, reg and firm. Her eye has been a "startled fawn," but they whom timidity quickly gives resistance. Her manner was

SUBDUED BUT COL

Her answers were given in a were all clear and to the point. to be treading on dangerous gr to give no answer at all.

The only sign of emotion th a quiver that often passed th of her jaw , she had spo ier teeth quickly and sharply

To complete the picture, her hair in a "bang" over complexion is rather sallow, b her mouth has rather a cons as if her lips met with difficult

Altogether, she might have young schoolmistress, intellig a little sharp, perhaps even a sloping magazine on to a moving belt. These were the machines, with their immediate successor, the Model 1 (which had a star-shaped base), which were put in by British newspapers. They were single-magazine machines and they were equipped for the setting of text only. Their challenge was to the news-text hand compositors and to the type-assembling machines which had been adopted by a number of newspapers (the Kastenbein by *The Times*, the Thorne, Empire and Hattersley mainly in the provinces). Even when the first Model 4 Linotype appeared, with its three magazines, its capacity 'for newspaper headlines' (as explained in the official Linotype handbook) was limited to founts of capitals with an upper size limit of 14pt. In 1908 the Linotype specimen book showed a few 'miscellaneous founts' within the size limit indicated; they were available in capitals only in various weights of news titling, an old style bold then known as Monarch, and some variations of sans (gothic). Clearly there was little here to disturb conventional newspaper headlining.

Indeed, the London morning newspapers continued to cling stubbornly to the traditionalist formula of *The Times* – the front page of 'smalls', the minimal news-titling headlines and so forth. An enterprising American newspaperman, Chester Ives, launched the halfpenny *The Morning* in 1892 with news on the front page, well-headlined in the light condensed sans capitals and lower-case decker style of the *New York Herald* (Paris edition). It failed; and Kennedy Jones, who had been on its staff, commented that what was wrong was that 'it did not look like a morning paper.' It was necessary, in short, to look like *The Times*, as did that paper's particular, and successful, rivals, the *Telegraph* and *The Standard*. The immense 'blanket sheet' of the latter paper in the 1890s has already been mentioned; even on a major news day the largest headline in the vast prairie of its main news page (the right-hand centre-spread) would be a single-column three-decker, without turn lines, in pica and long primer news titling. That was in 1897; in 1907 the basic titling style remained, though size and display had increased – the main heading was now a four-decker, with turn lines in the first and third decks, the size of the first deck having risen from pica (12pt) to two-line long primer (20pt).

Most remarkable of the obeisances to morning paper traditionalism was that forthcoming from Northcliffe's *Daily Mail*. The 'Northcliffe Revolution', heralded by the launching of the *Mail* in May 1896, was journalistic, not typographical. 'The Chief' was of exactly the same mind as his aide Kennedy Jones on the need to 'look like a morning paper'. While he insisted on editorial control of make-up (a radical attitude for those days), Northcliffe equally insisted on leaving type to the printer; 'you do not understand type' he told editorial men, 'Consult the craftsman who knows. Changing a type is a most serious thing. The effect on your readers may be disastrous.' Clearly he took no account of the long-standing typographic backwardness of the London newspaper trade, to which reference has already been made; indeed, he was probably quite unaware of it. So No. 1 of the 'penny newspaper for one halfpenny', the 'busy man's daily journal' appeared in regulation dress. The white-lined blackletter title sported the Royal arms; the front page was all advertisements; news titlings of varied weight and style were the sole ingredient of the cramped single-column decker headlines; where crossheads were used (in the small caps of the text) they were in the 'read-through' style already noticed in the case of the *News of the World*. The novelty of the *Mail* lay in its presentation of features (headed 'the Daily Magazine'), including fashion hints illustrated with line blocks, and above all in its closely sub-edited brevity. 'Conciseness and compactness' was its note, as an opening leader said. The seven-column page made an agreeable shape with the shorter cutoff already referred to; the paper was Linotype-set, was printed on the latest Hoe rotaries, and was thus technically able to exploit to the full its potential as the first mass-circulation daily. Its immense success is a matter of newspaper his-

◀ The un-revolutionary look of the revolutionary *Daily Mail's* main news page (May 1896).

THE FIRST STEP.

THE AMERICAN FLEET MOVES ON HAVANA.

SPAIN MOBILISES HER RESERVES.

UNITED STATES TROOPS HURRYING TO THE FRONT.

PRESIDENT TO CALL FOR 100,000 VOLUNTEERS.

Yesterday the first step was virtually taken in the war between Spain and America by the sailing of the American fleet from Key West.

Anticipating the receipt of the ultimatum cabled by President McKinley to General Woodford at Madrid, the Spanish authorities handed the Minister his passports, and notified him that diplomatic relations with the United States had been broken off. General Woodford quitted Madrid in the afternoon.

As the Spanish fleet was reported—erroneously it would appear—to have sailed from the Cape Verde Islands, the American squadrons at Key West and Hampton Roads were instructed to put to sea under sealed orders.

The former promptly sailed for Havana.

America's military expedition, it is reported, will leave for Cuba next week. Some 300 vessels have already been chartered for the transport of the troops from Key West to Havana.

About 80 per cent. of the National Guard of the various states have offered to go to the front.

Spain is busy mobilising her land forces.

RUPTURE OF RELATIONS.

SPAIN ACCEPTS THE AMERICAN CHALLENGE.

FROM OUR OWN CORRESPONDENT

(PER ANGLO-AMERICAN TELEGRAPH COMPANY.)

WASHINGTON, April 21.

As the result of the series of startling incidents which have occurred during the past twenty-four hours diplomatic relations between the United States and Spain are now completely severed.

From the present time forward events will move with amazing rapidity up to the climax of actual war.

The State Department this morning received a cable from General Woodford at Madrid, stating that the Spanish Government had handed him his passports, without giving him an opportunity of presenting Mr. McKinley's ultimatum demanding that the Spanish forces shall evacuate Cuba.

The Spanish Government had accepted the presentation of the ultimatum to the Spanish Minister at Washington as a formal announcement on the part of the United States.

Immediately upon receipt of the news the President called a special Cabinet meeting to consider the situation. The conference led to a decision that Spain's act virtually constituted an act of war, consequently rendering a formal declaration of war by Congress unnecessary.

The majority of the Senators consulted agreed with the President, and advised that a manifesto be sent to the Powers announcing that a state of war exists.

MOVING ON HAVANA.

UNITED STATES FLEET PUT TO SEA UNDER SEALED ORDERS.

(From Our Own Correspondent.)

NEW YORK, April 21.

The Board of Naval Strategy at Washington was in session all day, and reported to the President that an immediate move on the part of the fleet was absolutely necessary in view of the reports that the Spanish flotilla had left the Cape Verde Islands, bound for Cuban waters.

The Cabinet decided to lose no time in speculating whether the reports were correct, but determined to act at once.

Orders were consequently issued at three o'clock this afternoon for the flying squadron at Hampton Roads and the fleet at Key West to put to sea under sealed orders.

Although the exact destination of the vessels is kept secret, it is believed the flying squadron has been ordered to meet the Spanish flotilla off Porto Rico.

Captain Sampson, commanding the Key West fleet, received a telegram saying "Execute orders," which is generally understood to mean "Blockade Havana and the other Cuban ports."

The latest move of the Navy Department has caused intense excitement, and questions are now asked "Where will the first battle take place, and how long will the war last?"

The general opinion among American naval officers is that Spain will prove a formidable enemy, that the war will last much longer than is generally expected, and that several disasters to American warships will probably happen before it is over.

The Army is being rapidly concentrated in the vicinity of Key West. Every regiment of the regular forces is now on its way south.

Nearly eighty per cent. of the men of the National Guard regiments of the various States have offered to go to the front.

"A STATE OF WAR EXISTS."

WASHINGTON, April 21 (5 p.m.).

In the opinion of the State Department a state of war now exists between Spain and the United States.

Moreover, this in its view has been brought about by the action of Spain, which in notifying General Woodford that it had broken diplomatic relations thereby took the initiative.—Reuter.

TEXT OF THE ULTIMATUM.

HOW SPAIN ANTICIPATED THE BLOW.

WASHINGTON, April 21.

The following official statement of the text of the ultimatum was issued to-day:—

"Yesterday, about eleven in the forenoon, the Department of State served notice of the purposes of this Government by delivering to the Spanish Minister, Senor Polo de Bernabe, a copy of the instruction given to the United States Minister at Madrid, General Woodford, and also a copy of the resolutions passed by the Congress of the United States on April 19.

"After receipt of this notice, the Spanish Minister forwarded to the State Department a request for his passports, which were furnished to him yesterday afternoon.

"A copy of the instruction sent to General Woodford is herewith appended. The United States Minister at Madrid was at the same time instructed to make a like communication to the Government of Spain.

"This morning the State Department received from General Woodford a telegram, a copy of which is hereunto attached, showing that the Spanish Government had

BROKEN OFF DIPLOMATIC RELATIONS

with this Government. This course renders unnecessary any further diplomatic action on the part of the United States."

The following are the telegrams appended to the foregoing:—

Appendix I., April 20.—"To Woodford, Minister, Madrid.—You have been furnished with the text of the joint resolution voted by Congress of the United States on the 19th inst., and approved to-day, in relation to the pacification of the island of Cuba.

"In obedience to that act the President directs you immediately to communicate to the Government of Spain the said resolution, with a formal demand on the part of the Government of the United States that Spain at once relinquish its authority and government in the island of Cuba, and withdraw its land and naval forces from Cuba and Cuban waters.

"In taking this step the United States hereby disclaims any disposition or intention to exercise sovereignty, jurisdiction, or control over the said island, except for the pacification thereof, and asserts its determination when that is accomplished to leave the Government and control of the island to its people, under such free and independent government as they may establish.

"If by the hour of noon on Saturday next, the 23rd day of April inst., there be not communicated to this Government by that of Spain a full and satisfactory response to this demand and a resolution whereby the ends of peace in Cuba shall be assured, the President will proceed without further notice to use the power and authority enjoined and conferred upon him by the said joint resolution to such extent as may be necessary to carry the same into effect. "SHERMAN."

Appendix II.—Madrid, April 21. Received 9.2 a.m.—"To Sherman, Washington.—Early this (Thursday) morning immediately after the receipt of your open telegram and before I had communicated the same to the Spanish Government, the Spanish Minister for Foreign Affairs notified me that diplomatic relations have been broken off between the two countries, and that all official communication between their respective representatives have ceased.

"I accordingly asked for safe passports,

PLAN OF HAVANA HARBOUR.

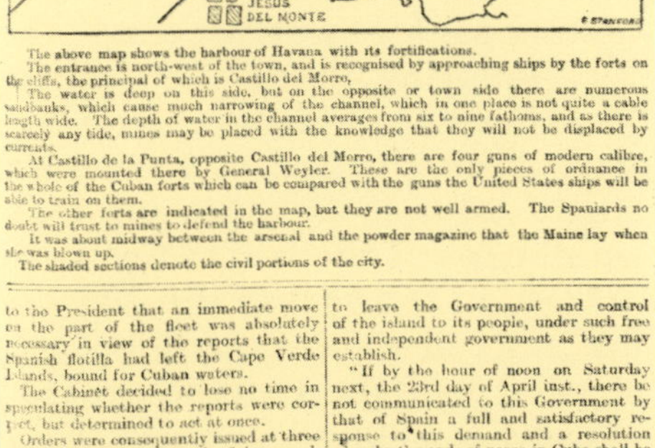

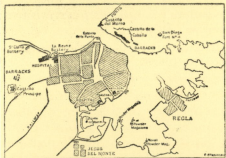

The above map shows the harbour of Havana with its fortifications.

The entrance is north-west of the town, and is recognised by approaching ships by the forts on the cliffs, the principal of which is Castillo del Morro.

The water is deep on this side, but on the opposite or town side there are numerous sandbanks, which cause much narrowing of the channel, which in one place is not quite a cable length wide. The depth of water in the channel averages from six to nine fathoms, and as there is scarcely any tide, mines may be placed with the knowledge that they will not be displaced by currents.

At Castillo de la Punta, opposite Castillo del Morro, there are four guns of modern calibre, which were mounted there by General Weyler. These are the only pieces of ordnance in the whole of the Cuban forts which can be compared with the guns the United States ships will be able to train on them.

The other forts are indicated in the map, but they are not well armed. The Spaniards no doubt will trust to mines to defend the harbour.

It was about midway between the arsenal and the powder magazine that the Maine lay when she was blown up.

The shaded sections denote the civil portions of the city.

BLOEMFONTEIN OCCUPIED.

ROBERTS ENTERS WITH HIS MAIN BODY.

CORDIAL WELCOME.

OUR FLAG FLYING OVER THE PRESIDENCY.

FLIGHT OF STEYN.

SALISBURY'S REPLY RECEIVED AT PRETORIA.

BOER DECISION.

REPLY OF THE GERMAN GOVERNMENT.

PRISONERS OFF TO ST. HELENA.

Lord Roberts, in a despatch received late yesterday evening, but sent off from Bloemfontein on March 13, announces that he has occupied the capital of the Free State without resistance. The leading citizens came forth and handed over to him the keys, and the people cordially welcomed the troops. The British flag, it is added, waves over the Presidency, vacated "by the late President of the Orange Free State."

The enemy's troops retired, probably to the north-east. According to Boer messages the capital of the Free State has been transferred to Kroonstad, on the railway 120 miles north-east of Bloemfontein. We fear, however, it will not be long before President Steyn has to make yet another move. The subjugation of the southern quarter of the Free State will now doubtless be rapidly completed, the small forces along the Orange River captured or dispersed, and the bridges at Norvals Pont and Bethulie repaired.

There cannot be fewer than 2,000 Boers at Norvals Pont, at Bethulie, and near Aliwal North. It is difficult to see how they are going to retreat with a large British army and a powerful cavalry force at Bloemfontein, and with Boshof and Jacobsdal in our hands.

Though rumours as to the relief of Mafeking are flying about, there is no definite news on this head. We may hope great things from Colonel Plumer, as it seems clear that the Boer force before Mafeking is weak. But for the exhausted condition of the garrison, Colonel Baden-Powell and his gallant men could probably cut their way out. With Colonel Plumer's help they should be much too much for "old Snyman."

Operations against the rebels in Western Cape Colony are being vigorously pressed under the indefatigable Lord Kitchener. His presence is a guarantee of a rapid pacification. An ample force is being poured into the district; the Canadians are at Prieska, where the rising had its beginning, and a large number of Yeomanry are also being employed. The insurgents are in no way formidable. They may try guerilla warfare, but in that case there are means of rapidly bringing them to their senses, which Lord Kitchener will, if necessary, employ. They have no artillery, and probably none too much ammunition.

General Cronje is actually to be sent to St. Helena with his principal officers. This, in their own interest, is best, since they can be given far more liberty than is possible at Capetown. As they have made attempts at escape they cannot legitimately complain.

The Boer report of the battle of Driefontein is amusing reading. We fancy that the Free Staters will want some explanation of the fact that, in spite of General Delarey's great victory, the British are at Bloemfontein. Two Boers are acknowledged to have been wounded. As over a hundred were found dead and buried on the field, this is a piece of superlative mendacity.

Our Pretoria correspondent, Mr. Story, informs us that the Boer Presidents are busy concocting a reply to Lord Salisbury's telegram. They intend to deny the annexations of British territory—a line which they have recommended to their auxiliaries in the British Press—but they will have hard work to get round certain announcements in their official journals, the "Volksstem" and the "Bloemfontein Express." Still, as mendacity is their particular forte, they may make out a good story for foreign consumption.

The Powerful's naval brigade from Ladysmith is to be given a splendid send-off from Capetown. We hope that on the arrival of the brigade in England it will be marched through the streets of London, when we may trust the public to do the rest. The Navy has been none too well treated in the past in the matter of honours.

The new and revised "Daily Mail" map (in colours) of the Boer Republics has reached a sale of 170,000 copies. It can be purchased of all bookstalls and newsagents, or direct from Messrs. George Philip and Son, 32, Fleet-street, price 1s., by post 1s. 1d. Orders should be marked "War Map."

ORANGE FREE STATE.

BLOEMFONTEIN OURS.

ROBERTS'S FORCE ENTERS THE FREE STATE CAPITAL

AND OUR FLAG FLIES OVER THE PRESIDENCY.

Lord Roberts has occupied Bloemfontein, the news being contained in the following telegram, which was issued about nine o'clock last night by the War Office.

It will be noticed that the occupation was effected on Tuesday evening:—

"BLOEMFONTEIN, March 13 (8 p.m.).

"By the help of God and by the bravery of her Majesty's soldiers, the troops under my command have taken possession of Bloemfontein.

"The British flag now flies over the Presidency, vacated last evening by Mr. Steyn, late President of the Orange Free State.

"Mr. Fraser, member of the late Executive Government, the Mayor, the Secretary to the late Government, the Landdrost, and other officials met me two miles from the town and presented me with the keys of the Public Offices.

"The enemy have withdrawn from the neighbourhood, and all seems quiet.

"The inhabitants of Bloemfontein gave the troops a cordial welcome."

Mr. John Fraser, late chairman of the O.F.S. Volksraad, was always a determined opponent of President Steyn in his home and foreign policy, and if he had won at the last Presidential election there would be no war to-day. He is the son of the Rev. Colin Fraser, who went out with Dr. Moffat from the Church of Scotland as a missionary to South Africa. He is a graduate of Aberdeen University, and a thoroughly progressive man. Paul Kruger hates him because he is in sympathy with the Uitlander. He is a lawyer by profession, and about forty-five years of age.

THREAT TO BOMBARD.

HURRIED FLIGHT OF PRESIDENT STEYN.

LARGE SEIZURE OF RAILWAY ROLLING STOCK.

(From Our War Correspondent.)

BLOEMFONTEIN, March 13 (6.45 p.m.).*

We have surprised and outflanked the enemy with irresistible force. The capital is glad to surrender.

The Boers are hurrying madly north of the Glen and Modder Rivers.

Overnight General French seized the railway north and south of Bloemfontein, while Lord Roberts despatched a prisoner on parole with a message that he would bombard the city at once unless it surrendered.

Thereupon the townsmen, mostly proprietors, grew alarmed, and all the enemy's organisation disappeared. President Steyn evacuated the place hastily, accompanied by the chief members of the Executive, and proclaimed Kroonstad as the capital.

He himself fled to Winburg.

At last only 3,000 fighting men remained, and in the morning many, finding themselves so weakened, broke their guns, while others, still fearing confiscation, fled north of the Modder, the majority returning to their farms.

The remnant still shelled General French at dawn, but the opposition soon collapsed, and at noon the Landdrost Poppinfust (? Papenfust), Attorney Fraser, Mr. Under-Secretary Collins, and the Mayor, Kelner, submitted.

They formally came to meet Lord Roberts outside the town.

Our General then perambulated the pleasant city, and was received with cheers.

The hoisting of the British flag over the Presidency was at once carried out.

C. E. HANDS.

BLOEMFONTEIN, March 13 (7.10 p.m.).

Bloemfontein has been occupied by our troops. There was no opposition; resistance was useless.

Kroonstad has been proclaimed the capital of the Free State.

It appears that the State Government behaved decently towards the British residents, who form the majority of the commercial population.

Eight locomotives and much rolling stock have been taken.

The battle of Driefontein has frightened the Boers, for, notwithstanding that their losses have been minimised, they know they have been outfought.

Their very organisation is collapsing.

The breach between the Transvaalers and Free Staters is widening.

Major-General Pretyman has been made Military Governor here.

Lord Roberts, accompanied by his staff, has ridden through the town, and been everywhere cheered, while "God Save the Queen" was enthusiastically sung.

The shops are gladly opening, and there is general rejoicing.

It is not expected that the Free Staters will fight again.

They say the Transvaalers, too, are "funking."

This is a pleasant country, and it is lovely weather.

The Boers in the vicinity are unlikely to need further fighting, and will probably gradually dissipate. C. E. HANDS.

NEW FREE STATE CAPITAL.

KROONSTAD SELECTED INSTEAD OF BLOEMFONTEIN.

PRETORIA, March 13.

The Bloemfontein correspondent of the "Volksstem" telegraphs that, in view of the military situation, the seat of government of the Orange Free State may be removed to Kroonstad.—Reuter.

This is very likely. Kroonstad is a township of 2,000 souls, mostly Boers, on the main line from Bloemfontein to the Transvaal.

It is on the Valsch River, a stream which is of some importance in wet weather, and not readily fordable, except in one easily fortified place, even in the dry season. There are rocks, kopjes, and trees on both sides of the river, and the place is much less open in position than is the erstwhile capital. It used to be a holiday resort for

*Copyright in Great Britain (and in the United States by the "New York Herald").

The Spanish-American War of 1898 produced the first *Daily Mail* double-column heading but for the Boer War the paper did not go beyond deep single-column deckers, with main lines in condensed grot capitals, as in this 1900 specimen.

tory; by the turn of the century it had passed the 700,000 mark and was soon to revel in the slogan '*Daily Mail* – Million Sale'.

As so often in the story of news display it took a war to shake the *Mail* out of its single-column whispers into something like a shout. The opening of the Spanish-American War of 1898 was reported by the *Mail* with a fine double-column five-decker – its first double-column headline, alternating a good bold condensed news titling with a light condensed, the whole heading fairly spaced. This was a notable innovation. Though this showed remarkable prescience on the *Mail's* part (it may have been unconscious) as to the ultimate significance of the entry of the United States into the path of imperialism, it did not become a permanency. The paper continued to take the Spanish-American War sufficiently seriously to instal a 'fudge' device on its presses, with 'Latest War News' as the heading in the forme over the 'fudge' space; but when the Boer War broke out the following year its news did not receive double-column treatment. Instead, like American Civil War sheets, the *Mail* turned to very deep single-column deckers, as many as ten decks, alternating bold condensed sans capitals (with turn lines often 'stepped') and condensed news titlings.

The bold and massive Boer War deckers did not survive the peace, however. The *Mail* retreated to its restrained news-titling style, playing a little more on the condensed version for main lines, raised from two-line brevier (16pt) to two-line bourgeois (18pt), and spacing more generously. The effect was exemplified when Joseph Chamberlain resigned from the Cabinet over the tariff reform issue in September 1903; the ensuing political crisis rocked the country and paved the way for the Liberal landslide and the emergence of the Labour Party as a major political force in the General Election of 1906. The sensational news was presented by the *Mail* with a single-column five-decker in the style indicated earlier in this paragraph, opening RESIGNATION / OF / MR CHAMBERLAIN. This was in sharp contrast with the headlining of the radical *Daily Chronicle*, which ran a double-column five-decker in a strong medium square Grot, alternating capitals and upper- and lower-case decks (having taken a leaf out of the book of the popular evenings); the opening line, in 18pt letter-spaced capitals, read A POLITICAL BOMBSHELL. Stemming from a local Clerkenwell sheet, the *Chronicle* had been acquired by Edward Lloyd in 1876 and built into an important morning paper; under the combined editorship of H. W. Massingham (who resigned because of his opposition to the Boer War) and Robert Donald it became strongly radical in tone, in effect the morning equivalent of *The Star*. Its later distinctly chequered political and financial career led to its absorption in 1930 by the *Daily News*, resulting in the *News Chronicle*.

▼ The Chamberlain political sensation of 1903 did not wean the *Daily Mail* from stiff and formal single-column news titlings, but the Radical *Daily Chronicle* produced a punchy sanserif double-column.

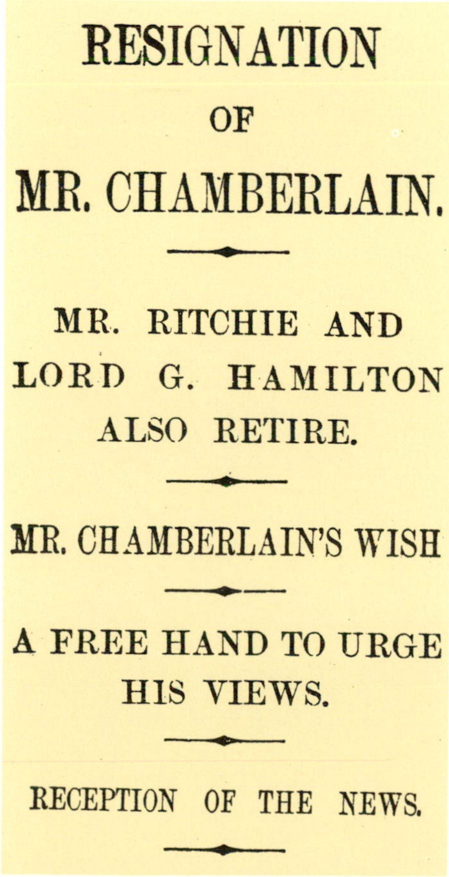
RESIGNATION
OF
MR. CHAMBERLAIN.

MR. RITCHIE AND
LORD G. HAMILTON
ALSO RETIRE.

MR. CHAMBERLAIN'S WISH

A FREE HAND TO URGE
HIS VIEWS.

RECEPTION OF THE NEWS.

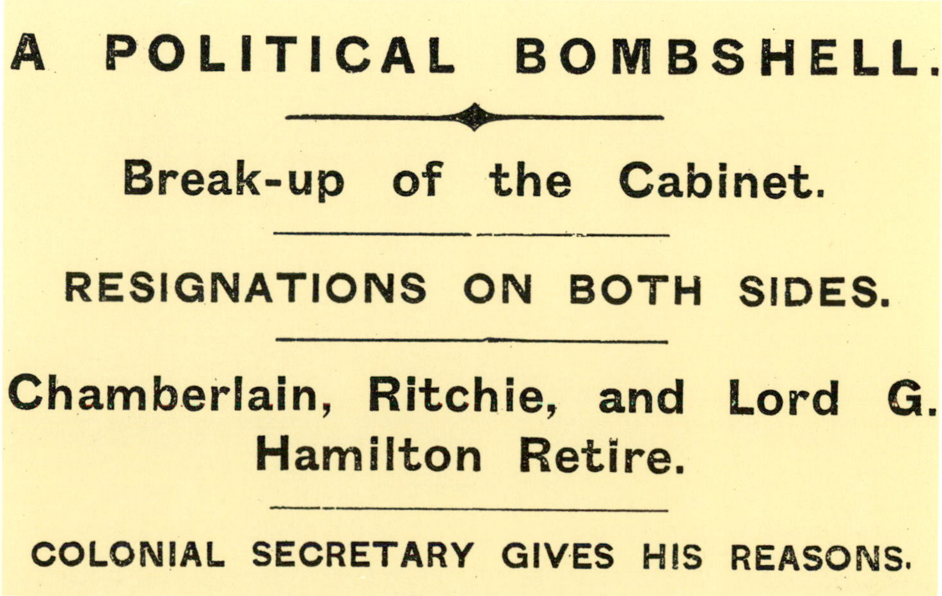
A POLITICAL BOMBSHELL.

Break-up of the Cabinet.

RESIGNATIONS ON BOTH SIDES.

Chamberlain, Ritchie, and Lord G.
Hamilton Retire.

COLONIAL SECRETARY GIVES HIS REASONS.

Daily Express

NO. 431. LONDON, SATURDAY, SEPTEMBER 7, 1901. ONE HALFPENNY

TO-DAY'S STORY.

SATURDAY MORNING.

Fair weather generally is predicted for to-day, but some local showers are probable.

King Edward has left Homburg. After a last massage, there was a general leave-taking, and his Majesty mounted his motor for Frankfort.

For the second time in twenty years an American President has been murderously wounded. While visiting the Buffalo Exhibition grounds yesterday, Mr. McKinley was twice shot with a revolver by a young Anarchist named Frederick Nieman.

Accounts of the circumstances under which the deed was perpetrated vary, but it is beyond doubt that Mr. McKinley received two serious wounds, and the latest reports cabled last night are that he is dying.

Mr. Choate is away in Scotland. The Lord Mayor of London last night cabled to America the horror which the deed inspires in England and the civilised world.

Only in the evening did the news reach New York, and leading business men at once met to devise measures to prevent a financial panic to-day. On the tragedy becoming known in London there was a striking demonstration of feeling in the West End. Should Mr. McKinley die Mr. Roosevelt will succeed.

Lord Kitchener reports that Colonel Scobell's column has killed or captured the entire commando of Lotter and all its stores. The prisoners number ninety-four. Our casualties were eighteen. Another Cape M.P. has been arrested.

M. Santos-Dumont has had bad luck. While making his trial spin yesterday with splendid success, his drag rope got twisted round a tree, and the jerk slightly strained the woodwork, necessitating his descent.

American opinion now fully recognises that the Cup is in danger. Fifty Boston citizens threaten to apply for an injunction against the exclusion of Independence. Shamrock II. took another spin yesterday. Columbia's record is described in detail.

Our budget of letters sympathising with the poor fisherfolk of Grimsby is again large. Many of them also enclose the help that sanctifies pity.

Aided and sustained by this sympathy and by the public support accorded in daily increasing measure, our task of feeding the famishing people goes steadily forward. More than 5,000 received food yesterday.

As yet, smack-owners and men have not yet mustered moral courage to vault that yawning abyss of a penny's width that still divides them. There is a general feeling, however, that prospects are brightening.

The Deputy-Adjutant-General's report upon the Imperial Yeomanry has at last been published. It tells in connected form the story of the raising, equipment, and despatch of a force which, in more senses than one, has done "yeoman service."

Still more interesting are the War Office Committee's proposals for the future of the force, which is to be reorganised on a scale constituting a proud monument to its work in South Africa.

For once Berlin has refused to bow to the imperious Kaiser. The magistracy has re-elected as second burgomaster Herr Kauffmann, whom the Emperor had refused to accept.

Apparently the Sultan seeks to steal a march on France by trying to settle direct with the Porte's French creditors behind the back of the Government.

Cranks have tried to draw a pro-Boer herring across the business of the Trade Union Congress but met with signal defeat, by more than two to one the Congress refused to discuss the question.

Hamburg is clouded by fear that before long America will ship coal to Germany. This is caused by the immense drop of freights.

Details of the fatal accident to Miss M. Trafford, in the Alps, show that her sister, unnerved by the occurrence, rushed frantically among rocks, where she was found unable either to advance or go back.

Enormous quantities of coal are to be stocked at Gibraltar. After the Atlantic manoeuvres the two fleets will enter the harbour to test its coaling capacity.

From drought, extensive districts of India have passed to a condition of flood. Heavy rains are still falling.

Railway companies are totting up their latest gains from the holiday season. Business has this year been largely in excess of the average.

Irish and Danish butter wage bitter war for the conquest of the British market. There is shortly to take place between them a grand challenge championship, of which the conditions are stated in detail.

For Gloucester next week will be one of music. The Festival of the Three Choirs begins to-morrow, and continues until Thursday evening.

For brutally assaulting a lady "fare" in [illegible] after midnight on Thursday a cabman named [illegible] has been sentenced to [illegible] months' imprisonment. His licence is also revoked.

[illegible] submarine is being built for the [illegible] in addition to the five Holland boats. It is understood to be by an English inventor.

[illegible]-generalship is to be created [illegible] in West Africa. Brigadier [illegible] R.A., will be the first occupant of [illegible].

[illegible] races, the downfall of [illegible] the most noticeable feature [illegible] fared disastrously. The [illegible] M. Davis, bought out of a selling [illegible] Handicap for Lord [illegible]. The September Sale [illegible] was won by Captain Kirk's Traviesa, [illegible] Nursery by Captain J. [illegible].—(Page 8.)

[illegible] B. Fry, in his "Football Gossip," [illegible] the difference between [illegible] and Southern football.—(Page 8.)

[illegible] scored a century in brilliant [illegible] against Yorkshire at the Hastings [illegible] Festival yesterday. Yorkshire [illegible] a considerable disadvantage.—[illegible]

There was a fairly steady tone in the Stock [illegible] with the exception of [illegible], which were weak on fears of dear money in America. Home Rails were irregular and the only feature in the Mining section was the renewed strength of Westralians.

PRESIDENT McKINLEY SHOT BY AN ANARCHIST

AT THE PAN-AMERICAN EXPOSITION.

TWICE WOUNDED.

STRUCK IN BREAST AND GROIN.

FATAL RESULT FEARED.

LORD MAYOR'S MESSAGE OF SYMPATHY.

THE NEWS IN LONDON.

"Express" Telegram.

NEW YORK, Friday, Sept. 6.

William McKinley, President of the United States, lies, it is believed, dying from the effects of two bullet wounds inflicted by an Anarchist with a fancied grievance.

The shooting took place at the grounds of the Buffalo Exposition this afternoon, where the Chief Executive was the honoured guest of the great city by the Lake.

The President was receiving the public in the Temple of Music. According to the American custom, he was shaking hands with the people who passed before him in a long line.

The would-be murderer approached with the pistol hidden under a handkerchief. He came up quickly, and while he grasped his hand fired the pistol.

Before the bystanders could move a second shot was fired by the Anarchist. He would have pulled the trigger again, but he was seized and disarmed.

The President sank into the arms of members of the committee. The floor was wet with his blood. It was believed that he was dying.

WILD EXCITEMENT.

Mr. McKinley was carried to the hospital on the grounds amid the wildest excitement. The report spread that he had been slain, and the people made a rush for the place where it was supposed the Anarchist was being held. There were loud cries of "Lynch him!" and "Kill the murderer!"

At the hospital Mr. McKinley, who, it is said, was unconscious, was undressed. The doctors found that he had been shot in the breast bone and in the groin.

The bullet was removed without difficulty from the breast; the other was not probed for. It is believed that an X-Ray apparatus will be used in locating it.

Alarming reports are in circulation as to the nature of the wounds, and at the moment of wiring it is feared that the result must be fatal.

There was extreme difficulty in getting particulars of the exact place where the shots were fired. One account of the murderous attack was to the effect that the President had not actually reached the Temple, but was on his way there and passing between a line of enthusiastic admirers, many of whom reached out to grasp the hand of the popular Chief Executive.

With him were Mr. Milburn, president of the Exposition, and Dr. Rixie, a member of the McKinley party.

As they passed a well-dressed man in a frock-coat and a tall hat stepped from the crowd of onlookers. He held out his hand, and the President smiled and extended his.

The stranger thereupon fired twice with a pistol that he had concealed from view, and the President fell with a cry of pain.

THE ASSAILANT.

After the shooting the assailant was taken to the police station. Great precautions were taken to prevent a lynching, which would have been inevitable had the infuriated people been able to find the miscreant.

He was identified as an Anarchist named Frederick Nieman, twenty-three years old, and a resident of Detroit.

He had gone to the grounds with the deliberate intention of carrying out the tenets of his creed and removing a Ruler from the face of the earth.

The news of the shooting reached Wall-street long after the close of business.

A conference of big financiers was held in New York to-night to devise means to prevent a panic at the opening of business to-morrow. It is likely that the bears will try to depress prices by pointing out the evil results that might befall the country in case of the death of McKinley and the succession of Vice-President Roosevelt for the remainder of the term—more than three years.

Roosevelt, it is pointed out, is a man of the "jingo" type who is continually advocating war.

The shooting of the President has evoked a loud cry for the suppression of the semi-crazy Anarchists, who are allowed a freedom of speech in the United States which the sensible public are beginning to believe is much too great.

The murderer of King Humbert came from Paterson, N.J., where the Anarchists were allowed to carry on their wild plots without let or hindrance.

McKinley has been denounced with so much vigour as an "Imperialist" and a "Czar" that many ignorant non-English speaking foreigners take the appellation of "Czar" literally, and class the President politically with the ruler of Russia or the German Empire.

There is some likelihood of a demonstration against the Anarchists in New York and Chicago. Some of them have openly advocated the killing of McKinley.

It is likely that the patience of the public will be found to be exhausted if men like Herr Most seek to glorify the scoundrel who shot at a man who is the model head of a Government.

The report which has just reached here that the Buffalo police defeated an attempt to lynch the murderous alleged Anarchist Nieman was received with profound regret.

The reports as to the location of the second bullet conflict. One statement is that it lodged in the groin, but later reports say that it struck Mr. McKinley in the abdomen, which puts a much more serious face on the matter. At his time of life a bullet in the abdomen must be of necessity most dangerous.

It is reported that it has been probed for.

Mrs. McKinley has not yet been informed of the probably successful attempt upon her husband's life. She is extremely frail in health, and her friends and the doctors fear the effect upon her of such dreadful news. They hesitate to break it to her.

"FATALLY INJURED."

NEW YORK, Friday, Sept. 6.

The President was shot in front of the Ethnological buildings on his way to the Temple of Music. He is fatally injured; one shot passed through the left breast, and the other entered the abdomen.—Reuter.

PROBING FOR THE BULLET.

NEW YORK, Friday, Sept. 6.

Dr. Parker, a prominent physician, is now probing for the bullet lodged in the abdomen. Police-Commissioner Cooper has had a conversation with Nieman, who then denied being an Anarchist.

NIEMAN ATTACKED.

ASSAILANT'S FACE CUT OPEN IN A FIGHT WITH TWENTY MEN.

NEW YORK, Friday, Sept. 6.

After Nieman fired, Detective Ireland, who was only 2ft. away, immediately jumped upon him, and brought him to the ground.

In an instant twenty other men precipitated themselves upon him, and when Nieman was rescued from their hands he had his face cut open and was covered with blood. He is now locked up at the police headquarters.

A physician who left the hospital a few minutes before six, reports that the respiration of the patient is easy, and the pulse good. An anaesthetic had been administered, and the probing for the second bullet had begun.

When shot, the President fell into the arms of Detective Gerry, to whom he coolly said: "Am I shot?"

The detective unbuttoned his vest, and, seeing blood, replied: "I am afraid you are, Mr. President."

It is now stated that soon after the outrage Nieman, on being asked why he shot the President, replied:—

"I am an Anarchist. I did my duty."

A PROFESSIONAL OPINION.

Mr. McKinley's wounds are reported to be in the chest and in the groin.

With regard to both, the immediate danger to life is first from shock and secondly from hemorrhage. Mr. McKinley has not succumbed to shock, and the danger of a fatal end from hemorrhage may be said to diminish in proportion to the length of time that elapses from the infliction of the wound. What is known as secondary hemorrhage is a later danger.

In the case of the chest wound, the ultimate result will be governed by its character. If the bullet is a small one the chance of surviving it is good.

The wound in the groin may entail serious consequences. The bullet here may have possibly penetrated some abdominal organ, and may be attended with septic inflammation of the peritoneum.

Modern surgery, however, is full of resource, and should the President survive the danger of hemorrhage he may pull through.

LORD MAYOR'S SYMPATHY.

HE WRITES A FEELING MESSAGE TO ALL AMERICANS.

The London correspondent of the "Philadelphia North American" conveyed the news of the shooting to the Lord Mayor of London, who showed great emotion, and wrote the following for transmission to America:—

"The Lord Mayor of London learns with feelings of the greatest possible indignation and consternation of the dastardly and cowardly attack made to-day upon the life of the President of the United States of America, and is confident that the citizens of London without exception will unite in one common sentiment of detestation and abhorrence at so horrible and unprovoked a crime.

"The Lord Mayor prays that so valuable a life may yet be spared to his country, and desires at the same time to offer the expression of his sympathy with all American citizens."

THE NEWS IN LONDON.

SAD AND STRIKING SCENES IN THE WEST END.

When the first rumours of the tragedy reached the West End shortly after ten last night it was received with shocked incredulity, which quickly gave place to deep consternation. Confirmation was soon to hand, and then the news flew from mouth to mouth along the streets.

At the Cecil a small party of Americans were sitting on the verandah discussing the America Cup race. One of the party had just offered to make a bet for a large sum when the news was told by a breathless messenger. All the gentlemen immediately arose and doffed their hats, the party breaking up forthwith.

At the Carlton, where a number of American millionaires are staying, the news created the greatest excitement.

Several gentlemen were standing in the hall when the news was made known.

They rushed at once to the tape machine, anxious to secure the later and fuller information, all hoping that subsequent details might minimise the seriousness of the original report.

For the remainder of the evening the hotel guests crowded round the machine. At one time, standing together, were seen no fewer than half a dozen millionaires, among them being Mr. John W. Gates and Mr. Morgenthaw, of the Steel Trust, Mr. Frick, Mr. French, and Mr. Frank Mackay.

MR. McKINLEY'S CAREER.

THE CHAMPION OF ULTRA-PROTECTION AND "IMPERIALISM."

William McKinley, who was shot down by a would-be assassin at the Buffalo Exposition, is serving his second term as President of the United States, having been re-elected last November on the Republican ticket.

He was born at Niles, O., on January 29, 1843, and is consequently more than fifty-eight years of age. He was educated at the public schools, in which he became a teacher. At the outbreak of the Civil War he enlisted as a private, and after passing through the intervening grades was breveted major of Volunteers by President Lincoln for gallantry in action.

After the bloody days of the war he studied law, and settled at Canton, Ohio, which has since been his home.

He was chosen Governor of Ohio in 1891, and re-elected in 1893.

At the Republican National Convention at St. Louis in 1896 he was nominated for the Presidency, receiving 661 out of 905 votes. He was elected by a popular plurality of 600,000 votes over William J. Bryan, Democrat. The issues which carried him through were high protection and sound money, as opposed to the tariff reform and free silver views of Bryan.

It was under McKinley that the Spanish-American war was declared, and the policy of so-called "Imperialism" inaugurated. These measures were popular. They secured the re-election of McKinley last November. Bryan again opposed him, but with a weak platform and a divided party, and no principles to speak of.

ROOSEVELT WOULD SUCCEED.

In the event of President McKinley's death the Presidency would devolve upon Theodore Roosevelt, the Vice-President.

Mr. Roosevelt cut a somewhat dramatic figure in the Spanish-American war. He resigned the Assistant Secretaryship of the Navy to lead a regiment of rough riders. Subsequently he became Governor of New York State, and was elected Vice-President last November.

OTHER SIMILAR ATTACKS

TWO UNITED STATES PRESIDENTS KILLED BY ASSASSINS.

The following list of the world's Rulers attacked by assassins during the nineteenth century and this century is taken from the "Royal Magazine" for February last:—

IN THE UNITED STATES.

President ABRAHAM LINCOLN, mortally shot in Ford's Theatre, Washington, April 14, 1865, by Wilkes Booth.

President JAMES A. GARFIELD, mortally shot by Charles Guiteau in Washington, July 2, 1881.

To which may now be added:—

President WILLIAM McKINLEY, shot at the Buffalo Exposition, on September 6, 1901, by Fred. Nieman.

OTHER RULERS.

GEORGE III. of England, attacked twice, May, 1800.
NAPOLEON I., attacked while First Consul, December, 1800; twenty killed and fifty-two wounded.
LOUIS PHILIPPE, King of France, shot at while driving along the Boulevard du Temple; forty killed.
QUEEN ISABELLA of Spain, stabbed, February 2, 1852.
KING VICTOR EMMANUEL of Italy, shot at, 1853.
FERDINAND CHARLES III., Duke of Parma, shot at, March 27, 1854.
KING FERDINAND of Naples, stabbed by a soldier, December 8, 1856.
NAPOLEON III., attacked by Orsini and others, many killed, January 14, 1858.
PRINCE DANIEL of Montenegro, killed, August 13, 1860.
KING OTHO of Greece, shot at by a student, 1862.
PRINCE MICHAEL of Servia, shot and killed, June 10, 1868.
ABDUL AZIZ, Sultan of Turkey, killed with scissors, June 4, 1876.
KING ALFONSO of Spain, shot at, October 25, 1878, and December 30, 1879.
EMPEROR WILLIAM I. of Germany, shot at by Hoedel, May 11, and by Dr Nobeling, June 2, 1878.
ALEXANDER II., Czar of Russia, blown to pieces with nitroglycerine while driving through St. Petersburg, March 13, 1881.
PRESIDENT CARNOT of France, stabbed to death by Caserio, or Pietro, Santo, June 24, 1894.
NASR-ED-DIN, Shah of Persia, killed May 1, 1896.
KING HUMBERT of Italy, attacked by Pietro Acciarito, April 22, 1897.
PRESIDENT FAURE of France, attacked with dynamite bomb, June 13, 1897.
PRIME MINISTER CANOVAS DEL CASTILLO of Spain, stabbed and killed by Rinaldi, August 8, 1897.
GENERAL BORDA, President of Uruguay, killed, August 25, 1897.
PRESIDENT BARRIOS of Guatemala, killed, February 8, 1898.
EMPRESS ELIZABETH of Austria, fatally stabbed while walking [illegible] her hotel in Geneva to the lake boat, September 10, 1898.
KING HUMBERT of Italy, shot three times and killed at Monza, by Gaetano Bresci, July 29, 1900.
Three attempts were made to kill QUEEN VICTORIA and two to kill the PRINCE OF WALES, but in no instance was anyone injured.

PAUL I., Czar of Russia, was assassinated during the night between March 23 and 24, 1801, but this murder cannot be classed among anarchical or Nihilistic crimes, as the murdered monarch was killed by adherents of the Court, at the instigation of certain members of the Royal Family.

ANARCHIST WAVE.

HOW FRENCH POLICE PROVIDE AGAINST OUTRAGE.

There appears to have been a strong wave of Anarchism overflowing both hemispheres since the assassination of King Humbert. The Continental police, however, are much more alive to the possibilities of outrages by Anarchists than seem the American police.

At the death of the Empress Frederick the German authorities took the greatest precautions to prevent the access of any suspicious person near the Imperial and Royal mourners.

The French police are no less energetic in providing for the safety of the Czar, as the following telegram shows:—

"Express" Telegram.

DUNKIRK, Friday, Sept. 6.

The police hunt for Anarchists hereabouts is being prosecuted with the utmost diligence and vigour. I understand that every new arrival here is made the subject of the most searching inquiry, and if a single member of the "Brotherhood of Blood" is able to find his way to Dunkirk from now on it will not be through any lack of vigilance on the part of the police.

Meanwhile, it is worthy of notice that Dunkirk embraces a big colony of militant Socialists, who are far from enthusiastic over the coming visit of France's "Ally and Friend." The revolutionary views of these inhospitable gentlemen, however, are not being so publicly expressed just now as usual, for the Paris detectives are everywhere, and a decree of expulsion could be enforced in a twinkling. As Socialists possess, like all the the rest of humanity, a considerable element of curiosity, they are not anxious to be turned out of Dunkirk when something is "going on," for the first time in many years.

LOTTER CAUGHT.

HIS COMMANDO AND BELONGINGS TAKEN.

NOTABLE PRISONERS.

TWO NOTORIOUS CAPE REBELS KILLED.

The War Office yesterday issued the following telegram from Lord Kitchener:—

"PRETORIA, Sept. 5, 10.30 p.m.

"I yesterday reported Scobell in pursuit of Lotter; am glad to say he has been entirely successful, having come up with him early this morning, and captured his entire commando—viz., 10 killed, 52 wounded prisoners, and 62 unwounded, together with all their belongings.

"Prisoners include Commandants Lotter and Breedt, Field Cornets Kruger and W. Kruger, and Lieutenant Shoeman.

"Among the killed were the two *Vasters, both notable rebels.

"Our casualties were 10 killed and 8 wounded, names being reported separately."

MATJESFONTEIN, Thursday, Sept. 6.

Colonel Scobell has captured Lotter's commando by a night attack. Nineteen Boers escaped.—Reuter's Special.

MIDDELBURG, Thursday, Sept. 6.

In the capture of Lotter's commando everything in the laager was taken, including 25,000 rounds of ammunition.—Reuter's Special.

* Voorsters according to a Reuter's Special telegram, which says they were Cape Colonials of the Middelburg district, and had given much trouble.

HOW LOTTER WAS CAUGHT.

CRADOCK, Friday, Sept. 6.

Further particulars of Colonel Scobell's coup show that Lieut.-Colonel Doran engaged Lotter on Monday at Garstler Kloof, when one Boer was killed and thirty horses were captured.

The Boers then attempted to escape over the mountains to Paardekraal, in Zwagershoek, attacking twenty-five men of the Midland Mounted Rifles who had been placed in a position to frustrate the attempt. The small force performed its part successfully, killing seven Boers and wounding one.

Failing to get away by this route, the Boers crossed a precipitous path over Ospad towards Pearston, reaching Strick's farm at midnight. On Tuesday afternoon the commando fled hastily, as four of Scobell's Scouts appeared, making for Petersburg.

Colonel Scobell, who had personally watched the proceedings from the mountain top, then made a night march, which resulted in the capture of an entire commando being effected for the first time in the Colony.—Reuter's Special.

LOTTER AND HIS CAPTOR.

The attack took place south of Petersburg, which is thirty miles east of Graaff Reinet.

Lotter, who, according to a Laffan telegram, was wounded, seems to have been notorious mainly for sending an unprintable reply to Lord Kitchener's proclamation. His commando, which has been looting and plundering in Cape Colony, has not been in close quarters with the British before.

Colonel Scobell, who has effected the capture of Lotter's commando, was originally employed in the purchase and transhipment of mules to South Africa.

After completing this work he rejoined the Scots Greys, and took his squadron through the engagements at Kimberley, Paardeberg, and Bloemfontein.

He subsequently took over the command of Brabant's Horse, and quite recently was gazetted to the 5th Lancers.

NATIVE TERRITORY INVADED.

A telegram from Lord Kitchener, dated Pretoria, September 5, says:—

"About 300 Boers crossed to south of Orange River, in native territory, near Herschell, early yesterday. Columns in pursuit."

CAPE M.P. ARRESTED.

CAPETOWN, Thursday, Sept. 5.

Legislative Councillor Vandenheever and his two sons have been arrested at Burghersdorp. Arms, ammunition, and foodstuffs were found beneath the flooring of their house.—Laffan.

CUP IN DANGER.

CURIOUS ACTION OF FIFTY BOSTON CITIZENS.

NEW YORK, Friday, Sept. 6.

The "Post" says: "Indisputably the Cup is in greater danger than ever, and should it go to Sir T. Lipton no one will begrudge the victory to so chivalrous and gallant a sportsman."

The "World's" Boston correspondent to-day states that fifty citizens have addressed a letter to the New York Yacht Club protesting against the right of the club to exclude Independence from the trial races, and threatening, in the event of Shamrock winning the Cup, to ask for an injunction from a United States Court to prevent the club from delivering the America Cup to Sir Thomas Lipton.

The letter says that Sir Thomas Lipton has been notified of the intention of the protesters.—Reuter.

It may be possible for the Boston protesters to get some judge to issue an injunction—injunctions are easily obtained in the United States—but the New York Yacht Club have only to show the deed of gift under which they hold the America Cup to override any injunction, and allow Sir Thomas Lipton, if he should win the series of races, to peacefully bring the Cup home in the cabin of the Erin.

A Newport telegram says Constitution will be kept in commission in case an accident happens to Columbia.

SHAMROCK TAKES A SPIN.

NEW YORK, Friday, Sept. 6.

Shamrock was out for an hour and a half's spin to-day to stretch her new mainsail.—Reuter.

CHERRYSTONE CAUSES DEATH.

VIENNA, Friday, Sept. 6.

The post-mortem examination of Prince Christian of Cumberland showed that his death was caused by his swallowing a cherry-stone.—Publishers' Press.

THE CZAR'S VISIT.

PRECAUTIONS AGAINST ROUGH SEAS.

ENGLISH INTEREST.

"Express" Telegrams.

PARIS, Friday, Sept. 6.

M. Loubet's Dunkirk, Compiègne, and Reims speeches have been prepared after consultation with M. Waldeck Rousseau, and have been telegraphed in cipher to the Czar, who will similarly communicate his replies.

The Council of State have granted the sum of £60,000 to defray the expenses caused by the visit of the Czar.

DUNKIRK, Friday, Sept. 6.

As the Dunkirk sea is noted for its tendency to be unruly when its good behaviour is most desired, the national authorities are making provision to secure the safest and most comfortable conditions for the visitors in the event of there being a particularly rough sea on the day of the Czar's arrival.

To this end the crew of the Cassini, on which President Loubet will go to meet the nation's guests, are being carefully trained in the manipulation of a vessel being brought alongside another in a heavy sea.

THE PRESIDENT'S GREETING.

If the arrangements are not changed on account of a rough sea, President Loubet will board the Imperial yacht as soon as the Cassini is moored alongside. He will be received by the Emperor at the foot of the main staircase of the yacht, the Czar wearing the uniform of a Russian admiral, with the sash of the Grand Cross of the Legion of Honour.

After an interchange of greetings the chiefs of the two States will ascend to the deck, and the presentation of their respective suites will follow. The Czarina will then receive the French President in the salon. Then M. Loubet will go aboard the Cassini, and, weather permitting, the Sovereigns will immediately return his visit, remaining upon the destroyer for the review, which will be preceded by an inspection of the submarines.

THE KING'S JOURNEY.

HE LEAVES HOMBURG IN HIS AUTOMOBILE.

"Express" Telegram.

HOMBURG, Friday, Sept. 6.

Last evening the King gave a farewell dinner party, to which were invited Sir Frank Lascelles, the British Ambassador at Berlin, and Mr. Bennett, Commercial Attaché at Vienna.

To-day was a general leave-taking day. In the morning the King, as usual, took the waters and was massaged at Dr. Hamel's establishment. Later he paid a visit to the studio of Professor Corrodi.

At midday his Majesty received the chief of the local police and several officers of the secret police and of the gendarmes, to whom he personally distributed the Victorian Order, Victoria medals, and presents of money in recognition of their trusty services.

The proprietor of Ritter's Park Hotel received a valuable present. His Majesty accepted a present of an Arab horse from the staff of the hotel.

In the afternoon the postmaster was presented to his Majesty, and received a decoration. After this ceremonial the King had a round of golf, and then returned to the hotel.

The King left in his automobile for Frankfort at 6.35 p.m., where the Royal saloon carriage with the Royal servants had already preceded him.

At 8.35 his Majesty departed from Frankfort in a special train, which will travel to Hamburg, whence he sails to Copenhagen.

The Homburg cure has greatly benefited his Majesty, who has expressed the intention of returning here next year.

MISHAP TO SANTOS-DUMONT.

"Express" Telegram.

PARIS, Friday, Sept. 6.

Although there was more wind to-day than yesterday, M. Santos-Dumont decided this morning to make a trial trip with his airship.

In the presence of a large assemblage of enthusiasts, he mounted to a height of 160ft., and, moving with great rapidity, crossed the Seine. The spectators were absolutely amazed by the speed attained and by the perfect control over the aeronef which M. Santos-Dumont manifested.

While they were still wondering, the balloon was suddenly seen to stop, the drag-rope being hauled taut. It was soon found that the rope was knotted about a tree in the park of the Chateau de Boulogne, belonging to Baron Rothschild.

This accident necessitated a rapid descent. Without alighting, M. Santos-Dumont discovered that the wooden frame was strained, requiring an immediate return to the shed.

Still remaining in the basket, the aeronaut superintended the towing of the balloon back to the Aero Club grounds.

On the day the rope caught in the telegraph wires, and the balloon collided with a house. This necessitated its deflation, and on descending the framework was broken.

PRINCE CHUN IN GERMANY.

"Express" Telegram.

BERLIN, Friday, Sept. 6.

The Kaiser has presented the Emperor of China's yellow silk letter to the Hohenzollern Museum.

The letter is a most interesting specimen of Chinese embroidery work. It consists of numerous pages, extending, when unfolded, into one length of three yards. Fantastic dragons, exquisitely embroidered, form the chief decoration, and the lettering is in black silk floral embroidery. Small ivory fastenings take the place of seals on the envelope, which is also ornamented with bright yellow dragons.

Prince Chun, after paying a visit to the Charlottenburg Schloss Park, and there laying wreaths on the tombs of the Emperor William I. and the Empress Augusta, left Berlin to-day for Danzig.

THE MISSION TO JAPAN.

YOKOHAMA, Friday, Sept. 6.

The Chinese Envoy has notified the Foreign Office, through the Chinese Legation, of the nature of his mission.

The Emperor's reception of the special envoy has not yet been arranged.—Reuter.

ANOTHER 5,000 FED.

"EXPRESS" RELIEVES HUNGER-STRICKEN GRIMSBY.

A GIGANTIC TASK.

The work of feeding famine-stricken Grimsby continued yesterday. At the headquarters of the "Express" Relief Fund at the Temperance Hall, Cleethorpes-road, rations were distributed to 989 families. As the families of the fisherfolk run to many children, this means that more than 5,000 persons who were actually hungry were provided with meals.

The distribution will continue to-day. Arrangements have been made to give supplies to 500 more families.

One thousand children were fed last night by the mission societies. These helpless little creatures were pinched by starvation, and many of them were in grievous suffering. Their joy at getting something to eat after their terrible privation melted the hearts of the volunteers who made the distribution.

The accounts of the suffering at Grimsby which have been published in the "Express" awoke the sympathy of many employers, who had no idea of the gruesome plight of their workmen. The sailors are proud men, who never before have had to call for charity, and it was not until the "Express" delved beneath the surface of things that their pitiable plight was laid bare. Some of the owners visited the famine districts yesterday, and expressed an earnest desire to end the strike. It is likely that employers and men will meet in a more amicable spirit now that the purely human side of the controversy has been brought to the front.

SICKNESS FEARED.

A matinée benefit performance was given at the Prince of Wales' Theatre, Grimsby, yesterday, in aid of the relief fund, and about £100 was realised.

The work of packing and sorting the provisions continued all last night at the Temperance Hall. The volunteers were preparing bundles of provisions to be given out to-day.

The Arlington Wesleyan Mission, which is running two large soup kitchens in the poorest district, received a donation of five sacks of potatoes from the "Express" supply depot.

Sickness is on the increase in Grimsby, and fever is spreading. It is feared that the next urgent call will be for nurses and doctors and medicines. An epidemic once started among the poor fisherfolk, weakened as they are by hunger and privations, might spread with awful rapidity.

There is a coal famine among the Grimsby sufferers. Contributions of fuel are urgently asked for by the local distributors of charity.

A mass meeting of the men may be held at the Prince of Wales' Theatre, Grimsby, this morning, at which a proposition will be submitted that the men go to work on the terms suggested by the owners until a final settlement can be made by arbitration.

The editor of the Grimsby "Daily Telegraph" wires to say that the work of the "Express" is deeply appreciated. The work to which he refers could not have been so successful had [illegible] for the cordial support of the [illegible] "Telegraph," whose proprietor and [illegible] worked unsparingly in organising the relief. These gentlemen placed their services and their local knowledge, their time and their pockets, at the disposal of the "Express" representatives, who are administering the relief.

CONTRIBUTIONS IN KIND.

Contributions continued to come in yesterday. The cash donations are acknowledged separately. Here is a list of some of the contributions of food:—

Seventy-two packets of Neave's Food from Messrs. Neave.
Package of porridge food from the International Plasmon, Limited.
One box of cocoa from Cave, Austin, and Co., Limited, Eastbourne.
216 half-pound packages of cocoa from the Imperial Steam-Users' Association.
Three cases of Nestle's milk, sent anonymously.
Twenty pounds of dairy butter given by the manager and assistants of the Uxbridge branch of the Home and Colonial Stores.

A shilling subscription was opened at the Mecca Café in Mark-lane. The establishment was yesterday opened after being redecorated, and at the ceremony a reference was made to the Grimsby relief fund established by the "Express."

Captain Frederick Barnes, R.N.R., in sending a donation, writes: "Please allow me to express my admiration of the splendid work the 'Express' is doing at Grimsby. I have been a seafaring man myself in my early years, and feel great sympathy for the wives and children of the fishermen."

DRAWING TOGETHER.

The Grimsby Dispute Committee yesterday decided to recommend the men not to accept the terms offered by the owners on Thursday, but to abide by their own terms, which only differ by a penny in the poundage.

The general feeling of the committee is that the disputants are now so close that by making a small sacrifice either side could end the dispute. At the same time the committee are very much afraid that the men will not ratify their decision on the ground that they are conceding too much.

A general feeling obtains that the outlook is growing brighter.

HELP FROM THE PUBLIC.

The following subscriptions were received at the "Express" office yesterday:—

[illegible]

The *Daily Chronicle's* break with the single-column, news-titling headline tradition was no isolated phenomenon. The new century had opened with a newspaper portent, the appearance in September 1900 of the *Daily Express*. The *Express*, a venture of a then well-known newspaper and magazine magnate, C. A. (later Sir Arthur) Pearson, had an interesting background story. It dated back to the ill-fated *The Morning* of 1892; that paper had survived Chester Ives's American styling by reverting to the ads-front-page, minimal headings of its contemporaries; its position was none too secure, however, and in 1898 its name was changed to *London Morning*, this being later modified to *Morning Herald* (recalling at least a historic predecessor). Under the last title it was acquired by Pearson, who remodelled it with front-page news and changed its title to the *Daily Express*. Not only did the *Express* put news on its front page, in which for years it ploughed a lone furrow among London mornings, but it completely abandoned the traditional news titlings in its headline typography. It alternated decks of Monarch and Venetian capitals (Venetian then ranked as a distinctly 'with it' jobbing type – put out by the typefounders as some sort of response to William Morris). Long stories were broken by flush-left sideheads in bold sans. More was to come; for the assassination of President McKinley in September 1901 induced the *Express* to lead with two lines double-column, in bold condensed sans capitals, reading into a single-column decker; shortly afterwards two double-column headings graced the front page. The move had begun away from the grim, grey pillars of single-column make-up to the horizontal stress of later days.

Progress had its zigzags, however. The drab old ways died hard. The most startling example was *The Tribune*, launched as a new Liberal morning during the General Election campaign of 1906. As a small boy of five I remember the enthusiasm with which my father, then thirty, greeted the paper; in this he typified the reaction of the young, radical Liberals. But *The Tribune*, which should have soared to success on the crest of the Liberal tidal wave, slavishly followed the ancient formula; a front page of 'smalls', minimal headlines in the old news titlings, it was a replica of *The Times* except for its title, which was in roman capitals instead of blackletter (but a poor piece of lettering, of no distinction). The paper began to slip; it tried to liven up its headlining with more decks and larger news titlings; but in February 1908 it folded.

◀ The first London morning with front-page news, the *Daily Express* of 1901 introduced double-column headlines as regular practice.

▼ Traditional news-titlings were the headline dress of the ill-fated Liberal morning *The Tribune* (1906–8).

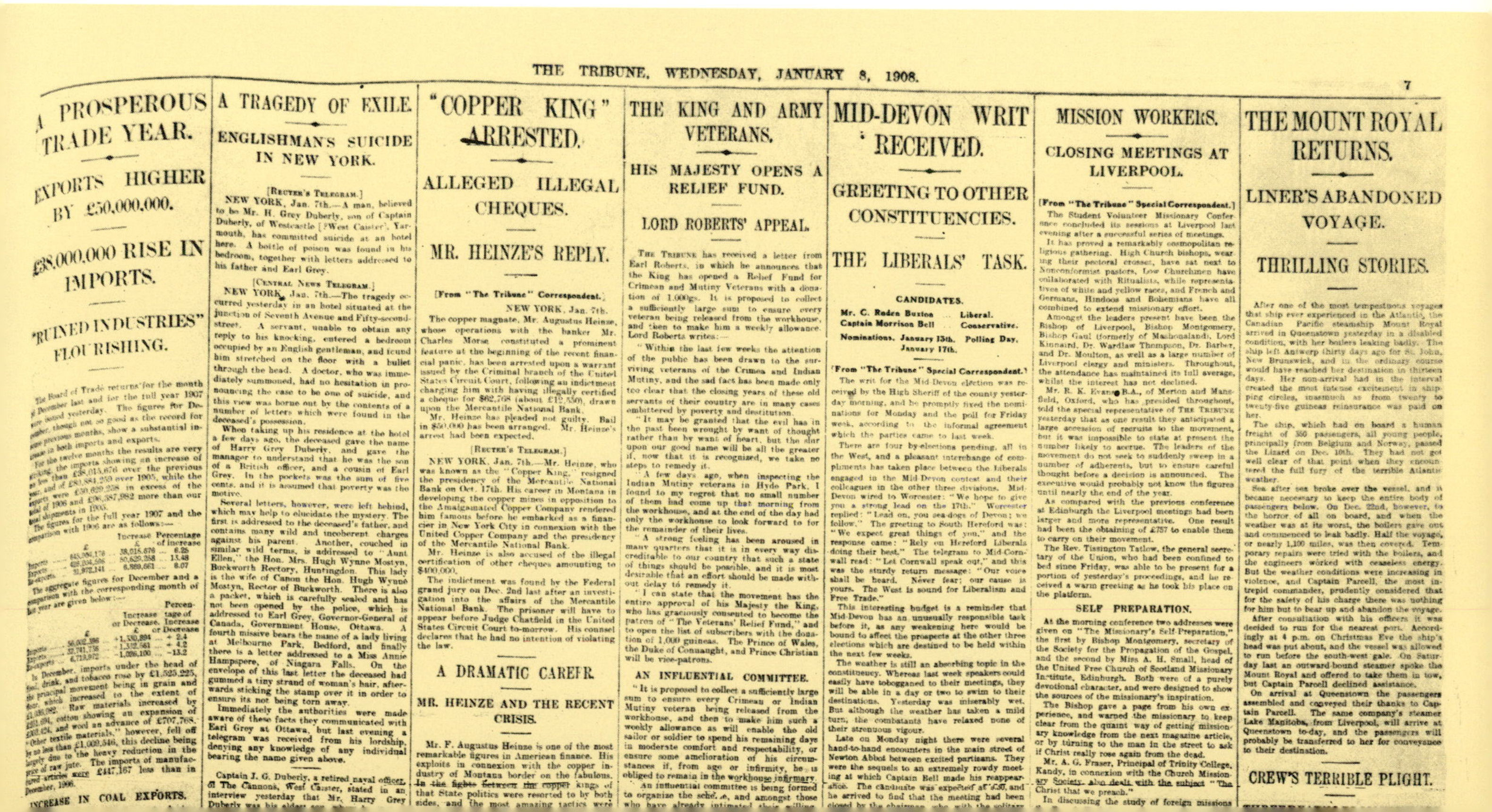

THE TRIBUNE, WEDNESDAY, JANUARY 8, 1908. 7

A PROSPEROUS TRADE YEAR. EXPORTS HIGHER BY £50,000,000. £38,000,000 RISE IN IMPORTS. "RUINED INDUSTRIES" FLOURISHING.

A TRAGEDY OF EXILE. ENGLISHMAN'S SUICIDE IN NEW YORK.

"COPPER KING" ARRESTED. ALLEGED ILLEGAL CHEQUES. MR. HEINZE'S REPLY.

A DRAMATIC CAREER. MR. HEINZE AND THE RECENT CRISIS.

THE KING AND ARMY VETERANS. HIS MAJESTY OPENS A RELIEF FUND. LORD ROBERTS' APPEAL.

AN INFLUENTIAL COMMITTEE.

MID-DEVON WRIT RECEIVED. GREETING TO OTHER CONSTITUENCIES. THE LIBERALS' TASK.

MISSION WORKERS. CLOSING MEETINGS AT LIVERPOOL.

SELF PREPARATION.

THE MOUNT ROYAL RETURNS. LINER'S ABANDONED VOYAGE. THRILLING STORIES.

CREW'S TERRIBLE PLIGHT.

LATE LONDON EDITION.

Will the Millennium Work? Page 10.

Daily Herald

Socialists and Socialism. Page 10.

THE LABOUR DAILY NEWSPAPER.

NO. 234. [REGISTERED AT THE G.P.O. AS A NEWSPAPER.] MONDAY, JANUARY 13, 1913. ONE HALFPENNY.

ASQUITH'S LAST CHANCE.

Will the Premier Speak Now?

WORKING WOMEN'S DEPUTATION.

Why Ministers Must Meet Them.

Our Special Commissioner announces that the leaders of the Cabinet will to-day decide whether the working women's deputation shall be received, and he urges upon the Premier to seize this last chance to make a declaration clearing himself from the charge of complicity in the Cabinet intrigue.

Failing the Premier, declares Our Commissioner, the deputation cannot be expected to accept anyone less than Mr. Lloyd George and Sir Edward Grey as spokesmen of the Government.

The concentration of the many Suffrage Societies into a powerful "middle party" of women is foreshadowed.

Labour and Socialist Societies are urged to bring utmost pressure upon Mr. Redmond and the Irish Whips.

From the "Daily Herald" Special Commissioner.

To-day the leaders of the Cabinet will have to make up their minds whether the working women's deputation organised by the Women's Social and Political Union shall or shall not be received, shall or shall not be given a full hearing and a fair reply. Before Ministers left town on Friday, not only had Members of the Government been sounded, but the Whips had had a good opportunity to ascertain the feeling among the Government's followers. I believe I am not revealing any secret in saying that the general feeling among Members is that this deputation of unenfranchised citizens should be properly received, and given some satisfactory assurance of the Government's intentions.

...

HUNDREDS KILLED.

Cyclone in Madagascar Wrecks a Town.

LINER AND TORPEDO-BOAT SUNK.

The real story of the Madagascar cyclone, which occurred recently, is only told now, on the arrival of news by mail, but it is a thrilling account of wholesale destruction of lives and property.

Three hundred people were killed, hundreds were injured, and the town of Diego Suarez was devastated. A French liner and a torpedo-boat were sunk, and a man-of-war only escaped by beaching in the shelter of a hill.

Many natives were killed at the opening of a Protestant church outside the town, but the Roman Catholic Cathedral practically escaped undamaged. ...

Millerand's Exit.

DREYFUS SEQUEL CAUSES DOWNFALL.

Indignation in Paris.

PARIS, Sunday.

At a meeting of Ministers last night, M. Millerand, Minister for War, again tendered his resignation, and the Cabinet declined to accept it; but at a Council of Ministers to-day, presided over by M. Fallieres, the resignation was accepted.

M. Lebrun, Colonial Minister, goes to the War Department, being replaced at the Colonial Office by M. Rene Besnard, present Under-Secretary of the Treasury, an under-secretaryship which is now dispensed with.

The affair is, of course, due to the reinstatement of Colonel du Paty de Clam, who figured in the *affaire Dreyfus*.—Central News.

Sensation in Paris.

PARIS, Saturday.

LIVES LOST IN GALE.

Ocean Liner's Terrifying Experience.

DUTCH CAPTAIN'S STORY OF A WRECK.

Severe loss of life has taken place as the result of the fierce gale that raged from mid-Atlantic to the North Sea. Seven lives have been lost on the East Coast of Scotland in a wreck, and a passenger on the "Celtic" died through fright at the fierce weather encountered by the liner on her eastward voyage.

Heavy weather is reported all along the coast, and as far south as Portugal several gallant rescues are reported by lifeboat crews.

OUR BIRTHDAY NUMBER.

Daily Herald

No. 312. [REGISTERED AT THE G.P.O. AS A NEWSPAPER.] TUESDAY, APRIL 15, 1913. HALFPENNY.

BELGIUM IN THE THROES OF A NATIONAL STRIKE.

The Rebels of the Coalfield Declare They Will Fight to the Last.

VANDERVELDE'S SPEECH.

Forty Thousand Men Cry "Vive La Greve Generale."

Industry is paralysed in Belgium by the national strike.

Troops are guarding the railways.

It is stated that some of the railway telegraph wires have been cut.

Traders are finding it difficult to supply the people with food.

So many soldiers have been called out for service that balls and other social gatherings have had to be postponed.

The strike is for equal Manhood Suffrage.

(From the "Daily Herald" Special Commissioner.)

BRUSSELS, Monday night.

To-day witnessed the opening of the great struggle for Universal Suffrage.

Already about half of Belgium's workers have downed tools, and to-night should see a big accession to the ranks of the strikers.

Here, in the capital, all is quiet as quiet can be. The trams are running, though how long they will continue nobody knows, and the only obtrusive sign of the upheaval is the presence of armed trops in the streets.

The Belgian Tommy Atkins.

The Belgian soldier is not a very formidable being to look at, it is true—there are only 47,000 of him all told, in times of peace—though he will doubtless do his "duty" if, as their opponents hope, the workers are provoked ...

...

"that the King is perfectly aware of the steps I have taken, and am taking. As to the consequences of my actions, as a constitutional servant of the Crown, I take them all upon myself. I, and I alone, am responsible."

At Brussels there is a complete stoppage in the principal industries, including the carriage and automobile works. It is believed that the movement will gain in force during the week.

TO-DAY'S CONTENTS.

The following are some of the contents of to-day's "Daily Herald":—

FRAGRANCE IN MUFUMBIRO.

Speaking at the Royal Geographical Society, last evening, on "The Mufumbiro Mountains," Capt. E. M. Jack, R.E., caused amusement by declaring that the most marked characteristic of the Batusi race was, generally speaking, a most pronounced and disagreeable smell.

All Bahima and Batusi had a smell, which varied in intensity, and was reminiscent of farmyards and cattle and milk. ...

LANSBURY MAY BE TRIED F_R TREASON.

Government Consider Question of Prosecuting Him for His Albert Hall Speech.

WHAT ABOUT KING CARSON?

Will the Home Office Try the Treason-Mongers in Ulster?

It has been freely stated that the authorities have had under consideration the question of proceeding against Mr. George Lansbury in connection with a speech he delivered in the Albert Hall on Thursday night.

The reports of the speech in the Press vary considerably, but in Friday's DAILY HERALD the following passages were quoted in a special descriptive report of the meeting:—

"Burn and destroy property, do anything you will; but teach the Government that this is a war for something bigger than the vote, a war for human freedom, in which there will be no regard for property of any kind. . . . Every window that is broken, every golf course that is attacked, every race-stand that is burned down, worries them more than hooting every woman that goes to prison is a bigger worry still."

What Lansbury Thinks.

In an interview yesterday George Lansbury said to the DAILY HERALD:—

"You ask me what I think of the statement that the Government are considering the question of prosecuting me for my speech at Albert Hall. Well, I think nothing about it. If they are so foolish as to start another attack on ...

...

BOMB AT THE BANK OF ENGLAND.

Milkcan Discovered Containing Three Ounces of Gunpowder and Some Hairpins.

A great sensation was caused at the Bank of England about three o'clock yesterday afternoon by the discovery by the police of a bomb which had been placed inside the railings at the main entrance to the Bank in Threadneedle-street.

The bomb was in the form of a milk-can which would contain about a pint of fluid.

In it was a large quantity of powder, which was connected with a fuse, communicating at the other end with a time-piece, a small clock or watch.

The bomb was removed to Cloak Lane Police Station.

There have been no arrests, and so far there is no evidence forthcoming as to who is responsible for placing the dangerous bomb in its position.

Smoke From the Milkcan.

About half-past three o'clock a policeman was seen to issue from the doors of the bank holding a milk can in his arms, from which smoke was issuing.

He proceeded to the fountain just in front of the Exchange, and plunged the can into the water, after which he went ...

UNSOLICITED TESTIMONIAL.

Copy of telegram received last night:—

Editor, "Daily Herald," Victoria House, Tudor-street, London, E.C.

Warmest birthday congratulations to "Daily Herald." Have read every number since birth, and could not do without it. Congratulations on the Workers' Daily, from Heraldite.

FRANCES EVELYN WARWICK.

Warwick Castle.

Set to Explode at Midnight.

MRS. PANKHURST HAS RELAPSE.

CHILD BURNED TO DEATH.

Four years later two new dailies, further on the Left, were born. In April 1912 the *Daily Herald* was launched by a committee of trade unionists and socialists in which a leading part was played by Ben Tillett, dockers' leader of 1889, and George Lansbury, just elected MP for the East End constituency of Bow and Bromley. The *Herald* revived the title, and the militancy, of the daily strike sheet issued in 1911 during the fiercely-fought London compositors' dispute. The 'Miracle of Fleet Street' lived from hand to mouth and when war came in August 1914 had to become a weekly, reviving daily publication in 1919; but that, and its sequel, is another story.

The original Lansbury *Herald* did not express its pugnacity in its typography, unless its eschewing of the conventional news titlings should be accounted a radical deviation. It was born a small broadsheet of five columns, with a traditional white-lined blackletter title; for its simple single-column decker headlines it alternated capitals and lower-case of Hawarden, a then popular jobbing face, resembling Cheltenham Bold in cut and colour, but less cleanly drawn.

This headline style did not last many months. By the beginning of 1913 the *Herald* had adopted a headline dress that for those days was positively elegant. It consisted exclusively of Shanks's Plantin, mainly in simple deckers of capitals and lower-case, but also running to double-column headings for the front-page lead, and occasionally even using upper- and lower-case for first decks. Plantin was a misnomer; the type was a modernised old face, broadly inspired by Caslon, cut in 1910 for the Bloomsbury typefounders P. M. Shanks & Sons Ltd by Edward Prince, who had been William Morris's punch-cutter. At this time, too, the paper's title was changed from white-lined to solid blackletter, in a somewhat florid style.

Bigger changes, however, were in store. Before its first birthday in April 1913 the *Herald* had changed to tabloid format. The half-sheet page was small, since the cutoff of its rotaries was only 20½ inches. This yielded a page format of four 12½-pica columns. Make-up was normally all single-column with American-style three- and four-decker headings, alternating gothic condensed capitals (the first deck usually stepped) with a squarer and lighter gothic lower-case. The American note was not surprising, since the then editor, the vehement Charles Lapworth – at the turn of 1913–14 he was sacked, with a £200 payoff, because Lansbury was distressed by his 'hate' spirit – had worked as a journalist in the U.S. Lapworth introduced contributors like Hilaire Belloc and G. K. Chesterton and, above all, the great cartoonist Will Dyson, whose daily drawings had a vitriolic power never equalled in any newspaper anywhere.

Lapworth's tabloid ran a full centre-spread, with a double-column leader (set in 10pt Antique) and a daily column flanking a four-column Dyson cartoon. It also carried one or two picture pages, the coarse halftones, probably 45 or 50 screen, reproducing not badly; blocks were run up to half- or full-page size, as in the two half-page stills from *Quo Vadis*, headed CINEMA FILM THAT COST £50,000 (30 April 1913). By the beginning of 1914, however, the picture pages had gone, no doubt for economic reasons. More often than not, by this time, the paper was only eight pages tabloid – four pages broadsheet equivalent – and the Dyson cartoon was as much as could be managed, alike in terms of space and money.

By January 1914, with Lapworth out, the Dyson cartoon was brought forward to fill the whole of the front page beneath the title, itself appearing in novel form. The blackletter was dropped in favour of a hand-lettered line in roman upper- and lower-case, inserting the definite article, and with something of an *art nouveau* flavour. It was the first lower-case roman line to be used as a British morning paper title – the picture papers apart. Headline style changed back to Plantin, with a distinctly old-world format of three 17-pica columns, though the four-column format was not long in returning for the right-hand news pages.

◀ The *Daily Herald* (January 1913) stylishly dressed in the then new Shanks's Plantin: note the play on upper- and lower-case.

◀ Converted to a tabloid, the *Daily Herald* of the spring of 1913 used decker headlines of obvious American inspiration.

▼ The January 1914 *Daily Herald* filled its front page with a Will Dyson cartoon: the title was changed from blackletter to hand-lettered roman upper- and lower-case.

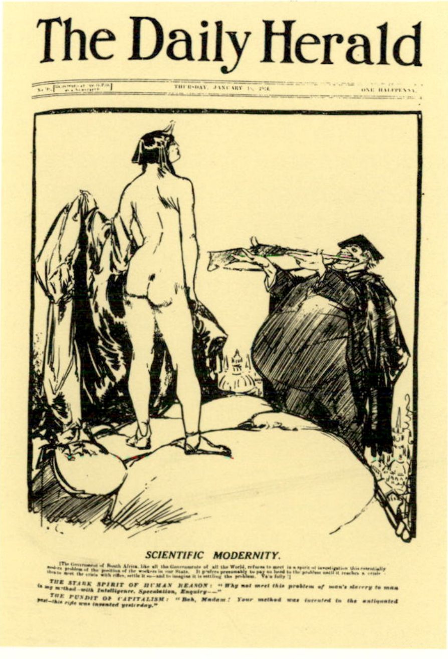

By April 1914 some main headings began to be set double- or three-column, in Plantin capitals; and similarly-set streamers, usually linking the two main inside news pages, appeared. They were slogan or 'thought' lines, not news headings. On 7 May 1914 streamer style was changed to upper- and lower-case (for the first time, so far as I know, in any London daily). This first effort, in 24pt Morland, was a full banner across two pages. It read: *Labour Leaders who Rub against the Golden Calf are Liable to Become Gilded.*

The rebellious and 'unofficial' tone of the *Herald* was displeasing to reigning circles in the Labour movement; and in October 1912 the official *Daily Citizen* was started. It was an eight-page seven-column broadsheet, conventional in aspect, from its blackletter title to its news titling decker headings. It struck no sparks and died in 1915.

GILES AND THE SQUIRE. See Page 4.

The Daily Citizen

THE ILLUSION THAT ENGLAND IS A FREE COUNTRY. See Page 4.

LATE LONDON EDITION.

LONDON. WEDNESDAY, JANUARY 8, 1913. MANCHESTER. ONE HALFPENNY.

LIBERAL SPLIT. MR. LLOYD GEORGE AND LAND. "INTERESTS" IN REVOLT. BAN ON PROMISED CAMPAIGN. CRITICAL SITUATION.

BIRTHDAY OF GREAT SCIENTIST.

FIRM FOR PEACE. POWERS' ATTITUDE ON BALKAN IMPASSE. BEHIND THE SCENES ACTIVITY.

VOYAGE OF TERROR. DESERTION OF TWO CREWS. TUG MANNED BY LANDLUBBERS.

SPRING IN WINTER. ROOKS BUSY AT THEIR NESTS. TOPSY-TURVY CLIMATE.

WEALTH & WANT. STAGGERING TRADE RETURNS. TRAGEDY OF RICHEST NATION'S POOR.

G.O.M. OF SCIENCE. DR. RUSSEL WALLACE 90 TO-DAY.

▸ The official Labour *Daily Citizen* (1912–15) was a conventional presentation in single-column news-titling deckers.

From the end of the Civil War to the turn of the century was a period of intense American newspaper development. It was the era of the mass-circulation, sensational 'Yellow Press', typified in the papers of those ruthless newspaper empire-builders William Randolph Hearst and Joseph Pulitzer. It also saw the growth of powerful dailies in the growing West, like the *Kansas City Star* in the Great Plains and the *Denver Post* in the Rocky Mountains. Hoes were already building rotaries with colour facilities and it was the first colour supplement (in Pulitzer's *New York World* in 1893) that gave rise to the term 'Yellow Press'; the supplement carried a cartoon, the start of a series, captioned 'the Yellow Kid', and printed in that colour.

The late 1870s likewise witnessed the establishment of big-city evenings, like the *St Louis Post-Dispatch* and the *Boston Globe* (a relaunch of a small sheet begun in 1872), which are still powerful and prosperous, when most of their once-mighty metropolitan contemporaries have vanished. The *Post-Dispatch* was the first big newspaper success of Pulitzer, a humble Hungarian immigrant to Missouri, on the strength of which he was able, in the mid-1880s, to move to Manhattan, acquiring the *World*. In their early days both the *Post-Dispatch* and the *Globe* took some advertising in the left-hand columns of their front pages, like the London evenings (except that they were display ads, even double-column display in the *Post-Dispatch*, which argues the early use of a rotary). Pulitzer would run up to four columns of advertising on his seven-column broadsheet front page. For news-display both papers used the already well-established, bold single-column multi-decker.

In newspaper typography this period was one, first, of the simplification and standardisation (better, perhaps, formalisation) of the single-column multi-decker headline and, second, of the institution of the full-page 'banner'. It is only necessary to compare the headlining in *The Sun* of the New York blizzard of 1888 and the sinking of

The Boston Daily Glo

BOSTON, THURSDAY MORNING, MARCH 7, 1878.

NOTICE to SMOKERS

CLOSING SALE. LADIES' LINEN, CAMBRIC & LAWN SUITS. JORDAN, MARSH & CO.

NEW HAMPSHIRE ELECTION. Democratic Prospects Flattering. REPUBLICANS DEJECTED. Favorable Reports from Concord. Legislative Gains Predicted.

RUSSIA AND TURKEY. A Synopsis of the Terms of the Treaty.

WASHINGTON

JORDAN, MARSH & CO. FLANNEL DEPARTMENT. SPRING, 1878.

UNAPPROACHABLE. W. Simmons & Son, Oak Hall, Boston.

▾ The *Boston Globe* of 1878 illustrated the then common U.S. big-evenings' style of splitting the front page between editorial and advertising.

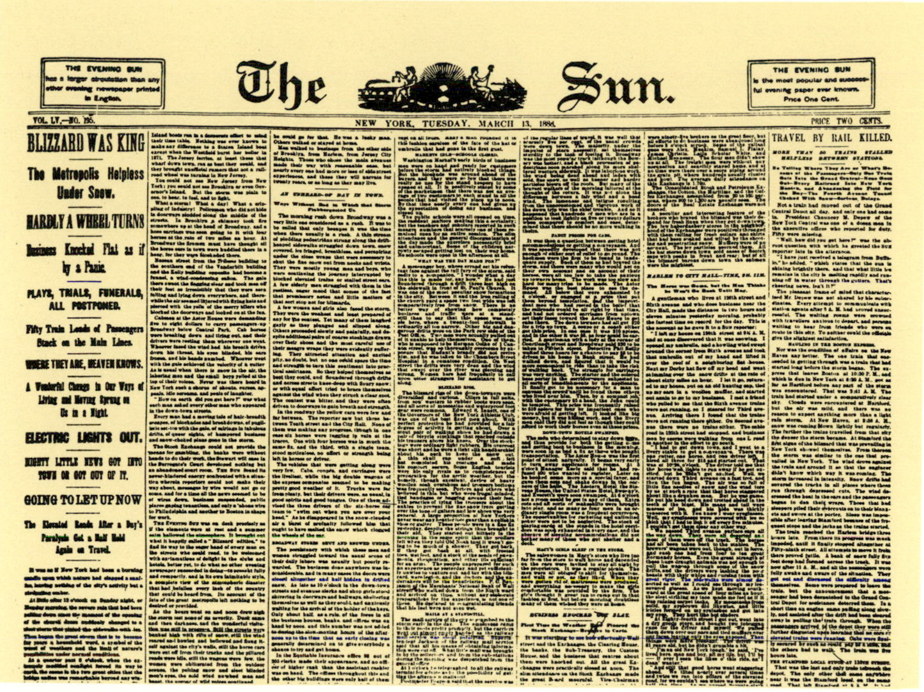

THE EVENING SUN has a larger circulation than any other evening newspaper printed in English.

The Sun.

THE EVENING SUN is the most popular and successful evening paper ever known. Price One Cent.

VOL. LV.—NO. 195. NEW YORK, TUESDAY, MARCH 13, 1888. PRICE TWO CENTS.

BLIZZARD WAS KING

The Metropolis Helpless Under Snow.

HARDLY A WHEEL TURNS

Business Knocked Flat as if by a Panic.

PLAYS, TRIALS, FUNERALS, ALL POSTPONED.

Fifty Train Loads of Passengers Stuck on the Main Lines.

WHERE THEY ARE, HEAVEN KNOWS.

A Wonderful Change in Our Ways of Living and Moving Sprung on Us in a Night.

ELECTRIC LIGHTS OUT.

MIGHTY LITTLE NEWS GOT INTO TOWN OR GOT OUT OF IT.

GOING TO LET UP NOW

The Elevated Roads After a Day's Paralysis Get a Half Hold Again on Travel.

TRAVEL BY RAIL KILLED.

The New York *Sun* (March 1888) showed a front page virtually headless apart from the immense single-column decker lead heading – and that heading a notable typographical jumble.

The Sun.

VOL. LXXIX.—NO. 224. NEW YORK, THURSDAY, APRIL 11, 1912. PRICE TWO CENTS.

TELLS OF RUSE TO GET KNIFE FROM F. O. BEACH

ONLY THE LAW WANTS WILL HOLLY PUNISHED

TITANIC DRAGS LINER FROM HER MOORINGS

TAFT PLATFORM GOES THROUGH

The decker style cleaned-up and formalised, with main lines in closely-stepped News or Headline Gothic capitals: the front page of *The Sun* in April 1912.

the Titanic in 1912 to observe the evolution from a typographic jumble as bad as, if not worse than, the decker headings of Civil War days to a simple but stiff and formal arrangement. Allowing for differences in type selection, this style of decker, suitably reduced or extended in the number and linage of its decks, was long the American standard (and can still be seen in the *New York Times*).

This developed and formalised decker headline put a premium on extra condensed capitals for its opening deck, written to two or three lines, either closely 'stepped' or full out to measure. Bold extra condensed faces, from the Cheltenham or Latin families, could be pressed into service, but suitably narrow sanserifs were the most popular, as *The Sun* example of 1912 shows. Faces of this sort, supplied by the typefounders and composing machine manufacturers, came to be designated news or headline gothics. The structure of these decker headings, both in the close-fitting main deck and the elaborate three-line inverted pyramid upper- and lower-case alternates, called for exceptional skill and care on the part of the headline writer; indeed, the typographic restrictions engendered a special jargon or headlinese language of three- and four-letter words.

San Francisco Chronicle.

VOL. LXVII. SAN FRANCISCO, CAL., WEDNESDAY, FEBRUARY 16, 1898. NO. 32.

BATTLE SHIP MAINE BLOWN UP IN THE HARBOR OF HAVANA.

A Terrific Explosion Rends the Magnificent Machine of War and Brings Death to Hundreds of the Brave Fellows Upon Her.

CAPTAIN SIGSBEE, COMMANDER OF THE MAINE.

Captain Sigsbee, who commanded the battle-ship Maine in Havana harbor, is one of the most trusted officers of the Navy. He has a splendid record, dating from his graduation from Annapolis in 1863, but the incident that brought him the most prominence was his presence of mind in New York harbor last year, when, by the quick handling of his ship, he saved the lives of a thousand river excursionists.

NEW YORK, February 16.—A cable to the World from Havana says: Captain Sigsbee says that one-quarter of his crew of 600 men are dead which is precisely the same estimate as that of Paglierei, Chief of Police of Havana.

Captain Sigsbee says he is not able to state officially the cause of the explosion until he has made an investigation among his officers. He said the magazine was well guarded, usual.

"Tell the American people," he said, "that nearly all the officers are saved."

The ship is lying near the head of the bay. Proof that it was not the magazine only that exploded is shown by the fact that the bow was entirely blown to pieces. The crew are in entire ignorance of the cause of the disaster.

The force of the explosion was something frightful. Part of the marines were taken on board of the Alphonso XII, the crew of which rendered very effective service in saving the lives of the American sailors. Others of the crew were picked up by a Ward Line steamer in the bay. There is much excitement here, but there is no riot and no danger to Americans.

DETAILS OF DISASTER.

A Terrific Explosion That Cost Hundreds of Brave Men Their Lives.

HAVANA, February 15.—At 9:45 o'clock this evening a terrible explosion took place on board the United States cruiser Maine in Havana harbor.

Many sailors were killed or wounded.

The explosion shook the whole city. The windows were broken in many houses.

The wounded sailors of the Maine are unable to explain it. **It is believed that the cruiser is totally destroyed.**

A correspondent says he has conversed with several of the wounded sailors and understands from them that the explosion took place while they were asleep, so that they can give no particulars as to the cause.

All the boats of the Spanish cruiser Alfonso XIII are assisting.

HAVANA, February 16.—**The wildest consternation prevails in Havana. The wharves are crowded with thousands of people.**

It is believed the explosion occurred in a small powder magazine.

The first theory was that there had been a preliminary explosion in the Santa Barbara (magazine) of powder or dynamite below the water.

Admiral Manterola believes that the first explosion was of a grenade that was hurled over the navy yard.

Captain Sigsbee and the other officers have been saved. It is estimated that over 100 of the crew were killed, but it is impossible as yet to give exact details.

Admiral Manterola has ordered that boats of all kinds should go to the assistance of the Maine and her wounded. The Havana firemen are giving aid, tending carefully to the wounded as they are brought on shore. It is a terrible sight.

General Zolano and the other Generals have orders by Captain-General Blanco to take steps to help the Maine's crew in every way possible.

A correspondent has been near the Maine in one of the boats of the cruiser Alfonso and seen others of the wounded, who corroborate the statement of those first interviewed **that they were asleep when the explosion occurred.**

Captain Sigsbee says the explosion occurred in the bow of the vessel. He received a wound in the head. Orders were given to the other officers to save themselves as best they could. The latter, who were literally thrown from their bunks in their night clothing, gave the necessary orders with great self-control.

At 1:15 the Maine continues burning.

THE NEWS IN WASHINGTON.

WASHINGTON, February 15.—The Secretary of the Navy received the following telegram from Captain Sigsbee:

Maine blown up in Havana harbor at 9:40 and destroyed. Many wounded and doubtless many killed and drowned. The wounded and others are on board a Spanish man-of-war and the Ward line steamer.

Send lighthouse tender from Key West for crew and the few pieces of equipment still above water. No one saved other clothes than those upon him.

Public opinion should be suspended until a further report. All officers believed to be saved. Jenkins and Merritt not yet accounted for.

Many Spanish officers, including representatives of General Blanco, now with me, express sympathy.

SIGSBEE.

The officers referred to in the above dispatch are Lieutenant

BATTLE SHIP MAINE BLOWN UP IN HAVANA.

OFFICERS OF THE MAINE

The Men Who Had Charge of the Splendid Warship Destroyed in Havana Harbor.

The officers of the Maine are:
CHARLES D. SIGSBEE, Commander.
RICHARD WAINWRIGHT, Lieutenant-Commander.
G. F. HOLMAN, Lieutenant.
JOHN HOOD, Lieutenant.
C. W. YUNGEN, Lieutenant.
C. W. BLOW, Lieutenant (junior grade.)
J. T. BLANDIN, Lieutenant (junior grade.)
F. A. JENKINS, Lieutenant (junior grade.)
J. H. HOLDEN, Cadet.
W. T. CLUVERIUS, Cadet.
AMOS BRONSON, Cadet.
D. F. BOYD Jr., Cadet.
L. G. HENEBERGER, Surgeon.
RYAN, Paymaster.
L. G. HOWELL, Chief Engineer.
E. C. BOWERS, Passed Assistant Engineer.
J. R. MORRIS, Assistant Engineer.
D. R. MERRITT, Assistant Engineer.
POPE, Cadet Engineer.
WASHINGTON, Cadet Engineer.
ARTHUR. GRENSHAW, Cadet Engineer.
J. P. CHADWICK, Chaplain.
A. W. CATLIN, Lieutenant of Marines.
FRANCIS E. LARKINS, Boatswain.
JOSEPH HILL, Gunner.
GEORGE HELMS, Carpenter.

The Harbor of Havana, in Which the Maine Was Destroyed.

MORRO CASTLE, HAVANA HARBOR

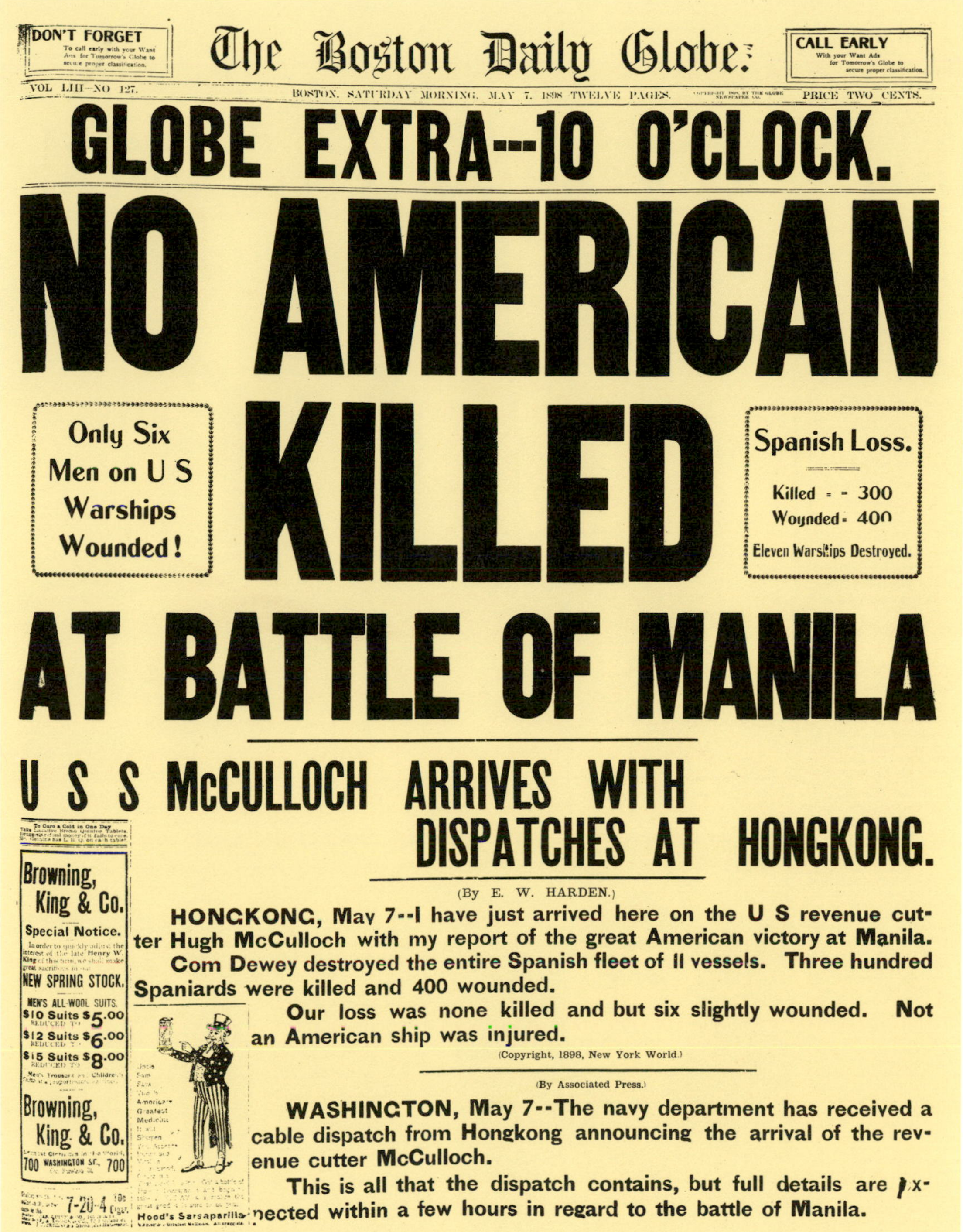

DON'T FORGET
To call early with your Want Ads for Tomorrow's Globe to secure proper classification.

The Boston Daily Globe.

CALL EARLY
With your Want Ads for Tomorrow's Globe to secure proper classification.

VOL LIII—NO 127. BOSTON, SATURDAY MORNING, MAY 7, 1898 TWELVE PAGES. PRICE TWO CENTS.

GLOBE EXTRA—10 O'CLOCK.

NO AMERICAN KILLED AT BATTLE OF MANILA

Only Six Men on U S Warships Wounded!

Spanish Loss.
Killed - - 300
Wounded - 400
Eleven Warships Destroyed.

U S S McCULLOCH ARRIVES WITH DISPATCHES AT HONGKONG.

(By E. W. HARDEN.)

HONGKONG, May 7—I have just arrived here on the U S revenue cutter Hugh McCulloch with my report of the great American victory at Manila.

Com Dewey destroyed the entire Spanish fleet of 11 vessels. Three hundred Spaniards were killed and 400 wounded.

Our loss was none killed and but six slightly wounded. Not an American ship was injured.

(Copyright, 1898, New York World.)

(By Associated Press.)

WASHINGTON, May 7—The navy department has received a cable dispatch from Hongkong announcing the arrival of the revenue cutter McCulloch.

This is all that the dispatch contains, but full details are expected within a few hours in regard to the battle of Manila.

How the banner could be made a poster: the *Boston Globe* reporting the capture of Manila in 1898.

The early banners were not always in sledgehammer gothics: this 1898 De Vinne Condensed style from the *San Francisco Chronicle* was not untypical.

The banner, a full-page heading usually (but not always) in large sans capitals, was a war product; or rather, initially, a warmongering product. When Hearst, fresh from his Pacific Coast blooding with the *San Francisco Examiner* (casually acquired by his millionaire father), bought the New York *Journal* in the mid-1890s, he set about whipping up anti-Spanish feeling and thus provoking the Spanish-American War of 1898. In pursuit of this campaign during 1897 the *Journal* ran its first banners. When the USS *Maine* was mysteriously sunk in Havana harbour the Hearst *Journal* bannered the incident into a casus belli – WARSHIP MAINE SPLIT IN TWO BY ENEMY'S SECRET INFERNAL MACHINE and the next day WHOLE COUNTRY THRILLS WITH WAR FEVER. The final victory at Manila, in the Philippines, turned the banner into a poster; the *Journal* took half its front page with the words MANILA OURS, and in Boston the front page of the *Globe* was even more imposing. The banner had made its entrance, though another and greater war was needed to make it a permanent, every day feature of American front-page make-up.

"All the News That's Fit to Print."

The New York Times.

THE WEATHER.
Unsettled Tuesday; Wednesday, fair, cooler; moderate southerly winds, becoming variable.
For full weather report see Page 23.

VOL. LXI...NO. 19,886. NEW YORK, TUESDAY, APRIL 16, 1912.—TWENTY-FOUR PAGES, ONE CENT In Greater New York, Jersey City, and Newark. | Elsewhere, TWO CENTS.

TITANIC SINKS FOUR HOURS AFTER HITTING ICEBERG; 866 RESCUED BY CARPATHIA, PROBABLY 1250 PERISH; ISMAY SAFE, MRS. ASTOR MAYBE, NOTED NAMES MISSING

Col. Astor and Bride, Isidor Straus and Wife, and Maj. Butt Aboard.

"RULE OF SEA" FOLLOWED

Women and Children Put Over in Lifeboats and Are Supposed to be Safe on Carpathia.

PICKED UP AFTER 8 HOURS

Vincent Astor Calls at White Star Office for News of His Father and Leaves Weeping.

FRANKLIN HOPEFUL ALL DAY

Manager of the Line Insisted Titanic Was Unsinkable Even After She Had Gone Down.

HEAD OF THE LINE ABOARD

J. Bruce Ismay Making First Trip on Gigantic Ship That Was to Surpass All Others.

The admission that the Titanic, the biggest steamship in the world, had been sunk by an iceberg and had gone to the bottom of the Atlantic, probably carrying more than 1,400 of her passengers and crew with her, was made at the White Star Line offices, 9 Broadway, at 8:20 o'clock last night. Then P. A. S. Franklin, Vice President and General Manager of the International Mercantile Marine, conceded that probably only those passengers who were picked up by the Cunarder Carpathia had been saved. Advices received early this morning tended to increase the number of survivers by 200.

The admission followed a day in which the White Star Line officials had been optimistic in the extreme. At no time was the admission made that every one aboard the huge steamer was not safe. The ship itself, it was confidently asserted, was unsinkable, and inquirers were informed that she would reach port, under her own steam probably, but surely with the help of the Allan liner Virginian, which was reported to be towing her.

As the day passed, however, with no new authentic reports from the Titanic or any of the ships which were known to have responded to her wireless call for help, it became apparent that authentic news of the disaster probably could come only from the Titanic's sister ship, the Olympic. The wireless range of the Olympic is 500 miles. That of the Carpathia, the Parisian, and the Virginian is much less, and as they neared the position of the Titanic they drew further and further out of shore range. From the Titanic's position at the time of the disaster it is doubtful if any of the ships except the Olympic could establish communication with shore.

Titanic Sank at 2:20 A. M. Monday.

In the White Star offices the hope was held out all day that the Parisian and the Virginian had taken off some of the Titanic's passengers, and efforts were made to get into communication with these liners. Until such communication was established the White Star officials refused to recognize the possibility that there were none of the Titanic's passengers aboard them.

But by nightfall came the message from Capt. Haddock of the Olympic to Cape Race, Newfoundland, telling of the foundering of the Titanic and of the rescue of 655 of her passengers by the Cunarder Carpathia, which, the wireless message said, reached the position of the Titanic at daybreak. All they found there, however, was lifeboats and wreckage. The biggest ship in the world had sunk at 2:20 o'clock yesterday morning.

Mr. Franklin admitted late last night that the Parisian and the Virginian, though they were among the first to answer the Titanic's calls for help, could not have reached the scene before 10 o'clock yesterday morning, seven and a half hours after the big Titanic buried her nose beneath the waves and pitched downward out of sight. The Carpathia, so the wireless dispatch from Capt. Haddock to Cape Race announced, reached the scene of the Titanic's foundering at daybreak, several hours before the expected arrival of the Virginian and the Parisian.

1,488 Lives Lost First Report.

It is unbelievable, so White Star Line officials were compelled to concede finally, that the Carpathia should have failed to pick up every lifeboat which still floated on the waves. If they failed to pick up more than 655 passengers, it was because the others of the ship's complement had gone with her to the bottom.

But it was not until nearly nightfall that the extent of the disaster was realized. Before that the reassuring nature of the bulletins issued by the White Star line was sufficient to quiet the fears of those who had relatives or friends aboard the unfortunate ship and to prevent widespread belief in a serious disaster.

Capt. Haddock's message from the Olympic, which is printed in another column of THE TIMES, strongly indicated that none but the 655 taken from life boats by the Carpathia had been saved. This message was relayed immediately to the White Star offices, but Mr. Franklin positively declined to make the text of the message public. He offered still the hope that passengers were aboard the Parisian and the Virginian, and even when the admission was wrung from him that there seemed little hope of the saving of any others than the 655 aboard the Carpathia, he clung to the hope that in some unexplained way there were other passengers abroad the two Allan liners.

First Reported Titanic in Tow.

Throughout the day there had been reassurances that the Titanic was being towed to port by the Virginian, and when Capt. Haddock's message proved this to be untrue only the admission was made at the White Star offices that the Titanic had sunk. Mr. Franklin said that Capt. Haddock's message was brief and "neglected to say that all the crew had been saved." But the inference was not that all the passengers had been saved. Rather it was that many of them had died, and presently Mr. Franklin admitted the fear that there had been a terrible loss of life on the Titanic.

This version of Capt. Haddock's wireless had been given at the White Star offices:

Capt. Haddock of the Olympic sends a wireless message to the White Star offices here that the steamer Titanic sank at 2:20 A. M., after all the passengers and crew had been lowered to life boats and transferred to the Virginian. The steamship Carpathia, with several hundred passengers of the Titanic, is now en route to New York.

At 9 o'clock, however, he modified this statement, declaring:

As far as we know the situation, there have been rumors from Halifax that three steamers were at the scene of the Titanic's sinking, namely, the Virginian, the Parisian, and the Carpathia. We have heard from Capt. Haddock of the Olympic, who says that the Titanic sank at 2:20 o'clock this morning. Haddock also informs us that the Carpathia has 675 survivors on board. It is very difficult to say whether the Virginian and the Parisian have any survivors on board until we can get a report from those vessels.

Fears Serious Loss of Life.

We have asked for that report from Capt. Haddock, and we are expecting a reply at any time. The Carpathia is proceeding to New York direct. We very much fear that there has been serious loss of life, but it is impossible for us to say definitely concerning this end part of the situation until we are able to reassure ourselves whether or not any of the Titanic's passengers are aboard the Allan liners.

We are hopeful that the rumors which have reached us by telegraph from Halifax that there are passengers aboard the Virginian and the Parisian will prove to be true, and that these vessels will turn up with some of the passengers. It is the loss of life that makes this thing so awful. We can replace the money loss, but not the lives of those who went down.

Another version of the message from the Olympic was current last night and included the sentence: "Loss likely total 1,800 souls." This sentence was not in the message received by THE TIMES from Cape Race nor in that sent to the White Star line offices.

Continued on Page 2.

The Lost Titanic Being Towed Out of Belfast Harbor.

CAPT. E. J. SMITH,
Commander of the Titanic.

THE PROBABLE LOSS.

Number Aboard.	
First cabin	325
Second cabin	285
Steerage	710
Crew, (estimated)	800
Total	2,120
Saved.	
By the Carpathia	866
Probably drowned	1,254

PARTIAL LIST OF THE SAVED.

Includes Bruce Ismay, Mrs. Widener, Mrs. H. B. Harris, and an Incomplete name, suggesting Mrs. Astor's.

Special to The New York Times.

CAPE RACE, N. F., Tuesday, April 16.—Following is a partial list of survivors among the first-class passengers of the Titanic, received by the Marconi wireless station this morning from the Carpathia, via the steapship Olympic:

Mrs. JACOB P. ——— and maid.
Mr. HARRY ANDERSON.
Mrs. ED. W. APPLETON.
Mrs. ROSE ABBOTT.
Miss G. M. BURNS.
Miss D. D. CASSEBERE.
Mrs. WM. M. CLARKE.
Mrs. B. CHIBINACE.
Miss E. G. CROSSBIE.
Miss H. ROSEBIE.
Miss JEAN HIPACK.
Mrs. HY. B. HARRIS.
Mrs. ALEX. HALVERSON.
Miss MARGARET BAYS
Mr. BRUCE ISMAY.
Mr. and Mrs. ED. KIMBERLEY.
Mr. F. A. KENNYMAN.
Miss EMILE KENCHEN.
Miss G. F. LONGLEY.
Mrs. A. F. LEADER.
Miss BERTHA LAVORY.
Mrs. ERNEST LIVES.
Miss MARY CLINES.
Mrs. SINGRID LINDSTROM.
Mr. GUSTAVE J. LESNEUR.
Miss GIORGETTA A. MADILL.
Mme. MELICARD.
Mrs. TUCKER and maid.
Mrs. J. B. THAYER.
Mr. J. B. THAYER, Jr.
Mr. HENRY WOOLMER.
Miss ANNA WARD.
Mr. RICHARD M. WILLIAMS.
Mrs. F. M. WARNER.
Miss HELEN A. WILSON.
Miss WILLARD.
Miss MARY WICKS.
Mrs. GEO. D. WIDENER and maid.
Mrs. J. STEWART WHITE.
Miss MARIE YOUNG.
Mrs. THOMAS POTTER, Jr.
Mrs. EDNA S. ROBERTS.
Countess of ROTHES.
Mr. C. ROLMANE.
Mrs. SUSAN P. ROGERSON. (Probably Ryerson).
Miss EMILY B. ROGERSON.
Mrs. ARTHUR ROGERSON.
Master ALLISON and nurse.
Miss K. T. ANDREWS.
Miss NINETTE PANHART.
Miss E. W. ALLEN.
Mr. and Mrs. D. BISHOP.
Mr. H. BLANK.
Miss A. BASSINA.
Mrs. JAMES BAXTER.
Mr. GEORGE A. BAYTON.
Miss C. BONNELL.
Mrs. J. M. BROWN.
Miss G. C. BOWEN.
Mr. and Mrs. R. L. BECKWITH.
Miss RUTH TAUSSIG.
Miss ELLA THOR.
Mr. and Mrs. E. Z. TAYLOR.
GILBERT M. TUCKER.
Mr. J. B. THAYER.
Mr. JOHN B. ROGERSON.
Mrs. M. ROTHSCHILD.
Miss MADELEINE NEWELL.
Mrs. MARJORIE NEWELL.
HELEN W. NEWSOM.
Mr. FIENNAD OMOND.
Mr. E. C. OSTBY.
Miss HELEN R. OSTBY.
Mrs. MAMAM J. RENAGO.
Mlle. OLIVIA.
Mrs. D. W. MERVIN.
Mr. PHILIP EMOCK.
Mr. JAMES GOOGHT.
Miss RUBERTA MAIMY.
Mr. PIERRE MARECHAL.
Mrs. W. E. MINEHAN.
Miss APPIE RANELT.
Major ARTUR PEUCHEN.
Mrs. KARL H. BEHR.
Miss DESSETTE.
Mrs. WILLIAM BUCKNELL.
Mrs. O. H. BARKWORTH.
Mrs. H. B. STEFFASON.
Mrs. ELSIE BOWERMAN.

The Marconi station reports that it missed the word after "Mrs. Jacob P." In a list received by the Associated Press this morning this name appeared well down, but in THE TIMES list it is first, suggesting that the name of Mrs. John Jacob Astor is intended. This supposition is strengthened by the fact that, except for Mrs. H. J. Allison, Mrs. Astor is the only lady in the "A" column of the ship's pasenger list attended by a maid.

NAMES PICKED UP AT BOSTON.

BOSTON, April 15.—Among the names of survivors of the Titanic picked up by wireless from the steamer Carpathia here to-night were the following:

Mr. and Mrs. L. HENRY.
Mrs. W. A. HOOPER.
Mr. MILE.
Mr. J. FLYNN.
Miss ALICE FORTUNE.
Mrs. ROBERT DOUGLAS.
Miss HILDA SLAYTER.
Mrs. P. SMITH.
Mrs. BRAHAM.
Miss LUCILLE CARTER.
Mr. WILLIAM CARTER.
Miss CUMMINGS.
Mrs. FLORENCE MARE.
Miss ALICE PHILLIPS.
Mrs. PAULA MUNGE.
Mrs. JANE ———
Miss PHYLLIS O. ———
HOWARD B. CASE.
Miss MINEHAN.
Miss BERTHA ———

Biggest Liner Plunges to the Bottom at 2:20 A. M.

RESCUERS THERE TOO LATE

Except to Pick Up the Few Hundreds Who Took to the Lifeboats.

WOMEN AND CHILDREN FIRST

Cunarder Carpathia Rushing to New York with the Survivors.

SEA SEARCH FOR OTHERS

The California Stands By on Chance of Picking Up Other Boats or Rafts.

OLYMPIC SENDS THE NEWS

Only Ship to Flash Wireless Messages to Shore After the Disaster.

LATER REPORT SAVES 866.

BOSTON, April 15.—A wireless message picked up late to-night, relayed from the Olympic, says that the Carpathia is on her way to New York with 866 passengers from the steamer Titanic aboard. They are mostly women and children, the message said, and it concluded: "Grave fears are felt for the safety of the balance of the passengers and crew."

Special to The New York Times.

CAPE RACE, N. F., April 15.—The White Star liner Olympic reports by wireless this evening that the Cunarder Carpathia reached, at daybreak this morning, the position from which wireless calls for help were sent out last night by the Titanic after her collision with an iceberg. The Carpathia found only the lifeboats and the wreckage of what had been the biggest steamship afloat.

The Titanic had foundered at about 2:20 A. M., in latitude 41:16 north and longitude 50:14 west. This is about 30 minutes of latitude, or about 34 miles, due south of the position at which she struck the iceberg. All her boats are accounted for and about 655 souls have been saved of the crew and passengers, most of the latter presumably women and children.

There were about 2,100 persons aboard the Titanic.

The Leyland liner California is remaining and searching the position of the disaster, while the Carpathia is returning to New York with the survivors.

It can be positively stated that up to 11 o'clock to-night nothing whatever had been received at or heard by the Marconi station here to the effect that the Parisian, Virginian or any other ships had picked up any survivors, other than those picked up by the Carpathia.

First News of the Disaster.

The first news of the disaster to the Titanic was received by the Marconi wireless station here at 10:25 o'clock last night [as told in yesterday's New York Times.] The Titanic was first heard giving the distress signal "C. Q. D.," which was answered by a number of ships, including the Carpathia,

All American newspapers during this period adopted the formalised decker headline but not all followed the path of Hearst/Pulitzer sensationalism. The outstanding example was the *New York Times*, which in those days was far indeed from being the imperishable institution we know today. When Adolph S. Ochs, a successful young publisher from Chattanooga (Tennessee) bought the *Times* in 1896 its circulation was 9,000. Hearst's *Journal* had 385,000, Pulitzer's *World* 370,000. Ochs proved himself a publisher of genius; with the famous slogan 'All the News that's Fit to Print', and a price reduction from three cents to a cent, he boosted the circulation to 75,000 before the end of the century; by the First World War the *Times* was on the quarter-million mark. By 1912 the basic style of *New York Times* headlining, as it continues today, had been settled; the later introduction of double-column headings and very occasional banners (always in restrained typography) does not invalidate the significance of the general point, which is without precedent in twentieth-century journalism.

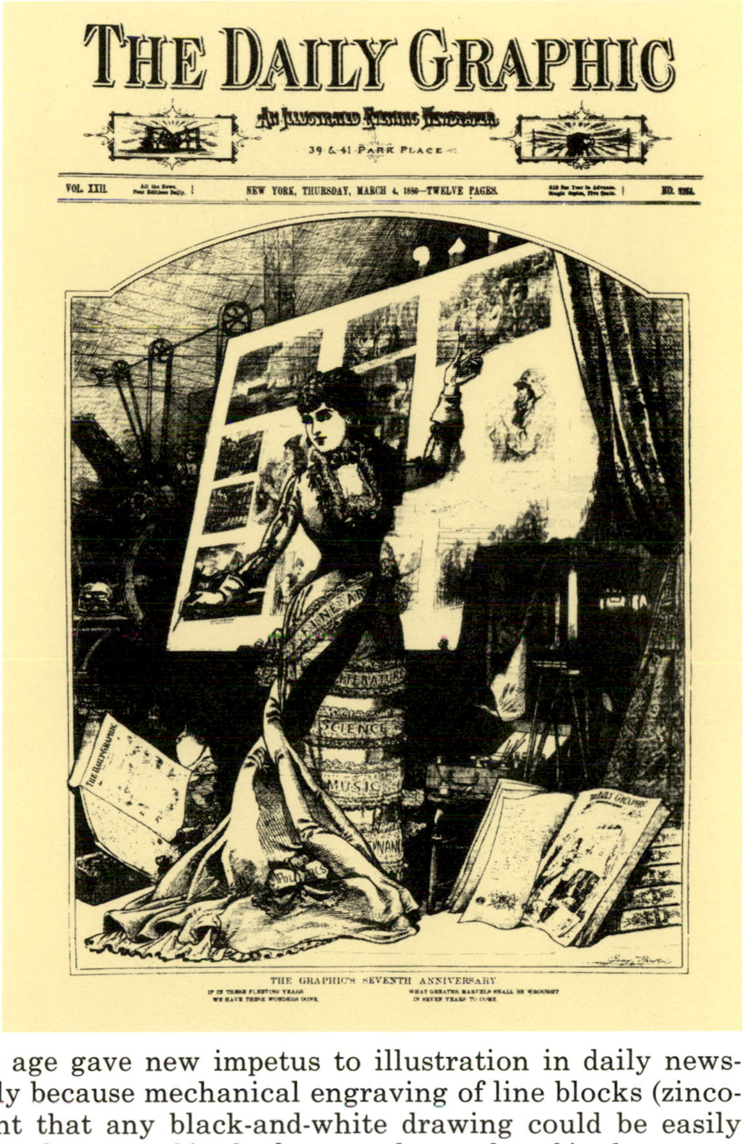
THE DAILY GRAPHIC
39 & 41 PARK PLACE
VOL. XXII. NEW YORK, THURSDAY, MARCH 4, 1880—TWELVE PAGES.
THE GRAPHIC'S SEVENTH ANNIVERSARY

▸ The New York *Daily Graphic* (1880), credited with being the first paper to run a halftone illustration.

◂ The Titanic disaster of 1912 found the *New York Times* with its decker style well established: the only subsequent change was to Latin Condensed for first decks. Note the restrained Cheltenham Bold multi-line banner and (for those days) the imposing halftone display.

The rotary age gave new impetus to illustration in daily newspapers, largely because mechanical engraving of line blocks (zincography) meant that any black-and-white drawing could be easily rendered in metal, mounted in the forme and reproduced in the stereoplates for the rotary presses. The slow hand process of wood-engraving, with the subsequent need to make electrotypes for the actual printing, was no longer necessary. In London Stead and Massingham were editors who pioneered line-illustration in their papers, using graphic artists of the standing of Joseph Pennell or cartoonists like Phil May.

On both sides of the Atlantic, too, daily papers specialising in illustration, and describing themselves as 'illustrated papers', began to develop. As it happens the pioneer in this sphere, the *Daily Graphic* of New York (1873–1884), used neither letterpress zincos nor web-fed rotary printing. The four of its eight pages devoted to illustrations were printed by a photo-lithographic process on lithographic presses direct from the stone; this must have been very slow, though the quality of reproduction of the drawings was very fine. Clearly these four picture pages must have been worked off first, and early. The sheets were then run through a Hoe type-revolver to complete the four news pages; there were three to four editions daily. Printed on an all-rag paper, the *Graphic* was a quality product and must have had a limited sale. Its cover price was five cents, a high figure for those days.[4]

The *Graphic's* photo-lithographic speciality limits the newspaper significance of its claim to have printed the first halftone illustration – the 'Shantytown' photograph reproduced in its issue of 4 March 1880. A straight-line halftone – the cross-line screen came later – this was the work of Stephen H. Horgan, an engraver on the *Graphic*, who is also credited with engraving the first halftone, cross-line screen, to

THE EVENING ILLUSTRATED NEWSPAPER.

No. 1.] LONDON, WEDNESDAY, OCTOBER 26, 1881. [ONE PENNY.

YORKTOWN CELEBRATION.—THE PARLEY PREVIOUS TO SURRENDER.

London's *Evening Illustrated Paper* (1881), which reproduced in line only.

be plated and printed in the normal way on a newspaper rotary (the *New York Tribune* in 1897). All these halftone priority claims have been contested but the controversy is a sterile one; the fact is that at that stage in newspaper printing techniques effective reproduction of halftones under normal rotary running conditions was not possible. Line-drawings were the only wear for London's curious *Evening Illustrated Paper* (1881) and even when photographs of big events were available they had to be re-drawn in line. Quite a technique developed in this connection. At the turn of the century the *Morning Leader* (absorbed in 1912 by the *Daily News*) was able to boast that it was thus able to have in the forme by 1 a.m. a double-column line block of the Grand National winner, of which a photo-still had only been 'received from the Bioscope News Reel at 11.5 p.m.'

THE DAILY GRAPHIC

An Illustrated Newspaper.

No. 1. LONDON, SATURDAY, JANUARY 4, 1890. [PRICE ONE PENNY.

The Weather.

"DULL AND DAMP."

PROSPECTS FOR TO-DAY.

Districts.		Forecasts.
1. Scotland,	N.	Southerly winds, fresh or strong; rain at times.
1. Do.	E.	South-easterly and southerly winds, light or moderate: fair, but damp, to rainy.
2. England,	N.E.	Same as No. 1.
3. Do.	E.	
4. Midland Counties,		
5. England, (London & Channel).	S.	South-easterly winds, moderate; dull and damp, perhaps rain later.
6. Scotland, (and Isle of Man).	W.	Southerly winds, fresh; rain at times. Wind shifting north-westward later.
7. England, (and N. Wales).	N.W.	Same as No. 6.
8. England, (and S. Wales).	S.W.	
9. Ireland,	N.	Very variable breezes; dull, rainy, unsettled.
10. Do.	S.	—Same as No. 9.

THE FOREST GATE FIRE.

A VISIT TO THE SCENE.

(BY OUR ARTIST COMMISSIONER.)

Even so late as Thursday evening a striking testimony was borne to the extent to which the calamity at Forest Gate is felt by individuals not directly connected with it. A large crowd of people, mostly of the poorer class, lingered long after the gates had been closed to interrogate and sympathise with those relations and friends of the children who from time to time issued from the building, and even the policemen at the gates were subjected to constant and eager inquiry. The presence of the crowd was the more striking because from the entrance gates there is so little to see; for the wards which were burnt form so slight a portion of the whole of the buildings as to be almost invisible from that point of view. The bodies, after the fire, were removed to an outbuilding, which is itself a ward. At one end of a passage in this outbuilding is a square room, whose schoolroom-like walls are gaily decorated with coloured pictures and prints, such as are dear to the hearts of children; and on the floor, lightly covered with blankets, are the little lifeless bodies. Their faces, in nearly every instance are discoloured; but, except in one sad case, where the arms are raised above the head, as in defence, there is no other visible evidence of the nature of their death, and we may happily believe that at least death was painless. So quiet and peaceful does one little fellow look, that, with the flickering gaslight to aid the illusion, one can fancy him asleep. And the contrast to this sad scene is that, at the other end of the passage, there is a corresponding room, with pictures on its walls, too, and children there, but alive, and happy and merry. Everywhere, indeed, there is this sad incongruity; and even in the entrance-hall, where, during the last few days, so many grief-stricken parents have waited to identify the victims, there still remain the mottoes with their good wishes of happiness for the New Year.

The Coroner's inquest was held on Thursday, in the Girls' Schoolroom, and the jury adjourned thence to the mortuary, so that there was no repetition of the painful scenes which attended the identification of the bodies by the parents; but, nevertheless, the sobs of some of the mothers, as their children's names were called out, rendered the occasion very saddening, formal as the inquiries were.

Of the origin of the fire there is no certain information, but it is supposed that it occurred from the over-heating of a stove-pipe, which ran from the basement of the building in which the fire took place, through the two dormitories above. This building is separate from the main structure, and is of three storeys. The first contains a needle-room and a wardrobe-room, in which the stove was situated; the second a dormitory, in which forty boys slept; and the third another dormitory, in which fifty-four boys slept. It seems that the first signs of fire were discovered by Miss Bloomfield, who slept on the ground floor of the building, shortly after twelve o'clock, when the bells would be ringing in the New Year. She awoke her colleague, Miss Terry, who slept in the room above, and Miss Terry in turn alarmed the whole house. The doors of the dormitories were locked, and in this circumstance lay the great danger of the situation. Mr. Duncan, the superintendent, was soon on the spot, and, with an extincteur on his back, succeeded in forcing his way to the door of the lower dormitory before he was overpowered by the thick smoke and fell downstairs. Mr. Duncan's heroic efforts to reach the children were seconded by the men connected with the building, and by the firemen who drove up soon after the alarm had been given. The suffocating density of the smoke, however, made it impossible to penetrate into the dormitory very far, and, to the unfortunate children in the remote corners of the room, no help could be carried. When the flames were subdued—and this was effected in a comparatively short time—it was found that 14 out of the 40 sleepers had perished. In the upper dormitory the tale of death, though heavy, was not so grave as that in the lower dormitory, only 12 out of 54 boys losing their lives. That this was so is due largely to the presence of mind of George Hare, a young man of twenty-two, who slept in a room adjoining the dormitory. Both rooms were already full of smoke when he was awakened by the cries of the boys. Turning to the main staircase, which leads to the dining-room, he found the smoke so dense that he was obliged to shut the door again between the dormitory and the stairs. But there was another staircase at the opposite end of the room leading into the yard, and to this he immediately ran, driving some boys before him, and calling to others to follow him. Happily the door at the bottom of the stairs had already been burst open, and the boys whom he had succeeded in taking with him thus found themselves beyond all danger at once. Groping his way back to the dormitory, he carried and led more of the boys into safety, and when all had thus been brought out, quick and dead together, the energetic young man ran to render assistance in another part of the building. At one end of the upper dormitory two of the female servants slept. Suddenly awaking to their peril, and seeing no help at hand, one of them with daring readiness climbed down the water-spout, while the other in desperation jumped from the window, being fortunate enough only to break her ankle. The boys themselves do not seem to have been awakened until the fire had made some progress, and even then they were slow to realise their extreme peril. Upon some the smoke seems to have exercised a stupefying effect, and, as far as can be gathered from the narratives of survivors, not only did they make no effort to save themselves, but actually declined to be saved. Many exhibited a curious anxiety about their belongings, one lad being smothered by the smoke while putting on his socks. Another lad of 12 succeeded in rescuing not only himself, but also his clothes basket which stood beneath his bed. Several of the boys, whose ages range between 6 and 12, showed great courage and disregard of their personal safety in helping their weaker comrades.

By three o'clock in the morning the fire was well in hand. All danger of its spreading was at an end, and then arose the terrible question, how many were missing? In the middle of the night, with the New Year but three hours old, the still terrified and excited lads were gathered together as well as might be, and the roll was called. Of the 64 names pronounced by Mr. Duncan, only 38 brought the customary response. Of those missing, two were found alive and well in the morning, but the remaining 24 would never answer to any roll call again on earth.

The news of the disaster, like all evil tidings, spread rapidly, and early in the morning many inquiries were made as to the names of the victims. From the fact that the inmates of the schools come from Whitechapel and Poplar, it was impossible that their nearest relatives should come so early, but by noon the doors of the institution were besieged by a pathetic crowd of anxious parents and friends, eagerly inquiring after those dearest to them. Far too many there were whose fears were confirmed, painful uncertainty being only changed for still more painful certainty; but if anything could relieve the terrible impressiveness of the scene, it was the joyful faces of those mothers who learnt that their children were spared to them. But a still more painful scene had yet to be enacted when the bodies came to be identified. The flames and the smoke had so charred and disfigured the bodies of some who had failed to escape from the fatal dormitories that it was impossible to distinguish them further than by a number; this circumstance adding another burden of grief to those who had already more than they could well bear.

It should be mentioned that great assistance was rendered to the firemen and schoolroom officials in the suppression of the fire by some men employed on the Great Eastern Railway, who happened to be passing when the alarm was given. That every effort was made to lessen the fatal character of the disaster evidence from all quarters unanimously shows. Mr. Duncan who himself did so much in rescuing the lads who slept in the lower dormitory, has had the burden of the terrible calamity, which one in his responsible position must specially feel, lightened by a pile of letters congratulating and thanking him for his conduct in the hour of peril. The closing act of this tragedy—the first event which the New Year has brought us—will take place on Monday at the West Ham Cemetery, when the bodies of the twenty-six children whose names are contained in the list of the dead will be interred together.

WHERE THE FIRE BROKE OUT.

THE BURNT-OUT DORMITORY.

THE FIRST ALARM.

THE ROLL CALL.

The *Daily Graphic* (London) mainly used line illustrations but in 1891 ran the first halftone photograph to appear in a British newspaper.

Early use of halftone blocks in daily publication was exceptional. The London *Daily Graphic*, a line-illustrated paper founded in 1890, printed its first halftone, a single-column portrait, the following year. But this was not in a normal newspaper rotary run. It was a *tour de force*; the process, though no technical account has survived, was said to be 'cumbersome' and slow. Elsewhere I have hazarded guesses as to what might have been the *Graphic's* procedure – either the sticking of a curved, thin original zinco on to a blank in the stereo-plate (a process patented by the *Bradford Telegraph* in 1883) or the use of the 'halftone press' then made by Hoe, a slow machine printing from curved electrotypes, with a separate reel running-in a blank setoff sheet.[5]

The real breakthrough to effective halftone reproduction in ordi-

THE DAY'S NEWS IN PHOTOGRAPHS—SEE PAGES 8 & 9.

The Daily ILLUSTRATED Mirror.

News in Photographs. See Pages 8 & 9.

News in Photographs. See Pages 8 & 9.

No. 71. Registered at the G. P. O. as a Newspaper. MONDAY, JANUARY 25, 1904. One Penny.

A CHARMING PHOTOGRAPH OF MISS MARIE STUDHOLME.

Photo by] The talented young actress who is playing one of the principal parts in "The Orchid" at the Gaiety Theatre. [Downey.

The "Daily Mirror," January 7, 1904.

LEAMINGTON AGAIN WINS THE RADIUM. See Page 6.

The Daily Mirror.

No. 56. Registered at the G. P. O. as a Newspaper. THURSDAY, JANUARY 7, 1904. One Penny.

◀ First issue of the *Daily Mirror* (January 1904) as a halftone picture paper; it will be seen that this whole page photograph has been 'lined' first, the halftones being grouped on the centre-spread of a 16-page tabloid. Thereafter all photographs were halftoned, the front page often displaying several news pictures (as imitated by the New York *Daily Mirror* later: see p. 99). The blackletter and the insertion of the word ILLUSTRATED in the title was only temporary. The paper soon returned to its original roman lower-case title (below), which it retained until its 'revolution' of 1936.

nary rotary-printed newspapers did not come till 1904, when Northcliffe's *Daily Mirror*, a grotesque fiasco as 'the First Daily Paper for Gentlewomen' was transformed into a popular and profitable picture paper. The achievement was due to the ingenuity of Arkas Sapt, an editor-cum-technician of Hungarian origin in the Northcliffe entourage. There is no satisfactory technical documentation of the way in which Sapt solved the problem of producing tolerable halftones on a newspaper rotary running with ordinary stereo-plates at speed, but the main features of his procedure are clear enough. They were:
1) Careful retouching of the original prints;
2) Deeper etching of coarser screen blocks (screens as coarse as 45 lines to the inch, later improved to 65);
3) 'Making-ready' the blocks with paper interlays cut to keep down the highlights and bring up the solids, the block then being placed on a solid base and 'bumped' by passing under a moulding press, which gave it something of a low relief surface;
4) Much closer attention to the stereotyping process, particularly the moulding.

Much technical advance was still required, for instance in respect of deep etching (the etching machine was yet to come) and stereotyping (the use of specially faced 'dry' flong instead of the conventional 'wet' flong, and moulding by direct platen pressure). Changes on the rotary press, like hard-surfaced packing of impression cylinders, different rollers, new ink formulations, plus the provision of smooth-surfaced newsprint, were also needed to give full flexibility of good halftone reproduction right through a paper. The sum of these complex technical requirements was not to be achieved until the 1920s.

Meantime Sapt had made possible the production of a half-sheet (tabloid) illustrated paper like the *Mirror*, with its pictures concentrated on four pages – front and back and the centre-spread. Thus the *Mirror's* principal halftones occupied only two formes, or two full printing plates; it was therefore possible to take special care with the moulding of these formes and with the blanket dressing of the impression cylinders for the plates. Sapt was emulated by the *Daily Sketch* (1909) and in Paris by Pierre Lafitte's *Excelsior* (1910), most brilliant of Edwardian picture papers. Interestingly enough, these European examples were not to be followed in America until after the First World War, as will be seen.

On the other hand, American newspapers were quick to react to the rotary photogravure process, then perfected in Germany, with its immensely superior reproduction of photographs. The *New York Times* introduced a photogravure section in 1914, printed in the sepia colour long thought inseparable from gravure work; and the 'roto' sections speedily became a feature of leading U.S. dailies. This, of course, sidestepped the problem of halftones in the body of the paper; these were still handled gingerly, both in Britain and America. By the end of this period the regular use of halftones in the body of a paper had not advanced beyond the use of portraits in single-column or half-measure – the thumbnail, or American newspaperman's 'pork chop'.

5: The First World War and its Aftermath

The revolutionising effect of war on newspaper typography has been a repeated theme of this book; by its magnitude the First World War, the Great War of 1914–18, had a far greater effect than its lesser predecessors. Of this the front pages of the *Daily Express* and the *Daily News* for 5 August 1914 provide striking evidence. They also present a summation of the typographic changes that had been making headway during the Edwardian decade. Both sported a banner, the full-page one-line streamer heading, cut off by a double fine rule (a style long to continue), and both had moved away from the news-titlings to newer display faces – the *Express* to Cheltenham Bold, the *Daily News* to Caslon Old Face Heavy (an innovation of the first decade of the century, devised in America by thickening-up 'Lining Caslon', a transatlantic bastardisation of the historic Caslon Old Face produced by cropping its descenders).

Oddly enough in the light of later history, the *Express* was much less advanced in its presentation than the *Daily News*. Its streamer was a 36pt upper- and lower-case of a strange jobbing type (which I have not been able to identify) and its headlines, none more than single-column, were all in capitals. The Cheltenham Bold alternated with Venetian and the condensed third decks were not set (as they might have been) in Cheltenham Bold Condensed, but in the 18pt size of Caslon's small series, Latin Compressed No. 2. The *Daily News* streamer was in 48pt Cheltenham Bold Extended with the double-column lead story headed in 60pt Grot No. 8, both capitals (Morison incorrectly transposed these sizes). But the significant thing was the incursion of upper- and lower-case decks; the lead story alternated such decks in Grot No. 9, while the run-of-the-page Caslon Old Face Heavy headings each followed a first deck in capitals with a second in lower-case.

The fortuitous typography of the early streamers is worth noting. We have already seen how the *Daily Herald* had turned to a jobbing type like Morland for its first upper- and lower-case streamers. Even white-lined or outline jobbing faces (in capitals) were elsewhere called on.

Slowest to be shaken out of its tranquil titlings was the *Daily Mail*, still the circulation leader. At the turn of July–August, when the war clouds were at bursting point – Austria had already declared war on Serbia – the *Mail* did no more than put one line double-column, in De Vinne Condensed capitals, over its single-column seven-decker lead heading in light news-titlings. A special Sunday edition on 2 August drove it to some headings in condensed sans (plus an interesting full page of well-reproduced pictures, no doubt taking advantage of the techniques which Sapt had developed two years before for the *Daily Mirror*, and strongly bannered in Cheltenham Bold Condensed capitals). But not until it had to report the British declaration of war did the *Mail* of 5 August go so far as to lead with a full double-column headline, in four heavy decks of Doric and sans condensed; even then it eschewed the full-page streamers of its competitors – its main news page was still inside, the right of the centre-spread – and retained the news-titlings for all other headings on the page.

The explosion of August 1914 was enough to crack the staid conservatism of Printing House Square. For some remarkable special Sunday editions *The Times* produced news on the front page; for

▶ The *Daily Express* greeted the 1914 war with a slogan banner.

Daily Express

NO. 4,470. LONDON, WEDNESDAY, AUGUST 5, 1914. ONE HALFPENNY.

England Expects That Every Man Will Do His Duty.

TO-DAY'S WEATHER.

Wednesday Morning.

The weather forecast for to-day is:—Rainy at first, then fair; southerly and south-easterly winds, shifting later to the westward or north-westward; remaining cool.

High water at London Bridge, 1.13 a.m., 1.49 p.m.

Lighting-up time, 8.42 p.m.

London weather: Official records for twenty-four hours ending 6 p.m. yesterday: Fair; rainfall, 0.02in.; shade temperature, highest 68, lowest 53.

THE KING TO THE FLEET.

"THE SURE SHIELD OF BRITAIN."

The following message has been addressed by the King to Admiral Sir John Jellicoe:—

"At this grave moment in our national history I send to you and through you to the officers and men of the fleets of which you have assumed command the assurance of my confidence that under your direction they will revive and renew the old glories of the Royal Navy and prove once again the sure shield of Britain and of her Empire in the hour of trial.

"GEORGE R.I."

The above message has been communicated to the senior naval officers on all stations outside of home waters.

FOR THE DEFENCE OF THE REALM.

THE KING'S INJUNCTION TO HIS SUBJECTS.

"The present state of public affairs and the extent of the demands on our military forces for the protection of the interests of the Empire do, in our opinion, constitute a case of great emergency."

These grave words appear in a series of proclamations by the King published yesterday calling out the Army Reserve, embodying the Territorial Force, continuing soldiers in Army service, and calling out the Militia Reserve of Jersey. A further proclamation was issued regarding the defence of the realm." In this the King says:—

The present state of public affairs in Europe is such as to constitute an imminent national danger."

The proclamation continues:—

"Now, therefore, we strictly command and enjoin our subjects to obey and conform to all instructions and regulations which may be issued by us or our Admiralty or Army Council, or any officer of our Navy or Army, or any other person acting in our behalf, for securing the objects aforesaid, and not to hinder or obstruct, but to afford all assistance in their power to, any person acting in accordance with any such instructions or regulations or otherwise in the execution of any measures duly taken for securing those objects."

PRIVATE WAR NEWS FROM THE "DAILY EXPRESS."

Owing to the enormous number of requests for war news received after going to press, the "Express" War News Service has been established to telegraph important information to those of its readers who require it.

The conditions will be as follows:—

12 word messages ... 1s. each. (including name and address)
24 word messages ... 1/6 each. (including name and address)

The telegrams can only be supplied on the following conditions:—

1. **The telegrams must be paid for in advance.**
2. **The "Daily Express" cannot accept responsibility for delay in transmission, nor can we guarantee delivery.**
3. **No messages can be sent to persons abroad.**
4. **The telegrams can only be supplied for private information, and not more than five messages can be sent in one day.**

All you need do is to send a request for a number of messages (indicating if they are to be 12 word messages or 24 word messages), together with a remittance to cover the cost to

THE "DAILY EXPRESS," PRIVATE WAR SERVICE, 8, SHOE LANE, LONDON, E.C.

TO-DAY'S DIARY.

Imperial Maritime League: Captain T. Acheson and J. E. A. Whitman at Budleigh Salterton.

Racing: Brighton.

Oversea Mails: To-morrow's arrivals and despatches will be found on Page 8.

AN APPEAL TO MEN TO JOIN THE ARMY.—See Page THREE.

WAR DECLARED ON GERMANY.

Great Britain declared war on Germany at eleven o'clock last night.

[This, allowing for the difference in time, was midnight in Berlin.]

The Foreign Office issued the following statement at 12.15 a.m. this morning:—

Owing to the summary rejection by the German Government of the request made by His Majesty's Government for assurances that the neutrality of Belgium would be respected, His Majesty's ambassador in Berlin has received his passports, and His Majesty's Government has declared to the German Government that a state of war exists between Great Britain and Germany as from 11 p.m. on August 4.

GERMANY STRIKES FIRST BLOW.

MINE-LAYER SUNK.

SEA FIGHT REPORTED OFF ALGERIAN COAST.

ALL RAILWAYS IN GREAT BRITAIN TAKEN OVER.

England declared war on Germany at eleven o'clock last night.

The tension is past. The die is cast. With one single sentiment the nation accepts the challenge of an arrogant foe, and with confident courage commits its cause to God.

Great Britain issued an ultimatum to Germany yesterday to expire at midnight. It was, "Hands off Belgium, or war." Germany's reply was a summary rejection.

This step, announced by Mr. Asquith to a House of Commons purged of party, to a nation united in the most righteous cause for which men have ever prayed to the God of Battles, was the inevitable sequel to Sir Edward Grey's clear and forcible exposition of British policy, honour, and obligation.

Perhaps Germany hoped to divide us, to part us from our friends; perhaps she presumed on her colossal ignorance of the spirit of Ireland, on the supposed tendencies of English Liberalism. Perhaps she thought we would not fight for honour and for justice. The point is not material any longer. Germany has overrun Europe, smashing treaties, violating neutral States, carrying fire and sword.

She has run against England at last.

ACTS OF WAR.

It is reported that the German fleet has sunk a British mine layer. It is also reported that a German cruiser, the Breslau, after bombarding Bona, a French Algerian port, fell into the hands of the British Mediterranean Squadron.

FROM OVERSEAS.

The Dominions have rallied with a splendid and absolutely united enthusiasm to the Empire's defence. The enemy finds a solid and unshakable Empire in his path. The King has sent a stirring message "to my people of the Overseas Dominions." He says: "I shall be strengthened in the discharge of the great responsibilities which rest upon me by the confident belief that in this time of trial my Empire will stand united, calm, resolute, trusting in God."

BELGIUM.

Scenes of extraordinary enthusiasm were shown in the Belgian Parliament when King Albert addressed the assembled chambers in common session. He made a speech full of dignity and resolution. Belgium will fight to a man for the independence of the country. M. Vandervelde, the famous Belgian Socialist, has joined the Ministry.

Meanwhile the German advance through Belgium is continued. Germany has gone to war with England on her right to break treaties and ravage neutral lands.

THE SPIRIT OF LONDON.

London remains calm, confident, and grim. All day yesterday troops were massing and moving. Crowds were in the streets encouraging the troops, demonstrating loyally before Buckingham Palace, reading eagerly the royal proclamations, couched in the gravest language, calling out the armed forces.

The spirit that moves the nation was seen in a rush of offers of military or civil service in defence of the country. A stream of men poured into the various recruiting offices and headquarters. Many doctors with large practices volunteered for service as surgeons with the Fleet.

The spirit showed itself, too, with a subtle and ennobling exaltation when an immense crowd in Birdcage-walk bared their heads as the colours of a regiment of Guards were brought on parade in the barrack square. Only a flag—and the phlegmatic Briton is not used to make displays of emotion before material things. But to-day—a symbol, a sacred thing, a whisper of England's soul, and the London crowd bared their heads.

IN THE CITY.

The great banking houses hummed with activity and the "bank holiday" only meant that there was no paying out and no receiving. The banks are working at the highest pressure, getting straight and making ready to deal with the financial situation to be disclosed when ordinary business is resumed.

It would surely be well at this juncture if a general moratorium were declared, and if the Bank rate were reduced once more to something like 6 per cent. This, with the suspension of the Bank Act, would do much to restore complete confidence.

THE FOOD SUPPLY.

Mr. Lloyd George announced in the House of Commons the steps which are being taken to insure and safeguard our food supplies. He spoke with quiet confidence. Mr. Asquith announced that steps would shortly be taken for controlling the distribution of supplies.

Meanwhile, at the great shops, considerable numbers of foolish persons are attempting to lay in large supplies. This conduct is both foolish and unpatriotic. There is no excuse for panic, none for a selfish abuse of the power of a long purse, which, indeed, may only bring peril on the household thus provisioned as though for a siege.

The large establishments are wisely and properly holding back the execution of all unreasonably large orders, and satisfying the needs of the more modest consumer. It is to be hoped that the Government will take the strongest measures to defeat the criminal folly of all public or private speculations in foodstuffs.

NEW SHIPS FOR ENGLAND.

The British Admiralty have taken over the two battleships of very high fighting efficiency just completed in this country for Turkey. They have been named, with an excellent aptitude, Agincourt and Erin.

ITALY'S ROLE.

The position of Italy is extremely interesting. Assurances have been given to her that will, we understand, prevent her under any circumstances joining with Germany and Austria, and it is probable that she will shortly announce a dramatic step which will be entirely in accord with the sentiment of her people.

THE RAILWAYS.

The Government have taken control of all the railway systems of the country.

IN SUPREME COMMAND.

SIR J. JELLICOE AT THE HEAD OF THE FLEET.

FIGHTING CAREER.

The Admiralty announced yesterday that, with the approval of the King, Vice-Admiral Sir J. R. Jellicoe has assumed supreme command of the Home Fleets with the acting rank of admiral.

Rear-Admiral Charles E. Madden has been appointed to be his chief of the staff.

It is just a year since Sir John Jellicoe taught Great Britain a lesson by striking hard in the course of manœuvres at vulnerable points on the east coast.

In a few days, with a force inferior to that opposed to him, he raided Grimsby, the Humber, Sunderland, and Blyth, poured troops ashore, and roused throughout the entire country a feeling of respect for his ability and of doubt whether an enemy might not repeat his success.

Now it falls to him to avert the danger.

Sir John Jellicoe is a clean-shaven, keen-eyed man of the sea, alert, vigorous, and

ADMIRAL SIR JOHN JELLICOE,
Commander-in-Chief of the British Home Fleets.

decisive. There is nothing spectacular about his plan of warfare.

Strike, strike hard, and strike again has always been his plan of campaign, and he has known what it is to be face to face with death.

He was in the Egyptian war of 1882. He was in the Victoria when she went down in the ghastly disaster off Tripoli, and was one of the few of the ship's company who survived to face the court-martial into the catastrophe.

He fought side by side with the Germans when the Allied Forces, under Sir Edward Seymour, went to the relief of the Peking Legations, and was severely wounded. And earlier in his career he won a medal for a gallant effort to save the lives of the crew of a steamer stranded on a sand bank near Gibraltar.

He was born on December 5, 1859, and entered the Navy on July 15, 1872. His subsequent career may be tabulated thus:—

Sub-lieutenant, December 5, 1878.
Lieutenant, August 23, 1880.
Commander, June 30, 1891.
Captain, January 1, 1897.
Rear-admiral, February 8, 1907.
Vice-admiral, September 18, 1911.

He has frequently served at the Admiralty, in the Ordnance Department, as Controller of the Navy, and as Second Sea Lord. His commands afloat have included the old Atlantic Fleet, now incorporated in the Home Fleets, and the Second Division of the Home Fleet.

Among his decorations is included the German Red Eagle.

Rear-Admiral Charles E. Madden, the chief of the staff, was until recently in command of the Second Cruiser Squadron. He is fifty-two years old, and has been a flag officer since 1911.

GERMAN FLEET SINKS BRITISH SHIP.

DESTROYED WHILE ENGAGED IN LAYING MINES.

The Government is understood to have received intimation that a British ship has been sunk by the German fleet while engaged in laying mines.

NO WOUNDED LANDED.

It was stated in a London evening newspaper last night that the wounded from a naval engagement in the North Sea had been landed at Cromarty, in the north of Scotland, and that special trains had been chartered to convey surgeons and nurses from Aberdeen to Cromarty. The Admiralty denied this report last night.

GERMAN CRUISER ATTACKS FRENCH PORT.

ENGAGED BY OUR FLEET IN THE MEDITERRANEAN.

PARIS, Tuesday, Aug. 4.

The Governor-General of Algeria reports that at four o'clock this morning a four-funnelled cruiser, thought to be the German cruiser Breslau, discharged eight broadsides at the town of Bona, sixty shells being fired.

One man was killed and some houses were damaged.

She then steamed towards the west, where she is said to have been engaged with the British fleet.—Reuter.

Bona is a fortified town in Algeria, and has the best harbour on the coast.

The Breslau is one of the smaller new German cruisers, and is the name ship of a class of four launched in 1911. Her displacement is 4,450 tons. She was reported on Monday going westward through the Mediterranean from Austrian waters.

LITTLE DAMAGE AT LIBAU.

LIBAU, Aug. 3.

An official communiqué issued to-day states that a German cruiser approached Libau yesterday and bombarded the town. Twenty shots, adds the communiqué, were fired, of which one hit the naval hospital and two struck private houses. The material damage was very small. There were no casualties. The cruiser subsequently disappeared.—Reuter.

The captain of this cruiser reported to Berlin on Sunday that he had bombarded this Russian port and that it was in flames.

ARMY BILLETS AND TRANSPORT.

The War Office last night issued copies of two Orders under the Army Acts made by the King and signed by Mr. Asquith.

One authorises any general or field officer commanding his Majesty's Regular Forces in any military district or place in the United Kingdom to issue a Requisition of Emergency requiring Justices of the Peace to issue warrants for the provision for the purposes mentioned in the requisition of carriages, animals, vessels, and aircraft.

In the other case he is authorised to issue a billeting requisition requiring chief officers of police to provide billets in such places and for such numbers of officers and soldiers and their horses and for such period as may be specified.

A MORATORIUM?

WHAT THE GOVERNMENT SHOULD DO AT ONCE.

REDUCE THE BANK RATE.

There is no doubt that a general moratorium, if declared at once, would greatly relieve the commercial world. A partial moratorium on bills, as declared the other day, is not sufficient. We strongly urge the Government to take steps at once in the direction of declaring a general moratorium.

It should be all or nothing.

It is felt, too, in the City that the financial situation does not warrant so high a Bank rate as 10 per cent. An immediate reduction to 5½ or 6 per cent. would be hailed by the business community with the greatest satisfaction.

GERMAN EMBASSY MOBBED.

HOSTILE DEMONSTRATION BY A CROWD.

A hostile demonstration was made outside the German Embassy last night.

A large crowd assembled about 9.30 p.m., and groaning and hissing were freely indulged in.

A message was sent to Cannon-row police station, and a force of foot and mounted men arrived shortly afterwards. They experienced considerable difficulty in restoring order.

MORE BATTLESHIPS.

NEW FOREIGN VESSELS BOUGHT BY BRITAIN.

Two more super-Dreadnoughts have been added to the British Fleet.

The Admiralty announced last night that the Government have taken over the ships building for Turkey by Messrs. Armstrong, at Elswick, and Messrs. Vickers, at Barrow, and the two destroyer leaders building for Chili by Messrs. J. S. White and Co., at Cowes.

The two battleships will receive the names of Agincourt and Erin, and the two destroyer leaders will be called Faulkner and Broke, after two naval officers famous in history for their bravery.

The Agincourt was laid down in 1911 as the Rio de Janeiro for Brazil. She was sold after her launch to Turkey and renamed Osman I. Her principal dimensions are:—

Displacement	27,500 tons
Length	652 feet
Speed	22 knots
Armament	14 12-in. guns
	20 6-in. guns

The Erin's previous name was Sultan Mehmet Rechad. Her principal dimensions are:—

Displacement	23,000 tons
Length	560 feet
Speed	21 knots
Armament	10 13.5-in. guns
	16 6-in. guns

ESPIONAGE ARRESTS.

THIRTY HOUSES RAIDED BY SCOTLAND YARD.

Scotland-yard detectives raided nearly thirty residences of Germans in London late last night, and made several arrests.

Observation has been kept on various "suspects" by officers of the special branch of Scotland-yard for several weeks past, and yesterday a large number of search warrants were obtained. These were being executed during the night by Chief Inspectors Ward and McBrien, Inspectors Hester, Riley, and Buckley, and a large force of detectives.

The persons arrested were taken to Bow-street Police Station. One of the prisoners is stated to be an ex-lieutenant in the German navy.

They will probably be brought before the magistrate at Bow-street this morning.

SIR JOHN FRENCH.

INSPECTOR-GENERAL OF THE FORCES.

Field-Marshal Sir John French has been appointed to the vacant post of Inspector-General of the Forces. He held this post from 1907 to 1911.

His aides-de-camp will be Lieut.-Colonel S. L. Barry and Major and Brevet-Colonel Lord Brooke.

Major A. F. Watt has been appointed his private secretary.

Mr. Luxmoore Drew, the coroner for West London, cannot return home from Norway, where he has been spending a holiday, and his deputy, Dr. Douglas Cowburne, has been called up by the military authorities.

The chairman and executive committee of the Children's Country Holidays Fund have been compelled to decide not to send away from London the second large party of children who should have left for the country to-morrow. The first party of 25,000 children, which left London on July 23, will return to-morrow as arranged.

WAR SPECIALS ON OTHER PAGES.

On Page THREE: Can Belgium Hold Out? By Lieut.-Colonel Alsager Pollock.

On Page FIVE: Assuring the Food Supply.

On Page TWO: Mobilisation Order. Russia's Cossacks.

DASH AGAINST THE FRENCH.

THE KAISER'S TROOPS MARCHING THROUGH BELGIUM.

LIEGE GUNS HEARD.

ANOTHER BATTLE AT SEDAN?

There is every indication that Germany has begun a rapid dash through Belgium with the object of hurling herself at the left wing of the French army, and gaining a decisive victory at the outset of the campaign.

German troops entered Belgian territory at several points yesterday morning, and in the afternoon the Belgian Government learnt that they were marching in the neighbourhood of Fleron, near Liège.

Later telegrams state that the guns of the Liège forts are in action, and that the Germans have captured Visé, in Belgian territory, where there is one bridge over the Meuse. This the Belgians have blown up. A siege of Liège, which is strongly fortified, will probably be begun at once.

Germany is carrying out her attack on France on precisely the lines expected by students of military strategy.

The advance into Luxemburg by way of the "Trou de Treves," which took place on Sunday, gives her the command of the south-east corner of Belgium, through which an army can enter France at her most vulnerable point—the sixty-miles line between Maubeuge and Verdun, where there is no fortified position of the first order.

All along the frontier down to Belfort, near the Swiss border, the attack is developing, but the main attack is likely to be in the vulnerable north, and a great battle may be fought again in the neighbourhood of Sedan.

An advance is being made from Luxemburg, and three columns are marching on the old-fashioned fortress of Longwy, a point above Verdun, Villerupt, eight miles to the south-east of Longwy, and Thionville, in Alsace-Lorraine, sixteen miles north of Metz.

The frontier has also been crossed at Mars-la-Tour, between Metz and Verdun—the scene of terrific carnage in 1870.

The following telegrams give the latest details of the German movements:—

THROUGH THE MEUSE VALLEY.

BRUSSELS, Tuesday, Aug. 4.

The Government have learnt this afternoon that the Germans are continuing their onward march through Belgian territory, and are in the neighbourhood of Fleron, near Liège.

They are, however, out of range of the forts, but are evidently desirous of reaching the Meuse, and following the course of that river.—Reuter.

FIGHTING AT LIEGE.

BRUSSELS, Tuesday, Aug. 4.

The "Etoile Belge" states that the Belgian and German troops have come into contact, and the firing of the guns at the Liège forts can be heard.

Belgian engineers have blown up bridges at Ardenteau and Hombourg.

A state of siege has been declared at Antwerp, Namur, and Liège.

The German forces are advancing from Luxemburg in three columns, one towards Longwy, another towards Villerupt, and the third towards Thionville.—Central News.

CHECKED BY THE BELGIANS.

AMSTERDAM, Tuesday, Aug. 4.

Visé has been taken by the Germans.

The Belgian engineers have blown up the bridge over the Meuse, and the Germans are building a new bridge.—Central News.

HISTORIC POINT INVADED.

PARIS, Tuesday, Aug. 4.

A German company is reported [illegible] in French territory near Mars-la-Tour, the scene of one of the most sanguinary battles of the war of 1870.—Reuter.

RUSSIAN ADVANCE REPULSED.

BERLIN, Tuesday, Aug. 4.

It is announced here that a portion of the garrison of Memel, on the East Prussian frontier, yesterday repulsed an advance party of Russia's frontier guards coming from the direction of Krottingen.—Reuter.

LORD HALDANE AT THE WAR OFFICE.

The statement that Lor[illegible]

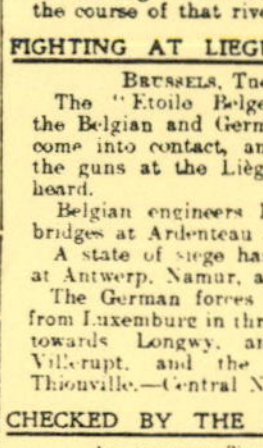

LORD HALDANE.
(Lafayette.)

Mr. Asquith, but ther[illegible] his becoming War Se[illegible] the Premier.

No official appointme[illegible] in the case of Lord Kit[illegible] he also has been in co[illegible] Mr. Asquith.

GERMAN ATTACK BY LAND AND AIR (Inset, the forts of Liege).

4.30 EDN

Daily News & Leader

No. 21,343. LONDON & MANCHESTER, WEDNESDAY, AUGUST 5, 1914. ONE HALF-PENNY.

GREAT BRITAIN & GERMANY AT WAR.

AT WAR!

Fateful Decision Last Evening.

KING'S MESSAGE TO NAVY.

"The Sure Shield of England and Empire."

FIRING IN THE NORTH SEA.

It was officially announced early this morning that war was declared between Great Britain and Germany last night.

This declaration followed a British ultimatum to which an answer was demanded by midnight.

The British action followed Germany's declaration of war on France and Belgium and the receipt of official news during the forenoon of the invasion of Belgian territory.

Germany is now at war with Great Britain, France, Russia and Belgium.

The Premier, in announcing the Government's momentous action to the House of Commons, stated that early yesterday morning Germany was asked for an assurance that her demand upon Belgium would not be proceeded with, and that her neutrality should be respected.

An immediate reply was asked for, and a message was received from the German Foreign Secretary to the effect that no Belgian territory would be annexed, but that Germany was compelled to disregard Belgian neutrality owing to fears of a French attack through that country.

News also reached London that the German Army was marching into Belgium.

Thereupon the British Government repeated its request for an assurance of Belgian neutrality on the same lines as that given by France, demanding that a satisfactory reply should reach London before midnight.

This grave announcement was received with loud cheers.

First news of Germany's declaration of war on Belgium reached London yesterday in a telegram from Mr. Ernest W. Smith, the special correspondent of "The Daily News" at Brussels. The German action was a reply to Belgium's firm refusal to allow the Kaiser's troops to cross her frontiers.

Great Britain is prepared for war. The Navy is mobilised and at sea; the Army is being mobilised. Men and youths are flocking to the colours, and crowds besiege the recruiting offices.

Admiral Jellicoe has been appointed to the supreme command of the Home Fleet, with Rear-Admiral Madden as his Chief of Staff. Sir John French has been reappointed to his former post as Inspector-General of the Forces.

The Admiralty has made a notable addition to the British Navy by the seizure of two battleships and two scouts, building in English yards. The battleships belonged to Turkey and the scouts to Chile.

The Lobby Correspondent of "The Daily News" says that Lord Haldane, the Lord Chancellor, is acting as Assistant Secretary for War, Mr. Asquith retaining the office of Secretary. Lord Kitchener's services, it is believed, will be available in this country.

The British railways have been taken over by the Government for military purposes, and it is notified that the ordinary services may be dislocated for some time.

Public fears as to food supply are groundless. An official statement by the Cabinet (See Page 5) shows that our supplies of corn and meat are ample, and that there is no justification for a rise in prices.

FIGHTING IN BELGIUM.

Germans Driven Back Near the Frontier.

BRUSSELS, Tuesday.

According to a wireless telegram received here, an engagement is said to have taken place near Liége between Belgian and German troops.

The Germans were driven back. Numbers of Belgians were wounded, and will be brought to Brussels.—Reuter.

GERMANS TAKE VISE.

AMSTERDAM, Tuesday Night.

Visé has been taken by the Germans.

The Belgian engineers have blown up the bridge over the Meuse, and the Germans are building a new bridge.

A state of siege has been proclaimed at Limbourg. Belgian engineers have blown up the bridges over the Amblève.—Central News.

MOVING INTO FRANCE.

Three Columns Pressing Forward from Luxemburg.

BRUSSELS, Tuesday.

The German forces are advancing from Luxemburg in three columns, one towards Longwy, another towards Villerupt, and the third towards Thionville.

A telegram from Givet states that the French and German troops are blowing up the French and German frontier stations.—Central News.

[Villerupt is a French village situated eight miles east-south-east of Longwy. Thionville (German, Diedenhofen) is situated in Alsace-Lorraine, 16 miles north of Metz on the Moselle.]

NEAR MARS-LA-TOUR.

PARIS, Tuesday.

A German company is reported to be in French territory near Mars-la-Tour, the scene of one of the most sanguinary battles of the war of 1870.—Reuter.

[Mars-la-Tour lies close to the German frontier, south-west of Metz.]

THE DECLARATION

BRITISH DEMANDS REJECTED.

OFFICIAL MESSAGE.

AMBASSADOR HANDED HIS PASSPORTS.

The following statement was issued from the Foreign Office at 12.15 a.m. to-day:

Owing to the summary rejection by the German Government of the request made by his Majesty's Government for assurances that the neutrality of Belgium would be respected, his Majesty's Ambassador in Berlin has received his passports, and his Majesty's Government has declared to the German Government that a state of war exists between Great Britain and Germany as from 11 p.m. on August 4.

There was some confusion in earlier messages, the first being to the effect that Germany had declared war, while a second stated that Great Britain had taken the fateful step.

From the above official announcement it appears that Germany committed the act of war in rejecting the British ultimatum, while Great Britain, on receipt of this decision, declared the state of war.

WILD SCENES.

How News of Declaration was Received.

In anticipation of the receipt of Germany's reply, huge crowds gathered in Whitehall and outside Buckingham Palace, and extraordinary scenes of enthusiasm were witnessed.

It had been intended to hold a midnight Council at the Palace, but owing to Germany's summary rejection of our ultimatum this gathering took place earlier.

It was preceded by a concentration of Ministers at 10, Downing-street, and each was loudly cheered as he entered the Premier's official residence.

Not for years—since Mafeking night—have such crowds been seen in London, and Whitehall, the Mall, and Trafalgar-square were all packed with excited throngs.

AT THE PALACE.

The enthusiasm culminated outside Buckingham Palace when it became known that war had been declared. The word was passed round by the police that silence was necessary, inasmuch as the King was holding a Council for the signing of necessary proclamations.

A lady came out of the Palace and announced that war had been declared.

This was received with tremendous cheering, which grew into a deafening roar when King George, Queen Mary, and the Prince of Wales appeared on the balcony shortly after eleven o'clock.

They looked down upon an extraordinary scene—a dense mass of excited people, many of whom had clambered on to the Victoria Memorial.

THE NATIONAL ANTHEM.

As if by general accord, the cheers gave way to the singing of the National Anthem, which was taken up lustily by the whole throng.

For fully five minutes the Royal Party remained on the balcony. They retired amidst a perfect storm of cheering, and although the crowd subsequently began to melt away, thousands remained.

They grew gradually less demonstrative, and it was noticeable that the news of the actual state of war had a sobering effect on many. Mafficking gave way to distinct seriousness.

THE GERMAN FLEET.

Bombardments in Baltic and Mediterranean.

An official message issued by the French Embassy informs Reuter that the German cruiser Breslau bombarded the town of Bona, in Algeria, at four o'clock yesterday morning, and afterwards steamed off at full speed in a westerly direction.

A Central News message from Flushing (received yesterday by an indirect route) makes the statement that several of the German warships were lying off that port.

A German cruiser has bombarded the Russian port Libau. According to a Russian official communiqué cabled by Reuter, one shot hit the naval hospital, and two struck private houses. The material damage was very small, and there were no casualties.

There is no confirmation of the report that German warships have seized the Aland Islands.

The "Daily News" War Telegrams arriving during the day will be published in "The Star."

A MAP OF THE NORTH SEA, SHOWING THE GERMAN NAVAL BASES.

GERMANS SINK BRITISH SHIP.

Reported Loss of a Mine-Layer.

Late last night we received the following:

The Press Association learns that there is no truth in the report of a naval engagement in the North Sea.

It is understood that the British Government has received intimation of the sinking of a British mine-layer by the German Fleet.

KING'S MESSAGE TO ADMIRAL JELLICOE.

The Navy, the Sure Shield of the Empire.

The following message has been addressed by his Majesty the King to Admiral Sir John Jellicoe:

At this grave moment in our national history I send to you, and through you to the officers and men of the fleets of which you have assumed command, the assurance of my confidence that under your direction they will revive and renew the old glories of the Royal Navy, and prove once again the sure shield of Britain and of her Empire in the hour of trial.

GEORGE, R.I.

The above message has been communicated to the senior naval officers on all stations outside of home waters.

NEW HEADS OF NAVY AND ARMY.

Admiral Jellicoe to Command the Fleet.

It was announced officially yesterday that Vice-Admiral Sir John Jellicoe has been appointed to the supreme command of the Home Fleet.

Field-Marshal Sir John French has been reappointed to his former position of Inspector-General of the Forces, which he resigned some time ago in connection with the General Gough incident in Ulster.

Sir John Jellicoe has been Second Sea Lord since December, 1912, and it was known several months ago that he had been selected to succeed Admiral Callaghan. He has had a most distinguished career, having served in the Egyptian war and in China. He was wrecked in 1893 in the Victoria, but was saved after sinking, and severely wounded at Peitsang. Among his many decorations is one conferred by the Kaiser. He is 55, and has been described as the Roberts and the Kitchener of the Navy.

Rear-Admiral Chas. E. Madden has been appointed Chief of Staff to Admiral Jellicoe. He has been Rear-Admiral Commanding the Third Cruiser Squadron since 1912; prior to that he commanded the Home Fleet, and he has also been Fourth Sea Lord.

GERMAN ADVANCE.

Guns Heard Ten Miles Within the Belgian Frontier.

BRUSSELS, Tuesday.

It was reported last night that the 6th German Army Corps had encamped in the territory of Moresnet, and was continuing its advance, massing between Moresnet and Eupen.

All Germans have been expelled from Liege and Namur.

Artillery fire has been heard at Aywaille.

Dutch Limburg, in North Brabant, is defended by a strong contingent of Dutch soldiers.

It seems probable that the Germans are desirous of reaching the Meuse, and following the course of that river.—Reuter.

[Moresnet is between the province of Liége and the Prussian Rhine province. Eupen is in the Rhine province, just on the Belgian frontier. Aywaille is in Belgium, on the Amblève, in the province of Liége, about ten miles from the German frontier. It is less than sixty miles east of the field of Waterloo.]

WAR DECLARED ON BELGIUM.

German Army Enters Her Territory.

KING'S SPEECH IN THE BELGIAN CHAMBER.

From Our Special Correspondent, ERNEST W. SMITH.

BRUSSELS, Tuesday.

I learn officially at the Ministry of War that Germany has declared war upon Belgium this morning.

M. de Broqueville, the Prime Minister, has announced in the Chamber that Belgian territory has been invaded at Verviers. He read the German reply to the Belgian Note, which said that Germany would take by force of arms the measures of security demanded by the situation.

I feel it my duty to pay a tribute to the splendid calm and restraint of the population in the days which preceded Germany's ultimatum with its tragic sequel—a state of war. Their attitude has been unprovocative and fired by the sole desire to defend the independence of the country. This little people has emulated the splendid calm reigning in Paris up to the time I left there.

I wired last night that events were moving quickly, but I confess I was unprepared for the dramatic turn which things took this morning. Thousands of people collected around the Royal Palace to cheer the King on his way to open Parliament, and when the news that Germany was at war with Belgium was known it spread like wildfire. I called at the Ministry of War, where I received confirmation, and thence to the Chamber, where M. de Broqueville, the Premier and Minister of War, was making a long declaration.

M. de Broqueville read almost textually Sir Edward Grey's statement made in the House last night describing Germany's demand and Belgium's answer. "We have waited till this morning for Germany's reply to the Belgian Note," said the Minister. "Germany has replied that she will take the measures which the situation imposes by force of arms." A murmur of incredulous astonishment ran through the Chamber. "This reply is beyond comment," added M. de Broqueville. "La parole est donc aux armes. We will do our duty, our whole duty. We may be beaten, but we shall never be cast down. The Belgian people will not fail to do their duty; of that I am convinced."

Later the Premier announced that Belgian territory had been violated. Great cheering greeted the announcement that M. Vandervelde, the Socialist leader, had been nominated Minister of State. Immense crowds ovated King Albert on his return to the Palace, and then promenaded the centre of the city amid tremendous scenes of enthusiasm and cries of "Vive Belgique, France, Angleterre."

This afternoon the aspect is almost normal except that many groups are discussing the situation.

KING GEORGE'S MESSAGE.

King George, before the rupture with Germany, sent a telegram to King Albert assuring him of his support and determination to respect and make respect (respecter et de faire respecter) the independence, integrity, and neutrality of Belgium.

The British Minister has arranged for a special dispatch of letters for England on Saturday morning.

KING ALBERT'S CALL.

Every Citizen Required to Do His Duty.

BRUSSELS, Tuesday.

The King delivered the following speech to the deputies:

"Never since 1830 has a graver hour sounded for Belgium. The strength of our right and the need of Europe for our autonomous existence make us still hope that the dreaded events will not occur. If it is necessary for us to resist an invasion of our soil, however, that duty will find us armed and ready to make the greatest sacrifices. Our young men have already come forward to defend the Fatherland in danger. One duty alone is imposed upon us, namely, the maintenance of a stubborn resistance, courage, and union. Our bravery is proved by our faultless mobilisation and by the multitude of voluntary engagements.

"This is the moment for action. I have called you together to-day in order to allow the Chambers to participate in the enthusiasm of the country. You will know how to adopt with urgency all necessary measures. Are you decided to maintain inviolate the sacred patrimony of our ancestors?

"No one will fail in his duty, and the army is capable of performing its task. The Government and I are fully confident. The Government is aware of its responsibilities, and will carry them out to the end to guard the supreme welfare of the country. God will be with us."—Reuter.

SEIZED FOR THE BRITISH NAVY.

Turkish Battleships and Chilian Scouts.

The Government have taken over the two battleships, one completed, and the other shortly due for completion, which had been ordered in this country by the Turkish Government.

The two destroyer scouts ordered by Chile have also been seized.

The battleships will be named Agincourt and Erin, and the scouts will be called Faulkner and Broke, after two famous naval officers.

ADMIRALTY TAKES OVER LINERS

MONTREAL, Tuesday.

The Canadian Pacific Railway Company announces that its liners, Empress of Russia, Empress of Japan, and Empress of Asia have been taken over by the Admiralty.—Central News.

CABINET & THE WAR.

Lord Haldane Assisting at War Office.

(By Our Lobby Correspondent.)

War has been declared, and the German Ambassador, Prince Lichnowsky, will call at the Foreign Office at 10.30 this morning, as a preliminary to leaving the country. It has been arranged that the United States will take over the affairs of the German Embassy.

Lord Haldane is acting in effect as Assistant Secretary of State at the War Office, and is in daily attendance there. This fact will be generally welcomed, since it is obvious that the Prime Minister requires the ablest assistance in his double duties, and the great reputation which Lord Haldane won at the War Office is fresh in everyone's memory.

Lord Kitchener's invaluable services will, there is reason to believe, be available in this country, but the suggestion which has been put forward in irresponsible quarters that he should be appointed Secretary of State was not very happy. Parliamentary experience is peculiarly necessary in a Minister of State at this juncture.

LIBERAL AND LABOUR FEELING.

The feeling among the Liberal rank and file yesterday was more solidly behind the Government in the course which events have inevitably thrust upon them. The German declaration of war against Belgium is resented by the Liberal Members who attended the meeting at which Mr. Ponsonby presided on Monday.

The Labour Party are now divided in feeling. Some hold that the Government must be supported in view of the accomplished fact. If an attitude of direct antagonism to the Government were adopted the party would not have a general support from the Labour Party in the country.

The Labour Conference which has been summoned for to-day will probably give its chief consideration to the steps which must be taken for the relief of distress if unemployment results. But there will also be a peace propaganda.

CABINET RESIGNATIONS.

Lord Morley and Mr. John Burns have tendered their resignations. It is not believed that Lord Morley will withdraw his resignation, but whether Mr. Burns will reconsider his position was in doubt last night. Mr. Trevelyan, Secretary to the Board of Education, has also tendered his resignation. No official announcements have yet been made, but neither Lord Morley nor Mr. Burns attended the Cabinet meeting yesterday.

About 60 members of the Opposition and 30 Ministerialists in the House of Commons are called up to the Army and the Reserves.

Mr. Balfour's contemptuous reference to Liberals who in this crisis have been wrestling with their conscience, as the "lees and dregs," when these Liberals included some of the most respected members of the party, is much resented. The less we have of Mr. Balfour in these high matters the better it will be for the country, which has not forgotten how he mismanaged a war.

THE SESSION AND HOME RULE.

It is rumoured that the session will be prorogued on Saturday. A new session could be begun and adjourned to keep Parliament in being if necessary. A prorogation instead of an adjournment is vital to the Government's position, since the Home Rule Bill must go formally on the Statute Book. Otherwise the situation in Ireland would be hopelessly prejudiced, and the effect of Mr. Redmond's fine speech nullified. The Government count on the patriotism of the Opposition to recognise this, and it is believed the Opposition leaders conferred on the subject yesterday.

The Arms Proclamation, it is stated, is about to be revoked in Ireland.

A. P. N.

STEPS WHICH LED TO THE WAR.

King of the Belgians' Appeal.

Mr. Asquith in the House of Commons yesterday made the momentous announcement that an ultimatum, expiring at midnight, had been presented to Germany in respect to the neutrality of Belgium.

Received with general cheers, the Premier said:

"In conformity with the statement of policy which was made by my right hon. friend the Foreign Secretary yesterday, a telegram was sent early this morning by him to our Ambassador in Berlin. It was to this effect:

The King of the Belgians has made an appeal to his Majesty the King for diplomatic intervention on behalf of Belgium. His Majesty's Government are also informed that the German Government has delivered to the Belgian Government a Note proposing friendly neutrality for maintaining a free passage through Belgian territory, and promising to maintain the independence and integrity of the kingdom and its possessions at the conclusion of peace, but threatening in case of refusal to treat Belgium as an enemy. An answer was requested within twelve hours. We also understand Belgium has categorically refused this as a flagrant violation of the law of nations. His Majesty's Government are bound to protest against this violation of a treaty to which Germany is a party in common with us, and must request an assurance that the demand made upon Belgium will not be proceeded with and that her neutrality shall be respected by Germany. (Cheers.)

We asked for an immediate reply. (Renewed cheers.)

BELGIUM INVADED.

"We received this morning from our Minister at Brussels the following telegram:

The German Minister has this morning addressed a Note to the Belgian Minister for Foreign Affairs stating that, as the Belgian Government had declined the well-intentioned proposals submitted to them by the Imperial Government, the latter, deeply to their regret, is compelled to carry out, if necessary by force of arms, the measures considered indispensable in view of the French menace.

"Simultaneously, or almost immediately afterwards, we received from the Belgian Legation here in London the following telegram from the Belgian Minister for Foreign Affairs:

General Staff announce that territory has been violated at Gemmenich, near Aix-la-Chapelle. Subsequent information tends to show the German force has penetrated still further into Belgian territory.

THE GERMAN REPLY.

"We also received this morning from the German Ambassador here a telegram sent to him by the German Foreign Secretary, and communicated by the Ambassador to us, which is in these terms:

Please dispel any mistrust that may subsist on the part of the British Government with regard to our intention by repeating most positively the formal assurance that even in the case of armed conflict with Belgium, Germany will under no pretence whatever annex Belgian territory. (Laughter.) The sincerity of this declaration is borne out by the fact that we have solemnly pledged our word to Holland strictly to respect her neutrality. It is obvious we could not profitably annex Belgian territory without making at the same time territorial acquisitions at the expense of Holland. (Laughter.)

Please impress upon Sir Edward Grey that the German army could not be exposed to French attack across Belgium, which was the plan, according to absolutely unimpeachable information. Germany has consequently to disregard Belgian neutrality, it being to her a question of life and death to prevent the French advance.

That is the end of the communication. I have to add this on behalf of his Majesty's Government:

We cannot regard this as in any sense a satisfactory communication. (Cheers.) We have in reply to it repeated the request we made last week to the German Government that they should give us the same assurance in regard to Belgian neutrality as was given to us and to Belgium by France last week—(cheers)—and we have asked that the reply to that request—a satisfactory answer to the telegram of this morning which I have read to the House—should be given before midnight. (Loud cheers.)

TO-DAY'S WEATHER.

London and Channel Forecast.—Southerly and south-easterly winds, shifting later to the westward or north-westward; rainy at first, then fair; remaining cool.

Lighting-up time, 8.48.

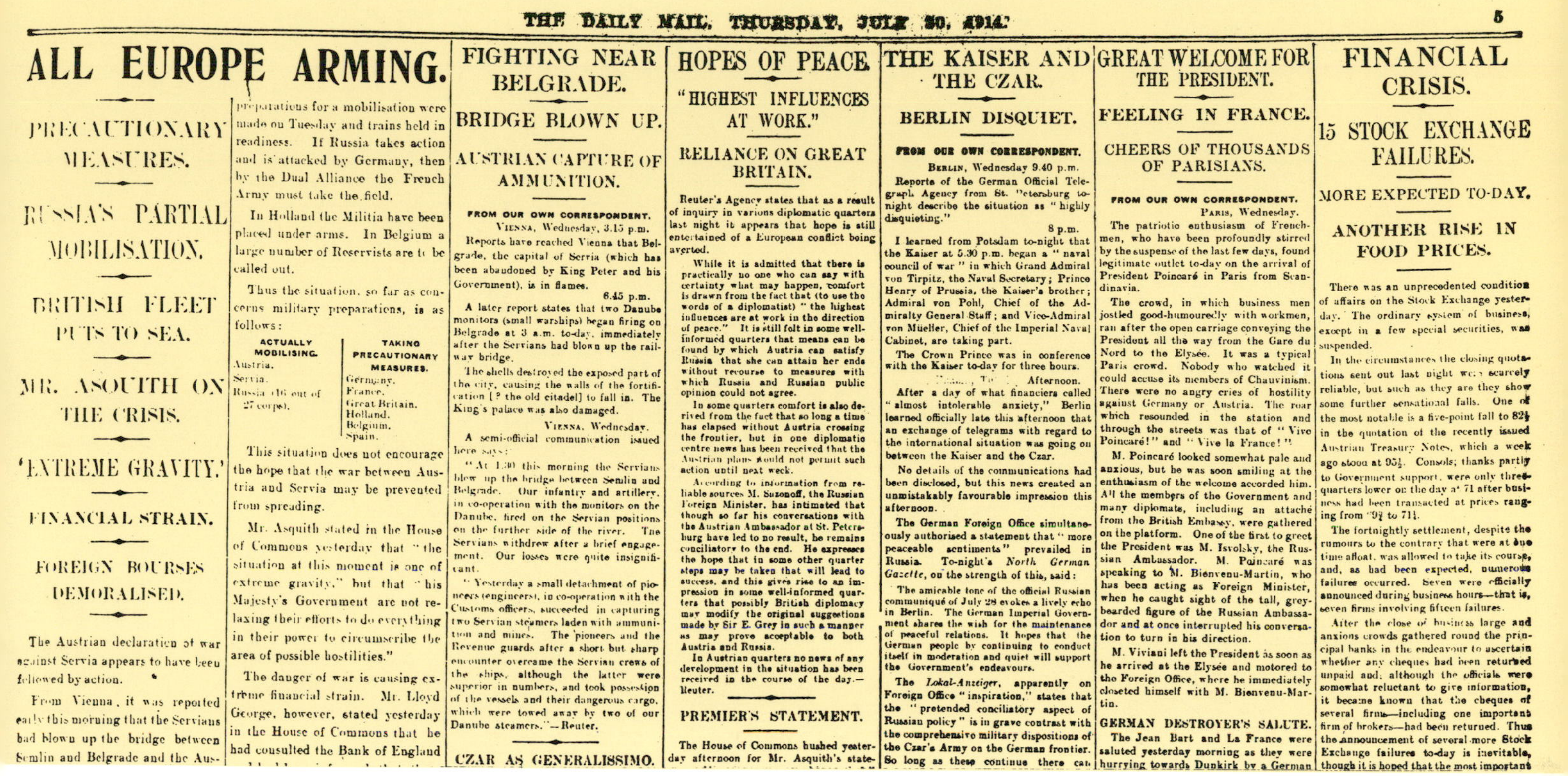

THE DAILY MAIL, THURSDAY, JULY 30, 1914. 5

ALL EUROPE ARMING.

PRECAUTIONARY MEASURES.

RUSSIA'S PARTIAL MOBILISATION.

BRITISH FLEET PUTS TO SEA.

MR. ASQUITH ON THE CRISIS.

'EXTREME GRAVITY.'

FINANCIAL STRAIN.

FOREIGN BOURSES DEMORALISED.

The Austrian declaration of war against Servia appears to have been followed by action.

From Vienna, it was reported early this morning that the Servians had blown up the bridge between Semlin and Belgrade and the Aus- … preparations for a mobilisation were made on Tuesday and trains held in readiness. If Russia takes action and is attacked by Germany, then by the Dual Alliance the French Army must take the field.

In Holland the Militia have been placed under arms. In Belgium a large number of Reservists are to be called out.

Thus the situation, so far as concerns military preparations, is as follows:

ACTUALLY MOBILISING.	TAKING PRECAUTIONARY MEASURES.
Austria.	Germany.
Servia.	France.
Russia (16 out of 27 corps).	Great Britain.
	Holland.
	Belgium.
	Spain.

This situation does not encourage the hope that the war between Austria and Servia may be prevented from spreading.

Mr. Asquith stated in the House of Commons yesterday that "the situation at this moment is one of extreme gravity," but that "his Majesty's Government are not relaxing their efforts to do everything in their power to circumscribe the area of possible hostilities."

The danger of war is causing extreme financial strain. Mr. Lloyd George, however, stated yesterday in the House of Commons that he had consulted the Bank of England …

FIGHTING NEAR BELGRADE.

BRIDGE BLOWN UP.

AUSTRIAN CAPTURE OF AMMUNITION.

FROM OUR OWN CORRESPONDENT.

VIENNA, Wednesday, 3.15 p.m.

Reports have reached Vienna that Belgrade, the capital of Servia (which has been abandoned by King Peter and his Government), is in flames.

6.45 p.m.

A later report states that two Danube monitors (small warships) began firing on Belgrade at 3 a.m. to-day, immediately after the Servians had blown up the railway bridge.

The shells destroyed the exposed part of the city, causing the walls of the fortification [? the old citadel] to fall in. The King's palace was also damaged.

VIENNA, Wednesday.

A semi-official communication issued here says:

"At 1.30 this morning the Servians blew up the bridge between Semlin and Belgrade. Our infantry and artillery, in co-operation with the monitors on the Danube, fired on the Servian positions on the further side of the river. The Servians withdrew after a brief engagement. Our losses were quite insignificant.

"Yesterday a small detachment of pioneers (engineers), in co-operation with the Customs officers, succeeded in capturing two Servian steamers laden with ammunition and mines. The pioneers and the Revenue guards after a short but sharp encounter overcame the Servian crews of the ships, although the latter were superior in numbers, and took possession of the vessels and their dangerous cargo, which were towed away by two of our Danube steamers."—Reuter.

CZAR AS GENERALISSIMO.

HOPES OF PEACE.

"HIGHEST INFLUENCES AT WORK."

RELIANCE ON GREAT BRITAIN.

Reuter's Agency states that as a result of inquiry in various diplomatic quarters last night it appears that hope is still entertained of a European conflict being averted.

While it is admitted that there is practically no one who can say with certainty what may happen, comfort is drawn from the fact that (to use the words of a diplomatist) "the highest influences are at work in the direction of peace." It is still felt in some well-informed quarters that means can be found by which Austria can satisfy Russia that she can attain her ends without recourse to measures with which Russia and Russian public opinion could not agree.

In some quarters comfort is also derived from the fact that so long a time has elapsed without Austria crossing the frontier, but in one diplomatic centre news has been received that the Austrian plans would not permit such action until next week.

According to information from reliable sources M. Sazonoff, the Russian Foreign Minister, has intimated that though so far his conversations with the Austrian Ambassador at St. Petersburg have led to no result, he remains conciliatory to the end. He expresses the hope that in some other quarter steps may be taken that will lead to success, and this gives rise to an impression in some well-informed quarters that possibly British diplomacy may modify the original suggestions made by Sir E. Grey in such a manner as may prove acceptable to both Austria and Russia.

In Austrian quarters no news of any development in the situation has been received in the course of the day.—Reuter.

PREMIER'S STATEMENT.

The House of Commons hushed yesterday afternoon for Mr. Asquith's state- …

THE KAISER AND THE CZAR.

BERLIN DISQUIET.

FROM OUR OWN CORRESPONDENT.

BERLIN, Wednesday 9.40 p.m.

Reports of the German Official Telegraph Agency from St. Petersburg tonight describe the situation as "highly disquieting."

8 p.m.

I learned from Potsdam to-night that the Kaiser at 5.30 p.m. began a "naval council of war" in which Grand Admiral von Tirpitz, the Naval Secretary; Prince Henry of Prussia, the Kaiser's brother; Admiral von Pohl, Chief of the Admiralty General Staff; and Vice-Admiral von Mueller, Chief of the Imperial Naval Cabinet, are taking part.

The Crown Prince was in conference with the Kaiser to-day for three hours.

[illegible] Afternoon.

After a day of what financiers called "almost intolerable anxiety," Berlin learned officially late this afternoon that an exchange of telegrams with regard to the international situation was going on between the Kaiser and the Czar.

No details of the communications had been disclosed, but this news created an unmistakably favourable impression this afternoon.

The German Foreign Office simultaneously authorised a statement that "more peaceable sentiments" prevailed in Russia. To-night's *North German Gazette*, on the strength of this, said:

The amicable tone of the official Russian communiqué of July 28 evokes a lively echo in Berlin. The German Imperial Government shares the wish for the maintenance of peaceful relations. It hopes that the German people by continuing to conduct itself in moderation and quiet will support the Government's endeavours.

The *Lokal-Anzeiger*, apparently on Foreign Office "inspiration," states that the "pretended conciliatory aspect of Russian policy" is in grave contrast with the comprehensive military dispositions of the Czar's Army on the German frontier. So long as these continue there can …

GREAT WELCOME FOR THE PRESIDENT.

FEELING IN FRANCE.

CHEERS OF THOUSANDS OF PARISIANS.

FROM OUR OWN CORRESPONDENT.

PARIS, Wednesday.

The patriotic enthusiasm of Frenchmen, who have been profoundly stirred by the suspense of the last few days, found legitimate outlet to-day on the arrival of President Poincaré in Paris from Scandinavia.

The crowd, in which business men jostled good-humouredly with workmen, ran after the open carriage conveying the President all the way from the Gare du Nord to the Elysée. It was a typical Paris crowd. Nobody who watched it could accuse its members of Chauvinism. There were no angry cries of hostility against Germany or Austria. The roar which resounded in the station and through the streets was that of "Vive Poincaré!" and "Vive la France!"

M. Poincaré looked somewhat pale and anxious, but he was soon smiling at the enthusiasm of the welcome accorded him. All the members of the Government and many diplomats, including an attaché from the British Embassy, were gathered on the platform. One of the first to greet the President was M. Isvolsky, the Russian Ambassador. M. Poincaré was speaking to M. Bienvenu-Martin, who has been acting as Foreign Minister, when he caught sight of the tall, grey-bearded figure of the Russian Ambassador and at once interrupted his conversation to turn in his direction.

M. Viviani left the President as soon as he arrived at the Elysée and motored to the Foreign Office, where he immediately closeted himself with M. Bienvenu-Martin.

GERMAN DESTROYER'S SALUTE.

The Jean Bart and La France were saluted yesterday morning as they were hurrying towards Dunkirk by a German …

FINANCIAL CRISIS.

15 STOCK EXCHANGE FAILURES.

MORE EXPECTED TO-DAY.

ANOTHER RISE IN FOOD PRICES.

There was an unprecedented condition of affairs on the Stock Exchange yesterday. The ordinary system of business, except in a few special securities, was suspended.

In the circumstances the closing quotations sent out last night were scarcely reliable, but such as they are they show some further sensational falls. One of the most notable is a five-point fall to 82½ in the quotation of the recently issued Austrian Treasury Notes, which a week ago stood at 95½. Consols, thanks partly to Government support, were only three-quarters lower on the day at 71 after business had been transacted at prices ranging from 69¾ to 71¼.

The fortnightly settlement, despite the rumours to the contrary that were at one time afloat, was allowed to take its course, and, as had been expected, numerous failures occurred. Seven were officially announced during business hours—that is, seven firms involving fifteen failures.

After the close of business large and anxious crowds gathered round the principal banks in the endeavour to ascertain whether any cheques had been returned unpaid and, although the officials were somewhat reluctant to give information, it became known that the cheques of several firms—including one important firm of brokers—had been returned. Thus the announcement of several more Stock Exchange failures to-day is inevitable, though it is hoped that the most important …

▲ On the very eve of war the *Daily Mail* was not urged to more than one double-column line in De Vinne Condensed capitals over the normal single-column news-titling decker.

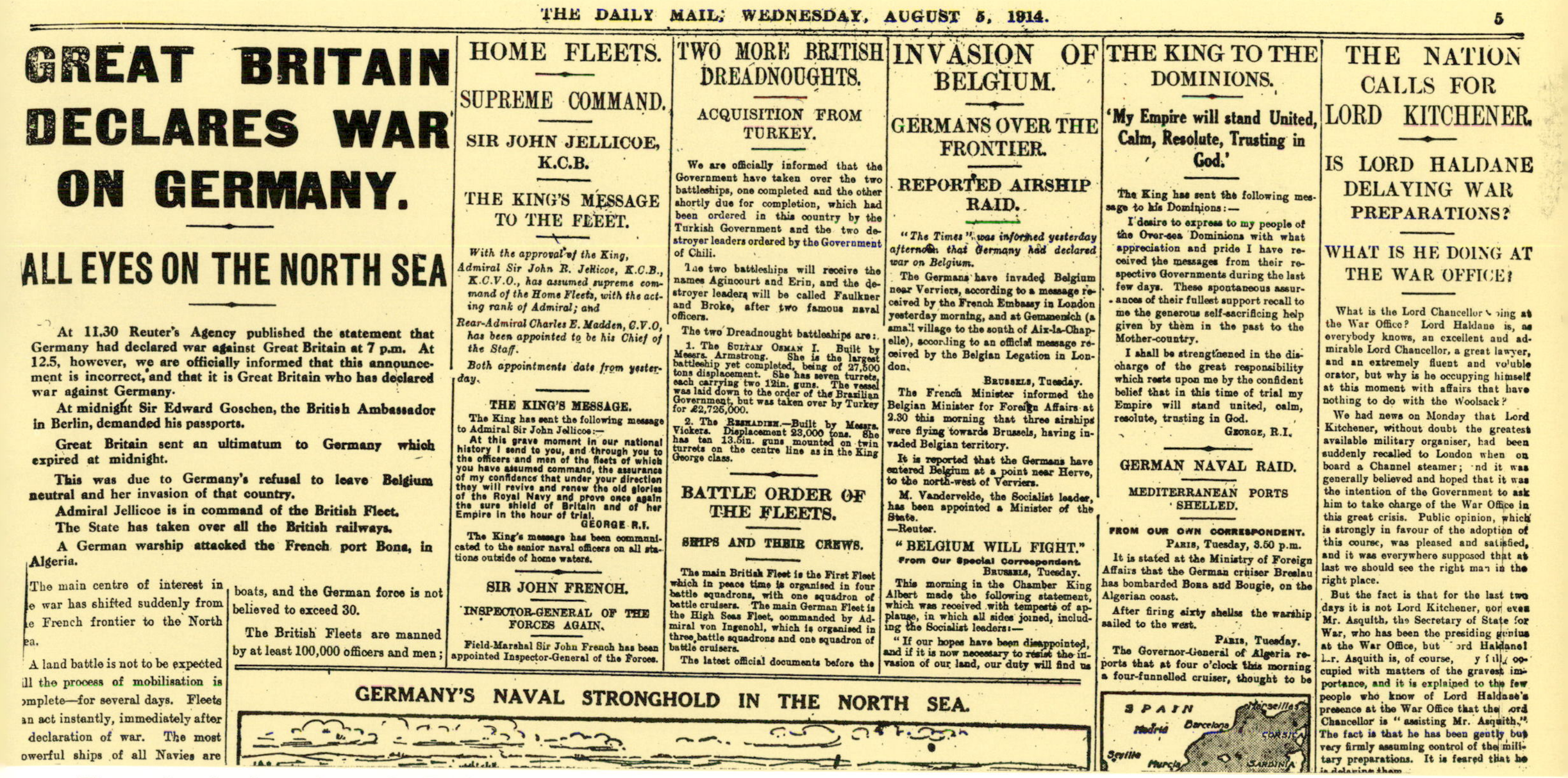

THE DAILY MAIL, WEDNESDAY, AUGUST 5, 1914. 5

GREAT BRITAIN DECLARES WAR ON GERMANY.

ALL EYES ON THE NORTH SEA

At 11.30 Reuter's Agency published the statement that Germany had declared war against Great Britain at 7 p.m. At 12.5, however, we are officially informed that this announcement is incorrect, and that it is Great Britain who has declared war against Germany.

At midnight Sir Edward Goschen, the British Ambassador in Berlin, demanded his passports.

Great Britain sent an ultimatum to Germany which expired at midnight.

This was due to Germany's refusal to leave Belgium neutral and her invasion of that country.

Admiral Jellicoe is in command of the British Fleet.

The State has taken over all the British railways.

A German warship attacked the French port Bona, in Algeria.

The main centre of interest in the war has shifted suddenly from the French frontier to the North Sea.

A land battle is not to be expected till the process of mobilisation is complete—for several days. Fleets can act instantly, immediately after declaration of war. The most powerful ships of all Navies are … boats, and the German force is not believed to exceed 30.

The British Fleets are manned by at least 100,000 officers and men; …

HOME FLEETS.

SUPREME COMMAND.

SIR JOHN JELLICOE, K.C.B.

THE KING'S MESSAGE TO THE FLEET.

With the approval of the King, Admiral Sir John R. Jellicoe, K.C.B., K.C.V.O., has assumed supreme command of the Home Fleets, with the acting rank of Admiral; and

Rear-Admiral Charles E. Madden, C.V.O., has been appointed to be his Chief of the Staff.

Both appointments date from yesterday.

THE KING'S MESSAGE.

The King has sent the following message to Admiral Sir John Jellicoe:—

At this grave moment in our national history I send to you, and through you to the officers and men of the fleets of which you have assumed command, the assurance of my confidence that under your direction they will revive and renew the old glories of the Royal Navy and prove once again the sure shield of Britain and of her Empire in the hour of trial.

GEORGE R.I.

The King's message has been communicated to the senior naval officers on all stations outside of home waters.

SIR JOHN FRENCH.

INSPECTOR-GENERAL OF THE FORCES AGAIN.

Field-Marshal Sir John French has been appointed Inspector-General of the Forces.

TWO MORE BRITISH DREADNOUGHTS.

ACQUISITION FROM TURKEY.

We are officially informed that the Government have taken over the two battleships, one completed and the other shortly due for completion, which had been ordered in this country by the Turkish Government and the two destroyer leaders ordered by the Government of Chili.

The two battleships will receive the names Agincourt and Erin, and the destroyer leaders will be called Faulkner and Broke, after two famous naval officers.

The two Dreadnought battleships are:

1. The SULTAN OSMAN I. Built by Messrs. Armstrong. She is the largest battleship yet completed, being of 27,500 tons displacement. She has seven turrets, each carrying two 12in. guns. The vessel was laid down to the order of the Brazilian Government, but was taken over by Turkey for £2,725,000.

2. The RESHADIEH.—Built by Messrs. Vickers. Displacement 23,000 tons. She has ten 13.5in. guns mounted on twin turrets on the centre line as in the King George class.

BATTLE ORDER OF THE FLEETS.

SHIPS AND THEIR CREWS.

The main British Fleet is the First Fleet which in peace time is organised in four battle squadrons, with one squadron of battle cruisers. The main German Fleet is the High Seas Fleet, commanded by Admiral von Ingenohl, which is organised in three battle squadrons and one squadron of battle cruisers.

The latest official documents before the …

INVASION OF BELGIUM.

GERMANS OVER THE FRONTIER.

REPORTED AIRSHIP RAID.

"The Times" was informed yesterday afternoon that Germany had declared war on Belgium.

The Germans have invaded Belgium near Verviers, according to a message received by the French Embassy in London yesterday morning, and at Gemmenich (a small village to the south of Aix-la-Chapelle), according to an official message received by the Belgian Legation in London.

BRUSSELS, Tuesday.

The French Minister informed the Belgian Minister for Foreign Affairs at 2.30 this morning that three airships were flying towards Brussels, having invaded Belgian territory.

It is reported that the Germans have entered Belgium at a point near Herve, to the north-west of Verviers.

M. Vandervelde, the Socialist leader, has been appointed a Minister of the State.

—Reuter.

"BELGIUM WILL FIGHT."

From Our Special Correspondent.

BRUSSELS, Tuesday.

This morning in the Chamber King Albert made the following statement, which was received with tempests of applause, in which all sides joined, including the Socialist leaders:—

"If our hopes have been disappointed, and if it is now necessary to resist the invasion of our land, our duty will find us …

THE KING TO THE DOMINIONS.

'My Empire will stand United, Calm, Resolute, Trusting in God.'

The King has sent the following message to his Dominions:—

I desire to express to my people of the Over-sea Dominions with what appreciation and pride I have received the messages from their respective Governments during the last few days. These spontaneous assurances of their fullest support recall to me the generous self-sacrificing help given by them in the past to the Mother-country.

I shall be strengthened in the discharge of the great responsibility which rests upon me by the confident belief that in this time of trial my Empire will stand united, calm, resolute, trusting in God.

GEORGE, R.I.

GERMAN NAVAL RAID.

MEDITERRANEAN PORTS SHELLED.

FROM OUR OWN CORRESPONDENT.

PARIS, Tuesday, 3.50 p.m.

It is stated at the Ministry of Foreign Affairs that the German cruiser Breslau has bombarded Bona and Bougie, on the Algerian coast.

After firing sixty shells the warship sailed to the west.

PARIS, Tuesday.

The Governor-General of Algeria reports that at four o'clock this morning a four-funnelled cruiser, thought to be …

THE NATION CALLS FOR LORD KITCHENER.

IS LORD HALDANE DELAYING WAR PREPARATIONS?

WHAT IS HE DOING AT THE WAR OFFICE?

What is the Lord Chancellor doing at the War Office? Lord Haldane is, as everybody knows, an excellent and admirable Lord Chancellor, a great lawyer, and an extremely fluent and voluble orator, but why is he occupying himself at this moment with affairs that have nothing to do with the Woolsack?

We had news on Monday that Lord Kitchener, without doubt the greatest available military organiser, had been suddenly recalled to London when on board a Channel steamer; and it was generally believed and hoped that it was the intention of the Government to ask him to take charge of the War Office in this great crisis. Public opinion, which is strongly in favour of the adoption of this course, was pleased and satisfied, and it was everywhere supposed that at last we should see the right man in the right place.

But the fact is that for the last two days it is not Lord Kitchener, nor even Mr. Asquith, the Secretary of State for War, who has been the presiding genius at the War Office, but Lord Haldane! Mr. Asquith is, of course, fully occupied with matters of the gravest importance, and it is explained to the few people who know of Lord Haldane's presence at the War Office that the Lord Chancellor is "assisting Mr. Asquith." The fact is that he has been gently but very firmly assuming control of the military preparations. It is feared that he is delaying them …

GERMANY'S NAVAL STRONGHOLD IN THE NORTH SEA.

▲ The outbreak of war drove the *Daily Mail* to a Doric capitals double-column lead.

◀ For the *Daily News* the outbreak of war rated not only a banner but a double-column splash.

THE BIRMINGHAM DAILY POST, WEDNESDAY, AUGUST 5, 1914.

WAR DECLARED BY BRITAIN.

GERMANY'S REPLY TO ULTIMATUM.

"UNSATISFACTORY."

THE NEUTRALITY OF BELGIUM.

WAR BEGUN.

REPORTED SINKING OF BRITISH SHIP.

It was announced last night that Great Britain had declared war on Germany.

THE DECLARATION OF WAR.

OFFICIAL STATEMENT.

The following official announcement was issued by the Foreign Office at 12.10 a.m.:—

"Owing to the summary rejection by the German Government of the request made by his Majesty's Government for the assurance that the neutrality of Belgium will be respected, his Majesty's Ambassador at Berlin has received his passport. His Majesty's Government have declared to the German Government that a state of war exists between Great Britain and Germany as from 11 p.m. on August 4."

GERMANY AND FRANCE.

THE FORMAL DECLARATION OF WAR.

ALGERIAN TOWN BOMBARDED.

ADVANCE FROM LUXEMBURG.

HOSTILE AIRCRAFT.

CAPTURED GERMANS.

OFFICER BURIED WITH FRENCH MILITARY HONOURS.

INSPECTOR-GENERAL OF THE FORCES.

SIR JOHN FRENCH APPOINTED.

THE POSITION IN THE MEDITERRANEAN.

DECLARATION OF WAR ON BELGIUM.

GERMANY'S VIOLATION OF THE TREATY.

KING ALBERT'S APPEAL.

BELGIUM'S ANSWER TO THE GERMAN NOTE.

DEMANDS REJECTED.

THE BELGIAN REPLY.

WAR NEWS.

The "BIRMINGHAM DAILY POST" will be sent to any address in the Midlands for delivery by the early morning post (with a few exceptions) for 10/- per quarter or 3/- for 4 weeks prepaid. Address, 38, New Street, Birmingham.

Saturday Night's late edition of the "MAIL" will be sent by post for delivery on Sunday morning for 1/- for 12 weeks prepaid. Address, 13, Corporation Street, Birmingham.

PATRIOTIC COLONIES.

A MESSAGE OF THANKS FROM THE KING.

AUSTRALIA'S OFFER.

ANXIETY IN SOUTH AFRICA.

COMMAND OF HOME FLEETS.

THE KING'S MESSAGE TO THE NAVY.

ITALY'S NEUTRALITY.

BIRMINGHAM AND A WAR RELIEF FUND.

THE KAISER'S SPEECH.

"NO LUST OF CONQUEST IMPELS US."

CREDIT OF £250,000,000.

BIG CREDIT VOTE.

RUSSIAN SPIES IN GERMANY.

ALLEGED ATTEMPT ON CROWN PRINCE'S PALACE.

GERMANY AND RUSSIA.

REPORTED REPULSE OF AN ADVANCE PARTY.

BOMBARDMENT OF LIBAU.

AUSTRIA AND BRITAIN.

"CONVINCED OF PEACEFUL ATTITUDE."

BRITISH ULTIMATUM TO GERMANY.

PREMIER'S STATEMENT.

NEUTRALITY OF BELGIUM MUST BE RESPECTED.

CALLING OUT THE RESERVES AND TERRITORIALS.

THE HOUSE OF LORDS.

AUSTRIA AND SERVIA.

INVADERS UNABLE TO CROSS THE DANUBE.

BRITISHERS IN WAR AREA.

▲ Armageddon could not shake the solid provincials from their staid single-column deckers: the *Birmingham Post* of 5 August 1914.

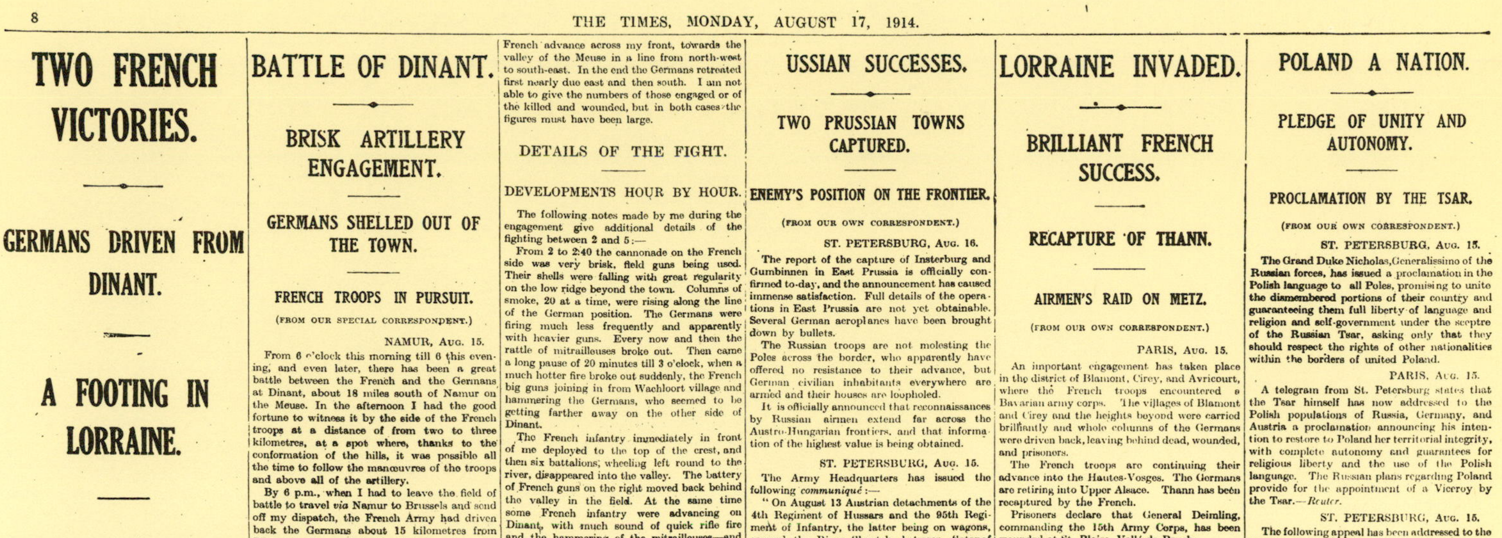

8 THE TIMES, MONDAY, AUGUST 17, 1914.

TWO FRENCH VICTORIES.

GERMANS DRIVEN FROM DINANT.

A FOOTING IN LORRAINE.

TSAR AND THE POLES.

One of the most important engagements of the war took place on Saturday in and around Dinant, on the River Meuse, about 18 miles due south of Namur. German troops occupying the town were driven out by a French force advancing from the north on the west bank of the Meuse. The action lasted from 6 a.m. to about 6 p.m., when the Germans had been driven about nine miles south to a point between Givet and Rochefort.

Our Special Correspondent at Namur witnessed this battle, which he describes in a dispatch published to-day. He bears witness to the excellence of the French artillery practice and the dash of their infantry. We publish a plan of the engagement.

The French troops also behaved brilliantly in an attack upon the German troops holding Blamont and Cirey, two posts on the Lorraine frontier due west of Strassburg ...

BATTLE OF DINANT.

BRISK ARTILLERY ENGAGEMENT.

GERMANS SHELLED OUT OF THE TOWN.

FRENCH TROOPS IN PURSUIT.

(FROM OUR SPECIAL CORRESPONDENT.)

NAMUR, AUG. 15.

From 6 o'clock this morning till 6 this evening, and even later, there has been a great battle between the French and the Germans at Dinant, about 18 miles south of Namur on the Meuse. In the afternoon I had the good fortune to witness it by the side of the French troops at a distance of from two to three kilometres, at a spot where, thanks to the conformation of the hills, it was possible all the time to follow the manœuvres of the troops and above all of the artillery.

By 6 p.m., when I had to leave the field of battle to travel *via* Namur to Brussels and send off my dispatch, the French Army had driven back the Germans about 15 kilometres from Dinant to the south in the direction of a point between Rochefort and Givet, and were pursuing them all the time.

The battle was divided in two parts, the first part occupying the day up to 2 p.m., and the second half the rest of the afternoon. It began, as I have just said, in the morning at about 6. At that time the Germans had taken possession of the part of the town of Dinant which is on the left side of the Meuse. At the same time a regiment of French infantry were advancing from the south to the north occupied the other side of the town—that is to say, the right bank. After that for some hours there were skirmishes between the two forces which extended as far as the villages of Houx and Sommière and other places.

The first part of the fight was spent in these operations.

THE ARTILLERY.

In the afternoon, from about 2 o'clock, it was principally an artillery engagement. The French infantry in the west and south of Dinant withdrew into the woods on this side of the Meuse, at six kilometres from the river, and the artillery took charge of the battle. At the same time a French regiment of infantry advanced along the Meuse, still on the right bank, coming from Houx, which is on the river, five or six kilometres north of Dinant. This force flung itself on the Germans who were in that part of the town which is on the other side of the ...

French advance across my front, towards the valley of the Meuse in a line from north-west to south-east. In the end the Germans retreated first nearly due east and then south. I am not able to give the numbers of those engaged or of the killed and wounded, but in both cases the figures must have been large.

DETAILS OF THE FIGHT.

DEVELOPMENTS HOUR BY HOUR.

The following notes made by me during the engagement give additional details of the fighting between 2 and 5:—

From 2 to 2.40 the cannonade on the French side was very brisk, field guns being used. Their shells were falling with great regularity on the low ridge beyond the town. Columns of smoke, 20 at a time, were rising along the line of the German position. The Germans were firing much less frequently and apparently with heavier guns. Every now and then the rattle of mitrailleuses broke out. Then came a long pause of 20 minutes till 3 o'clock, when a much hotter fire broke out suddenly, the French big guns joining in from Wachloort village and hammering the Germans, who seemed to be getting farther away on the other side of Dinant.

The French infantry immediately in front of me deployed to the top of the crest, and then six battalions, wheeling left round to the river, disappeared into the valley. The battery of French guns on the right moved back behind the valley in the field. At the same time some French infantry were advancing on Dinant, with much sound of quick rifle fire and the hammering of the mitrailleuses—and an occasional shot from the French siege guns in the wood behind the three batteries.

At 3.30 the middle French battery retired behind the first, swept round, and then advanced farther south, disappearing over the slope down towards the river. Five minutes later another French battery, from a much more advanced position, made much the same movement, apparently to join the one which had gone towards the river. Then one appeared on this side of the slope in front and opened fire at 3.45.

At 3.50 five French field batteries were in the shape of a V with the apex away from the Germans. Behind the apex of the V, which was situated on the swelling cornfields, at a distance of one or two kilometres further from Dinant, are the woods of Weillen, in a long line stretching away from Sommières on my right. In these were placed the French big field guns, and, I suspect, a strong body of infantry. This French position, which one could place by the sound of the big guns, is presumably the objective of the German big guns, as no shots had fallen near the batteries of French field guns in the fields in the centre of the picture.

THE GERMAN FIRE.

...

RUSSIAN SUCCESSES.

TWO PRUSSIAN TOWNS CAPTURED.

ENEMY'S POSITION ON THE FRONTIER.

(FROM OUR OWN CORRESPONDENT.)

ST. PETERSBURG, AUG. 16.

The report of the capture of Insterburg and Gumbinnen in East Prussia is officially confirmed to-day, and the announcement has caused immense satisfaction. Full details of the operations in East Prussia are not yet obtainable. Several German aeroplanes have been brought down by bullets.

The Russian troops are not molesting the Poles across the border, who apparently have offered no resistance to their advance, but German civilian inhabitants everywhere are armed and their houses are loopholed.

It is officially announced that reconnaissances by Russian airmen extend far across the Austro-Hungarian frontiers, and that information of the highest value is being obtained.

ST. PETERSBURG, AUG. 15.

The Army Headquarters has issued the following *communiqué*:—

"On August 13 Austrian detachments of the 4th Regiment of Hussars and the 95th Regiment of Infantry, the latter being on wagons, crossed the River Sbrutch between Satanof and Husiatyn, advancing eastward. By the River Smotritch, however, they were dispersed by the fire of the Russian troops, and beat a retreat, leaving their prisoners behind.

"On August 14 two German destroyers unsuccessfully bombarded Doune and Polangen.

"German cavalry is being concentrated in the radius of Pillkallen and Khomentovo, and the infantry near Stallupönen. German detachments of the Landwehr are advancing to the south from Schmalleningken."—*Reuter.*

AUGUST 16.

On Thursday the Russian cavalry near Kielce dispersed a body of troops which was supported by detachments of the 10th Austrian Dragoons. After this combat the enemy evacuated Kielce and Chęciny. On the same day detachments of the First German Infantry Division attempted an attack on the Russian front at Gutow, Bajohren, Eydtkuhnen, and Kybeiki, but were repulsed after an artillery engagement.

On Thursday also a German Cavalry Division with artillery attacked the Russian lines, but were forced by Russian cavalry to beat a hasty retreat.

On Friday the enemy again attacked Eydtkuhnen and were again repulsed. Skirmishes took place near Kreitingen and Alexandrovsk. Russian troops dislodged the enemy from several villages, which were burned by the Germans as they retreated. Russian cavalry, after having repulsed detachments of the 40th, ...

LORRAINE INVADED.

BRILLIANT FRENCH SUCCESS.

RECAPTURE OF THANN.

AIRMEN'S RAID ON METZ.

(FROM OUR OWN CORRESPONDENT.)

PARIS, AUG. 15.

An important engagement has taken place in the district of Blamont, Cirey, and Avricourt, where the French troops encountered a Bavarian army corps. The villages of Blamont and Cirey and the heights beyond were carried brilliantly and whole columns of the Germans were driven back, leaving behind dead, wounded, and prisoners.

The French troops are continuing their advance into the Hautes-Vosges. The Germans are retiring into Upper Alsace. Thann has been recaptured by the French.

Prisoners declare that General Deimling, commanding the 15th Army Corps, has been wounded at St. Blaise, Vallé de Bruche.

To mark this exploit of the troops two French airmen left Verdun and, flying over Metz, dropped two bombs upon the Frascati hangars, where the Zeppelin airships are lodged. After being exposed to more than 200 shots fired by artillery the airmen regained Verdun in safety, having accomplished their mission.

A new German aeroplane, containing two officers, has been captured near Bouillon. The pilot was wounded.

⁂ Avricourt, in Lorraine, is shown on the map of the French eastern frontier. Blamont and Cirey are on the French side about six and 12 miles respectively S.E. of Avricourt. Avricourt and Thann will be found in the map on page 7.

A BRILLIANT ENGAGEMENT.

AUG. 16.

The engagement at Blamont and Cirey, which has been already reported, was particularly brilliant.

One of the French divisions began the attack on Friday evening. The enemy was strongly entrenched behind field works in front of Blamont. Just at daybreak his advanced posts were thrown back and his attack arrested, and when dawn had broken the French resumed the offensive. They succeeded in carrying Blamont and Cirey by an infantry action sup- ...

POLAND A NATION.

PLEDGE OF UNITY AND AUTONOMY.

PROCLAMATION BY THE TSAR.

(FROM OUR OWN CORRESPONDENT.)

ST. PETERSBURG, AUG. 15.

The Grand Duke Nicholas, Generalissimo of the Russian forces, has issued a proclamation in the Polish language to all Poles, promising to unite the dismembered portions of their country and guaranteeing them full liberty of language and religion and self-government under the sceptre of the Russian Tsar, asking only that they should respect the rights of other nationalities within the borders of united Poland.

PARIS, AUG. 15.

A telegram from St. Petersburg states that the Tsar himself has now addressed to the Polish populations of Russia, Germany, and Austria a proclamation announcing his intention to restore to Poland her territorial integrity, with complete autonomy and guarantees for religious liberty and the use of the Polish language. The Russian plans regarding Poland provide for the appointment of a Viceroy by the Tsar.—*Reuter.*

ST. PETERSBURG, AUG. 15.

The following appeal has been addressed to the Poles by the Grand Duke Nicholas, Commander-in-Chief of the Russian forces:—

Poles.—The hour has sounded when the sacred dream of your fathers and your grandfathers may be realized. A century and a half has passed since the living body of Poland was torn in pieces, but the soul of the country is not dead. It continues to live, inspired by the hope that there will come for the Polish people an hour of resurrection, and of fraternal reconciliation with Great Russia. The Russian Army brings you the solemn news of this reconciliation which obliterates the frontiers dividing the Polish peoples, which it unites conjointly under the sceptre of the Russian Tsar. Under this sceptre Poland will be born again, free in her religion and her language. Russian autonomy only expects from you the same respect for the rights of those nationalities to which history has bound you. With open heart and brotherly hand Great Russia advances to meet you. She believes that the sword, with which she struck down her enemies at Grünwald, is not yet rusted. From the shores of the Pacific to the North Sea the Russian armies are marching. The dawn of a new life is beginning for you, and in this glorious dawn is seen the sign of the Cross, the symbol of suffering and of the resurrection of peoples.—*Reuter.*

THEATRES.

APOLLO. Henry Lowenfeld, Sole Proprietor. Tom B. Davis, Sole Lessee and Manager.

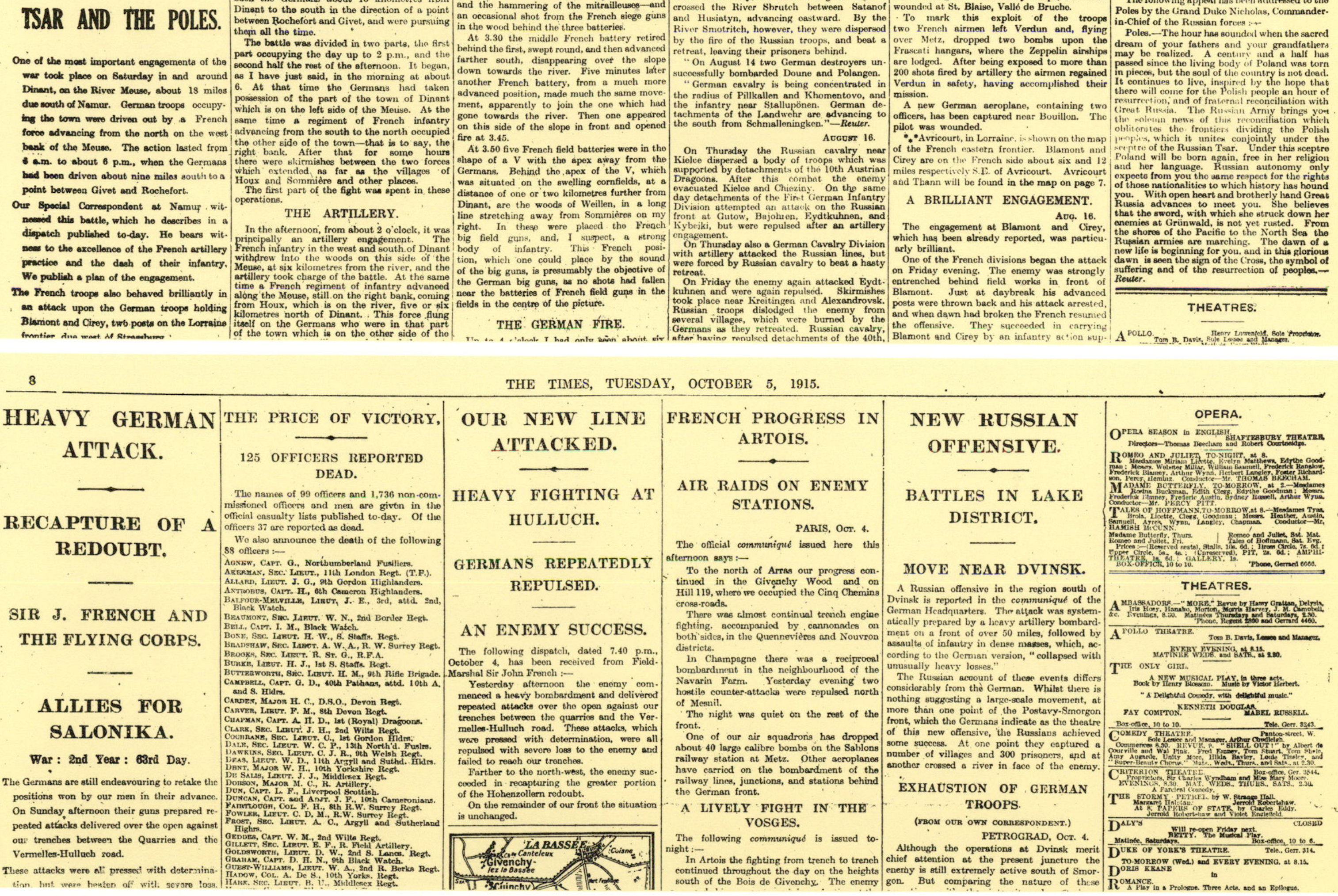

8 THE TIMES, TUESDAY, OCTOBER 5, 1915.

HEAVY GERMAN ATTACK.

RECAPTURE OF A REDOUBT.

SIR J. FRENCH AND THE FLYING CORPS.

ALLIES FOR SALONIKA.

War: 2nd Year: 63rd Day.

The Germans are still endeavouring to retake the positions won by our men in their advance. On Sunday afternoon their guns prepared repeated attacks delivered over the open against our trenches between the Quarries and the Vermelles-Hulluch road.

These attacks were all pressed with determination, but were beaten off with severe loss ...

THE PRICE OF VICTORY.

125 OFFICERS REPORTED DEAD.

The names of 99 officers and 1,736 non-commissioned officers and men are given in the official casualty lists published to-day. Of the officers 37 are reported as dead.

We also announce the death of the following 88 officers:—

AGNEW, CAPT. G., Northumberland Fusiliers.
AKERMAN, SEC. LIEUT., 11th London Regt. (T.F.).
ALLARD, LIEUT. J. G., 9th Gordon Highlanders.
ANTROBUS, CAPT. H., 6th Cameron Highlanders.
BALFOUR-MELVILLE, LIEUT. J. E., 3rd, attd. 2nd, Black Watch.
BEAUMONT, SEC. LIEUT. W. N., 2nd Border Regt.
BELL, CAPT. I. M., Black Watch.
BONE, SEC. LIEUT. H. W., 8. Staffs. Regt.
BRADSHAW, SEC. LIEUT. A. W. A., R. W. Surrey Regt.
BROOKS, SEC. LIEUT. R. St. G., R.F.A.
BURKE, LIEUT. H. J., 1st S. Staffs. Regt.
BUTTERWORTH, SEC. LIEUT. H. M., 9th Rifle Brigade.
CAMPBELL, CAPT. G. D., 40th Pathans, attd. 10th A. and S. Hldrs.
CARDEN, MAJOR H. C., D.S.O., Devon Regt.
CARVER, LIEUT. F. M., 8th Devon Regt.
CHAPMAN, CAPT. A. H. D., 1st (Royal) Dragoons.
CLARK, SEC. LIEUT. J. H., 2nd Wilts Regt.
COCHRANE, SEC. LIEUT. G., 1st Gordon Hldrs.
DALE, SEC. LIEUT. W. C. P., 13th North'd. Fusrs.
DAWKINS, SEC. LIEUT. C. J. R., 9th Welsh Regt.
DEAS, LIEUT. W. D., 11th Argyll and Suthd. Hldrs.
DENT, MAJOR W. H., 10th Yorkshire Regt.
DE SALIS, LIEUT. J. J., Middlesex Regt.
DOBSON, MAJOR M. C., R. Artillery.
DUN, CAPT. L. F., Liverpool Scottish.
DUNCAN, CAPT. and ADJT. J. F., 10th Cameronians.
FAIRCLOUGH, COL. F. H., 8th R.W. Surrey Regt.
FOWLER, LIEUT. C. D. M., R.W. Surrey Regt.
FROST, SEC. LIEUT. A. C., Argyll and Sutherland Highrs.
GEDDES, CAPT. W. M., 2nd Wilts Regt.
GILLETT, SEC. LIEUT. E. F., R. Field Artillery.
GOLDSWORTH, LIEUT. D. W., 2nd S. Lancs. Regt.
GRAHAM, CAPT. D. H. N., 9th Black Watch.
GUEST-WILLIAMS, LIEUT. W. A., 2nd R. Berks Regt.
HADOW, COL. A. DE S., 10th Yorks. Regt.
HAKE, SEC. LIEUT. H. U., Middlesex Regt.

OUR NEW LINE ATTACKED.

HEAVY FIGHTING AT HULLUCH.

GERMANS REPEATEDLY REPULSED.

AN ENEMY SUCCESS.

The following dispatch, dated 7.40 p.m., October 4, has been received from Field-Marshal Sir John French:—

Yesterday afternoon the enemy commenced a heavy bombardment and delivered repeated attacks over the open against our trenches between the quarries and the Vermelles-Hulluch road. These attacks, which were pressed with determination, were all repulsed with severe loss to the enemy and failed to reach our trenches.

Farther to the north-west, the enemy succeeded in recapturing the greater portion of the Hohenzollern redoubt.

On the remainder of our front the situation is unchanged.

LA BASSÉE ... Givenchy ... Cuinchy

FRENCH PROGRESS IN ARTOIS.

AIR RAIDS ON ENEMY STATIONS.

PARIS, OCT. 4.

The official *communiqué* issued here this afternoon says:—

To the north of Arras our progress continued in the Givenchy Wood and on Hill 119, where we occupied the Cinq Chemins cross-roads.

There was almost continual trench engine fighting, accompanied by cannonades on both sides, in the Quennevières and Nouvron districts.

In Champagne there was a reciprocal bombardment in the neighbourhood of the Navarin Farm. Yesterday evening two hostile counter-attacks were repulsed north of Mesnil.

The night was quiet on the rest of the front.

One of our air squadrons has dropped about 40 large calibre bombs on the Sablons railway station at Metz. Other aeroplanes have carried on the bombardment of the railway lines, junctions, and stations behind the German front.

A LIVELY FIGHT IN THE VOSGES.

The following *communiqué* is issued to-night:—

In Artois the fighting from trench to trench continued throughout the day on the heights south of the Bois de Givenchy. The enemy ...

NEW RUSSIAN OFFENSIVE.

BATTLES IN LAKE DISTRICT.

MOVE NEAR DVINSK.

A Russian offensive in the region south of Dvinsk is reported in the *communiqué* of the German Headquarters. The attack was systematically prepared by a heavy artillery bombardment on a front of over 50 miles, followed by assaults of infantry in dense masses, which, according to the German version, "collapsed with unusually heavy losses."

The Russian account of these events differs considerably from the German. Whilst there is nothing suggesting a large-scale movement, at more than one point of the Postavy-Smorgon front, which the Germans indicate as the theatre of this new offensive, the Russians achieved some success. At one point they captured a number of villages and 300 prisoners, and at another crossed a river in face of the enemy.

EXHAUSTION OF GERMAN TROOPS.

(FROM OUR OWN CORRESPONDENT.)

PETROGRAD, OCT. 4.

Although the operations at Dvinsk merit chief attention at the present juncture the enemy is still extremely active south of Smorgon. But comparing the nature of these ...

OPERA.

OPERA SEASON in ENGLISH. SHAFTESBURY THEATRE. Directors—Thomas Beecham and Robert Courtneidge.

ROMEO AND JULIET, TO-NIGHT, at 8.

MADAME BUTTERFLY, TO-MORROW, at 8.

TALES OF HOFFMANN, TO-MORROW at 8.

BOX-OFFICE, 10 to 10. 'Phone, Gerrard 6665.

THEATRES.

AMBASSADORS.—"MORE." Revue by Harry Grattan.

APOLLO THEATRE. Tom B. Davis, Lessee and Manager. EVERY EVENING, at 8.15. MATINEE WEDS. and SATS., at 2.30.

THE ONLY GIRL. A NEW MUSICAL PLAY, in three acts.

"A Delightful Comedy, with delightful music."

KENNETH DOUGLAS. FAY COMPTON. MABEL RUSSELL.

COMEDY THEATRE.

CRITERION THEATRE.

THE STORMY PETREL.

DALY'S. BETTY. The Musical Play.

DUKE OF YORK'S THEATRE. TO-MORROW (Wed.) and EVERY EVENING, at 8.15.

DORIS KEANE in ROMANCE. A Play in a Prologue, Three Acts, and an Epilogue.

▲ The shock of August 1914 brought a Venetian-Cheltenham reaction from *The Times* but by 1915 the sober news-titlings had come back.

these, and for the 'bill' page, it ransacked its advertising display cases for types with more colour and impact than the news-titlings. So its six-column broad gauge page – all other London dailies had long since standardised on seven-column make-up – was adorned with well-spaced headings in Venetian Condensed capitals, the lead story on the first column occasionally going up to the capitals of the then latest variant of the Cheltenham family, the Bold Extra Condensed (not the Bold Condensed, as Morison said). Such typographic radicalism must have been a severe shock to many readers of *The Times*; by 1915 it settled down to an improved news-titling style, with well-whited decker headings in a bold titling contrasting with a light version. Though wartime sensations often brought various bold jobbing types into headline play, this news-titling style remained, with some adaptation, until the Morison revolution of 1932.

REYNOLDS'S NEWSPAPER

Government of the People, by the People, for the People.

LONDON, SUNDAY, AUGUST 13, 1916.

PRICE ONE PENNY.

SPECIAL SUNDAY EDITION.

PENSION PROBLEMS.

CHEERY NEWS FROM ALL THE FRONTS.

BIG FRENCH SUCCESS.

STRONGLY ORGANISED GERMAN WORKS CAPTURED.

MAUREPAS ENTERED.

1,000 Prisoners and 30 Machine-Guns Taken North of the Somme.

ATTACK ON BRITISH FAILS.

WHERE THE ALLIES ARE ADVANCING

RUSSIANS STILL ADVANCING.

LEMBERG'S OUTER DEFENCES MENACED.

STANISLAU UNTOUCHED.

SECRET HISTORY OF TO-DAY.

GERMAN FOOD PROBLEM.

DAYLIGHT RAID ON DOVER.

SEVEN PERSONS INJURED.

BIG ATTACK FAILS.

SITUATION SATISFACTORY.

ENEMY LOSSES HEAVY.

WOOD PENETRATED.

ATTACKS FRUSTRATED.

A WEEK OF VICTORIES.

MOVE IN THE BALKANS.

VILLAGES CAPTURED.

VIGOROUS FIGHTING.

OPERATIONS IN EGYPT.

A CHANCE IN THE DARK.

LAST NIGHT'S NEWS ITEMS.

THIS WEEK IN PARLIAMENT.

The banner style had come to stay: a 1916 front page of *Reynolds's*.

FINAL NIGHT EDN.

THE PALL MALL GAZETTE

No. 16,883. [REGISTERED AT THE G.P.O. AS A NEWSPAPER] SATURDAY, JUNE 28, 1919. ONE PENNY.

PEACE SIGNED.

This afternoon at 3.12 the Peace between the Allied and Associated Governments and Germany was signed at Versailles, bringing to a formal end the hostilities which commenced by the declaration by Germany of war on Russia on August 1, 1914, and France on August 3, 1914; by the declaration by Britain of war on Germany on August 4, 1914; and by the declaration by America of war on Germany on April 5, 1917.

GREAT HISTORIC SCENE AT VERSAILLES.

GERMAN PLENIPOTENTIARIES SIGN THE TREATY OF PEACE.

MAIN DATES OF THE GREAT WAR.

1914.

Aug. 1.—Germany declares war on Russia.

Aug. 3.—Germany declares war on France.

Aug. 4.—Great Britain declares war on Germany.

LONDON'S JOY NIGHT.

SEARCHLIGHTS, GUNS, DINNERS, AND REJOICINGS.

An early 72pt banner: how the *Pall Mall Gazette* hailed the Versailles Treaty of 1919.

What may be called the streamer-and-double-column style now became general. A random example taken from *Reynolds's* exemplifies its adoption by the Sunday papers. Any sort of typographic consistency, or specialised development of display faces for uniform newspaper headlining, was yet to come; the specimen shows jobbing types like Hawarden, Windsor Bold Condensed, grot and condensed sans, all in play. That uniform styling could be achieved was indicated by the 1919 Versailles Treaty-signing issue of the *Pall Mall Gazette* (that once prosperous London evening had only four years to live). Headlining was throughout in Caslon Old Face Heavy deckers – all capitals still – with the Old Face Heavy Compressed as a convenient variant. The big streamer was a 72pt in the capitals of a blunt, bold jobbing type – the largest size of Haddon, a then popular product of the firm of that once-notorious maverick among typefounders, the late Walter Haddon (it resembled Stephenson Blake's Chatsworth); the retention of the full-point is noticeable. At this stage founders' type was unchallenged for the setting of headlines; for many papers it remained so for years to come. London's popular evening *The Star*, for instance, continued to use Stephenson Blake's Clearface Extra Bold, roman and italic, until the 1940s, Monotype-cast type was little employed (the Super Caster, with its up to 72pt capacity, did not appear until 1929) though the revived *Daily Herald*, which had the Monotype casters of the Pelican Press at its disposal, used Monotype Plantin 110 for upper- and lower-case decks to headings in condensed sans capitals.

The developments described above, it will have been noted, were all casual and chancy. For its weapons against the prim, weak newstitlings the campaign for bolder headlining laid hands on whatever display type there happened to be about. There was no re-thinking of overall headline and make-up styles. Such a planned, organised revolution in a newspaper's graphic presentation was to be pioneered in the U.S. Without doubt it was the biggest thing to happen in newspaper typography during the First World War, indeed the biggest thing until the radical changes of the 1930s and after, many of which it foreshadowed.

This great change took place on the *New York Tribune*, which in the five years up to 1914 had already made a number of format changes, first from six columns to seven, and then to eight (not to become general in Britain until after the outbreak of the Second World War in 1939). Until 1916, it was later observed, 'the notion that news printing could be a thing of practical beauty, far removed from the brashness of a screaming headline, had not dawned in America'.[1] In that year the conductors of the *Tribune* got their editorial and composing room chiefs to co-operate with a noted New York typographer, Ben Sherbow, in a lengthy series of typographic experiments aimed at discovering (with stop-watch control) which combinations of display types produced more pleasing, more striking and more quickly readable headlines. The experiments lasted nearly a year; the changes they suggested were introduced gradually in the course of 1917–18 – first an all upper- and lower-case style and finally this style in one type family throughout, Bodoni Bold roman and italic.

At this point it will not be out of place to quote the late John E. Allen's reminiscences of the now shadowy Sherbow at work in his New York office on some of his newspaper experiments. Allen, then a youngster working for Mergenthaler Linotype, told how during 1919–20 he

'used to drop in on Sherbow on Saturday afternoons to watch him at work and to do odd jobs of type checking and galley sorting for him. That experimenting typographer, a wide-hipped little man with a high-pitched voice, usually had a curved-stem pipe going full blast and a cloud of tobacco smoke about his head as he worked away on his unconventional newspaper pages. A brother of his who worked

ALL MERCHANDISE ADVERTISED IN THE TRIBUNE IS GUARANTEED

New York Tribune

First to Last—the Truth: News · Editorials · Advertisements

Vol. LXXVIII No 26,315 TUESDAY, DECEMBER 3, 1918

Wilson Asks United Congress to Support Peace Ideals, but Keeps Program Secret; Bills to Call Office "Vacant" Are Offered

Tear-Filled Eyes Greet Soldiers on Homecoming

Thousands Crowd Round Cunard Piers as Mauretania Docks With 4,069 Glad American Airmen

23 Left Wives On Other Side

Noisy Welcome in Broad Daylight Contrasts With Stealth of Departure for Overseas Service

1,600,000 Christians Massacred by Turks

Chile Recalls Army Reserves to Colors

First Forecast for U. S. Mail Fliers

Peace Plans Agreed On By Premiers

Fate of Ex-Kaiser Said to Have Been Discussed at London Conference

Guards Stationed At All Entrances

Consideration of Amount of Fine on Germany Reported Considered

New All-Russian Government Formed

Lansing Hints U. S. Seeks Indemnity For U-Boat Losses

Refusal to Explain Plan Disappoints

Future Opposition Shown in Demand by Cummins for Peace Committee

Real Enthusiasm Entirely Lacking

Leaders Declare, After Speech, It Failed to Clear Up the Situation

By Carter Field

Wilson Goes to Give Counsel To Allies on Fourteen Points

President in N.Y. To-day to Board Liner

Expected to Name R. S. Lovett to Head Railroads

Policies at Home Left To Congress

Advocates of Public Ownership Disappointed in Hint to Return Roads

By Theodore M. Knappen

Alsace Wanted in French Parliament

Solution of Rail Problem Is Sought by President

Men Who Helped Win War Are Highly Praised in Address at Joint Session of Congress

Wants Fruits of Victory Secured

Declares Women Have Deserved Ballot by Support of Government in the Most Crucial Days

President Reviews Great Events of Last Months

Nearly Two Million Men Sent Overseas to Fight

NOW THAT HE'S GONE

▲ After the Ben Sherbow revolution: the *New York Tribune* of December 1918 with the basic Bodoni Bold upper- and lower-case headline style which its successor the *Herald-Tribune* permanently retained.

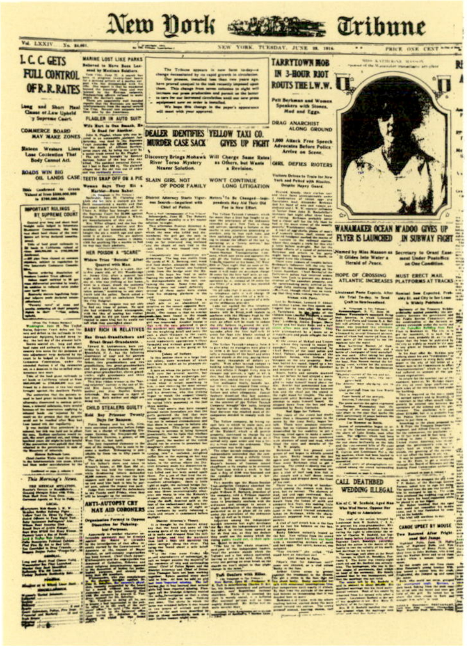
New York Tribune

NEW YORK, TUESDAY, JUNE 23, 1914. PRICE ONE CENT

I. C. C. GETS FULL CONTROL OF R. R. RATES

COMMERCE BOARD MAY MAKE ZONES

ROADS WIN BIG OIL LANDS CASE

IMPORTANT RULINGS BY SUPREME COURT

MARINE LOST LIKE PARKS

FLAGLER IN AUTO SUIT

TEETH SNAP OFF ON A PIE

HER POISON A "SCARE"

BABY RICH IN RELATIVES

CHILD STEALERS GUILTY

DEALER IDENTIFIES MURDER CASE SACK

SLAIN GIRL NOT OF POOR FAMILY

YELLOW TAXI CO. GIVES UP FIGHT

WON'T CONTINUE LONG LITIGATION

TARRYTOWN MOB IN 3-HOUR RIOT ROUTS THE I.W.W.

DRAG ANARCHIST ALONG GROUND

GIRL DEFIES RIOTERS

WANAMAKER OCEAN FLYER IS LAUNCHED

HOPE OF CROSSING ATLANTIC INCREASES

M'ADOO GIVES UP IN SUBWAY FIGHT

MUST ERECT MAIL PLATFORMS AT TRACKS

▲ The *New York Tribune* of 1914 in its version of the stiff American decker headline style.

with him often stood by playing a violin as Benjamin did his experimenting. And some of that music, it seemed, managed to get into his newspaper heads – always in capitals and lower-case.'[2]

Ben Sherbow's Bodoni lower-case restyling of the *Tribune* was not only revolutionary, but long-lived. After the merger with the *New York Herald* in 1924 it continued virtually unchanged as the style of the *Herald Tribune* until that paper's regretted demise in 1966 (and it still continues in the *Herald Tribune* Paris edition, now a joint venture of the *New York Times* and *Washington Post*). The Sherbow 'free' upper- and lower-case style was a direct challenge to the established formalism of American headlining, with its stiff opening decks in condensed capitals, though as it turned out that formalism was to die very hard. At the same time the single-family approach at once adumbrated an important principle and (by the choice of Bodoni Bold) represented the first attempt to exploit for headline purposes the new ranges of good display types then being made available in the U.S. The initiative here lay with the American Type Founders Co. and its talented design chief, Morris F. Benton, son of the celebrated Linn B. Benton without whose pantographic invention the mass production of matrices for composing machines would have been impossible. For the ATF, Benton undertook adapted revivals of the classics, like Bodoni, Cloister, Garamond, new display faces by Frederic W. Goudy (Goudy OS, Goudy Bold), numerous bold and condensed variants of the Century and Cheltenham families, and improved gothics like Franklin. Gradually these ATF display types found their way, with or without further adaptation, into the composing machine repertory, though that was to be a slower process in Britain than in America.

As I said, the formalism of the American condensed-capitals decker heading died very hard; some lone outposts were to survive to our own day. What Sherbow's radical pioneering did for American newspapers was to induce a progressive dilution of the all-capitals first-deck style. Papers began to alternate traditional decker headings opening in capitals with headings opening in upper- and lower-case, usually in condensed faces; multi-column lower-case headings were introduced, often in bold italics. What became common and constant in all American dailies as a result of the First World War was the banner – one, or even two, lines of large-size bold condensed sans capitals (in 72 or even 96pt) across the full width of the page.

▼ In America the big gothic banner became regular style, as in this 1919 *San Francisco Chronicle*.

THIS NEWSPAPER IS ONE HUNDRED PER CENT AMERICAN

Monarchies in Ruins
The crash of European thrones in 1917-1918 is presented in its full significance at a glance through the medium of maps in
NEXT SUNDAY'S CHRONICLE

San Francisco Chronicle
LEADING NEWSPAPER of the PACIFIC COAST
REG. U. S. PAT. OFF.

FAIR
WEATHER
SAN FRANCISCO, OAKLAND AND VICINITY
Thursday fair, except cloudy or foggy in morning; moderate west winds. E. A. BEALS, Forecaster.
Complete Weather Report on Page 79

FOUNDED 1865 SAN FRANCISCO, CAL., THURSDAY, APRIL 3, 1919 VOL. CXIV, NO. 78

JAPAN MAY BOLT WORLD LEAGUE, HUNDREDS DIE IN GERMAN RIOTS

COVENANT NOT FOR ASIATICS, SAYS MAKINO
Mikado's Delegate at Paris Demands Race Equality if Nippon Is to Join

Bark Albert Goes On Reef off Point Reyes, Total Loss; Captain Drowned
Course Lost in Fog; Crew Make Shore After Fight

MACHINE GUNS QUELL RIOTERS IN STUTTGART
Gas and Electric Service Is Shut Off and Food Situation Is Serious

Herbert E. Law Sued for Attack on Divorcee.
Dr. Northcott Faces Court for Murder of Nurse

RAIL WORKERS IN PETROGRAD

Two Boys Hide in Burning House and Die While Mother

S. F. PHYSICIAN GIVEN HEARING

MRS. MARGARET ROBBINS, plaintiff in a suit for $100,000 damages against Herbert E. Law.

WOMAN ASKS $100,000 FROM

First of the 'tabs': the New York *Daily News* of 1919, the picture paper that flopped, with (below) the style to which it changed.

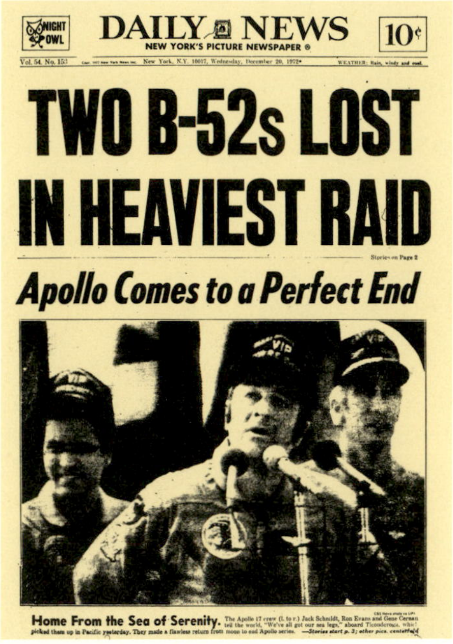

NIGHT OWL

DAILY NEWS

NEW YORK'S PICTURE NEWSPAPER ®

10¢

TWO B-52s LOST IN HEAVIEST RAID

Stories on Page 2

Apollo Comes to a Perfect End

Home From the Sea of Serenity.

Illustrated Daily News

No. 1 | New York | Thursday, June 26, 1919. | 2 Cents

GERMANS BLOCK SIGNING OF TREATY

Newport to Entertain Prince of Wales in August

A war made democrat is the Prince of Wales. He reviews the Naval Division and, in another intimate photograph, borrows a light from Lord Reading.

(By Marshall)

The post-war 'jazz era' in America, covering the decade from 1919 to the Wall Street crash and the start of the Great Depression in 1929, had a characteristic newspaper by-product. This was the emergence of the tabloids. The 'tabs', half-sheet papers making big play with halftones, were directly inspired by the London *Daily Mirror*. Joseph M. Patterson, associate of Robert R. McCormick in the proprietorship of the *Chicago Tribune*, had spent some time in England during his Army service overseas and had been impressed by the success of Northcliffe's *Mirror*. So in June 1919 he launched the New York *Daily News* as a picture paper copying the *Mirror*; the early issues had *Illustrated* in the title.

It was a worse flop than Northcliffe's original 'gentlewomen's' *Mirror*; at the end of its first two months circulation was a mere 11,000. Evidently the London-style 'picture paper' was no good for Manhattan. So Patterson changed the formula to the brashest and most bawling journalism attainable, exploiting sex appeal, scandal and sensation (of which there was no dearth in those prohibition, bootlegging, Al Capone days). To get horrific impact nothing was barred, as in the illegally-obtained picture of Ruth Snyder's electrocution at Sing Sing in 1928. The new formula paid off and was followed by Hearst when he started his competing *Daily Mirror* (now defunct) in 1924. The *Daily News* climbed steadily to the position it still enjoys of the largest daily circulation in the U.S. – around two million, with

Second of the 'tabs'; first issue of Hearst's New York *Daily Mirror*, closely copying its London namesake, in 1924.

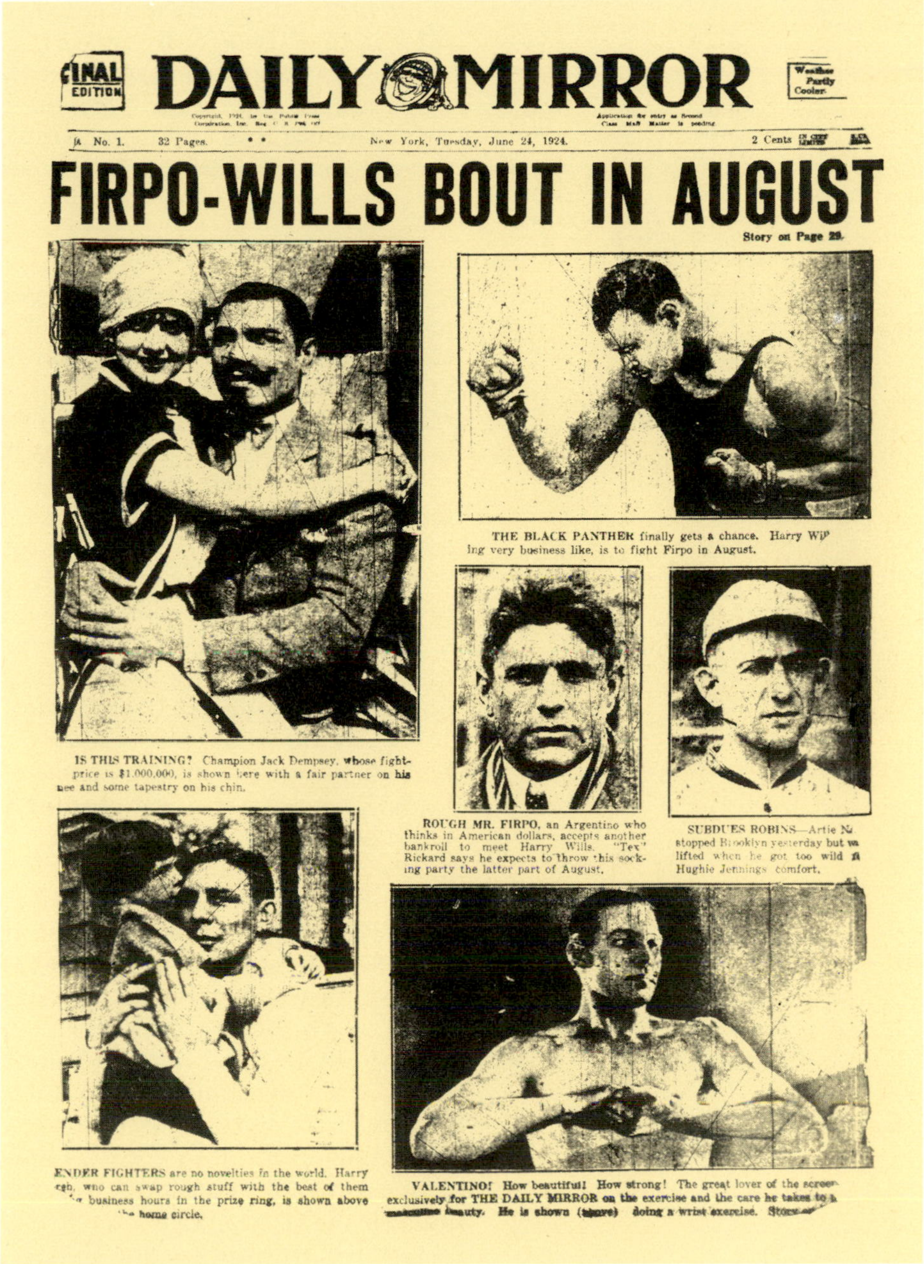

FINAL EDITION

DAILY MIRROR

No. 1. 32 Pages. New York, Tuesday, June 24, 1924. 2 Cents

FIRPO-WILLS BOUT IN AUGUST

Story on Page 29.

THE BLACK PANTHER finally gets a chance. Harry Wi ing very business like, is to fight Firpo in August.

IS THIS TRAINING? Champion Jack Dempsey, whose fight-price is $1,000,000, is shown here with a fair partner on his nee and some tapestry on his chin.

ROUGH MR. FIRPO, an Argentino who thinks in American dollars, accepts another bankroll to meet Harry Wills. "Tex" Rickard says he expects to throw this socking party the latter part of August.

SUBDUES ROBINS—Artie N stopped Brooklyn yesterday but wa lifted when he got too wild Hughie Jennings comfort.

ENDER FIGHTERS are no novelties in the world. Harry eb, who can swap rough stuff with the best of them business hours in the prize ring, is shown above home circle.

VALENTINO! How beautiful! How strong! The great lover of the scree exclusively for THE DAILY MIRROR on the exercise and the care he takes to beauty. He is shown (above) doing a wrist exercise.

many more on Sunday.

While making dramatic halftones a vital part of their presentation, the 'tabs' made their mark more with sledgehammer sans headlining, in the heaviest condensed gothics. Rather than picturing the front page the 'tabs' more often made it a poster, emulating and exceeding the treatments which, as we have seen, marked the victory in the Spanish-American War of 1898. The *Daily News* began with four wide columns on its small half-sheet, later modified to five. Contrast with the smashing sans headings was secured by the use of bold seriffed italic types from the Cheltenham or Ultra-Bodoni range.

Sherbow's *Tribune* revolution notwithstanding, the 1920s in both Britain and America were still a period without conscious and informed participation by editorial men in the determination of the typography of the newspapers they produced; indeed, years later (in the mid-1930s) I can recall overhearing the astute old chief sub-editor of a London Sunday, on which I was working, gravely warning a colleague to beware of 'young Hutt's' preoccupation with typography – 'there's no future in it', he said. Nevertheless there were signs, particularly in America, of a growing challenge to the Northcliffian 'leave type to the printer' attitude. In 1925 Adolph S. Ochs of the *New York Times* told students at the Columbia University School of Journalism: 'an apprenticeship in the composing room is an experience and qualification that helps to place the journalist in the front rank

Consideration of ease of reading is so essential in the planning of printed matter that every principle helping to achieve comfort in the assimilation of *the message conveyed by words* should always be in the forefront of the typographer's mind. On what does ease of reading depend? On the simpleness of the type design, on the length of the type lines and on their leading, on the spacing of words, *and on a principle either misunderstood or sadly ignored: that of appropriate choice of type face for the paper on which it is to be printed. Many type faces appropriate for the moderate*

A typical Modern (8pt), Intertype De Vinne.

of his profession. The make-up is the appearance of the newspaper. It is to attract the eye, to arrest the attention of the reader.'

The preceding chapter noted that the 1920s saw the completion of various technical improvements in process-engraving, stereotyping, rotary machining and newsprint, needed for overall good halftone reproduction, thus providing the basis for making the news photograph an integral part of newspaper design instead of an occasional pictorial additive. Some of these technical developments, however, were to have decisive repercussions in the sphere of newspaper text typography, to which no serious specialised attention had hitherto been paid. Dry-flong moulding subjected type to punishing pressures, while the steady rise in rotary press speeds (responding to circulation growth), with the attendant use of thinner inks and harder-surfaced rollers, resulted in papers whose broken-down texts printed either weak and grey or, if colour was increased, thick and smudgy.

The nineteenth-century moderns which had been the newspaper mainstay of the linecaster since its inception were clearly no longer adequate, the more so since American dailies were then mainly using 6pt and 7pt for text-setting. The standard news-text of this sort was Mergenthaler Linotype's Roman No. 2; from 1904 onwards there was a somewhat superior alternative, Century Expanded (an oddly-named variant of the famous improved modern introduced by Theodore L. De Vinne for the production of the *Century Magazine* in the 1890s; in appearance it was not expanded at all). Century, however, had only been taken up by some of the larger U.S. dailies; and its performance under the new stereotyping and machining conditions was little better than Roman No. 2.

The crucial year appears to have been 1922, when Linotype technicians, headed by the late C. H. Griffith, Mergenthaler's vice-president in charge of typographic development, began to address themselves to the problem. It is clear that they were so disillusioned with the modern face that they did not seek to revise or improve that design (a point to which we shall return in chapter 8) but looked instead to the strong strokes and open appearance of a slab-seriffed Victorian jobbing letter, stemming ultimately from the 'Egyptians', called Ionic. As Ionic, or Antique, it was still to be seen in British typefounders' specimen books as late as the 1930s. It was a strictly monotone letter, a point which must have worried the Mergenthaler men in the five successive versions they tried, ending in the finally issued Ionic No. 5.

Griffith himself warned that 'a purely monotone letter, all lines of equal weight, with large counters, would be fatiguing and monotonous for extensive reading.' He went on to describe Ionic No. 5, which was completed in 1925, as 'a fairly dark face, with just enough contrast in thick-and-thin lines to avoid the monotony of a monotone and still print with a vigorous colour and maximum legibility under adverse conditions'.[3] In fact the Mergenthaler Ionic did not have 'just enough' stroke contrast 'to avoid the monotony of a monotone'. This was tacitly conceded in the design of its successor, Excelsior, issued in 1931 to provide a competing newspaper with a text different from the Ionic installed by its rival. Excelsior related more to Modern; its 'thin-and-thick lines have slightly more contrast than in Ionic', as Griffith admitted.

Apart from its monotone drawing, Ionic was abnormally big on its body, reducing interlinear space to the point at which it required setting on a slug a halfpoint or even a point larger if it was to be easy on the eye. Excelsior had a more normal x-height. The exceptional x-height of Ionic must have been conditioned by the desire of its designers to overcome the problem of the small text sizes then common in America, as already mentioned; and the first size of Ionic to be cut was the 6½pt which, cast on a 7pt slug, was adopted early in 1926 as the main text type of the *Evening News*, Newark, New Jersey's leading evening (it closed down in 1972 as the sequel to a forty-five-week editorial strike).

Millions of words, in thousands of newspapers and magazines, are printed and read daily. All over the world news is necessary to the everyday routine of many millions of people. The public appetite for news is enormous, and the man who never reads a newspaper is news himself.

Type designs for this important area of printing are a class in themselves. To survive the effects of stereotyping and high-speed rotary printing the type face must be sturdy, and free from thin lines and delicate serifs. It must be designed with due regard for the tendency of thin inks to collect in the sharp angles and narrow openings.

Ionic (8 and 7pt).

Millions of words, in thousands of newspapers and magazines, are printed and read daily. All over the world news is necessary to the everyday routine of many millions of people. The public appetite for news is enormous, and the man who never reads a newspaper is news himself.

Type designs for this important area of printing are a class in themselves. To survive the effects of stereotyping and high-speed rotary printing the type face must be sturdy, and free from thin lines and delicate serifs. It must be designed with due regard for the tendency of thin inks to collect in sharp angles and narrow openings.

Excelsior (8 and 7pt).

Millions of words, in thousands of newspapers and magazines, are printed and read daily. All over the world news is necessary to the everyday routine of many millions of people. The public appetite for news is enormous, and the man who never reads a newspaper is news himself.

Type designs for this important area of printing are a class in themselves. To survive the effects of stereotyping and high-speed rotary printing the type face must be sturdy, and free from thin lines and delicate serifs. It must be designed with due regard for the tendency of thin inks to collect in the sharp angles and narrow openings.

Corona (8 and 7pt).

Ionic, however, had the biggest immediate success of any newspaper text type in history; within eighteen months of its debut at Newark it had been installed by 3,000 newspapers. After nearly half a century it is still widely esteemed, except in the U.S., where (with Excelsior) it survives in fewer than 15 papers, compared with around 390 using its successor Corona or Royal, the Intertype version of Corona (1970 figures). It continues to be the favoured text type of the London 'popular' nationals (the *Daily Mail* went back from Jubilee to Ionic in 1972) and of many British provincial dailies. The fact was that the over-strong colour of Ionic well suited the fast running of papers with many-millioned circulation; these machining conditions thinned it down so that its defects were much less perceptible. And, like the whole of the Linotype 'Legibility Group' of which it was the first, its open-cut and freedom from 'ink traps' made it print clearly.

The 'Legibility Group' was on all counts a remarkable contribution to newspaper text typography. The No. 2, Excelsior, has already been discussed. In 1935 two specialised variants, Opticon and Paragon, were devised to meet particular production conditions in certain American newspapers; they are no longer of practical significance. Finally, in 1940 came Corona, as a 'composite of the entire Legibility Group, with especial emphasis on the factor of space economy' (Griffith) – Ionic having been notably wide-set and square-ish. Additionally, or even perhaps principally, Corona was designed to overcome the extreme matrix shrinkage common in U.S. newspaper practice – as much as two-thirds of an inch or more across the width of a broadsheet page. To achieve this Mergenthaler developed 'a scientific formula of shrinkage factors and distortion characteristics of each letter'.

Discussion of these news-text developments has taken us beyond the period of this chapter; it is time to return to the 1920s and an examination of events in the other field of newspaper typography – headline display. Reference has already been made to the new ATF display ranges of the time and how they began to find their way into the composing machine repertory; that mechanical aspect of headline setting now requires analysis. There were actually two aspects; first, the extension of the display capacity of the linecaster, which had already begun; second, the growing use of the Ludlow machine, which cast slug display lines from hand-set matrices in a screw-locked 'stick'.

During the first half of the 1920s linecaster display developments varied in Britain and America. By this time Mergenthaler and Linotype & Machinery were functioning entirely independently, both in terms of machine development and of typographic programmes. Thus by 1923 a brilliant headline face like Bodoni Bold in upper- and lowercase up to the effective linecaster limit of 36pt (42pt and 48pt sizes were possible, but only in capitals) could be had from Mergenthaler; but that year Linotype & Machinery could only offer the less useful light weight of Bodoni, or some sizes of Cheltenham Bold and (for those obtuse enough to want that Edwardian aberration) Clearface Bold, even up to 42pt capitals.

By the turn of the decade things had changed. In the early 1930's Linotype & Machinery were showing full and varied ranges of headline faces like Cheltenham, Bodoni, Century and the new sans Metro, one of the many excellent types designed for the Linotype by the late W. A. Dwiggins. In America, elegant German-inspired sans types like Spartan and Erbar were made available for linecaster keyboarding. Details of the progressive development of the linecaster as a display machine, with the appropriate moulds, side-magazines with independent keyboards, saw trimmers for wide-measure slugs, do not call for extensive discussion. In one case, however, mechanical development was directly linked to the headline-setting needs of a particular newspaper, *The Times*.

Printing House Square had installed its first linecasters – Intertypes – in 1914. But the authorities of *The Times* required machines with eight magazines (four main, four side) so that all headlines could be keyboarded and cast in slug form. The second Printing Number of *The Times* (29 October 1929) disclosed that technicians of Linotype & Machinery had thus been encouraged to produce such a machine, the Model 6 SM. Machines of this sort were put in at Printing House Square from 1926 onwards; their magazine layout showed how they were able to cope with the full range of various news-titling styles then still forming the headline scheme of *The Times*. Since all these founts were capitals only, many of them condensed, it was possible to carry three in each main 90-channel magazine, one fount being accommodated in each of the three groups of channels (lower-case, figures and points, capitals).

Here we see some of the limitations of headline-keyboarding; magazine capacity can only be maximised when headlining is of the old-fashioned, comparatively small-size, capitals-only sort. Larger sizes in upper- and lower-case call for one, or two, magazines per fount. Further, while keyboarding is the best and fastest way of setting headlines (with automatic distribution) for single-column styles, or double-column if that comes within the normal 30-pica limit of linecaster measure, it is cumbersome with wider measures, having to be set 'two bars' or more. And the body-size limitation mentioned above should be recalled.

This was where the Ludlow machine came in. It could cast all sizes, in upper- and lower-case, up to 72pt (and 96pt in certain founts); it did not need an expensive magazine for each fount of matrices, which were laid in simple trays – like small, modified type-cases – in a cabinet, so that a large type repertory could be economically accommodated; it was flexible in operation, requiring no mould changes for its standard casting on a pica slug, buttressed by blanks for the larger sizes (the blanks, together with rules, leads and borders, provided in strip form by the ancillary Elrod machine); by the use of angle matrices it provided superior versions of italic.

The inventor after whom the machine was named, Washington Irving Ludlow, had begun with the idea of a simplified text-setting machine for smaller newspapers; but his manufacturing associate, William A. Reid (of Cleveland and later of Chicago) found that the notion was not commercially practicable and therefore turned the Ludlow Typograph Co. he had formed to the production of the basically display slug-caster that became universally known as the Ludlow. A batch of machines was produced in 1911 but there were matrix-making problems and it was 1913 before the first Ludlows were installed, in a Chicago newspaper. Not till ten years later did the Ludlow make a serious appearance in Britain; the then London Society of Compositors negotiated its first Ludlow agreement in 1923.

That year saw the beginning of what was to prove Ludlow's big breakthrough on the typographic front. The Chicago company took on a young Glaswegian immigrant, Robert Hunter Middleton, as type designer. He was to prove himself one of the most able, as well as most prolific, practitioners of the century. He supervised the production of fully varied ranges of existing types suitable for newspaper headlining, like Bodoni, Caslon (including the only tolerable Heavy italic), Century, Goudy (Old Style and Bold, designated No. 11 in the Ludlow list), and gothics like Franklin. He was also responsible for over a score of original designs, among which the immense Tempo Sans family, Record Gothic, Karnak (a good 'Egyptian'), Garamond, Cameo (an excellent shaded), Ludlow Black (resembling the smashing Cooper Black), may be mentioned for their newspaper display value.

The end of the aftermath of the First World War was now at hand, for both British and American dailies. On the eve of what was to be a revolutionary decade in newspaper design it is of interest to examine the display typography of five leading London nationals, together with the *Manchester Guardian*, then provincially-based but already national in standing. In 1930 the dress of these papers effectively summed up the changes in page presentation brought about by the 1914–18 War and the period immediately following. Only two of the six newspapers had news on their front page; only three had full-page streamers – no longer ruled off, but usually sporting a wide French dash before dropping-in to the double-column lead story. The decker headline remained universal, its decks separated by French dashes and/or short rules, and consistently set in capitals, bold and light alternating. To this continued clinging to capitals the *Manchester Guardian* was the sole exception; its deckers all alternated capitals and upper- and lower-case; instead of dashes and rules it was content to rely on ample white space.

The *Guardian* style was in general interesting and unusual. Evolved during the 1920s it remained constant until the changeover to front-page news in 1952. Here was a 'quality' paper, a 'heavy', which had abandoned news titlings for a colourful display face (Cheltenham Bold) and a contrasting lighter face (Transit), both with lower-case. Since the paper did not exceed double-column measure for lead stories, and carried no streamers, headlines could be keyboarded. Linotype Transit had been originally, and oddly, called Baskerville Old Style, though it bore no sort of relation to the designs of the Birmingham maestro; it had been shown under that title in pre-1914 Caslon specimen books. In fact it was a French design, very much of the *belle époque*, produced by the Deberny et Peignot foundry in Paris and called simply *Série 18*. Its text sizes were used in French bookwork and it was carried by Linotype in a complete range, from 6pt to 48pt, capitals inclusive, with italic up to 18pt; there was also a range, up to 14pt, duplexed with Cheltenham Bold (the *Guardian* combination).

▼ The Cheltenham Bold-Transit headline style established by the *Manchester Guardian* in the 1920s.

THE MANCHESTER GUARDIAN, TUESDAY, APRIL 28, 1931 9

AN EMERGENCY BUDGET

Mr. Snowden Finds Two Roosts to Raid

PETROL DUTY UP 2d.

Income Tax Device: You Pay Three-quarters in January

LAND VALUES TAX IN 1933

A "Baby" Motor-Cycle Concession to Help Makers

Mr. Snowden's third Budget resorts to the temporary expedients made familiar by his predecessor, Mr. Churchill. It imposes no new taxes, and increases only one—that on petrol.

MR. SNOWDEN'S SPEECH

Free Trade

AN UNREPENTANT DECLARATION

His Stop-Gap Measures

(From our Parliamentary Correspondent.)

WESTMINSTER, MONDAY NIGHT.

Mr. Snowden came into the crowded House of Commons from behind the Speaker's chair at half-past three, ten minutes before questions had been disposed of, and was received with a great cheer.

The Budget impressed the House by its simplicity and straightforwardness. Mr. Ramsay MacDonald's mystification of last Thursday was not cleared up until the end, but as Mr. Snowden described its solution as the main feature of the Budget, it may well come first here. Provisions are to be included in the Finance Bill for the taxation of land values, but as the preliminary valuation cannot be completed before 1933, and consequently the taxation cannot become effective until then, a separate resolution is to be submitted to the House to authorise a provision in this year's Finance Bill to give effect to any resolution in Committee of Ways and Means for taxation to come into operation after the expiration of the coming financial year. Then the resolution to impose the taxation—which is to be at the rate of a penny in

MR. SNOWDEN AS OPTIMIST

Bold Estimates

REVENUE WITHOUT TEARS

Churchillian Finance

(From our Financial Editor.)

LONDON, MONDAY NIGHT.

This is an emergency Budget. So exceptional does Mr. Philip Snowden consider present conditions that he is meeting £30,000,000 out of an estimated extra requirement of £37,000,000 by "raids." The remaining £7,000,000 he will raise by a 2d. addition to the tax per gallon on motor spirit.

The bulk of the required new revenue for this year is to be taken from a "dollar exchange fund" hitherto maintained by the Treasury as a reserve against the American debt payments. Mr. Snowden proposes to raid this fund for £20,000,000, whereby the "miscellaneous" revenue will be brought up from £35,000,000 to £55,000,000. This sum will be appropriated without any taxpayer being aware of it.

Taxpayers will be aware, however, of the second raid, by which £10,000,000 of extra revenue are to be brought into the receipts of the current year. Income tax, which is at present payable in two equal instalments on January 1 and July 1, is to be payable in instalments of three-quarters on January 1 and one-quarter on July 1. Thus without raising the standard rate

THE PRINCES HOME TO-DAY

Flying from Paris to Windsor

VISIT TO KING

A Stormy Voyage from Lisbon

The Prince of Wales and Prince George, who arrived in Paris yesterday evening from Bordeaux, will complete their return journey from South America to-day, when they will fly from Le Bourget to Windsor or Hendon.

The Prince of Wales, it is understood, would prefer to use Smith's Lawn, his private landing ground in Windsor Great Park, but if weather conditions make it desirable for Hendon to be used the Princes will motor immediately to Windsor Castle to see the King and Queen and report on the work they have done to stimulate British trade with the South American States. Wherever the Princes land the strictest privacy will be observed and there will be no public reception.

The Princes' 'plane will be escorted from the coast to London to-day by three flights of fighter machines of the 25th Squadron at Hawkinge, which will meet the City of Glasgow over the Channel and give an aerial salute.

Rough seas and stormy weather delayed the arrival at Bordeaux of the cruiser Kent, in which the Princes had

ARCTIC RESCUE FLIGHT

Search for Missing Englishman

A LONE OUTPOST

Left in Charge Last November

The Swedish airman Captain Ahrenberg expects shortly to leave Malmö for Greenland to search for Mr. Augustine Courtauld, son of the British silk magnate, Mr. S. A. Courtauld, who is lost in Greenland. Mr. Courtauld volunteered last November to man the central station on the ice cap in Greenland for the British Arctic Route Expedition, and has not been seen since.

The British Air Ministry were requested last week to help in the work of rescuing Mr. Courtauld. They

FIGHTING IN MADEIRA

Landing by Punitive Force

REBEL ROUT

Seaplane and Naval Bombardment

Seventeen prisoners were taken yesterday following upon a successful landing of the Portuguese Expeditionary Force on the Island of Madeira.

This information, says a Reuter telegram from Lisbon, is contained in an official statement issued in Lisbon, based upon a telegram received from the headquarters of the Expeditionary Force at Porto Santo, 50 miles from Madeira. According to this telegram, the Government forces effected a landing some ten miles from Funchal, with the object of dismantling the wireless station utilised by the rebels. A party of some 70 rebels was routed, the wireless station dismantled, and a sergeant and 16 rebel privates taken prisoners.

The insurgents opened fire with their artillery, on the Government vessels that were supporting the landing party, but the shore guns were soon silenced by bombardment from the sea and by most effective bombing from Government seaplanes, whose action proved the deciding factor.

REBEL TRENCHES

THE BUDGET

AN INCOME-TAX DEVICE

HEAVIER JANUARY INSTALMENT

NEW CONTROL OF COLLECTION

2D. ON PETROL

The Budget was introduced in the House of Commons yesterday by Mr. Snowden, the Chancellor of the Exchequer. Details of the statement of revenue and expenditure, which was issued as a White Paper, are given on page 9, and the Chancellor's speech is reported on page 8.

The main points in the Budget are as follows:—

LAND VALUES

Provisions for the taxation of land values (which Mr. Snowden said he regarded as the main feature of his Budget). The valuation is estimated to take two years, and to be available as a basis (subject to periodical revision) on which to charge an annual tax for 1933-34 and subsequent years. The Finance Bill to provide for a tax at the rate of 1d. in the pound on capital land value.

PETROL

The duty on petrol raised from 4d. to 6d. per gallon, yielding £8,300,000 in a full year.

TAX INSTALMENTS

Income-tax, at present payable in two equal instalments on January 1 and July 1, to be payable in instalments of three-quarters on January 1 and one quarter on July 1. (The instalment system of paying the tax was instituted in 1915.) The change applies to Schedules B, D, and E.

"EXCHANGE ACCOUNT"

£20,000,000 taken from the dollar exchange reserve, established during the War, and amounting to £33,000,000.

An annual tax of 15s., in lieu of the present rate of 30s., on light motor-cycles, to encourage the manufacture of a new type of light machine.

TAX COLLECTION

The appointment of income-tax collectors to rest in future with the Commissioners of Inland Revenue.

THE NEW REVENUE

The Chancellor budgets for £37,500,000 new revenue to meet a deficit of £37,366,000, yielding the nominal surplus of £134,000 shown in the table below. The additional revenue is obtained as follows:—

	£
Reduction of "exchange account"	20,000,000
Change in income-tax instalment system	10,000,000
Extra petrol duty (this year)	7,500,000
Total	£37,500,000

THIS YEAR'S REVENUE AND EXPENDITURE

The Treasury statement of ordinary revenue and expenditure for 1931-32 is as follows:—

ESTIMATED 1931 REVENUE

	£
Inland Revenue—	
Income-tax	258,000,000
Surtax	72,000,000
Estate Duties	90,000,000
Stamps	24,000,000
Excess Profits Duty / Corporation Profits Tax	2,900,000
Land Tax, &c.	800,000
Total Inland Revenue	447,[illegible]00,000
Customs and Excise—	
Customs	125,650,000
Excise	119,850,000
Total Customs and Excise	245,500,000
Motor Vehicle Duties—	
Exchequer Share	5,000,000
Total Receipts from Taxes	£697,[illegible]00,000
Post Office net receipt	12,200,000
Crown Lands	1,300,000
Receipts from Sundry Loans due to British Government	33,500,000
Miscellaneous	55,000,000
Total 1931 Revenue	799,500,000
Appropriation from Rating Relief Suspense Account	4,000,000
TOTAL	£803,500,000

ESTIMATED 1931 EXPENDITURE

	£
Interest and Management of National Debt	302,950,000
Payments to Northern Ireland Exchequer (including net share of reserved taxes)	6,350,000
Miscellaneous Consolidated Fund Services	3,000,000
Total	312,300,000
Supply Services—	
Defence— Excluding Pensions Army	31,150,000
Navy	42,509,000
Air Force	17,846,000
	91,633,000
Pensions Army	8,730,000
Navy	8,790,000
Air Force	234,000
	17,[illegible]
Civil—	
I. Central Government and Finance	2,097,000
II. Foreign and Imperial	3,763,000
III. Home Department, Law and Justice	16,313,000
IV. Education	56,351,000
V. Health, Labour, Insurance (including Old Age and Widows' Pensions)	119,396,000
VI. Trade and Industry	8,7[illegible]
VII. Works; Stationery, &c.	8,833,000
VIII. War Pensions and Civil Pensions	52,000,000
IX. Miscellaneous	92,000
X. Exchequer Contributions to Local Revenues	43,444,000
	317,812,000
Tax Collection—	
Customs and Excise and Inland Revenue Votes (including Pensions £910,000)	11,340,000
	438,016,000
Total 1931 Expenditure	£794,[illegible]
National Debt—Sinking Fund	32,[illegible]
Surplus	134,000
TOTAL	£803,500,000

SELF-BALANCING REVENUE AND EXPENDITURE

	£
Post Office—Revenue required to meet Post Office expenditure [illegible]	56,232,000
Road Fund—Motor Vehicle Duties appropriated to Road Fund	21,3[illegible]
Total	£881,362,000

MR. SNOWDEN'S SPEECH

HOPE IN ECONOMY COMMITTEE

MEETING THE DEFICIT

WESTMINSTER, MONDAY

The scene in the House of Commons to-day was distinctly less animated than is usual on Budget day. The House, indeed, rushed through questions, the answers to which were, as usual, silenced by a barrage of conversation. The floor and the galleries were crowded as usual by a distinguished audience, which included, in addition to members of Parliament, Mr. Montagu Norman, General Dawes, Mr. Dwight Morrow, Lord Reading, and Lord Snell—the latest migrant to the Peers' gallery. Mr. Snowden, who entered a few minutes before the end of questions, was received with loud and very general cheers, which were repeated when he ended his task. But during the interval the House was strangely restrained, partly out of delicate consideration for Mr. Snowden himself and partly because of the character of his Budget, which was frankly a Budget of postponement devoid of surprises and sparing in challenges, whether to the Opposition or to his own supporters.

REPERCUSSIONS OF 1930

MR. SNOWDEN asked for only one indulgence to his illness—namely, that the usual review of the past financial year should be printed instead of spoken. The House readily granted this indulgence, which was confirmed by the CHAIRMAN'S announcement that the Speaker assented, provided that no precedent was set. The past was therefore dismissed by Mr. Snowden with a claim (based on suppressing throughout his speech all reference to borrowing for the Unemployment Insurance Fund) that he had repaid £52,500,000 of debt, and that no other country had met the trade depression so well.

The past had, however, many repercussions. The first was a decision not to make up any more of the deficit of 1929-30, because £9,000,000, the proceeds of the German Mobilization Loan, had already been allotted to the Sinking Fund; and not to carry forward to this year's accounts last year's deficit of £23,000,000. Mr. Snowden, to justify this latter step, began a *motif* of confidence in the once barely tolerated Economy Committee which ran right through his speech. He declared that the economies which that Committee might suggest, together with some hope of successful conversion operations during the year, might in effect cancel out most of the past year's deficit, and that in any case it was better in times of depression to stimulate trade than to repay debt.

THE CURRENT YEAR

Passing to the current year, Mr. Snowden drew up as follows the prospective balance-sheet on the basis of existing taxation, excluding self-balancing services, but including £52,000,000 for the sinking funds:

Ordinary expenditure	£803,500,000
Ordinary revenue	£766,000,000
Deficit	£37,500,000

This figure, he sardonically observed, would be disappointing to the Jeremiahs, especially as it included £12,000,000 extra payable under the Derating Acts and unmet by the Suspensory Fund, and £8,000,000 more than was spent last year on the dole. He again hoped that the Economy Committee would make the figure of expenditure unduly pessimistic, and proceeded to explain why the figure of revenue was not unduly optimistic.

Income-tax, which was levied in respect of the depressed year 1930-31, would yield £8,000,000 less, in spite of the full operation of the 4s. 6d. rate. Surtax, which would not be levied on the same depressed period, would yield over £4,000,000 more, and death duties, helped by the full operation of the increased rates imposed last year, would yield £90,000,000, or nearly £7,500,000 more. Stamps would yield £3,350,000 more on the assumption of a revival of Stock Exchange activity. Direct taxation would therefore yield in all over £6,000,000 more. Indirect taxation (Customs and Excise) would yield about £7,400,000 less. Other receipts—such as the Post Office profit and receipts from loans—would yield about £3,400,000 more, but he could bring in only £4,000,000 (or £12,000,000 less) from the Rating Relief Suspense Account, so that over the whole field of revenue he would lose just under £10,000,000 as compared with last year.

LEGISLATIVE CHANGES

Before facing the resulting deficit of £37,500,000, Mr. Snowden paused to describe certain proposed legislative changes. Power would be taken to offer holders of the old issue of Savings Certificates a prolongation of the date of repayment. The tax on light motor-cycles would be halved as from next January 1. Owing to the calls of unemployment relief schemes the Road Fund needed more money, and this would be found by giving the Fund power to borrow. The collection of income-tax on dividends at the source in all cases would be put beyond doubt. Lastly, all future appointments to the post of collector of taxes would be made by the Commissioners of Inland Revenue. The collectors would thus become Civil servants, as was proper in their interests and the interests of the Exchequer. In reply to a query about the interests of the taxpayer, Mr. Snowden contended that a practice universal in Scotland and prevalent in 17 districts of England and Wales could not be injurious.

He then approached his deficit with grievous anxiety induced by the world depression, but was not thereby deterred from a violent attack upon the Conservative policy of tariffs. A revenue tariff was the first instalment of a high protective tariff, and would impose in effect an Excise duty on wages for the profit of manufacturers. "I shall never be a party to any such scheme," he cried amid the first excited cheers of the day.

COPYING MR. CHURCHILL

This scorn of one emergency weapon did not affect his recognition that an emergency existed, and he proceeded to borrow all Mr. Churchill's devices on the excuse that to-day's was the first real emergency. He found a reserve fund to raid in the so-called Exchange Account money advanced during the War and used by the Treasury in buying foreign exchange to finance payments of our obligations abroad. Arrangements had been made for our foreign debtors to pay [illegible] and [illegible] War Debts in dollars [illegible] at the Bank of International Settlements. These dollars could be used for our payments to the United States, and he could therefore take £20,000,000 of the £33,000,000 in the Exchange Account.

He next copied Mr. Churchill's juggling with payments of income-tax under Schedule A by proposing to collect next January three-quarters of the tax due under other schedules, leaving one-quarter to be paid in July, 1932. The effect of this is to collect one-and-a-quarter times the tax during 1931-32 on certain kinds of income; and Mr. Snowden estimated that it would give him an extra £10,000,000, while imposing not even inconvenience on the weekly wage-earner.

FINAL BALANCE-SHEET

The rest of his deficit he met by increasing the petrol duty from 4d. to 6d. a gallon. The fourpenny duty had neither decreased consumption nor prevented a fall in price. The increase would not decrease consumption and could only restore the price to that prevailing last February. He hated the tax, but it was the least injurious; stern necessity dictated some tax, and it would yield £7,500,000.

The final balance-sheet therefore read:—

Revenue	£803,500,000
Expenditure	£803,366,000
Surplus	£134,000

Mr. Snowden confessed that this narrow margin had been secured by ignoring possible supplementary expenditure; but he again called upon the House to note the hope that lay—and lay only in statesmanlike consideration of the forthcoming reports of the Economy Committee and—his one reminder of the point of the Royal Commission on Unemployment Insurance. He frankly confessed that he had only postponed difficulties for a year, but the postponement might be for ever if industry recovered and the House of Commons acted up to its professions of economy.

LAND VALUE DUTIES

Turning with obvious relief from putting industry on its honour to recover and the House of Commons on its honour to be wise, Mr. Snowden came to the titbit of land value duties. Amid tremendous Liberal and Socialist cheers, he forecast a duty of 1d. in the £ on capital land values, to be imposed when the necessary valuation was complete—say, in two years. A separate resolution would be necessary to justify including in the Finance Bill for this year provisions on which a tax in subsequent years would be based. Mr. Snowden excused himself from further explanation at the moment, but he gave a generous advance instalment of propaganda by claiming that the new tax would end a scandal, remove a crushing burden on industry, and provide a landmark on the road of social progress by emancipating the people from the tyranny of the private land monopoly.

The Conservatives showed traces of disputing this claim, although they had earlier equally shown traces of admitting Mr. Snowden's claim that the whole Budget was not as bad—except to the financial purist—as they had feared it might be. For the moment, however, the House amused itself by calling loudly for Mr. Churchill when Mr. Chamberlain rose to make a first comment. MR. CHAMBERLAIN paid a graceful compliment to Mr. Snowden's courage and expressed a graceful hope for his complete recovery; but his neatest point was the equivocal remark that Mr. Snowden had approached Mr. Churchill in practice, if not in principle. MR. LLOYD GEORGE harped blithely on the string which had rejoiced his heart, and the House melted away without more ado to gather ammunition for to-morrow.

THE KING AND QUEEN

RETURN TO LONDON POSTPONED

The Press Association stated last night that the King and Queen had cancelled their proposed visit on May 14 to Aldershot, where they were to stay for four days. It was also stated that the return of the Court to London, which had been fixed for Monday next, May 4, had been postponed, and that the King and Queen would stay on at Windsor Castle for a further short period.

The recent cold weather has prevented the King from getting out into the fresh air again after his recent attack of bronchitis, and therefore the Court will not return to London until the King has been able to enjoy some sunshine at Windsor.

This may mean that the King will not be present at the Royal Command Variety Performance (of which the approved programme is published on page 19) at the Palladium on Monday, May 11.

Yesterday King Alfonso motored to Windsor and saw the King and Queen. He remained to luncheon with their Majesties and afterwards returned to London.

SIR JAMES O'GRADY'S NEW POST

GOVERNOR OF FALKLAND ISLANDS

It is officially announced that the King has been pleased to approve the appointment of Sir James O'Grady to be Governor and Commander-in-Chief of the Falkland Islands in succession to Mr Arnold Weinholt Hodson.

Sir James O'Grady was Governor of Tasmania from 1924 to December, 1930, his term of office having been extended for one year. Sir James, who was formerly secretary of the General Workers' Federation, sat in the House of Commons as a Labour member from 1906 to 1924, representing successively East Leeds and South-East Leeds. In the spring of 1917 he was sent by the Government on a special mission to Russia. He was created K.C.M.G. in 1924.

MILITARY APPOINTMENTS

The War Office announces that Major-General H. Karslake, C.B., C.M.G., D.S.O., has been appointed Major-General, Royal Artillery, Army Headquarters, India, in succession to Major-General J. E. S. Brind, C.B., C.M.G., D.S.O., with effect from June next.

Major J. V. R. Jackson has been selected for command of the 1st Battalion, The Buffs (East Kent Regiment), in succession to Lieutenant-Colonel L. H. Smith, whose tenure expired yesterday.

OPENING OF THE OPERA SEASON

The Duke and Duchess of York attended the opening night of the opera season at Covent Garden last night, when *Der Rosenkavalier* was performed, Herr Bruno Walter conducting. A notice of the performance appears on page 14, and the names of some of those present and a description of some of the dresses are given on page 19.

COLLISION ON PARIS "METRO"

[illegible]

PARTY VIEWS

BID FOR LIBERAL SUPPORT

LABOUR LEFT WING DISAPPOINTED

From Our Parliamentary Correspondent

After all the preliminary excitement and the imaginative forecasts of its contents the Budget speech was regarded by members of the House of Commons as something of an anti-climax. The predominant feeling was that the Chancellor of the Exchequer, even at the risk of offending the Left Wing members of the Labour Party, had produced a Budget which would enable the Government to expect the continuation of the support of the Liberal Party for many more months unless an unexpected crisis developed.

The main proposals in the Budget—the raid on the Exchange Account, the decision to proceed with a land values scheme, and the increase of 2d. in the petrol duty—caused no surprise. In fact, the only point which had not been expected was the decision to collect three-quarters of the income-tax next January and a quarter in July in order to bring more money into the current financial year. Mr. Churchill, when he speaks to-morrow, may have something to say about Mr. Snowden's way of copying his best tricks. It is, by the way, one of the few points in the Budget which the Labour members are afraid will provoke criticism. They realize that even in normal conditions January is the worst month of the year for the middle-class taxpayer, and the imposition of a fresh charge at such a period, even though there will be compensation by a smaller demand note later in the year, is bound to cause irritation. Members of all parties were frankly surprised at the small amount of fresh taxation which had been imposed, for even the increase in the petrol duty was less than had been expected. The principal comment to be heard last night was that the Budget was the last throw of the desperate gambler. Mr. Snowden, having found that the limit of direct taxation had been reached, if not passed, decided to bank on two possibilities—that trade might improve and that economy might be practised.

LAND VALUES PROCEDURE

Mr. Snowden did not entirely clear up the mystery with which the Prime Minister surrounded the Budget procedure last week, and when the House rose it was assumed that there would be a full-dress debate on land values on Thursday. Arrangements were made at the Liberal Party meeting on that assumption that Sir Donald Maclean should be the principal Liberal speaker to-day, Sir Herbert Samuel to-morrow, and Mr. Lloyd George, on land values, on Thursday. But it is understood that the resolution which was handed in last night for discussion on Thursday deals solely with the question of procedure. New taxes can only be imposed in Committee of Ways and Means, and in the ordinary way the Finance Bill cannot impose taxation which is not to become operative in the financial year. The resolution which will be discussed in the House on Thursday is virtually a proposal to suspend Standing Orders, as it empowers the Committee of Ways and Means to proceed with a resolution imposing a tax on land values regardless of the fact that it cannot become operative for two years. Thursday's debate will accordingly be on questions of procedure, and if the resolution is carried the full-dress debate on land values will take place in Committee of Ways and Means next Monday.

While the Conservative section of the Opposition was relieved that the Budget contained no new proposals for immediate direct taxation, the back-bench members of the Labour Party were obviously disappointed that Mr. Snowden is unrepentant on the subject of economy and that he held out no hope of any extension of the social services. When the Liberals proposed the setting up of an Economy Committee, Mr. Snowden, though he did not resist the proposal, was not convinced that the Committee could serve any useful purpose. Now that the Committee has been set up the Chancellor of the Exchequer looks to it to rescue him from some of his difficulties.

UNEMPLOYMENT

The Left Wing members are also disappointed at his hint that the Government really intends to take action on any report which the Royal Commission on Unemployment Insurance may present, and they are wondering what "refreshing fruits" they can serve up in the constituencies beyond the promise of land values in two years' time—and there are few experienced members who really think that the work of compiling the valuation can be completed in two years. By deciding to include the valuation proposals in the Finance Bill instead of in a separate measure the Government have probably made sure of their passage into law, for nobody thinks that the House of Lords would reject the whole Finance Bill on such an issue even if it is not certified as a Money Bill by the Speaker. There was a general disposition last night to reserve criticism on the land tax proposals until the precise details are known. Members are anxious to know, for instance, whether they apply to agricultural land as well as to land which has improved in value as a result of urban developments.

The National Council of the I.L.P. last night adopted the following resolution:—

The I.L.P., while welcoming the proposal to tax land values in so far as it applies to urban land and secures unearned increment for the community, regrets that its operation is delayed until 1933 and that the tax is being limited to one penny in the pound. The I.L.P. views with apprehension the Budget statement in general, (1) as making no provision for extended social services (particularly in relation to old age and widows' pensions, unemployment allowances, and a national housing scheme); (2) as endangering existing social services by the reliance placed upon the anticipated recommendations of the Economy Committee and the Unemployment Commission.

TAX COLLECTORS

The Conservatives will strenuously oppose Mr. Snowden's proposal to alter the machinery for the collection of income-tax by bringing the local collectors under the control of the Board of Inland Revenue. It had been hoped that the protests which have been made in *The Times* from all parts of the country would have been enough to kill the proposal, but the fight will now be waged on the floor of the House of Commons.

Mr. Snowden remained at the House of Commons for some time after the House rose in consultation with his colleagues and then returned to 11, Downing-street, where he spent the night. He hopes to be in his place when the debate is resumed to-day to [illegible] to [illegible] a meeting of the Cabinet was not held in the morning. Mr. Snowden drove straight to the House of Commons from his home in Surrey and took luncheon in his room there.

THE PRINCES' RETURN

ARRIVAL IN PARIS

FLIGHT TO ENGLAND TO-DAY

FROM OUR OWN CORRESPONDENT

PARIS, APRIL 27

The Prince of Wales and Prince George arrived at Le Bourget at 6.10 p.m. to-day in the aeroplane City of Glasgow, after a flight of nearly 3½ hours from an aerodrome near Bordeaux, in a strong cross-wind under heavy clouds. As the time of their arrival was uncertain, only a few score people had collected at the aerodrome in the hope of seeing them. Elaborate precautions were taken to prevent their being photographed or approached, and strict orders were given that no one was to be allowed within the barriers.

Although one or two aeroplanes had flown off westwards in the hope of meeting it, the City of Glasgow came into sight alone, flying just below the clouds. On landing Major Olley turned the machine and taxied fast to one of the distant sheds far from the public enclosure, and the Princes disembarked out of sight of the crowd. Here they were received by the director of the aerodrome, who represented the Air Ministry, and other French authorities.

General Trotter had been waiting with the Princes' car behind the shed, and, while many people were still lingering to see the Princes at the main gate, it left the aerodrome by a side gate and sped away to Paris. A few people standing outside the gateway saw it pass and waved. The departure of the Princes was so quick and unobtrusive that the Minister and First Secretary of the British Embassy, who arrived by the main gate a few minutes after the unexpectedly fast aeroplane, did not see them and had to give chase in their car.

An hour after landing at Le Bourget the Prince of Wales and Prince George alighted from their car at the Hôtel Meurice. They both looked extremely well, though rather tired. Before going to their rooms they stood for a few moments in the hall talking with friends who had come to greet them.

According to present arrangements the Princes will leave Paris for England by air to-morrow afternoon.

ARRIVAL AT BORDEAUX

FROM OUR CORRESPONDENT

BORDEAUX, APRIL 27

H.M.S. Kent, with the Prince of Wales and Prince George on board, anchored a mile off Pointe-de-Grave at 11.30 this morning, and their Royal Highnesses landed immediately afterwards in the ship's cutter. They were greeted by M. André Bouffard, Prefect of the Gironde, representing the French Government, and other officials, the British Consul and Vice-Consul at Bordeaux, Group Captain Bone, Air Attaché at the British Embassy in Paris, Squadron Leader Brackley, of Imperial Airways, and Captain Broad, of the De Havilland Company. The two Princes also received a hearty welcome from a large crowd which had been waiting for several hours.

After a short address of welcome by M. Bouffard, the Prince of Wales replied in French, and both Princes then went by motor-car to Tegnac-Mérignac aerodrome, nearly 40 miles away. The Prince of Wales asked M. Bouffard to convey to the French Government his appreciation of the arrangements made for his reception. The City of Glasgow made a perfect take-off at 2.44 p.m., and, in company with two French machines acting as escort for part of the journey, soon vanished into the grey skies in the north.

TO-DAY'S FLIGHT

The aeroplane in which the Princes are travelling home is the City of Glasgow (G-EBLF), the first Argosy delivered to Imperial Airways, since brought up-to-date by the fitting of the newest type of Jaguar engine. It will continue the journey from Paris to Smith's Lawn in Windsor Great Park this afternoon.

The last stage of the flight will begin at 2.30 (B.S.T.) and should be completed before 5 p.m. The Prince of Wales, when he flew home from Marseilles in a Service aeroplane a year ago, made his landing in the same private flying field which has now been approved for the landing of the Argosy. Major H. G. Brackley (air superintendent of Imperial Airways) is in charge of the flight and the pilot is Mr. G. P. Olley.

The air liner will be escorted across the Channel by two Southampton flying-boats of No. 201 Squadron stationed at Calshot, and on crossing the English coast escort duties will be taken over by two fighter squadrons of the R.A.F.—No. 1, stationed at Tangmere, and No. 25, stationed at Hawkinge, both of which are equipped with Siskins. Their Royal Highnesses will therefore be accompanied by 18 military aircraft until they arrive at Windsor.

FREIGHTS ON PRODUCE FROM CEYLON

QUESTION OF SUEZ CANAL DUES

At the meeting of the Ceylon Association in London yesterday Mr. Walter Shakspeare, the president, said that they had approached the shipping lines respecting the freight rates on rubber, but they were met with the argument that shipowners were also passing through terribly hard times. The association then wrote to the President of the Board of Trade asking for his support in endeavouring to obtain from the Suez Canal Company a reduction of the dues levied on shipping.

They had, Mr. Shakspeare said, not abandoned hope of securing a reduction in the freight charges on both tea and rubber, and "would renew their application, perhaps more hopefully, in the event of the Suez Canal Company meeting the reasonable demands of British interests."

The meeting is reported in our City columns.

INVALIDS

The condition of Sir James Melville, K.C., M.P., was stated yesterday to be unchanged, and to be "very serious indeed."

The condition of Viscount Brentford is reported to be slightly improved.

Mr. J. J. H. Moses, M.P., who is suffering from pleurisy, is making good progress.

Mrs. Mary Holman-Hunt, of Melbury-road, Kensington, was knocked down by a motor-van yesterday afternoon while crossing Kensington High-street, and was taken to St. Mary Abbot's Hospital suffering from serious injuries. She is 84 years of age.

TROOPS LANDED IN MADEIRA

WIRELESS STATION DESTROYED

FROM OUR CORRESPONDENT

LISBON, APRIL 27

The Government received news this afternoon from Porto Santo, the base of operations against Madeira, that a detachment of Chasseurs had landed at Caniçal, a village about 12 miles north-east of Funchal, and at the eastern end of the island, where there was a wireless station. It was defended by a force of 73 rebels with four quick-firing guns.

On the approach of the Government forces the rebels retired, but a sergeant and 16 soldiers were made prisoners and

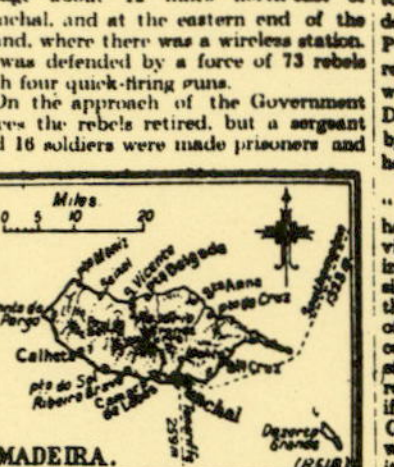

the wireless station was destroyed. The rebel artillery fired on the ships which were covering the landing, but they were silenced by the brilliant work of the seaplanes.

The Chasseurs afterwards returned to their ships. The moral of all the Government troops is said to be excellent.

PANICKY CONDITIONS IN FUNCHAL

LORD ULLSWATER'S IMPRESSIONS

Over 100 passengers from Madeira reached Southampton yesterday in the Union-Castle liner Armadale Castle. Among them were Lord and Lady Ullswater.

Lord Ullswater said that when he left Funchal last Thursday morning there was a panic among the people, and those who were able were going to the hills, as they feared a bombardment. The rebels had made great preparations. They had dug trenches, and the bridges were mined ready to be blown up should necessity arise.

The attitude of the islanders to the rebels (said Lord Ullswater) is more or less apathetic, and although they have several grievances against the Lisbon Government they are not a fighting lot and do not want bother. From my observations it is likely that they will follow whichever party is in the ascendancy. Lord Ullswater added that the rebel troops, wearing steel helmets, were in the streets, and motor-lorries were dashing about. Four big guns were mounted on the hills behind the town, and the rebels seemed to have an ample supply of machine-guns. No attempt had been made to molest British people.

THE SITUATION IN SPAIN

GENERAL BERENGUER ARRESTED

FROM OUR OWN CORRESPONDENT

MADRID, APRIL 27

The arrest and committal for trial of General Berenguer, the Prime Minister in succession to the Marqués de Estella, was decided upon at a meeting of the Cabinet held this evening after the return of Señor Alcalá Zamora from Barcelona. An officer was immediately sent to the General's home, and he was removed to the prison for officers.

Inquiries are continuously being made as to whether it is safe for travellers to visit Spain. To those who live in this country and are witnesses of the complete calm which has rapidly followed the proclamation of the Republic the question seems almost ludicrous. Everywhere the police are resting after the strenuous time they have experienced for the past year, and it should soon be possible to reduce their numbers. The students, whose studies have been so fragmentary for such a long time past, have all returned spontaneously and quietly to their lectures in order to make up for lost time and not lose the term, as seemed almost inevitable had the Revolution been delayed a little longer. There are no general strikes either in progress or threatening. Labour is acting as reasonably as the students, and now that its political object has been achieved work is resumed.

The contrast between the present tranquillity and the uncertainty of the past few years is indeed striking. One could not be certain then from one day to another of what might happen, and the streets were patrolled by fully armed guards both day and night. All that at least has now gone.

A requiem Mass was celebrated this morning in the Church of the Buen Suceso for the repose of the soul of the late Infanta Isabella. Almost the entire Diplomatic Corps, including the British Ambassador, Sir George Grahame, was present, and hundreds of members of the aristocracy. The concourse was so great that the doors had to be opened to allow the public to listen to the service from outside.

The fact that the Provisional Government of the Republic has handed over entirely the administration of the four Provinces of Barcelona, Lerida, Gerona, and Tarragona to the Generalitat is proof of the good will and confidence which inspires the Cabinet and should evoke a corresponding trust, and therefore greater moderation, in framing the Statute for Catalonia which is now being drawn up in Barcelona for submission to a plebiscite of the municipalities of all Catalonia. The Provisional Government is pledged to support the Statute in the Cortes, and is therefore anxious that it shall be of such a nature as not to offend opinion throughout the rest of Spain and provoke opposition.

LORD IRWIN

The Doncaster Town Council last night decided to confer the freedom of the borough on Lord Irwin, and also to give him a civic reception at Doncaster railway station next Saturday when he arrives on his way to visit his father at Hickleton Hall.

HENLEY REGATTA COURSE

Major Mackenzie has instructed Messrs. John D. Wood and Co., of Berkeley-square, to dispose of Fawley Court, an estate of 3,000 acres, which includes the whole of one bank of the Henley Regatta Course and Temple Island. Further particulars will be found in our Estate Market column on page 22.

VIOLENCE IN INDIA

GOVERNMENT AND CONGRESS

"A PLAIN WARNING"

FROM OUR SPECIAL CORRESPONDENT

SIMLA, APRIL 27

The main topic of discussion here to-day is the speech made by Sir Geoffrey de Montmorency, the Governor of the Punjab, at Khushab on Saturday [as was reported in *The Times* yesterday] in which, referring to serious breaches of the Delhi Pact which had been committed by the Congress, he said, "Our toleration has only in the end bred licence."

His Excellency indicated that the "Government would no longer hold its hand" in cases of violence, incitement to violence, or sedition. His speech was important enough in itself; but its real significance goes further. Ever since the signature of the Pact the Government of India has been acting in the closest cooperation with the Provinces in an effort to preserve a uniform policy in relations with the Congress. Even if the specific references in the Governor's review of the situation were confined to his own Province it is most unlikely that he would have made so grave a pronouncement without being in agreement with the Government of India, wherewith he is in constant telephonic communication. Relations between the Governments of India and of the Punjab are particularly close, as Simla is the summer seat of both. It is, therefore, not unreasonable to regard Sir Geoffrey's speech as a plain warning to the Congress not only within the bounds of the Punjab, but all over India.

Meanwhile here in Simla quiet work is being done to get the machinery of the Round-Table Conference going again, and it is expected that the expert committees on the North-West Frontier, on the Indian Sandhurst, and on Sind will be under way before the end of May. The discussion on Burma is unlikely to start for some time, as that question is still the subject of voluminous correspondence between Simla and Downing-street.

FEARS OF OUTBREAK AT CHITTAGONG

FROM OUR OWN CORRESPONDENT

CALCUTTA, APRIL 27

It is reported from Chittagong that another revolutionary outbreak similar to that in 1930, when the armoury was raided, is feared. The local authorities have, accordingly, taken precautions. Unlicensed meetings, processions, and the discharging of fireworks are prohibited, and people have been warned to stay indoors between 10 p.m. and 4 a.m. This application of a curfew is only temporary pending the completion of arrangements to protect the town.

There is some local irritation in consequence of these restrictions, but the authorities are doing their best to minimize the inconvenience. Two companies of the 8th Gurkhas, under Lieutenant-Colonel G. C. B. Buckland, D.S.O., have arrived from Shillong, and the streets are being well picketed and patrolled.

RED ACTIVITY IN INDIA

MOSCOW'S NEW ORDERS

FROM OUR OWN CORRESPONDENT

RIGA, APRIL 27

At the conference of the Ikki (Executive Committee of the Comintern), which ended in Moscow last week, attention was devoted to Communist agitation in India.

Agents of the Comintern in India are to be instructed to "organize a revolutionary offensive among the oppressed classes against English imperialism and the Indian National Congress, to stir up workmen and peasants, organize a mighty all-Indian Communist party and Red labour unions, and prepare a general political strike." It was also decided to intensify Communist activity in Germany and Poland.

The Ikki formed a new presidium composed of 30 members, including Stalin, Bela Kun, Manuilsky, Losovsky, Pollitt, Foster, and Randolph. The Presidium formed a new "political secretariat" of 13 members in which Manuilsky plays the leading part. This secretariat will exercise the functions of a president.

ENTERTAINMENTS INDEX

(For details see page 14)

OPERA		
Covent Garden	TRISTAN UND ISOLDE	7
THEATRES		
Adelphi	EVER GREEN	8.15
Aldwych	MARRY THE GIRL	8.15
Apollo	THE VENETIAN	8.30
Cambridge	CHAUVE SOURIS	8.30
Coliseum	WHITE HORSE INN	2.30 & 8.15
Comedy	NAUGHTY CINDERELLA	2.30 & 8.30
Criterion	AFTER ALL	2.30 & 8.30
Daly's	THE BELLE OF NEW YORK	8.15
Drury Lane	THE SONG OF THE DRUM	8.15
Duchess	THE GIRL ON THE PILLION	8.30
Embassy	THE CRIME AT BLOSSOMS	8.15
Fortune	BUSH FIRE	8.40
Garrick	MY WIFE'S FAMILY	8.30
Globe	THE IMPROPER DUCHESS	8.30
Haymarket	FIVE FARTHINGS	8.45
Hippodrome	STAND UP AND SING	8.15
His Majesty's	SAINT JOAN	8
Lyceum	BITTER SWEET	8.15
Lyric	AUTUMN CROCUS	8.15
Lyric, Hammersmith	THE DUENNA	8.30
New	TANTIVY TOWERS	8.30
Piccadilly	FOLLY TO BE WISE	8.15
Playhouse	THE CHURCH MOUSE	8.40
Queen's	THE BARRETTS OF WIMPOLE STREET	8.15
Royalty	THE WORLD OF LIGHT	8.30
Sadler's Wells	KING LEAR	7.45
St. Martin's	BLACK COFFEE	2.30 & 8.30
Savoy	WONDER BAR	8.30
Shaftesbury	MR. FAINT-HEART	8.30
Strand	IT'S A BOY	8.30
Vaudeville	THE CIRCLE	8.30
Victoria Palace	CHELSEA FOLLIES	8.15
Whitehall	GOOD LOSERS	8.30
Wyndham's	JACK O' LANTERN	8.30
VARIETIES		
Alhambra		2.30 & 8.15
Holborn Empire		[illegible]
Maskelyne's		[illegible]
Palladium		[illegible]
CONCERTS		
Queen's Hall	STOCK EXCHANGE ORCHESTRAL SOCIETY	[illegible]
Wigmore Hall	MISS MARI [illegible] / MME. EMMI LEISNER	[illegible]
EXHIBITIONS, &c.		
Crystal Palace		[illegible]
Olympia	IDEAL HOME EXHIBITION	[illegible]
Zoological Gardens		[illegible]
PICTURE THEATRES		
Astoria	PART TIME [illegible]	[illegible]
Capitol	CHARLIE CHAN CARRIES ON	[illegible]
Carlton	[illegible]	[illegible]
Dominion	CITY LIGHTS	[illegible]
Empire	[illegible]	[illegible]
Kensington	[illegible]	[illegible]
Leicester Square Theatre	[illegible]	[illegible]
London Pavilion	[illegible]	[illegible]
Marble Arch Pavilion	SONG OF THE [illegible]	[illegible]
New Gallery	[illegible]	[illegible]
New Victoria	[illegible]	[illegible]
Phoenix	[illegible]	[illegible]
Plaza	[illegible]	[illegible]
Polytechnic	[illegible]	[illegible]
Regal	[illegible]	[illegible]
Rialto	[illegible]	[illegible]
Stoll Picture Theatre	[illegible]	[illegible]
Tivoli	[illegible] KINGS	[illegible]

The main news page of *The Times*, the left-centre-spread 'bill page' (though the theatre 'bills' had been reduced to an 'entertainments index'), exemplified the evolution of that traditionalist newspaper's typography and make-up. Since 1921 the page format had been seven-column, though the old six-column format was retained for the leader page; the famous picture page was introduced in 1922, with halftones also discreetly appearing in the body of the paper; from 1923 the alternation of bold and light headlines had been systematised. Headlines never exceeded single-column and news titlings remained their sole ingredient. As we have seen, Linotype headliners had been installed from 1926 onwards, and the news titling founts available on those machines provided for the paper's increasing play on the bold condensed variants. The page illustrated may be regarded as the finally-established style of the old *Times* before the radical Morisonian changes to be discussed in the next chapter.

The common feature of the remaining four papers was the clinging to capitals already mentioned; only in the most gingerly fashion was an occasional heading, or deck, in upper- and lower-case embarked on; and, with the single exception of the *Express*, the persistence of varying weights and styles of news titlings was noteworthy. Both the *Daily Mail* and the *News Chronicle* were still using founders' type; the *Mail* banner and the alternate decks of its lead story were in the bold Sovereign Titling; the *News Chronicle* streamered in Old Face Heavy, with a jumble of Stephenson Blake types like Old Style No. 5 italics, Verona (actually the 1920 American indifferent display type Laclede Old Style, in no sense a suitable news heading letter), Clearface Extra Bold and italic.

Founders' type (Shanks's Plantin) was used for the four-column streamer of the *Telegraph*, then in its early years under Lord Camrose (who bought it in 1928), busily performing the feat by which he lifted the paper from under-100,000 moribundity to its position as the biggest-selling and most prosperous 'heavy' national morning in British

◀ The main news page of *The Times* (1931), still all single-column and in a classical arrangement of news-titling deckers.

▼ The *Daily Telegraph* (1931) added a streamer in handset Shanks's Plantin to its machine-set decker headings in Century and Century Bold.

THE DAILY TELEGRAPH, TUESDAY, APRIL 28, 1931 — 13

BUDGET INCOME TAX DRIVE

PETROL DUTY INCREASED BY TWOPENCE

LIGHT MOTOR-CYCLE CONCESSION

£20,000,000 RAID ON THE DOLLAR EXCHANGE ACCOUNT

INCOME TAX COLLECTION SPEED-UP

75 PER CENT. TO BE PAID AS THE FIRST INSTALMENT

MOVE FOR TAXATION OF LAND VALUES

The main features of the Budget which Mr. Snowden "opened" in the House of Commons yesterday, in a speech which lasted only 69 minutes, were:

INCOME TAX

No alteration in rates of taxation, but a speeding up to be effected in collection next January.

In the case of Schedules B, D, and E payment of 75 per cent. of the assessment will be required as the first instalment (instead of 50 per cent. as at present), leaving only 25 per cent. payable as the second instalment.

In the case of Schedule A (income from property) payment is already made in one instalment, while the tax on income from dividends (Schedule C) is deducted at the source.

Weekly wage-earners, on whom income-tax is assessed half-yearly, will not be affected by the change.

All collectors of income-tax to be placed under the control of the Inland Revenue.

PETROL AND MOTOR CYCLES

Petrol duty to be raised from fourpence to sixpence.

To encourage the development of light motor-cycles, the annual tax on machines with a cylinder capacity not exceeding 152 cubic centimetres to be reduced from 30s to 15s.

This reduction to take effect from Jan. 1 next.

LAND TAX

Provisions to be introduced in the Finance Bill for the taxation of land values.

Imposition is contemplated of a tax of one penny in the

MR. SNOWDEN'S DEVICES

AN OVER-ESTIMATE OF TAX YIELD?

UNIONIST COMMENT

By OUR POLITICAL CORRESPONDENT

A "wangling and gambling" Budget is how one would sum up the considered verdict of experienced Parliamentarians on Mr. Snowden's production.

The Chancellor of the Exchequer, finding himself in serious difficulties, has resorted, according to Conservative opinion, to dodges and devices which, had he been on the Opposition side, he would have condemned in his most acid tones.

The politicians who are really pleased with Mr. Snowden are the Liberals, who met in a committee-room after the speech and decided to give all-round support to his proposals.

Sir Donald Maclean is to speak for them to-day in the general discussion on the Budget plans, Sir Herbert Samuel is to take part in the debate to-morrow, and Mr. Lloyd George is arranging to intervene on Thursday during the consideration of the land taxation question.

If the Liberals have one regret it is that the "rare and refreshing" fruits of the unpost on land—to quote a phrase current when they were applauding over twenty years ago the ill-starred adventure in the same field of Mr. Lloyd George—will not become ripe for another two years.

SOCIALIST SATISFACTION

The Socialists, on the whole, are well satisfied with the Chancellor of the Exchequer. They are keen on a land tax, and, like the Liberals, are only chafing at the necessary delay in bringing it into operation.

The only passage in the Budget statement which excited alarm and distrust among them was the reference to economy. They foresee in the warning given by Mr. Snowden an intention on the part of the Government to reduce expenditure on the "dole," and to this they will be most bitterly opposed.

It was suggested in Conservative circles last night that the Chancellor of the Exchequer would not have introduced a Budget in which he gambles so heavily on the future if he expected to have to defend the results of his proposals from the Treasury Bench next year.

Be that as it may, there is no gainsaying the fact that in resolving to collect 75 per cent., instead of 50 per cent., of the income-tax in the first quarter of next year he is making the task of himself, or a successor, more difficult.

The demand that will be made upon the taxpayers to hand over to the Commissioners of Inland Revenue an additional

Parliament

"MAIN FEATURE OF PRESENT BUDGET"

Mr. Snowden and Land Tax

MOVE TO FORESTALL THE LORDS

Ideas Copied From Mr. Churchill

BY A STUDENT OF POLITICS

WESTMINSTER, Monday.

Mr. Snowden's Budget speech to-day lasted an hour and six minutes. Mr. Asquith made one of his Budget speeches in forty minutes, and the general opinion was that it was one of his best.

Mr. Snowden artificially shortened his speech to-day by missing out the elaborate review of the revenue and expenditure in the past year, and having it printed on a paper that was circulated.

Sir Robert Young from the Chair said that that must not be taken as a precedent. One hopes that it will become one. After all, everyone can read figures, and few can take them in when they are spoken. Most Budget speeches are far too long.

Mr. Snowden has never looked better for years than to-day, and his voice was stronger and more distinct than usual. The achievement, after so serious an illness, did immense credit to his doctors, of whom Mrs. Snowden was doubtless the most important. Mr. Snowden must have been pleased, and perhaps was surprised, by the evidence of his personal popularity to-day. There was a tremendous roar of welcome when he entered the House, and all parties joined in the cheering, both when he rose and when he sat down.

TARIFF DENOUNCED

It was in some ways not a characteristic speech. He spoke faster than usual and with fewer inflections of voice. The general tone of his argument was even and almost amiable. He let himself go somewhat in his attack on a general revenue tariff, and he almost shouted his declaration that he would never be a party to such a policy.

There was a dramatic moment when, after speaking for three-quarters of an hour, he paused, took a drink of water, and began: "And now I turn to the main feature of this year's Budget." This was the long section

AIR SEARCH IN GREENLAND

THE MISSING BRITISH EXPLORER

A SWEDISH AVIATOR'S OCEAN DASH

Capt. Ahrenberg, Sweden's leading airman, is to fly across the Atlantic to Greenland to search for the missing British explorer, Mr. Augustine Courtauld, who was left in the interior of the Greenland ice-cap last December on the understanding that he was to be relieved early in February.

Mr. Courtauld is connected with a private expedition which is seeking data for the organisation of an Arctic air route.

THE DAILY TELEGRAPH learns that repeated efforts have been made to relieve him by sledge parties and by light aeroplanes, with which the expedition is equipped for survey work.

Owing, however, to exceptionally bad weather conditions—always associated by Arctic explorers with the edge of an anti-cyclonic area such as an ice plateau—the efforts to locate his snow house have been unavailing. The light 'planes were badly damaged in the search.

THAWING DANGERS

During the months of May and June great difficulty may be experienced in using aircraft in the Arctic. There will not be sufficient clear water for the use of pontoons, while ice and snow will be thawing and the use of ski-undercarriage be consequently precarious.

Sealing vessels are unable to reach the east coast of Greenland until the end of July. Should a relief ship also be sent in the near future it would be necessary to use an icebreaker, for which, it is understood, tentative inquiries are being made in shipping circles.

In the event of Mr. Courtauld's food supply running short he must face alone the 180-mile journey from his inland camp to the expedition's base. From Nansen's account, the region is crevassed, and consequently dangerous to a single traveller, as there is no possibility of roping.

Mr. Courtauld is, however, an experienced traveller, and experts are of the opinion that, provided he is in good health, he should be able to extricate himself from his difficult position.

CAMBRIDGE MEN

The expedition is largely composed of Cambridge University men. Mr. Courtauld was at one time associated with Messrs. Buckmaster and Moore in the City, and is a member of the Thames Yacht Club. He is the son of Mr. S. A. Courtauld, head of the artificial silk company.

The expedition was not sent out by the Royal Geographical Society. Nearly the whole cost of the undertaking is being borne privately, the organisation being in the hands of Mr. H. J. Watkins.

DANGER FROM WOLVES

LONE PIONEER'S STORY

COPENHAGEN, Monday.

"I had to sing and make other noises

RETURN OF COURT POSTPONED

The Visit to Aldershot Cancelled

THE DAILY TELEGRAPH learns authoritatively that the King and Queen have cancelled their proposed visit to Aldershot on May 14.

Their Majesties were to have spent four days inspecting the mechanised Army and other troops.

THE DAILY TELEGRAPH also understands that the return of the Court to London, which has been fixed for Monday next, May 4, has been postponed, and that the King and Queen will stay on at Windsor Castle for a further short period.

Owing to the recent cold weather the King has been prevented from getting out into the fresh air again after his recent attack of bronchitis, and therefore the Court will not return to London until the King has been able to enjoy some sunshine at Windsor.

This will probably mean that the King will not be present at the Royal Command Variety Performance at the Palladium on May 11, though this is not yet definite.

King Alfonso yesterday motored down to Windsor again and saw the King and Queen. He lunched with their Majesties and afterwards returned to London.

A list of the artists selected for the Royal Variety Performance is on Page Fourteen.

THE PRINCES HOME TO-DAY

MESSAGE TO THE KING

After an absence from England of over fourteen weeks, the Prince of Wales and Prince George are expected to land at the former's private flying ground, Smith's Lawn, Windsor, late this afternoon on their return from South America.

FROM OUR OWN CORRESPONDENT

PARIS, Monday.

Smiling cheerily and apparently unwearied by their long day's travelling, the Prince of Wales and Prince George stepped from the Imperial Airways liner City of Glasgow at Le Bourget at 6.13 this evening. They arrived at their hotel in Paris a little more than an hour later.

During the journey from Bordeaux, the City of Glasgow was constantly in touch by radio with Le Bourget and other stations, and messages were sent by the Prince of Wales to the King and to the Air Minister announcing the safe arrival of himself and of Prince George in France.

Photographers were disappointed, for the Princes, who were met by Gen. Trotter, did not leave the aerodrome by the usual gate. A solitary English woman, who had driven out to Le Bourget in a taxi, happened to be standing near the gate by which they left, and when she waved her handkerchief the Prince of Wales waved

LISBON FORCES IN MADEIRA ATTACK

A LANDING MADE ON THE ISLAND

WIRELESS STATION DESTROYED

BOMB AND ARTILLERY ONSLAUGHT

FROM OUR OWN CORRESPONDENT

LISBON, Monday.

Hostilities were opened to-day by the Government forces against the rebels in Madeira. They took the form of

A landing at the easterly end of the island.
The dropping of bombs by a seaplane.
An artillery bombardment by warships.
The putting out of action of the wireless station used by the rebels.
The capture of a few insurgents and the infliction of an unstated number of casualties.

Funchal, the capital, was not involved, but it is reported to be under the guns of several Portuguese warships.

An official note issued by the Lisbon Government this evening says:

"A telegram has been received from the base of operations established at the island of Porto Santo, saying that a successful landing was effected by Government forces at Canical, five (?) miles north-east of Funchal. The object was to break down the wireless telegraph station installed there which the rebels have been using to broadcast their news.

REBEL FORCE SHELLED

"The rebel force was 73 men, which was strengthened by four machine-guns under the command of Lt. Rebelle, who defended the post. One sergeant and six men fell into the hands of the Government forces.

"The rebel artillery fired on the ship covering the disembarkation, but they were reduced to silence by the artillery of the warship and the efficacious action of the seaplane, which dropped bombs.

"The morale of the forces, both land and sea, is excellent."

From other sources it is stated that after the seaplane had flown over the island and dropped proclamations, a Government squadron, composed of the cruiser Carvalho Araujo and a transport, landed troops at Sao Lourenco (at the extreme easterly end of the island). After a brief struggle the wireless apparatus was wrecked and the troops withdrew, carrying prisoners.

Most of the wireless material was brought away by Government forces, which retreated to the ships. The Carvalho Araujo opened a heavy fire on the rebel positions, and the rebel troops fled, leaving casualties, it is added.

LORD ULLSWATER'S

Daily Express

TO-DAY'S WEATHER: Showers; Cold.

NO. 9,517. MONDAY, NOVEMBER 3, 1930. ONE PENNY.

Gordon's is REAL Gin and ITS not coloured

Royal Sovereign Pencils

THUNDERSTORM FREAKS ON SEA AND LAND.

GIANT WAVE STRIKES CHANNEL BOATS.

FOUR PASSENGERS INJURED.

RAIN, HAIL, SNOW AND LIGHTNING.

TWO WOMEN KILLED.

MOTOR-CARS BLOWN OVER.

SOUTHERN ENGLAND and a large part of the midlands were swept yesterday morning by one of the most violent and sudden thunderstorms on record for this time of the year.

SHATTERED WINDOWS.

MARQUIS OF WINCHESTER INTERVIEWED.

His Home In An Old French Chateau.

"I AM HERE."

By C. J. KETCHUM. "Daily Express" Special Correspondent.

"HIS OWN BUSINESS."

ENGLISH BUTLER.

DRIVE THROUGH THE STORM.

LOVELY GARDENS.

INDIGNATION.

"BETHUNE'S HORSE."

ABYSSINIA'S EMPEROR CROWNED AT DAWN.

SCENE OF BARBARIC SPLENDOUR.

CRIMSON ROBE.

PRIESTS IN VELVET AND GOLD.

THE EMPRESS OF ABYSSINIA.

Ras Tafari.

CORONATION COACH.

CATHEDRAL CEREMONY.

SECRET KINGS OF DRUG TRAFFIC.

TRAITORS DOOMED TO TORTURE AND DEATH.

HUGE FACTORIES.

MYSTERY JAPANESE.

NEW SEARCH FOR LOST VICAR.

WOMAN'S STATEMENT TO POLICE.

SOCIALIST DEFEATS IN ELECTIONS.

92 SEATS LOST; 79 WINS FOR CONSERVATIVES.

DO.X FLIGHT POSTPONED.

HUNTING WOMAN INJURED.

Pilot Knocks Out A Woman In The Air.

LATE NEWS.

FAMOUS SOLDIER DEAD.

ADMIRAL TAYLOR IN THE HOUSE TO-DAY.

FAMOUS BRITISH CAVALRY COMMANDER DEAD.

"My wife is my banker Mr Drage we pay 30/- only on the £75?"

DRAGES HIGH HOLBORN · LONDON · W.C.1

Still in strict decker styles, but with some lower-case, the *Daily Express* (1930) was simply dressed in Century and Century Bold roman and italic.

newspaper history. Beyond that, though, the *Telegraph* had begun to use the American Century and Century Bold – which meant Linotype or Ludlow – as a main headline element. The *Express* had gone further, styling its headings exclusively in Century and Century Bold, including the bold italic. The device of running the centre line of a three-line deck a size smaller will be noted (it was then not uncommon British practice), as also the adherence – as the page above shows – to the superfluous full point at the end of every heading, from streamer to down-page filler.

The final comment may be made that, while the new text types like Ionic had swept the U.S. the London nationals were still using the old-fashioned modern romans, usually duplexed with Doric; and the spattering of news-columns with 'black indent' paragraphs – not least in order to provide some colour amid the dim, grey mass of the text – was normal practice. A radical change was, however, at hand here as in the matter of headline typography and page make-up.

6: A Revolutionary Decade – The 1930s

BOTH in Britain and America the 1930s marked the Great Divide in the history of newspaper typography. The whole aspect of newspapers changed more radically than it had ever changed before. Freedom began to overthrow formalism in editorial display. Make-up emerged as a concept of overall page design, including illustrations and the relationship of editorial to advertising, not just the fixing of the 'tops' and shovelling in the shorts and fillers beneath them. Typography, that is to say the design and style of the type itself, was more and more seen as a central ingredient of headlines and text alike. Journalists started to get the upper hand in the choice, and use, of type; the old 'leave it to the printer' attitude died a deserved death; the ranks of the sub-editors (copy readers) gave birth to a new breed, the production journalist – the editorial man concerned with the typographic design of his paper.

Developments were unequal, and varied, both as between Britain and the U.S., and within the two countries. Nor was it a matter, as in the 1890s, of the London dailies merely modelling themselves on American headline styles. Though transatlantic inspiration was important, there was a good deal of cross-fertilisation. Thus by the middle of the decade the Hearst papers were copying some London headline styles, and were specifically under orders to study and emulate the typography of the *Daily Express*. American journalism textbooks were holding up the free and lively feature pages of the *Express* and the other Fleet Street 'populars' as models for their students.

The year 1929 presented some significant pointers to the developments that the ensuing decade was to witness. In America's *Linotype News*, the Mergenthaler house journal which was to earn itself the title of 'the nation's typographic laboratory', editor John E. Allen started campaigning for the 'streamlining' of newspaper headings by the introduction of the free flush-left style, lines ending at will, and using upper- and lower-case, in place of the stiff and formal decker with its play on condensed capitals. In Britain that September the Trades Union Congress agreed, not without heart-searching, to transfer the printing and publishing of the Labour movement's struggling *Daily Herald* (circulation not more than 250,000) to Odhams Press, a leading London newspaper and periodical printing concern. And in the Printing Number of *The Times* that October, already mentioned, the paper's new typographic adviser, Stanley Morison, contributed a critical survey of existing newspaper types which was in fact the first shot in the campaign that led to Printing House Square's typographic revolution of 1932.

Allen's 'streamlining' campaign followed the adoption of the flush-left headline style by the *Morning Telegraph*, a New York sporting daily, in December 1928.[1] Designer Heyworth Campbell (better known for his work in the magazine and book spheres) specified a simplified, 'free', decker style, all in upper- and lower-case. First decks were set flush-left in Ultra-Bodoni roman, second decks (and there were no more) in Bodoni Bold italic, indented even and ending at will. This radical innovation, however, found no echo in the big, general newspapers, though some small-town dailies began to adopt Allen's ideas.

In succeeding issues of the *Linotype News* Allen hammered away, demonstrating the possibilities of different type faces for his simpli-

BULLETINS

New Newspaper Home in Davenport

Front view of the building dedicated by the Davenport Times in October. See story on page two

The Reading (Pa.) Times has installed three Two-in-One Blue Streak Master Model 31 Linotypes, some twenty-five fonts of display matrices, and has adopted a modern head dress in Erbar Medium Condensed and Metromedium No. 2.

The Brooklyn Eagle has modernized its head dress and is now presenting most of its heads flush at the left in the Bodoni family.

The San Francisco Chronicle has adopted flush-left heads, most of them in Bodoni Bold or Poster Bodoni, and is departmentalizing news stories under such heads as "Foreign," "Science," "Education," "Crime," and so on.

The Kansas City (Mo.) Journal (formerly the Journal-Post) has installed many display sizes in the Memphis family and adopted a modern head dress that has attracted much favorable comment.

The Washington Star has installed twenty-five fonts of 7-point Ionic No. 5, many display fonts of Erbar Medium Condensed and Metromedium No. 2 with Italic, and is now presenting its heads flush at the left.

The Linotype News

VOLUME XVII | BROOKLYN, NOVEMBER, 1938 | NUMBER THREE

1938 THE YEAR OF LINOTYPE'S BLUE STREAK MASTER MODELS

K. C. Journal Picks Memphis For New Dress

Modern Heads and Classified News Win Readers' Praise

KANSAS CITY, Mo.—One of the first acts of Orville S. McPherson after he became president of the Kansas City Journal-Post Company and publisher of the Journal-Post was to plan an effective new head dress for his paper.

Mr. McPherson had had much experience in newspaper re-styling in other parts of the country and so was well qualified to give the Journal-Post an unusually effective new dress.

And when the new dress first appeared, October 4, it was greeted with enthusiasm by readers and advertisers, as well as by newspaper executives in many parts of the country.

The issues of the Journal (the word "Post" had been dropped from the nameplate and masthead) for the next three days presented messages of commendation from more than 200 people in various walks of life, with many comments such as "I like it," "A hundred per cent improvement," "Best thing I've seen for some time," "I want that paper on my porch every day," "You can put me down as a regular subscriber," "I like its modern treatment of news," and "It's the talk of the town today."

Most of the heads in the new Journal are presented flush at the left in members of the Memphis family. News heads are chiefly in Memphis Medium Condensed and Memphis Medium, and society and woman's-page heads chiefly in Memphis Medium and Memphis Medium Italic. On the sports pages many of the heads are in Memphis Bold Condensed, Memphis Bold and Memphis Bold Italic. The Journal's editorial page is unusually attractive, with a three-column cartoon centered at the top and

(Continued on page two)

Washington Post Adopts New Dress

WASHINGTON, D. C.—The Washington Post, Eugene Meyer, publisher, which recently modernized its head dress by adopting simplified flush-left heads in the Bodoni

For 5,000 Years From Now

Joe Mallen, Linotype operator who cast the famous slug, hands it to Grady Miller, foreman of the Tuckahoe Record plant

Small-Town Linotype Man Casts Slug for Year 6939

Five thousand years from now, barring too many earthquakes or other cosmic disturbances in the wrong place, a group of scientists will gaze on the handiwork of a small-town printer of today—on the work of Joe Mallen, Linotype operator with the Tuckahoe (N. Y.) Record.

September 23 a "time capsule"—an 800-pound metal cylinder that contains much information about us and our times—was deposited fifty feet below the surface of the ground at the New York World's ... the Westinghouse Electric & Manufacturing Company and deposited at the site of that company's exhibit at the fair, was made of a copper alloy known as cupaloy and has a pyrex glass crypt. The cylinder is seven and one-half feet long and [illegible] eight inches in diameter.

Can Opener and Woman's Hat

Among other things included in the "time capsule" are a can opener, a woman's hat of the latest style, a Bible, a toothbrush, a safety pin, a camera, a pipe, cigarettes, a foun-

Washington Star Adopts Modern Dress

Now Using Erbar, Metro for Heads, With Larger Ionic

WASHINGTON, D. C.—The Star of this city came out October 31 with a modern head dress in Erbar Medium Condensed, Metromedium No. 2 and Metromedium No. 2 Italic, and with body matter in 7-point Ionic No. 5 on an 8-point body.

As the Star's presses were turning out the first copies in the new dress, a radio broadcast announcing the change was made from the composing room. Those taking part in the broadcast were Newbold Noyes, associate editor; B. M. McKelway, managing editor; Charles P. Merkle, foreman of the composing room; Ralph McCabe, makeup editor, and "Bill" Coyle, radio announcer.

For the new dress, the Star installed twenty-five fonts of 7-point Ionic No. 5—twenty-four of them with Bold Face No. 2 and one with Italic—and fonts of 18-, 24- and 34-point Erbar Medium Condensed, and 12-, 14-, 18- and 24-point Metromedium No. 2 with Italic.

Typographically Revitalized

On the radio broadcast Newbold Noyes stated, in part: "Today when you pick up your copy of the Star in your office, in your home, or at the newsstand, you will find a Star that is typographically revitalized. The headlines and news stories sparkle with readability. The Star has lightened the optical task of absorbing the news."

Mr. McKelway: "One big advantage of the new headlines is that they can be written faster, for they are simpler; you can get more words in them, and you don't have to spend so much time making each line exactly the same length."

Mr. Merkle explained how the composing room got ready for and took care of the change: "Everything we did was gotten out of the way yesterday. We had a battery of machinists headed by our chief machinist, William T. Henderson, and under the supervision of Dave McCarty, news foreman."

Better Looking Paper

Mr. McCabe: "Our new dress enables us to put out a much better looking paper. There will be less eye strain."

A front-page story in the Star the day of the change stated, in part: "In changing the dress of the Star it is felt that the finest typographic

3 Blue Streaks, New Dress For Times of Reading, Pa.

READING, Pa.—The Times of this city has installed three Two-in-One Blue Streak Master Model 31 Linotypes, some twenty-five fonts of display matrices, and has adopted a modern head dress in Erbar Medium Condensed and Metromedium No. 2.

A front-page story in the Times the day of the change stated, in part: "Your Reading Times comes to you today dressed in still more modern clothes. Our headlines are streamlined. . . . The new style of headline setting, and the Erbar and Metro types which compose the lines, make for more comprehensive headline writing, and for speedier and easier reading. With the streamlined head type we also have modernized our masthead—that portion of page one above the dateline. While Father Time and his part of the picture remain the same, the modern side of the world's affairs has been redesigned to include later developments in industry, commerce and agriculture, among which is the airplane, skyscrapers and the streamlined train."

All three of the new machines are equipped with six-mold disks, two of them with Mohr Lino-Saws, and one with an automatic ejector set. A Reid magazine rack was included in the installation.

Fifteen Linotypes are now operated.

John H. Perry is president of the Reading Times Publishing Company, which publishes the Times. Earl A. Kettel is secretary-treasurer. Eagle Freshwater is manager. Abe Hurwitz is editor, and Charles W. Detweiler is advertising director. Harry Y. Sterrett is mechanical superintendent, and George Schaaber is Linotype machinist.

Mr. Perry, who recently purchased control of the Western Newspaper Union, is head of the John H. Perry Associates enterprises, which include the Jacksonville (Fla.) Journal, the Pensacola (Fla.) News and the Journal, the Panama City (Fla.) News-Herald, and radio station WCOA, Pensacola.

San Francisco Chronicle Modernizes Its Makeup

SAN FRANCISCO. — "The Newspaper You've Been Waiting For!" was the heading on the announcement by the Chronicle of this city that that paper had modernized its makeup and had departmentalized its news stories, classifying them under such heads as "Foreign," "Science," "Education," "Crime," "The Nation" and "Labor's Day."

Heads in the Chronicle are now set flush at the left, most of them in Bodoni Bold or Poster Bodoni.

In the issue for the day before the change "30" dashes throughout the paper were made up of the words "Tomorrow" and "Streamline," and an announcement was made that the change was coming.

W. D. Chandler, managing editor, stated, "We are delighted with the reception. The reaction has been much more favorable than we had hoped."

"There is no doubt that streamlining will increase circulation," stated G. E. Gilroy, circulation manager.

The changes in typography were made under the direction of Paul C. Smith, general manager. "We aim to classify news, to make it accessible and to make the relationship of one event to another readily discernible," Mr. Smith stated.

Inquirer Adds Model 29 And Fonts of Erbar, Metro

PHILADELPHIA. — The Inquirer of this city has added a Two-in-One Model 29 Linotype and fonts ... dent and general manager of the company, and Walter H. Annenberg is vice-president. John T. Curtis is

▲ America's *Linotype News*, which John E. Allen made into 'the nation's typographic laboratory' and propagandist for simplified headline styles; this 1938 issue demonstrated headings in the Egyptian-style Memphis of Mergenthaler Linotype.

fied headline treatments. He rapidly moved on from the simplified decker style to the multi-line single-decker, set flush-left, in upper- and lower-case; and he stressed that only one type family was needed for any newspaper's headline dress. By November 1930 he was emphasising, and showing, the importance of the simple light-bold contrast – which has appeared to be a special achievement of the 1960s – with an all-sans make-up in Metroblack and Metrothin.

It was absurd, Allen contended, that there should be 'virtually no changes in the physical treatment of news heads' when reading habits had so substantially changed; the stage had been reached, he asserted, when the newspaper reader 'doesn't read – he glimpses'. He noted the effect on the reader's visual consciousness of the superior typography attained by display advertising. His 'streamlined' headings, he argued, 'attract attention, save valuable space, are easy to write and to compose, and effect savings all along the line. They do away with tedious letter counting and line fitting.'

While Allen determinedly soldiered on – and he can hardly even have dreamed at that point that his advocacy would eventually transform the look of the newspapers of a nation in a way never before, or since, achieved by one man – an outside body took action which was to prove of major importance in the revolutionising of newspaper typography in the U.S. In 1931 a big Philadelphia advertising agency, N. W. Ayer & Son, Inc, introduced the first of its annual contests, open to all English-language daily papers in America, for excellence in typography, make-up and presswork. The Ayer Award, repeatedly won in its early years by the *New York Herald Tribune* (still in Ben Sherbow's Bodoni headline dress of 1918), was the first contest of the kind in the English-speaking world. It would be hard to overestimate the importance of the competitive spirit it stimulated in encouraging the development of good newspaper design. The Ayer sponsors were fully justified when, in 1968, they eventually wound up the Award on the ground that it had served its purpose.

By the early 1930s there was no sign that Allen's new ideas were

Saturday, January 6, 1934. DAILY WORKER 3

FEVER RAGES THROUGHOUT COUNTRY

Poverty And Drought The Chief Causes

DIPHTHERIA cases have increased in England by 29 per cent. in the last three months, as compared with the similar period of last year, while cases of scarlet fever have increased by no less than 85 per cent.

In October to mid-December, 1933, there were 17,691 cases of diphtheria registered, as compared with 13,755 in the similar period of 1932.

In October to mid-December, 1933, there were 53,428 scarlet fever cases, as compared with 29,348 in the similar period of 1932.

Deaths from influenza doubled in 1933, rising from 5,732 in 1932 to 11,434 in 1933.

Some of the recent epidemic of scarlet fever is due to the deterioration in the water supply, consequent on the prolonged drought.

But another exceedingly important factor is the decline in the workers' power of resistance, consequent on low wages and low unemployment relief.

Shipbuilders Menaced With Displacement

BOSSES TRY TO CREATE NEW TRADE

The joint conference between the shipyard trade unions and the employers' federation in regard to the dispute over the employers' proposals for the creation of a new class of electric welders, will be resumed in Edinburgh next Wednesday.

This new class of workers will displace boilermakers, riveters, blacksmiths, caulkers, holders-up, heaters and catchers.

Hardest Winter For British Working Class Since The War

Mounted Police, who are frequently in action against the Hunger Marchers.

Appeal For National Congress Sent Out

HAS YOUR BRANCH ELECTED DELEGATES TO BUILD UNITY

"THIS winter is the hardest for the British workers since the War. All the more necessary is it therefore that all our energy be directed towards achieving working-class unity in action as a means of driving back the new attacks.

"Because of the new starvation cuts, and the growing resistance of the workers, the Government is reorganising its forces of repression. Fascist methods are steadily creeping into the administration and into the police organs of capitalism, while Press propaganda in favour of Fascist suppression of the working-class is everywhere increasing. Further, numerous threats of war are increasing and intensifying."

The above is an extract from the manifesto calling the National Congress of Action.

The manifesto is signed by:—

Alex Gossip, General Secretary of the National Amalgamated Furnishing Trades' Association;

John Jagger, President of the National Union of Distributive and Allied Workers;

Harry Pollitt, Communist Party;

James Figgins, Executive member of the National Union of Railwaymen, 1931-33;

James Lee, General Secretary, Scottish Brassmoulders' Union;

James Maxton, M.P., Independent Labour Party;

John McGovern, M.P., Independent Labour Party;

Aneurin Bevan, M.P.;

Ted Hill, London delegate, Boilermakers' Society;

Jack Tanner, Organising District [illegible]

"We propose the calling of a great National Congress of employed and unemployed i. the New Year. A Congress of Action. We also propose the commencement of preparations for the organisation of a National March, and that we should endeavour to develop the preparatory campaign on a mass scale to ensure the successful carrying through of the March, with a view to arriving in London in ti ıe for the opening of the Great National Unity Conference.

"We propose that the Congress and the March shall lead the working-class fight against the Unemployment Bill, the Means Test and the Anomalies Act; lead the fight for free speech, the right of assembly and against the Fascist measures of the police; and will lead the fight for the restoration of the ten per cent. economy cuts and for an all-round increase in wages and [illegible]

WELL-KNOWN MILITANT ELECTED

Stokes Victory In Engineering Union

Comrade Stokes, of Coventry, a well-known militant in the Amalgamated Engineering Union, has been elected as president of the Coventry District of that union.

W. H. STOKES

The voting was W. H. Stokes, 429; A. Maddison, 394.

Comrade Stokes has been active

Part of the Fife Contingent during a Scottish Hunger March to Edinburgh.

TOBACCO COMBINE'S BIG PROFITS

But Chairman Hopes For More

A DIVIDEND of 7½ per cent. was declared by the British-American Tobacco Company at its 31st Annual Meeting, held in Westminster House, Millbank, yesterday.

Sir Hugo Cunliffe-Owen, who presided, complained about the chaotic state of foreign exchanges.

In many countries the exchange rate is nominal. In other countries you cannot remit at all, and in some countries you can only remit under the most [illegible]

Leeds Support For Heroic Fairdale Strike

STRUGGLE IN THIRTEENTH WEEK

THE Fairdale clothing strikers, who to-day start on their thirteenth week of struggle took a further step towards intensifying the fight on Thursday, when pickets were again put on the retail shops of Brian Walsh, where blackleg goods are sold.

Extensive retail shop picketing took place in the first two weeks of the strike under the leadership of the Strike Committee.

Many pickets were arrested and fined, and Magistrate Mead ruled that all picketing was illegal.

The higher union officials, who had got control of the strike, allowed this decision to pass unchallenged, and the picketing was dropped pending a "question in the House," which has still to be asked.

The indignation of the strikers at this state of affairs grew until, backed by the Solidarity Committee, they were able, on December 12, to force the officials to let them resume picketing at the retail shops.

The effect was immediate. The employers asked the same day for an "armistice" on terms including cessation of picketing. This was agreed to "for twenty-four hours," but on one pretext and another it was continued until last week, when the Strike Commitee put pickets on the factory once more.

The strikers now realise that they were tricked into taking pickets off the retail shops during the Christmas shopping season, and we are determined that they shall stay on now until the strike is won, especially as the January sales of Brian Walsh are almost as busy as the Christmas trade.

OFFICIALS' ARGUMENTS

The higher officials are telling the strikers that picketing is unwise, as it may prejudice the negotiations which are to be resumed next week. But the strikers have a clear idea now of what is wise and what is not.

▲ Portion of a London *Daily Worker* page in January 1934, showing early efforts at 'streamlining'.

evoking any response among British newspaper technicians. Newspaper promotion material issued by the Linotype and Monotype organisations at this time was still limited to suggesting arrangements of the manufacturers' types for conventional decker headings. The specimens shown continued to make their principal play on capitals for main decks. Monotype ingenuity, for example, was expended on a scheme of three weights of Baskerville Titling for news headlines, each weight in 14, 18 and 24pt, all accommodated in one die-case. Whether any newspaper ever so keyboarded its headlines on the Monotype I do not know; but on the scheme indicated they could only have been in all-capitals decker style.

Nevertheless, though I find it impossible to pinpoint precisely how, the 'streamlining' notions must have begun to filter through. I recall that, in a first modest attempt in 1934 to improve the typography of the then infant *Daily Worker* (born 1 January 1930) I specified flush-left headings in Caslon Heavy and Bodoni italic, both in upper- and lower-case. Whatever happened in the tiny *Worker* was unlikely to stimulate Fleet Street, though I did get an inquiry from the *Express* about the unusual-looking Bodoni italic I had put in. It was founders' type from the ancient Caslon establishment (then within three years of its final dissolution). Caslons had had a distorted Bodoni roman in their specimen books since the 1920s, described as 'from the original design of Giambattista Bodoni'; pretty far 'from', too. To this they later added a less distressing italic, which sported a peculiar non-kerning 'f'; it was this letter that had momentarily caught the eye of, or at any rate puzzled, the *Express*.

It is time now to backtrack for a while to the second of our significant pointers for the decade. The production of the 'new' *Daily Herald* by Odhams Press on 17 March 1930 caused an immense sensation in the London newspaper trade. Fleet Street's backwardness in make-up, text and machining was put to shame by a 'popular' paper – which immediately quadrupled circulation to around a million – with a consistently planned typography in the bold variants of one type family only (Cheltenham), with a strong-coloured text in the American Ionic discussed in the previous chapter – its first appearance in Britain – and with rotary presswork of a quality comparable only with that of *The Times*.

Daily Herald

No. 4,395 MONDAY, MARCH 17, 1930 ONE PENNY.

PREMIER WELCOMES THE NEW "HERALD"

HIS MESSAGE TO NATION

"While writing he was snapped."

Great Day in History of Labour

FORWARD!

Special Visit to Our Offices

MR. MACDONALD'S WISH

TO-DAY the new "Daily Herald" will be in the hands of over a million readers.

No one has watched with greater interest its organisation than Mr. Ramsay MacDonald, Labour's first Prime Minister. On the eve of the birth of the new paper he paid a special visit to its new home.

"I send cordial wishes for success," was the burden of his message specially written in the Editor's room. **"I hope that all supporters of Labour and all who wish to have Labour's case put fairly before them will buy it and read it."**

PRIME MINISTER'S GREETINGS

"I SEND MY CORDIAL GOOD WISHES"

The following is the text of Mr. MacDonald's Message to the "Daily Herald":—

TO-DAY [illegible] "Daily Herald" which [illegible] survived many difficulties [illegible] crises, starts out on a new [illegible].

This [illegible] for the first time, it will be [illegible] equipped to meet its competitors in the newspaper world [illegible] terms, and to supply [illegible] and services which [illegible].

A National Newspaper

I [illegible] all supporters of Labour [illegible] those, whatever their [illegible] wish to have the Labour [illegible] put fairly before them, [illegible] and read it.

There never was a **time when it was more necessary for the Labour Party to have a national newspaper devoted to its support; or for the public to have the Labour point of view continuously before it.**

Labour [illegible] now responsible for the government of the country, and has to deal daily with the urgent problems confronting it.

Friendly Pages

Our predecessors escaped their responsibilities in time and left for us to face a mass of ripening problems such as have never before confronted a Government.

It is therefore essential that the public should be able to learn of our doings and our sayings from a friendly page, and not exclusively from journals which are influenced by the wish to see our adversaries supplant us.

Cordial Good Wishes

To the old staff and the old readers who have supported the paper through thick and thin, and to the reinforcements who from to-day on will join that goodly company, I send my cordial good wishes.

The great newspaper can only be built up on close sympathy and understanding between those who write and those who read.

I hope that writers for and readers of the new "Daily Herald" will constitute together an ever-increasing force of instructed public opinion and good judgment which will be a strength to the Labour Party and an intelligent guiding influence in national policy.

HISTORIC HOUR AT NEW OFFICE

SCENES AND INCIDENTS OF HIS TOUR

MR. MACDONALD made history when he paid his visit to the offices of the new "Daily Herald."

Never before had a British Premier mingled so freely with the staff of a great daily journal.

He talked to reporters and sub-editors at their work, watched compositors, process workers, machinists and the host of others engaged in the task of producing a newspaper with a nation-wide sale.

The Prime Minister's visit was the outcome of a keen willingness to identify himself with the new enterprise.

There was present, too, a desire to see at first hand the great strides that have been made, after many months of hard work, to build up a newspaper organisation worthy of Labour's position in national affairs.

Well Equipped

Time after time, during the hour he spent at Wilson-street, Long Acre, he expressed satisfaction on finding that Labour's only daily newspaper in future will be as well-equipped as its rivals.

Having seen every phase of newspaper production, he met Mr. J. S. Elias, chairman and managing director of the "Daily Herald" (1929), Limited. They spent some time talking over the prospects of the new paper with Mr. William Mellor, the Editor.

Mr. J. S. Elias

Mr. Elias spoke enthusiastically of the vast amount of help given to the paper by all sections of the Labour Movement. The Premier wished Mr. Elias every success in the new enterprise in which he and the Trades Union Congress are so closely allied.

While writing his inspiring message at the Editor's desk he was "snapped" by a staff photographer, and took a souvenir copy of the picture away with him.

Mr. MacDonald, who was accompanied by Capt. H. B. Usher and Miss Rose Rosenberg, his personal private

(Continued on page two, column five.)

DON 'ALL OUT' TO-MORROW FOR A SPEED RECORD

PHONE TALK TO THE "DAILY HERALD"

FAITH IN HIS CAR

FOUR MILES A MINUTE —OR MORE?

By KAYE DON
In an interview by Trans-Atlantic Telephone

DAYTONA, Florida, Sunday.

IF conditions are favourable I am hoping to go all out for the world's record speed run on Tuesday.

Unless disaster—which I am not contemplating—overtakes the venture, it will, I hope, place Great Britain in possession of a record of something over 240 miles an hour—or four miles a minute.

I wish it was to be a fight for the honour with other countries and their cars in the struggle.

I am playing a lone hand, but the interest in the attempt I am making has become intense. The Americans are very excited and are packing every hotel in Daytona.

PLEASED WITH CAR

When I took the Silver Bullet out for a trial yesterday crowds of people watched her, and were delighted when they saw her in action. They tell me that she looks a picture of speed.

Certainly she has lived up to my expectations. I am very pleased with her. She steers easily and well, and holds the ground splendidly.

Conditions were far from ideal yesterday; in fact, there were many who thought it might be risky. Visibility was poor, and the sands were bumpy.

198 M.P.H. ATTAINED

Nevertheless, the Silver Bullet, in the southern run along the beach, reached a speed of 115 miles an hour, and 198 in the opposite direction.

This is only 33 miles an hour short of the record set up here by Sir Henry Segrave, and there was more than that in reserve in engine power.

I had still plenty of throttle left and am satisfied that the Silver Bullet, given the best conditions of weather and beach, **is capable of 250 miles an hour.** Perhaps she will do even better than this.

The sea was only about 12 fet away when I shot past. It was a moment of emotion, and one of the most exciting of my career.

Now I would like to wish the new "DailyHerald" and its readers the best of luck."

HEARD OVER 5,000 MILES AWAY

CLARITY OF FAMOUS DRIVER'S VOICE

Mr. Kaye Don's voice came over the 5,000 miles between the "Daily Herald" office in Wilson-street, Long Acre, and his hotel at Daytona with perfect clearness (writes a "Daily Herald" representative).

The call was put through to the minute, and a man's voice, with an American accent, announced, "You are through to Daytona."

A moment later Mr. Kaye Don called out, cheerily, "Hullo, 'Daily Herald,' how are you?"

It was afternoon in London, but Mr Don had only just got up for breakfast. English time is five hours ahead of American time.

He was his usual calm self, but talked almost excitedly about the weather.

"Fine in London, is it? It's raining here, and rather unpleasant, although it is quite warm.

"This is a marvellous line. I can hear you much better than is often the case with a trunk call in England."

MYSTERY HOTEL DEATH

CANADIAN FOUND SHOT IN LOCKED ROOM

Stated to be a prominent Canadian business man, William Hughes was found unconscious with a gunshot wound in his body in his room at the Midland Hotel, London yesterday.

On receiving no reply to her knocks, a chambermaid unlocked the door and found Hughes lying at the foot of the bed. A single-shot gun with a spent cartridge was near.

Hughes was rushed to hospital, but found to be dead. He had been staying at the hotel for three weeks, but had not slept in his bed the previous night.

JOCKEY HURT IN CAR SMASH

George Turner, the steeplechase jockey, was involved in a road accident at Worthing last night.

Turner has cancelled his engagement at Wye to-day, but he will be riding in the Grand National.

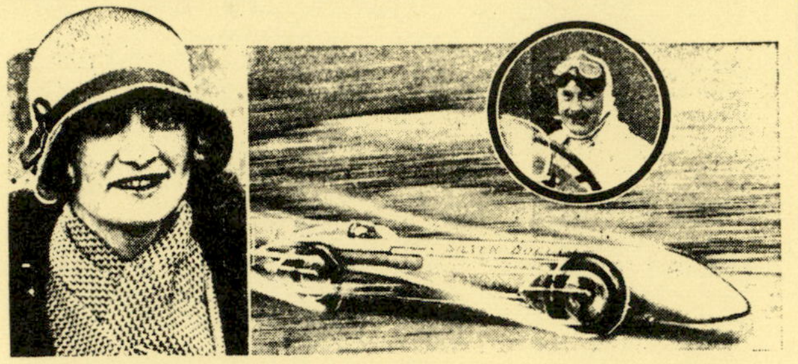

THE SILVER BULLET, in which Kaye Don will attempt to break the world's land speed record at Daytona, America, to-morrow. Left, Miss Rita Don, who is with her brother at Daytona.

PRIMO DE RIVERA FOUND DEAD

SURPRISE ARREST OF GIALDINI

HATRY'S COLLEAGUE TO BE TRIED IN ITALY

Giovanni Gialdini, the Italian associate of Clarence Hatry, was arrested late on Saturday evening in Milan.

The arrest was carried out by detective officers of the Special Judicial Police.

M. Gialdini

The Italian authorities (says our Italian correspondent) took action immediately on receiving the necessary evidence from the British Embassy.

There is no question of extradition, as the Anglo-Italian Treaty does not provide for the extradition of Italians to England or vice versa.

Gialdini will be charged under a section of the Italian penal code, which makes it a punishable offence for an Italian citizen to do anything abroad that may damage the prestige and reputation of the State.

The first stage will be an inquiry by a magistrate. If he decides that the evidence is sufficient Gialdini will be brought to trial.

It will probably be necessary to bring witnesses from London, and the case may be protracted.

Hatry's application for leave to appeal will be made in the Court of Criminal Appeal to-day.

FORD "BABY" CAR FOR £100

WHAT WILL BRITISH MAKERS DO?

By Our Motoring Correspondent

An interesting event is expected in the Ford motor family within the next few months—the birth of the Ford "baby" car.

Mr. Henry Ford plans to be the first "foreigner" to tackle Britain's most successful industry—the manufacture of "baby" cars.

Mr. Ford's ambition is to produce the first £100 car—an eagerly awaited event that has defied the efforts of British manufacturers so far. The two cheapest "babies" on the market at present both cost £130.

No confirmation of the report could be obtained from the Ford Company's London office. "A baby car is not even contemplated so far as we are aware," I was told.

British manufacturers of "baby" cars, despite the denial, are making preparations to fight this threat of competition from within—a threat to an industry in which Britain has always led.

TO-DAY'S 20 PAGES

PARIS HOTEL DRAMA

LONE PASSING OF THE EX-DICTATOR OF SPAIN

PREMONITION

From Our Own Correspondent

PARIS, Sunday.

GENERAL PRIMO DE RIVERA, ex-Dictator of Spain, died suddenly in Paris this morning.

The diabetes from which he suffered was aggravated by a sudden attack of influenza, and a heart attack finally caused his death.

The ex-Dictator was alone in his hotel when his end came.

SON'S DISCOVERY

His son Miguel, who recently slapped the face of a Spanish General for uttering public criticism of his father, and subsequently fought a duel in defence of his father's honour, was the first to discover that his father had died.

Both he and his sisters left the sick room this morning for the first time in several days. General de Rivera then appeared in better health.

Primo de Rivera

Returning from a walk a few minutes before noon, the son found his father lying on the bed in a dressing-gown.

His body was arched, as if in an effort to rise, and one foot hung over the side of the bed.

Before he died the General had apparently made an effort to write down his last wishes, for a writing-pad lay open on a table, but no message was scrawled on it.

HIS LAST WORDS

His last words to his son contained a tragic premonition of his [illegible] Spain has finished me"—but they were uttered in a jesting manner. Neither Miguel de Rivera nor his sisters dreamed that they were to prove prophetic within an hour.

The son has taken his father's words seriously, and declares that the treatment Primo de Rivera received at the hands of his Sovereign and of his political friends in Spain was responsible for his early end.

"SWEATING" IN SHOPS

FABULOUS PROFITS AT WORKERS' EXPENSE

Compulsory legislation was the only way to deal with the excessive hours in the distributive trades, said Alderman R. A. Taylor, M.P. for Lincoln, addressing a mass meeting of shop assistants at Cardiff on Saturday.

He predicted a majority for the second reading of the Shops (Hours of Employment) Bill.

Fabulous profits were being made by the great food retailing combines, and these profits were built up on systematic understaffing, overwork, long hours, and low wages.

WELSH COMPOSER DEAD

Dr. T. D. Edwards, of Portmadoc, the well-known Welsh musical composer, Eisteddfod adjudicator, and choral conductor, died on Saturday, aged 54.

BALLOON CHASE BY MOTOR-CAR

TALLULAH'S KISS FOR 'VARSITY AIRMEN

From Our Special Correspondent

HENLEY, Sunday.

"Have you seen the balloon?"

Several hundred Oxford undergraduates in fast sport cars made this inquiry on the roads between Oxford and Aldershot this afternoon.

I, too, had for a while joined in the chase of the balloon "Florence" which made the inaugural ascent of the Oxford University Balloon Club and came down safely near Princes Risborough at seven o'clock this evening.

Tallulah Bankhead and the aeronauts posed for the talkies and cameras. She kissed the balloonists good-bye several times.

At first the balloon would not rise. A crowd of undergraduates pushed it, but it bumped back to the ground. The three fliers took off their coats to lighten the load, but still it would not rise.

Finally, one of them had to get out, and, to a burst of cheers and laughter, the balloon rose quickly and in a few moments was lost in the clouds.

OUR £10,000 INSURANCE FOR READERS

EVERYDAY RISKS COVERED FOR ALL

REGISTER TO-DAY!

PROTECTION AT HOME, AT WORK AND AT PLAY

TO-DAY is the day on which every reader of the new "Daily Herald" with a stroke of the pen becomes eligible for our Great £10,000 Free Insurance.

Our readers are offered the great boon of a free insurance scheme which in point of comprehensiveness, practical features and liberal benefits is unsurpassed.

The long list of Benefits set forth on Page 15 shows how thoroughly the "Daily Herald" has done its work.

Thirty-one in number, the benefits range in amounts from £10,000 to £5—wonderful protection indeed.

The "Daily Herald" **has kept** closely in mind the everyday risk rather than the remote chance. The Benefits were framed for ***you***—and for your wife and children.

£10,000 OFFER

Under the new "Daily Herald" Free Insurance, £10,000 is offered in the event of a registered reader and his wife losing their lives in an accident to a rail-

Continued on Page Three.

First Odhams Press production of the *Daily Herald* in March 1930, uniformly headlined in Cheltenham Bold.

The reason for the technical novelty of the Odhams *Herald* was as simple as it was unusual. Odhams Press dated from 1847, when a *Morning Post* compositor named William Odhams, a Dorset man who had left his native Sherborne for London as soon as he was out of his time, set up on his own account; from the start the business specialised in newspaper production. The firm prospered and grew vastly but never deviated from its basic aim of printing, as distinct from publishing, newspapers. When Odhams became publishers, as not infrequently happened, it was only in order to retain the printing contract. The firm had never been interested in the power-potential of newspaper publishing in the fashion of the Harmsworths, Beaverbrook, the Berrys and the other Press tycoons.

The guiding principle of Odhams was – keep the presses running. The policy of the papers printed was of no concern. In 1906 the firm was anxious to print on contract the ill-fated Liberal *Tribune*. Twenty-odd years later its rotary press capacity had so greatly increased, first through meeting the once big run of the muck-raking *John Bull* of the monstrous Horatio Bottomley and then through the sensationalist Sunday *The People*, that a daily was needed to take up the slack. On the eve of the 1930s the head of the firm, Julius Salter Elias (later Viscount Southwood) was seriously disquieted by his machine-room's uneconomic working. He tried to get the ultra-Tory *Morning Post* and failing that the Lloyd Georgeite Liberal *Daily Chronicle* – both not far from their respective deaths – eventually settling for the only firm final prospect, the Labour *Daily Herald*, as recounted above.

It would be tempting to probe a little deeper into the Odhams set-up in general and the personality of Elias in particular; but it is beyond the purpose of the present work and has been admirably done elsewhere.[2] Suffice it to say that Elias, who had joined Odhams as a junior clerk in 1894 and worked his way painstakingly to the top, was an able administrator and charitable employer who could only be described as a caricatural suburban 'little man' of the most limited intellectual interests. Politically and editorially he was a disaster. He succeeded temporarily in pushing the *Herald* past the two million mark, the first national morning to do so, but it was only by means of the meretricious commercial device of a free-gift circulation 'war' so fantastic that the NPA eventually had to intervene to stop it.

The free-gift 'war' launched by Odhams was not without effect in conditioning and stimulating newspaper typographic experiment and development. It helped to enhance the impact of Odhams in the national morning field; of this an early sign was the realisation throughout Fleet Street that the old weak and smudgy modern romans would no longer do for text. By 1933 the other leading dailies had followed the *Herald's* example and installed Ionic, the *Express* leading the *Mail* and the *News Chronicle*.

As we have seen, the Odhams *Herald* scored from the start not only with its text but with its orderly headlining in a single type family, initially in traditional decker style, alternating capitals and upper- and lower-case. This headlining bore further witness to the progressive techniques of Odhams. At a time when founders' type for headings was still common in London newspaper composing rooms Odhams were early Ludlow enthusiasts. By 1930 the Odhams Ludlow repertory was easily the most extensive in Europe. The Odhams Ludlows provided the *Herald* with the Cheltenham heading dress of its first eight years in its new guise; after a while the Bold style was lightened in the middle range of sizes (18 to 42pt) by the introduction of the unusual Medium and Medium Condensed. Ludlow resources likewise coped with the *Herald's* radical change of May 1938, when the paper went over to an all-Bodoni heading style, in Light and Bold, each with roman and italic. Nor was the change limited to the new type-face. The 1938 *Herald* was 'streamlined', even if not in full John E. Allen style. Some headlines were flush-left, others centred; but decker heads had disappeared in favour of multi-line single-deckers; main headings

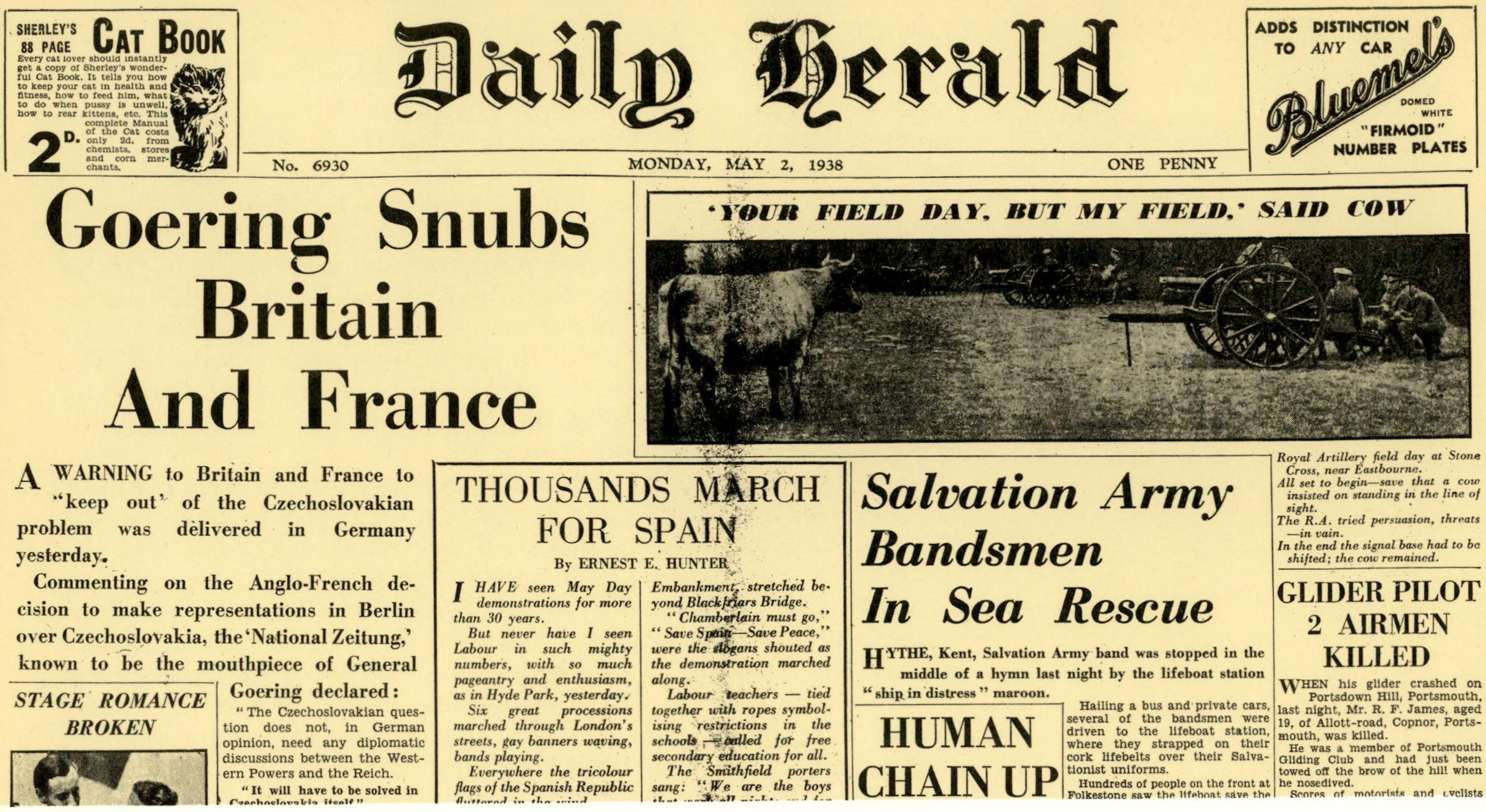

SHERLEY'S 88 PAGE CAT BOOK
Every cat lover should instantly get a copy of Sherley's wonderful Cat Book. It tells you how to keep your cat in health and fitness, how to feed him, what to do when pussy is unwell, how to rear kittens, etc. This complete Manual of the Cat costs only 2d. from chemists, stores and corn merchants.
2D.

Daily Herald

ADDS DISTINCTION TO *ANY* CAR
Bluemel's
DOMED WHITE "FIRMOID" NUMBER PLATES

No. 6930 MONDAY, MAY 2, 1938 ONE PENNY

Goering Snubs Britain And France

A WARNING to Britain and France to "keep out" of the Czechoslovakian problem was delivered in Germany yesterday.

Commenting on the Anglo-French decision to make representations in Berlin over Czechoslovakia, the 'National Zeitung,' known to be the mouthpiece of General Goering declared:

"The Czechoslovakian question does not, in German opinion, need any diplomatic discussions between the Western Powers and the Reich.

"It will have to be solved in Czechoslovakia itself."

STAGE ROMANCE BROKEN

THOUSANDS MARCH FOR SPAIN

By ERNEST E. HUNTER

I HAVE seen May Day demonstrations for more than 30 years.

But never have I seen Labour in such mighty numbers, with so much pageantry and enthusiasm, as in Hyde Park, yesterday.

Six great processions marched through London's streets, gay banners waving, bands playing.

Everywhere the tricolour flags of the Spanish Republic fluttered in the wind ... Embankment, stretched beyond Blackfriars Bridge.

"Chamberlain must go," "Save Spain—Save Peace," were the slogans shouted as the demonstration marched along.

Labour teachers — tied together with ropes symbolising restrictions in the schools — called for free secondary education for all.

The Smithfield porters sang: "We are the boys ...

'YOUR FIELD DAY, BUT MY FIELD,' SAID COW

Royal Artillery field day at Stone Cross, near Eastbourne.
All set to begin—save that a cow insisted on standing in the line of sight.
The R.A. tried persuasion, threats—in vain.
In the end the signal base had to be shifted; the cow remained.

Salvation Army Bandsmen In Sea Rescue

HYTHE, Kent, Salvation Army band was stopped in the middle of a hymn last night by the lifeboat station "ship in distress" maroon.

Hailing a bus and private cars, several of the bandsmen were driven to the lifeboat station, where they strapped on their cork lifebelts over their Salvationist uniforms.

Hundreds of people on the front at Folkestone saw the lifeboat save the ...

HUMAN CHAIN UP

GLIDER PILOT 2 AIRMEN KILLED

WHEN his glider crashed on Portsdown Hill, Portsmouth, last night, Mr. R. F. James, aged 19, of Allott-road, Copnor, Portsmouth, was killed.

He was a member of Portsmouth Gliding Club and had just been towed off the brow of the hill when he nosedived.

Scores of motorists and cyclists ...

The *Daily Herald's* change to 'streamlined' Bodoni and Bodoni Bold in May 1938.

were in upper- and lower-case; instead of the front-page full banner in capitals the lead heading was three lines across three columns in 72pt upper- and lower-case – a splash style many years ahead of its time.

Now for the third significant pointer already outlined – namely Stanley Morison's survey of newspaper types which marked the opening stages of his campaign for the typographic transformation of *The Times*. Morison had started as the paper's typographic adviser in the late summer of 1929, after insisting that it abandon the archaic, and then still general, practice of ending headings with a full point. His article in the Printing Number that October, referring to 'recently conducted experiments', suggested the direction of his own thoughts in the words 'the question of an ideal type is . . . one of the greatest difficulty, complexity and risk for any newspaper'. The complexity of the whole business was certainly to emerge in the course of the following year.*

The Times set up an office committee, under the chairmanship of assistant editor R. M. Barrington-Ward (later to be editor, from 1941 until his untimely death in 1948). In November 1930 this committee received from Morison a printed *Memorandum on a Proposal to revise the Typography of The Times*. This 38-page quarto presented a mass of historical and technical detail to argue the case for a 'new typography' for *The Times*, laying down that it must be 'masculine, English, direct, simple . . . and absolutely free from faddishness and frivolity'. The committee considered the results of the 'experiments', mentioned by Morison in 1929, which had continued; among the types tested were the new American newspaper texts like Linotype Ionic and Intertype Ideal (then recently adopted by the *New York Times*) and Monotype faces like Baskerville, a specially-cut 9pt of Eric Gill's Perpetua, and Plantin 110 – the famous 1913 re-cutting, from the Plantin office specimen of 1605, of a sixteenth-century face that had in fact not been used in the lifetime of the Antwerp master.

The Barrington-Ward committee's final directive to Morison (recorded in its minutes for 28 January 1931) specified a ' "modernised Plantin", i.e. Plantin . . . with sharper serifs'.[3] And this is exactly what Times New Roman, as it was initially called, turned out to be. Himself no draughtsman, Morison handed a specimen of Plantin to the late Victor Lardent (a skilled lettering artist in the publicity department of *The Times*) and supervised his drawing of the appropriate alphabets in accordance with the directive. There has been much speculation about the details of this design transaction, but really they seem

* Those were opulent, not to say Byzantine, days at *The Times*. Morison worked 'day and night almost for several weeks' to produce *The Typography of The Times*, a majestic folio set in 24pt Bembo, for which the matrices were specially cut, and illustrated with over forty collotype plates. One copy only was printed, for presentation to the Chief Proprietor (there was in fact a second copy, which Morison not unreasonably retained for himself, and which presumably was destroyed with the rest of his library when his Regent's Park flat was fire-bombed in 1941). Fortunately the collotype plates were preserved, to form the basis in 1953 of the limited edition *Printing The Times*, another massive folio for which the text was set in 24pt Times Wide 427.

quite beside the point. A simple comparison of Plantin 110 and Times Roman is sufficient proof of provenance.

12pt alphabets of Monotype Times New Roman (series 327) and (below) Monotype Plantin 110.

ABCDEFGHIJKLMNOPQRSTUVWXYZ&ÆŒ
ABCDEFGHIJKLMNOPQRSTUVWXYZ&ÆŒ

ABCDEFGHIJKLMNOPQRSTUVWXYZÆŒ

ABCDEFGHIJKLMNOPQRSTUVWXYZÆŒ

abcdefghijklmnopqrstuvwxyzfiflfffffiffl æœ
abcdefghijklmnopqrstuvwxyzfiflfffffiffl æœ

The new text type was elegant and urbane. It had a sensationally successful debut, in $5\frac{1}{2}$, 7 (increased in 1936 to $7\frac{1}{2}$) and 9pt, replacing the old ruby, minion and bourgeois modern, in *The Times* of 3 October 1932. Its old face character – for the 'modernisation' did not go beyond the sharpness of the serifs – reversed the newspaper text style of the previous 130 years and thus struck a note of novelty. It had a marked degree of condensation, upon which Morison had insisted for space-saving reasons; with long paragraphs in wide measure (*The Times* then had a 14-pica column) this was a factor of some significance, though as columns narrowed and paragraphs shortened the significance disappeared, as will be seen in Chapter Eight.

With hindsight it is possible to perceive that what the *History of The Times* not unfairly called a 'complete typographic novelty in journalism' had certain inherent defects as a newspaper text. Its design required careful presswork, possible with the comparatively slow running of *The Times* in the 1930s, on the good quality mechanical printing then specially manufactured for Printing House Square. When greatly increased circulation compelled fast running on light-weight ordinary newsprint Times Roman lost not merely its elegance but its readability. There was no sign of this in the early days, however; and, when after a year's exclusive use, *The Times* agreed to the general release of the face, it entered on its still successful career as the outstanding twentieth-century general text type, particularly for book and magazine work (a danger signal, in fact, for its newspaper viability) and particularly in its Monotype version.

The Monotype aspect of the design of Times Roman was, indeed, of considerable importance. Morison himself, the Monotype Corporation's typographic adviser since 1923, was a long-standing enthusiast for the single-type machine, which was undeniably superior and more flexible for fine bookwork. Unfortunately, the curious existence of a Monotype installation at *The Times* nourished in him the illusion that the single-type machine was practical in daily newspaper terms. The Monotypes in Printing House Square dated from 1909, immediately after Northcliffe's takeover, replacing the Kastenbein type-assembling machines which had been in use since 1872. Why 'the Chief', who had pioneered the Linotype when he started his *Daily Mail* a dozen years before, should have authorised the installation of Monotypes rather than linecasters, is entirely obscure. In those early years of the century, as newspapers mechanised their setting they invariably abandoned single-type, whether handset or from a type-assembler, for the make-up and quick-change advantages of slug, as well as the flexibility and speed of the linecaster in handling short takes of 'rush' copy.*

* In 1908, for example, the Sunday *Reynolds News* went over, somewhat belatedly for a national paper, from handsetting to the Linotype. When I joined the paper in 1936 there was still a whole line of old Model 1 single-magazine machines in the composing room.

These considerations soon began to have their effect in Printing House Square. In 1914, as Chapter Five has recounted, the first linecasters went in to *The Times*. By 1932 there was a battery of thirty-six linecasters and news headlines, as we have seen, were also being keyboarded. Apart from such tabular work as was needed, plus specialised advertisement setting, the contribution of the Monotypes to the general composition of the paper must long have been minimal. Thus it was odd, to say the least, that Morison should put the cart before the horse (in an article in *The Times* house journal) by suggesting that the Monotypes played the central part in setting the paper, 'supplemented' by the linecasters. It is hard to resist calling this Mono-mania, especially when the maestro further asserted that *The Times* 'necessarily' used Monotypes (which was no more than a historical accident, due to Northcliffe's unexplained decision) and 'naturally' turned to the Monotype Corporation to cut the first punches for Times Roman.*

That Times Roman was designed primarily for the Monotype – its first, and best, state was Monotype series 327 – meant that the linecaster version had an inbuilt technical defect from the beginning. The face not only had a certain condensation, as already noted; it was exceptionally close-set. With the individual square matrices of the Monotype this did not matter, but it meant that the linecaster matrices had sidewalls so abnormally thin that they rapidly broke down, producing disfiguring hairlines between the letters. To avoid this, constant and expensive matrix replacement was necessary. Eventually this defect so irritated newspaper publishers who had put in Times Roman that a Linotype news-text of old face character but with stout sidewalls was designed, as described in Chapter Seven.

So far we have been discussing Times Roman in its basic form, the normal weight in roman and italic, for it was in this form that it transformed the text of *The Times*. It is not necessary here to examine the specialised variants which were later developed, like the Wide (Monotype 427) for bookwork or the Semi-Bold (Monotype 421). But the companion Bold (Monotype 334) and the new headline types were of major importance, yet never documented and discussed as was the pristine roman. The point is of interest, because the Bold's design was quite different from that of the roman; its top serifs were flat, not angled, and in general its character was modern rather than old face; further, the thickening inside the letter was carried to the point at which the apparent condensation was markedly greater than in the roman. Indeed, it may be felt that the Bold was something of an afterthought. At first it had two versions, No. 1 and No. 2, which had appreciable differences in alphabet length. The Bold was of so little consequence for the general text of *The Times* that No. 1 was initially only produced in single-letter matrices for the linecasters; it was some time later before No. 2 (the Monotype 334) was duplexed with the roman.

Whether Lardent drew the Bold, or the various headline faces, for Morison, or whether they were the product of other draughtsmen, it is not now possible to determine. Morison would have been horrified to find the display sizes of Times Bold upper- and lower-case used for headlines, as they have been in *The Times* since September 1970. He was a firm adherent of titling capitals for headlines (as he made plain to me in a letter as late as 30 April 1959). In any event, Times Bold's exceptional degree of condensation, already mentioned, was to make it far too narrow and wordy a letter for multi-column headings. Its lower-case was slightly more condensed than that of Century Bold, with which it could be compared for width and weight, whereas its capitals were slightly wider; a certain disproportion between capitals and lower-case was a feature of the design of Times Roman.

Morison himself was later to assert that the main feature of the 1932 transformation of *The Times* was not the New Roman text; 'the most important difference in design . . . lies in the headlines' which 'depart radically from precedent.' By this he meant that a consistent

* *Monotype Recorder*, September–October 1932 (incorrectly numbered XXI, No. 246: it is XXXI, No. 247), p. 12. Considerable credit was taken at the time because 1,075 punches were rejected in the course of cutting the initial 5,973; a later generation may well feel that, instead of being a sign of virtue, this was either perfectionism of a most expensive kind or remarkable carelessness. The note may be added here that, when *The Times* opened its new building at the end of 1937 it renewed its Monotype installation, putting in fourteen keyboards and twenty-eight casters. On any showing the number of casters seems excessive.

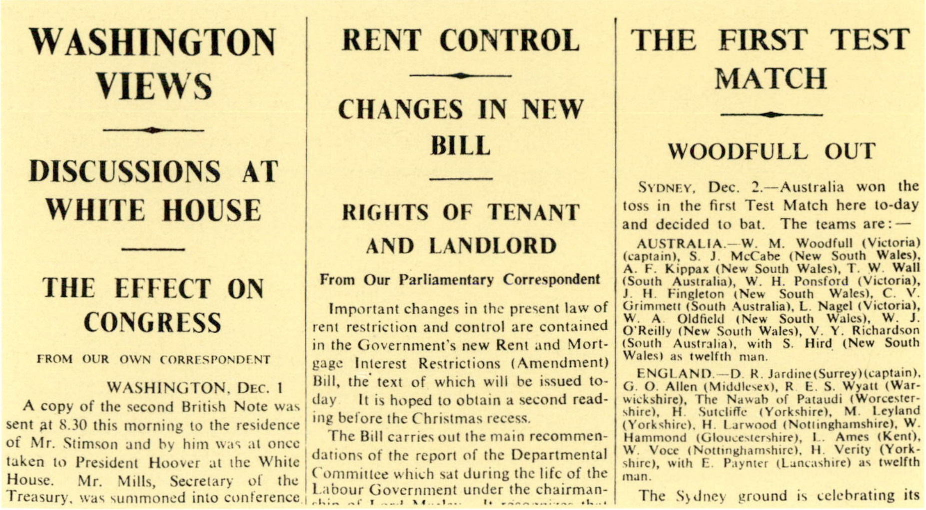

WASHINGTON VIEWS

DISCUSSIONS AT WHITE HOUSE

THE EFFECT ON CONGRESS

FROM OUR OWN CORRESPONDENT

WASHINGTON, DEC. 1

A copy of the second British Note was sent at 8.30 this morning to the residence of Mr. Stimson and by him was at once taken to President Hoover at the White House. Mr. Mills, Secretary of the Treasury, was summoned into conference

RENT CONTROL

CHANGES IN NEW BILL

RIGHTS OF TENANT AND LANDLORD

From Our Parliamentary Correspondent

Important changes in the present law of rent restriction and control are contained in the Government's new Rent and Mortgage Interest Restrictions (Amendment) Bill, the text of which will be issued to-day. It is hoped to obtain a second reading before the Christmas recess.

The Bill carries out the main recommendations of the report of the Departmental Committee which sat during the life of the Labour Government under the chairman-

THE FIRST TEST MATCH

WOODFULL OUT

SYDNEY, Dec. 2.—Australia won the toss in the first Test Match here to-day and decided to bat. The teams are:—

AUSTRALIA.—W. M. Woodfull (Victoria) (captain), S. J. McCabe (New South Wales), A. F. Kippax (New South Wales), T. W. Wall (South Australia), W. H. Ponsford (Victoria), J. H. Fingleton (New South Wales), C. V. Grimmett (South Australia), L. Nagel (Victoria), W. A. Oldfield (New South Wales), W. J. O'Reilly (New South Wales), V. Y. Richardson (South Australia), with S. Hird (New South Wales) as twelfth man.

ENGLAND.—D. R. Jardine (Surrey) (captain), G. O. Allen (Middlesex), R. E. S. Wyatt (Warwickshire), The Nawab of Pataudi (Worcestershire), H. Sutcliffe (Yorkshire), M. Leyland (Yorkshire), H. Larwood (Nottinghamshire), W. Hammond (Gloucestershire), L. Ames (Kent), W. Voce (Nottinghamshire), H. Verity (Yorkshire), with E. Paynter (Lancashire) as twelfth man.

The Sydney ground is celebrating its

The new headline style in *The Times* (December 1932).

grading and contrast of weight and style was offered by the three main ranges of headline Titlings: Times Heading (Titling 329 in the Monotype), Times Heading Bold Condensed (Bold Titling 328), Times Heading Bold (Extended Titling 339). The coarser, but not unattractive, Bold Titling (series 332) was not used till much later, while the Hever Titling 355 – a design of its own, named after the Chief Proprietor's country seat – was limited to the Court page and entertainment items. Morison described the headline Titlings as 'heavier versions of the capitals belonging to the text founts', though one commentator had perceptively categorised the Bold Titling 328 as 'a modern condensed letter, spruce rather than elegant'.[4]

While the Times Titlings of 1932 had some curious features – none of them were true full-face titlings, and series 329 was peculiarly aligned on its body, carrying a most marked beard at both head and foot – they made up extremely well. For the first time the paper had headings with strong colour, all robustly contrasting with the text. The Extended Titling in particular was an exceptionally fine letter, outstanding among bold roman capitals. From 1932–66 Morison's Titlings gave *The Times* the handsomest and most effective headlining in the traditional all-capitals decker style that had ever been seen. Shortly after the October Revolution the paper ran its first double-column heading (2 December 1932). Earlier that year Morison had uncompromisingly reaffirmed the 'right reason' of *The Times's* adherence to single-column make-up, since double-column treatment 'inevitably introduces the habit of artificial display'; but twenty years later he claimed that in devising the new Titling founts 'provision was made for the eventual appearance in *The Times* of headlines . . . designed to run across two columns'.[5] From 1939 and the opening of the Second World War double-column lead treatment became standard; not till July 1957 was this exceeded, when a treble-column lead story first opened the 'bill' page. For no fewer than thirty-four years, in fact, the headline typography of 1932 remained the basic style of *The Times*. Changes were marginal, for example in column-rule width or column measure, devised as wartime newsprint economy steps. The first full-page banner, in 36pt Bodoni Bold italic upper- and lower-case, appeared in July 1958 while types like Perpetua and Cochin were called on for certain feature headings; but news headlines were unchanged until May 1966.

The final feature of the 1932 revolution in *The Times*, and indeed the most instantly perceptible and challenging one, was the change of its front-page title from the long-standing blackletter to decent roman capitals. It was the one change that very nearly did not happen. Morison, as has been seen in Chapter Two, was highly critical of the original switch from roman capitals to blackletter for the title-line; his researches had conclusively shown that there was nothing 'traditional', as had been commonly supposed, about blackletter for

BRITISH NOTE TO AMERICA

DISASTROUS RECORD OF WAR-DEBT PAYMENTS

LAUSANNE SETTLEMENT IN DANGER

SUSPENSION NEEDED FOR WORLD REVIVAL

The following is a full Summary of the British Note of December 1, 1932, in regard to the British War Debt to the United States Government. The full text is published on page 7.

The British Note begins by saying that His Majesty's Government warmly welcome that part of the reply of the United States Government in which they express their willingness to facilitate discussions with a view to the adjustment of the British War Debt. Since the United States Government state that it does not appear to them that sufficient reasons have been given for their request for the suspension of the December instalment, the present Note sets out in greater detail the reasons of His Majesty's Government for the view that a resumption of War Debt payments would intensify the world depression.

1. Reparations and War Debts in Relation to the Economic Crisis

The causes of the depression may be manifold, but it has been generally recognized that War Debts and Reparations have been one of the major causes. While in some respects it may be difficult for Governments to remedy the troubles of the world, there are certain steps which it is clearly within their powers and their responsibility to take.

The vast requirements for War purposes far exceeded any normal means of payment and could only be financed by means of loans from the producing countries. The loans raised, whether they were market loans or Government loans, were taken, not in the form of money, but in the form of goods.

The United States made loans to the Allies (including the United Kingdom) totalling approximately £2,055,000,000; the United Kingdom made loans to its European Allies amounting to £1,600,000,000; the French Government had made similar loans equivalent (at par) to £460,000,000. In the aggregate these loans reached the colossal total of over £4,000,000,000. (Throughout this Summary dollars are translated into sterling at par.)

BURSTING OF THE STORM

If the course of commerce were deflected to the extent required to repay these War-time Debts, it would entail a radical alteration in the economy both of the debtor and of the creditor countries. For a time the payment of Reparations and War Debts was rendered possible by the flow of investment capital from the United States of America to Continental Europe. But the prosperity of the period from 1923 to 1929 was to a large extent illusory. Almost before the ink had dried on the agreements embodying the Young Plan for the final settlement of Reparations drawn up in the summer of 1929, the storm which had not then been visible had burst upon the world. Startled and alarmed, the lenders who had for five years so liberally poured their capital into Continental Europe withdrew such funds as were immediately recoverable. Towards the middle of 1931 something like a panic prevailed. Since then the world has been living under the stress of repeated shocks, which have completely undermined the confidence on which the system of private investment depended. Currencies are threatened with instability, if not with collapse, and the controls and restrictions intended to remedy the trouble have merely aggravated it. Everywhere taxation has been ruthlessly increased and expenditure drastically curtailed, and yet Budgets are in deficit or are balanced with ever increasing difficulty. The world cannot even begin to consider how to restore the monetary mechanism, without which the modern world cannot effectively conduct its daily life, until the causes which undermine confidence have been removed. One of the most important of these is the system of inter-Governmental debts.

EXPENDITURE ON DESTRUCTION

These inter-Governmental debts are radically different from the commercial loans raised by foreign Governments on the markets for productive purposes. Such market loans have converted whole territories from desolate swamps or uninhabited plains to flourishing provinces teeming with human life and producing great additions to the real wealth of the world. Such productive loans are self-liquidating. But Reparations and War Debts represent expenditure on destruction. Like the shells on which they were largely spent, these War loans were blown to pieces and have produced nothing to repay them. In the long run, international debts can only be paid in the form of goods or services.

The creditors, in so far as they have adopted a commercial policy which precludes payment in goods, have compelled their debtors to pay in gold. This has led to a drain on the gold reserves of many countries and has forced down the price of commodities in terms of gold currencies, causing widespread ruin to producers in debtor and creditor countries alike. This process has seriously increased the burden of commercial debts; but it has rendered intolerable the peculiar burden of unproductive War Debts.

Difficulties first became acute in Germany. The withdrawal of credits from Germany and the consequent movements of capital forced the United Kingdom to abandon the Gold Standard with world-wide results. Thus the baneful effects of these unnatural transfers in respect of Reparations and War Debts have gravely accentuated the difficulties of all five Continents. Confidence and credit cannot revive until an end has been put to these attempts to force the stream of capital to flow uphill.

2. The "Capacity to Pay" and the "Capacity to Receive"

The Secretary of the United States Treasury in his Annual Report for 1924-25 stated that a debtor Government must "be permitted to preserve and improve its economic position to bring its Budget into balance, and to place its finances and currency on a sound basis, and to maintain and, if possible, to improve the standard of living of its citizens." A resumption of War Debt payments in the present circumstances appears altogether inconsistent with the principles here laid down.

Experience has, in fact, shown that when dealing with international transfers of the character and of the unprecedented magnitude of Reparations and War Debts, the principle of "the capacity to pay" of the debtor—even if thus applied—can only be regarded as of secondary importance compared with an even wider principle, viz., that of the capacity of the world to endure the economic and financial consequences which those transfers would involve.

3. The Fiscal Sacrifice and the National Gain

Any remission of War Debts may be criticized as merely transferring the liability from the taxpayer in the borrowing country to the taxpayer in the lending country, and in this respect the taxpayers in the United Kingdom and in the United States of America are in much the same position. Before the Hoover Moratorium all the Reparation and War Debts receipts of the United Kingdom were required to cover the current payments due on its own War debt to the United States Government, and the United Kingdom taxpayer had each year to find from his own resources the amount of over £80,000,000 a year required for the interest on the internal loans out of which the advances (£1,600,000,000) were made by the United Kingdom to the Allies. In the case of the United States of America, the amount due from foreign Governments in respect of War Debts is now £55,000,000 a year, and if this is not received it would increase by that amount the burden on the American taxpayer, who also, of course, has to pay interest on the internal loans from which the advances by the United States Government to the European Allies were made. The interests of the two countries looked at from this standpoint are the same. But it would be taking altogether too narrow a view to regard those interests as being limited to securing payment of these War Debts from the borrowing Governments. Even a partial recovery of business activity in the creditor countries would result in additional receipts from taxation on the existing scale which would compensate the Exchequers of the creditor countries many times over for the loss of revenue involved in the revision of the War Debt settlements. It will not profit a creditor country to collect a few million pounds or dollars if it thereby perpetuates world disorder; and a War Debt settlement, however generous it may seem, would be repaid again and again by the contribution which it would make to world revival.

It is in the power of the Governments of the world, and particularly of the United States of America and of the United Kingdom as the two greatest creditor nations, if they unite in cooperation, to make the first and essential step towards averting disaster, financial, economic, and political.

4. The Past Record of the United Kingdom

Apart from these general considerations, H.M. Government hold the sincere conviction that this request for a re-examination of War Debts is fully justified on the grounds of the past record of the United Kingdom in the matter of inter-Governmental debts, and of their present position.

The total British War expenditure in the United States of America amounted to approximately £2,400,000,000. Of this total only about one-third was financed by borrowing from the United States Government. Approximately £600,000,000 was obtained by the sale of gold and of securities. In addition H.M. Government raised commercial loans on the United States market before the entry of the United States into the War to the amount of about £304,000,000.

Of these market borrowings £275,000,000 have been repaid, and in respect of indebtedness to the United States Government payments have been made both before and after the Funding Agreement amounting to £354,000,000, or £629,000,000 in all.

Meanwhile the advances made by this country amounted to £1,600,000,000 and had increased subsequently by the addition of unpaid interest to capital. Shortly after the War his Majesty's Government offered to join in any equitable arrangement for the reduction or cancellation of inter-Allied debts provided it was of an all-round character. That proposal was not accepted and his Majesty's Government were called upon to fund their debt to the United States of America.

RECEIPTS AND PAYMENTS

They then announced that they would limit their demands on their own debtors to the amount that they were themselves required to pay to their creditor. But in fact receipts of his Majesty's Government from their debtors have amounted to less than half their payments to their creditor. The relative position is that the United States of America made loans amounting to £2,055,000,000 and the United Kingdom made similar loans amounting to £1,600,000,000; the United States of America have received for the benefit of their taxpayers £434,000,000 and the United Kingdom have received for the benefit of their taxpayers nothing, have passed on all their receipts to the United States of America, and have paid out of the pockets of their taxpayers to the United States of America £134,000,000. In fact, when interest has been taken into account, some £200,000,000 has been found by the British taxpayer. While the British share of the total indebtedness to the United States of America is only 40 per cent., of the total debt payments made to the United States of America 80 per cent. has come from Great Britain. The efforts which this has involved to the British nation, coming as they did after the losses resulting from the War, constitute, in the view of his Majesty's Government, a strong claim to consideration on the part of the United States Government.

5. The Increase in the Burden

His Majesty's Government also call attention to the changes of circumstances which have increased the burden of their obligations.

In the first place the British debt is expressed in terms of gold, but the burden on the British people is measured in terms of sterling. The payment due on December 15 is owing to this circumstance increased from £19,750,000 to approximately £30,000,000.

In the second place the average wholesale price index in the United States of America during the period when the debt was incurred was 189, and is now under 94 (taking 1913 as a basis in each case). The debt therefore represents to-day in terms of goods not less than twice the amount which was borrowed.

In the third place the effect of the American Tariff has been to restrict the import of the manufactured goods which the United Kingdom produces. In 1923 when the British War Debt was funded, the War Debt annuity amounted to £33,000,000, or approximately half the value of the British domestic exports to the United States (£60,000,000). From 1933 onwards the annuity in respect of the War Debt would amount at present rates of exchange to approximately £60,000,000; whereas the British domestic exports to the United States of America this year are not likely to exceed £16,000,000.

The imports into the United Kingdom from the United States show an equally remarkable fall from £211,000,000 in 1923 to £59,000,000 in the first nine months of 1932. The total trade between the two countries from the time of the Funding Agreement has fallen from about £300,000,000 a year to £100,000,000.

6. Economic Reactions of Resuming War Debt Payments

The United Kingdom has up to the present generally been the best customer of the United States, but, if War Debt payments had to be resumed, the very heavy adverse balance of visible trade between the United Kingdom and the United States of America (£78,000,000 in 1931) would have to be reduced by adopting measures which would further restrict British purchases of American goods. To the extent, therefore, that payments were resumed to the United States Treasury a definite loss must follow to the United States producer.

Moreover, his Majesty's Government would also have to guard against the effects which would follow if the unique facilities offered by the British market to the world's goods were used by the other debtors of America to obtain sterling which they would then sell across the exchange in order to meet their obligations to the United States Government.

7. The Lausanne Settlement

His Majesty's Government take it for granted that preferential treatment would never be claimed for the War Debts due to the United States of America as compared with those due to this country; and a situation in which this country was required to continue War Debt payments while forgoing the War Debt payments due to it would be admitted at once to be unthinkable. Thus, if the payment of the sums due in respect of the British War debt to the United States Government were to be resumed his Majesty's Government would be obliged to reopen the question of payments from their own debtors—France, Italy, Portugal, Yugoslavia, Rumania, and Greece, and also the British Dominions, which have been suspended since the Lausanne Conference. The debtor countries would, in turn, have to demand the payment by Germany of her obligations under the Young Plan, and the United Kingdom would have to do likewise. Without a readjustment of War Debt obligations the Lausanne Agreement could not be ratified; the question of Reparations would remain unsettled; the improvement in confidence which followed the Lausanne Agreements would be undone; and fatal results might well be found to have accrued to the solution of many grave political, as well as financial, problems now under discussion.

8. The Payment due on December 15 in Relation to the Subsequent Discussions

His Majesty's Government emphasize their conviction that their proposal for a suspension of the December payment, a proposal which would in no way affect any ultimate settlement, is necessary in order to create the condition favourable to a successful issue of the subsequent conversations in regard to the revision of the existing Debt obligations. The difficulties of making the transfer in present circumstances are so great and would involve such far-reaching reactions, both financial and political, that the resulting doubts and anxieties in regard to the immediate situation would distract the attention of the Governments and peoples when the chief need was an objective and systematic approach to the problem to be solved.

9. The Transfer Difficulties

The reserves of his Majesty's Government in gold and in foreign exchange, though adequate for the purpose of mitigating exchange fluctuations for which they were designed, were not intended and would not suffice to cover, as well, the payment of $95,500,000 due on December 15. The exchange difficulty would remain even if the device were adopted of payment in sterling to a blocked account; for the existence of a large sum awaiting transfer would affect the market almost as seriously as an actual purchase of exchange.

The only remaining alternative would be payment in gold. Such a method of payment would involve the sacrifice of a considerable part of the gold reserves of the Bank of England, which are widely regarded as no more than sufficient for the responsibilities of London as a financial centre.

10. Conclusion

In conclusion his Majesty's Government state that they trust that the full statement of their views which they have now made will demonstrate clearly the ground upon which their request was based—namely, their own profound conviction that a resumption of War Debt payments as they existed before the Hoover Moratorium would inevitably deepen the depression in world trade and would lead to further falls in commodity prices with disastrous consequences from which no nation would be exempt.

They believe that a discussion between the United States Government and themselves upon these matters might bear fruitful issue for the revival of world prosperity. They are convinced that the prospects of success would be materially improved by the postponement of the December instalment, and they are prepared to consider with the Government of the United States of America any manner in which that postponement might be most conveniently arranged.

WASHINGTON VIEWS

DISCUSSIONS AT WHITE HOUSE

THE EFFECT ON CONGRESS

FROM OUR OWN CORRESPONDENT

WASHINGTON, DEC. 1

A copy of the second British Note was sent at 8.30 this morning to the residence of Mr. Stimson and by him was at once taken to President Hoover at the White House. Mr. Mills, Secretary of the Treasury, was summoned into conference there and the Note was discussed at length. Later in the morning Mr. Stimson went to the State Department, where he was joined by the British Ambassador. It was then announced that the text of the Note would be given to the Press soon after the Stock Exchange was closed for the day.

There is no reason to doubt that Mr. Stimson was able to convey to Sir Ronald Lindsay the conclusions which Mr. Hoover had reached and to indicate in general the nature of the President's recommendations to Congress next week, as these may have been affected by the arguments of the British Government. It is common knowledge that, independently of their presentation by London, these arguments are in a large sense found convincing not only by Mr. Hoover, but by all those whose executive position here gives them a knowledge of and a concern in the world situation. What effect the British Note, the recommendations Mr. Hoover will make, and the growing mass of opinion favourable to friendly adjustment will have upon Congress is still doubtful almost to the point of despair.

AGRICULTURISTS' VIEWS

It is true that some hold to the belief that a deeper impression was made upon those members of the Senate Finance and House Ways and Means committees who were called in by the President some time ago than could discreetly appear in the statement of views issued by Mr. Hoover soon after they had left him. If this is so these gentlemen have signally failed to make this evident. It is true also that the agricultural interests, for the relief of whose depression the President-Elect is now trying to devise means, are occasionally vocal on the debt question. The Houston Cotton Exchange, for instance, has passed a resolution calling upon the Government to "confer at once with foreign Governments with the view of finding a rearrangement of debts that can in fact be carried out without destruction of foreign buying power, on which our farmers' survival depends." If the example of the Houston exchange were more generally followed Congress would be a thousand times more likely to give heed than it will be when it reads Mr. Hoover.

Perhaps the willingness of members of the Senate and the House to discuss privately the possibilities of separate treatment of the British debt is a sign of a change of heart, for this willingness is perceptibly growing. Their reasons, however, are as dangerous as their conversion is partial. They appear, in fact, to be moved less by anxiety about the economic effect of British difficulties than by their determination that France shall not escape one cent of the payment either of the December annuity or of later instalments and by the hope that an Anglo-American compromise at this time would have the double effect of tending to isolate France and of persuading Japan to modify its Manchurian policy.

"POLICY OF DISUNION"

They might with advantage read Mr. Walter Lippmann's contribution to the *New York Herald Tribune* this morning, for, as he says, they are crying out "for a policy to divide, to disunite, or to disorganize the common action of the most advanced nations." How, he asks, "do they expect peace to return to this troubled earth if the British, French and American democracies get into a brawl over the immediate payment of a few dollars?" And, "What is the good of talking about disarmament and world economic conferences, and the maintenance of treaties in Asia, if at the very heart of Western civilization the democracies have not the sympathy, intelligence, and self-restraint to sit down like gentlemen and discuss a debt?" It is, he says, a "spectacle for the ironic gods."

The few Americans who have had the opportunity of reading the British Note and with whom there has been an opportunity of speech before this dispatch was written have been unhesitating in the expression of their admiration for its cogency and good temper. This notwithstanding, they find explosive possibilities in the statement that the "initiative in devising a settlement of reparations was taken by the creditor Governments at Lausanne with the cognizance and approval of the United States Government." They may be right, but events are moving with such rapidity that even the Democrats, who desire to charge Mr. Hoover with the making of a "deal" to the disadvantage of the American people, may not get an attentive hearing.

A message from our Paris Correspondent referring to the French reply to the United States, which was despatched last night, appears on the preceding page.

M. DOUMERGUE IN LONDON

M. Doumergue, former President of the French Republic, and Mme. Doumergue arrived at Victoria Station at 3.40 yesterday on a visit to London. They were received by the French Ambassador, Lord Derby, President of the United Associations of Great Britain and France, M. Bernheim, President of the French Colony in London, and other distinguished French residents.

M. Doumergue's speech last night at a dinner given by the United Associations of Great Britain and France is reported on page 16.

DEATH OF DAME ELIZABETH WORDSWORTH

We regret to announce that DAME ELIZABETH WORDSWORTH, D.C.L., the first Principal of Lady Margaret Hall, Oxford, died at her home in Oxford on Wednesday night at the age of 92.

A memoir will be found on page 20.

RENT CONTROL

CHANGES IN NEW BILL

RIGHTS OF TENANT AND LANDLORD

From Our Parliamentary Correspondent

Important changes in the present law of rent restriction and control are contained in the Government's new Rent and Mortgage Interest Restrictions (Amendment) Bill, the text of which will be issued to-day. It is hoped to obtain a second reading before the Christmas recess.

The Bill carries out the main recommendations of the report of the Departmental Committee which sat during the life of the Labour Government under the chairmanship of Lord Marley. It recognizes that private enterprise has now caught up with the demand for the best type of houses which were controlled under the original legislation. It is rapidly catching up with the second type of house, for the better-class artisan, but it has not yet solved the problem of providing cheap houses for the lowest-paid sections of the community. Where houses of this type are decontrolled the rent may jump up to 80 per cent. above the pre-War figure, and the Government recognize that for these houses full control must continue.

PLAN FOR FIVE YEARS

The Bill accordingly proposes that there shall be immediate decontrol of houses with a rateable value which in 1931 was more than £45 in the Metropolitan Police District, £35 in the rest of England and Wales, and £45 in Scotland. A period of six months will elapse before mortgages on these houses are decontrolled. Houses with a rateable value between £20 and £45 in the Metropolitan Police District, £13 and £35 in the rest of England and Wales and £26 5s. and £45 in Scotland will still be subject to decontrol when they become vacant. Houses with a rateable value below these figures will cease to be decontrolled when they become vacant, but houses which are already decontrolled will remain decontrolled. A register will be kept by local authorities of houses falling within these limits which are already decontrolled, and if a landlord does not register a house within a specified time it will be treated as controlled. The Bill will remain operative for five years, and if it is not renewed rent restriction will then come to an end.

It is hoped to deal with excessive charges by protected tenants to sub-tenants by a clause in the new Bill which sets out that the tenant must inform his landlord of any sub-letting, with particulars of accommodation and the rent charged. If the landlord considers the rent excessive he can apply to the local County Court for the ejection of the tenant, and if the Court grants the Order, from which there is no appeal except on a point of law, it will fix the proper rent payable by the sub-tenant, who will then become the direct tenant of the landlord. In such circumstances the house does not become decontrolled on the change of tenants. Where a Court has at any time fixed the rent, a protected tenant who attempts to charge his sub-tenant more will be liable to a fine of £100.

RECOVERING POSSESSION

Amendments will be made in the law as to recovery of possession. At present a landlord who has owned a house since 1924, and who requires possession for his own occupation or that of members of his own family, may apply for it on the ground of "greater hardship" without proof of alternative accommodation. This right will now be extended to any landlord who bought his house at any time before July 11, 1931, when the Marley Committee reported, and the onus of proving hardship will be transferred from the landlord to the tenant. In any case where a landlord desires possession he can obtain it on proving to the County Court that suitable accommodation is available for the tenant, whatever may be the reason of the landlord for requiring possession. Alternative accommodation includes a council house or a privately-owned house (either controlled or with like security of tenure) which is similar as regards extent and rental to a council house or is otherwise reasonably suitable to the needs and means of the tenant. It is now provided for the first time that a landlord can obtain possession if the tenant has been guilty of overcrowding.

MISCHIEF MAKERS IN COTTON DISPUTE

MONEY FROM "DOUBTFUL QUARTERS"

The Blackburn Weavers' Association report that over £64,000 was paid in members' benefit in the last quarter in connexion with the recent cotton trade dispute.

The committee state that "there are persons bent on creating disunity in our ranks and furthering the cause of an avowed insurrectionary movement financed from doubtful quarters."

"Happily," it is added, "these mischievous individuals are persons without influence among cotton operatives. The high character and intelligence of our members enables them effectively to resist the malicious propaganda of the people referred to."

INVALIDS

Sir Austen Chamberlain was reported last night to be much better.

The condition of Mr. J. C. Stobart, of the B.B.C., who is ill at his London home with diabetes, was stated yesterday to be about the same.

The Hon. Mrs. French, wife of Major the Hon. Edward Gerald French, who was knocked down by a car in Cromwell Road, Kensington, a few days ago, was stated yesterday to be progressing as well as could be expected in view of her serious injuries.

COMPANY MEETINGS

Reports of the following meetings appear in our City pages:—

London and Rhodesian Mining and Land.
Madeley Collieries.
New Zealand Loan and Mercantile Agency.
North Ashanti Mining Company.
Peruvian Corporation.
Rover Company.
Tobacco Securities Trust.

THE FIRST TEST MATCH

WOODFULL OUT

SYDNEY, Dec. 2.—Australia won the toss in the first Test Match here to-day and decided to bat. The teams are:—

AUSTRALIA.—W. M. Woodfull (Victoria) (captain), S. J. McCabe (New South Wales), A. F. Kippax (New South Wales), T. W. Wall (South Australia), W. H. Ponsford (Victoria), J. H. Fingleton (New South Wales), C. V. Grimmett (South Australia), L. Nagel (Victoria), W. A. Oldfield (New South Wales), W. J. O'Reilly (New South Wales), V. Y. Richardson (South Australia), with S. Hird (New South Wales) as twelfth man.

ENGLAND.—D. R. Jardine (Surrey) (captain), G. O. Allen (Middlesex), R. E. S. Wyatt (Warwickshire), The Nawab of Pataudi (Worcestershire), H. Sutcliffe (Yorkshire), M. Leyland (Yorkshire), H. Larwood (Nottinghamshire), W. Hammond (Gloucestershire), L. Ames (Kent), W. Voce (Nottinghamshire), H. Verity (Yorkshire), with E. Paynter (Lancashire) as twelfth man.

The Sydney ground is celebrating its jubilee this year, the first Test having been played at Sydney in 1882. A quarter of an hour before the start there were probably 30,000 people present. The weather was fine and invigorating. Thousands of fashionably-dressed women thronged into the Ladies' Enclosure and gave the ground an Ascot-like appearance.

Woodfull and Ponsford came out to bat first. Larwood opened the bowling to Woodfull, who made the first run off Larwood's second ball. Ponsford then made another single.

Voce took the other end, opposite the pavilion, and bowled a maiden over to Ponsford. Then Larwood followed with a maiden over. One of his balls struck Ponsford on the hip, and the crowd showed its displeasure.

Although neither team had then been chosen, it was announced yesterday that the doctors had declared D. Bradman to be unfit to play. It was stated late last night that he had been ordered a fortnight's rest. The doctors had said that he was thoroughly run down.

SLOW SCORING

Both batsmen were playing carefully, for Larwood and Voce were bowling well.

In bowling the fourth ball of his fourth over Voce slipped on the hard wicket and fell heavily to the ground on his back. He got up rubbing the knee that he injured on board the Orontes, but continued to bowl, apparently not affected by his spill.

Jardine made his first change when 10 had been scored, Allen coming on for Larwood, who had bowled four overs for four runs. Play continued to be very slow, and the first half-hour yielded only a dozen runs.

The third ball of Voce's fifth over clean bowled Ponsford—but it was a no-ball.

Then, after batting 38 minutes for seven runs, Woodfull fell into Voce's leg trap. He swung at a high ball, but only snicked it and it sailed over his shoulder to Ames, who held a fine catch.

Fingleton, who came in next, had scored two runs when he cut a ball from Voce and ran. Ponsford, however, sent him back. Allen quickly threw the ball in and Ames broke the wicket. There was a confident appeal, but it was not successful. Fingleton only just saved his wicket.

Voce had been bowling splendidly, but at 28 he was given a rest in favour of Hammond. Voce had one wicket for 12 runs in seven overs.

Jardine only gave his fast bowlers a few overs at a time, and when the score reached 30 he brought Larwood back and gave Allen a rest. Allen had bowled four overs for eight runs.

The first boundary came at 42, a leg-bye off Hammond. Twenty-one more runs were added before the luncheon interval.

Lunch score:—

AUSTRALIA—First Innings

Woodfull, c. Ames, b. Voce ..	7
Ponsford, not out	32
Fingleton, not out	13
Extras	11
Total (1 wkt.)	63

—*Reuter.*

COLONEL OF SCOTS GUARDS

THE DUKE OF YORK'S APPOINTMENT

The King has been pleased to approve the appointment of Major-General His Royal Highness The Duke of York, Earl of Inverness, K.G., K.T., G.C.M.G., G.C.V.O., Colonel-in-Chief 11th Hussars (Prince Albert's Own), The Somerset Light Infantry (Prince Albert's), The East Yorkshire Regiment, Royal Army Ordnance Corps, and The Leicestershire Yeomanry (Prince Albert's Own), Personal Aide-de-Camp to The King, to be Colonel, Scots Guards, in succession to the late Field-Marshal Lord Methuen.

BELGIAN NEUTRALITY

FROM OUR OWN CORRESPONDENT

BERLIN, DEC. 1

I learn that the London message recently published in the German Press, in which a vital passage in Major-General Sir George Aston's recent letter to *The Times* was mistranslated in such a way as to suggest that the British General Staff before the War had advocated a British violation of the neutrality of Belgium, whereas the original memorandum quoted in that letter strongly opposed either a British or a French invasion of Belgium, did not emanate from the London office of the semi-official Wolff Agency.

As no indication was given of the source of this message in the German newspapers which published it beyond a date-line, "London," its origin must remain a mystery; but its statement that Great Britain contemplated an invasion of Belgium remains in the minds of German newspaper readers.

THE GIMCRACK DINNER

Speaking at the annual Gimcrack Club dinner at York last night Sir Alfred Butt, who won the Gimcrack Stakes in August with Young Lover, said that the totalisator had so far failed in any way to help racing. The latest stage of the development of the totalisator was what is known as Tote Clubs, which, Sir Alfred said, are most harmful and injurious to the community. Sir Alfred also made several suggestions to the Jockey Club for the benefit of racing generally.

A report of Sir Alfred Butt's speech will be found on page 4.

TRANSPORT BILL

SLOW PROGRESS IN THE COMMONS

LORDS AND SPEED LIMIT

WESTMINSTER, THURSDAY

The House of Commons made very slow progress with the London Passenger Transport Bill to-day, the efforts of Ministers to placate opposition offering merely new occasions for obstruction.

The first Government amendment enlisted the Labour Party among the critics, for it proposed to take from the Minister of Transport the power to appoint members of the Control Board of the amalgamated London transport and vest it in appointment trustees. MR. PYBUS claimed that the change would free the machinery set up by the Bill from political interference, but MR. ATTLEE bitterly attacked him for removing the last vestige of public control of a monopoly. The *personnel* of the trustees then gave endless opportunities for amendments to secure representatives of special interests, and it seemed as though the Government will have to take expeditory measures if the Bill is to go through.

In the Lords, LORD BUCKMASTER returned to the attack upon "speed fiends" with a motion, which was agreed to, that all vehicles subject to a speed limit should be fitted with accurate speedometers. He was particularly severe upon omnibuses and lorries which drove too fast and upon employers who forced their drivers to break the law under pain of dismissal. He suggested the installation of instruments recording the speed at which vehicles travelled throughout a run, and that no licences should be issued unless they had at least a speedometer.

CARDINAL BOURNE ILL

ATTACK OF INFLUENZA IN ROME

FROM OUR OWN CORRESPONDENT

ROME, DEC. 1

Cardinal Bourne is lying seriously ill here with a bronchial cold and gastric influenza.

His Eminence arrived in Rome at 2.30 on Monday, and was then feeling so poorly that instead of staying as usual with the Redemptionist Fathers in the Via Merulana he went to the hospital of the English Sisters at Santo Stefano Rotondo, and took to his bed. At first his Eminence seemed to be holding his own, but yesterday Dr. Sabatucci became uneasy at his temperature remaining so persistently at 101 and at the quickness of his pulse. Dr. Bastianelli was therefore also called in, and the latest bulletin declares that, although the Cardinal's condition is serious, as yet there is no trace of pneumonia. I understand that his Eminence is in excellent spirits.

BOOKS OF THE WEEK

The first of a series of articles on Christmas Books, summarizing the successes of the season; and reviews of "War Debts and World Prosperity," by H. G. Moulton and L. Pasvolsky; "Philip II. of Spain," by David Loth; "Days of Endeavour," by Captain J. W. Harris; "Reminiscences of a Specialist," by Dr. Greville MacDonald; "The Story of the Borgias," by L. Collison-Morley; "The History of Piracy," by Philip Gosse; and of four recent volumes on fishing; together with other notices of new books, will be found on pages 8, 9, and 10.

ENTERTAINMENTS INDEX

(For details see page 12)

OPERA

Old Vic	THE MAGIC FLUTE	8
Savoy	THE MIKADO	8.15

THEATRES.

Adelphi	WORDS AND MUSIC	8.30
Aldwych	FIFTY-FIFTY	2.30 & 8.15
Alhambra	A KISS IN SPRING	2.30 & 8.15
Apollo	SPRINGTIME FOR HENRY	8.40
Coliseum	CASANOVA	2.30 & 8.15
Comedy	MIRACLE AT VERDUN	8.30
Court	THE SCHOOL FOR HUSBANDS	8.15
Criterion	MUSICAL CHAIRS	8.40
Drury Lane	WILD VIOLETS	8.15
Duchess	CHILDREN IN UNIFORM	8.30
Embassy	THE CATHEDRAL	8.15
Gaiety	POTASH AND PERLMUTTER	8.30
Garrick	WHILE PARENTS SLEEP!	8.40
Globe	FOR SERVICES RENDERED	8.40
Haymarket	ONCE A HUSBAND	8.30
Hippodrome	THE MERRY WIDOW	8.15
His Majesty's	THE DUBARRY	8.15
Little	GETTING MARRIED	8.15
Lyric	ANOTHER LANGUAGE	8.40
Phoenix	NEVER COME BACK	8.30
Playhouse	FIREBIRD	8.40
Prince of Wales	LA REVUE DE PARIS	2 to 11.30
Queen's	EVENSONG	8.30
Sadler's Wells	MACBETH	8
St. James's	BEHOLD, WE LIVE	8.30
St. Martin's	STRANGE ORCHESTRA	2.30 & 8.30
Savile	TELL HER THE TRUTH	8.30
Shaftesbury	ORDERS ARE ORDERS	8.30
Strand	NIGHT OF THE GARTER	8.30
Whitehall	ROAD HOUSE	8.30
Wyndham's	SERVICE	2.30 & 8.30

VARIETIES

Holborn Empire		6.30 & 9
Leicester Square Theatre		2 to 12
London Pavilion		2 to 12
Maskelyne's		3 to 10.30
Palladium		6.30 & 9
Piccadilly		2 to 11.45
Vaudeville		2 to 12
Victoria Palace		2 to 11.30
Windmill	REVUDEVILLE No. 17	1.30 to 11.30

CONCERTS

Aeolian Hall	MISS JESSIE KING	8.30
Grotrian Hall	MISS HELEN McGRAW	8.30
Royal College of Music	ORCHESTRAL CONCERT	8.15
Wigmore Hall	MISSES FLORENCE HOOTON AND DOROTHY MANLEY	8.30

EXHIBITIONS, &c.

Crystal Palace	10 to 10
Madame Tussaud's	10 to 10
Whipsnade Park Zoo	10 to sunset
Zoological Gardens	9 to sunset

PICTURE THEATRES

Academy	BARBARINA	1 to 11
Astoria	THE FLAG LIEUTENANT	12.30 to 11
Capitol	HAPPY EVER AFTER	12 to 11
Carlton	LOVE ME TO-NIGHT	11.45 to 11
Dominion	AMERICAN MADNESS	12 to 11
Empire	RED DUST	10 to 12
Kensington	THE BROKEN WING	2 to 11
Marble Arch Pavilion	RASPUTIN	2 to 11
New Gallery	AFTER THE BALL	12.15 to 11
New Victoria	TELL ME TO-NIGHT	12 to 11
Palace Theatre	GRAND HOTEL	2.30 & 8.30
Plaza	TIGER SHARK	10.15 to 11
Polytechnic	CONGORILLA	2.30, 5.30, 8.30
Regal	SLEEPLESS NIGHTS	12.40 to 11
Rialto	THE BLUE LIGHT	12 to 12
Stoll Picture Theatre	SCARFACE	12 to 11
Tivoli	ROME EXPRESS	12 to 11

◀ *The Times* transformed with Morison's new titlings, and with its first double-column heading (December 1932).

newspaper titles, which had only begun as a late eighteenth-century 'Gothick' fad. In a *Supplement* of 1931 to his general *Memorandum* of the previous year, he argued cogently for the abandonment of the blackletter title. This set the cat among the Printing House Square pigeons with a vengeance. A battle royal ensued between the conservatives and the Morison-led 'romanists'. Many designs were bandied to and fro. In the end Morison narrowly won, and it was decided to revive the original roman title of 1788.[6]

▶ The changed titles of *The Times*: the original blackletter, the first 'romanist' achievement (1932) and the Reynolds Stone design (1953), which lasted until the front-page news revolution of May 1966.

While Morison's victory was ultimately to revolutionise British newspaper title styles at all levels its immediate effect was nil. For years the London dailies retained their blackletter; indeed, so much did the trade still regard blackletter as an essential symbol that when Odhams took over the *Daily Herald* the title was immediately changed to a conventional white-lined blackletter. Since its revival as a daily in 1919, the *Herald* had followed the old roman title tradition of radical and left-wing newspapers; the version when the paper moved to Long Acre was a handsome piece of hand-lettering in inscriptional style.*

In 1932 Morison concluded *The English Newspaper* with the sentence: 'The community would unquestionably benefit if men of learning would extend their interest to the end that the tranquillity, exactitude, clarity and ease of reading, which have been secured in the English book, may also be obtained in that other category of printing, the fundamental economic character of which is more fully developed, and which is in consequence more widely distributed – the English Newspaper.' The paragraph which wound up with that sentence, however, had opened with a more prophetic observation. 'It seems likely', said Morison, 'that a period of active headline experiment will follow the realisation by newspapers that the radio has undermined their old position as the sole exploiters of news.' The extent to which that realisation was profound, or widespread, was of no great moment; newspapers were appreciating that their old monopoly position had gone and one of the ways forward – which was to bring the largest increases in both circulation and advertising revenue hitherto known – was 'active headline experiment'.

The *Daily Express* was the trail-blazer. In 1933 Lord Beaverbrook took a step far more important, not only to his morning newspaper but to the Press in general, than the *Express* changeover to Ionic text that year. He appointed one of his young Manchester executives, twenty-nine-year old Arthur Christiansen, as the paper's new editor. Unusually for his generation Christiansen was passionately type-conscious. Five years before he had advised a colleague: 'Study type. There are too few newspaper journalists who know type.' He had taken his own advice and attended technical courses in general typography. Now he had the chance to give a new graphic form to the editorial policy which a critic (Lord Francis-Williams) described as 'sophisticated escapism and the bright romantic treatment of news' and which was to achieve by far the largest circulation, eventually over four-million, that any broadsheet morning newspaper had ever known.

Christiansen took the Ludlow Century range already installed at the *Express* and handled it in a new way. He played particularly on the

* Morison designed two remarkable title-pieces, of Gill provenance, one in Sans Bold Titling for the *Daily Worker* (Barker, pp. 303–4), and one in Perpetua Bold Titling for *Reynolds News*.

Daily Express

WORLD'S LARGEST DAILY SALE

No. 11,976 | Friday, October 7, 1938 | One Penny

PREMIER HAS GREAT VICTORY FOR HIS PEACE POLICY—366 VOTES FOR, 144 AGAINST

MODEL GLIDER | SPECIAL 1 a.m. EDITION | Daily Express

The Daily Express declares that Britain will not be involved in a European war this year, or next year either

Mussolini draws up frontier | PEACE! | Commission to decide plebiscites

AGREEMENT SIGNED AT 12.30 a.m. TODAY

German troops march in tomorrow: Then occupation gradually until October 10

WHY THE DAILY EXPRESS HAS TOPPED 2,500,000

2,520,205 COPIES OF THE DAILY EXPRESS WERE SOLD EVERY DAY DURING SEPTEMBER.

This is the first occasion on which the sales of the Daily Express have passed the two-and-a-half million figure, and constitutes a remarkable new world record daily sale.

During the international crisis there was an immense and increasing demand for the Daily Express. Two things account for it:—

1. The policy of restrained optimism which the Daily Express maintained throughout, and which now has been abundantly justified.
2. The excellence of the Daily Express foreign news service. The Daily Express during the crisis kept more correspondents in foreign countries than any other newspaper. These men, from beginning to end, gave more comprehensive and balanced accounts of the advance of events than any others which appeared in the British Press.

The following is the auditors' certificate for the month of September:—

October 6, 1938.

We have examined the books and accounts of the London Express Newspaper, Ltd., and certify that the average net daily sale of the Daily Express at the recognised trade terms or published prices (as defined by and arrived at in accordance with the instructions of the Audit Bureau of Circulations, Ltd.) during the month of September 1938 was 2,520,205 copies.

DELOITTE, PLENDER, GRIFFITHS & CO., Chartered Accountants.

URGENT STEPS TO CLOSE GAPS IN DEFENCE

Inquiry while M.P.s holiday

By GUY EDEN

Daily Express Political Correspondent

ALL THE DEFENCE SERVICES—NAVAL, MILITARY, AIR, AND CIVIL—HAVE BEEN ORDERED TO PRESENT REPORTS TO THE CABINET ON WEAKNESSES REVEALED BY THE RECENT CRISIS.

These will be considered by a special committee of Ministers, and by the Committee of Imperial Defence, on which sit all the technical heads of the Services.

The consideration is regarded as a matter of urgency, and it is expected that definite decisions on the scope of further re-armament, and any new steps necessary, will be made by the time a new session of Parliament opens in November.

Announcement of the inquiry was made in the House of Commons yesterday by Mr. Chamberlain before M.P.s resumed their broken holiday until November 1.

Intensive inquiries will be made all over the country about the local working of A.R.P. plans, particularly in relation to the storage and distribution of gas masks.

A complete reorganisation of the methods of storing gas masks is likely to be decided on, to ensure that all the population receive their masks within twenty-four hours of an emergency being declared.

Masks will continue to be manufactured at the rate of 500,000 a week, for replacement purposes.

MASKS DECISION

A decision will be made soon about the masks already distributed to the public. The question whether it is worth collecting them for storage in Government warehouses is being considered.

Another question to be examined, with a view to a statement being made next month, is "national service."

Nothing more than the necessary preparations, such as registering the technical and other abilities of the population, is likely to be attempted. Nothing in the nature of compulsory military service will be proposed.

Premier says: No election, no conscription

Mr. Chamberlain's policy for peace was approved in the House of Commons yesterday by the large majority of 366 votes to 144. Here are points from his speech at the end of the four-day debate following the Munich Agreement:—

"I DO not want a general election now.

"One reason is that I do not want to capitalise the feeling of relief which is so conspicuous for the sake of obtaining some temporary party advantage."

★

"I HAVE previously stated that conscription or compulsory national service will not be introduced by this Government in peace time. That statement still holds."

★

"ANY one who has been through what I had to go through day after day face to face with the thought that in the last resort it would be I, and I alone, who would have to say that yes or no which would decide the fate of millions of my countrymen, of their wives, of their families—a man who has been through that cannot very readily forget it."

William Barkley's report begins on Page Eleven.

ASCOT BANNED WIFE

Divorce case in the list

Daily Express Staff Reporter

THE divorce list for the forthcoming law term, issued last night, contains the undefended petition of Mrs. Katherine Mary Follett against her husband, Mr. John R. Follett, racehorse owner.

Mrs. Follett's name was not disclosed when it was announced last June that a woman, regularly admitted to the Royal Enclosure at Ascot for the previous fifteen years, had been barred this year because she had filed a divorce petition.

Legal storms followed this announcement. It was contended that his Majesty's Comptroller for Ascot appeared to have obtained information from the Divorce Registry in Somerset House before the petition was made available to the public in the printed list issued last night.

NO DISCLOSURE

It was alleged that the premature disclosure to Court officials of information unavailable to the public raised important issues of the rights or individuals as against the Crown.

Inquiries have now revealed that no such disclosure took place.

Mrs. Follett, in accordance with the usual practice, will be readmitted to the Royal Enclosure after her divorce petition has been heard. Parties to divorce suits, whether innocent or guilty, are barred from the Royal Enclosure pending hearing of the petition.

Mrs. Follett was the widow of Sir Frederick Carmichael-Anstruther when she married Mr. Follett eight years ago.

Mr. Follett, son of Lady Mildred Fitzgerald, owns the racehorse Jovial Lad.

MRS. FOLLETT

Plebiscite surprise: Legion may not go

From SEFTON DELMER,

Daily Express Staff Reporter,

PRAGUE, Thursday.

THEY don't think in Prague tonight that there is much likelihood of seeing the British Legion boys in blue in Czecho-Slovakia.

The decisions of the International Commission in Berlin on what is to constitute Zone 5, to be ceded to Germany this week-end, seem to make a plebiscite superfluous.

The areas which at Munich had been contemplated as potential plebiscite territories have been assigned to the Germans without a plebiscite. With them, so it is

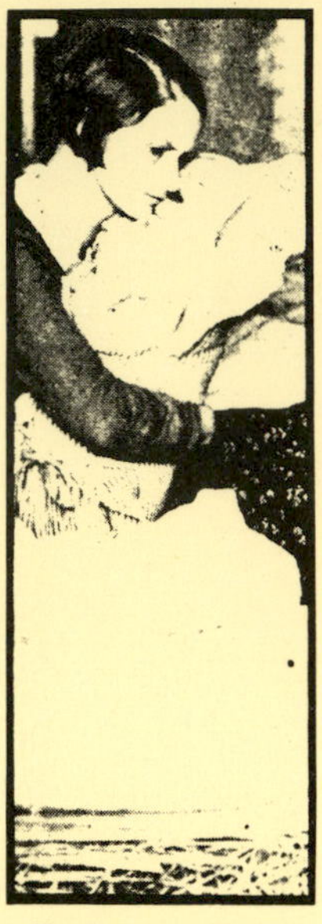

Refugee baby

Mrs. Vera Koudelova, nursing her crying nine-weeks-old baby, fled from home when the Germans entered Sudetenland, and is now one of 1,500 refugees being sheltered in a school at Steti, twenty miles north of Prague. Another picture on Back Page.

LATEST

CENTRAL 8000

JEWS FOR ABYSSINIA

[illegible] United Press.

Bette Davis has [illegible] retracted [illegible] divorce [illegible]

Weather: Gales (see page 13)

Ellerman heir doubles father's £18,000,000

Daily Express Staff Reporter

WHEN Sir John Ellerman, £37,000,000 shipping magnate, died five years ago, death duties left his son with the family fortune reduced to £18,000,000. After five years, the new Sir John Ellerman, now twenty-eight, is estimated to be worth more than his father ever was.

Yesterday the accounts of Ellerman Lines, Ltd., were published. The company control 104 ships trading to every country in the world.

Their profit last year was £1,177,906. That is 61 per cent. more than in 1936; and the 1936 profit was 23 per cent. more than in 1935.

So, for the first time since his father died, Sir John has decided to pay himself a dividend on the Deferred Ordinary capital, a modest ten per cent. The rest of the profits go back into the business.

£100 BECOMES £127

This will help to explain how Sir John has regained the millions that went to the State:—

One hundred pounds in a business earning 5 per cent. becomes more than £127 if you leave the profits alone for five years. A million pounds, similarly invested, becomes approximately £1,276,000.

But the earnings on much of Sir John's capital in the past year have been equal to 50 per cent.

His companies have an investment income of £4,000,000 and floating assets of £5,545,910.

A shipping expert said to me last night: "There is always money to be made in shipping somewhere.

"If one of his companies loses a bit another makes it up."

Sir John—a modest young man, devoted to his blackhaired young wife

PAGE TWO, COL. SIX

Three R.A.F. planes crashed, one bomber missing, ten men escaped by parachute—see Page Thirteen

Bette Davis wants divorce

"A friendly one"

...WOOD, Thursday. — Bette ... film star, announces that ... a suit for divorce from ... Mr. Harmon Nelson. ... a friendly divorce," she ... "There is no third ..."—Reuter.

... Davis's last picture was ... a big success in America ... "Of Human Bondage," ... Forest" (with Leslie ... and "Dangerous" are her ... films.

B.B.C. "Bishop"

... next year the Rev. J. W. ... thirty-eight-year-old principal ... John's College, York, will ... S. A. Iremonger as ... with the B.B.C.

MERCURY RACES FOR RECORD

Over Africa

Daily Express Air Reporter

Mercury, top half of Imperial Airways pick-a-back plane, is due to appear over Table Mountain and Capetown early tomorrow morning, non-stop from Scotland, with the world's 6,301 miles long-distance airplane record beaten.

Captain D. C. T. Bennett, at Mercury's controls, soared off mother-plane Maia's back over Dundee at 1.20 yesterday afternoon, bound for the Cape, 6,370 miles away.

Early today Mercury reported her position as near Melghir, in French North Africa. She had then covered 1,635 miles in ten hours.

Pictures on Back Page.

Communists quarrel with Daily Worker

THE secretariat of the Communist Party have fallen out with the Daily Worker, their official and only daily organ in Britain.

On Monday a leading article appeared in the Daily Worker entitled "The Lessons—Labour's Plain Duty."

It admitted that had it not been for the Munich agreement Britain would already have been at war.

In Wednesday's issue, immediately below its leading article, the Daily Worker published an announcement by the secretariat that Monday's leading article was "directly contrary to the policy of the Communist Party."

The secretariat, it was added, "expresses the hope that immediate and effective measures will be taken to prevent any recurrence of such completely wrong statements in the columns of the paper."

The Communist Party policy endeavours to show that the Chamberlain-Hitler Munich agreement means war, not peace.

BENNY LYNCH CONFESSES

BENNY LYNCH, ex-fly-weight champion of the world, today begins what he describes as "the greatest fight of my life—the fight with myself."

He starts the cure recommended to him by the National Sporting Club in an effort to regain his prestige, lost in recent fights.

Lynch made a full confession to John Macadam yesterday and says (on Page Five) "Now I'm going away from John Barleycorn."

◀ The Christiansen revolution in the *Daily Express* (1938), with, right, its post-war continuation (1959). ▶

DAILY EXPRESS

No. 18,310 THURSDAY APRIL 9 1959 3 a.m. forecast: Sunny spells; showers; hail Price 2½d.

Britain's new challenge in the Atlantic

SUPER-LINERS AHOY

Struggle for power goes on as . . .

Dr A lashes at Britain

From COLIN LAWSON

They will replace Cunard's Queens

By MONTAGUE LACEY

TWO super-liners are to be built with Government help to replace the Queen Mary and Queen Elizabeth. They will counter foreign competition now threatening the Cunard Company.

'RAB'S' COUSIN SWEPT FROM LEDGE

RAF hero saves ex-deb from waves

From RICHARD KILIAN

SALLY BUTLER

TROUBLE ALL THE WAY SAYS CRANKO

She disappeared

HIS NEED

PAUL RICHEY

POCKET CARTOON by OSBERT LANCASTER

2 women die on line

Picture to cap it all!

THREE COOL MEN ROB TRAIN—AND LEAP OFF

Express Staff Reporter

THREE well-dressed young men boarded the Caledonian Glasgow express at Euston station just before 4 p.m. yesterday—and on the way North sauntered forward to the mail van and rifled it.

Ideas . . . Speed . . . Power . . .

4.30 a.m. LATEST

TV BREAKDOWN

TREMOR

4,020,703

FLEet-street 8000

My New K Shoes

Up and coming dancer cossets her feet in light K Skips

FLEET-STREET, Midnight

SWEARING ROW HOLDS UP V-BOMBERS

WHO'S THIS?

TWIN SITS UP

SHARES SOAR

GRANNY'S LETTER

MAGIC NAMES

£600 TRIP

FIGHT IN HALL

LAMA LEAVES

Fiancé killed on new motor-cycle

Bold (roman and italic) and Bold Extended, running the sizes up to the then effective limit of 72pt; nowadays many Ludlow ranges are available up to 96pt and some beyond. His choice of Century was to have an influence on British headline typography as widespread as it was lasting; to this day the many variants of the American-originated Century family constitute the characteristic heading style of both London and provincial newspapers. Not least important was Christiansen's novel exploitation of the Bold Extended, which for multi-column headings and streamers secured maximum impact in relation to body size. This reversal of the traditional leaning towards condensed headline types – a by-product of the single-column style – was to prove in our own day one of Christiansen's outstanding innovations. Here the choice of Century was vital, since no other display face has so satisfactory a Bold Extended version; the squat and ugly Cheltenham Bold Extended did not compare with it.

There were roughly three stages in Christiansen's transformation of headline typography and make-up, which in varying ways his contemporaries were to follow. First there was the increasing accent on horizontal stress in make-up, the multiplication of multi-column headings, particularly below the fold. As against the old custom of letting a page slide into a grey mass of single-column shorts and fillers, the doctrine of 'strength below the fold' was enunciated. The next step was to loosen up the decker style, four decks reduced to two and finally to one. Finally, large upper- and lower-case, italic as well as roman, was introduced for main headlines. By 1936 the basic process was complete. One subsequent development, much admired and widely imitated, was the placing of a four-line lower-case sans heading – usually in Ludlow Gothic Medium Condensed – around the centre of the front page; against the Century this really kicked right out of the page and came to be called the 'kicker' (not to be confused with the term as used in American newspapers, where it means a smaller, contrasting strapline, usually underscored, over a main heading).

An integral part of Christiansen's transformation of the *Express*, and again one of the things which had an immediate and wide influence, was the building into the fabric of the paper of freely-treated feature, or magazine, pages. These pages were laid out in an open style, influenced by developed advertising typography. They used large display types, playing strongly on upper- and lower-case, of other than news heading style (Goudy, Caslon, Garamond, Cameo, Tempo). Bold illustrations in varying techniques – photographs, line or wash drawings, scraper board – were incorporated. Text was set indented to carry whites (usually a pica) instead of column rule and often ornamented with fancy drop letters and other decorative devices. Historically, this revolutionary *Express* style of feature presentation had been foreshadowed on the Left by the work of J. M. Flanagan for the *Sunday Worker* (1925–29). The feature pages of that short-lived Sunday showed 'free' layouts in Goudy Bold and Handtooled, in Caslon Old Face and other display types. Flanagan, who later made his mark on the *Daily Mail*, the *Daily Telegraph*, the *Observer*, among other papers, was among the very first editorial craftsmen in Britain to take type seriously; in his last years, until his untimely death in 1954, he so transformed the feature presentation of the *Daily Worker* that it won special praise from the Newspaper Design Award judges.

The *Express* transformation was already in progress when the 'tabloid revolution', an event in many ways even more significant and startling, burst upon Fleet Street. It can be dated from 1934, when Harry Guy Bartholomew, former process engraver and pioneer art executive of the *Daily Mirror*, became editorial director of that paper. The picture-paper formula which had paid off so handsomely thirty years before had gone dead; the *Mirror*, not helped by blinkered and unresourceful management, was sinking fast. 'Bart', roughest and toughest of all British newspaper tycoons, decided quite simply to

▸ ▾ Portions of four 1936 feature pages from the *Daily Express*, showing free and varied type treatments and the use of illustration.

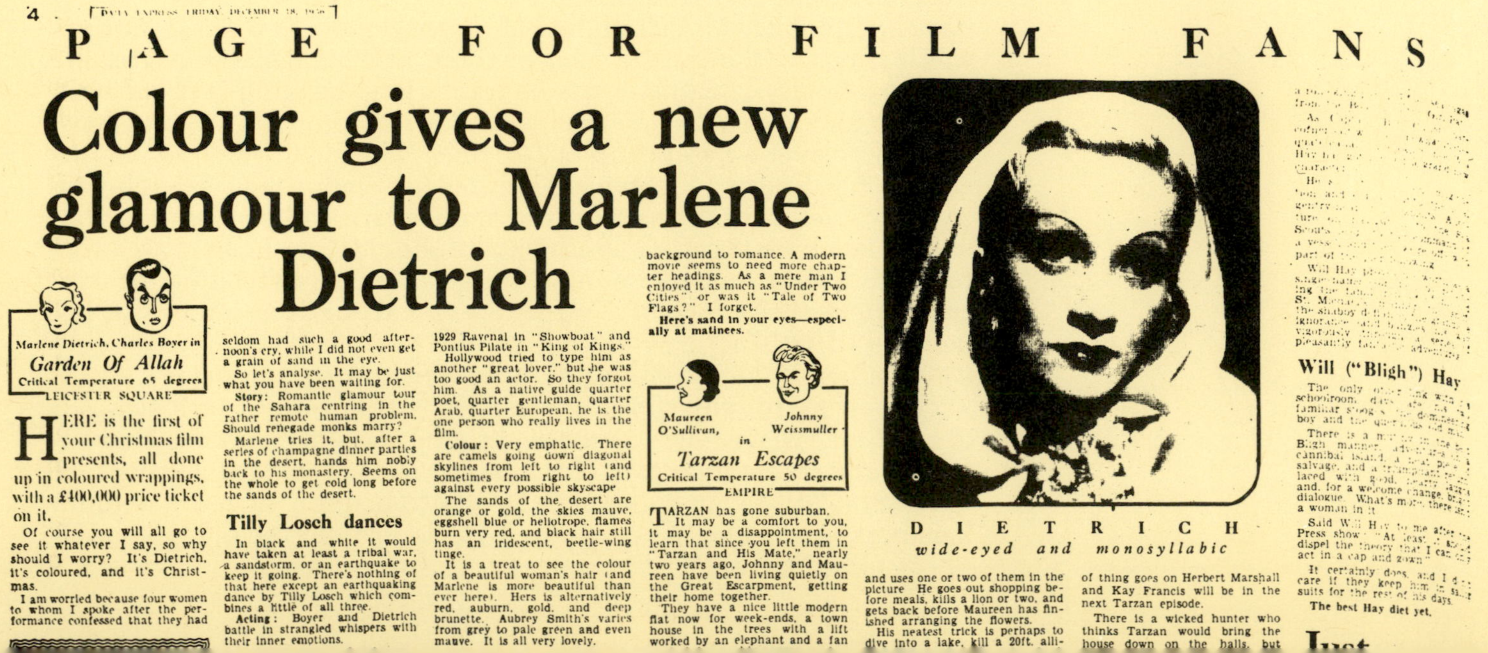

4

PAGE FOR FILM FANS

Colour gives a new glamour to Marlene Dietrich

Marlene Dietrich, Charles Boyer in
Garden Of Allah
Critical Temperature 65 degrees
LEICESTER SQUARE

HERE is the first of your Christmas film presents, all done up in coloured wrappings, with a £400,000 price ticket on it.

Of course you will all go to see it whatever I say, so why should I worry? It's Dietrich, it's coloured, and it's Christmas.

I am worried because four women to whom I spoke after the performance confessed that they had seldom had such a good afternoon's cry, while I did not even get a grain of sand in the eye.

So let's analyse. It may be just what you have been waiting for.

Story: Romantic glamour tour of the Sahara centring in the rather remote human problem. Should renegade monks marry?

Marlene tries it, but, after a series of champagne dinner parties in the desert, hands him nobly back to his monastery. Seems on the whole to get cold long before the sands of the desert.

Tilly Losch dances

In black and white it would have taken at least a tribal war, a sandstorm, or an earthquake to keep it going. There's nothing of that here except an earthquaking dance by Tilly Losch which combines a little of all three.

Acting: Boyer and Dietrich battle in strangled whispers with their inner emotions.

1929 Ravenal in "Showboat" and Pontius Pilate in "King of Kings."

Hollywood tried to type him as another "great lover," but he was too good an actor. So they forgot him. As a native guide quarter poet, quarter gentleman, quarter Arab, quarter European, he is the one person who really lives in the film.

Colour: Very emphatic. There are camels going down diagonal skylines from left to right (and sometimes from right to left) against every possible skyscape.

The sands of the desert are orange or gold, the skies mauve, eggshell blue or heliotrope, flames burn very red, and black hair still has an iridescent, beetle-wing tinge.

It is a treat to see the colour of a beautiful woman's hair (and Marlene is more beautiful than ever here). Hers is alternatively red, auburn, gold, and deep brunette. Aubrey Smith's varies from grey to pale green and even mauve. It is all very lovely.

background to romance. A modern movie seems to need more chapter headings. As a mere man I enjoyed it as much as "Under Two Cities" or was it "Tale of Two Flags?" I forget.

Here's sand in your eyes—especially at matinees.

Maureen O'Sullivan, Johnny Weissmuller in
Tarzan Escapes
Critical Temperature 50 degrees
EMPIRE

TARZAN has gone suburban.

It may be a comfort to you, it may be a disappointment, to learn that since you left them in "Tarzan and His Mate," nearly two years ago, Johnny and Maureen have been living quietly on the Great Escarpment, getting their home together.

They have a nice little modern flat now for week-ends, a town house in the trees with a lift worked by an elephant and a fan and uses one or two of them in the picture. He goes out shopping before meals, kills a lion or two, and gets back before Maureen has finished arranging the flowers.

His neatest trick is perhaps to dive into a lake, kill a 20ft. alli-

of thing goes on Herbert Marshall and Kay Francis will be in the next Tarzan episode.

There is a wicked hunter who thinks Tarzan would bring the house down on the balls, but

DIETRICH
wide-eyed and monosyllabic

Will ("Bligh") Hay

The best Hay diet yet.

"HERE WE ARE (AT IT) AGAIN."

LION PANTALOON: "OH, I SAY, HERE'S A JOLLY LARK! I'VE BEEN AN' ORDERED A LOT MORE DUCKS—"
KANGAROO CLOWN: "AH! BUT WHO'S GOIN' TO PAY FOR 'EM THIS TIME?"

Politics and BBC staff inquiries apart, what about the LISTENER?

To start with, do you know HOW to USE your radio? asks Paul Holt

PLEASE, I am trying to learn to listen-in. All over again. Ten years ago it was a point of domestic honour that the head of the house should twiddle the radio knob, just as the prehistoric

I think there's dance music at eight tonight."

Then you sit through seven minutes of a talk on social services, waiting for the music to begin, because you're too darned lazy to find anything else. And then you write to me:—

"Dear Paul,—CAN'T you tell them that a man, when he comes home from a hard day's work, doesn't want to listen-in to a lot of words? . . ."

I'M not blaming the B.B.C. I'm blaming you.

There is a gentleman at the B.B.C. called Mr. Howgill, whose job is programme planning. Some nights it seems that he throws all programme items for a night into a hat, pulls them out two by two, saying to himself the while, "Regional, National, Regional, NATIONAL, REGIONAL, National . . ."

It works out pretty well. And it would work better if Mr. Howgill had the full co-operation of a greater percentage of listeners.

Anyway, this arbiter of entertainment, this major-domo of a nation's pleasure, isn't the whole cheese.

I am told that most efficient all-wave sets can pick up a very fetching line in dance music, with announcements in perfect English,

caviare for breakfast, dinner, and tea.

I think I know the trouble. The spark of adventure is alight in you, and you say (perhaps you said last night), "Let's try Vienna! Some real music!" So you try, and the darned thing crackles at you spitefully.

And back you go, like a scuttling rabbit, to a home station, and get on with your knitting. Whereas anybody would tell you that noise is really an illusion. (Or rather, the human ear is highly selective.)

There can be a blasting calliope at work ten feet away on the merry-go-round, but if the gal on the next hobbyhorse is saying she loves you, you won't hear it. Stick to Vienna awhile and the crackles will fade away.

I am suggesting all this because I am just beginning to realise, all over again, that an evening's listening can be an adventure, not just a background, now blurred, now loud . . . to realise you can have the radio on less and listen more.

But stick to ONE station if

affected with incurable wanderlust. Seldom does he stay in one country for more than five minutes.

Not because, as you say in the case of Vienna, there may be crackling. But because he just can't leave that confounded knob alone. In fact, I regard the knob-twiddler as a potential home-breaker in disguise.

YOU mention a coupon-scanner who has the radio on at the same time. Why not?

Don't you watch a film and smoke a cigarette at the same time, deriving enjoyment from both?

No, Mr. Holt. We welcome you to the ranks of all-wave listeners.

But many of us—perhaps most of us—have passed through that first flush of glorious adventure you are now undergoing.

If we want to hear Hitler we tune deliberately to Germany. If we are home late, maybe we yawn a little over a Schenectady programme.

But in the main we are content to pick our B.B.C. play, our symphony concert, or our variety—according to a majority vote from our families—light our pipes, put our feet up, and listen.

If we have a book or a knitting needle in our hands, so much the

Evening Hair

...A little lavish, perhaps, but just now you ought to let yourself go...

PARIS, *Thursday.*

¶ I went to the hairdresser yesterday afternoon. When I have a little time to think about fashion I go to a chic "salon de coiffure," as I would go to a show or to a restaurant.

And while expert hands shampoo, pin, curl, uncurl, and put me through tortures under an electric drier, I can at leisure watch all the beautiful ladies gliding in and out, having their nails trimmed (by the way, use no more red varnish: pink or orange are the two favourites for the moment) and their hair done.

¶ But yesterday I did not only look about me: I interviewed one of the chief leaders of Paris fashion. I asked him, thinking about Christmas and the New Year: "Have you some new ideas for evening hair styles?"

"Rather," he answered. "It is absolutely impossible for an elegant woman to wear an evening dress with her hair done in the usual way.

"It is just as bad to have your hair done in an 'everyday' way for an evening outing as to wear sport shoes with an elaborate dress."

"But what a bother and how difficult it is to change! And what expenses it would lead me into!"

"Don't think that. For instance, I would advise *you*, because of your thinnish face, to have your hair done for a simple dark evening dress, like this girl." And he showed me the top right picture.

"If your cheeks were round, this one would be perfect (top left): forehead uncovered, hair off the face."

¶ Of course, this was only a prelude. I wanted to know more about what could be done with my hair . . . and with yours.

What followed made me think I was walking through fairy land. Think that for an elegant evening you may, if your hair is very fair, be a romantic young lady with black velvet flowers about your curls (bottom right picture).

If you don't mind being a little eccentric and have regular features, try yourself as Mercury, with a pair of small black shiny wings (bottom left picture). Don't forget that under bright electric light you need more colour on your face. Otherwise you will look pale and almost ill. Put on your rouge as shown in top right picture if your face is thin: that is high on your cheek-bones. And far off your ears and going down towards your lips if your face is round like the girl shown in top left picture.

¶ I noticed this week: A simple afternoon dress made of brown serge, trimmed with a velvet collar, and big velvet pockets and buttons (a good idea to make an old dress look new).

A hair-net of thick gold thread worn off the forehead with curls rolled all around.

Helene Gordon

Horoscope on Page Four

Gardeners' Plot

When looking over apples in store for signs of rot remember that decay very often starts at the cavity of the stalk.

The mistake is sometimes made of storing apples in the same place as potatoes. The potatoes must be shifted, because the apples take their flavour.

18/12/36. G. H. B. B.

kissing of horses in public?

Interviewed later, one of the horses said: "We are just pals, good pals."

A Thoughtful Idea

I HEAR that the publicity men are considering a scheme by which thousands of life-size wax models of Mrs. Dietrich will be driven about London at night, so that the people who have not yet been able to have hysterics within six feet of her may find consolation and new strength to continue the battle of life. In Kindness to the Public Week the wax models will be thrown to the mob, who will be allowed to tear them to pieces with glee tempered with respect.

Marginal Note

Fans, wild with excitement, burst the police barricades, and climbed on the roof and luggage grid of her car. Even the fur-collared chauffeur seemed afraid of the crowd.

THESE words, taken from a description of the first night of a film, prove that actors and actresses will soon have to go about armed.

Tail-Piece

The Adventures of CUBBY

THE proprietor of the circus was so pleased with Cubby that he engaged him to jump through the hoop every night for a week, on trial.

At the end of the week he said, "Well, Master Cubby, we must go on to the next village now. I hope you will sign on with my circus, and travel with us."

"Oh dear," said Cubby, "though I have no doubt that it would mean that I should make my fortune, I'm afraid I can't go with you. You see, I have a sick friend living near by, and I don't like to desert him."

"Tut, tut," said the proprietor, whose name was Robin, "your sentiments do you credit; but tut, tut, all the same. I should be sorry to lose you, so tell me some more about your friend."

★

"His name is Waterbutt-Willy, and he's an elderly seal."

"A seal, did you say? Why, we're looking for a seal. We need a new trainer." Robin sounded quite excited.

"Then Waterbutt's your man," cried Cubby, much relieved. "I know he's been in a circus in his youth. The only thing is that he has a stickleback, from whom he cannot possibly be parted. His job is to scratch Waterbutt whenever he itches."

"I know these *old* actors," laughed Robin. "They all have their foibles."

So Waterbutt, who was pronounced fit to travel by Dr. Vole, M.D., was engaged at a very good salary to teach the young seals their tricks. He and Cubby had contracts of their own, very grand and imposing documents with red seals over them (wax ones, of course).

Waterbutt was an old hand at circuses, and was soon tucked up in his bunk, but Cubby was much too excited to sleep. Most of all he wanted to ride on the traction engine which pulled the string of caravans and wagons chuff, chuff, along the road.

The traction engine couldn't go very fast because there were so many things for it to pull, so Cubby was able to jump from his caravan and catch it up as it rumbled through the country lanes.

"Sir, sir," cried Cubby to the traction engine driver, who happened to be Papa Podge, the baby elephant's father.

"Well?"

"Let me ride with you!"

"Who are you?"

"Cubby, the new hoop jumper."

"Why aren't you in bed, Cubby?"

"I'm much too excited! *Please* let me ride with you."

★

"Oh, well, jump up," said Papa Podge. "We've got to humour the youngsters, I suppose." And he stopped the engine in time for Cubby to leap up beside him.

"Would you like to start her up?" he asked.

"I'd *love* to."

"Pull that handle then."

So Cubby pulled, and with a great cloud of steam and a whirl of the flywheel and a beat of the piston in, out, in, out, the traction engine started pulling the long line of caravans and wagons.

"Hey! Not so fast," cried Papa Podge. "You'll have us in the ditch, man. Bless my soul, the old 'bus has never gone so fast before."

"That's because *I'm* driving," said Cubby proudly.

More Tomorrow

"More blessed to give than to receive"

SCIENCE PROVES IT

Buying presents for other people is a form of self-help. It does YOU good to give.

I WATCHED a man and his wife choosing Christmas presents in a big store the other day.

They were both prosperous and well dressed; the man wore a silk handkerchief and a gold wrist watch, his wife ran to an expensive fur coat. I put their income at something above the £1,000-a-year mark.

Yet when it came to choosing the presents the husband obviously wanted to save. "Wouldn't fifty cigarettes do for Kenneth," he said, "or we could send him the ashtray you won in the bridge tournament?"

"Well, perhaps fifty would be enough," said the wife.

So Kenneth got only fifty cigarettes. It was the same with the tobacco pouch they chose a moment later. The leather they picked on was nice, but hogskin would have cost only a few shillings more.

He finds it is a competitive market, he must never cease from spurring his travellers on to bigger sales figures.

Sometimes he has the unpleasant job of getting rid of one. Now and then he must sign letters to customers threatening to sue them if they do not pay.

None of these are very pleasant tasks, and George himself is not particularly fond of doing them. But once he is in the office he puts on a stern face and settles down to business. He has already got himself a reputation for being "a tough guy who won't stand for any monkey business."

Yet essentially George is a peaceful sort of person; he may push hard through the barrier to get a better seat on a train, but he is really quite fond of his fellow passengers.

Christmas is about the one time of the year he can show his

"Some people give presents they would like themselves."

BABES-IN-WOOD BOY RUN OVER

AS HE HID IN LEAVES

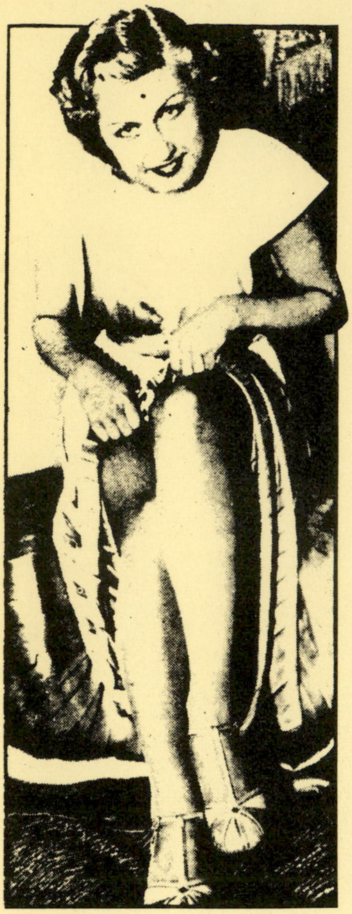

She's Got All Three

Good looks, a sense of humour and outstanding dancing ability. Stanley Lupino's search for a girl with these talents ended when he found Lu Anne Meredith, ex-Dorchester beauty. She's to be his leading lady in the film "Sporting Love."

BY A SPECIAL CORRESPONDENT

WORKMEN were lopping branches from the trees in New Park-road, Brixton, London, S.W., yesterday, to make room for new street lamps, and eleven-year-old Melvin Clack got a great idea for a game.

Finding a pile of leaves on the kerb near his home, he decided to play Babes-in-the-Wood, and told his friend Albert Swift. Albert was busy with a game of his own so Melvin went off alone.

He lay down and covered himself with leaves. The next moment the lorry collecting the leaves drove up—and went right over him.

"Great Fun"

When his companions returned to seek him they found him dead.

With tears streaming down his cheeks, his thirteen-year-old playmate, Albert Swift, told me how he was powerless to prevent the tragedy.

"I was not playing with the others," he said, "but modelling a head in clay. When Mel told me what he was going to do, I thought it was great fun.

"I was too busy with my modelling to watch the end of the game. I heard the lorry driving past, and when I looked up it was just passing over the pile of leaves where Mel was lying.

Awakened from Sleep

"Rushing forward, I parted the leaves, and saw him. . . ."

Poor Albert was too overcome to continue.

Mr. Harry Clack, father of the dead boy—there are five others—who works at night as a garage cleaner, was awakened from his sleep with the news that his boy had met with an accident.

He ran from Lafone-house, his home, to find him dead.

41,000,000 People

in France call him Monsieur le President Lebrun. His "last word" is law to all of them. But at home he's just "old grandpa" to these three—and it's their word that's law.

THE QUEEN'S HAREWOOD HOLIDAY PLANS CHANGED

Arrangements for the annual visit of Queen Mary to Harewood House, the home of the Princess Royal and the Earl of Harewood, have been altered.

It had been expected that she would go from Sandringham for her ten days' stay on Wednesday, but at Harewood yesterday it was stated that she would not be arriving this week.

It is understood that the Queen will be at Harewood during the first week in September.

WIDOW'S COIN HOARD

A hoard of silver coins of all denominations, worth about £100 and carefully wrapped in small paper packets, was found under the bed and in odd places in a room at Bayham-street, St. Pancras, London, where Mrs. Mary Jewell, aged sixty-five, lived.

She was a widow and an old age pensioner.

It was when she failed to pay her weekly rent at the usual time—a certain hour on one particular day—that her room was entered and she was found dead on the floor.

ISLAND ISOLATED BY CLOSING BRIDGE —SHIPS HELD UP

FROM midnight last night the Isle of Sheppey, off the mouth of the Thames, was cut off from the mainland by the closing for repairs of King's Ferry Bridge to road and rail traffic.

The bridge is the only means of communication with the mainland. To maintain normal living extra food supplies were taken into Sheerness yesterday.

While the bridge is being repaired passengers will be taken in motor-coaches from the stations in the island to the Sheppey end of the bridge. They will be allowed to walk over.

Because it is not possible to lift the bridge for vessels to pass through, several ships carrying cargoes are held up.

PIT DISASTERS: MINERS URGE DRASTIC STEPS

The Council of the Yorkshire Miners' Association, at Barnsley yesterday, urged on the responsible authorities the need for a searching inquiry, with a view to drastic steps being taken to prevent the recurrence of such disasters as that at Wharncliffe Woodmoor Colliery.

Little Dr. Tucker Swung for His 'Supper' Too Soon

An old favourite in a new version featuring a New Orleans, Louisiana, doctor, according to an epistle of Reuter.

Little Doctor Tucker
Golfed when work was done.
Entered for a tournament
To hole a ball in one.

He walked out to the contest-hole,
One-sixty yards in length,
Took an iron from his bag
And swung with all his strength.

A ping—the ball flew through the air,
Across the green it stole,
And, to the Doctor's great surprise,
Trickled down the hole

Rushing to the club-house
To claim the winner's "dime,"
He found the competition
Was in a fortnight's time.

B. J F.

£60,000 MORE EACH WEEK FOR WORKERS

WAGES are rising steadily. How much is revealed in a return issued by the Ministry of Labour last night.

The changes in rates which came into operation in July are estimated to have resulted in an increase of nearly £60,000 in the weekly full-time wages of over a million workpeople—and a decrease of about £3,800 in the pay of 44,000.

Trades Affected

The principal increases affected adult male workers in the engineering industry whose wages were raised by 1s. a week.

Of other increases, the more important affected gas workers, railway shopmen, municipal tramway and omnibus employees in the provinces and pottery workers

Crashed Air Liner Pilot "Best I Knew"

Drowning caused the death of one of the victims of the Cloud of Iona air disaster.

This was decided at the resumed inquest at Jersey yesterday on Ernest James Appleby, a passenger, after a doctor had stated that there was no evidence of injury caused by the crash.

Mr. Louis Greig, director and general manager of Jersey and Guernsey Airways, said that the pilot, Mr. Halmshaw, had joined the company after leaving the Royal Air Force.

"I do not think I ever met a better pilot."

DIED BECAUSE BROTHER WAS ABSENT

BECAUSE his cries for his elder brother went unanswered, twenty-nine-year-old Rochard Vosper, insurance agent, of Weston Mill, Plymouth, died in Plymouth City Hospital yesterday.

Doctors attending Vosper for internal trouble were unable to effect any improvement owing to his insistent calls for his "big brother."

As a last hope they sanctioned a radio S O S for the forty-three-year-old brother. Ernest, a naval pensioner, whose last known home was in Bodmin two years ago.

The S O S failed to reach Ernest—and Richard's parents, who had kept a day-and-night vigil by his bedside, went home broken-hearted.

Mrs. Vosper, mother of the two men, told the *Daily Mirror*:—

"They were great friends. Dick always turned to Ernest in trouble. If Ernest had been able to reach him, I think he would have lived"

MISSING GIRL SEARCH

Police have been asked to assist in the search for a fifteen-year-old girl, Elsie Newman, of Boswell House, Devonshire-street, Holborn, London, who has been missing from her home since August 2.

The girl is described as being 5ft. 2in. in height, with dark brown hair, grey eyes, of sturdy build, and with a round face.

▲ The 'tabloid revolution': a *Daily Mirror* page of 1936.

turn the *Mirror* and its companion *Sunday Pictorial* (now *Sunday Mirror*) into American-style tabloids. In this he was closely seconded by Cecil Harmsworth King of the paper's advertising department (a second-generation member of the famous family, nephew of Northcliffe and the first Rothermere). King suggested calling in a noted New York advertising agency to ensure accurate emulation of the American models. Morison was later to make the tart comment: 'One of the greatest of British journalistic revolutions was thus initiated, carried through and made successful by men who were not journalists. An art manager and an advertising manager were responsible.'*

The emulation of New York was thorough. There were the sledgehammer sans headings, exploiting the bold ranges of Ludlow Condensed Gothics, the sexy picture spreads, the strip cartoons. Strident sensationalism was combined with political and social radicalism – 'Forward with The People' – to put the *Mirror* circulation well ahead even of the mammoth *Express*. Actually the development to the ultimate *Mirror* tabloid formula was more gradual than might be supposed. The four 15-pica columns page of the picture paper remained until 1939; the seven 9-pica column page, which we regard as the national tabloid norm, was a product of the Second World War. In

NEWS CHRONICLE, Saturday, October 8, 1938.

St Ivel FULL CREAM MILK CUSTARD. CONTAINS THE MILK — SIMPLY ADD WATER 4½D PINT SIZE

News Chronicle

No. 28,841 ONE PENNY SATURDAY, OCTOBER 8, 1938

POSTAGE IN U.K., CANADA, AND NEWFOUNDLAND .. 1d. OTHER PLACES ABROAD 1½d.

be **sure** to enter the News Chronicle GRACIE FIELDS £1,000 SONGS CONTEST Closing Date: Friday, October 14

GERMANY GRANTS TURKEY CREDITS FOR 12 MILLION POUNDS

Bill To Offset Anglo-French Drive in Balkans

BERLIN, Saturday Morning.

IT is officially announced that an agreement for a German credit of £12,000,000 has been reached at Ankara between the Reich Minister for Economics, Herr Funk, and the Turkish Minister of National Economy, Shakir

London Balloon Barrage Test Today

LONDON will see its balloon barrage tested for the first time today.

From the forenoon until 6 p.m., the Air Ministry announced last night, balloons will be flown from many points in central and suburban London as a peace-time exercise of the

MERCURY NEARS CAPETOWN– AND 3 RECORDS

EARLY this morning flares were lit in Table Bay to guide the Mercury, upper component of the pick-a-back plane, which left Dundee on Thursday on a non-stop flight to the Cape, to a safe landing.

This came after news that the Mercury had been seen over Alexander Bay, 380 miles from Capetown.

She had then been in the air approximately 36 hours. The record for a flight from Britain to the Cape is 45 hours 2 minutes, made last year by Flying-Officer Clouston and Mrs. Kirby-Green.

£21,158 . 2 . 0

was last night's total of the News Chronicle Refugee Fund.

This is magnificent—but more is wanted still.

Contributions to: Czechoslovakia Relief Fund, News Chronicle, Bouverie Street, London, E.C.4.

(Details Page Thirteen)

P.C. CLINGS TO 50 M.P.H. STOLEN CAR

A NON-STOP car carried a police constable 5 yards on the running-board, knocked

LATE NEWS

COVENT GARDEN FIRE

den today after fire had broken out in a building in Floral Street. Many fire engines were rushed to the scene.

▸ *News Chronicle* headlining of the late 1930s: an essay in typefounders' sans – Granby.

those early days of the tabloid revolution the *Mirror's* inside pages were comparatively modest in their headline treatment, running up to 36 and 48pt capitals of the Medium and Condensed Gothics. Nevertheless the stage had been set for the giant double-spreads covering front and back, for the slogan 'the paper with two front pages' and the rest of the presentational heavy artillery.

The *Mirror* revolution had no imitators, at least in its first years; but the example of the *Express* proved infectious throughout the 'popular' broadsheet field. There was little direct imitation. Different papers fought their way to the new typographic freedom in different ways. The *Daily Herald*, as we have already seen, scrapped its Cheltenham deckers and adopted a streamlined all-Bodoni style in 1938. The *Daily Mail*, clinging to its famous solus display advertisement front page even after the staid *Daily Telegraph* had gone over to front-page news (April 1939), took some time to reduce a jumble of types to something like order; but by 1938 it, too, had a 'free' headline style in Century Bold Extended and Bodoni Bold italic, with substantial lower-case treatments, though streamers could be in contrasting type (e.g. Caslon Heavy).

Two newspapers which had never had Ludlow installations re-dressed their pages in ways unlike those of their contemporaries. The *News Chronicle* adopted a typefounder's modern sans – Stephenson Blake's Granby (with italic) and Granby Bold, as its main news headline ingredient; for contrast Linotype-keyboarded Century Bold italic was used. Headings were set flush-left and streamers, double-lined, kept two columns short of the measure of the page. The re-styling was the result of extensive collective discussion at upper editorial level, directed by the late Sir Gerald Barry, then the paper's editor and an enthusiastic type amateur.†

* *Penrose Annual* (1956), p. 24. Here it may be recalled that Bartholomew, who became chairman of the *Mirror* group in 1944, was ousted by King in 1951 and King himself was ousted from the chairmanship of the greatly enlarged International Publishing Corporation by a palace revolution in 1968. Two years later came a £225 million takeover by Reed, the newsprint concern, with Reed boss Don Ryder becoming the real ruler of IPC.

† For this information I am indebted to *News Chronicle* survivors Ralph McCarthy (later editor of *The Star*), Sir Paul Reilly and Tangye Lean. All agree that Barry was personally responsible for the Granby headline typography, indulging his own known liking for that type. I stress the point because I have previously asserted that the *News Chronicle* restyled itself at that time 'as advised by Stanley Morison' (*Newspaper Design*, 1st edn, p. 44); of this there appears to be no evidence. McCarthy and Sir Paul specifically say that they do not recall any involvement of Morison.

"REYNOLDS NEWS," May 3, 1936.

OUR ARTFUL TAX-DODGERS See Page 12

FIRE AND FRAUD See Page 8

REYNOLDS NEWS

GOVERNMENT OF THE PEOPLE, BY THE PEOPLE, FOR THE PEOPLE

4470 RADIO—Page 19 LONDON SUNDAY MAY 3 1936 TO-DAY'S WEATHER: Fair, local frost at night. PRICE 2d.

EMPEROR HAILE SELASSIE AN EXILE

Cheerio, Kids!

WHO COULD FORGET? The retiring matron of a Liverpool babies' hospital, Miss C. T. Emery, says farewell to two of her little charges.

Flight From Addis While Mob Shoot and Pillage

EMPEROR Haile Selassie of Abyssinia is now an exile. With the Empress, the Crown Prince, and other members of the Royal Family he fled the capital, Addis Ababa early yesterday, for Djibouti, the French Somaliland port.

This sensational message was flashed to the British Foreign Office by Sir Sidney Barton, our Minister at Addis Ababa. Immediately it was received Mr Anthony Eden, the Foreign Secretary, interrupted his week-end and returned to the Foreign Office to discuss the situation with his officials.

Although the Emperor was accompanied on his flight by his Foreign Minister, M. Herouy, and other officials of the Abyssinian Government, there is nothing to indicate that he intends to abdicate.

Reports of grave disorder in Addis Ababa have been received in London. Looting and shooting are taking place in the streets.

British subjects and other nationals have taken refuge in the British Legation compound about four miles outside the city.

News of the flight of the Emperor was received with incredulity at the Abyssinian Legation in London. "The Emperor will fight till he dies," it was declared.

A grave view of the situation is taken in London, but until the Italians have actually occupied the city the position is likely to remain obscure.

It has been suggested during the last few days, when the ultimate fall of the Abyssinian capital appeared daily more imminent, that the seat of the Abyssinian Government would be transferred westwards, but the flight of the Emperor has created an entirely new position.

End of the War

In Abyssinia Haile Selassie is himself the Government, and his flight means the collapse of all organised resistance to the Italians, although guerilla fighting may be expected.

ADDIS ABABA'S main street.

It is revealed that the Emperor on Friday had a personal interview with Sir Sidney Barton. What passed during that conversation is not known, but it is reported that it was not on the advice of the British Minister that the Emperor decided to take his departure.

Consultations between the Diplomatic Corps in Addis are being held to consider the next step to be taken in view of the fact that the occupation of the capital without resistance is now only a matter of a few hours.

It is suggested that Haile Selassie and his family may seek refuge in England and that the Emperor may make a dramatic appearance at the League of Nations Council meeting at Geneva on May 11.

It is generally expected that the loyal chieftains will make their own terms with the Italian forces. Afterwards will come the difficult task of deciding who shall rule a country disrupted by treason and bitter hatred of the invader.

Ras Gugsa, a son-in-law of the Emperor and now Governor of the Tigre Province, to which he was appointed in the name of the King of Italy, has strong claims on the Abyssinian Throne.

As Emperor he would smooth the way to the Italian penetration of territory remaining unconquered, which stretches west and south from Addis Ababa to the borders of Kenya Colony and the Anglo-Egyptian Soudan.

Italians Push On

Meantime two Italian columns which are pressing forward on Addis Ababa are now within striking distance.

Landslides and thunderstorms have delayed the advance of the main column over the Pass of Termaber. Workmen with spades and dynamite have had to clear a way for the lorries.

Marshal Badoglio is stated to have left Dessie and to be on his way south behind the main column with his staff to take part in the triumphal entry into Addis.

France regards the flight of the Emperor as justification for her "Go Slow" policy.

"It is the end," is the general opinion.

Message from Reuter and Central News.

MAIMED DOGS SENSATION

Feet Torn by Nails in Traps

"Reynolds" Correspondent

FIRST-CLASS sensation has [illegible] sporting circles as the result of the disclosure yesterday that there had been tampering, during the previous night's racing, with the traps from which the greyhounds are released.

Out of six traps, five had wire nails with sharp points standing straight up from the floor of the trap.

The nails had been driven in in such a manner that dogs, scratching at the door of the trap as the electric hare came round, would tear their feet on the points.

Two of the dogs, "Dark Night" and "Lindrum," had their forepaws badly torn.

The injuries to the dogs were discovered after a race, and then the nails were found.

THE SIXTH DOG

Mr. W. H. Hargreaves, the track manager, said to me, "We believe that members of some gambling gang are responsible for the outrage.

"We feel sure that it was intended to maim five of the dogs and leave the sixth uninjured so that it would win, and then back the sixth dog.

"We have placed the matter in the hands of the police, and a reward will be offered for information that leads to a conviction.

"Recently a similar attempt was made to injure the dogs by placing fragments of glass in the bottom of the trap, but we detected it in time."

MYSTERY FIRE INQUIRY

Outbreak In Flat When Tenants Were Absent

Detectives and fire experts were yesterday investigating a mysterious outbreak of fire in the early morning in a basement flat in Churchfield-mansions, Cristowe-road, New King's-road, Fulham.

Dense smoke awakened occupants of flats above shortly before two o'clock. They found that the dining room in the front of the basement flat was well alight, and that the two bedrooms at the back of the flat were also on fire.

The Fulham-road fire brigade extinguished the flames with a hydrant, but the dining room was practically burnt out.

The flat was fully furnished, but the occupants, a man and a woman, were not on the premises at the time.

On Other Pages

MAY DAY will be celebrated in Hyde Park to-day, but in many parts of the country the great Labour festival was yesterday.

£10 A WEEK MEN TO BE ON THE PANEL

New Plan Is Ready To Launch

"REYNOLDS" CORRESPONDENT

HUNDREDS of thousands of people with incomes above £250 will benefit by a new scheme of medical service to be launched shortly.

Under a group system financed on a weekly contribution basis families with an income not exceeding £500 a year will be able to obtain general and even specialist advice from a doctor of their own choice.

The scheme, which was exclusively forecast in "Reynolds" in January last year, was drawn up some time ago by the London Public Medical Service, of which Dr. Alfred Cox, for 20 years medical secretary of the British Medical Association, is secretary.

DOCTORS RELAX RULE

Delay arose because the B.M.A. would not relax its rule that no doctor could undertake "panel" or group treatment for those in receipt of incomes over £250 a year.

This rule was rescinded by special resolution at the last annual general meeting of the B.M.A., and the Association is now completing final arrangements with the London Public Medical Service H.Q. as to amounts of weekly contributions, benefits, and so on.

A detailed scheme has now been submitted to the British Medical Association, and will be formally considered at a meeting to be held during the next fortnight.

'PLANE CRASH THRILL

Gardeners Miss Smash By Inches

ONLY by crouching low to the ground were three gardeners able to escape a falling aeroplane which crashed near to their workplace at Fairfield Nurseries, Gosport, yesterday.

The machine whipped off the tops of four chrysanthemums which one of the three, Mr. George Mason, had just planted.

One wing of the plane hit a strawberry frame, and, after travelling about 50 yards, the machine turned over, the engine being flung clear of the other wreckage.

The pilot, Mr. Peter Nicholas, son of Admiral Nicholas, of Lee-on-Solent, managed to crawl out of the wreckage. He was cut from the nose to the lip, the lip itself being severed, and, after receiving medical attention in Gosport, was taken to hospital suffering from severe shock.

PIGS IN BLAZE

Two Farmers Overcome In Attempt At Rescue

Twenty-nine pigs, a dog and a goat were burned to death on the farm of Mr. J. Abbott and Mr. S. W. Patchesa, at New Duston, Northampton, yesterday.

Both men made desperate attempts to save the livestock from one of the three sheds which were ablaze, but were overcome after Mr. Patchesa had dragged Mr. Abbott into the open.

Villagers formed a chain with buckets of water to assist Northampton Fire Brigade.

NO 40-HOUR WEEK

Time Not Opportune, Says Council Committee

A suggested 40-hour week for all manual workers in the employ of Manchester Corporation, without reduction in weekly rates of pay, is adversely reported on by two of the Council's Committees.

It is pointed out that the estimated number of additional employees would be 3,353, and the additional annual cost £568,208.

In respect of non-trading departments the additional charge on the rates would be approximately 7d. in the pound.

"The time is not opportune to adopt the proposal," says the Finance Committee.

SMILING SENORITA LOSES TENNIS FINAL

First Century To Kimpton

"REYNOLDS" SPORTS EDITOR

THE biggest sports day of the year. Such was yesterday with the wind-up of the football season, the start of the cricket and baseball seasons, and the English golf championship at Deal.

In the hard courts tennis championship, at Bournemouth, the outstanding match—not excepting the Perry-Austin clash—was the appearance of dark, smiling little Senorita Anita Lizana, the Chilean star, in the women's final.

Could the Senorita win the British title? She would have done had not hard-hitting Kathleen Stammers, probably our most improved woman player, been in form

A £4,000 TOUR

Miss Stammers, a left-hander, won by 7—5, 7—5. She had to be at her best to counter the Senorita's subtle top-spinners.

Victory would have meant much to the Chilean girl. Her tour here has been financed by sports organistions in her native country. It will cost about £4,000. Had she won the championship her visit here would have been prolonged.

As it is, she will be at Wimbledon. And, on present form, must be ranked among the favourites.

Perry came through his first real test since his back injury in good form. He beat Austin 6—2, 8—6, 6—3.

Senorita Lizana

Langley

In the cricket world, Squires, the bespectacled Surrey batsman, had a race with R. C Kimpton, the Oxford player, for the honour of getting the season's first century.

Squires was going well against the bowling of Leicestershire at Leicester. With his score at 86 he was dismissed.

That left Kimpton, batting against Gloucestershire at Oxford, to go on to score 101 runs.

Baseball's bid to capture the South opened in the London area. Among the players for Streatham-Mitcham Giants was George Nepia, famous All-Black Rugby star.

Nepia is likely to be as big a personality in baseball as he is in Rugby. He learned the game when at school in New Zealand. A left-hander, he has shown in practice that he is among the best in the baseball game.

Nepia

Squires

Youth was beaten in the English golf championship. Eighteen-years-old James Langley, the boy title-holder, had swept through to the final at Deal, mowing down some of the best golfers in the country.

Then, yesterday, came his test with experienced Harry Bentley. And experience triumphed. Langley played pluckily, finishing level after the first 18 holes, but Bentley put on pressure in the second round to win by 5 and 6.

CUP FOR CASUALS

At football, beating Ilford by two clear goals, at West Ham, the Casuals won the replayed Amateur Cup Final.

In the Football League, Manchester United, by drawing 1—1 at Hull, assured themselves of the Second Division championship. They are promoted with Charlton Athletic, who took the points from Port Vale, to send the Hanley club into the Third Division.

Coventry City triumphed over Torquay United by the odd goal of three to become Third Southern champions.

HENDREN WILL BE THERE

"PATSY" HENDREN, the England and Middlesex batsman, is again to write regularly each week for "Reynolds News" on cricket topics during the season.

Hendren.

The first of his articles, appearing on Page 23, deals with the new leg-before-wicket rule—a law which vitally affects amateur cricketers this year.

With Graham Greenwood covering lawn tennis, and the usual gossip features, "Reynolds" leads the way in summer sport.

MEANS TEST CHANGES

Commons Battle Over New Regulations

Special to "Reynolds"

THE new Unemployment Assistance regulations governing the administration of the Means Test are now before the Cabinet, who hope to see them in force before Parliament rises at the end of July.

They are intended to replace the scheme which caused such a storm early last year that it had to be hurriedly withdrawn.

Certain concessions are being made, but now that a General Election is probably some years ahead they are not so generous as to satisfy the critics. Strong opposition is certain in the House of Commons.

It is understood that a minimum will be prescribed beyond which young people will not be forced to contribute to parents' maintenance, and which, if exceeded, will not involve a reduction of the unemployment allowance.

Rent allowance also will be more liberal in the new scheme than in the old.

LEPER HERO'S HOME-COMING

FORTY-EIGHT years after his death, the body of Father Damien, the heroic priest who devoted the greater part of his comparatively short life to the lepers of Molokai, Hawaiian Islands, in the Pacific, comes home to-day.

He died of leprosy in 1888, when he was 48 years old, and was buried on Molokai Island.

The body will be borne into Antwerp Harbour, in old-world splendour aboard the sail-driven Belgian cadet ship Mercator.

King Leopold III., at whose request the body was brought home, will be on the quay to receive it, along with the Prime Minister, M. Van Zeeland, and the Cardinal Archbishop of Belgium, Cardinal Van Roey. Britain will be represented by Father Dunstan Sargent.

In solemn procession the remains will be carried to the Cathedral of Notre Dame.

After a picturesque ceremony there, they will be taken through the principal streets—beflagged from end to end—to their last resting-place in the crypt of the Church of the Sacred Heart of Jesus and Mary at Louvain.

◀ Times Bold titlings and Bodoni Bold (Monotype Super Caster types) in the redesigned *Reynolds News*, 1936.

The case of the other paper, *Reynolds News*, was unusual from several points of view. In previous chapters we have made the acquaintance of this celebrated radical Sunday paper. It was in much reduced circumstances when, in 1930, it was sold to the Co-operative movement by the late Lord Dalziel, a cunning old Lloyd-Georgeite trafficker in newspapers. Coinciding as it did with the Odhams takeover of the *Daily Herald*, this quite opposite deal – a paper passing from capitalist to Labour movement ownership – had obviously great potentialities; it was common talk among leading Co-operators that it could be the forerunner of an independent Co-operative daily newspaper. The long and sorry story of the egregious failure of the blinkered and fumbling Co-operative leadership to realise these potentialities, eventually culminating in the closure of the paper (its name changed to the *Sunday Citizen*) in 1967, is beyond the scope of this book. What matters here is that an able and energetic young editor, Sydney R. Elliott, managed to push through a complete re-launch of *Reynolds News* in March 1936. From a poor half-sheet produced in a plant of startling antiquity (the stereo-plates were hand-cast, and pigeons nested in the foundry) it was transformed into a stylish broadsheet produced in a modern plant; this last was built and fully equipped, on a freehold site, for under £200,000, two lines of unused Goss three-unit rotaries, or four presses with colour units, having been picked up for the incredible figure of £25,000.

The next unusual feature, for a national, was that it had been decided to handset all headings, not from founders' type, but from type provided by a Monotype Super Caster, which was duly installed in a corner of the new composing room. I suspect that an important reason for this decision was the curious quirk then existing in the London compositors' Sunday paper scale by which, unlike morning and evening papers, advertisements could be set on time (not at piece rates) provided they were entirely handset from movable type. Since there was a good deal of house-setting of advertisements on *Reynolds* it was in the Printer's interest to have a constant and large supply of advertising text types, from 6 to 12pt, which could simply be re-melted after use. Hence the special value of the Super Caster.

There was, of course, the further advantage that, when Elliott entrusted me with the job of designing the 'new' *Reynolds News*, I had the full Monotype display range to call on. When he further briefed me with the words 'the chief aim is to produce a quality paper with a popular appeal and the typography must be in consonance with this aim' I did not hesitate. For the news headlines I chose Times Extended Titling 339 and Bold Titling 328, with Times Bold 334 – the first use of these types in a 'popular' newspaper – and Bodoni Bold 260 roman/italic as a companion letter. Since the Times Titlings then had a 30pt ceiling, the Monotype Corporation promptly cut the larger sizes up to 48pt (the 60 and 72pt came later). Some minor decker styles persisted and headings were mostly centred, not flush-left, but there were many three- or four-line single-deckers, and two-line streamers, sometimes in upper- and lower-case, not more than half the page measure, which I described as 'more flexible than the traditional single line of large capitals right across the page.'[7]

Morison designed a splendid title-piece for the paper, using 72pt Perpetua Bold Titling 200 (setting a fashion in title-line typography that has continued and is still to be seen). For the text Linotype Excelsior was chosen, after a number of trials including the old Moderns (Nos. 35 and 41). It was typical of the Times Roman euphoria of those days that I was most anxious to try Times for the text of the new *Reynolds*. But apart from any other snags in linecaster Times – which, out of ignorance, I did not consider – the available size range quickly quashed my hopes. For 8pt was required for the body of the paper and there was then no 8pt in the linecaster Times range; indeed, only in 1936, as already noted, did *The Times* introduce $7\frac{1}{2}$pt for its body size. When the Linotype organisation indicated that to cut the 8pt Times

TONIGHT Snow, colder; lowest 25.
TOMORROW Snow ... northwest winds.
Temperatures at Each Hour [illegible]

THE CLEVELAND NEWS

Home Edition

Exclusive Evening News and WIREPHOTOS of the Associated Press

VOL. 93—NO. 303 | WEDNESDAY, DECEMBER 19, 1934 | THREE CENTS

NAVAL PARLEYS BREAK UP AS JAPS DROP U. S. PACT

GOOD NEWS!

GOOD news today from all parts of the United States!

Business is better, dispatches from widely separated sections reveal.

The facts come from the men who know — steel leaders, merchants, manufacturers, bankers, utility executives, railroad men. They reflect a definite general advance, and hope for its continuance.

Following are a few of the day's "better times" straws in the wind:

Steel Hits 35½ Pct.

NEW YORK—Steel production has reached 35½ per cent on ingot capacity, according to Iron Age, the highest rate since June.

Christmas Buying Up

WASHINGTON—There will be at least a 16 per cent bulge in America's Christmas stocking this year that wasn't there in 1933. Reports from 70 cities say Christmas sales from Thanksgiving to the middle of December were almost equal to those in 1931 and the best in the three years since then.

Utility Earnings Rise

CHICAGO—(AP)—The Commonwealth Edison Co. announced gross revenues for November of $6,393,889, as against $6,367,549 for the same month of 1933. Net income was $828,415, compared with $512,306 for November, 1933. Gross revenues were $69,022,147 for the first 11 months of 1934, against gross revenues of $67,940,477 for the same period last year.

Glass Production Up

PITTSBURGH, Pa—Total production of polished plate glass by members of the Plate Glass Manufacturers of America for November was 6,587,386 square feet, as compared to 7,512,052 for October and 4,169,442 square feet for November, 1933.

Bank Deposits Rise

WASHINGTON — The controller of currency reports that on Oct. 17 deposits of 5,466 licensed national banks totaled $20,821,392,000, a gain of $888,732,000 over three months ago and $3,766,184,000 over a year ago.

Will Spend $1,600,000

DAYTON—(AP)—Prospects for the refrigeration and air conditioning industries are so bright for 1935 that Frigidaire Corporation has retooled its two plants here and installed new machinery at a cost of $1,600,000 to meet an anticipated record sales volume of 500,000 units.

More Electricity Used

SCHENECTADY, N. Y—(AP)—Gerard Swope, president of the General Electric Co., said the increased use of electrical appliances was partly responsible for the 30 per cent gain in 1934 in the electrical manufacturing business and the 7 per cent gain in the use of electricity throughout the United States.

Car Loadings Rise

NEW YORK—Railroad car loadings are rising. Figures on some reporting lines for the week of Dec. 15 and the previous week are: Rock Island, 20,908 and 19,830; Missouri Pacific, 20,997 and 20,182; Chicago, Burlington & Quincy, 21,145 and 20,405; Gulf Coast, 3,913 and 3,718; Wabash, 12,772 and 11,897.

$7,000,000 Nash Schedule

KENOSHA, Wis—(AP)—The Nash Motors Co. announced its January production schedule calls for about $7,000,000 worth of Nash and Lafayette automobiles against unfilled orders already received from distributors.

1,308 Dividends Paid

NEW YORK — (AP) — Favorable dividend actions this year up to Dec. 12, according to a compilation made by Standard Statistics Co., have totaled 1,308, compared with 807 in the corresponding period last year and only 559 in the like period of 1932, the leanest year of the depression.

More Cement Used

WASHINGTON — The Portland cement industry in November produced 5,779,000 barrels, shipped 5,664,000 barrels from mills and had in stock at end of month 20,086,000 barrels. Production in November showed an increase of 23.7 per cent and shipments an increase of 26.9 per cent over November, 1933.

Hat Profits Increase

NEW YORK—(AP)—Hat Corporation of America announced a net profit, after provision for federal income tax, of $618,051 for the fiscal year ending Oct. 31, against $222,178 for the previous year. The profit per share of outstanding preferred stock this year was $18.49 against $6.05 last year, and on outstanding common stock the profit was 85 cents a share against nothing last year.

Jewelry Sales Gain

CHICAGO—(AP)—John H. Malone, wholesale jeweler, reported an improvement in sales volume and attributed it rather to better times than to seasonal activity.

Restore Rail Pay

WASHINGTON —(AP)— Railroad brotherhood workers on Jan. 1 get back $15,000,000 of the $60,000,000 wage cut of 1932. On April 1 the last quarter of the 10 per cent cut will be restored, returning rail men to the basic wage.

Loans Urged For Teachers' '35 Salaries

Borrow if necessary to meet teachers' payrolls after the first of the year.

Officials of the teachers' organizations today announced they would make this request to the Cleveland school board if the schools feel a real pinch for funds in January or February.

"This plan offers the best solution to the whole problem," said Claude V. Benedict, president of the Cleveland Teachers' Federation.

"Our group takes the same position," said George Davis, the president of the teachers' union.

The schools, they said, could borrow against taxes at a rate of 5 per cent on a short-term loan. For the teachers to borrow as individuals it would mean paying interest ranging from 17 to 50 per cent. Teachers, they added, are now living on a week-to-week basis on extremely low salaries.

A check of the school treasury disclosed that there are sufficient funds to meet the coming payroll which is due just before Christmas.

The pinch will come, officials say, either late in January or early in February.

If salaries are paid in full through these weeks through the return from property taxes, there will be a race against time until the first returns are received from the newly-passed sales taxes.

Because the sales tax is not expected to go into effect before Jan. 15, few county officials expect any returns to the local subdivisions before March 1.

Toyshop Gifts

THE NEWS acknowledges herewith the following very welcome cash contributions to the Toyshop. Every contribution, however large or small, will help greatly in bringing Christmas happiness to the thousands of unfortunate children of Greater Cleveland.

Address all communications to The Toyshop, The News building, Superior ave. at E. 18th st. Contributions of cash or used toys in workable condition may be left at the Want Ad counter in the lobby of The News building every evening until 10 o'clock.

Previously acknowledged	$387.96
Cleveland News Benefit association	25.00
Cleveland News Bowling league	25.00
Emilie Grasselli	10.00
B. A. T. club	5.00
A Friend	3.00
Dr. B. M. Kohrman	3.00
Mrs. J. W. Dolf	2.00
Mr. and Mrs. R. E. Dague	1.57
H. C. Ralston	1.00
Louis Westerburg	1.00
Jane Bradner	1.00

Gin-Drinking Thieves Smash Concrete Safe

Joseph Ault came to work at the Syndicate Parking Co., 1805 Euclid ave., today to find a steel and concrete floor safe in the office smashed to bits. Near by lay a sledge hammer and a bottle of gin.

"The concrete sides of the safe, which was worth $500, were a foot thick," Ault told police. "They must have worked on it for three hours." The robbers got $150.

England Hangs Mother In Murder of Husband

HULL, England—(AP)—After appeals to the king and queen had failed to save her, Mrs. Ethel Lille Major, 42-year-old mother of two children, was hanged today at Hull prison.

She was the first woman to be executed in England in eight years. Until the end she maintained she was innocent of the charge of murdering her husband by poison.

Farrell's Sudden Death Ends Life Given Labor

THOMAS S. FARRELL

BY JACK B. CLOWSER

Thomas S. Farrell, whose brilliant leadership promised to carry organized labor far in its renaissance here, was dead today.

He died of a heart attack only five months after taking office as secretary and business representative of the Cleveland Federation of Labor.

Mr Farrell was a former city utilities director, former member of the board of elections and had been a state and national labor official since the early part of the century. He would have been 56 years old had he lived until Christmas day.

Although he had suffered from a heart ailment for some time, he stuck to his duties. He was at his desk until after dark yesterday and had even then confided to friends that he intended to go to a hospital for observation tomorrow.

Wife Rushes to Aid

The treatment that might have prolonged his life was delayed too long. He and Mrs. Farrell entertained friends last night at their home, 2538 Kemper rd., Shaker Heights. He retired shortly after midnight, saying he was "very tired."

A few minutes later his wife heard him moan and rushed to his room. Dr. A. S. Maschke was sum-

Turn to Page 4, Column 1

Black, Former Reserve Bank Chief, Dies

ATLANTA — (AP) — Eugene R. Black, 61, former governor of the Federal Reserve board, died at his home here today of a heart attack.

EUGENE R. BLACK

Mr. Black had been slightly indisposed the past three days. His wife and a nurse were at his bedside when death came.

An outstanding citizen of the south, President Roosevelt called Mr. Black to Washington on May 10, 1933, to become chairman of the Federal Reserve board. In that position he gained nationwide prominence in assisting the President in getting the New Deal under way.

He returned to his old post as governor of the sixth federal reserve district in Atlanta last June, but, at the request of the President, also acted as contact man for the Reconstruction Finance Corporation.

In that capacity he contacted banks through the country and stimulated the making available of credit as a part of President Roosevelt's general recovery program.

Christmas Music

NEXT Saturday, Dec. 22, The News will publish programs of music to be presented by the churches of Greater Cleveland on Christmas day. Pastors and music directors are requested to send programs to the Church Music Editor, The News, by 6 p. m. tomorrow.

More Yule Gifts, And Bigger, in '34

Christmas cheer flows through the Cleveland postoffice in a much larger volume than a year ago.

Postmaster Michael F. O'Donnell said today postal receipts yesterday amounted to $44,9?9, compared with $24,091 on Dec. 18, 1933.

"The difference is accounted for by the fact that people are mailing packages whereas they mailed postal cards last year," explained Mr. O'Donnell. "Also, they are sending larger packages than last year."

Quintuplets Lazy; Pep Up, Cry of Doctor

CALLANDER, Ont — (AP) — The Dionne babies are reducing.

The quintuplets were getting fat and fussy, and somewhat lazy, Dr. A. R. Dafoe said today, and henceforth they can take their food or leave it.

The quintuplets will make their radio debut at 8:15 p. m. tomorrow (Cleveland time). The broadcast will be given to the American public from the Dafoe hospital. The babies are expected either to coo or cry. The broadcast will be over WABC.

Quintuplets on Air

THE most famous babies in the world since Romulus and Remus — the Dionne quintuplets, or, as Dr. Dafoe has called them, "the quins" —will go on the radio tomorrow night at 8:15. WHK will carry the program here. They will be fed during the broadcast and may laugh or cry for their coast-to-coast audience.

"We are not compelling them to eat," the gray-haired physician, just back from the United States, said in explaining his desire to guard against the quintuplets' putting on too much weight. Their condition is excellent, he explained, and no change has been made in their feeding.

"They seemed to be getting a trifle lazy," Dr. Dafoe said, "and wanted to be waited on and played with. We want them to have more pep and more desire to eat without 'fooling around'."

"They got so they wanted to be sung to when they were taking the bottle. It didn't matter which of the nurses did the singing or how terrible it might be, the singing seemed to put the babies in a more amiable mood."

Amelia May Span Pacific in Plane

LOS ANGELES — (AP) — Amelia Earhart, the first woman to cross the Atlantic by airplane, may be the first to fly the treacherous water route from Honolulu to California.

When she sails next Saturday for Honolulu the noted flyer will take her airplane along. Her husband, George Palmer Putnam, publisher and motion picture executve, who will accompany her to Hawaii, said it was "very probable" she would fly the plane back to California.

Food Prices Here Drop 1 Per Cent

Retail food prices in Cleveland decreased 1 per cent during the two weeks ended Dec. 4, while the average price for the nation fell only three-tenths of 1 per cent, the U. S. bureau of labor statistics announced today.

The decline in Cleveland was the greatest registered in any north central city.

Roosevelt Favors City Power Loans

BULLETIN

WASHINGTON —(AP)— President Roosevelt and Mayor LaGuardia of New York laid the groundwork today for construction of a municipal power plant for the metropolis.

WASHINGTON —(AP)— President Roosevelt is ready to loan federal funds to New York or other cities for construction of municipal power plants if investigations prove they can be operated cheaper than by private companies.

This was made known today at the President's semiweekly press conference in giving his views on current topics.

The President took up the question with Mayor LaGuardia of New York and City Commissioner Davidson. They have refused bids of private companies for next year's power, saying they were exhorbitant. It was disclosed also that the navy is making a study to determine whether power can be obtained at less cost through construction of its own plants.

Finds Most of Securities Sound

In response to inquiries, the President commented on a proposal of the Edison Electrical Institute that the government joins in a test of the constitutionality of the federal power program, a proposal rejected by the administration.

The President said the overwhelming proportion of utility stocks and bonds are as sound as government bonds.

The water in utility financial structures, he said, is in the holding companies. It was emphasized the administration is determined to go ahead with its campaign for cheaper power.

The President said he regards the power question as largely one of simple mathematics—a question of whether it is cheaper to buy from private companies or construct one's own plant.

Non-Committal on Canal

Asked about proposals for construction of a canal through Nicaragua, President Roosevelt observed non-committally that his father years ago had invested in such a proposition. He added that his mother had enough Nicaragua canal stock to paper a whole room. Government construction of such a canal would not affect this stock.

The President said he was maintaining silence on his legislative program until it is presented to Congress Jan. 3. In all probability he will not make the radio report to the nation he had planned before Congress meets.

Guards Message Details

Carefully guarding details of his message to Congress, Mr. Roosevelt did disclose he would pursue his policy of the past and submit a series of separate messages on specific propositions after presentation of his opening report.

Mr. Roosevelt said he was hopeful of an early agreement within the steel industry on the new proposal for peace in the industry.

The three-point plan for maintenance of peace was not disclosed pending further talks between employers and employees.

Heavy Snow Falls Over Middlewest

CHICAGO—(AP)—A heavy blanket of snow covered middlewestern states today, giving promise of a widespread "white Christmas."

The storm struck Chicago at 3 a. m. (eastern standard time), and seven hours later the fall of wet, heavy snow was estimated at three inches. Weather bureau officials said snow was general, with as much as seven inches in parts of Illinois, Indiana and Missouri. All airplane service out of Chicago was suspended.

Iceland Repeals Dry Law

COPENHAGEN, Denmark—(AP)—Iceland has repealed prohibition, advices reaching here from Reykjavik said.

Poses as Gang Girl — Heroine — to Trap Dillinger Gunman

FEARLESS—Genevieve Roth of Booneville, Ind., who aided Deputy Attorney General J. E. Barce in trapping Edward ("Jerry") Burns, by posing as a "gang moll."

INDIANAPOLIS —(AP)— A 24-year-old southern Indiana girl who posed as a gangster's girl during three dangerous weeks of undercover investigation in Chicago underworld haunts was unconcerned today about any danger attached to her work.

Governor McNutt and state officials, however, hailed with satisfaction the results of the secret association with gang characters which led to arrest of John Burns, fugitive Indiana convict said to have been attempting a roundup of remnants of the Dillinger gang.

Never Frightened

"I wasn't scared at any time," Genevieve Roth said. "I was having a good time. Goodness, no. I wasn't frightened. I went with Burns to cabarets and dances. He was very neat and polite. He was a fancy dresser, but didn't care much for night clubs."

Miss Roth added she was worried about any anxiety she may have caused her mother, who lives in Boonville, Ind. She indicated her mother did not know she had been assisting J. Edward Barce, deputy Indiana attorney general.

Mr. Barce praised the girl, known

Turn to Page 9, Column 4

Warns Drivers Of Icy Streets On Way Home

Greater Cleveland's thousands of motorists who came to work backward, sideways and forward today over icy streets probably will go home the same way.

Caught in a sleetstorm, cars skidded into each other and into curbstones. Traffic jams formed at the foot of hills when cars were unable to get traction.

Rising temperatures relieved the situation after two hours of slipping and sliding in the city. In the suburbs salt and cinders reduced the hazard and speeded traffic.

150 Stalled on Ramp

The Eagle ave ramp and the Bulkley blvd. hill in Edgewater park were reported to be the worst stretches in the city. On the ramp more than 150 cars and busses stalled until Cleveland Railway Co. employees scattered sand and salt.

A sudden drop in temperature to below freezing was predicted for late today by Weatherman Ralph C. Mize. It will freeze the water remaining on the streets and the drizzling rain into more ice, duplicating conditions of the morning rush hour, he said.

Most of the ice disappeared by noon, when the temperature rose to 38 degrees. The lowest temperature tonight will be about 25 degrees, Mr. Mize said. Snow is expected, and it may be heavy enough to cover the ice.

Two men were injured in traffic

Turn to Page 9, Column 1

Liquor Stores Here Close on Christmas

Cleveland's liquor stores will be closed Christmas and New Year's days.

Director John A. Hughes said at Columbus that the state agencies will not be permitted to sell liquor on Christmas, but that to accommodate New Year's celebrators state liquor stores will remain open until 10:30 p. m. Dec. 31.

Meet Fails To Fix New Talk Date

LONDON—(AP)—The tri-power naval conversations broke up today, shortly after the Japanese privy council, acting in Tokyo, abrogated the Washington naval limitation agreement.

The delegates of the United States, Great Britain and Japan adjourned the naval parleys, in progress for the last three months, without setting a date for renewal of the discussions.

This was in accordance with a prior warning, served by the American delegates, that the onus for wrecking the conference must rest on Japan, as soon as Tokyo formally approved abrogation of the Washington treaty.

The naval conference delegates met in Prime Minister J. Ramsay MacDonald's room in the House of Commons and formally ended the conversations.

In many weeks of conversations the three delegations have been unable to agree to a new treaty to succeed the Washington pact of 1922, which Japan soon will denounce chiefly because Great Britain and the United States refused to grant the Japanese demand for full equality.

"Although the three governments represented in these conversations," said the communique issued at the close of the conference, "are in favor of a continuation of naval limitation with such reductions as can be agreed upon by all the powers concerned, the principles of the methods for achieving this in the future remained to be determined."

The British, as hosts to the parley, will continue explorations for a basis for an agreement through diplomatic channels and will arrange further conversations or a conference when "an opportune moment arrives."

Japan 'Ready to Meet Any Emergency'

TOKYO—(AP)—The Japanese government acted today to scrap the Washington naval treaty and expressed confidence in its "readiness to meet any situation which might arise" as a result.

The powerful privy council recommended abrogation of the limitation pact to Emperor Hirohito, whose speedy approval is expected. The action in effect constituted abrogation.

Speaking for the privy council, Baron Kiichiro Hiranuma, its vice president, said: "The imperial government desires continuation of clauses of the Washington treaty relating to limitations of fortifications and naval bases in the Pacific ocean, but if such clauses are terminated the government is prepared to cope with such a situation."

Assurances were made that the government would strive to conclude a new naval treaty replacing the Washington pact, with its 5-5-3 ratio odious to Japan—a new treaty

Turn to Page 9, Column 5

Deaf Man Admits Theft of Radio

Despite the fact that he is deaf, Arthur Hopson, 24, of 9206 Quincy ave., confessed today to Police Judge Merrick tha he stole a radio.

"Guilty or not guilty?" the judge asked. Hopson pointed to his ears. The question was written on a piece of paper. Hopson nodded, indicating his plea was guilty. He was referred for probation.

Yawning Wife Sleeps, Believed Recovering

STERLING, Ill—(AP)—Mrs. Harold McKee yawned once last night and went to sleep.

For more than eight days her strange marathon yawning affliction has necessitated the use of sedatives to bring sleep. But last night the yawn was natural and physicians said they believed her well along the road to recovery.

Shivery Crib Tenders Come Ashore Today

B-r-r-r! It was to be land ho! again for the Holzworth brothers today.

A tug was to plow its way through icy waves to the five-mile crib and back to the coast guard station, bringing the city's crib tenders, Arthur, Harry and Edward Holzworth, ashore for the winter and Christmas with their families.

Fun to Pack Old Timers' Toyshop Drive Friday

Today and tomorrow and then—WHAM!

The Cleveland News Old Timers—nobody knows how many of them—will be out on the streets of Cleveland, putting on the world's biggest vaudeville show, and the noisiest one, too, for the benefit of the Toyshop.

They'll sell souvenir copies of The News to anyone and everyone for any amount ranging from three cents up. And the entire proceeds will go into the Toyshop fund, to fill the Christmas stockings of the city's needy children.

Aim to Score a Double

The Old Timers raised $3,800 last year, as compared with $900 in 1932, their first year.

This year they aim to double the 1933 figure.

And they aim to have twice as much fun and furnish twice as much fun as last year, while they're doing it.

They would try to make twice as much noise, if that were possible. But it isn't.

It probably isn't possible to inject twice as much variety into their entertainment, but they're going to try it.

134 Already Lined Up

To date there are 103 of the original Old Timers, plus a determined band of 31 women, who imply they aren't afraid of the men's superior numbers.

There will be more Old Timers tomorrow. By Friday the list will have grown and grown. That's the way it always happens.

There will be quartets and trios and duos and soloists, to furnish

Turn to Page 5, Column 1

2 East Side Pupils Win $50 Expo Essay Prizes

Two East Side students today were announced as winners of the grand prizes in the essay contest on "Ten Reasons for Cleveland's Greatness."

First prize of $50 in the senior high division went to Alice Catterall, a 10-B student in John Hay High school.

Judah Rubenstein, an 8-B student in Alexander Hamilton Junior High, was the winner of the $50 first prize in the junior high division.

The other cash winners, who will split $105, were:

SENIOR HIGH DIVISION: second prize, $25, James Regan, John Marshall High; third, $10, Arthur Yaspan, Glenville High; fourth, $5, Marjorie Tryon, Villa Angela academy; fifth, $5, John E. Liedtke, Rocky River High, and sixth, $5, Margaret Ray, Shore High, Euclid.

JUNIOR HIGH DIVISION: second prize, $25, Donald Long, Addison Junior High; third, $10, Betty Mary Fier, Noble school, Euclid; fourth, $5, Phillip Schmidt, W. H. Kirk Junior High, East Cleveland; fifth, $5, Clifford Duffner, St. Ann's school, and tied for sixth, each receiving $5, Raymond Hach, St. Wenceslas' school, and Donald Toker, St. Aloysius' school.

In addition free tickets to the Cleveland Exposition, which opens in public hall Dec. 29, will be given to the English classmates of all students who finished among the 100 finalists.

The judges were Dr. A. Caswell Ellis, director of Cleveland college; George Q. Keeley, president of the

Turn to Page 4, Column 4

Roman would cost £400, on top of the price of the matrix founts, the provincial grocers on the board of the Co-operative Press Ltd hastily ran for cover; which, hindsight permits one to add, was just as well.

Returning now to America, we may recall that by the early 1930s John E. Allen's 'streamlining' campaign was only slowly evoking a response. The number of smaller dailies adopting his ideas continued to increase but the big-city papers remained proud and stiff. The first breakthrough came in 1934, from Ohio, when the *Cleveland News* 'streamlined' in the Allen fashion. Editor Earle Martin reduced decks to two, then to one, adopting the flush-left style of headline-setting with all lines ending at will. Martin commented that in its new dress his front page 'is as irregular as nature can make it. Every one of those chunks of irregular white lifts the page. White patches will help any page. They afford sharp contrasts. The left-flush-headline idea automatically forces the reader into the white.' He added that 'we are trying to make the headlines as nearly like conversation as we can. The big thing is that you can tell the story simply and naturally.'[8]

The experience of the *Cleveland News* showed that the substitution of the 'streamlined' single-deckers for the old, deep multi-deck headings saved an appreciable amount of space. Martin estimated this at two to two-and-a-half columns an issue (paging not stated). This, he claimed, offset the extra space taken by the extra leading of text he introduced as part of the general re-dress of the paper. The *Cleveland News*, whose body type was 7/7½pt, increased the leading to 7/8pt and later to 7/8½pt. Martin said that he 'gladly' sacrificed this space 'to get white back of that black. Whenever you get enough white you get a good page.'

◀ An Ohio big-city daily, the *Cleveland News*, was the first major American newspaper to adopt John E. Allen's 'streamlined' headlining in 1934.

▼ The big, bold banner continuing strongly in American dailies of the 1930s: an example from the *Chicago Tribune*.

2 CENTS PAY NO MORE!

Chicago Daily Tribune

THE WORLD'S GREATEST NEWSPAPER

FINAL EDITION

VOLUME LXXXX.—NO. 90 C — WEDNESDAY, APRIL 15, 1931.—38 PAGES — PRICE TWO CENTS IN CHICAGO AND SUBURBS — ELSEWHERE THREE CENTS

SPAIN A REPUBLIC; KING FLEES

11 AMERICANS SLAIN; SANDINO DECLARES 'WAR'

Seaport in Panic as Bandits Advance.

BULLETIN.

PUERTO CABEZAS, Nicaragua, April 14.—(AP)—Refugees who have spent two nights aboard the fruit steamer Cefalu prepared to board her again tonight, for a heavily armed group of insurgents was reported less than two miles away, preparing to attack. Ships and schooners in the harbor were ready to sail on short notice in case of trouble.

NEWS SUMMARY of The Tribune

[And Historical Scrap Book.] Wednesday, April 15, 1931.

FOREIGN.

King Alfonso of Spain sails for exile upon giving up his crown; republic set up headed by revolt chief. Page 1.

Spanish exiles coming home meet fleeing aristocrats at Hendaye on the French border. Page 1.

Eleven Americans reported slain in Nicaragua as Sandino bandits march on Puerto Cabezas. Page 1.

LOCAL.

Story of heroic rescue of firemen and workers from burning tunnel told at inquest; toll of fire is 11 dead and 54 injured. Page 1.

DOMESTIC.

STORY OF HEROIC TUNNEL RESCUE OF TRAPPED MEN

Save 16 from Fire; 11 Dead; 54 Hurt.

Crowd Waits at Tunnel.

THE GRIM MARCH OF PROGRESS

NOBLES RUSH TO FRANCE; CARRY JEWEL HOARDS

BY EDMOND TAYLOR.

[Chicago Tribune Press Service.]

Border Guards Step Aside.

Queen's Brother Arrives.

ALFONSO SAILS, YIELDING CROWN WITHOUT FIGHT

No Shots Fired as Monarchy Ends.

BULLETIN.

CARTAGENA, Spain, April 15 (Wednesday).—(AP)—King Alfonso XIII. and the Infante Alfonso, Spanish crown prince, left Spain before dawn today aboard the cruiser Principe Alfonso, bound presumably for exile in England. They came by auto from Madrid in seven hours. The cruiser was waiting with steam up and five days' provisions aboard. Alfonso and those with him went aboard without ceremony. Nobody was there to see them except a few newspaper men.

BULLETIN.

Washington, D. C., April 14.—(AP)—The Spanish embassy's first word from Spain said late tonight that terms of King Alfonso's abdication had specified he remain titular ruler until the new republican government officially was ready to take control. The message was received from Count Romanones, former minister of state.

BY JAY ALLEN.

F. E. DAVIDSON, ARCHITECT, DIES ON LOOP STREET

Cermak Opens Campaign for

THE WEATHER

ALL THE NEWS ALL THE TIME
LARGEST HOME-DELIVERED CIRCULATION
LARGEST ADVERTISING VOLUME
MAdison 2345
The Times Telephone Number
Connecting All Departments

Los Angeles Times

EQUAL RIGHTS
LIBERTY UNDER THE LAW
TRUE INDUSTRIAL FREEDOM

IN TWO PARTS — 42 PAGES
Part I — GENERAL NEWS — 20 Pages
TIMES OFFICES
202 West First Street
And Throughout Southern California

VOL. LV C MONDAY MORNING, AUGUST 31, 1936. DAILY, FIVE CENTS

Thousands Hunt Killers of Officers

Mob Apparently Bent on Lynching Trails Yreka Trio's Slayers

YREKA, Aug. 30. (AP)—Two law enforcement officers and a maritime pilot were shot to death at Horse Creek, isolated mining settlement near here, today in a battle with two prospectors, who fled before a rapidly growing citizen mob apparently bent on lynching.

Deputy Sheriff Martin Lange, Constable Joe Clark and Capt. Fred Seaborn, 50 years of age, a civilian pilot at the Mare Island navy yard, were shot down as they attempted to arrest John H. Bright, 35, and Coke T. Bright, 30, brothers.

POSSE ON TRAIL

The Brights vanished in the wilds of Horse Creek Canyon on buckbrush - covered mountain slopes thirty-five miles out of Yreka as a posse of officers reinforced by angry citizens started after them.

Several hours later a Forest Service lookout reported seeing the brothers at Donmore Meadows, twenty miles north of Horse Creek.

Possemen said they apparently are heading for Mt. Sterling, near the summit of the Siskiyou mountains, where they have a friend who doubtless will assist them. The posse was several miles behind them at the time.

BORDER PATROLLED

Two Oregon officers patrolled the State border, ready to stop the Brights if they ventured across the boundary line.

Yreka, scene of the lynching a year ago of Clyde Johnson, was virtually deserted as many of its 2200 residents deployed over the mountain wilds in the manhunt.

The posse, consisting of Sheriff Chandler, five deputies and two bloodhounds, trailed the brothers to Bull Meadows, at the head of Horse Creek, not far from the Oregon line.

Posse members said the Brights are armed with two rifles and still are in a killing mood. The boulders and buckbrush made ideal hiding places for them and the posse moved carefully, seeking to cut off their avenue of escape into Oregon.

ARREST ATTEMPT

Charles Baker, friend of Seaborn and survivor of the bloody battle, said the trouble started when he and the three victims

Turn to Page 8, Column 3

GOOD MORNING! MEET THE STREAMLINED 'TIMES'

We Trust Our New Type and Head Dress Meet With Your Approval

The Times presents a new typographical dress to the world this morning. Streamlined—it is the last word from the typographer's beauty shop and this newspaper trusts you will approve it.

The new type face which you are now reading is the result of exhaustive research carried on by the management of this newspaper for many months seeking a body type best suited to the eyes of the newspaper reader. Gilbert P. Farrar, typography expert for the American Type Founders Corporation, acted as counselor in the experimental work.

MODERN GOTHIC HEADS

The heads are from the modern Gothic family and designed to enhance legibility and at the same time give the copyreader an opportunity to tell the story and not devote the major portion of his efforts in searching for a combination of words to balance and fit a certain space. If white space results—so much the better. Air—white space—is restful to the eye and aids in the reading of a page.

In case you have forgotten, this paragraph is set in the body type used by The Times until today. Research and experiment have discovered this type to be too small for the text type of any newspaper, and the management of this newspaper believes the readers will appreciate the change.

The new text type is Paragon eight point set on a nine point base. The old type was a seven point set on an eight point base. Thus the body type of The Times from this day forward will be a point larger in size than the old and set on a point wider base. Both of these features, of course, add to the ease with which the eye can scan the text.

LAST WORD IN TYPE

The new typographical dress is termed streamlined because it has simplicity and grace; because it eliminates all obstacles to legibility both in heads and body type; and because it represents the last word from the type foundries of the land.

Thus another extra dividend has been declared for readers of The Times.

New neon-lighted signs worn by Times newsboys as protection from traffic hazards at night are pictured and described on Page 1, Part II.

RESIGNS

Mrs. Ruth Bryan Owen Rohde, recent bride, resigns envoy post.

Envoy-Bride Quits Post

Bryan Daughter's Resignation Disclosed on Roosevelt Train

RAPID CITY (S. D.) Aug. 30. (U.P.)—Ruth Bryan Owen Rohde has resigned as Minister to Denmark, it was announced tonight aboard President Roosevelt's special train.

Mrs. Rohde, America's first woman diplomat, and daughter of the late William Jennings Bryan, recently married Capt. Boerje Rohde of the King of Denmark's personal bodyguards, at St. James Episcopal Church at Hyde Park, N. Y. The President and Mrs. Roosevelt attended the ceremony.

ACTION EXPECTED

At that time it was expected the resignation would be forthcoming in view of the fact Mrs. Owen had become the wife of a foreigner. The couple now is in the United States honeymooning.

The following exchange of telegrams was given out:

"The President; desiring to

Turn to Page 3, Column 4

Col. Turner Crashes in New Mexico

Speed Pilot Seriously Injured in Wreck of Bullet-like Ship

His 1000-horsepower speed plane a tangled wreck on the desert wasteland sixty-five miles south of Gallup, N. M., Col. Roscoe Turner, with several ribs broken, was aboard the Santa Fe Chief last night en route to Los Angeles.

He will be taken from the train at 1:30 p.m. on a litter, his hopes shattered of winning the 1936 Bendix transcontinental race, for which he holds the record.

SHIP WRECKED

Turner's bullet-shaped ship, in which he took off from Union Air Terminal at 5:30 yesterday morning, was demolished in a forced landing at 9 a.m. on the edge of the Zuni Reservation.

His throttle broke, cutting off his engine and forcing him down in the inaccessible and sparsely populated mountain district at Gallup, he said, after he had ridden eighteen miles on a horse given him by Zuni Indians and then had taken an automobile into town.

BROKEN RIBS

Speaking from his hotel room he said he does not know just what is the matter with him but that he thinks he had some broken ribs. He was put aboard the Chief at 8:35 p.m.

Asked how badly his plane was damaged, he said:

"Bad enough that I'll just take the motor out and leave the rest of it there."

The scene of the mishap is approximately 100 miles west of Albuquerque and a few miles west of the Zuni mountain range, which, as the Continental Divide, towers more than 9000 feet at the point near the crash.

PHONES TO WIFE

It was almost nine hours after his ship struck the ground, traveling at terrific speed, before he was given medical aid. It was then he telephoned his wife, Mrs. Carline Turner, 2353 Hollyridge Drive, who was almost prostrate with anxiety over his mysterious disappearance.

"He was very nervous and excited," said Mrs. Turner, who received word from her husband at 6:45 p.m. "He told me he would

Turn to Page 3, Column 2

Spanish Plane Rains Bombs at United States Destroyer

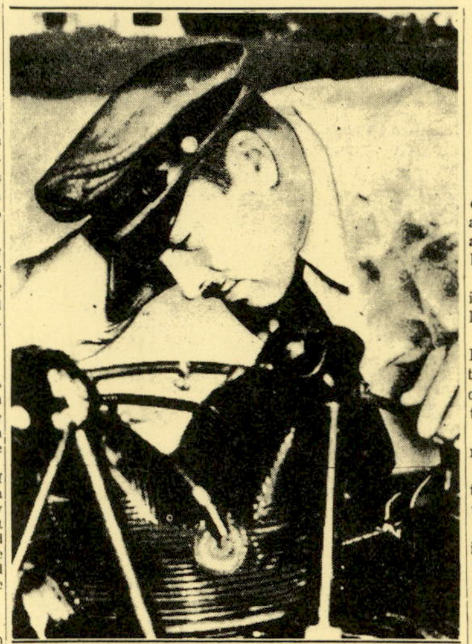

HUNTING FOR TROUBLE

Col. Roscoe Turner, who crashed yesterday in New Mexico, shown looking for motor trouble after he narrowly missed crashing at the airport Saturday. Times photo

U.S.S. Kane Returns Fire; Hull Warns Both Sides at Order of Roosevelt

WASHINGTON, Aug. 30. (AP)—An American destroyer—the U.S.S. Kane—was the target for six bombs from an unidentified monoplane off the coast of Spain today, and tonight a protest was being prepared for dispatch to both the Spanish government and the Spanish rebels.

The destroyer was not hit. It fired nine rounds from its anti-aircraft guns but the airplane flew away apparently without harm.

President Roosevelt by long distance telephone from Rapid City, S. D., directed Secretary of State Hull to frame the protests. The incident was brought to the attention of both participants in the civil war in Spain immediately through the American Embassy at Madrid.

Secretary Hull was at work tonight drafting formal representations.

The State Department said both sides will be asked to "issue instructions in the strongest terms" to both sides to "prevent another incident of this character."

The department made it plain it considered the bombing the result of mistaken identity of the American ship.

"Since both the government forces and the opposing forces in Spain in the friendliest spirit have made every possible effort to avoid injury to American nationals and American property," the department's statement said, "it can only be assumed that the attack on the United States destroyer Kane was due to its identity having been mistaken by a plane of one faction for a vessel of the other."

AMERICAN STATEMENT

The Department's statement:

"The United States destroyer Kane left Gibraltar at 8:12 August 30 en route to Bilbao, Spain, to assist in the work of evacuating American nationals from Spain. It will be recalled that since the inception of the present conflict in Spain, the American government has repeatedly urged all American nationals to proceed from Spain to places of safety and has provided vessels to remove them from Spanish ports.

"According to a report from the commanding officer of the United States destroyer Kane, at 4:10 p.m., (Spanish time,) August 30, at 36 degrees, 33 minutes north, 7 degrees, 35 minutes west, approximately forty miles off the Spanish coast, an unidentified tri-motored, low-winged monoplane flew over the Kane and dropped two bombs which exploded near the vessel.

FLIES AMERICAN FLAG

"The Kane, which was flying the American flag at her fore-mast head and in addition had an American ensign horizontal on top of the well deck awning, increased her speed to maneuver away from the plane.

"At 4:25 the plane again flew over the Kane and dropped a third bomb. At 4:26 the Kane's anti-aircraft gun fired two rounds in the direction of the plane.

"At 4:32 the plane again flew over the Kane and dropped three more bombs, making a total of six, none of which struck the Kane nor caused any damage to her.

"The Kane's anti-aircraft gun fired nine rounds in the direction of the plane during its approach and retreat.

IMPARTIAL ATTITUDE

"The attitude of the American government in respect to the unfortunate conflict in Spain is

Turn to Page 2, Column 3

Duce Gives War Warning to World

AVELLINO (Italy) Aug. 30. Italy's Mussolini warned a rearming world tonight he can mobilize 8,000,000 soldiers in the course of a few hours and after a simple order.

Speaking from this heart of mimic war to his fighting men and his people, the dictator rejected what he called "the absurdity of eternal peace," declared his army was sharpened by its African victory, and proclaimed:

"We must be strong! We must be always stronger! We must be so strong that we can face any eventualities and look directly in the eye whatever may befall!"

Il Duce stressed that Italy desires to live in peace and pledged "our lasting, concrete, contribution to the project of collaboration among peoples."

REARMING RACE

But he told the thousands who cheered him to the echo in Avellino's municipal square that the world is in the throes of an "irresistible" rearmament race.

He did not mention the six weeks' civil war in Spain, between a Socialist government and a revolting Fascist army.

But he did, just after declaring Italy must reject the idea of "eternal" peace—"foreign to our creed and to our temperament"—speak of "certain political situations which now are in the course of uncertain developments."

The armed forces of Italy (es-

Turn to Page 2, Column 3

County Tax Rate Raised to $1.27 for Each $100

Los Angeles county's final budget for 1936-37 carrying a figure for proposed expenditures that will necessitate a basic tax rate of $1.27 on each $100 of assessed valuation, 8 cents higher than last year, was adopted by the Board of Supervisors shortly before midnight last night, the time limit in which action could be taken.

As the budget stands after an analysis by a force of accountants in County Auditor Payne's department, the total to be raised by taxation is approximately $28,500,000. On top of this figure is approximately $19,000,000 more, this amount being paid in various revenues received by the county throughout the year.

The 8 cents increase over the $1.19 rate of last year is due primarily to two items. One item was the sum of $1,500,000 which had to be set up to meet a judgment recently obtained by school districts against the county for interest on school deposits held in trust by the County Treasurer. The court held the county had no right to use of the interest money and awarded the districts judgment.

Another item is that of $500,000 which had to be inserted in the budget to meet the expense of the coming general election in November.

These two items increase the figures of the final budget of last year $2,000,000. As each 4 cents of the tax rate represents $1,000,000, the increase of 8 cents is reflected in the two items.

The Board of Supervisors has tentatively agreed upon a 20-cent rate for the County Flood Control District, an increase of 1 cent over last year. The county library rate of 5 cents will remain unchanged.

The rates for the county, Flood Control district, library and school districts will be fixed by the board tomorrow.

After numerous conferences and hearings during the past week, the last one lasting all day

Turn to Page 2, Column 6

Head-on Auto Crash Takes Four Lives

MICHIGAN CITY (Ind.) Aug. 30. (AP) — Four persons were killed and six injured ten miles east of here today when two automobiles crashed head-on as they approached the top of a hill. The dead were: Orange W. Barrett, 43 years of age of Fort Wayne; Mrs. Maude Barrett, 40, his wife; Ray Reitter, 25, and Sarabelle Boltz, 23, of Chicago.

Six Chicago young people suffered critical injuries and were taken to a Laporte hospital. Attaches expressed a belief that Mary O'Brien, 21, and Alice Kuhn, 22, were dying.

Fiery Plane Kills One and Hurts Three

NEW YORK, Aug. 30. (AP)—A private plane crashed in flames in the midst of a group of Sunday picnickers today at Ferris Point, Long Island Sound, killing one woman and injuring three other persons.

The plane was destroyed by fire but two occupants escaped injury.

Sylvia Salmi, 29 years of age, of Manhattan, was killed.

In the plane were Herbert S. Ross of the Bronx, a commercial pilot, and Robert Bequiest of the Bronx, a student flyer.

Korean Typhoon Leaves 1104 Dead and 426 Missing

TOKIO (Monday) Aug. 31. (U.P.)—The Korean government announced today that 1104 persons were killed by a typhoon which struck Southern Korea Saturday. In addition, 1028 persons were injured and 426 were reported missing.

The gale has subsided and rivers are receding. All foreigners were believed safe.

Second Lightning Bolt Burns Barn

STERLING (Ill.) Aug. 30. (Exclusive)—Thursday night lightning struck the Frank Hinckel barn near Mount Carroll with little damage. Last night lightning again struck the barn and this time it was destroyed by fire.

APPEAL VOICED BY POPE PIUS

Prayers of Pilgrims Urged to Save World

CASTEL GANDOLFO (Italy) Aug. 30. (AP)—Pope Pius XI urged a group of pilgrims tonight to pray "lest the continued atrocities of men" result in a "grave affliction for Godless humanity."

Speaking to thirty Italians who came to pay him homage, the Pope, weakened by worry over the Spanish war, thanked them for coming to see "the father who not only grows older but is, indeed, old."

His seventy-nine years, he said, "are an imposing number and provoke many preoccupations."

After chatting briefly with the pilgrims, the Holy Father turned sadly to the theme which has harassed him in recent weeks.

"We thank you for your promises to continue your prayers, of which we have need with such menaces clouding the horizon; such a reason to hope for the mercy of God but also to fear—with the continued atrocities of man—lest menaces against God produce grave afflictions for Godless humanity."

SPOKANE MARKS STREET CAR'S PASSING TODAY

SPOKANE (Wash.) Aug. 30. (AP) — Spokane tomorrow will celebrate the ending of street railway traffic here.

The high light of the program will be the public burning of one of the last of the rattling trolley cars.

Soviet Troops Spurn Orders in Passive Rebellion

MOSCOW, Aug. 30. (Exclusive)—A passive revolt among Red army troops at Rizan who refused to obey their officers today added to the unrest resulting from the government's ever widening purge of anti-Stalin elements and persons formerly connected with Leon Trotzky, exiled Red army head.

The disobedience movement was quickly "reduced" by army authorities, it was reported. Reports continued to reach Moscow, however, of open anti-government agitation by peasants in the Ukraine, where troops are said to have received extremely severe orders to stamp out the protests.

Rizan, about 200 miles from the capital, is a peat center where troops were rushed recently to fight fires in the peat fields. Many victims were taken by the fires.

The government tonight arrested an undisclosed number of functionaries and civil workers in Moscow and the provinces as a result of the "Trotzky trial" at which sixteen persons were executed after being convicted of plotting to set up a "regime of terror."

ROOSEVELT DEDICATES HUGE MEMORIAL TO JEFFERSON

RAPID CITY (S. D.) Aug. 30. (AP)—Amid the Black Hills of South Dakota President Roosevelt today dedicated the Thomas Jefferson figure on the lofty Mount Rushmore Memorial, a monument which he said "can be an inspiration for continuation of a democratic-republican form of government, not only in our country, but, we hope, throughout the world."

From a valley far below the huge memorial, where the busts of Washington, Jefferson, Lincoln and Theodore Roosevelt are being hewn from a rocky cliff, he saw five thundering blasts of dynamite send tons of rock hurtling down the mountainside.

He saw a seventy-foot American flag drawn from the half-completed figure of the third

Turn to Page 5, Column 1

Alfonso's Son Reported Better

NEW YORK, Aug. 30. (AP)—Physicians attending the Count of Covadonga, former Crown Prince of Spain, reported today he spent a comfortable night at Presbyterian Hospital where he has been a patient since last Wednesday. Suffering from hemophilia, the Count was taken to the hospital after a hemorrhage that followed the lancing of a boil.

IN THE 'TIMES' TODAY

MONDAY, AUGUST 31, 1936

REMEMBER THIS

Dictators sprout from the forcing beds of mass stupidity.

OBSERVATIONS

By Irvin S. Cobb

SANTA MONICA, Aug. 30. Local travel bureaus report an increase of incoming tourists. But then again on the other hand, part of it may be due to returning residents who went hurriedly away when the papers started printing a certain romantic diary. If your sins do not always find you out at least they frequently find you getting out.

It's all over now and peace and quiet have been restored to our home-circles, but at the height of the rush one involuntarily was reminded of the ancient story of the Frenchman who bet with his friend he could prove every man, however outwardly pure, had a dreaded secret in his life. So, to test it, he sent to each of the ten most respected notables in Paris an anonymous telegram reading as follows: "All is discovered. Flee at once."

And, next morning, nine of them were gone and the tenth had committed suicide.

But, of course, that was just pure fiction. It couldn't happen here.

IRVIN S. COBB.

The first 'streamlined' paper to win the Ayer Cup, the *Los Angeles Times* (1936).

The interesting point about this last contention, of course, is that it raises a question of American newspaper practice which continues to be of importance. This is the increase of body size and/or the increased leading of newspaper text; in its turn this arose from the large x-height of the 'Legibility Group' of text types. Whereas British newspaper text designers like Walter Tracy sought to produce texts with sufficient interlinear white to enable them to be set solid, the Americans were content to treat big-on-the-body faces to extra leading; this was a luxury possible given American paging but scarcely practical under British conditions of newsprint economy.

This sort of text change was also a feature of the biggest Allen success of those days – the 'streamlining' of the mighty *Los Angeles Times* in the latter part of 1936. The Los Angeles paper increased its body size to 8pt (in Paragon, a late member of the 'Legibility Group') which was set on a 9pt slug. Headline style was in modern sans – Erbar and Metro, set flush-left. The paper's restyling was master-minded by Gilbert P. Farrar, an ex-compositor from Virginia (nicknamed 'the Deacon') who had turned to lecturing on typography and acting as a typographic adviser to advertising agencies; at the material time he was a consultant to the American Typefounders Co. Farrar, who went on to re-design around sixty newspapers, starting with the Scripps-Howard Ohio daily, the *Toledo News-Bee*, was a first-rate executant of the general line propounded by Allen. Twenty years later he was retained as a newspaper design consultant by the Mergenthaler Linotype Co. and in 1955 conducted a series of one-week seminars all over the U.S. on newspaper typography and make-up.

After the *Los Angeles Times* revolution a California publisher drew the lesson: 'Throw away the old condensed head letters, buy or use some of the open faces now in the shop, get larger body type, whiten up all the pages. Give readers a new, readable product.' And the year after the change, 1937, the *Times* achieved the supreme accolade of first prize in the annual Ayer Award. From that moment the Allen revolution never looked back. Allen himself linked the graphic changes with the whole question of departmentalising and summarising the news, so as to make it assimilable by a modern reader.[9]

7: War – and Peace – Again

The outbreak of the Second World War in September 1939 soon had an effect on British newspapers – more particularly the London nationals – that was both dramatic and traumatic. The British Press has long lived on substantial imports of newsprint; wartime's early, and severe, rationing of this basic raw material limited the mass-circulation 'popular' daily papers to four pages broadsheet (eight tabloid), with double that allowance for Sunday papers. This austerity did not end with the cessation of hostilities; it continued until 1946, and newsprint was not fully freed until the 1950s. In many ways the effect of these rigid restrictions was long felt; they certainly brought new precision working in British newspaper make-up, with the general introduction of accurate inch-scaled miniature page make-up sheets.

Since the 1890s the standard format of the broadsheet daily had been seven 13½-pica columns, usually with 8pt as the basic text size. This now changed to eight columns, usually in 7pt (the trend back to 8pt did not become marked until the late 1950s). Initially the eight-column page was based on an 11½-pica measure but there were later reductions to 11¼-picas and 11-picas. This reduction continued even after the war, when it was no longer a question of rationing but of continuous rises in newsprint price. It is evident that, for multi-million sale papers, a saving of a quarter of a pica a column, or two picas in the width of an eight-column page, adds up to a considerable annual tonnage of newsprint.

Many provincial papers went over to a nine-column page, with measures of around 10-picas; this remained after the war, and indeed the practice extended to papers which had hitherto stuck to their eight columns. The pressure here was economic; to increase the number of columns, and reduce the column measure, makes the advertiser pay more for his space. Mention has already been made of the wartime tabloid change to a seven-column page, which in the case of the *Daily Mirror* format meant a 9-pica column. To the extra-column trend now described there was one notable exception – *The Times*, which retained its seven-column make-up until April 1967, well after the Thomson takeover; up to that late date the only change made by *The Times* in column measure was to drop it from 14-picas to 13½-picas when it was able to return to a more generous column rule after a war-enforced reduction to the over-narrow 5pts.

The desire to economise in newsprint by savings in reel-width was a prime factor in inducing a general reduction in column rule widths. From the pre-war norm of 6pt many papers dropped to as little as 3pt; such a rule is too thin for satisfactory working or appearance and the three-pointers soon found it necessary to indent matter each end to avoid lateral overcrowding and consequent discomfort in reading. The same wartime departure from 6pt column rule was widespread in America, where some papers dropped below even 3pts to 2pt and 1pt column rules; rules of these last two bodies had to be made of steel, since type-metal so thin would be quite impracticable, and in any event papers using them were forced from the start to indent matter not less than 3pts each end to get a tolerable reading effect. The same result would have been achieved by retaining normal-width rules and setting to a narrower measure.

The drastic cuts in paging had a number of other typographic repercussions. A four-page paper was compelled to put news on its front page; so the *Daily Mail* succumbed, leaving *The Times* (until May 1966) as the only national with the antique front page of advertising. In November 1939, when the *Yorkshire Post* absorbed the *Leeds Mercury*, it went over to a news front page, though the other big regional dailies followed suit more slowly, the process taking ten years or so after the end of the war. The *Birmingham Post* changed over in 1946, followed by the *Manchester Guardian*, as the *Guardian* then still was (1952), the *Scotsman* (1957) and the *Glasgow Herald* (1958).*

Considerable impetus was given to the already marked development of upper- and lower-case styles for headlines. In addition to the claim of increased legibility the space-saving value of lower-case was obviously in its favour when two lines of lower-case display could easily cover the wordage of three lines of capitals. From this period, too, may be dated the appreciation, now all but universal, of the additional space-saving virtues of the even lower-case style for headings, as well as logical consistency and ease of reading. It is hardly necessary to rehearse here the arguments for the 'all down' lower-case headline style; it simply transfers to display the normal style of lower-case text – namely, that capitalisation is reserved for the opening word and for proper names. Here it may be noted that many American papers have resisted the complete 'down-style', contending that the opening word of each line of a heading should always be capitalised, to avoid an uneven look.

In two other respects wartime space-saving brought significant changes. One was in the style of page folios, or running heads. For these the standard style had long been either the title of the paper centred, with the date and the page number full out right or left as the case might be; or the title centred with the date and the page number full out at opposite ends, the whole line cut off with a full rule. In the years immediately before the war this style had begun to be modified for the feature pages, with the substitution of the 'open' style; that is to say, running the title with the date and the page number in double-column or less, full out right or left, and thus freeing the rest of the page from the constricting effect of the full rule across the top. This 'open' style now took over on news pages. The second change was in the style of the title-piece; aimed at saving space, this turned out to be the first serious blow to the blackletter tradition since Morison's 'romanising' of *The Times* title in 1932.

In July 1942 the *Daily Express* (and its Sunday stablemate) dropped the blackletter title, from which it had already removed the traditional, but unauthorised and superfluous, Royal arms, in favour of the line in roman capitals, designed by Morison, retained up until 1973. Morison himself described his *Express* title as a 'super-fatted and extended Perpetua', which is as good a description as can be given. Commenting further on his ideas in prescribing the new *Express* title he said: 'It should be black. And Simple. White lettering on a stippled ground shaded, shadowed, interlined or anything "featuresome" should be avoided'.[1] Between them, the *Daily Mail*, the *Daily*

* When the *Manchester Guardian* put news on the front page the old Cheltenham Bold/Transit headline formula was dropped in favour of a straight Century Bold decker style. The title was changed from blackletter to 42pt Perpetua Bold Titling, deleting the definite article. The Perpetua style, suitably increased in size, remained after the removal of 'Manchester' and the move to London in 1960; in 1969 it was changed to the present bolder and blunter hand-lettering.

▼ In 1942 the *Daily Express* dropped its blackletter title for this Morison design, partly as a wartime space-saver.

DAILY EXPRESS

No. 13,149 MONDAY JULY 20 1942 Black-out 10.52 p.m. to 5.21 a.m. One Penny

RUSSIA: Red troops retreat in south, fighting desperate rearguard actions while main army gets back to the Don

VOROSHILOVGRAD EVACUATED

Germans break through: Bock is driving on Rostov

MOSCOW announced in this morning's communiqué that the industrial city

While Soviet rearguards are fighting ferocious actions at close quarters to slow up the German advance, the main Russian forces are withdrawing in good order to the line of the Don, where they can make a determined stand

More News

THERE is more news than ever in the Daily Express today.

The old-fashioned typography of our title has been abandoned. In its place a bold but economical design appears.

More advertisements have been sacrificed, the size of headline types has been reduced, and other economies have been effected in the general lay-out and display.

Our readership, which is the largest in the world, will approve these developments in modern newspaper technique.

EGYPT: Auchinleck wins new ground

BIG ROMMEL SWITCH OVER

Troops in south withdrawn for centre battle

Express War Reporter ALAN MOOREHEAD

EIGHTH ARMY DESERT HEADQUARTERS, Sunday.

ROMMEL has been forced back to positions he occupied a fortnight ago—three days before the battle of Alamein began. His line, which once stretched 40 miles down from the coast to the Qattara Depres-

Herald and the *News Chronicle* failed to avoid this trap. When the *Express* introduced the new title it ran a promotion panel, headed 'More News', which specifically stressed the 'economical design' of the title. In comparison with the old blackletter it saved three-quarters of an inch right across the page, no fewer than 36 picas or over 60 lines in 7pt of single-column matter; in those days of fighting for every line of text this was an appreciable item.

As for the headline typography of individual newspapers under wartime stress and strain, *The Times* (as the previous chapter has indicated) adhered firmly to its revolutionised 1932 style. This served the paper well, with little more than minor changes in spacing, until 1966. The roman title-piece which had created such a furore in 1932 was reduced in depth and then (in 1953) displaced by an elegant new design, both of the title itself and the attendant Royal arms, by Reynolds Stone. The other change was the introduction in June 1951 of the space-saving $4\frac{3}{4}$pt size of Times Roman, nicknamed Claritas, in place of the original $5\frac{1}{2}$pt, for the classifieds, sports results, long lists of names, City prices and the like. Somewhat rounder and less condensed than Times Roman in its normal sizes, Claritas was the first effective micro-size of the kind for machine composition. Yielding 15 lines to the column inch it rapidly attracted attention far beyond Printing House Square. Space-starved publishers eagerly seized upon this new means of increasing their intake of lucrative 'smalls'. By the mid-1950s a number of leading London and provincial dailies were setting their classifieds in $4\frac{3}{4}$pt Claritas.

Here a brief excursus seems necessary, though it carries us forward to the end of the period covered by the present chapter. The extensive use of $4\frac{3}{4}$pt Claritas for 'smalls' setting soon gave rise to complaints. It was the old story of Times Roman, made more acute by the micro-size; namely, that the presswork and paper of Printing House Square was one thing, the fast running and common newsprint of ordinary dailies (especially the rush-produced evenings) quite another. Publishers were torn between their gratification over the financial returns of 15-lines-to-the-inch and their unease over the blurred look of the Claritas in their classified pages.

At this point the eyes of London newspaper advertising men began to be attracted by examples of practices that had developed in America. U.S. papers had discovered the virtues of small-size sanserifs for the mini-type items like Stock Exchange prices, sports tables, classifieds. One such type was Bell Gothic, a highly-condensed but very clear telephone directory face (as its name implies); this, however, was not made below 6pt, which in view of its condensation could in any event be regarded as its smallest practical size. Another was Spartan Book with Bold; this was a normally-proportioned light weight of the most popular Mergenthaler Linotype sans. Its square-ish aspect stood a reduction to $5\frac{1}{2}$pt, the traditional agate of American newspaper advertising; in this size it won wide popularity in the States for 'smalls' pages. In the latter part of the 1950s it was seen and admired by the classified advertising manager of the London *Evening News*, one of the dissatisfied users of Claritas. The *Evening News* promptly demanded Spartan Book, but in $4\frac{3}{4}$pt. An automatic reduction of this kind was not possible, so an adapted and revised design had to be undertaken. This was done for the British Linotype organisation by its designer, Walter Tracy; the $4\frac{3}{4}$pt that resulted was christened Adsans. Installed by the *Evening News* in 1959 it was soon adopted by other $4\frac{3}{4}$pt users and was flattered by imitation. The *Evening Standard*, also a Claritas user, was not to be outdone by its London competitor. It commissioned a similar $4\frac{3}{4}$pt sans from Intertype; but Standard Gothic, as the type was named, did not prove a satisfactory imitation and had a short life on the *Standard*.*

Returning now to wartime developments in headline typography, the mass-circulation 'populars' afforded some significant contrasts. Christiansen's Century revolution in the *Express* (and its emulation

DICTAPHONE TYPISTS required by a City Insurance firm. Salary according to ability. Luncheon vouchers. 5-day week. Permanent progressive posts. Box 5122.
DIC/T'S £11 up & 10-5 p.m. £10 up! St. Paul's Ag., 35 Copthall-av. **NAT 9494.**
DIE CASTING TOOLMAKER for Pressure & Gravity Dies. Immediate vacancy. Top rates. Phone or call A. B. & D. F. Ltd., 14 Gaskin-st., N.1. CAN 7141.
DIESEL FITTER required to look after maintenance bay for a fleet of 20 commercial vehicles. Write, giving full details of experience and salary required—Dock & General Transport Co., 74-82 Carnwath-road, Fulham, S.W.6.
DINING ROOM MAID required. Resident Post. Salary £7 1s 3d for 44-hour week less £2 11s 2d residential charges. Extra pay for split duties and Sunday working. Apply to Catering Officer, Royal National Orthopaedic Hospital, Bracknell, Berks.
AUST TAXIS, pet-dsl, low deps. BRI 5404.
AUST 12 '39, clean. £45. WOO 2550.
ESTATE CARS LTD., THE UTILITY SPECIALISTS. To buy or sell an estate car consult us the foremost name in estate cars in the country. 100 always in stock. 221 Upper Richmond-rd, Putney, S.W.15.

* From Standard Gothic the *Evening Standard* went for a time to 5pt Ionic for its classifieds, eventually returning to $4\frac{3}{4}$pt in the shape of Maximus.

in the *Mail*) proved entirely adequate to the strident demands of the war news. All that was needed was some adaptation, some development in terms of the established style – mainly through a generally freer handling, the extension of strapline treatment over main headings, the increasing use of the sans 'kicker'. The *Mail* did not follow the *Express* in abandoning its blackletter title (indeed, it never has); it tried a reverse version for a while and later had more than one re-drawing, including the simplification of the Royal arms, to which it still clings, alone among national mornings.* During the war the *Mail* tried a more sensational-looking presentation of major news, using large condensed gothic lower-case; after the war it dropped the practice, as it had dropped the condensed sans capitals of its Boer War deckers. Partly, no doubt, because of difficulties at that time in importing Ludlow matrices, the *Mail* was wont to draw on large sizes of founders' type. Thus in 1945, lacking the Ludlow Century Bold Extended it later acquired, it set the double banner on the Hiroshima atomic bomb story in the Bold Expanded capitals of Winchester, Stephenson Blake's curious Edwardian imitation of Cheltenham.

A founders' type banner (Winchester Bold Expanded) in the *Daily Mail* of 1945.
▶

Daily Mail

NO. 15,367 ONE PENNY • FOR KING AND EMPIRE TUESDAY, AUGUST 7, 1945

Most terrifying weapon in history: Churchill's warning

'THIS revelation of the secrets of nature, long mercifully withheld from man, should arouse the most solemn reflections in the mind and conscience of every human being capable of comprehension. We must indeed pray that these awful agencies will be made to conduce to peace among the nations, and that instead of wreaking measureless havoc upon the entire globe they may become a perennial fountain of world prosperity.' SEE BELOW.

ATOMIC BOMB: JAPS GIVEN 48 HOURS TO SURRENDER

Radios threaten Tokio: 'You can expect annihilation'

From JAMES BROUGH, Daily Mail Correspondent New York, Monday Night.

JAPAN is faced with obliteration by the new British-American atomic bomb—mightiest destructive force the world has ever known—unless she surrenders unconditionally in a few days.

Already Japan has felt the terrible effects of one of the bombs. Now she is threatened with being blown out of the Pacific. Soon after President Truman had released the sensational news of the atomic bomb this afternoon, reliable sources here said that a new ultimatum is to be sent to Japan.

ATOMIC POWER CAN CHANGE THE WORLD—OR DESTROY IT. By John Langdon-Davies PAGE TWO

ATOM BOMB CHIEF

IMPENETRABLE SMOKE

HIDDEN IN URANIUM

ATOM DECISION AT POTSDAM?

ZERO HOUR CAME ON JULY 16

Blind girl 'saw' the first big flash

Steel into gas

The risks

THEY TOIL IN SECRET CITIES

Their brains helped in the great search

FIRST VICTIM

CHURCHILL TELLS BRITAIN'S PART

Spies and commandos in battle of wits

WE BEAT NAZIS BY FEW MONTHS

Scientists' race

BRITAIN'S part in the atomic bomb researches, her ceaseless watch on German preparations along similar lines, and her Commando attacks against enemy plants in Norway were described in a statement from 10, Downing-street last night.

Began in 1939

JAP TOWN IS WIPED OUT

STALIN ON POTSDAM

'U 235' What it can do

The war and post-war typography of the *News Chronicle* and the *Daily Herald* was a very different story. Both papers were nearing the slippery slope which was to end with the demise of the *News Chronicle* (and its evening stablemate *The Star*) in 1960 and of the *Herald* in

* The *Daily Mail's* monarchist leanings were always pronounced. In 1926 it put up the line 'For King and Country' under its title, later changing this to 'For King and Empire' and finally to 'For Queen and Commonwealth'. The slogan disappeared with the changeover to tabloid format in 1971.

NEWS CHRONICLE, Saturday, July 6 1940

News Chronicle

No. 29,382 ONE PENNY SATURDAY, JULY 6, 1940 RADIO, PAGE 2 * POSTAGE IN U.K. .. 1½d ALL PLACES OUTSIDE UNITED KINGDOM .. 1d

Petain Government Breaks With Britain

By the Diplomatic Correspondent

THE Pétain Government of France has broken off diplomatic relations with Great Britain.

This was officially confirmed at Vichy, seat of the Pétain Government, yesterday afternoon, after reports of the rupture had come from Berlin and several other German-controlled sources.

Up to a late hour last night, however, no notification of the severance of relations had been received at the Foreign Office.

Nor had the French Embassy in London received any communication on the subject from the French Government, though it was pointed out that there is now considerable delay—often as long as twenty-four hours—in receiving cables from France. There is no disposition in French circles to doubt the truth of the reports.

During the afternoon, M.

British

BRITISH SAILORS ABOARD THE FRENCH WARSHIPS

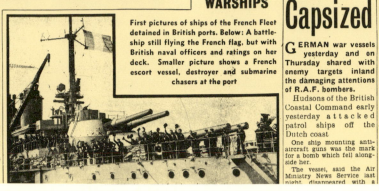

First pictures of ships of the French Fleet detained in British ports. Below: A battleship still flying the French flag, but with British naval officers and ratings on her deck. Smaller picture shows a French escort vessel, destroyer and submarine chasers at the port

German Ship is Capsized

GERMAN war vessels yesterday and on Thursday shared with enemy targets inland the damaging attentions of R.A.F. bombers.

Hudsons of the British Coastal Command early yesterday attacked patrol ships off the Dutch coast

One ship mounting anti-aircraft guns was the mark for a bomb which fell alongside her.

The vessel, said the Air Ministry News Service last night, disappeared with a

S. COAST BAN EXTENDED 100 MILES

Hants, Dorset: Not Brighton

FOUR far-reaching decisions in connection with the defence of Britain were announced yesterday.

They are:

1 The coastline and 20 miles inland from Hastings to Dorset has been declared a Defence area, extending the existing banned area by over 100 miles.

2 Regional Commissioners are, in emergency, to have absolute power to prohibit or curtail road traffic everywhere.

3 The flying of kites and balloons is forbidden. Signals by kites are believed to have greatly aided the enemy in Holland and Belgium.

4 Regulations, which may include a partial moratorium, are to be made for the relief of distress in evacuation areas.

In the extended defence area it is expected that the three Regional Commissioners concerned will shortly give directions limiting movement

NEWS CHRONICLE, Wednesday, Nov. 27, 1946

News Chronicle

No. 31,363 WEDNESDAY, NOVEMBER 27, 1944 ONE PENNY

LATE LONDON EDITION

Latest U.S. day raid concentrated on aircraft factories

BRUNSWICK WAS AGAIN MAIN TARGET

By RONALD WALKER
News Chronicle Air Correspondent

HUNDREDS of bombers and fighters concluded a continuous 48-hour offensive against the Germans in Western Europe when heavies of the United States Strategic Air Force again struck yesterday at military targets in Germany.

American headquarters announced at midnight that "very strong forces of heavy U.S. bombers escorted by almost equally strong formations of fighters attacked aircraft factories at Brunswick and major aerodromes with repair depots in North-West Germany.

"Nearly as many aircraft were employed in this second successive day of major offensive as participated in the assault on units of the German fighter aircraft industry on Sunday.

"Two airframe component factories at Brunswick which were badly damaged on Sunday were again attacked. Targets at Hanover and several large aircraft parks and other military installations near the Netherlands border were also attacked.

"Among the aerodromes were those at Bramsche, Ingen, Vechte, Quakenbruck, Diepholz and Ahlhorn.

"Our fighters shot down 33 enemy aircraft. Fifteen of our

The fall in fighters

It is estimated in Washington that German fighter output is down to 500 to 600 a month, insufficient to cover battle losses.

Estimates are based on the Eighth Air Force review for 1943 and a statement by Gen. Henry Arnold, Commander of the United States Army Air Forces, that the week-end raids had cut output by one-quarter.

Last October Gen. Arnold estimated German fighter production at 1,020 and only 880 in September.

STREET BATTLES

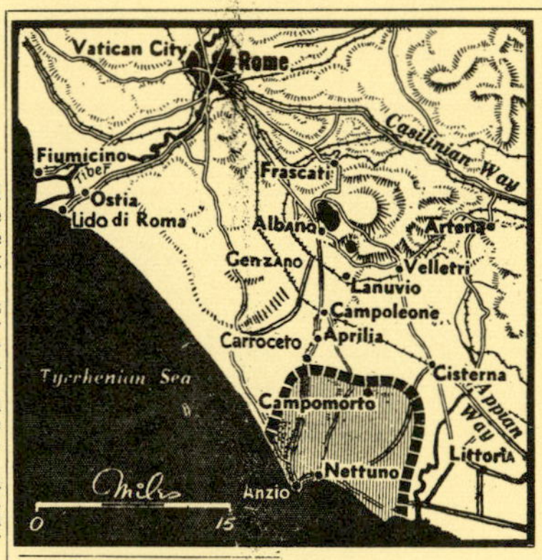

In London Tubes last

Nazi groups cut off at Anzio

COUNTER-ATTACKS BY ALLIED TANKS

BRITISH and U.S. armoured units have made penetrations in the Anzio bridgehead area and cut off German battle groups.

This was admitted in a broadcast last night from Berlin by the German war reporter, Lutz Koch.

He added the usual claim that German positions had been restored by counter-attacks.

This admission followed reports from different sources that the fighting had flared up in the past 24 hours and reached a new peak of violence.

Another Berlin report on the battle said that thousands of Allied guns had been pounding the German positions.

Lt.-Gen. Jacob Devers, Deputy C.-in-C., Mediterranean Forces, and Commander of the U.S. Forces in the bridgehead area, made this comment on the fighting: "Things look all right here: everybody is keen to get at those Germans — and that's the spirit that wins.

"It does not look as though

Nazis were pounded

PAASIKIVI HAS SOVIET TERMS

—Report

From Our Own Correspondent

STOCKHOLM, Monday.

PAASIKIVI is returning to Finland with Russia's armistice demands, it is reported here tonight.

The eventual conditions for peace between Russia and Finland are also said to have been discussed.

Paasikivi is still in Stockholm,

LATE NEWS

NEWS CHRONICLE

No. 32,298 FRIDAY, DECEMBER 2, 1949 ONE PENNY

LORDS: *Minister of Civil Aviation makes an apology and then counter-attacks his critics*

COMMONS: *Barnes defends Transport Commission, says long-term policies will end railway losses*

PAKENHAM STICKS TO IT

Resignation is demanded by Tory and Liberal peers

'TO RESTORE CONFIDENCE'

By E. CLEPHAN PALMER, the Parliamentary Correspondent

FACED in the Lords last night with demands for his resignation, Lord Pakenham, Minister of Civil Aviation, apologised for the way in which he made public his dissent from the findings of the court of inquiry into the Prestwick air disaster, but otherwise was quite unrepentant.

Instead of appearing in a white sheet, he counter-attacked his critics vigorously.

He claimed that he had the support of the aviation world in his refusal to accept the verdict of the inquiry that the ground staff was at fault.

He challenged the charge, put from Conservative and Liberal benches, that he had gravely shaken confidence, which could only be restored if he left his office

A SHIP OF THE LINE

H.M.S. Implacable, 152-year-old relic of Trafalgar, towed past the carrier Vengeance out of Portsmouth Harbour yesterday towards her last resting place on the sea bed

Bank gunmen snatch £17,600

News Chronicle Reporter

A FAT man with a revolver was among bandits who snatched £17,600 in workers' wages from the doorway of a bank yesterday.

The armed bandits' haul from the Commercial Bank, Motherwell, was almost the whole of the weekly wages withdrawal for Colville's Lanarkshire steel works.

Hugh Richardson, the firm's cashier, and Stewart Young, the security officer, were leaving with a two-handed bag between them when two men in dark raincoats rushed at them.

Grabbed bag

One stood back with a revolver covering them, while the other snatched the bag.

Then both raiders ran to a waiting car—which had false number plates—and were driven away.

1964, a date a good deal later than might have been anticipated, given the paper's lack of viability. Papers heading for the rocks have a habit of experimenting with their typography, under the delusion that in some magical way a change in form will prove an easy way out of their difficulties and will solve the problem of unappealing content. Sometimes, in an oddly symbolic fashion, the chops and changes were confined to the title-piece. Of this perhaps the most remarkable example was that of the *Daily Mail's* weekend companion, the *Sunday Dispatch* (the old-established *Weekly Dispatch* renamed), which, with several other Sundays, was in a tottering state after the war. Between the spring of 1957 and the autumn of 1958 the *Dispatch* changed its title-line no fewer than seven times. Of these essays five were variants of solid blackletter (up to then the paper had sported the traditional white-lined style), the last two in versions of Times Roman, upper- and lower-case, including a restoration of the Royal arms. The paper folded in 1961.*

◀ The 1940 wartime change of the *News Chronicle* to typefounders' Grot No. 9 and Grot No. 7 was abruptly altered in ◀ 1944 to a Ludlow Bodoni Bold style.

Both the *News Chronicle* and the *Herald* changed not only their title-pieces but the whole of their typography. So far as the title went the *News Chronicle* was the more conservative of the two; it stuck to its blackletter until 1949. Overall depth of the title-piece was reduced from 10 to 6½ picas by using a smaller line and Royal arms and eliminating one folio rule. For a short time the white line of the blackletter was shaded but this odd refinement – which must have perpetually tended to fill in on the run – was soon abandoned. The same risk of filling-in was apparent in the paper's first roman title, which ran from 1949 to 1956; a line of handsome inscriptional capitals was reversed to white on a dark tint ground, the shading being simplified early in 1955. When the paper made a last desperate effort, in 1956, to retrieve its failing fortunes by buying the Manchester *Daily Dispatch* from Lord Kemsley (its hopes of thus adding some 400,000 to its northern circulation proved vain) the unpractical reverse title was dropped. For its closing years the *News Chronicle* had a large upper- and lower-case title, handlettered in what looked like an attempt to produce a lower-case for the 'super-fatted and expanded Perpetua' of Morison's *Express* capitals. It was not a distinguished effort.†

For its wartime headline typography the *News Chronicle* began by seeking to strengthen its Granby style. It increased its splash headings to 60pt Granby Bold, upper- and lower-case, and introduced some sizes of the heavier Granby Extra Bold. The somewhat mannered Granby still seemed to lack sufficient impact; something harsher was called for. So in the summer of 1940 the paper changed to a scheme proposed by Robert Harling.‡ This provided the necessary punch by a simple arrangement of contrasting weights of sturdy Victorian grotesques, Stephenson Blake's Grot No. 9 and the thinner Grot No. 7. The style was apt for the times, it presented a good weight/colour variation and the paper exploited it well. When the paper installed Ludlows in 1942 it was able to continue the style by substituting the machine's Medium and Condensed Gothic ranges. It came as a considerable surprise when, early in 1944, with the war approaching its final stages, editor Barry carried out what can only be called a typographical *coup de main*. Admitting that they might think it 'too Palladian', which they certainly did, he presented his startled staff with another Harling scheme, a novel and elegant all-Bodoni arrangement. As a battledress for a newspaper the style was, to put it mildly, insufficiently bellicose; a protracted struggle began to escape from Bodoni, which was largely diluted with Gothic and (later) Tempo Heavy italic; at one desperate point in the late 1940s the thoroughly un-newsy Ultra-Bodoni (Bodoni Black) incongruously appeared, in 60pt capitals, as a splash streamer. By the early 1950s Barry had gone and so had Bodoni. The paper experimented variously with Century Bold and Bold Extended, initially in some quite old-fashioned decker arrangements. The appointed end, reached when the paper had a bare five years to live, was the by now hackneyed and unenterprising Fleet

Struggling to escape from the 'Palladian' Bodoni style the *News Chronicle* – changing its title from blackletter to a roman capitals reverse block – even ◀ tried Ultra-Bodoni banners (1949).

* Facsimiles of the whole gamut of *Sunday Dispatch* titles are reproduced in Hutt, *Newspaper Design* (2nd ed.), p. 250.

† In its closing years the *News Chronicle* used the colour seal to present the symbolic figure (in red) of a torchbearer, initially lettered PROGRESS, though the word was later deleted. After the 1960 absorption by the *Daily Mail* that paper somewhat incongruously continued the red torchbearer for a while.

‡ An outstanding typographer and designer, initially in advertising, Robert Harling edited the now legendary journals *Typography* (1936–39) and *Alphabet & Image* (1946–48) launched by the late James Shand. He advised the *Financial Times*, *The Times* (for a short period after the retirement of Morison), Kemsley Newspapers (continuing under Thomson) and has long played an active part in the design of the *Sunday Times*. He edits the glossy *House & Garden* and designed the italic for Stephenson Blake's Grot No. 9 and Grot No. 7 (Narrow Sans italic).

ASK FOR GRENVILLE SHIRTS they're really good

News Chronicle

AND *Daily Dispatch*

No. 35,291 © NEWS CHRONICLE LTD., 1959 MONDAY, AUGUST 24, 1959 PRICE 2½d.

BIG GRANTS FOR SPORT AND ART

Parties vie for young voters

By DAVID WILLIS

WITH an eye on the three and a half million young people who will vote for the first time in the coming General Election, the Conservative and Labour Parties are to make cultural and sporting amenities one of the key issues in their campaigns.

This week the Tories will reveal proposals for extending the arts and youth services and providing vastly increased facilities for sport and outdoor recreations.

Drama and music

Huge Government grants will be earmarked:

1.—To support the legitimate theatre, music and ballet; to improve and extend art galleries and museums and libraries and their collections, so that the demand created by higher education can be met adequately.

2.—To provide athletics, Soccer, Rugby, tennis, cricket and swimming with playing and training facilities on a scale which could put Britain back into the forefront of world sport.

3.—To help youth services and organisations like the Scouts and Guides to cater for an increasing number of youngsters and provide an outlet for their energies and enthusiasm.

Labour's plan may prove even more ambitious, but there is great unhappiness in the Labour Party that the Tories should be first in the field and publish their ideas when most of Transport House is away on holiday.

The manifestoes of both parties will stress the need to create conditions under which the young can best avail themselves of the opportunities for relaxation offered by shorter hours, higher wages and better living standards.

Labour, aware of the need to recruit the young—there are six and a half million voters in their twenties—has spent months preparing its 70-page policy document, "Leisure for Living."

Planned in secrecy

The Conservatives, in great secrecy, have rushed their own plans through, had them approved by Mr. R. A. Butler, and will publish them on Thursday.

As proof of Conservative intentions it will be suggested that if no election comes this autumn, then the foundations of their programme will be introduced into Parliament and legislation arranged.

In any event the next Government, whatever its political colour, will be pledged to do more for leisure than any in history.

Mr K sends personal letters to Western leaders

By William Forrest

LETTERS or messages from Mr. Khrushchev have been received by President Eisenhower, President de Gaulle and Chancellor Adenauer.

Reports from Bonn last night said that Mr. Macmillan has also received a letter from the Russian leader, but 10 Downing Street and the Foreign Office refuse to confirm or to deny these reports.

In Paris and Bonn the Khrushchev letter was delivered by the Russian Ambassador.

Ten days ago Mr. Malik, Russian Ambassador in London, called at the Foreign Office at his own request. Mr. Macmillan was then in Yorkshire, and Mr. Selwyn Lloyd had just left for a holiday in Spain.

Mr. Malik was received by Mr. John Profumo, Minister of State, and discussed "matters of mutual interest."

Since then there have been no statements

13 pages

From BONN George Vine telephoned last night: Chancellor Adenauer's letter from Mr. Khrushchev ran to 13 pages, it was officially confirmed today.

GRAND PRIX ESCAPE

Brabham tells of his crash at 100mph

From Alan Brinton

LISBON, Sunday.—Stirling Moss won the Portuguese Grand Prix here today.

It was his first championship victory of the present season.

As he stepped out of the Super Cooper Climax at the end of 210 gruelling miles with the temperature in the 90s, his first words were: "How's Jack?"

Jack Brabham, who writes exclusively for the News Chronicle, had been taken to hospital a third of the way through the race after his car had left the circuit on a right-hand bend and hit a telegraph post when he was lying second.

THIS IS BRABHAM'S OWN VERSION OF THE CRASH:

'Believe me, it's not funny lying in the middle of a race track with a chum bearing down on you at over a hundred miles an hour.

But that's what happened to me this afternoon and I reckon I'm lucky to be back in my hotel with only two grazed knees, a cut finger and a couple of bruises. This is the first real accident I've had, and I don't want another like it.

My Cooper is a nasty mess. John Cooper says it is scrap. There is a neat hole in the front that exactly fits the telegraph pole it hit.

And my crash cost me a useful second place that could virtually have decided the world

JACK BRABHAM

ous part of the whole episode was the drive in the ambulance. That driver was a madman.

He scared me like nothing else as he roared into Lisbon hospital.

They say bad luck comes in cycles of three. I started here by losing my wallet containing £50 at a bullfight. Yesterday I nearly tore off a toe-nail while boating. Now this.

Let's hope that's the end of it, and that the next round of the world championship—at Monza in three weeks—will see a change.

But well done, Stirling. And thanks for pulling up at the pits to tell my wife I was all right.'

Until the crash on the 24th

LATE NEWS

Priest locked out of church

BISHOP SAYS: HE

17 missing on boat trip to

▲ The *News Chronicle* ended its days with a hand-lettered lower-case title and an imitation of the *Express* Century headline style.

Street imitation of the successful *Express* Century formula, not forgetting the Gothic contrast, by way of Christiansen's single-column 'kickers' and otherwise.

While the *News Chronicle's* wartime headline evolution was from sans to Bodoni, that of the *Daily Herald* was from Bodoni to sans. We have already seen that, after the Odhams takeover of 1930, the *Herald* only made one basic change in its editorial display – from Cheltenham in conventional decker headings to a free, streamlined style in Bodoni. This remained the position at the end of its first Odhams decade; but then in the critical summer of 1940 a switch was made to Ludlow Gothics, including Franklin, Square, Condensed. The initial sans style seemed genuinely to have the makings, with its strong lead in large Franklin Gothic upper- and lower-case (which has become so widely popular in our own day) and good colour contrast from the medium-weight Square Gothic and the light Condensed, usually in capitals; the thinner and more condensed capitals of Gothic Headline were also called on. This style, with its distinct originality, did not long survive, however. From 1941 onwards the paper veered between Condensed and Square styles, in capitals, for its main headlines, latterly mainly the Square. The Condensed periods themselves varied from the heavy Medium (including its full-face extension to 84pt, Gothic Bold Condensed Titling) to the light Condensed, which contrived to give an extraordinarily dishevelled look to the front page when run in 72pt capitals as a multi-column multi-liner.

The erratic wartime course pursued by the *Herald* was also, and most strikingly, expressed in the frequent changes of its title-piece. Until the paper's demise in 1964 (that is to say, its transmogrification into the short-lived IPC *Sun*) these title-piece changes, allied to the amazing variations in headline typography that either accompanied them or more often took place between title changes, offered the most extraordinary example of newspaper typographic pathology that has ever been recorded. In June 1940, when the change began, the black-letter title of 1930 gave way to a reverse, white-on-tint title in heavy italic capitals (drawn to link the RA in *Herald*), run as a full-measure title, flanked by two advertising 'ears'. In March 1941 this was changed, presumably to save space, to a two-line double-column block,

"DAILY HERALD," Monday, June 3, 1940

DAILY HERALD

No. 7582 MONDAY, JUNE 3, 1940 ONE PENNY

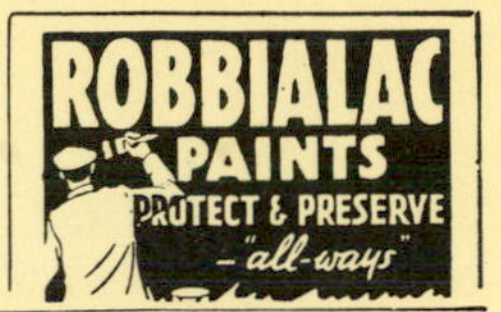

Eight Out Of Ten B.E.F. Men Saved

NAZIS DIE IN DUNKIRK FLOOD

"THANKS to the magnificent and untiring co-operation of the Allied navies and air forces, we have been able to embark and save more than four-fifths of that British Expeditionary Force which the Germans claimed to have surrounded."

This stirring news of the Allies' epic withdrawal from Flanders was broadcast to the world last night by Mr. Anthony Eden, Secretary for War.

"Germany," Mr. Eden said, "has made great strategic gains. The loss to us in equipment and in material has been heavy.

"But there is another side to the picture . . . the bulk of the B.E.F. has been saved."

Mr. Eden [*whose speech is reported on Page 3*] told of troops marching 35 miles in 24 hours; of nine divisions holding an 80-mile front.

"The B.E.F.," he declared, "still exists, not as a handful of fugitives, but as a body of seasoned veterans. . . ."

The withdrawal from Dunkirk was still going on last night. But the speed of evacuation had dropped.

Instead of the thousands who arrived at English ports on Saturday there was only a thin trickle of men, mostly French.

MOST DIFFICULT

This does not mean the withdrawal has ended: it means that the most difficult part of the Navy's job now lies ahead—the getting out of the last few thousand men.

The more troops there are withdrawn from Dunkirk the less the power of resistance of those who are left.

The critical hours of the evacuation are thus approaching.

Messages from Paris this morning say that the Germans have launched a supreme effort to capture Dunkirk, hurling masses of infantry through flood waters in successive attacks.

The infantry are supported by a ring of heavy artillery which now almost surrounds the city.

BEATEN BACK

Wading up to their waists in water, the German troops, in a reckless attempt to cross the flooded areas, are having great gaps mown in their ranks by the defenders' machine-gun fire.

Every man who falls, dead or wounded, immediately disappears beneath the mud and water.

The Germans are using 15 divisions in this onslaught, but, so far, they have been beaten back.

Enemy aircraft have almost flattened Dunkirk in successive bombing raids.

Fires are raging in the port, but the jetty over which thousands of men have walked the last 400 yards to the comparative safety of the ships is still intact.

NAZI ADMISSION

The Nazi forces are reported to be using between 900 and 1,500 planes in the Channel sector.

More than 100 Allied warships and 200 transport vessels are engaged.

The Germans themselves admit that the Allies are still stubbornly resisting.

More units of Gen. Prioux's rearguard have battled their way into Dunkirk.

With them were several detachments of Belgian troops who had scorned King Leopold's order to capitulate.

ENEMY PAYS TRIBUTE TO CALAIS DEFENDERS

FOR a week, a small party of British soldiers and Marines and a few Frenchmen, have held the 17th Century Citadel of Calais against seemingly overwhelming numbers of Germans.

The little garrison is still there this morning, surrounded by the enemy, its only link with home the machines of the R.A.F., which drop provisions, ammunition and water by parachute into the fortress.

Praise was given to the defenders yesterday by both the French and the Germans.

Behind Old Walls

"Fighting against big odds," said the French military spokesman, "they have beaten off all assaults against the walls. It is an exploit worthy of the most heroic examples of siege warfare.

"Having defended the town and port step by step, the detachment withdrew behind the old walls, and is holding off German forces very considerably larger in numbers.

Berlin newspapers, after referring to the "proven tenacity of the Anglo-Saxon race," described the Calais fighting as "the stiffest resistance of the war.

Answer Was "No"

"When the surrender of the Citadel was demanded," the German account continued, "the British commander replied, 'The answer is No!'

"Progress in the attack against the Citadel was slow. Furious fire beat on the Germans.

"Earlier, house by house had to be conquered in the town.

"The Englishmen had made every building a fortress."

In his broadcast last night, Mr. Eden made this reference to the siege:

"We now know, from certain information which we have received, that this gallant defence drew off powerful German mechanised forces which must otherwise have been free to attack the flank of the British Expeditionary Force, at that time dangerously exposed."

Built In 1641

The walls of the Citadel, which stands to the west of the town above the docks—to the right of the Channel steamer berth—have never been modernised since they were built for Cardinal Richelieu in 1641.

Deep casemates beneath the turfed earthworks are an excellent shelter from bombing, and in spite of breaches which have been made in the stone ramparts, the sheer drop from the top of the ramparts to the ground continues to provide an insurmountable obstacle to tanks.

REYNAUD AT FRONT

M. Reynaud, the French Prime Minister, and Marshal Petain and M. Dautry, Minister of Armaments, visited a sector of the Somme front yesterday.

"The morale of the troops has never been higher," they said afterwards.

It Pays To Carry Them

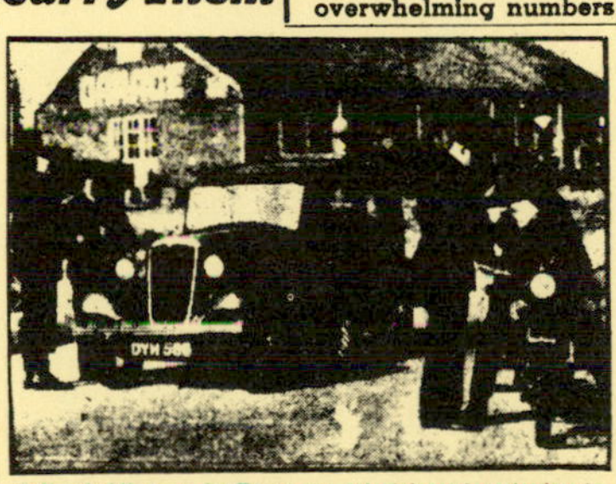

Police holding up traffic on an arterial road yesterday to inspect the identification cards of the drivers.

NAZI SOS for PILOTS

FOR the first time since the war began all German radio stations yesterday broadcast an urgent appeal for youths to enlist in the German Air Force.

Recruiting offices have been set up in Berlin, Vienna, Hanover and Munich.

The appeal stated:

"Our air force has proved to be of decisive importance. Its success, however, has been achieved by the spirit which animates the pilots.

"We therefore call on all German youths with an adventurous spirit to serve as pilots, wireless operators or gunners."

B.E.F. men back from Dunkirk say that many German airmen brought down are more than 40 years old.

TWO MEN ARE SHOT DEAD BY SENTRIES

TWO men who did not stop when challenged were shot dead by sentries during the week-end.

One was Joseph Henry Vaughan, aged 20, of Whitman House, Bethnal Green, E.

Vaughan, who had four young men with him, was driving a car near Abridge, Essex, between 10 p.m. and 11 p.m. on Saturday when police officers and soldiers, who were on guard, waved a light as a signal to stop.

The car went on, and the guard had to jump clear. Two of the sentries fired.

Vaughan and another man were injured. Both were taken to hospital at Romford, where Vaughan died yesterday.

The other man is still in hospital.

Shot by a sentry at an R.A.F. camp in a North Country town on Saturday, John Henry McDonald, aged 58, a master joiner, died a few hours later in hospital.

McDonald, who was employed at the camp, was riding on the pillion of a motor-cycle driven by Leslie Jones, another joiner.

Blackout To-night
9.37 p.m.–4.19 a.m.
MOON RISES 3.37 a.m.
SETS 6.20 p.m.

300 PLANES ON THE WAY TO BRITAIN

ONE HUNDRED United States bombers left the United States on Saturday for Britain.

Two hundred more planes, mostly bombers, and 150 aircraft engines were due to leave yesterday.

Yesterday, too, the first batch of American planes to be flown direct to the Allies by United States pilots took off from Roosevelt Field, New York, for Halifax.

Hitherto, United States pilots have flown machines ordered by the Allies to the Canadian border, where Canadian pilots have taken them over.

It was reported in Washington last night (says Reuter) that President Roosevelt has before him for consideration a proposal which would enable some older United States military and naval planes to be delivered to the Allies' immediately.

Among them are 200 twin-engined bombers belonging to the United States Army Air Corps, which are now being replaced by more modern types.

119 NAZIS DOWN IN TWO DAYS

ONE HUNDRED AND NINETEEN Nazi aircraft have been destroyed or seriously damaged by the R.A.F. over Dunkirk beaches since Saturday morning.

Seventy-eight were brought down by the R.A.F. on Saturday. Yesterday's figure of 35 certainties and six probables is provisional and incomplete.

It is believed that the Germans have lost nearly 3,000 aircraft since the war began—2,200 since May 10.

On Thursday and Friday alone we had accounted for more than 140 Germans.

We lost 16 fighters on Saturday and eight yesterday, but at least one of the pilots was very soon in the air again.

Walked Home

When his Hurricane was disabled in an engagement with a Messerschmitt, this pilot had to land on the beach, says an Air Ministry bulletin.

Carrying his parachute, he walked 15 miles to Dunkirk, got a lift across the Channel in a paddle-steamer, rejoined his squadron and was out on patrol again the next day.

"Squadron after squadron of Hurricanes and Spitfires flew high above the French fens all Saturday guarding the convoys which were bringing the B.E.F. rearguard home," said an Air Ministry bulletin.

"Huge formations of Nazi bombers escorted by fighters came out and attempted to sink the ships. They did not lack targets, for the sea was thick with craft of all kinds.

Bombs In Sea

"But when they attempted to bomb, our fighters attacked and drove them off. Most of the bombs fell into the sea.

"Many Junkers, Heinkels, Dorniers and Messerschmitts soon crashed into the sea after their bombs. 32 fighters were certainly destroyed. Two squadrons bagged 23 Messerschmitts.

Continued on Back Page.

UNARMED—BROUGHT BOMBER DOWN

ONE R.A.F. pilot proved over Dunkirk on Saturday that a British fighter can bring down a German without firing a shot.

The R.A.F. man had used all his ammunition when he met a Junkers bomber.

He got on the enemy's tail and persecuted him with daring manœuvres until the German pilot missed a turn and crashed into the ground.

HIS AIM IS TRUE

The R.A.F. gunner on right has accounted for eight Nazi aircraft on one patrol. His squadron of "Defiants" brought down 37 enemy aircraft in one day without loss.

Bombs On Norfolk Yesterday

IT was officially announced last night that early yesterday morning an unidentified aircraft passed over Norfolk.

No air raid warning was sounded, but searchlights immediately flashed into action, and then two bombs fell near a village.

German planes, which bombed Marseilles and Lyons on Saturday, again raided south-eastern France yesterday.

They swept down the Rhone Valley in three waves.

Bombs were dropped in the Lyons region, and there was a number of civilian casualties.

Last night's French communique said that 12 raiders, as far as have been counted up to the present, were brought down in Saturday's raids.

Fifty-six French civilians were killed and more than 100 injured by bombs on Saturday.

Two bombs fell in Marseilles itself, and two in the harbour.

Five towns around Lyons were bombed, and so was Nimes.

In Aix-les-Bains a hotel was destroyed.

A Reuter message says that among the Germans' objectives was a number of aircraft factories, and the Germans claimed last night that railways had also been "successfully" attacked.

DON'T LEAVE YOUR JOB—OFFICIAL WARNING

Stay quietly at your post: carry on with your normal work: don't listen to rumours.

This advice is given to dwellers in the south and east coastal areas in a Ministry of Home Security statement issued last night, following the evacuation of schoolchildren.

TO-DAY'S 'DAILY HERALD'

Dear Reader,

We hope you will like your "Daily Herald" to-day.

Papers have been reduced in size to conserve paper supplies.

But we think that the new style and type achieve our aim to make the "Daily Herald" more attractive and easy to read.

If you think so, please tell your friends. If not, tell us.

DUKE OF NORTHUMBERLAND KILLED IN FLANDERS FIGHT

THE 27-year-old Duke of Northumberland has been killed in action with the B.E.F.

His flag, the blue lion rampant, was half-masted on the keep of Alnwick Castle, Northumberland, yesterday.

An announcement was made by the Duke's chaplain and commissioner.

The Duke, who succeeded his father in 1930, was a lieutenant in the Grenadier Guards (Supplementary Reserve).

His heir is his brother, Lord Algernon Percy, who is 26.

Captain R. W. Porritt, aged 30, M.P. for the Heywood and Radcliffe Division of Lancashire, has also been killed in action.

He is the first M.P. to have died on active service in the present war.

He was recently gazetted captain. Before that he was a lieutenant in the Lancashire Fusiliers.

1 Dead, 3 Hurt In Rail Crash

ONE man was killed and three were injured in a collision between two trains on the G.W.R. branch line at Llangennech, near Llanelly, Carmarthenshire, yesterday.

The dead man was James Pumford, a guard.

The injured are engine driver Arthur T. Fry, fireman Edgar Jones and guard J. Griffiths, all of Llanelly.

Pumford was the guard in charge of a mineral train.

The driver and fireman of the second train, which consisted of empty passenger coaches, were unhurt.

WAR! DUCE IS RESOLVED

10,000 N.C.O.s Are Called Up

TENSION mounted in Rome during the week-end as Italy called up 10,000 non-commissioned officers to supplement the 50,000 recruited last autumn.

Italians are hastening home from Greece, Turkey, Rumania and Jugoslavia.

The Italian Air Line has cancelled its service between Rhodes and Basra and Italian steamship companies say they cannot guarantee sailings after June 15.

Mussolini yesterday received Count Manzolini, an armaments manufacturer, who showed him what are described as "new engines of war."

During the last fortnight the Allied Fleet concentration in the Eastern Mediterranean has been considerably increased, says Reuter.

W. N. EWER, "DAILY HERALD" DIPLOMATIC CORRESPONDENT WRITES:

Every sign now suggests that Mussolini means to take the plunge without further delay and that, within a few days, he will order the Italian people to war with the Allies.

BOILING POINT

The Fascist Press has been brought to boiling point.

And even usually responsible papers are now calling for war with Britain and France as Italy's "enemies for 50 years past."

Signor Ansaldo, who broadcasts every week to the Italian Army, announced yesterday that military preparations carried on since September had now reached their final stage and that mobilisation had been accomplished steadily and silently.

Most significant of all, the Fascist Grand Council, which

(Continued on Back Page.)

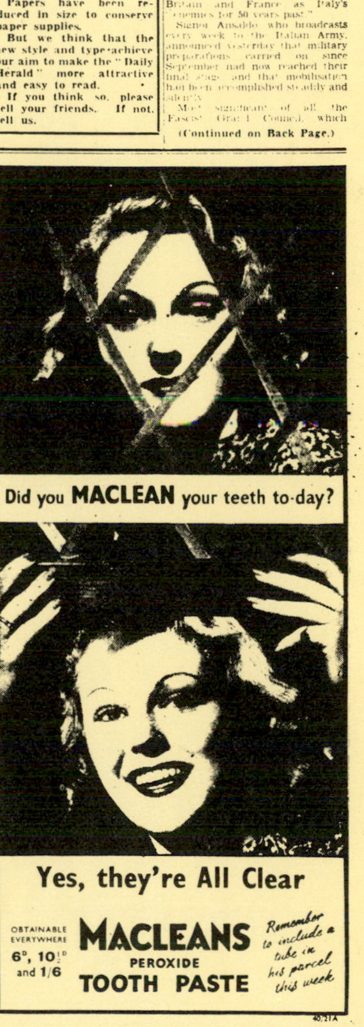

▲ First wartime change of the *Daily Herald* (June 1940), with an italic capitals title in reverse, and a bold/condensed gothic headline style.

DAILY HERALD

No. 7910 MONDAY, JUNE 23, 1941 One Penny

BRITAIN WILL GIVE ALL AID TO

'I warned Stalin,' says

MURMANSK
FINLAND
ARCHANGEL
HELSINKI
LENINGRAD

RAF again—30 yesterday

ANOTHER 30 Messerschmitt fighters were shot down yesterday when the RAF continued its big offensive over Nazi-occupied territory.

Large numbers of Hurricanes and Spitfires accompanied small forces of Blenheim bombers in sweeps over Northern France.

The Blenheims went 30 miles inland and bombed the marshalling yard at Hazebrouck, the big railway junction which handles the traffic to the Channel ports.

ONLY TWO OF OUR

DAILY HERALD

No. 8256 TUESDAY, AUGUST 4, 1942 One Penny

Caucasus Battles Grow Fiercer

RUSSIANS COUNTER-ATTACKING IN DON BEND AS BOCK OPENS NEW DRIVE

Dusseldorf After Its

TORIES TO TELL LADY ASTOR TO APOLOGISE

By MAURICE WEBB

WIDESPREAD resentment has been

"Daily Herald," Friday, Sept. 10, 1943.

LONDON BLACKOUT

7.59 p.m. to 5.57 a.m.
Moon Sets 1.18 a.m.
Moon Rises 5.33 p.m.
Lighting-up Time 8.29 p.m.

Daily Herald

No. 8598 ★ ★ FRIDAY, SEPTEMBER 10, 1943 ONE PENNY

STOP PRESS

SPITZBERGEN ATTACK

German radio said last night that Spitzbergen had been attacked by German naval units.—Associated Press.

Allies' 4 a.m. Invasion Fleet Covered 1,000 Square Miles Of Sea

FIRST GREAT BATTLE OF ITALY STARTS ON NAPLES FRONT

LANDING SHIPS

SMOLENSK
DNIEPER
Yartsevo
Viazma
Dorogobuzh
Elnya
Kaluga
Tula
Roslavl
Liubinovka
BRIANSK
Orel
Yelets
Gomel
Navlya

KIEV HEARS GUNS: PUSH

Imperial
FOR BETTER LETTERS
Made in England
IMPERIAL TYPEWRITER Co. Ltd., LEICESTER

DAILY HERALD

No. 11163 (A) PRICE 1½D

THURSDAY DEC 20 1951

MICHELIN the SUPPLE TYRE

up
BACON 10d. lb. MORE
CHEESE 10d. lb. MORE
down

WOOLTON RAISES PRICES: CUTS RATIONS

Miss Israel looks us over

London waits for new check on PoW list

By A. J. McWHINNIE Military Correspondent

IT will be several days before the War Office can communicate with the next of kin of men

---

Couple held—big hunt ends

'KIDNAPPED' BABY FOUND ALIVE

DAILY Herald

Monday, March 4, 1957 PRICE 2d. No. 12754 (D)

Caroline steals the balcony scene

EIGHT ARE TRAPPED

DAILY HERALD

No. 12933 (D) Monday, September 30, 1957 PRICE 2d.

Last night's eve-of-Conference tip on the Big Issue

SHARES PLAN WINNING

WE SAY

Where we're going!

of similar style (but with the lettering in roman), ranging the words *Daily* and *Herald* on the left. Three months later this title was reduced in both width and depth, the lettering somewhat more condensed, with the word *Daily* little more than one-third as deep as the word *Herald*. This mini-version evidently proved unsatisfactory – it was a couple of picas less than double-column – for by August 1941 the full double-column reverse had reappeared, with its two words of equal size, except that *Daily* was now centred on *Herald*, instead of both being ranged left. It must be presumed that the difficulty of making-up a broadsheet page without a free run across its eight columns, led to the *Herald's* next move – the abandonment in 1942 of the double-column, tabloid-style reverse title-piece for a normal cross-page title, with 'ears' (though used for editorial, not advertising).

◀ 1941 (June): a reduced top-corner reverse title succeeded the double-column reverse of March 1941: headline note is bold condensed gothic.

The new *Herald* title-line was almost certainly the most amateurish and indifferent that had ever graced (or rather disgraced) a London national; it was a pathetic performance, in more or less Egyptian slab-seriffed style, but so crude and poor in its drawing that it is surprising any publisher should ever have accepted it. Indeed the Odhams authorities evidently were soon dissatisfied, for they approached Stanley Morison, fresh from his successful *Express* title, to advise them. He prescribed a title in carefully letter-spaced Baskerville Bold Titling, which was introduced in 1944 and was to last over a dozen years, until 1957, by far the longest-lived of any *Herald* title.

◀ 1941 (August): back to the full double-column reverse title – with a 'dishevelled' condensed gothic heading style.

It may well be wondered why the *Herald*, so often so eager to emulate the *Express*, did not do so in the matter of its Morison title. The *Express*, as has been noted, clung for a generation to the Morison prescription; and, even if the Baskerville Bold Titling had not quite the originality of the 'super-fatted Perpetua' – the evidence is that Morison's heart was not in the *Herald* job – nevertheless it was a distinctive and effective line. In the spring of 1957, however, it fell a victim to the combination of the paper's continued decline and the complex internal politics of the Odhams set-up.

◀ 1942: an amateurish Egyptian lower-case title with a square gothic headline flavour.

Coinciding with a more than usually severe crisis in the affairs of the *Herald* – there was even talk of a merger with the *News Chronicle* – came a series of sweeping staff changes, from the editor downwards. The new editorial broom swept away the Morison title and in March 1957 substituted an unusual shortened title; this was a three-column box, with the word *Daily* small (around 14pt) in letter-spaced sans italic capitals and the word *Herald* large (over 72pt) in a tolerably lettered medium-weight slab-serif. Brightened by the use of the colour seal to revive in red the old challenging chantecler symbol of the independent *Herald* of yore, this title-box was positioned in the top right-hand corner of the front page. This left space, as had the short title-blocks of 1941–42, to take the lead story to the top of the page. Such an arrangement is always a restrictive factor in broadsheet make-up, though acceptable for tabloids. Nevertheless the *Herald* repeatedly experimented with the short-title device (which its successor, the *Sun*, adopted throughout its brief career) as a supposed means of overcoming the handicap of the Odhams 21-inch cutoff. This historical hangover from the firm's earlier periodical commitments produced a shorter and squarer broadsheet page than that of its $23\frac{9}{16}$-inch contemporaries. More, it meant a comparative loss of around a column of front-page matter; hence the urge to maximise editorial space on the front page by reducing the title space.

◀ 1944–57: Morison's Baskerville Bold title, with the Tempo Heavy/Century Bold heading style of the early 1950s.

◀ 1957 (March): a three-column boxed title, with a *Mirror*-style of heavy gothic headlining.

The three-column boxed title did not last many months; before 1957 was out its place had been taken by a normal cross-page title in roman capitals faintly evocative of Morison's *Express* title, though more squat and more expanded. It was not an unsatisfactory line and lasted for four years, accompanying the two stages of the Odhams struggle to remove the links with the TUC – by way of a joint operating company – which had been part of the original *Herald* arrangement of 1930. The issue was a sham; the Odhams assertion that the TUC connection had hampered the paper's growth was a mere excuse, since

◀ 1957–61: a normal measure title in sharp-seriffed expanded roman capitals, somewhat reminiscent of Morison's *Express* title of 1942. Typography in Record Medium and square gothic.

DAILY HERALD

THE PAPER THAT CARES

No. 13416 (C) Thursday, April 23, 1959 Price 2½d.

Is there a fiddle? ask angry MPs

TV STARS CALL-UP

Five killed in pit blast

Herald Reporter

DAILY HERALD

[redacted]EPENDENT [redacted]TSPOKEN

No. 13833 (D) Thursday, August 25, 1960 Price 2½d.

Historic decision by TUC General Council gives independence to the Herald

OUR FUTURE

'UP FOR T' CUP' FIRE CHIEF IS SACKED

CUP-TIE fever gripped Norwich when the local team was just one step from magic Wembley.
Even Fire Chief Gerald Hinde — no great football fan—fell

Kruschev challenge to China

TOP COMMUNISTS GET 'BACK ME' MESSAGE

DAILY HERALD

No. 13878 (D) Monday, October 17, 1960 Price 2½d.

FAIR AND FREE

A NEW CAR MUST BE WON —See Page 8

Excessive? Oh no, say brasshats, but exercise casualties top first day's toll in Suez war

MPs IN ARMY STORM

Babies rescued

Daily Herald

No. 14026 Tuesday, April 11, 1961 Price 3d.

Excitement mounts as Moscow awaits news

HAS K LAUNCHED

The world this morning

● Excitement at rumours that the Russians had fired, or were about to fire, the first man into space.

Excitement rather than surprise. The dogs and the apes have ascended and returned. The first manned flight was known to be near. The only question has been whether a Russian or an American would make it.

There can be nothing but congratulations if the Russians are first to write this epic page of history.

The BBC television strike continues. Programmes last night were again messed about. Cliff Michelmore, out in the rain, up an iron emergency staircase, found enough light to get "Tonight" on the screen.

It was nearly the Dark Programme.—THIS PAGE.

No. 14261
Friday,
January 12, 1962

Daily Herald

3D

POSTMEN MAKE PEACE

The world this morning

● President Kennedy put all his authority behind proposals for a tariff-reduction policy to forge "a trading partnership with vast resources for freedom" between the U.S. and Europe *(this page)*.

A great conception, but will the U.S. Congress agree?

POSTMEN'S OFFER

The Post Office Union offered to end its work-to-rule if the

PRINCE CHARLES RUSHED TO HOSPITAL

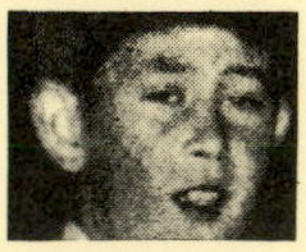

MONDAY, FEBRUARY 12, 1962

Daily Herald

No. 14287 THREEPENCE

The world this morning

Kruschev

1 a.m. operation

from the start the Odhams-appointed editorial director had had full authority over the conduct of the *Herald*. Nevertheless the link was loosened in 1957 and finally severed in 1960, a couple of years before the emergence of the giant, *Mirror*-based International Publishing Corporation which took over Odhams among other large printing and publishing concerns.

It can only be presumed that the turmoil associated with these events (which had begun with the *Mirror* takeover of the Amalgamated Press, the original Harmsworth magazine concern, in 1959) was somehow reflected in the substitution of a deeper Perpetua Bold upper- and lower-case title-line for the space-economising roman expanded capitals. The Perpetua line was blown up to around 84pt and wide letter-spaced, contrary to normal criteria for lower-case display. First used straight, with a red chantecler seal (soon dropped), in March 1961, the line had three successive changes in presentation by means of varying tint underscores. The Perpetua period lasted less than a year, giving way in February 1962 to the last of the *Herald* short titles.

By this time the *Herald* had developed a front-page news summary, 'The World this Morning', run at the top of the last two columns; the heading for this was now incorporated in a double-column short title-piece. The new title was perhaps the *Herald's* ugliest, though not quite as amateurish as the 1942–44 semi-Egyptian. The two lines *Daily* and *Herald* were set in the crude-looking Tempo Black Extended, upper- and lower-case, ranged left and flanked by a red decorative device which included that persistent chantecler, in reverse. After a few months the decorative device was simplified, the two lines of the title centred and 'The World' heading, in Karnak Heavy italic, reduced from 24pt to 18pt. But there must have been acute dissatisfaction with this poor affair; before the end of 1962 it was abandoned for a cross-page title, decently lettered in the upper- and lower-case of an extended antique. This was the last title-piece of the *Daily Herald*, continuing until its death in September 1964 and the birth of the ill-fated *Sun*, to which further reference is made in the final chapter.*

As already indicated, the unprecedented kaleidoscope of the

SATURDAY, JUNE 29, 1963 THREEPENCE No. 14714

Daily Herald

My love life—by Christine's friend

MANDY NAMES LORD ASTOR

Model, 18, and Cliveden peer

LORD AND LADY ASTOR

By DON CASSELL

PRETTY 18-year-old Marilyn Rice-Davies said in court yesterday that while she was living at a flat with Dr. Stephen Ward she had intercourse with Lord Astor.

Macmillan says: I'll lead again

By HAROLD HUTCHINSON
Herald Political Correspondent

IN a shock statement on television last night, Mr. Macmillan reasserted his hope of leading the Conservative Party at the next election.

Asked if he still held to what he had told Conservative backbenchers on April 10 when he said he hoped to lead the Party at the next election, Mr. Macmillan replied:

"Yes. I said that all being well, if I keep my health and strength, I hope to lead the Party into the election."

Though that statement is qualified, it is the Prime Minister's first indication since the Profumo

saying in a speech in Northumberland that if Mr. Macmillan insists on staying "it will mean civil war in the Conservative Party."

But Lord Lambton is one of the Prime Minister's strongest opponents. The "Mac must go" group are leaderless and can put forward no successor who has the unqualified approval of the Party as a whole.

So the prospects are that the majority of Conservative M.Ps, however angry, will choose to accept Mr. Macmillan rather than split the Party.

SUPPORT

Mr. Macmillan was interviewed

The world this morning

The court hearing of vice charges against Dr. Stephen Ward opens. Miss Mandy Rice-Davies and Christine Keeler give evidence. In the dock Ward scribbles and sketches, and occasionally shakes his head *(this page, P.8 and P.9).*

He hopes

Mr. Macmillan prepares to do a Canute. Health and strength permitting, he declares, he hopes to lead the Tories at the next election. *An explosion is expected among the Tories who thought he was on the way out (this page).*

Reality

Lord Hailsham — this time in his role as Minister for the North-East — calls the area "a land of opportunity." *He'll have to work hard to make the reality match that one (P.2).*

Prodigy

Miss Caroline Glyn is 15 and has written her first novel. *Frederick Laws thinks she is a much better writer than her grandmother, Elinor Glyn, one-time queen of sexy, slushy romance (P.4).*

Black mark

Teachers should make deliberate mistakes, says a headmistress. Always being right is bad for them. *But is it good for the children when teacher is wrong? (P.5).*

Simple life

The new Viscount Alanbrooke lives in a transport cafe and does not intend to let his title change his

▲ 1962 (end): the last title, a cross-page line in Antique Extended lower-case. Headlining settled for heavy gothic and variants of Tempo.

* The *Herald* rang an exceptional series of changes on its red colour seal. Sometimes it was used, conventionally, as an edition indicator, sometimes (in bold reverse) for the date, sometimes for a slogan ('The Paper That Cares' was one of these; and after the 'liberation' from the TUC in 1960 a deep seal with the words FAIR AND FREE appeared for a while), sometimes for a symbol, the chantecler of the ancient Lansbury days. This bird kept popping in and out of the title-piece like the cuckoo from a clock; in 1962 it became a fixture until the end in 1964.

◀ A spring 1959 outcrop of Gill Bold Titling in the then manner of the London *Evening News*.

◀ The *Mirror* tabloid style returned in 1959 with a bang – in the shape of specially-cut 120pt poster gothics.

◀ In the autumn of 1960 this emergence of a Caslon Bold banner presaged a temporary adoption of *Express* headline typography.

◀ 1961 (March): the title changed to letter-spaced Perpetua Bold lower-case, first unadorned and then with three successive variants of a heavy tint underscore. Headline style now the *Express* Century formula.

◀ In the spring of 1961 the Century Bold Extended lead style was switched to this 96pt Tempo Bold Condensed.

◀ 1962 (February): a double-column title in Tempo Black, red-bordered (a simpler border and a change in setting style shortly followed). Headline style was again tabloid gothic.

Daily Mirror

MON SEPT 22 1947

ONE PENNY

FORWARD WITH THE PEOPLE

No. 13,646

Registered at G.P.O. as a Newspaper.

RUSSIA LOSES ROUND 1 IN THE BATTLE OF THE VETO

AMERICA last night beat Russia in Round 1 of the battle to limit use of the big-Power veto in the Security Council.

Over Russian protests, the United Nations' Steering Committee at Lake Success, New York, voted to put the U.S. proposals to have a "little Assembly" of fifty-five nations—made by Secretary of State Marshall last Wednesday—before the General Assembly.

The "little Assembly" would sit the year round to deal with any threats to peace, and would have power to recommend meetings of the full Assembly

Mr. Gromyko fought the plan on the ground that it violated the United Nations' Charter and was an American attempt to side-track the Security Council.

He said the U.S. apparently did not want the Council to have basic responsibility for peace "because the Council does not accept all proposals made by the U.S.

"Who Will Show Respect?" He Asks

"But we must not base the Council's work on the convenience of one country.

"If the big Powers ignore the Charter, who will respect it?"

America's Warren Austin declared: "A small minority—Russia and its big-Power veto—has rendered the Security Council futile in protecting world peace."

Twelve nations voted against Russia and Poland. Britain abstained.

Russia was defeated again when the committee voted for Assembly debates on revision of the Italian treaty and on the U.S.-Soviet dispute over Korea.

Britain raps "terror" in two countries

Britain's Foreign Office last night condemned the suppression of freedom and rule by State police in Bulgaria and Rumania.

A spokesman said that further "flagrant denial of human rights" would constitute a breach of the peace treaties.

"Denial of the fundamental freedoms, dissolution of Opposition parties, arrests without charge are condemned by British opinion," he said.

"In Hungary, too, affairs are giving rise to grave concern," he said.

Flying baby is doing "nicely, thank you"

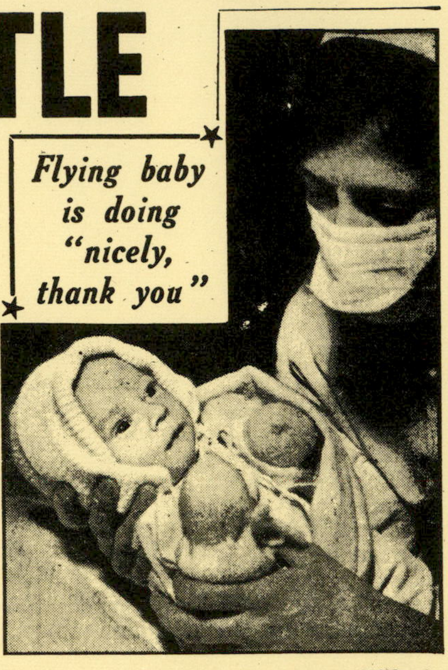

A night nurse at the Great Ormond-street Children's Hospital, London, makes a record-breaking little patient comfortable for the night. He is David, son of Captain and Mrs. V. Palmer, who was flown from Berlin to London on Friday—when he was one day old—for an abdominal operation. It was performed when he was thirty-six hours old. Last night he was "progressing favourably."

Wife, daughter helpless as he baled all night to save drifting yacht

AS his seasick wife, daughter and a man lay helpless in a cabin, Mr. Thomas Lethbridge fought desperately, single-handed, on deck to keep his drifting yacht from sinking.

All Saturday night the ten-ton yacht Zoraida had drifted in bad weather in the Strait of Dover, her engines broken down.

And all the time Mr. Lethbridge, who lives in Cambridge, baled out the water. He did not tell the others of their plight.

He hoisted a bucket to the masthead as a distress signal.

Then early yesterday Fred Upton, Walmer lifeboat coxswain, saw the signal and put out in his own motor-boat.

He found Mr. Lethbridge exhausted with the water rapidly filling the boat, which he towed into Ramsgate.

JUST IN CASE

The U.S. Army is burying 200,000 tons of bombs "to be dug up if and when needed."

B.U. rationing system to be 'tightened up'

MEASURES to tighten up the bread rationing system are believed to be before the Cabinet, writes a Political Correspondent.

Slackness in the administration of B.U.s is to be overcome, and a closer check on flour supplies may be re-introduced.

At present, it is understood, it is not proposed to reduce bread rations, but supplies of cakes and pastries may have to be reviewed.

If the wheat supply situation abroad makes it necessary to reconsider differential rationing, heavy workers and children would not suffer cuts.

Ex-18B man is charged after street meeting

EDWARD JEFFREY HAMM, former 18B detainee and a leader of the British League of Ex-Servicemen and Women, was arrested at the close of a London East End street meeting last night.

Hamm, whose address was given as Arundel-gardens, W., was taken to Dalston police station and charged under the Public Order Act with insulting words and behaviour.

He was released on bail of £5 and will appear in court today.

In the crowd at the meeting in Ridley-road, Dalston, were a number of Labour M.P.s.

Seeing a youth in the crowd holding a knife in one hand and a knuckle-duster in the other, one of the M.P.s asked him his age. The boy was fifteen.

WIDOW FOUND DEAD IN RIVER

Mrs. Elizabeth Felix, 60, widow, who went from London to Aberystwyth three weeks ago to stay with her brother, was found dead in the River Rheidol at Aberystwyth yesterday.

Her husband, who had a dairy business, died last July.

MR. CRICK, THE PERFECT HUSBAND, GIVES HIS WIFE A 5-DAY WEEK

MRS. ELEANOR CRICK, 32, of Cricklewood (London), housewife with a five-day week, sipped morning tea in bed yesterday and said: "My husband is wonderful."

And Mr. Eustace Crick, 34, washing up and preparing a dinner of roast beef, veg., apple souffle and caramel, said: "My wife is wonderful."

The Cricks, winners of Willesden's one-rasher flitch in the "happy couples" contest this week-end, say that the secret of happy marriage lies in sharing everything—money, thoughts, leisure.

"When I got a five-day week job," said Eustace, conductor on a No. 60 bus, "I saw that Eleanor had a five-day week, too.

"On Saturdays I do the family wash—Eleanor irons—and on Sundays I cook.

"I have never bought a tie, a shirt, a pair of socks or a suit myself. My wife knows my taste perfectly."

He Buys Her Hats

And Mrs. Crick has never bought any hats, clothes or shoes. Mr. Crick does that.

"In winter," said Mrs. Crick, "I suffer from cold feet. So my husband puts his feet on mine, warms them up and I can go to sleep quicker."

Mr. Crick gets up in the night to attend to the children—Brian, 9, and Angela, 3—never drinks or smokes, and never goes out alone.

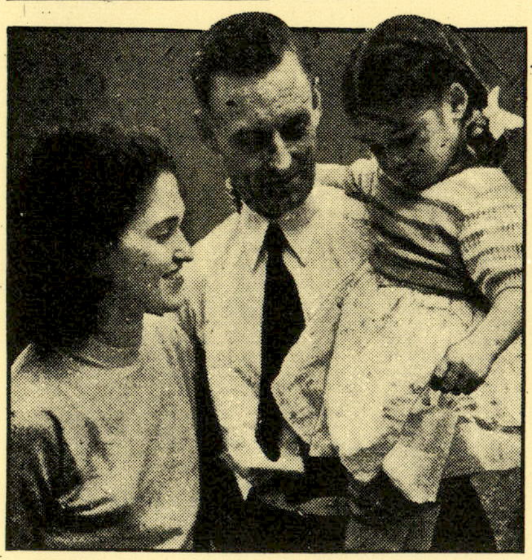

Mrs. Eleanor Crick and Mr. Eustace Crick with their daughter, Angela.

NO, THANKS

CAPETOWN RAF Association has refused £200 from a lawyer who last week protested against the Sunday showing of the film, "First of the Few." The show was banned under the Lord's Day Observance Act.

Boy hugging 5 pigeons falls 100ft. to his death

WITH five pigeons—one still alive—stuffed between his shirt and jacket, Harry Simpson, 13, of Swanfield-road, Bilton, Hull, was found dead at the foot of a 100ft. high spire yesterday.

The spire, practically all that remains of the bombed St. Stephen's Church, Hull, is a sanctuary for pigeons.

It is thought that the boy may have been a pigeon-lover and tried to climb the spire in search of pets.

He waited till gas lamps near the spire were put out at midnight on Saturday before starting to climb, it is believed.

A flashlamp was found near his body.

Goalkeeper dies

A goalkeeper burst an artery and died during a match at Nancy, France, yesterday.

His delayed tip was £1.000

A wealthy Can

Harry F. McLean,

guest farm near C

South Africa, early this year, told the manager and his wife how much he appreciated their welcome.

This week-end the manager was advised that £1,000 had been placed to his credit by Mr. McLean.

Boy falls 30 feet

John Morgan, 5, of Burnham-road, Dagenham, fell thirty feet from a railway bridge at Dagenham on to the track yesterday and was badly injured.

Cut increasing horde of officials, says M.P.

THE increasing "horde of officials" must be drastically reduced if workers were to get a new deal, Mr. Geoffrey Cooper, Labour M.P. for West Middlesbrough told his constituents yesterday.

The workers must get a chance to fit themselves now for greater responsibility to replace the raw deals of the past, he said.

But the ever-growing number of officials were becoming the "new parasites on the backs of the production workers."

The Government must completely reorganise the inflated Civil Service and transfer their wasted man-power into productive work.

COLONEL SHOT

Lieutenant-Colonel I. R. T. Irvine, who was found suffering from a shot wound at his home in Meloncroft-drive, Caldy, Wirral (Cheshire) on Saturday, was critically ill last night.

BULLET-PROOF CAR FOR BEVIN

MR. ERNEST BEVIN arrived in Paris by air yesterday to preside at today's sixteen-nation meeting to discuss the Marshall Plan.

France has given him a 20h.p. car for use during his visit. It has bullet-proof glass.

Advertiser's Announcement

The girl who put herself on the shelf

The years passed by and the men passed her by. Yet she had only herself to blame. If only she had gone to her dentist, he would have told her that she was guilty of Oral Offence.

Scientific tests prove that in 7 cases out of 10 Colgate Dental Cream stops Oral Offence that originates in the mouth. 1/3 Inc. Tax

PLAY SAFE! USE COLGATE TWICE A DAY

▲ How a newsprint-rationed tabloid packed the news in: a *Daily Mirror* front page of 1947.

THE STANDARD, WEDNESDAY, JUNE 23, 1897.

THE QUEEN'S JUBILEE.

CELEBRATIONS ABROAD.

THE UNITY OF THE EMPIRE.

THE QUEEN'S HEALTH.

THE UNITED STATES.

PRESIDENT KRÜGER AND THE UITLANDERS.

SPAIN AND CUBA.

THE QUEEN'S MESSAGE TO HER PEOPLE.

"From my heart I thank my beloved people. May God bless them.—V.R. and I."

TURKEY AND GREECE.

An English 'blanket sheet': the main news page of the morning *Standard* of 1897, with eight wide-measure columns and a sheet of 22½-by-26½-inches.

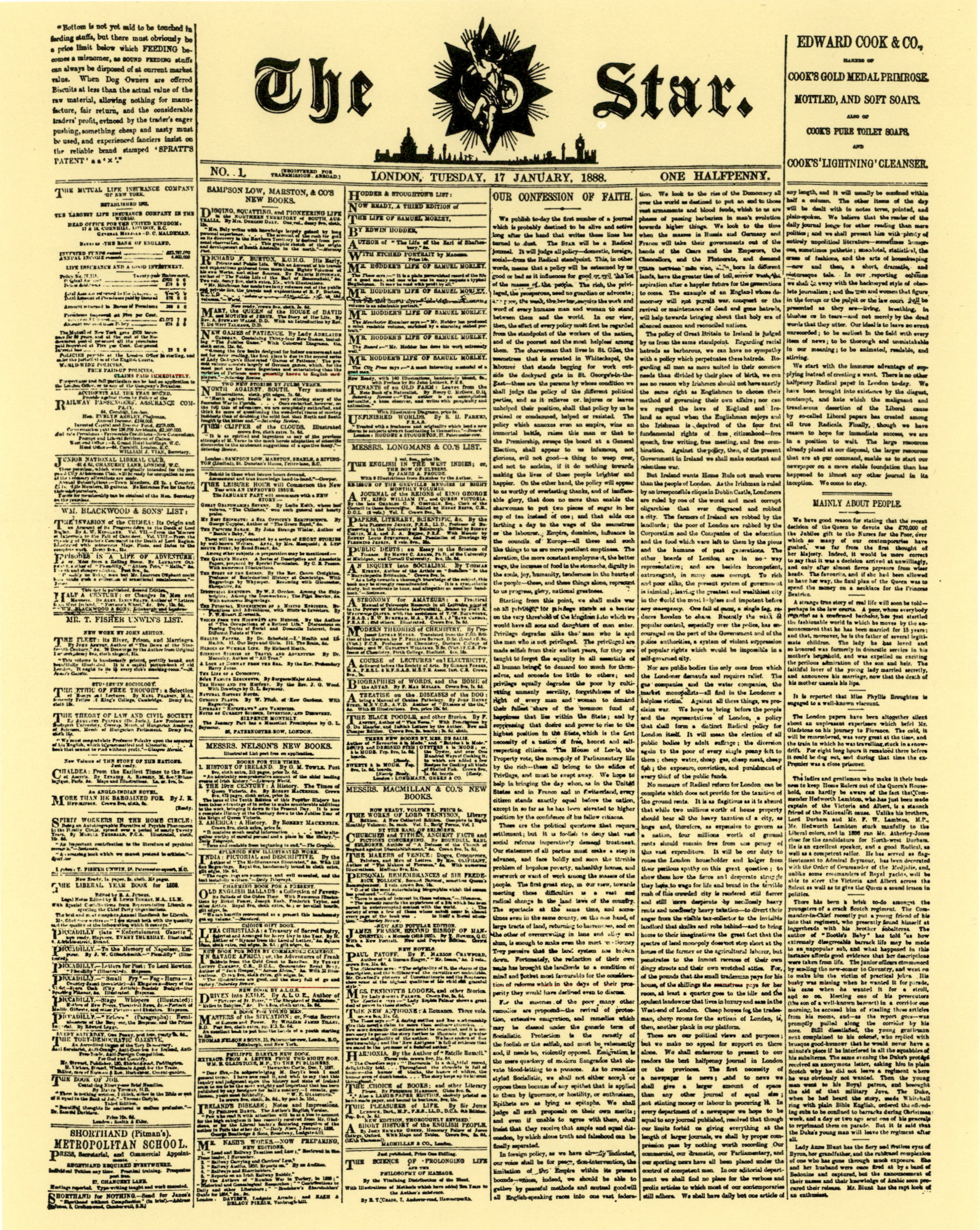

"Bottom is not yet said to be touched in feeding stuffs, but there must obviously be a price limit below which FEEDING becomes a misnomer, as SOUND FEEDING stuffs can always be disposed of at current market value. When Dog Owners are offered Biscuits at less than the actual value of the raw material, allowing nothing for manufacture, fair return, and the considerable traders' profit, evinced by the trader's eager pushing, something cheap and nasty must be used, and experienced fanciers insist on the reliable brand stamped 'SPRATT'S PATENT' and a 'X'."

The Star.

NO. 1. (REGISTERED FOR TRANSMISSION ABROAD.) LONDON, TUESDAY, 17 JANUARY, 1888. ONE HALFPENNY.

EDWARD COOK & CO.,

MAKERS OF

COOK'S GOLD MEDAL PRIMROSE, MOTTLED, AND SOFT SOAPS.

ALSO OF

COOK'S PURE TOILET SOAPS,

AND

COOK'S 'LIGHTNING' CLEANSER.

OUR CONFESSION OF FAITH.

We publish to-day the first number of a journal which is probably destined to be alive and active long after the hand that writes these lines has turned to dust. The STAR will be a Radical journal. It will judge all policy—domestic, foreign, social—from the Radical standpoint. This, in other words, means that a policy will be esteemed by us good or bad as it influences for good or evil the lot of the masses of the people. The rich, the privileged, the prosperous, need no guardian or advocate; the poor, the weak, the beaten, require the work and word of every humane man and woman to stand between them and the world. In our view, then, the effect of every policy must first be regarded from the standpoint of the workers of the nation, and of the poorest and the most helpless among them. The charwoman that lives in St. Giles, the seamstress that is sweated in Whitechapel, the labourer that stands begging for work outside the dockyard gate in St. George's-in-the-East—these are the persons by whose condition we shall judge the policy of the different political parties, and as it relieves or injures or leaves unhelped their position, shall that policy by us be praised or condemned, helped or resisted. The policy which annexes even an empire, wins an immortal battle, raises this man or that to the Premiership, sweeps the board at a General Election, shall appear to us infamous, not glorious, evil not good—a thing to weep over, and not to acclaim, if it do nothing towards making the lives of these people brighter and happier. On the other hand, the policy will appear to us worthy of everlasting thanks, and of ineffaceable glory, that does no more than enable the charwoman to put two pieces of sugar in her cup of tea instead of one; and that adds one farthing a day to the wage of the seamstress or the labourer. Empire, dominion, influence in the councils of Europe—all these and such like things to us are mere pestilent emptiness. The elevation, the more constant employment, the better wage, the increase of food in the stomachs, dignity in the souls, joy, humanity, tenderness in the hearts of the people—these, and these things alone, represent to us progress, glory, national greatness.

Starting from this point, we shall make war on all privilege, for privilege stands as a barrier on the very threshold of the kingdom into which we would have all sons and daughters of men enter. Privilege degrades alike the man who is and the man who is not privileged. The privileged are made selfish from their earliest years, for they are taught to forget the equality in all essentials of all human beings, to demand too much for themselves, and concede too little to others; and privilege equally degrades the poor by cultivating unmanly servility, forgetfulness of the right of every man and woman to demand their fullest share of the common fund of happiness that lies within the State; and by suppressing that desire and power to rise to the highest position in the State, which is the first necessity of a nation of free, honest and self-respecting citizens. The House of Lords, the Property vote, the monopoly of Parliamentary life by the rich—these all belong to the edifice of Privilege, and must be swept away. We hope to help in bringing the day when, as in the United States and in France and in Switzerland, every citizen stands exactly equal before the nation, except in so far as he has been elevated to higher position by the confidence of his fellow citizens.

These are the political questions that require settlement; but it is foolish to deny that vast social reforms imperatively demand treatment. Our statesmen of all parties must make a step in advance, and face boldly and soon the terrible problem of hopeless poverty, unhealthy homes, and overwork or want of work among the masses of the people. The first great step, in our view, towards meeting these difficulties is a vast and radical change in the land laws of the country. The spectacle at the same time, and sometimes even in the same county, on the one hand, of large tracts of land, returning to barrenness, and on the other of overcrowding in lane and alley and slum, is enough to make even the most reactionary Tory perceive that the land system has broken down. Fortunately, the reduction of their own rents has brought the landlords to a condition of mind and pocket most favourable for the consideration of reforms which in the days of their prosperity they would have declined even to discuss.

For the miseries of the poor many other remedies are proposed—the revival of protection, extensive emigration, and remedies which may be classed under the generic term of Socialistic. Protection is the remedy of the foolish or the selfish, and must be vehemently and, if needs be, violently opposed. Emigration is the mere quackery of modern Sangrados that elevate blood-letting to a panacea. As to remedies styled Socialistic, we shall not either accept or oppose them because of any epithet that is applied to them by ignorance, or hostility, or enthusiasm. Epithets are as lying as epitaphs. We shall judge all such proposals on their own merits; and even if unable to agree with them, shall insist that they receive that ample and equal discussion, by which alone truth and falsehood can be finally separated.

In foreign policy, as we have already indicated, our voice shall be for peace, non-intervention, the limitation of the Empire within its present bounds—unions, indeed, we should be able to gather by peaceful methods and mutual goodwill all English-speaking races into one vast federation. We look to the rise of the Democracy all over the world as destined to put an end to those vast armaments and blood feuds, which to us are phases of passing barbarism in man's evolution towards higher things. We look to the time when the masses in Russia and Germany and France will take their governments out of the hands of the Czars and the Emperors, the Chancellors, and the Plutocrats, and demand peace between men who, while born in different lands, have the greater ties of toil, sorrow, and the aspiration after a happier future for the generations to come. The example of an England whose democracy will not permit war, conquest or the revival or maintenance of dead and gone hatreds, will help towards bringing about that holy era of silenced cannon and reconciled nations.

The policy of Great Britain to Ireland is judged by us from the same standpoint. Regarding racial hatreds as barbarous, we can have no sympathy with a policy which perpetuates these hatreds. Regarding all men as more united in their common needs than divided by their place of birth, we can see no reason why Irishmen should not have exactly the same right as Englishmen to choose their method of governing their own affairs; nor can we regard the laws of England and Ireland as equal when the Englishman enjoys and the Irishman is deprived of the four first fundamental rights of free citizenhood—free speech, free writing, free meeting, and free combination. Against the policy, then, of the present Government in Ireland we shall make constant and relentless war.

But Ireland wants Home Rule not much worse than the people of London. As the Irishman is ruled by an irresponsible clique in Dublin Castle, Londoners are ruled by one of the worst and most corrupt oligarchies that ever disgraced and robbed a city. The farmers of Ireland are robbed by the landlords; the poor of London are robbed by the Corporation and the Companies of the education and the food which were left to them by the pious and the humane of past generations. The other boards of London are in no way representative; and are besides incompetent, extravagant, in many cases corrupt. To rich and poor alike, the present system of government is inimical; leaving the greatest and wealthiest city in the world the most helpless and impotent before any emergency. One fall of snow, a single fog, reduces London to chaos. Recently the want of popular control, especially over the police, has encouraged on the part of the Government and of the police authorities, a system of violent suppression of popular rights which would be impossible in a self-governed city.

Nor are public bodies the only ones from which the Londoner demands and requires relief. The gas companies and the water companies, the market monopolists—all find in the Londoner a helpless victim. Against all these things, we proclaim war. We hope to bring before the people and the representatives of London, a policy that shall form a distinct Radical policy for London itself. It will mean the election of all public bodies by adult suffrage; the diversion again to the poor of every single penny left to them; cheap water, cheap gas, cheap meat, cheap fish; the exposure, conviction, and punishment of every thief of the public funds.

No measure of Radical reform for London can be complete which does not provide for the taxation of the ground rents. It is as flagitious as it is absurd that while two millions worth of house property should bear all the heavy taxation of a city, as huge and, therefore, as expensive to govern as a nation, four millions worth of ground rents should remain free from one penny of this vast expenditure. It will be our duty to rouse the London householder and lodger from their perilous apathy on this great question; to show them how the fierce and desperate struggle they have to wage for life and bread in the terrible rush of this crowded city is rendered still fiercer and still more desperate by needlessly heavy rents and needlessly heavy taxation—to divert their anger from the visible tax-collector to the invisible landlord that skulks and robs behind—and to bring home to their imaginations the great fact that the spectre of land monopoly does not stop short at the house of the farmer or the agricultural laborer, but penetrates to the inmost recesses of their own dingy streets and their own wretched attics. For, of the pounds that the small tradesman pays for his house, of the shillings the seamstress pays for her room, at least a quarter goes to the idle and the opulent landowner that lives in luxury and ease in the West-end of London. Cheap houses for the tradesman, cheap rooms for the artisan of London, is, then, another plank in our platform.

These are our political views and purposes; but we make no appeal for support on these alone. We shall endeavour to present to our readers the best halfpenny journal in London or the provinces. The first necessity of a newspaper is news; and to news we shall give a larger amount of space than any other journal of equal size; not stinting money or labour in procuring it. In every department of a newspaper we hope to be equal to any journal published, resolved that though our limits forbid us giving everything at the length of larger journals, we shall by proper compression pass by nothing worth recording. Our commercial, our dramatic, our Parliamentary, and our sporting news have all been placed under the control of competent men. In our editorial department we shall find no place for the verbose and prolix articles to which most of our contemporaries still adhere. We shall have daily but one article of any length, and it will usually be confined within half a column. The other items of the day will be dealt with in notes terse, pointed, and plain-spoken. We believe that the reader of the daily journal longs for other reading than mere politics; and we shall present him with plenty of entirely unpolitical literature—sometimes humorous, sometimes pathetic; anecdotal, statistical, the crame of fashions, and the arts of housekeeping—now and then, a short, dramatic, and picturesque tale. In our reporting columns we shall do away with the hackneyed style of obsolete journalism; and the men and women that figure in the forum or the pulpit or the law court shall be presented as they are—living, breathing, in blushes or in tears—and not merely by the dead words that they utter. Our ideal is to leave no event unrecorded; to be earliest in the field with every item of news; to be thorough and unmistakable in our meaning; to be animated, readable, and stirring.

We start with the immense advantage of supplying instead of creating a want. There is no other halfpenny Radical paper in London to-day. We have been brought into existence by the disgust, contempt, and hate which the malignant and treacherous desertion of the Liberal cause by so-called Liberal papers has created among all true Radicals. Finally, though we have reason to hope for immediate success, we are in a position to wait. The large resources already placed at our disposal, the larger resources that are at our command, enable us to start our newspaper on a more stable foundation than has happened to almost any other journal in its inception. We come to stay.

MAINLY ABOUT PEOPLE.

We have good reason for stating that the recent decision of the Queen to devote the £70,000 of the Jubilee gift to the Nurses for the Poor, over which so many of our contemporaries have gushed, was far from the first thought of her Majesty. Indeed, it would be more correct to say that it was a decision arrived at unwillingly, and only after almost fierce pressure from wiser heads. The favourite, and if she had been allowed to have her way, the final plan of the Queen was to spend the money on a necklace for the Princess Beatrice.

A strange true story of real life will soon be told—perhaps in the law courts. A peer, whom everybody regarded as a confirmed bachelor, has just startled the fashionable world in which he moves by the announcement that he has been married for 15 years; and that, moreover, he is the father of several legitimate children. The lady he has loved and so honored was formerly in domestic service in his mother's household, and was expelled on exciting the perilous admiration of the son and heir. The faithful lover of the young lady married secretly, and announces his marriage, now that the death of his mother unseals his lips.

It is reported that Miss Phyllis Broughton is engaged to a well-known viscount.

The London papers have been altogether silent about an unpleasant experience which befel Mr. Gladstone on his journey to Florence. The cold, it will be remembered, was very great at the time, and the train in which he was travelling stuck in a snow-drift. For eight long hours it remained there before it could be dug out, and during that time the ex-Premier was a close prisoner.

The ladies and gentlemen who make it their business to keep Home Rulers out of the Queen's Household, can hardly be aware of the fact that Commander Hedworth Lambton, who has just been made captain of the Victoria and Albert, is a staunch friend of the Nationalist cause. Unlike his brothers, Lord Durham and Mr. F. W. Lambton, M.P., Mr. Hedworth Lambton stuck manfully to the Liberal colors, and in 1886 ran Mr. Atherley-Jones close for the candidature for North-west Durham. He is an excellent speaker, and a good Radical, as well as a competent sailor. He has served as flag-lieutenant to Admiral Seymour, has been decorated with the Order of Commander of the Medjidie, and, unlike some commanders of Royal yachts, will be able to steer the Victoria and Albert across the Solent as well as to give the Queen a sound lesson in politics.

There has been a brisk to-do amongst the youngsters of a crack Scotch regiment. The Commander-in-Chief recently put a young friend of his into that regiment, who presently found himself at loggerheads with his brother subalterns. The author of "Bootle's Baby" has told us how extremely disagreeable barrack life may be made to an unpopular sub, and what happened in this instance affords good evidence that her descriptions were taken from life. The junior officers commenced by sending the new-comer to Coventry, and went on to make him the victim of practical jokes. His busby was missing when he wanted it for parade, his cane when he wanted it for a stroll, and so on. Meeting one of his persecutors (the son of a well-known baronet) in a corridor one morning, he accused him of stealing these articles from his rooms, and—as the report goes—was promptly pulled along the corridor by his nose. Still dissatisfied, the young gentleman next complained to his colonel, who replied with brusque good-humour that he would never have a minute's piece if he interfered in all the squabbles of his subalterns. The same evening the Duke's protégé received an anonymous letter, asking him in plain Scotch why he did not leave a regiment where he was obviously not wanted. Then the young man went to his Royal patron, and besought the aid of that military Jove. The Duke, when he had heard the story, made Whitehall ring with plain Bible English, ordered the offending subs to be confined to barracks during Christmas week, and a day or two ago sent one of his generals to reprimand them on parade. But it is said that the Duke's young man will leave the regiment after all.

Lady Anne Blunt has the fiery and fretless eyes of Byron, her grandfather, and the rubicund complexion of one who has gone through much exposure. She and her husband were once fired at by a band of Bedouins and captured, but the announcement of their names and their knowledge of Arabic soon procured their release. Mr. Blunt has the rapt look of an enthusiast.

First number of *The Star*, in January 1888: exemplified the London evenings' practice of splitting the front page between advertising and editorial, with the Mainly About People gossip column prominently placed.

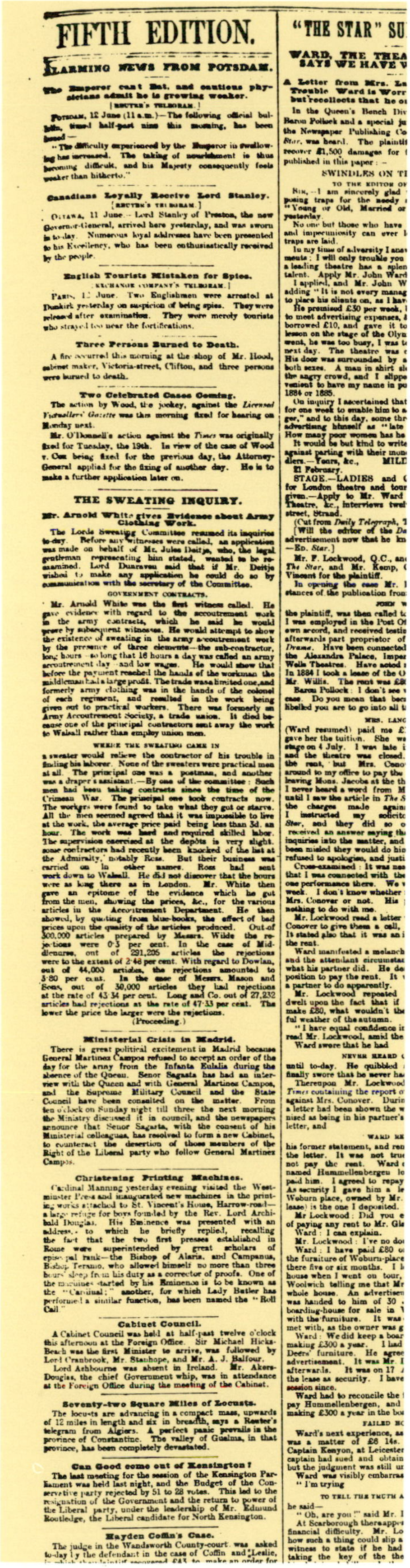

FIFTH EDITION.

ALARMING NEWS FROM POTSDAM.

The Emperor can't Eat, and cautious physicians admit he is growing weaker.

[REUTER'S TELEGRAM.]

POTSDAM, 12 June (11 a.m.)—The following official bulletin, timed half-past nine this morning, has been issued:—

"The difficulty experienced by the Emperor in swallowing has increased. The taking of nourishment is thus becoming difficult, and his Majesty consequently feels weaker than hitherto."

Canadians Loyally Receive Lord Stanley.

[REUTER'S TELEGRAM.]

OTTAWA, 11 June.—Lord Stanley of Preston, the new Governor-General, arrived here yesterday, and was sworn in to-day. Numerous loyal addresses have been presented to his Excellency, who has been enthusiastically received by the people.

English Tourists Mistaken for Spies.

[EXCHANGE COMPANY'S TELEGRAM.]

PARIS, 12 June. Two Englishmen were arrested at Dunkirk yesterday on suspicion of being spies. They were released after examination. They were merely tourists who strayed too near the fortifications.

Three Persons Burned to Death.

A fire occurred this morning at the shop of Mr. Hood, cabinet maker, Victoria-street, Clifton, and three persons were burned to death.

Two Celebrated Cases Coming.

The action by Wood, the jockey, against the *Licensed Victuallers' Gazette* was this morning fixed for hearing on Monday next.

Mr. O'Donnell's action against the *Times* was originally fixed for Tuesday, the 19th. In view of the case of Wood v. Cox being fixed for the previous day, the Attorney-General applied for the fixing of another day. He is to make a further application later on.

THE SWEATING INQUIRY.

Mr. Arnold White gives Evidence about Army Clothing Work.

The Lords Sweating Committee resumed its inquiries to-day. Before any witnesses were called, an application was made on behalf of Mr. Jules Deitje, who, the legal gentleman representing him stated, wanted to be re-examined. Lord Dunraven said that if Mr. Deitje wished to make any application he could do so by communication with the secretary of the Committee.

GOVERNMENT CONTRACTS.

Mr. Arnold White was the first witness called. He gave evidence with regard to the accoutrement work in the army contracts, which he said he would prove by subsequent witnesses. He would attempt to show the existence of sweating in the army accoutrement work by the presence of three elements—the sub-contractor, long hours—so long that 16 hours a day was called an army accoutrement day—and low wages. He would show that before the payment reached the hands of the workman the middleman had a large profit. The trade was a limited one, and formerly army clothing was in the hands of the colonel of each regiment, and resulted in the work being given out to practical workers. There was formerly an Army Accoutrement Society, a trade union. It died because one of the principal contractors sent away the work to Walsall rather than employ union men.

WHERE THE SWEATING CAME IN

a sweater would relieve the contractor of his trouble in finding his laborer. None of the sweaters were practical men at all. The principal one was a postman, and another was a draper's assistant.—By one of the committee: Such men had been taking contracts since the time of the Crimean War. The principal one took contracts now. The workers were found to take what they got or starve. All the men seemed agreed that it was impossible to live at the work, the average price paid being less than 3d. an hour. The work was hard and required skilled labor. The supervision exercised at the depôts is very slight. Some contractors had recently been knocked of the list at the Admiralty, notably Ross. But their business was carried on in other names. Ross had sent work down to Walsall. He did not discover that the hours were as long there as in London. Mr. White then gave an epitome of the evidence which he got from the men, showing the prices, &c., for the various articles in the Accoutrement Department. He then showed, by quoting from blue-books, the effect of bad prices upon the quality of the articles produced. Out of 300,000 articles prepared by Messrs. Wilde the rejections were 0·3 per cent. In the case of Middlemore, out of 291,205 articles the rejections were to the extent of 2·46 per cent. With regard to Dowlan, out of 44,000 articles, the rejections amounted to 3·80 per cent. In the case of Messrs. Mason and Sons, out of 30,000 articles they had rejections at the rate of 43·34 per cent. Long and Co. out of 27,232 articles had rejections at the rate of 47·33 per cent. The lower the price the larger were the rejections.

(Proceeding.)

Ministerial Crisis in Madrid.

There is great political excitement in Madrid because General Martinez Campos refused to accept an order of the day for the army from the Infanta Eulalia during the absence of the Queen. Senor Sagasta has had an interview with the Queen and with General Martinez Campos, and the Supreme Military Council and the State Council have been consulted on the matter. From ten o'clock on Sunday night till three the next morning the Ministry discussed it in council, and the newspapers announce that Senor Sagasta, with the consent of his Ministerial colleagues, has resolved to form a new Cabinet, to counteract the desertion of those members of the Right of the Liberal party who follow General Martinez Campos.

Christening Printing Machines.

Cardinal Manning yesterday evening visited the Westminster Press and inaugurated new machines in the printing works attached to St. Vincent's House, Harrow-road—a large refuge for boys founded by the Rev. Lord Archibald Douglas. His Eminence was presented with an address, to which he briefly replied, recalling the fact that the two first presses established in Rome were superintended by great scholars of episcopal rank—the Bishop of Alaria, and Campanus, Bishop Teramo, who allowed himself no more than three hours' sleep from his duty as a corrector of proofs. One of the machines started by his Eminence is to be known as the "Cardinal;" another, for which Lady Butler has performed a similar function, has been named the "Roll Call."

Cabinet Council.

A Cabinet Council was held at half-past twelve o'clock this afternoon at the Foreign Office. Sir Michael Hicks-Beach was the first Minister to arrive, was followed by Lord Cranbrook, Mr. Stanhope, and Mr. A. J. Balfour.

Lord Ashbourne was absent in Ireland. Mr. Akers-Douglas, the chief Government whip, was in attendance at the Foreign Office during the meeting of the Cabinet.

Seventy-two Square Miles of Locusts.

The locusts are advancing in a compact mass, upwards of 12 miles in length and six in breadth, says a Reuter's telegram from Algiers. A perfect panic prevails in the province of Constantine. The valley of Guelma, in that province, has been completely devastated.

Can Good come out of Kensington?

The last meeting for the session of the Kensington Parliament was held last night, and the Budget of the Conservative party rejected by 51 to 28 votes. This led to the resignation of the Government and the return to power of the Liberal party, under the leadership of Mr. Edmund Routledge, the Liberal candidate for North Kensington.

Hayden Coffin's Case.

The judge in the Wandsworth County-court was asked to-day by the defendant in the case of Coffin and Leslie,

▲ American-style lower-case decks introduced in *The Star's* headlining (June 1888).

a late news device for racing results, using Linotype slugs. Passing rapidly from one axe-grinding owner to another *The Globe* died shortly after the end of the First War.*

The other 'pennies' were an interesting group typographically; they emphasised their selective and (as we would say) 'up the market' appeal by using bookish old style type throughout, in sharp distinction from the conventional newspaper modern and their title-pieces were in roman, not blackletter. Produced in half-sheet – 'tabloid' – format, their leisurely page make-up was usually three-column, with editorial pages in two wide-measure columns. By modern standards their circulations were derisory. On one exceptional big-news night *The Globe* reached a 125,000 peak, which it never came in sight of again. The others appear to have rated an average of no more than around 20,000 at best.

Among this group only the *Pall Mall*, under the sensational editorship of W. T. Stead, made an important contribution to the 'New Journalism'. The other vital contributors were the two new 'halfpennies' of the 1880s, the *Evening News* and *The Star*, especially the latter. Discussing the 'New Journalism' in chapter XV of *The English Newspaper* Morison stressed the part played by these three evenings and noted that their innovations were American in inspiration. The *Pall Mall*, for example, was the first to introduce what orthodox London journalistic opinion thought the distinctly shocking American device of the interview; it was in an interview with the *Pall Mall* that T. P. O'Connor, editor of the newly-born *Star*, said that 'in many respects the American paper will be my model.'

Morison's view reflected the opinions voiced forty years earlier by the best-informed journalistic observers of the time. In 1892 Henry W. Massingham, himself later to edit successively *The Star* and the *Daily Chronicle*, remarked that *The Star* 'represents the most complete adaptation to this country of the method which gives the American Press its vast circulation and immense popularity'. The three examples of 'Americanisation' cited by Massingham were the personal paragraph (the 'Mainly About People' column pioneered by *The Star* had become extremely popular), the descriptive report and the descriptive headline. Of the descriptive report which 'aims at giving a picture rather than a literal rendering', he said:

'Within certain limits there can be no doubt that this method presents a healthy break to the dullness of English reporters. The American reporter not only works a great deal harder for his money than his English brother but he puts much more observation, surface cleverness and literary knack into his work. The result of the opposite course pursued by the greater part of the English Press has been to banish dash, force and even verisimilitude from the English newspaper. You get from it not a picture of men and women, but a dry clatter of words, words, words.'

On headlining Massingham thought that 'the American practice might be partially adopted without offence to good taste.' He noted that the multi-decker American heading amounted to a 'shorthand description' of the following text, thus conveniently allowing the reader to get the gist of the news by glancing at the headlines; this 'clearly rids the hasty reader of such generic descriptions as "Extraordinary Affair" and "Strange Occurrence", which really indicate little but the sub-editor's inability to use his own language.'[3]

The process of 'Americanising' the headlines was gradual. It took Stead's 'Maiden Tribute of Modern Babylon' sensation – exposing the scandal of the purchase of little girls for prostitution – and his subsequent imprisonment, to shake the gentlemanly *Pall Mall* into bolder headings; but the effect was unmistakable. When the paper got an exclusive political story of the first importance early in 1894 it led its three-column main news-page with a three-decker of four lines in bold Grot, condensed and square, well-spaced and followed by a brief,

* The paper's plant in the Strand survived for a while as the Globe Rotary Press Ltd and was to print the first Communist Party daily paper to be issued in Britain – the *Communist Daily*, a sheet which appeared for three days during the General Election of November 1922.

IMPENDING RESIGNATION OF MR. GLADSTONE.

GRAVE POLITICAL CRISIS.

DISSOLUTION PROBABLE.

We have reason to know, from an authority which we are not able to disclose, but in which we have every confidence, that Mr. Gladstone has finally decided to resign office almost immediately. We understand that the letter announcing his resolution will be sent to the Queen before the reassembling of Parliament. This decision is due to a sense of his advanced age and to the great strain of the late arduous session. He is also deeply disappointed at the rejection of the Home Rule Bill, and at the opposition which the Parish Councils Bill has encountered. Domestic pressure, moreover, has not been without considerable influence in determining his mind at last. Who will succeed him? And what will be the result?

THE MATABELE CAMPAIGN.

SETTLEMENT ROUND BULUWAYO.

BARBAROUS CRUELTY BY A WITCH DOCTOR.

On the return of Sir John Willoughby and Hon. Maurice Gifford's from searching for Captain Williams's body, they met the Induna whose impi destroyed Major Wilson and his party, and received confirmation of the details already given of the gallant defence and death of Wilson and his men. Mr. Cecil Rhodes has promised that if the patrol party which has gone out under Colonel Goold-Adams to seek for the bodies of Wilson's party is successful in its search, he will bear the cost of the conveyance of the remains to Zimbabye, as well as of the burial and the erection of a monument to the memory of the gallant dead. Heavy rains have set in. Numerous settlements are being made round Buluwayo. Prospectors are active, and one claims the discovery of an alluvial field near Inyati. All the farms between Buluwayo and Tati have been secured. The Bechuanaland Police have been placed at the disposal of the Chartered Company, who are administering the whole country.

HORRIBLE TORTURE OF A WOMAN.

Sir Henry Loch, the High Commissioner, has received a report from Colonel Goold-Adams announcing that he has captured a notorious witch-doctor who has visited the kraals in the vicinity of Shiloh and carried off many women and children. In one instance a woman who fell into his hands was murdered in the most horrible manner. Her hands and feet were bound together, and the doctor then pricked out her eyes with needles. She was afterwards thrown into the Khami river, where she was torn to pieces by crocodiles. On hearing of this atrocity, Colonel Goold-Adams ordered the arrest of the witch-doctor and the victim's husband, and they were both tried for murder and condemned to be shot. The other women and children seized by the witch-doctor were set at liberty. Colonel Goold-Adams states that the natives in the district are engaged in sowing.

LIEUTENANT MIZON BANQUETTED

THE DREAM OF OTHER DAYS REALIZED.

PARIS, Wednesday.—The Industrial and Commercial Society of the Colonies gave a banquet yesterday evening to Lieutenant Mizon, the explorer. Addressing those present, Lieutenant Mizon said what formerly had been regarded as a dream, had become a reality, and that was the junction in the vicinity of Lake Tchad, of the French African possessions of Algeria, Senegal, and the Congo. He briefly sketched the work of the French explorers, Monteil, Le Maistre, and De Brazza, and then referring to Adamawa, he stated that this kingdom had been placed by treaty under the protection of the Republic, and a military post had been established at Yola, while he himself had governed Mouri and Bachama for a year. The dream of other days had thus been realized. M. Mizon concluded by extolling the advantages of colonies for the mother country.—*Reuter*.

ENTRY OF THE DUKE OF COBURG INTO GOTHA.

GOTHA, Wednesday.—To-day being the day fixed for the State entry of the new Duke of Saxe-Coburg-Gotha into this capital, the town is everywhere gaily adorned with flags and banners, and decked with draperies of bunting in the German, Coburg, and British colours. The houses are almost without exception decorated with bright-coloured hangings of all kinds, and the whole presents a pretty spectacle. The streets to be traversed by the Ducal procession are lined by rows of tall Venetian masts, decorated with flags and streamers and joined one to another by garlands of fir-cuttings. From an early hour crowds of sightseers have been pouring into the town from the surrounding districts, and the streets are thronged with spectators in holiday attire. The sky is overcast, but there is no rain at present.—*Reuter*.

THE CAPTURE OF JABEZ BALFOUR.

DECISION OF THE NATIONAL GOVERNMENT.

THE ACT OF INTERNATIONAL COURTESY.

(FROM OUR OWN CORRESPONDENT.)

[PER THE EASTERN TELEGRAPH COMPANY, LIMITED.]

BUENOS AYRES, Wednesday.—The National Government has ordered the Governor of Salta to send Jabez Balfour here.

LONDON OFFICER LEAVES FOR ARGENTINA.

All the additional warrants, documents, papers, &c., having now been prepared and completed, Sergeant Craggs, of the Criminal Investigation Department, will proceed from Liverpool to-day by the Pacific liner *Britannia*. So far as is at present known, no other officer of the Metropolitan Police will go to the River Plate.

TEXT OF THE EXTRADITION TREATY.

An Order in Council, dated "At the Court at Osborne House, Isle of Wight, the 29th day of January, 1894," is published in yesterday's *London Gazette*. The Order embodies the whole of the Extradition Treaty made with the Argentine Republic on the 22nd May, 1889, of which ratifications were exchanged at Buenos Ayres on the 15th December, 1893; and orders that, in accordance with this treaty, the Extradition Acts of 1870 and 1873 shall apply to the Argentine Republic from and after the 9th February, 1894. This date has obviously been fixed in compliance with an article of the treaty which provides that it shall come into force "ten days after its publication, in conformity with the forms prescribed by the high contracting parties." It is therefore evident that Jabez Balfour has not been arrested under the Extradition Treaty, and the original announcement is confirmed, that "the arrest was made, not as implying any right on the part of the British Government to demand it, but as an act of international courtesy." The question of retrospective action is not in any way referred to in the treaty.

LIABILITY OF THE CONVICT WRIGHT.

In the Queen's Bench Divisional Court, yesterday afternoon, Mr. H. S. Theobald applied in the matter of the Liberator Building Society and H. G. Wright, convict, to have an appeal put down as urgent in the paper for Thursday. Counsel said there were proceedings in the City of London Court against Wright, seeking to make him liable for a considerable sum of money. He had taken out an appeal for security for costs, and it was most desirable that the appeal should be heard at once. As was well known, Jabez Balfour was expected in England before long, and when he came it would be necessary for the books of the Liberator Society to be handed over to him so that he might have an inspection of them. That would practically be preventing them from getting a hearing, as the books could not in the event be produced in the City of London Court. The other side did not in terms object or consent. The appeal was for costs, while in the meantime the whole proceedings were hung up. The Court granted the application, with liberty to the other side to reply.

THE REVOLUTION IN BRAZIL.

INTERVIEW WITH ADMIRAL BENHAM.

RIO DE JANEIRO, Tuesday Evening.—Admiral Benham, in the course of an interview on yesterday's incident said: "On Friday the batteries on Cobras Island fired at an American ship. Admiral da Gama claimed in defence of this proceeding that blank shots were first fired, warning the vessel that it was within the danger line. I ordered him, however, to cease. Nevertheless, on Saturday the fort on Cobras Island and the cruiser *Trajano* both fired at the barque *Agate*. I warned Da Gama that if he repeated this firing on American vessels I would fire back. If Admiral da Gama touches an American ship or American goods he is pirate. I will protect American vessels absolutely except against chance shots. I also notified Admiral da Gama unofficially that firing at the wharves for the purpose of terrorizing traders, and enforcing a blockade would not be permitted as far as it affected Americans. Admiral da Gama returned no answer. Three American vessels afterwards wanted to go to the wharves. I notified Admiral da Gama that I meant to convoy them at sunrise on Monday, and

THE FLEET WAS CLEARED FOR ACTION.

Two of the vessels, after all, declined to come in, but the *Amy* did so, escorted by the *Detroit*. I thought a fight was possible, and made every preparation for one. The cruisers *New York*, *Charleston*, and *Newark* were assigned to deal with the ironclad *Aquidaban* and the cruiser *Almirante Tamandare*, and the cruisers *Detroit* and *San Francisco* with the cruisers *Trajano* and *Guanabara*. The last-named fired a musket shot at the *Amy* whereupon the *Detroit* fired two shots at the *Guanabara* and *Trajano*. All opposition to the convoy of the *Amy* to the wharves at once ceased.

THERE WAS NO NECESSITY TO USE THE HEAVY GUNS.

The reason the other two vessels stayed out was that they were persuaded to do so by the captain of the *Julia Rollins*, who is believed to be the agent of an English firm which is furnishing the insurgents with money. Later in the day Admiral da Gama conferred with his officers on the question of surrendering to the *Detroit* in consequence of the musket shots fired at the *Guanabara* and *Trajano*, but it was decided not to do so. The insurgent leader may, however, surrender yet. Admiral da Gama is in a bad way. The compromise considered at the conference on board the *New York* was rejected by the Government. Admiral de Mello's prolonged absence has given rise to a rumour that he is dead. There are sixteen foreign warships now here, of which five are American and four British. The French commander has congratulated Admiral Benham on the vigorous action taken by him yesterday. The Austrian commander cleared for action in readiness to assist Admiral Benham, in the event of an engagement with the insurgent warships.—*Reuter*,

REPORTED DEFEAT OF GOVERNMENT TROOPS.

BUENOS AYRES, Tuesday Night.—According to intelligence from Rio de Janeiro, Curutiba, Paranagua, and Antonina are in the hands of the insurgents. The Government troops are stated to have fled, abandoning their arms and ammunition. Admiral De Mello is at Curutiba, and is reorganizing the administration of the province.—*Reuter*.

THE INSURRECTION IN MEXICO.

DEFEAT OF THE REBELS.

MEXICO, Tuesday Night.—The insurrection in the northern part of the Mexican Republic has been crushed by the Federal troops. The filibusters Ochoa and Lugan were overtaken in the Sierra Neguracbie where they made a determined stand. The fight between the insurgents and the Government forces lasted eleven hours. The rebels lost thirty men killed, and twenty-five wounded, while of the Government troops one officer and seven men were killed and twelve wounded. Ochoa escaped and fled.—*Reuter*.

THE REBELLION IN HAYTI.

NEW YORK, Wednesday.—A despatch from Port au Prince states that the Haytian revolutionists are despondent. General Manigat, the leader of the Haytian revolutionary cause, was arrested at Kingston as he was about to enter a boat to be rowed to a steamer of which he was to take command, and which had been purchased for him by his agents in America. The arrest of their leader upsets all the plans of the revolutionists for their contemplated invasion of Hayti.—*Dalziel*.

MILITARY INTELLIGENCE.

PORTSMOUTH, Wednesday.—The hired transport *Bothnia*, sailed at eight o'clock this morning for Karachi with military reliefs under Major Taylor, of the Derbyshire regiment, numbering 39 officers, 570 rank and file, 24 soldiers' wives, and 14 children. She will call at Queenstown, where she will embark 600 more troops.—*Reuter*.

CORDITE PATENT IN CHANCERY.

THE "PALL MALL'S" CHARGES TRIED.

Upon the resumption to-day of the hearing of the Nobel Explosives Company's action against the Government for the infringement of their ballistite patent in the Ordnance Department's manufacture of cordite, Sir Charles Russell continued to cross-examine Dr. Odling, the Oxford Professor of Chemistry, who had declared cordite and ballistite to be, as Mr. Noble alleges them to be, practically the same thing. But Sir Charles was not the cross-examining terror that he usually is on the Queen's Bench side of the courts. Sir Charles is a specialist in human nature, but in matters of patent law he is a child in comparison with Mr. Fletcher Moulton, who leads for the plaintiff, or with Sir Richard Webster, who, ex-Attorney-General as he is, has been briefed by the Government to reinforce the Attorney-General's own not very formidable forces. Sir Charles was as far away from home in this case as Mr. Moulton might be on a sporting trial; but of course so great an advocate was not and could not be at anything like a loss for tactics. He had been well crammed with the technicalities of the matters in dispute. It was only in resourcefulness and facility of handling that his leading opponent showed to so much greater advantage. Mr. Moulton could doubtless conduct the whole case without any documents to refer to, and did, indeed, open the case exhaustively without notes. Sir Charles Russell does not dare to take a single step without consulting his voluminous references, unless it was upon a whispered suggestion from Sir Richard Webster that he proceeded.

THE POINT OF DIFFERENCE.

It was difficult to follow the line of the cross-examination, but it seemed to suggest that the nitro-cellulose employed in the cordite was of a more soluble variety than that employed in ballistite, enabling cordite to be manufactured in a manner altogether different from that of ballistite. Witness admitted that, according to the specification of ballistite, it was an essential that the substance in course of manufacture should be pressed between heated rollers, while in the manufacture of cordite no heated rollers were used, nor was there any pressure at all in the same sense, although in the kneading process used in cordite-making there was necessarily and obviously a certain degree of compression.

So far from heat being used at Waltham Abbey, a contrivance is resorted to in order to avoid heat?—Yes.

While in the manufacture of ballisite the rollers are heated to 100 degs. Centigrade, or boiling point?—That is so.

Other distinctions which Sir Charles elicited from the witness were that in cordite there was no camphor, but there was vaseline; while in ballistite there was no vaseline, and the use of camphor in the manufacture was optional. Sir Charles also put to the witness that while immersion in alcohol would reduce ballistite to a jelly, the same treatment applied to cordite would leave sticks of insoluble gun-cotton. Witness believed this to be so, but had never made the experiments.

THE RE-EXAMINATION.

All this while Mr. Moulton, who is a Senior Wrangler with the uncultured habit of continually wetting his pencil on his tongue, had been making voluminous notes, and it was he who re-examined Dr. Odling. He did it with the air of one revelling in these abstruse and highly technical matters. The case seems to be a scientific debauch for Mr. Moulton. Witness stated that the camphor used in ballistite-making was merely to facilitate the combination of the other ingredients. In the specification, acetone was mentioned as an alternative to camphor, and acetone was used in making cordite. What was used was driven off in the final stages in the making of both cordite and ballistite. Vaseline was used in cordite making, but before it was added the ingredients were thoroughly incorporated for 3½ hours. The vaseline did not alter the character of the union of nitro-cellulose and nitro-glycerine. There was no essential difference between the method and the result of the manufacture of the two things, beyond the one difference of the high temperature rolling in ballistite making.

Much has been made of the different results obtainable by the solution of the two things in alcohol. Is the great object for which they are made to put them into alcohol?—No.

Their use is as propellers of projectiles?—Yes.

And the immersion in alcohol fulfils absolutely no use except for test purposes?—That is so.

THE CLOSING OF BRUSSELS UNIVERSITY.

STUDENTS' DISORDERLY CONDUCT.

BRUSSELS, Wednesday.—Three hundred of the students have addressed a protest to the Pro-Rector, expressing their sympathy with their expelled comrades, and declaring that they will not enter the University until the present Council is dismissed. The twenty-two students of the University who have been expelled gave the Pro-Rector a hostile reception yesterday, in which they, aided by about two hundred of their companions, hooted him vigorously. So threatening did their attitude become that the Pro-Rector had to be protected by the professors who accompanied him The Pro-Rector announced that the University would be closed until further notice, whereupon the students formed themselves into a procession and paraded the principal streets of the city, singing and shouting, and headed by a banner bearing the words "The Unemployed." The demonstrators strongly support the attitude taken by Dr. Denis, the late Rector, who resigned owing to the action of the Council, and Professor Greef. The latter, it is said, will hold his class outside the University, probably in the Freemasons' Hall. It is expected that when M. Elisée Reclus, the cause of all the trouble, comes to Brussels to deliver his lectures, his presence will give rise to Socialist disorders.—*Dalziel*.

A REGISTRATION AGENT'S DIVORCE SUIT.

The further hearing of the case of White v. White and Bovington was resumed this morning before Sir F. Jeune in the Divorce Division, it being the petition of Mr. Edward White, a Liberal registration agent in London, for a dissolution of his marriage with the respondent on the ground of her misconduct with the co-respondent. Mrs. White, the respondent, entered the witness-box and denied that she had been guilty of adultery.

ATTEMPTED SUICIDE THROUGH LOVE.

A young man named Green attempted to commit suicide last night at Chatham by cutting his throat. When discovered he moaned, "It is all for the love of her." He now lies in St. Bartholomew's Hospital, Rochester, in a critical condition.

WRECKS AND CASUALTIES.

During last night's gale a large iron vessel, laden with a general cargo bound for Glasgow, struck on Thorn Island at the entrance to Milford Haven. The vessel is partly submerged, the bows alone being above water and the forecastle is on fire. The crew were saved by the *Angle* lifeboat and rocket apparatus.

The large steamer, *Henry Fisher*, which ran ashore at Hayle during Monday night's gale, remains high and dry, and it is feared that unless the weather abates it will be difficult to tow her off.

IN THE LONDON BANKRUPTCY COURT TO-DAY.

JOHN LUTTMAN.

The Official Receiver reported to-day upon the affairs of John Luttman, who states that since 1871 he has carried on business as a financial agent, company promoter, and accountant, having an office from 1888 until October last at No. 1, Gresham-buildings, City. The liabilities amount to £9,899, and the assets are returned at £10. The debtor, who admits that he has been insolvent for some years past, has been adjudged bankrupt.

Herald's title changes was matched by the successive changes in its headline typography. We have charted something of its erratic gothic course during the war. With the coming of peace the sans variations were abandoned in favour of an all-Century style, later enlivened with gothic 'kickers', *Express* fashion; but the general style bore little sign of any consistent attempt to copy the *Express*. The overall effect of the Century make-up was curiously flat, largely because of the excessive use of the Bold Extended in the smaller down-page headings. The horizontal spread of the Extended exaggerated the squareness and shortness of the page, arising from the 21-inch cutoff. It resembled the way in which a horizontally striped frock exaggerates the figure defects of a short, stout woman.

In 1951 sans reappeared as a major ingredient of the paper's headline style, in the form of Tempo Heavy capitals; these mated well with Century Bold lower-case, particularly the italic. It looked as if the paper had at last arrived at a strong, well contrasted, flexible headline style of its own. But the Odhams authorities, casting anxious and envious eyes on the success of the *Mirror* in winning working-class readers, were only too willing to be persuaded, by *Mirror* men they had recruited, that it was merely necessary to give the broadsheet *Herald* the sledgehammer sans treatment of the tabloid. This was duly done. It at least provided a permanent object lesson in the error of thinking that what works with a tabloid will automatically work with a broadsheet. Equally it must have caused critical reactions among the paper's controllers, for from the autumn of 1957 a much more moderate sans style was adopted, playing on the medium-weight Square Gothic and for lead headings the capitals of Record Gothic Bold Medium Extended, apart from a strange outcrop in the spring of 1959 of the large-size Gill Bold Titling fancied by the London *Evening News*. Later in 1959, however, the *Mirror* style was resumed, and even more stridently; extra-large sizes, e.g. 120pt, of smashing poster sans, heavy and condensed, were specially cut in duralumin by Joyce, the wood-letter manufacturers.

This super-*Mirror* treatment continued into 1960; but that autumn what can only be called an *Express* faction temporarily got the upper hand. The news typography of the paper was radically changed to a fair copy of the *Express* Century Bold, Bold Extended style, after an odd start with the front-page streamer in Ludlow Caslon Bold capitals, a vapid letter for a main news heading. Still there was to be no permanency, though. In the spring of 1961 the *Express*-style Century Bold Extended streamers were displaced by two-line streamers in the 96pt capitals of Tempo Bold Condensed. Certainly this was a medium-weight type, but in so large a size the somewhat mannered drawing of Tempo – the splayed 'M' and the cut of the 'S', for example – betray only too clearly its origin as an advertising display letter. Yet the Century was gradually phased out and for the last two years of its life the *Herald* drew mainly on various weights and styles of Tempo for its news headings, with the exception of the front-page lead. Here heavy Gothic Condensed capitals, usually in 84pt, took the place of the Tempo Bold Condensed.

The above analysis of the astonishing typographical manifestations which accompanied the decline and fall of the *Daily Herald* has taken us rather far, in terms both of space and time. Attention must now be given to the general picture of war and immediate post-war developments in newspaper presentation. There was very little in the way of any radical approach to the problems, apart from a striking scheme by Robert Harling for a new kind of tabloid front page. Harling's *Daily Sketch* proposal, prepared while on leave from the Navy in 1942, was clearly much too *avant-garde* for Lord Kemsley and never got beyond the dummy stage. In the continuing period of newsprint rationing in the late 1940s the *Daily Mirror* showed great ingenuity in close-packing a page while keeping it brisk and vigorous; as the newsprint situation eased during the 1950s the 'presentational heavy

▼ Robert Harling's 1942 *Daily Sketch* dummy displayed a radically new approach to news presentation, but did not get beyond the proof stage.

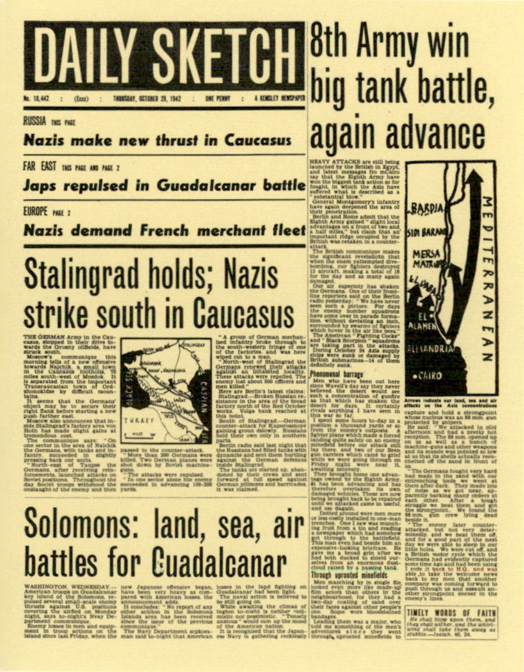
DAILY SKETCH

No. 10,442 : (Exxx) : THURSDAY, OCTOBER 29, 1942 : ONE PENNY : A KEMSLEY NEWSPAPER

RUSSIA THIS PAGE

Nazis make new thrust in Caucasus

FAR EAST THIS PAGE AND PAGE 2

Japs repulsed in Guadalcanar battle

EUROPE PAGE 2

Nazis demand French merchant fleet

Stalingrad holds; Nazis strike south in Caucasus

Solomons: land, sea, air battles for Guadalcanar

8th Army win big tank battle, again advance

Arrows indicate our land, sea and air attacks on the Axis concentrations

TIMELY WORDS OF FAITH

He shall blow upon them, and they shall wither, and the whirlwind shall take them away as stubble.—Isaiah, 40, 24.

ARE THEY ALL LIARS AND SCAREMONGERS?

- **IS SIR ANTHONY EDEN PLANNING A WAR WITH EGYPT? GREAT NEWSPAPERS AND FAMOUS PEOPLE IN THIS COUNTRY ARE DEEPLY CONCERNED ABOUT HIS SECRET PLANS.**
- **HERE ARE THEIR VIEWS:**

'Risks greater than those it would cure..'

From The Economist, August 25, 1956, edited by Mr. Donald Tyerman:

There is in Britain one school of thought which reckons that, failing negotiation, the only way to prevent this triumph and its consequences is to pull President Nasser up short by means of a quick military operation designed to upset him and strengthen his Asian enemies.

But would this act yield such a result? There is another and more sober school which holds that such an operation would invite risks greater than those it would cure.

Mr. Donald Tyerman, Editor of The Economist and formerly assistant editor of The Times.

Mr. Laurence Cadbury, chairman of the News Chronicle.

'Playing a dangerous game'

From the News Chronicle of Sept. 1:

Mr. Gaitskell's new request [for a recall of Parliament] reflects growing irritation among Labour leaders at the Government's failure so far to make its policy clear.

They are inclined to discount a good deal of the war talk, because they feel no administration would start a war which would be disapproved by the Opposition, part of the Press, and perhaps a majority of the public.

But they feel that the Government is playing a dangerous game—even if it is largely bluff—by allowing the impression to grow that it 'means business.'

Mr. Hugh Gaitskell, leader of the Labour Party.

'RECENT TROOP MOVEMENTS . . .'

Report from the Daily Herald yesterday:

"Mr. Hugh Gaitskell, Leader of the Opposition, speaking in Leeds on Sunday night, urged the Government to make it plain that recent troop movements were purely for self-defence, and that no action would be taken in conflict with the United Nations Charter.

"He called on the Government to denounce reports 'coming from Whitehall' suggesting that force might be used to find a Suez solution."

Daily Mirror
2d FORWARD WITH THE PEOPLE
No. 16,401
TUES SEPT 4 1956

Mr. David Astor, the Editor of The Observer.

'Wild man' in the background?

From The Observer, September 2:

It seems to be the deliberate policy of the British and French Governments to continue military preparations against Nasser without publicly specifying the conditions for taking military action.

Probably Sir Anthony Eden thinks that his show of force will help the negotiators, allowing them to explain that **they** are reasonable people, but that there is a wild man in the background.

Sir Vincent Tewson, General Secretary of the T.U.C.

'Force should not be used until...'

This emergency resolution will be put to the Trades Union Congress annual conference at Brighton this week:

Congress . . . hopes that the proposals of the eighteen Governments now being submitted by the committee of five to the Egyptian Government will lead to a speedy and satisfactory settlement. Should the talks break down, force should not be used until the question has been referred to the United Nations and with its consent.

'Poised to attack'

Here is an extract from Mr. Richard Crossman's column on Page 4 of today's Daily Mirror:

Britain and France are now preparing to take the law into their own hands. We are poised to attack Nasser if he does not do our bidding. And the trouble is that Sir Anthony has staked his whole personal prestige on a triumph over Nasser.

What will be the cost of this policy?

From the Manchester Guardian editorial, August 31:

The Government seems to be preparing to go to war immediately if Mr. Menzies's mission fails...what will the Government's policy cost?

A damaged American alliance, a broken Commonwealth, the waste of many British and Egyptian lives, economic isolation of Britain and France or the end of the United Nations, no oil, and an open door for Russia in the Middle East.

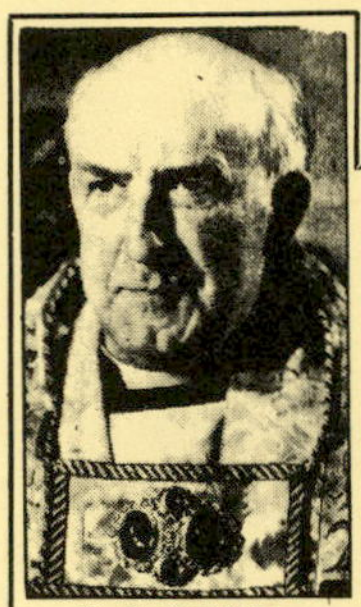

Dr. Geoffrey Fisher, Archbishop of Canterbury.

DR. GEOFFREY FISHER, the Archbishop of Canterbury, addressing the TUC delegates at Brighton on Sunday:

In the field of international politics, everyone knows that war is no longer compatible with civilisation: that when nations dispute with one another, the appeal should always be no longer to force against force, but to reason against reason.

But to change from the one to the other is terribly difficult and risks disaster. Right-minded statesmen know the fierceness of the dilemma. . . .

If the answer to unreason must not be found in force, then it must look to the co-operation and partnership of all the reasonable and right-minded...

That is the principle which is directing the foreign policy of this and other freedom-loving nations.

Mr. A. P. Wadsworth, Editor of the Manchester Guardian.

'War with whole Arab world?'

From a speech on Sunday by Mr. John Strachey, M.P., who was War Minister in the Labour Government:

Unless Labour stops it, this Tory Government will get us into war with the whole Arab world.

Of all the foolish things the Government has done over Suez, inviting French troops to Cyprus is the most dangerous.

We risk being involved in the hopeless attempt of the French to crush the Arab movement for independence in Algeria.

I demand the immediate recall of Parliament before the British Army is used to support the last attempt to maintain an outworn French imperialism — for that is what it amounts to.

THE TIME HAS COME FOR EDEN TO TELL THE NATION

- **Is he planning a war with Egypt?**
- **If so, under what conditions would he use military power?**

Daily Mirror, Tues. Sept. 4, 1956.

Printed and Published by the DAILY MIRROR NEWSPAPERS, Ltd., at Geraldine House, Fetter-lane, London, E.C.4. Tel. Holborn 4321, and at Mark-lane, Manchester, 4. Tuesday, September 4, 1956.

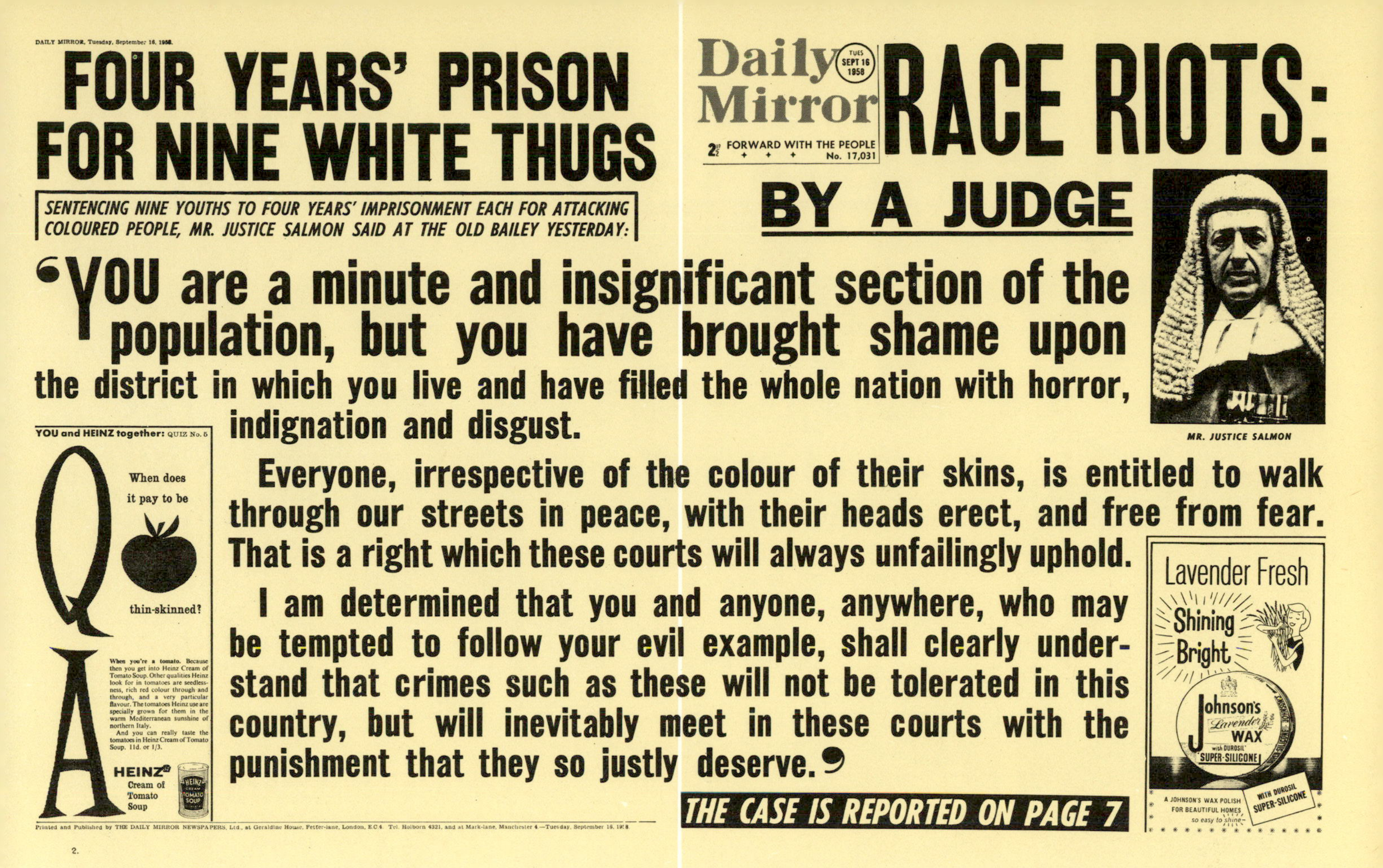

DAILY MIRROR, Tuesday, September 16, 1958.

FOUR YEARS' PRISON FOR NINE WHITE THUGS

SENTENCING NINE YOUTHS TO FOUR YEARS' IMPRISONMENT EACH FOR ATTACKING COLOURED PEOPLE, MR. JUSTICE SALMON SAID AT THE OLD BAILEY YESTERDAY:

Daily Mirror — TUES SEPT 16 1958 — 2d FORWARD WITH THE PEOPLE No. 17,031

RACE RIOTS: BY A JUDGE

MR. JUSTICE SALMON

'YOU are a minute and insignificant section of the population, but you have brought shame upon the district in which you live and have filled the whole nation with horror, indignation and disgust.

Everyone, irrespective of the colour of their skins, is entitled to walk through our streets in peace, with their heads erect, and free from fear. That is a right which these courts will always unfailingly uphold.

I am determined that you and anyone, anywhere, who may be tempted to follow your evil example, shall clearly understand that crimes such as these will not be tolerated in this country, but will inevitably meet in these courts with the punishment that they so justly deserve.'

THE CASE IS REPORTED ON PAGE 7

Printed and Published by THE DAILY MIRROR NEWSPAPERS, Ltd., at Geraldine House, Fetter-lane, London, E.C.4. Tel. Holborn 4321, and at Mark-lane, Manchester 4.—Tuesday, September 16, 1958

2.

▲ A thunderous *Mirror* front-and-back (or back-and-front) double-spread of 1958.

◀ Suez (1956) provoked this broadsheet tabloid: a good example of *Mirror* 'presentational heavy artillery'.

▼ By 1959 the *Sunday Express* was firmly established in the square gothic headline style which it has retained.

artillery', as the previous chapter called it, came into effective play.

Among the Sunday papers the long-established 'heavies' settled down quickly to a lucid, if conventional, style. The *Observer*, with a strong title in roman capitals (flanked by the Royal arms each side) adopted two basic ingredients, Caslon Heavy and Bodoni Bold roman and italic, which worked tolerably well together. The *Sunday Times*, after experiments with Bodoni deckers and flush-left Century Bold upper- and lower-case, evolved a Century Bold and Bold Extended decker style; in the early 1950s it dropped its blackletter title and, after a brief trial of a medium-weight roman capitals line of Century aspect, settled for a version of Times Extended Titling, surmounted by the Royal arms (flanked by the date and other details) in the manner with which we are now familiar. Among the 'populars' the *Sunday Express* adopted the simple sans presentation, mainly in Square Gothic, with occasional Medium Condensed contrast, which it still retains. Of its mass-sale contemporaries it is only necessary to notice

SUNDAY EXPRESS

JULY 5 1959 — Lighting-up Time 9.48 p.m. to 4.21 a.m. (Mon.). — Founded by LORD BEAVERBROOK — Moon Rises 4.38 a.m. Sets 8.28 p.m. — PRICE 4d.

October 15—and a big win for Tories?

Sunday Express Political Correspondent

THE General Election will now almost certainly be held on Thursday, October 15.

Mr. Harold Macmillan has had three dates for polling day in mind—October 8, 15, or 22.

The Prime Minister will plump for the middle date, I understand, unless some big, unexpected development—for instance, Summit

Four-hour crisis meeting ends in 'no-progress' report —then comes blunt talking from both sides

THREE-DAY REPRIEVE

But little hope of papers after that

Sunday Express Reporter

NATIONAL daily newspapers and the London evening papers are to go on printing until Wednesday. After that, the outlook is bleak.

That was the position which emerged last night after day-long discussions by

88° And bathers go in at midnight

Sunday Express Reporter

IT was the hottest day of the year with temperatures high in the 80's yesterday. And the hottest night too.

At Wimbledon it was 88 in

FOUR STEPS SET A ROYAL POSER

COUSINS WILL INSIST: STOP MAKING BOMB

by LLEW GARDNER

DOUGLAS, Isle of Man, Saturday.

AT his union conference in Douglas next week Mr. Frank Cousins, secretary of the Transport and General Workers, will demand that Britain should cease to manufacture the H-bomb.

Plane hunts tourist's killer

Sunday Express Reporter

INNSBRUCK, Saturday.

AN Austrian Army major flew in a helicopter among the mountains near Innsbruck today hoping to spot a clue leading to the gunman who murdered a British tourist and

NEWS of the WORLD
AND EMPIRE NEWS
SUNDAY, NOVEMBER 20, 1960 No. 6,106 PRICE FOURPENCE

FIND BRENDA NASH —NOW £5,000

News of the World doubles reward

BRENDA NASH MUST BE FOUND. OVER THREE WEEKS AGO THE 12-YEAR-OLD GIRL GUIDE VANISHED FROM HESTON, MIDDLESEX. WIDESPREAD SEARCHES HAVE BEEN UNSUCCESSFUL. ANOTHER HUNT BY 800 CIVIL DEFENCE WORKERS AND POLICE IS DUE IN THE STAINES AREA TODAY. BRENDA'S DISAPPEARANCE HAS DETECTIVES BAFFLED. HER PARENTS ARE SICK WITH GRIEF AND WORRY.

Her father, Mr. James Nash, said yesterday he would sell his few possessions to offer a £500 reward to anyone finding his daughter alive. An anonymous person has already offered a reward of £2,000.

The News of the World wants to help the Nash family. So today we announce, with the full approval of the authorities and the parents, that we offer a reward of £2,500 to the first member of the general public who in the Editor's opinion gives information which leads directly to the discovery of Brenda alive.

We thus double the reward, bringing the total to £5,000.

News of the World readers who believe they can throw any light on Brenda's disappearance should contact their local police-station immediately. Do not phone or call at the News of the World as this may cause delay.

Information will be treated with absolute secrecy. If, as a direct result of such assistance, Brenda is found alive, the News of the World will pay the sum of £2,500 to the person who first gave the information. No clue is too small.

The Editor's decision on who should be rewarded is final.

This moving story from GRAHAM STANFORD shows why Brenda must be found NOW:—

BRENDA NASH

The anguish in a little girl's home

HESTON, Middlesex, Saturday.

IN the kitchen of his home in Bleriot-road, here tonight, James Nash told me of the three weeks of hell that he and his wife have endured.

He was deeply grateful, pathetically grateful, for the gesture of the News of the World in raising the reward offer of £2,000 from an anonymous source and £500 from himself to £5,000.

"It's something practical," he said. "I've scraped together all I can and now with these two other sums we may get results.

"We are grateful for all the sympathy we've received; for all the publicity. But so far there's been nothing; no clue to give us a hope. It's just possible that all this money may help."

Mr. Nash, strained and tense, apologised for not inviting me to his sitting-room. "I know you'll understand," he said. "The wife's in there with the two children (Carole, aged 14, David aged seven) and she doesn't want to see anyone.

"Of course, the TV's on. It always is. But it's on for the children. She really doesn't know whether it's on or not. This has been her worst day, by far her worst day since Brenda went.

CHANGE

"She takes pills, of course, but I don't know how much good they do. I don't know how many more days like this she can stand."

I told Mr. Nash not to talk unless it would help. "That's all right," he said. "Maybe it will help. He looked round the kitchen with its brightly decorated walls, its refrigerator, washing machine and with a boy's toy gun propped in the corner.

"It's just as though this

Continued on Page Eleven

Hinds in handcuffs

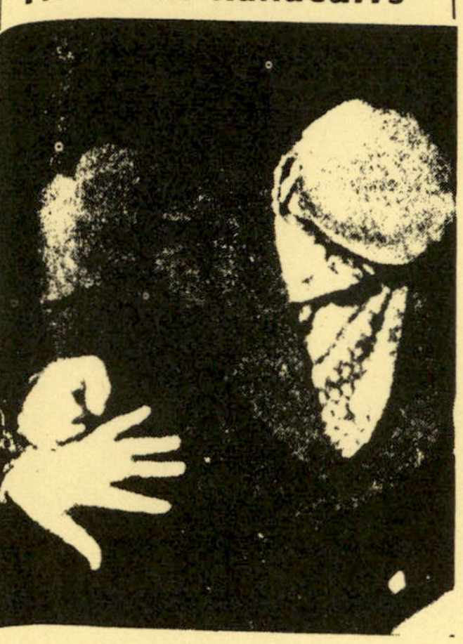

ALFIE HINDS . .

. . . AND LILA

He'll still prove he's innocent—Lila

By JOHN BALL

MASTER gaol-breaker Alfred Hinds flew into London last night and was welcomed at the airport by the strictest security precautions I have ever seen.

Three squad cars plus a score of uniformed police and C.I.D. men surrounded the Viscount airliner as it taxied to rest.

When the stairway was pushed against the aircraft a policeman jumped on to it immediately.

The door opened and Hinds, handcuffed to two Flying Squad men, was led down the steps.

He held his head down and covered his face with a green cap.

Squad car

A squad car was driven swiftly to the foot of the stairway and Hinds was put into the back.

He was then driven off at high speed to Chelmsford, Essex. The whole operation took a matter of seconds.

The next passenger out of the plane was his wife Lila. She told me: "Alfie will never give up hope of proving his innocence."

During the hour and a half flight from Belfast, Lila sat across the gangway from Alfie.

"We talked the whole time about new moves to prove his innocence," she said. "Alfie is going to lodge an appeal to the House of Lords.

"The policemen were very sweet to let me sit so near him. It's the longest chat I have had for some time with him. We didn't touch hands, but before the plane landed I kissed him goodbye. The flight was really wonderful because I could be so near him."

I asked Lila if she thought Alfie would try and make another break for freedom.

She smiled and said: "I may get into trouble but I will say this. When Alfie's free he is able to voice his opinions against this wrongful conviction. I'm looking forward to the next time he escapes."

Hinds was charged at a late night court in the Shire Hall, Chelmsford, with escaping from Chelmsford Gaol in June, 1958. He was taken from the police-station to the court by an underground passage.

After evidence of arrest was given by Det. Insp. Gardiner Hinds was remanded to Brixton prison until tomorrow week when he will again appear at Chelmsford.

Earlier yesterday Hinds failed in another bid for freedom when, through his wife, he asked a Belfast court for his conditional release.

The object of his application made to the Northern Ireland High Court yesterday was to test the validity of a Scotland Yard warrant. He was arrested on this warrant on Friday seconds after he was freed from Belfast Prison where he had served a sentence for smuggling cars. The application was dismissed.

"Tom Brown's schooldays were never like this, eh?"

Lady C for top forms only

SPECIAL conditions have been laid down at Rugby School for boys who wish to buy copies of the unexpurgated edition of "Lady Chatterley's Lover."

The school's main bookshop has been told to sell it only to fifth and sixth form boys who have notes from their housemasters.

DEARER CARS ARE LIKELY

By KEITH CHALLEN

EXPECT a rise in the cost of lower and medium price cars during the next few weeks if sales do not improve.

A British Motor Corporation spokesman said yesterday: "The low volume of production coupled with increased wages and other overheads is a threat to retail prices.

"I cannot see the present selling prices holding if current conditions are maintained. But every manufacturer, anxious to increase his sales, will put off the date of price rises until the last moment."

At Dagenham, car production lines at Britain's biggest vehicle factory, Ford's, which ground to a halt late on Friday, will remain idle tomorrow unless the 1,500 men involved in the wildcat strike change their tactics.

Nearly 20,000 workers have lost their pay as a result of the wildcat action but last night there was hope of an early return to work.

Mr. Henry Ford II., who is trying to get full control of British Fords, gave an assurance in a statement issued in London yesterday that despite the £128,000,000 offer the company will continue as British. Development plans would not be affected.

The offer would be made in sterling at 145s. 6d. a share, subject to Treasury consent. This is 6d. more than the previously reported offer of 145s. a share.

TOP POP . . .

ROCK 'N' ROLL SINGER Marty Wilde is a father. His 19-year-old wife Joyce gave birth to a seven-pound daughter in Chiswick Maternity Hospital, London, yesterday. They're calling her Kim.

. . . NEW CHAMP

ANOTHER new Dad yesterday was Henry Cooper, British and Empire heavyweight champion. It's a boy—and he weighed-in at 7lb. 6oz.

Sir Winston's back is less painful

LORD MORAN, Sir Winston Churchill's personal physician, spent half an hour with him last night. As he left he said: "There's no fresh news. The position is exactly as before."

Earlier, a bulletin said that though Sir Winston had not had a very good night the pain of his injury was less.

He is confined to bed at his home in Hyde Park-gate, London, after breaking a small bone in his back in a fall on Tuesday.

Sir Winston spent a quiet evening yesterday and there were no social callers.

But a nurse arrived by car. Carrying a bag, she rang the front door bell and was quickly admitted.

Then a grey-haired woman physiotherapist called. She left after an hour and said: "He is a wonderful patient. He could not be a better patient. He's getting along."

Another visitor during the day was Professor H. J. Seddon, director of the Royal National Orthopaedic Hospital. He stayed 90 minutes.

Two schoolboys die for a dare

TWO schoolboys died for a dare on the railway at Harold Hill, Romford, Essex, last night. In darkness, lighted only by the gleam of a torch, they raced across in front of a train. The object: To see who could escape by the narrowest margin.

Watching children heard screams and ran for help. Twenty-year-old Andrew Lee and Mr. Frank Tolson, from a general store in Harold Court-road, hurried to the line.

They found Barry Moore, aged 13, of Fairford-way, and 14-year-old Alan Andrews, of Oakley-drive, Harold Hill, lying dead.

A third boy, 14-year-old Richard Moyes, of Stratton-road, escaped with cuts and bruises. He was able to go home after hospital treatment.

Andrew Lee's father, Mr. Arthur Lee, a railway clerk, of Harold Court-road, said: "I've often been to the railway bridge to warn children and send them away. But they usually ignore me."

Gilbert Harding's last wish

TWO Irishmen spoke the thoughts of millions over a deserted grave in Kensal Green Cemetery, London, yesterday: "There'll never be another Gilbert."

They were the words of 30-year-old Bill Kehoe as he and 45-year-old Jimmy Grace, from New Ross, Co. Wexford, took up their shovels to perform their last melancholy duties.

At the bottom of the grave as they sombrely filled it in lay a plain oak coffin and a solitary spray of roses.

It was by Gilbert Harding's own wish that all flowers for his semi-secret funeral had been sent to cancer hospitals.

The mourners consisted only of close friends and relatives, like Gilbert's aunts, Miss Dorothy Harding and Mrs. Constance Clarke, who had driven up from Hampshire.

Roger Storey, Gilbert's devoted private secretary, wept as the priest sprinkled holy water into the grave.

Miss Harding said to me: "Gilbert expressly wished a very quiet and small funeral."

An hour earlier Eamonn Andrews, associated with so many of Gilbert's TV shows, had sadly left the church of St. Charles Borromeo, Ogle-street, Marylebone, where a simple Mass had been said.

Gilbert Harding lived in a welter of publicity and upheaval. It was in quiet solitude which he would have appreciated that Jimmy Grace and Bill Kehoe covered with a green sward the last mortal glimpse of the man known to 50,000,000.

HARDING — the man behind a TV mask—Page 10.

LIFE, LOVE AND LOREN!

THIS IS IT. The Sophia Loren story. The story you've waited for. Told by the girl herself. The girl Frank Sinatra once summed up in two words: "THE MOST."

This is the LOT. Her struggle from a slum home to fame and riches. Her battle with the small men who sought to exploit her exciting beauty. Her tender love story with the great man who coaxed into full flower a sparkling talent to match that beauty.

NOW TURN TO PAGES 4 AND 5 FOR THE FIRST FASCINATING INSTALMENT.

WEEK-END WEATHER

- Rain after early morning fog. Skies will clear later as winds freshen. Average temperatures.

Further Outlook.—Continuing changeable.

Lighting-up Times (G.M.T.).—
London 4.34 p.m. to 6.58 a.m.
Southampton 4.42 to 7.01
Dover 4.30 to 6.51.
Cambridge 4.31 to 7.00.

◀ The jolly jumble of founders' type in the 1960 *News of the World*: here are Granby Elephant, Grot No. 9, Clearface Bold, Old Style No. 6 (Stephenson Blake), Royal Gothic, Bodoni, Minster Bold (Stevens, Shanks). Clearface Extra Bold, roman and italic and Cheltenham Bold were among other faces to be seen in the paper at this time.

that peculiar institution the *News of the World*, which at the turn of the 1950s and 1960s suddenly dropped both its institutional Latin Elongated deckers and its splendid, scrolled 'music hall' title-piece. Briefly retaining the figure of Britannia (central feature of the old title), with a title-line in that odd white-lined American Doric, Comstock, it soon abandoned the lady and settled for its present plain title in heavy antique capitals. For its headlines the typefounders supplied a positively Gallic riot of movable type – heavy Doric (roman and italic). Grot No. 9 italic, Clearface Extra Bold, Cheltenham Bold, Winchester Bold italic, Bodoni, plus some keyboarded faces like Century and Metroblack (roman and italic). It was the last great jumble of the kind.

Here it should be noted that two important new news-texts made their appearance in the mid-1950s. These were Walter Tracy's Jubilee, designed for the British Linotype organisation, and Edwin W. Shaar's Imperial, designed for Intertype in America. The aim of Jubilee – so named because it was completed in 1953, the fiftieth anniversary of the incorporation of Linotype & Machinery Ltd – was to meet the demands of publishers who by this time were complaining of the technical defects of Times Roman but wanted a news-text of comparable old face character. First installed in 1954 by the *Glasgow Herald* (which still uses it) it was adopted by a substantial number of dailies and weeklies, including the *Daily Worker* (whence it descended to the *Morning Star*, to show its capabilities for web-offset) and later the *Daily Telegraph* and *Daily Mail*. The well-produced Beckett group of South Coast weeklies substituted it for their Times Roman.[2]

Millions of words, in thousands of newspapers and magazines, are printed and read daily. All over the world news is necessary to the everyday routine of many millions of people. The public appetite for news is enormous, and the man who never reads a newspaper is news himself.

The well-designed news face makes the best possible use of space. It must be compact and yet not look crowded. This is achieved by careful distribution of the white space in and around the letter so that it actually looks bigger than it is.

Points of difference between similar letters are deftly emphasized, and individual letters are drawn so that they will knit firmly together into words and aid the swift movement of the eye as it skims the column.

Jubilee (8 and 7pt).

Intertype Imperial was not, like Jubilee, an attempt to provide an acceptable news-text of old face origin that could take the place of Times Roman. What Edwin Shaar did was to smarten up the strong-coloured, near-monotone texts long familiar in the 'Legibility Group' and its Intertype counterparts. Imperial was, in effect, a more stylish and sharper cut Excelsior, embodying (as Shaar said) certain transitional characteristics designed to avoid, or reduce, any monotony. It sought to resolve the conflicting demands of larger body and narrower measure; fractionally bigger on its body than Jubilee, it was fractionally less wide than Excelsior, at least until above 8pt. Like Jubilee, Imperial had an excellent italic (in both faces this was smoother and better-fitting than many linecaster italics) and a good bold. It was adopted by a number of provincial papers in Britain, but it did not enjoy the success it had in the States, where it became the most popular Intertype news-text, narrowly leading the already popular Intertype Royal. Its most spectacular score came in the 1960s, when its $8\frac{1}{2}$pt was chosen by the *New York Times* to replace Ideal as its body type.

When only three sizes of Imperial were off the matrix manufacturing floor to show as advance specimens of this important new type face, Imperial was chosen and installed as the new newspaper body face. In rapid succession, additional sizes were completed to extend the range from $5\frac{1}{2}$ point to 10 point inclusive.

When only three sizes of Imperial were off the matrix manufacturing floor to show as advance specimens of this important new type face, Imperial was chosen and installed as the new newspaper body face. In rapid succession additional sizes were completed to extend the range from $5\frac{1}{2}$ point to 10 point inclusive.

Imperial (8 and 7pt).

In 1954 Britain's counterpart of America's Ayer Award, the Annual Award for Newspaper Design, was established on the initiative of James Moran, then editor of *Printing World*. The Award was jointly sponsored, as it still is, by that trade weekly and the British Linotype Group. Both these organisations were represented on the Award's administrative committee, which also included representatives of the Newspaper Society (the association of provincial publishers), the British Federation of Master Printers and the Council for Industrial Design. This committee selected for each year three judges, two of them from the printer/journalist/typographer field, the third – though this was not always achieved – being an eminent layman with a general interest in design. The Award had three categories: Class 1 (Dailies, i.e. mornings, and Sundays), Class 2 (Evenings), Class 3 (Weeklies). Until 1963 there was an overall top prize, a bronze plaque for the 'best-designed newspaper of the year'; experience showed that this system produced too many anomalies and it was abandoned in favour of a plaque for each of the class 'firsts' together with a Special Award for a single outstanding feature in a paper which might not otherwise qualify for a prize.

THE CAIRO SEE-SAW
see page two

Daily Worker
(7027) 2d ★ ★
WEDNESDAY APRIL 14 1954
THE ONLY DAILY PAPER OWNED BY ITS READERS

EDEN AGREES TO 'A NEW KOREA'

Attlee says Yes, Bevan says No, to Indo-China action

From PETER ZINKIN

LABOUR M.P.s' shouts of "Another Korea" interrupted Mr. Anthony Eden, Foreign Secretary, in the Commons yesterday as he read a statement showing that he and Mr. Foster Dulles had agreed to joint action in Indo-China.

"There will be no national unity on this intervention," Mr. Ellis Smith (Lab, Stoke-on-Trent S.) called out, while another of his colleagues accused Mr. Eden of prejudicing the Geneva talks.

Leaping to his feet, Mr. Aneurin Bevan told the Foreign Secretary that his statement "would be deeply resented by the majority of the people in Great Britain."

He was loudly cheered by Labour M.P.s.

"It will be universally regarded as a surrender to American pressure," Mr. Bevan continued. "In Asia, people will interpret it as an attempt to form an organisation to preserve European Colonial rule in South-East Asia."

These points were made as a result of Mr. Eden's declaration that he and Mr. Dulles had agreed to study with interested countries the setting up of a "N.A.T.O. Organisation" for the West Pacific and South-East Asia.

Most Labour M.P.s were quick to see that this was merely an excuse for Mr. Eden's support for Mr. Dulles' plan for a full-scale war in Indo-China, which might become an excuse to make war on China.

In contrast to the Labour M.P.s' reactions, **Mr. Attlee's** welcome of Mr. Eden's statement showed that he had lost any authority he may have won during the H-bomb debate last week.

BEVAN BACKED

Mr. Attlee welcomed Mr. Eden's statement which only the Tories had cheered. He warned the Foreign Secretary that if it was to succeed, "It should not be built up in any way that it may be represented as a defence of obsolete colonisation."

But it was Mr. Bevan who obviously had the support of the majority of Labour M.P.s by his sharp attack on Mr. Eden made immediately after Mr. Attlee's welcome.

Other Right Wing leaders, including **Mr. E. Shinwell** (Lab, Easington), were more cautious in questioning Mr. Eden's statement.

Mr. Shinwell asked for an assurance that the Government would not commit the country to any project without any consultation.

Mr. Desmond Donnelly (Lab, Pembroke) asked Mr. Eden whether it was not a fact that the proposed "defensive alliance in South-East Asia could not possibly be effective in a military way for several months.

SABOTAGE

"Is it not clear that this statement is made for political purposes to sabotage the Geneva conference which is to open in a few weeks?" he asked.

To loud Tory cheers, while Labour M.P.s sat glumly silent, **Mr. Stanley Evans** (Lab, Wednesbury) came to Mr. Attlee's support.

He declared that Mr. Attlee's restrained questions about the statement would command the overwhelming support of the majority of the Parliamentary Labour Party.

A CHALLENGE

Mr. Evans' declaration was regarded by Labour M.P.s as a challenge to the Left, which could not be ignored

Mr. Bevan's followers were considering an attempt to call a special Parliamentary Labour Party meeting to discuss this question before the House rises for the Easter recess tomorrow

They believe that a majority of Labour M.P.s would be opposed to Mr. Eden's agreement with Dulles because they see it as a threat to world peace.

Labour M.P.s were collecting signatures to a motion protesting against Mr. Eden's statement on South-East Asia yesterday. Their motion regretted that it should have created the impression that the Government had committed itself in South-East Asia before the Geneva conference.

It also attacked Mr. Eden for acting without prior consultation with other Commonwealth countries concerned.

EDITORIAL

Eden bows to Dulles

DULLES has achieved some success in dragging Britain toward participation in the dirty imperialist war in Indo-China. That is the meaning of Eden's statement in the Commons yesterday.

Eden has accepted every American lie about the real situation in that country.

The Democratic Republic of Viet Nam, which has been firmly established since 1945, controls most of the area of Viet Nam and is successfully guiding the country in a progressive direction.

This Republic is referred to in the statement as "the Communist forces," and the puppet Government functioning in the confined territory held by the French is referred to as the legitimate Government of Viet Nam.

The Dulles-Eden statement declares that the "Communist forces" have been increasing their attacks on the French in view of the coming Geneva conference.

Smashed

In fact, the Democratic Republic months ago suggested a cease-fire and negotiations but was completely ignored by the French.

The French High Command has, with American aid, been carrying out an offensive—the so-called Navarre plan—against the Democratic Republic.

That plan has been smashed by the People's Army which has now moved to the offensive.

Dulles and Eden now propose to set up an organisation in South-East Asia which they say will be similar to the American war alliance in Europe—the so-called North Atlantic Treaty Organisation.

This organisation will, in the [illegible] of South-East Asia, [illegible] of the white imperialist Powers—U.S., Britain and France and Australia—and a few wretched Asian puppets like the Philippines.

It is safe to say that none of the larger, semi-independent States in Asia will participate in what they know is basically a white imperialist alliance directed against the independence of all Asian countries.

Right!

This agreement, unless annulled by the action of the British people, will mean that Britain will be dragged into America's war in Indo-China.

Those Labour Members who shouted "Korea" were correct. Dulles is dragging us into another war of imperialism against an Asian people.

In endorsing Eden's statement, Attlee committed an act of treachery to Socialist principles and helped to bring Britain nearer war.

The rank and file of British Labour will never tolerate British lives being sacrificed for this purpose. Attlee's statement must be repudiated. Otherwise the Labour Party will be helping to sabotage the Geneva conference.

Times change

LESS than a year ago the presses of The Times began printing the U.S. Air Force Daily, complete with strip cartoons.

Now the American invasion of Printing House Square has gone a stage farther.

Yesterday's Times carried a large advertisement inserted by the U.S. News and World Report.

Splashed across almost half a page, it reproduced a bombastic editorial in the current issue of that magazine, warning Britain and France of the dire consequences of not obeying American orders on Indo-China.

If America's "dispirited allies" do not toe the line, it warned, "then Americans generally will begin to feel they had better . . . let Europe worry along the best she can."

If The Times cares to earn £750 or so by carrying this advertisement—well, that's their business.

But would John Walter the Second, or Thomas Barnes, or J. T. Delane have allowed three columns of "The Thunderer" to be fouled with a Yankee snarl at the British people?

In a leading article of 1836, making a comparison of the Press of London and of Paris, The Times wrote:

"With the Press of the United States we will not descend to a comparison."

The Times has changed. But not, we fear, for the better.

Best talks ever gloats Dulles

By Our Diplomatic Correspondent

THE U.S. Secretary of State Mr. Dulles left London yesterday declaring his complete satisfaction at the outcome of his talks with Mr. Eden on intervention in Indo-China.

"I have had the best series of talks in 48 hours that I have ever had," he declared before boarding the plane for Paris.

"We have come to an agreement which I think will be full of value in the future. I feel this agreement is entirely satisfactory to myself, as it is to Mr. Eden."

His assertion of the existence of an agreement was in striking contrast to Mr. Eden's repeated claims in the House of Commons that he had entered into no agreement.

The joint statement issued yesterday after the talks repeated American propaganda about Indo-China.

Puppet regime

It claimed that "Communist forces" were seeking to overthrow "the lawful government which we recognise," which means the puppet Bao Dai regime.

They were said to be "endangering peace and security of the entire area of South-East Asia and the Western Pacific."

"Accordingly," it added, "we are ready to take part, with the other countries principally concerned, in an examination of the possibility of establishing a collective defence to assure the peace, security and freedom of South-East Asia and the Western Pacific."

Atom talks

The statement also mentioned that atomic energy matters had been discussed and the calling of an early meeting of the U.N. Disarmament Commission Sub-Committee.

On his arrival in Paris, Mr. Dulles declared that "all members of the free world" concerned with Indo-China "must unite to end the war," and he made it clear that he intended it to be ended in the American fashion.

LABOUR PROTEST STARTS

By Our Political Correspondent

LABOUR M.P.s tried to get their leaders to support a protest motion against intervention in Indo-China after Mr. Edens' statement yesterday.

Headed by Mr. Ben Parkin (Paddington N.) and Miss Jennie Lee (Cannock) a few M.P.s drafted a motion which they sent to the Parliamentary committee for approval.

Others were Mr. Stephen Swingler, Mr. John Baird, Mr. Julian Snow, Mr. D. W. Jrones and Mr. William Warbey.

Their motion regretted that Mr. Eden had failed to make clear in his statement that the Government was not committed to support French colonial policy in Indo-China.

ATTACKS EDEN

It attacked the Foreign Secretary because he had made his statement without first consulting India and other interested parties.

The Parliamentary Labour Party meets tonight, when Mr. Attlee will open the discussion by stating the Parliamentary Committee's views on Indo-China.

After meeting last night the committee—the Labour M.P.s' executive—asked the M.P.s to await tonight's meeting before putting their motion.

6 FRENCH ATTACKS REPELLED

SIX French attempts to recapture the five hillocks taken by the People's Army on the eastern side of the centre of the French fortress of Dien Bien Phu have been thrown back, the Viet Nam radio reported yesterday.

The report contradicts the French claim to have retaken one of the hillocks.

Three French companies were wiped out and three 18-ton American-built tanks destroyed by the People's Army at Dien Bien Phu in seven days fighting up to and including Monday, the radio said. An American-built bomber was also shot down.

Mr. Richard Casey, the Australian Foreign Minister, arrived in Singapore yesterday on his way to Indo-China.

American warships and Chiang Kai-shek warships, with jet planes, bombers and marines, yesterday took part in manouevres in the Formosa Straits, it was reported from Taipeh.

Ship dividends

Cammell Laird and Co., the Birkenhead shipbuilders, yesterday announced a final ordinary dividend of 10 per cent, making 15 per cent, less tax, for 1953.

Navy jets 'not grounded'

The Navy's Sea Venom and R.A.F.'s Venom jets are being modified after a small crack was found in the wing of one aircraft.

An Admiralty spokesman said it was hardly correct to say they had been "grounded"

WEATHER: Cloudy, showers, bright intervals.
Lighting-up time: 8.53 p.m.

Our Alfie

'I bet they convert 'em into workers' flats and put the rent up.'

ELECTRICIANS NOT HAPPY WITH ½d

Angered by award

From GEORGE SINFIELD

CONTRACTING electricians last night gave a hostile reception to an Industrial Disputes Tribunal award granting them an increase of ½d an hour

On March 15 the Electrical Trades Union obtained 2d an hour in partial settlement of the pay dispute which had gripped the industry for months.

Widespread guerilla strikes and other stoppages were staged to bring the employers to reason.

As the original claim was for a substantial increase—generally interpreted to mean 4d an hour at least—the E.T.U. accepted the 2d. and put its case for the remainder to arbitration.

The award of ½d and the negotiated 2d will together yield 9s 2d for a week of 44 hours.

Although this is several shillings more than received by some other manual workers recently, it will not satisfy the 45,000 electricians and their leaders, who fought so long and so well against an obstinate set of employers.

Witch-hunting and threats of reprisals strengthened their determination to secure a rise adequate to meet rising living costs.

WON RESPECT

Earlier, the employers had endeavoured to split the workers' ranks with a pay offer limited to certain areas, and with a proposal to cut overtime rates for all.

The electricians, in defeating that move, gained more than an increase of 2½d; they won the respect of all trade unionists for their fighting stand.

The award will take effect as from March 15.

Jagan calls on people to disobey

Daily Worker Special Correspondent

GEORGETOWN, Tuesday.

BEFORE he was sentenced to six months imprisonment yesterday for attending his dental patients outside Georgetown, Dr. Jagan, the elected Prime Minister of this country, said:

"Justice has been dead since the troops arrived. British Guiana is a vast prison. There is little difference if I am in or out of jail.

"I advise all to disobey these laws (the fascist emergency laws under which he was sentenced) and to wear mourning on the Queen's birthday."

Dr. Jagan was also fined 100 dollars for "holding an illegal procession"—when people followed him home from court after an earlier hearing.

Police hurled tear-gas bombs at people meeting in Port Mourant last night to protest against the sentence on Dr. Jagan, who was their M.P. in the dissolved House of Assembly.

Top U.S. atomic scientist suspended

BECAUSE he opposed the development of the H-bomb in 1949, America's top atomic scientist, Dr. Robert Oppenheimer, has been suspended from all his official posts and is being subjected to a special investigation.

This latest move in the U.S. witch-hunt hysteria was disclosed by the New York Times and New York Herald Tribune yesterday on the basis of documents in their possession.

At the same time it was announced in New York that three associate professors at Hunter College for Women had been suspended on charges that they had been in the Communist Party in the 1930s.

'SUPPOSED'

Part of the allegations against Dr. Oppenheimer also consist of vague charges of "supposed association with Communists" in 1940 and contributions to anti-fascist organisations.

Another "charge" is that he fell in love with an alleged Communist and married another former Communist.

The situation has got so bad that even ex-President Truman has attacked the witch-hunt in a speech at Westminster College in Fulton, Missouri, because he said it was trying to destroy the concept that a man was innocent until proved guilty.

This is exactly what is being done in the case of Dr. Oppenheimer.

The charges were conveyed to him in a letter from the General Manager of the U.S. Atomic Energy Commission, General Nichols, on December 23 last year.

'REPORTED'

Each allegation began with the stock phrase now used in all these witch-hunts — "It was reported that . . ."

On March 4, this year, Dr. Oppenheimer replied in a 43-page letter, in which he denied that he had lobbied against the development of the hydrogen bomb after President Truman had ordered its development.

He also denied that he had given secret information to any unauthorised person.

One of the world's most brilliant mathematicians and scientists, Dr. Oppenheimer lectures with Dr. Einstein at Princeton University, where he is director of the Institute of Advanced Studies.

He has been a member of President Eisenhower's Science Advisory Committee, consultant to the Atomic Energy Commission and adviser to the U.S. State Department, Defence Department and National Security Council.

One of Australia's leading atom scientists, Prof. Oliphant, said in Canberra yesterday that it was "incredible" that Dr. Oppenheimer had been guilty of any un-American activity.

Dr. Oppenheimer, he said, was a man concerned for America and for humanity, and the witch-hunting to which he was being subjected was a terrible thing.

Britons-stay-in-Europe pact signed

PARIS, Tuesday.

THE six countries of the proposed European Defence Community and Britain today signed here an agreement on British co-operation with the planned European Army.

Details of the agreement were not disclosed.

The text will not be published till tomorrow, but informed quarters here believe it binds Britain to keep troops on the Continent and to consult the E.D.C. before any withdrawal.

It is also believed to put British units on the Continent under the same command as E.D.C. forces and to ensure British representation on all the chief organs of E.D.C.

The Gaullist Ministers in the French Cabinet, who protested to the Premier on Monday at the "weakness" of the British guarantees saw M. Laniel again and complained that a fait accompli had been created by the French signing today.

DOCTORS TO EAT BETTER

The "reasonable" suggestions made in March by resident medical staff at Preston (Lancs) Royal Infirmary, who have refused to eat hospital meals, are to be implemented.

Yesterday only ten out of 120 resident nurses had breakfast but, after a meeting with the matron, 60 turned up for lunch.

Leaflet call to lost soldier

A ship left Japan yesterday with 100,000 leaflets which will be dropped over the jungles of New Guinea calling on a Japanese soldier to return home.

The soldier was reported killed in action, but his parents believe he is in hiding, unaware that the war is over.—Reuter.

STRIKE STAYS

No settlement in the strike on Liverpool's overhead railway was reached after a five-hour meeting yesterday between employers, Ministry of Labour officials and the union

MAN OF TODAY

John Gollan, the Communist candidate at the Motherwell by-election where polling takes place today.

RENT RISE WILL MEAN POVERTY

MPs condemn Tory Bill

THE Tory Rents Bill will create such hardships as to force many more people on to National Assistance, Mr. A. Blenkinsop (Lab, Newcastle-on-Tyne E.) declared in the Commons yesterday.

Leading the attack on the Third Reading of the Bill, he said it would lead also to renewed demands for wage increases to meet the additional 4s or 5s a week which will go on the rents.

"If we do fail to prevent this Bill from becoming law," he declared, "we shall do all we can to defend the tenant against increases which we consider will be unjust and wholly unwarranted."

'Don't pay until . . .'

Mr. Geoffrey de Freitas (Lab, Lincoln) declared: "Tenants should not pay one penny of rent increase until they have made certain that the landlord is really entitled to that increase."

The Labour Party, he said, would organise tenants "as they have never been organised before."

"So far as possible, in every village and town, we shall set up rent bureaux to see that what little justice is provided for the tenant can be given to them."

The Bill, he added, "makes owning of slum property respectable and economically worth while."

Moving the Third Reading on behalf of the Government, **Mr. Ernest Marples,** Parliamentary Secretary Ministry of Housing and Local Government, said he found it hard to say anything new.

But he announced that the Government would erect a house on a sight in Oxford Street, London, for three months in the summer "to demonstrate what can be done in the way of repairs and conversions."

In the debate **Mr. Albert Evans** (Lab, Islington S.W.) said there were not enough local government officials to cope with the thousands of applications for certificates of disrepair which would flood the town halls.

Seaside blaze

The Ritz Theatre, Weymouth, and a neighbouring dance hall were badly damaged by fire yesterday. Nearby steamers in the harbour were moved to a bay.

He'll be there

Colonial Secretary Oliver Lyttelton will leave London by air for Uganda on April 26, to be there when the Queen arrives.

This is Gollan's line

From LLEW GARDNER

MOTHERWELL, Tuesday.

AT enthusiastic eve-of-the-poll meetings in Motherwell and Wishaw tonight, John Gollan pledged himself to continue, in and out of Parliament, to fight for the interests of the people.

"I ask you with confidence to vote for me," he said.

"What I have called for will triumph as sure as night follows day," the Communist candidate in the most important by-election for years told his listeners.

The meetings came as the climax to the magnificent campaign that has been waged in the constituency by the Communist Party. A campaign that focused attention not only here but throughout Britain on the vital issues facing this country.

An inspiration

"A victory for my policy tomorrow will be a political event of lasting importance," he said, continuing:

"It will be an inspiration to all that is best in the British Labour movement, who only want to live in peace and friendship with the peoples of the world.

"It will be a fitting answer to Dulles and his new war plans.

"It will give the old people a guarantee that they have a champion on the floor of the House of Commons.

Only solution

"It will let young people know that their demands will be placed before the nation as never before and everything possible done to safeguard their interests in industry, reduce conscription to one year, and endeavour to get better sport and cultural facilities in Motherwell.

"In this vital by-election as the candidate of the Communist Party, I have been concerned with one aim — the deadly seriousness to the people of Motherwell of the political and econmic situation—and I advance the only policy which can solve all the problems which face them.

"They can give a lead to the whole Labour movement by returning me as the Member of Parliament for Motherwell.

Vital issues

"In the course of the election campaign I have advanced a policy that is most constructive and practical.

"It is a policy based on the vital issues of wages, employment and unemployment, with the urgent need to help the old age pensioners.

"It has shown how houses can be built at rents within the capacity of the workers to pay.

"It has called for the banning of the atom and hydrogen bombs, rallied the people's opposition to a new Nazi army, and shown how the basis of a lasting peace can be secured by negotiations and the reduction of armaments.

"I have placed before [illegible] great importance of [illegible] trade for Motherwell, and how, if it is carried through, it can guarantee full employment in Motherwell for many years to come.

"In addition to fighting to end the domination of British affairs by the Americans, I have demanded a Scottish Parliament so that more attention can be devoted to Scottish affairs, and the present unequal and unfair treatment of Scotland by the British Parliament brought to an end.

"And as a Scotsman, I have fought for the right of the Colonial peoples to govern themselves, for the solidarity of the British workers with all Colonial peoples struggling to be free.

Sure of support

"I have not been concerned with personalities, but only with politics.

"I am confident that my campaigning has brought all these issues of the day before the people of Motherwell in a manner that could not have taken place if I had not been adopted as the Communist candidate.

"I am sure that I am going to get your support, and I pledge myself that I will fight for your interests inside and outside of Parliament in the same way that William Gallacher did for 15 years for the working people of West Fife."

Burchett tells of France's conquest efforts

IT'S U.S. INTERVENTION

From WILFRED BURCHETT

SOMEWHERE NORTH VIET NAM, Tuesday.

THE plan of General Navarre, the French C.-in-C., for the reconquest of Northern Indo-China, must be considered part of American intervention in the French dirty war here.

It was worked out with American advisers, approved by Washington and given great publicity build-up by the American Press agencies.

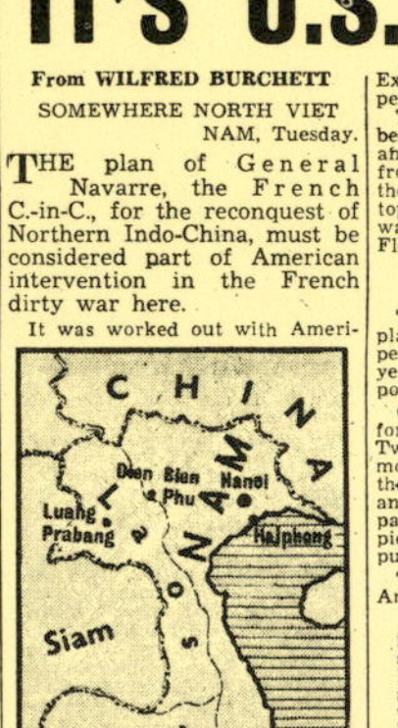

General Navarre followed in the sorry footsteps of General Salan, the previous French C.-in-C., who followed General Chansons, who followed General de Lattre, and so on, righ back to General Le Clerc, who first commanded the French Expeditionary Corps to crush the people's power in Indo-China.

The "dirty war" has not only been the burial ground for the annual output of French officers from St. Cyr Academy, but also for the careers of the cream of France's top-ranking generals, just as Korea was for the MacArthurs and Van Fleets of the American Army.

Four points

The much-publicised Navarre plan, which was to crush the people's resistance within two years, consisted of four main points.

One was to regroup the French forces and create mobile reserves. Two to take the initiative with the mobile reserves to break through the People's Army line of resistance to the rear areas. Three, to pacify the rear areas of the occupied zones; and four, to build up puppet troops.

The last was the pet of all the American schemes.

General Navarre was appointed in the summer of 1953 after the spring offensive of the Viet Nam's People's Army had liberated Son La Province in the western region of North Viet Nam and Laos. The Lao Liberation Army freed the adjoining province of Sam Neua in Laos.

The balance sheet of Navarre's activities, as shown in the inexorable red and blue flags on military maps, is that he succeeded in re-occupying over 2,000 square miles in the operation called "Atlanta." south central Viet Nam.

Pinned down

In the same period the Viet Nam People's Army and Lao Liberation Army in co-ordinated offensives drove Navarre's troops out of over 35,000 square miles of territory and attached it to the already firmly liberated areas.

They extended guerilla bases and zones in scores of thousands more square miles.

Exclusive No 3

This is the third of an exclusive series of dispatches from our special correspondent Wilfred Burchett, the only British newspaperman in Liberated Viet Nam.

Instead of building up "mobile reserves," Navarre's forces were pinned down in isolated posts. In order to regroup and create these reserves, Navarre started by evacuating some isolated posts and transferring troops to the Red River delta region for initiatives elsewhere.

He had 20 battalions in the delta at the time. But now even after voluntarily abandoning important posts, he only has 17 battalions in the delta region.

The Viet Nam People's Army initiative has forced him to immobilise his reserves elsewhere.

In operation "Mouette," Navarre struck out from the western edge of the Red River delta toward an important Vietnamese base and communications centre.

Pulled back

Using some of his newly acquired reserves he managed to reach the centre, burn a few hundred houses, but within three weeks after the operation started he was forced to pull his forces back.

The Viet Nam People's Army did not allow the operation to upset their schedule for an offensive. They dispersed supplies from the centre and used only regional troops and guerillas to harass Navarre's troops, inflicting over 2,000 casualties.

Vietnamese offensives against Laichau Province took place on

★ *continued on p. 3*

◀ The 1954 issue of the *Daily Worker* which won it first place in the first Newspaper Design Award jointly with *The Times*, whose presentation was basically the same as it had been after

The contest for the Annual Award soon became, as its sponsors said, more of a 'movement to improve newspaper design by promoting a greater interest in it'. In the first year there were 203 entrants; by 1959 these had risen to 277 and during the 1960s passed the 300 mark, once even going beyond 380. From the start the judges' reports were sound and stimulating contributions to the theory and practice of good newspaper design. In 1954 the judges, headed by Brooke Crutchley, the Cambridge University Printer, opened their report with the words: 'A well-designed paper explains itself at a glance. The typographical treatment distinguishes different kinds of news stories, and separates news from features. Further, it maintains interest throughout. There should be a dynamic quality right through the issue and covering each page.' Developing these points the report added that the judges looked for 'lucid and orderly layout of news and features; good choice of types and intelligent use of type variation to provide emphasis and differentiate between kinds of matter; appropriate use of white space in the display headings and elsewhere; absence of visual confusion between editorial and advertising matter; good use of pictures; high standard of reproduction of pictures; efficient and even machining; good taste in the display of front-page titles and special headings; a pleasant and intelligible appearance generally, giving an impression of easy readability.'

With this penetrating presentation of the general problems of newspaper design, it is instructive to cite, as one of the constant criteria of the contest, an early briefing of judges by the administrative committee (1958). This directed the judges to 'pay due regard to the *nature of the readership* in each case' and concluded: 'They will not place undue merit on rare typography or typographical refinements that cannot be seen to serve some practical purpose; neither will they penalise any entry that departs from accepted typographical practice in order to serve its readers' interests more fully.'

The 1954 judges made a sensation with their principal choice, in Class 1. 'Two newspapers', they reported, 'stood out as by far the most distinguished and thoughtfully designed – *The Times* and the *Daily Worker*, and as it was impossible to make a direct comparison between two papers of such different styles, the judges decided to give the class award to these two jointly.'* *The Times*, in the developed form of Morison's 1932 headline dress and with Reynolds Stone's new title-piece of 1953, also received the 'best-designed newspaper of the year' bronze plaque. The *Daily Worker*, as I re-designed it in 1948 for standard broadsheet, had a title in specially-arranged large Ultra-Bodoni italic upper- and lower-case; its news headlines combined Caslon Heavy with Bodoni Bold italic (Grot No. 9 for sans contrast), its features used Goudy Bold roman and italic.

Most significant of the 1954 judges' other choices was that of the *Shoreham Herald*, one of the Beckett Group already mentioned, in the weekly class. This paper was a stablemate, and typographical compeer, of the *Worthing Herald*, specially praised by the 1955 judges because it was 'designed as a whole . . . the style is consistent from beginning to end'. From this point on successive judges were repeatedly to stress the importance of a 'sense of unity', of a 'unified structure of good typographical detail', of a 'plan that embraced not only the front page but went right through to the back'. Judges of the 1970s regretfully echoed the conclusion of their predecessors of 1960 that there are 'too many newspapers which present spectacular front pages to the world and then fall to pieces on the inside pages'.

The Beckett papers were not subject to this stricture; it was the unified planning of the *Worthing Herald* which in 1958 gained it the distinction of being the first and only weekly to win the 'best-designed of the year' bronze plaque. The creator and principal executant of this planned design was Frank Cave, then editor-in-chief of the Group. In 1955 he expounded his views at length, basing them on a score of years experience in charge of the Beckett papers. He specially

* It appears that the judges at first favoured awarding the first prize in Class 1 to the *Daily Worker* outright but then came to feel that they could hardly relegate *The Times* to second place. In 1956 the judges awarded the *Worker* an unqualified first.

WORTHING HERALD

No. 2039 FRIDAY, MAY 29, 1959 PRICE 4d.

WIND AND TIDE RIGHT, BUT

Hitch in the trawl for seaweed

WIND and tide were just right yesterday (Thursday) morning for the first trawl of the seaweed beds off Worthing, in an effort to release the weed before summer gales tear it up and dump it on the beach.

So the trawler *Girl Pat*, of Shoreham, under her skipper, Mr J. Howell, of Brighton, hired by the Corporation which has ben voted £1,000 for exploratory work in clearing the weed, began her first sweep of the marked 1,000 yards by 300 yards plot.

But the *Girl Pat* was soon in trouble. By 11 o'clock on one of her earliest runs from just off the end of the Pier to the other end of the plot off Heene-road, her speed dropped to less than one knot. Then she stopped dead and despite full power from her 25 hp engine she failed to overcome the obstruction her trawling chains had fouled on the sea bed.

So round she swung, retraced her course, and then hove to while her crew manhandled the trawl wires and eventually released the chains. Afterwards, trawling continued steadily.

Holidaymakers watching from the Promenades saw occasional pieces of seaweed fluttering from the trawl wires as they were hauled aboard.

THE PLAN

Watching, too, from the Promenade was Mr D. G. Sutton, chief assistant engineer of the Borough Engineer's department, who described the Corporation's plan for the preliminary sweep.

"After today's trawling, expected to take about three hours, we shall make another survey of the beds and see how effective it has been," Mr Sutton told the HERALD.

"The Brighton, Hove and Worthing Sub Aqua Club made eight dives for us at Whitsun weekend, taking photographs of the beds, and will be making another dive for more photographs after this sweep so that we can compare the two sets of prints.

"We hope they will be able to

Continued page 9, column 2.

Findon fears loss of identity

AN outline application for building 61 bungalows at The Vale, Findon-road, Findon, was refused by Worthing Rural Council on Tuesday because "further residential development in this area between Findon and Worthing would be likely to lead to the coalescence of the two communities."

The Planning Committee, recommending refusal, said that development would lead to the loss of the separate identity and village character of Findon and would be detrimental to the character and visual amenities of the locality.

Other reasons given were that the site was in an area of great landscape value and was contrary to development plan provisions; and that further development beside this unrestricted part of the Worthing-London road would be a source of danger and inconvenience.

SUNNIEST SINCE JUNE, 1957

WORTHING is having its sunniest month since June, 1957. Up to Wednesday, May had recorded 237·2 hours, compared with the average for 1st-27th of 192 hours, and Sunday, with 14·8 hours, was the sunniest day since June last year.

Two years ago May recorded 270 sun hours.

With 22 rainless days and a fall of only ·79in., the month has been the driest May for three years. Worthing's average May rainfall is 1·65in. No rain has fallen since the 20th.

Since the weekend temperatures have dropped 12 deg. Sunday recorded 70 deg., but Tuesday's reading of 58 deg. was 4 deg. below average.

Hurt in collision

After a collision with a car while walking in Brighton-road, near the junction with York-road on Wednesday, Mrs Ethel Ruff, of 7 Sussex-road, was taken to Southlands Hospital, Shoreham, with a broken thigh. Yesterday (Thursday) she was stated to be quite comfortable.

IN THE UNIFORM of Ottway's Regiment, as the Royal Sussex Regiment was known in 1759, Pte. V. Dunne (right), of Worthing, and Pte. E. Harrington wait to play their part in the regiment's Royal Tournament display.

MOTHER OF THREE DISAPPEARS

A SOMPTING husband is waiting anxiously for news of his wife whom he has not seen for a week.

Mrs Jessie Bertha Booth, aged 33, of 32 Halewick-lane, disappeared last Friday after sending her three children, Iris, aged 13½, Maureen, aged 12, and Eric, aged eight, off to the pictures.

The children were waiting for him alone when their father, Mr Roy Booth, aged 40, returned from his job as a builder's labourer at about 6 p.m. on Friday.

She had taken a small suitcase and an open work plastic bag with her, and Mr Booth thought she would return by the weekend.

Sunday night came and she had not returned. Then Mr Booth began making inquiries. He found that she had not gone to relatives.

He also checked with her employers, the Southern Services Laundry in Lancing, and found that she had left her job there the previous Wednesday.

Mr Booth has informed the police. He thinks that she may have gone to Wallasey, Cheshire, where she had been evacuated as a child. Many times she had spoken of returning there, but he knows of no address there to which she could go.

MRS BOOTH

Two lunch hour raids

MORE than £60 in cash was stolen from an office and a shop within a few hundred yards of each other in the Rowlands-road area during the lunch hour yesterday (Thursday).

The sum of £12 8s. in a green cash box was stolen from Messrs Potter Bailey's ironmongery shop in Crescent-road, and £49 14s. 4d. in cash and a cheque was stolen from the office of John Barclay, estate agents, at 33 Rowlands-road.

The raids took place between 1 p.m. and 2.15 p.m. while the premises were closed for lunch.

A duplicate key is believed to have been used to gain entry in each case.

£119 CLOTHES RAID

Four suits and a jacket, together worth £119, were stolen from Hector Powe Ltd., Chapel-road, on Tuesday night, some time between the closing and opening hours of the shop.

Entry was obtained by forcing a rear window open. Nothing else was taken.

ON THE SPOT

A passing ambulance pulled up seconds after Mrs Doris Gathern, aged 45, of 26 Orme-road, had been involved in a collision with a car while riding her moped in West-parade on Wednesday.

Mrs Gathern was taken to Worthing Hospital with a knee inury, but was allowed home after treatment.

PRISON CAMP SOUVENIRS

AN idea of conditions that prevailed in Malayan prisoner-of-war camps during the 1939-45 war is given in a display in one of Jones and Tomlin's windows in Chapel-road.

Arranged by two members of Worthing District and West Sussex Far Eastern Prisoner of War Social Club, Mr C. J. Banham, chairman, and Mr. J. Garnham, welfare officer, it heralds the National Federation of Far Eastern Prisoner of War Clubs' 1959 National Conference which will be opened by the Mayor, Coun. H. W. Bradley, at the Richmond Room tomorrow.

It will be the first time that the conference has been held in Worthing.

Mr Banham told the HERALD that the two Japanese swords and a Japanese soldier's full uniform used in the display were lent by ex-prisoners who brought them back as souvenirs.

Photographs taken at one of the camps are included in the display.

About 130 delegates from 45 clubs throughout the country are expected to attend the conference.

Mr Garnham dressing a model

FEWER OUT OF WORK

UNEMPLOYMENT in Worthing is lower than at any time since last September. On Monday, the local employment exchange recorded 476 people out of work, 380 men and 96 women, compared with 539 on the corresponding day in April.

There is still a problem in trying to find work for older people, commented a Ministry of Labour and National Insurance official. It was difficult to persuade some local employers to take on people over 50.

The unemployment in Worthing has been largely seasonal, and there are increasing numbers of vacancies in hotels and catering.

The scope for clerical work is still limited.

Assault on councillor

HAROLD WILLIAM VENIS, aged 34, an asphalt worker living in Maybridge-crescent, Goring, was at the adjourned Quarter Sessions at Chichester on Tuesday sent to prison for six months for assault.

He pleaded not guilty and conducted his own defence.

Mr Geoffrey Lawrence, Q.C., the chairman, told Venis, "It was a disgraceful and lawless piece of conduct. You deliberately assaulted a man at least 20 years older than yourself in a particularly brutal way, generally behaving in an arrogant and bullying fashion."

Mr A. McCowan, prosecuting, said that Mr Richard Paton Purchase (57), a Chichester rural councillor, was assaulted by Venis in the car park of the Regnum Club at Chichester on December 17.

Venis, he said, twisted Mr Purchase's arm behind him and pushed him against a car.

Venis, in evidence, denied that he ever touched Mr Purchase, apart from snatching some papers from him after Mr Purchase refused to give him his name.

Venis admitted two previous findings of guilt at Worthing for larceny; and one previous conviction for taking and driving away a car without the owner's consent.

Why weeds surround new church

THE striking modern building which is Findon Valley Free Church stands on a prominent main road site. The surrounds, untended, are overgrown with weeds—and the subject of adverse comment.

Church members want to lay out the land, but are concerned at the delay in the making-up of the service road which is to be continued south from the Findon-road parade of shops.

The Borough Engineer, Mr G. H. Kempton, told the HERALD that no provision for the construction of the continuation was made in this year's estimates, and the matter was likely to remain as it is for some time.

But, he added, there was nothing to stop the church from laying out its grounds.

The minister, the Rev. H. Bonser, told the HERALD that it was hoped the road would be put in before the land was laid out.

The church architect said that they planned to raise the level of the ground so that the laid-out part of the site would be higher than the road.

The absence of any road would make it difficult, as they did not want to go to the expense of walls if this could be avoided; and there would be nuisance from weeds.

"But we are getting out costs and schemes for doing our corner," he added.

BUBBLE CAR OVERTURNED

Mrs Elizabeth Doig, of 6 Malvern-close, was treated at Worthing Hospital yesterday (Thursday) morning after the three-wheel "bubble" car in which she was travelling overturned at the junction of Ham-road and Chesswood-road.

She was taken to hospital by ambulance and allowed to go home after treatment.

Her daughter, who was in the car with her, was shaken but unhurt.

Good in parts

A 1937 Ford 8 — like "the curate's egg" — is one of the scores of bargains offered in the classified advertisements on pages 32 to 39 of this issue.

The 1958 *Worthing Herald*, one of the Beckett group of South Coast weeklies, which was the first (and only) weekly to win the bronze plaque as 'best-designed newspaper of the year'.

stressed the importance of the co-ordination of advertising and editorial planning (which he succeeded in operating in a way attained by very few papers). 'Positioning of half-tones, size and placing of headings and general balance of the page all demand the closest co-operation between editorial and advertising', he said. Headline typography must be simple (there was 'great danger in having too wide a variety of faces'); the Beckett *Heralds*, all tabloids, used Century Bold for news headings with Tempo Heavy (not larger than 42 or 48pt) for the front-page lead; features were differentiated with Century Bold Extended, Caslon Heavy, Bodoni. The 'fundamental aim' of all newspaper presentation was 'clarity and ease of reading for the reader. We are not engaged in the creation of patterns solely for our own satisfaction or enjoyment.'

Cave concluded that while 'the content of a newspaper is paramount', make-up was 'much more than a veneer. It is something to be *used* . . . used to help express the paper's individuality or character' but always 'fundamentally simple and conducted to arouse and retain the interest of the reader and facilitate his journey through the pages.' To this he added: 'A newspaper benefits from establishing a style and, essentially, sticking to it, so that the paper is recognisable at a glance. This is not to say that one conceives a style or general appearance, executes it and then, metaphorically, goes on perpetual holiday. There must always be room for experiment and change within the style.'[3]

The comment may be offered here that the 'heavies' have been the Design Award's principal scorers, both in the overall bronze plaque days and, since, in the Daily/Sunday Class 1. In eight out of the first ten years of the Award the bronze plaque for 'best-designed newspaper of the year' went to *The Times* (twice), the *Observer* (three times), the *Sunday Times*, the *Scotsman* (twice). In the nine following years the first three papers named have between them won seven of the nine first prizes in Class 1; and of the remaining two, one was another 'heavy', the *Guardian*. The point has to be noted that, with the exception of some of the 'heavies' the London nationals have throughout stood aloof from the Design Award contest. This has been particularly the case with the mass-sale 'populars', both morning and Sunday; their line, when expressed, has been either that they are perfectly satisfied with their own design achievement, regarding it as *hors concours*, or that it would be 'bad for the paper's image' to enter without a certainty of a prize (as one editor blandly put it). The one and only exception was the *Daily Mail*, in 1966.

The war and post-war period in America saw the Allen revolution rolling triumphantly on. In the year of John E. Allen's untimely death (1947) the results of the Ayer Award were significant. Over three-quarters of the winning papers set their headings in upper- and lower-case, while over a half had turned to Allen's flush-left style.* Allen was succeeded as editor of *Linotype News* by Edmund C. Arnold, who later became head of the graphic arts department of the School of Journalism at the University of Syracuse (NY). Author of a number of works, including the standard textbooks *Functional Newspaper Design* (1956) and *Modern Newspaper Design* (1969), Arnold has long been a leading figure in American journalist education and newspaper design.

The United States, of course, is a continent not a country. With 2,000 or so English-language dailies at the material time, it is impossible to do more here than pinpoint certain trends. The massacre of Manhattan – which left America's number one newspaper city cut back to two mornings, one evening, by the end of the 1960s – had yet to be unleashed, though there had been mergers. In 1949 the main casualty was the *New York Star*, the re-named *PM*, a remarkable evening venture begun in 1940 by Marshall Field III, reigning multi-millionaire head of the famous Chicago department store dynasty. Edited by Ralph Ingersoll, an outstanding personality in American journalism, *PM* combined a stand for total independence – its aim was to run without accepting advertising – with the most elegant typography ever seen in a newspaper in America, or anywhere else. Its text was set in Caledonia, the modernised and stylish derivation from Scotch Roman devised for Mergenthaler Linotype by W. A. Dwiggins; the body size chosen was 9pt, thus presaging the movement to larger body sizes which during the next quarter of a century was to sweep the U.S. daily press. For *PM* headlines Dwiggins cut Caledonia Bold, roman and italic, in a full range of display sizes up to and including 36pt; in addition to the normal 18, 24 and 30pt the unusual between-

* It should be noted that from the start the Ayer Award had three categories, determined by circulation: i) Over 50,000, ii) 10,000–50,000, iii) under 10,000. A fourth category, for tabloid format papers, was introduced in 1939. Thereafter there were eleven Ayer winners a year, namely the winner of the Ayer Cup, three 'honourable mentions' (first, second and third) in each of the three circulation categories, a single 'honourable mention' for the tabloids.

6 PM, FRIDAY, APRIL 2, 1948

THE WORLD

What's Behind The Crisis in Berlin

By Frederick Kuh

(Copyright, 1948, by Chicago Sun-Times and The Newspaper PM, Inc.)

LONDON

Behind the grave crisis which has blown up in Berlin is a secret report which reached the Soviet Military Governor, Marshal Vassili Sokolovsky, several days ago, according to which the U. S. A. and Britain had begun to remove machinery and stores from Berlin to the American-British zones.

The information received by the Soviet commander stated that the Americans and British were transporting valuable industrial installations and stocks of materials from their sectors of Berlin to Western Germany.

There was no confirmation from the U. S. or British authorities that such removals were in fact started nor, if so, what their purpose was.

One version suggested that, foreseeing an imminent Soviet bid for the sole mastery in the German capital, Gen. Lucius D. Clay, U. S. Military Governor, and the British commander, Gen. Sir Brian K. Robertson, decided that certain industrial equipment and supplies were to be withdrawn rather than run the risk of having them fall into Russian possession.

According to the same account, which emanates from Soviet official sources, the Russians then attempted to impede or prevent these removals by tightening inspection and control of the American-British rail traffic from Berlin from Wednesday midnight.

It was confirmed in British quarters last night that Germans have been transferring their property to the West in order to bring it to safety.

A Tass, Soviet news agency, message said between Mar. 20 and 30, 79 freight cars laden with goods were carried from Berlin westward by rail. More than half of this material belonging to German private firms was alleged to have been transported illegally to the U. S.-British-French zones.

In addition, according to Tass, 1175 tons of materials were shipped by barges.

The Soviet command has warned the German municipal administration of Berlin that speculators are destroying the city's economic foundation by these concealed exports to the West. The Russians have indicated that they would crack down on German officials if such manipulations were not stopped.

U. S. Offers Plan for Regime in Trizonia

(Copyright, 1948, by Chicago Sun-Times and The Newspaper PM, Inc.)

LONDON

The U. S. government has submitted to Britain and France a detailed plan for early establishment of a single German government in the three western zones.

Gen. Lucius D. Clay, U. S. Military Governor, and Ambassador Robert Murphy are reliably reported to have produced this project in confidential negotiations with top-ranking British and French representatives in Berlin.

The scheme has met some opposition.

The main features of the American plan are:

¶ General election to be held soon in Western Germany for the establishment of a parliament.

¶ The parliament is then to designate members of a new government.

¶ At a later stage a Constituent Assembly is to be convened to prepare and adopt a constitution.

French Doubtful

The U. S. intention was to have everything set to start creating a West German government in case Russia established a rival government in the Soviet zones, possibly claiming that such a government represented all Germany.

The French Government has expressed serious doubts concerning the U. S. proposal.

France would prefer to use the existing German Economic Council with 104 members and its smaller executive body as the skeleton from which the future government shall evolve. The French, moreover, have askd that the American plan be thrown into discussion when the U. S. A. and West European Powers resume their conference on Germany in London, probably Apr. 19.

France also fears that if the German Government is established now, French claims, particularly regarding the Ruhr, may be subordinated to German political events. Consequently, the French want clarification of Allied control of the Ruhr to precede the emergence of a German government.

Britain, while more sympathetic to the American scheme, is understood also to favor the transfer of these negotiations from Berlin to the coming London meeting.

Allies Defy Soviet Curb; Fly Food To Berlin

By United Press

BERLIN

The Russians withdrew late last night from a control station they set up in the British sector of Berlin after 400 British troops, supported by nine armored cars, surrounded them on three sides.

The British victory in a new war of nerves came after a tense day during which U. S. and British Army chieftains defied a virtual Soviet blockade of Berlin by ordering their air forces to set up emergency service for passengers and freight between the capital and their occupation zones.

Milk Rationed

U. S. headquarters announced that two transport planes had brought in 15,000 pounds of food in the first fulfillment of the promise of Gen. Lucius D. Clay, U. S. Military Governor, that U. S. troops and civilians here would be fully supplied by plane if necessary.

But as the result of the Russian strangehold on the city's communications Allied authorities were compelled last night to ration milk at their commissaries. Milk was is-

U. S. Wives Start Run on Milk

By Associated Press

BERLIN

American housewives in Ber-

THE BERRYS

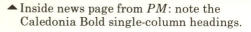

▲ Inside news page from *PM*: note the Caledonia Bold single-column headings.

PM Daily FIVE CENTS

(Copyright 1948, by The Newspaper PM, Inc.)

Vol. VIII — No. 248

Friday, April 2, 1948

☆ COMPLETE EDITION

Chet Bowles Opposes Truman, Wallace—Suggests Eisenhower, Douglas, et al.

Story on Page 3

Russia Charges Britain Stalls On Trade Deal

Story on Page 9

By Frederick Kuh:

What's Behind Berlin Crisis

Official Soviet sources in London say Russians heard U. S. A. and Britain had begun to remove machinery and supplies from Berlin to Western Germany and therefore tightened inspection and control on rail traffic. In Berlin, British troops force Russians to withdraw from control point near Gatow airport (*see map* ▼) in British zone. U. S. planes fly in food.

Stories on Pages 6 and 7

Special Session of UN Assembly Called On Palestine

USSR and Ukraine abstain as Security Council approves U. S. resolution for session "to consider further the question of the future government of Palestine." Council unanimously approves U. S. resolution calling for immediate peace in Palestine and truce talks.

Story on Page 8

Truman Delays Coal Move; May Fear T-H Loopholes

White House hesitates over seeking Taft-Hartley injunction to halt soft coal stoppage. One theory is that John L. Lewis has found loopholes in the new law which demonstrate that its "national emergency" sections are less effective than Congress hoped.

Story on Page 3

▶ A Tempo-styled front page from the later years of the New York evening *PM*; this was a post-war change from the Bodoni Bold it had previously used.

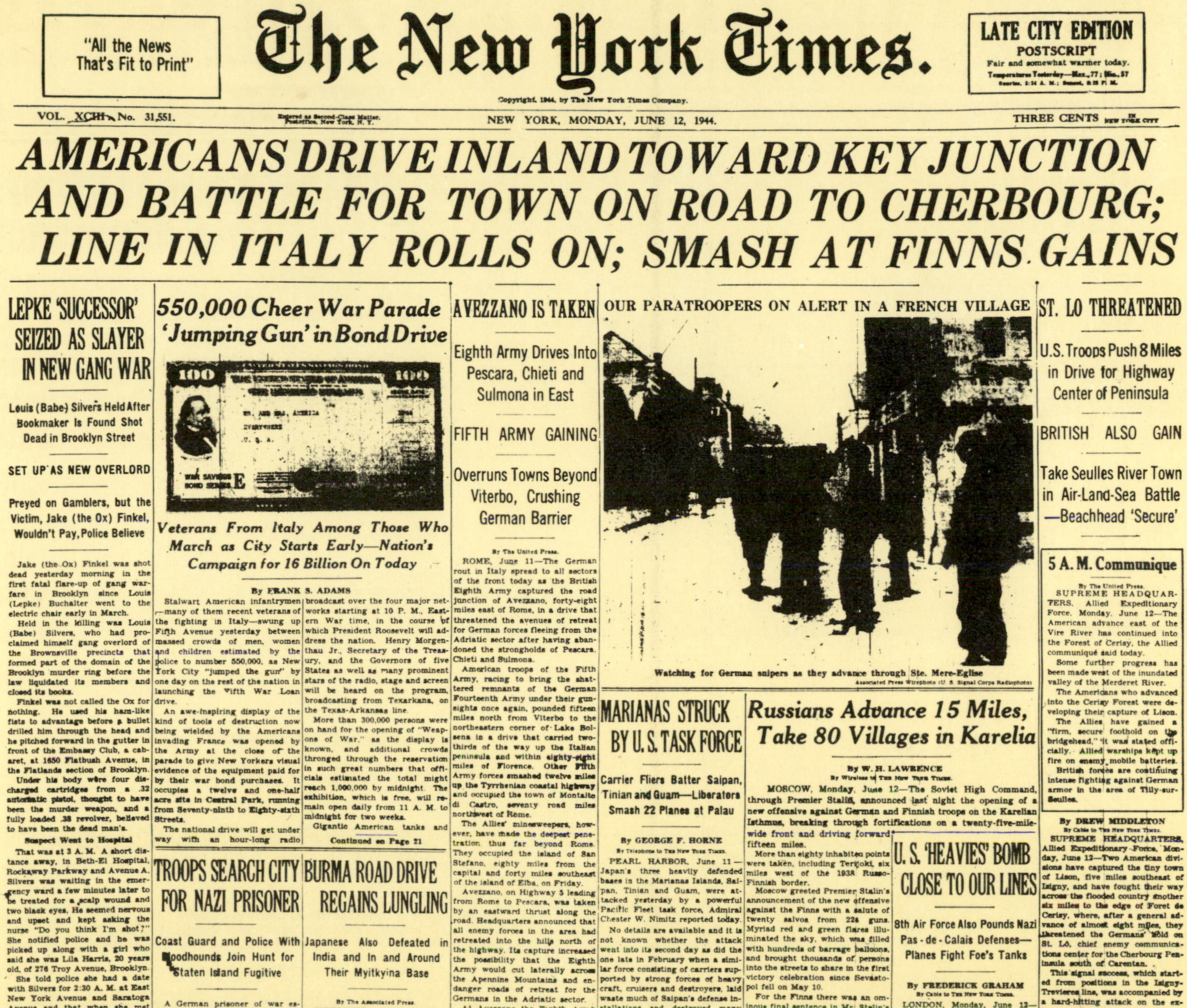

"All the News That's Fit to Print"

The New York Times.

LATE CITY EDITION
POSTSCRIPT
Fair and somewhat warmer today.

Copyright, 1944, by The New York Times Company.

VOL. XCIII...No. 31,551. NEW YORK, MONDAY, JUNE 12, 1944. THREE CENTS

AMERICANS DRIVE INLAND TOWARD KEY JUNCTION AND BATTLE FOR TOWN ON ROAD TO CHERBOURG; LINE IN ITALY ROLLS ON; SMASH AT FINNS GAINS

LEPKE 'SUCCESSOR' SEIZED AS SLAYER IN NEW GANG WAR

Louis (Babe) Silvers Held After Bookmaker Is Found Shot Dead in Brooklyn Street

SET UP AS NEW OVERLORD

Preyed on Gamblers, but the Victim, Jake (the Ox) Finkel, Wouldn't Pay, Police Believe

Jake (the Ox) Finkel was shot dead yesterday morning in the first fatal flare-up of gang warfare in Brooklyn since Louis (Lepke) Buchalter went to the electric chair early in March.

Held in the killing was Louis (Babe) Silvers, who had proclaimed himself gang overlord of the Brownsville precincts that formed part of the domain of the Brooklyn murder ring before the law liquidated its members and closed its books.

Finkel was not called the Ox for nothing. He used his ham-like fists to advantage before a bullet drilled him through the head and he pitched forward in the gutter in front of the Embassy Club, a cabaret, at 1650 Flatbush Avenue, in the Flatlands section of Brooklyn.

Under his body were four discharged cartridges from a .32 automatic pistol, thought to have been the murder weapon, and a fully loaded .38 revolver, believed to have been the dead man's.

Suspect Went to Hospital

That was at 3 A. M. A short distance away, in Beth-El Hospital, Rockaway Parkway and Avenue A, Silvers was waiting in the emergency ward a few minutes later to be treated for a scalp wound and two black eyes. He seemed nervous and upset and kept asking the nurse "Do you think I'm shot?" She notified police and he was picked up along with a girl who said she was Lila Harris, 20 years old, of 276 Troy Avenue, Brooklyn.

She told police she had a date with Silvers for 2:30 A. M. at East New York Avenue and Saratoga Avenue and that when she met him he said he had been beaten up by two men.

The police knew that Silvers' car, registered in the name of his wife, Mrs. Florence Silvers, was parked across the street from the Embassy Club at the time of the killing, and in Miss Harris' handbag they found the car's keys.

At 9 o'clock last night Silvers was formally "booked" on a homicide charge at the Vandeveer Park police station in Brooklyn. He is due to appear in the line-up this morning, after which he will be arraigned in Brooklyn Felony Court. The police said they would

550,000 Cheer War Parade 'Jumping Gun' in Bond Drive

Veterans From Italy Among Those Who March as City Starts Early—Nation's Campaign for 16 Billion On Today

By FRANK S. ADAMS

Stalwart American infantrymen—many of them recent veterans of the fighting in Italy—swung up Fifth Avenue yesterday between massed crowds of men, women and children estimated by the police to number 550,000, as New York City "jumped the gun" by one day on the rest of the nation in launching the Fifth War Loan drive.

An awe-inspiring display of the kind of tools of destruction now being wielded by the Americans invading France was opened by the Army at the close of the parade to give New Yorkers visual evidence of the equipment paid for by their war bond purchases. It occupies a twelve and one-half acre site in Central Park, running from Seventy-ninth to Eighty-sixth Streets.

The national drive will get under way with an hour-long radio broadcast over the four major networks starting at 10 P. M., Eastern War time, in the course of which President Roosevelt will address the nation. Henry Morgenthau Jr., Secretary of the Treasury, and the Governors of five States as well as many prominent stars of the radio, stage and screen will be heard on the program, broadcasting from Texarkana, on the Texas-Arkansas line.

More than 300,000 persons were on hand for the opening of "Weapons of War," as the display is known, and additional crowds thronged through the reservation in such great numbers that officials estimated the total might reach 1,000,000 by midnight. The exhibition, which is free, will remain open daily from 11 A. M. to midnight for two weeks.

Gigantic American tanks and

Continued on Page 21

TROOPS SEARCH CITY FOR NAZI PRISONER

Coast Guard and Police With Bloodhounds Join Hunt for Staten Island Fugitive

A German prisoner of war escaped early yesterday morning from Halloran General Hospital on Staten Island and became the quarry in one of the most intensive manhunts ever conducted in the New York metropolitan area.

Within a few hours, machine guns manned by soldiers had been set up at all the bridge and ferry exits from the island; the police were stopping trucks and wagons, while Coast Guard cutters and police launches churned the waters separating Staten Island from the New York and New Jersey mainland and from Long Island.

Two bloodhounds, brought by

BURMA ROAD DRIVE REGAINS LUNGLING

Japanese Also Defeated in India and In and Around Their Myitkyina Base

By The Associated Press.

CHUNGKING, China, June 11—The complete occupation of Lungling, the second most important Japanese base in Yunnan Province, was announced tonight by the Chinese communiqué, which called it "the greatest success to date for our troops in the Salween offensive."

Personally led by Maj. Gen. Sung Hsi-lien, troops of an Eleventh Army group, who stormed through the city yesterday, were mopping up trapped remnants of the Japanese garrison, the communiqué said. They also were pressing attacks of extermination outside Lungling

AVEZZANO IS TAKEN

Eighth Army Drives Into Pescara, Chieti and Sulmona in East

FIFTH ARMY GAINING

Overruns Towns Beyond Viterbo, Crushing German Barrier

By The United Press.

ROME, June 11—The German rout in Italy spread to all sectors of the front today as the British Eighth Army captured the road junction of Avezzano, forty-eight miles east of Rome, in a drive that threatened the avenues of retreat for German forces fleeing from the Adriatic sector after having abandoned the strongholds of Pescara, Chieti and Sulmona.

American troops of the Fifth Army, racing to bring the shattered remnants of the German Fourteenth Army under their gunsights once again, pounded fifteen miles north from Viterbo to the northeastern corner of Lake Bolsena in a drive that carried two-thirds of the way up the Italian peninsula and within eighty-eight miles of Florence. Other Fifth Army forces smashed twelve miles up the Tyrrhenian coastal highway and occupied the town of Montalto di Castro, seventy road miles northwest of Rome.

The Allies' minesweepers, however, have made the deepest penetration thus far beyond Rome. They occupied the island of San Stefano, eighty miles from the capital and forty miles southeast of the island of Elba, on Friday.

Avezzano, on Highway 5 leading from Rome to Pescara, was taken by an eastward thrust along the road. Headquarters announced that all enemy forces in the area had retreated into the hills north of the highway. Its capture increased the possibility that the Eighth Army would cut laterally across the Apennine Mountains and endanger roads of retreat for the Germans in the Adriatic sector.

At Avezzano the Eighth Army

Continued on Page 6

OUR PARATROOPERS ON ALERT IN A FRENCH VILLAGE

Watching for German snipers as they advance through Ste. Mere-Eglise

Associated Press Wirephoto (U. S. Signal Corps Radiophoto)

MARIANAS STRUCK BY U. S. TASK FORCE

Carrier Fliers Batter Saipan, Tinian and Guam—Liberators Smash 22 Planes at Palau

By GEORGE F. HORNE

By Telephone to THE NEW YORK TIMES.

PEARL HARBOR, June 11—Japan's three heavily defended bases in the Marianas Islands, Saipan, Tinian and Guam, were attacked yesterday by a powerful Pacific Fleet task force, Admiral Chester W. Nimitz reported today.

No details are available and it is not known whether the attack went into its second day as did the one late in February when a similar force consisting of carriers supported by strong forces of heavy craft, cruisers and destroyers, laid waste much of Saipan's defense installations and destroyed many

Continued on Page 11

Russians Advance 15 Miles, Take 80 Villages in Karelia

By W. H. LAWRENCE

By Wireless to THE NEW YORK TIMES.

MOSCOW, Monday, June 12—The Soviet High Command, through Premier Stalin, announced last night the opening of a new offensive against German and Finnish troops on the Karelian Isthmus, breaking through fortifications on a twenty-five-mile-wide front and driving forward fifteen miles.

More than eighty inhabited points were taken, including Terijoki, six miles west of the 1938 Russo-Finnish border.

Moscow greeted Premier Stalin's announcement of the new offensive against the Finns with a salute of twenty salvos from 224 guns. Myriad red and green flares illuminated the sky, which was filled with hundreds of barrage balloons, and brought thousands of persons into the streets to share in the first victory celebration since Sevastopol fell on May 10.

For the Finns there was an ominous final sentence in Mr. Stalin's special order of the day. He ended with the declaration: "Death to the German and Finnish invaders!" Previous orders of the day had named only German invaders.

U. S.-Soviet Pact Celebrated

Finland several weeks ago turned down Soviet peace proposals despite pleas from President Roosevelt, the King of Sweden and many others who thought the Russian proposals were generous.

The first official news of the offensive against the Finns was given yesterday by the Foreign Commissar, Vyacheslaf M. Molotoff at a luncheon celebrating the

U. S. 'HEAVIES' BOMB CLOSE TO OUR LINES

8th Air Force Also Pounds Nazi Pas-de-Calais Defenses—Planes Fight Foe's Tanks

By FREDERICK GRAHAM

By Cable to THE NEW YORK TIMES.

LONDON, Monday, June 12—The non-stop aerial support of the Allied armies in France continued through Saturday night and yesterday along the lines of the three-phase operations developed by American and British air power—heavy bombing of main Nazi traffic centers and vital defense points, tactical bombings closer to the battle area and far-ranging fighter and fighter-bomber cover.

[The weather in the Channel area turned clear and warm Monday morn. with good visibility.

[Nearly 7,000 Allied planes flew over France Sunday in operations that included running bat-

War News Summarized

MONDAY, JUNE 12, 1944

Important advances scored yesterday on the Normandy front expanded the Allied beachhead to nearly 600 square miles with a maximum depth of thirteen miles at two points. This area won during the first week of the invasion was believed to make the foothold secure.

Italy bombed targets throughout the Balkans. The first shuttle group to reach Soviet bases returned to Italy, with Lieut. Gen. Ira C. Eaker in one plane, and bombed Nazi airfields in Rumania. The Black Sea port of Constanta was also blasted. [8:1]

ST. LO THREATENED

U. S. Troops Push 8 Miles in Drive for Highway Center of Peninsula

BRITISH ALSO GAIN

Take Seulles River Town in Air-Land-Sea Battle—Beachhead 'Secure'

5 A. M. Communique

By The United Press.

SUPREME HEADQUARTERS, Allied Expeditionary Force, Monday, June 12—The American advance east of the Vire River has continued into the Forest of Cerisy, the Allied communiqué said today.

Some further progress has been made west of the inundated valley of the Merderet River.

The Americans who advanced into the Cerisy Forest were developing their capture of Lison.

The Allies have gained a "firm, secure foothold on the bridgehead," it was stated officially. Allied warships kept up fire on enemy mobile batteries.

British forces are continuing intense fighting against German armor in the area of Tilly-sur-Seulles.

By DREW MIDDLETON

By Cable to THE NEW YORK TIMES.

SUPREME HEADQUARTERS, Allied Expeditionary Force, Monday, June 12—Two American divisions have captured the tiny town of Lison, five miles southeast of Isigny, and have fought their way across the flooded country another six miles to the edge of Foret de Cerisy, where, after a general advance of almost eight miles, they threatened the Germans' hold on St. Lô, chief enemy communications center for the Cherbourg Peninsula south of Carentan.

This signal success, which started from positions in the Isigny-Trevieres line, was accompanied by a hard-hitting attack on the extreme right wing of Lieut. Gen. Omar N. Bradley's army. The doughboys are fighting to the north and south of Montebourg, sixteen miles southeast of Cherbourg, and are across the Merderet River, northwest of Carentan, as General Bradley extends his flank along the coast.

Hold 600 Square Miles

These American advances were matched yesterday morning by the British capture of Tilly-sur-Seulles, after a short and fierce battle in which the fire of two British cruisers, the Argonaut and the Orion, at 20,000 yards, helped to crumble up

▲ War tensions did not shake the *New York Times* from its Latin Condensed single-column deckers, but brought regular use of the multi-line Century Bold italic banner.

sizes of 16, 21 and 27pt were provided. It was a beautiful face, perhaps too beautiful for daily paper impact. Nevertheless, *PM* itself had an undeniable impact, especially in newspaper circles; for four years running (1941–44) it won first place in the Ayer Award's tabloid division.

As to the rest of the New York scene at this time, the *Herald-Tribune* continued, splendidly unchanging, with its Sherbow Bodoni style, its one concession to 'streamlining' being that some two-line headings were set flush-left, the lines ending at will. Expert approval of this now historic style was aptly reflected in the fact that by the mid-1950s the paper had won the coveted Ayer Cup no fewer than nine times. The magisterial *New York Times* also stuck to its style of Latin Condensed/Gothic deckers, with Cheltenham italic (Bold or Bold Condensed) for double-column headings; its one concession to wartime news stress was the regular use of full-page banners – but presented in suitably staid fashion in a not-too-large size of Century Bold italic capitals, normally in three lines, written with the utmost care to secure a fractional step line by line. By the beginning of the 1940s the evening *New York Post* had a smart, 'streamlined' sans headline dress, mainly of

The Weather—
Hot, humid through tomorrow with scattered showers tomorrow. High 85-93. Details on Page 30.

The Gazette and Daily

The news all the time without fear or favor, bias or prejudice.

Vol. 144—No. 23084 | York, Pa., Saturday Morning, July 18, 1959 | Price 5c—25c a Week

Conferees OK Foreign Aid Bill Slashing Military

Senate-House group cut $200 million from Eisenhower's $1.6 billion arms aid request. Conferees call on President to have specific plans next year on how to cut foreign grants. Both houses to act soon on measure.

Washington (AP)—A bill putting a $3,556,200,000 ceiling on foreign aid this year—$353,200,000 less than President Eisenhower asked—won approval yesterday from a Senate-House Conference committee.

The conferees, fitting together the versions passed by the Senate and House, also called on the President to come up with specific plans next year on how to start cutting off foreign grants.

The biggest cut in the adjusted version was $200 million from Eisenhower's request for $1.6 billion in military aid. This was achieved by those who argue that the administration is relying too much on arms aid, rather than economic.

The legislation is to be called up in the House Wednesday, and in the Senate soon thereafter. It provides only an authorization for foreign aid in the fiscal year which began July 1; the actual appropriation must be voted later and it could be under the authorized ceiling.

In addition to holding the military aid total to $1.4 billion, the compromise bill eliminates a Senate earmarking of $893,670,000 for countries in the North Atlantic Treaty Organization (NATO). This would permit more to be spent on non-NATO countries, including Korea and Formosa.

It also provides that no more than $67 million may be spent on military assistance to Latin American countires, the same amount as last year.

(Continued on Page Thirty-One)
See Foreign Aid Bill

City Will Allot $21,500 To Hire Planners Directly

A bill introduced in city council yesterday appropriated $21,500 to complete center city planning by hiring planners directly. The money will come from a loan made in 1958.

The plan of hiring the planners directly was devised by City Solicitor John W. Heller III after he had ruled that council under state law could not channel the money through York Redevelopment authority, which is handling the project.

Heller's new plan has been upheld by the city's bond counsel, Townsend, Elliott and Munson, according to Mayor Fred A. Schiding.

Planners Maurice Rotival and Dr. Ernst Jurkat are to handle the final phases of blueprinting.

Navy Admits It Made Mistakes Costing Millions

General Accounting Office says errors in negotiating contracts contained more than $12 million in excess charges.

Washington (AP) — The Navy admitted yesterday mistakes were made in negotiating contracts which, the General Accounting Office says, contained more than $12 million in excess charges.

"We made mistakes both in these cases, and in our relations with the GAO," Asst. Secretary of the Navy Cecil P. Milne told the House Armed Service Investigations subcommittee.

Milne said a number of the contracts dated back to the rush and pressure of Korean war days. He said negotiating methods have been vastly improved since then.

But the Navy stood firm in its refusal to give the GAO, the ac-

(Continued on Page Thirty-One)
See Navy Mistakes

Barton Introduces Bill To Demolish Park Farmhouse

Parks director proposes to raze architecturally historic structure in Memorial park unless some civic group will finance restoration.

Demolition of the architecturally historic farmhouse in Spring Garden Memorial park is authorized in a bill introduced into city council yesterday by Parks Director Jack H. Barton.

Barton told council that before having the building torn down he would wait a "reasonable" length of time to see if any civic group decides to finance the cost of restoring the two-story brick building.

Barton made the statement in reply to Mayor Fred A. Schiding, who asked Barton if he would be willing to give "people interested in restoring the building" sufficient time to make proposals.

The bill authorizing the destruction of the farm house is scheduled to come up for final passage when council meets next Friday. Barton told a reporter he is willing to wait even beyond that date before beginning demolition.

The Junior Service League of York has given up the idea of taking on the project of restoring the house, league spokesmen indicated yesterday after hearing of council's action.

"But the community should do something to prevent things like this from happening in the future," one of the spokesmen said.

"We recognize the architectural significance of the farmhouse but we could not restore it ourselves," she explained, adding: "We feel that as one of the early American farmhouses it should be preserved."

Restoration of the two-story brick building has been recommeded by Pennsylvania Bureau of Museums, Historical Sites and Properties and by the City Planning commission.

(Continued on Page Thirty-One)
See Farmhouse

Castro Quits Post, Accusing Urrutia Of Failing Revolt

Cuban Prime Minister and leader of revolution tells nation President Urrutia became hostile because he was denied leave of absence and neglected his duties. Castro criticizes U.S. Senate committee for calling Diaz Lanz to testify.

BULLETIN

Havana (AP)—President Manuel Urrutia resigned last night.

The council of ministers immediately named Osvaldo Dorticos, a lawyer in his 40's, as Cuba's new president. Dorticos, a relative unknown in Cuban politics, was made minister of revolutionary laws in last month's cabinet shakeup.

Havana (AP) — Fidel Castro resigned as prime minister of Cuba last night, accusing President Manuel Urrutia of immobility and of failing to discharge his duties.

This in turn, Castro told a television audience, has created "discrepancies of moral order."

Urrutia was not available for comment. At the presidential palace he refused to receive newsmen.

"In the midst of the Diaz Lanz blackmail game," Castro declared, "The President suspiciously pictures himself as the champion of anti-communism."

(Castro referred to the escape to the United States of former Air Force chief, Maj. Pedro Luis Diaz Lanz, who testified this week before a Senate committee headed by Sen. James O. Eastland (D-Miss.). Diaz Lanz called Castro a Communist and his government a Communist dictatorship.)

Plans Defamation Drive

Castro said Urrutia had begun "an elaborate plan of defamation against the government similar to the one of Pedro Diaz Lanz."

Castro also criticized a U. S. Senate committee in connection with the Diaz Lanz case. He said the committee, which heard Diaz Lanz testify in Washington, "descended to the low of calling a traitor to testify."

"Our enemies abroad, those sinister personages in the Senate or who knows where, these reactionary interests were poised for the blow against us," Castro said.

"I have always rejected Communist support and I believe all true revolutionaries should reject Communist support," Castro said.

"In the U.S.A. itself there is a Communist newspaper (the New York Daily Worker). Why then are we expected to go after the Communists? No, sir. We recognize freedom of all.

"We mobilized the forces of the nation to free man from fear of political dogma without dictatorship or terror of any kind. Capitalism kills a man with hunger. Com-

(Continued on Page Thirty-One)
See Castro Quits

Racial Unit May Act On Bunche Discrimination

Although Nobel Prize winning Negro considers West Side tennis incident closed, city race commission may force private clubs to make membership lists public.

New York (AP)—Dr. Ralph J. Bunche was ready yesterday to drop his complaint against the West Side Tennis club. But a city racial commission was less willing to forgive and forget.

After hearing the Nobel Prize-winning Negro, the city's Commission on Intergroup Relations said it may seek to force private clubs to make their membership lists public.

The commission also went ahead with plans to interrogate representatives of the tennis club, which operates the Forest Hills arena in Queens where many championship matches are held.

Dr. Bunche, a United Nations undersecretary, originally inquired about the possibility of joining the tennis club so his 15-year-old son would have a place to practice the game.

Bunche said he was told by club president Wilfred Burglund that Negroes and Jews were not eligible for membership.

Earlier this week, Burglund restatement saying it considers membership applications without regard to race, creed or color.

The club invited Bunche and his son to submit formal applications and promised them every consideration. Bunche said he is interested now in joining. His son still is thinking the matter over.

Before yesterday's meetng with the commission, Bunche said:

"This has not been a pleasant experience and I am glad it is over. But I will never give aid and comfort and religious intolerance whenever and wherever I encounter it, by withholding from the public information that it is entitled to have.

"In this community, happily, bigotry cannot long stand the heat of public exposure.

"So far as I am personally concerned, that statement (by the club), which is admirably to the point of all counts, winds up the West Side tennis story. Should I be asked, I will inform the commission to that effect."

After the meeting, the commis-

(Continued on Page Thirty-One)
See Racial Unit

State Seeks To Halt $900,000 Tax Refund For Manu-Mine Co.

Washington (AP) — The Pennsylvania Turnpike Commission yesterday appealed to the Supreme Court in its effort to keep a $900,000 federal income tax refund from going to the Manu-Mine Research & Development Co.

The commission asked the court to review a circuit court of appeals decision that the case is one for state court rather than federal court. jurisdiction.

In the appeal, counsel for the commission noted that the president of the Reading, Pa., firm, had been convicted of conspiracy to defraud and obtaining money by false pretenses in connection with a large mine-filling contract for the northeastern extension of the Pennsylvania turnpike.

"The defrauding corporation . . . obtained possession of the money by fraud, used it to pay the income taxes on the money so obtained, and then applied for the refund which the defendant district director was about to make," the commission's appeal said.

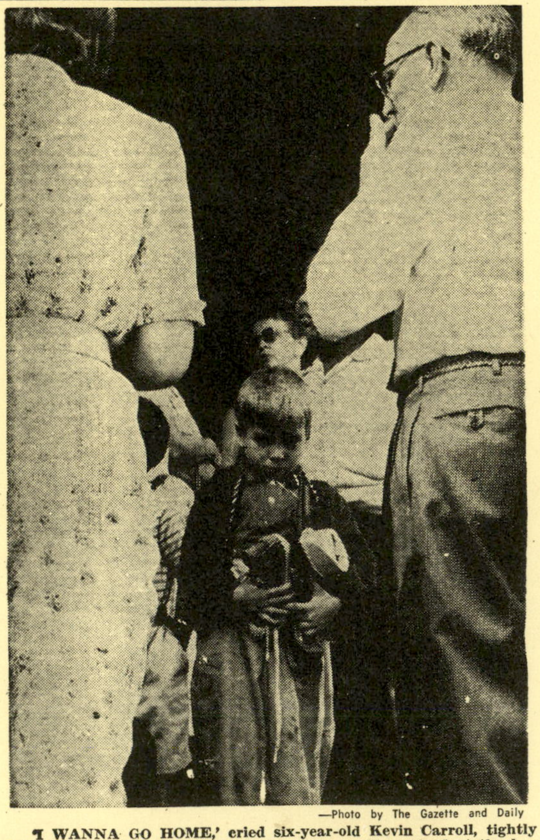

—Photo by The Gazette and Daily

'I WANNA GO HOME,' cried six-year-old Kevin Carroll, tightly clutching his tennis shoes and plastic airplane. He arrived at the bus depot here with 36 other "fresh air" kids who came from New York City for two-week vacations with York county families. But Kevin was not in a holiday mood. He cried bitterly for his mother and his home in the Bronx. For the outcome, see page three.

State Senate To Vote Monday On Reform Of Minor Judiciary

(By a Staff Reporter)

Harrisburg — Pennsylvania's 50 state senators face Monday the squeamish job of taking a final vote on proposed constitutional amendments to reduce in number and put on a salaried basis the state's fee-collecting magistrates.

Their votes will, in effect, indicate the senators' choice between advancing the cause of justice for their constitutents and Pennsylvanians as a whole or yielding to the pressure of the small, but politically powerful minor judiciary.

Through their state-wide organization, the magistrates — aldermen and justices of the peace — have been lobbying aggressively in Harrisburg for defeat of the amendment.

When they act on the amendments, the senators will be weighing also political pressure against a recommendation of experts for better government. The experts were members of the Commission on Constitutional Revision which was set up by an act of the legislature. They included some sena-

(Continued on Page Thirty)
See State Senate

Censorship Lifted For Reports On Nixon's Soviet Trip

Washington (AP) — The Soviet government has agreed to lift censorship for newsmen accompanying Vice President Richard M. Nixon on his good will visit to Russia this month.

Nixon's office disclosed this yesterday after weeks of backstage negotiation with Moscow on the issue.

Some 80 American reporters are assigned to cover Nixon's activities when he arrives in Moscow next Thursday for a two-week tour.

About 50 will accompany him from Washington, leaving Wednesday in a brand new jet airliner which is to make the first American nonstop flight to Moscow.

Nixon said the Soviet government has agreed that newsmen may file dispatches "freely and without delay" from Moscow and a half dozen other Russian cities he will visit.

WEATHER
Cloudy, warmer tonight; lowest in city about 28, in suburbs 20. Moderate temperature cloudy tomorrow followed by light snow.
Call WEather 6-1212 for latest forecast and hourly temperature.—Advertisement.

New York Post

NIGHT EXTRA

Founded 1801. Volume 139. No. 88.
Copyright 1940. New York Post, Inc.

NEW YORK THURSDAY FEBRUARY 29 1940

THREE CENTS

FINNS FALLING BACK 4 MI. FROM VIIPURI

ON GUARD: A FINNISH OUTPOST on the edge of a lake in the path of the Red advance.

GOP Aims to Appease Mayor

May Cut Mandatory Costs for Tax Loss

By ROBERT G. SEWELL
Post Staff Correspondent

ALBANY, Feb. 29.—The Republican-controlled Legislature today prepared to play ball with Mayor LaGuardia on cutting New York City's mandatory expenses in order to put over its plan for avoiding Gov. Lehman's proposed $15,000,000 income tax boost.

Under the GOP plan to trim nearly $6,000,000 of Gov. Lehman's $396,700,000 budget, thus bringing its total slightly below the current year's Republican economy budget and making the economy issue safe for District Attorney Dewey's Presidential drive, New York City will lose about $800,000 in state aid for schools.

But the city's major loss will result from decision to keep the state-collected bank tax which now goes to localities. The metropolis now gets about $3,000,000 annually from this tax. To offset that loss, Speaker Heck of the Assembly and Majority Leader Hanley of the Senate announced that legislation enabling the city to make an equal saving elsewhere would be passed.

Transit Board Plan

Part of the total will be made up by transferring to the state the cost of maintaining the Transit Commission, about $900,000 annually. However, the Republicans will also seek to wield the economy ax on the Transit Commission, thereby avoiding increasing the state's budget by the whole sum.

Just where the rest of the city's savings will be made was not clear today, but a series of suggestions were being made. They include transfer to the state of the cost of building armories, which the state bears outside the city; legislation to speed court and county consolidation, and to enable cutting of salaries of judicial attaches.

Legislative leaders, some New York City Republican legislators and representatives of the LaGuardia administration are expected to confer shortly, possibly tomorrow, on concessions to the city. The city's spokesmen are expected to insist that the shift of functions or revenue allocations be of a sort which will be permanent and not one-year affairs.

Try Again on Insurance

In ducking the income tax boost, Republican legislators used a bagful of fiscal tricks. One—taking over unclaimed insurance funds—was tried last

Continued on Page 4, Col. 1

Reds Bend Second Line Of Defense

City's Position Perilous—25 to 30 Divisions Reported Attacking

HELSINKI Feb. 29 (UP).—A war comunique today admitted that strong pressure by the Red Army had forced Finnish troops to fall back between the Bay of Viipuri and Lake Vuoksi, on the western end of the Mannerheim Line.

The communique indicated that the Russians had bent the second line defenses at some points and created a highly dangerous situation for the defenders of Viipuri (Viborg), although it was not admited that the city was lost.

(A Red Army communique claimed that the Russians had reached a point four miles from Viipuri.)

Huge Forces Attack

The Red army was throwing huge forces against the western end of the Finnish line in an

Germany Recalls Its Citizens in Holland

24-Hr. Notice Given—Siegfried Line Extension Seen

OLDENZAAL, Dutch-German Frontier, Feb. 29 (UP). — German officials today warned a number of persons who live in the Reich but have been temporarily sojourning in Holland to return to Germany before to-form the entire length of the Belgian and Dutch frontiers to the North Sea.

A number of persons of Dutch descent live across the frontier on German territory, and some of these have recently to cross the frontier will be canceled.

The order presumably was in connection with the reported extension of the German defense line.

This report coincided with in- Belgian and Dutch frontiers, probably tomorrow.

Tightening of border control was believed intended to prevent spying on the German defense works. Passes permitting lim-

City Bakery Strike Threatens

Intra-Union Conflict Dates Back to 1934

By KARL BOSTROM

Scales for other employees are the old-line AFL locals, was

▲ The 'streamlined' *New York Post* of 1940; it had just dropped its blackletter title and conventional condensed gothic/Cheltenham Bold headline style.

medium weight, with a distinctively designed sans upper- and lower-case title-line, shaded on the left. The paper later turned tabloid, but retained the new title.

There was now a general trend among newspapers favouring sans headline styles towards the lighter weights available in the Spartan, Erbar and Tempo families. There was a movement away from the heavy condensed gothics, the banners in 120pt and 144pt capitals; and the bold Franklin Gothic lower-case, though still to be seen in multi-column streamers, was being played less. There was also a movement away from sans altogether, particularly for broadsheets; and here the trend, most marked during the 1950s, was towards Bodoni. Century and Cheltenham Bold, though still to be seen, were growing less common. There were, of course, the odd men out, as the Ayer contests showed; thus of two small-town Cup winners, the *Rutland Herald* (Vermont) had a Granjon-Garamond heading dress – an appropriately academic design by the Yale University Printer, Carl P. Rollins – while the *Emporia Gazette* (Kansas), famous as the more-than-local voice of the late William Allen White, used the Venetian-style Ludlow Eusebius. But the general trend was unmistakable. By 1960 the Ayer winners showed Bodoni leading seven to two over sans (Erbar/Spartan).

The spread of tabloid format had also become marked. The word *format* is stressed; it was not the strident shouting of the tabloid New York *Daily News* or *Daily Mirror* that spread, but the half-sheet paper, presented with normal, and often quite quiet, display typography. The Ayer Award authorities did not institute their new tabloid division just before the war because they expected a rush of big-city bludgeoning 'tabs' but because they felt it necessary to provide for the local dailies that were adopting tabloid format. The innovation paid off; tabloid entries grew; and in 1958 the *Gazette and Daily* of the historic city of York (Pennsylvania) became the first tabloid to win the Ayer Cup; in the late 1940s it had already twice come top of the tabloid division. Neatly and attractively headlined in the more modest sans style indicated above, the *Gazette and Daily* showed how complete was the fidelity of many American papers to John E. Allen's textbook specimen headlines; its main single-column style adopted the three lines of 34pt Erbar Light Condensed, upper- and lower-case, set flush-left, which Allen had suggested. Precisely the same style appeared in the Cup winner the following year, the broadsheet *Goshen*

◀ This Pennsylvania local daily was the first tabloid to win the Ayer Cup, in 1958: its headings were styled in Tempo and Erbar.

News, an Indiana small-town daily with a circulation of under 10,000.

The page-format of these tabloids was mostly five columns, though there were signs of a move to six columns. In this period, however, it was in the broadsheet field that the introduction of an extra column – the change from eight to nine columns – became an important feature. Many local dailies were finding that advertising pressure was forcing them to increase their paging to the point at which it went beyond the straight-run capacity of their rotaries; thus not only were they enduring an uncomfortably expensive increase in their newsprint costs but were driven to the slower production of collect running. Hence the advantage of the nine-column format. It was mainly done by dropping the column measure (12 or 11½-picas) by a nonpareil, rarely a pica, and getting down to plate width by super-shrinkage of stereotype mats, with column rules dropped to 3pt or 4pt.

There was nothing new about the American practice of stereotyping shrinkage, which has been discussed in an earlier chapter. The nine-column format simply put a premium on the practice and emphasised its distorting effect on type. It will be recalled that Corona, the last and long the most popular of the 'Legibility Group' in the U.S., had been designed with an eye to overcoming the distorting effects of the extreme matrix shrinkage. The shrinkage factor apart, a further restricting effect on news-text type developed in America during the 1950s with the general spread of TTS wire service; this became a major factor in the next decade, and is discussed in the following chapter.

A last word on the first item – the title-piece. As in Britain, the blackletter title has a long history in America, and some papers still cling to it. But blackletter was already on the way out when the post-war period opened. By 1958 the eleven Ayer winners only rated three blackletter titles, in 1959 only four, in 1960 none.

8: An Epoch of Change

Economic and technical advance

From preceding chapters it will have been gathered that there are no absolute lines of division in the history of newspaper typography. New styles are started, trends develop, but they co-exist with the old methods for longer or shorter periods. By its nature, and by the widely varying circumstances of newspapers themselves, newspaper design is a perpetual phenomenon of unequal development. Nevertheless it is possible to see the year 1960 as the opening of a notable epoch of change; during the whole decade, and continuing strongly into the 1970s, newspaper design has been in the throes of a new revolution.

The design developments which will be discussed in this chapter are not things in themselves, not concepts emerging in isolation from the real world of newspaper publishing and production. They relate directly to the radical changes, both economic and technical, that have been a feature of the newspaper industry during the whole period. These changes have been complex and far-reaching and cannot be presented in any detail here; but it is essential to comprehend at least their main outlines.

Economically, the merger movement, the concentration of newspaper publishing into larger and larger units, has marched parallel with the often lethal competitive threat of new mass media like television. The mass-circulation metropolitan papers, whether the London nationals or the New York dailies, were the most at risk. The situation was highlighted by the catastrophe of the *News Chronicle* and *The Star* in October 1960; this, the first national daily closure for a generation, shook Britain and led to the appointment of the second Royal Commission on the Press (1961). Like its predecessor of 1947–49 this Commission produced an interesting and informative report and little else (the establishment of the Press Council does not relate to our concerns). In America the massacre of Manhattan, mentioned in Chapter Seven, was completed. No longer were there any Scripps-Howard or Hearst dailies in the newspaper metropolis of the U.S. Hearst's tabloid *Daily Mirror* and the venerable *Herald-Tribune* were the last to go. In their stead arose influential suburban dailies like *Newsday*, a Long Island evening which had begun to make its mark in the 1950s (when it was five times a winner of the Ayer tabloid award), though now it was to advance much further following a revolution in its design.

Concentration was more spectacular in Britain than in America. In 1959 Roy Thomson (now Lord Thomson of Fleet) had taken over the old Kemsley empire, including its extensive regional interests following his acquisition of the *Scotsman* and of Scottish Television (his 'licence to print money'); the consolidation of the Thomson Organisation was sensationally crowned in the autumn of 1966 by its takeover of *The Times* and the linking of the famous daily and Sunday in Times Newspapers. The establishment of the giant International Publishing Corporation has already been mentioned. IPC, with its linking of newspapers, consumer and technical periodicals, with large printing interests, was the largest concern of the kind in the world. Apart from its gold mines, like the *Mirror* papers and the *Sunday People* it inherited, with Odhams Press, the tottering *Daily Herald*, as described in the previous chapter. In 1964 IPC converted the *Herald* into the

Sun, an operation generally regarded in Fleet Street as the most bungled affair in national newspaper history; after an indifferent start the paper improved substantially in the quality of its presentation, but it was far too late.* Since 1962 the two papers had cost IPC around twelve million pounds and the end came in the autumn of 1969; the title was sold, for a modest sum, to the Australian publisher Rupert Murdoch, a newcomer to Fleet Street.

Murdoch, son of Sir Keith Murdoch, a famous Australian publisher, had been actively building a newspaper empire in the Antipodes (including the founding of the Commonwealth's first national daily, *The Australian*, at Canberra) when he appeared on the London scene at the end of 1968. He bid against Robert Maxwell, Czech-born head of Pergamon Press and former Labour MP, for control of the *News of the World* and its associated interests, and won. This yielded him both the large Fleet Street plant needed for the 6,000,000 weekly run of the *News of the World*, and substantial subsidiary newspaper and periodical concerns, notably the Berrows Organisation, with its string of evening and weekly papers in the South West Midlands and the West Country. On this basis he was able to launch his own *Sun*, very economically, as a brash tabloid morning which proceeded to peel hundreds of thousands off the circulation of the *Mirror*, and within three years to approach a three-million daily figure.

Of the other principal publishing groups Associated Newspapers (the Rothermere-*Daily Mail* concern) felt most keenly the cold wind of crisis, at least in respect of its national interests; its subsidiary string of provincial evenings, from Swansea to Hull, from Stoke to Exeter, continued to return substantial profits. In 1971 Associated closed down the tabloid *Daily Sketch* and converted the shrinking broadsheet *Daily Mail* to tabloid format, as described in more detail below. By the early 1970s, too, its London *Evening News* was in difficulties; its circulation, once around 1,750,000, had dropped to below 900,000 and, more seriously, it had fallen badly behind in the metropolitan evening paper advertisement race. The lead here had been decisively won by the Beaverbrook *Evening Standard*, whose own typographic revolution is discussed later.

The *Standard* scored by being first in the field with an elaborately-organised telephone-ad department, paying off in heavy daily paging of classifieds; at the same time its 'up-the-market' appeal put it in a strong position for attracting high-grade display advertising, including the lucrative full-colour advertising which it presented with striking success in gravure, preprinted in register (an important technical advance of a period which had begun with colour preprint in the unregistered 'wallpaper' style). Thus, with a circulation of around 515,000 the *Standard* steadily led the London evening field, frequently reaching its maximum of fifty-six pages tabloid; this figure exceeded by up to eight tabloid pages the normal paging of its competitor. The *Standard* is therefore a highly profitable unit of the Beaverbrook group which continues, since the death of its founder, to be a strong organisation. It is directed by Beaverbrook's son, Sir Max Aitken, Bt, who used the statutory procedure to divest himself of his father's title, on the understandable grounds that there could never be another Beaverbrook. The *Daily Express*, now the only 'popular' broadsheet national morning (since the disappearance of the *Herald–Sun* and the conversion of the *Mail*) has suffered some of the circulation shrinkage which has affected all the 'populars', in contrast to the 'heavies'. Nevertheless it is still, with its Sunday companion, the only national produced in three centres – London, Manchester and Glasgow – and the group has a many-millioned capital investment schedule for the 1970s. Interestingly, this capital investment is to be in hot-metal and rotary letterpress (as are the parallel plans of Murdoch for his *News of the World–Sun* operation).

The two nation-wide provincial groups, Westminster Press and United Newspapers, have both consolidated and extended. Their

* The *Sun* used two different title-pieces, both grey-tinted and in a style of poster sans; one was double-column, condensed and gauging about eighteen lines pica, the other was three-column, square and squat, gauging just over seven lines pica. The idea was that these title-blocks might 'float', as some American papers do with their titles; the experiment was not a success.

strength continues to be in the provincial and local weekly field, though between them they now have three regional mornings. As a subsidiary of the Cowdray interests (Pearson Longman Ltd) Westminster is linked with the prestigious *Financial Times*, but United have never had any national involvement (which is one of the reasons why they are consistently in the front rank of profitability among British newspaper groups). In 1969 United absorbed Yorkshire Post Newspapers, the independent and influential Leeds morning-evening publishers. Here it is worth adding that, the national groups apart, the early 1970s saw an important trend to regional mergers and groupings of local weeklies, particularly in the prosperous and suburbanised South East. Of these the outstanding example is the *Surrey Advertiser* group, of Guildford, which has acquired so many local papers in Surrey, Sussex and over to the Hampshire border that its overall circulation now exceeds 200,000 a week, making it by far the largest purely weekly group in the country. Also significant is the Morgan-Grampian group, a periodical publishing concern which has taken over a number of the main weeklies in suburban Kent, on the south-eastern outskirts of London, and the Sussex coast; among these is the old-established and many-editioned *Kentish Times*, whose 103,000 circulation has long been among Britain's highest weekly figures.*

Turning now to the radical technical changes, the 1960s can be shortly summarised as the period in which computerised typesetting, photo-composition and web-offset printing began to transform substantial sections of the newspaper industry, both in Britain and America. The purpose of the computer in typesetting is simply to increase productivity by providing justified and hyphenated tape from unjustified ('idiot') tape produced by high-speed keyboarding. Computerised tape can be used equally well to drive TTS linecasters or photo-composition machines (for the faster and more sophisticated of the latter its use is obligatory). But in practice, certainly in Britain, by far the greatest number of computerised typesetting installations have been associated with photo-composition, as an integral accompaniment of the changeover to web-offset production. That for web-offset newspaper production there are certain technical advantages in repro-proofing from hot-metal – ease of correction, speed of changing, superior typographic resolution – has hardly checked the trend of web-offset newspaper printers to photo-composition, which has its own technical (and, more particularly, financial) advantages.

It is necessary to get web-offset and its potentialities into proper perspective. Experience has taught us much; the early euphoria has worn away and few now believe that web-offset is a universal cure-all for all newspaper production ills. In Britain and America alike web-offset has been adopted by small and medium run papers but not by the big city dailies. The 300-odd British web-offset weeklies had an average run of under 25,000 and of 13 web-offset evenings a dozen had runs ranging from 22,000 to something over 50,000; the exception was *The News* (Portsmouth) which, with its well over 100,000 run, was known to have met substantial operational snags. In the States the ANPA returns for 1970 showed the heaviest concentration of web-offset dailies (135) in the circulation range of under 15,000, with 84 of these in the under-10,000 range; there were 26 in the 25,000–50,000 range but a mere 3 above that level. The fact is that certain negative features of web-offset working, both technical and economic, escalate sharply with the size of the run. These include i) *technical* – slower speed, slower get-away (a serious matter with tight transport schedules for a big run), more frequent and longer down-times (for blanket wash-up or changing), ii) *economic* – dearer plates, dearer ink, dearer newsprint, a much higher percentage of paper waste. For these reasons big-city dailies, with six-figure runs, seem likely to stay rotary letterpress for a considerable time to come. To most newspapermen in Britain it appears improbable that the costly venture of IPC in Glasgow – changing the over-500,000 tabloid *Daily Record* and the near-

* In July 1973, Morgan-Grampian sold their weekly paper interests indicated above, to Westminster Press for £5,350,000.

800,000 *Sunday Mail* to computerised photoset web-offset – will be repeated.

It is not necessary to penetrate what has been called 'the phototypesetting jungle', or to survey the mass of different makes of web-offset presses on the market, to reach broad conclusions about the impact of this mode of production on newspaper design. Allowing for the variations in precision of typographic resolution and in output capacity of the many display and text photosetters (the range of text speeds can be from 35 to 160 normal newspaper 8pt lines a minute) the principal design facilities offered by web-offset are:

i) *Halftones.* – The superior reproduction resulting from the fine-screen offset halftone is accepted as an outstanding advantage of the process. It means that high fidelity is possible both in small pictures and in large (especially when the latter have massive detail) as compared with the indifferent quality usual with the stereotyped coarse-screen halftones of rotary letterpress. Thus web-offset papers have been to the fore in exploiting photographs, not as a pictorial additive to the page, but as an integral part of the make-up.

ii) *Full process colour.* – It is a commonplace that web-offset is incomparably superior to rotary letterpress for four-colour process work (three primaries and black). With satellite units, using a common impression cylinder, accurate register is guaranteed. On the other hand, the initial enthusiasm for web-offset process colour is now somewhat muted. It was too often used as a mere confection, and there has come to be a general appreciation that editorial full process colour only fulfils a genuine function when colour adds a real dimension to the news picture. Full-colour facilities for advertisers can be an obvious advantage; but web-offset full colour on newsprint has a certain flatness about it; it only attains brilliance when heat-set on coated paper, which is scarcely practical for the normal newspaper.

iii) *Spot colour.* – Editorially, the design possibilities of spot (line) colour are greater, it would seem, than those of full process colour. Spot colour capacity can be had on the letterpress rotary, though Britain has always lagged well behind Europe in its use; but it is an accepted and easier facility of web-offset. Much remains to be done in its effective development. Spot colour is thrown away, or rather reduced to absurdity, when it is spattered about pages in vari-coloured headlines. It has great potential when consciously and deliberately used for editorial emphasis, by way of bold coloured rules or borders.

iv) *Reverses and tints.* – Ease of production of all types of reversing (white lettering on any ground) and of tints, is a major advantage of web-offset, that is to say, of the principle of photo-offset, over letterpress. With reverses only requiring simple negative photography and a bromide print, with tints simply produced by laying down the appropriate strips of screened transparent tape on the final page paste-up, the complex blockmaking procedures of letterpress are dispensed with. Ranging from substantial portions of display or text reversed out, to tint borders or cutoffs, or headings differentiated with a tint ground, many effects can be economically and expeditiously obtained which in practice could not be contemplated in letterpress. The design implications of all this are obvious.

This book does not aim to discuss in detail the many technical aspects of web-offset newspaper production, but it will be useful to note one or two additional points here. Thus there are two distinct methods of halftone working – the stripped-in negative and the screened bromide positive techniques. In the first a blank space is left in the page paste-up for each halftone; the individual screened negatives are then affixed to the clear 'windows' thus provided in the page negative and the whole then printed down on the plate. In the second a screened bromide positive is made from each individual negative; these positives are stuck in their required places on the page paste-up before the making of the page negative and the printing down. Both techniques have their adherents. For the first it is claimed that it gives better halftone presswork, since it uses the original negative without re-photographing from a positive. For the second it is argued that the flexibility of the positive, which allows for last-minute size alterations, for dropped-in headings or captions, for stripping-in transfer lettering and the like, outweighs what is said to be a negligible inferiority in reproduction quality.

One other item, whose design significance is perhaps marginal, is the late news device; here letterpress has the edge, and a pretty big edge, over web-offset. British evening papers in particular have leaned for generations on the Stop Press or 'fudge' device, i.e. the separate small cylinder with separate segments or 'boxes' which can be filled with linecaster slugs or specially-cast small plates, to get late news items speedily into the paper without stopping to replate pages. The 'fudge' has become traditional for the rapid conveying of race and other sporting results. No lithographic late news device has yet approached the speed and simplicity of the letterpress 'fudge'; and web-offset evenings have been largely driven to such inadequate and primitive procedures as cutting typewriter stencils for stamping-in after the papers have been printed. Only one large web-offset concern known to me, the East Midland Allied Press at Peterborough, ingeniously decided to make the best of both technical worlds by having an ordinary letterpress 'fudge' head built into the web-offset press which prints their *Evening Telegraph*.[1]

Having outlined the main new features of photoset, web-offset production it seems logical at this point to conclude by discussing the principal design developments in the web-offset field. For the technical reasons indicated above, the web-offset papers, particularly the fruitful crop of fresh local evenings, tend to form a distinct group. The 1971 Newspaper Design Award judges spoke, almost pejoratively, of the 'photoset, web-offset "look"'; by this they meant the general trend of the web-offset evenings to sans headline typography, in the range of grots and gothics, light and bold, square and condensed, variously available on the different display photosetters, plus an occasional use of Century (usually in the Schoolbook variant, considered below) for contrast. Another aspect of the 'look' was the omission of rules, both column and sometimes cutoff, to save the time and care needed to scribe, or strip-in, rules on a page paste-up. In place of column rules at least a pica of white (and occasionally more) is carried, measures being sufficiently narrowed to enable this to be done. Other considerations apart, the general omission of rules is apt to cause confusion; this is especially true of the omission of cutoffs, though this practice was advocated in America many years ago.[2]

By the mid-1960s web-offset weeklies and the pioneer evening *Shropshire Star* (1964) began to attract the Design Award judges' commendation; but it was not till 1968 that there came the breakthrough to a major award. In that year the *Evening Echo* (Watford), one of the two evenings produced in the Thomson Hemel Hempstead plant, won the bronze plaque 'first' in its class. For four out of the five ensuing years, up to 1972, the first prize went either to the *Echo*, its stablemate the *Evening Post* (Luton) or the joint Thomson-Westminster *Evening Mail* (Slough); and in the fifth year the *Evening Mail* won the Special Award for editorial use of spot colour – the bold red heading-and-boxing of a dramatic front page story. The 1968 panel of judges happened to be of exceptional standing – *Sunday Times* editor Harold Evans, London College of Printing Principal Leslie Owens and Arnold Quick, then an IPC divisional chairman. In awarding the first prize to the 'dashing and dramatic' *Evening Echo* they praised the way in which it 'boldly demonstrates the web-offset possibilities (particularly in decorative feature treatments) that would be impossible in hot metal'. Their main criticism was of defects in display photosetting ('word spacing in headings needs attention'); this criticism was to be echoed by their successors (e.g. in 1969).

KENT MESSENGER

THE PAPER FOR MAIDSTONE TOWN AND DISTRICT

5p

19 JANUARY 1973

Shocked gasman: I quit

It's a gas fiddle, say

CASE ONE

MRS Joyce Keari of 36 Wolfe Road, Maidstone.

"This man called at the door asking to look at my gas equipment. I thought he was some kind of engineer. He then tried to sell me a gas fire. I was very angry.

"This man got into my home under false pretences. If he was a salesman he should have said so."

Flashback to last week's KM

A SEGAS engineer has decided to quit his job, because of the way North Sea Gas conversion has been handled in Maidstone.

The engineer, who wants to remain anonymous, said: "I have seen a lot of people who have been taken for a ride by gas board salesmen.

"Many have ended up buying equipment which they never needed."

He confirmed high pressure salesmanship revealed in the Kent Messenger last week.

"The salesmen are working on a commission basis.

"This means they are not as eager to explain the full situation to the customer as clearly as possible."

Even the oldest gas cooker, could be converted, free, by the gas board," he said.

The engineer also pointed to another alarming situation.

Segas say portable room heaters cannot be converted, are dangerous and must be removed.

People who own such heaters receive a £3 voucher, when the heaters are removed.

The engineer said he had heard of old age pensioners being left without any heating."

"Engineers have called, seen a portable heater in use, and a week later removed it, leaving the home without heating, just a £3 gas board voucher."

The Kent Messenger Breakthrough team is investigating.

Segas said yesterday that they were investigating cases highlighted in last week's disclosures.

Patients are in peril, say nurses

By JONATHAN COE

STAFF at Oakwood Hospital, Maidstone, claim a shortage of nurses is putting patients' lives in danger because adequate supervision cannot be maintained.

Two patients have committed suicide in the past three weeks. Nurses say both would still be alive today if more staff had been available.

Leaders of the nurses' union – the Confederation of Health Service Employees – Oakwood Hospital principal staff and officials of the regional hospital board met at their Croydon headquarters yesterday to discuss the allegations.

ANGUISH

The two patients who died were 18-year-old Jane Hodge, of Church Avenue, Sidcup, and 38-year-old John Ward, of St. James Avenue, Sutton.

The inquest into the death of Jane Hodge was held last week. She took her own life by swallowing between 20 and 30 tablets. Mrs. Adoration Farrow, a ward sister at Oakwood told the inquest there was no reason to suspect that Jane would commit suicide.

According to a male nurse at Oakwood, Mr. Ward committed suicide after a female patient alleged he had raped her.

"This caused him a great deal of anguish," he said. "Doctors had emphasised that this patient should receive supervision and full support of the staff, yet on the night he committed suicide there were no night nurses on duty in his ward.

More staff and this man would be alive today."

This was not stated at yesterday's inquest into Mr. Ward's death when Pathologist Dr. Patrick Farnan said Ward had swallowed over 100 aspirin tablets, and deputy charge nurse Daniel McCashin said there was no reason to believe he would take his life.

But the coroner, Mr. Gerald Coombe, asked ward doctor Fouad Ghali, if it was true that allegation had been made against Ward which would have caused him a certain amount of emotional stress.

Dr. Ghali replied that it would not have caused Ward's death: "No threats were made."

Coroner: "We are not suggesting that any threats were made but was any allegation made to Mr. Ward that would have caused him some stress?"

Dr, Ghali: "Yes."

Nurses also claim that the lack of staff was one of the main causes of the murder last year of State Enrolled Nurse Cecil Winter.

The hospital has been cleared of blame.

And the nurses want restrictions placed on the drinking habits of patients. The patient in the Cecil Winter case had been drinking from 6.30 to 11.00 that evening.

They also want certain members of the hospital management committee sacked because "they are working against the interests of the hospital by constantly sweeping things under the carpet."

The nurses want urgent action to either cut down the number of patients or recruit more staff.

All these allegations were put to two of the top men at Oakwood – Hospital Secretary Emil Marchesi and Principal Nursing Officer Bede Mullen.

Mr. Marchesi said: "It is very difficult to see what more we can possibly do. Of course we are short of staff. We have 500 – we need 800.

"We are doing all we can to get them. We are about to launch a massive publicity campaign in Maidstone and we hope to get a leaflet through every letter box in the town advertising for nursing staff.

AMAZED

"Suicides, like the past two we have had, are unfortunate. But with open door and progressive nursing, patients are given a great deal of freedom.

Mr. Mullen said: "I am astonished that anyone could say members of the management committee hushed things up."

HOSPITAL secretary, Emil Marchesi: "It is very difficult to see what more we can possibly do."

PRINCIPAL Nursing Officer, Bede Mullen: "I am astonished that anyone could say members of the management committee hushed things up."

OPHTHALMIC IS 'SUB-STANDARD'

PARTS of Maidstone's prestige Ophthalmic Hospital have been described in an official report as "seriously sub-standard." The Audiology and Hearing Aid Department, housed in converted cottages at the back of the main building, is said to be "cramped and completely unacceptable."

A visiting member of the district management committee, Mr. Kenneth Scrase, wrote in the report: "Converted cottages, which presumably have been condemned for private occupation cannot be considered as suitable accommodation.

"The narrow steep stairs are dangerous and the tiny rooms which are either too cold or too hot for comfortable working conditions make it essential to consider some alternative."

His report is being studied by the members of the management committee and will be discussed at their next meeting.

£40,000 BLAZE AT HOSPITAL – Back Page

THE gates at Oakwood are left open so that patients can come and go. Now they have been warned of the dangers of drinking alcohol while taking drugs.

Drinking: The drug danger

THE situation at Oakwood was raised at the Maidstone and District Hospital Management Committee meeting at Preston Hall on Tuesday.

Dr. Barry Durrant, from Oakwood, was quoted as having given an assurance that the danger of drinking alcohol while taking drugs had been stressed to all patients.

MONEY

The Committee also discussed the installation of an alarm system for night staff which should be completed shortly.

Oakwood was criticised at the meeting for underspending on its professional and technical services. The hospital still has £5,000 to spend.

Mr. Marchesi explained that the money had been allocated for an occupational therapy unit. The actual building to house that unit had not yet been completed, but it should be finished in three months.

Redstart Ward at the hospital came under fire from two visiting members of the district management committee. They had investigated the bathing arrangements in August and returned to see what improvements had been made.

They found that 27 elderly women have to share three baths with a nearby male ward.

The report, discussed in a confidential session of the management committee, was presented by Mr. M. Edwardes-Evans and Mr. J. Ormrod.

WARDS

They found no improvement in the "hopelessly inadequate facilities". Side wards were still overcrowded, they added.

The hospital, however, maintained new baths wou'd be ready within three months.

THIS WEEK IN THE PAPER WITH PEOPLE IN MIND

Breakthrough!

HOUSEWIFE Margaret Cracknell was disappointed when she found her old cooker was unsuitable for natural gas conversion. She was even more disappointed when her new one failed to reach expectations. And she was disgusted when the necessary replacement parts had not arrived after 11 weeks. So she she rang BREAKTHROUGH, the Kent Messenger hot line to action. The full story is on Page 6.

If you need help with a special problem, ring BREAKTHROUGH — on Maidstone 77880, extension 244. We are waiting to hear from you.

It's your county . . .

IT'S been a long time since the prospect of local government re-organisation first dawned.

Now the pace is quickening as we find ourselves in the run-up year to the important changes which will herald a new era for council's in Kent.

Inside today's paper, you will find a 20-page supplement called What Does It All Mean?

You owe it to yourself to find out.

KENT county cricket club achieved its best - ever financial result last season. Figures issued this week show a surplus of £18,000.

The county won the John Player League and were runners-up in the county championship.

Full details in today's sports page, which also include the weekly comprehensive coverage of Kent soccer and other major sports.

FIRM VANISHES WITH TEACHER'S £760 DEPOSIT

TEACHER Mrs. Phyllis Bailey paid £760 for home improvements. And she is still waiting for workmen to call six months after parting with her money.

For the company, Aspacia Construction Ltd., have disappeared from its offices at 34 High Street, Maidstone.

Although it has been using a basement in College Road, frequent calls by a KM reporter have found no one in.

Mrs. Bailey teaches at Maidstone Technical High School for Girls. She wanted her house in Northdown Close, Penenden Heath, converted into four bedrooms. Three to be sub-let as bedsitters.

She wanted extra income to cushion the early retirement forced on her husband Reginald, 61, after a heart attack.

In May 1972, she accepted an estimate of £1,460 from Aspacia. After her building society agreed to extend her mortgage, she paid a 10 per cent deposit.

In July she was told that the council had approved the conversion plans. Work would begin immediately the company received a first stage payment of £614.

Mrs. Bailey handed a cheque to director Mr. David Higson. Since then nothing has happened. Mrs. Bailey has asked solicitors to try to recover the money.

This week a KM inquiry revealed that Mr. Higson was also involved with another Maidstone firm, Save-A-Move Extensions Ltd., Albion Place. After a number of complaints it went into liquidation last year.

He has a number of County Court judgments against him stretching back to 1966. The most recent was April 1970 for £225.

It is understood that the Sheriff of Kent has had a writ of execution against the company. But this has proved fruitless because of the "absence of any seizable goods."

Neighbours at his Dymchurch address have not seen him for 13 months.

One said "You're not the only one who wants to see him. There have been a string of callers since he went."

The old folk who face risk alone

ONE elderly woman died and another is very ill in hospital after two fires in Maidstone this week.

Miss Ivy Williams, 77, was found dead on Monday – slumped by her electric fire in a smoke filled back room of her Tonbridge Road home.

And at Milton Street, paraffin blew up in the face of 85-year-old Mrs. Jessie Piddock which she was trying to heat on a stove, to warm herself.

She was dragged out of the blazing kitchen by her son-in-law Mr. Albert Port, who lives next door but one to her.

Miss Williams was found by Mrs. Iris Lehmann, of Terminus Road, who saw smoke billowing out of the back room, which Miss Williams used as a bedroom.

She said: "It was impossible to get into the room, so I dashed out to telephone for the police and fire brigade."

Miss Williams had lived alone since the death of her two brothers. She was arthritic and had been receiving medical treatment.

TIME and again we hear how old people, living on their own have met with tragedy. But the real tragedy is that nobody seems to care until it's too late. Read BARRIE CLEMENT'S report on Page 9.

One of the first people on the scene was a neighbour, Mrs. Edith Jury, 84.

"Miss Williams should never have been living on her own," she said. "She has fallen down many times to my knowledge.

"She was a very lonely old woman and never went out on her own. Sometimes people would call to see her and occasionally take her out."

Another neighbour said Miss Williams had been living in the house for 20 years, since her family gave up running the nearby Fountain Inn.

"She certainly never went out on her own and had few real friends," she said.

"As far as I know she has no living relatives. Nobody around here really seems to know very much about her."

Neither police nor fire brigade officials would say what caused the fire or how Miss Williams died.

After the fire on Tuesday, Mr. Albert Port said: "The whole place enveloped into a sheet of flame – and I had to fight my way through the smoke to get at her."

Mr. Port took Mrs. Piddock into his house and then dashed back and turned the gas off.

Meanwhile Mrs. Dulcie Port ran to a shop down the street and phoned the fire brigade.

Mrs. Port said: "I can't think what got into her, she certainly wasn't confused when I saw her last night.

"Luckily we live very close to her.

End of the road for a driving instructor

IT WAS the day Mrs. Ann Chitty failed her driving test – for the second time – that she became suspicious.

Was her driving instructor all he seemed?

And a police probe proved to be the end of the road for Leonard Hutchcraft.

For Hutchcraft, Bearsted magistrates, heard on Wednesday, did not hold a Ministry licence to instruct drivers."

Hutchcraft, now employed as a deep freeze sales manager earning £1,200 a month, of Leonard Close, Allington Park, pleaded guilty to giving driving lessons for payment, and not being an approved driving instructor, or holding a Ministry instructor's licence. He was ordered to pay a total of £48.60 in fines, costs and restitution.

Mrs. Ann Chitty of Coxheath complained to police after taking 13 lessons at £1.50 a time, and failing her tests.

ILLEGAL

She had told them that the night before the first test, she had been shown how to make an emergency stop. It was the first time she had ever done it.

Hutchcraft said he had been teaching driving for 10 years. Eight of those covered the period before it became illegal to teach without a Ministry licence.

He had taken the written part of the Ministry examination, and had applied for the practical test and licence.

Mrs. Chitty had made an application for restitution of lesson fees; totalling £28.50.

Hutchcraft said: "She had expert tuition from me, and a deduction for petrol and insurance should be made."

Kray swaps jails

ONE of the three Kray brothers, Charles, has been transferred to Maidstone Prison.

Kray was sentenced to 10 years' jail in March 1969 at the Old Bailey for being an accessory after murder.

A bride's smile ends a nightmare

THE smile on a bride's face tomorrow will hide eleven months of pain and worry.

When Gillian Thompson, 23, of Skye Close, Maidstone, walks down the aisle of All Saints Church, Loose, she will be leaving behind months in hospital after being badly injured in a car crash in South Africa.

She and her husband-to-be, Alistair Mathers of Farnham, Surrey, were travelling in the outback when a tyre blew out and turned their drive into a nightmare.

Driver Gillian had arm and leg fractures and serious internal injuries. Alistair got away with shock and a few scratches.

"It is wonderful to be able to forget all that now and get on with arrangements for the wedding. With me in hospital, we had to cancel our first wedding date until now.

"The accident happened miles from anywhere.

"It was near Christmas and there were no ambulances available to take me to a doctor.

"The doctor even said he could not come out to me. I would have to find my way to him.

"In the end a police van arrived and the officers did a stupid thing, picked me up and put me in the back of their van.

"I was taken to a doctor and later transferred to a hospital. But the ambulance broke down on the way."

There is just one slight disappointment. Gillian's only brother Geoffrey, is living in Australia, and is unable to come.

"But I hope I will be able to have a few words with him over the telephone," she said.

Gillian and Alistair . . . all smiles now.

Long hair fireman banned from a funeral

A FIREMAN was told yesterday he could not officially attend the funeral of Gillingham fireman Neil McCulloch because his hair was too long.

But he went, anyway, taking time off that was owed him.

He protested to the Fire Brigades Union, and a spokesman was meeting "C" Division Commander May, yesterday afternoon, to discuss the length of fireman William Vine's hair. Commander May said there was no question of suspension.

"It was simply a situation that developed because many of the men wanted to attend Fireman McCulloch's funeral.

ROTTEN JOB

"It was decided that fireman Vine's hair was too long. He didn't come up to the standard required as a representative of Maidstone Fire Station."

"We don't line the men up and get out a measuring rod, but some men resist getting their hair cut. A question of safety is involved."

Fireman Vine, 31, who lives at Crows Hole Farm, Charing, said: "I am upset about this because it makes a mockery of a friend's funeral."

His wife, Lyn, thought the officers had their priorities wrong.

"They have to be very responsible and shouldn't be treated like children over haircuts."

ON PROBATION

Phillip John Ellery, 17, no fixed address, admitted at Maidstone to taking tea making equipment valued at £10. He was given three years' probation.

Quote

. . . from Bearsted Parish Council: First member: "A stile on one of our public footpaths is so dilapidated that it has disappeared."

Second member: "We must go and have a look at it."

BURGLARS STRIKE TWICE

West Malling newsagent and tobacconist Mr. Stanley Brown was burgled twice in two days last week.

Each time thieves broke into a back storeroom of the Town Newsagency.

False alarm call was revenge

A MAN who claimed he had not been allowed to see his children for two and a half years took revenge by calling the fire brigade to his former wife's house.

Joseph Malloy, 53, of Beaconsfield Road, Tovil, made the false alarm call on Saturday night, Maidstone Magistrates heard yesterday.

He admitted making the false call and to using a quantity of electricity at the telephone box. He asked for the theft of a drill in 1971 to be considered.

Malloy, now divorced, but a father of six children, said he was supposed to see his children periodically under a court order, but his former wife had stopped him.

The magistrates were told that Malloy, who is selling his house, had several personal problems and was moving from the area to try to sort them out.

Sentence was deferred for six months.

Kent's family plan 'the worst'

KENT has one of the worst Family Planning Services in the country.

This is the accusation of a member of the Birth Control Campaign, a nation-wide organisation urging free contraceptives.

Mr. Ian Watson, who lives with his wife Beryl and 20-month old-son Neil, at St. Lukes Avenue, Maidstone, said: "Kent County Council provides the least comprehensive family planning service it can possibly get away with.

"It is certainly the least expensive form of service. Out of the six recommended types of service suggested by the Ministry of Health, Kent has chosen the minimum."

Mr. Watson thinks the most comprehensive should be introduced. This is the scheme used by ten London boroughs, Birmingham and areas of Scotland, he says.

It gives free contraceptive advice and supplies, with no restriction on medical grounds or on where people live.

The Kent scheme gives free contraception advice and supplies on medical grounds only to those who live in the local authority area.

Mr. Watson says it is embarrasing for a woman to go to a clinic and have to "Qualify for free contraceptives and advice."

Mr. Watson also thinks the County Council avoid publicity of their birth control services because if a lot more people knew about it, they would be unable to cope with the demand.

A spokesman said yesterday that the county council will need time to prepare a full and detailed reply to Mr. Watson's criticism.

◀ A photoset, web-offset weekly, the *Kent Messenger*, remarkable for its eleven-column make-up, its use of spot colour and its play on Bold Extended for main headlines.

▶ The Slough *Evening Mail*, typical of the new British breed of photoset, web-offset local evenings, with the front page which won it a first prize in the 1972 Newspaper Design Award.

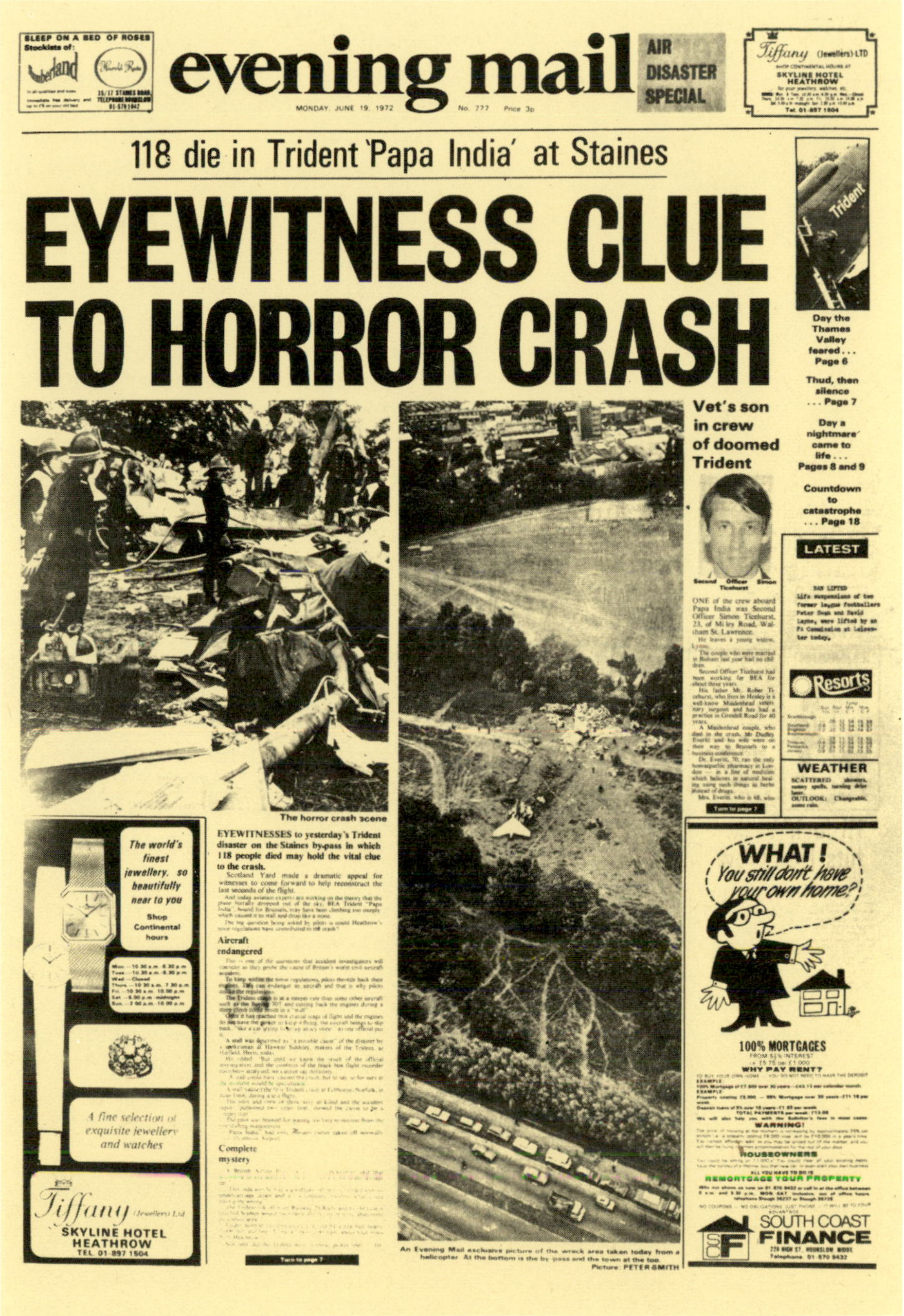

evening mail

MONDAY, JUNE 19, 1972

AIR DISASTER SPECIAL

118 die in Trident 'Papa India' at Staines

EYEWITNESS CLUE TO HORROR CRASH

Day the Thames Valley feared... Page 6

Thud, then silence ... Page 7

Day a nightmare came to life ... Pages 8 and 9

Countdown to catastrophe ... Page 18

Vet's son in crew of doomed Trident

LATEST

WEATHER

The horror crash scene

EYEWITNESSES to yesterday's Trident disaster on the Staines by-pass in which 118 people died may hold the vital clue to the crash.

Aircraft endangered

Complete mystery

The world's finest jewellery, so beautifully near to you

A fine selection of exquisite jewellery and watches

Tiffany (Jewellers) Ltd SKYLINE HOTEL HEATHROW

WHAT! You still don't have your own home?

100% MORTGAGES

SOUTH COAST FINANCE

It was the outstanding handling of halftones in the web-offset evenings, in addition to the exploitation of the other possibilities of the process, that now began notably to impress the judges. In 1970 the *Evening Post* was placed No. 1 not only because of the 'admirable light-bold balance' of its headlining ('between the punchy Grot No. 9 and Univers Medium Condensed, the Century Schoolbook and Bold') but because 'the dramatically deep double-column halftone and the effective use of reverses and tint backgrounds contributed to a striking page.' The point was well summed up in the 1972 award of the first prize to the *Evening Mail*, which 'has a remarkable instinct for a good picture' but does not stop at pictures as such; it won 'the top position because of its lively and successful integration of headlines, pictures and text'.

Passing references have been made above to typefaces that first appeared in newspaper work during this latest period. It is now time to examine them in some detail, and it is convenient to take the text types first. The previous chapter has told of the micro-size developments of the 1950s, following the appearance of $4\frac{3}{4}$pt Times Roman (Claritas) for 15-lines-to-the-inch setting of classified advertisements. It will be recalled that $4\frac{3}{4}$pt Adsans, inspired by the common American

ROVER 2000, 1966, one owner, radio; mint condition; £1075. — Cranmore Bros. Ltd., Hagley Rd. Bea. 2311.
VAUXHALL CRESTA de-luxe, 1966, fitted radio and Cinturatos, as new condition. £750 for quick sale.—Phone Sol. 7063.
VICTOR 2000, new, finished in burgundy with black interior, four-speed gearbox, immediate delivery. — B.M.T. Services Ltd., College Garage, 504-508, College Road, Erdington, 22C. Phone Erd. 2542.
VOLKSWAGEN 1200, 1958, registered 1963; £150 o.n.o.—Phone Aco. 6861.
VOLKSWAGEN 1300, 1966, serviced to date, very good condition, one driver, colour seasand/black: £750, o.n.o. — Fisher, 44, Shipston Road, Stratford-on-Avon. Telephone 4178.

Maximus with bold (4¾pt).

style of smalls-setting in sans – 5½pt Spartan Book – enjoyed substantial success. Nevertheless it was clear that a number of papers did not favour the sans style for their classifieds. There was need for a seriffed 4¾pt which would withstand rough presswork better than Claritas and would not be liable to such rapid matrix breakdown. This need was met by Maximus, a 4¾pt seriffed letter of stout and open cut, designed by Walter Tracy for Linotype and installed in December 1967 by the *Daily Telegraph*, the national morning with the largest classified paging, in place of Claritas.

Maximus represented a new approach in micro-size design. Tracy realised that to secure improved legibility and printability in such minute sizes it was necessary to increase the set-width of the face as well as to keep the letter-design open (the lower-case 'g', for instance, having an open tail instead of the conventional closed bowl). Duplexed with Bold or a good open Doric – actually the adapted Bold of Adsans – Maximus was not only wider than any preceding 4¾pt types – its lower-case alphabet rated 88pts as against the 79pts of Claritas – but wider even than 5pt Ionic or 5½pt Times Roman, which both rated 84pts. In addition to the typographical advantages of the greater width it was evident that the increase in paid linage would be to the advantage of the publisher. The *Telegraph* found Maximus a satisfactory solution of its smalls-setting problems; and the face adapted admirably to the paper's subsequent change to a 10-column make-up for its classified pages.*

It will take only one cursory glance at this new, clean-cut typeface to evaluate its remarkable ease of reading. Extensive study and research ultimately resulted in this typeface with all the essential inherent qualities so necessary in the appearance and production of today's crisp, clean looking newspaper page: good design, maximum readability, space saving, sparkling colour, sharp reproduction. Those are the reasons why we here at Intertype feel that Royal IS something special.

It will take only one cursory glance at this new, clean-cut typeface to evaluate its remarkable ease of reading. Extensive study and research ultimately resulted in this typeface with all the essential qualities so necessary in the appearance and production of today's crisp, clean looking newspaper page: good design, maximum reading ability, space saving, sparkling colour, sharp reproduction. Those are the reasons why we here at Intertype feel that Royal IS something special.

Royal (8 and 7pt).

The first significant change of the period in body types, in Britain, was the introduction of Intertype Royal by the *Scotsman* in 1960. Royal was Intertype's close copy of Linotype Corona, described in Chapter Five as the summation of the famous 'Legibility Group'. For the *Scotsman* a certain number of alternative characters were devised, with minor differences in drawing, so that this version could be called Scotsman Royal. Royal was adopted as the text type of the *Sunday Times*, of the *Guardian* and a number of regional newspapers. In 1970 the *Financial Times* changed over to Royal from the Times Roman that it had been using since 1946. The note may be added here that by 1970 Corona, with Royal and Regal (another Intertype face of similar character) had entirely displaced the earlier members of the 'Legibility Group', especially Ionic and Excelsior, as favoured texts of American newspapers.

As the 1960s drew to their close it became apparent that some British nationals were suffering, typographically, from the lightweight newsprint enforced by increased paging. This was particularly true of the *Daily Telegraph*, which had introduced Jubilee for its text in 1959 but was now finding that the cut in colour resulting from the lighter newsprint was producing much too grey a page. During 1966 Walter Tracy and I had been discussing the possibility of developing and adapting the modern face; this ended with Tracy's design of Linotype Modern, drawing its inspiration from the first Didot Modern of 1784, which was introduced by the *Daily Telegraph* and its Sunday stablemate in the summer of 1969. This Modern has since been adopted by the *Cork Examiner* group in Ireland, by the *Evening Echo* (Southampton) and has been re-drawn for the Linotype V-I-P photosetter.

Tracy's Modern admirably adapted the crispness and contrast inherent in the stroke variation and serif structure of the modern style. This was a modern suitably revised to print clearly and colourfully with the restricted inking usual under current production conditions. It was a remarkable, though in fact unconscious, fulfilment of a prophecy made thirty years before by Stanley Morison himself. In the course of a searching criticism of the Mergenthaler Linotype Ionic, Morison wrote early in 1936: 'Ionic is materially better, technically, than most of the "modern" founts made available during the past 40 years to line-composed newspapers. It is open and clear in design; it is well drawn and perfect in cut. But a similarly high degree of technical ability given to the old-fashioned "modern" would have trans-

* Intertype Royal was also provided with a 4¾pt, duplexed either with Bold or a clear, re-designed Doric; its lower-case alphabet rated 84pts. Classad, an Intertype copy of Maximus for the *Sunday Times*, exceeded its prototype with a lower-case alphabet rating of 92pts.

Linotype Modern is a fresh and original design, not a variation of an existing newspaper type. It owes something to the general characteristics of the 'modern' (Didone) class of design; but the designer has adapted the style to the practical requirements of today's newspaper and periodical printing.

Modern is not only an original design in itself; it is the result of a thorough re-examination of the requirements of modern letterpress production, and proper recognition of the fact that high-speed moulding and printing on absorbent newsprint inevitably erode the profiles of letters, with consequent loss of crispness and quality. The design of Modern *allows* for that process.

Linotype Modern (8 and 7pt) is now designated Telegraph Modern.

formed it into a very desirable face. It is more than probable that such a revised "modern" would be more readable than the admittedly readable American Ionic.'

If Tracy's Modern was thus a dramatic demonstration of the accuracy of Morison's forecast of the 'very desirable' face that could result from an appropriate revision and transformation of the old modern style, in one respect it radically rebutted one of Morison's central contentions about news-texts. This was, as noted in Chapter Six, that they must save space by their relative 'slenderness', they must have a distinct degree of condensation; as we have seen, relative condensation was one of the special virtues Morison claimed for Times Roman. Tracy was able to show that this contention had ceased to be relevant, given the current newspaper practice of frequent paragraphing in narrow-measure columns of 11-picas or thereabouts. While Linotype Modern was by no means as wide as Ionic or Excelsior (it was very close to Corona), it was substantially wider than Times Roman and appreciably wider than Jubilee – its lower-case alphabet in 8pt rating 117pts as against Jubilee's 113pts. But when a *Telegraph* page of eight 22-inch columns, set in Jubilee, was reset in Modern, the wider type only made an extra line at three points in the entire page. The break-lines made by the frequent paragraphing, in short, had been able to absorb the wider text. The significance of this discovery for news-text design needs no emphasis.[3]

By the time the *Telegraph* switched to Modern *The Times* was facing a crisis in its own text typography. Times Roman was failing to stand up to contemporary production conditions. Morison's famous face had always needed the precise presswork and high-grade mechanical printing provided by Printing House Square. Lacking these two essential conditions, other papers turning to Times Roman had never been able to do it justice, as the previous chapter has explained. When the technical conditions at PHS began to approximate those of the general run of dailies, Times Roman lost its virtue in the very paper for which it had been designed. This decline in the type's printability was seen as a further minus point, on top of the chronic technical defect, already mentioned, of the rapid breakdown of the ultra-thin matrix sidewalls, with constant and heavy replacement costs.

There were stages in the process. For twenty years from 1936 the paper's body size had been 7½pt. By 1956, however, it was felt that more colour was needed; the 7½pt in mass was looking too grey. To increase colour, without increasing body depth, the descenders of the 8pt were cropped by half a point, so that this point size could be cast on a 7½pt slug.* This ingenious notion appeared to work well for a while; but in 1966, when news was at last brought on to the front page, the 8pt was cast on its own body. By now, however, it was becoming plain that the deterioration could not be arrested by size-changes, even with the setting of all front-page matter in 9pt. The substantial increase in circulation which followed the changes of 1966, and more especially the Thomson takeover at the end of that year, was the last straw. Fast running on ordinary newsprint put paid to any possibility of careful presswork. By 1970 the Board of Times Newspapers, not uninfluenced by my critical 'reassessment' that summer, was persuaded that the day of Times Roman was done.[4] The question was: what to do? Should *The Times* switch to an existing, more practical, news-text? It was, after all, now linked with the *Sunday Times*, set in Royal, and the transfer of its printing to the *Sunday Times* plant was in prospect. Or should consideration be given to the creation of an entirely new design appropriate for Times Newspapers as a group, that is to say, not only for *The Times* and its *Supplements* but for the *Sunday Times* as well?

The rest of the story can be briefly told. An office committee was set up, following the precedent of its 1930–31 predecessor, chaired by Barrington-Ward; this one had *Sunday Times* editor Harold Evans as

* This neatly demonstrated the truth of the established view of the optical importance of the ascender (and lack of importance of the descender). The same 8/7½pt treatment was later given to Jubilee and 5½pt 'smalls' faces were adjusted to cast on 5pt slug.

THE graphic design of a newspaper is not a thing in itself. The good newspaperman does not assemble type in a page merely to make an agreeable pattern, or as an exercise in display for its own sake. Typography and make-up in a

THE graphic design of a newspaper is not a thing in itself. The good newspaperman does not assemble type in a page merely to make an agreeable pattern, or as an exercise in display for its own sake. Typography and make-up in a newspaper are only a vehicle for journalism and it is

THE graphic design of a newspaper is not a thing in itself. The good newspaperman does not assemble type in a page merely to make an agreeable pattern, or as an exercise in display for its own sake. Typography and make-up in a newspaper are only a vehicle for journalism; and it is journalism that is the most important. If it is poorly presented,

Times Europa (9, 8 and 7pt).

chairman, and in place of Stanley Morison as typographical consultant there was Walter Tracy. This meant that, when the decision was taken to proceed with a new design, the work was done by a linecaster expert; thus there was no danger that a new face would have the linecaster shortcomings of Times Roman, arising from its initial design for Monotype. After long discussion and numerous experiments a decision was reached, by the end of 1971, in favour of a new design by Tracy to which the name Times Europa was given, by way of a reference to Britain's EEC entry. Cut in 7, 8 and 9pt, Times Europa took its place in *The Times* on 9 October 1972, almost exactly forty years after the appearance of Times Roman.

Europa immediately showed its accord with the criterion the committee and Tracy had set themselves, namely to produce a news-text both technically satisfactory and with the distinctive, indeed distinguished, note necessary for Times Newspapers. It is a robust and well-rounded letter, wider than Times Roman (it approximates to the width of Corona) with good stroke-contrast and crispness of cut, giving it sufficient strength and colour to survive thin inking and fast running on lightweight newsprint. Its x-height is such that it provides the interlinear white essential when lengthy texts are presented. Tracy himself has said that the design of Europa is 'hybrid'; broadly, perhaps, it may be labelled transitional, namely of that order of letter-design between old face and modern of which Baskerville is the outstanding example. It may be recalled that Baskerville was one of the types Morison tried during *The Times* experiments of 1930–31. Europa's 8pt is as large in appearance as, and stronger in impression than, 9pt Times Roman (their lower-case alphabet widths, at 118 pts, are the same). Cast on 9pt body, it has shown its capacity to cope with wide-measure settings, as in the Business News leaders. For the 7pt, which is being extensively used, Tracy adjusted the x-height to be fractionally greater, in proportion, than that of the 8pt.

It will be noted that only the three basic text sizes of Europa were cut for the 1972 changeover. Times Roman survived, in the 5½pt and 4¾pt sizes, for classified advertisements, long lists of names, sports results and the other accustomed purposes of these micro-sizes. The 14pt Times Roman was likewise retained for front-page intros. Headlines also remained in the uniform Times Bold roman, upper- and lower-case, style, with a normal ceiling of 36pt, that was introduced in September 1970, as described below.

Apart from one or two continental news-texts of no significance for the British/American market, the only further news-text to be created during the current period was Olympian, issued by Mergenthaler Linotype in 1970. American-manufactured, Olympian was the work of an English designer, Matthew Carter, then associated with Mergenthaler in New York. To appreciate the face it is necessary to relate it to the technical effect of TTS wire service requirements on type design, already touched on at the end of the previous chapter. The main point is the simple one that to correlate the justification of the originating tape perforators, at the news agency's central office, with the actual matrix-assembly on receiving newspapers' linecasters, using varying typefaces and even varying measures, it was necessary to bring all matrices for TTS setting to a single, national standard.

This was achieved by the introduction of a unit system. The matrix of each character in a TTS fount was allotted one of 11 possible widths, each width being a multiple of a unit, itself 1/18th of the set. These widths were uniform, whatever the typeface; a capital 'A' always 14 units, a lower-case 'a' always 11 units and so on. For America's now all-but-universal 11-pica measure body matter, whatever the face size, had to be 8-set; that is to say, it must have the lower-case alphabet width of a unit-cut 8pt. Clearly this involved a sort of typographical Bed of Procrustes. Papers setting their body matter below 8pt, say in 7 or 7½pt (though they are now a negligible number) required a degree of expansion in their matrix characters; those set-

This is Olympian, a new series from Mergenthaler, a true design departure, traditional only in its legibility under newspaper conditions.

The majority of the world's newspapers are typeset in one or another of the traditional Linotype 'Legibility Group', and most of the rest in their derivatives.

This is Olympian, a new series from Mergenthaler, a true design departure, traditional only in its legibility under newspaper conditions.

The majority of the world's newspapers are typeset in one or another of the traditional Linotype 'Legibility Group', and most of the rest in their derivatives.

Olympian (9pt 8 set and 8pt 8 set).

ting above 8pt, say in 8½ or 9pt – the latter being the most popular – required a degree of condensation. Unit-cut adaptations of the 'Legibility Group' (Aurora, Majestic) made their appearance. Corona, as the most widely-used news-text in the U.S., was likewise adapted; the face now has no fewer than twenty-nine varieties of size and set, the leaders being the 9pt 8-set and the 8½pt 8-set. Some idea of the importance of the unit-cut matrix founts in American newspaper practice can be gathered from the fact that by 1970 their sales were ten times greater than those of 'normal' founts.

These were the circumstances in which Matthew Carter and his Mergenthaler colleagues approached the design of a new news-text. As he told the Newspaper Design Congress of the Association Typographique Internationale in London in 1971, they soon discovered that there was no future in pursuing the modern-style of Corona, with its vertical stress. In the 9pt 8-set version, which was their principal concern, the verticality of the modern letter produced what Carter called a 'picket fence' effect after undergoing around an 11 per cent degree of condensation. The answer to this problem proved to be the oblique stress of old face; thus Olympian could be classed with Times Roman and Jubilee, among twentieth-century news-texts, as basically old face in design.[5]

Olympian, however, was an old face of a distinctly new kind. Its drawing, seen notably in its serifs, was sturdy, with a generous x-height and wide open counters. Mergenthaler publicity described it as 'based on the wedge, not the slab'; a fair point, since the tapering stroke, as well as the oblique stress, of Olympian gave it a lively appearance. The companion Bold was designed on the same principles as the normal weight (unlike Times Bold, for example) and thus provided a harmonious emphasis. Additionally, Carter and his colleagues had web-offset in mind as well as rotary letterpress, with its problems of stereotype shrinkage and high-speed running. The full 6–12pt range of Olympian was available on the various Linotype photosetters before it could be had for hot-metal machines.

Of sixteen American dailies that have already adopted Olympian as their text face, it is significant that eleven have done so for photosetting (Linotron or V-I-P), one – the medium-size *Fort Luderdale News* in Florida – for both Linotype hot-metal and Linotron photosetting, and four for hot-metal only. The last category, however, includes the famous *Philadelphia Inquirer*, the oldest daily paper in the U.S. (founded 1771). Among the Olympian users, covering papers at all circulation levels, are a noteworthy number of leading metropolitan sheets – the *Evening Star* (Washington, DC), the *Commercial Appeal* of Memphis (Tennessee's principal daily and a key link of the Scripps-Howard chain), and such old-established large Ohio dailies as the *Cincinnati Post & Times-Star* and the *Columbus Dispatch*.

Turning now to headline types and styles the 1960s showed some noteworthy developments, apart from the continuing trend away from capitals and towards all upper- and lower-case. Of exceptional importance for the evolution of heading styles and make-up was a new understanding of the essentially optical factors involved in effective typographic contrast on a newspaper page. It came to be seen that the simple Light/Bold contrast, in roman and within a given type family or at least a given style (e.g. sans), was the most satisfactory from the standpoint of reader-comfort, of ease-of-reading. Bold italic declined in favour as the main contrast with bold roman; one American expert said bluntly in 1971 that since 'italics are harder to read than roman . . . they make no sense in newspaper headlines'.

For some time Century, particularly the Bold with its relatively condensed lower-case, had dominated British newspaper headline style (as had Bodoni in America); now there came a revival of an early Century variant which was to attain wide popularity. This was Century Schoolbook and its companion Bold. Schoolbook was slightly wider, and with somewhat less stroke-contrast, than the normal weight of Century (Century 'Expanded'); its Bold was substantially wider than Century Bold, most noticeably in the lower-case. Schoolbook Bold did not seem to have the crispness in lower-case headings of Century Bold, but its greater width was in its favour. It stood somewhere between Century Bold and Bold Extended; thus it accorded well with a significant trend away from condensed, and towards wide, types for headlines. This trend was a natural result of more multi-column headlining, where wide letters made for punchier headings but condensed letters led to verbal padding-out and loss of sharp impact. Hence, in addition to the enthusiasm shown for Schoolbook Bold, much more extensive use was made of Century Bold Extended, especially in upper- and lower-case (hitherto it had been mainly used in large-size capitals for banners).

The facility for Light/Bold contrast, together with the development of extended variants, also marked additions to the sans field. While the established families – Franklin Gothic and its Extra Condensed, Ludlow Medium and Condensed Gothic, Grot No. 9, Tempo, Futura and, in the U.S., Spartan – continued in wide use, the 'modernised' grots began to play a significant part in headline styles. Most prominent among these were Adrian Frutiger's Univers and Ludlow Record Gothic – both of which included extended versions of various weights – Helvetica and Monotype Grotesque 215/216. Display photosetting brought Anzeigen, a German-originated sans face, of immense x-height and blackness, which could be described as a coarser version of Monotype Placard 515; its violence won it considerable popularity with the new photoset, web-offset evenings.

Most of the types mentioned, or versions of them, were soon available, in varying degrees of fidelity, on the different display photosetters and the display extensions to text photosetters. In the sans field this applied, among others, to Univers, Grot No. 9, Futura; it also applied to Century Schoolbook and Bold, and to Century Bold Extended. Schoolbook's success likewise brought it unusually rapid and general availability. It could be had in founders' type (ATF), Monotype (series 650 and 651), Ludlow (designated Century Modern) and Intertype (up to 30pt). The note may be added that the large-size availability of the heading types cited – the photoset versions could be enlarged up to 96 or 120pt, in some cases to 144pt – helped to break the dominance, not to say tyranny, of the formal full-page banner. Extra-large sizes, particularly in upper- and lower-case, could be powerfully used banked across three or four columns for lead stories, while leaving the rest of the page much freer and more flexible than in the old full-streamer days.

The 1960s were not only a period of rapid technical advance, of the introduction of new types, both for text and headlines; even more significant, perhaps, was the expression in Britain of the understanding that more was needed for the general development of newspaper design than the empirical, rule-of-thumb approach hitherto reigning among newspapermen who shared the traditional national aversion to 'theory'. It was now seen, as I put it in 1960, that there was a 'need for some serious theory – that is, an exposition of general principles and the mode of their application – to illuminate and improve the practice'.* This did not apply in America, where journalist training had long been highly organised at university level, and where the textbooks of Allen, Arnold and others had fully provided the necessary 'exposition of general principles and the mode of their application'. British journalism textbooks, typified by the works of the late F. J. Mansfield (*Sub-Editing* 1931, *The Complete Journalist* 1935), had so far dealt with typography in a fashion at once incidental and conventional.

The publication of my *Newspaper Design* by Oxford University Press in 1960 may be taken as the first milestone on the path indicated.[6] The following year the International Press Institute published *The Active Newsroom* by Harold Evans (who had conducted a training

* Hutt, *Newspaper Design* (1960, 1st edn), Preface, p.v. Here I may recall that I had prepared a synopsis for a full-scale study of newspaper typography soon after the end of the war; it was vetted by Stanley Morison in November 1945 (not 1947, as incorrectly stated in *Newspaper Design*). But no publishers were interested and at last, much frustrated, I took what I had written so far as the basis for a series of articles in *The Journalist*, September 1949–February 1950. These were then collected and published by the NUJ in April 1950 as a forty-eight page booklet entitled *An Outline of Newspaper Typography*. It quickly sold 5,000 copies at 2s (as 10p then was). Morison wrote to me on 22 May 1950: 'I am very grateful for the *Outline*. This is a very modest description of what is, in fact, an encyclopaedia of the greatest benefit to the capable journalist. It would have been vastly useful to me 20 years ago.' The booklet was later incorporated in the 'Typography and Make-up' chapter of *The Practice of Journalism* (1963).

tour in India); though this was an elementary general manual it gave prominence to design, including picture-handling. In 1961, also, journalism training became obligatory in Britain (apart from Fleet Street) and the publisher-union joint National Council for the Training of Journalists began to provide teaching in newspaper typography, which was duly featured in its first textbook, *The Practice of Journalism* (1963). Experienced production journalists became notably articulate; of these the most radical was Clive Irving, who transformed the *Observer*, as described below, pioneered the 'Insight' feature in the *Sunday Times*, and was a key man on IPC magazines, before becoming a consultant to America's *Newsday*. Irving's views, which included the prophecy that newspapers must become 'hybrid' ('part newspaper and part magazine in format'), were summed up in 'Can newspapers move from the Stone Age to the Space Age?', a detailed and penetrating study in *Penrose Annual* for 1967. Here Irving stressed that newspaper design was primarily 'a job of communication', that the idea came first and the layout second, that since the newspaper designer's job 'can never be separated from the editorial purpose of the paper' he must first and last be 'a very good journalist'. Underlining the point he remarked that 'by the designer one means not simply a typographer or layout man, but essentially a journalist who understands the function of a newspaper.' He concluded that newspapers 'can no longer afford the often amateur and sometimes philistine and very British attitude that design is decoration and has very little to do with function. Designers, for their part, will have to accept a thorough apprenticeship in modern journalism.'

During the 1960s the Newspaper Design Award consolidated itself into an institution, despite the continued aloofness of most of Fleet Street; leading production journalists figured frequently among the judges – Irving (1966), Evans (1968), Leslie Sellers (1969). Sellers, who revolutionised the broadsheet *Daily Mail* as will be seen later on, became a star lecturer for the NCTJ on newspaper design; and a good deal of typographic know-how featured in two journalism manuals he produced in 1968 – *Doing it in Style* and *The Simple Subs' Book*. The London Congress of the A TYP I, devoted to the theme of newspaper design, has already been mentioned; at its sessions a team including Evans, his Design Director Edwin Taylor, Harold Keeble (*Daily Express* veteran and consultant to the *Daily Mail* for its tabloid transformation), Walter Tracy, Matthew Carter and myself, presented the various facets of the theme. Early the following year there appeared the first book (*Newsman's English*) of a five-volume manual by Harold Evans carrying the general title *Editing and Design*. Sponsored by the NCTJ, the succeeding books are II: *Handling Newspaper Text*, III: *News Headlines*, IV: *Picture Editing*, V: *Newspaper Design*.

In the light of the foregoing it is scarcely surprising that the latest period has seen emerging certain new approaches to design procedure and certain new design concepts. Thus the designer-journalist relationship has come to have a somewhat different emphasis. The primacy of journalistic criteria, stressed by Clive Irving in the quotations already given, was interpreted in some quarters (including myself) in a rather one-sided and mechanical fashion. According to this interpretation the production journalist must be the fount of design, and there was in effect no room in newspapers for the graphic designer. A more balanced view was voiced in 1964 by Cliff Hopkinson, then production editor of the *Observer*. He remarked how havoc could be wrought 'by journalists with insufficient design theory and by the occasional imported designer with insufficient newspaper background'. He concluded that 'eventually a new animal will evolve to look after this work . . . He will come, obviously, from an amalgam of the graphic designer and the production journalist . . . He cannot germinate in the subs' room alone, or in the art department, but he must know both.' Adopting this approach, Harold Evans in 1968 appointed a magazine designer, Edwin Taylor (formerly associated with

Time-Life) as Design Director of the *Sunday Times*; the record shows that Evans found Taylor a 'valuable revolutionary', able, because he was an outsider, 'to challenge . . . a whole range of newspaper practices which had always been taken for granted.'[7] Evans therefore spoke from experience when he told the 1971 A TYP I Congress that 'we do not solve the problem of editorial responsibility for design simply by saying that editorial must always have the last word. Still less that designers as such must be kept out of the way . . . What we need in newspaper design is not hairy-chested reassertion of journalistic prerogative, but more of a dialogue with typographers and designers – first about the format of a newspaper and secondly about the way we can use ink on paper to communicate . . . Design is not a craft apart. It is part of journalism. Design is not decoration. It is communications. . . . Newspaper design is not window-dressing. It is part of the product.'[8]

What Harold Evans called the 'partnership' between designer and journalist was the basis for the development of 'Newspaper graphics', the title of a major article he contributed to *Penrose Annual* (1970) and of the contribution made by Edwin Taylor at the A TYP I London Congress. Evans observed that a single drawing or a single photograph were not in themselves graphics 'but both become graphics if sign systems or words or symbols are made an integral part of the drawing or photograph'. In developed graphics, he went on, 'symbols and art together diagnose a complicated issue more succinctly than is possible in words alone.' These were 'fact graphics'; there were also the evocative 'flavour graphics' where artwork and lettering combine to make a distinctive departmental label or feature heading. Both styles had been pioneered for the Beaverbrook (*Express*) group at the turn of the 1950s and 1960s by three talented young designers – Raymond Hawkey (now *Observer*), Michael Rand (now *Sunday Times*), Arthur Hacker (*Evening Standard*). Hawkey may be taken as typical and the following passage sums up his achievement:

'After a high art school qualification in graphic design, the start of membership in the Society of Industrial Artists and Designers, he worked as art editor and designer of a number of magazines (including *Vogue*) and then became Design Director of the *Daily Express* in 1959. The link between his magazine experience and his newspaper work was well formulated by the *Express* authorities when they said that what they wanted was "the introduction into the paper of a magazine flavour, polished, sophisticated, modern". The aim was "primarily journalistic – to make the paper more attractive and more immediate in its impact." . . . What Hawkey did was to build up a team of graphic designers who could tackle, in the shortest possible time on edition, the graphic illustration of major news-stories, as well as the more leisurely embellishment of features.'[9]

The next design concept to become firmly established during the 1960s was the integration of the news photograph with the typographic elements of the page to make a dynamic whole. The photograph, in short, ceased to be a mere pictorial additive; it became part of the page's texture. This development was naturally helped by the superior halftone reproduction made possible by web-offset; and the web-offset evenings, in particular, scored with their picture-integration, as related above. But the approach to picture-integration transcended the production process. Skilful sizing for a dramatically deep double-column (or a dramatically shallow six-column) could be done just as well for a coarse-screen letterpress zinco as for a fine-screen offset negative or bromide. It was the rotary letterpress *Evening Gazette* (Middlesbrough) which in 1966 was placed first in its class by the Newspaper Design Award judges for its 'excellence of picture presentation'. Editor William Heeps later explained that, in carrying out its policy of strong play on pictures, the *Gazette* took 'great care in the vital matter of their positioning – "around the heart of the page".'

This 'heart of the page' approach to picture-positioning can be seen generally in newspapers nowadays, whether letterpress or offset. The down-from-the-top, off-centre placing of a well-sized half-tone is a main way in which news photographs are really integrated with the page, forming a true part of its design, and adding notably to its sense of movement.[10]

Finally, it came to be accepted that the organisation of a paper's contents, including such departmentalising or sectionalising as was thought necessary and useful, was as much an element in its design as its typography. If a paper gathered all its classifieds into one central pull-out section, as a number of provincial evenings and weeklies did, this was rightly seen as a contribution to the paper's overall design. The Evans-Taylor partnership performed operations of this sort on the *Sunday Times* in the late 1960s and early 1970s. They took the classifieds off the back of the Weekly Review (the separate magazine section whose launching in 1958 had been a significant step in Sunday newspaper design) and put the TV Guide, daringly made up across the page, in their place. They took sport off its supposedly sacrosanct place on the back page of the news section and ran comment features there instead: sports page design was itself reorganised and improved. The internal organisation of a newspaper, as already noted, covers the appropriate departmentalising or sectionalising of its news and features. Such sectionalising is a main aid to the reader in his perusal of the paper and it calls for good 'signposting', to quote the apt expression of the 1972 Newspaper Design Award judges (F. H. K. Henrion, Ruari McLean, Geoffrey Cannon). The *Guardian*, with its labelling of HOME NEWS, WOMAN'S GUARDIAN and the like in simple boxes of a smaller size of the bold, rough capitals used for its title-line, provides a good example. The *Financial Times*, as the 1972 judges said, is 'exemplary' in its signposting of its various sections: 'on this ground alone', they added, 'it can serve as a model to most other papers.'

HOME NEWS

OVERSEAS NEWS

Design developments in practice

Now that the general newspaper design background of our period has been substantially outlined, we can turn to the details of change in individual newspapers. It is proper to take first the national Sundays, since the transformation of the *Observer* was the earliest in point of time and the most important in terms of influence. In 1962 Clive Irving changed the paper's old Caslon Heavy/Bodoni Bold (roman and italic) news headline mixture to a straight Light/Bold treatment in the then novel Century Schoolbook and its Bold. All upper- and lower-case, the style initially included Schoolbook italic for additional contrast, but this was later dropped. The simple all-roman headline style, in the two weights of Schoolbook, has shown itself both flexible and varied, has married well with the development of 'graphics' and, in short, has meant that whatever problems the *Observer* may have, design is not one of them. Together with Schoolbook the paper introduced a modernised grot (Monotype 215 and 216) for subsidiary lines in feature work.

A change was earlier made in the *Observer's* title-piece. Still flanked at each end by the Royal arms, in a new and somewhat lighter version, the title-line appeared in an elegant, sharp-seriffed, drawn letter, slightly less deep but proportionately wider than the plain roman capitals that had followed the long-standing blackletter in 1942. With this new title, whose face-depth was no more than 48pts, the dateline was run in a 24pt light Clarendon (evidently the Consort Light of Stephenson Blake). Despite the elegance of the new title, its comparatively modest size was presumably felt to be insufficiently competitive;

▼ The *Observer* of 1959 in its established post-war style of Caslon Heavy, Bodoni Bold, roman and italic, with title in plain roman capitals.

▼ After Clive Irving's Schoolbook/ Schoolbook Bold re-design of 1962: note the sharp and stylish new title.

▶ Opposite is the *Observer* of today, with the larger and heavier title.

so at the turn of 1966–67 a much larger title was introduced. A heavy modern roman, virtually slab-seriffed, this title gauged nearly 72pts in depth and was around seventeen picas wider than its predecessor. The Royal arms were cut to one, on the left, and much reduced in size; the dateline was likewise reduced, to 14pt Grot 215, and overall about a pica was saved in the total depth of the title-piece, giving it a distinctly more crowded air than before. The only subsequent change, following a reduction in column measure and thus in page width, has been a necessary adjustment in the depth and width of the title, which is now 60pt full face.

THE OBSERVER

London, Sunday, July 5, 1959

Established 1791: No. 8,766

Price 5d. Postage 2½d. Abroad 3½d.

National Press Gets 3-day Respite

Union Agrees to Ink Pooling: Papers Continue Half-size

No Progress Made at Ministry Talks

By A Staff Reporter

THE national newspapers will continue to publish at least until Wednesday. The National Society of Operative Printers and Assistants, the union concerned, agreed yesterday to allow them to share stocks of printing ink, the redistribution of which will enable them to print small editions to-morrow and for two days after that.

The provincial papers and the printing trade generally were, however, still stopped. The three parties to the dispute which has kept them idle for three weeks met for 3½ hours at the Ministry of Labour yesterday, but did not agree. They left amid recriminations and without arranging to meet again.

The unions are demanding a pay rise of 2s. in the £ and a 40-hour week. The employers have offered 6d. in the £ and a 42½-hour week, and would also like to discuss a 22-point document for more efficient working submitted jointly by the British Federation of Master Printers, representing the printing trade in general, and the Newspaper Society, representing the provincial papers.

The unions' spokesman, Mr. G. G. Eastwood, general secretary of the Printing and Kindred Trades Federation, said as he left the Ministry: "We see little hope of progress and we say this present situation has been created by the continuing adamant attitude of the employers." Later he stated that the secretaries of the 10 unions concerned would meet in London on Wednesday.

Mr. R. W. Briginshaw, general secretary of Natsopa, whose members are involved in both dis-

enjoy a 40-hour week. Consequently, our executive council have agreed to co-operate with them in arranging a

—THE OBSERVER—

Notice to Readers

To-day's issue of "The Observer," like that of other Sunday papers, has been heavily reduced in size because of an industrial dispute in which we are not directly concerned.

We regret that some regular features and many advertisements have had to be curtailed or omitted.

★

Books	11	Letters	15
Bridge	15	Music	10
Chess	15	Nation's Business	2
Church Services	4	Political Diary	9
City Notes	2	Radio Notes	10
Commonwealth and Foreign	3	Sayings	7
Cookery	6	Sport	15 & 16
Editorial	8	Table Talk	7
Everyman	15	Television	10
Feiffer	13	Theatres	10
Films	10	The Week	5
Galleries	10	Women's Page	6
		Ximenes	13

TO-DAY'S RADIO AND TV PROGRAMMES: PAGE 10

GeorgeBrown Pins Blame on Macleod

MR. GEORGE BROWN, chairman of the trade union group of Labour M.P.s, said at Ripley, Derbyshire, yesterday, that not for many years had the credit of arbitration machinery stood so low with workers.

"It will not help to go into the printing dispute in public," he said. "But one thing requires saying in the strongest way. Not for the first time we see plainly the consequences of Mr. Macleod on industrial relations.

THE PEACEFUL PICKETS OF ESSEX ROAD

PETER KEEN

Pickets equipped with chairs relax outside the printing works of W. R. Royle and Son, Ltd., in Essex Road, Islington, London.

Demonstrators Barred from

Bonus Share Issue for Mr. Fraser

A-Test Experts Still Split

GENEVA, July 4.—Nuclear experts

COLOUR MAGAZINE: MACMILLAN AND SUEZ

THE OBSERVER

London, Sunday, June 19, 1966

ESTABLISHED 1791 No. 9,128 PRICE 8d.

Yugoslav party bosses to abdicate

They will no longer control Government

by LAJOS LEDERER, who has just returned from Belgrade

Tito: New revolution.

MARSHAL TITO is calling on the Central Committee of the Yugoslav League of Communists to meet next week to discuss and endorse the most radical measures of democratisation ever taken by a Communist Party in power.

At this meeting the Communist Party, which has dominated the country since Tito's assumption of power in 1945, is expected to abdicate from exclusive executive power and content itself with acting as a guide and stimulus.

The intention is to "disestablish" and "de-professionalise"

The war against the bad

LBJ: No wavering on Vietnam

from our own Reporter

WASHINGTON, June 18

PRESIDENT JOHNSON today made his firmest commitment yet to an all-out American war effort in Vietnam.

Brushing aside all recent rumours of peace feelers, he told a Press con-

Photographs by JANE BOWN

Wilson to call in troops for power stations

by DAVID HAWORTH, our Industrial Reporter

The second Test Match at Lord's between England and the West Indies is producing a rare and moving conjunction of two totally opposite tribal types: vanishing rural whites of the old school, equipped with buttonholes, straw-hats, umbrellas, riding mackintoshes, hip flasks, binoculars; and expanding urban blacks in open-neck shirts and Harlem-style headgear — two tribes participating in the only rite they share.

At close of play the West Indies were 18 for 1 in reply to

CONTRACEPTION: PAUL FERRIS'S INQUIRY Weekend Review	
U.S. stopped Britain quitting Singapore	3
China's new leap forward	5
Profile: Woodrow Wyatt	11
TV via satellites	12

Established 1791

THE OBSERVER

28 JANUARY 1973

No. 9,470 Price 8p

IN COLOUR
COLETTE THE INNOCENT LIBERTINE

INSIDE A TEENAGE GANG Page 29

BE A WHISTLEBLOWER
JOIN THE MAGAZINE CAMPAIGN TO IMPROVE THE QUALITY OF LIFE IN BRITAIN

The Vietnam tragedy, pp 9-12 • The £4,000-million share slide / How to keep your head, pp 13-15 • Katharine Whitehorn: Jobs for the girls, p 31 • VAT ups and downs, p 31

Pan Am wants its Concorde money back

by ANDREW WILSON

PAN AMERICAN AIRWAYS, whose option to buy the supersonic Concorde expires on Wednesday, is demanding the return of a £1 million deposit from the British Aircraft Corporation.

It claims that the makers have failed to produce an aircraft to the economic standards specified in its contract signed in 1963. Though the sum is small beside other Concorde figures, the demand for its repayment raises an important matter of principle.

BAC is almost certain to resist the claim, which could be taken up by Trans World Airways and other American customers who have indicated their intention of terminating their options soon.

I understand that nothing has happened to alter Pan Am's intention to end its options on Wednesday. It still sees no reason to accept any extension, and plans an announcement on Wednesday night or Thursday morning.

The Pan Am decision, which even an outright gift of the aircraft might not now reverse, is only one gust in a gathering storm whose Wagnerian dimensions cannot be much longer concealed from Parliament and the country.

The first intimation of the seriousness of the crisis over Concorde could come with a fresh investigation of its still spiralling development costs by the Commons Committee of Public Accounts.

This is likely to follow last Thursday's disclosure by Sir David Pitblado, the Auditor-General, that BAC's share of the development cost of the £1,000 million plane is now £222,700,000, 79 per cent more than the estimate given to Whitehall three years ago.

Among his disclosures was the cost of one item, crew seats, developed under sub-contract. This came out at £351,000, compared with an original estimate of £54,000, and would have been higher still but for Government intervention.

A widespread belief in Whitehall that the Government intends to impose a fixed price for the remaining development work on the plane has not been dispelled by a denial yesterday by the Aerospace Minister, Mr Michael Heseltine.

A fixed-price contract could prove crippling to the manufacturers, who may well see moves for it as the end of the Government's commitment to put Concorde on the world market at whatever cost.

BAC has not issued any formal statement on its 'negotiations' with Pan Am in New York last week, but I understand that Sir George Edwards, the corporation's chairman, met the Pan Am president, Mr William Seawell, on Tuesday. This followed a presentation by BAC salesmen of Concorde's costs and earning capabilities to the consortium of 38 bankers who recently granted Pan Am a two-year extension of the airline's vital operating loan.

Mr Seawell told Sir George that the aircraft now offered by BAC was quite inappropriate to Pan Am's needs. Sir George then asked if Pan Am would object to hearing any alternative proposals.

Mr Seawell said that Pan Am could hardly refuse to listen, but made it clear that the airline's verdict on Concorde's economics was unlikely to be altered.

Sir George then left Washington for the west coast to talk, it is believed, with another customer airline.

Pan Am's rejection of Concorde has already brought reactions from other American airlines, whose favour has hardly been won by BAC's declared hope of forcing them to buy an uneconomic aircraft by competition from the State-ordered purchases of Concorde by BOAC and Air France.

Significantly, on Tuesday, the *Wall Street Journal* published an interview with Mr Charles Tillinghast, president of TWA, in which he said that he saw 'nothing that could persuade TWA, faced with a 28 February deadline, to execute its options to buy Concorde at this time.'

As for Pan Am, Mr Tillinghast said he was certain Pan Am 'can't and won't' decide in favour of the plane.

His remarks were interpreted in Wall Street as a signal that Pan Am can terminate its options in the secure knowledge that TWA will not move in to take its place on the order list.

American Airlines and Eastern Airlines have also reiterated their intention not to buy.

Even more interesting reactions have taken place within BOAC and Air France. I can now disclose that last year the head of Air France, M. Pierre Cot, told a senior member of the French National Assembly that if Pan American did not order Concorde, Air France would not operate the plane either.

(*Continued on page 2*)

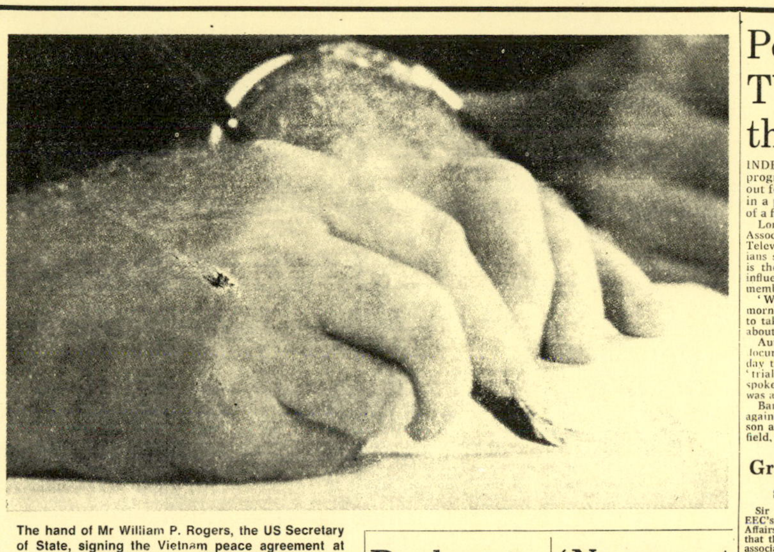

The hand of Mr William P. Rogers, the US Secretary of State, signing the Vietnam peace agreement at the Hotel Majestic in Paris.

America rings bells for peace and prayers

CHURCH BELLS rang out in the United States to signal the start of the ceasefire at midnight last night.

In Saigon traffic came to a halt in the city centre. People stood to attention in the street as a Government loudspeaker truck played the National Anthem. Women knelt.

By President Thieu's order bells, drums, gongs and cymbals rang throughout South Vietnam at the moment of the cease-fire to mark 'this historic day.'

In the United States President Nixon led the nation in a day of prayer and thanksgiving.

But there were reports that a battle was still raging in the Cambodian border city of Tay Ninh Cit, 25 minutes after the cease-fire.

The Vietnam war was fought right up to the dead-line with a final night of ground battles and American bombing.

Saigon airfield was shelled just before peace came and an American was killed earlier in the day, probably the last one to die in a war that cost nearly 46,000 US lives. He was believed to be Air Force Sergeant John Rucker, aged 21, of Texas, killed in a rocket attack at Da Nang during the morning.

In New York peace was flashed to Americans in rain-swept Times Square. National television cameras relayed the single word 'Peace' as it circled the Reuters lighted sign.

The names of the first United States servicemen on a prisoner-of-war list provided by the North Vietnamese were released last night by the Pentagon who began notifying their families that they were safe.

4-party signing in Paris

from ROBERT STEPHENS

PARIS, 27 January

THE ceasefire agreement officially ending at midnight all warfare on land, sea and in the air was signed here earlier today.

With its 23 articles and numerous protocols, formally closing a conflict that has lasted intermittently for 27 years, it was signed in two ceremonies by the Foreign Ministers of the four parties concerned—the United States, North Vietnam, the Saigon Government of South Vietnam and its Communist-led rival, the Provisional Revolutionary Government of South Vietnam set up by the Vietcong.

The signing ceremonies took place in the International Conference Centre, formerly the Hotel Majestic, near the Arc de Triomphe. Here for four years formal peace negotiations continued fruitlessly until the deadlock was broken by parallel secret talks elsewhere in Paris

(*Continued on page 2*)

Nixon ends conscription

from WILLIAM MILLINSHIP

WASHINGTON, 27 January

THE United States today announced the immediate end of conscription, five months before plans to put the services on an all-regular basis were due to take effect.

The outgoing Defence Secretary, Mr Melvin Laird, said in a message to senior Pentagon officials: 'I wish to inform you that the armed forces henceforth will depend exclusively on volunteer soldiers, sailors, airmen and marines.'

America has had conscription since 1940, except for 13 months in 1947 and 1948.

At the peak of the Vietnam war, in 1966, more than 380,000 Americans were called up. But the Government stopped sending conscripts to Vietnam last year, and the total call-up this year would have been down to 5,000.

The end of conscription will not mean a cut in the Pentagon budget. The total strength of the armed forces, which rose to 3,500,000 during the Vietnam war, will be down to 2,288,000 by the end of June. However, military pay and allowances have been sharply increased to attract recruits.

Barber to cancel tax cuts for rich?

by NORA BELOFF
our Political Correspondent

SOME Conservative MPs and some economic analysts would not be surprised if the Budget on 6 March stopped, at least for a year, the new tax concessions on unearned income and surtax.

The new rates, announced in last year's Budget, are due to apply from 6 April this year. If he stopped them, the Chancellor, Mr Barber, would use some of the revenue saved to help the poor.

In his 1972 Budget, Mr Barber reduced taxes by £1,211 million and of this £300 million represented the cost under the new unified tax system of concessions on surtax and unearned income. It is on this £300 million that Mr Barber is believed to have his eye.

If the tax concessions come in as planned the well-to-do will get their bonanza just when wage-earners are being asked to make do with £1 plus 4 per cent. The Shadow Chancellor, Mr Denis Healey, has already pointed out that the tax concessions would make Mr Heath—whose salary is £20,000 a year—£350 a year better off, whereas Phase Two of the prices and pay policy restricts wage increases to £250. In view of Treasury anxiety about the rapid growth of public expenditure, the Chancellor might not match the revenue saved with precisely equal spending. But it is expected that he would use at least some of it to meet the Government pledge, constantly reaffirmed by the Prime Minister, that the new prices and incomes package will be 'fair' and that there will be special provisions for the needy.

Additional funds might be found for the Family Income Supplement—or for extra provisions for pensioners, the disabled or the child allowance. This would meet some of the mounting indignation over the Government's refusal to intervene directly on the price of fresh foods.

Taking from the rich and giving to the poor would be electorally appealing, just as its failure to materialise would be a boon to the Opposition. But there would be a good deal of hostile comment and disappointment among Conservatives in the local associations. They are already worried about Mr Heath's shift from his earlier confidence in the market economy.

Right-wing back-benchers are already reflecting this disquiet and in a singularly hostile speech yesterday Mr Richard Body, MP for Holland with Boston, denounced the whole Government prices and incomes policy as 'doomed to failure.' He pointed out, as many Tories are now doing, that Mr Heath's policy cannot really be compared to the successful Nixon initiative, on which it is supposed to be modelled, as this went hand in hand with a monetary squeeze whereas the British Government has been increasing both public spending and the monetary supply. Other Tories point out that whereas the monetary circulation in the United States increased during the Nixon freeze by about 7 per cent, money supply in Britain went up last year by 24 per cent.

'No spy at Chequers'

MR HAROLD WILSON yesterday denied allegations, put forward at the Pentagon Papers trial at Los Angeles, that a secret United States agent was present at Chequers during his talks with Mr Kosygin on Vietnam in 1967.

Mr Wilson did not deny the presence, unknown to his Russian visitor, of the American diplomat Mr Chet Cooper, who has written his own account of the incident. But he denied that Mr Cooper was told details of the conversations between himself and Mr Kosygin, and also that the British Secret Service tapped a telephone talk between Mr Kosygin in London and Mr Brezhnev in Moscow.

Ulster bomb misfires

Shoppers in Dungannon, Co. Tyrone, had a narrow escape yesterday when a 15 lb. bomb planted in a store failed to go off.

A call to Portadown telephone exchange said a bomb had been planted at Wellworths, a firm with many branches in Northern Ireland, but the call was traced to Dungannon.

When the bomb was found, the detonator had burnt out.

Poulson: TV strike threat

INDEPENDENT television programmes may be blacked out for a time tomorrow night in a protest over the banning of a film on the Poulson affair.

London members of the Association of Cinematograph, Television and allied Technicians said: 'We believe this ban is the result of direct political influence being exercised on members of the IBA.

'We are meeting on Monday morning to decide what action to take. We feel very strongly about this.'

Authority chiefs who saw the documentary decided on Thursday that it might appear to be 'trial by television.' But an IBA spokesman denied that there was any political pressure.

Bankruptcy proceedings against architect Mr John Poulson are due to resume at Wakefield, Yorks, tomorrow.

Greece stays out, says Soames

Sir Christopher Soames, the EEC's Commissioner for External Affairs, said in Brussels yesterday that the EEC would keep Greece's associate membership 'frozen' while the regime there remained in power.—Reuter.

Pornography raids

Police visited 50 premises in London yesterday and last night a spokesman said nine men were 'assisting police with inquiries regarding serious assaults committed in connection with pornography. A large quantity of pornographic materials has been taken away.'

'We shot Israeli'

CAIRO, 27 January.—The Palestinian Black September organisation claimed today it had executed an Israeli intelligence officer 'by firing squad' in Madrid yesterday.

Police sources in Madrid reported yesterday that a 36-year-old Israeli was killed by two shots fired by an unidentified man outside a tobacco kiosk.—Reuter.

Heroin seized

TORONTO, 27 January.—Police seized 70 lb of heroin valued at up to £16 million on the illegal market here today. Nine men were charged with conspiracy to import narcotics.—Reuter.

All Blacks beaten

The Barbarians beat the All Blacks 23-11 at Cardiff yesterday in the last match of the New Zealanders' tour of Britain.

Nalgo weakens unions' stand on Phase Two

by DAVID WILSON, our Labour Correspondent

TRADE union opposition to the Government's anti-inflationary measures was weakened yesterday by the National and Local Government Officers' Association, the fourth largest union in the TUC.

By 45 votes to 15, its executive council rejected the TUC line of outright opposition to the Government. It decided instead to conduct its own evaluation of Phase Two and to try to make the TUC change its mind.

A resolution, carried by 36 votes to 16, affirmed 'the need for continuing consultation between the TUC and the Government on economic policy' and instructed the union's economic committee to examine 'the possibility of obtaining further concessions from the Government in the light of the proposed early Budget.'

Nalgo, which is widely regarded as the leading voice for moderation in the TUC, has in fact hedged its bets. It also said it opposed wage controls; and Mr Walter Anderson, the general secretary, said: 'There has not been a specific Yes or No on whether we should be represented on the prices and wages boards. Until this is cleared through the TUC, we would not want to take action that would flout TUC policy.'

He also felt that the chance of Nalgo persuading the TUC to change its mind was unlikely.

Some union leaders are planning to make Thursday, 15 February, a day of massive demonstrations against Phase Two. They hope for support from civil servants, teachers, hospital workers, busmen and gas and water workers.

If they succeed in co-ordinating their protests throughout the public sector, the disruption could be massive and many other unions might join in.

Pressure was mounted first by the National Union of Teachers, which approached all public sector unions asking them to send three representatives to a strategy conference.

But the Civil and Public Services Association hopes the TUC will sponsor the campaign. Yesterday Nalgo decided to support the teachers only if the TUC refused to take over leadership.

Although the campaign is split, some union leaders, especially in the National Union of Public Employees, want to embark quickly on industrial action, because of Government limits—of £1 plus 4 per cent—on wage increases. NUPE got an overwhelming vote for strike action from hospital staff in a ballot announced on Friday. Token stoppages, coinciding with the strategy conference, are favoured.

Mini-Trog
BERNARD LEVIN BILL COULD TOP £200,000

'Levin? Who's'e play for?

ON OTHER PAGES

Girl shot dead

NEW YORK, 27 January.—A policeman in civilian clothes shot and killed a 16-year-old girl in a Brooklyn street today after her companion, another 16-year-old girl, pointed a shotgun at him. The second girl was arrested.—Reuter.

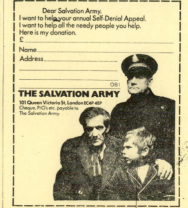

Dossier S. ticks away under Pompidou

by a Staff Reporter

A POLITICAL scandal involving a prominent Gaullist MP, which could have damaging repercussions for President Pompidou's Government in the crucial March elections, is looming in France after last week's publication of a book enigmatically entitled 'Dossier S . . . .'

Written by a young campaigning French journalist, Jean Montaldo, and published by an avant-garde Parisian publisher, 'Dossier S . . . is a case-study of the manipulation of political power in the early days of Gaullist rule. It revolves around the powerful personality of Alexandre Sanguinetti, a Gaullist MP, former Minister and 'S . . . of the title.

The book, which could be dynamite for a Government already reeling under the impact of a series of scandals, is being studiously left alone by the French Press. Only *Minute*, the right-wing anti-Gaullist newspaper, has written about it so far.

Normal distributors refused to touch it and it was sent out to bookshops throughout the country by a fleet of private vehicles. The publisher, Alain Moreau, has printed 4,000 copies and expects reprisals.

The core of the book is a series of documents, apparently leaked from the Ministry of Justice, which plot the process by which Sanguinetti, a staunch Gaullist of colourful plumage, was granted an amnesty in 1959.

Sanguinetti had been discharged as a bankrupt and barred from managing companies in 1954. The amnesty, introduced by de Gaulle as an act of clemency for war veterans to grace the birth of the Fifth Republic, halted and nullified criminal proceedings against him for fraudulent bankruptcy, falsification of company records and fraud. 'Dossier S . . . ' is an account of how this happened.

Sanguinetti denied the charges at the time and Montaldo does not seek to establish that they could have been proved. His main allegation, supported by documents and a detailed interpretation, is that the amnesty process involved the exertion of pressure on the Public Prosecutor's department by Sanguinetti's political allies in high places.

After erratic political and disastrous commercial careers, Sanguinetti had been rewarded for his services to the Gaullist cause in February 1959 with the important post of *Chef de Cabinet* to Roger Frey, de Gaulle's first Minister of Information. In July, Parliament approved the amnesty law. A week later a strongly worded application on Sanguinetti's behalf had been filed, demanding that the matter should be expedited in the shortest possible time.'

The most interesting document in 'Dossier S . . .' is the Public Prosecutor's reply two

(*Continued on page 2*)

DUCKHAM'S NOL MOTOR OILS

July 5 1959 Established 1822

THE SUNDAY TIMES

No. 7103 A KEMSLEY NEWSPAPER PRICE 5d.

PRINT TALKS LAST 5 Hrs.

Union Chiefs Gloomy As Meeting Adjourns

FLEET ST. INK POOLED

BY THE SUNDAY TIMES INDUSTRIAL CORRESPONDENT

EMPLOYERS and printing trade union leaders met at the Ministry of Labour yesterday for five hours. A Ministry statement said that both sides clarified their positions and would consider the views expressed.

NEW HOPE OF ARMS PACT

Big Four Accord Likely

By NICHOLAS CARROLL, Diplomatic Correspondent of The Sunday Times

THE international atmosphere is so changed today that there is every likelihood of the Big Four agreeing in principle at a Summit conference to the composition of a new Disarmament Commission whose creation would be brought about in the next session of the United Nations General Assembly.

Its first task would be to tackle the key question of nuclear disarmament before the "nuclear club" becomes unmanageably large. This development would take much of the wind out of the sails of the "non-nuclear club" movement in Britain.

An agreement between the United States, Britain and Russia

N.U.T. ACCEPT PAY AWARD

Minister Criticised

By KATHLEEN GIBBERD, The Sunday Times Education Correspondent

A SPECIAL conference of the National Union of Teachers

Walmar "Your fitting" Hats

THE SUNDAY TIMES

PRINT TALKS LAST 5 Hrs.

Union Chiefs Gloomy As Meeting Adjourns

FLEET ST. INK POOLED

NEW HOPE OF ARMS PACT

N.U.T. ACCEPT PAY AWARD

BOW GROUP URGE AFRICA REFORM

Make a note – Harrods Sale begins on Saturday July 11th

▲ Evolution of the *Sunday Times* from the decker headings and eight-column page of 1959 to the light/bold/extended style and wide-measure front page of today (opposite page). ▶

After the Thomson takeover in 1959 the *Sunday Times* continued into the next decade with little change from its Century decker style described in the preceding chapter. Much of the headlining was in capitals, and there were plenty of italics. The title-piece, with advertising 'ears', remained in the version of Times Extended Titling, with a small Royal arms centred above it, which Robert Harling had devised in the early 1950s. The first major change was to an all Century Bold roman upper- and lower-case style for news headlines. When the separate Business News section was started it was effectively headlined in Franklin Gothic Extra Condensed, securing variety by size only. After the appointment of Harold Evans as editor in January 1967 (and his own naming of Edwin Taylor as Design Director the following year) evolution was rapid. The 'ears' were dropped from the title, whose main line was re-drawn in a bolder and closer-fitted style, while retaining the general flavour of its predecessor; the dateline details, formerly flanking the Royal arms in a decorative 30pt Perpetua upper- and lower-case, had descended below the title in a modest 10pt Century Bold, but they now rose again to flank the Royal arms (much reduced) in a light Record Gothic.

Under Evans the *Sunday Times* evolved from the Century Bold only news style (the light Century Expanded was restricted to the features in the separate Weekly Review) to the Light/Bold contrast style pioneered by the *Observer*. This contrast was secured, without recourse to Schoolbook and Schoolbook Bold by simply moving the Century Expanded to the news pages; additionally, Century Bold Extended was introduced for lead stories. Main features in the body of the paper were headlined in Franklin Gothic Extra Condensed with a light Record Gothic for contrast; in the Weekly Review the cultural and literary features were headed in Record Gothic Medium Extended and its Bold counterpart. For certain special features, like Insight or Spectrum or Atticus, the sledgehammer Ludlow Black proved more useful than might have been thought; this blunt, fat face could be used in comparatively modest sizes, thus saving space, and yet pack a formidable punch. Reference has already been made to Evans's advocacy of 'graphics'; equally novel was his approach to the front page of the *Sunday Times*. While the general page format of the paper remains at eight 11-pica columns, the front-page is made up in seven columns, six of them 12-picas and column one a wide measure of 15-picas. This 15-pica column accommodates the News Digest, each item headed in graded sizes of Record Gothic Bold Medium Extended, from 24pt and 18pt down to 14pt.* A frequent Newspaper Design Award prizewinner, the *Sunday Times* was unanimously voted first in its class by the 1972 judges, who said that the paper 'continues, beyond question, to be entirely outstanding among British newspapers. Apart from the consistently high quality of its journalism, one of its secrets is that it works to a discipline which yet allows for great variety; other papers may often achieve variety, but lack consistent typographical discipline.'

* The page one news summary notion, placed in the first column with bold sideheads, was originated by the *Financial Times* as part of its successful transformation from a purely City sheet into a general newspaper. It has been developed by the *FT* into quite an elaborate affair, occupying the top of columns one and two, with its own reverse block 'signpost'.

MAY 13 1973 No 7822 Price 9p

THE SUNDAY TIMES

Nixon and the corrupt election 4-page special begins on p 14

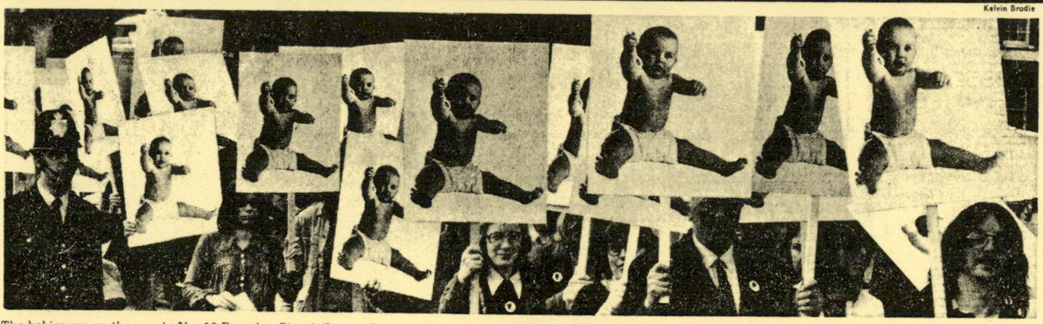
Kelvin Brodie

The babies are on the way to No. 10 Downing Street (home of a non-father) to make a point about population; report, page 3

NEWS DIGEST

May 13 1973

Gunboats open fire as Iceland gets tougher

GUNBOATS acting on the personal order of Iceland's Prime Minister went into action at dawn yesterday and fired warning shots across the bows of two British support tugs. This new tough policy in the Cod War was decided on Friday at a secret meeting between the gunboat skippers and the Prime Minister, Olafur Johannesson.

Only a few days before, Mr Johannesson had told gunboat captains to show restraint and provide an opportunity for talks between the British and Icelandic governments. The swift turnabout suggests that the Premier has felt obliged to give way to the demands of militant MPs and the feelings of impatience in Iceland's Coast Guard.

The Icelandic government was talking last week about a possible meeting between Sir Alec Douglas-Home, British Foreign Secretary, and Einar Augustsson, Iceland's Foreign Minister, in Strasbourg this week at the Council of Europe. Whether or not this was ever a real possibility, any early resumption of peace talks now appears unlikely.

Until yesterday's flare-up, there had been a week of uneasy peace in Icelandic waters following the talks between Lady Tweedsmuir, Minister of State at the Foreign Office, and the Icelandic Government. But at the same time, it was clear that gunboat skippers were frustrated by their government's moderation and MPs felt that Mr Johannesson's attempts to reach a settlement with Britain were fruitless.

The British Trawler Federation is disappointed by the Icelandic action. "I am not surprised but I heartily condemn their use of gunboats," the federation chairman, Austen Laing, said yesterday. "I am sorry they could not wait for further talks between our governments. But if they choose to escalate the war, then they will reap a bitter harvest."—*David Blundy.*

Living heart taken across Paris

A HEART was taken from a 16-year-old traffic victim in Paris yesterday, and rushed across the city to another hospital where it was transplanted into an unnamed man of 26. This is the first time a heart has been taken from one hospital to another; normally the donor is moved before the operation.

The heart, which was escorted by motorcycle police with sirens screaming, was kept in good condition by being chilled at 39 deg F (4 deg C). After a four hour operation the patient was said last night to be in good condition. *AFP*

Police 'ignored' 999 rescue call

TWO POLICEMEN are to be disciplined for not acting on a 999 call which gave the location of the four schoolboys missing last month in Snowdonia three days before they were rescued.

A Cambridge couple on holiday, Mr and Mrs Derek Jongsma, saw the boys on Saturday, April 21, the day after they were reported missing, and made the call to Llandudno police station. Police officers later denied receiving it, but the Post Office in Chester confirmed it had been made.

Tit-for-tat Tahiti

IF AUSTRALIA and New Zealand carry out their threat to boycott French ships and planes in protest against France's nuclear bomb tests in the Pacific, the French Polynesian Trade Union Federation in Tahiti will refuse to service Australasian ships and planes. Charles Taufa, federation president, said yesterday: "Our action is not political, but an economic and social defence of French Polynesian workers."—*AP*

A-test dangers, page 8

Beirut round-up

LEBANESE security forces yesterday arrested 38 suspected *agents provocateur* in a series of pre-dawn raids in Beirut, while along the Syrian border air force jets again attacked guerrilla positions and troops battled with commandos who crossed the border. —*Agencies*

Peter Pringle, page 9

Party-colour clash

LIBERAL Party headquarters are investigating a complaint that Liberals used Labour's colours on some local election cards in Birmingham last week in an attempt to capture the votes of the Indian population.

Freezer death: car found

A BLUE Hillman car owned by the missing husband of Mrs Denise Fairbairn, who was discovered dead in the freezer of her home in Feltham, Middlesex, on Friday, was found by police in North London early yesterday. Police are anxious to trace the husband, Brian Fairbairn, aged 34.

Guillotine again

AN IMMIGRANT labourer from Tunisia, convicted of murdering a seven-year-old French girl, was executed by guillotine at Marseilles yesterday — the third since President Pompidou took office. The man, Ali Benyane, 32, refused the traditional glass of rum and was stated by his lawyer to have died with "rare courage and rare sang-froid." —*Associated Press*

Haile Selassie in London

THE LION of Judah—Emperor Haile Selassie of Ethiopia — arrived in London yesterday, bound for Washington, where he is to have official talks with the US Government. In London he has no official engagements, but is expected to visit his son, who is undergoing medical treatment. —*Reuter.*

New TUC for Wales

TWO HUNDRED Welsh trade union representatives, meeting at Aberystwyth yesterday, reaffirmed a decision taken in February to set up a Welsh TUC, despite opposition from the British TUC. The new organisation will come into being next January 1, with a general council of 30 members.

Pension 35 years late

A GROUP of war widows is to start receiving pensions in October—35 years after their husbands died. They are women mostly over 70, who married after the end of the First World War and whose husbands died before September 3, 1939.

Pope sees Viet Cong

POPE PAUL had his first meeting yesterday with a representative of the Viet Cong. He received in private audience Nguyen Van Hieu, a Minister in the Viet Cong's Provisional revolutionary government, and his adviser, Le Van Loc.—*Reuter*

Sunday Times prices overseas

Republic of Ireland	15p	Holland	D.Fl.2.50
Austria	A.Sh.22	Italy	Lire600
Belgium	B.Fr35	Malta	10c4
Canada	$1.25	Norway	N.Kr. 5.00
W.Prov.	$1.50	Portugal	Esc.20
Canaries	Psts.50	Spain	Psts.50
Denmark	D.Kr.5.00	Sweden	S.Kr. 4.00
Finland	F.Mk.3.50	Switzerland	S.Fr4.00
France	Fr4.00	USA	$1.25
Germany	DM3.20	Western States	$1.50
Greece	Dra.30	2nd class postage paid at New York.	

Why Provos shot their own double agent

Hammond: exposed embezzlers

By Paul Eddy and Chris Ryder

THE BRITISH Army deserter who was left for dead in a Belfast alley two weeks ago was not shot because he spied on the IRA. Although 19-year-old Louis Hammond did pretend to work for Army intelligence for seven months last year, he was, in fact, a double agent planted by the IRA.

The reason he was beaten for three days and shot with four bullets by the Provisionals was that he gave information to The Sunday Times about the wholesale embezzlement of IRA funds. He did not give the Army any significant military information about the Provos.

Five weeks ago Hammond helped us to reveal that at least £150,000 had been stolen from IRA funds, mainly by officers serving in the Provisionals' First Battalion. Although he knew he was taking a risk, Hammond helped us because "somebody has got to speak out about the hard men who are lining their pockets, not fighting for the cause."

He believed that during his brief and bizarre terrorist career he had served that cause well, and was in no danger from the movement. But two weeks ago—a few days before his 19th birthday—he nearly paid the traditional price that the IRA extracts from informers. Four Provisionals, one of them a close friend of Hammond, lured him into a house in Joy Street, Belfast.

They beat him for three days, and interrogated him about the information he had given to us during the three months we had known him. Finally, on Saturday, April 28, as he lay unconscious from the continued beatings, he was shot three times in the head and once in the stomach.

His body was taken to Ormeau Road, half a mile away, and just before midnight he was dumped in the entrance to an alley and left for dead.

Astonishingly, he survived, although one of the bullets passed through his head, two lodged in his skull and the fourth in his liver. For eight days he lay critically ill in a heavily-guarded ward in the Royal Victoria Hospital, Belfast, but by last Friday he had recovered sufficiently to be able to get out of bed for an hour.

Hammond is now partially paralysed, and will almost certainly lose the sight of one eye, but he is now well enough to be moved, for his own safety, to another, better-guarded hospital.

It was comparatively easy for the would-be killers to abduct Hammond because he thought he had nothing to fear from the "dedicated Provisionals" who he believed shared his anger and disillusionment over the embezzlement.

HAMMOND was a boy soldier with the British Army. At 16 he joined the Royal Irish Rangers, and after basic training was posted to Watchet in Somerset, where he gained some knowledge of guns during infantry training. He was recruited by the Provisionals while he was on leave at his home in Andersonstown, Belfast, and was posted as absent without leave when he failed to return to his unit in January, 1972.

By then Hammond had been promoted by the Provos—because of the mass round-ups of their senior officers during internment swoops—to Intelligence Officer of E Company of the First Battalion.

IRA Provo chiefs milk £150,000 from funds

From The Sunday Times, April 8

A year ago today, on May 13, Hammond was arrested by the army while he was on vigilante duty, manning one of the street barricades in the no-go area of Andersonstown. The security forces soon realised that he was a deserter, but Hammond bought himself immunity from prosecution by offering to work as a "spy" for the army.

This was a pre-arranged Provo plan. At that time the Belfast Brigade was anxious to get information on the British army's secret and increasingly effective weapon—the plainclothes surveillance groups, code-named MRF. Provisional volunteers, including Hammond, and two other men we know about, Seamus Wright and Kevin McKee—had been instructed, if arrested, to offer their services to MRF and then become double agents.

Hammond's offer was accepted, and he went to live with nine other informers, including Wright and McKee, in two secluded houses—9 and 10 Harwell Road—inside Palace Barracks, six miles from Belfast.

MRF stands for Military Reconnaisance Force (*not*, as the IRA believe, Military Reaction Force). It is essentially the Army's CID.

Until last week the army has steadfastly refused to discuss the force or its activities, but last Friday in a frank briefing by a senior officer at the Lisburn headquarters we were told:

- MRF is made up of regular soldiers who volunteer for "these dangerous duties."
- They always wear plain clothes and patrol Belfast in civilian cars or, on occasions, bogus commercial vehicles.
- Their main job is surveillance of suspected terrorists, but they are always armed and "will certainly fire back when shot at."

The officer told us: "The unit is part of the normal military chain of command, but I do not want to go into details. We would like to retain the benefit of some doubt in the matter."

When we asked about the use of civilians he refused to comment, and said we were "getting into deep matters." But we know that the civilian operatives made up the "Provisional Section," and at the time that Hammond was involved they came under the command of a Captain "Big Jim" Moore. The soldiers worked in a separate section, at that time under the command of Captain James McGregor, of the Parachute Regiment.

In the first week of March this year Captain McGregor was charged with the unlawful possession of a Thompson submachine-gun, the IRA's traditional weapon. On May 4 the charge was withdrawn after it had been said in court that he had possessed the weapon in "authorised circumstances."

The informers were used to "screen" suspects who had been arrested and taken to MRF's headquarters, the former Interogation Centre—a corrugated iron compound inside Palace Barracks. They also went out on patrol in armoured vehicles pointing out "safe houses," weapons dumps and IRA sympathisers in the areas where they had formerly operated as Provisionals.

Continued on Page 2

Heath names Scottish oil watchdog

Sunday Times Reporter

IN a new and dramatic move to allay anxieties in Scotland over the social, economic and environmental consequences of the North Sea oil bonanza, Mr Heath yesterday announced the appointment of an official troubleshooter to tackle all problems of oil exploitation and development north of the border. He is Lord Polwarth, Scottish Office Minister of State, and he will have direct access to the Prime Minister.

Lord Polwarth, who is 56, prefers troubleshooter to descriptions like overlord or oil supremo. He will be backed up by a task force of officials from United Kingdom departments concerned with the oil industry. "One of my jobs," he said, "will be to put the heat on to release bottlenecks."

Announcing Lord Polwarth's appointment at a conference of Scottish Conservatives at Perth, Mr Heath said: "The development of the oil industry is one that requires an attitude of mind, a scale of thinking and a speed of action more in line with a vast war-time operation, than with the normal processes of a manufacturing economy. So far as the Government is concerned, it is clearly important that all the various aspects of this massive and complex operation should be seen and dealt with as a whole."

Mr Heath said the Scottish people were confronted with the greatest economic challenge since the industrial revolution.

Lord Polwarth, a former chairman of the Bank of Scotland, served for 17 years as chairman of the Scottish Council and was chiefly concerned with development and industry. His appointment should give a boost to the Government's popularity in Scotland, where Conservative fortunes have been at a low ebb. A recent Commons select committee report put the spotlight on what many Scots saw as mistakes and misjudgments in exploiting North Sea oil and gas.

Since the beginning of the North Sea development Lord Polwarth has urged Scotland's particular rights in the new industry and, as Minister of State, he has already helped to secure a substantial share of capital expenditure on the north-east coast and in the shipbuilding industry. One ambition was to make the Bank of Scotland a major force in the oil industry. A Cambridge man, he served in the Lothian and Border Yeomanry during the war, and held for a time the historic post of Brigadier, the Royal Company of Archers. His home is near Hawick in the Borders.

The oil boom has already created an estimated 3,600 jobs in Scotland and is expected to provide about 10,000 more. Some estimates put the North Sea output at three-quarters of Britain's oil needs by the 1980s. On present prices, profits could be between £500 million and £600 million by the end of this decade.

Oil experts have consistently upgraded the importance of the North Sea oilfield since the early strikes confirmed sizeable oilfields in the late 1960s.

Mr Heath's speech to Conservatives emphasised the Government's determination to give Scots more say in their affairs. He recalled his speech at Perth five years ago when he called on the Labour Government to set up a constitutional committee to examine government in Scotland.

"I pledged then, and I repeat the pledge today, to give the people of Scotland genuine participation in the making of decisions that affect them all—within the historic unity of the United Kingdom."

He said Labour had refused to set up a committee, but the Conservatives had done so. The Conservative Party's commitment to the people of Scotland was to put forward proposals in the lifetime of the present Parliament.

Polwarth: looking for bottlenecks

So that's why my phone clicked

By Henry Brandon

THE NEW YORK TIMES LAST week reported that my telephone had been tapped. I was not the only one thus honoured—one fellow reporter suggested that having your telephone tapped is the next best thing to getting a Pulitzer Prize.

I can no longer remember when I first noticed that my telephone gave a funny click and took much longer than usual to make a connection, but my wife remembers my drawing her attention to it.

I also remember how vehemently she resented this invasion of her privacy, but she gradually developed a sort of sympathy for the invisible listeners as they learned about our 14-year-old's Latin homework, about the insurrection music by James Taylor that his rock band favoured, as well as the secrets of our 12-year-old daughter and the tragedies that befell the rabbit of our eight-year-old. And what did they make of my wife's conversations about such highly sensitive electronic devices as vacuum cleaners, toasters, ovens, etc.? Codewords?

Here's to Nixon - The Last 10 Days..
CALMAN

The New York Times assums one of its writers was bugged after an article he wrote on the SALT talks. Perhaps I was bugged for an article I also wrote on the talks last May.

It would be fascinating to find out, by taking these telephone-tapping cases to Court, whether the Government could sustain what would no doubt be its contention that "national security" was involved. If they could not, it might not only cost them a lot of money, but also make them more cautious about tapping journalists' telephones.

- The former acting FBI Director, Patrick Gray, has told Senate Attorneys that he warned President Nixon last July that White House aides were interfering with the Watergate investigation, three American newspapers reported yesterday. Nixon said on April 30 that, until two months ago, he was unaware of any "effort to conceal the facts."

Yesterday's reports said Gray has told Senate investigators that he told Mr Nixon last July 6 that he was concerned that the FBI and the CIA were being "used" by people close to the White House in the Watergate probe. The Daily News quoted Gray as saying: "Mr President, I want to warn you that people around you are wounding you."

The News said Mr Nixon replied: "Well, Pat, you continue pressing the investigation as hard as you can."

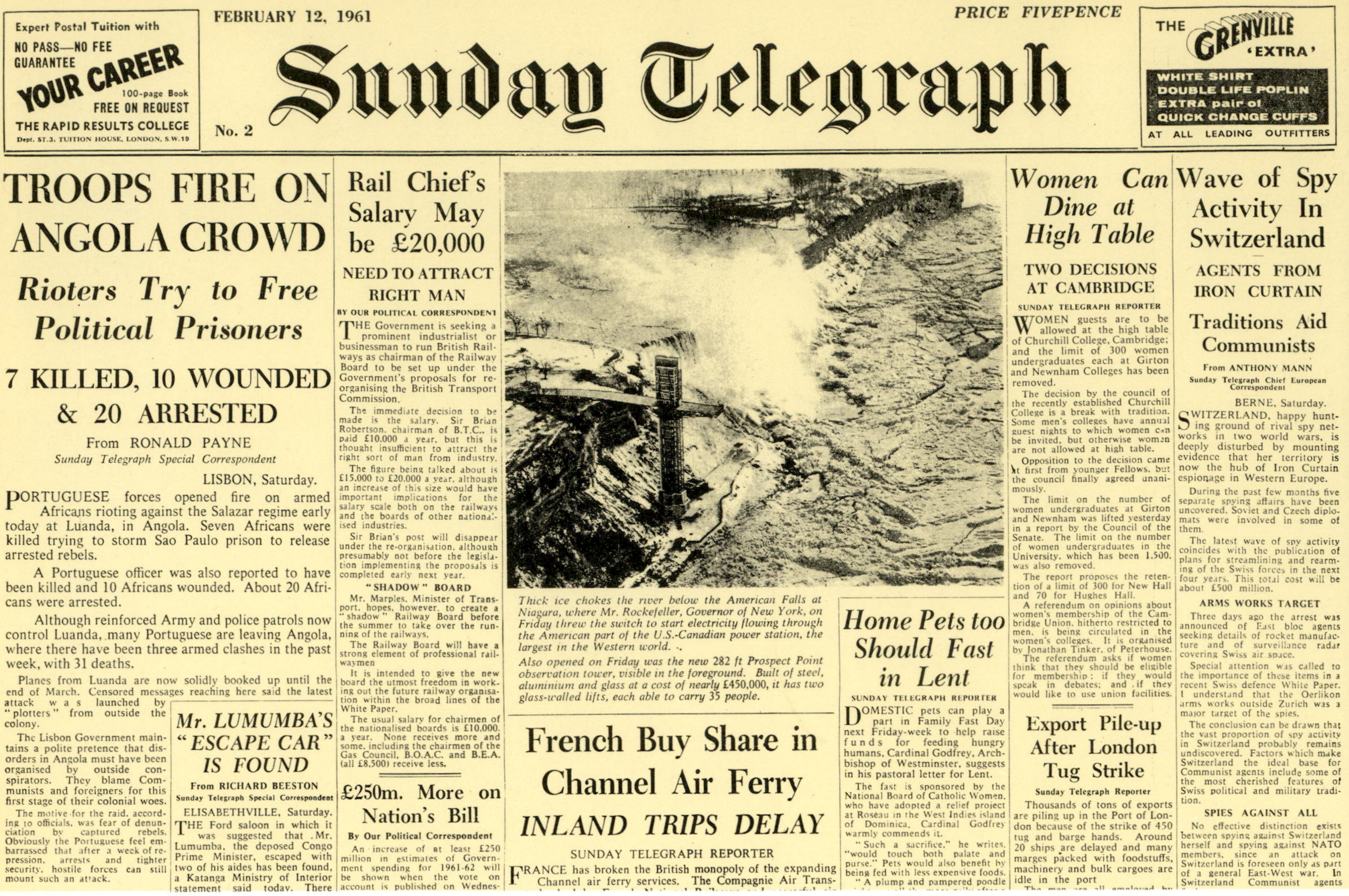

FEBRUARY 12, 1961
No. 2
PRICE FIVEPENCE

Sunday Telegraph

TROOPS FIRE ON ANGOLA CROWD

Rioters Try to Free Political Prisoners

7 KILLED, 10 WOUNDED & 20 ARRESTED

From RONALD PAYNE
Sunday Telegraph Special Correspondent

LISBON, Saturday.

PORTUGUESE forces opened fire on armed Africans rioting against the Salazar regime early today at Luanda, in Angola. Seven Africans were killed trying to storm Sao Paulo prison to release arrested rebels.

A Portuguese officer was also reported to have been killed and 10 Africans wounded. About 20 Africans were arrested.

Although reinforced Army and police patrols now control Luanda, many Portuguese are leaving Angola, where there have been three armed clashes in the past week, with 31 deaths.

Planes from Luanda are now solidly booked up until the end of March. Censored messages reaching here said the latest attack was launched by "plotters" from outside the colony.

The Lisbon Government maintains a polite pretence that disorders in Angola must have been organised by outside conspirators. They blame Communists and foreigners for this first stage of their colonial woes.

The motive for the raid, according to officials, was fear of denunciation by captured rebels. Obviously the Portuguese feel embarrassed that after a week of repression, arrests and tighter security, hostile forces can still mount such an attack.

Mr. LUMUMBA'S "ESCAPE CAR" IS FOUND

From RICHARD BEESTON
Sunday Telegraph Special Correspondent

ELISABETHVILLE, Saturday.

THE Ford saloon in which it was suggested that Mr. Lumumba, the deposed Congo Prime Minister, escaped with two of his aides has been found, a Katanga Ministry of Interior statement said today. There

Rail Chief's Salary May be £20,000

NEED TO ATTRACT RIGHT MAN

BY OUR POLITICAL CORRESPONDENT

THE Government is seeking a prominent industrialist or businessman to run British Railways as chairman of the Railway Board to be set up under the Government's proposals for reorganising the British Transport Commission.

The immediate decision to be made is the salary. Sir Brian Robertson, chairman of B.T.C., is paid £10,000 a year, but this is thought insufficient to attract the right sort of man from industry.

The figure being talked about is £15,000 to £20,000 a year, although an increase of this size would have important implications for the salary scale both on the railways and the boards of other nationalised industries.

Sir Brian's post will disappear under the re-organisation, although presumably not before the legislation implementing the proposals is completed early next year.

"SHADOW" BOARD

Mr. Marples, Minister of Transport, hopes, however, to create a "shadow" Railway Board before the summer to take over the running of the railways.

The Railway Board will have a strong element of professional railwaymen

It is intended to give the new board the utmost freedom in working out the future railway organisation within the broad lines of the White Paper.

The usual salary for chairmen of the nationalised boards is £10,000 a year. None receives more and some, including the chairmen of the Gas Council, B.O.A.C. and B.E.A. (all £8,500) receive less.

£250m. More on Nation's Bill

By Our Political Correspondent

An increase of at least £250 million in estimates of Government spending for 1961-62 will be shown when the vote on account is published on Wednes-

Thick ice chokes the river below the American Falls at Niagara, where Mr. Rockefeller, Governor of New York, on Friday threw the switch to start electricity flowing through the American part of the U.S.-Canadian power station, the largest in the Western world.

Also opened on Friday was the new 282 ft Prospect Point observation tower, visible in the foreground. Built of steel, aluminium and glass at a cost of nearly £450,000, it has two glass-walled lifts, each able to carry 35 people.

French Buy Share in Channel Air Ferry

INLAND TRIPS DELAY

SUNDAY TELEGRAPH REPORTER

FRANCE has broken the British monopoly of the expanding Channel air ferry services. The Compagnie Air Trans-

Home Pets too Should Fast in Lent

SUNDAY TELEGRAPH REPORTER

DOMESTIC pets can play a part in Family Fast Day next Friday-week to help raise funds for feeding hungry humans, Cardinal Godfrey, Archbishop of Westminster, suggests in his pastoral letter for Lent.

The fast is sponsored by the National Board of Catholic Women, who have adopted a relief project at Roseau in the West Indies island of Dominica. Cardinal Godfrey warmly commends it.

"Such a sacrifice," he writes, "would touch both palate and purse." Pets would also benefit by being fed with less expensive foods.

"A plump and pampered poodle

Women Can Dine at High Table

TWO DECISIONS AT CAMBRIDGE

SUNDAY TELEGRAPH REPORTER

WOMEN guests are to be allowed at the high table of Churchill College, Cambridge; and the limit of 300 women undergraduates each at Girton and Newnham Colleges has been removed.

The decision by the council of the recently established Churchill College is a break with tradition. Some men's colleges have annual guest nights to which women can be invited, but otherwise women are not allowed at high table.

Opposition to the decision came at first from younger Fellows, but the council finally agreed unanimously.

The limit on the number of women undergraduates at Girton and Newnham was lifted yesterday in a report by the Council of the Senate. The limit on the number of women undergraduates in the University, which has been 1,500, was also removed.

The report proposes the retention of a limit of 300 for New Hall and 70 for Hughes Hall.

A referendum on opinions about women's membership of the Cambridge Union, hitherto restricted to men, is being circulated in the women's colleges. It is organised by Jonathan Tinker, of Peterhouse.

The referendum asks if women think that they should be eligible for membership: if they would speak in debates; and if they would like to use union facilities.

Export Pile-up After London Tug Strike

Sunday Telegraph Reporter

Thousands of tons of exports are piling up in the Port of London because of the strike of 450 tug and barge hands. Around 20 ships are delayed and many marges packed with foodstuffs, machinery and bulk cargoes are idle in the port

Wave of Spy Activity In Switzerland

AGENTS FROM IRON CURTAIN

Traditions Aid Communists

From ANTHONY MANN
Sunday Telegraph Chief European Correspondent

BERNE, Saturday.

SWITZERLAND, happy hunting ground of rival spy networks in two world wars, is deeply disturbed by mounting evidence that her territory is now the hub of Iron Curtain espionage in Western Europe.

During the past few months five separate spying affairs have been uncovered. Soviet and Czech diplomats were involved in some of them.

The latest wave of spy activity coincides with the publication of plans for streamlining and rearming of the Swiss forces in the next four years. This total cost will be about £500 million.

ARMS WORKS TARGET

Three days ago the arrest was announced of East bloc agents seeking details of rocket manufacture and of surveillance radar covering Swiss air space.

Special attention was called to the importance of these items in a recent Swiss defence White Paper. I understand that the Oerlikon arms works outside Zurich was a major target of the spies.

The conclusion can be drawn that the vast proportion of spy activity in Switzerland probably remains undiscovered. Factors which make Switzerland the ideal base for Communist agents include some of the most cherished features of Swiss political and military tradition.

SPIES AGAINST ALL

No effective distinction exists between spying against Switzerland herself and spying against NATO members, since an attack on Switzerland is foreseen only as part of a general East-West war. In Switzerland Communist agents

▲ The Caledonia Bold, roman and italic, decker headings of the *Sunday Telegraph* (1961), soon abandoned for the 'streamlined' Bodoni style it now has. ▶

Founded in this period (February 1961) the *Sunday Telegraph* made an unusual and interesting but, as it turned out, abortive typographical start. It was the first, and the only, British newspaper to use Caledonia Bold exclusively for its news headlines. This very stylish Linotype face, one of the outstanding designs of the late W. A. Dwiggins, was originally cut for the ill-fated *PM* of New York, as already mentioned; since then a number of U.S. local dailies had used it as a headline type and it was eulogised by American authorities. Specified by John Dreyfus, it was installed by the *Sunday Telegraph* in a full range of sizes, up to its ceiling of 36pt (in roman) and 24pt (in italic). Many factors, however, soon told against it. Thus it was used in conventional decker style, when the day of the capitals-lower-case-capitals decker was already done. With the natural urge of the time to bigger headings, which affected even the 'heavies', the size limitation was serious. Above all, its own stylish elegance was seen to be somehow wrong even for a serious paper aiming to strike a note of some distinction. Caledonia Bold, in short, had beauty; it did not have news impact. Thus the *Sunday Telegraph* soon changed to a free style in Bodoni Bold, roman and italic, mainly in upper- and lower-case, with Bodoni Light for occasional contrast (usually in capitals). Lead stories normally carried a deep three-column heading, leading in 72pt Bodoni Bold roman; all headings were set flush-left, except down-page where Caledonia Bold survived, in 12pt capitals, on the one-par fillers, following the 18pt Caslon Heavy used for the shorts. A title-line in bold modern roman capitals – more Didot than Bodoni in its flavour – early replaced the blackletter of the first issues.

Of the 'popular' Sundays there is little to be said. The *Sunday Express*, as Chapter Seven has noted, continues faithfully, and rightly, with its long-evolved Square Gothic style; it has introduced incidental changes in its feature headlining – including Record Gothic variants like Bold (with italic) and Bold Extended. The two sensationalist circulation-leaders, Murdoch's *News of the World* (which in 1961 at last installed Ludlows) and the IPC *Sunday People*, call for a passing mention in respect of their typographical antics of the early 1970s.

REBECCA WEST: Why I am for Women's Lib—P.6

SUNDAY TELEGRAPH

No. 617 December 24, 1972 Price 5p

UNITED PICK UP THE PIECES P.28

WORSTHORNE
SEASON FOR ILL-WILL P.16

Nixon may halt bombing over Christmas

Public pressure

By DAVID ADAMSON in Washington

PRESIDENT NIXON was understood yesterday to be considering ordering a halt to the bombing of North Vietnam over Christmas. This would help to soothe the increasingly-alarmed feelings of Congress and the American public.

At the same time, it would give the North Vietnamese time to re-group and strengthen their air defences around Hanoi and Haiphong in readiness for the resumption of raids.

It would also cut the limited time which the president has available in which to prove that he can bomb the North Vietnamese into adopting a satisfactory attitude at the negotiating table.

Congress resumes on Jan. 3 and Mr. Nixon, will find it extremely difficult to maintain the offensive after that—particularly if heavy losses of aircraft continue. The international outcry over civilian casualties and widespread damage to the cities must also be reckoned with.

American uncertainty

As the Administration ponders the next step in the uncertain situation caused by the stalling of the Paris peace talks, the most prevalent impression is that no one has any clear views on what to do next.

There is no indication so far that the bombing is persuading the North to make the unspecified decision that Dr. Henry Kissinger said eight days ago was all that was required to unblock the road to peace.

In Paris, the North Vietnamese appear to be waiting for the Americans to give up and return to the talks about the so-called agreement.

Yesterday Hanoi's representatives walked out of a Paris meeting of experts at which they were to have discussed technicalities of the truce negotiations with America.

The North Vietnamese left after denouncing "frenzied air and naval attacks." They declared: "We are obliged to postpone once again the meeting of the representatives and experts until another day."

Heavy losses

One new element in a here-we-go-again situation is the unexpectedly heavy losses sustained by the American Air Force.

There is evidence that the admitted shooting down of 10 of the 100 B-52 heavy bombers used in the operation has disquieted the civilian and military planners. One senior official was reported to have said that losses on this scale could not be sustained for long.

However, there is a belief that the North Vietnamese, who claim to have destroyed 17 B-52s, have expended so many missiles that they are now digging deep into their reserves. The supporting fighter-bombers are also beginning to have some effect in their attempts to suppress the North's defence.

The bombing is controlled by computers manned by a dozen officers at Tansonnhut Air Base, near Saigon. It is an amazingly complex and detailed operation. Reconnaissance aircraft, B-52s, Phantom planes equipped with laser guided smart bombs, layers of patrolling fighters, tankers, aircraft crammed with electronic equipment and rescue helicopters move in and out on their missions with split-second timing.

The defence against this force is fittingly the toughest in the world. Its successes against the B-52s are not attributed to any new development in electronics or missiles although the techniques used have been improved.

Round the clock

The huge bombers are being used for pattern bombing. From a height of seven miles they blanket areas to which they are guided by the computers in Tansonnhut. The raids take place practically around the clock.

Against this force, the North Vietnamese fire volleys of missiles. Experts say that the three-day warning given by President Nixon after the breakdown of the negotiations that Hanoi and Haiphong would be bombed gave the defenders time to prepare.

Civilians were moved out and new missiles and other weapons were moved in. Radar equipment that had been put out of action earlier by Shrike missiles was again in operation.

The area under attack is relatively small. As a result, the defences can be closely grouped, with deadly effect.

Gen. Giap reported killed

By PETER GILL in Saigon

NORTH VIETNAM'S Minister of Defence and C.-in-C., Gen. Giap, 60, is dead, according to reports by South Vietnamese intelligence officers.

They claimed yesterday to have evidence that the General, architect of the French defeat in Indo-China in 1954 and planner of successive attempts to overthrow American-backed régimes in Saigon, was killed on Friday during an inspection tour of military installations at the main North Vietnamese port of Haiphong.

Haiphong, heavily defended by Russian-made S.A.M. 2 missiles, is one of the main targets of the new American bombing campaign against the North.

Kissinger in two minds, and Editorial comment P.16.
Wall Street—P.20.

Hundreds of aircraft have ranged over the city since Monday to dump thousands of tons of bombs on military and industrial installations and to drop new mines into the harbour.

It is said that Gen. Giap died when he trod on a delayed-timing mechanism during a visit to an arms depot to assess damage caused by the bombing. The device could have been a stray American mine intended for the harbour.

The intelligence reports provided little other information. It was not known whether others had died with Gen. Giap. Nor were there any details available on how the information reached Saigon.

'GOOD SOURCE'

In a telephone conversation with a South Vietnamese Army officer attached to the aptly named General Political Warfare Department, I was told last night that the origin of the report was "a very good intelligence source."

The American command in Saigon anounced that two more B-52 bombers, worth more than £3 million each, were lost near Hanoi on Friday morning. This brings the total of B-52 losses to 10 in five days. North Vietnam claims even more.

Denial by N. Vietnam

By Our Staff Correspondent in Paris

The report of the death of Gen. Giap is a product of the psychological warfare services of the United States and South Vietnam, the Hanoi delegation to the Paris peace talks said yesterday.

The comment, it was emphasised, was the only one the delegation "would lower itself" to make.

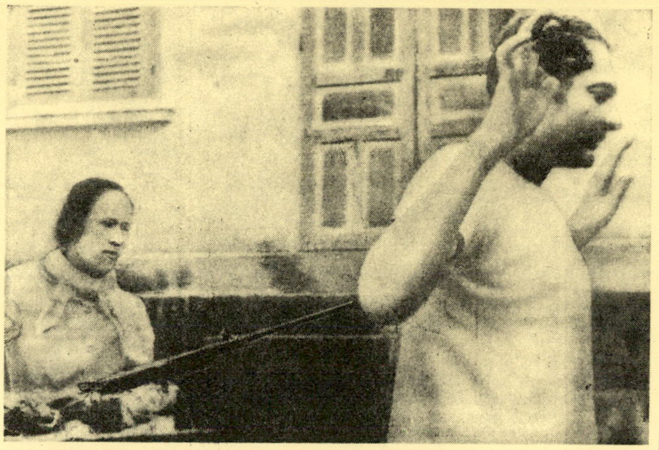

A NORTH VIETNAMESE militiawoman in the Kim Anh district, Vinh Phu Province, North Vietnam, guarding her captive, a shot-down B52 pilot, said by a North Vietnamese source to be U.S. Air Force Major Richard Edgar Johnson.

DRINK-DRIVE WARNING TO CIVIL SERVANTS

SUNDAY TELEGRAPH REPORTER

MORE than 500,000 civil servants throughout Britain, including all Environment Department staff, have been warned not to drink and drive during Christmas. The warning has been circulated to every district office of the department and even driving test centres.

Although it is couched in pleasant terms—"as a reminder to set an example," said the department yesterday — it nevertheless amounts to an order.

Every civil servant is now obliged to report to his superior this week if he has been breath-tested over Christmas.

Under the Civil Service disciplinary code any member who brushes with the law and risks prosecution must report this. Such would be the case of a civil servant failing a breath-test. He must report it.

Many involved

The code also states that a civil servant must report his actions if they are likely to result in publicity, such as a breath-test case could in court. Almost certainly details would be noted on his personal record file, I am told.

He could face a reprimand and in an extreme case such as a drink-driving prosecution involving a death, could lose seniority and therefore suffer a loss of promotion prospects, or he could be moved to an obscure position.

Any second case involving drinking would be regarded as very serious and special Civil Service disciplinary action would follow.

An Environment Department official added: "There are really many people in other jobs who are somewhat similarly placed—policemen, ambulance staff, even bus and train drivers all risk jeopardising their careers if they drink and drive."

PRINCESS OUT AGAIN WITH HUNT

Sunday Telegraph Reporter

PRINCESS ANNE was out with the Duke of Beaufort's Hunt at Foxley, Wiltshire, yesterday despite the controversy which followed two earlier appearances in the hunting field.

Major Gerald A. Gundry, joint master with the Duke of Beaufort, said: "The Princess seemed to enjoy herself thoroughly. She was right up with the hounds most of the time."

About 140 riders were out but there was no kill. "It was not a good day for scent," said one rider. "Although two or three foxes were found they were all lost."

As on the first occasion the Princess's escort was Lieut. Mark Phillips, 24, of the Queen's Dragoon Guards. She travelled to Wiltshire on Friday and stayed with his parents, Major and Mrs. Peter Phillips, at The Mount, in the village of Great Somerford, near Chippenham.

Last night Major Phillips, speaking to me in his centuries-old manor house, said that the Princess and her horses returned to Windsor in the early evening. "I understand they had a very good day."

'UP TO HER'

Lieut. Phillips, an Olympic equestrian gold medallist, now stationed at Catterick, rode his Great Ovation, on which he won at Badminton this year and last.

By following the Zetland and Bedale Hunts earlier, the Princess broke what had been an unwritten rule for nearly 50 years—that the Royal Family should steer clear of controversy by not playing an active part in hunting. The Duke of Windsor rode regularly when Prince of Wales.

A spokesman for the R.S.P.C.A. said yesterday that the society "very much regretted" that the Princess had been hunting again as she was a "trend-setter," and others would follow her example.

He added: "If she wants to ride to hounds it's up to her. We have to accept that."

A Buckingham Palace spokesman said: "We have no comment. It's entirely an individual decision whether a member of the family goes hunting or not."

TRUMAN 'IN COMA'

By Our Staff Correspondent in Washington

Former President Truman, 88, went into a coma last night and was completely unresponsive to any kind of stimulus, doctors at the Research Hospital, Kansas City, said. But later they said that he showed slight improvement, though still critical.

UNITED DRAW

Tommy Docherty, Manchester United's new manager, saw his team draw yesterday 1-1 with Leeds at Old Trafford.

United pick up the pieces—P.28

SUNDAY TELEGRAPH

Owing to industrial action by members of the National Graphical Association in the composing room, many readers last week received an edition of *The Sunday Telegraph* not appropriate to the area in which they live. We apologise to them for any inconvenience.

35 killed in air crash

A Norwegian internal airliner crashed 12 miles from Oslo yesterday with the deaths of 35 of the 45 people aboard. Most of the passengers, all Norwegians, save for one Dane, were flying from Aalesund to Oslo to celebrate Christmas.

The plane ran into fog just before crashing in "difficult terrain." Rescuers found the wreckage five hours later when cries were heard from survivors.

There were three crew. The passengers were 19 women, 18 men, four babies and another child.—Reuter.

ANDREI TUPOLEV

Andrei Tupolev, the Russian aircraft designer, has died, Tass news agency reported yesterday. He was 84.—A.P.

Obituary—Page 4

LATE NEWS

CRICKET

(See Page 29)

Australia 466 for 6 at lunch against Pakistan at Adelaide today.—Reuter.

Frauds spree hits Access

By PETER GLADSTONE SMITH

SHOPKEEPERS and security experts said yesterday that the new Access credit card organisation faces massive losses from fraud and bad debt. Cards that went astray when 3,400,000 were distributed two months ago and others that have been stolen have been used for fraudulent spending sprees.

Most shops accepting Access cards are authorised to sell goods worth up to £30 without checking the cardholder's credit.

Shopkeepers say it is quite clear that many young people issued with cards they did not seek have spent beyond the limit of their normal capacity to repay.

The Joint Credit Card Company, issuers of Access, is so concerned about fraud that it has assembled a team of ex-Scotland Yard detectives. At the head is ex-Det. Sgt. Ray Mogg, formerly of "T" Division, with former Det. Sgt. Alfred Laughlan of the Flying Squad.

Other Flying Squad men have been recruited in addition. Overall responsibility for security is in the hands of Mr. Dick Richardson, a former National Westminster Bank inspector.

One shopkeeper estimated the Access losses at 50 per cent.—"a figure so nonsensical we refuse to make any comment," said an Access spokesman.

Beyond limit

Other credit card companies estimated Access losses from fraud and bad debt at ¾ per cent, a figure which no credit card company can carry and remain profitable.

Operation of a credit card system, with the paper work and staff involved, is so expensive that a change of ¼ per cent. of turnover in profitability can make

Continued on Back Page, Col. 7

OTHER PAGES

10m. ITEMS OF MAIL HELD UP

Sunday Telegraph Reporter

MORE than 10 million letters and cards, posted late or badly addressed, were stockpiled at Post Offices last night, ready for delivery on Wednesday. Last deliveries for Christmas were made late yesterday morning.

Much of the stockpiled mail is cards and letters posted second class on Thursday, Friday and yesterday. All mail posted second class by last Monday and first class by Tuesday had been delivered by yesterday afternoon, according to the Post Office.

A Post Office spokesman told me: "We have done our damnedest to get mail, posted on time, to its destination and we have achieved our objective this year.

"Inevitably there are people who post late, but we have no figures on the precise numbers of letters and cards stockpiled for delivery next week." Letters posted yesterday will be sorted on Tuesday when the postmen return to work.

100,000 CASUAL STAFF

Normally the 100,000 delivery and sorting staff handle 35 million items of mail a day. During the past week they, with 100,000 casual staff have dealt with 110 million a day.

This year's Christmas mail has broken all records, with 670 million letters and cards and nine million parcels.

To make matters worse, there is no Christmas Eve delivery. This is the day the Post Office traditionally attempts to clear all undelivered mail.

"This is only the first of a dozen exciting presents I'm giving you over the next 12 days."

Turkey sales record 7½m.

By Our Agricultural Correspondent

The last of a record 7,500,000 Christmas turkeys were sold yesterday in a market which has seen the most stable prices for years. Some supermarkets sold oven-ready birds at 22p a lb., 1½p below last year's prices.

"There has been a steady demand for turkeys and other poultry and there has not been a last-minute rush," said a supermarket spokesman.

'5,000 dead' as quake and fire hit city

By Our Staff Correspondent in Washington

AT least 5,000 people were killed and thousands more injured in an earthquake yesterday which destroyed a large part of the city of Managua, the Nicaraguan capital, according to reports.

The reports, picked up from amateur radio operators, said that fires were raging, electricity supplies cut and that there was a shortage of drinking water.

The health ministry of Costa Rica said it had received a report broadcast by the Nicaraguan health ministry that at least 18,000 people were killed.

Other reports from amateur radio operators put the death figure at 30,000. Of the city's 300,000 inhabitants, 40,000 more were said to be injured and many thousands homeless.

One radio operator said: "Managua has disappeared from the map . . . We don't know how many are dead and we never will know because we'd have to remove the foundations of the city to get at the bodies."

Four tremors

The operator said he counted four major earth tremors. Many buildings that did not collapse were burned to the ground. The army had taken control of the city.

Among the buildings known to be destroyed in the lakeside city were an 18-storey hotel in the city centre, at least two hospitals and a large bank. A number of other hospitals were also damaged.

The American Embassy was reported to have been "flattened," although when a reconnaissance plane flew over the area it appeared that the walls

Continued on Back Page, Col. 4

I.C.I. sign ex-head of M.I.5

By JOHN WEAVER

SIR MARTIN FURNIVAL JONES, the former head of M.I.5, has taken control of a review of security for Imperial Chemical Industries. He retired last April as Britain's Director General of Security.

His task will be to guard the company against industrial espionage and to protect its investment secrets. Fortunes could be made by unscrupulous competitors who obtained prior knowledge of I.C.I.'s activities.

He will pay particular attention to its patented discoveries and to the international movements of its £1,500 million shares. He will also screen the company's 140,000 employees in Britain and keep a close eye on its connections with the manufacture of explosives.

HELP INQUIRY

In January, I.C.I. explosives experts collaborated with Northern Ireland security forces helping them to identify the source of explosives used by the I.R.A.

The firm asked Sir Martin, 60, to head a review of its security when he retired from M.I.5. His appointment started on Sept. 1, but he took time off to give evidence to the Franks Committee review of the Official Secrets Act, Section 2.

A company spokesman said: "We are using Sir Martin's experience in a review of our security arrangements. This covers everything from the theft of an office typewriter to investment movements. We tend to buy the best."

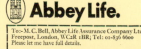

Daily Mirror

NEW POULSON CASE SENSATION

● Lord George-Brown blasts 'hush hush' holiday story

● Anthony Crosland hits out over gift of antique silver

EUROPE'S BIGGEST DAILY SALE

3p Tuesday, January 30, 1973 No. 21,474

I PROTEST!

THE Poulson bankruptcy affair, which has already led to the resignation of a Home Secretary, caused two more sensations yesterday.

They were the involvement in the case of top Labour politicians Anthony Crosland and Lord George-Brown.

Both hit back last night at the way they have become entangled in the resumed bankruptcy hearing at Wakefield, Yorks.

By EDWARD VALE

Mr. Crosland, the Shadow Environment Minister, told a Press conference at the House of Commons that it was "absolutely scandalous" that people should be named in such circumstances without having the right of reply.

Then Lord George-Brown added his voice to the criticism of statements made yesterday during the questioning of former international architect John Poulson.

Lord George-Brown, former Cabinet Minister and Deputy Leader of the Labour Party, denied that he had been given a holiday in Majorca by Mr. Poulson.

Lord George-Brown said he had never met or corresponded with Mr. Poulson.

He declared: "I would like to protest in the strongest possible terms against reference to public men of a damaging character being made by supposedly responsible lawyers without any attempt to communicate with them to verify the facts, particularly since no remedy in libel is available."

The marathon bankruptcy hearing led to the resignation from the Cabinet of Home Secretary Reginald Maudling, whose name had been linked with Poulson companies.

The new storm blew up over questions put to Mr. Poulson by Mr. Muir Hunter, Q.C. for the bankruptcy trustees.

Mr. Poulson told Mr. Hunter that he gave Mr. Crosland an antique silver coffee pot which cost about £100.

Incognito

The gift was made after Mr. Crosland—then the Education Secretary—performed a school opening ceremony.

Mr. Hunter told the hearing that Mr. Crosland had written a letter of thanks.

The letter added: "I tremble to think how much it cost."

The reference to Lord George-Brown came later in the hearing. Mr. Hunter spoke of a Mr. and Mrs. George Brown going incognito on holiday to Majorca in 1964.

He read from a letter said to have been written by Mr. Poulson to Mr. T. Dan Smith, a prominent figure in the North East of England.

The letter said that accommodation for Mr. and Mrs. George Brown had been booked at the Formentor Hotel in the name of Mr. and Mrs. T. Dan Smith "to ensure there is no undue publicity."

Mr. Hunter asked Mr. Poulson which George Brown he had been writing about.

Lord George-Brown.

'That damn coffee pot'

ANTHONY CROSLAND said last night that until his name was mentioned at the Poulson hearing, he did not remember receiving "that damn coffee pot."

Asked what the pot looked like Mr. Crosland, pictured last night, above, replied: "I don't know. I haven't seen it for seven years."

But he said his wife had now found it in a cupboard and he intended to send it to the bankruptcy trustees.

By VICTOR KNIGHT

He said he did not wish "to d[...] the creditors of anything they [...] receive."

Mr. Crosland added: "All I wan[...] get rid of the damn thing."

He said he would be amazed if t[...] fetched anything like the value[...] tioned during the hearing.

Mr. Crosland said it was a custo[...] Ministers performing public fu[...] should receive a memento.

Fifteen Britons die in plane crash

AT least fifteen British holidaymakers were killed last night when an airliner crashed in northern Cyprus.

They were among thirty-seven passengers and crew who died when the aircraft hit a wooded mountainside.

The plane, an Egyptian-owned Ilyushin turbo-prop, was on a scheduled flight from Cairo to Nicosia.

Some witnesses said it exploded in mid-air before crashing in flames.

Ridge

The plane was making its landing approach when it hit the top of a 2,000ft. mountain ridge twelve miles north of Nicosia.

All the passengers aboard were Europeans.

The Britons, believed to have been mostly middle-aged couples were on a £175 package tour organised by the holiday firm of Wings Ltd., of Welwyn Garden City, Herts.

They had flown to Cyprus from Gatwick Airport on January 18, then left for Cairo and Luxor, in Egypt, the next day.

When the crash happened they were flying back to Nicosia to continue their journey to London.

The ill-fated plane had flown over Nicosia airport and was taking a wide turn ready for its landing approach when it crashed.

Blaze

The Nicosia control tower lost contact with the plane after the pilot said he was coming in to land.

Late last night firefighters were tackling a forest blaze caused by the crash.

Two R A F helicopters were among rescue services which went to the scene of the crash.

▲ The *Daily Mirror* of the early 1970s continued the formula it had long pioneered.

Typographical difference in *The Sun* lay in the substitution of Tempo Heavy Condensed for the gothics of the *Mirror*. ▶

THE Sun

FORWARD WITH THE PEOPLE 3p

Tuesday, January 30, 1973

NEW POULSON CASE SHOCK

MINISTER AND THE '£500 COFFEE POT'

All I want to do is to get rid of the bloody thing, says Crosland

By MICHAEL McDONOUGH and GORDON BROOME

A TOP Minister in the last Labour Government was named yesterday in the Poulson bankruptcy case.

The Minister, Anthony Crosland, received a silver coffee pot after he opened a school designed by architect John Poulson.

Labour's former deputy leader, Lord George-Brown, was also mentioned during the hearing.

It was suggested that he had a holiday at Mr Poulson's expense. But he and the architect denied this.

'KARATE CHOP'

Last night Mr Crosland said he was sending his gift back.

"All I want to do is to get rid of the bloody thing," he said.

He added: "I feel like somebody innocently walking through Hyde Park and somebody gives him a karate chop."

He said he would return the coffee pot to Mr Poulson's bankruptcy trustees.

"I don't care twopence about the pot and, if this is stirring up trouble somewhere, the trustees can have it," he said.

"I don't care. It is of no interest to me in the slightest degree, this damned pot."

Asked if the pot would harm his political reputation, he replied: "I would think it would be treated as a storm in a teacup, which it is."

During yesterday's court hearing, at Wakefield,

Continued on Page 5

Ex-striptease star Rusty Humphreys with her husband

STRIPPER IN PLOT CASE

By ROBERT TRAINI

FORMER Soho stripper "Rusty" Humphreys will appear in court with 10 men today following the massive porn swoops by Scotland Yard.

Mrs Humphreys was charged last night with offering £2,000 to the victim of an attempted murder not to give evidence.

She was also accused of conspiracy to cause grievous bodily harm.

Mrs Humphreys, whose husband, James, is believed to be in Spain, will face magistrates at Old Street Court. Mrs Hum-

Turn to Page Two

PAY AND PRICES—VIC FEATHER HITS BACK

The TUC is not a rubber stamp!

THE TRADE UNIONS believe that there must be a policy against inflation. We have been saying this for years, and not just yesterday.

What the trade union movement does not accept is that wages and salaries are the only factor affecting prices.

The freeze on wages has not brought about a freeze on prices. There were hundreds of price rises during the freeze and there will be thousands during Phase Two.

It is not wages—of farm workers or shop assistants—that pushed up the price of beef or that are now pushing up the price of chicken.

And you can't blame today's pay packets for the soaring cost of houses built 40, 50, and 60 years ago.

If British goods are not selling well enough in the world's markets, it is not because all our competitors are paying lower wages. Wages here are only at about the average for industrial countries, and in the past 10 years our rate of increase has been below the average.

VIC FEATHER replies to yesterday's Sun leader.

It is not true to say that new moves have been suggested by the Government and the TUC said "we cannot talk about them."

We went on talking, at Downing Street and Chequers, as long as there was a point in it. But there is not much point in talking about shaping Phase Two, when decisions have already been made by the Government. We want a better choice from the Government than "any policy you like—so long as it's ours."

Positively, we want direct action

Continued on Page Two

16 BRITONS KILLED AS PLANE HITS MOUNTAIN

SIXTEEN Britons on a package holiday died last night when an airliner crashed on a mountainside in Cyprus.

They were among 37 people aboard the plane—a Soviet-built Ilyushin 18—operated by the Egyptian airline Misrair. There were no survivors.

The Britons—15 holidaymakers and a tour company representative—were on a scheduled flight from Cairo to Nicosia, the capital of Cyprus. They were to have spent two days there before returning home.

The jet crashed on a 2,00ft-high ridge on the heavily wooded slopes of the Kyrenian Mountains in North Cyprus.

After the crash, flames burst from the plane. A rescue team found bodies scattered among the wreckage.

Nicosia airport officials said the plane crashed as it took a wide turn on its way in to land.

£200 disaster — Page Seven

NORWICH ARE MASSACRED! —See Back Page

NEWS OF THE WORLD

SUNDAY, APRIL 29, 1973 WORLD'S LARGEST SUNDAY SALE No. 6,752 PRICE 5p

SHOWPAGE SPECIAL
THE NEW TV STAR WHO SWITCHES ON THE GIRLS
PAGE 12

VICE KINGS EXPOSED

Landlords get £150 a week from 'sin for sale' girls

This is Emmanuel Francis Coleiro. He is Maltese. He is greedy. He profits from vice. We name him today as an evil spider in a web the police must tear apart.

SHOCK INVESTIGATION BY TREVOR KEMPSON, JOHN LISNERS AND A TEAM OF REPORTERS

TODAY the News of the World exposes London's new kings of vice. After months of painstaking work, we start naming the men who have become rich by cashing in on the booming sin-for-sale trade.

Outwardly, they are respectable, wealthy businessmen, moving in influential circles, living in opulent homes and running property companies.

But these men have not prospered solely by the conventional development of housing estates or industrial sites. They have grown rich trading on human vices by letting flats at sky-high rents to prostitutes.

They let some apartments for £35 a week and tiny, single rooms for £12.50 to ordinary tenants. Pricey, perhaps. Yet not exorbitant by today's Soho or Mayfair standards.

But they rent many others only to girls who sell sex.

FLATS

And for each of these small flats used by call girls to entertain their clients, the vice landlords collect fantastic rents of £130 or more every week.

Three men control most of this undesirable property empire.

Today and over the next next few weeks, our investigators will:

- Name these vice landlords;
- Detail how thousands of pounds are paid in cash to them by the prostitutes each week;
- Outline the methods they use to avoid police attention;
- And reveal the location of some of the properties and the identities of the girls who use them.

The News of the World, of course, undertakes to give the fullest co-operation to Scotland Yard.

A 10-man team, led by

TURN TO PAGE 3

NEXT WEEK

- We name another vice king and his associates
- We tell how the cash flows from the girls to the coffers of the sex supremos

DON'T MISS THE SECOND SENSATIONAL REPORT

NIXON FIGHTS FOR HIS LIFE ON TV

From RAY KERRISON in New York

PRESIDENT NIXON is expected to go on television this week to bare his soul and give America his own account of the Watergate Affair — the bugging sensation that threatens to shatter his future.

Only a political miracle can now save his scalp as the scandal has not so much knocked at his door but blown it from its hinges.

Even one of his greatest admirers, millionaire economist William F. Buckley, Jnr, fears there may soon be a move by Congress to impeach and punish the President.

Says Buckley: "Even those who decline to believe that Nixon had foreknowledge of the affair believe that his supervision of the Watergate investigation was at best self-serving, at worst criminal.

Evidence

"It is likely that a considerable majority of American people believe Nixon knew way before April 17 that people surrounding him were conspiring to obstruct justice."

[On April 17 Nixon suddenly ordered his staff to give sworn evidence to a Senate inquiry into the Watergate scandal.]

But, says Buckley, it is imperative to defeat any motion to impeach Nixon because it could only reflect on the State. Impeachment is trial by the Senate, which could sack the President.

Instead, he urges Congress simply to censure the President if

TURN TO PAGE TWO

Seeing double

WHEN you see something good—look again. It will be twice as good if it's the Evans twins.

Dayle and Nicola are already the tops Down Under when it comes to TV commercials.

They are still only 16 and work 9-to-5 in a New South Wales bank. What odds they will soon interest some film producer as a profitable investment?

HEATH IN NEW UNION TALKS

TALKS between Mr Heath and the trade unions are expected to take place soon after Tuesday's May Day protest strike.

This new move to involve the TUC in managing the country's economy—which I forecast a month ago—emerged last night (*writes David Roxan, Our Industrial Correspondent*).

Tough bargaining is expected, with the unions demanding action on high food prices, bigger old age pensions and changes in the Industrial Relations Act.

In return, the Prime Minister will seek some limitation of wage demands once the present limitation of £1 plus 4 per cent is phased out.

Several million people will stop work on Tuesday. But the May Day TUC strike, planned as a national stoppage, will be only patchy.

Some factories and offices, however, may have to close because of the difficulties of getting to work.

Trains

This was the weekend round-up of what will happen:

ENGINEERING: Many large firms will be hit, including a number in the car industry. But some workers will keep the lathes going.

TRAINS: Nearly all will be at a standstill.

BUSES: Some provincial services will be hit. In London most are expected to run. Half the Underground services will be cut.

AIRLINES: Few planes will take off because of the maintenance men's strike.

NEWSPAPERS: No national or London evenings. Few provincial newspapers will come out.

MAY DAY MADNESS —Page 4

ORDEAL OF DEAD 'ANGEL'

THE HELL'S ANGEL whose bound and weighted body was found in a harbour was still alive when his killers hurled him in.

The macabre news was given by a pathologist yesterday to detectives hunting the murderers of 16-year-old coffee bar cowboy Clive Olive.

Now more tests are being carried out to discover how long the torture in the water lasted.

Detective Chief Superintendent Jim Marshall, who is leading the hunt said: "In view of the way he died it's important that anyone who knew him should come forward.

"The killing was a particularly dastardly crime."

Olive's body was found 11 days ago at Shoreham, Sussex. His wrists and ankles were tightly lashed with rope and weights were tied to his ankles.

Weather

SUNNY spells and showers, rather cold. Max temp 11 deg C (52 deg F). OUTLOOK: Sunnier.

TOP PEOPLE IN 'SEX RING' PROBE

By PETER EARLE

TWO police inquiries into alleged corruption have been launched by Sir Robert Mark, the Commissioner of the Metropolitan Police, News of the World investigators can reveal today.

The first follows allegations that girls attached to a model agency have been procured for immoral purposes for well-known public figures.

Silence

We can reveal that stories about a "top people's sex ring" began to emerge when police raided pornographic bookshops in London.

Detectives' inquiries have been met by silence from many high-level people who wish to hush up the whole affair.

Police are again to interrogate several girls they have already interviewed. One now has a police guard.

The second corruption inquiry involves the police themselves—and accusations against dozens of London's officers, some of them high-ranking.

This follows sensational allegations of graft against more than 30 officers in a dossier sent to Scotland Yard by the ex-strip king Jimmy Humphreys.

Police are seeking Humphreys—believed to be abroad—to question him about a number of matters.

Throughout his Soho career, Humphreys kept a detailed diary of his meetings with both criminals and policemen. Pictures of some pages of this diary are in our possession with names censored out by Humphreys himself.

Humphreys is said to have returned to Britain twice recently.

CAUSE FOR CONCERN Page 4

The super-tabloid sledgehammer style adopted by the nine-column *News of the World*. The *Sunday People* is comparable.

Going over to a nine-column make-up, they competed with each other in presenting their front pages as if they were, not broadsheet, but bloated super-tabloid. Multi-line headings above 96pt, vast reverse blocks, the whole heavy battery of Ludlow Gothics and Tempo (including Black Extended) – these performances have made tabloids like the *Sunday Mirror* look positively restrained. At this point it may be noted that for the tabloids in general, more particularly for the two mornings, the *Daily Mirror* and the *Sun*, there has been no radical change in the tabloid design formula so brilliantly devised and executed by the *Mirror* over many years. Typographically Murdoch's *Sun* echoes the *Mirror*, simply using Tempo Heavy Condensed instead of the Gothics; the difference between the two papers, and the reason for the *Sun's* success, lies in brash journalism, not in design.

MANCHESTER GUARDIAN

No. 33,053 MONDAY SEPTEMBER 29 1952 Price 3d

STATE BUSES HELD "ABOVE THE LAW"

Ministry Refuses Equal Terms to Private Services

PROBLEM FOR CABINET

NAHAS TO FACE CHARGES

Minister's Attack on Wafd Leader

NEW ATTEMPT AT KOREAN TRUCE

U.N. Proposals on Repatriation

TRIPLE CHOICE

PUBLIC AUDIT BY DEMOCRATS

Union Contributors to Illinois Funds

LABOUR SEARCH FOR UNITY —AND A PROGRAMME

Trials Ahead on Foreign Policy

When the *Manchester Guardian* went to front-page news in 1952 the title was changed from blackletter to Perpetua Bold Titling with a simple Century Bold decker heading style. This continued (below) after the 1959 dropping of 'Manchester'.

THE GUARDIAN

35,520 Manchester Tuesday September 13 1960 Price 3d

M. LUMUMBA STILL AT LARGE

Appearance at radio station after warrant for arrest

NEW PREMIER'S PLANS

"DOWNRIGHT LYING" BY SECURITY OFFICER

Dr Reeves deported from South Africa

THE GUARDIAN

Monday May 6 1963 Price 4d

Tories challenged to name companies

Which to protect—and which supply funds?

BY OUR PARLIAMENTARY STAFF

Dominican troops on border

Guard on Chinese cafes

A Labour defeat in co-op vote

With the *Guardian* producing in London from 1960 the heading style began to change to Century lower-case, with Garamond Bold for contrast.

In the broadsheet daily field the development of the *Guardian* was of particular interest, even though it did not attract the attention accorded to the transformations of the *Daily Mail* and *The Times*, discussed later. The previous chapter made a brief reference to the *Manchester Guardian's* change to front-page news in 1952. The style changes then effected were simple. Advised by me the late A. P. Wadsworth (then editor) changed the news headline dress from the long-used Cheltenham Bold and Transit to Century Bold, roman and italic, retaining the conventional decker style. The title was changed, deleting the definite article, from blackletter to 42pt Perpetua Bold Titling. The title-style, increased to 48pt, continued after the dropping of *Manchester* in 1959 and the decker headings initially survived the opening of production in London the following year. Page format was still the old seven columns. By the spring of 1963 format was changed to eight columns and the decker headings, with their main lines in capitals, supplanted by upper- and lower-case styles, somewhat gingerly at first. The italic as well as the roman of Century Bold continued to be used, there was some retention of subsidiary decks, Century Bold Extended was called on in 14pt and 18pt for single-column and minor double-column headings, and the distinctly unnewsy Garamond Bold (in 30pt) as a principal single-column contrast style. A process of rationalisation resulted, by the opening of the 1970s, in an all-Century style, in roman, Bold, Light and Bold Extended (in the larger sizes). Features, which had been set in a variety of bastard measures, with immense and space-wasting rivers of white,

LEGGE Locks

THE GUARDIAN

London Saturday January 27 1973 5p

STEEL PLATES 2,000 tons in stock S.M.THOMPSON LTD. STEEL STOCKIST MIDDLESBROUGH 45161

Council houses hit hardest in rates leap

By JOHN ARDILL, Regional Affairs Correspondent

A massive rates increase throughout the country, now being put as high as 30 per cent to 40 per cent in places, will fall hardest on council house tenants and other people in lower-valued houses.

Figures produced by one Midlands council show that an increase of 10 per cent in the council's total rate levy would mean an increase of 34 per cent for a typical council house. With no increase at all in the levy, a typical council house would have to pay 20.14 per cent more than last year, and a council flat 6 per cent more.

TV film on Poulson banned

By Nicholas de Jongh

Shares slide again

Bombs to the last

From Martin Woollacott

The £3M haul of Mr Big

By PETER HARVEY

CEASEFIRE DAY in Vietnam—but in Cambodia the war continues. A soldier carries two wounded children to safety after a Communist attack near Romeas

Chicken flutters on to the prices bandwagon

By PETER RODGERS

Kidnap victim freed

From our Correspondent in Madrid

Rethink on Maplin traffic

By DAVID FAIRHALL, Air Correspondent

Ellen's life of loneliness and heartache

Help the Aged

Spreads Your Goodwill

Help the Aged, Room G7 8 Denman Street, London W1A 2AP

TV, radio—2, 3

The final style was a Century and Bold lower-case simple contrast with a heavy hand-lettered title.

and headed in minimal sizes of Goudy Old Style and Bold, were reasonably standardised and headed in well-controlled sizes of Ludlow Black (whose utility has been noted above in connection with the *Sunday Times*).

Early in 1969 the Perpetua title was supplanted by the 'bold rough capitals' already mentioned in reference to the paper's 'signposting' of its sections. Its news headlining emphasised the Light/Bold contrast, easing out the Bold Extended; normal size of page one lead headings was raised from 48pt to 60pt Century Bold. In 1971 the *Guardian*, a frequent place-winner in the Newspaper Design Award, was for the first time named First in its class. The judges (Raymond Hawkey, Lord Redcliffe-Maud, Tony Bernard Smith) said: 'The *Guardian* possesses the essential quality of impact. It is adept at handling its simple typography. . . . We wonder a little why it makes a practice of putting excessive white beneath main news headings. It is an exceptionally well-organised and well-labelled paper, so that the reader can find his way about easily and speedily.' To which the note may be added that, at around 330,000 a day, the *Guardian* runs neck-and-neck with *The Times*; in 1959, just before the move to London, its circulation was 180,000 (and that was more than three times its 1939 figure).

Daily Mail MORNING SPECIAL

NO. 19,240 FOR QUEEN AND COMMONWEALTH FRIDAY, FEBRUARY 28, 1958 PRICE 2½D.

Heath, Hammersley, Bellson guilty—sentence today

RIDGE FREE ON BAIL

Comment

WEAKENING BRITAIN

Reinforcing

Recruiting

Conferring

Kiss for warder after his 'agony'

By LOUIS KIRBY

CHARLES Feild Williams Ridge, the 59-year-old Chief Constable of Brighton, was last night acquitted of conspiring to obstruct the course of justice.

He was released on bail amid dramatic scenes at the Old Bailey after being on trial for 19 days.

As he ran down the steps from the dock he embraced one warder and kissed another, weeping and saying over and over again: "Thank God, thank God."

Lyons is cleared

He was bewildered

Jubilant

THIS MAN LAWRENCE DOES IT AGAIN

Two-page Daily Mail fine focus on the Brighton Affair—Pages 4 and 5

35 die in day-trip plane disaster

£750,000,000—and all on HP

Brother killed

Kenneth Horne has stroke

The rebel inch

The vanished £15,000 bonds

MRS BUSBY BREAKS THE NEWS TO MATT

By MONTY COURT

TWO H-bombs fired by Russia

THE PRIEST

THE NAMES

THE TRUTH

Congratulations, Sir Winston

MP to quit

TV backs Hallé

Cheaper tyres

This is the show of shows

Win your ideal home

DR. FUCHS: 130 MILES TO GO

Family Fitness in March winds and April showers

MARMITE for goodness and flavour

▸ The *Express*-style Century/gothic formula, with full banner, as established in the *Daily Mail* by the late 1950s.

The *Daily Mail* revolution of 1964–66 is of special interest, even though the paper, in its broadsheet form, no longer exists. For the *Mail* was the first major paper to follow the *Observer* in taking Century Schoolbook and Bold for its main headline ingredient; demonstrating the potentialities of this type for bold 'popular' layout; and it has to be added that Schoolbook has continued as the principal heading style of the tabloid – or, as it is officially termed, 'compact' paper – into which the *Mail* was transformed in 1971. The *Mail's* revolution was also significant because of its precursor, the importation in 1963 of an outside graphic designer. The droll circumstances of this episode were recounted in an address I gave to the Wynkyn de Worde Society on 26 September 1968:

'The contribution of the *Mail's* imported "typographical expert" (as they called him) was to spatter its news and features pages with an extraordinarily eclectic mixture of Monotype jobbing faces. Cheek by jowl were New Clarendon 617, Grot 215 and 216, Placard Condensed 515 and that true nineteenth-century spindle-shanks, Victoria Condensed Titling 181. Stirred in with the paper's then existing Ludlow Century Bold and Bold Extended style, this astounding *mélange* made

Daily Mail
News Chronicle
NO. 21,725 FOR QUEEN AND COMMONWEALTH 4 SATURDAY, MARCH 5, 1966 PRICE 4d.

Napkin girl goes home to mother

By Daily Mail Reporter

THE TEN-YEAR-OLD girl who was sent to a children's home in the school cutlery row was reunited with her mother yesterday afternoon.

She was driven from the home and handed over to her mother at the Surrey County Council's children's department at Tolworth Tower, Tolworth.

After the reunion, the mother, who is 38, said: "She will be going back to school on Monday.

"I don't know which school I will be sending her to. I have not decided.

"But I hope to send her to a school where they will let her take serviettes to dinner. Otherwise I shall send her to a restaurant for dinner."

On Wednesday a juvenile court at Kingston, Surrey, took the girl from her mother's care because the mother refused to promise to send her to school. They sent her to a children's home for a fortnight.

The mother had kept her eight months at home because the headmaster had banned the girl from cleaning her cutlery at school meals with a napkin.

On BBC 2 on Thursday, Mr. Robert Aitken, Kingston's deputy education officer, explained why the headmaster of St. Andrew's and St. Mark's School, Surbiton, had refused to allow the girl to use a napkin.

He said: "The habit spread. Children were spitting on cutlery and wiping it with napkins or handkerchiefs, sometimes not clean handkerchiefs. The head felt he had to stop it."

The girl, who was moved to a second children's home on Thursday after a special meeting of the juvenile court, was released after Mr. John Riley, Kingston's children's officer, had talked with Mr. William Parsons, chairman of the council's children's committee, and the Home Office.

Agreed

Mr. Roy Jenkins, the Home Secretary, later phoned Mr. Parsons and told him he agreed with his decision to send the girl home.

Mr. Riley, 47-year-old father of four young children, said last night: "I mulled this over all day yesterday and decided it was best for the girl to go back to her mother.

"I told my chairman and the town clerk what I thought and they backed me up. We then contacted the Home Office and later Mr. Jenkins broke off a lunchtime appointment in London to telephone my chairman and say he fully approved of our decision.

"I have applied to the

Comment

Harold the Second

WHEN MR. WILSON gave his eve-of-battle address to his MPs this week, one of them staggered out exclaiming: "It was like King Henry V before Agincourt!"

The honourable member had mistaken the play. The PRIME MINISTER was, of course, drawing freely on a little-known Shakespearean work (one of the Histories) known to scholars as *Harold The Second—Part Two.*

It bears a strong likeness in places to other of the Bard's works. For instance, there is the scene where Harold, whipping his men to a frenzy before the battle of Westminster, ends: "Cry God for Harold, Jim and Brother George!"

This follows the soliloquy in [illegible]h Harold paces alone [illegible] the messengers have ar[illegible]ed hot-foot bringing polls. He chews a pipe-stem and speaks:

"I have not stopped mine ears to their demands,
I have not been desirous of their wealth,
Nor much oppressed them with great subsidies,
Then why should they love Edward more than me?"

Alarums

[illegible]CALLS in his advisers:
"[illegible]ll thing! That [illegible]llaghan
Whom now I keep in service;
He does make our fire,
Fetch in our wood and serve in offices
That profit us. What ho! Slave! Callaghan!"

There is a council of war in which Harold shows the festering doubts that belie

COMING DOWN YOUR WAY MORE OFTEN . . . A GPO TV DETECTOR CAR

BBC squeezes the bilkers

By BRIAN DEAN

A NEW WAR is being waged on TV-radio licence dodgers who rob the BBC of £10 million a year. The Post Office has doubled its fleet of detector vans to trap pirate viewers.

Other steps include putting all licence records on to computers.

The lost income would help the BBC—now £8 million in the red—to fulfil its guarantee to the Postmaster-General, Mr. Wedgwood Benn, to retain the licence at £5 for the next two years.

Plans to catch the dodgers are being drawn up in top-level talks between the BBC and the Post Office.

A GPO official said last night: "Our detector vans are quite effective. When one moves into an area there is a rush to buy licences."

Jon

"At least we'll be able to see the politicians blush when they make their promises."

SAILOR KILLED BY SHELL

ROYAL NAVY Petty Officer Kenneth McKenzie was killed last night when a war-time shell he was defusing exploded.

He died after being taken to Poole General Hospital, Dorset.

Granada joins Levin's attack on the political switch-off

By Daily Mail Reporter

GRANADA Television last night rebelled against the rules on TV debates laid down by the three main political parties. The company attacked the three-party agreement as an attempt "to preserve television as a medium of official persuasion and not of open democratic debate."

The Granada statement is the first challenge by a television company to the rules on pre-election TV debates agreed by the Labour, Conservative and Liberal parties.

You needn't wait

Dora Bryan will be new 'Dolly'

By Daily Mail Reporter

COMEDIENNE Dora Bryan last night accepted an offer of the title role in the Drury Lane musical *Hello, Dolly!*

The offer came from the managing director of the company presenting the show after a personal recommendation from the present "Dolly," Mary Martin.

The 52-year-old American star saw Miss Bryan's appearance on the *Eamonn Andrews Show* on television two weeks ago and immediately said: "That's my successor."

Miss Martin is leaving *Hello, Dolly!* in May for a holiday.

Miss Bryan, who is 42, said last night: "It's lovely — I'm thrilled."

She has been starring in her own show at Liverpool, *The Dora Bryan Show*, which closed last week after a ten-week run.

DORA BRYAN

Mary Martin has been Dolly of the London show since its opening on December 2. Before that she was the star of a production which toured America.

After last night's performance, her husband, Mr. Richard Halliday, said: "This is wonderful news about Dora. Mary saw her on television and immediately remembered her so vividly. She would be a great Dolly, she said.

"She called Binky Beaumont (the managing director) and said: 'For heaven's sake why hasn't anyone done anything about this wonderful woman? Why are we looking to America for the next Dolly when we have one right here?'"

Zsa Zsa to wed

LOS ANGELES, Friday
Zsa Zsa Gabor, divorced from her fourth husband yesterday, announced today that she was marrying a Texas millionaire, Mr. Joshua Gosden.—BUP.

Airman on bunker blaze charge

By Daily Mail Reporter

DETECTIVES investigating a £1 million fire which killed three firemen at an RAF station, arrested an airman yesterday.

The man, Leading Aircraftman John Cheeseman, 21, appeared before a special court at North Walsham, Norfolk, later, and was remanded in custody for a week.

He was accused of setting fire to a building at the RAF's secret radar and signals station at Neatishead on February 16.

Detective - Superintendent Tom Smith, head of Norfolk CID, said the charge was connected with the fire which broke out that day in an unoccupied technical room 60ft. under the station.

The RAF said after the hearing that Cheeseman, father of a six-month-old child, of RAF Horsham St. Faith's married quarters, near Norwich, was not a technician but he did work in the station's underground radar bunker.

DAILY MAIL, FLEET ST. 6000

LATE NEWS

SHIP RIDDLE
Police [illegible] death of 50-year-old seaman found in locker on board tanker Eddyfirth at Gosport, Hampshire.

GARAGE RAIDS
Two men, one with shotgun, held up Caffyns Garage, Sevenoaks, and Darenth Service Station, near Farningham, Kent. Escaped in white Triumph sports car.

● WEATHER: Cloudy at first. Details: Page NINE.

LATE WIRE.—Best from Haydock: SOME ANGEL (1.45 nap) and SANDY ABBOT (4.15).

▲ The Schoolbook/Schoolbook Bold revolution in the *Daily Mail*. First the 'split splash' make-up.

a sort of obscene porridge of the editorial display. I say nothing of the language of the stonehands of a fast-moving, many-editioned daily paper, wrestling with loose type after years of the safety and speed of slug make-up. The casehands, I gather, developed a remarkable occupational vertigo which regularly afflicted them on reaching the random and led them to pi an inconvenient number of anxiously-awaited headings. So the *Mail* was very shortly driven, with the wry admission that "the typographical expert is rarely also a working journalist with a feel for news", to turn (as it said) to "the journalist with an interest in the use of type".'

The journalist was present in the person of Leslie Sellers, then the paper's production editor, mentioned earlier in this chapter for his contributions to the theory and practice of newspaper design. It was Sellers who carried through the Schoolbook revolution (which involved the special cutting of the larger sizes above 48pt). The new type was phased in discreetly and gradually, the first Schoolbook Bold upper- and lower-case front page lead heading appearing at the end of July 1964. This was one of the main aims of the exercise – to break the tyranny of the full-page banner in dominating capitals and to free the

BROOKS LEADS THE INDUSTRY

Daily Mail

News Chronicle

NO. 22,062 FOR QUEEN AND COMMONWEALTH FRIDAY, APRIL 7, 1967 PRICE 4d.

YESTERDAY ROBIN GOODFELLOW gave a 27-1 double . . . TOMORROW a four page bonus SPORTSMAIL on the Grand National

Comment

Curb these stupid tongues

THE crassness displayed by MR. OTTO SHAW in asking a youth charged with motoring offences if he had slept with his girl friend would be unbelievable if we had not been conditioned by a flow of bizarre statements and actions by magistrates and coroners.

The temptation to play God and deliver moral judgments while dispensing justice must be overwhelming to some of the well-intentioned men and women who are appointed Justices of the Peace.

That a number should succumb to this temptation is all the more unfortunate because, on the whole, the magisterial system works well.

Some 16,000 magistrates administer more than 90 p.c. of Britain's criminal law and they do it with humanity but without fuss.

And, although being made a J.P. is cynically known as acquiring a "poor man's knighthood," they perform their often burdensome duties for a total material benefit of 12s. 6d. a day subsistence allowance.

Professional

HOWEVER, performances such as MR. SHAW'S can only result in increasing pressure to have the magistrates replaced by mini-

Storm over secret BBC 'spy bug'

By JOHN SPICER and MICHAEL LITCHFIELD

A BBC bugging device was hidden in the handbag of a woman who went to see a council welfare officer about her accommodation troubles.

Their conversation was monitored and recorded in a taxi parked outside the council offices in Fulham Broadway, London, S.W.

In the Commons yesterday an MP protested about the incident. And the leader of Hammersmith Council said the BBC's action was "deceitful and undesirable."

The council had agreed to help the BBC in a programme about the homeless, but did not know

Runaway sailor gives up

By Daily Mail Reporter

NAVY deserter Michael Goldsworthy, 21, finally gave himself up last night after nearly a year on the run.

ALL NEXT WEEK IN THE DAILY MAIL

The Health Kick

Ban on speech by Aden UN man

By JOHN DICKIE, Daily Mail Diplomatic Correspondent

THE United Nations mission in Aden was banned from the television screens last night by the Federal Government of South Arabia — only 15 minutes before it was due to go on the air.

Federal Ministers ordered the ban after the prepared text was issued because they were humiliated by the mission's insistence on dealing only with the British Government.

Mr. Hussein Ali Bayoomi, Acting Minister of Information, went on TV instead and said: "If the UN wants to use the Federal Government's facilities it will have to apply to us.

"But it cannot go through the British High Commission to get permission. It must come to us or it will not go on radio or television—not at any cost."

The text of the broadcast contained an extraordinary anti-British outburst by Dr. Manuel Perez-Guerrero, of Venezuela, leader of the three-man mission.

Britain may protest against it to U Thant, UN Secretary-General.

Cassandra, by Wilson

Cassandra, the *Daily Mirror* columnist, who died yesterday, was described by Mr. Harold Wilson last night as "a great craftsman, utterly incorruptible, a dedicated warrior against injustice, complacency and cant."

Cassandra, whose real name was Sir William Connor, will be buried on Monday at the village church at Hambleden, Buckinghamshire. He was 57.

Cassandra by Bernard Levin — Page EIGHT.

DAILY MAIL NORTHCLIFFE HOUSE, E.C.4 FLEET ST 6000

LATE NEWS

▲ A *Daily Mail* straight presentation in Schoolbook/Schoolbook Bold.

Mail from its emulation of the *Express*. Editor Mike Randall (now of the *Sunday Times*) said: 'What we set out to get away from was the old seven or eight-column splash banner which appeared relentlessly every day. Not merely because this was anyone else's technique but because by slavish adherence to it you cannot avoid the false emphasis which it gives. . . . The whole system creates a straitjacket from which you cannot escape. What we have been evolving is a system which allows flexibility.'

From this arose the style of the 'split' splash, of which Randall was very fond; in its developed form this ran the second main story with a seven-column line in Schoolbook, reading into columns one and two, with the splash itself centralised, under a deep, banked Schoolbook Bold heading, either across three or four columns, and often boxed. This style, however, created its own 'straitjacket' and did not survive Randall's departure from the editorial chair; but the Schoolbook typography had proved its worth for Light/Bold contrast, combined with Century Bold Condensed (both for single-column tops and down-page shorts) and with Ludlow Gothic Medium Condensed taking the place of the Monotype Placard when sans was called for. As part of the revolution the *Mail* changed its text from Ionic to Jubilee, saying that it was 'a clearer, cleaner type, easier on the eye' (in 1972 the tabloid *Mail* reverted to Ionic).*

Of the 'compact' *Daily Mail* launched in April 1971 there is little to say. The continuance of the Schoolbook headline style in the new format has been noted; and it works well. There is, after all, no reason why a half-sheet paper should be tied to traditional tabloid typography in the *Mirror–Sun* manner. But the tabloid format adopted by the new *Mail*, with a page of seven $8\frac{1}{4}$-pica columns does not make for easy setting or easy reading; and it is noteworthy that on many occasions the *Mail* has correctly found it necessary to use wider, bastard measures. The one other point arising was the novel headline style for lead stories; extra-large sizes were specially cut of the capitals of Hermann Zapf's Melior Bold Condensed, a letter which seems too mannered for a news heading, certainly in a London paper.

* In 1966 the *Daily Mail* entered for the Newspaper Design Award, the only 'popular' national daily ever to do so. It won the first prize in its class. The judges (Clive Irving, Herbert Spencer, Woodrow Wyatt) said that 'beyond any doubt' the 'radical simplification of the paper's headline typography' deserved the premier award.

Daily Mail

MONDAY, MAY 3, 1971 3p

Curb on car HP is to be lifted

MAIL EXCLUSIVE
By MICHAEL KEMP
Motoring Correspondent

THE Government is planning to remove all hire-purchase controls on car sales.

Finance and motor trade officials are expecting an announcement this month.

The decision will implement the recommendations of the Crowther Report, which recently called for statutory controls to be lifted so that HP sales could more fairly be based on people's credit-worthiness.

Insist

It will mean an end to the present minimum of 40 p.c. deposit and 24 months for repayments and in theory will give traders the freedom to sell cars on a '£10 down and drive away' basis.

But the Finance Houses Association is expected to advise members to insist on 20 to 25 p.c. deposits, with repayments over 33 months.

A man buying an £810 Mini Clubman today on HP must find £324 deposit and pay the balance of £486 plus interest over 24 months. On a 20 p.c. deposit basis he could buy the car for £162 down.

Child dies in M1 pile-up

By Daily Mail Reporter

A WOMAN and a child died last night in a three-car pile-up on the M1. Several people were seriously injured.

The accident happened near Hatfield, Hertfordshire, on a two-lane section between the Bury Grove and St Albans exits.

A car is believed to have crossed the central reservation and hit two others. Mr Ralph Moss, who lives close to the motorway, said: 'One car had been chopped into three sections.'

Nasser man fired

CAIRO: Vice-President Ali Sabry, 50 — former Prime Minister and close friend of Nasser — has been dismissed, a semi-official news agency said. Mr Sabry has strong links with Soviet leaders.

SPY SCANDAL IN BRITAIN'S DEFENCE HQ

THE DEFENCE MINISTRY IN WHITEHALL — SECRET PHONE NUMBERS WERE LEAKED TO . . .

. . . RUSSIA'S EMBASSY IN KENSINGTON PALACE GARDENS — SPY HQ IN BRITAIN

MAIL EXCLUSIVE
By JOHN DICKIE
Diplomatic Correspondent

BRITISH security has broken a Russian phone-tap on the telephones of top officials in the Ministry of Defence.

Counter-espionage agents discovered that the Soviet Embassy obtained the secret telephone numbers of many highly placed Civil Servants who in certain circumstances have to discuss classified information in telephone conversations from their homes.

The security leak will cause a Whitehall scandal. A number of Civil Servants have been questioned and charges under the Official Secrets Act are expected shortly.

Since the Soviet penetration was discovered

Welcome to your new 40-page Daily Mail

MR Vere Harmsworth, chairman of Associated Newspapers Group Ltd., holding an honorary union card, starts the presses to launch the new Daily Mail last night.

Exclusive news

LONDON AIRPORT cuts back on police security — Page 2. THE danger in school swimming pools — Page 9. REVOLUTION in the Civil Service—out goes job security—Page 19.

Inside news

HOW a Daily Mail reporter lived the news on the car production lines to find out what makes car workers strike — Centre Pages. WALTER TERRY, Britain's foremost political commentator, attacks the Westminster ostriches — Page 6.

City firsts

PATRICK SERGEANT, Britain's most influential City Editor, examines new rules for bank loans — Page 26.

Picture Impact

Ministers demand rise from Hea[th]

By GORDON GREIG

SEVEN junior Ministers have told Mr Heath that they may have to quit unless they get a pay increase by the autumn.

They are the hard core among 20 middle- and senior-ranking Ministers who claim they are finding it difficult to make ends meet.

The pay rebels are pinning new hopes of a rise on a Select Committee set up last month under Lord Boyle, to review the Queen's Civil List.

This would include their salaries as well as those of top Civil Servants and heads of nationalised industries.

Most of the Ministers are in the £5,000-£7,250 a year bracket. Nearly all of them earned far more in private business before the Tories came to power last June.

The rebels made a personal appeal to the Prime Minister in his room at the Commons. There was no ultimatum but September appears to be the deadline.

Mr Heath was sympathetic, but held out little hope of an early pay rise.

His message: you will have to take your turn in the queue with the rest of the country.

Plight

Some of the Government's most talented juniors are said to be finding that Whitehall pay has left their families on the breadline.

Among them: Mr Anthony Grant (Trade and Industry), Mr Dudley Smith (Employment), Mr Eldon Griffiths

▲ In April 1971 the tabloid (or 'compact') *Daily Mail* imitated America's *Newsday* with round-cornered boxing of its seven-column page – the 'ring job' as they call it on Long Island – but this was soon dropped (right) and the page opened up with wider-measure setting. ▶

Daily Mail

SATURDAY, JANUARY 27, 1973 3p

RICKMAN'S HAT-TRICK OF NAPS PAGE 40

'Teachers were in pubs instead of the class

They shouted at each other in front of pupils

Boys were hit and allowed to play truant'

FEUDING STAFF SHUT SCHOOL

By JOHN WEBB

A SCHOOL has been closed because of bitter rows between teachers.

Three teachers have been attacked in a letter signed by others and accused of disloyalty, drinking in a pub when they should have been at school and shouting criticisms to other teachers in front of pupils.

The dissension led to a High Court hearing yesterday when the three unsuccessfully sought an injunction to stop the school governors continuing an inquiry into complaints by staff.

During the hearing further allegations were mentioned: that one of the three struck some boys, smoked with others, and condoned truancy.

The school, for 100 educationally sub-normal boys, is the Edward Seguin School in Finsbury Park, North London.

The three teachers are Mr Eric Peagam, 31, of Westcombe Hill, Blackheath, S.E., and Mr and Mrs Edwin Burt, of Ockenden Road, Islington, N. In their application to the court, they claimed that the governors were not conducting the inquiry according to the rules of natural justice and that they had no chance to prepare their case.

Mr Raymond Kidwell, counsel for the governors, told Mr Justice Brightman that the school was closed 'because the other members of the staff cannot work with these three teachers.'

The trouble came to a head on the last day of the Christmas term when Mr Burt, 40, who is the elected teacher-governor, and his wife, Gwyneth, 42, a class teacher, were given copies of a letter of complaint.

The letter, signed by nine other members of the staff, detailed 17 allegations against Mr Peagam and the Burts, including one that they left classes unattended for long periods.

The governors began their inquiry into the letter last Thursday, but the three teachers decided to seek an injunction because, they said, the deputy headmaster, Mr George Ball, took the opportunity to make fresh charges.

'Insolent'

Their counsel said Mr Ball claimed Mr Peagam was insolent, hit boys, allowed some to play truant and left his classroom in an indescribable mess.

Mr Peagam—who is president of the North London branch of the National Union of Teachers—was also accused of smoking with boys at the gate and in a cinema and showing a total disregard of school discipline.

The judge, Mr Justice Brightman, decided that the governors had not acted with impropriety and that the three teachers were not entitled to stop the inquiry.

The school, for pupils aged between ten and 16, closed on Tuesday evening. An ILEA spokesman said last night that it would reopen next Tuesday.

'Sell at any price' panic in City

By PATRICK SERGEANT
City Editor

THIS has been one of the worst weeks millions of savers, insurance policy holders, pension fund managers and private investors have ever known.

The great Stock Market slide has knocked thousands of millions of pounds off the value of shares. Leading company shares are down on average by a tenth since Mr Heath launched his battle against inflation on January 17.

Dealers' attempts yesterday to mark up prices was overwhelmed by a flood of selling. Brokers reported clients pouring out instructions 'sell at any price.'

Banks were said to be pressing speculators to sell shares they had borrowed money on.

As share prices have sunk back to their level of December 1971, people have scrambled to make profits, to get out of takeover gambles that don't look like coming off and to turn sinking shares into cash.

Root cause is uncertainty—about whether Mr Heath's fight against inflation will succeed.

HOSPITALS: Union leaders of 250,000 cooks, cleaners, ward orderlies and other manual staffs last night rejected a £1·84 pay rise offer.

Mr Alan Fisher, general secretary of the 400,000-strong National Union of Public Employees, warned that there could be unofficial strikes next week and that 'it would be much more serious than a token stoppage.'

Banks 'shielding crooks'—Yard

By PETER BURDEN

A SCOTLAND yard police chief hit out at banks last night for unwittingly allowing criminals to hide stolen loot in safe deposit boxes.

He urged that banks should, in future, keep a full record of the contents of boxes and the customers who rent them for £5 or more a year.

Detective Chief Superintendent Robert Chalk made his plea at a Press conference after the jailing of four men for their part in the daring robbery of the safe deposit vault at Lloyds Bank in Baker Street, London, in September, 1971.

It is estimated that the gang netted a record £3 million in cash and jewellery during the tunnel raid, though the 268 customers who rented boxes at the bank would admit to losing only £1,500,000.

Mr Chalk, who led the investigation into the audacious crime in the heart of Sherlock Holmes territory, said:

'Many people told us privately the exact sums they had in their boxes but would only agree to a far smaller amount being recorded on paper.'

Chief Supt. CHALK

He added that eight depositors who had been robbed would not allow the bank to reveal their names.

Mr Chalk said: 'I am going to ask "why?" The banks must know their boxes are being used by thieves, but I suppose, to be fair to them they say it is none of their business what goes into the boxes.

'Surely banks must be made to realise that nearly all the cash stolen in this country is going to end up in a safe deposit box somewhere along the line. Banks should insist on knowing what goes into their customers' safe deposit boxes.'

A Midland Bank spokesman said last night: 'It is quite possible that criminals are putting stolen property in deposit boxes. But there are all sorts of reasons why people should be reluctant to disclose the contents of boxes.'

But Mr John Hunsworth, of the Banking Information Service, said: 'I do not have any evidence at all that safe deposit boxes are being used by criminals. I would think it is pure speculation.'

The four members of the bank gang jailed at the Old Bailey yesterday received a total of 44 years.

But approximately half

Turn to Page 2, Col 2

The 'spy at Wilson-Kosygin summit'

Daily Mail Correspondent
in Los Angeles

THE BRITISH Government hid a U.S. secret agent at an Anglo-Russian summit meeting, the Pentagon Papers trial was told yesterday.

It was said to have happened in 1967 when Prime Minister Mr Harold Wilson had secret talks with Russian Premier Alexei Kosygin at Chequers.

Subject of the summit: How to end the war in Vietnam.

The planted spy was named as Mr Chester Cooper.

It was also claimed that the British intercepted a private phone call between Mr Kosygin and Communist Party Leader Leonid Brezhnev in Moscow.

The story of the Chequers summit came out as papers known as the 'Negotiation Volumes' were made public for the first time during the trial of researcher Daniel Ellsberg, 41, and a fellow worker at the Rand Institute, Anthony Russo.

Brigadier-General Paul Gorman said: 'This is documentary evidence from a high-level American source that the British operated throughout that summit meeting hand-in-glove with the U.S.'

Brigadier-General Gorman is second in command of the investigation into how the secret documents were leaked to the Press.

Ellsberg and Russo are accused of stealing papers from the Rand Corporation in 1969.

INSIDE—Femail 12, Mac 13, Win a Mini 16, Prize Crossword 19, TV Guide 20 & 25, Holidays 21-24, City 32-36, Classified Adverts 28, 30, 31, 39, Amusement Guide 38

LONDON
TUESDAY
MAY 3 1966

THE TIMES

NO. 56,621
PRICE 9D.
ROYAL EDITION

London to be new H.Q. for Nato

Mr. Thomson to pursue talks with allies today

FROM OUR DIPLOMATIC CORRESPONDENT

London will be the new headquarters of the North Atlantic Treaty Organization. This is the firm conclusion of Nato experts directly concerned, although they emphasize that no final decision is likely to be taken or announced until the spring meeting of the organization, which opens in Brussels on June 6.

This conclusion of the experts is based on a study of the possible alternatives and supported by the known attitude of British Ministers most closely involved, notably Mr. Michael Stewart, the Foreign Secretary, and Mr. George Thomson, who was recently given responsibilities which make him in effect Minister for Europe and Nato.

The alternatives before Nato have throughout been limited to the United Kingdom or the Benelux countries, but neither the Netherlands nor Luxembourg has a suitable site to offer.

This has limited the choice to London or Brussels (or conceivably Antwerp, which has the advantage of being on an American supply line to Germany). However, London is favoured as being much the better centre for air communications with the other Nato capitals.

There are already communications systems between the Supreme Allied Commander, Atlantic, at Norfolk in the United States, and the Commander-in-Chief, Eastern Atlantic Area, at Northwood, Middlesex, and across the Channel from the Channel Committee in London. In many other ways also London is said to be the most convenient centre.

First of visits

The Belgians, though prepared to offer a site, are not pressing their claims, and M. Harmel, the new Belgian Foreign Minister, is likely to make this clear when Mr. Thomson visits him in Brussels today—significantly, this is the first of several visits which Mr. Thomson is to make to Nato capitals.

After this talk M. Harmel is expected to consult with his Benelux colleagues in the special committee which they set up between themselves after the French decision to withdraw from the Nato organization.

The relocation of the council will be further discussed on Friday and Saturday when Signor Fanfani, the Italian Foreign Minister, visits London. Italy acts as *rapporteur* for the sub-committee of the Fourteen on relocation. The other sub-committees (with their *rapporteurs*) are:—

Military consequences of the French decision (United States).
Reorganization (Britain).
Financial consequences (Germany).
Infrastructure (Canada).
French personnel (Signor Brosio, Secretary General of Nato).
French troops in Germany (Germany).

These sub-committees are expected to present their reports to the permanent representatives in Paris by the middle of May, and at the same time Mr. Thomson, and possibly other Nato Ministers, will be holding private talks, so that as many decisions as possible can be reached at the meeting in June.

Speed required

There is a need for early decisions to avoid any appearance of hesitation or disarray at the meeting, which will be followed by President de Gaulle's visit to Moscow. That is why a final decision on London as Nato headquarters is now firmly expected.

The proposal for the new organization of Nato, which is now most widely discussed, is based on suggestions put to the Fourteen (the Nato members other than France) by Sir Evelyn Shuckburgh, the British representative on the council. It provides that the council should be located with the "higher planning part" of Nato.

This will include the military committee on which sit the Chiefs-of-Staff of Nato members in Washington. (The standing group—or inner committee of which the United States, Britain, and France are members—would be eliminated.) Also in London would be the nuclear consultation committee, which will be established from the temporary so-called McNamara committee.

Nato action by Mr. Johnson awaited, page 7.

BRITAIN LOOKS AT PROSPECT IN E.E.C.

FROM OUR EUROPEAN ECONOMIC CORRESPONDENT

BRUSSELS, MAY 2

The first direct inquiry in Brussels into the prospects of British membership of the Common Market takes place tomorrow when Mr. George Thomson, the British Minister with special responsibility for European affairs, meets M. Pierre Harmel, the Belgian Foreign Minister.

The number of unofficial contacts being made suggests that the pre-negotiation period is already getting under way. European financial circles believe that Britain hopes to join the European Economic Community by the end of 1967, when substantial repayments to the International Monetary Fund fall due, and this in turn would entail an application to the community at the end of 1966.

The main purpose of Mr. Thomson's present meeting is to discuss the crisis in Nato, but he will also have the opportunity to learn at first hand how the situation looks in the community.

Early decisions

Events are now beginning to gather pace. In particular, two big decisions are expected in the coming days which will have an important bearing on the attitude of the British Government.

First, the treaty association between Nigeria and the Common Market is on the verge of being settled. This will be the first time an English-speaking country succeeds in negotiating a direct link with the Common Market, and the agreement is likely to set the pattern for the rest of the African Commonwealth.

Secondly, this month is expected to mark the Common Market's agreement on the financial terms of its common agricultural policy. This is of crucial importance to Britain.

Mr. Thomson's main concern, however, is to gather any pointers he can on French intentions towards British membership.

11 girls in hospital after Paris trip

Eleven out of 20 pupils from Harrow County School for Girls who visited Paris at Easter, are in West Hendon Hospital suffering from paratyphoid B. Four are ill, and the remaining seven are infected and carriers of the disease.

BOOMERANG BRINGS A RUGBY BAN

SYDNEY, May 2.—Richmond Rugby League in northern New South Wales have cancelled all further matches at a ground where an aborigine stalked on to the pitch and threatened the referee with a boomerang.—*Reuter.*

Mr. Callaghan, the Chancellor of the Exchequer, at work in his study at No. 11 Downing Street, yesterday. With him are Mr. G. Mackenzie, his Parliamentary Private Secretary (left), and Mr. P. Vinter, Third Secretary.

MR. BROWN AT PRE-BUDGET CABINET

FROM OUR POLITICAL CORRESPONDENT

The Budget Cabinet meeting at 10 Downing Street yesterday lasted two hours and 15 minutes. Mr. Brown attended for the first time since he left hospital, and he let his colleagues know that he meant to plunge into work without delay.

The only Cabinet Ministers absent were Mr. Stewart, Foreign Secretary, who was in Strasbourg, and Mr. Greenwood, Minister of Overseas Development, who was in Stockholm.

There is no doubt that a decision in principle has been reached by the Cabinet on the findings of the Kindersley review body on doctors' and dentists' pay, but no date has been given for a Government announcement or for publication.

In many parts of the country yesterday motorists renewed their car road fund licences in a pre-Budget rush.

Big dollar sale by Britain

FROM OUR CITY EDITOR

The British Government have agreed to sell a further $83m. (£29,700,000) of the official portfolio of dollar securities, which in March stood at £180m. after the Treasury had liquefied a large portion in order to bolster sterling area reserves. The proceeds, though, will not be reflected in the gold and foreign currency figures to be published today.

The Hess Oil and Chemical Corporation has agreed to buy 1,242,824 shares held by the Government in the Amerada Petroleum Corporation, one of the larger domestic oil producers in the United States. It is not known whether this block, representing nearly a tenth of the issued capital outstanding, is the full extent of the British official interest.

Taking Friday's closing price on the New York stock exchange, $66¼, the transaction would be worth over $83m.

SIR A. FORBES TO REST

Sir Archibald Forbes, chairman of the Midland and International Banks Ltd. since 1964, and chairman of Spillers, has had a slight coronary disturbance and has been advised to rest. He will not be fulfilling any engagements for the time being.

The Duchess of Argyll was admitted to the Victoria Infirmary, Glasgow, last night for a minor operation.

Mr. Sydney Silverman, Labour M.P. for Nelson and Colne, who is in the Royal Free Hospital, London, is maintaining excellent progress.

Clash between the major fuel industries

Minister's role to umpire on rival claims

FROM OUR POLITICAL CORRESPONDENT

Behind-the-scenes pressures on Mr. Marsh, the new Minister of Power, to give the coal industry a more hopeful future within the Government's national plan are now going to be felt by Mr. Cledwyn Hughes, the new Secretary of State for Wales, and Mr. George Thomas, his Minister of State. After a meeting at the Commons the Welsh group of Labour M.P.s have invited both Welsh Ministers to face their questions and demands in a private discussion.

The pressure is also being brought to bear on Mr. Wilson and Mr. Brown in the Commons. Mr. Leo Abse, Labour M.P. for Pontypool, has put down a question asking for the creation of an interdepartmental committee of the Ministers of Power and Labour, the Board of Trade and the Welsh Office "charged with the task of ensuring no pit is closed without alternative employment being available for any redundant miners".

New campaign

This must be seen as the beginning of a new campaign that is likely to be much more immediately troublesome to Mr. Marsh than drafting the Bill to renationalize steel. For the consequences of the Government's fuel policy are now being felt throughout all mining areas. There are unmistakable signs that Lord Robens, chairman of the National Coal Board, is using his private influence in general support of the National Union of Mineworkers' demands.

The consequences are also being felt in the nationalized gas and electricity industries. Every visit Lord Robens pays to Mr. Marsh's room to fight the case for coal brings counter-visits from Sir Henry Jones, chairman of the Gas Council, and Sir Ronald Edwards, chairman of the Electricity Council. Mr. Marsh's role is that of umpire. Lord Robens would like to see the Government insist on more coal-fired electricity generating plants. Sir Ronald warns Mr. Marsh how many more millions of pounds a political commitment to coal would involve.

Looking ahead, the gas interests of course would like to be able to take advantage of any large-scale find of natural gas on the Continental shelf. But when the Ministry of Power ask how certain such a large-scale find may be the answer comes that there is no certainty yet to be had. Mr. Marsh and the Government in all their fuel policy planning are bedevilled by the familiar political problem of making fateful decisions where some of the essential factors can be only guessed at.

Costs compared

Sir Henry Jones has categorically asserted that making gas from coal is more expensive than making it by the new oil processes or by natural gas importation. He told the Select Committee on Nationalized Industries last December that the Gas Council were anxious to get away from coal as quickly as possible from the financial point of view, but for no other reason.

Sir Ronald Edwards and his colleagues have also told the politicians that coal is most expensive. Coal is 0.54d. a unit on the coalfields, oil 0.52d., and nuclear 0.47d. The council have for the present agreed to give preference to coal, although they expect that preference to diminish year by year as the coal industry rationalizes itself.

Lord Robens, for the N.C.B., has never concealed his hostility to the treatment of the coal industry in the national plan, which predicted that the market for coal in 1970 might not be above 180m. tons. He complains that the plan provides for substantial increases in everybody's business except the coal industry's.

N.C.B. were asked, against his advice, to publish a list of closures of pits up to 1970 and also a list of possible closures. As a consequence, the N.C.B. have lost men at the rate of 1,000 a week.

DUKE OF EDINBURGH IN OSLO

From Our Correspondent

OSLO, MAY 2

The Duke of Edinburgh arrived here today for a two-day visit on the occasion of the British trade fair "Britain 66". The Duke was met at the airport by King Olav of Norway and by Sir Ian Dixon Scott, the British Ambassador.

The remarks by Mr. Douglas Jay, the President of the Board of Trade, at his press conference on Saturday about Norway acting contrary to the spirit of the European Free Trade Association drew critical comments from two Oslo newspapers in leading articles today.

Starfighter jet crash

FROM OUR OWN CORRESPONDENT

BONN, MAY 2

An F 104 G Starfighter of the Bundesmarine crashed this morning near Doerstedt, west of Kiel.

The pilot, a naval lieutenant, escaped with his ejector seat but died soon after landing

This is the fifty-second aircraft of this type to crash since the beginning of 1961.

RENAULT HOPE FOR SOVIET FACTORY

FROM OUR OWN CORRESPONDENT

PARIS, MAY 2

The Renault car company, which, like Fiat, has been engaged in negotiations with the Russians since last summer for the setting up of a giant factory in the Soviet Union, professes to be confident that it will be Renault, not Fiat, that will eventually get this large order. It is even suggested that General de Gaulle's trip to Moscow next month might clinch the deal.

4,000 U.S. drugs to be checked

FROM OUR OWN CORRESPONDENT

NEW YORK, MAY 2

The Food and Drug Administration is to investigate the effectiveness of some 4,000 drugs now being sold in America. Mr. James Goddard, the F.D.A. Commissioner, has announced that the investigation will begin this summer under the auspices of the National Research Council.

The withdrawal of hundreds of throat lozenges was ordered recently by the commissioner on the ground that they were not effective, as the manufacturers claimed, against sore throats.

ON OTHER PAGES

Seamen back decision to strike

The National Union of Seamen yesterday unanimously decided to support the executive council's decision to call a strike on May 16 over a pay and hours claim. Delegates stood and applauded the decision at the union's annual conference at Worthing.

Mr. F. B. Bolton, president of the Chamber of Shipping of the United Kingdom, said last night that the strike would be disastrous for the nation as well over 90 per cent in value of Britain's external trade goes by sea.

He added: "The effect on imports would be less immediately apparent, but, nonetheless, devastating over a fairly short period, for a nation so dependent on imports, including the whole of our oil supplies."

Mr. Ford Geddes, chairman of the Shipping Federation, said: "The strike is a critical one for a country like Britain. It is to try to enforce demands that would cost 17 per cent. We have gone a long way to try to meet the demands of the N.U.S. It is out of the question to concede the claim in full."

Conference report, page 16.

12,000 WILL BE LAID OFF

FROM OUR CORRESPONDENT

COVENTRY, MAY 2

Twelve thousand workers employed by Standard Triumph International in Coventry, Birmingham, and Liverpool will be laid off tomorrow because unofficial strikes by 60 Coventry machinists have stopped supplies of cylinder heads and blocks. Three factories in Coventry will close tomorrow and only about half the 9,300 people laid off will be able to restart on Wednesday.

The strikers, who caused 6,500 to be laid off for two days last week, are in dispute over piecework prices and did not work on Friday and today.

The company said that provided they restarted tomorrow it would meet the trade unions on Thursday.

Priest 'in hands of kidnappers'

FROM OUR OWN CORRESPONDENT

ROME, MAY 2

A letter said to have come from Mgr. Marco Ussia, the missing ecclesiastical counsellor at the Spanish Embassy to the Holy See, was delivered to police headquarters today. It said that he was well, but in the hands of kidnappers.

Mgr. Ussia disappeared on Friday night. A theory that he might have suffered an attack of amnesia was soon abandoned in favour of the view that he was in the hands of an anti-Franco movement, promptly labelled as anarchist. The fact of his kidnapping was confirmed during the day in reports from Madrid.

ROB ROY AS LARGE AS LIFE

If you would like a life-size marble statue for your home you can have one of Rob Roy. It is by Stuart Burnett, dated 1854. It is on view in London and is advertised in today's "Personal" columns on page 2.

REBUFF TO A RHODESIAN MINISTER

No assurances on 'social visit'

From Our Commonwealth Staff

Mr. Pieter Van der Byl, the Rhodesian Deputy Minister of Information, made an informal inquiry last week whether it would be possible for him to visit Britain for social reasons. The approach was made through a third party, and not directly through an official.

In reply, the Commonwealth Relations Office said that they could give no assurances in a hypothetical situation. The matter must depend upon the visitor's behaviour when in Britain.

No question arises, apparently, of Mr. Van der Byl's undertaking any negotiations, formal or informal, for the Rhodesian Government, nor is it the policy of the British Government to recognize any members of the rebel regime, or give them any facilities.

Mr. Van der Byl has been on leave for some weeks, travelling in Europe.

British airlift to Zambia ending

FROM OUR DIPLOMATIC CORRESPONDENT

The British airlift of oil supplies to Zambia will be ended in mid-May.

This decision has been taken because the supplies now reaching Zambia by road through Mozambique, which—somewhat ironically—travel from Beira, and then through Malawi, are now sufficient to meet all current needs in Zambia, and permit the storage of a surplus.

Lord Cameron for print inquiry

FROM OUR LABOUR STAFF

Lord Cameron, the Scottish Lord of Session, is to be chairman of an inquiry into the problems associated with the introduction of web-offset printing techniques. The inquiry has been set up by Mr. Gunter, Minister of Labour, and as well as looking at general problems it will also inquire into disputes at Southwark Offset Ltd., London, and the Co-operative Press, Manchester.

Talks continued throughout yesterday in an unsuccessful attempt to find a solution to the manning problems at Southwark Offset. Because of the dispute the £2,250,000 plant was closed last Friday and 350 employees were dismissed. The talks will be resumed today.

Sitting with Lord Cameron on the inquiry will be Mr. David Basnett, national industrial officer of the National Union of General and Municipal Workers, Mr. D. J. Flunder, group industrial relations officer of Dunlop Rubber Company, and Mr. Gerard Wood, of Erwick Orr and Company.

STOWAWAY IS TAKEN OFF LINER

Police were called to the liner Queen Elizabeth at Southampton last night to escort ashore a Polish American who had been found in a fan room during the voyage from New York.

POLISH BAN ON FOREIGNERS EASED

PILGRIMS CROWD BLACK MADONNA SHRINE

FROM OUR CORRESPONDENT IN EAST EUROPE—CZESTOCHOWA, MAY 2

Pilgrims cheered and applauded when Cardinal Wyszynski stepped out of his car to walk to the Black Madonna sanctuary at the Jasna Gora monastery this evening. Arriving at the festivities of Poland's Christian millennium, which the Church is consecrating to the Virgin Mary, the Cardinal was welcomed as the legate of the Pope.

In the medieval Jasna Gora monastery, which towers over this industrial town and is the only remaining architectural reminder of its long history, thousands of pilgrims have been flocking in since the early hours of today to celebrate with prayers and devotions the one-thousandth anniversary of Christianity in Poland.

An earlier decision to stop foreign pilgrims from coming has been slightly altered, and a group of Polish Americans arrived here by bus today. Their numbers have been drastically reduced, but nobody can now say that no foreign pilgrims were allowed, nor indeed could it be said that obstacles were placed in the way of Polish pilgrims to stop them from coming.

On the ramparts that surround the cloisters, the outdoor altar, at which Mass is to be celebrated tomorrow, and two thrones, one bearing the papal and the other the Polish Primate's coats of arms, dominate the green square outside where crowds of pilgrims have gathered already, many to spend the night in the open

Peasant women wrapped in shawls carrying blankets and baskets with food, young people in national costume marching and singing religious songs, men dressed in their Sunday suits, cripples and beggars and salesmen who have spread out their merchandise offering pictures of the Black Madonna, photographs of the Cardinal and of the Pope, sweets and fruits, give the solemn occasion an air of colourful informality and of contrast with the austere background of medieval walls and church towers of the Black Madonna sanctuary.

Door ajar

True, red flags and party slogans that adorn the streets serve as reminders that the regime also has a stake in Czestochowa, and that while it has decided not to interfere in the church celebration it, nevertheless, wishes to demonstrate that Czestochowa has a secular as well as a religious history. But the fact that no parallel state ceremony has been organized, that the authorities have placed no obstacles and that, apart from security checks on the roads, official surveillance is discreet, shows that after the heat a calmer atmosphere is setting in.

The festivities which began this evening are to continue until Wednesday; then on May 8 the Church moves to Cracow for another Christian commemoration.

The Pope's visit could not take place, but there are indications that the Government is anxious to allay the impression of having slammed the door and, even if for the moment it is difficult to envisage such a possibility, the fact remains that the door is being kept ajar perhaps for a future date.

The throne upon which the Pope was to have sat will now be occupied by his legate. But, as no foreign cardinal or bishop has been allowed in, the Polish primate will represent the Pope.

Thus, when he arrived this evening Cardinal Wyszynski was welcomed at the Lubomirski gate, the main entry into the monastery, as the Pope's legate as well as the Primate of the Polish Church. There was no doubt that this was yet another personal triumph for the Cardinal.

The Polish Government has only itself to blame for it because by stopping the Pope from coming to Czestochowa and then refusing to allow entry to all foreign cardinals and bishops it left no alternative to the Holy See but to delegate Cardinal Wyszynski as official representative of the Pope. Thus the Government has in fact helped to raise the status of the Polish primate.

◀ Front-page news in *The Times* (May 1966) started with stress on lower-case headings. Note the new Berthold Wolpe title-line.

May 1966 marked perhaps the most startling newspaper design event of the period; for at long last *The Times* took the plunge and changed the classic front page of classifieds to a front page of news. This in itself was revolution enough, but it was by no means all. As Sir William Haley, then editor, observed: 'The days when *The Times* could be satisfied with addressing a small national élite are gone.' So the whole typographic presentation of the paper was changed. The famous multi-deck headings, all in the various Times Titlings, vanished; where some deckers remained, their decks were cut from three to two, and the second deck was in upper- and lower-case; main headings were normally specified in Times Bold lower-case (to justify this change the paper characteristically commissioned a special report from the Medical Research Council on the superior legibility of lower-case – as if this had not been common knowledge among printers beyond the memory of man). Certain headline types of minor significance, like the Hever Titling used on the Court page and the light Titling 329, were scrapped.

Among other changes was a restructuring of the leader page, the leaders being doubled up and each given a double-column heading, while the 'turnover' article was promoted from double to three-column, with the newly-instituted Diary beneath it. This arrangement was temporary, since with the 'bill' page – facing the leaders – no longer needed as the main news page, it was able to accommodate more than one article of the 'turnover' type as well as the Diary. Features, starting with the women's page, entered on an exceptional period of free experimentation. As new feature sections, like the Saturday Review, developed, it appeared that the graphic presentation of this part of the paper was more concerned with virtuosity – indeed, was strongly flavoured with what Morison would have called 'faddishness' – than with making reading easy.

Directed by two talented women, Sue Puddefoot and Jeannette Collins (who was later named the paper's Design Editor), the feature pages began to use rules and other devices, both vertically and horizontally, in often distracting fashion. There were heavy rules (of varying weights) and treble rules, though the May 1966 Style Manual specifically said: 'All rules throughout the paper, both horizontal and vertical, are single rules, i.e. no thick and thin or "tramlines", and the weight (thickness) is standardised.' The current ease of photographic reproduction of any lettering, no matter how obscure its origin, provided *The Times* features not only with acceptable lines of period *avant-garde* style (like A. M. Cassandre's Bifur of 1929) but with an incredible clutter of late Victorian monstrosities of the sort that compositors in my young days used to call 'winklebag'.

The inner conflict of
T. E. Lawrence

Holiday '69

The colour for you

ST LAURENT VENET FERAUD

Pooter talks to Sidney Bernstein

▶ Some of the 'winklebag' type styles to be seen in feature pages of *The Times* in the late 1960s.

HOME NEWS

Abbot rebukes critics of the Pope

Critics of the Pope's encyclical on birth control were sharply rebuked by the Abbot of Downside, the Right Rev. Wilfrid Passmore, at the national pilgrimage of Roman Catholics at Walsingham, Norfolk, yesterday.

The abbot said there was a state of confusion because many people had expected one thing, but had got another. For five years they had been urging and challenging the Holy Father to speak, and now he had spoken clearly and emphatically.

"Do you want the Pope to give his judgment as the Vicar of Christ, or do you want the Pope to approve your own private views?" he asked. "That is the issue, and don't run away from it."

The encyclical was not a mere document, but an expression of the mind of the church centred on the Pope in a unique and particular way. All the Pope had done was to restate the teaching not only of the Roman Catholic Church but of Christendom.

The abbot criticized non-Catholic newspapers for conducting the controversy in insulting terms—particularly one "expensive periodical" which had described the Pope as "an Italian bachelor". He commented: "Surely we who know what the Holy Father means to each of us must resent such a way of treating the sovereign pontiff."

He called upon members of the laity to profess their faith publicly, to help and encourage their own pastors in their loyalty to the Holy See, and to help those who were passing through difficulties "with which we may sympathize, but which we cannot condone."

The pilgrimage was led for the first time by the Bishop of Northampton, the Right Rev. Charles Grant.

The abbot's statement came on a day when several priests in the south of England made public their opposition to the encyclical. One of them, the Rev. Andrew Beer, aged 45, assistant priest at St. Dunstan's, Woking, Surrey, told his parishioners from the pulpit at Mass that he could not accept the Pope's ruling on birth control. He was speaking after obtaining permission from his bishop, the Right Rev. David Cashman, Bishop of Arundel and Brighton.

Father Beer, who has not been allowed to preach or hear confessions for two weeks, said: "I am not able in conscience to accept the teaching of the Holy Father's encyclical.

"The traditional arguments of the natural law which have just been restated seem to me to be arguments from reason which are not reasonable, and which are shot through with inconsistencies. I do not believe that contraception is necessarily sinful and I do not see how I can in honesty impose that teaching on others."

Announcing that he is going away for two or three months at the bishop's request to think things over, Father Beer continued: "The bishop is not treating me as a rebel. He has not suspended me, and is not imposing any penalty. These past two weeks have been a time of strain and unhappiness, and in my present state of mind I cannot accept the Pope's ruling.

"I hope desperately that I do not have to leave the priesthood, which means more to me than anything else in the world. But I cannot exercise it in bad faith." He asked the congregation to pray not only for him, but for those priests and members of the laity who are torn in conscience.

Many members of the congregation were strong in their support for Father Beer. "Whatever happens to him now, we still think he is right and that contraception is not sinful," said one of a group within the Woking church. The local Roman Catholic organizations have made no statement yet.

The Pope's encyclical, on July 29, reiterated the Roman Catholic Church's prohibition on all forms of artificial birth control. It said that contraception might present a "wide and easy" road to a lowering of morality.

Father Beer also said in a radio interview yesterday: "We are not trying to wreck the church. We are all concerned for the church, I am sure there is this large, deep feeling on behalf of the laity, who are looking to the clergy for a lead."

He has been in the ministry six years, and came from Eastbourne to Woking two years ago. He served with the R.A.F. during the war, and was later in the Civil Service.

Another priest in the diocese of Brighton and Arundel, the Rev. Anthony Burnham, aged 31, curate at the Church of the Assumption of Our Lady, Englefield Green, Surrey, told his parishioners in the parish newsletter, circulated from the vestry yesterday, that he was also unable to accept the Pope's teaching about contraception.

"The Pope's encyclical has led to a great deal of heart-searching and anxiety among very many Catholics, both laity and priests," he wrote. "I have been one among them because I found, and find, myself unable to accept the Holy Father's teachings that it always is wrong for married people to use artificial means of contraception, and so could not in conscience impose this teaching on others.

"When I informed the diocesan authorities over a fortnight ago of my state of mind, I was told that I should not preach nor hear confessions until I had seen Bishop Cashman. This I have now done, and the bishop thinks that I should spend some weeks away from the parish to pray and think about my position. In the meantime, I am not under any ecclesiastical censure."

Father Burnham was not available for further comment yesterday, but a spokesman at the presbytery said he would be going away for a few weeks from next Friday. This coincided in part with Father Burnham's normal holiday.

The Rev. Laurence Duprez, parish priest of St. Cecilia's, North Cheam, Surrey, told his congregation yesterday that there was "nothing peculiar or strange" about the dissension within the Roman Catholic Church. "The present difficulties will be no more than a comma or a footnote in the history of Catholicism," he said.

St. Cecilia's is the parish where the Rev. Paul Weir was suspended for opposing the Pope's ruling. A letter from Chancellor Henderson at Archbishop's House, Southwark, was read by Father Duprez from the pulpit at St. Cecilia's. It said that the two petitions from North Cheam parishioners asking for the reinstatement of Father Weir would be considered by the Archbishop of Southwark, Dr. Cowderoy, when he returns from holiday.

In Salisbury, Mr. Kevin Moore, aged 34, a pharmacist, and his wife, Eunice, aged 33, a teacher, have decided to cut their normal £1 a week contribution to St. Osmund's church, to 5s., in protest against the encyclical. They are sending the rest to children's charities, and in a letter to their parish priest, they claimed it was "to alleviate suffering bound to be caused by the Pope's ruling".

Their parish priest refused to comment, as did the local canon and the bishop. But at the neighbouring Church of the Most Holy Redeemer—attended by friends of Mr. and Mrs. Moore who have joined their protest—the Rev. Timothy Berry said: "People who do things like this are very much in the minority. As Catholics they have the duty, not in charity but in justice, to support the church. It is rather a sulky attitude. I just do not understand it."

Mr. Moore said at his home in St. Clair Road, Salisbury: "I have already returned my supply of weekly collection envelopes for next year. We are giving 5s. towards the living of the priest—we do not want him to be hurt."

At the Church of Our Lady of Peace, Burnham, Buckinghamshire, the "talk-in" on the encyclical which began last Sunday continued yesterday.

The Rev. David Woodard, parish priest, has said that he and two curates, the Rev. Nicholas Lash and the Rev. Vincent McDermott, share responsibility for a sermon preached in the church a fortnight ago disagreeing with the Pope. During the "talk-in", each paragraph of the encyclical is discussed at length by the congregation.

Only 16 paragraphs have so far been dealt with. The talk-in will continue next week.

Test for the Pope, and Priests Defend Oppressed, page 3.

Talks on conscience issue

FROM OUR CORRESPONDENT—Portsmouth, Aug. 18

One of the youngest bishops of the Roman Catholic Church, the Bishop of Portsmouth, the Right Rev. Derek Worlock, aged 48, is to hold meetings with his priests next month, to discuss "conscientious difficulties" and other aspects of the papal encyclical.

He announced this today after issuing a pastoral letter which pointed out that the Pope's words constituted a "definite directive", but said also that birth control was scarcely the acid test of Christianity.

The letter urged people to discuss difficulties of conscience frankly with parish priests.

"These last days have seen a storm within the family of the Church", the Bishop wrote. "The publication of the encyclical has called forth a spate of comments, official and personal, responsible and some less responsible. On occasion, the sincere pursuit of truth has through forceful speech come close to uncharity."

People who loved the Church had read with distress the reports of rift. "It is important that we should see this question within the whole context of the Christian life, for it is scarcely the acid test of being for Christ or against him.

"It is praiseworthy that we should be quick off the mark in defence of conscience, though we owe it to others as well as to ourselves to make sure that our conscience is properly informed. The Pope's carefully worded statement demands deep study and reflection by the whole Church."

The Pope's words constituted a definite directive. Some people had been quick to emphasize that it was not an infallible pronouncement. But the Pope had made clear his authority, and "we receive his ruling in that light".

He urged Roman Catholics, as Cardinal Heenan had done, not to stay away from the sacrament.

"For some, there may still remain certain difficulties of conscience. I hope that such persons will discuss these frankly with their priests. Married couples should not hesitate to seek this help and forgiveness in accordance with their culpability.

"There are other immense problems we must face in carrying the message of Christ to the world, and in bringing spiritual truth and material relief to those who hunger after God's justice. We shall do these things better by our efforts now to raise our moral standards and by the exercise of discipline and self-denial."

A Roman Catholic bishop preaching in an Anglican cathedral said yesterday that there was more need than ever for unity although the Pope's pronouncement had been seen as a threat to the movement.

The Auxiliary Bishop of Westminster, the Right Rev. B. C. Butler, president of the Social Morality Council, said in Guildford Cathedral: "The Pope's message was addressed not only to Roman Catholics but to all men of good will. Thus it was certain to be disputed.

"The rights of conscience—a conscience that has tried to instruct itself adequately—are absolute. And wherever conscience is aroused there is bound to be heart searching and fierce debate; all the more when what is involved is not only happiness but the basic conditions of human existence and social happiness."

Most people, Roman Catholics or not, would agree on the need for a general reawakening of conscience about the role of marriage and sexual relations in society.

"What is called the decline of morals is largely an expression of moral uncertainty. A reexamination of fundamentals needs to be undertaken not only by Christians but jointly by all men and women of good will.

"And in our open society this is the best way to tackle other great moral issues too: world poverty, international peace and race relations, for instance. So we must keep open the channels of communication, particularly in our western world, between Christians, Jews, and humanists."

10s 2d rate strike over grants

FROM OUR CORRESPONDENT—Folkestone, Aug. 18

Mr. Archibald Edwards, aged 57, a civil servant, will go to Folkestone Magistrates' Court tomorrow to explain why he is refusing to pay 10s. 2d. of a rate demand for £40 12s. on his home in Walmer Way, Folkestone.

He will tell the magistrates that he calculates 10s. 2d. to be the amount of his rates normally spent by Kent County Council in student grants. He based his estimate on information from the county council that 3 per cent of its net expenditure on education goes towards the grants. He does not think the students are worth it.

"I am not biased. I have nothing personal against them", said Mr. Edwards, who had a grammar school education. "I am pleased they have such wonderful opportunities today. But I refuse to pay anything towards their grants until I am satisfied that the taxpayer is getting value for money."

Students' grievances were probably well-founded, but he objected to the way they were trying to resolve them.

"All these protest marches and sit-ins are a lot of nonsense. When the students sit down with the proper authorities to discuss their grievances sensibly, then I shall pay up happily."

Mr. Edwards said he felt that other people might follow his lead by withholding part of the rates. "My little effort may light a fire that will blaze up into something really big", he added.

Doctors told of patients' calls for help

Attempted suicide is becoming a fashionable mode of behaviour in cases of depressive illness, and many patients swallow a handful of tablets in order to signal their distress and to call for help, according to Professor Kenneth Rawnsley, Professor of Psychological Medicine at the Welsh National School of Medicine.

He estimates, in a report on the early diagnosis of depression, published today, that 820 persons in a million in an urban area attempt suicide each year.

One of his conclusions is that many suicide attempts among people suffering from depression could be prevented by development of better methods of diagnosis for the general practitioner.

He says that depressive illnesses are widespread and potentially fatal through suicide. Most of these illnesses are treated solely by the general practitioner.

Although it is easy to diagnose severe cases and recommend specialist treatment, there are many patients with milder symptoms which are more difficult to detect.

Only a proportion of attempted suicides are suffering from depressive illness, but it is important to recognize them since they are among the most treatable diseases in medicine. Failure to make a diagnosis may lead to another suicide attempt.

The rate of admission of patients with depressive conditions to psychiatric hospitals has risen greatly. Increasing numbers are treated in psychiatric outpatient clinics. But the group which is treated by specialists for depression constitutes only a minority of those who seek help from their general practitioner.

As the practitioner is the first doctor to see most patients suffering from depression, Professor Rawnsley believes new methods are needed in screening. The difficulty confronting the practitioner is how to diagnose a depressive illness when the patient deliberately avoids the central issue.

Professor Rawnsley describes how a patient may visit his doctor to talk about a backache, stomach pains or insomnia. This is the admission ticket which the patient will offer the doctor because he thinks it is acceptable. The astute clinician may quickly pick up the clue which enables him to proceed with the real business.

The prevalence of depressive illness increases from the age of 30, reaching a peak between age 55 and 64 for both sexes. It is commoner in women than men.

There is no ready-made screening test that the general practitioner can give to all patients at regular intervals. But Professor Rawnsley believes that the Beck depression inventory, a psychological questionnaire relating to 21 aspects of depression, is an instrument which may be capable of development for some work in general practice.

Professor Rawnsley's report is published by the Office of Health Economics, an independent organization for research into economic aspects of medical care and social problems established six years ago by the Association of the British Pharmaceutical Industry.

Also published today by the office is a paper on the early diagnosis of cancer of the cervix by Dr. O. A. N. Husain, consultant pathologist at the regional cytology centre, St. Stephen's Hospital, London. He puts the cost for a screening service of the female population over the age of 25 at five-yearly intervals at over £3m.

Outlining the methods of collection and analysis of cervical smears, he suggests how the services run by the public health authority, hospital laboratories, and general practitioners could best work in harmony.

From evidence of cervical screening in other countries Dr. Husain shows the importance of the role of the general practitioner if screening tests are to gain a wide acceptance. By wide acceptance he means well over 80 per cent of the population at risk accepting the service.

He suggests that a successful screening campaign would double the immediate bed requirements if it was followed by adequate treatment. In the long term, the number of hospital beds used for the disease should diminish by about two-thirds because early detection and treatment require a shorter time in hospital.

Bus strike brought forward

From Our Correspondent

Bolton, Aug. 18

Bolton's 800 bus workers will strike from noon on Tuesday, five days earlier than recommended by their branch committee, unless the corporation transport committee agrees tomorrow to backdate their frozen £1-a-week pay award to last December.

The bus crews' decision, approved by a large majority, was announced early today by Mr. Frank Owen, the union branch secretary, after a two-hour meeting.

He said: "The mood of the members was very militant and some wanted us to strike before our meeting with the transport committee. I would have preferred a little more time for manoeuvre, but the men feel angry and frustrated."

Alderman H. Wood, chairman of the transport committee, said: "I am a bit disappointed that the bus crews should make this so urgent a matter."

Lightning strike. — Three hundred busmen in Grimsby and Cleethorpes are to stage strikes until their disagreement with the joint transport undertaking over the controversial £1 pay award is resolved.

Only one busman knows the date on which the first strike is to occur. Mr. Cyril Harmer, aged 47, of Lime Street, Grimsby, drew the date out of a hat. Mr. Harmer, chairman of the busmen's works committee, said: "I am sorry about the inconvenience, but this is the only way we will get results—by using an element of surprise."

Back to work.—Northampton corporation buses began operating again yesterday after a six-day strike. The bus crews, members of the Transport and General Workers' Union, decided by 208 votes to two on Friday night to call off their stoppage. They accepted an offer of the Northampton transport committee to give them a £1-a-week pay rise on December 26, backdated to December 14 last year, provided this is legal.

During the strike, trade slumped in Northampton shops. Many shopkeepers reported at the weekend that their takings had fallen by at least half compared with a normal week.

Teacher told to quit house

From Our Correspondent

East Grinstead, Aug. 18

Mr. Ivor Cook, aged 53, the teacher whose allegations of brutality led to the closing of Court Lees approved school, faces legal proceedings unless he leaves his tied staff house at South Godstone, Surrey.

Mr. Alan Waite, deputy clerk to Surrey County Council, said at the weekend: "Mr. Cook was required to vacate the house on Friday, August 9. He appears to have ignored this notice to quit and gone away on holiday. Unless he can be persuaded to leave the house voluntarily on his return we will consult his solicitors with a view to instituting legal proceedings."

Lorries delayed at docks 'for days'

Some lorry drivers are complaining that they have to wait for days to get unloaded at the Royal Group of London docks where, in spite of more mechanical handling of loads, increased congestion is reported.

Much of the trouble is due to many dockers being allowed to take their holidays at the same time under the new charter scheme.

Before the dockers got their charter, holidays started in May and finished in October and it was possible to have an average number of men away each week. The new system often causes an acute shortage of labour.

Hundreds of cars belonging to dockers and other port workers parked near the quays help to cause further congestion.

A dock policeman said: "Quite a bit of the blame must be taken by the shippers themselves who send in exports at the last moment thinking the last into the hold will be the first out.

"It has been urged for some time that haulage firms should be banned from the docks and made to offload at warehouses on the outskirts of East London, so that the Port of London Authority or other stevedoring firms can themselves bring the cargoes into the docks when they are needed.

"Lorry drivers are not without blame. Some of them know just when to arrive so they will not have a chance to unload that day. They draw special sleeping-out expenses for each day they cannot get their loads cleared.

"A ticket system has been introduced to prevent lorry drivers queueing but this is not foolproof.

"Transit sheds where cargoes must be delivered several days before a ship is due to leave would be the real answer", the policeman suggested, "and would prevent traffic jams if only the stevedoring firms ferried the stuff to the ships."

"It could even mean a revival of river traffic", he added. "With work being found for the lightermen who in recent years have become redundant.

"It would be far easier to send in cargoes by barge than jam up the roads around the docks with lorries."

Back in union under protest

Mr. George Holt, aged 43, a lockman, who defied a closed-shop agreement in the docks, has rejoined the Transport and General Workers' Union under protest. Mr. Holt, of New Road, Leigh-on-Sea, Essex was one of a group of lockmen at Tilbury who broke away from the T.G.W.U. and joined the rival National Union of Portworkers.

But in April the Port of London Authority told staff in its marine services that from June 1 it would be a condition of employment that they belonged to the T.G.W.U.

The clock beats three women athletes

FROM OUR NORTHERN CORRESPONDENT—Dungeon Gill, Aug. 18

Three women athletes who insisted on competing in one of the toughest endurance events in Britain were forced to retire this afternoon. But they said they could have completed the course if they had had more time.

Mrs. Hazel Hill of Scartho, Grimsby, Miss Sophie Rex from Guildford, Surrey, and Miss Carol McNeil from Dunoon, Argyllshire, entered the Lake District Mountain Trial, which involves running, walking and climbing, 17 miles of fell country, with a total vertical distance of 8,000ft.

Officials of the association that has organized the trial for the past 17 years tried to discourage them from entering. They said the trial was by tradition "men only", but the women said they would take part in any case, even if they had to follow other competitors.

In order to avoid the danger of the women being stranded on the mountains without rescue or radio cover, Mr. Gerry Charnley, the association's secretary, decided to allow the women to enter as guest competitors, starting early. Special instructions were sent to radio control points to look after them.

A seven-hour time limit was set for the race, however, and all three women had to retire after advice from check points. Mrs. Hill, and Miss Rex reached five out of the six points; Miss McNeil gave up after four.

"It was a very tough course indeed," Miss McNeil said. "But I think I could have completed it if I wasn't racing against the clock."

The course was from Dungeon Gill to Black Crag, the summit of Castle How, Scafell and on to Great Knott.

When the three women returned to the hotel tonight, they denied that there had been any friction over their entry. "We just decided we wanted to try a tough event like this and put in our entry in the normal way", Mrs. Hill said.

Two of the three women, Mrs. Hill and Miss McNeil, are members of the team selected for the world orienteering championships in Sweden next month.

The Lake District Mountain Trial is not strictly an orienteering event, which usually involves the use of map and compass over short events, but it does call for precise navigation.

The winner was Mr. Chris Fitt, aged 27, a motorway engineer, from Kendal, who completed the course in 4 hours 22 minutes.

Team set Channel record

A team of six long-distance swimmers returned to Dover by boat last night after swimming from Dover to France. They claimed a new record time for the Channel relay crossing.

The six said they had done the swim, much of it in rough seas, in 10hr. 37min. The previous record from England to France was 11hr. 20min., set up by Rotherham Swimming Club.

The team were John Koorey, aged 24, of Australia; Hedy Schmidt, aged 24, a Canadian girl; Ted Erikson, the American holder of the Channel both-ways non-stop record; Peter Ritchie, of Australia; Rosemary George, aged 29, of Dover, who has swum the Channel in both directions; and Tom Hetzell, a New York police officer.

Mr. Hetzell said: "Most of us have been waiting around Dover for several weeks to make individual swims, but the weather has been bad.

Firm's fumes killed cows, farmer says

At villages around Edgcott, Buckinghamshire, trees have shed their leaves and grass and foliage have withered. The London Brick Company admits that the cause is emission of sulphur fumes from its works.

The company blamed freak conditions, but some farmers dispute that. One, Mr. Dennis Hook, said that 18 of his cows have died because sulphur fumes polluted the area over a long period. He added "I have lost many thousands of pounds because of the fumes, and I will soon be making a claim for compensation."

A veterinary surgeon who carried out a post-mortem examination on Mr. Hook's cows said he was sure the initial cause of their death was sulphur in the air. It had affected the breathing of the animals, causing bronchitis.

The London Brick Company said: "We have no comment on the effect of the fumes on the cows. But we consider the freak weather conditions during the last week caused the burning of foliage in Edgcott. This is a very rare occurrence with any of our factories."

Blocks of ice fall through roof

From Our Correspondent

Maidstone, Aug. 18

Several large blocks of ice, believed to have fallen from an aircraft, crashed through the roof of a house at The Meadway, Sevenoaks, today and made a hole several feet across. Lumps of ice also landed in the garden.

Mrs. J. Williamson, who lives there, said: "I heard an aircraft passing overhead then, suddenly, the ice came crashing down on my home".

In Brief

Two die in fire

From Our Correspondent

Swansea, Aug. 18

A girl, aged 17, and her boy friend died today when fire almost completely destroyed the girl's home in Carmarthen Road, Cwmbwrla, Swansea.

The bodies of the couple, Jeanette Price and Terence Provine, 19, were found in a bedroom. Firemen said they believed the boy, who was staying with the family, had gone into the room to try to rescue the girl. He could have jumped to safety from his own bedroom window.

Two rescued in Solent

A father and son clung to their dinghy for over an hour yesterday in rough seas after the dinghy capsized in the Solent near Elbow Buoy. Mr. Geoffrey Kirkham, aged 48, and his son, Leslie, aged about 19, of Woodbury Avenue, Bournemouth, Hampshire, were picked up by a yacht and transferred to the Yarmouth, Isle of Wight, lifeboat. They were treated in hospital for exposure and exhaustion.

News at Ten gets award

The National Viewers' and Listeners' Association award for 1968 is to be presented to the Independent Television's news programme News at Ten. Mrs. Mary Whitehouse, general secretary of the association, said yesterday that the award was being given to "the most responsible current affairs programme".

Student banned from university

Mr. Tom Fawthrop, of Stanbury Crescent, Folkestone, Kent, a student at Hull University who tore up the first paper in his finals and boycotted the other four, will not be readmitted to the university. But he has been told that he can take part II of his finals in political studies and sociology next June.

Mr Heath's office gets new head

Mr. John MacGregor, who has been head of Mr. Heath's private office for the past three years, is to take up a business appointment after the Conservative Party Conference in October. He will be succeeded by Mr. Douglas Hurd, aged 38, head of the foreign affairs section of the Conservative research department.

Police search for 'immigrants'

Police and customs officers were yesterday examining a 36ft. motor cruiser in which four illegal immigrants are believed to have landed at Itchenor, near Chichester, Sussex, at the weekend. A customs officer at Itchenor said there was "every indication" that three or four Pakistanis or Indians had been on board the vessel.

Mother of twins 'satisfactory'

The mother of the Siamese twin girls who died on Saturday night was said at the City Maternity Home, Lincoln, yesterday, to be in a satisfactory condition. The twins, born on Friday, were joined at the chest and abdomen and had severe cardiac disorders.

Pop singer is accused

Patrick James Cahill, lead singer in the Flower Pot Men pop group is due to appear at South Western Magistrates' Court today accused of being in possession of a prohibited firearm and a quantity of cannabis.

Four injured at Tate

Four people were treated at Westminster Hospital for slight injuries yesterday after part of a hoarding surrounding an open air Henry Moore exhibition collapsed at the Tate Gallery.

Scientologists hear Hubbard message

By TIM JONES

The stage at the international scientology congress was bare but for flowers and a bust of Mr. L. Ron Hubbard, the founder, which stood like some Roman God in the corner. His jowled features were spotlit and from hidden amplifiers his tape-recorded voice addressed the people who packed the hall.

Yesterday was the second day of the congress which was held at Croydon, Surrey. As the founder of the movement spoke of truth, understanding and power, there were occasional gasps of acknowledgment from the audience.

To the uninitiated, the philosophy expounded by Mr. Hubbard, liberally interspersed with scientological jargon, was difficult to follow and well-nigh impossible to interpret. It was equally difficult to discover from the students what they thought of it.

People kept referring me to the press officials and seemed unwilling to talk. An official who admitted that students had been told not to communicate with the press explained that it was, "in case they fall foul of loaded questions".

One man, when asked if he believed that scientology had benefited him, replied: "I do not have to believe what I know to be true".

A colour film which showed a pretty girl registering for a course on a ship anchored in a Spanish port and then urging others to follow her footsteps was cheered loud and long.

In spite of the Government's immigration ban on delegates to the congress, it was estimated that half of those at yesterday's meeting were non-British.

Many had come from America, Australia, New Zealand, France, Germany, Canada and the Scandinavian countries.

Mr. Scott Lealand, aged 31, an American at present living in Copenhagen, said: "I just walked through". He flew into Heathrow airport on Friday specially for the congress, and was staying in Britain for the weekend. He said that in America he was a teacher of English. In Copenhagen he is engaged full time in scientology.

Mr. David Gaiman, a spokesman of the cult, said the ban had considerably affected attendances at the congress.

The organizers are angry about the action taken by Mr. Robinson, Minister of Health, to exclude visitors.

An official said: "If we are harmful, which we do not accept, then we are certainly no worse than other minority groups, such as Jehovah's Witnesses or the Plymouth Brethren, who are left to live and practise in peace.

"If the Minister says he has good reasons for banning us then he should tell us what they are and we challenge him to disclose them without using the privilege of the House. At this rate he will turn around tomorrow and without giving any reason ban Roman Catholics."

Another scientologist said he intended to bring a private summons against Mr. Robinson on the grounds that he had, by his action, practised religious discrimination.

Writs served.—Two members of East Grinstead urban council have been served with writs for alleged slander by the Church of Scientology of California. A third, Mr. Ivor Jones, has received a writ for alleged libel. Mr. Jones said today: "I shall strenuously resist the writ."

The other two councillors, Mrs. Eileen Mead, of Windmill Lane, Ashurst Wood, and Mr. Tony Old, of Gorse Cottage, North End, East Grinstead, said: "Individual writs are not unexpected after the council's recent resolution calling on the Health Minister to ban scientology from the country."

Published daily except Sundays, December 25 and 26 and Good Friday by TIMES NEWSPAPERS LIMITED, London, E.C.4. Second Class Postage paid at New York, N.Y. [illegible] Subscription U.S. [illegible] yearly. 200 East 42nd Street, New York, N.Y. [illegible] Telephone [illegible] Inland and Air Edition Subscription rates on request.

With the change from seven to eight columns in April 1967 the alternate Bold Titling 332 was drawn on for lead headings.

◀ In 1968 *The Times* adopted this straight Times Roman/Times Bold contrast style for headlines.

LATE LONDON EDITION
TUESDAY APRIL 11 1967
NO. 56,912 SIXPENCE

THE TIMES

IN BUSINESS NEWS TODAY: NEW DEAL FOR BIG CONTRACTS

BIG GUERRILLA THREAT IN SOUTH AMERICA

Strongly fortified Castro-type base in jungle

Evidence that communist guerrillas have established themselves in strength in the Bolivian jungle, with the possibility of raids into neighbouring countries, has been given by the Bolivian Army's discovery of a strongly fortified mountain base.

The guerrillas, believed to have links with the Cuban regime of Dr. Castro, appear to be well equipped and far more skilled in jungle fighting than the troops opposing them. A field hospital formed one part of the base.

REPLY TO U.S. DOUBTS

From MURRAY SAYLE, Nachabhuazu, Bolivia, April 10

I have just returned from the four-day jungle patrol with the 1st Battalion, Fourth Division of the Bolivian Army, which discovered the strongly fortified base of Castro-type communist guerrillas deep in the jungle.

Our find is the first positive proof that communist guerrillas have in fact established themselves in strength in this politically explosive country in the heart of South America, bordering on virtually unmapped parts of Argentina, Brazil and Paraguay.

This vast new extension southwards of communist guerrilla activity came to light by accident when a patrol of six men under a lieutenant of the Bolivian Army was wiped out on March 23 in a skilfully set ambush in a gorge in the foothills of the Andes.

Two days later another patrol of 14 men and two officers, sent to look for the missing men, was ambushed, taken prisoner and released after 48 hours.

Bearded Russians

The returning prisoners, who were illiterate Bolivian conscripts, told fantastic stories of bearded Russians and Chinese. Most Bolivians believed that the guerrillas were, in fact, a band of cocaine or marijuana smugglers, as both drugs grow freely in this wild part of the world. Foreign observers suspected that the Bolivian Government had invented or magnified the guerrillas

seats for patients to wait outside, all made of jungle timbers bound together with creepers.

In a pile of rubbish near the hospital I found files of patients identified by their first names, and receipts from La Paz medical suppliers for $5,000 worth of medical equipment bought between November 8 and November 20 last through a fictitious firm. A hundred yards farther on was the dormitory area.

In this area were more than 50 home-made hand grenades. These had been welded up in a clandestine factory somewhere from empty fruit juice cans and lengths of gas pipe filled with sticks of dynamite and fired by detonators. These grenades, which were neatly painted green, had been used with deadly effect on the wiped-out patrol.

Among the rubbish neatly raked from the dormitory area I found a picture of Dr. Che Guevara [the former lieutenant of Dr. Castro] taken in a jungle and a copy of a speech by General Vo Nguyen Giap, of North Vietnam, translated into Spanish.

It was impossible that these could have been "planted" as I found them myself in the rubbish and the Bolivian patrol with me had never heard of Giap.

Documents burnt

The guerrillas' camp showed every sign of an orderly evacua-

Mr. Callaghan leaving 11 Downing Street yesterday for his pre-Budget meeting with the Queen at Windsor. He also gave the Cabinet an outline of his speech in the Commons, which starts at 3.30 p.m. today.

Inter-cities helicopter project

A plan to operate a daily intercity air service between towns across southern England with Russian-built helicopters is to be put to the Air Transport Licensing Board.

Mr. Maurice Posgate, managing director of Postgate Aviation Services at Gatwick, said yesterday

Bolivian troops probe an oven in the guerrillas' field kitchen, searching for booby traps. This picture and others on page 14 were taken by Murray Sayle.

Taxi protest stops the traffic

BY A STAFF REPORTER

More than 2,000 taxicabs converged on the House of Commons yesterday carrying taxi drivers to lobby M.P.s about "unfair competition" from minicabs in the London area.

For more than two hours there was a traffic jam: at one stage Lambeth, Westminster, and Waterloo bridges were blocked. Parliament Square was jammed solid, and queues nearly two miles long stretched along Victoria Street, Millbank, Whitehall and beyond.

About 1,000 drivers left their cabs near Regent's Park while their colleagues operated a shuttle service to get them to the Com-

MR BROWN KEEPS ADEN SECRETS

Farce in emergency debate

By WILLIAM NORRIS, Parliamentary Correspondent
Westminster, Monday

They may have blood and bullets in Aden. United Nations missions may come and go. But in the Palace of Varieties, that is the House of Commons, where these grave matters led to an emergency debate tonight, the spirit of the Whitehall farce lives on.

There in the centre of the stage was Mr. George Brown. His finger wagging severely, his arms cutting great swathes of air, Mr. Brown made his position plain.

"I haven't the slightest intention of telling the House what the present situation is", he said, "because if I did I would obviously mess up and complicate the consultations now going on."

That, in a nutshell, was Mr.

Move to end

Rail bonus dispute gets amber light

Settlement basis agreed

BY OUR LABOUR STAFF

Agreement was reached yesterday on a basis for settling the freight train drivers' bonus dispute, which at one point lately seemed likely to dislocate all British Railways services.

The Government, in effect, told British Railways to stop worrying about how to pay for productivity bonuses for the 20,000 footplate men and guards who do not already get higher pay in recognition of their acceptance of single-manning of locomotives. If it takes a year or so longer to realize the full savings of single-manning, the Government will see British Railways through.

The talks, which broke down when British Railways said they could not see how to extend the benefits of a productivity bonus scheme to 5,000 of the 20,000 men, are to be resumed on Thursday and on the understanding that all the men will eventually get something.

Selected depots

Pilot schemes are to be started in about a month's time at six selected depots, so that British Railways and the unions can see how the scheme works in practice. If it is satisfactory, with or without amendment, it will be applied to the rest of the men from about August.

Mr. Gunter, Minister of Labour, presided at yesterday's talks, which were attended by representatives of British Railways, the Associated Society of Locomotive Engineers and Firemen, and the National Union of Railwaymen.

Attack on British girl in Geneva

GENEVA, April 10.—A London girl was in hospital here today after being bundled into a car and left injured in a Geneva street soon afterwards, police said. They named her as Miss Geraldine Hosier, aged 19, understood to be working as an au pair girl. She had slight facial injuries.

Police cars gave chase after a local resident heard Miss Hosier crying for help shortly before midnight. She was found by a passer-by, lying in a street in another

New shots in Tennessee riots

NASHVILLE, TENNESSEE, April 10.—Rioting by Negroes continued last night in the neighbourhood of Fisk University and Tennessee State University, and shots were again exchanged with police.

Officials said the number of students involved declined sharply, but many more townspeople became involved as the violence intensified.

A Negro youth who was wounded near Tennessee State University told police he was shot by a car load of whites.

At least 70 people have been arrested since the trouble began over a Negro ejected from a city restaurant.—*Reuter*.

Picture, page 7

ON OTHER PAGES

Dr. David Stafford-Clark: Drugs and society—an analysis of man's dependence on artificial stimulants and comforts, including alcohol and tobacco 11

Louis Heren: Conflict of split personality in Alabama 10

A change in the title-piece was notable. It was felt necessary to dispose of the Royal arms and this was interpreted to mean the dropping of the handsome Reynolds Stone title of 1953. A new title-line by Berthold Wolpe was an agreeable and dignified piece of lettering, as might be expected from the designer of types like Albertus, but scarcely an exceptional advance on its predecessor. The dateline, edition indication, price and the like were neatly cornered left and right of the title; later these items were concentrated on the left, with the right corner used for a bold 'signpost' to important pieces in the day's issue.

It is evident that the new lower-case main heading style (the first deck in 36pt Times Bold) was soon felt to be inadequate. The 1966 Style Manual provided what was called an X heading ('reserved for the occasional special main lead, on front page only') whose first deck was the coarser, series 332, version of Times Bold Titling mentioned in Chapter Six. This formula rapidly moved from the 'occasional special' to the normal, thus virtually amounting to a change in general style. The Manual also prescribed 'for the rarest occasions' a front-page 'emergency' banner style, comprising a 60pt Bold Titling line across six or seven columns with strong following decks across three columns. This 'Major Disaster Headline' was soon called on, with the wording MR BROWN QUITS THEN RETURNS (21 July 1966). The curious may conclude that there was not perfect clarity in Printing House Square as to the nature of the 'disaster' – whether it was the going or the coming of Mr George Brown (as he then was).

These changes took place with a continuing seven-column page; in April 1967, following the Thomson takeover at the end of 1966, the eight 11-pica columns format was introduced. The bold X headings now began to extend across three columns with occasional, and curious use of Perpetua Bold Titling. Meantime Clive Irving prescribed simple Light/Bold all upper- and lower-case flush-left headlines, in his *Observer* manner but using Times Roman 327 and Bold 334, for the newly-launched separate Business News section (a Thomson venture which was intended to give the *Financial Times* a run for its money, but only succeeded, at vast expense to *The Times*, in increasing *FT* circulation). This style worked very well in the Business News and in August 1968 was carried right through the paper, making the third style change since May 1966. Many then thought that, given such a well-tried and flexible formula, *The Times* could take its graphic form for granted and concentrate on its editorial content; true, both weights of Times lacked the roundness and width which made Century Schoolbook and its Bold so successful, but their condensation was little more than that of normal Century Bold. However, Printing

Wednesday February 16 1972
No 58,403 Price 5p

THE TIMES

The IRA's separate roads to united Ireland, p 14

Photographed by Harry Kerr

Miners and union supporters pressing forward as policemen struggle to hold back demonstrators at the St Stephen's entrance to the Houses of Parliament yesterday. Every off-duty policeman was called in

1.2m laid off as power cuts are increased

As factory and office power cuts bit more deeply yesterday, 1,200,000 people, or a twentieth of the working population, were laid off. Imperial Chemical Industries gave a week's notice to all 60,000 of its weekly-paid staff as a "precautionary measure". Government figures showed that gas works were within a week of total exhaustion of coal stocks.

The TUC's "inner cabinet" last night rejected a government appeal to persuade the miners to relax their picketing and allow coal into power stations. The request was made earlier at a Downing Street meeting between the Prime Minister, Mr Carr, Secretary of State for Employment, and Mr Victor Feather, TUC general secretary.

The public were excluded from a court in Dunfermline, Scotland, yesterday, when 13 pickets arrested during incidents at Longannet power station on Monday were remanded in custody on charges of mobbing and rioting. The public were barred after scuffles between policemen and miners trying to enter the court. Thousands of miners marched from Tower Hill to lobby MPs at Westminster yesterday. About 12,000 gathered outside the Commons. All police leave was cancelled.

In evidence to the Wilberforce inquiry yesterday, Mr Lawrence Daly, general secretary of the National Union of Mineworkers, called for future employment guarantees and an agreement that miners would not face forced redundancy in any new deal.

The Central Electricity Generating Board, which made 6 per cent voltage reductions on top of rota cuts yesterday, said that from today every "high risk" area would definitely have a cut instead of standing a one-in-three chance of escaping a switch-off, as before. Rota cuts would be stepped up from 10 to 15 per cent today and there would probably be voltage reductions (details, page 4). From yesterday Londoners were given warning of impending power cuts by a brief interruption in supplies five minutes before the main cut.

The Meteorological Office's long-range forecast, issued yesterday, predicted a cold spell in all areas early in the 30-day period. (Forecasts, page 2.)

TUC refuses to urge pickets to let coal go to power stations

By Paul Routledge
Labour Correspondent

TUC leaders yesterday rejected Government overtures to press miners to relax picketing and allow coal stocks to be channelled into power stations.

Instead, the congress's powerful "inner cabinet", the Finance and General Purposes Committee, reaffirmed the instruction to union members not to cross NUM picket lines, and called on unions to give "maximum practical aid" to the striking miners.

The committee also asked trades councils to join the miners' local leaders in organizing demonstrations by workers laid off because of power cuts. (CBI seeks priority for industry after strike, page 4.)

The appeal for TUC help came in a meeting at 10 Downing Street between Mr Heath and Mr Feather, TUC general secretary, earlier in the day. The Prime Minister asked that the TUC's influence should be used to bring a speedy end to the six-week-old strike.

But after a two-hour meeting later in the day, the committee issued a statement that said: "The committee, whilst recognizing the seriousness of the situation, emphasized that the responsibility for the widespread dislocation of industry lies squarely on the Government's dogmatic attitude and inept handling of the situation.

"Millions of work people will be laid off and enormous damage will be done to the economy as a consequence of the Government's misjudgment of the situation, and its inflexible and insensitive attitude to wage claims."

Union leaders went farther and demanded that ministers should not make public statements or speeches arguing the need for the "national interest" to be taken into account by the Wilberforce inquiry, which opened yesterday.

The committee urged Lord Wilberforce and his two colleagues to work speedily to produce a report that would recognize the merits of the miners' case and give an acceptable base for a resumption of work.

"To this end the Government itself must be prepared to take whatever action is necessary to enable the coal board to meet the demands for a substantial improvement in the wages and working conditions of the mineworkers."

The committee also "noted"—that is, tacitly approved—the decision by the miners' executive yesterday to reduce the size but not the effectiveness of pickets.

After the NUM executive meeting, Mr Gormley, union president, said: "We do not think there will be a cat in hell's chance of getting these men off the picket lines until the report of the court is available. And, by God, if it is not favourable, I hesitate to think what could happen to Britain."

Job security demand, page 4
Business News, page 17

Power cuts for all high-risk areas

By a Staff Reporter

There will be more power cuts from today. All electricity boards will be increasing their planned rota cuts from 10 to 15 per cent, the Central Electricity Generating Board said last night.

The board made 6 per cent voltage reductions throughout Britain yesterday. A similar reduction is expected today on top of the extra rota cuts.

Every area at high risk in the cuts "rota" will definitely have a power cut during the day. "Under the 10 per cent cuts consumers in high-risk areas had a one-in-three chance of not being switched off under the rota, but under the new 15 per cent cuts everyone in a high-risk area will definitely have a cut", the CEGB said.

From today the rota power cuts will not start until between 6.30 and 7 am. "We are working towards only 17 hours a day of cuts, between 7 am and midnight, instead of the present 18 hours between 6 am and midnight", the Electricity Council said yesterday.

The delay in the starting of the cuts had been caused by operational difficulties in stopping large amounts of power suddenly at 6 am, the council said. "Starting disconnexions from 6 am has been posing severe technical problems for the CEGB."

The London Electricity Board yesterday began to give a five-minute advance warning of rota cuts by interrupting supplies for a few seconds. The LEB is the only board giving warning "because London is a relatively compact area with only six main switching stations".

British Rail cancelled more than 1,500 electric trains in a further attempt to conserve fuel. Southern Region was again the worst affected, with 909 trains cancelled out of 4,917.

London Transport's Underground system was not affected as it generates its own power supplies.

Milk deliveries continued almost normally, the Milk Marketing Board said.

ICI gives 60,000 week's notice as 'precautionary measure'

By Our Industrial Staff

The number of workers laid off in Britain reached 1,200,000 yesterday as power cuts affected more and more factories and offices. This was half as much again as on Monday and means that one worker in 20 was instructed to stay at home.

The nation's largest basic industrial enterprise, **Imperial Chemical Industries**, whose activities span chemicals, fibres and textile goods, issued a week's notice to its 60,000 weekly-paid staff. The company said the action was a "precautionary measure".

No lay-offs of ICI workers have occurred so far, but the company has given a warning that stability of earnings cannot be guaranteed, although all workers will be paid normal salaries up to the end of next week.

The national total of workers sent home was issued last night by the Department of Employment. Estimates suggested that about 360,000 people were affected in the Midlands, with about 30,000 in each of the South-west and Welsh regions. **In Scotland, the figure was put at between 55,000 and 110,000.**

With power station coal stocks down to two weeks' supply and four million tons stockpiled at pitheads, industrialists are worried on another front. Major industries are big users of coal in their own right and their stocks are fast diminishing, adding to worries even if emergency electricity supplies underwrite short-time working.

Companies are now taking many individual troubles to the Department of Trade and Industry regional centres, which are coordinating the operation of emergency fuel regulations. Meanwhile, the CBI was keeping an eye on the operation of the restrictions to document its plea for consecutive three-day working and other adjustments to present controls.

At the Central Electricity Generating Board efforts were being made to receive in due course some coal imports, coming by way of Amsterdam and Rotterdam from around the world. But the amount remaining under existing import contracts is only 500,000 tons of the four million tons ordered in December, 1970, when the Government lifted the long-standing ban on foreign coal supplies.

No new contracts have been negotiated because the Government has the reimposition of the ban, which had been due, under review.

While more than a few industrialists have hesitated to introduce maximum lay-offs and production cutbacks, a series of heavy manpower reductions is certain even if the chances of an early settlement rise.

This is because of the statement in the Commons on Monday that electricity restrictions will last for weeks after the resumption of normal coal mining.

British Leyland continued yesterday to be the worst affected group in the motor car sector, with more than 37,000 workers laid off out of a work force of 135,000.

In BLMC's Austin-Morris group of factories 17,000 employees were not at their jobs, including 7,800 at Longbridge, Birmingham, where no cars were built during the day. Production is expected to start at the works this morning with the return of assembly workers from a pay claim strike. About 2,700 workers at Castle Bromwich should also arrive back today.

At Cowley 2,250 employees

Continued page 4, col 4

Thousands stage noisy but peaceful procession with some of the pageantry of a Durham gala

By Philip Howard

Several thousand miners, their wives and other trade unionists marched through London to lobby members of Parliament yesterday.

It was a noisy but peaceful procession with some of the pageantry of a Durham miners' gala. Brass bands, including a children's band from South Wales led by a girl drum major twirling a staff, made the cliffs of the City echo with booming, oldfashioned music such as "Great Little Army" and "Colonel Bogey".

Huge scarlet and gold banners were held upright in the tearing wind by guy ropes fore and aft. They were emblazoned with the names of famous pits from South Wales to Yorkshire and Durham, with embroideries of mining scenes and inspiring mottoes.

At Tower Hill, Mr Alex Eadie, Labour MP for Midlothian, told the miners to march with their heads held high "to demonstrate to the people of London that the miners have an unanswerable case for more cash".

A band from Nottinghamshire, dressed in dinner jackets and displaying a banner showing Robin Hood, led the march playing "The Standard of St George". Police shepherded the procession through the City and across Waterloo Bridge.

In South Bank Gardens and on the embankment in front of County Hall the procession was halted and broken into irregular contingents which were allowed up the steps on to Westminster Bridge at intervals.

They were funnelled between police lines into the Houses of Parliament. Some were diverted through Westminster Hall. St Stephen's entrance had to be shut once and there was some pushing and shouting from those left outside in the rain.

Inside the House miners were dispersed around different committee rooms and corridors to be addressed by Labour MPs. The Leader of the Opposition made a circuit to give them a little touch of Harold in the night.

He told a group of Yorkshire miners: "You have the full support of the Parliamentary Labour Party. The condition for the miners going back to work is that the Prime Minister should go back to work first and do his duty.

"As soon as this strike is settled honourably, I want you to go back to work as quickly as possible so that your fellow workers in other industries can also get back to work. The solidarity of the Labour movement behind the miners in this strike will go down in Labour history."

Mr Hugh Scanlon, president of the Amalgamated Union of Engineering and Foundry Workers, told the miners: "You miners have done over the last weeks what should have been done by the trade union movement months ago."

Mr Harold Lever, Opposition spokesman on fuel and power, told a group: "I fervently believe that the miners have been unjustly treated in the postwar years. I resent the suggestion that your problems are not also the problems of the Government or the country."

The central lobby was crowded all the afternoon, and thundering cheers and claps made the dome ring when the lights went out.

Many awards for troops' bravery in Ulster

More than fifty men have been awarded honours for brave or distinguished service in Northern Ireland, the Army announced yesterday.

Only a bare list of names and regiments was released by the Department of Defence. The ministry said no further information was being provided "in the interest of the personal security of the recipients and their families".

Operational awards included the DSO for Lieutenant-Colonel R. Eccles, The Green Howards, and Lieutenant-Colonel R. K. Guy, The Royal Green Jackets.

The Military Cross was awarded to Major I. D. Corden-Lloyd, Lieutenant C. L. Burrage and Second Lieutenant M. Smith, all of The Royal Green Jackets, and Major P. H. Kingston, The Parachute Regiment.

Brigadier Frank Kitson, who won the Military Cross in Kenya in 1956, was appointed CBE for gallantry.

Other awards included: OBE for gallantry: Lieutenant-Colonel C. R. Huxtable, The Duke of Wellington's Regiment, Lieutenant-Colonel Geoffrey Howlett, Commanding Officer, 2nd Battalion, The Parachute Regiment.

MBE for gallantry: The Rev G. E. Weston, chaplain: Warrant Officer I. T. B. Latham, The Green Howards: Captain A. R. Redwood-Davies, The Duke of Wellington's Regiment. MBE for meritorious service: Major P. W. Graham, Gordon Highlanders.

George Medal: Captain Alan Clouter, bomb disposal expert; Warrant Officer T. J. Green; Captain D. Markham, all Royal Army Ordnance Corps.

Military Medal: Colour Sergeant E. Bright, The Royal Green Jackets; Corporals E. W. Fisher and G. Crossland, The Green Howards: Corporal R. Chinn and Private C. J. Butler, The Queen's Regiment: Corporal B. Togg and Private P. S. Burlace, The Parachute Regiment; Sapper A. G. Young, Royal Engineers.

Another 28 were mentioned in dispatches.

Other Irish news, page 2

Warning to car industry on foam plastic fires

By Clifford Webb

The Department of Employment has issued a warning that expanded or foamed plastic, used extensively by the car industry to pad dashboards to reduce injuries in accidents, produces dense smoke and poisonous gases when ignited.

The department's warning is being circulated widely in a leaflet

It follows extensive testing of the plastics, of which about 60,000 tons a year are used in Britain. About three quarters of this is in the form of polyurethane foam and the rest is polystyrene. The car industry's consumption, which is increasing all the time, accounts for about 10,000 tons a year.

A Ford Motor Company official said last night that the danger of the plastic foam catching alight in cars was very small. "The quantity used in a car is comparatively small and in any case is always covered by vinyl, which is a fire-retardant material," he said

The Department of Employment said that the tests were made because of increasing concern about the fire risks.

Mr A. W. Grimsey, superintending factory inspector for the Midlands, said: "Plastics generally have been involved in many serious fires and there has been considerable loss of property."

Prince Richard to marry Danish girl

Prince Richard of Gloucester, the Queen's cousin, who is 27, announced his engagement yesterday to Miss Birgitte van Deurs, aged 25, a Danish secretary. He met her six years ago while he was studying architecture at Cambridge University.

Prince Richard is tenth in line of succession to the throne. The Queen has given her formal consent to the marriage, which is necessary under the Royal Marriages Act, 1772.

The couple will marry this summer at the village church of St Andrew's, Barnwell, Northamptonshire, where the Gloucesters have their family home.

Miss van Deurs, whose parents were divorced when she was five, took her mother's maiden name when she grew up. She will leave her job in June.

Photograph, page 16

Ecuador leader overthrown in Army coup

Quito, Feb 15.—Ecuador's President Velasco Ibarra was overthrown in a coup by the armed forces tonight, Defence Ministry sources said here.

The sources said that his successor as president would be Brigadier-General Guillermo Rodriguez Lara, and that the ousted President would go into exile into Argentina.

The President had left Quito suddenly for Guayaquil tonight, announcing that he would make a nation-wide television broadcast from there, but the channel due to transmit it went off the air saying it was forced to do so by "very strong reasons"

President Velasco Ibarra dismissed Congress and the Supreme Court in June, 1970, and took dictatorial powers but said Ecuador would be restored to democracy in a year. Reuter

Sir Alec called back from tour to vote on EEC Bill

By Our Political Editor

Sir Alec Douglas-Home, the Foreign and Commonwealth Secretary, has abruptly ended his Far East tour on being called home by Government business managers to vote in Thursday night's division on the second reading of the European Communities Bill. A planned three-day visit to Japan will not take place.

It is an unmistakable sign of the Government Whip's determination to bring home every available vote in a division that may reduce the Government majority to single figures. Westminster has noted that the date of the division was known before Sir Alec left London, but no steps were taken until 24 hours ago to alter his arrangements.

The implication may well be that Mr Pym, the Government Chief Whip, having taken soundings among his anti-Market backbenchers, now realizes that the division will be tighter than he originally expected.

Estimates of the Government's majority are extremely difficult to make at a time when voting intentions are being concealed or hedged, but there is a widespread assumption that a small number of pro-Market Labour backbenchers may be willing to abstain at the eleventh hour if the Bill is clearly seen to be in peril.

For the present, the Government looks like having a majority of between 10 to 20.

Rippon reassurance, page 7
Britain's problems in Asia, page 9
Diary, page 14

Philharmonia's principal flautist quits

By a Staff Reporter

Mr Gareth Morris, chairman of the New Philharmonia Orchestra and its principal flautist, has resigned because of irreconcilable artistic differences. A joint statement issued yesterday said he had so decided in the best interest of the NPO and his career.

Mr Morris, aged 51, has been a member for nearly 24 years.

Mr Nixon's campaign manager named

Washington, Feb 15.—Mr John Mitchell today resigned as Attorney General to become manager of President Nixon's reelection campaign, the post that he held in the 1968 Presidential race.

Soviet employee of UN on spying charge

New York, Feb 15.—The United States Government today asked for bail to be set at $500,000 (£196,000) for Valeriy Markelov, a Soviet citizen employed at the United Nations, who is accused of espionage

Mr Markelov, a translator, aged 32, was arrested yesterday in a Long Island restaurant after allegedly obtaining secret documents on the new F-14 naval aircraft.

The Federal Bureau of Investigation alleged that Mr Markelov had made the acquaintance late in 1970 of an engineer of the Grumman Aerospace Corporation, which is building the F-14 for the Navy. The engineer co-operated with the FBI and had 11 separate meetings with Mr Markelov before allegedly handing over the secret material.—Reuter.

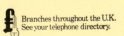

The rest of the news

◀ The 'modular' make-up introduced in September 1970, with an exclusively Times Bold headline style (normal ceiling 36pt). Note the changed title-line, re-drawn from Times Bold capitals.

House Square was racked by anxiety. Thomson had saved *The Times* but the paper was still heavily in the red. Evidently there was a feeling that something more radical than an existing formula, no matter how effective other papers were finding it, had to be devised.

The changes in the summer of 1968 had included some simplifications in setting; the traditional use of caps and smalls for proper names in leaders was ended; the poor showing of Times Roman text induced an extension of 9pt as the basic size from the front page to all news pages. But this was incidental; what finally emerged in September 1970 was a complete revolution in the paper's headline typography and make-up. News headings were now exclusively in Times Bold, upper- and lower-case, set flush-left, and limited to a size range of 12pt to 36pt, the last being the largest size in ordinary use for front-page leads. Matrices of these sizes were cut for slug-casting. Make-up was more strongly horizontal than had ever been seen before and extreme multi-column headlining seemed sometimes to fracture the page. With what came to be called a 'modular' make-up of this sort the use of 24pt and 30pt Times Bold for, say, three-liners across three columns, or two-liners across four or five, inevitably produced padding-out and verbosity in the headline writing. The official theory was that the generous letter-count would make for more 'literate' headings; in practice it tended to make them wordy and wandering.

On the day of the changeover (21 September 1970) the first leader developed the argument that it was 'very wasteful' for a newspaper to 'clamour for attention'. It went on: 'Big headings, large white spaces, blown-up pictures, all take space away from the most scarce source of journalism, the written word. By redesigning in a tighter and more classical style it becomes easier to give the news in full.' Later, as has been observed above, this desire to economise in space led to the cutting of a 7pt for the new Times Europa text. In 1970 a system of page 'signposting' was introduced that was not notably economical. The fully cutoff page running head was retained, with a page-width heavy rule beneath it, and opening with the words Home News, Overseas, etc., originally in 18pt Times Roman lower-case, later upped to capitals.

Accompanying the 1970 revolution was a further restructuring of the leader page. The leaders now spread across three columns, the remaining four (for the page retained the seven column make-up, as it does to this day) being allotted to the Letters to the Editor. Lead letters were headed in Times Roman lower-case – and grouped letters were separated only by a white, not a heading – with other letters headed in Times Bold; thus the handsome Times Extended Titling 339 (Times Heading Bold) lost its last foothold. The title-line was again changed, Berthold Wolpe's line was supplanted by one of the same 60pt face depth but around seven picas shorter; the new line was redrawn with some modification from large-size capitals of Times Bold, one difference being in the style of the 'E'.

The remaining national dailies require no very detailed survey. Even in a much-trumpeted re-vamp of March 1973 the *Daily Express* did not depart from its basic Century formula; it simply increased the play on Bold Extended and (contrary to modern practice) Bold italic, upper- and lower-case. Pages were strongly 'signposted', in an extra condensed gothic, with heavy rules and plenty of white. The conventional cutoffs between stories were dropped in favour of white space only; column rules were increased in weight, approximating those of the *Evening Standard*. The big surprise was the abandonment of the famous Morison title-line of 1942, which had become the paper's distinctive symbol, for a line in heavy slab-seriffed roman, comparable in flavour with the line introduced by the *Observer* in 1966–7 or the *Guardian* in 1969 (the *Sunday Express* retained the Morison line). Breaking sharply with national newspaper custom, the front-page solus advertisement was upped from double- to treble-column.

The *Financial Times* has already been mentioned in respect of the

DAILY EXPRESS

THE VOICE OF BRITAIN

No. 22,625 Monday March 19 1973 Weather: Dry; cloudy and warm Price 3p

Dilemma over Bermuda security

TOUR ALERT FOR CHARLES

By Chapman Pincher

THE PERSONAL security of Prince Charles is to be discussed by a three-man Cabinet team, following the assassination of Sir Richard Sharples, the governor of Bermuda, it was disclosed yesterday.

This has become necessary because the Prince is scheduled to return to Bermuda next month for a two-to-three-week stay.

After touring Caribbean islands, his ship, the 2,500-ton frigate Minerva is due at the old dockyard on Ireland Island for essential maintenance.

The Minerva visited Bermuda last month at the start of the Caribbean tour and Prince Charles took the same late night walk in the gardens of Government House that Sir Richard and his aide Captain Hugh Sayers were enjoying when they were shot dead.

Lord Carrington, the Defence Secretary, Mr. Robert Carr, the Home Secretary, and Sir Alec Douglas Home, the Foreign and Commonwealth Secretary, are to meet to decide the best course of action for the Heir to the Throne.

Action

Lord Carrington is responsible for the Prince's safety while he is aboard Minerva but the responsibility passes to the Home Secretary as soon as Prince Charles sets foot on land.

Sir Alec is concerned because Bermuda is still a British Colony.

The Queen will be consulted before the "considered view" is given to the Prince through the Minerva's captain, Commander John Garnier.

The decision is hedged with sensitive political and personal issues. Three courses of action are possible.

ONE: The Prince could return to Bermuda with the ship as planned and rely on the tightened security of the island when he goes ashore.

This would put great strain on the Bermuda Administration, even if extra security men were flown out from Britain.

Safer

The Prince's presence might be accepted as a challenge by Black Power gunmen who regard Bermuda as one of the last remaining symbols of British imperialism.

It is not considered feasible that he could stay on board the frigate during the whole period it is scheduled to be there.

TWO: Prince Charles could stay behind in Barbados or some other safer island or be flown home when the ship sails for Bermuda.

I understand that the Prince does not like either of these solutions because he wants to be treated like his ship mates.

Further, his absence could be claimed as something of a moral victory for the Black Power movement which is suspected of being responsible for the assassinations.

THREE: The ship could cancel its visit to Bermuda and put in for maintenance at an American port, such as Norfolk, Virginia.

Slight

This seems to be the likeliest move, though it would not be popular with the 53,000 Bermudans, most of whom are opposed to becoming independent of the British crown, and the Bermuda Government might regard it as a slight because Bermuda is the headquarters of the Navy's West Indies Squadron.

Meanwhile the scheduled dates of the arrival of Minerva at various Caribbean islands, including Bermuda, are to be kept secret.

The Daily Express Tomorrow's paper

TODAY THE Daily Express has a bolder title at the top of this page and the Crusader a firmer jaw.

More important the Daily Express has a change of voice—The Voice of Britain, but with a surprising new emphasis.

The Daily Express is an independent paper.

WE WILL put the views of the trades unions as well as those of Government and the employers.

We will be a voice for the silent majority. We will find space for the voice of dissent.

The Daily Express believes in youth. Eager young men and women helped my father to make this paper exciting, challenging, successful.

Now the Daily Express speaks for a new generation, for its lively ambitions and its concerns, especially its social awareness of those in need.

THIS IS a more thoughtful generation than mine.

That means, from today, a bigger Daily Express with more news in it. And a balanced paper with more thought in it—more thoughtful writing, more thoughtful photography, more thoughtful lay-out.

I know our 9,500,000 readers will like the changes in the Express.

I commend them to the Daily Express readers of tomorrow. Because the Daily Express is tomorrow's paper.

Max Aitken

CAR DEATH RIDDLE

Murdered man's car . . . no bullet holes

Double life of the A4 gun victim

By Colin Pratt

THE MYSTERY double life of a man shot dead at the wheel of his sports car was being probed by detectives last night. They believe that he may have been killed by an enemy he made in car dealings.

By day, Barrie Page, a 25-year-old bachelor, worked for an American-owned catering firm at London's Heathrow Airport.

But in his spare time he imported secondhand cars from the Continent to sell.

Detectives yesterday began sifting through records of car sales and H.P. deals in which Page was involved.

Detective Superintendent Philip Fairweather, the man leading the murder hunt, said: "We feel sure this is not a case of a man being ambushed for no reason. Almost certainly it was something to do with his car dealings."

Smashed

Page's £7,000 red Aston Martin veered off the A4 Colnbrook by-pass as he drove towards Slough, Buckinghamshire, on Saturday evening.

As it smashed into a hedge on the opposite side of the road, a car close behind it revved up and roared away.

Another motorist stopped and called an ambulance, thinking that it was an ordinary road acident.

But at Wexham Park Hospital, near Slough, two bullets from an automatic pistol were found in the body.

One thing puzzling police is just how the fatal shots were fired. The car doors and windows were closed and there were no bullet-holes.

The theory is that he stopped to talk to someone in another car. As the shots were fired, he slammed the door and tried to drive off but died after travelling a short distance.

Page, short and thick-set, of

Barrie Page

Oakfield Avenue, Slough, travelled from job to job in America, including a spell as a Hollywood stunt man, before joining Marriott's Inflite Catering at Heathrow.

Page's landlord and personal friend, Mr. Colin Shrubb, said: "He told me he had made a lot of enemies in the second-hand car trade.

"The exact operation, he kept to himself. He was a tough boy who could look after himself, but I think he must have got in a bit too deep."

The dead man's father, Mr. Albert Page, 53-year-old B.E.A. welfare officer and a magistrate, said: "It seems someone had a grudge, but we don't know why."

Guerrilla alert

Police surrounded an Amsterdam-bound airliner at Heathrow Airport yesterday and passengers were checked following a Black September threat made in New York. The plane was cleared.

Guard dogs panic girl fans

Picture by Steve Wood

An Alsatian leaps and the young pop fans cringe in fear

THIS WAS Popland '73 in London yesterday, a scene of snarling dogs and frightened young fans.

It happened as the Cassidy cult reached a new hysteria peak.

Several girls had their clothes torn by the dogs. Another was hit by a car—though not badly hurt—in the stampede to get away.

One man—a member of the Cassidy entourage—said he was bitten.

Scene of it all was the Esso Motor Hotel, 500 yards from the Empire Pool, Wembley, where singing idol David Cassidy was appearing last night.

Hotel manager Brian Holt said: "The safety of my guests is my concern—that's why the dogs were there.

"The handlers did a good job as far as I'm concerned, although there was a lot of barking and snarling, no one was bitten."

Said dog-handler Leigh Williams: "My dog didn't bite anybody—it's more than my job's worth."

But Cassidy's public relations officer, Tony Barrow, said: "It was a disgrace. We have our own security arrangements and we wouldn't dream of including dogs in this arrangement. It's barbaric."

Beatle back

Former Beatle Paul McCartney made his first "live" return to London last night with his group. Wings, at the Hard Rock Café.

Plane firms set for giant merger

By Keith Thompson

BRITAIN'S "Big Two" planemakers are to merge.

Drive and initiative to get the Hawker Siddeley aerospace companies and British Aircraft Corporation together has come from the Government.

The £220 million merger—creating Europe's most formidable and powerful aerospace firm—is likely to take a year or more to complete.

To encourage it, the Government has promised financial partnership in a range of new projects, including Hawker's new HS 146 "commuter" airliner.

The work force of the new set-up will be about 70,000. And it is most probable that new jobs will be created, with new projects in the pipeline.

There should be no redundancy fears for the unions.

Fears

So far no formal talks have been held between Hawker Siddeley and British Aircraft Corporation. But there have been a number of off-the-record chats between Hawker boss Sir Arnold Hall and B.A.C.'s Sir George Edwards.

Both firms are financially in a happy state. Their joint turnover last year was around £750 million.

The Common Market has been a major factor in getting the two firms closer. There have been growing fears about the expansion of the French aerospace industry.

The link up would give Britain a powerful stepping-stone into Europe and world markets.

LATEST

BETTER JOBS

There is a better Job for you in the Daily Express. See Pages 14 and 15.

PHONE STD CODE 01
353 8000
TELEX 21841

In today's 24-page Express

ALL THE news and picture reports appear in the front part of your bigger Daily Express today.

Page 2, for example, has **political and industrial** news.

Pages 4 and 5 carry the **Express World News** report . . . including a despatch by Hugh McIlvanney from Uganda.

Also on Page 4:—

The America Column

. . . with a new name—John Ellison, formerly in charge of the Paris bureau. Start reading him today ON PAGE 4.

On the same page—a new, enlarged **weather service.**

Then come the special articles and features.

TV programmes are on Page 10

William Hickey is on Page 11

And there are two pages of City news on Pages 18 and 19.

Here is your easy-to-find guide to the 24-page Express.

J. R. EVE & SON
• Chartered Surveyors
LAND AND PROPERTY CONSULTANTS
LONDON · BEDFORD · BRISTOL · HITCHIN
FINANCIAL TIMES
No. 25,791
Saturday June 24 1972
6p
MAENSON
CLOTHES FOR MEN
Superbly made from the finest cloths with immediate fit at all the best shops and stores
MAENSON
NEWS SUMMARY
Gilts rise £2½, 30-Share up 15
£ just over $2.50 in New York
Intense pressure on dollar
$2,600m. spent on sterling support
Talks in Paris today
£ float may last till EEC entry
BY WILLIAM KEEGAN, ECONOMICS CORRESPONDENT
F.T. INDUSTRIAL ORDINARY INDEX
Holidaymakers abroad hit
BY ARTHUR SANDLES
Concerned
Quotations
Sterling Area deals curbed
BY MICHAEL BLANDEN
GENERAL
UN meets over Mid. East crisis
BUSINESS
Unions urge steel talks

▲ Simple Times Bold headlining and effective reverse 'signposting' (as in the news summary) were the mark of the *Financial Times*.

change of its text to Royal and in respect of its excellent 'signposting'; this last is done by page-width, shallow reverse blocks, the Times Bold section labels in white on a dark tint ground. The paper is headlined throughout in Times Bold upper- and lower-case, roman for news, italic for features. When the front-page lead heading was raised to 60pt the Perpetua Bold Titling title-line was suitably upped in size without encroaching on width by the simple device of deleting the definite article. The title had been prescribed by Robert Harling in 1953 to make a bolder show than the large but light Perpetua Titling adopted from the *Financial News*, when that paper was taken over in 1945, to replace the under-scrolled bold Script title which dated from 1893.

The *Daily Telegraph*, whose million-and-a-half circulation and mass

Evolution of the *Financial Times* title – bold Script (1893–1945), Perpetua Titling (1945–53), Perpetua Bold Titling (1953, now increased in size and with 'The' deleted). ▶

The Financial Times.

Incorporating The Financier and Bullionist.

THE
FINANCIAL TIMES
Incorporating THE FINANCIAL NEWS

◀ The *Express* re-vamp of March 1973 continued the basic Century formula, but with more play on the Bold Extended lower-case: a heavy roman, not unlike the title of the *Observer*, supplanted Morison's long-standing line.

THE FINANCIAL TIMES
INCORPORATING THE FINANCIAL NEWS
INDUSTRY · COMMERCE · PUBLIC AFFAIRS

The Daily Telegraph

WEST RIFT OVER RUSSIAN TALKS

REASON FOR VISITS BY MR. DULLES

BONN & PARIS OPPOSE EARLY CONFERENCE

CYPRIOT INJURED IN GUN MISHAP

HUME BREAKS DOWN UNDER QUESTIONS

93 ABOARD SHIP GIVEN UP FOR DEAD

▲ At the start of the 1960s the *Daily Telegraph* was still in the traditional decker stage, including some ancient news-titlings, but by the 1970s it had evolved a 'free' Bodoni Bold style, with strong stress on lower-case. ▶

The Daily Telegraph

No. 36607. LONDON, SATURDAY, JANUARY 27, 1973. FINAL 4p

IRA TO PUT MacSTIOFAIN ON TRIAL

'He will have a lot to answer for'

By GERARD KEMP in Dublin

SEAN MacSTIOFAIN, the former chief of staff of the Provisional IRA who is serving a six-month sentence at the Curragh military camp, will be court-martialled by the IRA when he is released in April.

He will be charged with disobeying the Provos order that IRA men should not recognise a civil court, north or south of the border, and with "bringing the movement into disrepute."

MacStiofain is said to have recognised the Special Criminal Court in Dublin in November when he was found guilty of being a member of the IRA. Although he refused to plead he made several statements in court.

Mr Rogers, United States Secretary of State, being welcomed by Tan Van Lam, South Vietnamese Foreign Minister, when he arrived in Paris last night for the signing of the Vietnam ceasefire agreement.

POULSON TV FILM BANNED

Hospital staff refuse Phase II pay offer

By BLAKE BAKER, Industrial Correspondent

LEADERS of 230,000 hospital ancillary workers yesterday rejected a pay offer by the management of the National Health Service of £1·84 a week more from March 14.

U.S. CAN STILL HIT HO TRAIL

Dearer holidays, fish and meat

CHINESE FREE LAST BRITONS

BRITAIN TAKING ADVANTAGE, SAYS ICELAND

FIXED PRICE FOR CONCORDE WORK DENIED

ARK ROYAL MAY GO IN 1975

WORRYING DAY FOR INVESTORS

£17m TAKEOVER BID 'TOO LOW' SAYS BENTLEY

BILL WILL CURB INSURANCE FIRMS

J. CARROLL NAISH

CANADA DATE

TIGER ATTACKS SAFARI WARDEN

LEVIES ON BEEF STAY SUSPENDED

ULSTER GIRL HELD UNDER TERROR LAW

SOLDIER SHOT

LATE NEWS

INDEX TO OTHER PAGES

BRENTFORD'S REVOLUTIONARY OFFER! CELLULAR BLANKETS

NYLON FITTED SHEETS

of classifieds has won it esteem as the most successful 'heavy' in British newspaper history, is commonly thought of as a paper lacking in design. This is untrue. During the past decade the *Telegraph*, whose notable initiatives over its text types we have noted, simplified and improved its display typography in effective fashion. Maybe it is because the paper's presentation remains unsensational that these changes have not attracted the attention they deserve. At the start of the 1960s the *Telegraph* was still in the traditional all-capitals decker era, combining Century with Century Bold, Bodoni Light with antique news-titlings; decks were divided by dashes or short rules. Occasional lower-case decks were set in Transit. Ten years later both this mixture, and the deckers, had vanished. The paper had developed a uniform style in Bodoni Bold, roman and italic, with marked play on upper- and lower-case; where a second deck survived, as in the lead heading, it was in lower-case and separated from its top deck by white only. The only exceptions to the Bodoni style were three-column lead headings, set in Century Bold Extended, and down-page fillers, where the hangover of the *Sunday Telegraph's* Caledonia Bold experiment was used, in 12pt and 14pt capitals, in place of the news-titlings. Front-page lead headings had a normal ceiling of 42pt capitals. The *Telegraph* stuck stoutly to its blackletter title; this, however, had been

The current London *Evening News* contrasted with its style of 1960 (below). ▶

BIGGEST EVENING SALE IN THE WORLD

Evening News

London Wednesday January 3, 1973 No. 28,277 3p

Come and see the News light up London

David Greig

Protests grow as banker tells of 'anxiety'
Giant store cancels £500,000 drinks order

HIGH STREET BAN HITS DISTILLERS

Evening News Reporter

ONE of Britain's High Street giants this afternoon attacked the Distillers Company in the thalidomide compensation controversy.

Chiefs of the David Greig grocery chain —who buy Distillers' products worth half a million pounds every year—said they would buy nothing more until "a reasonable thalidomide settlement is offered."

The news, from Mr. Peter Green, joint managing director of the Wrenson Group, which owns Greigs, was handed to Distillers' chairman Sir Alexander McDonald when he arrived in London for crisis talks with bankers and legal advisers.

Moves in the U.S.

The GLC — holding 350,000 Distillers' shares — meanwhile joined the City's call for an extraordinary general meeting of shareholders to discuss the board's handling of the issue.

And in the United States, moves were afoot to

GLC join the big shares revolt

By LEONARD VIGARS

LOST! TWO TEETH ON A VITAL DAY

'Mercy' plea for mercy killers

Fantastic value for money!

ON WEDNESDAY December 27, Allders of Croydon had a front-page advertisement in the Evening News for their sale starting on Friday, December 29.

The Evening News INCORPORATING THE STAR

World's largest evening sale

No. 24,507 LONDON, TUESDAY, OCTOBER 18, 1960 PRICE 2½d.

THE EVENING NEWS Incorporates THE STAR And
The DAILY MAIL Incorporates The NEWS CHRONICLE

CALLING LONDON!

This Is THE REASON WHY

What The News Means To YOU

TO-DAY The Star, one of London's three evening newspapers, has been incorporated in The Evening News.

Similarly The News Chronicle has been incorporated in the Daily Mail.

Thus to-day is a momentous occasion both for the millions who read The Evening News and the millions who read The Star.

From now on they will be able to get a joint newspaper combining the best contents of both in the field of NEWS and FEATURES, PICTURES and SPORT—in short a newspaper for men and women, young and not-so-young.

The result will be that *The Evening News*, which has always led the field in its NEWS coverage, will do so even more with its greatly increased resources as *The Evening News and Star*.

Sturdy Rival

MURDER CHARGE FAILS... AND HER 20-YEAR SECRET HELL IS OVER

Mummy Widow Is Not Guilty

Mrs. Sarah Harvey

COCA COLA RAIDER GETS A MILLION

Bird Attacks Baby

YOUR WEATHER

CLOSING PRICES PAGE 2

MERCY FLIGHT

GIANT TANKER

re-drawn in much simpler style, somewhat reduced, and was now a clean and commendable version of this sort of letter. Noteworthy, too, was the way in which it unusually kept the back page for news; thus whatever the paging the reader could easily turn from front to back to follow 'turn' stories; in this way the front page was kept busy and varied, since stories of front-page weight but exceptional length could be given their due prominence and turned to run at will, without gobbling up precious page one space.

The position of the two surviving London evenings was touched on at the beginning of this chapter. Apart from incidental changes in recent years like the substitution of a neat, modernised grot title-line for its old blackletter, the *Evening News* has hitherto never appeared to have a consistent design policy. Its composing room practice has retained uncommon features, like handsetting certain headlines in founders' type (Grot No. 9, for example). Towards the end of 1972 there were certain signs of design activity, mainly exemplified by sledge-hammering the readers with poster-size Grot No. 9 capitals for front-page lead headings, but also seeking for some colour contrast in its all-sans style by playing up the medium-weight Ludlow Square Gothic.

Far different was the case of the *Evening Standard*, which had

Gothic and Century Bold style as established in the London *Evening Standard* by the 1960s. Note the small-sized, solid blackletter title.

600 GEORGE COHEN'S for PLANT and MACHINERY Tel: SHEpherds Bush 2070

Evening Standard

WEST END FINAL CLOSING PRICES

Drambuie

44,166 TUESDAY, JUNE 21, 1966 4d.

Hundreds of millions to be spent

NORTH SEA GAS TEXAS STYLE!

SIR HENRY JONES

It could be really cheap

PETER FAIRLEY

The North Sea gas strike could be as rich as the oil strike in Texas.

SEAMEN'S LEADERS ATTACK PREMIER

Evening Standard Reporters

Injured Roche has easy victory

BARRY NEWCOMBE

WIMBLEDON, Tuesday. — Before an audience of the world's Press, and with cameras rigidly focused on his every move, Australia's Tony Roche, the second seed in the All England Lawn

ENGLAND STRUGGLE—THEN COMES RAIN

England were first hampered and then helped by the rain after they had been set a target of 284 runs in 240 minutes in the Second Test at Lord's today.

Two early hold-ups ruined their victory

WEST INDIES. First Innings (Nurse 64; Higgs 6—91)

Second Innings

evolved its own Gothic (Franklin/Medium Condensed) and Century Bold style; it had made a minor change in its blackletter title, from white-lined to solid. Then, in 1969, the authorities at Shoe Lane called in a well-known advertising agency, Colman, Prentis and Varley to carry out what was called an 'up-the-market' typographic transformation of the paper. It was not surprising that the agency's choice fell on Century Schoolbook and Schoolbook Bold for the *Standard's* headline style, since the Irving and Sellers innovations in the *Observer* and the *Mail* had confirmed Schoolbook as high typographic fashion. What was surprising was the nature of the incidental CPV prescriptions, which turned out to be a textbook example of the remoteness from newspaper reality of the non-journalist graphic designer.

Thus the title was restyled in 72pt Century Bold italic, upper- and lower-case, adjusted to an extremely close fit; it was too large for the *Standard's* tabloid page and the close-fitting gave it a constricted look. For column rules and cutoffs the standard fine rule was supplanted by thicker medium ($1\frac{1}{2}$pt) rules, with all cutoffs – in this heavier weight – run full measure; pages with many shorts at once assumed an odd stepladder look. For main horizontal rules throughout the paper a double 12pt/3pt was specified; the effect of such bludgeoning blackness was funereal. In contrast, all crossheads and sideheads were styled in lightweight Century, which just faded away against the heavy-coloured Ionic text of the paper. For good measure the paper's most famous feature was headed in the supposedly *dernier cri* (but in fact over forty years out of date) even lower-case style – *londoner's diary*.

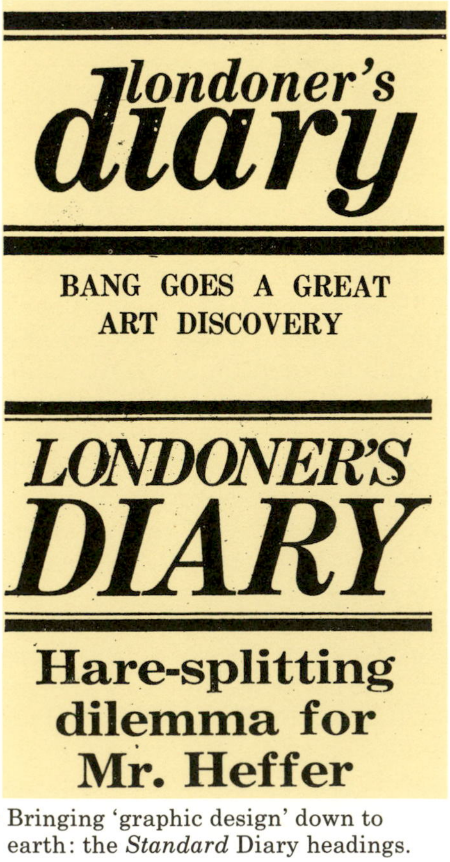
londoner's diary

BANG GOES A GREAT ART DISCOVERY

LONDONER'S DIARY

Hare-splitting dilemma for Mr. Heffer

Bringing 'graphic design' down to earth: the *Standard* Diary headings.

The CPV changes, as described, were introduced in the *Standard* early in October 1969; but within a couple of months the editorial staff had successfully grappled with the worst of the agency efforts. The title was reduced to 60pt, with normal setting to replace the over-close fit of its first version. Cutoffs were reduced from full measure to the normal broken width. The 12pt/3pt rules were reduced to an acceptable 9pt/$1\frac{1}{2}$pt. Bold was restored for crossheads. The Diary heading was restyled in Century Bold italic capitals, and the feature's subsidiary headlines were upped to Century Bold Extended. While there was some regret at the phasing-out of Century Bold, it was soon appreciated that the Schoolbook/Bold lower-case style could be handled to make attractive pages. There was one exception – the front page, where the upper- and lower-case Schoolbook, even in specially-cut 96 and 120pt, simply did not have the impact for evening paper street sales. Large sizes were cut of Bold Condensed roman capitals, resembling in weight and colour Stephenson Blake's Edwardian jobbing face, Chatsworth Condensed, but with more of the modern in their cut. These capitals (they have a remarkably ugly lower-case) sorted very fairly with Schoolbook and have certainly proved themselves to have ample impact.

So far as regional dailies are concerned a typical selection only can

NEW DIRECT LINE FOR CLASSIFIEDS 01-353 2345 9 a.m.-8 p.m.

Evening Standard

CLOSING PRICES

45,196 London: Thursday October 16 1969 6 5d.

BBC 'all-out' strike call

GEOFFREY HOBBS

DEMANDS for an all-out stoppage which would cripple BBC TV and radio services were made when about 3000 striking technicians met in a Hammersmith cinema today.

The total strike call is to be considered later today by the men's union, the Association of Broadcasting Staffs.

But the union executive will probably reject a complete strike in favour of continuing the lightning walk-outs which have hit scheduled programmes and studio production work over the past few days.

The men, on strike since 5.30 last night, went back to work after the meeting—in time to join the previously announced overtime ban at noon.

MOST EFFECTIVE ACTION

ABS general secretary Mr. Tom Rhys told the men that lightning strikes were the most effective action they could take against the BBC.

Such action gave the BBC no time to organise strike-busting measures. "It might not be a nice, gentlemanly way to fight, but it is the only way to fight," said Mr. Rhys.

The ABS was still prepared to negotiate with the BBC.

Appealing for all members to join the noon overtime ban, he said: "The more effective it is the sooner we shall get down to talking about an improved offer."

The four per cent pay rise offered by the BBC was not the maximum permitted by the Government, he claimed. Neither did it reflect the

Continued Back Page Col. 3

Biafra 'set for peace talks'

Libreville, Gabon. Thursday.

THE LEADER of breakaway Biafra, Major-General Ojukwu, was reported today to have agreed to another round of talks aimed at ending the 27-month-old Nigerian civil war.

Authoritative sources said the general had sent a letter to Gabonese President Bongo saying he was ready to negotiate without pre-conditions with the Federal Government and to take part personally in the talks.

He also suggested that the talks should be accompanied by a ceasefire. The sources said the letter was delivered in Libreville yesterday by Biafran envoy Sir Louis Mbanefo.

BONGO'S PLAN

The Organisation of African Unity has been making a fresh attempt towards ending the bloody conflict which has dragged on since July 1967, when hostilities broke out between the two sides two months after General Ojukwu declared Biafra's secession from Nigeria.

Several abortive attempts have been made since then to end the fighting.

President Bongo, whose government is among four African states to recognise an independent Biafra, said he might accompany General Ojukwu to new talks, so long as the OAU's previous resolutions on Nigeria were considered null and void, the sources said.

President Bongo might also contact President Ahmadou Ahidjo of Cameroun, current chairman of the organisation, and President Felix Houphouet-Boigny of the Ivory Coast before the talks, they said.

President Ahidjo had a meeting in Lagos on Tuesday with Major-General Yakubu Gowon, the Federal Nigerian leader, on ways of ending the war.

He told reporters: "I am very hopeful for peace talks, not only in the interest of the fighting sides but also in the interests of Africa."

The OAU Secretary-General, M. Diallo Telli, has been sounding out African leaders on the

Continued Back Page Col. 1

Now—£58 flights to New York and back

A FARE of £58 return between London and New York, the lowest offered on scheduled trans-Atlantic air services, was announced today by BOAC.

The fare for group travel, will apply from November 8, subject to Government approval.

It will be available to affinity groups of 130 and over travelling from Britain, and representing a saving of £44 on the lowest affinity group fare now available.

DEPOSIT

The new group fare follows the announcement yesterday by BOAC that a new low individual fare of £83 return between London and New York is being considered for introduction in 1970 by the International Air Transport Association in Lausanne.

This fare will be valid off-peak and will require four months' notice of booking and a non-refundable deposit.

British captain freed by China

FREE at last, Will, 46, arrive[d] from China. [...] his luggage t[...] been detained [...] he was taken [...] gunpoint in a [...] May last year.

He is the [...]

London home loans at 18

PAGE TEN

B-test: Another 'loophole'

PAGE EIGHTEEN

▲ The October 1969 advertising agency transformation of the *Standard* with (below) the modifications soon effected by the editorial staff and now the permanent style of the paper. ▶

WEATHER: Rather cloudy. Lighting-up time: 5.22 p.m. Full details—Back Page

Evening Standard

CITY PRICES

45,241 London: Monday December 8 1969 4 6d.

£100,000 RAID IN MAYFAIR

Standard Crime Reporter

SAFE-CRACKERS cut their way to a haul worth well over £100,000 in a raid on a post office in the heart of Mayfair discovered today.

They escaped with about £7000 in cash and an estimated £100,000 in stamps, postal orders and other stock.

The break in was discovered this morning when cleaners arrived at the Post Office in Albemarle Street.

They found a small hole cut in a safe, and oxy-acetylene cutting equipment the gang had left behind.

Alarm by-passed

Detectives were baffled as to how the gang managed to by-pass the post office alarm system. They immediately started checking on workmen who recently completed repairs to the roof.

Scotland Yard fingerprint and forensic science experts made a detailed check inside while police stood on guard outside turning away scores of people who use the busy main post office.

A notice was posted on the door telling customers that "due to unforeseen circumstances" the office was closed. They were advised to use other post offices nearby.

Weekend closing

GPO officials called in to make a detailed check to discover what stock had been stolen were expected to take several hours before they could reach an accurate value.

The raiders had all weekend to cut open the safe as the post office closes on Friday night and does not open again until Monday morning.

They will probably be able to sell the large amount of stamps they took, but other post office stock, such as postal orders and insurance stamps, will be difficult to dispose of.

● The nearby New Bond Street showroom of furriers Schonbeck and Miller were raided twice over the weekend — and the thieves got furs worth no more than £1000.

But the showrooms were smashed up—"just out of spite, it seems to me," a member of the staff said today.

Police disturbed the first gang of thieves on Friday night and they got nothing.

Because the burglar alarm system had been put out of action all the valuable furs were taken away for safe-keeping.

So when the raiders came back last night—detectives believe it was the same gang—there was not much left for them to steal.

Probe into rail line blaze

POLICE are investigating a fire which broke out on the track near Falconwood Station, Welling, late last night. The current between Falconwood and Eltham Park was turned off for about 10 minutes while firemen tackled the blaze.

SHOCK REPORT ON CHILDREN IN HOSPITAL

Scandal in the wards

By MICHAEL JEFFRIES and ALAN MASSAM

THE HEAT was on today for a full-scale inquiry into the treatment of sick children in all Britain's hospitals.

For the criticisms levelled against Paddington General Hospital by a special Health Service tribunal over the death of seven-year-old David Tomlinson, of Willesden, apply to many.

They are old and dilapidated—a potential hazard to good treatment for other child patients.

Doctors and nurses are scarce, particularly at night and weekends. Arrangements for calling out specialists in emergencies need tightening up.

This was the picture after I talked with leading doctors, health officials and welfare organisations today.

The British Medical Association is urgently considering backing demands for a full inquiry by the Department of Health.

Dr. James Cameron, chairman of the General Medical Services committee said if the allegation that the boy died of a virus infection through bad conditions at the hospital was true, they would press for an inquiry.

VULNERABLE POSITION

"I don't think anybody can generalise unless there is a proper survey and inquiry into hospitals," he added.

"There are many old hospitals up and down the country where to maintain a high standard of treatment is extremely difficult."

My own inquiries reveal criticism of at least two other London hospitals' children's wards—mainly due to lack of space.

The Council for Children's Welfare is backing the demand for a full-scale inquiry.

Chairman, Mrs. Leila Campbell, said: "Cases like this are always likely to happen because the hospital service is terribly overworked and inadequate.

"The position of children in hospital is most vulnerable."

Shadow Health spokesman Mr. Maurice Macmillan is considering the tribunal's report to decide whether or not to press the Government in the Commons for action.

TALKS SOON ON REPORT

The report is to be the subject of urgent talks with the hospital authorities.

This was disclosed today when the Department of Health and Social Security released the report of the official inquiry into the death of David Tomlinson aged 7, on July 9, 1967.

A Department official said that Baroness Serota, Minister of State, is to hold the talks with the governing body of the hospital as soon as possible.

The report records that David was admitted to Ward A1, the children's ward, at Paddington General Hospital as it was then called.

The diagnosis was probable acute appendicitis.

At about 11 p.m. on the same day his appendix was removed but it appeared normal. Shortly after 8 a.m. on Sunday, July 9, 1967, David died of "an overwhelming viral infection of unknown origin."

The Department of Health official said criticism of the report had centred on the fact

Continued Back Page Col. 1

M-way crash: 5 dead 100 hurt

AT LEAST five people are feared to have been killed and about 100 injured in a horror pile-up on the M6 motorway near Wigan, in thick fog today.

About 100 vehicles were involved in the series of concertina crashes, and one particular pile-up stretched more than 200 yards.

Teams of ambulances ran a shuttle service, taking 70 of the injured to Wigan Infirmary. Others were taken to St. Helen's Hospital.

Local firemen were also on the scene helping to cut people free and clear the wreckage.

Lancashire County police sealed off both lanes of the M6 between Leyland and Warrington and drafted extra men from as far away as Blackpool.

At one stage visibility on the M6 was down to 20 yards.

At least eight cars were in another pile-up just off the motorway at Standish as traffic piled up in the fog.

As fog came down suddenly in South Derbyshire, reducing visibility in places to 25 yards, between 30 and 40 vehicles were involved in multiple crashes on the main A38 road near Burton-on-Trent.

In one crash, 20 vehicles were involved. The injured were taken to hospitals in Derby and Burton by a fleet of ambulances.

Stone's girl told: Wed or quit the country

Anita Pallenberg with her son Marlon.

Standard Reporter

ANITA PALLENBERG, blonde actress girl friend of Rolling Stone Keith Richard, said today that she has been ordered by the Home Office to leave the country unless she gets married.

"It's just like living in a police state," she said at Heathrow airport as she waited for Keith to arrive from the United States. In her arms she cradled their four-month-old son Marlon.

Said Anita, who holds an Italian passport: "I asked for a new visa in July, but the Home Office have held my passport ever since. They won't let me have it back and have told me that I must either get married or get out.

"They have not named a time limit. I think it is disgraceful. I am not going to get married just in order to suit them. I would like to get married—round about 1975."

Keeping quiet

Anita said she had been keeping quiet about the trouble, but now felt "it is time people got to know about it." She said she had instructed solicitors to take up her case.

Keith Richard said as he flew in with another Stone, drummer Charlie Watts, from their open-air concert in California: "We've got to talk about this business and try to get it sorted out. But first of all I want some sleep."

Frayed

Keith Richard, speaking of the concert, said it was "basically well handled. But a lot of people were very tired and a few tempers got frayed."

Charlie Watts said: "I wouldn't mind doing another concert of this sort but not quite in the same way." They said that Mick Jagger would fly home in two days' time.

Said Keith Richard: "I don't think he has taken any notice of what has been said about Marianne Faithfull. He's not listening to anything that is being said."

● Miss Faithfull, 24, said in Rome recently that she had found her "Prince Charming" in a 33-year-old Italian film director Mario Schifano. She said she would keep away from her old boy friend, Mick Jagger.

Soccer attack—7 in court

SEVEN people, including a 16-year-old girl, were appearing at Bow Street today after a hunt for soccer hooligans who beat up a plain clothes police officer after Saturday's match between West Ham and Manchester City.

GLC told: 'Scrap that plan'

PAGE SEVEN

4 London clubs get luck of Cup draw

PAGE THIRTY-EIGHT

Misery line worse

PAGE NINE

THE EVENING STANDARD today introduces a new headline type, especially designed for this newspaper.

It is bolder and more dynamic than the type previously used, but in the same family.

Further major developments in the evolution of the Evening Standard will take place in the New Year.

Tel: 01-353 3000

FOR EVERYTHING MUSICAL
WILLIAMS · Darlington

The Northern Echo

No. 28,446 FOUNDED 1869 THURSDAY, AUGUST 3, 1961 THREEPENCE

CHOOSE YOUR ENGAGEMENT RING FROM OUR EXTENSIVE SELECTION
Bramwell & Harbron
90 NORTHGATE, DARLINGTON

MR. MACMILLAN'S CALL TO BRITAIN

Join vanguard of movement towards greater unity in the free world

NO DOUBTS ABOUT COMMON MARKET

BY OUR PARLIAMENTARY CORRESPONDENT

A SUPREME effort to win support in Parliament and the country for Britain's entry into the Common Market was made by the Prime Minister in the Commons last night.

Gone were his former hesitations and doubts. In confident, buoyant mood, he minimised the dangers, discounted the fears, and called on Britain to "join in the vanguard of the movement towards a greater unity in the free world."

A packed House listened in rapt silence (Sir Winston Churchill cupping his hand to his ear) as the Prime Minister faced the difficulties and measured them against the "tremendous advantages."

It was left to Mr. Gaitskell, Leader of the Opposition, to emphasise the doubts and disadvantages—a formidable list—but the real challenge to the Prime Minister's prospectus came from Sir Derek Walker-Smith, a former Tory Minister of Health.

In an impressive speech, punctuated with resounding cheers from both sides of the House, he urged closer economic and political association with the Commonwealth and said that Britain should seek only "an association" with the Common Market.

Political union

The cheers were warmed when Sir Derek warned that political union was the ultimate object of the European Economic Community, a direct contradiction of the Prime Minister's interpretation...

...it to open formal negotiations for admission to the Community.

The Prime Minister's appearance matched his manner. Alert, businesslike, and once again in full command of the House, he listed all the doubts and fears and cut them down to size in this confident analysis.

Farming's place

Agriculture: The Government reaffirmed its pledge to stand by the 1957 Agricultural Act (making provision for subsidies) for the remainder of this Parliament. Once in the Common Market, however, we might have to shift from a system where much of farmers' support came from the Exchequer to one which secured that the market itself provided a fair return to the producer.

"It is our purpose to have a prosperous, stable and efficient agricultural industry, but we must be ready to examine carefully and dispassionately all methods of achieving that end. It that is the will, I do not think that the working out of satisfactory arrangements to meet our requirements should prove an impossible task."

Commonwealth: It was wrong to regard the Commonwealth and European interests as conflicting. Basically, they must be complementary. Britain could best serve...

Mr. Fell's apology

HE STILL SAYS 'A NATIONAL DISASTER'

By J. E. D. HALL, Political Correspondent

MR. Anthony Fell, Conservative M.P. for Yarmouth, yesterday wrote to the Prime Minister apologising for his attack upon him after the Common Market statement last Monday.

...

Onus transferred

...

POLICE FIND LOST BABY

MRS. Bernard Francis holding her six-month-old baby son, Christopher John Francis, after he had been returned to her yesterday. Police with tracker dogs had searched for him after he was reported missing with his pram from outside his home in South-West London. He was found unharmed on the seventh floor landing of a block of flats.

20 TOURISTS MISSING AFTER BUS PLUNGES INTO LAKE LUCERNE

TWENTY American tourists were feared to have died yesterday when their bus ran off a road and plunged into the Lake of Lucerne.

There were 38 people on the bus—35 American tourists, the driver, and the Swiss courier and his wife. Eighteen people were saved and one body was recovered.

Hospital officials said that none of the survivors was in danger.

RESERVES DROP

Burnham Committee sticks to £47m.

THE Burnham Committee yesterday rejected the Minister of Education's £42m. "maximum" pay rise for primary and secondary school teachers in England and Wales from next January.

In a statement issued after a three-and-a-half hour meeting at Church House, London, the committee, consisting of teachers and representatives of local authorities, recommended instead approval of an already submitted agreement for an increase of £47½m.

The statement also suggested that there would be "great advantage" if the committee could have the opportunity of discussing the matter with Sir David Eccles.

Endorsed action

A report of the meeting was heard last night by the Executive Committee of the National Union of Teachers. A spokesman said later that they unanimously endorsed the action of their representatives on the committee.

He added that it would be possible to call a special meeting of the Executive if the need arose before the normal meeting in September.

The statement by the Burnham Committee referred to the award of an increase of 14 per cent. in Scottish teachers' pay from July 1, 1961, and claimed that the terms of this agreement, if applied to the teachers they represented, would cost the Government £8m. more than the increase they were seeking.

Could not understand

Although they understood the Minister's concern at the difficult situation which arose following the Chancellor of the Exchequer's statement, they could not understand why the Government "are only prepared to approve a settlement at the level of £42m. which has the effect of being £21m. below the level which would obtain if the terms of the Scottish settlement...

New factory and 600 jobs for Tyneside

'SHOWPIECE,' BIGGEST OF KIND IN EUROPE

A NEW factory, which will be the biggest of its kind in Europe, is to be built on the Team Valley Trading Estate at Gateshead by Thomas De La Rue and Co. Ltd., who produce currency notes for 93 countries and central banks.

The factory, which will eventually absorb the present factory engaged on a note-finishing process in Gateshead, will create jobs for more than 600 people, in addition to present workers.

Some 60 per cent. of these vacancies will be for women in semi-skilled jobs and the rest for technicians.

Plans for the factory are already being made and it is expected that building will start early next summer. It is hoped that the factory will be in full production by the late summer of 1964.

Move from Leeds

The new factory, which will cover some 300,000 square feet, will replace the existing factory at Leeds. A spokesman for the firm told The Northern Echo that permission had been sought to build the new factory at Leeds, but this had been refused by the Board of Trade because of full employment in Leeds. Now the whole of the Leeds and Gateshead personnel, together with the additional staff, would be combined in the one main factory at Gateshead, which would eventually employ, in all, about 1,000 people.

The new plant will be the most advanced and up-to-date for the production of banknotes in the world.

Mr. S. A. Sadler Forster, chairman of the Industrial Estates Corporation of England, commented: "This is immensely important and I am delighted by the news. The detailed planning has yet to be settled, but I am officially informed that the factory will be a showpiece."

North-East showpiece

"One of the reasons why Team Valley has been chosen is that De La Rue were anxious to have a...

Boy of 9 drowned in Ouse

NINE-YEAR-OLD Malcolm Philip Clark, of Cawood, near Selby, was drowned yesterday in the fast-flowing River Ouse just 100 yards from his home in Rythergate.

He and two boys on a camping holiday from Leeds had been playing on a launch tied up against the river bank at a Cawood boat yard.

The boys heard a splash and saw Malcolm's head bobbing in the water as the tide whipped him down the river. Then he disappeared from view.

Men from the boat yard and police searched the river in two speedboats and dragged the river bed, but without success. Malcolm could not swim.

Boy's story

One of the boys, 13-year-old Anthony Bell, said: "The three of us were clambering about the boat. Malcolm must have thought we were chasing him because he jumped on to the deck and must have slipped."

be given. Outstanding in our period was the *Northern Echo* of Darlington, a North-Eastern morning published by the Westminster Press. In the early 1960s it was Harold Evans's first editorship. Apart from a sensationally successful campaign to clear the name of Timothy Evans (wrongly convicted and executed for London's Rillington Place murders) editor Evans undertook a complete re-design of the *Echo*, spread over more than three years. The process was complete by 1965. An adapted Clarendon line took the place of the blackletter title, with the clearing-out of the advertising 'ears' (at a cost of £2,000 p.a.). Bodoni Bold was retained for news headlines, but all in upper- and lower-case with no decks, and carefully whited (Evans later said: 'A standard of white space was laid down – but sometimes it looked wrong. When, for instance, there were no ascenders and descenders between two lines of headline, the standard whiting looked excessive. We learned on these occasions to trust our eyes.') In place of the banner in capitals, with its following 'dog's leg' italic line lumbering around the columns, the lead story carried a three-column banked heading in Century Bold Extended – the only departure from Bodoni; the new splash heading style, incidentally, saved five square inches of space. The leader page, which had been all single-column with column rules, was transformed by clearing away radio programmes and ads, setting the leader wide measure, removing the rules and placing extra white between the columns, and adopting a uniform style of heading in Goudy Bold.

Evans put the central points of the whole operation very clearly. After stressing that the changes had to be appropriate to the character of a regional morning like the *Echo*, he declared that 'function' was fundamental, adding: 'It would be worse than useless to create pretty patterns with type and pictures if they clogged the production machinery or confused the reader. To function properly the design must convey the news clearly and with a sense of proportion. It must be economical in the time of both the editorial and printing departments, and the newspaper's space, and it must be amenable to quick changes.'[11]

A spectacular case was the salvage of the *Western Daily Press* of Bristol. In 1960 this centenarian independent morning was a dying derelict, editorially and mechanically antiquated and with a circulation of not more than 12,000. Then taken over by the prosperous and well-equipped *Evening Post* its editorship was entrusted to the *Express*-trained Eric Price. Adopting what someone called 'vintage Christiansen' typography – a vast advance on what the *Daily Press* had been – with a bold Egyptian title in place of the ancient black-

◀ How Harold Evans revolutionised the *Northern Echo*: the front page (left) before and (right) after. ▶

The Northern Echo
No. 29,979 (Founded 1869)
THURSDAY, JULY 14, 1966
FOURPENCE
Mr. Cousins sets stage for Prices Bill fight
OUR POLITICAL CORRESPONDENT
MORE than 50 Labour rebels have set the stage for an attack on the Prices and Incomes Bill in its later stages. The Bill will be debated in the Commons today but there will be no open revolt in tonight's division.
From Russia with camera
BUT LOOK AT THEIR SOUVENIR SUBJECT—
NEWSPROBE
Buying pep pills seems so easy
Northern Echo reporters
Two's a crowd
Back to 1961
Car insurance to cost less—if you're good
OUR MOTORING CORRESPONDENT
—IT'S YASHIN, FROM RUSSIA WITH BOOTS
Our Sunderland staff
Not liable

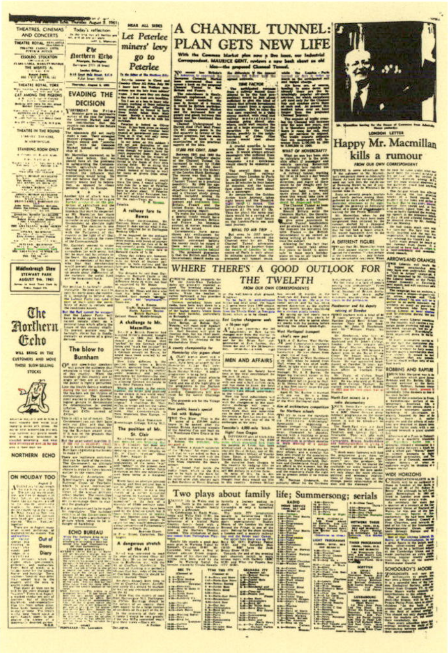

▲ Transforming the leader page of the *Northern Echo*. ▶

The Northern Echo
Wednesday, September 29, 1965
MEN AND SHIPS
Living on the edge of a volcano
Why do people go on doing it all over the world?
by ALLAN REDITT
Maurice Wedgewood, Deputy Editor of The Northern Echo, just back from Dublin, says
There's a revolution in Ireland
Ireland old and new — a German-owned factory making cranes and excavators in the heart of beautiful Kerry, overlooking the lakes of Killarney. Ireland has no direct restrictions governing sites, although planning committees keep an eye on "amenities."
North-East parallels
Out-of-Doors Diary
September 28
DANGEROUS DAYS
WIND-HOVER.
TODAY'S REFLECTION
WILLIAM FEATHER
FIRST FOR SLASHED LEEKS? NEVER!
HEAR ALL SIDES
YOUR VIEWS

The *Western Daily Press* (Bristol) presented one of the most spectacular transformation scenes.
▶

choose
FURNITURE
at
NEWBERY & SPINDLER LTD

The Western Daily Press
AND BRISTOL MIRROR

BRISTOL, SATURDAY, MAY 7, 1960

TWOPENCE HALFPENNY

See Our Usual
SPECIAL SHOW OFFERS
of TARPAULINS & SHEETS
BATH & WEST SHOW
YEO BROS. PAULL LTD.

'Bomb in the Abbey' hoax call

AERO ENGINE MEN IN WALK-OUT

Overtime ban now in force at Patchway

HONEYMOON SHIP SAILS OFF INTO THE NIGHT

End to a happy day

FROM THE WORLD'S NEWS

JAMES PHILLIPS
GOLDEN OPPORTUNITY
SALE
NOW ON

WESTERN
Daily Press
LATE CITY

TIMES & MIRROR

THE PAPER THAT FIGHTS FOR THE WEST

WEDNESDAY, JANUARY 31, 1973

Join the moneybuilding society
BRISTOL & WEST
BUILDING SOCIETY

Alderman Major Peter Sturgis opens Malmesbury's by-pass with Captain Alec Francis and the Mayor and Mayoress. Page 3: Snip, And A Town Is Quiet at Last

Trader Mr. Peter Flannery outside his shop at the bottom of Bath's New Bond Street. Page 7: Doomed Georgian Shops Are Given New Hope

HEATH: I'LL BACK CONCORDE

Is someone in fear on M5 bridge?

By Garth Pearce

MONTHLY progress reports on the delayed Avon M5 bridge will be prepared by Easton-in-Gordano parish council, near Bristol.

BRISTOL IS IN ON RATES

He is off to see Nixon

By Preston Witts

MR. HEATH will fight for Concorde during his U.S. visit.

Hospital strike leader goes...

The Post Office runs out of forms

By Nicholas Walker

I could be Mr X, says county planner

By Mary Wright

ALDERMAN Major Ernest Mealing, agreed last night that he could be the Mr. X referred to in the Commons by Mr. Charles Loughlin early yesterday.

letter, and transforming the paper editorially, Price had pushed the circulation to over 70,000 and viability by the end of the decade.

Of three remaining noteworthy examples the *Scotsman* was already an established Design Award winner. The distinguished Edinburgh morning, the first Thomson acquisition here, had twice carried off the original Bronze Plaque as best-designed newspaper of the year (in 1959 and 1963). Its headline typography was uniformly Bodoni Bold, in classical decker style. Its halftone reproduction was outstanding and its presswork good. But it began to feel that deckers, with the stress on main lines in capitals, were outmoded; in 1966, therefore, it followed the general trend and went over to all upper- and lower-case, still in Bodoni Bold. The front-page lead heading was set in 60pt, in three lines usually across four columns. By late 1972, however, it was clearly felt that the elegant Bodoni packed insufficient punch for a splash heading, whose style was therefore changed to 72pt Century Bold. This, together with a long-standing use of Ludlow Caslon Light for contrast with the Bodoni Bold, meant that the paper's front page at any rate acquired a distinctly mixed look.

Ludlow Caslon, but mainly in the Heavy and the Bold with Light

▶
Opposite: the *Scotsman*.
Above: the classical decker style which repeatedly won it top awards.
Centre: change (1966) to upper- and lower-case multi-liner headings, in Bodoni Bold, with (below) the 1972 introduction of 72pt Century Bold for the lead headline.

THE SCOTSMAN

No. 35,947 EDINBURGH, WEDNESDAY, AUGUST 13, 1958 PRICE 3d.

COMET SETS NEW RECORD

6¼-hour flight from New York

AVERAGE SPEED 558 M.P.H.

Flying at an average speed of 558 miles per hour, a de Havilland Comet IV turbojet airliner yesterday set up a new unofficial record for civil aircraft by covering the 3500 miles from New York to Hatfield, Hertfordshire, in six hours 16 minutes.

This is one hour 28 minutes faster than the previous record, set up by an El Al Britannia prop-jet aircraft between New York and London.

The Comet, one of 19 ordered by B.O.A.C., made its record flight when returning from Idlewild Airport, New York.

The flight was made to normal B.O.A.C. rules, with a load equivalent

CAPTAIN REJOINS U.S. SUBMARINE BY HELICOPTER

Commander W. R. Anderson, captain of the U.S. submarine Nautilus, being lowered from a helicopter on to the deck of the submarine near the Shambles Lightship prior to the Nautilus docking at Portland.

"BRITAIN AND U.S. HAVE GIRDED THE EARTH"

Ambassador welcomes Nautilus

In one year Britain and America have girded the earth with the two

EISENHOWER TO ADDRESS U.N.

1800 U.S. Marines withdrawing from Lebanon to-day

LLOYD HOPES FOR END TO "RADIO WAR"

President Eisenhower will address to-day's emergency session of the United Nations General Assembly on the Middle East, it was announced by the White House yesterday. After delivering the United States opening speech, the President will return to Washington leaving Mr Dulles, Secretary of State, in charge as permanent working head of the American delegation.

A few hours earlier it was also announced that the United States was pulling one battalion of Marines out of Lebanon to-day. The withdrawal of 1800 men, which will leave more than 13,000 in Lebanon, had been widely forecast in Washington as a move to counter Soviet charges at the Assembly meeting.

The Soviet Union last night tabled a draft resolution which it will submit to the Assembly asking the Secretary-General to reinforce the U.N. observer group in Lebanon, and to send a group of observers to Jordan with a view to supervising the withdrawal of American and British troops. The resolution calls for the withdrawal of the troops

AN ANTI-MISSILE MISSILE

U.S. nuclear blast

THE SCOTSMAN

No. 40,278 EDINBURGH, FRIDAY, JUNE 30, 1972 3 a.m. news PRICE 4p

Seven killed as blazing plane ploughs into holiday-camp chalets

Seven people died when a blazing executive jet ploughed through ten chalets at Pontin's Holiday Camp, Blackpool last night. All the dead were in the aircraft, a twin-engine Hansa which had just taken off from Squires Gate Airport bound for Munich.

The plane struck a landing-light support and bounced off a railway track on to two rows of chalets which were demolished and set on fire by blazing fuel. The holidaymakers who would normally have been in the area were just beginning their evening meal in the camp's central restaurant when the crash

---

THE SCOTSMAN

No. 40,400 EDINBURGH, MONDAY, NOVEMBER 20, 1972 3 a.m. news PRICE 4p

SPD biggest party in Bundestag

Brandt coalition return in election triumph

BONN, Monday.—Chancellor Willy Brandt won a convincing victory in the West German elections last night and said: "The majority has confirmed that we are on the right course."

Lord Grant killed in A9 pile-up

Lord Grant, Lord Justice-Clerk of Scotland, was killed in a crash involving two cars and a lorry on the A9 Perth-Inverness road, about three miles north of Kingussie, yesterday afternoon. Three people died in the accident.

Also among the dead was a 29-year-old father of three, Mr John Davie, of Alness, whose wife and three children were severely injured and taken to Raigmore Hospital.

Late last night Inverness police named the third person killed in the crash as Thomas Whyte, a relative, who lived with the Davies.

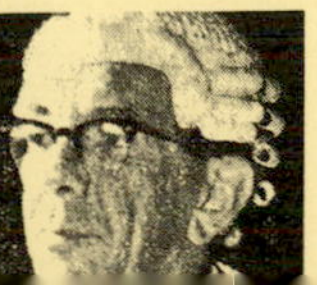

Appleyard FOR BMC SERVICE
APPLEYARD OF LEEDS LTD., NORTH ST. Tel. 32731

The Yorkshire Post

ESTAB. 1754 No. 36,922 * * * LEEDS THURSDAY FEBRUARY 10 1966 PRICE 4d. TEL. LEEDS 32701

WHITE SALE
WONDERFUL LINEN BARGAINS IN THE DEPT. ON THE 2nd FLOOR
OPEN ALL DAY SATURDAY
MARSHALL & SNELGROVE
BOND STREET, LEEDS
TELEPHONE 30001

'COAL CAN BE CHEAPER'

£30m. plan to reduce electricity bills

Lord Robens tells how to cut costs by 9s. a ton

LORD ROBENS, chairman of the National Coal Board, spoke last night of a survey that showed

Mr. Heath attacks 'smear campaign'

By GORDON LEAK, Yorkshire Post Parliamentary Correspondent

MR. HEATH, Leader of the Opposition, last night launched an unprecedented attack on the Government. He accused Mr.

WOMAN'S DEATH: MAN CHARGED

In court today

Yorkshire Post Wakefield Staff

A MAN was arrested yesterday and charged with the murder of Miss Ida Hinchliffe, 62, of Atherold Street, Ossett, Yorkshire.

Det. Supt. Godfrey Oldfield,

Vent-Axia Best value in unit ventilation.
5, Dolly Lane, Leeds, LS9 7TT (Leeds 22985)

YORKSHIRE POST

ESTAB. 1754 No. 38,864 * * * LEEDS WEDNESDAY MAY 17 1972 PRICE 4p Tel. LEEDS 32701

Hess Walker
creative hairstyling
artists in colour
beauté guerlain

Town Hall ombudsman likely for Yorkshire

Special report by NIGEL DUNCAN

YORKSHIRE may be given its own ombudsman to investigate complaints of maladministration in local government.

Consultations which the Government is having with local authority associations and staff interests to establish a system of local ombudsmen aim at a minimum of nine commissioners, each responsible for one area of England.

On this basis Yorkshire seems certain to be allocated its own local watchdog.

The Government is proposing an independent statutory commission for local administration to operate from April, 1974 when the new councils come into being.

The aim is to give people the same rights of complaint in local government as they now have through the Parliamentary Commissioner in the field of central government.

Although appointed by the Crown, the commission would be financed by local government and responsible to a body representative of local government. The present thinking is that on this basis local government would be keeping its own

Bribe charge detectives cleared

TWO DETECTIVES cleared of bribery charges yesterday had, on their own showing, "behaved with almost unbelievable stupidity," a judge said in Leeds Crown Court.

Det.-Sgt. John Mather and Det. Const. Anthony George Salisbury, of Leeds City Police, were found not guilty of corruptly accepting

MISS MOLLOY and Mr. Moran last night. (A Yorkshire Post picture.)

Former nun to marry man from monastery

Yorkshire Post Reporter

A FORMER nun is to marry a former lay brother of a monastic order later this month.

She is Miss Catherine Molloy, 25, who for three years has worked as a nurse at St. James's Hospital, Leeds.

There, a year ago, she met her fiance, Mr. Mark Gerald Moran, also 25, after he joined the nursing staff.

The couple, who are now staying with Mr. Moran's parents in Broughton Terrace, Harehills, Leeds, will marry on May 27 at Coatbridge, Lanarkshire — Miss Molloy's home town.

She was a nun for seven years with the Little Sisters of the Poor, spending three years at the Order's convent in Headingley, Leeds.

Mr. Moran was a lay brother for six years with the Brothers of St. John of God, a nursing order, at Scorton, near Richmond, North Riding.

"We did not know each other until we met at St. James's, then it all just happened," Miss Molloy said.

"We had both taken temporary vows, including that of chastity, but there was an automatic dispensation from these when we left our Orders."

Mr. Moran said he had intended becoming a monk "but it didn't work out. I took temporary vows but decided to leave before committing myself for the rest of my life. Only a few of the lay brothers do actually stay on to become monks."

There was nothing unusual if a lay brother who left became married. "It is not frowned upon at all," he said.

Miss Molloy will limp to the altar because she was kicked on the leg by a police horse at Elland Road when queuing to see her first football match — Leeds United's defeat of Chelsea on May Day.

It happened as a mounted policeman tried to control the boisterous crowd.

"I still cannot walk without pain but I am determined to go through with the wedding," she added. "I am having heat treatment for the injury and the hot sunshine in Spain should help."

Whitelaw's car kicked by crowd

THE CAR carrying Mr. William Whitelaw, the Secretary for Northern Ireland, was punched and kicked during his 'meet-the-people tour of Newry, Co. Down, yesterday.

A crowd waving placards and singing Republican songs surrounded the car and one woman screamed at Mr. Whitelaw: "Now you know what it's like to be hated."

The incident happened as the motorcade left the

INSIDE TODAY

A page-by-page guide to your Yorkshire Post:

Home News

3 Blueprint for playground of the North; Police to seek 13 per cent. pay rise; Widow without a penny gets £30 a week.

6 Electrical power struggle; 600 police needed for pop festival; Change policy on Ulster or we mobilise, says Craig.

11 Railman blamed for crash; Two-year plan to get Yorkshire moving.

Parliament

Food prices rise by 17 per cent

Parliamentary Correspondent

FOOD PRICES have risen by more than 17 per cent. since the election, Mr. James Prior, Minister of Agriculture, revealed in the Commons yesterday.

His announcement — the exact rise being 17.2 per cent. between June 1970 and March 21 this year — led to angry exchanges with Labour MPs and cries of "disgraceful" and "resign."

Mr. William Price (Lab., Rugby) demanded: "Don't you understand what this figure means to millions of pensioners and lower paid workers who regard you as the biggest disaster in this Government in spite of all the competition?"

Mr. Norman Buchan, from the Opposition Front Bench, accused the Minister of "throwing the housewives of the country entirely to the forces of the market."

In reply Mr. Prior said that although prices were still going up, they were doing so much more slowly than during the last two years or more and he believed this improvement would continue over the next few months.

"It is a little too early to give the really good figures that I think are becoming available," he said, but added: "In the last six months the increase in non-seasonal foods was 3.8 per cent. compared with 7.3 per cent. in the previous six months."

There were further angry outbursts from Labour MPs when Mr. Prior blamed inflationary wage demands for much of the increase.

In the past year some 30

Work with us—plea by Heath

By JOHN FISHER, Political Correspondent

MR. HEATH last night called on both sides of industry to collaborate more closely than ever before with the Government to overcome the major national problems of unemployment and inflation.

The Prime Minister made his appeal at the annual dinner of the Confederation of British Industry at the Hilton Hotel, London

▲ Substituting fat face for blackletter in its title, the *Yorkshire Post* adopted an upper- and lower-case headline style in Ludlow Caslon (Heavy, Bold, Bold Condensed).

and Bold Condensed contrast, was the typographic basis for the *Yorkshire Post's* changes of the summer of 1968. The Leeds morning dropped streamers in capitals and decker headings, adopting an all upper- and lower-case headline style, set flush-left. The blackletter title, deleting the definite article, was changed to Fat Face capitals gauging around 60pt face; later this depth was fractionally reduced and spacing between the letters better adjusted. With the installation of 'hybrid' (letterpress/offset) presses at the paper's new Leeds plant in 1971, part of each day's edition is usually photoset and printed web-offset. Text of the *Yorkshire Post* and its stablemate the *Evening Post* – which in October 1969 changed from a Gothic–Cheltenham–Caslon mixture to an all-Sans light/bold style – is in Royal.

The *Birmingham Post* made a thorough change, over the four years from 1964 to 1968, from traditional capitals and lower-case deckers, in Bodoni Bold (roman and italic), to an all lower-case, flush-left headline style. Starting this in Bodoni it ended by switching to Century Bold, with Bold Extended for main multi-column headings. Comparable play on Extended was seen in the *Liverpool Daily Post*.

The American scene from 1960 on embraced both the continuance

The *Birmingham Post* moved from traditional deckers in Bodoni Bold to a flush-left, lower-case style in Century Bold, with stress on the Bold Extended. ▸

▾ Strong play on Century Bold Extended was a feature of the design evolution of the *Liverpool Daily Post*, which also (below) modernised its title-piece.

NO U.S. LOANS, BAPTISTS DECIDE
Page B 1

The Courier-Journal

DEAN GINGER STEPS DOWN
Page B 3

VOL. 223, NO. 179 ******* LOUISVILLE, TUESDAY MORNING, JUNE 28, 1966 38 PAGES 10 CENTS

Jefferson School Budget May Jump $9 Million, Mostly for Pay Raises

By JAMES DRISCOLL
Courier-Journal Staff Writer

The Jefferson County School Board last night approved a tentative budget for fiscal 1966-67 of $37.8 million, an increase of about $9 million over the present fiscal year.

Most of the additional money will be used for salary increases for virtually all school employes.

The new budget, a record high, is not as exact as usual because school officials don't know how much money they will receive from local property taxes after reassessment of property at full cash value.

Supt. Richard Van Hoose and his staff estimate, however, that the property tax will produce a little more than $12 million, an increase of about $1.8 million over this year's total.

Most of the increase in this category would come from the 10 per cent boost in local property tax receipts which is permitted this year under a law passed by the Kentucky General Assembly.

Van Hoose estimates that the new county school-tax rate for the general fund will be 62.7 cents per $100 of assessed valuation. There will be a different rate—estimated at 57 cents per $100—for the specially-voted building tax.

The rest of the extra money will come from two other sources—about $3 million more from the state and about $5 million from the new occupational tax of one-half of one per cent of wages and net profits.

The total in new money will be almost $10 million, but the school system expects to lose the $700,000 it received this year from the Jefferson Fiscal Court for rental of playgrounds.

Salary Schedule Approved

Fiscal Court made that payment last year to help the financially pressed schools. Since then, the occupational tax and the property-tax increase have been authorized.

Teacher salary increases will account for about two-thirds of the extra $9 million in the budget. The board last night approved a salary schedule for

County school board rejects the request of 12 families in the Kenwood Hills area who wanted to send their children to Gottschalk Junior High School. Page B 1.

teachers which is exactly the same as the one previously approved by the Louisville Board of Education.

Under the schedule, a beginning teacher with a bachelor's degree will earn $5,100 a year.

At the top of the schedule, a teacher with 15 years of experience and a master's degree plus 30 hours of academic credit will receive $8,976 a year. Teachers with 20 years of experience will receive an extra $250.

Last year's teacher salaries ranged from $4,800 to $7,200.

The board also approved increases for principals and supervisors.

Van Hoose said that all other school employes—cafeteria workers, painters, carpenters, drivers, janitors, and so on—would receive pay increases of 10 to 12 per cent.

In another action, the board approved a one-year rental contract of $2,891 for data processing equipment of the Honeywell Corp. The action came after a two-year staff study of data processing needs.

Grayson said the equipment may lead

Col. 3, back page, this section

Staff Photo by Charles Darneal

TIRED of Louisville's heat wave, four-year-old Paul Adams of 2466 Grinstead Drive makes some cool waves in the kiddy pool at Hogan's Fountain in Cherokee Park yesterday.

Associated Press Wirephoto

Highland Lassies

MONTAGNARD militia girls wearing camouflage suits form part of the honor guard at a recent military awards ceremony at Pleiku in the Central Highlands of South Viet Nam. Among 10 Americans decorated were Capt. Bill Carpenter and Spec. 5 Charles Lose, who both received the highest Vietnamese government award. (War developments, Page A 3.)

Kentuckians Sizzle Again; No Relief Near

Kentuckians continued to bake yesterday in an unseasonal heat wave which has turned most of the Eastern United States into an oven of stagnant air.

Cooling thunderstorms moved through parts of Kentucky, Indiana, Illinois and Ohio, but no immediate relief is in sight for most of Kentucky. Rain fell on a line from north of Louisville to Maysville but it was barely measurable.

Scattered sections of Kentucky yesterday registered their highest temperatures of 1966. The mercury reached 99 at Bowling Green, 97 at Lexington, Paducah and Pikeville, and 95 in Louisville, Covington and Fort Campbell.

The Weather Bureau predicts the heat wave will continue at least through tomorrow, with "warm nights and hot days." Temperatures in Western and Central Kentucky are expected to reach 94 to 99 degrees, and 95 is the expected high in the eastern part of the state.

Several public utilities reported record high electrical outputs as Kentuckians turned to electric fans and air conditioners for relief from the heat.

A spokesman for the Louisville Gas & Electric Co. reported that between 2 and 3 p.m. the firm generated 859,000 kilowatts of electricity—an all-time peak load.

The previous high was 823,000 kilowatts last Aug. 16, when the temperature reached 92. The spokesman said the new record was due to the expanded service to homes and industry—and of course, the heat.

A Louisville Water Co. spokesman said the demand for water in the Louisville area "is increasing every day," primarily

Col. 2, back page, this section

Health Chief Optimistic

Easy Kentucky Debut Forecast for Medicare

By PAUL BULLEIT
Courier-Journal Staff Writer

Despite concern over hospital crowding, the birth of Medicare this week will go smoothly in Kentucky, the state's commissioner of health said yesterday.

"There will be no uproar," Dr. Russell E. Teague predicted at a conference of state and regional authorities in Louisville.

Dr. Hasty Riddle, executive director of the Kentucky Hospital Association, said the KHA is estimating a 5 to 10 per cent rise in admission requests in July.

He said a "critical shortage of beds in the Louisville area is being approached," and that a "tight" situation

Medicare's biggest squeeze on the nation's health facilities is still six months off—second in a series, Page A 6.

exists in the Hopkinsville-Paducah, Somerset-Middlesboro, Frankfort-Maysville and Elizabethtown-Danville areas.

But the tone of the session was that almost everyone involved with Medicare in Kentucky is ready—except the prospective patients.

For instance:

✔ Most of the state's hospitals have been, or are being, certified for participation.

✔ The "vast majority" of physicians are determined to see that this new program for the aged and indigent "works in the most proficient manner."

✔ Fourteen Social Security Administration offices in the state declared their readiness, as did all insurance intermediaries involved.

But the public faces a period of misunderstanding, most at the session agreed.

"Hospitals are deeply concerned," said Riddle, "that the limitations in the Medicare program are not understood by the public and that if this is true our institutions will receive unfavorable re-

Col. 1, back page, this section

Think Cool

Furnished by the U.S. Weather Bureau

LOUISVILLE area—Warm nights and hot days through tomorrow; 10 per cent chance of rain; high 95, low 68.

KENTUCKY—Clear to partly cloudy and continued hot; a few showers in north and east this afternoon; high today in the 90s, low in the upper 60s.

INDIANA—Sunny and hot through tomorrow; high today 88-95, low 65-72.

Standiford Field Readings

7 A.M.	69	1 P.M.	92	7 P.M.	90
8 A.M.	75	2 P.M.	93	8 P.M.	85
9 A.M.	82	3 P.M.	94	9 P.M.	82
10 A.M.	86	4 P.M.	95	10 P.M.	81
11 A.M.	90	5 P.M.	94	11 P.M.	80
12 M.	91	6 P.M.	92	12 P.M.	79

High yesterday, 95; low, 66.
Year Ago: High, 90; low, 69.
Sun: Rises, 5:22; sets, 8:10.
Moon: Rises, 9:21 p.m.; sets, 2:10 a.m.

Weather map, Page A 14.

Moves Threaten Coup

Argentine Army Chief Defies Plan to Fire Him

From AP and L.A. Times-Washington Post Service Dispatches

BUENOS AIRES (Tuesday) (AP)—The commander in chief of Argentina's army early today defied an attempt by President Arturo Illia to fire him. There were reports the country's military leaders had demanded that the president resign.

The 65-year-old country doctor, who was elected to the presidency three years ago, ordered Lt. Gen. Pascual Pistarini dismissed from the army command, but Pistarini said the dismissal order was "totally without value."

Presidential press secretary Luis A. Caeiro told newsmen that army troops were marching on Buenos Aires to seize Government House, where Illia was meeting with his cabinet. Caeiro said the troops were from the 10th Armored Cavalry Regiment at the Campo de Mayo Garrison, 30 miles west of the capital.

Confer With Defense Chief

The troops halted two blocks from "Casa Rosada," the pink stone seat of the government, while the commanders of the navy and air force entered the president's office after a conference with Defense Minister Leopoldo Suarez.

Illia ordered Pistarini's removal after the army commander in chief forced the resignation of the army secretary, Brig. Gen. Eduardo Castro Sanchez.

No violence was reported.

There was doubt Illia could enforce his order against Pistarini. It appeared the commanders of all four corps of the army would back the commander in chief, and reliable sources said the navy and air force would back the army.

The sources said the air and navy com-

Col. 4, back page, this section

Cities' Officials In Mississippi Accused by U.S.

From AP and UPI Dispatches

WASHINGTON—The Justice Department yesterday filed a lawsuit charging Philadelphia, Miss., officials with failure to provide adequate protection for civil rights marchers last week.

The suit, filed in U. S. District Court in Jackson, supplements similar legal action against Philadelphia officials by Negro leaders of the march, which ended at Jackson Sunday.

It asks an injunction to protect Negroes and other civil rights demonstrators who are in Philadelphia now or may be in the future.

If granted, the injunction would make city officials subject to contempt-of-court prosecution if its terms were violated.

The Justice Department complaint centers on violence that broke out in Phila-

Col. 1, back page, this section

On Inside Pages

Study on Food Calls for Curb On Big Mergers

WASHINGTON (UPI)—The National Commission on Food Marketing yesterday called for a tight rein on mergers by big food firms and urged creation of a new federal consumer protection agency.

The controversial report, presented to President Johnson and Congress, ended an 18-month study of the $91-billion-a-year food industry. The commission is composed of five senators, five House members, and five public members appointed by the President.

Johnson accepted the report—and sharply worded dissents from six commission members—as "a good beginning" to the problem of achieving greater abundance in America.

He promised that the report would receive careful attention and described the dissenting views as "healthy reflections of the complexity and importance of the issues."

The majority report described the huge food industry as generally efficient and progressive.

The report cited as an exception, the "inordinately costly" distribution of some foods from the plant to the grocer's shelf.

It also struck at advertising designed to promote one product or company among comparable brands of firms, declaring: "It is highly unlikely that costs thus incurred add value to goods purchased by consumers."

The commission placed trading stamps in that category. It said the $680 million spent for stamps by retailers was a

Col. 1, back page, this section

On 1964 German Junket

Dodd Admits He Intended to Aid Klein

By RICHARD HARWOOD
Los Angeles Times-Washington Post News Service

WASHINGTON—Sen. Thomas J. Dodd, D-Conn., acknowledged to the Senate Ethics Committee yesterday that he intended—"if the opportunity arose"—to promote public relations man Julius Klein's business interests in the course of an official trip to Germany in April 1964. But Dodd denied every charge of official misconduct brought against him in three days of public hearings.

"I was anxious," he said, "to do anything I could to help Gen. Klein straighten out what I thought was an injustice. . . . He had been depicted (in Germany) as a criminal . . . I had known him a long time. . . . I thought well of him and if I could in any wise make known the facts (of his case) I was willing to do so."

Klein and his public relations firm were at odds with their West German clients as a result of unfavorable publicity arising out of the Senate Foreign Relations Committee's investigation of foreign lobbyists in 1963. Testimony showed that Klein badgered the senator repeatedly to go to Germany and testify to Klein's good reputation in Washington.

The hearings recessed yesterday afternoon for at least two weeks. The next

Dodd: A surprise in the Senate. Page A 7.

witness—about July 15—will be Klein, who is now in Germany.

There were innumerable letters, phone calls, visits and telegrams from Klein, Dodd related to the committee. Some of them had a demanding tone and others were blunt and insulting.

"He is a very aggressive man," said Dodd, who tried repeatedly to clarify his relationship with Klein.

Sen. John Sherman Cooper of Kentucky, one of the three Republicans on the committee, was curious about Dodd's response to an insulting letter from Klein in November 1963. Klein was dissatisfied with Dodd's failure to come to his defense more vigorously after the Foreign Relations Committee hearings. "What are you afraid of?" Klein wrote. "Do you consider friendship a one-way street? All I can say is I am ashamed of you."

Dodd responded immediately with an

Col. 4, back page, this section

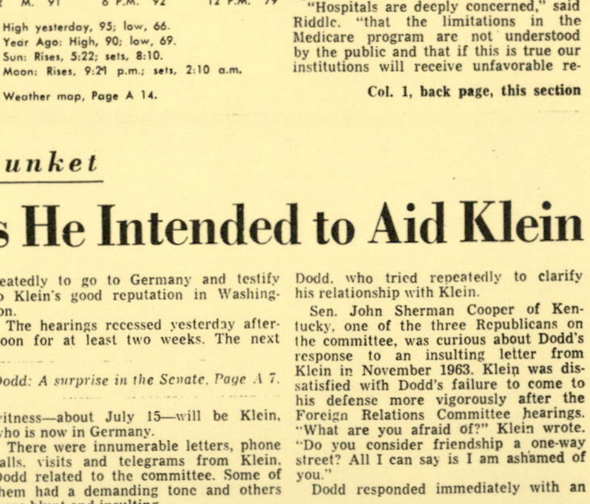

Associated Press Wirephoto

COVERING HIS MOUTH and eying his client is attorney John F. Sonnett, representing Sen. Thomas J. Dodd, left, as the Senate Ethics Committee yesterday delved into misconduct against the Connecticut Democrat. Dodd testified for three hours.

He Nearly Got Into Viet Nam War

4-F a Proud American in Borrowed GI Uniform

By JOSEPH GALLOWAY

SAIGON (UPI)—Red-faced with anger, a brigadier general chewed out David Stucki as a disgrace to his uniform.

Maybe so, but in the few days he wore it, David Stucki for once felt useful and needed and proud to be an American. And they'll never take that away from him, even if it was only a masquerade.

Somewhere there is a real GI in trouble. But this is not his story. It is the tale of a 21-year-old who was 4-F but wanted to go where the action is.

He explained: "I wanted to join the Army. It's something I lacked. I wanted to fight here."

Ten days ago David was punching buttons as a business-machine operator on the night shift on the San Francisco campus of the University of California. He lived with a roommate.

An Army buddy of his roommate, escorting home the body of his cousin who had been killed in Viet Nam, visited them. The soldier said he was fed up.

"I wish I could take your place," Stucki said, jokingly.

But the joke became an idea and suddenly there stood David Stucki at the Oakland Army terminal in the soldier's uniform and with his transportation orders.

Where was his identification card and record of immunization shots?

"Oh, I lost my wallet," David told the sergeant. "I'm going to apply for new ones when I rejoin my unit in Viet Nam."

"OK, OK." The sergeant approved him for transportation to the 25th Infantry Division, Engineer Battalion, Cu Chi, Viet Nam.

That was June 18. Thirty hours later, the first real "private" soldier to come to Viet Nam arrived in Saigon.

As he wandered around trying to find out how to get transportation to the Engineer Battalion, a brigadier general came along.

David did not cut much of a soldierly figure. He needed a shave after the trip, his hands were in his pockets, his haircut was strictly civilian and he didn't know about generals.

"You are a disgrace," the general bellowed. "What kind of a soldier are you?

"Well, dammit, are you going to salute me or not?"

David gave it the John Wayne touch and snapped a salute that pacified the general. He walked away. Close call.

David made it to a helicopter pad and signed on for a trip to his adopted

Col. 1, back page, this section

◀ The *Courier-Journal* (Louisville, Kentucky) in the six-column format it adopted in 1965.

WESTERN MAIL

Wednesday, July 22, 1970 — THE NATIONAL NEWSPAPER OF WALES — No. 31,429 — Price 6d.

Macleod job may go to Barber

Six ministers hold secret talks on plea for special probes

Britain runs into Market snags

BRUSSELS, Tuesday. MR. ANTHONY Barber quickly ran into snags today over Britain's proposals for joining the Common Market.

Guidance

Withheld

Three ships beat dock strike in Welsh port

Troops in?

Get tough on arms sales, U.N. told

150 protest

WEATHER

INSIDE

SUN KEEPS FARMERS FROM THE SHOW

£1,000 down

Franco police kill strikers

After Everett

DEVLIN MAY TAKE THE OATH IN CUSTODY

JOTHAMS SALE STARTS TOMORROW 23rd. JULY

Men's Clothing at VERY SPECIAL LOW PRICES

PLUS

ALSO

JOTHAMS LTD. 26 St. Mary St. and 12 Duke St., Cardiff

STEEL TUBES FROM STOCK

Frequent regular deliveries to South Wales by road

LE BAS TUBE COMPANY LIMITED

Kingswinford 4545

▲ The *Western Mail* (Cardiff) was the only daily here to emulate Louisville's six-column style.

of existing tendencies – for instance, the trend to nine-column broadsheet format described in the previous chapter – and the emergence of new ones. A most striking common factor was the move to larger text sizes, that is to sizes above 8pt for the body of a paper. During the decade the use of 8½ and 9pt for text rose from twenty-six per cent to over seventy-one per cent; the ANPA figures for 1970 showed the following number of newspapers using body sizes from 8pt upwards – 8pt: 203, 8½pt: 168, 9pt: 381. It will be recalled that American practice is normally to set newspaper text on a slug 1pt or 1½pts above face size.

Not unconnected with the trend to larger text sizes, particularly to 9pt, was a development the exact contrary of the nine-column format. This was the move from an eight- to a six-column news page (retaining eight or nine columns for the classified advertisements). In 1965 the nationally-esteemed morning and evening papers of Louisville (Kentucky), the *Courier-Journal* and *Louisville Times*, went over from eight 11-pica columns to six 15-picas; column rules were abolished, around a pica of white being shown between columns by the device of a standard indention on all lines. The papers' Vice-President and Executive Editor, Norman E. Isaacs, listed the advantages as 'the ease of reading, the distinct improvement in headline construction, the pick-up in typesetting speed, and the overall more handsome appearance.' A year later he reported that 'reader reaction remains excellent'.

Louisville's example was significantly followed. The *Christian Science Monitor* went still wider – to five columns of just over 17-picas, with its text size raised from 7½pt to 9pt; a leading Michigan daily, the *Detroit News*, likewise turned to five-column format, though with a less wide measure (and the *News* was only able, for advertising reasons, to use the five-column format on its front and a few key pages inside). By the turn of the decade over forty local dailies, ranging from Illinois to Florida, from Indiana to Mississippi, had turned to the six-column format. Evidently they all overcame the advertising problem, both technical and economic, which is cited as the reason for avoiding such deviations from usual measure. Nor did any advertising snags, as it happens, check the one British daily to emulate Louisville – the *Western Mail* of Cardiff; in 1970 Thomson's Welsh morning successfully went over to the six-column format, with a strong headline style in lower-case Century Bold and Bold Extended.

One other deviation from the newspaper norm has been tried in the U.S. In 1963 the leading Colorado daily, the *Denver Post*, adopted the fashionable book and periodical style of unjustified setting, claiming among other things that it increased linecaster output. In the narrow 11-pica column, and with the text in 9pt Corona on 10pt slug, there were in fact few ragged lines; the greater part of the setting, in short looked as if it were normal justified composition, to which the *Post* returned late in the 1960s when it, too, went over to the six-column format. No other American newspaper has so far tried unjustified setting, though it has appeared in some experimental dummies for projected newspapers. Experiments in Europe have proved uniformly abortive. Holland's *Rotterdamsche Nieuwsblad* had to abandon a changeover to unjustified setting introduced with great enthusiasm in 1967, while the *Observer*, which tried unjustified setting in January 1969 for one of its most popular columns, had immediately to revert to normal setting following a revolt by the readers and the columnist. Some papers, like the *Daily Mirror* have adopted unjustified setting for double-column leaders.

The America-wide success of the Allen revolution has already been indicated in these pages. By this latest period Allen's successor Edmund C. Arnold has been occupied with what may be called mopping-up operations in the pockets of resistance to be found here and there. Arnold performed an operation of this sort with the prestigious *Kansas City Star* in 1970. Missouri's celebrated evening, one of the oldest and most influential dailies of the West, was still dressed in

THE KANSAS CITY STAR

MAIN EDITION

VOL. 90. NO. 331 ★ KANSAS CITY, FRIDAY, AUGUST 14, 1970—34 PAGES To Subscribe Call 421-1200 For Classified Ads Call 221-5500 PRICE 10 CENTS

U.S. CUTS TROOP LEVEL

Units Totaling 15,000 Men in Saigon Military Region to Be Brought Home—Big Base at Tay Ninh Is Taken Over by South Vietnamese

A MAJOR MOVE

Americans Reshuffle Forces, Pull Back From Border

GREAT PROGRESS CITED

Reds Cannot Mount Offensive in Area, Commanders Declare

Saigon (AP)—American forces in the Saigon military region are being cut by about 15,000 men as the result of a major reshuffling of Allied units and the transfer of a large base to the Vietnamese, official sources disclosed today.

The sources said two full brigades plus other units would be shipped home from Saigon and the 11 surrounding provinces of the 3rd military region. Men who have not completed most of their 12-month tours in Vietnam will be transferred to other units.

Security regulations prohibit publication of the units to be sent back to the United States until the U. S. command announces them.

Ambushes in North

Elsewhere in the war, small ambush actions and mopping up operations were reported along the northern coast.

The largest Allied casualties reported today occurred about 65 miles northwest of Saigon when mortar rounds, fired by an American unit accidentally landed on a South Vietnamese position. Eleven government troops were killed and 24 Vietnamese and two American advisers were wounded.

U. S. B-52 bombers pounded North Vietnamese forces threatening Fire Base O'Reilly near the Laotian border. Thirty B-52s dropped 900 tons of bombs on North Vietnamese positions.

One harassing action was reported in Cambodia. A spokesman in Phnom Penh said the Viet Cong and North Vietnamese apparently were occupied with integrating reinforcements.

Abrams Is Back

Gen. Creighton W. Abrams returned from convalescent leave with his family in Thailand and resumed his duties as commander of U. S. forces in Vietnam. His gall bladder was removed in Japan July 3.

In the major reshuffle of Allied forces in the Saigon region, all American combat units except one brigade have been

BULLETINS

Washington (AP)—A federal district judge refused today to forbid the sea-bottom burial of 2,675 tons of deadly nerve gas 282 miles off the Florida coast.

Judge June L. Green coupled her denial of a temporary restraining order with an "urgent request" that the Defense department designate a different site for the dumping.

She said she had "serious misgivings" about the selected site. Sinking of the ship hulk at a depth of 16,000 feet, she said, posed the danger of a sudden and simultaneous crushing of all of the concrete-encased gas containers.

The Weather—Fair and Mild

Continued fair and mild tonight with light southwesterly winds is the weather bureau's forecast for Kansas City and vicinity. The temperature will drop to the lower 80s by midnight and to 70 by tomorrow morning. Increasing cloudiness tomorrow afternoon with a high in the 90s and chance of showers tomorrow afternoon with shifting winds. Probability of rain will be about 30 per cent tomorrow afternoon.

12 midnight	77	9 a. m.	78
1 a. m.	77	10 a. m.	81
2 a. m.	76	11 a. m.	*82
3 a. m.	76	12 noon	90
4 a. m.	74		
5 a. m.	74		
6 a. m.	73		
7 a. m.	74		
8 a. m.	75		
9 a. m.	78		

*Unofficial.

Relative humidity, 6 a. m., 66 per cent.

Barometer reading, 6 a. m., 29.92 inches.

River stage today 6.9 feet, fall of .1 of a foot.

Lake of the Ozarks, 6 a. m., 2.6 feet below full reservoir.

NIXON TO NEW ORLEANS

President Will Meet With Desegregation Officials

Washington (AP)—President Nixon departed for New Orleans today to venture his greatest involvement in Southern school desegregation. He will meet with advisory councils from seven states on twin goals: Bolstering the effectiveness and prestige of the state desegregation advisory councils, and emphasizing his commitment to enforcing wide-scale voluntary integration in the South this fall.

Accompanying the President were Mrs. Nixon, George P. Shultz, vice-chairman of the cabinet Committee on Education, Secretary Elliot Richardson of the Welfare department, John N. Mitchell, attorney general, and several top aides.

SQUALLS IN ATLANTIC

VOTE EDGE CUT IN KANSAS BID

Wyandotte County Canvass Reduces Richard Rome Lead to 111

A GAIN FOR STEINEGER

State Senator Awaits Final Results Tuesday

Topeka (AP)—Richard J. Rome of Hutchinson retained his lead in the race for the Democratic nomination for lieutenant governor but his margin over State Sen. Jack Steineger (D-Muncie) has been cut almost in half by the canvass of Wyandotte County's complete official returns.

Steineger, whose home county is Wyandotte, picked up 106 votes over the unofficial figures compiled for the August 4 primary, while Rome added 11 votes to his Wyandotte total.

Rome's state-wide lead is now 111 votes, down from the 206 he held earlier.

The complete, unofficial statewide total is 32,790 votes for Rome to 32,679 for Steineger. The official state canvass is scheduled Tuesday.

In the Republican race for lieutenant governor, State Sen. Reynolds Shultz (R-Lawrence) picked up 77 votes to raise his statewide margin over L. A. (Bud) Billings of Overland Park to 1,306.

Official Wyandotte County figures gave Billings 2,462 votes and Shultz 1,001. The Billings total was 365 votes less than reported earlier.

Billings lost 56 more votes in the official Wyandotte County canvass. The Shultz total was 21

UNDERBRUSH WAS BURNED AWAY by the swirling flames of "foo gas" dropped on the perimeter of Fire Support Base Maureen in the A Shau Valley by helicopter. A mixture of oil, gasoline and explosives, the incendiary material destroys cover used by infiltrating Communist forces—(Wirephoto).

A Soldier's Letter Becomes His Epitaph

Wright, Kas. (AP)—Gregg Steimel was to have been 20 years old yesterday but there was no celebration in Wright. Instead, the more than 500 persons who attended, remember his funeral.

NEW SNAG IN CEASE-FIRE

Israeli Jets Hit Targets in Jordan in Retaliation for Assistance Reportedly Given by That Nation to Palestinian Guerrillas

EGYPT CHARGED

Soldiers Accused of Violating the Truce, Too

Jerusalem (AP)—Israeli air force planes struck at Jordanian army positions today, the military command said, in further deterioration of the Middle East cease-fire.

The military said the raid was launched against Jordanian army strongholds which have given assistance to Palestinian guerrillas in attacks against Israeli frontier settlements.

Says Army Aids Terror

A spokesman said the Jordanian army "assists terrorists and makes it possible for them to act against Israeli civilians."

A spokesman earlier had announced that Israeli Air Force jets crossed the border and bombed and strafed Arab guerrilla targets inside Jordan for the second straight day today. The Tel Aviv spokesman said those raids were in response to mortar attacks on two Jewish settlements.

The planes all returned safely after hitting objectives adjacent to Israel's Beisan valley, he said. Beisan valley settlements of Maoz Haim and Yardena came under mortar fire last night but no damage was reported.

This was the second Israeli air strike inside Jordan since the Middle East cease-fire went into effect a week ago. The guerrilla organizations have disowned the truce initiated by the United States as a preliminary to peace talks.

An Israeli newspaper, the Tel Aviv Yediot Aharonot, reported that Egyptian soldiers fired across the Suez canal in a second minor violation of the cease-fire yesterday.

Reports from Amman said Jordanian authorities have tightened security measures to prevent Arab commandos from kidnaping diplomats, foreigners or government officials. An informant said the guerrillas may resort to this tactic to sabotage the U. S. peace plan.

Fear Assassination Plot

Two Beirut newspapers also reported that King Hussein of Jordan has warned his armed forces to be on the alert because subversives were plotting to assassinate him and other Jordanian officials.

The ruler said the assassins might be disguised as Jordanian soldiers, according to the reports published by Al Ahrar and Al Kifah, purporting to be the

Cyclamate Ban Expected by FDA

Washington (AP)—The Food and Drug administration is expected this afternoon to reverse its disputed decision of six months ago and bar use of cyclamates in artificially sweetened diet foods.

The FDA said there will be an announcement on the controversial sweetener after stockmarkets close. Extension of the cyclamate restrictions to all food would have considerable economic impact.

Informed sources said top FDA officials decided to remove the sweetener from all foods on recommendations of a special medical advisory panel. The committee only a few months ago suggested the opposite course.

But more than a month ago, apparently in anticipation of today's announcement, Charles C. Edwards, FDA commissioner ordered regional offices to stop processing applications for permission to use cyclamates in diet foods.

FBI THWARTS HOLDUP

Two Men Are Shot and Wounded by Agent as They Leave Park National Bank After Robbery

Bill Vaughan Says

Prefabricated housing is booming again. "One more word out of you, young man, and you can go to your module without any supper."

Critic Backs State Study Of Deposits

Carthage, Mo. (AP)—State Sen. Richard M. Webster (R-Carthage) today approved a plan by the Missouri state treasurer to seek methods of reforming deposit procedures of that office.

William E. Robinson, state treasurer, has announced he will call in experts to aid in determining the amount of money the state should keep in interest-free checking accounts.

Earlier this week Webster was highly critical of deposit procedures in a debate in Carthage with leaders of the administration of Gov. Warren E. Hearnes. He made refer-

(Continued on Page 2.)

To Trim Speed Limit on Turnpike Monday

ON A STAKEOUT

Officer Assigned to Surveillance Duty in Area

An agent of the Federal Bureau of Investigation on a stake-out across the street from the Park National bank, 4632 Troost avenue, today shot and wounded two bandits who had robbed the bank moments earlier.

The agent is one of a corps of FBI employees who are foregoing their normal luncheon hours to watch over banks here from 11 o'clock each morning until 2 o'clock in the afternoon. That is the time interval in which several recent bank holdups here have occurred.

The two wounded men were struck by shotgun pellets. They were taken to the General hospital, where identities and conditions were not learned immediately.

Two other men arrested near the scene were being questioned by officers in an effort to determine whether they also were involved.

Mason Working, special agent in charge of the FBI office here, who said that "law-enforcement officers are fed up" as a result of the recent rash of robberies

▲ The *Kansas City Star* in its long-standing decker style with (opposite) its 1970 change to lower-case Tempo prescribed by Edmund C. Arnold.

▶

traditional deckers, with main lines in Gothic Condensed capitals. For this Arnold substituted a simple flush-left all sans lower-case style, using Tempo Bold up to 72pt. The comparatively modest weight of Tempo Bold (to get what would normally be considered boldness it is necessary to ascend a stage to Tempo Heavy) was a significant feature of Arnold's head schedule for the *Star*. It expressed a headline typographic trend that for some time had been gaining ground in American newspapers.

This trend was simply summed up in the words 'From Big Black to Medium', a headline in the fourth (1964) edition of the house Manual of the *Chicago Sun–Times* to a survey of the typographic evolution of that paper from the mid-1940s on. The *Sun–Times* was a merger of the tabloid *Chicago Sun*, founded by Marshall Field (who, it will be recalled, was the begetter of the New York *PM*), with an older Chicago tabloid, the *Daily Times*. The Manual, compiled by the late Quentin P. Gore, managing editor, is worth a mention as the most remarkable internal type specimen and style book, and detailed guide to newspaper typography, ever issued by any newspaper. In seventy-eight profusely-illustrated pages in the full format of the paper it examined in depth everything from make-up (there were hundreds of reduced page facsimiles) to text type. The *Sun–Times* was then one of the handful of American newspapers using Times Roman for text, calling it Sun–Times Roman, since it had had certain modifications made in the design; by 1967, however, it felt the disadvantages of the face, as others had done, and changed to Imperial.

The opening paragraphs of this chapter briefly mentioned the suc-

THE KANSAS CITY STAR

VOL. 91, NO. 10 | MAIN EDITION | ★ ★ | KANSAS CITY, SUNDAY, SEPTEMBER 27, 1970 | 202 PAGES IN FOURTEEN SECTIONS INCLUDING STAR MAGAZINE | 30¢

Air Alert

A South Vietnamese helicopter crew keeps watch as about 20 boats move along the Bassac river carrying South Vietnamese marines and army forces to an operation in Eastern Cambodia.

(Wirephoto)

Hostages Freed

From The Star's Press Services

Amman radio announced last night that 32 more airline hostages had been freed and were under the protection of the Jordanian army. All are Americans.

The list of freed hostages, as listed in a broadcast by Amman radio, included Capt. Carroll D. Woods, T. W. A. pilot, 6517 Granada drive, Prairie Village, Kas.

Earlier, the Popular Front for the Liberation of Palestine, the Arab guerrilla group that had been holding the hostages since the highjacking of three western airliners of the Jordanian desert September 6, had announced that 38 remaining hostages would be freed within 24 hours.

There was no immediate explanation of the discrepancy in the number of those released and the announcement by the guerrillas.

Sixteen non-American hostages, including eight Britons, were released Friday and flown to London last night.

It was possible, however, that several of the persons included among the 38 listed on the T. W. A. passenger list had been the highjackers and joined the guerrillas when the plane landed in Jordan.

T. W. A. officials said at the time of the highjacking they could not identify those persons who commandeered the plane.

Radio Amman gave no indication that any of the hostages were still being held by the guerrillas.

The brief announcement by Amman radio was made by Field Marshal Habes Al-Majali, the Jordanian military commander, who said the 32 newly-freed hostages were under the protection of the Jordanian armed forces. He did not elaborate.

There was some speculation that the 32 Americans would be flown to Cairo but there was no confirmation of any evacuation plans.

The announcement by the Popular Front was made to newsmen at the Intercontinental hotel by an aide of the Egyptian embassy here in Amman. It said there would be no conditions attached to the release of the hostages, a few of whom are believed to hold dual U. S.-Israeli citizenship.

Prime Minister Edward Heath sent a message to King Hussein of Jordan thanking him for help in freeing the British hostages.

See ARABS Page 6A

CAPT. CARROLL D. WOODS . . . T. W. A. pilot of Prairie Village, reported freed by guerrillas.

Hussein to Cairo

From The Star's Press Services

King Hussein of Jordan is expected to arrive in Cairo today to respond to questions from leaders of other Arab nations on the bitter conflict between his army and Palestinian guerrillas.

The report of Hussein's visit to the Egyptian capital came from an Egyptian spokesman last night. If the trip is made, it will be an effort to placate Arab critics who have accused him of plotting to liquidate the guerrillas.

Meanwhile, an uneasy cease-fire persisted in Amman, the Jordanian capital.

Hussein said the guerrillas had built concrete blockhouses inside the walls of private homes in Amman, and said his army officers were amazed at the speed with which his opponents had built elaborate fortifications within the capital. He said he considers such careful preparations evidence that the Palestinians planned to overthrow his regime.

The guerrilla reply to Hussein's charge came in an announcement last night in Beirut, Lebanon, that the Palestine Liberation organization intends to bring Hussein to trial on a charge of genocide.

A spokesman said "evidence of the king's role in the last nine days of mass extermination of Palestinians will be piled up in an indictment which will be issued by the P. L. O. in Beirut in the next two days.

"That will be our last resort. We are serious about the trial. We expect to topple him soon and in this case he will be tried and condemned in Jordan."

If that is not possible, the guerrillas plan to set up a tribunal representing all Arab countries and try the king in absentia. The trial possibly will be held in Libya, Syria or Iraq, the spokesman said.

Hussein named a new government yesterday, apparently hoping to placate his critics.

Ahmed Toukan, chief of the royal court and former deputy prime minister, was named prime minister. Toukan is a Palestinian but the king kept military men in key positions. It was guerrilla rage over the naming of a military regime that helped touch off the civil war last week.

O earth,
earth,
earth,
hear the word
of the Lord.
JEREMIAH 22:29

Campus Violence Scored

By Joe Lastelic
Of The Star's Washington Bureau

Washington — Condemning all violence, the President's Commission on Campus Unrest yesterday called for a national cease-fire, a return of respect for law, individual responsibility and tolerance for each other and told President Nixon he must lead the way toward a reconciliation of all Americans.

"We utterly condemn violence," the commission said in its report to the President and the nation. "No grievance, philosophy or political idea can justify the destruction and killing we have witnessed."

The commission spent three months investigating the deaths, bombings, assaults and turmoil on America's college campuses and why they occurred. It came down hard in criticism of students, professors, administrators, police, National Guardsmen, politicians, the self-righteous and the excuse-makers, the hard-liners and the name callers, those who preach permissiveness and those who demand repression.

"Students who bomb and burn are criminals," the commission said. "Police and National Guardsmen who needlessly shoot or assault students are criminals. All who applaud these acts share in their evil. Crimes committed by one do not justify crimes committed by another.

"There can be no place in our society for vigilantes, night-riders or militants who would bring destruction and death upon their opponents. No one serves the law by breaking it. Violence must stop because it is wrong. It destroys human life and the products of human effort."

The chairman, William W. Scranton, former Pennsylvania governor, presented the inch-thick report to President Nixon at the White House. He told the President the report explores the history and causes of campus unrest and contains recommendations for meeting the problem.

It is expected that the self-examination and criticism of so many segments of society and the university in particular will be debated for a long time. Some of what the commission recommends will cost money, such as more aid for higher education, special equipment for National Guardsmen and training of campus police. But the thrust of the recommendations go toward communication and correction.

The commission took into account what students, faculty, administrators, police, sociologists, politicians and others told them. They examined the causes of violent student activity and from that fashioned these recommendations and observations:

"The university must pull itself together. It must develop that sense of community which has often been sadly lacking. The university must clearly distinguish between those forms of protest which it will permit and defend and those it will prohibit.

"We recommend that every college or university that has not recently done so examine its internal rules of conduct with a view toward making them consonant with principles of free speech and due process, as well as more explicit in defining what the university considers to be impermissible conduct.

"Faculty members who engage in or lead disruptive conduct have no place in the university.

"Students must be worthy of the mature treatment they rightfully claims as adults. The administration is not always wrong, and more students must be willing to say so.

"In general, there is no reason for a university to refuse to discuss grievances with students involved in a disruption—even when the students' request comes in the form of a list of 'non-negotiable demands.'

"Students . . . must become

See VIOLENCE on Next Page

Democrats Nudged

By Henry Clay Gold
The Star's Missouri Correspondent

St. Louis—Democratic ward leaders here have told Lt. Gov. William S. Morris of Kansas City and True Davis of St. Joseph to announce their intentions soon if they plan to become candidates for governor in the 1972 election.

Davis, now head of a bank in Washington, accepted the advice and said last night he will make his plans known after the November 3 general election and before the end of the year. Morris also indicated his plans will be made public soon after the November election.

Leading Democrats are here for the St. Louis observance of Harry S. Truman days, which was marked last night by a speech by Sen. Birch Bayh (D-Ind.) and the giving of a Truman day award to Sen. Stuart Symington (D-Mo.).

Davis said he was extremely encouraged by his two days of meetings here with Democratic party officials who gave their views on his possible candidacy for governor. The meetings, Davis said, included a majority of the Democratic ward leaders in St. Louis and members of the party from other parts of the state.

In the 1968 contest for U. S. senator, Davis failed to announce as a candidate until most leaders of the Democratic party had pledged their support to one of two other candidates. He was repeatedly advised here not to wait and to return to Missouri soon if he expects to win his party's nomination for governor.

By withholding their plans until after November 3, the candidates for governor will leave the spotlight on Symington and Haskell Holman, state auditor, who are seeking re-election.

Morris, who has been lining up support for governor for several months, told Young Democrats here last night that Missouri needs a new state constitution. He outlined the procedure for calling a constitutional convention.

One of the more widely discussed developments among Democrats here was a St. Louis move to elect state Sen. John

See DEMOCRATS on next page

On Inside Pages

URSCHEL

Charles F. Urschel, an oilman and philanthropist who was the victim of a famous kidnaping in 1933, dies in San Antonio where he had chosen to live to avoid the public eye. His careful attention to details while a prisoner led to the arrest of the Machinegun Kelly gang as his kidnapers. Page 1B.

Foes of Home Rule for Jackson County move quietly to defeat charter legislation. 3A.

General Motors and United Auto Workers negotiators hold a weekend session but it gets nowhere. 1B.

Our Environment: A special report. The effects of air, water, land and noise pollution in Greater Kansas City, and measures to abate them . . . Section F, No. 29 in the Background for Better Understanding series.

Colorado pulls off the biggest upset of the day in the collegiate ranks with an overwhelming 41-13 triumph over the Nittany Lions of Penn State. The loss wipes out the longest winning streak—23 games—in college football . . . The Air Force, not to be outdone, builds a 30-0 half-time lead over Missouri and walks away with a 37-14 victory in St. Louis . . . Kansas finds the winning touch against Syracuse with a rousing 31-14 triumph . . . Bob Johnson hurls a 4-hitter against the Minnesota Twins and picks up a 5-0 victory in the Municipal Stadium.

The baseball scores:

AMERICAN LEAGUE
New York 2, Detroit 1.
Baltimore 7, Cleveland 4.
Milwaukee 9, Chicago 5.
Boston 6, Washington 3.
Oakland at California, night.

NATIONAL LEAGUE
San Francisco 7, San Diego 6.
Cincinnati 6, Los Angeles 3.
Houston 5, Atlanta 2.
Pittsburgh 4, New York 3.
Philadelphia 7, Chicago 1.
St. Louis 7, Montreal 2.

Prosperity can be measured by demands from people for more meat, milk and eggs, writes Roderick Turnbull, The Star's agricultural editor. If world consumption could be boosted American grain producers would benefit. The leading editorial. 10D.

Deaths are on Page 3B.

Index by Page and Section

Bill Vaughan Says:

A complete physical for airline passengers as they board would not only prevent highjackings but improve worldwide health standards.

K-State to Defer Action Against Nixon Hecklers

By The Star's Own Service

Manhattan, Kas.—Authorities at Kansas State university announced yesterday that no university disciplinary action will be taken at this time against hecklers of President Richard Nixon at his Landon lecture here September 16.

Ron Innes, Riley County attorney, also said:

"I have concluded that I will at this time defer . . . any prosecution of the individuals who have been identified."

Dr. James A. McCain, K-State president; Pat Bosco, student body president, and Charles Hall, president of the faculty senate, said in a joint statement: "Because of the unique conditions under which the convocation was held, the university has less evidence than would be normally required as a basis for disciplinary action.

"Nevertheless, students who may have been involved have been notified by the dean of students of the university's attitude toward this behavior and the consequences of such behavior in the future."

Dr. McCain, Bosco and Hall also said that "in behalf of students, faculty and administration, we commend K-State students for their magnificent response to President Nixon's address and strongly condemn the crude scurrilousness of a tiny minority."

Innes said:

"Against the backdrop of events and after careful consideration of the evidence and of the other aspects of this particular incident, it is my thought that to provide the individuals identified with an additional public forum (trial) at this time (would) in fact give them an opportunity to further attempt to inappropriately portray themselves as martyrs and perhaps as truly representative of a substantial faction of the K-State student body, while in fact they are not."

Both the county attorney and university officials said they have reviewed the Kansas Bureau of Investigation and all other information currently available. They conferred to discuss the evidence twice, but their decisions were arrived at independently.

Black Union Clear at K.U.

By The Star's Own Service

Lawrence, Kas.—Two state agencies that conducted investigations of the University of Kansas Black Student union have found no misuse of state money, Max Bickford, executive officer of the Kansas Board of Regents has announced.

The probe was ordered by Gov. Robert Docking of Kansas after it was revealed that Laverta Murry, B. S. U. chairman, had written a check for $120.62 on a Lawrence bank account to purchase ammunition in Kansas City.

Bickford said the regents investigated B. S. U. accounts at K. U.

"This office," Bickford wrote, "made an immediate survey of all vouchers paid by the university for activities sponsored and approved for the Black Students union. Examination of these vouchers revealed none of these funds has been used for other than approved purchases."

The attorney general's report concluded that "It would appear that the monies collected in the private account are from donations, either in cash, currency or check." Identity of the individual contributors is not known.

The largest deposits made to the account during the period 1970, were $89.47 in cash last May 28 and a $50 check from the Roger Williams fellowship account in the First National bank of Lawrence.

The largest withdrawal was the $120.62 check for the ammunition, which was purchased July 19, the day after Rick Dowdell, of Lawrence, a Negro youth, was killed by a police bullet.

The regents in their September 18 meeting unanimously adopted a report by a special subcommittee which investigated use of student activity fees at K. U.

One clause states:

"Each organization should be required to declare all funds available for use by the organization and that failure to meet this requirement would mean automatic ineligibility for student activity funds."

The Weather

Fair today and tomorrow with slowly rising temperatures is the weather bureau's forecast for Kansas City and vicinity. Light and variable winds. Probability of precipitation near zero throughout the period. High today in the upper 60s to lower 70s, low tonight in the mid 40s. Tomorrow's high in the lower 70s.

(Map, State Forecasts and World Temperatures on 26A).

Temperatures

1 p. m.	60	8 p. m.	57
2 p. m.	62	9 p. m.	57
3 p. m.	64	10 p. m.	55
4 p. m.	64	11 p. m.	53
5 p. m.	65	12 Midnight	52
6 p. m.	64		
7 p. m.	63		

Missouri river stage at 7 p. m. yesterday, 8.9 feet, a fall of .7 of a foot from 12 hours earlier.

Handwork

Intricate gables, fretwork and wrought iron encrust the Vaile mansion at 1500 North Liberty street, Independence. The mansion is one of 22 buildings most in need of preserving on a list by the city's historical preservation committee. (Story on pages 4A and 5A)

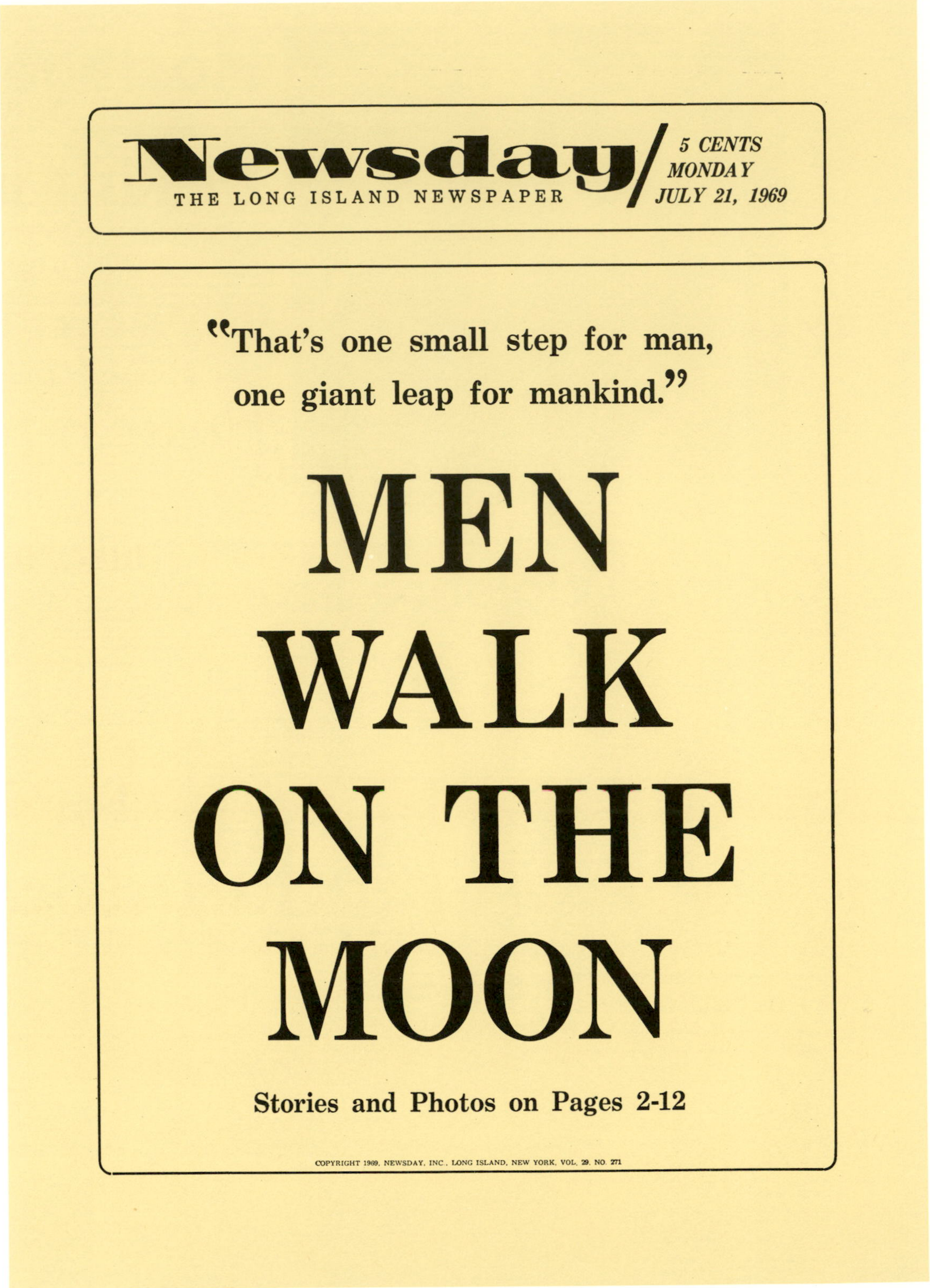

Newsday
THE LONG ISLAND NEWSPAPER

5 CENTS
MONDAY
JULY 21, 1969

"That's one small step for man,
one giant leap for mankind."

MEN
WALK
ON THE
MOON

Stories and Photos on Pages 2-12

COPYRIGHT 1969, NEWSDAY, INC., LONG ISLAND, NEW YORK, VOL. 29, NO. 271

cess of *Newsday*. It is now time to examine the case of this Long Island evening, still rotary letterpress, in more detail. For *Newsday* presents a success story that is also a design story; the success and the design have gone together. Radical innovations in design have helped to build *Newsday* into its powerful and prosperous position as America's outstanding suburban daily and seventh largest evening, with 430,000 circulation; by the same token they have established the paper as the front-runner in U.S. newspaper design. It all dates only from 1968, when Director of Design Paul Back laid hands on what had so far been a conventional American tabloid daily, though with unusual features, like setting its text in the elegant Electra instead of a standard news-type.

'I redesigned *Newsday*', said Back, 'to desensationalise it'; and indeed, as Harold Evans puts it, the paper is now 'an advanced example

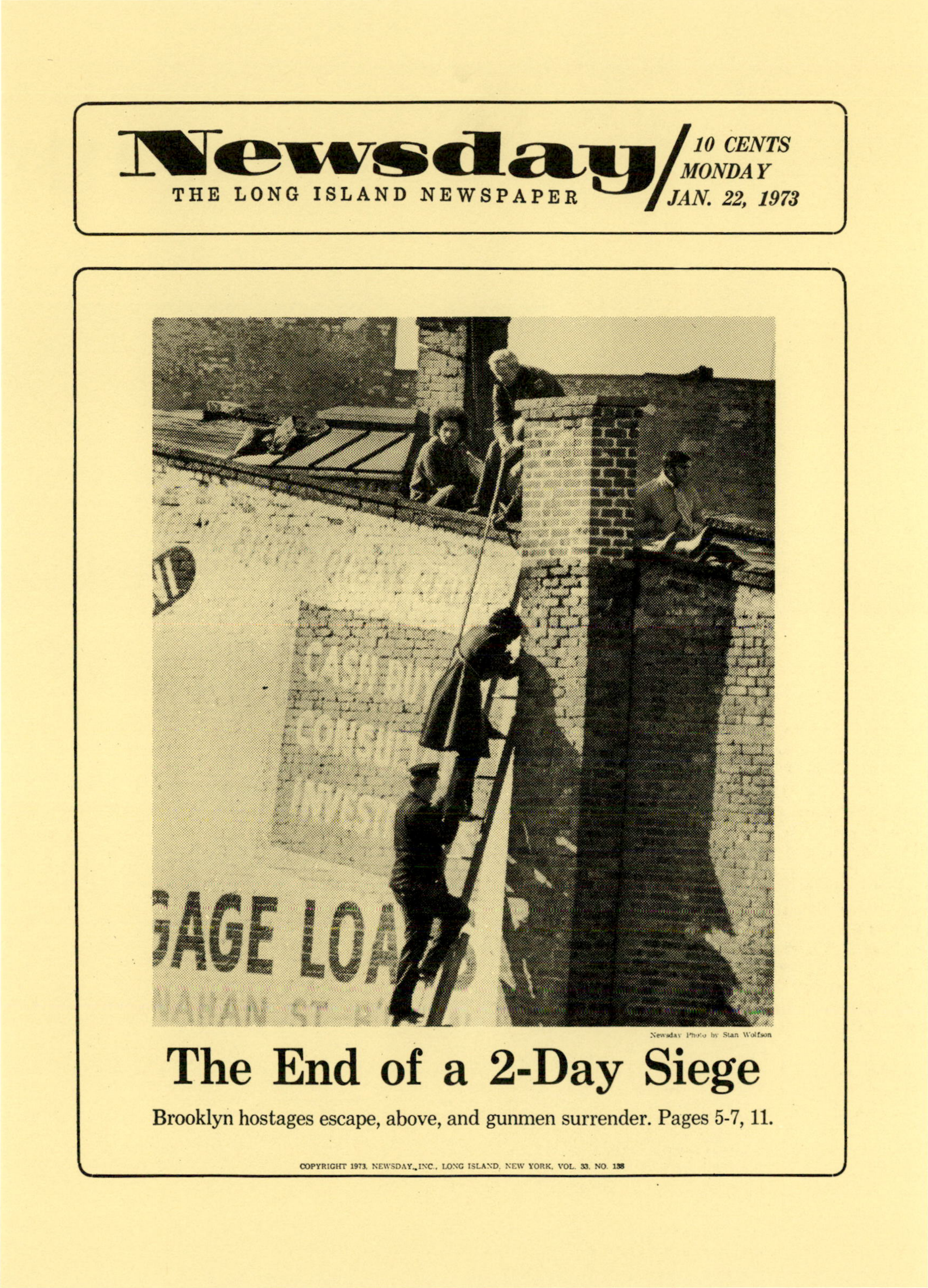

Newsday
THE LONG ISLAND NEWSPAPER
10 CENTS
MONDAY
JAN. 22, 1973

Newsday Photo by Stan Wolfson

The End of a 2-Day Siege

Brooklyn hostages escape, above, and gunmen surrender. Pages 5-7, 11.

COPYRIGHT 1973, NEWSDAY, INC., LONG ISLAND, NEW YORK, VOL. 33, NO. 138

Three front pages of *Newsday*, the Long Island tabloid evening, exemplify its three basic front-page styles – i) all type, ii) picture and type, and (on p. 210) iii) picture and text. Note the 'ring job' round-cornered boxing of the title and the page.

of what a serious tabloid might be'. The underlying concept tended more towards a news-magazine than a conventional newspaper. Back prescribed a three-column make-up (19-picas measure) for main news pages, four columns (14-picas measure) for subsidiary pages, retaining six $9\frac{1}{2}$-pica columns for the 'classified' pages. The widest measure was 23-picas for double-column measure, allowing, e.g. on the front page, ample white between the columns and each end for medium rule-boxing, used a good deal throughout the paper. Always with rounded corners (the 'ring job') these boxes added a distinctive and attractive note.

These format prescriptions were given a framework of a new kind by *Newsday's* then publisher, Bill Moyers. He decided that the 60-plus editorial pages of daily issues that could run to 200 pages or more were to be freed from the casual and anarchic intrusion of display

Newsday / 10 CENTS FRIDAY JAN. 19, 1973

THE LONG ISLAND NEWSPAPER

Newsday Photo by George Argeroplos

The managers: Project heads Peter Waters and Vincent Tizio with AX model

The AX: Victory For Republic

By Myron S. Waldman and Drew Fetherston

Fairchild Republic Division and Long Island emerged the victors yesterday in the competition for the Air Force's AX close-support plane.

But the carefully worded announcement said that an agreement is still to be negotiated before even the first installment of 10 planes is built. The work on those 10 planes would keep Fairchild's Farmingdale plant humming until late 1975 and could lead to a hoped-for $1 billion contract for 600 planes that would mean 19,000 more jobs for Long Island.

The news caused cheers from workers and pops from champagne corks when it blared over the plant's public address system at 4:03 PM. Nassau and Suffolk officials and the Long Island Association of Commerce and Industry reacted with enthusiasm. Suffolk County Executive Klein said the news was "the biggest, finest shot in the arm that the economy of the Island has had in the past 15 years." Fairchild had said it might have to close if it didn't receive the contract.

No price for the initial 10-plane contract was announced, but congressional sources said it would be about $200,000,000. "That's about the right order of magnitude," said Col. James E. Hildebrandt, head of the Air Force's AX program.

The announcement, made in Washington by Air Force Secretary Robert C. Seamans Jr., made it clear that the Air Force would not commit itself to full production until late 1975, and then only if exhaustive testing of the aircraft and the new 30-mm. cannon that is being developed for it prove that the plane would work. Maj. George

—Continued on Page 5

advertising. In magazine fashion, advertisements were grouped in whole pages, maintaining throughout the paper a clear barrier between editorial and advertising – no more small solus positions, no pyramid make-up. When display advertising was placed on an editorial page it was always in a complete rectangle, usually a vertical half-page.

Both the text and the headline typography were simple and economical. Century Schoolbook was chosen for the text, in 9/10pt (with 10/11pt for the front page, for occasional main intros and editorials). For the lower-case, flush-left headings Schoolbook Bold, with Schoolbook roman and italic (and some Century Bold italic) was the sole style. Whites were used throughout in place of column rules.

The daily edition is divided into two parts, Part II being the magazine, run as a centre section. The paper's presses have been fitted with

Scientists Cast Doubt on the Waters

By Larry Eichel

White Plains—Long Islanders may have no one to blame but themselves for the pollution of the western part of Long Island Sound. At least, they may not be able to blame New York City, if some tentative scientific findings turn out to be accurate.

Oceanographers from the State University at Stony Brook said here yesterday that the net flow of water between Long Island Sound and New York Harbor appears to be out of the Sound and into the Harbor. Long Island ecologists have often said that the flow was in the opposite direction, and scientists had theorized that fresh water and pollutants might flow from the Hudson River to the East River, and thence into the Sound.

David Jay, a graduate student who took part in the testing, said that "just the sloshing back and forth [of the water] would have some effect in polluting the Sound [regardless of the net flow].

Stony Brook oceanographers presented their findings at the annual Long Island Sound Conference of the New England River Basins Commission. But they stressed that their conclusions are tentative. All they are certain of, they said, is that on one day—September 23, 1972—about 10 per cent more water flowed into New York Harbor from the Sound than flowed in the opposite direction. Even on that day, discounting underwater currents, the net flow of water on the surface was into the Sound. They got their results on Sept. 23 by stationing about 100 persons in 13 boats and at 14 land stations to chart the flow of surface and underwater currents and to test the water content for salt and pollutants, such as coliform bacteria and heavy metals. The river basins commission is a joint body with representatives of seven northeastern states and the federal government. It is conducting a three-year, $3,500,000 study of the Sound that is scheduled to be completed by 1975.

Malcolm Bowman of the Marine Sciences Research Center, at Stony Brook, said he expected to reach conclusions in a few months about what happens at other times of the year. He said he would use observations of harbor conditions compiled by other scientists. He said the results found on any one day might be totally explained by the wind or tide conditions on that day, and might not be representative.

In other papers presented at the conference, a Cornell University ecologist listed four undeveloped areas along the Long Island shoreline as "most important to preserve in their natural state." Paul Spitzer said that Plum Island, the salt marshes at Orient, the Mashomack Forest on Shelter Island, and the Caumsett State Park on Lloyd Neck all had especially high educational, recreational, esthetic and scientific value.

And Donald Matchett, a Boston engineer, said that the electric power plants already built along the Sound have raised the average water temperature by half a degree Fahrenheit. If all the plants scheduled to open by 1980 do open on time, he said, the temperature would be further raised by .15 degree Fahrenheit.

Matchett said the temperature increases would be higher near the plants themselves. His conclusions were the result of a study done for four power companies, including the Long Island Lighting Co.

About 100 scientists, environmentalists and planners attended the all-day conference.

Bus Firm Wants to Keep LI-City Run

LIRR Beckons To Commuters With Fare Offer

The Long Island Railroad, attempting to get commuters to return to the line," will sell tickets today and tomorrow good for the rest of the month at the price of a weekly ticket.

The line said that unused December monthly tickets purchased before the 50-day strike began can be retained and used for the rest of January. November tickets may be used through Monday or turned in for a refund. Holders of weekly tickets that expired Dec. 1 can use those tickets today or tomorrow and then may return the ticket for a cash refund. They may apply the ticket value toward the purchase of the reduced commutation ticket.

LIRR stations open tomorrow in Nassau are Hempstead, Rockville Centre, Baldwin, Freeport, Bellmore, Wantagh, Massapequa, Mineola, Westbury, Hicksville, Lynbrook, Long Beach, Valley Stream, Great Neck, Manhasset and Port Washington. In Suffolk, stations open are in Amityville, Babylon, Bay Shore, Patchogue, Southampton, Ronkonkoma, Huntington, Northport and Port Jefferson. In Queens, open stations are in Flushing, Woodside and Jamaica; in Brooklyn, Flatbush, and in Manhattan, Pennsylvania Station.

Newsday Photo by Don Jacobsen

Back in the ticket line at Hicksville

At least one bus company that ran emergency service during the Long Island Railroad strike is seeking a franchise to continue the extra service now that the strike is over. The plans of other bus lines surveyed ranged from "maybe" and "we'd like to" to "no way."

The company that has indicated that it will ask the state for a certificate to operate the emergency service permanently is Alert Coach Corp., which has been running buses from Kings Park, East Northport, Greenlawn and Amityville to Shea Stadium. Steve Harrington, fleet safety engineer for the firm, was unable to give the status of the firm's application.

James Smith, an officer of Babylon Transit, said "a lot of people have asked us, saying they would like to continue." Babylon Transit ran buses from Babylon into the Van Wyck Expressway subway stop in Queens during the strike. But Smith said, "We have found from past experience that, once that train whistle blows, you lose them all. As long as they don't have an express bus lane on the expressway, there's no sense trying to compete. They just don't have faith the bus is going to make it on time, because of traffic tie-ups or breakdowns." So Babylon Transit has no plans to apply to the State Transportation Department to keep their emergency service running after the strike.

But Alpha Beta Coach of Port Jefferson is thinking seriously of turning what was an emergency service into a routine. "Our attorney's working on it to find out what legal problems [may exist]," companys manager Jay Day said. The firm has been running express buses between the Port Jefferson and Stony Brook railroad stations and midtown Manhattan, on a charter basis. "The people really seem to enjoy it," he said. "They get in there faster than by train. There's one fellow who started a committee and they got over 100 names for two buses."

Tom Perfect of Port Jefferson, the commuter who organized the two daily charter buses from Day's firm, said: "I chartered the buses and I work it out with the people. There's 41 people in each bus. I have another 25 or 30 who are interested. Right now, we negotiated a contract at $20 a head . . . I feel that after this [strike] is over, we'll make better time than with the train. We make it to New York, even with this heavy traffic, in two hours and five minutes."

A Day to Work Out Kinks

—Continued from Page 11

kowski of Bay Shore, waited in line at the Babylon station yesterday morning. "I'm happy it's over," he said of the longest strike in the railroad's history. "But they haven't actually settled the strike, and if they jack up the fare I'll go back to my car pool," he added.

Many other commuters seemed to feel the same way. They were willing, they said at stations across the Island, to return to the line, but not at higher prices. For Mrs. Virginia McKullen of North Babylon, the 50-day strike was "pretty miserable." But not miserable enough to make her love the rails. "If they raise the fare too high I'll go back to my motor pool," she said.

Still Need Accord

Trainmen also were unhappy. Robert Thompson of Hicksville, who has worked as an engineer for four years, was pessimistic about the temporary agreement. "The strike really didn't accomplish anything. I feel that there's just going to be another strike in 90 days. If they couldn't settle it in 16 months, what's another 90 days?" he said. He also said: "You know they gave us orders that we can't run the trains over 30 MPH over the weekend. I know it's for safety reasons, but would you come back if you knew the train wasn't going to be on time?"

LIRR spokesmen yesterday refused to comment on when workers who struck would receive a six per cent increase, retroactive to January, 1972, that was agreed upon Wednesday. Anthony D'Avanzo, general chairman of the Brotherhood of Railway Carmen and spokesman for the 12-union coalition, said the worers' pay would be increased beginning Thursday, but said they would not receive a check for the pay until a settlement is reached. A line spokesman, however, said the payments would be made as soon as checks were ready.

Sunday, January 21, 1973

13

An inside news page of *Newsday*, showing three- and four-column make-up.

an ingenious 'thumb centre punch' device, which punches a semi-circular opening in the centre of the fore-edge of the first half of the news section, so that the reader can instantly and easily detach the magazine. Part II is notable for its good graphics and photographs and for its attention to typographical detail, as in the careful presentation of the small-type, narrow-measure 'preview' columns on entertainments and local events. The Sunday edition, which can reach 350-plus pages, is an elaborate affair of four alternating tabloid and folded broadsheet sections, with a gravure magazine and a television programme-magazine (also gravure) in addition. Both gravure magazines were the province of Clive Irving, who spent a year with *Newsday*, up to the end of 1972, as a consultant.*

As it happened, Irving was not the only British consultant employed by an American newspaper; a total re-design of the *Minne-*

* The news-magazine approach adopted by *Newsday* was also exemplified in the radical redesign of the Sunday edition of the *New York Herald Tribune* in the mid-1960s, shortly before that famous paper's lamented demise. The redesign, by Peter Palazzo, presented a strongly sectionalised but typographically unified paper (headline display was changed from the daily Bodoni Bold to Caslon Old Face). The front page featured a wide-measure news summary in column one, with the rest of the space taken by a single main story, powerfully pictured. An account of Palazzo's redesign, with facsimiles, is given in Harold Evans, *Newspaper Design* (1973), Book V of the author's *Editing & Design* Manual, pp. 184–86.

The Minneapolis Tribune

TUESDAY

Vol. CIV—No. 177 Copyright 1970 Minneapolis Star and Tribune Company MINNEAPOLIS, MINN., TUESDAY, NOVEMBER 17, 1970 ** Price 10c

Black Sit-in Ended at St. John's

9 Arrested; Students Sought Financial Aid

By GREG PINNEY
Minneapolis Tribune Staff Writer

COLLEGEVILLE, Minn. — Nine black students from St. John's University and the College of St. Benedict were arrested Monday after they took over the office of the St. John's president.

Approximately 20 students occupied the office of the Rev. Colman Barry for about 2½ hours before seven Stearns County sheriff's deputies entered the room. The nine refused to leave and were arrested.

The students had barricaded the doors by nailing up boards, but they took the barricade down to permit the deputies to enter.

The nine were arrested after District Judge Paul Hoffman of Stearns County issued an injunction ordering them to leave the office.

The nine students, five men from St. John's and four women from the College of St. Benedict, are being held in the Stearns County Jail on charges of contempt of court. Arraignment is scheduled for this morning. Bail was set at $1,000 each.

Father Colman Barry, president of the Roman Catholic men's school and seminary, was in St. Paul at the time of the takeover, and his staff left the room when the students took it over.

The Organization of Afro-American Students, which consists of black students from both St. John's and nearby St. Benedict, a Roman Catholic women's school, had demanded that the University establish a $10,000 fund for the black organization, and that the organization be guaranteed financial aid each year in

St. John's
Continued on Page Four

Minneapolis Tribune Photo by Richard Olsenius

As sheriff's police cleared the president's office at St. John's University, a black student briefly confronted the Rev. Colman Barry, university president.

Death Rode Bengal Waves

OFFICIAL PAKISTAN STORM TOLL PASSES 55,000

By ARNOLD ZEITLIN

DACCA, Pakistan (AP)—Relief officials said Monday that the confirmed death count from the cyclone and tidal waves that tore through the Bay of Bengal coast late last week has passed 55,000.

Radio Pakistan said not one person was left alive on 13 islands near Chittagong.

Pakistani officials spoke of a final toll of about 300,000 in the densely populated area, which would make the storm one of the world's worst natural catastrophes.

The government promised that no effort would be spared to aid the stricken. "All will be done, no matter if the death toll is 300,000 or 500,000," said Information Secretary Syed Ahamed after President Agha Mohammed Yahya Khan made a 135-minute flight over the stricken areas.

The storm hit Friday with 150-mile-an-hour winds, churning up 20-foot waves that smashed offshore islands and crashed into the Ganges River delta in East Pakistan.

Nearly two million people live in the area.

Survivors of the disaster were threatened with disease because of polluted water supplies and a breakdown in sanitation facilities.

A relief official said cholera was spreading on the offshore island of Hatia. Three ships attempting to dock with medical supplies were unable to do so because of the fast current, he said.

The world's worst disaster on record is the 1887 flood that took 900,000 lives in China's Honan Province.

Historians say 300,000 persons perished in the Bay of Bengal area in a storm and tidal waves in 1737. The area is frequently hit by cyclones, usually with heavy death tolls.

A flight over the stricken southern zone yesterday gave this picture:

Devastation is virtually complete in the southern half of Bhola Island, the largest island in the Bay of Bengal, where more than 1 million people lived. The island's rice crops and those on neighboring Hatia Island and

Pakistan
Continued on Page Four

FIRST IN 20 YEARS

'Lame Duck' Congress Opens

WASHINGTON, D.C. (Reuter)—Congress began its first post-election session in 20 years Monday with Senate Democratic Leader Mike Mansfield calling for continuation of the Senate's watchdogs role on Indochina and for a healing of political wounds at home.

Senate Republican Leader Hugh Scott of Pennsylvania said he thought the post-election session would be an unmitigated disaster, with little meaningful business transacted before the new Congress convenes in January.

He said he thought there would be a great deal of political posturing as a result of the presence of 10 senators and 50 members of the House who were defeated in the congressional election and will lose their seats at the end of the year.

Mansfield raised the Indochina issue, one which played a minor role in the recent campaign, during a speech criticizing Vice-President Spiro T. Agnew's sharp attacks on senators who voted for amendments to limit future American military involvement.

Mansfield was speaking to a closed-door caucus of Senate Democrats who were meeting to discuss the issues coming up in the "lame duck" session.

He said an amendment introduced by Sens. John Sherman Cooper, R-Ky., and Frank Church, D-Idaho, and passed by the Senate June 30 "emphasized the importance which the Senate attached to the uninterrupted withdrawal of American servicemen from the misbegotten adventure in Vietnam."

The amendment has been pigeonholed in a joint conference committee with the House, whose members support the administration in opposing the move to require congressional approval for future military involvement in Cambodia.

Mansfield told his Democratic colleagues: "You defeated opponents in the face of what can best be de-

Congress
Continued on Page Five

Auditor Calls MOER Books Mismanaged

By SAM NEWLUND
Minneapolis Tribune Staff Writer

Hennepin County's anti-poverty agency was suffering—as of a year ago—from badly mismanaged controls over its spending, an independent accounting firm has reported.

Mobilization of Economic Resources (MOER), according to an audit of its books, incurred "questioned" costs totaling $223,175 during the program year ending Nov. 30, 1969.

The audit by Elmer Fox & Co., St. Paul, was completed late last week. A copy was made available Monday to The Minneapolis Tribune.

The audit contains no accusation of wrongdoing, nor does it reflect MOER's current status under new fiscal management.

But it is important to the poverty agency's future because its completion—and presumably acceptance of the findings—was one of the conditions for continued federal support laid down earlier this year by the federal Office of Economic Opportunity (OEO).

MOER's existence has been in jeopardy for several months, largely because OEO demanded assurances

Sunburg Shocked by Slaying of 5

Family Well Liked, Industrious

By ROBERT HAGEN
Minneapolis Tribune Staff Writer

SUNBURG, Minn.—The feelings of shock and disbelief were fading in Sunburg Monday after the killing of the James Fremberg family on their farm.

In some, initial reactions changed to frustration and anger.

Fremberg

Some were afraid.

"My wife wanted me to lock the door last night," said John Solonski, manager of Simmond's Feed Mill in Sunburg.

Wayne Thorkelson,

Associated Press

The bodies of Mr. and Mrs. James Fremberg and their three children were found in this farmhouse near Sunburg, Minn.

found dead Sunday morning.

Each had been shot in the head.

Senate Panel Votes Cutbacks

19-Year-Olds May

▲ The *Minneapolis Tribune* as it was and, on the opposite page, the re-design (April 1971). ▶

apolis Tribune in April 1971 was the work of Frank Ariss, an Associate of the Royal College of Art. The before-and-after facsimile pages shown here tell the story. Headline style is now exclusively Helvetica Medium, 14pt to 72pt, set lower-case flush-left. Text is uniformly 9pt Imperial on 9½pt slug, set either single-column or double-column only (the one exception is the leader-setting, in column-and-a-half). There is no paragraph indention and full whites are carried between paragraphs; as these are normally extremely short, the horizontal breaking of the columns is obsessive. The paper's typesetting (still hot-metal for rotary letterpress) is computerised, so that the paragraph-whiting is automatic. Hand-leading, said Ariss, has been eliminated: 'we justify when necessary with white space at the foot of a column or at the end of a type block.'

The title has substituted an elaborately contrived piece of sans lettering for the old somewhat skimpy blackletter; it incorporates a symbol, repeated frequently in reduced form elsewhere in the paper, which according to Ariss can be viewed either 'as an open newspaper in the hands of a reader or as a web of newsprint flying through a press'. Remarking that the primary aim of the re-design was to give the paper a 'clean fresh appearance' he added that it 'also involves graphics engineering', since the design is 'built on a grid – with precise vertical and horizontal measurement for every element on a page – which establishes a basis for computerised make-up'. He concluded with the hope that the re-design had 'achieved an attractive and functional relationship between contemporary graphic design and changing newspaper production technology'.

Minneapolis **Tribune**

Monday
April 26
1971

3
Sections
15c Single copy

Volume CIV
Number 337
M . .

Others take up protest of war after big march

Tribune Wire Services

Washington, D.C.
Police arrested 124 Quakers who were holding a peace vigil at the White House Sunday. Not far away, other groups were discussing more militant action following Saturday's giant demonstration against the Indochina war.

The developments yesterday:

- The Quakers, who had a permit for 100 persons to hold a religious service on Pennsylvania Av. in front of the White House, were arrested when the crowd grew larger.

- Organizers of the People's Coalition for Peace and Justice set up camp in West Potomac Park. They plan to use it as a base for a campaign leading up to what they call "massive civil disobedience and strikes" May 5.

- Organizers of Saturday's protest said 500,000 persons had attended it. The official police estimate was 200,000 but policemen and reporters who were at the rally said the number was probably higher. Only a handful of incidents was reported.

The Quaker vigil was held to disagree with President Nixon's statement that he, as a Quaker, is working for peace in Indochina. Mr. Nixon, who was at Camp David, Md., did not return to the White House until night and apparently was unaware of the demonstrations.

Those arrested were charged with crossing police lines, which carries a $25 penalty. Those who remained continued the vigil across the avenue in Lafayette Park.

Starting today, the People's Coalition plans a week-long "people's lobby" leading to planned nonviolent disruptions next week.

The People's Coalition is an umbrella group with a more militant cast than the National Peace Action Coalition, which was the main organizer of Saturday's rally.

The People's Coalition also has broader aims, seeking such things as a $6,500 guaranteed income

Protest
Continued on page 3A

Staff Photo by Kent Kobersteen

Fans cheer winning Stars

Minnesota North Star fans, 15,363 of them, stood and roared encouragement in the final moments of play as the Stars stunned Montreal 5-2 Sunday in National Hockey League Stanley Cup play-offs and evened the best-of-seven series 2-2. News report, page 1C.

Russ claim Soyuz success

United Press International

Moscow, U.S.S.R.
The three-man crew of Soyuz 10 expressed "complete satisfaction" with the two-day space flight that ended early Sunday following a docking with the unmanned Salute satellite.

A Soviet space expert called the Soyuz flight a "research and test flight."

It was the briefest manned Soviet space flight since the fatal Soyuz I crash of April 23-24, 1967, and the Russians moved quickly to dispel suspicions of failure.

They quoted the three cosmonauts as expressing "their complete satisfaction with the flight" and described the five-hour docking experiment as a major breakthrough toward "a huge flying multipurpose laboratory" of the future.

Tass said Soyuz 10 parachuted onto a pre-set landing target in Soviet central Asia at 2:40 a.m.

Its crew — Col. Vladimir Shatalov, Alexei Yeliseyev and Nikolai Rukavishnikov — was aboard and in good health, Tass said. There was no indication in the reports of the docking experiment that any of them had explored Salute by space-walk or internal transfer during link-up.

Moscow Radio quoted the three as telling a news conference that they had achieved "a new stage in the mastering of a cosmic space station" by mastering new docking equipment.

Space
Continued on page 15A

Staff Photo by Richard Olsenius

A 23-year-old Vietnam veteran, a former heroin addict, took a dose of methadone at Halfway Inn.

North Side 'Brotherhood' offers hope to drug addicts

By Sam Newlund
Staff Writer

They call themselves a Brotherhood, and they mean business.

Their enemy is drug addiction and their aim is to save their black brothers and sisters from its evils.

"Hey, man—drugs? They offer you nothing but oblivion," one of them said last week.

The Brotherhood is a tough-minded corps of north Minneapolis black men, most of them former addicts, who have set up a drug-fighting Halfway Inn at People's Church, 1001 Penn Av. N.

To enter the program, addicts must sign a pledge agreeing, among other things, to abstain from hard narcotics, to attend group meetings, to submit to spot chemical tests and to commit no crimes.

Those who break the rules must answer charges before a tribunal of their peers.

About half the 13 who had signed the pledge last week are on a methadone-maintenance program. Methadone is a synthetic narcotic used to break heroin addiction.

The group also plans to spread the word—to youngsters, parents or anyone who will listen—that drug addiction is a monstrous cop-out.

The Brotherhood grew out of alarm in the North Side black community over a recent rash of deaths from drug overdoses and deaths related to illicit drug traffic.

With the help of People's Church's white minister, the Rev. Rolland Robinson, a program was written and an application for a $30,000 subsidy was submitted to the State Crime Commission.

Mr. Robinson estimates there are 900 North Siders using opiates (including heroin) and cocaine, and that one in five of them is addicted.

Halfway Inn rules provide that members using methadone take their daily doses in the presence of two of the Brotherhood's four leaders and a registered nurse.

Methadone is picked up twice daily from nearby Pilot City Health Center and brought to the church for swallowing. Efforts are under way to set up a permanent "kick pad" where addicts trying to break their drug habits can live during the time they are suffering from withdrawal sickness.

A telephone is manned around the clock to help any call-

Brotherhood continued on page 12A

School board candidates talk money

By Greg Pinney
Staff Writer

Analysis

The Minneapolis school system is a huge financial operation, and its costs have risen rapidly in recent years. The school board takes the biggest single bite out of the city's property-tax revenue.

Because school finances touch all taxpayers — and touch them hard — all of the major candidates in the school board election campaign have felt compelled to talk about the issue.

But they have come up with very few substantial ideas for rescuing the taxpayer.

The first round of the biennial election campaign will be over on Tuesday when voters in the primary election narrow the 13 candidates down to four nominees. Those four will run in the general election on June 8 when two will be elected to serve six-year terms.

Because no candidate has come out for higher taxes, only one side of the issue is available, and all the candidates have tried to find a toe hold somewhere on its often slippery slopes.

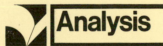

As a result, campaign oratory on finances is frequently more emotional than substantive. Some statements have been reasonable, but many others have been misleading, vague, picayune and occasionally inaccurate, although apparently not intentionally dishonest.

In the absence of any known less-than-disastrous way of making substantial cuts in the school district's $73-million operating budget, many candidates have resorted to deploring the size of the budget and then joining all the voters who also deplore it. Candidates frequently dis-

Schools continued on page 10A

College GOP dumps vocal Agnew critic

By Dale Fetherling
Staff Writer

The College Republicans of Minnesota Sunday defeated the reelection attempt of Chairman David Kaiser, a University of Minnesota junior and a vociferous critic of Vice-President Spiro Agnew.

Kaiser, 21, was defeated on the second ballot in a four-man race by David O'Connell, 20, a Macalester College junior.

O'Connell is considered to be as liberal as Kaiser, and the election was

GOP
Continued on page 10A

State's attorney may be indicted in slaying of two Chicago Panthers

United Press International

Chicago, Ill.
A special grand jury investigating the 1969 raid in which two leaders of the Black Panther Party were killed scheduled a meeting today. There were reports that it would indict Cook County State's Attorney Edward Hanrahan on charges of obstructing justice.

The 14 policemen who went to the West Side apartment before dawn Dec. 4, 1969, with a warrant to search for weapons were assigned to Hanrahan's office and worked under his direction.

Chicago newspapers published reports in their Sunday editions that the grand jury had voted to indict Hanrahan and to name Chicago Police Supt. James B. Conlisk Jr. as an unindicted coconspirator.

It was expected that the grand jury would issue its report today. However, Barnabas Sears, a lawyer who served as special prosecutor for the grand jury, would say only that the jury was to meet. He would neither confirm nor deny published reports that a witness, possibly Hanrahan, would testify

Panthers
Continued on page 12A

Edward V. Hanrahan

Inside news

Foreign

Communists fired 130 rocket and mortar shells into six American bases in South Vietnam. There were no reported American deaths, but 30 Americans were wounded, the U.S. command said. There were several clashes in South Vietnam, including two near Saigon. Page 2A.

The allied operation in South Vietnam's A Shau Valley is surrounded by a veil of secrecy, leading some informants to wonder if something has gone wrong or if Operation Lam Son 720 is only a training exercise for new Saigon troops. Page 2A.

The Ceylon government announced that its military forces had captured Deniyaya, the largest city held by rebels. It said normal conditions were returning to Alpitiya, once a rebel stronghold. Troops continued to patrol other areas and the capital was under heavy guard. Page 7A.

Local

Sixty-eight percent of persons interviewed by the Minnesota Poll said that the federal government should share its revenue with state governments, but most disapproved of both President Nixon's revenue-sharing program and a plan offered by Democratic National Chairman Lawrence O'Brien under which the federal government would take over the entire cost of welfare. Page 4A.

Emphasizing that they are not planning a metropolitan police force, members of the Metropolitan Council are nonetheless examining the crime problem in the Twin Cities area. The Council is considering providing police protection for small communities in the area on a 24-hour basis, establishing a single emergency telephone number and other proposals aimed at improving law enforcement. Page 1B.

The six new members on the Metropolitan Council—the first new blood since its formation in 1967—are beginning to get their feet wet in the river of "plannerese" jargon of staff reports and memoranda. The new members also appear intent on mending fences with local communities and seeking broader support in the metropolitan area. Page 2B.

Sports

Milwaukee, led by Lew Alcindor's 27 points, won 102-83 at Baltimore to take a 2-0 lead in the best-of-seven National Basketball Association playoff finals. Page 1C.

In two Sunday pitching starts this season, left-handed Jim Kaat of the Twins has not allowed a run. Kaat pitched a two-hitter and the Twins defeated New York 8-0 behind two home runs by Tony Oliva, who leads the American League with six homers. Page 1C.

Index

A future hunter

Features

A group of future hunters underwent the final phase of the Minnesota Sportsmen's Club firearms safety course—they walked with guns through fields, swamps and woods, encountering actual hunting conditions. Page 1B.

In a new book entitled "If They're So Smart, How Come You're Not Rich?", John L. Springer discusses how you, the prudent stock investor, can distinguish sound investment guidance from incompetent, "get-rich-quick" advice. Tribune columnist Sylvia Porter reports on Springer's recommendations. Page 13A.

Almanac

**Monday
April 26 1971
116th day
249 to go this year
Sunrise 6:11 am
Sunset 8:13 pm**

Today's weather

Cool

Details page 7B

Sunday's temperatures

am	1	2	3	4	5	6	7	8	9	10	11	Noon
temp	44	43	43	41	38	37	37	43	45	47	52	54
pm	1	2	3	4	5	6	7	8	9	10	11	Midn
temp	55	56	57	59	59	58	53	51	49	49	47	45

Variable cloudiness and continued cool weather through Tuesday are predicted for the Twin Cities area. The chance of rain today is 10 percent. The predicted high today is 56; the low for tonight is 35. Tuesday's high should be 55.

Predicted highs today: Minnesota, 46 to 58; North Dakota, 42 to 52; South Dakota, 40 to 56; Wisconsin, from the lower 50s in the extreme north to the lower 60s in the extreme south.

A question of etiquette

A 3-year-old girl attended a birthday party and brought her party hat home. "Why did I have to wear this hat?" she asked her mother. "To keep the cake out of my hair?"

The Weather

Today — Partly cloudy and breezy, high near 70, low tonight in the 40s. The chance of rain is 20 per cent today. Friday—Fair, high in the 60s. Temp. range: Yesterday, 69-41; Today, 70-49. Details are on Page C6.

The Washington Post

Times Herald

FINAL

144 Pages—8 Sections

96th Year ···· No. 163 · THURSDAY, MAY 17, 1973 · Phone 223-6000 · Classified 223-6200 Circulation 223-6100 · 15c Beyond Washington, Maryland and Virginia 10c

Vast GOP Undercover Operation Originated in 1969

By Carl Bernstein and Bob Woodward
Washington Post Staff Writers

The Watergate bugging and the break-in into the office of Daniel Ellsberg's psychiatrist were part of an elaborate, continuous campaign of illegal and quasi-legal undercover operations conducted by the Nixon administration since 1969, according to highly placed sources in the executive branch.

There are more instances of political burglaries, buggings, spying and sabotage conducted under White House auspices that have not yet been publicly revealed, according to the sources.

Although the undercover operations became most intense during the 1972 presidential campaign, such activities as the Watergate bugging and the break-in in the Ellsberg case, which previously had appeared to be isolated, were regarded in the White House as components of a continuing program of covert activity, according to the sources.

The clandestine operations, the sources said, were at various times aimed at radical leaders, student demonstrators, news reporters, Democratic candidates for President and Vice President and the Congress, and Nixon administration aides suspected of leaking information to the press.

The sources said that many of the covert activities, although political in purpose, were conducted under the guise of "national security," and that some of the records relating to them are believed to have been destroyed. Some of the activities were conducted by the FBI, the Secret Service and special teams working for the White House and Justice Department, according to the sources.

Most of the activities were carried out under the direct supervision of members of President Nixon's innermost circle, among them former White House deputies H. R. (Bob) Haldeman, John D. Ehrlichman and John W. Dean III; former Attorney General John N. Mitchell, and former Assistant Attorney General Robert C. Mardian, the sources said.

Although most of the clandestine operations are still shrouded in secrecy, they are known to include:

- The use of the Secret Service to obtain information on the private life of at least one Democratic presidential candidate in 1972.
- The possession of Sen. Thomas Eagleton's confidential health records by Ehrlichman, former White House domestic affairs chief, several weeks before the information was leaked to the news media.
- The use of paid provocateurs to encourage violence at antiwar demonstrations early in the first Nixon administration, and again in the 1972 presidential campaign.
- Undercover political activities against persons regarded as opponents of the Nixon administration conducted by "suicide squads" in the FBI. The term is a bureau euphemism for teams of agents engaged in sensitive missions which, if revealed, would be disavowed by the FBI and the White House.
- The use of paid-for-hire "vigilante squads" by the

See WATERGATE, A16, Col. 1

2d Candidate Declines Job As Prosecutor

By John P. MacKenzie
Washington Post Staff Writer

Warren M. Christopher yesterday removed himself from consideration as special Watergate prosecutor, the second candidate in two days to drop from the list of prime prospects drawn by Attorney General-designate Elliot L. Richardson.

This development which came at the end of a day of increased signs of Senate resistance to Richardson's view of the prosecutor's proper role, appeared to deepen the uncertainty over Richardson's nomination itself.

Coupled with Tuesday's rejection by New York Federal Judge Harold R. Tyler Jr. of Richardson's offer of the post, Christopher's action cut the candidate list to two—Justice William H. Erickson, 49, of the Colorado Supreme Court, and David W. Peck, 70, retired New York state appellate judge.

Christopher, Erickson and Peck each met in separate sessions yesterday with Richardson, who is still Secretary of Defense, in his Pentagon office. Richardson's controversial guidelines were discussed at each meeting but no formal offer of the job was made to anyone.

The day's fruitless proceedings left the Pentagon, the Justice Department and members of the Senate Judiciary Committee all in a quandary. The committee, which suspended Richardson's confirmation hearings to give him time to land a special prosecutor, had no plans to meet for the remainder of the week.

All sides agreed that Richardson's confirmation turns on his ability to convince the Senate that his elusive special prosecutor has the ability and authority to restore public confidence in the prosecution of the Watergate scandals — even if the pursuit should reach the highest levels of the White House.

Some committee members expressed mounting dissatisfaction with Richardson's refusal to agree to give the prosecutor a freer hand.

Sen. Quentin N. Burdick (D-S.D.) said the Richardson nomination, "may be in jeopardy" and that he hoped the nominee would "rethink" his position because "his judgment is placed in doubt when he insists on having ultimate power over the actions of the prosecutor."

Majority Whip Robert C. Byrd (D-W.Va.), an influential committee member, said he had not made up his mind on the nomination and that his vote could depend on the prosecutor's independence.

And Sen. John V. Tunney (D-Calif.) said he would wait

See PROSECUTOR, A16, Col. 1

2 Top Aides Said Facing Indictments

By Lawrence R. Meyer and Timothy S. Robinson
Washington Post Staff Writers

The lawyers for H. R. (Bob) Haldeman and John D. Ehrlichman told a federal judge here yesterday that the two former top White House aides "may be indicted" as a result of the federal grand jury's investigation into the Watergate affair.

The statement, contained in a formal motion filed with U.S. District Judge Charles R. Richey, was accompanied by sworn statements from Haldeman and Ehrlichman in which they say that they have been formally notified by the prosecution that they are "subjects of the investigation" and that their statements could be used in "subsequent proceedings."

Although it has been previously reported that both Haldeman and Ehrlichman had testified before the grand jury here, their affidavits and the statement of their lawyers yesterday were the first formal acknowledgement that the former presidential aides may be defendants in a criminal trial.

The motion filed with Judge Richey asks him to delay scheduled depositions of Haldeman and Ehrlichman set for May 22 in connection with the $6.4 million civil suit brought by the Democratic National Com-

See PROBE, A20, Col. 4

Watergate Probe on TV

All three commercial television networks (channels 4, 7 and 9 in Washington) will begin live coverage of the Senate select committee Watergate hearings today at 10 a.m. WETA (channel 26) will televise a taped version at 8 p.m.

Schedule on Page B3.

United Press International

Former CIA Director Richard Helms arrives to testify before a Senate subcommittee.

Nixon Name Used To Pressure CIA

By William Claiborne
Washington Post Staff Writer

Several high White House aides invoked the name of President Nixon when they asked the Central Intelligence Agency to help cover up the Watergate scandal and assist key conspirators, Sen. John L. McClellan (D-Ark.) disclosed yesterday.

For that reason, McClellan said, Richard M. Helms, who was then CIA director, and other intelligence officials did not inform either Congress or the President about the requests.

McClellan said they "wanted to go as far as they could to accommodate the President" because the requests had come from such high offices of the Executive Branch.

"Some things went too far and they put a stop to it," McClellan said after listening to three hours of testimony by Helms in a closed Senate Appropriations subcommittee hearing.

Helms, who is now ambassador to Iran, emerged from the hearing room with his jaw tightly clenched and bored through a crowd of newsmen to a waiting car without making a comment about the first of at least three scheduled appearances before Watergate-related investigating panels.

But McClellan later reviewed Helms' testimony, and then angrily accused the White House of violating the National Security Act by trying to pressure the CIA into covering up financial manipulations connected with Watergate.

Referring to the 1947 act that prohibits the CIA from domestic intelligence work, McClellan said, "I'm satisfied the CIA made a mistake. I'm satisfied that the CIA was imposed upon."

McClellan also implicitly criticized Helms for his silence over a two-year pe-

See HELMS, A20, Col. 1

President Authorized 17 Wiretaps

By Murrey Marder
Washington Post Staff Writer

President Nixon personally authorized the use of 17 wiretaps on officials and newsmen between 1969 and 1971 although the practice was reportedly spurned by the Kennedy-Johnson administrations as too "damaging" to use.

The dispute over the secret monitoring of telephone calls by the Nixon administration rebounded yesterday as the White House acknowledged President Nixon's role in the wiretapping.

A White House spokesman said that President Nixon "authorized the wiretap procedure to solve a national security problem," namely, security breaches through news leaks. From among those whose telephones were tapped, however, came the charge that the administration used wiretaps to test "political loyalty" or "to find excuses to fire people" who disagreed with the President.

The political charge has been hovering over the wiretap controversy since Acting FBI Director William D. Ruckelshaus on Monday disclosed that the telephones of 13 government officials and four newsmen were tapped between May, 1969 and Feb. 1971 on White House orders.

All or most of the officials whose telephones were tapped reportedly worked on the National Security Council staff directed by presidential security adviser Henry A. Kissinger. Many former members of Kissinger's staff suspect or claim that the unadmitted ulterior motive for the wiretapping was that their political liberalism made them the "enemy" in the eyes of such top presidential assistants as John Ehrlichman and H.R. Haldeman.

There was indeed a mixture of security and political

See WIRETAP, A10, Col. 1

SEC's Chairman Quits in Wake of Vesco Indictment

Cook Cites A 'Web' Of Factors

By Jack Egan
Washington Post Staff Writer

The chairman of the Securities and Exchange Commission, G. Bradford Cook, resigned yesterday, saying he found himself in a "web of circumstances" connected with his role in the agency's investigation and prosecution of financier Robert L. Vesco.

"The web of circumstances that I find myself confronted with has made me feel that the effectiveness of the agency might be impaired," Cook told a press conference after he delivered a letter of resignation to the President's chief of staff, Gen. Alexander M. Haig Jr.

Cook, 36, the youngest chairman in the history of the SEC, has only been in the post since March 2. No successor was immediately announced, and Hugh F. Owens, senior member of the commission, will serve as acting chairman until a new one is appointed.

Cook's resignation is certain to have an impact on the chief project undertaken during his brief tenure—a major restructuring of the nation's security markets.

Cook said at his press conference that he had been considering the move for "four or five days."

The chairman has been under mounting congressional pressure to resign since announcement of a federal grand jury indictment in New York last Thursday against Vesco, former Attorney General John N. Mitchell, Nixon campaign finance chief and former Commerce Secretary Maurice H. Stans and former New Jersey politician Harry L. Sears for conspiring to influence, obstruct and impede the SEC proceeding against Vesco.

Vesco and 41 others have been accused in an SEC civil suit with looting $224 million from a group of foreign-based mutual funds.

The indictment charged that Stans "did cause" Cook "to delete all specific refer-

See COOK, A21, Col. 1

By Douglas Chevalier—The Washington Post

Cook: "Effectiveness of the agency might be impaired."

'Dean Report' Came From Ehrlichman

By Carroll Kilpatrick
Washington Post Staff Writer

President Nixon did not talk with John W. Dean III before declaring last Aug. 29 that an investigation by Dean showed that no one then on the White House staff was involved in the Watergate scandal.

In making that disclosure yesterday, White House press secretary Ronald L. Ziegler said that the President ordered the investigation through "senior" aides and received Dean's report orally in the same way.

Other sources confirmed a New York Times report that the information regarding the investigation—an investigation Dean said he never made—was given to the President by former aide John D. Ehrlichman, whose resignation Mr. Nixon accepted April 30. Dean was fired the same day.

Dean said in interviews over the weekend that he was "flabbergasted" when he heard the President say in his Aug. 29 press conference that on the basis of a Dean investigation he could say categorically that no one then on the staff was involved in Watergate.

In those interviews, Dean said that he never produced the report which Mr. Nixon mentioned and had not had any word about it from the President before the press conference.

Ziegler said yesterday that in the months that followed the Aug. 29 press conference he himself had many conversations with Dean about the investigation and never heard him say he had not made one.

"There was no question in any of our minds that an appropriate investigation had been undertaken," the press secretary said, adding that

See PRESIDENT, A20, Col. 8

Cooling Down May Permit 2d Launch Delay

Scientists Work on Skylab Sunshade

By Thomas O'Toole
Washington Post Staff Writer

HOUSTON, May 16—The overheated Skylab space station had cooled down tonight to the point where the launch of the first crew of Skylab astronauts will almost surely be postponed from Sunday to Friday, May 25.

The five-day postponement would be the second straight delay for astronauts Charles (Pete) Conrad, Joseph Kerwin and Paul Weitz, but it would buy valuable time for the Skylab astronauts and engineers to develop and test out a sail-like sunshade that can be carried into space by the crew and deployed around the workshop to cool it down to a more comfortable temperature.

"I don't want to go on Sunday and we don't want to go on Sunday," Johnson Space Center Director Christopher C. Kraft said in an interview today. "If the spacecraft can remain reasonably intact without hurting the food and materials inside, then it's preferable to wait until Friday," he said.

Early in the day, engineers at the Johnson Space Center in Houston had maneuvered the 80-ton workshop to where it was tilted 55 degrees away from the sun. This position supplied enough sunlight to the working solar panels to charge the workshop batteries at the same time that it appeared to move the space station out of the full glare of the sun.

Temperatures inside the workshop fell today to 109 degrees, a drop of 11 degrees from the peak temperatures reached Tuesday night.

"We feel certain they are are not going to go any higher," Flight Director Don Puddy said tonight. "We also feel there is a decreasing trend and we may actually be able to get down to about 100 degrees."

The heat inside the workshop had climbed to 120 degrees Tuesday night, while engineers were still tilting the space station around to find the best position to cool the workshop and still get power from the sun. This was hot enough to spoil some of the canned food, fog up some of the ultraviolet film and ruin as many as half the 62 drugs and medications placed aboard the spacecraft to treat the astronaut crews during the planned 28 and 56-day missions.

Doctors at the Johnson Space Center said tonight that tests showed that pro-

See SKYLAB, A4, Col. 1

Concealed Gifts, U.S. Charges

Humphrey Donor Accused

By Morton Mintz
Washington Post Staff Writer

The Justice Department yesterday began a criminal prosecution of a leading Wall Street stockbroker for using the names of eight other persons to conceal contributions of $48,000 to last year's campaign of Sen. Hubert H. Humphrey for the Democratic presidential nomination.

An eight-count information filed in Federal Court in New York City named John L. Loeb, 70, senior partner of Loeb, Rhoades & Co. The maximum possible penalty on conviction is a year in prison and a $1,000 fine on each count. Arraignment was set for May 29.

A criminal information makes formal charges without action by a grand jury and is used for misdemeanors.

The prosecution, said by election law experts to be the first of its kind against a contributor, originated officially last June 5 with a report to the Justice Department by Congress' General Accounting Office.

The GAO said that Loeb and his wife, Frances, had committed a "possible" violation of a provision of the election financing disclosure law that bans giving or accepting contributions in the name of another person.

Subsequently, the Finance Committee to Re-elect the President and affiliated Nixon fund-raising groups reported receiving at least $62,000 from Loeb. His son, John L. Loeb Jr., was listed for an additional $10,000.

The elder Loeb was a White House guest Tuesday night at the state dinner given by the President for Emperor Haile Selassie of Ethiopia. A contingent of campaign contributors customarily has been invited to such affairs, on the basis of lists prepared in the office of former White House staff director H.R. Haldeman.

The criminal information said that on May 12, 1972, Loeb "unlawfully, wilfully

See LOEB, A10, Col. 2

The Weather

Today—Rain, high in the 70s, low around 60. Chance of rain is 60 per cent today and 70 per cent tonight. Thursday — Rain, high in the 70s. Temp. range: Today, 77-61; Yesterday, 80-52. Details are on page C9.

The Washington Post

Times Herald

FINAL

112 Pages—5 Sections

Amusements	B 9	Financial	E11
Classified	C11	Metro	C 1
Comics	B16	Obituaries	C 8
Crossword	B 8	Sports	E 1
Editorials	A18	Style	B 1
Fed. Diary	B17	TV-Radio	B15

96th Year .... No. 169 © 1973, The Washington Post Co. WEDNESDAY, MAY 23, 1973 Phone 223-6000 Classified 223-6200 Circulation 223-6100 15c Beyond Washington, Maryland and Virginia 10c

Concern for National Security Limited Watergate Investigation, Nixon Says

By Carroll Kilpatrick
Washington Post Staff Writer

In an extraordinary, 4,000-word statement yesterday, President Nixon said national security problems of "crucial importance" caused him to pay insufficient attention to warning signals of a Watergate cover-up and led him to order limitations to the Watergate investigation.

Acknowledging that there were "apparently wide-ranging efforts to limit the (Watergate) investigation or to conceal the possible involvement of members of the administration," he confessed that he had not adequately pursued indications of wrongdoing he received.

"With hindsight, it is apparent that I should have given more heed to the warning signals I received along the way about a Watergate cover-up and less to the reassurances," Mr. Nixon said.

However, he asserted again: "I will not abandon my responsibilities. I will continue to do the job I was elected to do."

In two statements, the President reviewed the history of the investigation and asserted his innocence. He again declared that he never offered clemency to Watergate defendants, that he never tried to implicate the CIA and that he did not know until two months ago that funds were provided the Watergate defendants.

Modifying his earlier definition of executive privilege, Mr. Nixon said it will not be invoked in any testimony concerning possible criminal conduct in matters now under investigation.

While conceding that unethical and illegal activities had taken place, the President charged that recent disclosures have given a "grossly misleading" impression of many facts relating to his role.

None of these unethical or illegal activities "took place with my specific approval or knowledge. . . .

"I have found myself accused of involvement in activities I never heard of until I read about them in news accounts," Mr. Nixon said.

The President's two statements were handed to newsmen at the White House in the late afternoon. Mr. Nixon was not present to answer questions, but presidential counsel Leonard Garment, special counsel J. Fred Buzhardt and Press Secretary Ronald Ziegler were.

They were subjected to a 70-minute barrage of questions that ended in a shouting match. Garment heatedly denied that the statement indirectly acknowledged that the President participated in the cover-up.

In the lengthier of the two statements, the President sought to separate secret investigations initiated earlier in his term from the Watergate break-in.

He told how J. Edgar Hoover, the late FBI director, refused in the last years of his life to cooperate with other federal intelligence agencies.

Hoover's refusal to cooperate, the President said, led him to establish a special investigating unit in the White House to check on subversive activities and on leaks of national security documents.

See PRESIDENT, A9, Col. 1

Text of President's statement. *Page A10.*

McCord Offer Directed by Dean, Panel Told

Nixon Tells Of Forming Secret Unit

By Laurence Stern
Washington Post Staff Writer

In his Watergate statement of disclaimer yesterday, President Nixon ac-

'Top Level' Promised Clemency

By Lawrence Meyer and Peter Osnos
Washington Post Staff Writers

John J. Caulfield, self-described former investi-

Pace-setter in the exposure of the Watergate scandal, the *Washington Post* in 1973 found that the weight of the news frequently called for full-page two-line banners (above), though still in its standard large-size Bodoni Bold upper- and lower-case. For many years the lead-story style of the *Post* had been a three-line three-column heading on the right of the page (left). While adhering to its classic single-column decker heading, the *New York Times* (right) has been developing its double-column – and even three-column – headlines in Cheltenham Bold italic.

"All the News That's Fit to Print"

The New York Times

LATE CITY EDITION

SECTION ONE

VOL. CXXII ... No. 42,120 NEW YORK, SUNDAY, MAY 20, 1973 50 CENTS

Extensive Fraud Charged In Europe Farm Subsidies

Export Rebates, Under Control of Market Countries, Said to Be Granted Without Adequate Checking—British Irked

By CLYDE H. FARNSWORTH

CAULFIELD IS SAID TO CONNECT DEAN TO CLEMENCY BID

He Reportedly Asserts He Acted on Instructions of Ex-White House Counsel

UNSURE OF NIXON ROLE

Caulfield Quoted as Holding He Can't Remember if He Used President's Name

By DAVID E. ROSENBAUM

Leonid I. Brezhnev, Soviet leader, meeting in Bonn with Chancellor Willy Brandt

Brezhnev and Brandt Sign 10-Year Pact

By CRAIG R. WHITNEY

Mr. Nixon on pier where the Independence is docked

Nixon Demands Hanoi Tell Fate of Missing Americans

By R. W. APPLE Jr.

Conservatives Expecting Sandman to Win in Jersey

By DONALD JANSON

Charles W. Sandman Jr.

GOVERNOR URGES DELAY ON CHARTER

Wants Public Vote Deferred 2 Years for More Study —City Favors Move

By M. A. FARBER

Authority to Develop Land Is Termed a Public Right

By GLADWIN HILL

Rhode Island Boat Capsizes and 12 Die

MITCHELL REJECTS ROLE OF 'FALL GUY'

Says He Did Nothing Wrong 'Mentally or Morally' in the Watergate Scandal

Mrs. Johnson to Pursue A Selective Public Life

By ROY REED

AFTER ABORTIONS: Women resting in Women's Medical Services, Inc., clinic in Philadelphia. Despite recent court rulings, women in many areas of the country find problems persist in getting an abortion. Details, Page 53.

Today's Sections

Index to Subjects

Secretariat Is Winner

The whole trend of the present study of development in newspaper typography, of the history of newspaper design, suggests that the concept implied in the preceding quotation is mistaken. The problem is not one of a relationship between 'contemporary graphic design' and 'changing production technology'. What about the central figure, the journalist? The problem, as indicated in this chapter's earlier exposition of the views of Harold Evans and others, is how to achieve an integration of journalist and designer – eventually creating what Evans calls a 'new breed' of journalist-designer or designer-journalist – so that newspaper design may be still more effective in its essential function of the visual communication of news. Certainly all design, including newspaper design, is a balance of form and function; but function always comes first. This is the central message of Evans's exhaustive and brilliant *Newspaper Design*, the fifth book in his five-volume *Editing and Design* manual mentioned above, which has appeared as these lines are written (February 1973). It is significant that he warns against what he calls the 'fashionable fallacy', in these technological days, that it can all be left to the engineer. The computer and the cathode ray tube, he stresses, are in themselves irrelevant to design. 'The basic essential is still the organised communication of ideas and not the proliferation of free-form patterns.'

Glossary

Agate: American name for 5½pt, used as the unit for U.S. advertising linage.

Banner: a main headline across the full width of the page.
Blackletter: the 'Gothic' letter developed in the late Middle Ages in Germany and the normal text type in Northern Europe in the early years of printing. Here commonly called Old English.
Blanket: the sheet of composition (rexine, rubber) used to cover the impression cylinder of a printing machine. Also the similar sheet used to cover the flong when making a stereo mould from a forme.
Block: an illustration, halftone or line, as engraved in metal for printing.
Bourgeois: pronounced 'burjoyce', old name for 9pt.
Box: an item ruled off on all four sides, usually with heavy rule or border.
Brevier: old name for 8pt.
Brief: news item of a few lines.
Broadsheet: a page the full size of a rotary press plate.
Canon: old name for approximately 48pt. In England usually called French Canon. The French had two – *Double Canon* and *Gros Canon*, whose respective size-equivalents were 56pt and 44pt.

Caption: the descriptive matter accompanying an illustration: sometimes loosely, and incorrectly, used as a synonym for headline.
Casting-off: calculating how much space a given amount of copy will take in a given type size and measure.
Chase: the steel frame in which type is assembled to make a page.
Column rule: the light-faced rule used to separate columns.
Comp: usual abbreviation for compositor.
Cossar: the most popular web-fed, flatbed, British newspaper press. Named after its Scottish inventor. Manufacture now discontinued in favour of the Duplex, q.v.
Counter: space wholly or mainly enclosed by the strokes of a letter.
Crosshead: a centred sub-heading in the text.
Curtain: a headline ruled off on three sides only. Sometimes called 'hood'.
Cut-off: a full rule across one or more columns; also the depth of a rotary-printed broadsheet.

Deck: a separate portion or section of a headline, usually applied to the subsidiary sections following the main headline.
Decker: a headline composed of two or more decks.
Drop letter (*Drop initial*)*:* usually indicated 'dp' or 'dp ltr', an initial letter covering two or three lines of text type.
Duplex: an American web-fed, flatbed newspaper press resembling the Cossar, q.v.

Ear: the advertising space (or spaces) beside the front-page title-line.
Egyptian: a type, of monotone drawing, with heavy, slab serifs.
Elrod: a rule- and lead-casting machine, associated with the Ludlow, q.v.

Fat Face: a heavy type, with hairline serifs, originated in Regency days (c. 1810) by London typefounders Thorne and Thorowgood. Modern versions are usually called Ultra-Bodoni.
Flong: the sheet of papier mâché used to make a mould from a forme for casting a stereotype plate.
Folio: a side of copy; the running headline of a page; a tabloid (q.v.) sheet.
Forme: the completed page of type locked up in a chase.
Fount: pronounced 'font' – the complete set of type of one particular face and size: applied also to the set of matrices in a composing machine magazine.
Fudge: the attachment for running stop press news on a rotary press.

Gothic: the correct name for blackletter (q.v.). More commonly used today for the nineteenth-century angular sans types developed in America for news headlines.
Grot: abbreviation of grotesque, a generic nineteenth-century term for sanserif type; usually square in cut.

Half-double: the rule or dash half the width of the column used to indicate the end of a story: traditionally a double rule, thick and thin, but now usually a single rule (formerly differentiated as a 'half single').
Half-stick: small portrait block half the column measure; also called 'thumbnail', and in the US 'porkchop'.
Half-tone: process by which continuous tone is simulated by a pattern of dots of varying size.
Hanging-indent: an indented setting

where the first line of each paragraph is set full out to the column measure and the remaining lines indented 1 em; thus this setting is sometimes indicated as '0 and 1'.

Hot metal: general term for composing machines casting type from molten metal, as opposed to photocomposition (sometimes called 'cold type').

Indention: any setting short of the column measure, e.g. for panels, normally indented 'nut each end', or for black or italic paragraphs indented in text, which are set with the appropriate indention on the front only (indicated as '2 and 1', i.e. 2 ems indent the first line, then 1 em).

Intertype: composing machine similar to the Linotype.

Kern: the part of a letter which overhangs the shank.

Lead: the main news story in the paper or the opening paragraph of any news story.

Lead: pronounced 'led' – the strips of type metal or brass used to space out headings and text. Normal sizes in newspaper work are $1\frac{1}{2}$pt ('thin'), 2pt, and 3pt ('thick').

Letterpress: the primary form of printing, taking an impression on paper from an inked, raised or relief printing surface.

Linecaster: generic term for all keyboard-operated slug-casting composing machines, Linotype or Intertype.

Linotron: a high-speed photocomposing machine which uses the cathode ray tube as part of its fast setting technique.

Linotype: the first keyboard-operated composing machine to employ the principle of the circulating matrix and to cast type in solid lines or slugs. Invented by the German-American engineer Ottmar Mergenthaler and first used in 1886.

Lithography: printing from a damped, flat surface using greasy ink, the principle being the mutual repulsion of oil and water. Originally the printing surface was a porous stone but later a grained zinc plate was used.

Long Primer: old name for 10pt.

Lower-case: the small (minuscule) letters in a fount of type.

Ludlow: machine which casts display sizes of type on a slug from hand-assembled matrices.

Magazine: the case holding the matrices on a Linotype or Intertype.

Make-up: the sheet indicating the placing of the various items on a page; the process of actual assembly of the page.

Mat: short for matrix, meaning (a) the stereotypers' flong after moulding; (b) the individual brass letter moulds on a composing machine.

Matter: MS or copy to be printed, type that is composed.

Minion: old name for 7pt.

Modern face: type-face having vertical stress, strong stroke contrast and unbracketed fine serifs.

Monotype: composing machine which casts single types.

Nonpareil: old name for 6pt, used as an indicator for measure or spacing, indicating half a pica (12pt) em.

O.C.R.: Optical Character Recognition – a device for the electronic scanning of copy and thus its conversion into photoset matter without keyboard operation (i.e. dispensing with the human element in composition).

Offset: the development of lithography by which the image is not printed direct from the plate but 'offset' first on to a rubber-covered cylinder, which then performs the printing operation.

Old Face: type forms originating in the sixteenth century, characterised by diagonal stress and sloped, bracketed serifs.

Overmatter: matter set but superfluous to the requirements of a given edition or issue.

Panel: a short item indented either side, usually in bold-face or italic type, with a rule or border top and bottom.

Pearl: old name for 5pt.

Perfector: a press which prints both sides of the paper at a single pass. All letterpress rotaries and web-offset machines are perfectors.

Photocomposition: the production of display line and text, on film or paper, by photographic means. Photocomposing machines assemble lines of letters from various forms of photomatrix; they are usually operated by tape, justified and hyphenated on a computer, originated from keyboarded tape-perforators.

Photogravure: the process of printing from a photo-mechanically prepared surface in which ink is contained in recessed cells.

Photon: a range of photocomposing machines very popular for newspaper work. Initially a French invention, called the Lumitype, its letter forms are carried on a revolving disc, through which they are photographed at extreme speeds.

Photopolymer plates: sensitised plastic plates on which negatives can be printed down and, by a chemical wash-out, a printing surface in relief is formed. Thus photocomposed pages can be converted into letterpress printing surfaces, either printing direct from the photopolymer plate or moulding from it to make stereoplates.

Pica: pronounced 'pieker', old name for 12pt. The pica em is the unit for measurement in setting, e.g. a 14-em column means a column 14 picas wide.

Plate: the curved metal plate cast from a stereotype mat for printing on a rotary press.

Platen press: a press which brings paper and printing-surface together as plane surfaces.

Point: the standard unit of type size, 0·01383 in. or approximately 72 to the inch (British-American system). The continental (Didot) point is differently calculated.

Rotary: a reel- or web-fed newspaper press 'perfecting' from a cylindrical printing surface. Papers are delivered folded and counted, ready for dispatch.

Ruby: old name for 5½pt.

Run: the period of printing an edition.

Run-on: where matter is not to be broken into paragraphs.

Sans serif: a type face without serifs and usually with no stroke contrast.

Screen: The number of dots to the square inch of a half-tone process block; the lower the number the coarser the reproduction. Usual newspaper screens are 55 or 65 for rotary and 85 for flatbed or Cossar.

Serif: small terminal stroke at the end of the main stroke.

Sidehead: a sub-heading in text set flush left.

Slug: a line of type or a blank line set on a Linotype, Intertype or Ludlow.

Slug machine: generic term for Linotypes and Intertypes.

Smalls: the run-on classified advertisements in a newspaper, usually set in 6pt or below.

Space: the non-printing graded units for spacing out a line of type, classified as hair, thin, mid, thick.

Stereo: a flat plate made by stereotyping from type or blocks, usually applied to advertisements supplied in plate form.

Stone: the smooth iron or steel surface on which pages are made up: originally of marble, hence the name.

Strap: a subsidiary headline placed over a main headline.

Streamer: a multi-column headline leading a page, but not necessarily across its full width: see Banner.

Style: the special requirements of a given newspaper for the preparation and setting of copy in respect of capitalisation, punctuation, contractions, variant spellings, and the like.

Super Caster: a Monotype machine which casts large sizes of types for headlines, rules, borders, and leads.

Tabloid: a page half the size (the folio or single fold) of a broadsheet.

Titling: a headline type available in capitals only.

Transitional: type forms of the mid-eighteenth century which are neither old face nor modern. Exemplified by the types of P. S. Fournier, in France, and more especially those of John Baskerville, in Britain.

TTS: abbreviation for Teletypesetter, in which a linecaster is operated by perforated tape. The device was initially exploited for long-distance control of typesetting but is now more used for increasing productivity. A TTS-controlled linecaster has an output two to three times that of a manual machine.

Turtle: the segmental chase in which movable type was locked up in columns for printing on a type-revolver, the mid-nineteenth century newspaper presses which introduced the principle of the rotary, i.e. a rotating instead of a flat, printing surface.

Type-revolvers: the mid-nineteenth century newspaper presses, devised by Hoe in New York and Applegath in London, which were the first 'rotaries' i.e. printing from a rotating drum on which the columns of type were locked in 'turtles' (q.v.). They were sheet-fed, however, and were not 'perfectors' (q.v.).

Upper-case: the capital letters in a fount of type.

Web-offset: an offset press working from the web or reel of paper, delivering newspapers folded and complete, like the letterpress rotary.

White: the generic term for the non-printing part of a printing surface. It covers the space disposed around and through display lines, e.g. headings.

Bibliographical References

CHAPTER ONE

1. Stanley Morison, *The Origins of the Newspaper*, inaugural lecture to St Bride university extension series on 'The Press' (London, 1954: privately printed), pp. 13-28.
2. Morison, *Origins*, pp. 29-30.
3. Morison, *The English Newspaper* (Cambridge, 1932), pp. 19, 28, 32.
4. Text quoted in Harold Herd, *The March of Journalism* (1952), pp. 18-19.

CHAPTER TWO

1. Joseph Moxon, *Mechanick Exercises* &c Davis and Carter edition (1958), folding plate following p. 480.
2. An excellent facsimile of the 'tombstone' *Pennsylvania Journal* was reproduced in John E. Allen, *Newspaper Designing* (New York, 1947), p. 19.
3. The most detailed study is the monograph by Clifford K. Shipton, *Isaiah Thomas, Printer, Patriot, Philanthropist*, in the Printers' Valhalla series published by the Printing House of Leo Hart (Rochester, NY, 1948).
4. Allen Hutt, *Newspaper Design* (2nd ed.), p. 247.
5. Morison, *Printing The Times* (1953), pp. 103-4.
6. William E. Ames, *A History of the National Intelligencer* (University of North Carolina Press, 1972). Unfortunately Prof. Ames gives no details of the paper's typography nor any facsimiles of its pages.

CHAPTER THREE

1. *Printing The Times*, p. 61.
2. Rollo G. Silver, *Journal of the Printing Historical Society*, No. 7 (1972), pp. 29-36.
3. Robert W. Jones, *Journalism in the United States* (New York, 1947), pp. 228-30.

CHAPTER FOUR

1. Rollo G. Silver, *Efficiency Improved: the Genesis of the Web Press in America* (American Antiquarian Society, Worcester, Mass., 1971).
2. Morison, *The English Newspaper*, p. 279.
3. H. W. Massingham, *The London Daily Press* (1892), pp. 182-85.
4. Stephen H. Horgan in *Penrose Annual*, Vol. XXXV (1933), pp. 23-4.
5. Ken Baynes (ed.), *Scoop, Scandal and Strife: a Study of Photography in Newspapers* (1971), pp. 34, 58ff.

CHAPTER FIVE

1. *New York Herald Tribune*, 28 February 1937.
2. John E. Allen, *Newspaper Designing* (New York, 1947), p. 31.
3. All C. H. Griffith quotes from Allen, op. cit., pp. 80-7.

CHAPTER SIX

1. John E. Allen, *Newspaper Designing*, pp. 318-20.
2. Francis Williams, *Dangerous Estate* (1957), chapter XIII.
3. Nicolas Barker, *Stanley Morison* (1972), p. 291. Generally on Times Roman see Barker, chapter 12 *passim*; James Moran, *Stanley Morison: his typographic achievement* (1971), pp. 123-38; Peggy Lang, *Alphabet & Image No. 2* (September, 1946), pp. 5-17.
4. *Printing The Times* (1953), pp. 69-70: Peggy Lang, op. cit., p. 17.
5. *The English Newspaper* (1932), p. 318: *Printing The Times*, p. 70.
6. Barker, pp. 293-98: *Printing The Times*, p. 68.
7. *Monotype Recorder*, XXXV, No. 1 (Spring, 1936), pp. 10-11.
8. John E. Allen, *Newspaper Designing*, p. 333.
9. Allen, p. 337: *Typography No. 5* (Spring, 1938), pp. 37-42.

CHAPTER SEVEN

1. Barker, op. cit., pp. 400-1.
2. Hutt, 'A new face for newspaper text' (*Penrose Annual*, 1955), 'Walter Tracy, type designer' (*Penrose Annual*, 1973).
3. Quoted in Hutt, *Newspaper Design* (2nd ed.), pp. 159-63.

CHAPTER EIGHT

1. Web-offset evening papers' late news problems were authoritatively discussed by John Beverley, group managing editor of Westminster Press, in 'Typewriters to the rescue' (*Penrose Annual*, 1971).
2. Allen, *Newspaper Designing*, p. 123.
3. Hutt, 'A "Modern" for News' (*Penrose Annual*, 1970): *Monotype Recorder*, XXXV, No. 1 (Spring, 1936), pp. 3-6.
4. Hutt, 'A re-assessment of Times Roman', *Journal of Typographic Research*, Vol. IV, No. 3, pp. 259-70.
5. Matthew Carter's exposition, well illustrated, was given fully in the international quarterly of graphic design, *Interpressgrafik 7* (Budapest), pp. 42-7.
6. *Newspaper Design* was commissioned by Oxford in 1957, on the recommendation of Hugh Williamson, the success of whose *Methods of Book Design* had persuaded the Press that there was a market for works on typography. The first edition was greeted, among many others, by Arthur Christiansen (who said that it was 'a bridge over the ocean' between design and production) and Morison (who wrote on 10 November 1960 that it 'is destined, I am already sure, to remain the standard treatment of the subject in the English language'). By the autumn of 1961 the first impression was selling out and a second impression, bearing a brief author's updating note after the Preface, appeared. An extensively revised second edition was published in November 1967 and four years later this had to be reprinted, with a revised and updating Preface.
7. *The Pearl of Days* (1972), the official *Sunday Times* 150th anniversary history, p. 480.
8. *Interpressgrafik 7*, pp. 3-10.
9. Hutt, *Newspaper Design* (2nd edn), p. 232.
10. Hutt, 'Design', a section of *Scoop, Scandal and Strife* (1971), pp. 58-70.
11. Harold Evans was invited by the Society of Industrial Artists and Designers to describe the *Echo* changes in the *SIA Journal*, March 1966, pp. 4-5. Early stages of the transformation were illustrated in *Penrose Annual* (1964), pp. 80-1.

Index

NOTE: Type-faces are indexed under the heading 'types'.
Italic figures indicate illustrations